The Balkans since 1453

M

The BALKANS
since 1453

L. S. Stavrianos

WITH A NEW INTRODUCTION BY
Traian Stoianovich

 New York University Press
WASHINGTON SQUARE, NEW YORK

This edition first published in the U.S.A. in 2000 by
NEW YORK UNIVERSITY PRESS
Washington Square
New York, NY 10003

Library of Congress Cataloging-in-Publication Data

Stavrianos, Leften Stavros.
    The Balkans since 1453 / L.S. Stavrianos ; with new introduction by Traian Stoianovich
      p.   cm.
    Originally published: New York : Holt, Rinehart, and Winston, 1965, c1958
    Includes bibliographical references and index.
    ISBN 0-8147-9766-0 (paper : alk. paper) — ISBN 0-8147-9765-2 (cloth : alk. paper)
    1. Balkan Peninsula—History. I. Title
DR36.S83 2000
949.6—dc213--dc21   99-053351
                                                            CIP

Printed in Malaysia

Preface

ERHAPS THIS BOOK should be preceded by an apology rather than a preface—an apology for presumption in undertaking single-handed a history of the Balkan Peninsula. This task, under ideal circumstances, should be assumed by an international team of scholars. And even such a team could not hope to produce anything approaching a definitive work without a good many years of cooperative research and deliberation on the numerous basic problems in Balkan history that still remain unresolved.

I began this study almost a decade ago with the hope that the inevitable shortcomings of the final product might be balanced by certain positive features. More specifically, two objectives have been kept in mind throughout the preparation of this volume. One was to synthesize and to make more generally available the great amount of monographic and periodical literature that has appeared since the period following World War I, when the currently available general Balkan histories were written. The nature and extent of this literature is indicated in the bibliography, where an attempt also has been made to point out the most pressing needs and the most promising research areas in contemporary Balkan historiography.

The other objective has been to make manifest the broader significance of Balkan history by emphasizing the interrelationship of Balkan, general European, and world history. During the past century, particularly, Balkan developments are explainable to a significant degree in terms of the impact of the dynamic, industrial Western society upon the static, agrarian Balkan society. The instability and turbulence of Balkan politics in the modern period become meaningful when interpreted as a local manifestation of the world-wide problem of the adjustment of backward areas to the Western industrial civilization that has enveloped the globe.

Early in the preparation of this study certain basic questions of definition and delimitation had to be decided. One concerned geography—how far north do the Balkans extend? The decision here—arbitrary of necessity—was to exclude Hungary and include Rumania. Another question was whether the approach to Balkan history during the Ottoman period should be primarily local or imperial. The latter had certain important advantages, particularly

pedagogically. The Ottoman period of Balkan history has been viewed traditionally from Constantinople, and this treatment undoubtedly is more adaptable to the familiar patterns of general European history. On the other hand,
a Balkan approach to the Ottoman period is desirable precisely because it has
been hitherto neglected. But this in turn immediately raises the problem of
current Balkan historiography for the Ottoman period. Yugoslav historians,
who have devoted far more attention to the prenational era than any of their
Balkan colleagues, are still debating elementary questions of interpretation
and even of fact.

At the risk of falling between two stools, an attempt has been made to
combine the imperial and local approaches. Ottoman imperial history is surveyed in Parts II and III, though the analysis is deliberately "slanted" toward
the Balkans. For example, the conquests of Selim I in Syria and Egypt are of
basic significance for the general history of the Ottoman Empire; yet they are
only briefly summarized here because they did not directly affect the Balkans.
For the same reason much more emphasis is placed on Suleiman's campaigns
in Central Europe, where Balkan frontiers were involved, than on his equally
important expeditions into Persia and the western Mediterranean. At the same
time, Parts II and III include chapters devoted to Balkan institutions and
trends during the Ottoman period, and also the "national" chapters in Part IV
include background surveys of pre-nineteenth century developments and
conditions.

The nineteenth century also posed a problem of delimitation. Should
this study concern itself with the various crises and wars arising from the intrusion of the great powers into the vacuum created by Ottoman decline? For
example, both the Near Eastern crises of the 1830's and the Crimean War did
not originate in the Balkans and the military operations were not waged in that
area. This would appear sufficient reason for concluding that these episodes
have no place in a Balkan history. Yet the events of 1875–1878 obviously
must be considered, and if they are to be considered meaningfully it is clearly
necessary to trace the diplomatic threads back to the earlier crises. Thus the
decision again was in favor of broader coverage, so that the so-called Eastern
Question is here examined comprehensively to the Lausanne Treaty of 1923.
In fact, the Question is traced through to the post-World War II period, for
the maneuverings, declarations, and doctrines of Churchill and Stalin and
Roosevelt and Truman are but the contemporary manifestation of the age-old
Question that in the past involved Greeks, Persians, Romans, Slavs, and
Turks.

It gives me pleasure to take this opportunity to acknowledge the
friendly and unstinted help of the following scholars who read and criticized
portions of the manuscript: Professor Sinasi Altundag of the University of
Ankara, Professor George Arnakis of the University of Texas, Professor C. E.
Black of Princeton University, Professor Michael B. Petrovich of the University of Wisconsin, Professor Carl Roebuck of Northwestern University, Professor Jozo Tomasevich of San Francisco State College, and Dr. Peter Top-

ping, Director of the Gennadius Library of the American School of Classical Studies in Athens. Other scholars, including Professor Sydney N. Fisher of The Ohio State University, Professor Charles Jelavich of the University of California at Berkeley, Professor William L. Langer of Harvard University, Dr. Philip E. Mosely of the Council on Foreign Relations, Professor Henry L. Roberts of Columbia University, and Professor Wayne S. Vucinich of Stanford University, responded generously to the innumerable questions that arose in the course of preparing the manuscript. I am indebted also to the following authors who kindly allowed me to read their works while still in manuscript form: Dr. John C. Campbell of the Council on Foreign Relations (*French Influence and the Rise of Roumanian Nationalism*), Dr. George Coutsoumaris (*Possibilities of Economic Development in Greek Agriculture*), Professor Roderic Davison of The George Washington University (*Reform in the Ottoman Empire 1856–1876*), Professor Adamantios Pepellasis of the University of California at Davis (*Socio-Cultural Barriers to the Economic Development of Greece*), Professor Howard A. Reed of Wallingford, Pennsylvania (*The Destruction of the Janissaries by Mahmud II in June, 1826*), Dr. Ernest E. Ramsaur, Jr. (*The Young Turk Revolution, An Inquiry into the Origins of the Turkish Revolution of 1908*, published in 1957 by the Princeton University Press as *The Young Turks: Prelude to the Revolution of 1908*), Professor Henry L. Roberts of Columbia University (*Rumania: Political Problems of an Agrarian State*, published in 1951 by the Yale University Press), Professor Traian Stoianovich of Rutgers University (*L'économie balkanique aux XVIIe et XVIIIe siècles*), Professor Lewis V. Thomas of Princeton University (*Ottoman Awareness of Europe, 1650 to 1800*), and Professor Jozo Tomasevich (*Peasants, Politics and Economic Change in Yugoslavia*, published in 1955 by the Stanford University Press). While this work was in the press, Dr. George C. Soulis, Librarian of Dumbarton Oaks and member of the Faculty of Arts and Sciences, Harvard University, kindly informed me of a number of studies that had escaped my attention. These have been added to the bibliography section, with the notation in each case that they have not been consulted in the preparation of the manuscript. Mr. Justin Kestenbaum, formerly Hearst Fellow in American History at Northwestern University and presently a member of the history department at Wright Junior College, photographed the illustrative materials with expertness and care.

The directors and staff members of the libraries in which I have worked have been most helpful and courteous. I am grateful to them all, and particularly to those of the National Library of Greece, the Gennadius Library in Athens, the Library of Congress, the New York Public Library, and the libraries of Harvard University, Princeton University, Columbia University, Stanford University, the University of California at Berkeley, and the University of Chicago. The staff of Deering Library at Northwestern University responded unfailingly to repeated requests throughout the preparation of the manuscript.

I should also like to extend my thanks to the John Simon Guggenheim Memorial Foundation for a fellowship that enabled me to devote without interruption the year 1951–1952 to this study, and also to the Committee on Research of the Graduate School of Northwestern University for generous and successive grants-in-aid which facilitated the preparation of this book.

Finally it gives me the greatest personal pleasure to express my appreciation and gratitude to my colleague, Professor Gray C. Boyce. I am indebted to him not only for his helpful comments concerning portions of the manuscript that he read, but above all for his selfless and perceptive consideration in smoothing the way during the preparation of this study. The measure of my indebtedness will be best appreciated by my colleagues who also are associated with Professor Boyce in his department.

L. S. S.

Evanston, Illinois

Contents

PART III.   AGE OF OTTOMAN DECLINE: 1566–1815

sion) · Social and Cultural Trends (Variations, Food and
Housing, Health, Emigration, Education, State Administra-
tion) · Political Trends (Pattern, Agrarianism, Dictatorships,
Communism)

Photographs

Maps

A Dialogic Introduction by Traian Stoianovich (1999)

WHAT IS THE function of an introduction to another person's, a friend's and colleague's, book? In part, it may show the author that the book has had consequences that he initially may not have intended. Good books acquire an independence of the author. The author shapes the thought of the book. At some moment, however, the yet unfinished book begins to shape the thinking of the author. Book and author affect each other but remain separate. Later, as the author undergoes other experiences, he may begin to think different-ly—create some distance between the thought that was both his and not his. The book, on the other hand, affirms not only the meaning that the author consciously or unconsciously sought to put into it but also the meaning that the progressive ordering of information gives to a book.

A book's meaning depends, furthermore, on the varying experiences of its readers, who assign other meanings to it. An introduction may facilitate that process. The writer of an introduction says: let me relate my reaction to the book. The prospective reader's response may be: let me read the book. Is this guy right? Is that what L.S. Stavrianos says? The reader's conclusions may be less important than the fact that the introduction has moved him/her to think. To the degree that an introduction is dialogic, engaged in a dialogue with author and readers alike, to the extent that it incites readers to be critical, it serves its purpose.

The present book is part of a trilogy—three books that Stavrianos wrote over a quarter of a century in terms of the long-term historical relationship between a particular dependent region, the Balkans, and the not fully independent world around it, upon which that region has nevertheless been dependent, or between the world as a whole and its interdependent parts: *Balkan Federation: A History of the Movement toward Balkan Unity in Modern Times* (1942); his present book, *The Balkans since 1453* (1958), and *The World since 1500: A Global History* (1966). The lesson that one may draw from the trilogy is that the meaning of local, provincial, regional experiences cannot be fully understood without a knowledge of the wider world and that the wider world cannot be fully apprehended without the diverse regional and local contexts of which it is a part.

Professor Stavrianos embraces both the world and a comparative approach to history and society. His *Balkans since 1453* represents an itinerary in world history. It provides readers with a view of time and space in a Balkan perspective but also with a vision of how to look at other regions of the world, and how to perceive the world itself as a unit composed of diverse spatial, temporal, and cultural components.

Balkan geography lays the region open to movement to and from three continents—to cultural exchange with, and invasion from, the Mediterranean, the forests of the northwest, the rivers and steppes of the northeast, and the Anatolian plateaux. "The Pyrenees", affirms Stavrianos, "effectively separate the Iberian Peninsula from the rest of Europe, and the Alps likewise shut off the Italian peninsula. In contrast, the Danube River is not a barrier but rather a link between the Balkans and Central Europe. It is a broad highway over which Slavs and Goths and Huns and Bulgars have crossed southward through the centuries into the Balkans lands." Open to a multiplicity of cultures from the outside—Mediterranean, Islamic, Eurasian, Central European, and Western European—the local Balkan cultures often are closed off from each other by a "rugged and complex topography" and a scarcity of easily navigable rivers (pp. 1-5). They are simultaneously exposed to several different great cultures—historians often call them civilizations—but also often isolated from, and insulated to, each other.

Several questions may perplex the reader. How valid is the contrast between the Balkan peninsula, so named only since the Napoleonic wars, and the two other great peninsulas of the northern Mediterranean? How accurate is the conception of the Danube as a facilitator of communication, both along its course and across it? Does it facilitate equally the communication of goods, people, and information? How does it compare in this respect with the Rhine, Dnieper, Volga, and yet other great rivers? Is geography a given, or is it part of an interdependent relationship of geography, history, and technology? Stavrianos later answers some of these questions, but the reader should think ahead of, anticipate, the author.

No region is fully open or fully closed to the rest of the world. Nor is every region equally open to the movement of people, goods, information, money, and capital, not to the same extent over time. Stavrianos alludes to this problem in his portrayal of the early-sixteenth-century contest between Portugal and the Ottoman Empire for the control of trade routes to and from the Indian Ocean, and of the movement to Europe and the Mediterranean of Asian silks, pepper, and other spices. He compares the all-maritime traffic of the Portuguese by way of the Cape of Good Hope and the partly overland, partly maritime, Ottoman trade with Europe by way of the ports of the eastern Mediterranean. The shift of trade to the all-maritime route was not decisive, at least not in the sixteenth century.

A map of "Ottoman Conquests, 1481-1683" (p. 68) suggests as one reason for the ability of the Ottoman Empire to maintain an important share in the trade of Europe with the Indian Ocean for a long time, its own expansion along the Mediterranean and adjacent seas by means of six wedges of penetration: westward by land almost to Vienna, across Mesopotamia to the Persian Gulf, southward along the eastern coast of the Red Sea to Aden, up the Nile valley, westward across the Mediterranean coast of Africa, and eastward across the northern Black Sea coast of the vassal khanate of Crimea toward the Volga and the Golden Horde.

How close the Ottomans came to reaching the Atlantic in their struggle with the Habsburgs of Austria and Spain is suggested by a German sixteenth-century folksong about the Turk(s) that Stavrianos cites (p. 77):

> *From Hungary he's soon away,*
> *In Austria by break of day,*
> *Bavaria is just at hand,*
> *From there he'll reach another land,*
> *Soon to the Rhine perhaps he'll come.*

The Ottoman Empire was then a fearsome enemy. Its greatest success probably derived from its ability to organize men. It formed armies superior to those of any European state or any other neighboring state. It opened careers to converts to Islam. It divided up the fiefs of many great lords among holders of small benefices, Christians and Muslims alike. It won the support of many Christians by extending privileges or local autonomies to groups who agreed to police Ottoman routes, mountain passes, and river traffic along the Danube. It recognized Jews, Orthodox Christians, and Armenians as separate self-governing communities in matters pertaining to the large sphere of religion. As a result, there were virtually no ethno-religious revolts among Balkan Christians until the 1590s.

The obstacle to further Ottoman expansion was its overexpansion. The wars of the tricontinental state became not only longer, exceeding the usual three-year maximum of the conquest period (p. 136), but ever more costly. Being both a land and sea power, the Ottoman Empire needed both land and sea forces. Forced sometimes into two-front or three-front wars of long duration, it could not wage them effectively. Its territorial overextension made the acquisition of booty more dubious, depriving its soldiery of one of the incentives for organized war, if not for razzias.

The loss of Ottoman superiority in the organization of men was partly the product of an expanding world money economy, marked by the export of some of the newly-discovered American silver to eastern Mediterranean ports during the latter part of the sixteenth century in payment for Europe's imports. Much of that silver flowed eastward from the Ottoman Empire to pay for European and Ottoman imports from India and places yet further east. In the Ottoman Empire itself, in combination with urban and demographic growth and rising taxes, the arrival of this dear money for which there was a strong demand—by the government, by merchants, and by Persia, India, and Asia in general—brought down the value of coin that was already in circulation. The concomitant rise in the price of Ottoman wheat exports to Europe provoked a rise in the price of other Ottoman goods (p. 126).

Inflation and the long land wars waged against the Austrian Habsburgs (beginning with Ottoman razzias in 1592 and waged systematically between 1593 and 1606) and against a revived Persia (1602-1612, 1616-1618) together represent a turning point in Ottoman history. But what are historical "turning points" (p. 893)? Superficially, a turning point resembles an economic crisis between a short-term rising and a short-term falling economy or between a short-term falling and a short-term rising one. But the historical turning points that Stavrianos situates are conjunctures of relatively long duration between a long rising and a long stagnating or declining polity and social order, or between a long stagnating and a long rising polity or social order.

Professor Stavrianos postulates a strong connection not only between political-military power and technology but between political-military power, technology, and the changing forms of money power. Possessing a strong intra-imperial trade and developing a trade with Europe and Asia that was set for the most part in terms of imperial needs until the later part of the sixteenth century, the Ottoman Empire enjoyed a century of relative well-being after the completion of most of its Balkan conquests in the 1490s. The use of the term *Pax Ottomanica* (pp. 112-115) to identify a time of internal well-being, an era during which, in the Balkans, there was no ethno-religious opposition to Ottoman rule, and which passed without other internal disorders that the central government could not quickly suppress by means of its monopoly of arms, is appropriate only to this period.

A first long upward phase began around 1430 with the Ottoman occupation of Saloniki, followed by the acquisition of new resources (in particular, rich Serbian, Bosnian, and Greek silver and other mines). These successes enabled Ottoman rulers by the 1490s to augment the tax base of the state. The extension of the upward phase to almost every aspect of the polity and economy continued thereupon for a century. Then came a conjuncture of retrenchment, stagnation, and decline despite brief moments of recovery.

Characterizing this downward phase was the forcible conversion to Islam of mountain hamlets in Albania, Bulgaria, and the recently conquered island of Crete, a weakening of the organizational power of the central government, and a *de facto* transfer of authority to taxfarmers, contractors, subcontractors, and provincial and local notables. In the sixteenth century—and even in the seventeenth, which continued to be interpreted by Europeans on the basis of what sixteenth-century observers had said—the Ottoman Empire served in much of continental Europe as a model for absolutism, or the concentration of political power in the state, replacing the previous dispersion. In the fifteenth and sixteenth centuries, the Ottoman Empire had not opposed importing or imitating foreign skills. Selective and critical, its cultural borrowing had been an act of cultural dynamism. Its openness subsequently declined. Replacing it was a reluctance to innovate and a hostility to European ideas and material culture. Under the stress of war and military defeat, a reserved resumption of openness marked the 1770s and, intermittently, the 1790s and 1800s. No persistent effort in that direction occurred, however, until after 1830, following another major defeat.

Faced with the difficulties of direct tax collection, the Ottoman Empire satisfied its needs in the seventeenth and eighteenth centuries, much like many other states, by relying on the services of taxfarmers and contractors. Professor Stavrianos discusses in particular the role of Orthodox Christian Greeks known as Phanariotes, who played an especially important role in that capacity both within the Ottoman Empire proper and in the vassal principalities of Wallachia and Moldavia (pp. 270-272). Such middlemen provided the State Treasury with cash payments in advance in return for the right to collect certain taxes or derive revenues from the purchase of monopoly rights to the sale or manufacture of a particular commercial product in a particular district or province. Taxfarmers and holders of provincial monopolies often subcontracted their rights to others buyers.

Contracting and subcontracting were also ways of recruiting soldiers from among young unmarried males. Made up mostly of Muslims but also of some Christians, such males usually lacked property in land. If they were able to steal or buy a handgun or musket, however, they could offer their services to a captain contractor, who might take them in charge. When the need for such soldiers and captains subsided, many of the armed ex-soldiers took to pillaging one countryside after another.

While only vaguely hinting at the foregoing process (pp. 218-219, 366), the author explicitly draws attention to the rise of the chiflik form of land tenure during the seventeenth and eighteenth centuries in the maritime districts of the Balkans and several of the river valleys. By lending money to holders of small military benefices or timars, for example, a contractor obtained a right not to the revenue rights of the holder of the benefice but to a portion of the product of the benefice's tithe-paying peasants. The benefice holder continued to obtain a tenth of the crops produced on the land, while the contractor claimed an equal and often a much greater amount. By his ability to provide work animals, the holder of chiflik rights could draw labor to the farms under his control. To defend his claims, he could hire armed men to ward off the raiders of rivals and, in turn, organize raids against them. Various forms of sharecropping spread in this manner to many areas. After 1804 in the pashalik of Belgrade and after 1830 elsewhere, the system declined. It continued to be practised, however, until the early decades of the twentieth century (pp. 138-141, 144, 236, 244, 366, 376, 478, 677).

This peculiar form of "privatization", along with the development of the economy of Habsburg Hungary, aided the emergence of other forms of private enterprise, that of Balkan peddlers, especially Greeks and Vlachs, Ottoman Serb pig and cattle merchants, Habsburg Serb wheat merchants, and Ottoman mariners and ship captains (Greeks, Albanians, South Slavs), who delivered to Europe or redistributed within the Habsburg Monarchy some locally produced products—cotton, pigs, and cattle by land and wheat by sea and by way of the Danube and Sava rivers—for which there was a regional or European demand. Local Ottoman notables and holders of chiflik rights had a particular incentive to promote the trade in cotton and wheat.

The growth of Ottoman urban life during the sixteenth century similarly had fostered the growth of a money economy. It had encouraged the government to give advantageous trading rights to Europeans. It had favored the enterprise of well-to-do Greek, Jewish, and Armenian merchants in the intra-imperial trade between large cities. The activities of the merchants who were added during the seventeenth and especially eighteenth century, on the other hand, extended primarily to bringing Balkan products to Europe or engaging in the carrying trade with Europe and Russia.

The emergence of this second category of merchants laid a foundation for the beginning, by the 1770s, of a literary revival and the introduction of Enlightenment thought among the Greeks and Vlachs of the western regions (Thessaly, Epirus, and southwestern Macedonia), among the Greeks of the circum-Mediterranean provinces of the Aegean, Ionian, and Pontic seas, and among the Habsburg Serbs, residents of a culturally European land. The Hungarian Serbs occupied territories peripheral but adjacent to the Ottoman Empire. The circum-Mediterranean Greek and adjacent continental Greek and Vlach districts were, in some respects, central to the Ottoman Empire. While a center, however, this region was also a margin. Its people, mostly Christian Greeks, were the provisioners of the capital. By their commercial intercourse by land and sea alike, however, they were also closely linked to western and central Europe and to Russia. The acceptance of Enlightenment ideas by at least a portion of the elites of these two regions marks, in effect, the beginnings of the turning away of some of the Orthodox Christian elites from the Ottoman model of culture toward European models. Between the 1770s and 1830s or 1840s, the turn was made.

The attachment to Enlightenment thought both in its romantic and rational forms, which strengthened and deepened during the nineteenth century, represented the adherence of the Balkan Orthodox Christian elites to the goal of rejoining the Balkan cultures to what Edgar Morin (in his *Penser l'Europe* [(Paris)]: Gallimard, 1987, pp. 127-129) calls the "dialogic(al) culture" of Europe. That culture is a culture of multiple discourse among persons who both think and are well informed. Its initial formation dates back to the twelfth and thirteenth centuries. One may also relate it to what Anthony Giddens calls "dialogic democracy," with beginnings in the seventeenth century and a penchant to deny some or every form of fundamentalism or embodiment of the "refusal of dialogue" (in his *Beyond Left and Right: The Future of Radical Politics* [1994], pp. 115-124).

May I hazard the hypothesis, however, that the diffusion of Enlightenment and French revolutionary ideas to Balkan elites was of comparable significance to the spread of Christianity among the Balkan Slavs in the ninth and tenth centuries, that second coming of Christianity to the Balkans, which were the first European region to embrace Christianity? Professor Stavrianos may or may not concur. He does draw attention, however, to the impact upon Greeks and Balkan Slavs of the French occupation of the Ionian Islands and of Napoleon's subsequent expedition to Egypt and later brief alliance with the Ottoman Empire and occupation of Dalmatia, Istria, and Dubrovnik (pp. 152-153, 198-213). He also identifies the beginnings several decades earlier of "a new intellectual climate" among ethnic and cultural Greeks (especially Vlachs and Orthodox Albanians) and Habsburg Serbs. He further ascribes that new climate not just to "more education" but to the spread of "a new type of education . . . no longer primarily religious" but, instead, "profoundly influenced by the current Enlightenment in Western Europe" (pp. 145-149). In a seminal article, "Antecedents to the Balkan Revolutions of the Nineteenth Century," *Journal of Modern History*, XXIX (December 1957), 335-348, he explains the interconnections in the Balkans between the Enlightenment and revolutionary thought.

Coinciding with this change in the outlook of culturally Orthodox Christian thinkers was the changed outlook of the Austrian political leadership toward the

Ottoman Empire. Reacting after 1791 to revolution in its own territories, Austria temporarily gave up the idea of dividing the European territories of the Ottoman Empire with Russia and/or other European states. In 1797, after discovering an anti-Ottoman plot by Greek revolutionaries to transform the Ottoman Empire into a pseudo-Jacobin republic, the Austrian government arrested the conspirators. It handed over their leader, Rhigas Pheraios, to the Turks in Belgrade, where Rhigas was executed (pp. 184-185, 193-197, 278-279). At the same time, in reaction against the Enlightenment call for liberty and the revolutionary call for fraternity among free peoples, the higher echelons of the Orthodox ecclesiastical hierarchy vigorously spoke out in defense of the Ottoman social order (pp. 149-153). Several years later, amidst the turmoil of the Napoleonic wars, distrustful of popular rebellion, Austria denied aid to the Serb rebellion against provincial misrule in the Ottoman pashalik of Belgrade.

Lending their support to the Serbian uprisings (1804-1813, 1815) and the Greek war of independence (1821-1829), Serb and Greek thinkers were able to begin giving firm institutional foundations to their European cultural models only during the 1830s and 1840s by their adherence to the concept of constitutional government—to the thesis that freedom cannot be maintained without an order of law based more and more on the experiences of the new post-1789 and less and less on the experiences of the old pre-1789 Europe (pp. 251-256, 285, 292-294). But joined to the question of individual freedom was that of whether the rights of citizens have a basis in the wills of individuals, in the will of the state or inferred collective aspiration of the inhabitants of a politically distinct territory, or in the will of the nation. If their basis is the will of the nation, can there be individual freedom until or unless nation and state are one? If the answer is no, must the Balkan ministates not strive to bypass the old barriers of religious division—but also benefit from the community of religion—in order to incorporate in their territories, and emancipate, all people who fulfill the linguistic, cultural, symbolic, and/or historical and mythical criteria with which their respective intellectual gurus associate their own nationhood?

There were obstacles to the realization of this goal. How does one determine a community of language? Should it have a basis in urban or in rural speech? Should it be current, or may it be archaic? Can one avoid a selectivity of symbols and history? What is a sufficient basis for nationhood? An obstacle of a different type was the presence of mixed populations in individual communities and extensive regions alike, and of linguistic and ethnic differences between urban and rural populations. As the elites of more and more ethnic groups shifted their focus from the partly universalizing principle of religion—Orthodoxy in particular—to the nation that they aspired to form, the problems grew more complex. That shift further required a de-emphasis alike of the religion that drew people together and the localism and clannishness that kept them apart. A further impediment was the collective reluctance of the great powers to permit the collapse of any of the empires that were products of the old or pre-1789 Europe, whether Ottoman, Habsburg, or Russian, which bore the brunt of the attack by the new thinking.

Instead of promoting the idea of one or more federations or confederations of new states to replace one or more of the empires, the great powers pursued, at least until the Balkan wars of 1912 and 1913, a policy of "balkanizing" the "Balkans," setting limits upon the viability of the states—Greece, Serbia, Montenegro, Egypt, Wallachia, Moldavia (the last two later unified as Rumania), and Bulgaria—that arose from the partitioning of the Ottoman Empire. These objectives were included in the provisions of the Congress of Berlin (1878). By its terms, the great powers prevented the establishment of a Great Bulgaria. They obstructed the goal of a Great Serbia by simultaneously authorizing Austria-Hungary to occupy Bosnia-Hercegovina and setting limits to Serbia's southward expansion. They held Greece's ambitions in check by preventing its annexation of Epirus, Crete, and Macedonia. They denied the aspirations of Albanian elites, who, in anticipation of a further partitioning of the Ottoman Empire, aspired to a Great Albania including Metohija, Kosovo, Macedonia, and Epirus—territories to which Serbia, Bulgaria, and/or Greece likewise laid claim.

As constituted between 1829 and 1875 or 1878, the Balkans were a product of the treaty of Adrianople (1829) and of the succeeding treaties by which the Ottoman Empire and successor states were fully opened to the commerce of the European states, bringing to fruition the process that Russia had begun by its victory over the Turks in 1774. The products of the Black Sea coasts ceased to be confined to the satisfaction of local needs and the needs of the Ottoman capital. As a result, Wallachia, Moldavia, and Bulgaria converted their primarily pastoral economies to the production and export of cereals. European demand for cereals brought up the price of wheat and maize. That rise boosted in turn the price of land. European merchants heretofore had generally limited their direct trade to Aegean and Mediterranean ports, depending on Balkan middlemen (usually Greeks, Vlachs, and Jews) to dispose of their products at the active Balkan fairs. They now established warehouses filled with their manufactures (mostly textiles, hardware, and glassware) at key sites across the Balkans. At the same time, the old Ottoman monopoly rights of guilds were suppressed. European manufactures began to enter more deeply into the Balkan interior.

Accompanying the foregoing economic changes and commercial growth was the flowering between the 1830s and 1870 of Bulgarian market towns like Gabrovo, centers that also served as the nuclei of educational development. As a result, the hegemony of Greeks was curtailed in the realm of ideas as in the domain of material culture (pp. 191-197, 343, 371, 444). Bulgaria, too, joined the Enlightenment.

By the 1870s, having greatly developed their manufactures, all the western and central European states were in keen competition with each other for demand markets. At the same time, the entry into world trade of areas with a superior raw-material base—wool, cotton, cereals—made it difficult for Balkan raw materials to compete effectively in the world market. Moreover, in the Balkans as in most of the rest of the world, a sufficiently developed infrastructure to allow a continuing importation of European manufactures was lacking. The "dynamic and expanding civilization of Western Europe," observes Professor Stavrianos, "impinged upon the Balkan Peninsula and undermined the latter's self-sufficient natural economy." The post-1870 impact of the West upon the Balkans, however, was "unprecedented in nature and revolutionary effect." To cope with the new circumstances, Europe became between the 1870s and 1914 "the banker as well as the workshop of the world." To enhance its own slowed-down economic growth, it had to make the Balkans and other relatively undeveloped regions of the world politically dependent upon its own capital markets. It persuaded them to solicit government loans in order to modernize, thereby making them financially dependent; also to borrow in order to build railways, which brought into the area "an influx of Western machine-made goods." Earlier "economic intercourse with the West" had been "virtually limited to foreign ships calling at the seaports." The new way encouraged them to borrow funds from the capitalist European states in order to build "roads, ports, docks, tramways, irrigation works, and lighting and power plants." This new relationship between political-military power, technology, and money power, this "new imperialism," swayed the economically less developed portions of the world to promote the growth of the hegemonic economy of capitalism in the hope that they, too, would have a share in its growth (pp. 413-419).

Interrupted during the 1870s and 1880s, the post-1830 upward economic trend yielded after 1914 to stagnation. The problems that beset the Balkan states were too numerous: war reconstruction costs; the need to redistribute land—transfer it from formerly privileged ethnic or ethno-religious groups to deprived elements of the politically dominant nationality in order to dissuade them from social revolution; low agricultural prices; a low export level and continuing population growth, which together discouraged improvements in labour productivity; a slow pace of industrialization; territorial-administrative and monetary reorganization and/or problems of population exchange; the prevalence of malnutrition, disease (pellagra, malaria, tuberculosis, anemia, scurvy), infant mortality, and invalids of war; illiteracy; the rise of agrarian parties known as peasant parties in the fertile Danubian and formerly Habsburg regions of Romania and Yugoslavia that were narrowly nationalist or regionalist in orientation; the threat of communism; an exacerbation of questions of national identity; the institution of royal or military dictatorships in reaction to the foregoing problems; and a growing German penetration of the economies of the Balkan states.

Many of the problems were directly or indirectly related to the war itself, which both in its narrow Balkan-Danubian aspects and in its broader world aspects was a product of the crisis of capitalism. Successful in reviving and intensifying its economic penetration of the Balkans after the crisis of the 1870s and 1880s, European capitalism was unable to induce a Balkan economic growth much beyond the level attained by 1910. At the same time, nationalist divisions arose even in the ranks of internationally oriented communists. In 1924, the Communist International proclaimed "the right of every nation to self-determination, even to the extent of separation." It called in particular for "the political separation of oppressed peoples from Poland, Rumania, Czechoslovakia, Yugoslavia, and Greece." Its program included the separation of Macedonia and Thrace from Greece; Macedonia, Croatia, and Slovenia from Yugoslavia; and Transylvania, Dobruja, Bessarabia, and Bukovina from Rumania. But Greek and Serb/Yugoslav communist leaders contested Stalin's program of putting revolution ahead of the question of nationhood (pp. 614-615). Two and a half decades later, another Yugoslav communist, Josip

Broz Tito, also broke with Stalin over the issue of the role of individual nations or states in the propagation of social revolution. The rebels then advocated "separate roads to socialism."

In the era between the two world wars, the breakdown of the Versailles treaty system began with the assassination in Marseille, in October 1934, of King Alexander of Yugoslavia. Following this event, France was reluctant to support a small ally, victim of a state terrorism orchestrated and subsidized by Mussolini's Fascist Italy and of Macedonian terrorists protected in Bulgaria and Croatian terrorists trained in Hungary. The response of the League of Nations was similarly lethargic. Its ineffectiveness was apparent before Italy's war against Ethiopia and before the Spanish civil war. The French alliance system was subverted.

What Italy could do, Hitler's Germany did better. On July 31, 1940, after having conquered Poland, the Netherlands, Belgium, and France, and, heeding the advice of his top army and navy commanders that a successful invasion of Britain was unlikely that fall, Hitler decided to do what was necessary "to eliminate all factors that let England hope" that it would be able to obtain aid from "*Russia and the United States*" (here and in the rest of the paragraph, Stavrianos's italics of Hitler's words). If Russia drops out of the picture America, too, is lost for Britain, because elimination of Russia would tremendously increase *Japan's power* in the Far East. ... *Russia is the factor on which Britain is relying the most.* ... *With Russia smashed, Britain's last hope will be shattered.* Germany will then be master of Europe and the Balkans. *The sooner Russia is crushed, the better....*If we start in May 41, we would have five months to finish the job in" (p. 749).

In September 1940, to enforce the foregoing decision, Nazi Germany negotiated an agreement with Japan and Italy known as the Tripartite Pact or Berlin-Rome-Tokyo Axis. By this accord, the three powers defined the establishment of a new order in Europe as the responsibility of Germany and Italy and of a new order in Greater East Asia as the task of Japan. The three also agreed that if one of them was attacked by a country not currently at war with them—presumably the United States, for the accord did not apply to the Soviet Union—the others would come to its aid.

In October, however, Italy, which a year and a half earlier had occupied Albania, attacked Greece without first informing Germany of its intention. Having suffered a series of reverses, it complicated Germany's plans for the conquest of the Soviet Union, which required the absence of any Balkan country from which Britain might be able to strike at Germany. Obtaining the adherence of Rumania and Bulgaria to the Axis Pact, Germany moved troops into these countries. In March 1941, a Yugoslav delegation similarly signed the pact subject only to the requirement that it remain neutral in order to facilitate Germany's occupation of Greece. The Serbs of Yugoslavia, however, rose up in protest, calling for a rejection of the pact. A military coup d'état brought into existence a new government, with which, however, Hitler refused to negotiate. On April 6, Germany bombarded Belgrade. Within less than two weeks, German, Hungarian, Bulgarian, Italian, and Albanian troops occupied Yugoslavia and proceeded to partition it. German troops overran Greece.

As World War II drew to a close in Europe, two seemingly contradictory events foreshadowed the future Cold War. The first was the Moscow Conference of Stalin and Churchill in October 1944, which the American ambassador to Moscow, Averell Harriman, attended as an observer. At this meeting, Stalin and Churchill agreed to the following distribution of great-power influence in the Balkan states: 10 per cent Russian in Greece, 50 per cent in Yugoslavia and Hungary; 75 per cent in Bulgaria, and 90 per cent in Rumania, 90 per cent British (in accord with the United States) in Greece, 50 per cent in Yugoslavia and Hungary, 25 per cent in Bulgaria, and 10 per cent in Rumania. At Yalta, on the other hand, in February 1945, the Big Three—United States, Soviet Union, and Britain—agreed to "free elections responsive to the will of the people" in the liberated countries of eastern Europe. Perhaps the second agreement did not annul the respective degrees of influence previously adhered to. But the decision, under the leadership of the United States, to read Yalta as if there had never been a spheres of influence agreement made the Cold War inevitable.

Stavrianos places World War II as a turning point on a par with the Ottoman conquests of the fifteenth century. It allowed the expansion of communism just as the Ottoman conquests heralded the expansion of Islam. The Ottoman Empire's "ultimate fate was decided by its inability to keep pace with the dynamic West, which was being transformed by the Renaissance, the discoveries, the Commercial Revolution, the scientific advances, and the rise of the absolutist monarchies" (pp. 839-840). In an Epilogue, Stavrianos takes a long view of the future as he has done of the past. Writing in the late 1950s, he observed: "We are now witnessing in the Balkan Peninsula two different and rival approaches toward the solution of the traditional problems. One set of procedures is being followed in the Communist-dominated northern Balkans and a very different set in Western-oriented Greece." He saw this as a contest to determine which of the two, the northern group of states—Rumania, Bulgaria, Yugoslavia, and Albania—or "the Western type of society in Greece," would "prove more adaptable and more capable of coping with the traditional problems that have plagued all underdeveloped areas." Which effort would succeed—the attempt to create a new social order by means of a "thoroughgoing political and economic revolution" or the "gradualism" or reform of "existing institutions," along with massive Western financial and technical aid? "A Balkan society that is incapable of adaptation to its world setting," he wrote, "is doomed irrevocably to the same fate that befell the Ottoman Empire" (pp. 841-845).

In an epilogue to the Epilogue, with some knowledge of what has happened between 1989 (the ambivalent celebration of the bicentennial of the French Revolution, the celebration of the six-hundredth anniversary of the Battle of Kosovo by the visit to Kosovo Polje of a million Serbs and other Yugoslavs, and the bringing down of the Berlin Wall and subsequent unification of East and West Germany and demise of the Soviet Union) and 1999 (the NATO war against the rump Yugoslavia, ostensibly in defense of human rights, following the earlier NATO intervention against the Serbs of Bosnia and Hercegovina), one might offer the suggestion that power is also destructive of itself, that the hegemony of the apparent winner—achieved in part by the ability of the hegemonic world power to maintain economic growth by devoting heavy investments to the technological-scientific waging of war—might not long outlast the *Pax Ottomanica* in duration.

Without intending to commit Professor Stavrianos to the suggestion, I ask, was there no connection between the sixteenth-century wars of the Ottoman Empire and Portugal and of the Ottoman Empire and the Habsburgs of Spain and Austria, and the ensuing decline both of the Ottoman Empire and of Portugal and Spain? May one not see a connection between the growing strength of Austria and the rise of another power, Russia, which likewise challenged Ottoman power? New groupings of states, new alliances, periodically arise. New challenges follow. The challenge that states continue to refuse to meet, however, is the challenge of the violence of ever more costly wars, leading mankind to divert, deplete, and pollute the world's resource base.

In the Epilogue to what I have called the third book of his trilogy (*The World since 1500*, pp. 660-668), Professor Stavrianos raises this question: Is "man as a species sufficiently pliable to adjust to an environment that he is so rapidly transforming" by the pollution of the earth with his own kind, with the ecologically detrimental wastes, poisons, and encumbrances of his own production, the consequential social tensions, the threat of nuclear, chemical, and biological warfare, and the dangers of manipulating human, animal, and plant life, and even human thought, posing the threat of human regimentation by the very social systems that pretend to be the defenders of human rights?

An age of perils, it is also an age of yet unseized opportunities. But to one question there is no comforting answer. We do not know whether there can be any limit to human violence so long as any state or group of powers prizes human lives differentially, devaluing the lives of Jews, Slavs, and Roma (Gypsies), as did Nazi Germany; devaluing the lives of Iraqis, as did America's allies in the Persian Gulf War; devaluing the lives of Serbs, as did NATO in its war for NATO credibility in 1999, a foreboding prelude to the twenty-first century, in the American-led war of nineteen states against Serbia/Yugoslavia; or devaluing the lives of Kosovars, as did some Serbs in that war in defense of the integrity of Kosovo as part of Serbia/Yugoslavia. Do not the capitalist great powers behave like Stalin's Soviet Union, excommunicating states that deviate from great-power policies? Do they not even unilaterally create a category of "rogue states," that is, states whose policies deviate from great-power versions of an acceptable globalization?

More seriously yet, has not Europe itself—partly by its overvaluation of economic growth, perhaps an Asian idea, to which both communism and capitalism have been attached—deviated from its own project of a dialogic culture? Balkan elites joined in that project between the 1770s and 1830s, a period that marks the beginning not only of nation states but of the inclusion of southeastern Europe as part of the dialogic European civilization. Has that dialogic culture come to an end? Can it be reinvigorated and reinforced?

October 1999

Note on Spelling and Place Names

IN THE SPELLING OF NAMES I have sought to render the originals as nearly as possible as they are actually pronounced. I have, therefore, eschewed the conventions of modern transliteration systems which, however logical in themselves, give to the nonspecialist an entirely false impression of the sounds they are intended to convey. For this reason I have preferred to render Enver Hoxha as Enver Hoja, and Nikola Pašić as Nikola Pashich. Likewise I have followed common usage rather than consistency in choosing between the original or Anglicized forms of personal names. Nikola Pashich, for example, has appeared frequently enough to be preferable to Nicholas Pashich, whereas King George obviously is more appropriate than the original Georgios. In short, I have tried to follow common-sense procedures in the hope of being helpful to the reader.

Closely related to the problem of spelling is that of the choice of place names. Zagreb obviously should be referred to as Zagreb rather than as Agram, its German name. Yet the term "Agram Trial" will be found on several occasions in the text. The reason is that the use of the term "Zagreb Trial" in place of the "Agram Trial" of 1909, appeared to be as incongruous as the use of the term "Fall of Istanbul" would be for the "Fall of Constantinople" in 1453. The lack of uniformity may prove grating for some readers, but it should not be difficult to deduce from the text and the maps that Agram is Zagreb, that Constantinople is Istanbul, and that likewise Adrianople, Üsküb, and Dedeagach are known today as Edirne, Skoplje, and Alexandroupolis, respectively.

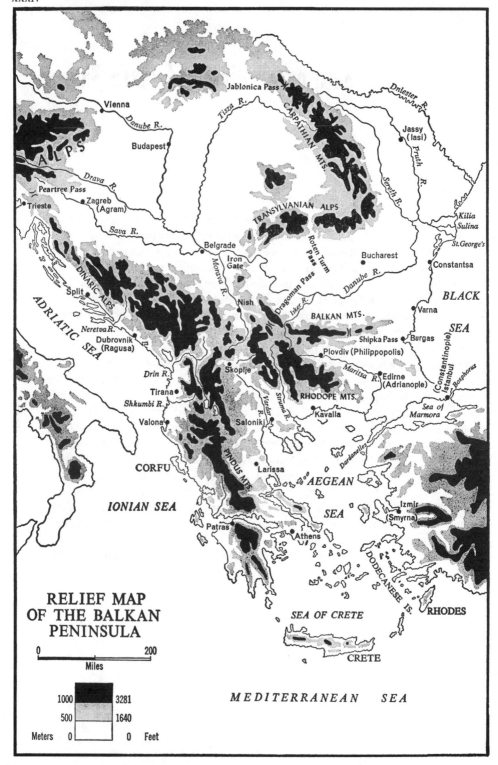

RELIEF MAP
OF THE BALKAN
PENINSULA

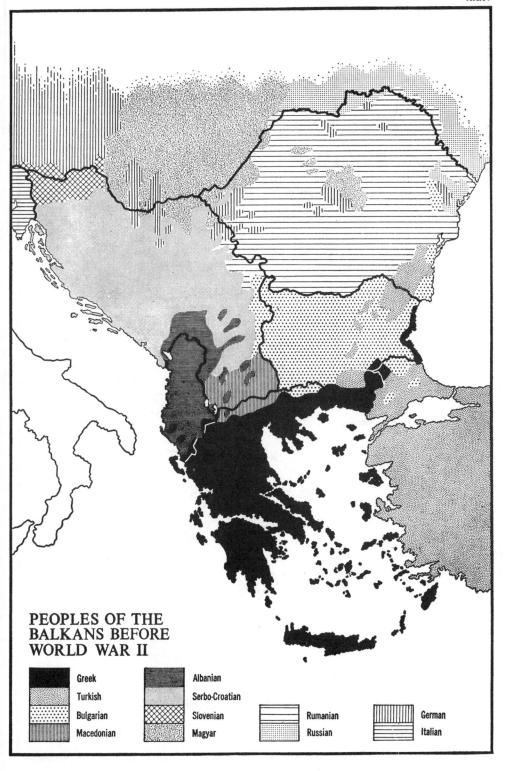

PEOPLES OF THE BALKANS BEFORE WORLD WAR II

■ Greek	Albanian		
Turkish	Serbo-Croatian		
Bulgarian	Slovenian	Rumanian	German
Macedonian	Magyar	Russian	Italian

BALKANS AFTER WORLD WAR I

- ■ Greek acquisitions from Bulgaria
- Greek acquisitions from Turkey by Sèvres Treaty
  (restored to Turkey by Lausanne Treaty)
- Yugoslav acquisitions from Austria-Hungary
- ‖ Yugoslav acquisitions from Bulgaria
- ‖ Rumanian acquisitions from Austria Hungary
- ≡ Rumanian acquisitions from Russia

CZECHOSLOVAKIA

U. S. S. R.

Vienna

Danube R.

AUSTRIA

Budapest

HUNGARY

TRANSYLVANIA

MOLDAVIA

BESSARABIA

SLOVENIA
(Agram)
Zagreb

CROATIA

Drava R.

SLAVONIA
Sava R.

VOIVODINA

BANAT

RUMANIA

Ploesti

YUGOSLAVIA

Belgrade

WALLACHIA

Bucharest

Zara

BOSNIA

Danube R.

DOBRUJA

HERZEGOVINA

SERBIA

Nish

Lagosta I.
to Yugoslavia
from Italy

MONTENEGRO

BULGARIA

Sofia

Plovdiv
(Philippopolis)

Pelagosa
Islands

Scutari

ALBANIA

Skoplje
(Üskub)

MACEDONIA

Midye

Edirne
(Adrianople)

Istanbul (Constantinople)

ITALY

Tirana

Ohrid

WESTERN
THRACE

Bosphorus

Saseno I.
Valona

Kavalla

EASTERN
THRACE

Sea of
Marmora

to Albania
from Italy

Yanina

GREECE

Larissa

Saloniki

Enez

TURKEY

Dardanelles

Izmir
(Smyrna)

Athens

DODECANESE IS.

BALKANS AFTER
WORLD WAR II

CRETE

■ Greek acquisitions from Italy

▍ Bulgarian acquisitions from Rumania

▤ Russian acquisitions from Rumania

░ Yugoslav acquisitions from Italy

Part I. Introduction

1. The Land and the People

A TRAVELER making his way through the Balkan lands is impressed above all by the countless signs of a long and varied past. He may unexpectedly pass by an old Roman bath or walk along a Roman road. He may stop to admire the medieval frescoes in a Byzantine church or the graceful minarets of a Moslem mosque. On the Dalamatian coast he might drive along roads built by Napoleon Bonaparte. If he passes through Split or Spalato (the dual name reflects the town's Slavic-Italian heritage), he will see the remains of Emperor Diocletian's palace, still forming the center of the town, with alleyways and streets cut through the palace rooms between slender columns of vaulted arches. In Greece he can see the classical temples of Athens, the Frankish castles of the Peloponnesus and the crumbling Venetian fortifications of Corfu and Crete. Everywhere in the Balkans the past jostles the present—a present symbolized by modern office buildings in the capital cities and by hundreds of thousands of peasant huts in the countryside.

LOCATION

This variety in historical background is explained in large part by the intermediate location of the Balkan Peninsula. Jutting southward into the eastern Mediterranean, it constitutes an integral part of Europe. Yet at the same time it faces Asia across the narrow Aegean Sea, and its southern capes stretch down toward the coast of Africa. This location at the crossroads of three continents gains added significance because of the peninsula's unusual accessibility. In this it differs from its two sister peninsulas in the Mediterranean. The Pyrenees effectively separate the Iberian Peninsula from the rest of Europe, and the Alps likewise shut off the Italian Peninsula. In contrast, the Danube River is not a barrier but rather a link between the Balkans and Central Europe. It is a broad highway over which Slavs and Goths and Huns

1

and Bulgars have crossed southward through the centuries into the Balkan lands.

Likewise to the west a mere fifty miles separate the heel of the Italian boot from the coast of Albania. In the south the island of Crete serves as a natural steppingstone between Greece and Egypt. And to the east, the island-studded Aegean has been easily crossed in both directions by colonists and invaders on countless occasions since the days of Troy.

This central location of the peninsula explains why it has been traditionally a bridge or a battleground of empires and cultures. The ancient Greeks who developed the first great center of civilization in the peninsula owed much to their proximity to the Nile and Tigris-Euphrates valleys. When the Roman Empire was divided in A.D. 395, the line of demarcation between East and West cut across the Balkans. This line corresponded closely to that which divided the Catholic world from the Orthodox when the Christian church split in the medieval period. Likewise when the conquering Turks were finally stopped at Vienna in the sixteenth century the frontier between the Cross and the Crescent again followed the old furrow. With the rise in modern times of the Russian land empire and the British sea empire, the peninsula was again a zone of conflict throughout the nineteenth century. And today, with the division of the world following World War II, the Balkans once more are a battleground between East and West. Thus the location of the peninsula has in large part determined its history from the earliest times to the present.

TERRAIN

Almost as important as the location is the complex terrain. An airplane traveler may view in close succession fertile valleys, barren limestone wastes, level steppes, inaccessible mountain forests, Norwegian-like fiords, and hundreds of islands, large and small, set in the blue Aegean and Adriatic seas. The prevailing impression, however, will be of the overwhelming predominance of mountains. In fact, the name "Balkan" is derived from the Turkish word for mountain.

Unlike the Italian Peninsula with its relatively simple arrangement of the Alps in the north and the Apennines running the length of the boot, the Balkan Peninsula is crisscrossed with mountain ranges running in all directions. If we disregard the complexities of geologic origins and local terrain, the main features of Balkan topography stand out clearly and simply.

In the far north the Carpathian Mountains swing around in a great curve, with the Danube River breaking through at the Iron Gate, a narrow gorge at the western apex of the curve. Geographers usually consider the Danube as the northern limit of the Balkan Peninsula. From the physiographic viewpoint this is understandable, but for the historian it is unsatisfactory because it excludes the trans-Danubian Rumanian lands whose development has been part and parcel of general Balkan history. Accordingly we will consider the dividing line between the peninsula and the rest of

Europe to run the length of the Sava River to its junction with the Danube at Belgrade, then down the Danube from Belgrade to the Iron Gate, and finally around the Carpathians to the Russian frontier to the northeast. This line should not be taken too literally. Geography and politics rarely are in accord in the Balkans, and today we find that Yugoslavia at one point protrudes northward above the Danube, and that Rumania extends far beyond the Carpathians to include the whole province of Transylvania. For most of the course of Balkan history, however, the line delineated above will be found to be the most meaningful.

Considering next the mountains south of the Danube, we encounter first the Balkan range, which runs east and west to the south of the Danube and which is really the southward extension of the Carpathians. This range reaches a maximum height of nearly eight thousand feet in the center, but in its eastern section it gradually decreases in height until it levels down to low hills at the shore of the Black Sea. It is important to note that the Balkan range offers no serious obstacle to penetration from the north. The invader may skirt the range at its eastern end by pushing down the Black Sea coast. Or he may advance further to the west through any one of several passes, including the Shipka, the Isker, and the Baba Konak, all of which are relatively easy to cross.

South of the Balkan range lie the Rhodope Mountains. The two chains meet in the region of Sofia in the heart of the peninsula. From that point the Rhodope Mountains run in a southeasterly direction, gradually decreasing in altitude until they become low foothills when they reach the Aegean. Between the Balkan and Rhodope ranges is the broad valley of the Maritsa (Evros) River. This is one of the most considerable tracts of lowland in the peninsula, and it continues as an undulating plain beyond the Maritsa to Istanbul. A similar, though interrupted and narrower, belt of plain is to be found between the Rhodope and the Aegean.

In the western part of the peninsula the mountain chains run parallel to the coast line. In the long stretch from Trieste to the southern tip of Greece they are divided into three well-defined sections. The northernmost, known as the Dinaric Alps, extends the length of the Adriatic coast of Yugoslavia in a southeasterly direction. This is followed by the Albanian Mountains which run almost due north-south from the mouth of the Drin to Valona. At the latter point the mountains resume a southeasterly course and cross into Greece, where they are known as the Pindus Mountains. These extend the length of Greece and finally swing around to a west to east direction, when they emerge from the Aegean to form the island of Crete.

The northern half of these western mountains is of limestone formation with very thin surface soil and frequent patches of exposed bare rock. Running water is usually absent, as most of the streams, after a short distance, sink through the porous limestone into underground cavities and emerge later as full-grown rivers at the sea margin or even as springs bubbling up on the sea floor. Consequently this region is extremely difficult to cross because of the almost complete lack of continuous river valleys to serve as natural routes. These ranges not only form a barrier between the sea and the interior but also offer little sustenance for human habitation because of their poor soil and meager resources. Thus this western mountain area is noted for its poverty and isolation.

The rugged and complex topography of most of the peninsula has profoundly influenced its political development. It has prevented unification and encouraged isolation and particularism. A comparison of Italian and Balkan history will illustrate this point. There were Greeks in antiquity in south Italy and Sicily as well as in the Balkans, and beyond were the barbarians—Latins in the one case, Thraco-Illyrians in the other. Why did the Latins succeed in forming a state and an empire while the Thraco-Illyrians failed? Why also did the Greeks fail to produce a unified state? One important factor was the far greater geographic diversity of the Balkans, which tended to the formation of local units rather than a unified state or empire. Nowhere in the peninsula is there to be found a natural center around which a great state might crystallize. Thus Balkan unity in the past has not risen from within but has been forced from without by foreign conquerors, first the Romans and then the Turks.

RIVERS AND ROUTES

The mountainous character of the peninsula enhances the importance of its rivers as natural routes of penetration. Of all the Balkan rivers the Danube is by far the most outstanding, both in length and in historical significance. Rising in southern Germany, it runs through Austria, Czechoslovakia, and Hungary before reaching the peninsula. Then it flows quietly through the north Yugoslav plains until it reaches the Carpathians, where it narrows suddenly to a quarter of its previous width and rushes through the famous Iron Gate with towering granite walls rising twenty-five hundred feet on either side. Beyond, it resumes its leisurely course eastward, with the broad Rumanian plains on the left and the rolling Bulgarian hills to the right. Suddenly and perversely it shifts to the north, thereby ending its function as a natural frontier between Rumania and Bulgaria and so giving rise to endless disputes and periodic wars between the two countries. Finally, about one hundred miles to the north it shifts once more eastward, finally reaching the Black Sea.

This magnificent river, the longest in Europe with the exception of the Volga, is navigable for most of its course. Thus from prehistoric times it has served as a natural highway, beckoning invaders and settlers and merchants, and linking the peninsula with Central Europe to the west and with the Russian steppes to the east.

Several tributaries flow from the interior of the peninsula into the Danube. From the northwest the Sava River runs due east until it joins the Danube where Belgrade is located. About twenty miles further down the Danube the Morava River flows in, making its way northward from the center of the peninsula. Still farther to the east a number of short Bulgarian rivers empty their waters into the Danube, the most important being the Isker, which connects Sofia with the Danubian lowlands.

Considering next the rivers that flow south to the Aegean, the chief ones in order from east to west are the Maritsa, the Struma (Strymon), and the Vardar (Axios). The Maritsa for most of its course runs between the Balkan and Rhodope ranges in a southeasterly direction as though it were to end in the Black Sea. Then it turns suddenly due south at Adrianople and flows into the Aegean, and in doing so it fairly draws Bulgaria down to the coastal region. This twist of the Maritsa, like that of the Danube, has had lasting political repercussions. It has encouraged the inland Bulgarians to eye the ports of Kavalla and Alexandroupolis (Dedeagach) and thus has brought them into conflict with the maritime Greeks determined to maintain their grip on the coast. At the other end of the north Aegean coast the Vardar River and the great port near its mouth, Saloniki, form the natural outlet for the Macedonian hinterland. Here again there is conflict, in this case further complicated by the fact that Serbians as well as Bulgarians seek to reach the sea through the usual fringe of Greek settlement along the coast.

On the western coast of the peninsula the rivers are infrequent and unimportant. Since the ranges there run parallel to the coast, the rivers are usually short and find their way to the sea only after many twists and falls. Thus, despite the length of the coast, the only rivers worth noting are the Neretva (Narenta) half way up the Adriatic, the Drin and the Shkumbi in north and central Albania respectively, and the Acheloos in Greece. None of these approach the central or eastern Balkan rivers in their influence on the history of the peninsula.

With the exception of the Danube, most of the Balkan rivers are of little value for navigation, for they shrink to shallow streams during the hot summers and their mouths are blocked by silt carried down from the uplands. Since prehistoric times, however, the river valleys have served as natural routes for penetration into the interior. As noted above, the Danube has been the traditional route traversed by peoples moving westward from Asia. The great open road leads all the way from Mongolia and the Gobi Desert, through Chinese and Russian Turkestan, around the northern end of the Caspian Sea, and along the north coast of the Black Sea to the Danube Valley, and then either south to the Balkans or further up the valley to Central Europe.

For those who during the course of the centuries have turned southward, a number of routes have pointed the way to the warm water and blue skies of the Aegean. At the northwestern tip of the peninsula, the Peartree Pass opens a passage southward to the ports of Trieste and Fiume on the Adriatic Sea. In the center of the peninsula the Morava River offers passage southeast to Constantinople and also directly south to Saloniki. Starting at Belgrade, one may journey up the Morava to the city of Nish, cross the mountains to Sofia, follow the Maritsa Valley to Edirne (Adrianople), and then strike across the Thracian plateau to Istanbul (Constantinople). This route, originally one of the most famous of the Roman roads in the Balkans, is now followed by the internationally known Orient Express. Almost as important in Balkan history is the north-south route, which follows the Constantinople road from Belgrade to Nish, where it strikes southward across the watershed to the Vardar Valley and down that valley to the port of Saloniki. In the eastern part of the peninsula one can follow the Black Sea coast from the mouth of the Danube southward to Constantinople, thus avoiding the Balkan and Rhodope ranges. Finally there is the all-water route passing Constantinople from the Black Sea through the Bosphorus, the Sea of Marmora, and the Dardanelles to the Aegean.

These routes have always figured prominently in Balkan history because the mountain barriers of the peninsula constitute the great natural obstacle separating the land powers of Central and Eastern Europe from the Mediterranean Sea. It is not surprising, therefore, that Trieste, Saloniki, and Constantinople, the termini of the overland Balkan routes, traditionally have been contested by the maritime powers seeking to retain control of the Mediterranean and by the land powers attempting to expand to the sea. Thus in the nineteenth century the Italians eyed Austrian-held Trieste while the British were always ready to block an Austrian move toward Saloniki or a Russian move to Constantinople. Likewise during the "Cold War" that followed World War II, the Western powers consistently sought to keep Russia out of the Mediterranean by bolstering the Italians in Trieste, the Greeks in Saloniki, and the Turks in Constantinople.

CLIMATE AND RESOURCES

Next to location and terrain, the factor which has most deeply influenced human life on the peninsula is the climate, mainly through its effect on natural vegetation and cultivated crops. The whole peninsula is situated within the Temperate Zone, but the climate varies sharply with differences in altitude and in proximity to the Mediterranean.

Disregarding local variations, two main types of climate prevail, the Mediterranean and the Continental. Included within the area of the Mediterranean climate are the southern part of Greece and two narrow coastal strips along the Aegean to Constantinople and along the Adriatic to Trieste. The remaining interior, which constitutes by far the larger proportion of the peninsula, is subject to the Continental climate.

The distinguishing characteristic of the Mediterranean climate is the long dry summer, with one sunny day regularly following another. This appeals to the tourist, though the temperature at midday soars high and the local peoples take refuge in their siesta. In the late afternoon cool breezes blow off the sea, the temperature drops, and life begins to stir once more. Hence the late dinner hour and the prolonged night life typical of the Mediterranean world.

In the autumn the first rains fall and the parched earth suddenly turns green. This is the time for sowing, and the harvesting must be completed before summer, when the drought once more sets in. The constant fear of the farmer is that the autumn rains may come late or that the drought may start prematurely in the spring. This explains why the traditional Mediterranean products are olives, grapes, figs, and citrus fruits rather than grain cereals, which require more regular rainfall. Likewise the lack of forests and grassy pastures means that the goat and the sheep in the Mediterranean areas take the place of the cow and the pig in the central Balkans. It is quite natural, therefore, that the tourist will be treated to roast suckling pig and plum brandy in Belgrade, and to skewered lamb and wine in Athens.

The Continental climate differs from the Mediterranean in two principal respects: the rainfall is distributed more evenly through the year and the winters are much colder and more prolonged. It follows that the vegetation of the interior is correspondingly different from that of the coastal areas. In contrast to the rocky and denuded mountains of the south, the central highlands are covered with forests, both deciduous and evergreen. Likewise the valleys are sufficiently well watered to grow wheat, rye, oats, corn, flax, and other products typical of the whole of Central Europe. Further north the broad Danubian plains of northern Yugoslavia and particularly of Rumania are reminiscent of the fertile Ukraine or of the American Midwest. Corn, oats, and especially wheat are grown in such quantities that this region traditionally has been the breadbasket of Western Europe, though in recent decades it has suffered severely from overseas competition.

The central and coastal areas differ markedly not only in their climate and vegetation but also in their mineral resources. Greece on the whole is poorly endowed in this respect, though she does possess considerable quantities of bauxite, nickel, chromite, and some lignite. Furthermore, recent investigations indicate that a thorough geologic survey might reveal far richer resources than hitherto suspected. In the northern Balkan countries the mineral output is much more varied and valuable. This is especially true of Yugoslavia, which produces copper, lead, zinc, bauxite, iron, chrome, antimony, gold, silver, and lignite, and is generally considered to possess many rich deposits still unexplored. Likewise Rumania is noteworthy for her oil fields, by far the largest of the Continent west of the Caucasus.

At this point it should be noted that the economy of the peninsula and the living standards of its peoples have been affected to a surprisingly slight degree by this mineral wealth. The reason is that many of these resources have been exploited by foreign capital, with much of the profit and most of the raw material exported abroad. As an example, bauxite is found in Greece close to the hydroelectric power necessary to transform it into aluminum. Nevertheless, the bauxite up to the present time is shipped to Western Europe for refining while Greece continues to use her scanty foreign exchange to import the finished product and the large rural surplus population continues to be tragically underemployed.

This situation has prevailed in the past throughout the peninsula, thereby explaining the predominantly rural complexion of its population. On the eve of World War II three out of every four people in the Balkans were dependent upon agriculture or forestry for their livelihood. Even in Greece, with its abundant ports and unique opportunities for trade, two thirds of the people live in the countryside. This dependence upon agriculture has produced dire results because the amount of land is limited and the birth rate in the peninsula is one of the highest in Europe. This combination of circumstances has led to a constantly increasing rural overpopulation which the puny industrial system has thus far been unable to absorb. As will be noted in the concluding chapters, this is one of the most urgent and basic problems confronting Balkan governments and peoples today.

PEOPLE

This leads us to consideration of the several ethnic groups inhabiting the peninsula at present. Who are these Balkan peoples, where did they come from, and where do they live? A glance at an ethnographic map of the peninsula shows that Balkan ethnography is as complex as Balkan terrain. Closer examination reveals a pattern of four principal races and several scattered minorities.

The most numerous of the four races are the South Slavs, who have settled in a great belt across the central Balkans from the Adriatic to the Black seas. These Slavs are divided into four subgroups: the Slovenes at the head of the Adriatic, the Croatians further to the southeast, the Serbians in the central Balkans around the Morava River, and the Bulgarians in the remaining territory to the Black Sea. The other three races are the Rumanians to the north of the Slavs, and the Greeks and the Albanians to the south.

The circumstances in which these races appear in the Balkans will be considered in detail in the following two chapters. Suffice it to note here that in classical times the ancient Greeks inhabited the southern part of the peninsula as their descendants do today, and that to the northwest and the northeast were two barbarian peoples, the Illyrians and the Thracians, respectively. The Illyrians originally inhabited most of present-day Yugoslavia but later were forced southward by the Slav invaders. Thus today the descendants of these Illyrians, known as the Albanians, occupy only a small mountainous area along the southern Adriatic coast. The Thracians fared even worse at the hands of the Slavs. They were so effectively dispersed or absorbed that only a few survivors remain today. These are known as the Vlachs, a wild and largely nomadic group of shepherds and cattle breeders who are to be found scattered in mountainous areas throughout the peninsula. Their total number at the beginning of this century has been estimated at 140,000. Since then they have steadily dwindled because of assimilation with their sedentary neighbors.

The people to be considered next in chronological order, the Rumanians, are the descendants of the early Dacians, who were subjected to Roman rule A.D. 107 to 274. During this period they were Romanized to a considerable degree, intermarrying with their conquerors and adopting their language. Hence the origin of the term "Rumanian" and the basically Latin character of the modern Rumanian language. Nationalistic Rumanians have considered themselves with pride as a Latin island in a sea of Slavic barbarians. In actual fact the Roman strain has been greatly diluted through centuries of successive invasions, and Slavic and Asiatic elements are prominent both in the present-day Rumanian people and in their language.

The most radical change in the racial composition of the peninsula occurred in the sixth and seventh centuries with the invasions of Slavic tribes originating in the low-lying areas north of the Carpathians. By sheer weight of numbers they pushed back or assimilated the Illyrians and Thracians, and at times even menaced the East Roman or Byzantine Empire with its capital at Constantinople. As noted earlier, these newcomers gradually settled down in the central Balkans and developed as separate Slovenian, Croatian, and Serbian peoples. Toward the end of the seventh century some of these Slavs were conquered in turn by the Bulgarians, an Asiatic people related to the earlier Huns. The Bulgarians, however, were few in number and soon were so completely assimilated by their subjects that only their name persists to the present. The modern Bulgarians, therefore, are considered one of the South Slavic subgroups, and are, in fact, completely Slavic in language, general culture, and physical appearance.

In this manner the peninsula acquired its basic ethnic pattern over one thousand years ago. Since then several minority groups have appeared in varying circumstances. The Turkish domination of the Balkans from the fifteenth to the early twentieth centuries led to a scattering of isolated Turkish ethnic islands. With the recession of their empire, most of these Turks returned to their homeland, so that insignificant remnants are left in the peninsula today. The only exception is to be found in the area immediately to the west of Constantinople. This area, known as Eastern or Turkish Thrace, is the only part of the peninsula remaining to the Turks, and its population of about half a million, or one million if Istanbul is included, is almost entirely Turkish.

Turkish rule in the Balkans had a more permanent effect in the religious field. Although the Turks did not attempt forcibly to convert their Christian subjects, some nevertheless accepted Islam in order to escape certain disabilities to which all non-Moslems were subject. Consequently sizable Moslem minorities are to be found in the Balkans today. One and a half million are in Yugoslavia, most of them in Bosnia. Another 720,000 are in Albania, where they constitute the majority of the total population of slightly over 1,000,000. Bulgaria has 100,000 so-called Pomaks who are Bulgarian-speaking Moslems whose Slavic ancestors were converted in the seventeenth century.

Balkan ethnography was further complicated by the practice of the Turkish and Austrian governments of deliberately planting colonies along their frontiers as a defense against the enemy. The Hapsburgs, for example,

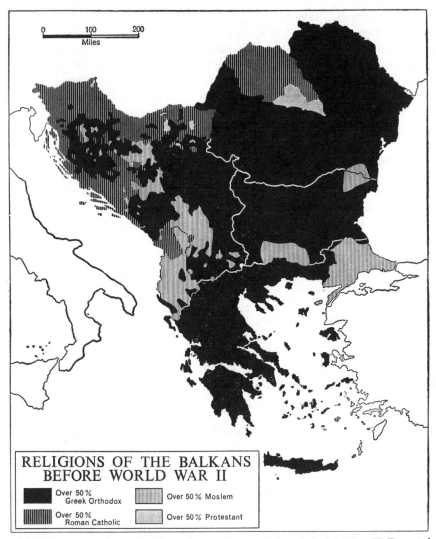

RELIGIONS OF THE BALKANS
BEFORE WORLD WAR II

- Over 50% Greek Orthodox
- Over 50% Roman Catholic
- Over 50% Moslem
- Over 50% Protestant

settled Germans along the Danube, so that prior to World War II Rumania had a German minority of about 750,000 and Yugoslavia had about 500,000. Similarly, the Turks settled Moslem Tatars in the Dobruja to guard the route to Constantinople, and over 170,000 are still to be found there.

Jews have also played an important role in the economic life of the peninsula, particularly during the Turkish period. Before World War II about 1,000,000 were living in Rumania, where they had migrated from Russia and Poland in the seventeenth and eighteenth centuries. Approximately another 170,000 were scattered in Bulgaria, Yugoslavia, and Greece, most of these being descendants of sixteenth-century refugees from Spain and Portugal, who were given asylum by the Turks.

Another small minority are the gypsies, numbering approximately

500,000. Some of them are nomadic, but the majority inhabit quarters on the outskirts of towns and villages and eke out a miserable livelihood as smiths, peddlers, musicians, porters, and scavengers.

Finally it should be noted that the two world wars served to simplify this ethnic intermixture somewhat, though at appalling cost to the hapless minorities that were uprooted or in some cases exterminated. Following World War I, Greece, Turkey, and Bulgaria agreed to exchange their respective minorities, and a total of 400,000 Turks, 250,000 Bulgarians, and 1,300,000 Greeks were repatriated. During the German occupation of the Balkans in World War II a large proportion of the Jews were shipped to the extermination camps of Germany and Poland. Following the war many of the surviving Jews sought refuge in the new state of Israel. Paradoxically enough, the other Balkan minority that was greatly reduced as a result of World War II was the German. Some of the Yugoslav and Rumanian Germans enlisted in the *Wehrmacht* and few of them returned. Others fled with the retreating German armies in the closing months of the war. Many of those who remained behind were forcibly transported to Russia. Thus Hitler's attempt to win "breathing space" in Eastern Europe for the German people led rather to the decimation of centuries-old German colonies in the Balkans.

It is apparent from this survey that Albania, Greece, and Bulgaria are ethnically homogeneous countries, particularly as a result of the exchange of minorities after World War I. Albania has a small Greek minority in the south, and Greece has an equally small Slav enclave on her northern frontier, but these are insignificant exceptions, even though diplomatically troublesome. Bulgaria also has a small Moslem minority, but this is disappearing as a result of emigration to Turkey precipitated by repressive measures adopted by the Bulgarian government in 1950.

In contrast, Rumania and Yugoslavia inherited large minority groups in the provinces they acquired from the Hapsburg Empire. According to the 1948 census, Yugoslavia has a total population of 15,751,935, of which 14,-000,000 are South Slavs. The principal minority elements are 400,000 Hungarians, an equal number of Albanians, 180,000 Rumanians, and 100,000 Italians. The Yugoslav population also is divided in its religious affiliations. The Orthodox Christians (mostly Serbs) constitute 50 per cent, the Roman Catholics (Croatians, Slovenes, and Italians) 33⅓ per cent, the Moslems 11 per cent, and the Protestants, Jews and Greek Catholics the remaining 5⅔ per cent.

Rumania, according to the 1948 census, has a total population of 15,872,624, in contrast to almost 20,000,000 in 1939. The decrease is due mainly to the loss of Bessarabia and Bukovina to the Soviet Union and to the drastic reduction in the number of Jews and Germans. The principal minorities now are the 1,499,851 Hungarians (1,387,719 in 1930), the 343,913 Germans (720,000 in 1930) and the 138,795 Jews (1,000,000 in 1930). The minority peoples at present constitute 13 per cent of the total population, in contrast to approximately 25 per cent before World War II. The Rumanians, like the Yugoslavs, are also divided in their religious affiliations, although the proportion of Roman Catholics is much less than in Yugoslavia with its Catholic Croatians and Slovenes. According to 1946 estimates, 81 per cent of the Rumanian population is Greek Orthodox, 9 per cent Greek Catholic, 7 per cent Roman Catholic, and 3 per cent Jews, Protestants and Moslems.

BALKAN AND WESTERN ETHNOGRAPHY

A relevant question is why four major racial strains and several minor ones have persisted in an area not quite the size of Texas. The geographic factors analyzed earlier provide a partial explanation. The location and the accessibility of the peninsula have led to frequent and prolonged invasions from the outside. The struggle against these invasions undoubtedly has hindered the process of racial assimilation which has been the characteristic development in Western Europe. The complex terrain is also an important factor. If the peninsula had been a plateau instead of a highly mountainous and diversified region it is probable that the various races would have amalgamated to a considerable degree. A common Balkan ethnic strain might have evolved, which certainly would have varied in composition from one locality to another, just as the Genoese differ markedly from the Neapolitans, yet would have constituted a unit in place of the present separate peoples.

Differences in historical background and in cultural tradition also have contributed to ethnic separatism. The Balkan races do not have the bond of a common Roman cultural tradition as do Western Europeans. When the Christian church split in the eleventh century into its Eastern and Western branches, the Slovenes and the Croatians were left in the realm of the Pope of Rome while the Greeks, Serbians, Bulgarians, and Rumanians fell to the Patriarch of Constantinople. When the Turks later conquered most of the peninsula this cultural cleavage was deepened. During most of four centuries the Croatians and the Slovenes lived under Hapsburg rule while the other Balkan peoples lived under that of the sultan. Such basic and lasting separations in government, religion, and general culture inevitably have left deep marks. To the present day a cultural dividing line runs across the peninsula, with Catholic Christianity, the Latin alphabet, and a Western cultural orientation on the one side, and Orthodox Christianity, the Greek alphabet, and a Byzantine cultural pattern on the other. The internal dissension in Yugoslavia in the period between the two world wars bears witness to the lasting significance of this cleavage.

These factors help to explain the fundamental difference between the ethnic evolution of Western Europe and the Balkans. Western Europe is inhabited today by large, homogeneous national groups such as the French, the Spaniards, the Germans, and the British. It does not follow, however, that there are fewer racial strains in the West than in the East. If we look behind the façade of national unity we find Iberian, Ligurian, Frankish, Norman, and Gallic strains in the French; Slavic, Celtic, Baltic, and Teutonic strains in the

Germans; and Celtic, Anglo-Saxon, Scandinavian, and Norman strains in the British. In other words, the difference between East and West is not in the number of component strains but rather in the particular circumstances which made possible the unification of several strains into a national unit in the one case, and which prevented such a unification in the other.

Thus the unique feature of Balkan ethnic evolution is that virtually all the races that have actually settled there in the past, as distinguished from those that have simply marched through, have been able to preserve their identity to the present. The significance of this may be illustrated by imagining a Balkan type of ethnic development in England. Had that occurred we would meet, in a journey through England today, Britons speaking Welsh, Romans speaking Latin, Angles and Saxons speaking their Germanic dialects, Scandinavians speaking Danish, and Normans speaking Old French. Furthermore, religious diversity would match the ethnic. Some of these peoples would be Roman Catholic, others Anglican, and still others Nonconformists of various types.

In an English setting such a situation seems fantastic. And yet this preservation of ethnic groups through the centuries is precisely what has happened in the Balkans. This is one of the unique and fundamental factors that has influenced the historical development of the peninsula to the present.

NONGEOGRAPHIC FORCES

The influence of geography upon history having been noted it should be emphasized now that geography is only one of several factors. Otherwise we run the risk of geographic determinism, which can be as misleading as economic determinism. Certainly various nongeographic forces have made their influence felt strongly from the outset. This will become apparent as we trace the course of Balkan history in the following chapters. However, the most important of these factors will be mentioned here, to be kept in mind as guideposts.

First it should be noted that the past—even the very distant past—and the present are side by side in the Balkans. Centuries chronologically remote from each other are really contemporary. Governments and peoples, particularly intellectuals, have based their attitudes and actions on what happened, or what they believe to have happened, centuries ago. The reason is that during the almost five centuries of Turkish rule the Balkan peoples had no history. Time stood still for them. Consequently when they won their independence in the nineteenth century their point of reference was to the pre-Turkish period—to the medieval ages or beyond. Thus the Rumanians have looked back with pride to their Latin origin in Roman times, the Greeks to the classical period and to the great Byzantine Empire, the Serbians and the Bulgarians to their respective medieval empires controlling a large part of the peninsula, and the Albanians to their Illyrian background and to their fifteenth-century hero, George Skanderbeg.

This obsession with the past has its ludicrous aspects. Alexander the Great is claimed by the Greeks as a Macedonian Greek. He is also claimed by the Albanians, who issued coins bearing his image. And he is claimed by the Bulgarians, who exhorted their armies in World War I "to revive the fame of the great Bulgarian, Alexander the Great." More serious have been the political repercussions of this living in the past. Peaceful inter-Balkan relations were scarcely likely in the face of simultaneous attempts to revive the medieval Greek, Bulgarian, and Serbian empires. Thus historical tradition has been an important factor, and usually a disturbing factor, in Balkan affairs in the modern period.

Equally significant has been the influence of the great powers. At times this influence has been unconscious, as when French Revolutionary ideology, Romanticism, Pan-Slavism, socialism, and communism seeped into the peninsula from the outside to affect its destinies decisively. At other times the great powers have intervened purposefully to enthrone Balkan kings, to determine Balkan frontiers, and to cajole or force Balkan governments into alliance systems or even into war. Whether deliberate or not, the influence of foreign powers runs like a red thread through Balkan history from the days of the Crusades to the days of the Cominform and the Truman Doctrine.

The final factor to be kept in mind is the changing economic relationship between the Balkans and the West. In the ancient and medieval periods the Balkan area was an important center of industry and commerce while Western Europe was a relatively primitive agrarian region. With the Turkish conquest and the Commercial and Industrial Revolutions this situation was reversed. The Ottoman Empire and the succession Balkan states became in the modern period virtual economic appendages of the West. They have served as a source of raw materials for Western factories and as markets for Western capital and manufactured goods. Thus the Balkan economy became passive and predominantly agrarian. This economy has been unable to meet adequately the needs of the rapidly growing Balkan population. The result has been a profound economic and social dislocation which in turn has affected political institutions. Thus Balkan history in the modern period is explainable in large part in terms of the impact of the dynamic, industrial Western society upon the static, agrarian Balkan society. In this sense the Balkan problem is merely a local manifestation of the world-wide problem of the adjustment of backward areas to the Western industrial civilization that has enveloped the globe.

2. Historical Background

THE BALKAN STATES are newcomers in the family of European nations. Four of the five states made their appearance in the course of the nineteenth century, while the fifth did not materialize until the beginning of the twentieth. It does not follow, however, that the Balkan peoples lack a sense of historical consciousness. Precisely the opposite is the case. For over four centuries the Balkan peoples were under the domination of the Turks. These centuries became a blank in their histories, so that when they were once more free they naturally looked back to their respective periods of imperial power and glory: the Bulgarians to their Tsar Simeon, the "Autocrat of the Greeks," the Serbians to their great Dushan, conqueror of most of the peninsula, and the Greeks to their Byzantine emperor, Basil the Bulgar-Slayer, or further back still, to the glories of their classical age. These traditions are alive and real, and are taken quite seriously, particularly in supporting territorial claims. For a Western parallel to modern Balkan territorial aspirations based on such historical precedents, one must imagine a British statesman citing the empire of Edward III as justification for claiming half of modern France. Such have been the force and the persistence of historical tradition in the Balkan Peninsula.

GREEK PERIOD

The first great civilization of the Balkan Peninsula—and of the Western world—developed on the shores and islands of the Aegean Sea. This was the part of the peninsula that was closest to the fertile, sheltered valleys of the Nile and the Tigris-Euphrates, where the earliest civilizations of mankind were born. This was also the part of the peninsula that has felt from time immemorial the stimulating influence of the Mediterranean Sea.

In few regions of the world does the sea hold such attractions for man. First there is the Mediterranean itself, with its clear skies, light summer winds, and few strong currents. Nowhere else are waters so safe and climatic

15

conditions so favorable for primitive vessels propelled by oars or sails. Then there is the deeply indented coast of southern Greece, with its uninterrupted succession of channels, gulfs, and harbors; and in the distance, one island following another to the coast of Asia Minor. The mariner can scud along, from point to point, from island to island, never losing sight of land, never feeling lost between the sea and the sky. And finally there is the rugged mainland, almost entirely lacking in spacious plains, and divided by a jumble of mountain chains into a series of valleys hemmed in on all sides save that facing the sea. The people penned up in these valleys, or on the islands, were literally driven to the sea: to trade if they had a surplus of wine or oil; to colonize if their lands could not support them.

This natural environment helps to explain the distinguishing characteristics of the earliest Balkan civilization, that of the Greeks, with its maritime trade and colonization that were novelties in human history up to that time; its sovereign and self-governing communities that contrasted so markedly to the absolutist monarchies of the Orient; its lack of political unity and susceptibility to foreign invasion; and its contacts with overseas cultures from which it borrowed freely but never imitated slavishly.

The first great center of Greek culture flourished on the island of Crete from 3400 B.C. to 1100 B.C., a period of over two thousand years. Crete is situated some sixty miles from the Balkan Peninsula, four hundred miles from Egypt, and a little over one hundred miles from Asia Minor. This central location made the island the natural intermediary in the transmission and transmutation of the Egyptian and Mesopotamian cultures to the Balkan mainland.

The precise nature and extent of Cretan influence upon the Balkans have not been determined. It is not known, for example, whether the Cretans actually emigrated and founded settlements on the mainland. There is no question, however, about the influence of Cretan culture upon the mainland inhabitants. These were the Achaeans, the vanguard of a roundheaded Alpine people known as the Hellenes, who migrated in successive waves from Central Europe into the Balkans. The comparatively backward Achaeans quickly adopted the main features of Cretan culture and developed a center of their own at Mycenae, in the northeastern part of the Peloponnesus. Mycenaean culture gradually spread from the coastal areas to the interior of Greece.

The Mycenaeans eventually became sufficiently strong to turn against their tutors. About 1400 B.C. they assaulted and overran Crete. Then they conducted a combination of piracy, trade, and colonization in the Aegean and Mediterranean, and on to Syria and Asia Minor. About 1200 B.C. they launched their famous expedition against Troy, memories of which have been preserved for posterity in the *Iliad* and *Odyssey* of Homer.

Meanwhile, the pressure of the barbarian Thracians and Illyrians in the north had forced the Dorians into the southern Balkans. The Dorians were of the same Hellenic race as the Achaeans and spoke a dialect of the same language. About 1100 B.C. their slow infiltration turned into an invasion.

Although barbarians in comparison to the Mycenaeans, the Dorians were invincible with their iron weapons. Central Greece, the Peloponnesus, Crete, and the Aegean isles fell to the conquerors. Whereas the Achaeans had adopted and preserved the Aegean civilization of Crete, although in a coarser form, the Dorians destroyed all that remained of it. The Aegean world passed into a "Dark Age" from which gradually emerged the civilization of classical Greece.

Homer's epics reveal the primitive agricultural and pastoral society of the early Hellenes. This Homeric Age, as it is commonly called, began to give way in the ninth century under the impact of new forces. Homeric Greece was tribal, aristocratic, agricultural, and confined to the Aegean Basin. By the end of the sixth century all this had changed. The tribe had given way to the city-state; other social classes had risen to equality with the nobility; industry and commerce had come to play a considerable role; and Greek colonies were to be found scattered on all the Mediterranean shores.

With these changes the way was cleared for the Classical Age beginning in the fifth century. The Greeks now made their unique and well-known contributions to Western civilization. Although handicapped by their incurable particularism and by the poverty of their technology, they succeeded nevertheless in emancipating the human mind from the supernaturalism and intolerance which had characterized ancient Oriental civilization. Following the lead of philosophers rather than of priests or prophets, they created a new art, ethics, and literature, and established criteria of behavior based on secularism and humanism. Historically viewed, their contributions unveiled a new world for Western man.

Our concern, however, is with the progress of man in the Balkan Peninsula rather than with the evolution of Western civilization. Considered from this viewpoint, the significance of classical Greece can easily be exaggerated. Whereas the Roman Empire was continental in character, the Greek world was maritime and coastal. It was confined to the southern tip of the Balkan Peninsula and to a thin coastal strip along the Aegean, Adriatic, and Black seas. The city-states remained city-states. They did not attempt territorial expansion, and their influence did not penetrate deep into the hinterland. We will, therefore, now consider the non-Hellenic peoples of the interior who, sharing none of the stimulating experiences of the Greeks on the Mediterranean shores, were separated from them by a wide gulf.

MACEDON DOMINATES THE BALKANS

Two non-Hellenic peoples lived in the Balkans at this time, the Illyrians and the Thracians. The Illyrians, who occupied most of present-day Yugoslavia, were the least affected by Greek culture, partly because of the uniniviting nature of the Illyrian coast with its lack of harbors, and partly because of the strength and ferocity of the Illyrian tribes. Whereas the Thracians tolerated Greek colonies and taxed them after their establishment, the

Illyrians excluded them from their shores altogether until a late period. Thus the few Greek colonies were never able to extend their influence far into the interior. They established metallurgic, pottery, and glass works on the Dalmatian coast, and traded these products, together with various manufactured goods from the homeland, for the raw materials of the Illyrian tribes. Despite this commerce Illyria remained a comparatively self-contained and conservative region, with its tribes living in a state of intermittent warfare with their neighbors and with one another.

The Thracians occupied the territory bounded roughly by the Morava-Vardar Valley in the east and the Rhodope Range in the south. Like the Illyrians, their culture was quite different from that of the Greeks, and they constituted a distinct race, although of the same Indo-European stock. The Greeks were unable to understand their language and accordingly dubbed it barbarian. The Greeks were impressed by the light complexion and red hair of the Thracians. A typical observation was, "The Ethiopians are black and snub-nosed; the Thracians light-haired and grey-eyed." The interior of Thrace, like the interior of Illyria, held little attraction for the Mediterranean Greeks. Instead, as early as the late seventh century B.C., the Ionians began to fringe the Black Sea with their colonies. One of them, Byzantium, was destined to be for centuries the capital of the Byzantine and Ottoman empires.

The Greeks also made their way up the Danube and founded colonies along its banks. Only ten miles east of Belgrade, on the right bank of the river, archaeologists have unearthed rich classical findings—the remains of the Greek colony Vincha. Thus, the Greeks influenced the peoples of the Balkan hinterland by commercial operations from the Dalmatian coast on the east, the Black Sea coast on the west, and the Danube Valley in the north. They also exerted influence directly from the south, through the medium of the semi-Hellenized Macedonians.

The Macedonians were located between the Thracians and the Greeks, inhabiting the fertile plains drained by the Vardar and Struma rivers. From antiquity to the present the question has been debated as to whether these early Macedonians were Greeks or barbarians. The Macedonian rulers claimed to be the descendants of Heracles and therefore genuine Greeks, a claim which the orators of the Athenian assembly scoffed at and rejected. The debate has continued to the present day, enlivened by the conflicting claims of modern Balkan states to the Macedonian lands. Recent philological and archaeological research indicates that the ancient Macedonians were in fact Greeks, whose civilization had not kept up with that of the tribes which had settled further to the south. Their language closely resembled the classical Greek from which it differed no more than one English dialect from another. Various non-Greek peoples apparently had come under the rule of the Macedonian nobles and kings, but these latter definitely were Greeks in language and outlook, and invited Greek men of learning to their courts.

At the beginning of the fourth century B.C. the Macedonian state was primitive and loosely organized, still retaining the tribal monarchy of Homeric times and a peasant type of culture. All this was changed during the reigns of Philip II (395–336 B.C.) and of his son, Alexander the Great (336–323 B.C.). Philip overran the divided Greek city-states while Alexander went on to conquer a fabulous empire—Asia Minor, Phoenecia, Syria, Egypt, Mesopotamia, Persia, and the Punjab. He was grappling with the problem of organizing an effective administration for his enormous domains when he died at Babylon in 323 at the age of thirty-three.

Alexander's untimely death ended what small chance there was of unifying this vast empire. For a generation and a half his successors fought for the spoils. The Greco-Macedonian world disintegrated and presently returned very much to the political shape it had had before Alexander, though under different rulers and a different civilization. By 275 B.C. three monarchies were well established; the Seleucids ruled much of what had been the Persian empire in Asia; the Ptolemies, Egypt, and the Antigonids, Macedonia, including Greece. These monarchies ruled the Near East during the so-called Hellenistic period between the death of Alexander and the Roman conquest. Continual wars during the third and second centuries so weakened the Hellenistic monarchs that when the Roman legions appeared in the eastern Mediterranean they had little difficulty in taking final possession of Alexander's legacy.

For the Balkan Peninsula the Macedonian or Hellenistic Age was one of profound changes in all fields. Politically it was characterized by the atrophy of the city-state and a trend toward larger political units. For a brief period Philip and Alexander united a considerable portion of the peninsula under their rule. Philip not only subjugated the Greek city-states but also defeated the Illyrian tribes and annexed part of their country. Likewise, Alexander marched northward to the Balkan Mountains and on to the Danube in order to subjugate the unruly Thracian tribes.

The Hellenistic period also witnessed the remarkable diffusion of Greek culture eastward with the conquests of Alexander and the creation of Greek cities throughout the Asiatic domains. In the Balkans, Greek culture penetrated to a greater degree than heretofore, though in this respect also the peninsula was far from being united. The Thracians were only slightly influenced and the Illyrians almost not at all. The Macedonians, however, became thoroughly Hellenized in the third century. They dropped their native dialect for Attic Greek and their native pantheon for the gods of Olympus. Despite their mixture of blood, the Macedonians were now one people and their country was an integral part of the Greek world.

In the economic field the Greek part of the peninsula lost its primacy during these years. With the tremendous expansion eastward, the main commercial centers shifted to the points where the land routes of the Orient met the sea routes of the Mediterranean, as at Alexandria in Egypt, Antioch in Syria and Ephesus in Asia Minor. Most of the old Greek cities declined, although Corinth, with its favorable geographic position, continued to secure its share of trade. Furthermore, thousands of Greeks emigrated to the eastern areas that were now controlled by Macedonian rulers, and found there enticing opportunities as merchants, soldiers, administrators, and fiscal agents. Indeed, the exodus to the newly opened lands was so great that parts of Greece and Macedonia were depopulated. The general economic decline and the social struggles of the homeland were thereby sharpened, with the result that by the time Greece fell to the Romans its vital energies had been exhausted. Apart from the cultural prestige that still adhered to cities like Athens, Greece declined to the status of a comparatively insignificant Roman province.

ROME UNITES THE BALKANS

The Romans conquered the Balkans during the third and second centuries B.C. First they subjugated the Adriatic Coast, then they defeated the rulers of Macedon, and finally they destroyed the Achaean League of Greek states. Having overrun the peninsula the Romans proceeded to construct a network of paved highways similar to those that they built in Gaul, Britain, Spain, and other parts of their empire. These magnificent roads, raised considerably above the level of the ground, and with a deep ditch on each side, were in themselves eminently defensible and enabled troops to be massed at any threatened point with security and dispatch. In this manner the Romans built the Via Egnatia from the Adriatic coast to Saloniki, providing direct entry from Italy to the heart of the Balkans. Other roads crisscrossed the peninsula in all directions, following natural routes used by primitive men in earliest times and by railway engineers today. Along these roads the Romans erected forts and planted colonies which were merely fortified outposts on a larger scale. A number of modern Balkan cities trace their origins back to these Roman colonies, including Edirne (Adrianople), Nikopol (Nicopolis), Sofia (Sardica), Nish (Naissus), and Belgrade (Singidunum).

In the realm of politics the Romans consistenly applied the policy of divide and rule. They partitioned natural regions and isolated individual sections. They weakened leagues and combinations which might have proved dangerous to their authority. They ended the Achaean League, for example, though later they permitted its revival for restricted purposes. Finally they encouraged the propertied classes whose interests were bound up with Roman supremacy.

The material results of Roman rule varied greatly. Greece suffered a steady economic decline due to the ravages of Roman civil wars fought on her soil and to the diversion of trade following the establishment of direct communications between Italy and the Levant. The most lucrative enterprise left to the Greeks was pasturage in large domains, but this enriched almost exclusively the wealthier citizens and widened the breach between the classes. Certain new industries were developed to meet the needs of Roman luxury. Greek marble, textiles, and table delicacies were in great demand. Yet the only cities that really flourished were the Italian communities planted at Corinth and Patrae, and the old city of Athens.

Commerce languished in general, and such wealth as remained was amassed in the hands of a few great landowners and capitalists. The middle class declined and the great bulk of the people earned a precarious living supplemented by frequent doles and largesses. Thus Greece sank to the level of an obscure and neglected province. In the following centuries Greek history dwindled to a mere record of barbarian invasions, which, in addition to occasional plagues and earthquakes, seem to have been the only events worthy of record by contemporary chroniclers.

The Illyrian lands, in contrast, rose from their former obscurity and backwardness and flourished under the rule of Rome. A prosperous textile industry was established, vine cultivation became widespread, and mining and lumbering proved profitable in Bosnia. The commercial cities along the coast grew wealthy, and Latin civilization spread to the interior. Illyricum became one of the best recruiting grounds for the Roman legions. In troubled times, more than one Illyrian soldier fought his way up from the ranks to the imperial purple. Claudius, Aurelian, and Diocletian are the best known of the emperors who started out as sons of Illyrian peasants.

The influence of Rome upon the culture of the Balkans likewise varied. In the Greek part of the peninsula there was no question of Romanization; rather, as a Latin poet put it, "Captive Greece led captive her rude conqueror." The Romans were scornful of Greek political aptitude but at the same time were very conscious of the greatness of Greek civilization. Within a comparatively short time their upper classes, at least, acquired a veneer of Greek culture. More Greek was learned in Rome than Latin in Greece. Culturally speaking, Greece remained Greek. It is true that in time the Greeks became so accustomed to their subject political status that they called themselves "Romaioi" or Romans, and continued to do so in modern times; yet in language and culture they remained Greeks.

Rome made a greater impression on the backward peoples of the Balkan hinterland, though even here there was no outright Romanization. Where the Roman went he took with him Latin as the language of government, but he also took with him Greek as the language of culture. It was a Greco-Roman culture that was diffused through the Balkans in the Roman period, with Greek influence predominant in the northeast and Latin influence in the northwest. The Illyrian lands were the most thoroughly Latinized, though the native dialect persisted in the inaccessible valleys of the southwest. It also survived the later Slavic invasions and is spoken today by the people of Albania, though with a heavy overlay of Latin, Greek, Slavic, and Turkish words. The Thracians, in contrast, failed to preserve their cultural identity, their Vlach descendants today speaking a Latin language akin to the modern Rumanian north of the Danube.

The Romans drew their northern frontier in the Balkans along the Danube, with the exception of a brief period when they extended their rule across the river to include the kingdom of Dacia. The inhabitants of Dacia were a Thracian people who had attained a modest degree of civilization before the Roman conquest. They engaged mostly in agriculture and cattle breeding, but also worked gold and silver mines in Transylvania and carried on a considerable foreign trade.

The Dacians incurred the wrath of the Romans with their continual raids into Moesia, the province immediately to the south of the Danube. Emperor Trajan conducted a number of victorious campaigns against the Dacians, pursuing them far into the Carpathian Mountains, and ended by incorporating their kingdom into the empire (A.D. 107). In the following years the Romans built highways and forts in the new province of Dacia, and imported colonists to cultivate the land and work the mines. For over a century and a half, from A.D. 107 to 275, Dacia remained a province of the empire and became so thoroughly Romanized that today the descendants of the Roman colonists and native Dacians call themselves Rumanians and speak a Romance language.

Nevertheless, the Roman hold over Dacia was never very firm. The province across the Danube proved a vulnerable outpost, and the successors of Trajan looked upon it as a strategic liability. Emperor Hadrian (A.D. 117–138) seriously considered its abandonment and was deterred only because of the plight of the numerous Roman settlers. A century later the Goths crossed the Carpathians and drove the Romans out of most of Dacia, leaving them only a few fortified positions. Finally Emperor Aurelian (A.D. 275) withdrew his troops altogether from the exposed province and evacuated many of the Roman settlers to Moesia. Thus Dacia, the last won, was also the first lost of the Roman provinces in the Balkans.

ROME TO BYZANTIUM

The retreat from Dacia was but one of the many manifestations of the widespread disintegration within the Roman world in the third century. The disintegration was more marked in the western provinces than in the eastern. The East, with its multitude of well-established cities and their numerous artisans and merchants, was better able to withstand the dry rot that was undermining the imperial edifice. The difference was recognized by Emperor Constantine when he moved (326) his seat of government to the old Greek colony Byzantium, on the European side of the Straits. To emphasize the significance of the shift, he renamed the city New Rome, but from the outset it was popularly called the city of Constantine, or Constantinople.

The transfer of the capital to Constantinople increased the importance of the Balkan Peninsula. It now took the place of Italy as the leading province of the empire. In the deluge of barbarian invasions that swept over the empire in the fifth century, the frontier of the Balkans held more firmly than those of the western provinces. Some of the tribes did succeed in breaking through the Danube defenses. The West Goths under Alaric conducted destructive raids from which hardly a section of the peninsula was spared, but about A.D. 400 they moved westward and descended upon Italy. Ten years later occurred the memorable sack of Rome at the hands of Alaric. In subsequent decades other German tribes—Franks, Vandals, East Goths, Angles, and Saxons—overwhelmed all the western provinces. Finally (A.D. 476) the barbarian chief Odoacer forced the boy-ruler, Romulus Augustulus, to retire, ending the shadowy remains of imperial rule in the West.

The deposition of Romulus Augustulus did not mark the end of the Roman Empire. It was, rather, the beginning of the end. For one more century the tradition of imperial unity persisted, inspiring the Eastern emperors to gallant but foredoomed efforts to restore a past that was beyond restoration. This was the case especially with Justinian (527–565), who won Africa from the Vandals, Italy from the Ostrogoths, and a part of Spain from the Visigoths. But in the century following his death the western provinces were irrevocably lost, the Slavs poured across the Danube to begin their process of crystallization into individual Balkan nations, and the Arab tribesmen, fired by the faith of Mohammed, burst across northern Africa and up the Levant to the borders of Asia Minor. The flimsy foundations of Justinian's imperial structure were demolished. Accordingly we may consider the first half of the seventh century as the period in which the Eastern Roman Empire became distinctively Byzantine.

COMING OF THE SLAVS

The all-important development in the Balkan Peninsula during this transition period was the influx of the Slavic peoples. They began to move southward from Central Europe into the Danube Valley in significant numbers in the fourth century after Christ. The process was a gradual drift and infiltration rather than a sudden invasion. By the sixth century the Slavs firmly occupied the Danube Basin and began to cross into the Balkans. At the same time other peoples were appearing intermittently upon the scene, including the Mongolian Huns and Avars, who swept into the Balkans from the steppes of Asia. But they were marauders rather than settlers, and did not pause long enough to obtain a permanent foothold. The agriculturally minded Slavs, in contrast, sank roots into the Balkan soil and took possession of lands which remain theirs to the present.

By the early seventh century, when Emperor Heraclius finally was able to dispose of the Persian danger and turn to the Balkans, he found the Slavs occupying and cultivating wide areas laid waste by war. Making a virtue of necessity, he assigned to them definite districts, in return for which they acknowledged his suzerainty and agreed to pay annual tribute. This arrangement did not bring complete order and peace to the Balkans. Some tribes occasionally refused to pay tribute, others spread beyond their stipulated territory, and still others were forced to move once more by fresh migrations from across the Danube. Yet the seventh century is significant as the period when the Slavic newcomers changed gradually from invaders into settlers. By the end of the century they were in possession of the Adriatic Coast and its hinterland, and large areas of the central Balkans between the Aegean and the Danube.

These Slav migrations reduced the number of the older Balkan races and crowded them into smaller areas. Part of the Illyrians were assimilated and part were forced southward into present-day Albania. The Greeks held their own in the southern part of the peninsula and rapidly assimilated the Slavic tribes that had settled in their midst. The Latinized Thracians and Dacians of the central Balkans and trans-Danubian lands were dispersed by the Slavs and forced to find refuge in isolated mountain areas. For centuries no mention of them occurs in the meager contemporary records. Then gradually they reappeared as the scattered nomadic Vlachs south of the Danube and the much more numerous Rumanians north of the Danube. In this manner the Balkan Peninsula developed in the early medieval period its present ethnic pattern.

With the passing of a few centuries, the Balkan Slavs, widely scattered and loosely organized as they were, developed along different lines and crystallized into four major groups: the Slovenes at the head of the Adriatic, the Croatians between the Drava River and the Adriatic, the Serbs in the central Balkans between the Adriatic and the Danube, and the Slavs in the remaining territory to the Black Sea, who shortly were to adopt the name of their Bulgarian conquerors. The latter two groups organized great though short-lived medieval kingdoms which borrowed their culture from Byzantium. In contrast, the Slovenes and Croatians, because of their position in the western part of the peninsula, became subjects of the Holy Roman Empire and were influenced by Rome rather than Constantinople in their cultural development.

MEDIEVAL BALKAN EMPIRES

These Slavic newcomers organized a number of powerful empires in the Balkans during the medieval period. The first of these was the creation of the Bulgarians, a people who were not Slavs, but rather Finno-Tatars related to the Huns. Like their Asiatic predecessors in the Balkans, they had no taste for agricultural pursuits. They preferred to leave these to their Slavic subjects, whom they were able to subdue by virtue of their superior organization under military leaders or khans. The Bulgarians, it should be noted, never equaled the Slavs in numbers. Within a comparatively short time the Bulgarian minority was assimilated and became Slavic in everything but name. Today the Bulgarians are considered a Slavic people, and are in fact Slavic in appearance, in language, and in customs.

The Bulgarians first crossed the Danube into the Dobruja in the second half of the seventh century. Later, under the leadership of their great Khan Krum (808–814), they were able to advance southward, destroy a number of Byzantine armies, and, on one occasion, even besiege Constantinople itself. Another great Bulgarian leader, Khan Boris, accepted Christianity from Constantinople rather than from Rome in return for Byzantine rec-

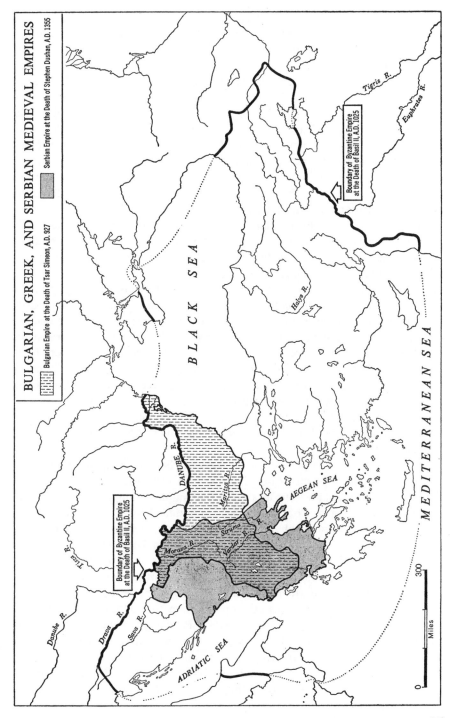

BULGARIAN, GREEK, AND SERBIAN MEDIEVAL EMPIRES

Bulgarian Empire at the Death of Tsar Simeon, A.D. 927

Serbian Empire at the Death of Stephen Dushan, A.D. 1355

Boundary of Byzantine Empire at the Death of Basil II, A.D. 1025

Boundary of Byzantine Empire at the Death of Basil II, A.D. 1025

BLACK SEA

AEGEAN SEA

MEDITERRANEAN SEA

ADRIATIC SEA

Tigris R.

Euphrates R.

Halys R.

DANUBE R.

Maritza R.

Struma R.

Vardar R.

Morava R.

Danube R.

Tisza R.

Drava R.

Sava R.

Danube R.

0   300
Miles

ognition of the Bulgarian conquests. Boris obtained a national church with its own bishops and archbishops, the only limitation being that an honorary recognition was to be accorded to the patriarch as the supreme head of the Orthodox Church.

Having removed the threat of Byzantine domination, Boris felt free to encourage the work of the Greek missionaries. In the following years they provided the Bulgarians with an alphabet, translated the Scriptures into their language, and prepared a Slavonic liturgy. Henceforth Slavonic rather than Greek was the official language of the Bulgarian church. Thus were laid the cultural foundations of the Orthodox Slavs of the Balkans.

About the same time the Serbian tribes were also converted to Orthodoxy. Further to the west the Latin church prevailed in Croatia and Slovenia. For a period Byzantine missionaries held their ground in Croatia, but the combined influence of the Franks and the old Roman cities of Dalmatia finally prevailed. Byzantine influence petered out in the western Balkans, and the Croatians and the Slovenes in the future followed in the wake of their Catholic neighbors, Italy, Hungary, and Germany.

The medieval Bulgarian state reached its high point during the reign of Boris's second son, Simeon (893–927). His years of education in Constantinople imbued him with a deep respect for Greek culture and he encouraged its diffusion among his backward subjects. Greek books were translated into Slavonic, the arts were patronized, and palaces and churches were built. At Preslav, Simeon sat on. his throne, girt with purple, arrayed in pearl-embroidered robes and surrounded by a dazzling suite of nobles. This munificence and culture exerted influence far beyond the borders of Bulgaria. Indeed, Preslav served as a funnel through which Byzantine culture poured into Serbia, Rumania, and Russia, dominating the civilizations of these countries for centuries.

Simeon's accomplishments on the battlefield were equally impressive, though in the long run disastrous. He had it in his power to unite the South Slavs under his rule and to form a great Balkan Slavic empire. Instead he fell victim to the dream of Constantinople. He assumed the proud title "Tsar of the Bulgars and Autocrat of the Romans [Greeks]," and squandered his soldiery to make this dream a reality. He conquered Nish and Belgrade, and overran Macedonia, Albania, and Thrace, but the walls of Constantinople and the wiles of Byzantine diplomacy cheated him of his prize. When he died he was master of the northern Balkans, including the Serbian lands, but his country was exhausted and his empire was soon to crumble. Before the end of the century it was overrun by Magyars, Pechenegs, Russians, and finally the Byzantines, who made Bulgaria their province. It was on this occasion that a redoubtable Byzantine emperor, known to history as Basil the Bulgar-Slayer, annihilated a Bulgarian army and blinded fourteen thousand captives.

Byzantium was now dominant over the Orthodox Slavs of the Balkans. But her domination had come too late. The Slavs of Bulgaria and Serbia no longer were barbarians susceptible to assimilation or expulsion. They now were peasants, tilling the soil, professing Christianity, and cherishing memories of which the names of Boris and Simeon were the flaming symbols. They would therefore submit to Greek domination only so long as Constantinople remained the inviolable capital with power adequate to control the peninsula. By the late twelfth century this was no longer the case. The attacks of the Seljuk Turks, the commercial competition of the Italians, the disturbances of the Crusaders, and, to crown it all, the ineptitude of the Angelus dynasty, combined to bring Byzantium to an obvious state of decay. In these circumstances the Serbians were able to found an imposing Balkan empire and the Bulgarians to revive their past glory.

The Serbians were the Slavic people who, in the period of the migrations, settled in the central Balkans. In the early ninth century they formed an incipient state that soon passed under the control of the Bulgarians. About the same time the Serbians adopted the Byzantine form of Christianity. This helped to develop a sense of kinship among the scattered tribes and, by the eleventh century, they were consolidated into two rudimentary states, Zeta along the Adriatic and Rashka in the interior. It was the latter state that was the nucleus of future Serbian greatness.

In the second half of the twelfth century Stephen Nemanja, head or the Great Zhupan of Rashka, united the Serbian people for the first time. In a series of successful wars with Byzantium and Bulgaria he conquered the whole of Zeta and extended the frontier of Rashka to the Morava Valley, thus establishing the territorial basis of the future Serbian kingdom. His son and successor, Stephen Nemanja II (1196–1228), was a prudent diplomat and warrior who realized the dream of Serbian independence without striking a blow. Hitherto the Serbian rulers had been at least nominally the vassals of the emperor and bore the title of Great Zhupans rather than kings. This relationship ended with the fall of Constantinople to the Crusaders in 1204. Stephen promptly exploited the opportunity and played off the pope against the patriarch. From the one he obtained the title of king and from the other a Serbian archbishopric that made the Serbian church autonomous. The head of the new church was the king's brother, a legendary figure who was to be revered by future generations as the holy and miracle-working St. Sava. With a free state and church the Serbian people were now well launched on the road to nationhood.

In the meantime the Bulgarians also had profited from the decline of Byzantium to regain their independence. Several brief uprisings had failed in the eleventh century, but in 1185 the brothers Peter and John Asen successfully raised the flag of revolt. The occasion was the imposition of a new and burdensome tax, designed, it was rumored, to provide for the wedding festivities of the emperor himself. With the help of the Cumans beyond the Danube and of the Vlachs, who were now reappearing after four centuries of refuge in their mountain fastnesses, the Asen brothers repulsed the feeble efforts of the emperor to reassert his authority. Their successor, Kaloyan (1197–1207), made Bulgaria a formidable rival of Byzantium. In fact, the blows he dealt the tottering empire helped to make it fall a ready prey to the Crusaders.

For a period in the thirteenth century, during the reign of Kaloyan's successor, John Asen II (1218–1241), Bulgaria was the leading power in the Balkans. Like the rulers of the first Bulgarian state, John Asen II cherished hopes of imperial grandeur. He assumed the coveted title "Tsar and Autocrat of all Bulgarians and Greeks," and extended his domain to include northern Albania, Macedonia, and Western Thrace. But he was no more successful than his predecessors in capturing the imperial city, and his kingdom disintegrated soon after his death. His weak and inexperienced successors were unable to maintain his conquests, and the declining kingdom reached its nadir with its defeat by the Serbs in 1330. Thus Bulgaria became vassal to Serbia, which now emerged, for a brief period before the Turkish tidal wave, as the major power of the Balkans.

A year after the defeat of the Bulgars, Stephen Dushan the Mighty, the greatest of the Serbian medieval rulers, ascended the throne. As a military strategist and lawgiver, Stephen Dushan has been compared to Napoleon. He is remembered not only for his conquests but also for his famous code issued in 1349. This is of interest for us because of the picture it gives of the medieval Serbian civilization.

The reign of Dushan also witnessed a modest development of Serbian culture. Church architecture flourished. At first crudely Byzantine, it was gradually modified by Western influences, and by Dushan's time had developed its own characteristics. Monasteries became centers of learning. Serbian literature, inspired by Greek models, made its appearance and reflected a feeling of national unity. This was particularly true of the great popular epics that were now beginning to be sung and that were exclusively and peculiarly Serbian, owing nothing to Byzantium.

Neither the political nor the cultural institutions of medieval Serbia had an opportunity to develop to the full. The foreign enemies were too many and Dushan's ambition was too great. Like so many South Slavic rulers, he envisioned himself on the imperial throne in Constantinople, and his vision proved his people's undoing. His conquests were quite impressive. He strengthened his hold on Bulgaria, overran Albania, Macedonia, Thessaly, and Epirus, and proclaimed himself "Tsar of the Serbs and Autocrat of the Greeks." To ensure his success against Constantinople he sought the aid of the Turks, the Italians, and the pope. In 1355 he marched on Constantinople with every hope of success, but on the march he died.

With him died his empire, leaving behind only a memory that was to inspire Serbian patriotism for centuries. His empire broke into fragments because it was too diverse. There were Bulgarians, Italo-Dalmatians, Vlachs, Albanians, and Greeks as well as Serbs. Some were Orthodox Christians, others Catholic, and not a few were Bogomil heretics. Dushan's empire lacked both the time and the cultural tradition needed to fuse, or at least to weld together, these disparate elements.

The collapse of the Serbian empire created a political vacuum in the Balkans, a vacuum that was filled not by a resurgent Byzantium as had happened so often in the past, but rather by the all-conquering Turks, who overran the whole peninsula—even the hitherto invincible Constantinople—and held it in their grip for almost half a millenium. Before turning our attention to the new masters of the Balkans we will pause briefly to view Byzantium in its decline, for this decline and the inability to stage one more recovery, rather than their strength at arms, explain the dazzling successes of the Turks.

EVE OF THE TURKISH CONQUEST

In 1019 Basil the Bulgar-Slayer had captured the last Bulgarian fortress and stood victorious on the Danube. This marked a high point in the fortunes of Byzantium. But within fifty years after the death of Basil, the Normans had overrun the imperial possessions in Italy and the Seljuk Turks had permanently occupied Asia Minor. The latter loss was the more serious, permanently impairing Byzantium's strength. Anatolia in the past had been the great reservoir of manpower for the imperial armies. It had provided Basil the troops with which he had destroyed the Bulgarian empire. Now, with the Turks ruling the area from the Sea of Marmora to the Euphrates, Asia Minor had become instead a dagger pointed at the heart of the empire.

Byzantium was undermined also by a steady economic decline. The loss of the rich Asiatic provinces had deprived the empire of a principal source of tax revenue. Equally serious was the tightening strangle hold of the Italian merchant adventurers upon the commerce of the empire. The refusal of Byzantine capitalists to invest in risky maritime ventures left the Italians in almost complete control of overseas trade. This foothold in Byzantium's economy was extended to ultimately fatal proportions when the Normans attacked Durazzo, the Byzantine fortress on the Adriatic. The attack was repulsed, but only with the help of the Venetian fleet. And the price of this help was a treaty (1082) granting Venetian merchants a quarter in Constantinople and complete freedom from tolls or duties throughout the empire. Later emperors tried to withdraw or reduce these privileges but the Byzantine navy was no match for that of Venice and the grip was maintained. Thus Byzantium was deprived of the duties which contributed so greatly to her revenues, and a hatred was engendered between Greeks and Latins which contributed in no small measure to the final catastrophe.

Such was the situation in the empire when it was faced by the onslaught of the Fourth Crusade. Although organized originally to attack the infidel in Egypt, the Crusade was directed instead against Constantinople on the insistence of the Venetians and the blandishments of the Byzantine pretender. The latter was placed upon the throne with little difficulty, only to be unseated a few months later by a popular anti-Latin uprising. There followed the second siege of Constantinople, the capture of the capital on April 13, 1204, and the three days' looting of this wealthiest of Christian cities.

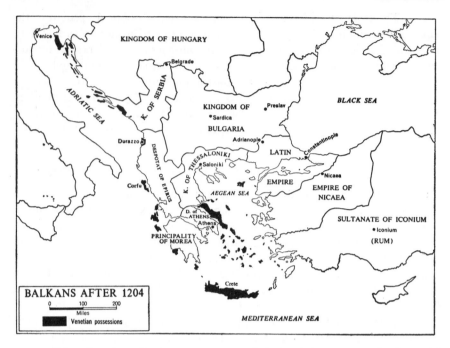

The victorious Latins now set up their feudal states on the imperial ruins. They established a Latin empire at Constantinople, a Latin kingdom at Saloniki, and several Latin states in Greece, of which the most important were the duchy of Athens and the principality of Morea in the Peloponnesus. The commercially minded Venetians rounded out their empire by occupying a whole quarter of Constantinople and annexing numerous islands and ports strategically located on their route to the Levant.

This Latin occupation represents a brief and comparatively unimportant interlude in the history of the peninsula. The new states were doomed from the outset. They received little support from the fanatically Orthodox population, particularly in Constantinople. Furthermore, they controlled only the fringes of the peninsula and were surrounded on all sides by enemies. They faced not only the still formidable Bulgarian and Serbian kingdoms in the northern Balkans, but also several Greek succession states. Of these the most important were the empire at Trebizond on the southern shore of the Black Sea, the despotat of Epirus on the Adriatic, and the empire across the Straits at Nicaea where a member of the deposed dynasty, Theodore Lascaris, had himself crowned by the Patriarch as "Emperor of the Greeks." Under these circumstances the only question was to which one of these states the Latins ultimately would succumb.

The answer was given when the able emperors of Nicaea conquered much of Asia Minor and Eastern Thrace, and became by far the most powerful of the Greek rulers. By skillful diplomacy and force of arms they reduced the Latin empire until only the capital remained. Finally in 1261 the

Latin emperor, together with the Latin Patriarch and the Venetian settlers, fled from Constantinople without resistance. The Nicaean emperor, Michael Palaeologus, made a solemn formal entry into the city, and, amidst popular acclamation, took up his residence in the imperial palace.

The outlook for the restored Byzantine Empire was scarcely more promising than that of its Latin predecessor, despite the ability and diplomatic triumphs of Michael. In Asia it faced the formidable Turks, and in Europe it was surrounded by Latins in Greece, the despotat of Epirus in the West, and the Serbians and Bulgarians in the north. Thus Michael was left with the pitiful remnant of an empire. Confined to a few islands in the Aegean, to the northwestern corner of Asia Minor, and to the insignificant portion of the Balkans between Saloniki and Constantinople, his realm reminds one of post-Versailles Austria. Both states were like shrunken bodies with enormous heads—Constantinople in the one case and Vienna in the other.

To these external dangers were added internal difficulties. Economically the empire was bankrupt. The Italians continued to drain its lifeblood. In the mid-fourteenth century the Genoese quarter in Constantinople was collecting 200,000 solidi annually in customs revenues while the imperial government collected only 30,000. The emperors were reduced to debasing their currency and pawning their crown jewels with Venetian bankers. When they increased taxes to meet state expenses, the rich frequently escaped by judicious bribing, while the poor, already in desperate straits, rose in revolt against the aristocracy of birth and of wealth. The large cities were torn by bloody social strife. In fact, for seven years (1342–1349) Saloniki was virtually an independent republic ruled by revolutionary leaders known as the Zealots. Particularly deplorable was the rapid growth of large estates which absorbed the holdings of the soldiery-peasantry.

Another basic factor in Byzantine decline was the religious issue. Hoping to obtain Western aid against the ever-increasing Turkish menace, the emperors decided on an agreement with the Papacy. In 1439 Emperor John VIII attended the church council of Florence, where he solemnly accepted the supremacy of the pope and the union of the two churches. The concession was in vain. The West gave insignificant aid while the terms of the agreement caused bitter controversy in Constantinople. The Byzantine clergy and the devout masses fiercely rejected any compromise with the hated Latins as a betrayal of Orthodoxy. Even on the eve of the Turkish conquest, for many the pope rather than the Turk was the real enemy. The first minister of the empire was only expressing popular sentiment when he declared that he would rather behold in Constantinople the turban of Mohammed than the tiara of the pope or the hat of a cardinal.

Thus with diminished territory, laboring under financial exhaustion and military weakness, rent by social and religious strife, and battered by Serbs, Bulgars, Latins, and Turks, the Byzantine empire sank slowly into hopeless impotence before the oncoming Turks.

BYZANTIUM IN RETROSPECT

On coming to the end of the Byzantine era we may look back and consider its significance for Balkan history. This may be illustrated by comparing the peninsula over which Justinian ruled in the sixth century with that which the Turks conquered in the fifteenth. When this is done the change that stands out most obviously is in the ethnic composition of the Balkans. In Justinian's day the Greeks, Illyrians, and Thraco-Dacians of antiquity still held their ground in the peninsula. By the fifteenth century the Slavs were in firm possession of a broad belt from the Adriatic to the Black seas. The dispossessed Illyrians were concentrated in present-day Albania and the scattered Thraco-Dacians were reappearing as the nomadic Vlachs of the central highlands and as the Rumanians of the newly emerging trans-Danubian states, Moldavia and Wallachia. This ethnic distribution that took place in the Byzantine period has persisted with slight changes to the present.

The modern culture of the Balkans also had evolved by the fifteenth century through a process of Byzantinization and Christianization. For the South Slavs, and the Albanians and Rumanians for that matter, Byzantium was what Rome had been for the Germans—the great educator, the great initiator, the source both of religion and of civilization. Her missionaries spread the gospel among the barbarians, and with it they brought Byzantine legal ideas, literature, art, trade, and everything else that constitutes a distinctive civilization. During the future centuries of Turkish rule Balkan Christianity contributed to the preservation of Balkan nationality. For the church became the center of national life and the ecclesiastical organization was entrusted by the Turkish overlord with some of the functions of civil government.

Finally, the Byzantine period witnessed the development of the imperial idea in the Balkans, in contrast to the city-state particularism of antiquity. Whereas in the West feudal decentralization, loosely organized monarchies, and imperial illusions prevailed, in the East there came an extreme development of absolute monarchy and of highly centralized imperial bureaucracy. All authority was in and from the emperor. The patriarch, in contrast to the pope, lived in the shadow of the imperial palace. Thus the medieval political institutions of the West laid the basis for the national state system, while those of the East preserved the imperial tradition of Rome and of the Orient, and passed them on to the new Turkish master of the Balkans.

To 1566

Part II. Age of Ottoman Ascendancy

3. Coming of the Ottoman Turks: to 1402

THE EFFECT OF THE TURKS on the development of the Balkans and of the Near East may be compared, generally speaking, with that of the Germans on the development of Western Europe. In the fourth and fifth centuries A.D. successive waves of German barbarians gradually overwhelmed the Western Roman Empire and prepared the ground for that fusion of Germanic, Roman, and Christian elements known as Western civilization. Likewise from the eighth century onward, Turkish tribesmen streamed out of their central Asian homeland into the Near East, overwhelmed the Islamic and Byzantine empires, and eventually founded the Ottoman Empire, with its blending of several Near Eastern cultures upon an Islamic base. In this chapter we shall analyze the factors explaining the success of the Turks, and trace their career of conquests until the beginning of the fifteenth century, when they had gained a firm grip on the Balkan Peninsula.

PRE-OTTOMAN TURKS

Much less is known of the origins of the Ottoman Empire than of the Merovingian and Carolingian kingdoms in the West. The early Turks were too busy with the sword to have time for the pen. Not until the fifteenth and sixteenth centuries, when their empire had been fought for and won, did Turkish chroniclers concern themselves with their early history. By that time fable had taken the place of fact. Of necessity the chroniclers accepted and recorded a mythology of their origins analogous to the Romulus myth of the Romans and the sun-goddess myth of the Japanese. Only in the past few decades have serious attempts been made to lift the colorful veil of legend, but in the absence of reliable records much still remains obscure.

We hear of the Turks first from Chinese sources. They were then the inhabitants, strong and predatory, of the Altai plains in Siberia and Mongolia. By the sixth century A.D. they had established a vast khanate stretching across the continent of Asia as far west as the Sea of Azov. Like most nomadic empires this khanate collapsed almost as soon as it was created, and the various Turkish tribes divided into a western and an eastern branch. The western group, located in Turkestan, was subdued in the eighth century by the Moslem Arabs advancing from the south, and in the following two centuries the Turks adopted the Islamic faith of their conquerors.

The condition of the Islamic world at this point was similar to that of the Roman world when the German tribes were pressing on its borders. The great empire conquered by the crusading Arab disciples of Mohammed in the century following his death (632) had become a hollow shell. Spain and North Africa had seceded from the empire and virulent sectarianism had disrupted the monolithic faith of the Prophet. Faced with this crisis the caliphs of Baghdad turned to the Moslem Turks for support, just as the Roman emperors under similar circumstances had turned to the Germans.

As early as the eighth century the Turks had begun to infiltrate the Islamic Empire. Employed first as mercenaries, they soon became the predominant element in the armies of the caliph. In the tenth century, Mongol pressure in the rear forced more Turkish tribes to move into the empire. It was these newcomers who captured Baghdad in 1055, thereby founding the brilliant though short-lived Seljuk Empire.

These Seljuk Turks reanimated the moribund Islamic world. They united once more the vast territory from the shores of the Mediterranean to the borders of India. They successfully repulsed the attacks of the Crusaders in the Holy Land. Above all, they broke the traditional frontier of Asia Minor along the Taurus Mountains—the frontier that had sheltered Rome and Byzantium for fourteen hundred years. They accomplished this when they defeated the Byzantine army in the fateful battle of Manzikert in 1071. This victory proved a turning point in the history of Asia Minor. Large numbers of Turkish settlers migrated northward in the wake of their victorious soldiers, and the native Anatolian population gradually lost its thin veneer of Greek culture. Between the eleventh and thirteenth centuries the larger part of Anatolia was transformed from a Greek and Christian to a Turkish and Moslem region, and it remains so to the present day. It should be noted that this Turkification of Asia Minor meant that the Turks who later conquered the Balkan Peninsula were far from purely Turkish in ethnic composition. Many were of Greek origin and probably some were Armenians.

In the meantime the Seljuk Empire had disintegrated into a patchwork of independent principalities or sultanates, one of these comprising the newly conquered Asia Minor area. This was known as the sultanate of Rum, by virtue of its former Roman ownership, and also as the sultanate of Konya, after the name of its capital Iconium (Greek) or Konya (Turkish). Thanks to the capture of Constantinople by the Latins in 1204, the Seljuk sultans of Konya were able to add to their domains the ports of Adalia on the Mediterranean and Sinope on the Black Sea. This opened their kingdom to a profitable trade with the Italian city-republics. The resulting riches made possible the development of a brilliant court at Konya, the extraordinarily high culture of which has been revealed by recent excavations.

No sooner did the sultanate of Rum reach its peak than it declined precipitously. The main reason seems to have been the practice of granting hereditary fiefs in return for military services. This led to the development of independent or semi-independent states, especially when the central government was weak. This occurred all too frequently, for the Turks had no tradition of strong autocratic government comparable to that of the Byzantines. The disintegration of the Rum sultanate was completed when the great Mongol conqueror, Genghis Khan, burst into Asia Minor, routed the Seljuk forces in 1243, and temporarily occupied the capital. The great khan did not stop to establish his personal rule. He contented himself with levying tribute and he allowed the Seljuk sultans to remain tributary rulers. But the sultans henceforth lacked even the feeble authority they formerly had possessed.

The disorder was heightened by new bands of Turkish immigrants forced westward by the Mongol invaders. Thus Asia Minor in the late thirteenth and early fourteenth centuries sank into a state of near anarchy, with most of the country controlled by virtually independent local chieftains or emirs. One of these was a certain Osman, memorable in history as the founder of the Osmanli or Ottoman Empire, destined to carry the banner of Islam to the walls of Vienna and to dominate the entire Near East to the twentieth century.

OSMAN: FOUNDER OF THE OTTOMAN EMPIRE

Legend has it that Osman's father, Ertoghrul, led a small company of four hundred and forty-four horsemen with their families across the mountains of Armenia to the Anatolian plateau. There he came unexpectedly upon a battle in which one side was sorely pressed. He rallied his followers to the aid of the losers and won the battle with an impetuous charge. The warrior that he had saved from defeat proved to be none other than the Seljuk sultan himself, who gratefully rewarded Ertoghrul with a grant of land along the Byzantine frontier. The story savors of myth but it is not without interest in that it demonstrates how the nomadic Turkish tribes were establishing themselves at this time throughout Asia Minor. We can well believe that the Seljuk sultan welcomed Ertoghrul and the other Turkish chieftains as allies to resist the pressure of the Byzantines in the west and the Mongols in the east.

Ertoghrul's fief was located on the extreme northwestern fringe of the Seljuk territory, less than fifty miles from the Sea of Marmora and not a hundred miles from Constantinople itself. Here Ertoghrul was to be a Warden of the Marches, to hold his territory for the sultan and to extend it for himself if he could. Hardly had he settled down when the sultan's authority dwindled to the point where the newcomers were virtually on their own. Ertoghrul's son, Osman, is reputed to have declared his independence in 1299, but this could have been nothing more than formal affirmation of patent fact. In the same year Osman took up his residence at Yenishehir, or New City, located halfway between the prosperous Byzantine cities of Brusa and Nicaea. From this strategic base Osman set out upon his career of conquest. Before following his path we need to consider how a small group of comparatively primitive Turkish tribesmen were able not only to capture large walled cities but also to consolidate their domains and organize them into a base for still further expansion.

BASES OF OTTOMAN POWER

The source of Ottoman power still remains obscure in many respects. But one cardinal point stands out clearly. The popular conception of Ottoman power originating in an overwhelming invasion of Asia Minor by hordes of central Asiatic Turks who swept on into the Balkans as single-minded apostles of Islam—all this may be discarded with assurance. The story of Ertoghrul leading his four hundred and forty-four horsemen obviously is related more to the sacred number four than to actual fact. But it does express the popular belief that his orginal followers were a mere handful. This is quite significant. Great Asiatic conquerors like Attila and Genghis Khan won their vast empires at the head of large nomadic armies, but Osman and his successors started with virtually nothing. And yet they accomplished much more. The Osmanli Empire endured to our own times, in contrast to the other Asiatic empires that almost invariably disappeared with their founders. We need to explain, therefore, not the simple and common occurrence of an overwhelming Asiatic invasion, but rather the complex combination of factors that made possible the emergence of a lasting new state out of the remnants of the decaying Seljuk and Byzantine empires.

An important factor was religion. Osman and his successors owed much of their strength to the steady stream of ghazis, or warriors of the faith, who poured in from all parts of Anatolia to do battle against the enemies of Islam. Osman's position near the Byzantine capital attracted an exceptionally large number of these warriors. Whereas the other emirs had consolidated their holdings and stabilized their borders at an early date, Osman was forced to fight much longer and harder to overcome the Byzantine strongholds that he faced. This attracted to him a continuous supply of ghazis, so that although he ruled a domain smaller than those of other emirs, he possessed a disproportionately large striking force. The ghazi hosts not only made possible the early successes against the Byzantine cities in Asia Minor, but also virtually forced Osman's successors to conquests further afield. The ever-increasing numbers of Islamic warriors who were attracted to the expanding Osmanli frontier state had to be kept occupied in some manner. The obvious solution lay across the Straits, where infidel Balkan kingdoms, feeble and divided, promised rich spoils for the ghazis and new glory for the faith.

Another important factor explaining the expansion of the Osmanlis was the unprecedented weakness of the Byzantine defenses in the face of the ghazi onslaught. The imperial outposts in Asia Minor traditionally had been manned by special frontier troops known as akritai. These rough and ready guards originally had defended the empire with great courage and energy, but in later years they had become wealthy and lax. When the Byzantine emperors returned to Constantinople in 1261 they virtually wiped out the akritai by means of taxation and conscription. The latter promptly revolted, and, although they were suppressed, the defense system remained completely disorganized. Henceforth the Byzantine emperors could muster at the most an army of only ten to twelve thousand men, of which a large part was unreliable.

In addition to these military considerations there were important economic factors behind the Osmanli triumph. The late thirteenth and early fourteenth centuries were years of economic and social disintegration in the Byzantine provinces. Most of the land was held by monasteries and absentee landowners. The destitute peasants were driven to acts of lawlessness, raiding the large estates for foodstuffs and sometimes even appropriating land by forceful means. When the Turks appeared, many of these Christian peasants accepted and even hailed them as deliverers from their unbearable lot. And contemporary evidence indicates that the peasants' lot did improve. Anarchy and terror in the countryside gave way to peace and security. In the place of the former absentee landowners was a new class of small farmers who naturally identified their well-being with Turkish rule.

The economic appeal of the Turks probably was heightened by their Akhi brotherhood. This consisted of corporations of craftsmen, devoted to Islam and to the idea of chivalry, and practicing a communal life reminiscent of Christian monasticism. Their golden rule was "put the other man above thyself." The famous Arab traveler, Ibn Battuta, experienced the hospitality of these Akhis when he journeyed through Asia Minor in 1333. "Nowhere in the world," he reported, "will you find men so eager to welcome travellers, so prompt to serve food and to satisfy the wants of others. . . . A stranger coming to them is made to feel as though he were meeting the dearest of his own folk." [1]*

Contemporary Christians must have been impressed by the contrast between this benevolent brotherhood and the institutions and practices within Byzantium. The fact that the Akhi and all the other Turks were Moslems did not influence the Christian Greeks as much as might be expected. In contrast to the nineteenth century, when conflicting nationalist awakenings aroused religious fanaticism in Moslems and Christians alike, the distinctions between the rival religions at this time were blurred to a surprising degree. The Moslem Bektashi order, for example, put little store by doctrinal differences and ceremonial practices, and aimed at the reconciliation of Christianity and Islam. Likewise, not a few shrines in Asia Minor were frequented

* Numbered notes begin on page 847.

indiscriminately by both Christians and Moslems. It may be assumed, then, that many Christians in this period found not only that apostasy was expedient but also that it required only a slight adjustment of their beliefs and practices.

Finally, Turkish expansion was aided by the fact that Osman's principality was situated astride the main routes from Constantinople to central Anatolia. As a result, the Osmanli lands had more intimate contact with the Moslem interior than did the other Anatolian emirates. This in turn ensured a steady supply of ulema or Moslem doctors in law who interpreted the Koran and who assumed the vital role of organizing the administration of the new territories that were being conquered. This ensured order and stability and thereby contributed to the strength and permanence of the rising state.

In the light of these various factors the success of the Osmanlis against mighty Byzantium becomes comprehensible. First they captured Brusa in 1326, when Osman lay on his death bed. Then his son and successor, Orkhan, won the two remaining large Byzantine cities in Asia Minor, Nicaea and Nicomedia, in 1331 and 1337, respectively. None of these cities was taken by assault or by battle beneath its walls. Rather, they were abandoned to their fate by the feeble emperors in Constantinople. The Turks were permitted to settle in the surrounding countryside and to cut off the trade upon which the prosperity of the cities depended. Years went by with no effective relief from Constantinople. In the end the Greek townspeople chose submission as the sole alternative to economic ruin.

ORKHAN PREPARES FOR CONQUEST

Having broken the power of Byzantium in Asia Minor, Orkhan penetrated to the coast, opposite which rose the majestic imperial capital. Before attempting to span the narrow chasm of the Straits, Orkhan paused to consolidate his gains. Being now the ruler of a greatly expanded domain, he dropped the title of emir to assume the more ambitious one of "Sultan of the Ottomans." * In accordance with this new sense of sovereignty he coined money in his own name to take the place of the Byzantine and Seljuk currency hitherto used.

His most important measures had to do with his army. The Osmanli forces heretofore had consisted of volunteer horsemen who served for the duration of a campaign and then returned to their villages. With a rapidly expanding territory and with ambitions for further conquests, a permanent and well-disciplined force was needed. This was achieved by organizing a cavalry militia associated with land tenure. The land was divided into fiefs, the smaller ones known as timars and the larger as ziamets. The holders of these fiefs (timariots and ziams) were obliged to serve in the event of war,

---

* The word "Ottoman" is derived from the Turkish name "Osman," which becomes "Othman" in Arabic. Hence the adjectives "Osmanli" in Turkish, "Othmani" in Arabic, and "Ottoman" in common Western usage.

and to come with their followers, horses, and equipment in proportion to the size of their fiefs.

This resembled the feudal system then prevailing in Western Europe, though with certain important differences. The fiefs were small in extent and were not, as a rule, hereditary. The timariots and ziams owed allegiance to none but their ruler, from whom they directly held their land. And in contrast to the Western European limit of forty days' annual service the timariots and ziams were liable to be summoned for service for any length of time and at any moment. Thus the sultan was assured of a large body of cavalry, dependent entirely upon him for its material welfare, and always ready to march under his banner.

In addition to these feudal levies, Orkhan's successor, Murad I (1359–1389), organized the body of infantrymen known as the janissaries, a term derived from the Turkish "yenicheri" or "new force." In later centuries these janissaries were to win international fame as the scourge of Christendom. The janissary corps consisted of slaves who were either prisoners of war or were bought from slave traders. In order to distinguish them from other troops the slave guards were provided with tall white caps, which later became the distinctive headgear of the janissaries.

Such a body of slave soldiers was by no means uncommon among Moslem rulers at this time. But one feature rendered the janissary corps unique. This was the introduction of the devshirme, or child-tribute, as a means of recruitment. At some uncertain date, probably during the reign of the same Murad I, the Turks began to fill the ranks of the janissaries by forcibly recruiting and training the children of their Christian subjects. This practice, discussed in Chapter 6, probably started as a special levy and then became regularized, with one fifth of the Christian children being recruited every five years.

These military developments converted the nascent Ottoman state into a most powerful engine for war. Orkhan was now ready for expansion, and his line of advance was already foreshadowed. He could hardly strike back into Asia Minor, occupied as it was by Moslem principalities. To have done so would have been to sin against Islam. But to the west was the rich but feeble Byzantine Empire, and beyond it other still weaker Christian states. Not only was the Balkan Peninsula open to invasion, but the whole of Christendom in the fourteenth century was weakened and divided to an unprecedented degree. The Ottomans hardly could have selected a more propitious moment to begin their advance across the Straits into Europe.

STATE OF CHRISTENDOM

The Ottomans were aided in the first place by the paralyzing effect upon Europe of the terrible Black Death. Pestiferous Genoese galleys spread the disease from Black Sea ports to Constantinople in 1347, and in the following year to harbors throughout the Mediterranean. Thence the disease spread all over Western Europe and east to Poland and Russia. In every country whole sections of the population were carried off. The economic and moral effects of this disaster were incalculable. Communications with the Levant were partially cut off, and were not fully resumed until after the Turks were firmly rooted on the European side of the Straits. The plague also contributed much to the outbreak of the Jacquerie in France (1358) and the Peasant Revolt in England (1381). Countries suffering such calamities were not likely to concern themselves with events occurring at the other end of Europe. The following sequence of events suggests some relationship between social fragility in Christendom and Ottoman success in Southeastern Europe: 1354, first Turkish settlement on the Gallipoli Peninsula; 1358, Jacquerie in France; 1381, Peasant Revolt in England; 1389, Serbian defeat at Kosovo; 1514, Peasant Revolt in Hungary; 1523, Peasant Revolt in Germany; 1526, Hungarian defeat at Mohacs; 1529, Turks besiege Vienna.

England and France were also absorbed during these crucial decades in their ruinous Hundred Years' War. The dates of this conflict are significant. It started in 1338, a year after Nicomedia in Asia Minor fell to Orkhan, and it lasted to 1453, when the Ottomans capped their Balkan conquests by taking Constantinople.

Conditions in Italy were equally unpromising. Its two great commercial powers, Venice and Genoa, were interested only in destroying each other and in advancing their trading interests in the Levant. To attain the latter they did not hesitate to sign commercial agreements and even outright alliances with the growing Ottoman power. Likewise the Papacy, which hitherto had been the driving force behind the Crusades against Islam, was at its lowest ebb during these decades. The Babylonian Captivity, the Great Schism, and the Conciliar Movement all diverted the attention of fourteenth-century popes from the growing peril of Islam in the East. Even had circumstances been more favorable, the popes would have been little disposed to rally Western Christendom to the rescue of the Byzantine heretics.

Finally, there was the helpless impotence of Byzantium herself. The destructiveness of the Latin occupation, the hard blows of the Serbian Dushan, the economic strangulation by the Italian merchants, the dynastic conflicts, and the economic distress and social strife—all these ailments, which we noted in the preceding chapter, made it impossible for the empire to rally once more as it had so frequently in the past.

Nor were the other Balkan kingdoms in a more vigorous state. Both the Serbs and Bulgars were wracked by rival pretenders, warring nobles, and deep-rooted social and religious strife. The popularity of the revolutionary Bogomil heresy, a dualistic creed that was widespread in Bulgaria and Bosnia, attests to the social fragility of the South Slav states. According to the testimony of a contemporary opponent of the Bogomils, ". . . they blaspheme the wealthy . . . ridicule the elders, condemn the nobles, regard as vile in the sight of God those who serve the tsar, and forbid all slaves to obey their masters." [2] In this attack we can discern the significance of the Bogomil movement, arising from the common people, led by ordinary parochial priests, and seeking to bring relief and liberation to the oppressed multitudes. Persecuted by the Catholics and the Orthodox churches alike, many of these Bogomils, as will be seen in the next chapter, turned to Islam and welcomed the Turks as their deliverers.

We may conclude that the entire Balkan Peninsula on the eve of the Turkish invasion was socially as well as politically ripe for conquest. In the words of a modern authority, "A feudal society, grinding the peasants, was surprised by the shock [of the Turkish onslaught] and crumbled before it. . . . This social reality explains the ravages and startling successes of the conquerors. . . . The conquest, wiping out the great landholders, was from certain viewpoints, a 'liberation of poor devils.' " [3] Another historian has emphasized this point as follows:

Again and again gifted Serbians, or Bulgarians, or Greeks, who in their own country could not rise from the position in which they were born, found an open way to wealth, honour and power, a path to the saddle of a Beyler Bey (Commander-in-Chief), or to the carpet of a Vizier, and perhaps to the golden cage of one of the daughters or sisters of the Sultan himself! It seems a paradox to say that the Turks opened new horizons to the people of the Balkan Peninsula. Yet their political system, a combination of absolute despotism with the very broadest democracy, had much in it that was novel and acceptable. To the notions of an average Greek, and especially to the notions of an average Serbian or Bulgarian, that system was not more unnatural or more disagreeable than the feudal system which secured all the good things of the world only to the nobles and the priests.[4]

Thus the fabulous successes which awaited the Ottomans become comprehensible. They were due only in part to the strength and single-mindedness of the invaders. More important was the disorganization and division of Western Europe, which precluded a united Christian resistance, and the fatal weakness of the Balkan states themselves, which created a vacuum quickly filled by Ottoman power.

CROSSING TO EUROPE

The Osmanlis first entered Europe not as conquerors or as settlers but as mercenaries. In 1345 an ambitious Byzantine official, John Cantacuzenus, solicited the help of Orkhan to support his bid for the imperial throne. He offered Orkhan the hand of his daughter, Theodora, in return for the services of six thousand soldiers. The offer was accepted, the Ottoman troops crossed the Hellespont, and took part in a campaign that carried them to Adrianople, to the Black Sea, and, as allies of the usurper, into Constantinople itself. Four years later came a second invitation, this time for twenty thousand soldiers to help save Saloniki from Stephen Dushan. Orkhan again responded and his troops, having effected their purpose, once more returned home. Still a third time Cantacuzenus, now engaged in civil war,

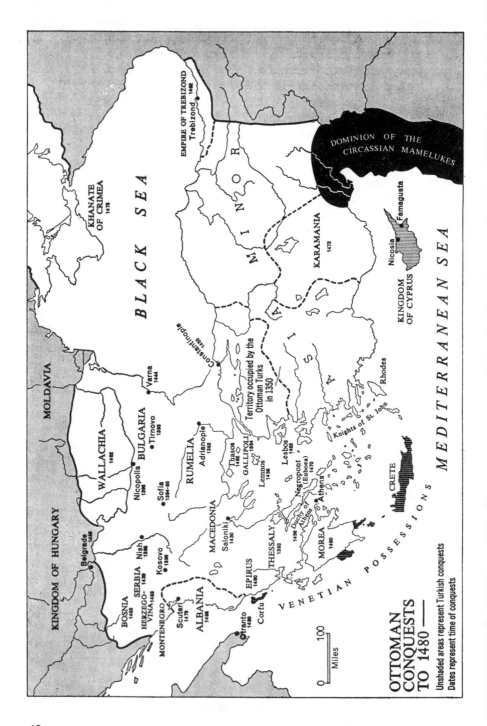

OTTOMAN
CONQUESTS
TO 1480 ——

Unshaded areas represent Turkish conquests
Dates represent time of conquests

MEDITERRANEAN SEA

BLACK SEA

DOMINION OF THE
CIRCASSIAN MAMELUKES

KHANATE
OF CRIMEA
1475

EMPIRE OF TREBIZOND 1462
Trebizond

MINOR

KARAMANIA
1473

Nicosia
Famagusta

KINGDOM
OF CYPRUS

ASIA

Constantinople 1453

Rhodes

Knights of St. John

Lesbos 1462

Thasos 1462

GALLIPOLI 1354

Lemnos 1456

Negropont (Euboea) 1470

Athens

Duchy of
Athens 1456

MOREA 1460

CRETE

VENETIAN POSSESSIONS

Varna 1444

BULGARIA
Tirnovo 1393

Adrianople 1362

RUMELIA

MOLDAVIA

WALLACHIA 1462

Nicopolis 1396

Sofia 1384–85

MACEDONIA
Saloniki 1430

THESSALY 1393

EPIRUS 1480

KINGDOM OF HUNGARY

Belgrade 1456

Nish 1396

SERBIA 1459
Kosovo 1389

BOSNIA 1463

HERZEGO-VINA 1483

MONTENEGRO
Scutari 1479

ALBANIA 1468

Otranto 1480

Corfu

Territory occupied by the
Ottoman Turks
in 1350

0   100
Miles

42

sought the help of the Ottomans, robbing the churches of Constantinople of their plate to pay Orkhan the money he demanded.

Having thus learned of the wealth and attractions of Europe, and also of its disunion and weakness, the Ottomans soon took the next logical step. In 1354 Orkhan's son led a body of troops across the Hellespont, not as mercenaries but as invaders. He seized the city of Gallipoli near the Aegean end of the Straits, where he constructed strong fortifications and stationed a large garrison. Gallipoli now became a strong Ottoman base for further expansion into the Balkans.

Cantacuzenus has fared badly at the hands of historians for his collaboration with the Turks. It is doubtful, however, that his invitations sensibly hastened the coming of the Ottomans. The fact is that had he not called them to Europe, they would have come of their own volition. Furthermore, Stephen Dushan also was seeking an alliance with the Turks, and the Genoese and Venetians likewise were not averse to such a move. Cantacuzenus merely anticipated his rivals, and in doing so he probably delayed rather than hastened the fall of Constantinople. If he had followed a hostile policy toward the Turks, and the latter had retaliated by siding with the Serbs or the Italians, it is unlikely that Constantinople could have held out for another century. As it was, Byzantine diplomacy diverted the Turks against the other Balkan states, and during the following decades Orkhan's successors advanced not against Constantinople, but around the city into the Balkan interior.

MURAD DEFEATS THE SOUTH SLAVS

The next Sultan, Murad I (1359–1389), did not long leave the world in doubt about his intentions. Marching suddenly to the northwest, he overran large parts of Thrace and compelled the emperor to relinquish title to the province. In 1362 he captured Adrianople, the great emporium and fortress commanding the route up the Maritsa Valley into the central Balkans. Significantly enough, he made this European city his capital in place of Brusa in Asia Minor, and it remained the Ottoman capital until the conquest of Constantinople. Thus the Turks established themselves firmly in the Balkans. They entrenched their position by systematic colonization measures, removing large numbers of the native population to Asia Minor and settling Turkish settlers in their place.

The Central European states, whose borders the Turks were approaching, now became alarmed. It was scarcely more than a century since the Mongols had swept through Eastern Europe, overrunning Hungary, Poland, and Germany. And now a new host of Asiatic conquerors was marching on Central Europe from the southeast. At the instigation of Pope Urban V, a crusading army of Hungarians, Serbians, Bosnians, and Wallachians was formed, and in 1364 it set forth to recapture Adrianople. It marched undisturbed to the Maritsa, but there it was surprised by a night attack and cut to pieces.

The Christian defeat on the banks of the Maritsa hastened the fall of Bulgaria. This country was divided politically among three pretenders and religiously by three creeds—Orthodox, Catholic, and Bogomil. It was also harassed from the north by King Louis of Hungary, who aspired to Bulgarian territory under the pretext of the defense of the Catholic faith. The atrocities of Hungarian soldiers and the forceful proselytism of Franciscan missionaries prepared many Bulgarians for willing submission to the Turks as the lesser of two evils. Thus Murad overran the country with little opposition, and compelled its leaders in 1366 to become his vassals.

The Serbians offered stiffer resistance but with no more success. Their great Dushan had died in 1355, and his weak successor was ignored by the nobles, who plunged the country into near anarchy. Nevertheless, the Serbs resolved to stop the Turks in the valley of the Maritsa and marched as far as Chernomen, between Philippopolis and Adrianople. There, at dawn on September 26, 1371, a greatly inferior Turkish force surprised them and slaughtered large numbers. So great was the carnage that the battlefield is still called "the Serbs' destruction."

Macedonia was now at the mercy of the Turks. Kavalla, Drama, and Serres fell into their hands as they marched west to the Vardar. In 1372 they crossed the Vardar and made raids into Bosnia, Albania, and Greece. But these were still raids, not permanent conquests. The Turks next pushed northward into the central Balkans, capturing the key city of Sofia in 1384 or 1385. This opened the route to the Serbian town of Nish, which fell in 1386. But most of Serbia was allowed to remain under its Prince Lazar on the condition that he become vassal to Murad, pay tribute, and furnish troops when demanded. Precisely the same arrangement had been forced upon the Byzantine emperor a few years earlier.

In fact, a definite pattern is discernible in the Ottomans' strategy of conquest. First they established their suzerainty over neighboring rulers, requiring them to pay tribute and to furnish troops when required. Murad's successor, Bayezid I, was the first sultan who took the next step, imposing direct rule by eliminating the native dynasties, dividing the land among his followers, and recording the population and resources into official registers or defterdars. At this point it should be noted that the obligations assumed by the native rulers during the first stage were by no means nominal. Over and over again the Ottomans won victories with the aid of substantial Christian contingents.

This was true of the great battle which in 1389 destroyed the remnants of Serbian independence. Murad had been called to Anatolia by disorders in his Asian domains. Lazar seized the opportunity to combine forces with the king of Bosnia, Tvrtko, for a final bid for independence. In 1388 the two leaders defeated the Ottomans in three successive battles. These victories drew together a coalition of Bosnians, Serbians, Bulgarians, Wallachians, and Albanians. Murad meanwhile had pacified Asia Minor and hurried back with all his forces. He summoned to their duties his south Serbian, Bulgarian, and Albanian vassals, and on June 15, 1389, fought a great battle on the Kosovo Plain near the Serbian-Bulgarian border.

It was the culminating conflict, an irretrievable disaster for the South Slavs. The story of the struggle has become the subject of legend to such an extent that we do not know exactly what happened on the battlefield. Sultan Murad was assassinated during or after the battle by a faithless ally, a deserter, or a wounded soldier. But assassinated he was, and the Ottomans avenged their leader by killing the common prisoners as they captured them and executing Lazar and the other Christian princes after the battle.

To complete the tragedy of the day, Bayezid, on hearing of the death of his father, and his own consequent accession to the throne, gave orders for the immediate murder of his brother Yakub. There was to be no question of the succession to the throne. For the next two centuries it was the settled practice for the sultans, upon their accession, to put to death their brothers and other collaterals lest they should dispute the accession.

BAYEZID THE THUNDERBOLT

Before his accession Bayezid I (1389–1402) had earned by his prowess on the battlefield the title Yilderim or "Thunderbolt." As sultan he lived up to this reputation. During the thirteen years of his rule he firmly established Turkish domination over the Balkans and paved the way for the capture of Constantinople a half century later. Bayezid followed up the great Kosovo victory by forcing Stephen, the successor of Lazar, to sue for peace. The terms agreed upon provided that Serbia should be an autonomous state, recognizing Ottoman suzerainty, paying an annual tribute, and providing a contingent of five thousand soldiers for the use of the sultan. Bayezid calculated that these lenient conditions would assure him Serbian support in future campaigns, and he was not mistaken. In the great battles of Nicopolis against the Western crusaders, and of Ankara against the Mongols, Bayezid had no more loyal soldiers than the Serbians led by Prince Stephen in person.

Having come to terms with Serbia, Bayezid turned his attention to Asia Minor. It is a curious and important fact that the Ottoman Empire at this point was more European than Asiatic. Its greatest extent lay to the west of the Straits and its capital had been moved from Brusa to Adrianople. This westward orientation had been due partly to the strength of the Anatolian emirates, in contrast to the weakness of the Balkan states, and partly to the reluctance of earlier Osmanlis to fight fellow Moslems. The latter consideration was of no concern to Bayezid, and as for military strength, his state now possessed far greater resources than any Anatolian emirate. Accordingly in 1390 he began his conquests in Asia Minor.

It is important to note that the ghazis or warriors of the faith, who had spearheaded the onslaught on the Christian Balkans, were reluctant to participate in a campaign against Moslem states. This was due not only to obvious religious reasons but also to the more mundane consideration that looting and pillaging could not be practiced so freely in Moslem lands. Thus Bayezid was forced to rely mostly on the janissaries and on Serbian and Greek contingents. This use of Christian infidels against Moslem states scandalized the faithful and later boomeranged fatally against Bayezid at a critical stage of his fortunes.

Despite these complications Bayezid had little difficulty in occupying the Aegean coastlands and penetrating into the interior. By 1394 he had overrun Karamania, the leading Anatolian emirate, and also had absorbed by various means several others, thereby extending his frontier to Sivas. His Asiatic domains now were bordered by the weak Christian states, Armenia, Georgia, and Trebizond, and by friendly Moslem kingdoms in Syria and the Tigris-Euphrates Valley. The only menace to the Ottomans was from the aggressive Mongols, who were approaching Asia Minor from the east led by their formidable conqueror Timur the Lame or Timurlane. But Timur at this point turned away from Asia Minor, embarking instead on his whirlwind campaigns through southern Russia, Turkestan, Persia, India, and Syria. Bayezid thus had a respite of seven years, during which time he extended his domain in the Balkans.

The strength and boldness of Bayezid is shown by the fact that while campaigning in Asia Minor he had at the same time overrun eastern Bulgaria and Wallachia and laid siege to Constantinople itself. Eastern Bulgaria hitherto had enjoyed an independent existence, but on July 17, 1393, its capital, Tirnovo, fell to a large Turkish army. This event completed the servitude of the Bulgarian people. Their entire country now was under Ottoman rule.

Although the exact sequence of events is obscure, the latest research [5] indicates that the Turks overran Wallachia following their successes in Bulgaria. Wallachia was a newly formed Balkan state situated on the northern bank of the Danube. Its inhabitants, the Latin-speaking Rumanians, were the descendants of the Daco-Roman stock of the ancient period. After centuries of barbarian invasions and periods of Bulgarian, Hungarian, and Tatar overlordship, the Rumanians had succeeded in the first half of the fourteenth century in forming two principalities, Wallachia along the Danube and Moldavia to the north. It was the ruler of Wallachia, Prince Mircea, that Bayezid defeated on May 17, 1395. Bayezid withdrew after Mircea agreed to pay tribute and to cooperate against the Hungarians. The latter point is important. The Wallachians faced two enemies, the Hungarians as well as the Turks. Of these, the former probably were considered the more dangerous. The kings of Hungary were determined not only to reduce Wallachia to political servitude but also to impose the Catholic faith on its Orthodox population. The Ottomans, in contrast, granted their Bogomil and Orthodox subjects liberty to practice their own rites to an extent inconceivable to pious Catholic rulers. The Turks were also indifferent to the constitution or leadership of their vassal states so long as they paid regularly the tribute of money and men. These considerations helped to explain the ambivalence of Mircea and his Wallachians when the Western crusaders appeared a few years later.

Meanwhile Emperor John V had died in 1391, and his son, Manuel, who had been kept virtual hostage at Bayezid's court, secretly fled to Constantinople, where he was installed on the throne. Bayezid promptly sent an envoy to the new emperor with the following message: "If you wish to execute my orders, close the gates of the city and reign within it; but all that lies outside belongs to me." [6] This was not an idle threat. For four years Bayezid compelled the emperor to do his bidding, even to the point of forcing him to join in the Asia Minor campaigns. Manuel accepted the humiliation in the hope of thereby saving Constantinople. But in the end he realized that appeasement would not suffice and that the sultan aimed at nothing less than the conquest of what remained of the empire. Manuel then decided to break definitely with Bayezid and turned to the West for support. Bayezid in turn sent an army to ravage the Peloponnesus while he himself began about 1395 the first Turkish siege of Constantinople. For nearly eight years he invested the city, until Timur's invasion forced him to march eastward to his doom. Only the weakness of the Ottoman navy, which was unable to cut Byzantine contact with the outside world, enabled Constantinople to survive the ordeal of these years.

NICOPOLIS CRUSADE

Bayezid's conquests were not confined to the Balkans. He also captured the fortresses of Nicopolis, Vidin, and Silistria, thus opening the way into Hungary, while his akinjis, or mounted scouts, spread terror over the Hungarian plains, burning and destroying villages, and carrying off their inhabitants as slaves. King Sigismund of Hungary at first resorted to diplomacy. He sent an embassy to Bayezid to ask by what right he had invaded Bulgarian lands which were ancient possessions of the Hungarian crown. Bayezid led the ambassadors to his arsenal, pointed to Bulgarian weapons hanging on the walls, and replied that so long as he could seize such arms, he had right not only over Bulgaria, but also over Hungary itself.

Sigismund appealed to the Western princes for assistance. He was supported by Pope Boniface IX, who called for a crusade against the infidels. The enthusiastic response, reminiscent of earlier Crusades against the Saracens, was due in part to the growing fear of the Turks, but probably more to the temporary cessation of the Hundred Years' War, which left the undisciplined chivalry of Europe unoccupied and restless.

Nobles and their attendants came from all parts of France, Germany, England, and the Netherlands. In the spring of 1396 they joined the Hungarians at Buda. A part of the Hungarian force marched through the Transylvanian mountains to Wallachia with the intention of forcing the hesitant Prince Mircea to join their ranks. In this they succeeded, and the two forces crossed the Danube near Nicopolis, where they met the main body, which had followed the shorter and easier route down the Danube Valley. Even in Catholic Germany and Hungary the crusaders had behaved disgracefully. When they entered the Balkans they treated the Orthodox peasants as though they were the enemy. The clergy urged the leaders to check the pillaging and debauchery, but the response, as they ruefully observed, was as though they had been talking "to a deaf ass." The whole army, in fact, was in a state of indiscipline and disorder, boastfully contemptuous of the enemy, and spending its time in gambling and in riotous living with the large numbers of courtesans.

For two weeks the crusaders besieged Nicopolis. They did not attempt an assault, being undecided whether they should go further to seek the Turkish army or to await its coming. Bayezid did not leave them long in uncertainty. Summoning his Christian allies he descended upon the crusaders and prepared for battle on the plain before Nicopolis. The two armies were of approximately equal strength, though their numbers remain disputed, estimates ranging from twenty thousand to a hundred thousand on each side.

The Western knights repeated the worst tactics of Crécy and Poitiers. Refusing to heed the advice of Sigismund, who had experience with Ottoman strategy, they charged recklessly against the Turks and to their own destruction. They broke the first line of the enemy but this consisted only of irregulars. When they came upon the veteran and disciplined Ottoman regulars, their energy was spent and their horses were tired. The outcome was inevitable; the proud nobles perished in droves and the remainder were forced to surrender. The Hungarian infantry fared no better, while the Wallachians, seeing how the battle was going, discreetly withdrew from the field without a fight. Only the Hungarian center under Sigismund held out, but its fate was sealed when the Serbians under Prince Stephen came to the aid of Bayezid at a critical moment.

The main body of the Western army fled in utter confusion. Those who escaped across the Danube suffered at the hands of the outraged peasantry as they crossed the Carpathians to Hungary. The prisoners were executed by order of Bayezid in retaliation for the massacre of the Turkish irregulars by the French knights. Only a handful of Christian leaders were spared, for whose release Bayezid later exacted a ransom of 20,000 pieces of gold. Thus ended the ill-fated Nicopolis crusade. Not only was the disaster a humiliation for European chivalry. It sealed the fate of Constantinople, confirmed the grip of the Ottomans upon the Balkans, and prepared the way for their later advance to Buda and Vienna.

TIMUR THE LAME

Bayezid's overwhelming triumph at Nicopolis contributed, ironically enough, to his defeat and death at the hands of Timur a few years later. The explanation is to be found in the very ease with which Bayezid had defeated the Western knights. This so emboldened him, and led him to overestimate his strength so grossly, that he became arrogant and insulting in his relations with the great Mongol conqueror. The result was the outbreak of war between Bayezid and Timur in 1402.

Timur came from a minor Turkish noble family in Turkestan. After long and relentless fighting he restored the vast empire of Genghis Khan. He subdued Central Asia, the Golden Horde in southern Russia, India, Persia, Mesopotamia, Syria, and then turned against the arrogant sultan of the Ottoman Empire. When hostilities began, it soon became apparent that Bayezid's position was not as strong as it seemed to be on the surface. His use of Christian forces against the Anatolian emirates now told decisively against him. A number of the deposed Moslem rulers were to be found in Timur's camp. Also, the local Anatolian levies proved to be unreliable when the final test came with the battle of Ankara in July, 1402. Bayezid placed the inferior Anatolian troops in the front line in accordance with the established Ottoman practice that had proved so successful at Nicopolis and elsewhere. But in this case the tactic proved his undoing. The Anatolians showed no desire to fight for the Ottoman sultan, and being out in front they were able to desert in a body to Timur. Since they comprised a full quarter of Bayezid's army, their defection decided the issue. The Serbian levies fought bravely and loyally for the sultan but to no avail. Timur won an overwhelming victory, capturing Bayezid himself as he attempted to flee.

Timur followed up his triumph by overrunning the greater part of Asia Minor and reinstating the Anatolian emirs who had been dispossessed by the Ottomans. In order to forestall a future resurgence of Ottoman power he gave the Karamania emirate much more territory than it had controlled before. Its new frontiers jutted northward, serving as a barrier between the reduced Ottoman state and the interior of Asia Minor. The unfortunate Bayezid, despairing of the future of his empire, committed suicide in March, 1403, while still in captivity.

It is interesting to speculate how different the course of events might have been if the Nicopolis crusade had not occurred until the time of Timur's victory. Instead of perishing on the Danube, the crusaders might have reached the Straits and ended Ottoman rule in Europe forever. As it was, precisely half a century after Bayezid's suicide, Mohammed the Conqueror was able to realize Bayezid's ambition by taking possession of Constantinople.

4. Conquest of the Balkans: 1403–1481

HE YEAR 1403 marked the nadir of Ottoman fortunes. With Bayezid dead and his sons fighting for the succession, it appeared that Timur had destroyed the rising Ottoman power with one stroke. Yet within a decade the empire was restored and the career of conquest resumed. And half a century later the Turks captured Constantinople, ending the city's millenium of suzerainty over the domains of Byzantium. Mohammed II, the conqueror of Constantinople, then proceeded to establish direct Turkish rule over virtually the entire territory from the Black Sea to the Adriatic, and from the Carpathians to the Aegean. Thus the Balkans came fully and indisputably under Ottoman domination before the end of the fifteenth century.

OTTOMAN RECOVERY

The restoration of the Ottoman Empire following Timur's great triumph was not due entirely to good fortune as is sometimes assumed. Timur's departure from Asia Minor in 1403 and his death in China a few years later certainly aided the Ottoman cause. The Mongol conqueror left nothing behind him, neither an army nor an administration. A power vacuum was created, which the Ottomans quickly exploited to re-establish their authority. But they were by no means able to do so simply by virtue of Timur's death. Other parties might have taken advantage of the situation, including the Westerners who had been defeated at Nicopolis, the Balkan Christians who had only recently been subjected to Turkish rule, and the Karamanians who had been built up by Timur as a counterweight to the Ottomans. The question remains why none of these parties asserted themselves whereas the Ottomans were able to do so.

The answer is to be found in the ghazi domination of the Balkan Peninsula. The warriors of the faith had disapproved of, and refused to participate in, Bayezid's campaigns against the Anatolian emirs and against

Timur. Furthermore, Timur had not crossed the Straits; hence the ghazis remained the unchallenged masters of the peninsula. This explains why Bayezid's defeat and death were not followed by a Western invasion of the Balkans or by an uprising of the Balkan peoples themselves. Thus the ghazis provided the basis necessary for the resurgence of Ottoman power. In fact, they also decided in large measure who was to be the successor to Bayezid.

Of all Bayezid's sons, it appeared at first that the oldest, Suleiman, was to succeed his father. Following the disaster at Ankara, Suleiman was able to escape across the Straits and establish himself at Adrianople. A little later he also secured Timur's approval of his rule of the Balkans. By contrast, his youngest brother, Mohammed, was precariously maintaining a holding in Asia Minor, threatened constantly by both Timur and the Karamanians. Yet in the end it was Mohammed who prevailed and became the sultan of the Ottoman Empire. The reason is that the Balkan ghazis preferred him over Suleiman. The latter was rather effeminate and yielding, as is evidenced by the many concessions that he made to Christian rulers in order to consolidate his position. To the Byzantines he surrendered Saloniki, Thessaly, and certain islands, while to Venice he gave certain ports in Albania and the Peloponnesus.

The ghazis viewed these measures with deep revulsion. As fighters for Islam they wanted a ruler who would lead them against the infidel, not one who yielded territory already conquered. It was this opposition of the ghazis to Suleiman that eventually proved decisive during the internecine war among Bayezid's sons. On February 17, 1411, Suleiman was killed in a battle near Sofia and Bayezid's youngest son succeeded to the throne as Mohammed I (1413–1421).

In view of the circumstances of Mohammed's succession it is not surprising that his reign witnessed the renewal of Ottoman pressure against Christendom. Ghazi hosts once more were let loose on Hungary and Styria. At the same time, however, it was demonstrated that the Turks were not yet ready to meet the Christians at sea. The Turks had been building for some time a naval base and arsenal at Gallipoli. This caused the Venetians much concern because of the threat it represented to the passage of their Black Sea trading fleet. In May, 1416, an unusual concentration of Ottoman warships at Gallipoli led to friction with the Venetians which culminated in a naval battle in which the bulk of the Turkish fleet was captured or destroyed. Mohammed recognized the superiority of the enemy and wisely negotiated an honorable peace. This naval engagement was the prelude to the great maritime wars that were to be fought a few decades later after the Turks had served their apprenticeship at sea.

MURAD II

Mohammed's successor, Murad II (1421–1451), was a stern and aggressive ruler who continued the ghazi tradition. His three decades on the throne were years of continual warfare. By the time of his death he had decisively defeated the European powers, re-established undisputed control over the Balkan Peninsula, and isolated the Byzantine capital so completely that its final downfall no longer could be postponed.

At the time of Murad's accession, the aged Byzantine emperor, Manuel II, withdrew from state affairs in favor of his son, John VIII. The latter lacked his father's experience in dealing with the Turks and rashly decided to support a claimant to Murad's throne. The pretender's revolt failed and Murad determined to avenge the perfidy by capturing Constantinople and putting an end to the troublesome Greek empire. In 1422 he besieged the city closely though without success. The cannon, then used for the first time by the Ottoman army, were not as yet effective against the great walls of the capital, and the Turkish navy was not able to cut off Constantinople from the outside world. The appearance of a new pretender forced Murad to raise the siege and turn to Asia Minor, where he reduced the hostile emirs to complete subjection. On the death of Manuel in 1425, Murad, in lieu of renewing the siege of Constantinople, forced upon Emperor John a new treaty exacting heavy tribute and stripping him of almost every possession beyond the walls of his capital.

Murad now turned his forces against the naval might of Venice. This great commercial power traditionally had been careful to placate the Ottomans for fear of jeopardizing its trade interests in the Levant, especially the vital grain supply from the Black Sea region. In pursuance of this policy Venice had negotiated a commercial agreement with the Turks as early as 1388. It had also refrained from committing itself to any anti-Turkish coalition, a precaution which had drawn upon it the denunciation of Christendom, particularly during the Nicopolis crusade. At this time, however, Venice was forced to stand firm against the Turks. The growing sea power of the Ottoman Empire and its steady advance into Albania and toward the Adriatic coast confronted the Venetians with the nightmarish prospect of Turkish control of the Otranto Strait. To forestall such an eventuality the Venetians extended their coastal possessions in Albania and the Peloponnesus, and in 1423 gained control of the great Macedonian outlet, Saloniki.

This large city had been governed by one of Emperor John's brothers who, realizing that he could not hold it against the Turks, handed it to the Venetians with the stipulation that they would "protect and nourish it, raise its prosperity, and make it a second Venice." But Saloniki remained Venetian for only seven short years. The Turks refused to tolerate an Italian outpost in Macedonia and started a naval campaign against Venetian establishments throughout the Aegean. The Ottoman navy was now shown to have caught up with and surpassed the Venetian in the decade since the defeat of Mohammed's fleet at Gallipoli. Venice was also handicapped by a war which broke out with Milan. The Turks thus were able to ravage the Venetian stations in the Aegean, capture Saloniki in 1430, and force Venice to sue for peace.

Having disposed of the Venetians, Murad proceeded to settle accounts with the Hungarians. First he invaded Serbia, whose prince, George Brankovich, had attempted to assert his independence by seeking the support of the Hungarians and ceding to them the fortress of Belgrade. After a brief campaign in 1439 Serbia was once more a Turkish province and Brankovich a refugee across the river in Hungary.

A new figure now arose to check for a time the Ottoman advance. John Hunyadi was a Rumanian who had entered the service of Hungary and fought with such success against the Turks that he became a Hungarian national hero. The "white knight of Wallachia," as he was called on account of his silver armor shining in the van of battle, became a master of frontier warfare and for twenty years was the terror of the Ottoman armies. In fact, he might be described as a Christian ghazi, dedicated to fighting against the hosts of Islam. He began his victorious career when, following his appointment as governor of Transylvania in 1441, he defeated the Turks several times on the slopes of the Carpathians and in the neighborhood of Belgrade. These victories aroused great enthusiasm in Europe and inspired another crusade to drive the Ottomans back to Asia.

VARNA CRUSADE

Pope Eugenius tried to mobilize Christendom against the Turks but the usual dynastic rivalries prevented a united effort. In the end a coalition was formed led by Vladislav, king of Hungary and Poland, and including Prince Vlad of Wallachia, the exiled Brankovich of Serbia, and a considerable number of French and German knights. Though nominally led by Vladislav, the Christian host actually was under the command of the renowned Hunyadi. In 1443 he took the offensive, defeated two Turkish armies in Serbia, captured Nish, crossed the Balkan range in winter, and advanced to Sofia. By January his supplies had run short, so he returned to Buda to display his trophies and receive a conqueror's triumph.

Murad decided to come to terms with the Christians because the Greeks in the Peloponnesus had revolted, the Albanians were also up in arms, and trouble had broken out in Asia Minor. Accordingly he signed a ten-year truce in June, 1444, in which he recognized the independence of Serbia and abandoned Wallachia to Hungary. Having secured peace with these concessions, Murad left the Balkans to campaign in Asia Minor. The Hungarians noted that Murad was absent and that only about seven thousand Turkish troops were left in Thrace. So, with the encouragement of the pope, they broke the truce and resumed the crusade. The Hungarians planned to march quickly through the Balkans while the Venetians prevented the Turks from recrossing the Straits and the Greeks made diversionary attacks in the Peloponnesus.

Only the Greeks fulfilled their task and for this they later paid a heavy price. The Venetians were prevented by unfavorable winds from sealing the Straits, and Murad was able to bribe the Genoese to transport his army to the European shore on barges. Meanwhile the Hungarians and their allies started their advance later than planned and without the support of Brankovich, who was unwilling to risk his newly regained throne. The reduced Christian army invaded Bulgaria, descended the Danube to the coast, and thence marched to Varna. There they were confronted by a superior Turkish army led by Murad, who had hastily returned from Asia Minor. The ensuing battle, on November 10, 1444, was a repetition of Nicopolis. Despite their inferior numbers the Christians at first had the advantage. But in the end the Turks won out because of their greater discipline. King Vladislav, less fortunate than Sigismund, perished on the battlefield, while Hunyadi saved himself only by ignominious flight.

The Varna battle stands out prominently in the history of Turkish-Western relations. It shattered the belief of the Christians that they were capable of driving the Turks back into Asia. Christian princes took the defeat as a judgment of God against Vladislav for having broken the peace. The Varna crusade represented the last attempt of Western Europe to rescue the sinking Byzantine Empire. Now Constantinople was left to its fate. Meanwhile the Turks encased Vladislav's head in a barrel of honey and sent it to Brusa, where it was stuck on a pike and carried jubilantly in the streets. In the month in which the Varna battle was fought, Murad retired from the throne as he had done several years earlier for a brief period, and went to a luxurious retreat in Asia Minor to spend his remaining days.

In August, 1446, he returned to the throne for reasons that remain obscure. At once he swung into action as of old. First he invaded the Peloponnesus and compelled its Greek princes to become his vassals. Then in 1448 he again defeated Hunyadi on the same field of Kosovo where in 1389 Murad I had subdued the Serbians. In contrast to the first Kosovo battle, the Serbians under their wily Prince Brankovich now refused to join Hunyadi and remained neutral. This cautious policy earned Serbia a few more years of precarious autonomy, though it did not prevent the final annexation of the country by the next sultan.

Only in distant Albania did Murad fail to impose his rule. There a primitive pastoral people, under the inspired leadership of their great national hero, George Kastriotis—more commonly known as Skanderbeg—fought a fierce and successful guerrilla warfare against successive Ottoman armies.* In fact, Skanderbeg was on his way to join forces with Hunyadi when the latter was defeated by the Turks at Kosovo. Despite this setback, Skanderbeg was able to hold his own in the mountains of his native land.

Murad's failure in Albania was trivial in comparison with his outstanding accomplishments elsewhere. He more than held his own against the naval might of Venice. He firmly buttressed the Danube frontier with his victories at Varna and Kosovo. And he left Constantinople completely surrounded by Turkish territory, without hope of relief from any quarter.

* See pages 496-501.

MOHAMMED'S PREPARATIONS

The new sultan, Mohammed II (1451–1481), was determined that the imperial prize that awaited him on the shores of the Bosphorus should not elude him as it had his forebears, Bayezid I and Murad II. Contemporary travelers described Constantinople as a city still awe-inspiring with its splendid imperial traditions, still impressive with its tiers of mighty fortifications, but with negligible inner resources to maintain this glittering façade.

It is very strong walled in a way that is a marvel to see. . . . the walls are very high and are made of great marble blocks bound together. . . . The city is sparsely populated. . . . The inhabitants are not well clad, but sad and poor, showing the hardship of their lot. . . . The Emperor's Palace must have been very magnificent, but now it is in such a state that both it and the city show the evils which the people have suffered and still endure. . . . properly regarded, he [the Emperor] is like a Bishop without a See. . . . I believe that God has spared it [Constantinople], more for the holy relics it contains than for anything else.[1]

Mohammed was not a man to be deterred by either holy relics or marble walls. During the winter 1452–1453 he made elaborate preparations for the siege. In 1452 he completed the Rumeli Hissar, or Castle of Europe, at a narrow point on the Bosphorus north of Constantinople and opposite the older Anadol Hissar, or Castle of Asia. This assured freedom of passage between Anatolia and Europe, and closed the Bosphorus to Constantinople. Mohammed also had the services of a certain Urban, of Hungarian or Wallachian origin, who cast for him enormous bronze bombards firing stone balls thirty inches in diameter. Mohammed was the first sovereign in history to possess a real park of artillery: fourteen batteries consisting of thirteen great bombards and fifty-six smaller cannon. These were dragged by oxen to Constantinople, where they played a decisive role in the battle. Mohammed's army is estimated at roughly a hundred and fifty thousand, the core being the formidable janissaries, who at that time were recruited exclusively from Christian families. In addition to the janissaries and the regular levies from the European and Asiatic territories, there were about one hundred thousand irregulars and camp followers eager for the sack of the city.

This was the force that faced the hitherto impregnable walls of Constantinople. The city is built in the shape of a triangle, bounded on the north by its harbor, the Golden Horn, on the south by the Sea of Marmora, and on the west by the plains extending to the foothills of Thrace. On all sides the city was protected by a massive wall which was strongest on the land frontage, where three walls rose in successive tiers. The outer wall was a breastwork surmounting a moat some forty feet wide and fifteen feet deep. The second wall was twenty-five feet high, the third forty feet, and each of these was furnished with towers capable of sheltering considerable numbers of soldiers. Between these walls were enclosures sixty feet broad, in which the defending forces could assemble their arms and supplies and march from one section to another. These powerful fortifications, built by Emperor Theodosius II in the fifth century, had protected the city through twenty sieges. But now, two factors tipped the scales for the first time against the defenders: the artillery of the Ottomans and the unprecedented weakness of the Greek forces.

The capital's population by this time had sunk to about sixty to seventy thousand. Of this number some five thousand were ready to bear arms against the Turks. Emperor Constantine's appeal to Europe produced few recruits. In the hope of winning the support of Western Christendom, earlier emperors on three separate occasions had agreed to the submission of the Orthodox Church to the pope (Unions of Lyons, 1274; Rome, 1369; and Florence, 1439). But each agreement for union proved meaningless in the face of the undying hatred of the Orthodox Greeks for the Catholic Latins— a hatred intensified by the barbarities of the Fourth Crusade and the merciless strangle hold of the Italian merchants. At this time, therefore, the pope's reply to the emperor's plea was to send Cardinal Isidore to Constantinople with a total of two hundred soldiers. When the cardinal arrived he proceeded to St. Sophia, the great church of the Orthodox world, where he read a solemn promulgation of the union dictum of the Council of Florence and celebrated the union liturgy, including the name of the pope. This so agitated the populace that it raised the cry "Better Islam than the pope"—a bitter and defiant answer to the Latins' "Better Islam than schism." This exchange had often been heard before, but this time Islam was at the gates, ready and able to accept the invitation.

The papal contingent was followed by others from Italy and Spain, the most important being seven hundred Genoese under Giovanni Giustiniani, a brave and experienced soldier of fortune who proved to be the main support of Constantine. The total force available for the defense of the city amounted to no more than eight thousand, a number totally inadequate to man the series of walls and to repair the breaches pounded by the enemy cannon. Yet Constantine proceeded with the defense of the city with a courage, energy, and devotion worthy of a last emperor of thousand-year-old Byzantium. He collected supplies from the neighboring countryside, strengthened the walls which had been badly repaired by fraudulent contractors, and called on his subjects to fight for the faith and for the "city protected by God."

FALL OF CONSTANTINOPLE

On April 2, Easter Monday, the Turkish guns were dragged near the edge of the moat and amidst the beating of drums and the shouting of thousands of excited men the first mass bombardment in history began. It was a slow affair, the great bombards requiring two hours to load and firing only seven times a day. The huge balls gradually tore breaches in the ancient walls, and on April 18 Mohammed ordered an assault down the Lycus Valley at approximately the mid-point of the land walls. Giustiniani was in com-

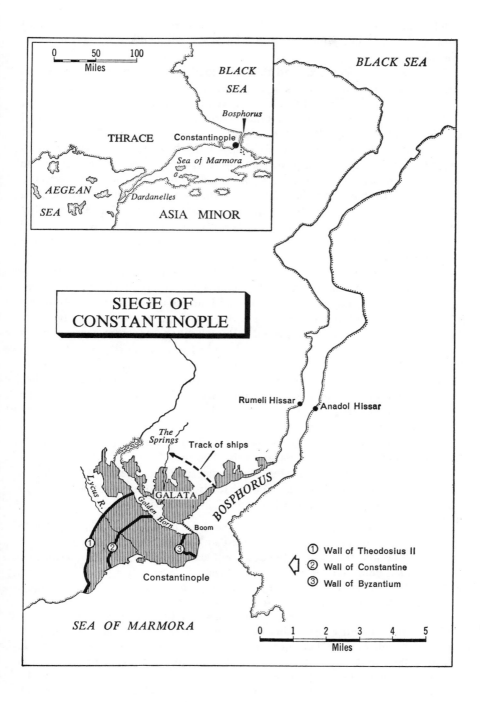

SIEGE OF
CONSTANTINOPLE

BLACK
SEA

Bosphorus

THRACE   Constantinople

Sea of Marmora

AEGEAN

SEA   Dardanelles

ASIA MINOR

0   50   100
Miles

BLACK SEA

Rumeli Hissar   Anadol Hissar

The
Springs   Track of ships

Lycus R.

GALATA

Golden Horn

BOSPHORUS

Boom

① Wall of Theodosius II
② Wall of Constantine
③ Wall of Byzantium

Constantinople

SEA OF MARMORA

0   1   2   3   4   5
Miles

mand at this critical sector and, with a withering fire from harquebuses, wall guns, bows, and catapults, he swept back the attackers after a four-hour struggle.

Two days later occurred the only good fortune which the Christians experienced during the whole siege. Three large Genoese ships and an imperial transport, loaded with soldiers and munitions, gallantly fought their way to the Golden Horn through a mosquito fleet of a hundred and fifty small Turkish ships. The spirits of the defenders soared high and for a moment they imagined the city was saved. Two days later they beheld an extraordinary and terrifying spectacle: Turkish ships were riding in the upper part of the Golden Horn despite the heavy boom which still held firm at the mouth. Mohammed, probably on the advice of Italian engineers, had constructed a wooden runway from the Bosphorus to a stream called The Springs that flowed into the Golden Horn. Some seventy or eighty ships were dragged over the greased planks by oxen, slipped quietly into the stream, and floated down into the harbor in the rear of the boom.

This stratagem forced the Greeks to stretch their thin lines still further to man the menaced sea wall. Meanwhile the bombardment had continued unabated, and Mohammed ordered an assault about the Romanus Gate on May 7 and again on May 12. Both were beaten back by Giustiniani with great slaughter. These repeated failures and the constant rumors that a Hungarian army was nearing Constantinople from the north and the papal fleet from the south led the Turks to lose heart. Moreover, their overwhelming numerical superiority was creating a serious supply problem. Unless they could win the city by the end of the month they would have to abandon the siege as so many other armies before them had been forced to do in the past. Even Mohammed grew doubtful and, failing to induce the emperor to surrender the city on terms, he summoned a council of war on Sunday, May 27, to ascertain the opinions of his generals. The grand vizir, Khalil Pasha, declared in favor of abandoning the siege, whereupon a general, Zagan Pasha, replied with a speech that described perfectly why Constantinople was even now a doomed city despite the heroism of its defenders.

Thou, O Padishah, knowest well the great dissensions that are raging in Italy especially, and in all Frankistan [Christian Europe] generally. In consequence of these dissensions the Giaours [infidels] are incapable of united action against us. The Christian potentates never will unite together. When after protracted efforts they conclude something like a peace amongst themselves, it never lasts long. Even when they are bound by treaties of alliance, they are not prevented seizing territories from each other. They always stand in fear of each other, and are busily occupied in intriguing against each other. No doubt they think much, speak much, and explain much, but after all they do very little. When they decide to do anything, they waste much time before they begin to act. Suppose they have even commenced something. They cannot progress very far with it because they are sure to disagree amongst themselves how to proceed. . . . Therefore, O Padishah, do not lose hope, but give us the order at once to storm the city! [2]

Mohammed was won over and he ordered a simultaneous assault on the land and sea walls for Tuesday, May 29. The main attack was to be in the Lycus Valley about the Romanus Gate, where the middle wall was practically leveled for a length of four hundred yards and the moat partly filled by the debris of the wall and by fascines. The attack was to be pressed without let or pause, night and day, until the defenders were so exhausted that the final assault would prevail. Mohammed further proclaimed to his troops that when the city was captured it would be given up to them to sack at their will for three days. They received this with tumultuous shouts of delight and awaited impatiently the order to advance.

Very different was the atmosphere within the doomed capital. A few days earlier a small scout ship had slipped into the harbor with the report that there were no signs of the promised papal fleet. This news shattered the last hopes of the weary defenders, now reduced to a bare four thousand. In the midst of the gloom the emperor maintained his courage and dignity. At the close of a religious procession through the streets he exhorted his people to remember that they were "the descendants of the heroes of ancient Greece and Rome" and to so conduct themselves that their memory would be as glorious as that of their ancestors. On Monday evening a solemn service was held in St. Sophia, memorable as the last Christian service before its conversion into a mosque. One who was present wrote, "If a man had been made of wood or stone, he must have wept at the scene."

In preparation for the attack the emperor decided to concentrate his remaining forces in the enclosures between the inner and middle walls. When the men had taken their posts the great gates of the inner wall were closed and locked. There was to be no retreat. Either the Turks would be repulsed or the defenders annihilated.

The attack began between one and two o'clock Tuesday morning. First came the irregulars, the least skilled of the army, to exhaust the strength and munitions of the besieged. After they had suffered heavy losses Mohammed withdrew them and sent forth the Anatolian infantry. Some broke into the enclosure but were driven back by the defenders led by Giustiniani. Mohammed now personally led the final attack with the elite of his army—the twelve thousand janissaries supported by archers, lancers, and picked infantrymen. They tore at the stockades, but the defenders fought back stubbornly and held their ground. At this crucial moment Giustiniani was gravely wounded and one of the gates of the inner wall was opened to allow him to be carried out. With him departed some of his Genoese soldiers. This loss caused confusion and dismay, which the experienced eye of Mohammed quickly perceived. He shouted to his troops, "We have the city! It it ours! The wall is undefended!" They rushed the stockade and fought their way into the enclosure. The emperor, seeing that all was lost, threw himself into the melee and died fighting. The Greek and Italian soldiers, trapped between the walls, were massacred to a man. The Turks now made their way easily through the undefended inner wall and the promised three-day sack began.

AFTERMATH

In this moment of triumph Mohammed showed himself to be a statesman as well as a conqueror. Had he so wished he could have destroyed Constantinople and massacred its citizens, as the Mongols had done repeatedly with even more populous cities. This, in fact, would have been in accord with the precepts of Islam for a city that had resisted to the end. But after the three days of merciless pillage and murder, which was the custom of the time and probably not as destructive as the handiwork of the Christian crusaders in 1204, Mohammed firmly restored order. He had decided to make his prize the capital of his empire and did not wish to be left with a hollow shell.

He set about immediately to repeople the city, whose numbers for long had been dwindling during the decline of the empire. Many citizens who had fled before and after the siege returned on the promise of protection to their property and religion. Thousands were deported en masse from Serbia, Albania, and Greece to repeople Constantinople. Thousands more arrived in the following decades as slaves, prisoners of war, religious refugees from the West, and voluntary immigrants attracted by the opportunities in a flourishing and expanding capital. Thus the ancient city experienced not extinction but rejuvenation, its imperial borders expanding suddenly from its own battered walls to the Danube River and the Taurus Mountains.

Mohammed was equally farsighted in matters of religion. The attitude expressed in the cry "Better Islam than the pope" had been his powerful ally in the taking of the city and he wisely resolved to nourish it further. He selected an eminent Greek clergyman, Gennadius, to be the Patriarch of the Orthodox Church and he assured him "all the privileges of your predecessors." * He exempted the clergy from taxes, allowed the church full autonomy in its administration, and permitted religious services to be freely celebrated. He even paid repeated visits to the new patriarch, discussed theology with him, and requested him to write a tract on Christianity. This toleration, so far ahead of current practice in Western Christendom, was not youthful romanticism but enlightened statesmanship. By satisfying the religious aspirations of his non-Moslem subjects he had perpetuated the schism between Western and Eastern Christianity and assured himself the stable rear necessary for the further conquests he planned.

The fall of Constantinople shocked Christian Europe, particularly since Mohammed had been considered a weakling because he had permitted his father to depose him. A chorus of lamentation arose in the West, even though little had been done to avert the loss. Many schemes for driving the infidel back to Asia were propounded during the following decades. Constantinople and Greece now took the place of Jerusalem and the Holy Land as the objectives of the proposed crusades. Successive popes sought to arouse

* See Chapter 7 for a discussion of the Patriarchate of Constantinople under the Ottoman Empire.

Christendom, and a series of diets or congresses met to organize expeditions, but all to no avail. By the mid-fifteenth century the state of European society no longer was propitious for a revival of the crusades. Pope Pius II realistically depicted the contemporary Christian world in his well-known letter written in 1454:

> People neither give to the Pope what is the Pope's, nor to the Emperor what is the Emperor's. Respect and obedience are nowhere to be found. Pope and Emperor are considered as nothing but proud titles and splendid figureheads. Each State has its particular Prince, and each Prince his particular interest. What eloquence could avail to unite so many discordant and hostile powers under one banner? And if they were assembled in arms, who would venture to assume the general command? What tactics are to be followed? What discipline is to prevail? How is obedience to be secured? Who is to be the shepherd of this flock of nations? Who understands the many utterly different languages, and is able to control and guide the varying manners and characters? What mortal could reconcile the English with the French, the Genoese with the men of Aragon? If a small number go to the Holy War they will be overpowered by the infidel, and if great hosts proceed together, their own hatred and confusions will be their ruin. There is difficulty everywhere. Only look at the state of Christendom.[3]

Some Westerners hoped that the possession of the great imperial prize would satisfy and preoccupy the youthful sultan and turn his thoughts from further conquests. This was soon proved to be an illusion. Mohammed considered the taking of Constantinople the beginning rather than the end of his career. He viewed himself the heir of Byzantium and he resolved to reclaim what Byzantium had possessed in its prime and lost in its decline. The princes of Serbia, Bosnia, and the Peloponnesus had hastily offered their submission to him following the capture of Constantinople. But Mohammed was not content with this prevailing system of vassal states paying tribute and retaining their autonomy. He decided upon the complete and direct subjection of the entire Balkan Peninsula, and after that, he would deal with the European powers that had poached upon the preserve of declining Byzantium.

MOHAMMED SUBJUGATES THE BALKANS

Bulgaria had been incorporated as a province of the Ottoman Empire half a century earlier, and Mohammed now set out to reduce Serbia to a similar status. Before the siege of Constantinople he had humored the Serbian prince, George Brankovich, and assured him his autonomous status, but now Mohammed claimed the country through his stepmother, a Serbian princess. No sooner had he set siege to some Serbian fortresses than the Hungarians, alarmed for their own safety, came to the aid of the Serbs. John Hunyadi, the veteran enemy of the Turks, renewed his raids into the central Balkans, using Belgrade as his base. In June, 1456, Mohammed gathered his army and dread artillery before Belgrade, boasting that within a fortnight the town would be his. But Hunyadi, with the assistance of a fiery Franciscan friar, John of Capistrano, led an army of peasant crusaders through the Turk-- ish lines into the beleaguered city. Not only did they repulse the repeated assaults but, in a bold sortie, they charged to the mouths of the enemy can- non and broke the Turkish lines. Mohammed himself was wounded in the struggle and retreated in disorder to Sofia. Pestilence now broke out in the Hungarian camp, taking the lives of both Hunyadi and Capistrano and pre- venting the victors from following up their advantage. Belgrade was saved for Hungary but Serbia was doomed. The aged Prince Brankovich died late in 1456 and the ensuing dynastic strife, complicated by Catholic-Orthodox rivalry, left the country open to the Ottomans. By the summer of 1459 all Serbia, excepting Belgrade, had become a Turkish pashalik.

To the west of Serbia lay two other Slavic kingdoms, Bosnia and Herzegovina, which now attracted the attention of Mohammed. The Slavic tribes that had settled in these territories were constantly pressed by powerful neighboring states—Hungary, Croatia, Venice, and Serbia. Occasionally the Bosnians and Herzegovinians had been able to win a few years of independ- ent existence. More frequently they were forced to acecpt the suzerainty of one or another of their neighbors. Another important factor in the history of these peoples was the prolonged conflict over religion. Being situated on the frontier between Orthodox and Catholic Christianity, the Bosnians and Herze- govinians were torn between the two creeds. In contrast to the Serbs, who were located in the central Balkans and were solidly Orthodox, the people of Bosnia-Herzegovina never allied themselves permanently with either the pope or the patriarch. Many of them, instead, became ardent Bogomils. We have seen that Bogomilism was not only a heresy akin to that of the Albigen- sians in the West and the Paulicans in the East, but also a revolutionary movement of social protest. Hence the fierce persecution to which the Bogo- mils were subjected by both the Western and Eastern churches. In 1325 Pope John XXII wrote thus to the king of Bosnia:

> To our beloved son and nobleman, Stephen, Prince of Bosnia,—knowing that thou art a faithful son of the Church, we therefore charge thee to exter- minate the heretics in thy dominion, and to render aid and assistance to Fabian, our Inquisitor, forasmuch as a large multitude of heretics from many and divers parts collected hath flowed together into the principality of Bosnia, trusting there to sow their obscene errors and dwell there in safety. These men, imbued with the cunning of the Old Fiend, and armed with the venom of their falseness, cor- rupt the minds of Catholics by outward show of simplicity and the sham assump- tion of the name of Christians; their speech crawleth like a crab, and they creep in with humility, but in secret they kill, and are wolves in sheep's clothing, cover- ing their bestial fury as a means to deceive the simple sheep of Christ.[4]

The Bosnian rulers enforced the pope's injunction to the full. Forty thousand Bogomils fled from Bosnia to neighboring countries, and others who did not succeed in making their escape were sent in chains to Rome. But this violent persecution did little to diminish the strength of the heretics. Instead, it caused them to look for relief to the Turks, especially since the latter proclaimed themselves the champions of the poor as against the native Balkan aristocracy which they consistently and ruthlessly exterminated. In a letter written in 1463 by Stephen, the last king of Bosnia, to Pope Pius II, we find these remarkable words: "The Turks promise freedom to all who side with them, and the rough mind of the peasants does not understand the artfulness of such a promise, and believes that such freedom will last forever; and so it may happen that the misguided common people may turn away from me, unless they see that I am supported by you." When Mohammed did invade Bosnia, Stephen's fears proved all too justified. The Bosnian peasantry refused to take up arms against the Turks, saying, "It is not our business to defend the king; let the nobles do it." [5] By the end of 1463 Bosnia had become another Ottoman dominion and twenty years later the same fate befell Herzegovina.

This conflict of religions is important in explaining not only the easy triumph of the Turks but also the later history of the South Slavs. With the establishment of Ottoman rule the majority of the peasants accepted Islam. Contemporary travelers almost invariably remarked that about three fourths of the population of Bosnia-Herzegovina was Moslem and the remainder Catholic or Orthodox. The Slav nobles also accepted conversion as a means of retaining their lands and feudal privileges. Thus Bosnia-Herzegovina, in contrast to Serbia, presents the curious phenomenon of a ruling landholder class, Slav by race yet Moslem by religion. These landholders, or beys, became in the course of generations more fanatical than the Turks themselves. The peasants, as we shall see later, became predominantly Orthodox during the eighteenth and nineteenth centuries, while their nobles remained aggressively Moslem. This explains why the Serbian nationalist awakening in the nineteenth century could develop only in Serbia proper where the population, being solidly peasant and Orthodox, had both social and religious unity. In contrast, Bosnia-Herzegovina, with its Moslem Slav ruling caste and its Christian Slav peasantry, remained a stronghold of Turkish power long after Serbia had regained its freedom.

Returning to the days of Mohammed, we find him next in another Serbian land, where a totally different reception awaited him. Serbia, Bosnia, and Herzegovina had fallen, but Montenegro, a barren and mountainous natural fortress, successfully defied the Moslem hosts in this dark hour of Serbian history. Stephen Crnojevich, the founder of Montenegro, had spent his life defending his country against Mohammed's father, Murad. His son, Ivan the Black, continued the struggle with indomitable spirit. When his position became impossible with the fall of Bosnia in the north and Albania in the south, he went up to lofty Cetinje, which thereafter remained the capital of his people. There, he and his descendants established a tiny mountain commonwealth which the Turks often invaded but never permanently conquered.

In Albania, also, Mohammed met with a resistance typical of a united mountain people. Albania in the preceding century had formed a part of Dushan's Serbian empire. Upon his death in 1355 all central authority disappeared and the country fell under the control of local chieftains. At the same time a feudal social system was developing, particularly in the coastal areas. In fact, serf revolts broke out in 1343 and 1351 because of the heavy exactions of the lords. But this social cleavage was not so widespread and acute as to leave the country divided when the Turkish invaders appeared. On the contrary, a remarkable unity and steadfastness was shown under the inspired leadership of the famous chieftain, George Kastriotis, popularly known as Skanderbeg.

Skanderbeg organized in 1444 a League of Albanian Princes which pooled resources and manpower for the resistance struggle. With this support Skanderbeg built fortresses throughout the countryside and also organized an extremely mobile defense force. When the Turks attacked they found it necessary to disperse their troops because of the scattered fortresses. This left them vulnerable to the hit-and-run tactics of the Albanians, who could move more swiftly about the mountainous terrain than the more heavily armed Turks. Skanderbeg also received some assistance from Venice, Naples, and the Papacy. Thus he was able to repulse thirteen invasions between the years 1444 and 1466. Only after his death in 1468 were the Turks able to conquer Albania. In the following centuries the majority of the Albanians accepted Islam and, together with the Bosnian Moslems, they became the bulwark of Turkish power in the western Balkans.

In Greece there was neither the leadership nor the will to resist. The Duchy of Athens, which was held by a Florentine merchant family, surrendered to the Turks in 1456. The ancient Parthenon, originally a pagan temple and later the Church of the Holy Virgin, now was turned into a mosque. Further to the south, in the Peloponnesus, utter anarchy prevailed. Thomas and Demetrius, the worthless brothers of the gallant Emperor Constantine, were heedlessly fighting each other for supremacy. Thus Mohammed's army met with little opposition as it passed through the Peloponnesus, besieging and capturing the petty strongholds. By 1460 the sultan possessed the whole area with the exception of a few seaports in the hands of the Venetians. The last spark of Greek independence had passed away, and for almost half a millenium the sons of the ancient Hellenes were to remain under the rule of the Turk.

It remains to speak of the fate of the Rumanian Christians at the other extreme of the Balkan Peninsula. In Chapter 2 we saw that in the fourteenth century they had organized the Principalities of Moldavia and Wallachia and maintained a precarious autonomy against their aggressive neighbors, the Hungarians in the west and the Turks in the south. Mircea, the prince of Wallachia, had participated in the battles of Kosovo and Nicopolis, and following these disastrous defeats, was forced to accept Turkish suzerainty. This arrangement was unsatisfactory to Mohammed for strategic reasons. So long as he did not firmly control the Principalities, his empire remained open to invasion from Hungary through Transylvania and Wallachia, or from Poland through Moldavia. Furthermore, an aggressive Wallachian prince, Vlad IV, had come to power in 1456 and refused to pay the customary tribute. After a fierce struggle, in which the Turkish armies suffered several defeats, Mohammed was able to install a ruler who could be depended upon to heed his wishes.

This procedure was repeated in Moldavia where, some years later, an outstanding ruler, Stephen the Great, defied Mohammed by invading Wallachia and dethroning its vassal prince. When the Turkish armies retaliated, Stephen resisted stoutly and held his ground. He realized, however, that he could not hold out indefinitely and, having failed to enlist the support of the neighboring Christian states, he advised his son to submit to the Ottoman power. This was done upon the accession of Mohammed's successor in 1512, and henceforth the Rumanians of both principalities were definitely under Turkish control. They were allowed, however, more freedom than the Christians to the south of the Danube, including the privilege of electing their own princes. This privilege, however, was later withdrawn, as will be shown in Chapter 7.

WAR WITH VENICE

Mohammed was now the master of the Balkans from the Black Sea to the Adriatic and from the Carpathians to the southern tip of Greece. The only exceptions were the independent principality of Montenegro; the city-republic of Ragusa (Dubrovnik), which was autonomous though tributary to the sultan; the provinces of Slovenia and Croatia, which were under the Hapsburgs and Hungarians, respectively; and a number of ports in Dalmatia, Albania, and Greece which the Venetians controlled together with several islands in the eastern Mediterranean. These Venetian possessions represented the only significant challenge to Ottoman hegemony in the Balkans. Having been wrested from declining Byzantium they were now coveted by Byzantium's vigorous successor.

For Mohammed, it was not a case of war for the sake of war, or of barbaric disregard for the benefits of trade. Immediately after the capture of Constantinople he had confirmed the vast trading privileges which the Venetians and Genoese had enjoyed under the Byzantine emperors. Thus, when he reached out for the string of Venetian ports and islands, his concern was for the balance of power in the Balkans and the eastern Mediterranean. The disappearance of Byzantium brought the expanding Ottoman land power into almost inevitable conflict with the intrenched Venetian sea power, in the same manner that centuries later the disintegration of the Ottoman Empire was to set tsarist Russia against imperial Britain.

The war with Venice began in 1463 and dragged out its course for sixteen weary years. There were no decisive battles because the Venetians dared not come to grips with the powerful Ottoman fleets. Mohammed besieged and captured the Venetian outposts one after the other, while Venice struck back by raiding the Anatolian coasts and inducing the Albanians and the Persians to attack the Turks. These diversions proved inadequate and in

1470 Mohammed captured the strategic island Negroponte or Euboea, off the eastern coast of Greece. In the following years he wiped out the Venetian outposts in Albania and sent raiders to the very outskirts of Venice. Deeply discouraged by these losses and by the failure of Western Europe to provide assistance, the Venetians sued for peace in 1479. They surrendered several stations in Albania, the Negroponte and Lemnos Islands in the Aegean, and agreed to pay annually the sum of ten thousand ducats for the privilege of resuming their commerce in the Levant.

The end of the Venetian war left Mohammed free to launch two new naval expeditions in the following year. The first landed an army in Italy itself, where it stormed the city of Otranto and laid waste the surrounding countryside. The second set siege to Rhodes, the island fortress of the Knights of St. John, who for years had harassed Turkish communications in the Aegean. The heroic defense of the knights inflicted upon the Turks a setback reminiscent of their defeat before Belgrade years earlier. Mohammed's death the following year relieved both Rhodes and Naples, and ended what appeared to be a carefully planned campaign for the conquest of all Italy.[6]

5. Ottoman Empire at Its Height: 1481–1566

THE CONQUESTS OF MOHAMMED had left the Ottoman Empire as much European as Asiatic. Mohammed's grandson, Selim I, altered the balance by overrunning Syria and Egypt and extending the Ottoman Empire to the Nile and Mesopotamian valleys. Selim's son and successor, Suleiman the Magnificent, renewed the westward expansion at the expense of Christendom. He thrust the Ottoman frontiers deep into the heart of Europe, conquering Hungary and besieging Vienna itself. At the same time Suleiman's armies fought against the Persians in the East while his fleets engaged the Portuguese in the Indian Ocean and the Venetians and the Hapsburgs in the Mediterranean. It was under Suleiman that the Ottoman Empire reached the dazzling height of its fortunes. The Ottoman leaders were all too aware of their pre-eminence, considering themselves infinitely superior to the infidels of the West. One of Suleiman's vizirs haughtily addressed a Christian envoy on a state occasion as follows: "Do you not know that our Master is like the sun and that, as the sun rules the heavens, so he rules the earth." [1]

BAYEZID II

The brilliant reign of Mohammed was followed by the prosaic rule of Bayezid II (1481–1512), the least significant of the first ten sultans of the Ottoman dynasty. The two outstanding events of his reign were the manner of his accession and the successful war with Venice which consolidated the Ottoman control of the Balkans.

Bayezid's accession was complicated by the fact that no custom or law defined a fixed line of succession. The practice, rather, was for the reigning sultan to decide which of his sons should follow him, and then to appoint him to a strategic post near the capital. In order to avoid civil war Mohammed had extended legal sanction and even compulsion to the practice of fratricide adopted by many earlier rulers. ". . . whoever among my illus-

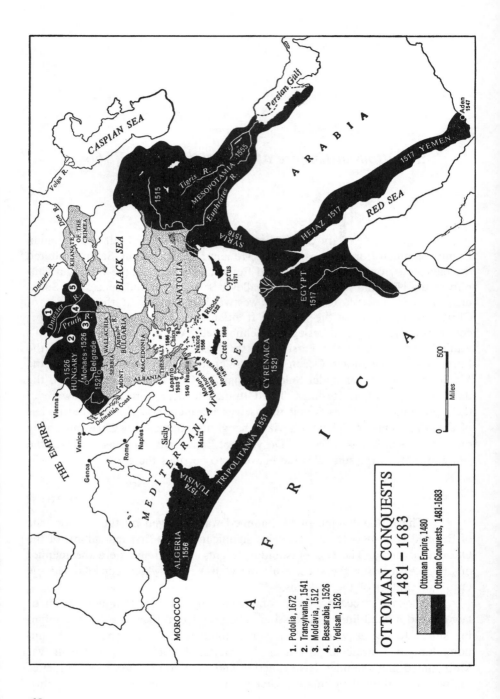

OTTOMAN CONQUESTS 1481–1683

- Ottoman Empire, 1480
- Ottoman Conquests, 1481–1683

1. Podolia, 1672
2. Transylvania, 1541
3. Moldavia, 1512
4. Bessarabia, 1526
5. Yedisan, 1526

CASPIAN SEA

Volga R.

Don R.

Dnieper R.

Dniester R.

KHANATE OF THE CRIMEA

BLACK SEA

THE EMPIRE

Vienna

Venice

Genoa

Rome

Naples

Sicily

Malta

Dalmatian Coast

MOROCCO

ALGERIA 1556

TUNISIA 1574

TRIPOLITANIA 1551

A   F   R   I   C   A

MEDITERRANEAN SEA

HUNGARY 1526

Mohacs 1526

Belgrade 1521

SERBIA

BOSNIA

MONT.

ALBANIA

MACEDONIA

BULGARIA

Danube R.

WALLACHIA

Pruth R.

THESSALY

Lepanto 1503

Nauplia 1540

Modon 1503

Coron 1503

Monemvasia 1540

Chios 1566

Naxos 1566

Crete 1669

Cyprus 1571

Rhodes 1522

ANATOLIA

SYRIA 1516

MESOPOTAMIA

Tigris R.

Euphrates R.

1515

1555

Persian Gulf

A   R   A   B   I   A

RED SEA

HEJAZ 1517

YEMEN 1517

Aden 1547

EGYPT 1517

CYRENAICA 1521

1   2   3   4   5

500

Miles

0

68

trious children and grandchildren may come to the throne," he decreed, "should, for securing the peace of the world, order his brothers to be executed. Let them hereafter act accordingly." [2] This Draconian law was enforced for well over a century, as the numerous little coffins in the royal mausoleums bear tragic witness. Although it prevented in definitive fashion the protracted dynastic wars common in Western Europe at the time, it also created a situation of unstable equilibrium as soon as the sons of a sultan began to grow up. Each knew that he must either seize the throne or follow his father to the grave.

In the case of Mohammed it appears that he had decided in favor of his younger son, Jem, who was a more forceful and attractive personality than the sober Bayezid. The latter, however, was the first to arrive in Constantinople, where he found that the janissaries had instituted a reign of terror, having murdered the grand vizir and plundered the houses of Christians and Jews. The janissaries greeted Bayezid by asking forgiveness for their excesses, but they asked for it in battle array, and accompanied their petition by a demand for an increase of pay and a large present on their new sovereign's accession. Bayezid complied, and thus he was able with janissary support to defeat his brother. But a precedent had been established, and henceforth the distribution of large sums of money upon every accession was expected and always forthcoming.

The war with Venice (1499–1503) broke out partly because of the numerous incidents that occurred between the Venetian maritime empire and the Ottoman land power all along the line from Istria to Rhodes. Another cause was Venice's acquisition by bequest in 1489 of the strategic island of Cyprus. Bayezid wished to develop Turkish sea power and therefore resolved to prevent Cyprus from becoming a new and powerful Venetian base in the Levant.

The course of the war demonstrated the decline of Venice and the rise of Turkey as a naval power. The Ottoman fleet of three hundred ships included vessels of eighteen hundred tons—at that time the largest in the world. The fleet was commanded by Kemal Re'is, a seaman of probably Greek origin who became the first great admiral of the Turks. He had distinguished himself in 1483 when he ravaged the coasts of Spain in support of the hard-pressed Moors of Granada. In this war with Venice he won a hard-fought battle of Lepanto in 1499, and in the following year he held his own against the combined fleets of Venice, Spain, and the Papacy. On land the Turks captured Lepanto, Modon, and Koron in the Peloponnesus, while ten thousand of their horsemen raided Venetian territory as far as Vicenza. These defeats forced Venice to sign a treaty in which she ceded the stations she had lost, though she still kept Nauplion in Greece and some of the Ionian Islands, as well as Cyprus and Crete. Despite these possessions Venice no longer was the dominant power in the Levant. This war marked the beginning of the Ottoman supremacy in the eastern Mediterranean that was to last for almost three hundred years. The sea approaches to the Balkan Peninsula were now under Turkish control, and a few decades later Suleiman the Magnificent was to lead his armies across the Danube into the heart of Europe without fear of a rear attack from the south.

SELIM I AND THE TRADE ROUTES

Bayezid's son and successor, Selim I (1512–1520), stands out in Ottoman history as the conqueror of Syria and Egypt. The details of his audacious campaigns do not concern us here because they did not directly affect the Balkans. Suffice it to note that a combination of dynastic and religious factors embroiled him in a war with the powerful Shah Ismail of Persia. Selim emerged victorious, whereupon the Mameluke ruler of Egypt and Syria aligned himself with the shah in order to redress the balance of power in the Near East. Selim retaliated with his customary impetuosity. In a whirlwind campaign he invaded Syria, defeated and killed the Mameluke Sultan Kansuh in the battle of Marj-Dabik (August 23, 1516), and triumphantly entered Cairo on January 30, 1517.

At this point it is worth pausing to consider the relationship between Selim's conquests and the immensely significant shift that was now occurring in East-West trade routes. For centuries spices and other commodities that Asia supplied to Europe had been funneled mostly through the Mameluke ports in Syria and Egypt, where they were purchased by Venetians and other Italian middlemen for resale throughout Western Europe. This transit trade became the lifeblood of the Mameluke economy, providing not only government revenue in the form of customs duties, but also a source of livelihood for thousands of merchants, clerks, sailors, shipbuilders, camel drivers, stevedores, and all the rest who were directly or indirectly connected with the trade. Certainly this commerce was in large part responsible for the great wealth and high culture of the Mameluke Empire.

Suddenly this flourishing empire was struck in its vitals when Vasco da Gama sailed into Calicut Harbor, India, on May 22, 1498, ten months after leaving Portugal. At last the Western Europeans had direct access to fabulous India and to the coveted spice islands of the East Indies. Lengthy as the voyage was on the all-water road around the Cape of Good Hope, it still was infinitely more economical than the old course through the Mameluke ports in the eastern Mediterranean. The latter route involved several loadings and unloadings to traverse the land barrier separating Alexandria from the Red Sea, and the Syrian ports from the Persian Gulf. Also, there were customs duties to be paid at several points along the route, as well as Bedouin marauders who had to be placated by money or wares or both. This combination of high transportation costs, customs dues, and outright extortions raised the price of spices in Alexandria to more than 2,000 per cent above their original cost in India. And there still remained the Italian merchants to levy their far from modest charges before the goods finally reached the consumer in France or England or Germany. It is not surprising, then, to find that in the four years 1502–1505, the Venetians were able to obtain an average of only 1,000,000 English pounds of spices a year at Alexandria, whereas in the last years of the fifteenth century they had averaged 3,500,000 pounds. Conversely, Portuguese imports rose from 224,000 pounds in 1501 to an average of 2,300,000 pounds in the four years 1503–1506.[3]

The Turks frequently are held responsible for this shift in the trade routes. According to this theory Selim conquered Syria and Egypt and then proceeded to interfere with the flow of spices through those countries to such an extent that Western Europe suffered a serious shortage. Hence the efforts of the Portuguese captains to find a direct route to the Far East, culminating in the successful voyage of Vasco da Gama around the Cape of Good Hope. This reasoning is palpably incorrect because, as we have seen, Gama reached Calicut in 1498; Selim overran Syria and Egypt eighteen years later in 1516–1517. Not only did the Turks have nothing to do with the appearance of the Portuguese in the Indian Ocean; on the contrary, they made every effort to drive the Portuguese out in order to revive the prosperity of their newly won Syrian and Egyptian possessions.

Selim did not live long enough to turn his attention to the Portuguese, but Suleiman sent several naval expeditions to the Indian Ocean to clear out the interlopers. These efforts all proved ineffective. The Turks and their Levantine subjects were at home in the Mediterranean, but in the Indian Ocean they were no match for the Portuguese seamean, trained in the school of Henry the Navigator, and tested on the long voyage around Africa.

The failure of the Turks had far-reaching repercussions for the entire Near East. It marked the beginning of the end of Levantine predominance in world commerce. The stress should be on the word "beginning." The old routes did not disappear overnight. After the first shock of the Portuguese intrusion a gradual recovery occurred. There even were years when the volume of trade through the Levantine ports surpassed that which rounded the Cape. In fact, it can be said that throughout the sixteenth century both routes were used, with now the one prevailing and now the other. The survival of the old channels is surprising in view of the natural advantages of the all-water route. The explanation seems to have been the excessively high rates set by the Portuguese and the corruption of Portuguese officials, who were willing for a consideration to permit cargoes to enter the Red Sea and the Persian Gulf. It was not until some time in the seventeenth century, after the penetration of the more efficient Dutchmen into the Far East, that the balance swung decisively in favor of the Cape route. Only then did the Levantine ports sink into that insignificance and obscurity out of which they were not to emerge until the late nineteenth century.

This shifting of trade routes, gradual though it was, marked the beginning of a changing relationship between Western Europe and the Near East, and indeed between Western Europe and the rest of the world. At a time when the Turks were steadily advancing from the Balkans into Central Europe, the Portuguese were outflanking the entire Moslem world by opening the sea route to India. In 1498 Ottoman advance guards were pushing into Venetia but in the same year Vasco da Gama landed at Calicut. In 1503 Venice lost Modon, Koron, and Lepanto to the Turks, but in 1509 the Portuguese destroyed an Egyptian fleet that had been sent to drive them out of the Indian Ocean. Thus at the time when the strongest Moslem state was spearheading ever deeper into Central Europe, the Westerners were executing a vast outflanking movement and attacking the Moslem world in its "soft underbelly." This development not only had important strategic implications but also involved infinitely more significant economic and political repercussions. It dealt a severe blow to the economic development of the Near East, it opened up vast new vistas for the Western world, and it cleared the way for European economic penteration of the vast Asian continent, which in turn led eventually to a political domination that was to prevail until the twentieth century.

SULEIMAN THE MAGNIFICENT

Selim left behind him only one son, Suleiman, surnamed by Christian writers "the Magnificent," and by his own people "El Kanuni" or "the Legislator." Suleiman occupies a position in his country's history comparable to that of Louis XIV in France. During his long reign (1520–1566) he added enormously to his empire. Belgrade, Rhodes, nearly the whole of Hungary, the Crimea, great parts of Mesopotamia and Armenia taken from Persia, Yemen and Aden in the Arabian Peninsula, a wide extension of Egypt in the direction of Nubia, and the coast of North Africa from Egypt almost to the Atlantic—these were the contributions that he bequeathed to his successors. Suleiman's talents and unceasing labors were in part responsible for his successes. Also, he had the good fortune to appear on the historical stage at precisely the right moment: following the great contributions of Mohammed II and Selim, and preceding the many symptoms of decay that were to become so evident by the end of the century. Finally, Suleiman had the ability to select gifted advisers and the sense to keep them in office as long as they were useful. His first vizir and great favorite, the Greek Ibrahim, served from 1523 to 1536; after him came the Bulgarian Rustem from 1544 to 1553 and 1555 to 1561; and finally the Bosnian Sokolli (Sokolovich), from 1565 to 1579. Suleiman delegated authority to all these men to an unprecedented degree. In effect, they were vice-sultans with unlimited powers so long as they enjoyed their master's confidence. This system worked well with a strong ruler like Suleiman, who knew how to control his advisers as well as to select them. His weak successors could do neither, thereby depriving the empire of that unity and decisive leadership that had been the envy and despair of the Western powers.

Suleiman first turned his attention to the northwestern frontier along the Danube. There the Hungarians still held Belgrade and other strategic fortresses, but their grip was weakening. No longer were they able to fulfill their traditional role of Christendom's bulwark against Islam. Their king,

Louis II, who was also ruler of Bohemia, was a dissolute youngster and was regarded by all his subjects as a foreigner because of his Polish descent. Besides, the Hungarians were weakened by religious dissension between Catholics and Lutherans, and by a deep social cleavage between the nobility and the landless peasantry. Finally, there was the added distraction of the Hungarian "nationalist," party which demanded a native dynasty for Hungary. Its leader was John Zapolya, a Transylvanian magnate who cherished personal ambitions concerning the proposed native dynasty and who was to ally himself with Suleiman when these ambitions were frustrated.

It is to these circumstances that we must attribute the astonishing fact that when Suleiman reached the Danube he found no army, whether Hungarian or Bohemian, to oppose his advance. He had to deal only with the garrisons of the towns he besieged, their governors having appealed in vain for relief from Buda or Prague. Thus Suleiman was able in the summer of 1521 to reduce without distraction several Hungarian fortresses on the Danube and the Sava. Then he surrounded Belgrade itself, and on August 29 the city that had defied so many Turkish armies in the past accepted his liberal terms for surrender.

From Belgrade, Suleiman turned to Rhodes, the island fortress of the Knights of St. John. Rhodes at this time was probably the most strongly fortified position in the world. Having repulsed Mohammed II forty years earlier, the grand masters of the island had lived ever since in constant fear of a new attack. All the spare funds available from the order's commanderies throughout Europe had gone into stone and mortar. The defenses were of the most modern style, specially designed to withstand artillery fire, and manned by a resolute force of about six thousand men. These precautions now proved fully justified. Suleiman was determined to destroy the stronghold that sheltered a swarm of Christian pirates who preyed on Turkish shipping. And Western Europe was too engrossed in the French-Hapsburg war to offer any aid.

The siege began on July 28, 1522. Week after week Suleiman pressed the siege, using every means at his command: artillery fire, underground mines, and constant assaults. It was not until late December that the grand master agreed to surrender, and even then it was shortage of ammunition that decided the issue. Suleiman's terms were generous: the knights were to be free to leave the island with all their personal property, while the native inhabitants were to be relieved of taxes for five years and were to enjoy free exercise of their religion. So ended the last outpost of militant Christendom in the eastern Mediterranean.

Suleiman had captured the two outposts of Christendom that had defied the conqueror of Constantinople. But in doing so he had not accomplished something original or unexpected. He was merely following in the footsteps of his predecessors and completing their work. At this point occurred an incident that changed completely Turkey's position in Europe and started a new era in the history of Ottoman relations with the West.

OTTOMAN EMPIRE AND CHRISTIAN EUROPE

Prior to this time Turkey had not been regarded as a member of the European family of nations. The medieval idea of the solidarity of Christian Europe precluded acceptance of a Moslem empire. Rather, Christian princes were expected to propagate the true faith and to exterminate the enemies of Christendom. Hence the long series of Crusades against the Moslems of the Holy Land and later against the Turks after they had overrun the Christian Balkans. But by the fifteenth century this crusading spirit had evaporated. Both the Hungarians at Belgrade and the Knights of St. John at Rhodes discovered this when they begged the Christian monarchs for aid against Suleiman. A more dramatic demonstration of this drift away from Christian unity was the appeal that Suleiman received in December, 1525, from Francis I, the king of France. The appeal was for a Turkish attack upon the Holy Roman Emperor and head of the House of Hapsburg, Charles V! And this was from the "Eldest Son of the Church"—from the king of the country with the most glorious crusading traditions!

The explanation is to be found partly in the influence of certain new forces that had gradually transformed the medieval world and shattered its unity. The most important of these were humanist concepts, dynastic interests, nationalist considerations, and the Protestant Reformation. Another factor that exerted a more immediate influence in the sixteenth century was the overwhelming increase in Hapsburg power and territorial possessions. At the time when Selim was conquering Syria and Egypt, all the accumulated heritages of Spain, Austria, and Burgundy, together with the crown of the Holy Roman Empire, were falling into the lap of Charles V. The only serious rival of the Hapsburgs was the king of France, but he was taken prisoner by the victorious emperor at the battle of Pavia in 1525. Francis looked around in desperation for a power strong enough to restore the balance in Europe. There was only one possibility, the Ottoman Empire. Hence the appeal to Suleiman and the beginning of that cooperation between Turkey and France that was to last for nearly three centuries. This relationship was denounced at the time as the "impious alliance" and "the sacrilegious union of the Lily and the Crescent." But it continued nonetheless, for it was as much to the interest of Suleiman, as of Francis, to put a stop to Hapsburg expansion. Thus the Ottoman Empire became an accepted and active participant in European affairs, and remained so until its disintegration four centuries later. Francis, it should be noted, played a double game throughout his reign. He posed as an eager defender of Christendom when that seemed advisable; yet he remained secretly allied to Suleiman, whose interests, however, he never hesitated to sacrifice when it was profitable to do so.

VICTORY AT MOHACS

Suleiman responded to Francis' appeal for aid by crossing the Danube in 1526 and overrunning Hungary. The invasion was calculated to ease the pressure on Francis and at the same time to satisfy the janissaries, who were openly rebellious after four years of inactivity. The Hungarians, on their part, were in no better condition to resist the Turks at this time than in 1521. The same internal cleavages still divided them, while the loss of Belgrade and of the other fortresses made defense more difficult.

There was little likelihood of assistance from the outside to bolster the Hungarians. Poland had just concluded a peace settlement with the Turks Venice had been able to obtain a favorable commercial treaty in 1521 and now was unwilling to risk losing its benefits. In fact, Venice congratulated Suleiman on the capture of Rhodes. The pope, although anxious to stem the advance of Islam, was able to contribute only limited funds. There remained only the two Hapsburg rulers, Emperor Charles and his brother Ferdinand, who ruled the Austrian domains. Both men had a personal interest in supporting Hungary, Charles because of his position as temporal head of Christendom, and Ferdinand because King Louis was his brother-in-law, and, more important, because the fall of Hungary would bring Suleiman's armies to the Austrian frontier. Yet neither Charles nor Ferdinand was able to contribute much, thanks to the multitude of pressures and crises that were ever arising in their sprawling empire.

Emperor Charles's policy was first to restore Christendom's unity within a new Holy Roman Empire and then to turn against the infidel Turks. But powerful interests in Christendom were unwilling to accept unification under Hapsburg aegis. At this very moment, for example, France, the Papacy, and the Italian states were combined in the powerful League of Cognac to drive the Hapsburgs out of Italy. Thus Charles was constantly preoccupied by the opposition of his Christian rivals and was unable to send significant forces to the East.

Likewise in Germany there was great reluctance to give aid to the Hungarians because it was generally believed that the Turkish danger was exaggerated. Otherwise, it was asked, why did not Charles aid King Louis of Hungary who was his own cousin? Furthermore the Romanists and the Lutherans in Germany were at each other's throats. In fact, the Lutherans opposed any efforts against the Turks because they might redound to the advantage of the Papacy. Luther went so far as to say, "To fight the Turks is to resist the judgment of God upon men's sins." [4] Under these circumstances the German Diet that met in the summer of 1526 refused to vote aid to Hungary until the religious issues had been settled. Finally Ferdinand promised that a conciliar council would meet within eighteen months to consider church reform, and that in the interval everyone "would live, act, and rule their subjects in such wise as each one thought right before God and his Imperial Majesty." [5] Having obtained what it wanted, the Diet voted 24,000 men for the defense of Hungary and then adjourned on August 27. Four days later the Hungarians suffered fatal defeat at Mohacs.

Suleiman had set out from Constantinople at the head of his army in April, 1526. By the end of July he had stormed the fortress of Peterwardein on the south bank of the Danube. He continued his march along the river until he reached the junction of the Drava and the Danube in mid-

August. Here he expected to find the Hungarians drawn up on the other bank, prepared to resist his further advance. Instead, they were immobilized by contentious councils on the plain of Mohacs thirty miles to the north. Some urged retreat until expected reinforcements had arrived; others opposed the surrender of most of the country without offering resistance. The latter group prevailed, and on August 29, 1526, the fateful battle of Mohacs was fought: 25,000 to 28,000 Hungarians and assorted allies on the one side, and on the other 45,000 Turkish regulars supported by 10,000 to 20,000 lightly armed irregulars.

The issue was never in doubt. Only a freak of chance could have saved the Christian army, rent as it was by dissension and its several parts acting independently. The heavily armed Hungarian cavalry broke the Turkish center, but was then held up by the Ottoman artillery, while the strong Turkish wings outflanked the Christian army. Within an hour and a half the battle was decided. The Turks took no prisoners and few of the defeated escaped.

What Kosovo had been for Serbia, Mohacs was now for Hungary. Not only the bulk of the army but almost all its leaders, including the king, had perished. Suleiman was able to advance to Buda and to enter the capital without opposition. He stayed only two weeks and then started with his army on the road back to Constantinople. He had decided not to annex Hungary but to make it a tributary principality like Wallachia. In this design he was aided by the scheming and ambitious Hungarian nobleman, John Zapolya.

The death of King Louis left Bohemia and Hungary without a sovereign. The obvious candidate for both thrones was Ferdinand of Hapsburg, brother of Emperor Charles and brother-in-law to Louis. With the use of judicious bribery Ferdinand persuaded the Bohemian nobles to proclaim him their king. But in Hungary he had to contend with Zapolya, the leader of the Nationalist party, who had occupied Buda after the departure of Suleiman. Ferdinand easily defeated the disorganized forces of Zapolya, and by the end of 1527 he had won the crown and gained control of most of the country. Zapolya now followed Francis' example and appealed to Suleiman for support.

The sultan, having conquered Hungary, was not disposed to sit back and permit the Hapsburgs to reap the fruits of his victory. He had undertaken the expedition to check the Hapsburgs, not to add still another kingdom to their empire. Since Suleiman did not wish to annex Hungary directly, a dependent Zapolya in Buda was the obvious solution. Accordingly he promised Zapolya the throne and assured him of his support.

This marked the beginning of the struggle between the Hapsburg and Ottoman empires that was to continue to the end of the eighteenth century. Hitherto Venice and Hungary had borne the burden of the Turkish onslaught. But Venice was now thoroughly intimidated and Hungary destroyed. Only the Hapsburgs had both the land and the sea power necessary to take the place of Venice in the Mediterranean and of Hungary in Central Europe.

Henceforth the Hapsburg Empire was the march of Western Christendom against the Moslem world. Indeed, the menace of the ever-victorious Turk became a matter of growing concern in Central Europe, as the following German folk song attests:

> From Hungary he's soon away,
> In Austria by break of day,
> Bavaria is just at hand,
> From there he'll reach another land,
> Soon to the Rhine perhaps he'll come. . . .[6]

DEFEAT AT VIENNA

Suleiman left Constantinople for Hungary on May 10, 1529. On the Mohacs Plain he met Zapolya, who paid him homage and contributed a considerable cavalry force to the expedition. Continuing northward, Suleiman recaptured Buda with little trouble, and on September 18 he reached the Austrian border. Ten days later he arrived before Vienna and the siege began. Meanwhile Ferdinand had been desperately seeking to scrape together money and men for the defense of his capital. His brother, the emperor, being still at war with Francis, was able to spare only a small number of Spanish infantry. The German princes were more helpful, while Luther had abandoned completely his earlier unconcern now that Suleiman was approaching the borders of Germany. "I fight," Luther declared, "until death against the Turks and the God of the Turks." [7]

All in all, nearly twenty thousand men were gathered in the city before the Turks cut it off from the outside world. Most of the defenders were professional soldiers and, under the leadership of the seventy-year-old veteran, Nicholas von Salm, they fought off the superior Turkish forces with courage and skill. Suleiman sorely missed the heavy artillery that he had been forced to leave behind because of the torrential rains that plagued him from the outset. The light cannon that remained made little impression on the city walls. He resorted to mining operations and repeatedly ordered assaults upon the breaches opened by the mines. But the attacks invariably were repulsed. The Turkish soldiers became so dispirited that their officers had to drive them forward with staves and sabers. With the failure of a final assault on October 14 Suleiman raised the siege and ordered retreat.

The expedition had been successful at least politically. Suleiman had driven Ferdinand out of Hungary and installed in his place an obedient vassal. But more significant was the fact that a Turkish army had been beaten back before the walls of Vienna by a force much inferior in numbers. This may be considered the beginning of the end of Ottoman military superiority. In the past the feudal cavalry of Persia, Egypt, and Hungary had been no match for the Turkish military machine with its disciplined janissaries and deadly artillerists. But at Vienna Suleiman discovered that Western artillery was equal to his own and that Austrian and Spanish foot soldiers, with their harquebuses and long pikes, were, if anything, superior to his janissaries. There were still many triumphs in store for Suleiman and his successors, but the days of easy victories had passed.

It should be noted that geographic factors played an important role in this and other Turkish campaigns to the north of the Danube. Ottoman armies destined for Central Europe traditionally left Constantinople on April 23, the day of the holy man corresponding to St. George. They needed about two months to reach southern Hungary; hence, allowing a similar period for the return, only eight to ten weeks remained for trans-Danubian operations. Thus the distance involved, together with the difficult terrain and unpredictable weather, protected Central Europe from the domination of Constantinople.

TRUCE ON THE DANUBE

If the Western monarchs were equal to Suleiman in the art of war, their political disunity still kept them hopelessly inferior in the conduct of war. This became painfully evident when Ferdinand attempted to follow up his success at Vienna. With the Turkish army recuperating from its losses and obviously incapable of a winter campaign, Ferdinand could have taken the offensive, driven Zapolya out of Hungary, and perhaps even recaptured Belgrade. But most of the troops provided at Vienna came from princes that were intensely jealous of the growing power of the Hapsburgs. They were willing to cooperate in a war against the common enemy but they refused to help Ferdinand win the Hungarian crown. Most of them, indeed, hoped for the success of Zapolya despite his Moslem patronage. Ferdinand likewise could not count on the support of his brother Charles. The harassed emperor had just made peace with Francis but was now hastening northward to deal with the Lutherans. First he would punish the Protestant heretics within the empire and then the Moslem infidels without.

Under the circumstances Ferdinand had no choice but to send envoys to Constantinople to seek peace. Suleiman, however, was determined to avenge the humiliation he had suffered at Vienna and was already preparing another expedition. In April, 1532, he left Constantinople at the head of an immense army, openly avowing that he would march to Vienna and give battle to the head of Christendom, the Emperor Charles. Faced with this imminent danger, Charles hurriedly made concessions to the Lutheran heretics. It is paradoxical that an invading Moslem army should have contributed so much to the cause of Protestantism in its critical formative stage. The restoration of peace enabled Charles to gather a large army, contingents arriving from Spain, Italy, Austria, the Netherlands, and the Germanies. Vienna was much better prepared to withstand Suleiman than on the previous occasion three years earlier.

This may explain why the siege never materialized. Leaving Belgrade on June 25, Suleiman crossed the Drava and then, instead of following the Danube northward to Buda and Vienna, he turned westward to the narrow strip of Hungarian territory still held by Ferdinand. Perhaps his strategy was to lure the imperial army out of Vienna and onto the Hungarian plains, where there would be a chance for a second Mohacs. But Charles refused to budge and Suleiman was left free to devastate the countryside, though he carefully avoided another exhausting ordeal before Vienna. After besieging the small town of Güns in desultory fashion for twenty days Suleiman turned aside, ravaged Styria, and then led his army homeward. Thus the anticipated duel between the sultan of the East and the emperor of the West never took place.

Suleiman now was ready for peace. While he had been campaigning in Hungary, the emperor's Genoese admiral, Andrea Doria, had captured the fortress of Koron in the Peloponnesus and ravaged the adjacent coasts. Much more worrisome was the outbreak of fighting with Persia on the eastern frontier. Suleiman could not hope to wage war simultaneously on the Hungarian plains and on the Persian plateau. He decided, therefore, to make peace in the West in order to be free for a campaign in the East the following year. On June 22, 1533, he signed the first Turkish-Austrian treaty with Ferdinand. The terms were that Zapolya should remain king of Hungary but Ferdinand was to keep the third of the country he occupied at the time. This settlement was with only one of the Hapsburg brothers. Charles V was not a signatory, so that in the following years Suleiman waged a naval war against the emperor and a land war against the shah of Persia.

PERSIAN AND MEDITERRANEAN EXPEDITIONS

We consider the Persian campaigns separately at this point only for the sake of convenience. Actually they were part and parcel of the intercontinental wars of these decades. The shah was in league with the emperor in the same manner that the sultan was with the king of France. Suleiman's invasion of Persia was inconclusive though by no means fruitless. His grand vizir, Ibrahim, occupied the shah's capital, Tabriz, on July 13, 1534. The following year Ibrahim, together with Suleiman, took over Baghdad from its Persian commander, who treacherously surrendered the city. The shah, however, was by no means beaten. Taking a lesson from his father's unfortunate experience at the hands of Selim, he avoided battle and instead harassed the Turkish army with hit-and-run tactics. Suleiman suffered heavy losses pursuing the elusive shah until he realized the futility of attempting to pin him down. Then he evacuated Tabriz after thoroughly sacking the city, and returned to Constantinople in January, 1536. This proved to be only the beginning of a protracted struggle that was to drag on intermittently for twenty years. Suleiman led new expeditions against Persia in 1548 and 1553, but with the same inconclusive results. Finally, he ended the tedious and costly war by accepting a peace settlement in which he abandoned all claim to the Tabriz region but kept lower Mesopotamia, including Baghdad and a frontage on the Persian Gulf.

In the meantime Ottoman fleets under the leadership of the famous

North African corsair, Khaireddin Barbarossa, had spread terror throughout the Mediterranean. In 1533 Suleiman had appointed Barbarossa to the post of Kapudan Pasha or Lord High Admiral, thereby combining North African Moslem sea power with the resources of the Ottoman Empire. During the following years Barbarossa successfully fought against the combined fleets of the Holy League—Venice, the Papacy, and the Empire. Following Barbarossa's death in 1545 his veteran captains continued his work. By 1562 Moslem vessels were sailing through the Straits of Gibraltar, venturing out into the Atlantic as far as the Canaries, and preying upon the treasure-laden galleons from the New World. The Turks suffered a setback in 1565 when they failed to take Malta, the last remaining stronghold of the Knights of St. John. Yet the fact remains that during his reign Suleiman had added the entire North African coast to his empire, the sole exception being the small stretch from Oran westward, which belonged to the Spaniards.

The year after the failure at Malta, Suleiman, now seventy years old, was carried in a litter, at the head of his army, on his thirteenth march out of Constantinople. The destination once more, as so frequently in the past, was the disputed kingdom of Hungary. Many events had occurred in that unfortunate country since 1533, when Suleiman concluded an agreement with Ferdinand of Hapsburg in order to be free against Persia. Most important had been the death in 1540 of his vassal king of Hungary, Zapolya. Ferdinand immediately marched in from the west to make good his claim to the whole country. Suleiman, in turn, invaded from the south, ostensibly to defend the interests of Zapolya's infant son. But as soon as he entered Buda, Suleiman proclaimed Hungary an Ottoman province and established his direct imperial administration. Ferdinand had no choice but to accept the *fait accompli,* and for nearly a century and a half almost all of Hungary was in Turkish hands.

Now, in 1566, Suleiman was heading north once more. The failure of the Malta expedition weighed heavily on his mind and he was determined to end his career with a success as signal as that against Belgrade in the first year of his reign. Also, he had a score to settle with the new emperor, Maximilian II, who had permitted raids upon Turkish territory. So Suleiman was borne northward from Constantinople to Sofia, Belgrade, Semlin (Zemun), and finally Szigeth. There he halted on August 5 to lay siege to the strongly fortified city that had successfully resisted him before. Exactly a month later, while his guns were thundering against the obstinate defenders, the great sultan died, a fitting end for the old warrior. His body was embalmed and carried in the royal litter, while orders continued to be issued over his name. For three weeks his death was kept secret from the army, until arrangements had been completed for the peaceful accession of the new sultan, the besotted Selim II.

6. Ottoman Institutions

ULEIMAN THE MAGNIFICENT represents the great divide in the history of the Ottoman Empire. Before his reign, Ottoman history was one of victories and expansion; after his reign it was marked by defeats and contraction. The decline admittedly was not uninterrupted. We shall note brief periods of recovery and even of expansion. But the general trend was downward, culminating finally in the partition of the empire after World War I.

Our Western world is more aware of these later centuries of decadence than it is of the earlier centuries of strength and efficiency. This is understandable, for the various European states that suffered the blows of the Turks in their prime have long since disappeared. In contrast, the present-day great powers came into close contact with the Turks only after the evils and weakness of their empire had become apparent. Thus the word "Turkish" became associated in the Western mind with such phrases as "Sick Man of Europe," "Bulgarian atrocities," and "Armenian massacres."

This association is as unsound as it is unjust. The Roman Empire admittedly was feeble and decadent in the fifth century A.D., but this does not detract from its splendor and contributions in earlier centuries. Likewise, the Ottoman Empire was a dying organism in its later years, and Tsar Nicholas I was fully justified in referring to it as the "Sick Man of Europe." But it should be recalled that a Spanish ambassador used precisely the same phrase to describe England in the sixteenth century, and that during the same century the Ottoman Empire was regarded by Western Europeans with a combination of awe, respect, and fear.

Ogier Ghiselin de Busbecq, the judicious and observant Hapsburg ambassador in Constantinople at the time of Suleiman, compared the sultan to a thunderbolt—"he smites, shatters, and destroys whatever stands in his way." [1] As late as 1634, well after the decline of the empire had set in, a thoughtful English traveler concluded that the Turks were "the only modern people great in action," and that "he who would behold these times in their greatest glory, could not find a better scene than Turkey." [2]

An empire that commanded such respect obviously had little in common with the weak and degenerate "Sick Man" of popular conception. In this chapter we shall examine the conditions and institutions of this empire at its height—its vast domains with their polyglot peoples, its formidable armies, its advanced culture and exceptional religious freedom, and, above all, its unique administrative system based exclusively upon slaves of Christian origin.

LANDS AND PEOPLES

The Ottoman Empire sprawled over three continents. In Europe it included the Balkan Peninsula to the Danube River, together with the following provinces north of the river: Transylvania, Moldavia, Wallachia, most of Hungary, Podolia in Poland, and the entire north coast of the Black Sea. In Asia it embraced Asia Minor, Armenia, most of the Caucasus, the Tigris and Euphrates valleys down to the Persian Gulf, the western coast of the Persian Gulf, and all the lands on the eastern coast of the Mediterranean together with a wide strip running down the entire length of the Arabian Peninsula to the Gulf of Aden. Finally in Africa, the empire encompassed Egypt, Tripoli, Tunisia, and Algeria. And to complete the picture we should add Crete, Cyprus, and the islands of the Aegean.

Within this vast empire lived peoples of diverse strains and creeds. The Turks, Tatars, Arabs, Kurds, Turkomans, Berbers, and Mamelukes all belonged to Islam, together with large numbers of Bosnians, Albanians, and Bulgarians who had apostatized to the conquering creed. The remaining ethnic groups—Greeks, Hungarians, South Slavs, Rumanians, Armenians, Georgians, and Egyptian Copts—all belonged to the various Christian churches, of which by far the most important was the Orthodox. In addition there were the Jews who at this time were migrating in large numbers to the lands of the sultan because they found there a degree of religious tolerance unknown and unimaginable in the Christian Europe of that day. All in all, a population of approximately fifty million compared to the five million in contemporary England.

SULTAN AND SLAVES

The sultan was the supreme ruler of these lands and peoples. Although he was generally regarded as a despot, his despotism in fact was rigidly limited by a specific and immutable constitution. This constitution, known as the Sheri or Sacred Law of Islam, was based upon the word of God—the Koran—and upon the sayings of Mohammed—the Hadith. The Sheri was not merely a religious law like the canon law of Christendom. It left no scope for secular laws to regulate mundane affairs. It was theoretically adequate to govern the Islamic world and to regulate minutely the social, ethical, religious, and economic life of all its members.

In actual practice the Sheri soon became obsolete, at least as a political constitution. It was designed to regulate the primitive society of the Arabian Peninsula rather than the world empire that Islam soon conquered. Furthermore, this sacred law, believed to be of divine origin, was unchangeable by its own provisions. Judges and jurists attempted to provide elasticity through interpretation, but this procedure by itself was insufficient. Accordingly, the sultans supplemented the sacred law by decrees of their own known as kanuns. These decrees did not constitute a secular law rivaling the Sheri. They were merely regulations applying to matters undefined by the Sheri, with the precepts of which they could not conflict. These kanuns allowed the sultans a certain latitude, though it was quite limited and rigidly circumscribed. No kanun could be effective unless it received the support of the conservative Moslem population and unless it was approved by the decisions of the established heads of law and religion, known collectively as the ulema. The latter, in fact, more than once forced the deposition of sultans who were judged to have violated the sacred law.

These restrictions left the head of the Ottoman Empire with little legislative power. But his administrative authority was virtually absolute; the reason was that the administration and the standing army were composed almost entirely of slaves over whom the sultan had the power of life and death. The use of slaves was not uncommon in Moslem states, especially for military purposes. The Ottoman rulers from an early period maintained a standing army of slaves in addition to a feudal cavalry force composed of freeborn Moslem landholders. The slaves either were purchased or, more commonly, were taken prisoners in the campaigns against the Christian infidels. But, as we noted in Chapter 3, Murad I (1359–1389) hit upon a new expedient, namely a periodic levy of the male children of his Orthodox Christian subjects. The children were taken from their parents at between the ages of ten and twenty, reduced to the status of slaves, and trained for service to the state. This system had two great merits in the eyes of the sultans: the child slaves cost nothing, and they were completely dependent upon their master. These advantages led to a further development. In the earlier days the administration of the growing empire had been conducted by free Moslems; these were now replaced almost without exception by the sultan's slaves. The long line of able and energetic rulers who preceded Suleiman perfected this unique system to the point where it became the solid foundation of the empire. The slaves were carefully selected, thoroughly trained, and then sent out to fill the ranks of the regular army and the administration. This vast slave organization, together with its imperial master who owned and controlled it, is commonly known as the Ruling Institution.

RECRUITING AND TRAINING OF SLAVES

The Ottoman sultans had much precedent in Islamic history for using slaves in their administration and armed forces. But they were quite original in using these slaves to the exclusion of free Moslems. Thus we have the paradox of a great Moslem empire being governed and, in part, defended, by slaves of Christian origin. This in turn meant that the freeborn Moslems could enter only the legal, religious, and educational institutions of their empire. Those who did so are commonly referred to collectively as the Moslem Institution in contradistinction to the Ruling Institution.

We shall consider later the composition and function of the Moslem Institution in more detail. To return to the Ruling Institution, it should be noted that not all of its slave members were recruited as children from Orthodox families. Others were captured in war and still others were purchased in the slave markets. These markets were kept supplied by two sets of professional slave raiders: the Barbary corsairs who preyed upon the shipping and exposed coasts of Southern and Western Europe; and the Crimean Tatars who devastated the steppe lands of Poland and Muscovy. It is estimated that seven to eight thousand slaves entered the sultan's service annually, of which about three thousand were from the child-levy.

Upon joining the sultan's great slave household the recruits were first examined and classified by highly trained officials. About 90 per cent were sent to Asia Minor to spend several years in the service of feudal landholders. There they were expected to learn Turkish, to master the art of war, and to be converted to Islam. Then they returned to Constantinople to enter one of the military corps. Meanwhile, in the famous Palace School established by Mohammed the Conqueror, the remaining 10 per cent, who were selected for their handsome appearance and apparent ability, were being trained to become the great men of the empire. After graduation they usually filled minor posts in the provinces. From then on they were free to rise, on the basis of merit, through the ranks of the hierarchy to the most exalted positions in Constantinople.

It is easy to arouse moral indignation against the practice of buying slaves in the market place or of taking young children away from their parents. But if we consider these practices in the light of contemporary conditions and mores they appear more natural and understandable. We should keep in mind that slavery in Islam was a very different institution from slavery in the West. The Moslem master recognized no color line. Normally he maintained warm personal relations with the slaves. Frequently he freed them as a meritorious act enjoined by the Koran. And not uncommonly he gave his daughters in marriage to those of his slaves whom he held in highest esteem. Thus slavery under Islam involved servitude but very little social inferiority. And in the Ottoman Empire, where the most favored slaves were at the same time the actual rulers, the use of the word "slave" is perhaps unavoidable but certainly unfortunate and misleading.

Contemporary evidence concerning the child-tribute is significantly contradictory. Some observers emphasized the reluctance of Christian parents to part with their sons. Stephen Gerlach, the chaplain to the Hapsburg ambassador in Constantinople, noted in 1577 that Christians "give wives to their sons in their eighth or ninth year, only so that they may be freed from the Turkish child-levy, for married ones are not taken." [3] In contrast, the Venetian ambassador reported a century earlier that Christian parents regarded the child-tribute a boon which provided their sons with an opportunity for advancement.

Both these attitudes undoubtedly prevailed. Certainly the imperial capital opened horizons for the new recruit that he could not have imagined in his native village. Indeed, there were instances of Moslem parents so anxious to enter their own freeborn children into the sultan's slave family that they bribed their Christian neighbors to exchange children surreptitiously. It is true that a Christian family of deep religious convictions could never countenance the loss of children to Islam, whatever the rewards might be. But here again we must recall that religious lines at this time were considerably blurred. It was not until the later centuries of Ottoman weakness and Western aggression that both Moslems and Christians became fanatical and intolerant. Of the long list of insurrections against Turkish rule, we know of only one minor disturbance that can be ascribed specifically to this child-levy. It is significant that Suleiman the Magnificent issued a decree in which, after listing the peoples—Russians, Persians, Gypsies, and Turks—from whom boys were not to be levied, he added: "If any officer recruits any of these, either for a bribe or at someone's request or because of the intervention of people in high places, and adds them to the number of my loyal slaves, may the curse of God and the hundred and twenty-four thousand prophets be upon him." [4]

The net result of this remarkable system was that a great Moslem empire was based upon Christian brawn and Christian brain. During the period from 1453 to 1623, when the empire was at its height, only five of the forty-seven grand viziers were of Turkish origin. The remaining forty-two consisted of eleven Albanians, eleven South Slavs, six Greeks, one Circassian, one Armenian, one Georgian, one Italian, and ten of unknown origin. Contemporary Western observers could not help being impressed and overawed by this unique system which took humble Christian peasant boys and transformed them into the great leaders of Islam and the most feared enemies of Christendom. Observed Ambassador Busbecq:

> In Turkey every man has it in his power to make what he will of the position into which he is born and of his fortune in life. Those who hold the highest posts under the Sultan are very often the sons of shepherds and herdsmen, and, so far from being ashamed of their birth, they make it a subject of boasting. . . . Thus among the Turks, dignities, offices, and administrative posts are the rewards of ability and merit; those who are dishonest, lazy, and slothful

never attain to distinction, but remain in obscurity and contempt. This is why the Turks succeed in all that they attempt and are a dominating race and daily extend the bounds of their rule. Our method is very different; there is no room for merit, but everything depends on birth. . . .[5]

ARMED FORCES AND ADMINISTRATION

The armed forces and the administration are considered together here because they were inseparable and to a large degree identical. With few exceptions all administrative officers were soldiers and all army officers had administrative duties. The explanation for this merging of functions is that the Turks were warriors before they were administrators. When they conquered territories they gave administrative duties to their officers who at the same time retained their original military titles and duties.

The greater part of the Ottoman armed forces consisted of a feudal territorial cavalry known as spahis. These were meritorious Moslem soldiers to whom the sultan granted the right to collect certain taxes from specified villages. This was the equivalent of a settled income, in return for which the incumbent was required to reside on the land and to be ready to give war service at a moment's notice. The size of the fief determined the number of extra armed horsemen that the spahi was required to bring to battle. During Suleiman's reign the enfeoffed lands in Europe supplied about 80,000 cavalry and those in Asia about 50,000.

This arrangement superficially resembled the feudal system of Western Europe. In practice it was much more centralized and efficient when the empire was at its height. The spahis were required to serve as long as they were needed, in contrast to the limitation of forty days a year common in the West. The spahis also paid allegiance to only one lord, their sultan, and no subinfeudation was allowed to weaken this relationship. Furthermore, the spahis were directly supervised by the sultan's slaves sent out from Constantinople to administer the provinces. These officials were of several ranks, the highest being the sanjakbey, who governed a district or sanjak, and the beylerbey, who had authority over all the beys of his province.

The central government did not pay these administrators regular salaries from the treasury. Instead, it attached fiefs to the offices, and the proceeds of the fiefs were available for the support of the officeholders. The latter, therefore, were feudal landholders themselves, but only in a limited sense—only by virtue of their office and for the duration of their tenure. Fiefs were set aside not only for administrative offices but also for numerous military posts, for members of the imperial family, and for the sultan's private domain. Thus the spahis, who alone enjoyed hereditary rights, controlled less than half of the enfeoffed land. This in turn meant that Ottoman feudalism was correspondingly more centralized than that in the West. In later days, as we shall see, provincial potentates did arise who successfully defied the authority of Constantinople. But rarely were they rebellious spahis. Rather, they usually were powerful officeholders who refused to relinquish their posts and the attached lands to a government that had grown lax and feeble.

We need to note also that the sultan's slaves who were sent to govern the provinces were responsible not only for administrative but also for military duties. In time of war they acted as military officers, assembling the spahis of their districts and leading them to the meeting place set by the sultan. Originally these warrior-administrators had been drawn from the Moslem landed families, but with the adoption of the child-levy the sultan replaced them with his slaves. In doing so he assured his authority over the feudal spahis, whether scattered over the countryside or gathered for war.

Not only did the sultan control the feudal cavalry by appointing his slaves to the command posts; he also controlled the regular standing army because its entire membership from top to bottom consisted of his slaves. This standing army comprised two great sections: the infantry known as the janissaries and the regular cavalry known as the spahis of the Porte—to be distinguished from the feudal cavalry or spahis. The spahis of the Porte were an elite corps, noted for their magnificent dress and accouterments, and respected for their incomparable skill as horsemen and bowmen. Under Suleiman they numbered ten to twelve thousand, and, with their attendant horsemen, who also rode into battle, they totaled forty to fifty thousand.

The most famous and feared unit of the Ottoman military machine was the corps of janissaries, in which were included smaller groups of armorers, artillerymen, and transport troops. Numbering ten to twelve thousand men in Suleiman's time, the janissaries possessed a discipline and *esprit* that made them the terror of the Christian world. They were almost as feared, however, within their own empire, for they had a strong sense of what they considered to be their rights and privileges. They caused much trouble and anxiety to as strong a ruler as Suleiman. In later centuries they dominated weak sultans to the point where they became a menace to the order and security of the empire they were supposed to protect.

THE MOSLEM INSTITUTION

We have seen that a basic difference between the Ruling and Moslem Institutions was that the former was slave-manned, whereas the latter of necessity was exclusively Moslem. The core of the Moslem Institution comprised those true believers who were experts in their knowledge of the Koran and who served as teachers, as judges, and as jurist-theologians.

The teachers taught in schools which were usually attached to mosques and which were in three grades: primary schools (mektebs), colleges (medressehs), and law schools of university grade (higher medressehs). The graduates of the colleges were eligible to teach in the primary schools and to attend to ecclesiastical duties. Those who completed the long and arduous course in the law schools could choose one of several callings: they might become professors of law in their turn, or they might join the select and distinguished class of jurists, or enter the judicial system. In the latter case they would be appointed as judges or kazis, of which there were numerous and complicated categories, culminating in the kaziasker or chief judge of Rumeli (Europe) and the kaziasker of Anatolia (Asia). The kazis might be compared to the judges of Western courts. The law they administered was the sacred law supplemented by the kanuns of the sultans and the customs of the regions in which they served. Contemporary Western observers were impressed by the speed and definiteness with which the kazis settled their cases, though they also reported that bribery and corruption were as common as in their own countries.

Those university graduates who became jurists ranked the highest in public esteem. These jurists or muftis were assigned as counselors to the kazis of every important city and to the sanjakbeys and beylerbeys. The function they fulfilled had no exact parallel in Western society. Appointed for life, the muftis lived in retirement and could not take the intiative on any issue. Rather, they served as a sort of court of appeal or of reference. If a judge or a bey or any private citizen faced a problem involving knowledge of the sacred law he would refer it to the mufti. The latter, after careful consideration, gave his professional opinion or fetva, which usually settled the case. The mufti of Constantinople, known as the Sheik ul-Islam, was the highest religious and legal authority of the empire. His position might be compared to that of the Supreme Court in the United States. He interpreted and defended the sacred law, the Ottoman equivalent of the American Constitution. In a sense he stood above the sultan himself. He could pass judgment, if requested, upon any action or legislation by the sultan, and if he found it in violation of the sacred law, the sultan then could rightfully be deposed.

This greatly simplified description of the Moslem Institution gives some notion of its extraordinary authority and influence. All these teachers, judges, and jurists, known collectively as the ulema or learned men, had an identical training and a common philosophy of life. They were the exponents and guardians of the sacred law. And since this inflexible body of doctrine was essentially hostile to change and progress, the Moslem Institution became the instrument of a blighting bondage upon the empire and its peoples. Whereas the Western world emancipated itself from a comparable scholasticism, the Ottoman Empire, partly because of the influence of the Moslem Institution, remained in servitude until the nineteenth century. In short, the ulema gave the empire a monolothic unity which at first was impressive and effective but which in the long run proved a fatal millstone.

THE DIVAN

Having considered both the Moslem and Ruling Institutions, we turn finally to the Divan, the body that brought them both together and gave unity to the organization of the empire. The early sultans presided in person over the meetings of the Divan, but Suleiman and his successors usually delegated this function to their grand viziers. The latter were the sultans' "burden-bearers" in fact as well as in name. They supervised the entire imperial administration, both central and provincial. They controlled the army and were expected to lead it in the field if necessary. Together with the kaziaskers they served as a supreme court of justice. And throughout the year they presided over long sessions of the Divan four days each week.

The Divan consisted of ex officio members who represented both Institutions. The kaziaskers of Europe and Asia represented the Moslem Institution. Their counterparts from the Ruling Institution were the two administrative heads, the beylerbeys of Europe and Asia, and the two financial heads, the defterdars of Europe and Asia. The latter were the treasurers of the empire, responsible for all incoming and outgoing funds. The janissaries were represented by their general or agha, and the naval forces by their admiral or kapudan pasha. Finally there was the nishanji, the head of the imperial chancery, which made and preserved a record of every act of the government.

The Divan transacted an enormous amount of business with efficiency and dispatch. Discussion was brief and to the point, the Turks being traditionally close-tongued. All decisions were subject to the approval of the sultan, but when this was given they were irrevocable. Since the sacred law was the constitution of the empire, the Divan had no legislative authority. But it was the top judicial and administrative organ of the state—the capstone of the Moslem and Ruling Institutions.

STATUS OF NON-MOSLEMS

The Ottoman Empire was unique not only for its slave system of administration but also for its unequaled degree of religious tolerance. In a period when Catholics and Protestants were massacring each other and when Jews were being hounded from one Christian state to another, the subjects of the sultan were free to worship as they wished with comparatively minor disabilities.

The explanation is to be found partly in the religious law of Islam and partly in Ottoman political strategy. The sacred law recognized the Christians and Jews as being, like the Moslems, People of the Book. Both had a scripture—a written word of revelation. Their faith was accepted as true, though incomplete, since Mohammed had superseded Moses and Jesus Christ. Islam therefore tolerated the Christians and Jews. It permitted them to practice their faith with certain restrictions and penalties.

Islam also laid down exact rules for all the concerns of life. It was both a religious and a civil code. Consequently, in tolerating the religions of the non-Moslems it also accepted their usuages and customs. This was implemented by permitting non-Moslem subjects to organize into communities with their own ecclesiastical leaders. These communities were known as millets, of which there were as many as there were religious groups. Thus the theocratic Ottoman Empire was organized not on the basis of ethnic groups but rather of ecclesiastical communities. The Ottoman authorities divided their subjects not into Greeks or Bulgarians or Rumanians, but rather into the following millets: Orthodox, Gregorian Armenian, Roman Catholic, Jewish, and Protestant.

The most privileged of these millets was the Orthodox, partly because of its superior numbers but also because of certain political considerations. After conquering Constantinople, Mohammed II sought to perpetuate the rift between Orthodox and Catholic Christianity by encouraging his Orthodox subjects to regard him as their benefactor and protector against the pope. For this reason he arranged for the election of a new patriarch to head the Orthodox Church, and granted the patriarch ecclesiastical and secular jurisdiction which in certain respects exceeded that which had been allowed by the Byzantine emperors.

In the following chapter we shall examine the precise degree of religious autonomy enjoyed by the Balkan Christians under Ottoman rule. We shall note also that they did not have full religious equality. Among other discriminations they were required to pay a special capitation tax and they were also subject to the child-tribute, which was enforced until the seventeenth century. But granting all this, the position of the nonconformist was much more favorable in the Ottoman Empire than in Christian Europe.

The most striking evidence of Ottoman tolerance is the large-scale immigration of Jewish refugees following their expulsion from Spain. The newcomers were welcomed and were accorded the same privileges enjoyed by other non-Moslems. This unprecedented reception stimulated new waves of Jewish immigration until a total of approximately one hundred thousand found refuge under the star and crescent. As merchants, artisans, and professional men, they soon played an important role in the affairs of the empire. A certain Joseph Nasi exerted such influence upon Selim II that foreign ambassadors respectfully courted this "Great Jew" and reported his comments and actions. Jewish traders and craftsmen were to be found in almost every city in the empire. Jewish physicians, interpreters, and financiers made themselves indispensable to Ottoman officials. Lady Mary Wortley Montagu, wife of the British ambassador, was so impressed by the unique position of the Jews that she described it at length in a letter to her sister on May 17, 1717:

> I observed most of the rich tradesmen were Jews. That people are an incredible power in this country. They have many privileges above all the natural Turks themselves, and have formed a very considerable commonwealth here, being judged by their own laws, and have drawn the whole trade of the empire into their hands, partly by the firm union among themselves, and prevailing on the idle temper and want of industry of the Turks. Every pasha has his Jew, who is his homme d'affaires; he is let into all his secrets, and does all his business. No bargain is made, no bribe received, no merchandise disposed of, but what passes through their hands. They are the physicians, the stewards, and interpreters of the great men.[6]

OTTOMAN CULTURE

Of the many popular misconceptions concerning the Ottoman Empire, the most common have to do with its culture. It is widely believed that the empire was large and powerful but backward and barbarous, and that the literature and arts it did possess were the product not of the Turks but rather of the Greeks, the Syrians, the Egyptians, and the other subject peoples.

Considering first the question of the ethnic origins of Ottoman culture, we find that the Turkish contribution was not as predominant as might be expected. But it should be remembered that the Turkish people were a small minority in their empire, and furthermore, a minority whose energies were concentrated to a great extent upon war and conquest. Perhaps an analogy may be drawn here between the Turkish warrior and the American frontiersman. The conquest of an empire may have left as little time and inclination for cultural pursuits as the conquest of a wilderness.

Whether or not this analogy is tenable, there remains the basic question of the validity of considering the numerous writers and artists of non-Turkish origin as Greeks or Syrians or Armenians or whatever their ethnic strain might have been. For illustration we may take the case of Sinan Pasha, the most famous architect of the Ottoman Empire. Born in 1589 of an obscure Christian Greek family in Asia Minor, he was inducted into the janissary corps through the child levy. He rose quickly through the ranks because of his skill in devising ferries and building bridges during the campaigns. Soon he was engaged exclusively in building mosques and palaces commissioned by the rulers and grandees of the empire. During his long lifetime of ninety years he worked with such energy and distinction that he gained an international reputation as the "Turkish Michelangelo." In every part of the empire, from Bosnia to Mecca, he left the imprint of his genius. Before his death at the age of ninety he had erected no less than 343 buildings, including 81 mosques, 55 schools, 50 chapels, 34 palaces, and 33 baths. Two of his pupils, it might be noted, later were responsible for the Taj Mahal.

The significance of Sinan's career is that it demonstrates why Ottoman culture cannot be considered simply the sum total of several individual national contributions. Sinan was definitely an Ottoman rather than a Greek architect. He was so not only because his style was distinctively Ottoman but also because his training, his promotions, and his amazing productivity are explainable only within the context of the Ottoman Empire with its wealth and its unique opportunities for advancement. Sinan Pasha was an Ottoman rather than a Greek architect for the same reason that Carl Sandburg is an American rather than a Swedish poet.

Turning from the origin of Ottoman culture to its content, we find that it was far from being scanty and inferior. Instead, it was sophisticated, highly advanced, and important in the life of the empire. On the other hand, it cannot be placed in the first rank of world civilizations. It lacked the originality and creativeness of a truly great culture like that of the ancient Greeks.

One reason was the stultifying influence of Islamic religious taboos. The strict injunction against the reproduction of the human form precluded any work in sculpture and painting. Perhaps an even greater handicap was the overpowering influence of the Persian, Arabic, and Byzantine civilizations to which the Turks fell heir. So massive and overwhelming was this heritage that in the long run it acted as an anesthetic rather than a stimulant. Important branches of Ottoman culture never freed themselves from the numbing influence of the past.

Ottoman literature provides the classic example of this cultural bondage. Until the mid-nineteenth century it consisted almost exclusively of poetry, prose being reserved for utilitarian purposes. An outstanding feature of this poetry was its immense popularity. Indeed, it was socially indispensable. Just as the Western gentleman of this period quoted Latin and Greek authors, so the Ottoman gentleman garnished his speech with Persian quotations. If he were able, in addition, to write verse of his own, then his social status and advancement were assured. The imperial court swarmed with poets, many of whom received handsome pensions or comfortable sinecures. It was not uncommon for sultans to hold literary competitions and to participate in the brilliant repartee and extemporaneous versifying. Many of the sultans—twenty-one of the thirty-four—have left verses of their own composition. By the seventeenth century this passion for poetry had become a veritable craze. One grand vizir wrote his reports from the battlefield in verse, and the sultan in reply sent his instructions also in verse.

Despite its popularity and honored position, Ottoman poetry remained artificial and unoriginal. It was almost entirely Persian in tone, form, and sentiment. The Seljuk Turks first adopted the highly developed Persian culture and then transmitted it to their Ottoman successors. Unfortunately the creative genius of Persia had by that time become sterile. The Ottomans therefore inherited a literature that was subtle and brilliant yet static and stultifying.

Ottoman poets wrote their verses in Persian meters and Persian forms. They dropped the simplicity of early Turkish verse in favor of metaphors, similes, homonyms, anagrams, and a host of other rhetorical embellishments. They faithfully repeated the traditional phrases and associations. "The 'moon-face,' the 'cypress-form,' the 'ruby-lip,' occur with wearisome repetition. . . . When the 'nightingale' is mentioned we may be sure the 'rose' is not far away, and if we read of the 'moth' in one line we may feel safe about meeting the 'taper' in the next." [7]

The themes likewise were those of the Persian masters. Although only a score in number, these traditional themes were presented again and again with ever-increasing beauty of language and ever subtler ingenuity of phrase. Even the language did not escape the overmastering Persian influence. The original rugged Tatar dialect became a marvelous literary language —brilliant, harmonious, subtle—but so artificial and so far removed from everyday speech that it became incomprehensible to all but the educated

Ottoman gentleman. And he, of course, represented only a small percentage of the total population.

THE OSMANLI AND THE TURK

Ottoman poetry was a class poetry. This was true also of the other arts practiced and patronized by the ruling circles in Constantinople. Although the empire was democratic in the sense that the classes were not rigid and exclusive, the fact remains that they did exist. Class distinction was clear and sharp, especially in cultural matters. This is strikingly evident in the different meaning of the two words "Osmanli" and "Turk." An Osmanli was an educated gentleman of broad intellectual interests who used the refined literary language heavily encrusted with Persian and Arabic words. A Turk, by contrast, was an unlettered provincial of Asia Minor who spoke the purer but cruder and despised Turkish idiom. The Osmanli looked down upon the Anatolian peasant Turk, calling him Kaba Turk or rough Turk, and Eshek Turk or donkey Turk.

Evliya Chelebi, the noted seventeenth-century traveler, is a good example of the Osmanli gentleman. His writings reflect a deep-seated and unaffected feeling of superiority reminiscent of a nineteenth-century British colonial official. Evliya came by his attitude naturally. He had behind him three centuries of successful empire building as well as the basic contempt of a devout Moslem for all infidels. He looked with scorn upon the Christian subjects of the empire. He loathed the Persians because they were schismatic Moslems. He had few favorable comments to make when he journeyed through Germany, the Low Countries, Scandinavia, and Poland. Yet with all his prejudices, Evliya was a man of considerable culture. Like his fellow Osmanlis he had a thorough knowledge of the sacred Islamic literature and he could quote freely from the Persian classics. He appreciated the arts and was a fine musician. He was typical of his class in his love for country life, animals, gardening, and sports. He himself was an expert horseman, archer, and swimmer. For all his mysticism and piety, Evliya was very much the gourmet, describing with relish the choicest viands and sweets and indicating precisely where they might be found. As a good Moslem he disclaimed any firsthand knowledge of wines; yet he showed himself thoroughly familiar with the best brands consumed by the unbelievers in the taverns across the Golden Horn. In short, Evliya was an all-round man—a typical Osmanli.

The Turk, on the other hand, had different training and different tastes. The literary language and the sophisticated poetry were for him a closed book. Instead, he obtained his amusement at the popular Punch and Judy show commonly known as Karagioz. This was a marionette show performed at night against a white linen screen lighted from behind to show off the figures. These were made of tinted camel hide and manipulated at the end of strings by the master of the show. Every evening as soon as it grew dark, crowds gathered in the innumerable coffeehouses where the shows were usually held. There they watched the moving silhouettes of the puppets and roared with laughter at the humorous sallies in the dialogues. There was much ribaldry and coarse joking, but not infrequently this was a cover for political and social satire. The principal character, Karagioz, was the embodiment of the plebeian Turk. Seemingly naïve and crude, he was in reality shrewd and cunning. In the end he invariably bested his more sophisticated rivals. His foil was the pompous Hadjievat, who had acquired a smattering of "culture" and who decorated his speech with elegant Arabic phrases. These were incomprehensible to Karagioz, and in mocking imitation he turned them into crude indecencies and puns to the delight of the sympathetic audience.

The guilds also played an important role in the social life of the Turks who lived in the towns and cities. Evliya Chelebi has left a vivid description of a roisterous three-day procession before the sultan in Constantinople in 1638. The various guilds participated—seven hundred and thirty-five in all— and Evliya describes them for us as they file past the imperial pavilion. Each guild is preceded by its band, followed by several wagons bearing symbolical groups representative of the particular craft or profession. As the wagons roll along, the occupants scatter sweets in all directions and amuse the spectators by shouting, dancing, gesticulating, grimacing, and bantering in carnival fashion.

There were the scavengers who paid "for the right to search the city dunghills for coins, nails, precious stones and other small articles"; the miners, mostly Armenians, "a foul-smelling set of men, yet indispensable in sieges"; the Chief Executioner "girt with a fiery sword, his belt bulging with all the instruments of his craft"; "the corporation of thieves and footpads, a very numerous one who have an eye to your purse"; "the corporation of pimps and bankrupts who are also without number"; and the night-watchmen who, as they pass along, "strike their staves on the ground and cry out, as if they were after a thief: 'Hie! Catch him! Don't let him get away! There he goes!' and, by way of a joke, they lay hold of the nearest spectators giving them a thorough fright, all in fun. The crowd, at their approach, open out on both sides so as to give a wide berth to their frolics."

We see the divers who spit oil from their mouths to mirror the bed of the sea, and who adorn their ears with mermaids' hairs; also the lion keepers, the bear leaders, the coffeehouse storytellers, the Greek charcoal burners, the snowmen from Mount Olympus with sacks of snow to provide the palace with iced drinks, and the Turcomen syrup sellers who, "with their sugar-sweet tongues . . . succeed in wheedling themselves into the hearts of women and obtaining from them the sweetest of favors. Such sly fellows are these wily Turks."

More prosaic were the guildsmen connected with the market: the cooks, dried-garlic merchants, butchers, mustard merchants, sherbet sellers, pastry makers, fishermen and fish cooks, textile merchants, honey dealers, goldsmiths, fruit merchants, watchmakers, poulterers, furriers, tanners, shoe-makers, brewers, and tripe sellers—the latter not without significance, for Evliya gives us a preventive for a hangover: tripe soup, to be eaten last thing before retiring. All in all, a brilliant and fascinating pageant of the Ottoman Empire at its height.[8]

7. Balkan Peninsula under Ottoman Rule

N<small>O</small> PERIOD of modern European history remains so obscure as the five centuries of Ottoman rule in the Balkans. Contemporary Western observers, fascinated and awed by the ever-expanding Ottoman Empire, wrote detailed accounts of what they saw and experienced. But most of these accounts are limited to Constantinople and to a few other cities. The travelers who ventured into the Balkan lands seldom strayed from the great European road running from Vienna through Budapest, Belgrade, Sofia, Adrianople, and on to the Ottoman capital. Very few contemporaries had any contact with, or interest in, the mass of Christian peoples living in the Balkan countryside. Accordingly, we are well informed about the institutions of the empire but largely ignorant of its subjects. We know much about the sultans and their courts and armies but very little about the Christian peasants and how they fared under Ottoman officials and Turkish feudal lords.

The Balkan peoples themselves have left few records of this period of their history. Having lost their ruling class, which alone was educated and articulate, they were left leaderless, anonymous, and silent. Even their clergymen were largely illiterate. The few who did have a smattering of learning contented themselves with ecclesiastical discourses and fanciful chronicles. Thus for centuries the Greeks, Albanians, Rumanians, and South Slavs were "peoples without a history." And when at long last they recovered their independence they turned their backs on the preceding Ottoman period as one of national humiliation and ignominy. Instead, their historians wrote of earlier periods of glory and greatness. The Greeks recounted the illustrious achievements of their classical and Byzantine ancestors; the Bulgarians turned to their great tsars, Simeon and Samuel; and the Serbians to their Stephen Dushan. Consequently five centuries of Balkan history still remain in large part blurred and indiscernible.

Inadequate as our knowledge is of Ottoman rule in the Balkans, we can at least dismiss as myth five centuries of unrelieved tyranny and oppres-

96

sion. The origins of this myth are natural and understandable. It was fostered in the nineteenth century by the various Balkan peoples who, fired by their newly awakened national consciousness, rejected and denounced everything connected with their past servitude. It was accepted and reinforced by Westerners who were more familiar with the empire of Abdul Hamid than that of Suleiman the Magnificent. Hence it came to be considered a fact that for five hundred years the Balkan Christians had been despoiled and persecuted. This interpretation is a typical example of modern nationalist mythology but it bears little resemblance to historical fact. The purpose of this chapter is to analyze as clearly as our present knowledge will allow the actual position of the Balkan peoples during the half millenium of Ottoman rule.

MIGRATIONS OF PEOPLES

The Balkan Peninsula did not change radically in its ethnic composition during the Ottoman period. It did not experience mass migrations comparable to those of the Slavs during the Byzantine era. But it did undergo considerable change in the details of its ethnic configuration. Certain Asiatic Moslem peoples settled in appreciable numbers in various localities, and the Balkan peoples themselves shuffled back and forth under the pressure of economic necessity and historical events.

The Turkish conquerors settled in the Balkans in comparatively small numbers. Those who resided in the towns as administrators and soldiers naturally withdrew with the shrinking of the Ottoman frontiers during the eighteenth and nineteenth centuries. The only Turks that remained were those who had actually settled as agriculturists. Most of these were to be found in the Constantinople area, in Bessarabia, the Dobruja, southern and eastern Bulgaria, and in certain valleys in Macedonia and Thrace. It is estimated that on the eve of World War II approximately one million Turks resided in Constantinople and its environs, and another million were scattered about in isolated settlements in the various Balkan states.

Certain other Moslem peoples appeared in the Balkans, the most numerous being Tatars who came from the Crimea in the late eighteenth century, and Circassians from the Caucasus about a century later. Both these groups settled in the Dobruja and in eastern Bulgaria. Another significant immigration was that of the Jewish refugees who came from Christian Europe in the fifteenth and sixteenth centuries. Constantinople received thirty to forty thousand of the newcomers, Saloniki fifteen to twenty thousand. Almost every other Balkan town had its community of Jews, invariably engaged in trade, crafts, and the professions.

These additions to Balkan ethnography did not affect the dominant position of the native peoples—the Greeks, Albanians, South Slavs, and Rumanians. Of these peoples, the Greeks emigrated to foreign countries in largest numbers, particularly during the long series of Turkish-Venetian wars. Some settled in Dalmatia, Venetia, southern Italy, Corsica, Sicily, and Malta, where they were gradually assimilated by the native inhabitants. Others migrated to Italian cities, where they founded communities which later made important cultural and economic contributions to the motherland. With the growth of trade in the seventeenth and eighteenth centuries, thousands of Greek merchants settled in the urban centers of the northern Balkans, Central Europe, and southern Russia. These communities also contributed greatly to the Greek awakening that preceded the national revolution in 1821.

At the same time that the Greeks were going abroad, large numbers of Albanians were migrating southward into Greece. These agriculturists and stockbreeders settled large areas in central Greece, the Peloponnesus, and even a few islands near the mainland. Since they were an unlettered people, and of the same religion as the Greeks, they were gradually Hellenized by the Greek church and Greek schools. As late as the mid-nineteenth century, however, one could find many villages where the women and young children knew only a few words of Greek. The Albanians also expanded during the eighteenth and nineteenth centuries into "Old Serbia," particularly the Kosovo region. Since many Serbians already had migrated northward, the Albanians were able to assimilate those that remained behind. Thus this area has remained predominately Albanian, even though it is now a part of the Yugoslav state.

The most extensive migrations during the Ottoman period occurred among the Serbian people. With the conquest of Serbia in the fifteenth century, large numbers crossed the Danube to Hungary while others migrated to Dalmatia, Bosnia, and Croatia. More Serbians crossed over into Hungary at the end of the seventeenth century following the defeat of the Hapsburg armies that they had supported. These migrations, together with the ravaging effects of the Austrian-Turkish wars, left northern Serbia sparsely populated. The mountaineers of "Old Serbia" and western Macedonia took advantage of the opportunity for better land and migrated in large numbers into the area between the Morava and Drina rivers. At the same time other mountaineers were migrating westward from Bosnia and Dalmatia to western Slavonia, and from Montenegro and Herzegovina to western Croatia. These population movements had important repercussions. They extended the sway of the Serbian people considerably further to the west and to the north, and they established in southern Hungary a large Serbian population that was to contribute as much to the awakening of the Turkish-ruled Serbs as the overseas Greek communities did to their compatriots at home.

In addition to these individual waves of migrations there was a common tendency among the Balkan Christians to move out of the urban centers in order to avoid the Turkish officials and garrisons. As a result the towns became denationalized. During most of the Ottoman period they reflected the nationality of those who held political and economic power. Accordingly, the towns, regardless of their location, consisted largely of Turkish artisans, administrators, and soldiers, and of Greek and Jewish traders and artisans. Western travelers, between the sixteenth and eighteenth centuries, described the principal Balkan cities as follows: Belgrade—"A mass of buildings and extensive suburbs inhabited by various races, Turks, Greeks, Jews, Hungarians, Dalmatians, and many others"; [1] Sofia—"A place so wholly Turkish, that there is nothing in it that appears more antique than the Turks themselves"; [2] Philippopolis—"Almost wholly inhabited by Greeks"; [3] and Adrianople—"Most of the rich tradesmen are Jews." [4]

When a Serb, Rumanian, or Bulgarian, went into a town in his native land he found himself a foreigner. This anomalous situation continued until these people gained their independence and until trade and industry gained momentum. Then the towns grew fairly rapidly and in doing so drew their population from the surrounding countryside. In this manner the national character of the towns gradually changed until the nationality of the land recaptured the towns. This transformation caused serious frontier disputes in border regions. In southern Albania and Macedonia the Greeks claimed certain regions because of their past or even continued control of the urban centers, while their opponents pointed to the predominantly non-Greek population in the countryside.

ADMINISTRATION

The Ottoman Empire was divided into two parts for administrative purposes. The European section was headed by the beylerbey (lord of lords) of Rumelia and the Asiatic by the beylerbey of Anatolia. With the great expansion of the empire under Selim and Suleiman this simple division became administratively cumbersome. The number of beylerbeys was then steadily increased until by the end of the sixteenth century, when the empire reached its greatest extent, they numbered about thirty-five. At the same time their title was changed from beylerbey to veli, and the territories they administered were known as eyalets rather than beylerbeyliks. A typical eyalet in the Balkan Peninsula comprised a considerable area: for example, Morea, Bosnia, or Temesvar. Each veli had a staff for the administration of his eyalet. This included a mufti (interpreter of the Koran), a reis effendi (recording secretary), a defterdar (treasurer), and a considerable number of clerks.

Below the veli in the administrative hierarchy stood the sanjakbey, who administered a sanjak, of which there were several in each eyalet. Each sanjakbey had a number of assistants corresponding to those of the veli. In the smaller towns the sanjakbeys were represented by the subashis, who were supplied with a sufficient number of janissaries to maintain the peace.

The position of the Christian peasants governed by these officials varied considerably from region to region. When the Turks overran the Balkan Peninsula they abolished the feudal arrangements prevailing under the former Byzantine, Latin, Serbian, and Bulgarian rulers. In their place they introduced a feudal system of their own which was more lenient and centralized. They granted fiefs in the newly conquered lands to their most deserving warriors. As noted in an earlier chapter, these fief holders, or spahis, were of two ranks, the ziams with large fiefs (ziamets) and the timariots who held small fiefs (timars). In time of war each spahi was required to report for service with a number of armed followers proportionate to the size of his fief. When the empire was at its height, there were approximately twelve thousand fiefs in the Balkan lands.

Turkish immigrants settled down and actually occupied the land only in certain localities noted above. In the rest of the peninsula the Turks normally parceled out the most fertile plains areas as fiefs to the spahis. This in turn caused a considerable number of Greek and Slavic peasants to migrate to nearby mountainous regions. Peasants who lived in the mountainous areas that were not divided into fiefs paid taxes directly to the government tax farmers. The taxes consisted primarily of the light head tax required from all non-Moslems and also the tithe which normally took one tenth of the farm produce. Peasants on the military fiefs paid taxes to the spahi or to his representative. These taxes were similar to those paid to the government. They comprised the head tax—which the spahi transmitted to the treasury—the customary tithe, and light money dues depending on the amount of land the peasant cultivated.

Many peasants lived on fiefs not held by spahis. In fact, the spahis controlled less than half the enfeoffed land of the empire. The remainder comprised fiefs that were set aside for the support of higher administrative officers, members of the imperial family, and the sultan himself. Another large category of peasants lived on land known as vakf, which was not under feudal tenure. Vakf land was designated for the support of religious, educational, and charitable enterprises, such as schools, libraries, public baths, mosques, and convents for dervishes. Some of this land originally had been set aside by sultans. Private individuals later contributed more parcels of land. Since no vakf property could be confiscated, it increased steadily in extent until it included, according to one estimate, a third of all the arable land of the empire.

The average Balkan peasant during the early Ottoman period tilled his land under better conditions than his counterpart in Christian Europe. One advantage was the lighter tax burden. He had hereditary use of a definite tract of land, which he regarded as his own and for which he paid only the head tax, the tithe, and a few minor additional imposts. Another advantage was the freedom from the feudal services and seigniorial jurisdiction characteristic of Western feudalism. The spahi had no legal right of lordship and justice over the peasants living in his fief. He was not allowed to eject them by force or, theoretically at least, to prevent them from moving and settling elsewhere. He was permitted only to collect the customary dues in return for which he gave military service in time of war. In other words, the Balkan peasant enjoyed the great advantage of being regarded simply as a source of revenue. This basic difference between Western and Ottoman feudalism explains the favorable position of the Balkan peasant—a least for as long as Ottoman feudalism remained vigorous and unimpaired. Undoubtedly there was considerable difference between the theory and the practice of Turkish feudalism, even when the empire was unimpaired. Nevertheless, the bulk of contemporary evidence indicates clearly that the Balkan peoples at this early period enjoyed substantial advantages denied to their counterparts in the West.

AUTONOMOUS REGIONS

The administrative and tax system described above is a simplified blueprint of Ottoman rule in the Balkans. But the blueprint does not apply to all sections of the peninsula. Regional conditions varied too greatly to make complete uniformity possible. Also, Ottoman administration developed in an *ad hoc* fashion. During the period of conquest special local arrangements and concessions were common. Once made, they were likely to be perpetuated by the inertia and conservative spirit of the empire. Thus we find in every section of the peninsula numerous variations and exceptions to the general pattern of government.

Ottoman authorities customarily granted special privileges to groups, villages, and even entire districts that they considered to be contributing in some manner to the welfare and security of the empire. Groups that received partial or complete tax exemption included miners, bridge builders, ferryboat operators, rice cultivators, official couriers, and guards of bridges, forests, and mountain passes. Also, certain villages were freed from taxation because they produced some valuable commodity and shipped a stipulated portion of their output to Constantinople. Other villages were granted complete self-government as well as tax exemption in return for direct contributions to the armed forces. Examples of this arrangement were certain Bulgarian villages that provided the Ottoman army with regular and auxiliary troops, and also certain Greek islands that sent an annual quota of sailors to the Ottoman navy. Some areas—Athens and Rhodes, for example—were removed from the regular imperial administration and enjoyed a large degree of self-government because they were the permanent appanages of members of the royal family. Finally, certain regions received at the time of their conquest special concessions that were observed thereafter. Typical examples were the city of Yanina in northwestern Greece and the Timok area along the Danube. In the latter place hereditary Serbian leaders dispensed justice, collected taxes, and retained armed guards with no Turkish interference until 1833.

The most significant exceptions to regular administrative procedure were to be found in certain inaccessible mountain areas that the Turks could not subjugate completely or did not deem worth the effort to do so. This was true in northern Albania, where the Ottoman authorities encountered so much resistance that in the mid-sixteenth century they granted complete autonomy and tax exemption in return for contingents of fighting men. A similar situation prevailed in Montenegro. Until the late seventeenth century the Montenegrin mountaineers paid the head tax with reasonable regularity and in return were allowed to manage their own affairs. But in 1688 they began their long struggle for independence, which they continued with varying fortunes until their final success in 1799. Turkish authority was equally tenuous in the mountainous Souli and Cheimarra districts of northwestern Greece and in the Mane district of southern Greece. The inhabitants of these areas paid with much reluctance and irregularity an annual tribute to Constantinople. But in their internal affairs they enjoyed complete autonomy, recognizing the authority only of their own tribal chieftains.

The regions we have considered to this point were included in the customary eyalet administrative units. Theoretically they were subject to the regular imperial government, though in practice their only connection with Constantinople was the periodic tribute. We will consider now the status of four remaining regions: Moldavia, Wallachia, Transylvania, and Ragusa. These were unique in that they were not divided into eyalets and were not under jurisdiction, actual or theoretical, of Ottoman officials.

The Principalities of Moldavia and Wallachia may be considered together, since they were both inhabited by Rumanians and both stood in a similar relationship to Constantinople. We noted in Chapter 4 that the Turks overran Wallachia in the fifteenth century and Moldavia in the sixteenth. They granted complete autonomy to the two principalities in return for the payment of tribute. They also allowed the Rumanian nobles or boyars to elect their own princes or hospodars. Although this practice continued for some time, it soon became meaningless. The candidates for office customarily bribed the sultan's ministers for their favor, which was decisive. Thus the hospodars followed one another in quick succession to the profit of the officials in the capital who pulled the strings. When Peter the Great approached the principalities at the head of his army in 1711, both hospodars proclaimed themselves in his favor. From then on the Ottoman government appointed to the two thrones only members of a group of Greek administrators and financiers known as Phanariotes. Since these Phanariotes came from Constantinople they could be appointed and removed without any difficulty. This arrangement continued until the Greek revolution of 1821, after which the Phanariotes were replaced once more by native Rumanian hospodars. But by that time the Ottoman government no longer held undisputed domination over the principalities. Russian influence and intervention were becoming increasingly strong until the Crimean War made possible the creation of an autonomous and united Rumanian state in 1861.*

The third of the four autonomous Balkan dependencies of the Ottoman Empire was the kingdom of Transylvania. Its population was predominantly Rumanian, though with large Hungarian and German minorities. Before the Turkish conquest Transylvania had been a province of the Hungarian kingdom. When Suleiman overran Hungary he granted Transylvania an autonomous tributary status. His successors respected this arrangement, allowing the native nobility to elect their kings with little interference. After the

* See Chapter 18.

failure of the Turks to take Vienna in 1683 their influence declined in Transylvania. A few years later, by the Treaty of Karlowitz in 1699, they ceded the entire area to the Austrians. It remained under the Hapsburgs until World War I, after which it was incorporated in the enlarged Rumanian kingdom.*

The fourth and final Balkan dependency of the Ottoman Empire was the tiny city-republic of Dubrovnik or Ragusa. Founded in the seventh century by fugitives fleeing before the invading Slavs, it soon became the leading commercial center of the Dalmatian coast. For centuries its merchants and literary men played a leading role in the economic and cultural life of the peninsula. But it never possessed the resources necessary for complete independence. Accordingly, the Ragusans paid tribute to the most powerful neighboring state in order to be free to carry on their trade. First they recognized the sovereignty of Venice, then of Hungary, and finally of the Ottoman Empire. The Turkish conquest of the Balkans proved a boon for the Ragusans. The numerous customs barriers erected by the former rulers were replaced by low and uniform duties applying to the whole peninsula. Thus the Ragusans not only accepted Turkish overlordship but actively opposed Venetian attempts to gain control of adjacent territory. This mutually satisfactory relationship with the Turks lasted until the early nineteenth century, when Napoleon acquired all Dalmatia and incorporated Ragusa in his newly created province of Illyria. In 1815 the city passed to the Hapsburgs and remained under their rule until it became a part of the new Yugoslav state in 1918.

In conclusion, the rule of the Ottoman sultans in the Balkans might be compared to that of the Chinese emperors in Eastern Asia. The lands south of the Danube were ruled, with certain exceptions, directly from Constantinople, just as the territory south of the Great Wall was ruled, with similar exceptions, directly from Peking. Likewise, the status of Moldavia, Wallachia, and Transylvania resembled that of Mongolia, Sinkiang, and Tibet. So long as the central government remained strong, these outlying regions acknowledged its sovereignty and paid the customary tribute. But when it became weak, these autonomous regions were the first to come under the control or influence of powerful neighboring empires—Russia and Austria in the case of the Balkans, Russia and Britain in the case of Eastern Asia.

PATRIARCHATE

It is an irony of history that the patriarch of Constantinople enjoyed greater ecclesiastical and secular jurisdiction under the Ottoman sultans than under the Byzantine emperors. One reason for this anomalous situation was the desire of Mohammed II to perpetuate the rift between the Catholic and Orthodox worlds. Accordingly, he arranged for the election to the patriarchal seat of Gennadius Scholarius, an eminent Orthodox jurist and a strong oppo-

* See Chapter 30.

nent of the Latin church. Mohammed also granted Gennadius a berat or ordinance defining the new status of the church.

The berat declared the patriarch to be "untaxable and irremovable." It assigned to him and to his synod the authority to settle all matters of doctrine, to control and discipline all members of the church, to manage all church property, and to levy dues on laity and clergy alike. The berat also granted full freedom of conscience. Orthodox Christians were free to keep sacred books and icons in their homes and to attend church services unmolested. Finally, the berat invested the patriarch with considerable civil authority as the head not only of the Orthodox church but also of the Orthodox community or millet. Ecclesiastical tribunals could pass on matters concerning marriage, divorce, and inheritance. Gradually they extended their jurisdiction to all civil cases since Christian litigants usually preferred the verdict of the bishop to that of the Turkish kadi. Thus the Orthodox bishops functioned in their dioceses virtually as prefects over the Christian population as well as ecclesiastical prelates. And the patriarch in Constantinople was not only the head of the Orthodox Church and of the Orthodox millet, but also a recognized Ottoman official, holding the rank of vizir, and serving as intermediary between the Orthodox Christians and the imperial government.

The other factor explaining the increased authority of the patriarch was the sudden extension of the imperial frontiers from the environs of Constantinople to the valley of the Danube. This made possible a corresponding extension of the frontiers of patriarchal jurisdiction. During the preceding centuries the trend had been in the opposite direction. The decline of Byzantium and the rise of the Bulgarian and Serbian empires had led to the establishment of independent Bulgarian and Serbian churches and to the corresponding contraction of the Constantinople patriarchate. Conversely, the disappearance of the Bulgarian and Serbian states with the Turkish invasion was followed also by the disappearance of their respective churches. The Bulgarian patriarchate, which had been established originally in the time of Tsar Simeon, came to an end in 1393. Likewise, the Serbian patriarchate, which had arisen under Tsar Dushan, was abolished in 1459. During the following centuries the ecclesiastical center of the Balkan Slavs was the Bulgarian Archbishopric of Ohrid, which retained a certain degree of autonomy. But the seat of ecclesiastical authority was now definitely in Constantinople. The jurisdiction of the patriarch, like that of the sultan, was unchallenged throughout the Balkans.

It remained unchallenged until 1557, when the Grand Vizir Mohammed Sokolli (Sokolovich), who was of Serbian origin, used his influence to establish the Serbian Patriarchate of Ipek (Pec). For over a century this patriarchate played an important role in Serbian national life. During the series of Hapsburg-Ottoman wars in the late seventeenth and early eighteenth centuries, the patriarchate threw in its lot with the Hapsburgs. But the latter finally were forced to withdraw across the Danube, leaving the Ipek patriarchate in an impossible position. At this time when the Serbians had been discredited, the Phanariotes and other Greek elements were gaining influence in Constantinople. This combination of circumstances led to the abolition of the Ipek patriarchate in 1766 and of the Ohrid archbishopric the following year.

The Constantinople patriarchate once more reigned supreme in the peninsula. It continued to do so as long as the Balkan peoples remained subject to Ottoman authority. But with the rise of national consciousness and the establishment of independent nation-states we note a repetition of what happened in the late Byzantine period. The imperial frontiers shrank back toward Constantinople and the scope of patriarchal jurisdiction contracted correspondingly. One after another the various Balkan states gained independent or "autocephalous" churches until, by the end of World War I, the Constantinople patriarchate exercised authority only in Constantinople and its environs.

In retrospect, the position of the Orthodox Church under Ottoman rule appears extraordinarily favorable. But a distinction must be drawn between paper privileges and actual practice. The Christians had a substantial degree of religious freedom but this did not mean religious equality. Non-Moslems were forbidden to ride horses or to bear arms. They were required to wear a particular costume to distinguish them from the true believers. Their dwellings could not be loftier than those of the Moslems. They could not repair their churches or ring their bells except by special permission, which was rarely granted. They were required to pay a special capitation tax levied on all non-Moslem adult males in place of military service. And until the seventeenth century the Orthodox Christians paid the tribute in children from which the Jews and the Armenians were exempted.

In addition to these discriminatory obligations and disabilities, non-Moslems were always subject to illegal violations of their privileges. The sultan might confirm the institutional rights of the church but this was no guarantee against outbursts of Moslem fanaticism or arbitrary actions by provincial officials. Church property all too frequently was confiscated and the clergy humiliated and persecuted. The sultans themselves changed their attitude toward the Orthodox Church as they came to realize that there was no danger of a united Christian assault. Their former deference to an esteemed ally therupon changed to scorn for a powerless subject.

BALKAN CHRISTIANITY

Ottoman religious policy is one of the major factors determining the historical development of the Balkan peoples. We have seen that the position of the Orthodox Christians under the Moslem Turks was far from ideal. They suffered from various disabilities and discriminations. In later years they suffered also from arbitrary exactions and occasional violence. Despite this, they enjoyed much more freedom than did the various religious minorities in contemporary Christendom. By way of illustration it is sufficient to mention the plight of the Huguenots in Catholic France, the Catholics in Anglican England, the Orthodox in Catholic Poland, the Moslems in Catholic Spain, and the Jews in all Christian lands.

More revealing is the difference in the manner with which the Turks and the Venetians treated their Greek Orthodox subjects. The Venetians invariably forbade the appointment of Orthodox bishops, compelled the lower clergy to obey the Catholic hierarchy, and supported the latter in their efforts to convert the population to Catholicism. When the French traveler Motraye landed at Modon on the west coast of the Peloponnesus in 1710, he discovered that the townspeople were extremely hostile toward their Venetian overlords, who had gained possession of the Peloponnesus by the Treaty of Karlowitz in 1699. A major grievance was the unceasing proselytism of the Catholic clergy. One of the local inhabitants complained to Motraye that "their priests come to us to talk against our religion, bothering us incessantly and urging us to embrace theirs, something that the Turks never dreamed of doing. On the contrary, they gave us all the liberty that we could have wished for. . . ." [5]

The significance of this difference between Ottoman and Western religious policy is that it explains in large part the success of Balkan Christianity in surviving the centuries of Moslem rule with remarkably few losses. Mass conversions to Islam occurred only in a few parts of the peninsula, the most important being Albania and Bosnia. In both regions the majority of the population had turned away from Christianity by the middle of the seventeenth century. The inhabitants of certain parts of Bulgaria also accepted Islam and came to be known as the Bulgarian-speaking Pomaks. Among the Greeks the only large-scale shift occurred on the island of Crete. The Turks captured the island in 1669 and within a century half of its inhabitants had become Moslems. This shift did not have a permanent effect because the Cretan Moslems emigrated to Turkey when the island passed under Greek control.

In some cases special local circumstances explain these conversions. The large number of Bogomils, harried by both the Orthodox and Catholic churches, contributed greatly to the Islamization of Bosnia. The Cretan islanders appear to have been influenced by the striking contrast between the rapacity and intolerance of their former Venetian masters and the easygoing, laissez-faire policy of the Turks. In other parts of the peninsula a combination of factors prompted the acceptance of Islam. Some Christians wished to escape the child-tribute and the financial exactions, though the latter were never as burdensome as the taxes imposed by the Venetians in their Balkan possessions. Other Christians were driven to Islam by the apathy and ignorance of some of their clergy. Still others committed apostasy lightheartedly because of a tendency toward cultural assimilation between Christian and Moslem communities. This was especially true in Albania, where contemporary observers noted that many Moslems baptized their children, became the godfathers of Christian children, and attended the festivals for Christian saints.

Whatever the combination of factors that prevailed in specific regions, the important point is that the Balkan Christians were never subjected to systematic and sustained proselytism. They never experienced the persecution that the Moslems and the Jews suffered in Spain. Had they done so, the religious map of the Balkans probably would be quite different today. At least two sultans, Selim I and Murad III, did consider seriously the mass extermination of all Christian subjects who refused to embrace Islam. They were dissuaded from their project by the arguments of their religious advisers and also by the prospect of losing the revenue from the capitation tax. But if they had carried out their plan it is difficult to believe that they would not have been substantially successful, given the defenselessness of the Christians and the prestige and attraction of Islam at the time.

If Islam had tirumphed in large areas it would have involved more than simply a shift in the balance of religions. Religious affiliation frequently has determined national consciousness in the Balkans. Thousands of Albanians and Vlachs became Hellenized through their membership in the Greek Orthodox Church. Likewise, thousands of Greeks on the island of Crete considered themselves Turks and chose to emigrate to Turkey because of their Moslem faith. Thus if a large portion of the Balkan peoples had become Moslems, not only their religious but also their cultural and political development would have been altered to a fundamental degree.

It is often stated that the great contribution of Orthodoxy during the Turkish era was that it preserved the religion and culture, and hence the national identity, of the Balkan Christians. This claim is valid, but it should be noted at the same time that the Orthodox Church was able to accomplish its mission because it functioned under conditions which, if not favorable, at least were not uncompromisingly hostile as in the West. Therein lies the significance of Ottoman religious policy for the historical development of the Balkan peoples.

FOLK CULTURE

The Turks had little influence on Balkan culture. One reason was that they were separated from their subjects by religious and social barriers. Another was that the Turks resided mostly in the towns. Accordingly, their cultural influence was limited largely to urban institutions. In fact, Balkan towns took on a marked Oriental character with their bazaars and mosques and narrow streets lined by flimsy wooden houses. Turkish influence on the Balkan languages was substantial. The few books written in the Balkan vernaculars during or immediately following the Turkish period contain a high percentage of words of Turkish origin. These words were gradually eliminated during the decades following liberation, so that eventually they were limited mostly to matters relating to urban life. Thus an American who dines in a Greek or Serbian restaurant in the United States today will find a large proportion of Turkish words on the menu—pilaf for rice, shish-kebab for meat grilled on skewers, moussaka for eggplant pâté, and dolma for vine leaves stuffed with chopped meat.

The superficiality of Turkish influence allowed the Balkan peoples to develop their respective cultures freely. In each case they made their most important contributions in their folk literature. This was usually anonymous, composed in the vernacular, and passed on from generation to generation by word of mouth. Certain characteristics are common to all Balkan folk songs. Most striking is the personification of nature. Mountain peaks dispute with each other; plants and animals hold allegorical conversations; and birds bring aid, give advice, and deliver love messages.

Some of the most artistic and lively of the Greek folk songs are known as the klephtika. These extol the feats of the klephts, or Robin Hood outlaws, who took to the mountains and started a guerrilla resistance that lasted until the winning of national independence. Among the most popular of these songs is "The Death of the Klepht," a piece that is typical not only in its militancy but also in its fearless and nonmetaphysical attitude toward death and the afterlife.

> Eat and drink, my comrades, rejoice and let us be gay,
> nothing ails me but a wound!
> How bitter is the wound, how venomous the bullet!
> Come, lift me up and set me yonder.
> Come, some of you brave lads, and take me
> and carry me up to a high hill.
> Strew green branches; then set me down,
> and from the priests fetch me sweet wine
> to wash the wound, for I am hurt,
> and take my knife, my silver scimitar,
> and dig my grave and build my coffin,
> wide, long, roomy enough for two
> to stand erect, fight, take cover, reload,
> and on my right side, leave a window,
> so that birds may fly in and out, the nightingales of Spring.[6]

Most Balkan ballads are of moderate length or quite short. The one exception is Serbian epic poetry. This is one of the most artistic creations of all the ballad literature of Europe. The epics usually are divided into nine cycles that present a fascinating picture of the history of the Serbian people. Starting with the medieval kingdoms, they continue through the Turkish conquest and occupation, the resistance of the haiduks (corresponding to the Greek klephts), the struggle for independence in the early nineteenth century, and finally the events of the postliberation period. The Serbian heroes in these epics were adopted by the neighboring South Slavic peoples and glorified in their respective literatures. This is particularly true of the burly, blustering, impulsively chivalrous haiduk, Marko Kraljevich. Marko is a spoiled child. He is strong, self-willed, capricious, at times cruel, but always brave, always fighting and hating the Turks, and always protecting the weak and the friendless. Marko also is a fabulous drinker, and so is his steed, Sharatz. Neither touches anything but wine. "Half he drinks himself, half he gives to Sharatz."

These qualities endeared Marko to all South Slavs, and he became their greatest hero. One evening his mother asked him to settle down.

> Weary is thy mother of washing from thy shirts the crimson stain
> But do thou now yoke ox to plow, and plow the hill and the plain.

Humbly Marko promises to obey his mother. The next morning he goes out with oxen and plow. But he knows nothing about husbandry. He starts the oxen cross country and tears up the "tsar's highway."

> Some janissaries come thereby; three packs of gold had they:
> "Plow not the tsar his highway, Prince Marko," said they then.
> "Ye Turks, mar not my plowing!" he answered them again.
> "Plow not the tsar his highway, Prince Marko," they said anew.
> "Ye Turks, mar not my plowing!" he answered thereunto.
> But Marko was vext; in anger he lifted ox and plow,
> And the Turkish janissaries he slew them at a blow,
> And their three packs of treasure to his mother he bore away:
> "Lo, mother, what my plowing hath won for thee to-day!" [7]

ECCLESIASTICAL CULTURE

Turning from the folk arts to the written literature and formal learning of these centuries, we enter another world utterly different in every respect. Here again we find certain common characteristics prevailing throughout the peninsula. The most basic was the all-pervading influence of the Orthodox Church. In the theocratically organized society of this period it naturally dominated education, written literature, and general intellectual life. The few teachers invariably wore priestly robes. The few books, with unimportant exceptions, were theological treatises. In place of several Balkan literatures there existed only one Orthodox ecclesiastical literature, written either in a debased classical Greek incomprehensible to most Greeks, or in an archaic Church Slavonic incomprehensible to most Slavs.

A second common characteristic was the terribly low level of learning. Among the Greeks, for example, the most distinguished scholars had fled to Italy with the Turkish invasion. Patriarch Gennadius attempted to maintain standards by establishing in 1454 the Patriarchal Academy. For centuries this institution fulfilled a most important function in training the Phanariote administrators who filled the top posts in both empire and church. But even this school operated with difficulty, being forced to close down periodically because of lack of funds. In the Greek provinces conditions were infinitely worse. Church schools appeared sporadically in a few towns, struggled along with meager means, and then closed down. The level of learning declined from generation to generation, reaching a low point at the end of the sixteenth century. Persons with even a modicum of education were so scarce that church positions remained vacant. Many villages in central and northern Greece were left without priests. Even archbishops had difficulty in writing their own names correctly.

Similar conditions prevailed amongst the non-Greek peoples of the peninsula. Before the Turkish conquest the outstanding cultural center in the northern Balkans was the Bulgarian capital, Tirnovo. The Bulgarian patriarch, Euthymius, was the most learned Slav of his time. Pupils came to his monastery from Serbia, Rumania, and Russia. Tirnovo came to be known as the Athens of the South Slavs. But in 1393 the Turks captured Tirnovo, forcing Euthymius and his disciples to flee to neighboring countries. In the following centuries learning throughout the northern Balkans sank to the same low level we noted in the Greek lands. The Bulgarians, who formerly had been the most advanced, now were left the farthest behind. The Rumanians had the advantage of a certain degree of autonomy which later allowed their more enlightened princes to endow schools and establish printing presses. The Greeks and the Serbians could look forward to economic aid and intellectual stimulus from their more fortunate compatriots living in foreign countries. But the Bulgarians had neither autonomy at home nor the prospect of assistance from abroad. This explains in part why the Bulgarians were to lag behind the Greeks and the Serbians in developing a sense of national consciousness and in winning their independence.

A third common cultural characteristic was the phenomenon of bilinguism. This arose because of an important difference between the linguistic development of the Latin West and the Greek East. Classical Latin was too closely identified with the Roman Empire to be able to survive its collapse. Hence the development of several Romance languages during the medieval period. In the East, on the other hand, the survival of the Byzantine Empire to the fifteenth century, together with the enormous prestige of the classical language and literature, combined to prevent the ancient Greek language from developing along the same lines as classical Latin. Instead, the ancient language was preserved in a corrupted form known as the katharevousa or "pure" language. This was the language of the cultured Greeks, in the same manner that literary Turkish was the language of the cultured Osmanlis, mentioned in the preceding chapter. But the katharevousa was as unintelligible to the Greek peasant as literary Turkish was to the Anatolian peasant. During the intervening centuries a demotic or vernacular language had developed with simplified grammatical constructions and with a certain number of Slavic, Albanian, Turkish, and Italian words. This demotic language differed as much from ancient Greek as modern English does from that of Chaucer's time. Nevertheless the katharevousa remains the official Greek language to the present day, creating serious educational and literary problems.*

* See Chapter 34.

Bilinguism was a problem in the northern Balkans as well as among the Greeks. In addition to their respective cultures, the South Slavs and the Rumanians had an artificial literary language known as Church Slavonic. This language dates back to the ninth century when the Bulgarian Tsar Boris accepted the Byzantine form of Christianity and encouraged the missionary work of Clement and his followers. These missionaries translated the Holy Scriptures and church books into an archaic Slavic permeated by Greek construction forms and ecclesiastical terminology. This Church Slavonic language continued to be used for centuries. It became the official ecclesiastical and literary language, not only of the Bulgarians, but also of the other peoples who adopted Orthodox Christianity—the Serbians, the Rumanians, and the Russians. For these people the Church Slavonic was as artificial and incomprehensible as the katharevousa was for the Greeks. But whereas the Greeks retained their "pure" language under the influence of their classical tradition, the other Orthodox peoples were less attached to the Church Slavonic and from the seventeenth century onward gradually dropped it as a literary language.

The fourth and final characteristic of Balkan culture was its anti-Westernism. The church itself was profoundly hostile to the West. Gennadius became the first patriarch under the Turks precisely because he was irreconcilably anti-Catholic and anti-Western. He and most of his successors opposed the West as the home of Catholicism and Protestantism and as the birthplace of the Renaissance. They rejected vigorously everything the Renaissance represented—the exaltation of reason in place of dogma, the turn to Greek antiquity, and the preference for Plato rather than Aristotle. In short, Balkan Orthodoxy opposed the West not only because it was heretical but also because it was becoming modern. The inevitable result of this opposition was the intellectual isolation and stagnation of the Balkan peoples.

The one exception, significantly enough, was in Ragusa and in the Venetian-held Greek islands. There we find an entirely different civilization—secular, sophisticated, individualistic, and maintaining close ties with the West. Its written literature was not church-dominated as was the case on the mainland. Instead, it consisted of epic poetry, lyrics, and drama, comparable to the literature of Italy at this time. The greatest literary creation of the modern Greek people is the epic poem *Erotokritos* composed about 1650 by the Cretan writer, Vincenzo Kornaros. It is noteworthy that this work is written in the vernacular demotic rather than in the artificial katharevousa favored by the church on the mainland. Likewise in Ragusa, Ivan Gundulich wrote a famous epic poem, *Osman,* in which he glorified his beloved city and anticipated the liberation and unification of all South Slavs.

Such writing and such ideas were completely foreign to the peoples of the mainland. Their intellectual horizon did not extend beyond the concepts of faith and local community affairs. Living in a static and self-contained Orthodox theocracy, they remained oblivious to the new learning, the scientific advances, and the burgeoning of the arts that were transforming and revivifying the Western world.

The hostility of Balkan Orthodoxy to the West might be compared with the opposition of Russian Orthodoxy against Peter the Great. In fact, Patriarch Dositheus of Jerusalem actively participated in the campaign against the tsar's Westernization program and particularly against his plan for an Academy of Sciences organized on Western lines. The Orthodox leaders failed in Russia because in that country the state power was arrayed against them. But in the Balkan Peninsula the Ottoman officials were uninterested and the peasantry inert. Consequently, the Orthodox hierarchy was the unchallenged arbiter in all matters intellectual. And it remained unchallenged until the eighteenth century, when, as we shall see in Chapter 9, new forces produced new classes with new ideas that spelled the beginning of the end of the age of theocracy.

"PAX OTTOMANICA"

One of the most common myths relating to Balkan history is that the five centuries of Turkish rule were centuries of unrelieved tryanny and oppression. It is often stated that during that period the Christians had yearned for freedom and had awaited impatiently for an opportunity to rise against the infidel conqueror. This interpretation fails to explain the actual course of events. The various Balkan peoples admittedly outnumbered the Turks. They lived in compact groups and retained their languages and religions. If they had been oppressed and ready for revolt, they would have caused more trouble for the Turks than they actually did. But for most of this period the Turks had less trouble ruling their Christian subjects in the Balkans than their Moslem subjects in Asia.

The explanation is that the coming of the Turks was for many Balkan peasants a boon rather than a disaster. The preceding Byzantine emperors, Greek despots, Frankish nobles, Venetian signors, and Bulgarian and Serbian princes had for two centuries ravaged the peninsula with incessant wars and severe exploitation. The Ottoman conquerors wiped out these dynasties and ruling classes, and put an end to their feuds and extortions. It does not follow that the Ottoman invasion was a pleasant or painless experience. Massacres and mass enslavement were all too common. But once the shock of conquest had passed, the condition of the subject peoples in most regions took a turn for the better.

Much contemporary evidence supports this conclusion. Most impressive is the testimony of Michael Konstantinovich, a Serbian who was taken prisoner in battle with the Turks in 1454. He was forced to enter the janissary corps and for nine years fought under their banner in Asia Minor and the Balkans. In 1463 he escaped to the Hungarians and later settled in Poland. There he wrote his memoirs in which he exhorted "all peoples who honor Jesus Christ" to "help the [Balkan] Christians against the pagans." Konstantinovich was a Serbian patriot and an ardent Christian who clung to his faith despite generous treatment and rapid promotion by the Turks. It is all the more significant, therefore, when he concedes that "amongst these pagans there is great righteousness, they are just to themselves and among each other and also toward their subordinates, whether those were Christians or Jews . . . because the Tsar [Sultan] himself looks sternly to it. . . ."

Konstantinovich also describes from his personal experience how the Ottoman armies were scrupulously respectful of private property and paid fair prices to the Christian peasants for provisions.

Extraordinary taxes they [the Christians] never give, neither to the Tsar nor to their masters [the spahi feudal lords]. But when the Tsar's army is passing by, no one may go through the green crops nor make any damage, nor take away from anyone anything against his will. And if someone should take something from anyone without his will, the other pagan masters would not let him do it, nor would they forgive each other, because they don't wish the damage of the poor, and if one should take only one hen by force, one would lose his head. Because the Tsar wants under no condition that evil should be done to the poor. When the Tsar orders the Christians, they must send many thousands of *samars* or horses, who carry food; and they will sell where they are ordered to, each sepparately, because the things are priced justly without damage to them.

If it is recalled that this was a period when Western armies almost invariably behaved in a barbarous manner, respecting neither the persons nor the property of their own Christian peasants, then the import of Konstantinovich's testimony may be appreciated. To illustrate the stern justice of the "pagan masters," Konstantinovich relates the following incident, which it is to be hoped is apocryphal but which is not without significance in its context.

Thus it happened during Tsar Murad that a woman accused an Azab [irregular infantryman] that on the road he took milk away from her and drank it. Then Tsar Murad ordered that he be caught and his belly be cut open, so that one may see whether there is milk in the stomach, and they found that there is although he denied it; and if there wouldn't be found any the same would happen to the woman; and thus the poor soldier was left without a head and the woman without milk; and that happened near Plovdin going to Chrnomen.[8]

We may conclude that the Turks ruled the Balkans as long as they did because they satisfied the needs of their subject peoples to an acceptable degree. In later centuries their administrative institutions deteriorated and became corrupt and oppressive. But in doing so Ottoman rule became less dangerous for the Balkan peoples. It did not threaten their national identity and cohesiveness. Its inefficiency and flabbiness eliminated the possibility of denationalization and gave assurance for the future of the subject Christians.

The significance of this point becomes clear if we compare the rule of the Turks on the mainland with that of the Venetians in the Greek islands and in the Peloponnesus. The Venetians levied much heavier taxes, allowed no self-government, controlled commerce strictly, and encouraged proselytism. In almost every respect their rule was more oppressive and more unpopular. Contemporary observers were nearly unanimous on this point. Stephen Gerlach, the chaplain of the Hapsburg embassy in Constantinople, noted in his diary in 1575 that "the Venetians kept their subjects in Cyprus (like the Genoese theirs in Chios) worse than slaves. . . . After the Turks came, the poor people are freed of their burden and are equally free, but their masters, who had tortured them, were caught and sold in Turkey." [9]

Venetian rule was not only more oppressive but also more threatening. The Venetians incited dissension among their subjects deliberately and effectively. They treated the aristocratic landowners generously, permitting them to retain their estates and titles. The latter responded by identifying themselves with their foreign masters rather than with their own countrymen. On the island of Crete the native nobles either remained neutral or actively supported the Venetians during the peasant revolt of 1567–1573. Likewise, in the Ionian Islands the cleavage among the Greeks was so complete that the peasants in 1638 revolted against their native landowners rather than against the Venetians. This "divide and rule" strategy was so successful that its effect continued to be felt long after the Venetians departed.

The Turks, by contrast, unwittingly strengthened the group solidarity of their subjects. They did so by granting a large degree of communal autonomy, by imposing regulations separating Moslems from non-Moslems, and by exterminating the native aristocracies. The latter policy deprived the Balkan peoples of their leaders but also freed them from social differentiation and strife. During the long centuries of Ottoman rule they continued to exist as a peasant mass—separate, homogeneous, and united.

It is interesting to speculate how different the course of Balkan history might have been if the Turks had followed the contemporary Venetian policy of "divide and rule" or the contemporary Western policy of forceful religious conformity. Either course would have strengthened very considerably their hold over the peninsula. The fact that they adopted neither explains in large part why the Balkan peoples were able to retain their unity and identity, and eventually to win their independence.

In conclusion we may dismiss the myth of five centuries of "darkness and slavery" as a part of the folklore of Balkan nationalism. Turkish rule in the early period was in many respects commendable. It provided the Balkan peoples with a degree of peace and security that previously had been conspicuously absent. It permitted them to practice their faith and to conduct their communal affairs with a minimum of intervention and taxation. Any comparison with Venetian rule in Greece during the same period is largely favorable to the Turks. In the following chapter we shall note that the situation later changed drastically. The deterioration of the Ottoman imperial structure inevitably had its effect on the subject peoples. In contrast to the former discipline and efficiency, they now were subjected to the rapaciousness of government officials and to the violence of uncontrolled soldiery and robber bands. Indeed, the plight of the Christians during this period was no worse than that of the Moslems. But imperial degeneration is not a phenomenon peculiar to Turkish rule. And it should not be allowed to obscure the role and significance of *Pax Ottomanica* in the history of the Balkan peoples.

1566–1815
Part III. Age of Ottoman Decline

8. Decline of the Ottoman Empire

THE OTTOMAN EMPIRE reached the height of its power and prestige during the reign of Suleiman the Magnificent. But in 1622, little more than half a century after Suleiman's death, the British envoy in Constantinople, Sir Thomas Roe, reported that the empire was in a state of disintegration.

> . . . it is impossible that the empire can endure, though no stranger had a finger to help forward their disintegration. . . . all the territory of the grand signor is dispeopled for want of justice, or rather by violent oppressions, so much as in his best parts of Greece and Natolia, a man may ryde 3, and 4, sometimes 6 daies, and not find a village able to feed him and his horse; whereby the revenew is so lessened, that there sufficeth not to pay the soldiour, and to mayntayne the court. . . .
>
> I can say no more, then that the disease yet works internally that must ruyne this empire: we daily expect more chaunges, and effusion of bloud: the wisest men refuze to sitt at the helme, and fooles will soone runne themselves and others upon the rocks.[1]

Fortunately for the empire, the "fooles" did not succeed one another in uninterrupted succession. In times of direst crisis, strong sultans or grand viziers appeared to ride out the storms. They even staged short-lived comebacks such as the conquest of Crete in the mid-seventeenth century. But the fact remains that after Suleiman we come to a period of general decline—a period in which the Ottomans ceased to be feared and began themselves to fear. Roe was correct in his prediction that "the disease yet works internally that must ruyne this empire." Our problem now is to diagnose this disease. What was the ailment which, despite repeated efforts at cure, poisoned the vitals of the empire and eventually brought about its downfall?

DEGENERATION OF THE DYNASTY

The Ottoman Empire was essentially a military machine. The engine that powered this machine was the Ruling Institution. The person who directed the Institution was the sultan. Hence the critical importance of the sultan's personality in Ottoman history. For two and a half centuries a remarkable succession of ten outstanding rulers had led the empire from victory to victory. After Suleiman, an equally remarkable succession of incapable sultans lost control of the empire to such a degree that it was left leaderless and powerless. The well-known Turkish proverb "The fish stinks from the head" emphasizes the significance of this dynastic degeneration.

The cause for this degeneration probably had little to do with laws of eugenics. Inbreeding certainly could not have been a factor. The mothers of the sultans continued to be drawn from all countries and ethnic strains. The decisive factor appears to have been the system of succession, which in turn was responsible for the appalling manner in which the royal princes were trained for their duties. We noted in Chapter 5 that Mohammed II issued a Draconian fratricide decree enjoining his successors to execute their brothers in order to avoid civil strife. The decree was obeyed until the end of the sixteenth century. Then it was modified in two ways which together proved disastrous. First the slaughter of royal princes was halted and, instead, all of them, with the exception of the sons of the reigning sultan, were confined to special quarters in the palace and denied all communication with the outside world. These pathetic creatures spent their lives in the company of a few eunuchs, pages, and sterilized harem inmates. Inevitably they became mental and moral cripples, pitiful victims of a vicious environment. Yet it was these very individuals who, by a change in the law of succession, were placed upon the imperial throne and entrusted with the destiny of the empire.

The change in succession occurred following the death of Sultan Ahmed I in 1617. The sultan's sons were not of age, and since no minor had ever sat on the imperial throne, Ahmed's brother was chosen as successor. At the same time a decree was issued stipulating that henceforth the throne should pass to the oldest member of the imperial house. This meant that future sultans were to be drawn not from the royal princes, who were raised under relatively normal circumstances, but rather from the brothers, uncles, and cousins, who had passed their lives in the degenerating seclusion described above.

These individuals were unequal to the tremendous responsibility of their position and also were incapable of selecting worthy advisers. It was only natural that they should continue to depend upon the peculiar companions of their boyhood. These worthies now became imperial favorites, using the puppet sultans as tools for the plundering of the empire. By the end of the sixteenth century the sultan as the actual governing power had passed from the scene, reappearing on a few rare occasions as a phenomenon with **no** lasting effect. Ottoman history henceforth was the history of endless strife between various individuals and cliques seeking to gain the confidence of the sovereign, and through him, the control of the empire. The "eldest male" system of succession, it should be noted, persisted from 1617 until the fall of the dynasty in 1924. But the practice of incarcerating the princes was gradually abandoned during the nineteenth century.

CORRUPTION OF THE ADMINISTRATION

The degeneration of the dynasty was accompanied by the corruption of the administration. When the Ruling Institution functioned properly it received from the Palace School a steady supply of superbly trained slaves. These were appointed to administrative posts throughout the empire and advanced on the basis of merit. This system proved extraordinarily efficient until the end of the sixteenth century. Then it deteriorated rapidly, partly because of the failings of the dynasty, but also because of certain other factors which probably would have taken their toll regardless of what went on in the palace.

The Ottoman slave bureaucracy could function effectively only so long as two conditions prevailed. One was that war should be waged continually and successfully, for war provided many of the slaves who were to become the administrators, and also provided the booty to support these administrators and their imperial master on the munificent scale to which they had become accustomed. The other condition was that the Moslem-born population should continue to accept a system whose distinguishing characteristic was that it excluded them from participating in the administration of their own empire.

Toward the end of the sixteenth century neither of these conditions was met. Wars continued, but they were becoming increasingly defensive and unsuccessful. Instead of yielding slaves and booty, they imposed burdens which became heavier as defeats became commoner. Likewise, the Moslem population was successfully challenging the slave monopoly of its government. In 1594 a Venetian ambassador reported that "the native Turks continue to sustain the greatest dissatisfaction, from seeing the government reposed in the renegades." The ambassador added his opinion that "one may reasonably hope . . . for some notable revolution within a short time." [2]

The revolution occurred, perhaps not in as dramatic a fashion as the Venetian anticipated, but with a most far-reaching and devastating effect. The sultans and their ministers began to accept "gifts" from candidates for office. The practice began in the latter part of Suleiman's reign, when the imperial finances were strained by continual war and an increasingly luxurious court. At first the competence of the candidates counted for more than their ability to pay. Gradually and inevitably the financial consideration prevailed. One result was that the merit system gave way to the bribe system. Another was that the Moslems, who previously had been excluded from their government, now were free to participate in it if they had the means or the influence to secure a post.

These two developments completely destroyed the basic features of the old bureaucracy: its merit system and its slave personnel. A fundamentally different administrative system developed, one in which every important position was available to the highest bidder. The bidders were numerous and eager, for everyone now could aspire to office. Indeed, the number of candidates was so much greater than the supply of offices that appointments began to be made for one year only in order to redress the balance and, incidentally, to increase the number of gifts. Only the subordinate officials continued to hold their positions and to receive promotions according to the old criteria of satisfactory service and seniority.

The tax collection system was equally unsatisfactory. Government officials originally collected the taxes directly. But so many of those officials proved dishonest that Mohammed II substituted a tax-farming arrangement. Henceforth all taxes were farmed out to the highest bidders, usually courtiers or high officials. These individuals in turn sold their concessions piecemeal. The process frequently was repeated several times, each vendor making a substantial profit. The crushing burden of this oppressive structure rested finally upon the helpless peasant population, Moslem as well as Christian.

We may conclude that from the seventeenth century onward the typical Ottoman official holding a position of any importance regarded it as a private investment from which he was justified in deriving as large a return as possible. Western observers, who formerly had noted that the sultan's subjects were justly ruled and lightly taxed, now began to report precisely the opposite. Likewise, the more public spirited of the Ottoman officials recognized and deplored the defects of the system under which they operated. Mehmed Pasha, who rose to be the treasurer of the empire at the beginning of the eighteenth century, described the effects of the all-pervading bribery in the darkest colors.

> Bribery is the beginning and root of all illegality and tyranny, the source and fountain of every sort of disturbance and sedition, the most vast of evils and greatest of calamities. . . . If it becomes necessary to give a position because of bribes, in this way its holder has permission from the government for every sort of oppression. Stretching out the hand of violence and tyranny against the poor subjects along his route [of travel] and spreading fire among the poor, he destroys the wretched peasants and ruins the cultivated lands. As the fields and villages become empty of husbandmen, day by day weakness comes to land and property, which remain destitute of profits and revenues and harvest and benefit.[3]

DISINTEGRATION OF THE ARMED FORCES

The corruption of the bureaucracy extended to the armed forces. In this case also, one of the important factors was the inability to extend further the imperial conquests. The Ottoman armies hitherto had been ready and eager for war because war invariably had meant rich booty, valuable slaves, and more land to be divided into fiefs. In fact, the Ottoman expansion in the Balkans was to a considerable degree the work of frontier soldiers who, like the American frontiersmen, kept pushing westward with little regard for central authority. Both Mohammed II and Bayezid II were unable to prevent raids across the border into the countries with which they were anxious to maintain peace. Sir Thomas Roe observed in 1623 that

the Turkish soldiour is not only apt, but desirous to make invasion; because all things are prey, and all kinds of licence given them; and his hope is more upon booty and prisoners, then upon conquest; every boy or girle slave being here the best merchandize, and worth 100 dollars; so that every village is to them a magazine, and they retorne rich.[4]

When war brought defeat rather than victory, and destruction instead of plunder, the Turks no longer were "desirous to make invasion." The English diplomat Sir Paul Rycaut accompanied the Ottoman army in its campaign against the Hapsburgs in 1665. He noted that after several setbacks the Turkish soldiers became demoralized and refused to fight.

The Souldiery was greatly terrified and possessed with a fear of the Christians . . . and having Wives and Children and Possessions to look after, were grown poor, and desired nothing more than in peace and quietness to return to their homes, so that nothing could come more grateful to this Camp, no largesses nor hopes could pacifie the minds of the Souldiery more than the promises and expectations of Peace. And this was the true cause that brought on the Treaty of Peace between the Emperor and the Turk.[5]

Ottoman military strength declined not only because of this external pressure but also because of certain domestic developments. Some of these developments affected primarily the standing army of janissary infantrymen and others the feudal army of spahi cavalrymen. Considering first the janissaries, we have noted that during their golden age they were exclusively of slave origin, superbly trained, formidable in war, but also notoriously prone to rebellion. With the advent of weak rulers the janissaries became increasingly unruly and at the same time they made themselves almost unassailable by sinking roots into the Moslem community.

This process involved several steps. Some time in the first half of the sixteenth century the formerly celibate janissaries won permission to take wives and raise families. This at once raised the problem of financial support. Even without family dependents this had become acute. Between 1350 and 1600 janissary pay had increased four times but the cost of living had risen ten times. Thus the married janissaries were quite incapable of supporting their families and therefore were allowed to supplement their meager allowance by engaging in trade and industry. Then in 1574 they won the right to enroll their sons in the corps. But these sons also continued in their fathers' respective professions. The outcome was that the most famous and feared unit of the Ottoman army gradually changed into a militia of city traders and artisans. This trend was hastened by the influx of many civilians who bribed their way into the corps in order to gain the tax-exemption privilege traditionally enjoyed by the janissaries. In many cities the various janissary companies became virtually guilds of bakers, butchers, cobblers, armorers, and so forth. This trend reached such proportions that in Saloniki at the end of the eighteenth century the janissaries and their families comprised fully one half of the total population of sixty thousand.

The child-tribute that formerly had filled the janissary ranks obviously was anachronistic in these new circumstances. Recruits from the Christian population were desired neither by the government, which was embarrassed by the expense of the greatly inflated corps, nor by the janissaries themselves, who regarded newcomers as interlopers and competitors. Hence the child-levy was enforced less and less frequently, the last recorded case being in 1637.

The transformation of the corps was now complete. The janissaries started as the slaves of the sultan, owing allegiance solely to him, and dependent upon him for everything. By the seventeenth century they had become a privileged and self-perpetuating caste, recruited from the Moslem population, and assured of its support. The effect on the empire was deplorable. Although the janissaries increased from twelve thousand under Suleiman to over one hundred thousand by 1825, only two thousand of the latter were actually trained. The corps had become useless as a fighting force, and yet it could not be disbanded. No other standing army existed to challenge its primacy. In case of emergency it could draw upon the enormous reserve force of the urban population of which it had become an integral part. More than one sultan and grand vizir who sought to neutralize or abolish the corps discovered at the cost of their lives how firmly entrenched was this monstrous vested interest.

The deterioration of the janissaries was paralleled by that of the spahis or timar-holding cavalrymen. In this case the difficulties arose from various abuses in the granting of fiefs. One of these abuses was the diversion of the fiefs or timars to dummy holders. Palace favorites and provincial officials obtained by devious means timars for their own retainers and then collected the revenue which normally would have supported spahi horsemen. This subterfuge became a serious matter when some individuals accumulated as many as fifty timars and in return contributed nothing to the armed forces.

Another abuse was the practice of adding timars to the imperial domain. This was occasioned by the increasing indebtedness of the government after Suleiman's reign. Since timar revenues went to the spahis rather than to the treasury, the government frequently refused to reassign timars that fell vacant. Instead it assimilated the property into the imperial lands and auctioned the revenue to the tax farmers, thus obtaining sorely needed funds. This practice brought some relief to the government treasury, but it weakened correspondingly the feudal army. These abuses, and others of a similar nature, explain the decline in the number of spahis and of the horsemen they were required to furnish. The total dropped from two hundred thousand in the time of Suleiman to no more than twenty-five thousand by the eighteenth century.

We may conclude that after the sixteenth century Ottoman military strength deteriorated rapidly. The janissaries had degenerated into a privileged social class interested more in their immunities than their duties, while the feudal spahis bore little resemblance to the great cavalry armies that at one time had swept irresistibly through the Balkans and across the Hungarian plains to the walls of Vienna. The government was forced to contend against the growing strength of neighboring powers by using Tatar horsemen from the Crimea, untrained levies, and undisciplined volunteers. These motley forces frequently did more damage to the inhabitants of the villages through which they passed than to the foreign enemy. We noted in Chapter 7 Konstantinovich's testimony that if a soldier "should take only one hen by force, one would lose his head." That was in the mid-fifteenth century. A little more than two hundred years later the Ottoman official, Mehmed Pasha, deplored the indiscipline and excesses of the imperial armies.

> Practicing brigandage, they are not satisfied with free and gratuitous fodder for their horses and food for their own bellies from the villages they meet. They covet the horse-cloth and rags of the rayas [peasants], and if they can get their hands on the granaries they become joyful, filling their sacks with barley and oats for provisions and fodder. While they behave in this way and make thus a habit of ruin, setting themselves to harm and oppress, the sighs and groans of mankind attain the heavens and it is certain that they will be accursed.[6]

RULING OLIGARCHY

The deterioration of the dynasty, the corruption of the administration, and the weakening of the armed forces combined to transform the once formidable Ottoman Empire into a flaccid and rickety structure ruthlessly exploited by a small clique entrenched in Constantinople. This clique consisted of courtiers and high officials who used the puppet sultans as a screen for their operations. At rare intervals a sultan showed up who attempted to exercise his prerogatives and to follow an independent policy. On such occasions the oligarchy usually aroused the janissaries and used them to depose the sultan and to put a more tractable person in his place. It is not without significance that the great majority of the janissary revolts were engineered from above.

The oligarchy used similar methods to secure compliant grand viziers. Only when the empire was in danger of complete destruction did they accept men of ability and will power. The assumption of office in 1656 by the masterful Mohammed Kiuprili is explained in precisely these terms by a contemporary English observer.

The Government was so broken, and things so unsettled, that a Vizir could scarcely hold his place to the end of a year; whereby things came to a very bad pass, soldiers not to be governed, and the revenue anticipated above five years beforehand; and then as the properest remedy for those evils, a rigid, cruel-natured fellow was found out, and made Vizier, who was the famous old *Cuperli* [Kiuprili]; a man so obscure that he was even known to few, and had been employed only in some petty *Bashalik,* and at that time was poor and in debt.[7]

Such men as Kiuprili were able to ride out the storms and to keep the empire afloat. But they were not able to eliminate the evils that were the basic cause of the difficulties. They were not able to destroy the janissaries, wipe out the corruption, and remove the palace favorites. In short, they failed to transform a decaying military machine into a modern state capable of holding its own in the new Europe that was emerging. The more time passed, the greater became the disparity between the Ottoman Empire and the West, a disparity that gradually forced the empire into a semicolonial status and eventually into oblivion.

ECONOMIC SUBSERVIENCE TO THE WEST

In analyzing the reasons for the decline of the Ottoman Empire it is necessary to consider not only the internal factors but also the external. The decline cannot be studied as though it occurred in a vacuum. Contemporary developments in Western Europe must also be taken into account. The very concept of the decline of the empire is relative in nature—relative, that is, to what was happening in the West. Furthermore, the developments in the West created new conditions and released new forces that affected the Ottoman Empire in numberless ways and completely altered its relations with the rest of Europe.

Considering first the economic conditions and relations, we find that until the mid-sixteenth century the Ottoman Empire was at least abreast of the Christian European countries. The vast extent and varied climes of the empire assured it of virtual self-sufficiency. The fertile plains of Hungary, Wallachia, Asia Minor, and Egypt produced an abundant supply of food-stuffs and raw materials. The skilled artisans of Constantinople, Saloniki, Damascus, Baghdad, Cairo, and other ancient cities turned out a multitude of handicraft products. The empire also possessed large timber resources and important mineral deposits, particularly iron, copper, and lead. All these goods were bought and sold without hindrance in the vast free-trade area provided by the far-flung Ottoman frontiers. The empire's strategic position at the junction of seas and continents also promoted a substantial foreign and transit trade. Various minerals were exported to the Middle East. Silks, velvets, rugs, leather, copper, and dyestuffs were sent westward through the Balkans to Poland, Austria, and Venice. And despite the opening of the Cape route in the early sixteenth century, Baghdad, Aleppo, and Cairo continued to attract the products of Persia, India, the East Indies, the Arabian Peninsula, and the Sudan.

The prosperity of the empire was reflected in the annual surplus left in the treasury. Suleiman's revenues in the early part of his reign totaled about six million ducats and his expenditures about four and a half million ducats. In his later years, after he had conquered large areas in Europe and Asia, the amount of revenue increased to seven or eight million ducats, a substantially larger sum than that collected by Charles V.

This vast amount must be attributed to the wealth and flourishing state of the empire rather than to an excessive rate of taxation. We have seen that the average Christian peasant paid a small head tax, a tithe of approximately one tenth of the produce of his farm, and, if he was a tenant on a feudal fief, certain additional obligations to his spahi overlord. These dues were far from burdensome. Contemporary travelers frequently remarked that the Balkan peasants were less heavily taxed and were generally better off than their counterparts in the Western lands.

There is little doubt that this was actually the case. We have much evidence that Ottoman rule had a great attraction for many people in neighboring Christian countries. When Barbarossa raided the Italian coasts he found considerable pro-Turkish feeling, even to the point of revolts in his behalf. Likewise, Martin Luther observed that "one finds in German lands those who desire the future of the Turks and their government, as well as those who would rather be under the Turks than under the Emperor and the Princes." [8] A considerable number of those who "would rather be under the Turks" did cross the frontier into the Ottoman Empire, especially after the series of peasant revolts in Central Europe in the first half of the sixteenth century.

Despite this impressive beginning, the Ottoman economy fell far behind that of Western Europe within a comparatively short time. The explanation for the unexpected reversal is that the Ottoman Empire did not experience the so-called Commercial Revolution which basically transformed Western economic institutions and practices between the fifteenth and eighteenth centuries. During that period the restricted noncapitalist economy of medieval Europe gave way to the expanding and dynamic capitalist economy of modern times.

In commerce this meant the gradual disappearance of the old merchant guilds operating on a local, or at the most, a continental scale, and imposing numerous restrictions on prices and profits. In their place appeared the joint-stock companies trading on a world-wide basis and making as large profits as possible. This change in commerce affected industry. The old craft guilds were quite incapable of meeting the demands of the new world markets. Gradually they gave way to the entrepreneur who used his capital to buy raw material, to hire labor, and to sell the finished product at the market price rather than at a regulated price. These developments in commerce and industry were part and parcel of the general expansion of the European economy until it attained world-wide proportions.

The Ottoman economy was remaining static during this period when

Western capitalism was enveloping the entire globe. It was not the Ottoman merchants who exploited Western Europe. Rather, it was the French, the English, and the Dutch who organized their respective Levant companies and exploited the resources of the Ottoman Empire. The first to appear were the French. In 1535 they negotiated a treaty which provided the legal basis for their trade in the Levant. By this treaty French subjects were permitted to reside and trade in the Ottoman Empire without being subject to Ottoman taxation or to the jurisdiction of Ottoman courts. These special privileges or "capitulations" were extended in 1583 to the English and the Dutch. As a result, Western merchants during the sixteenth century obtained an increasingly large proportion of the eastern Mediterranean trade formerly monopolized by Italian middlemen.

This development of direct trade with Western Europe proved detrimental to the economy of the Ottoman Empire. French, English, and Dutch merchants loaded their ships with foodstuffs and with raw materials needed by their home industries. In return they brought various native and colonial products, and, during the sixteenth century, large quantities of bullion that originated in the New World. But the bullion did not remain in the sultan's domains. Instead, it was exchanged for the spices and the fine fabrics that were brought in across the eastern borders. Thus the Ottoman Empire, like Spain, found itself in an unenviable position in international trade. It had become merely a funnel through which the bullion from the West flowed on to the Middle and Far East.

The results were as injurious for the Ottoman economy as for the Spanish. The most obvious manifestation was the marked inflation after the mid-sixteenth century. Contributing causes were the debasement of currency, the increasing extravagance and corruption of the government, and the heavy burden of wars which no longer were as successful and profitable as in earlier times. It is significant, however, that between 1550 and 1600 the price of wheat rose approximately five times in the Ankara region of central Anatolia and ten times in the Aegean coastal area. A similar price trend is noticeable in the case of other commodities which were being shipped to the West. The net result was a vicious circle so far as the Ottoman economy was concerned. The scarcity and high price of raw materials seriously handicapped Ottoman industry, and this in turn stimulated the inflow of manufactured goods and the outflow of bullion.

The imperial government was slow to take action, lacking as it did the experience and the mercantilist traditions of the West. In 1563 it ordered one hundred and fifty thousand pieces of canvas for the fleet but discovered that the order could not be filled because of the shortage of cotton thread. Likewise, the Ottoman officials found it increasingly difficult to obtain food supplies for the capital and for the army. Consequently, the government deemed it necessary in the latter part of the sixteenth century to ban the export of bullion to the East and various materials to the West, including cotton, cotton thread, lead, gunpowder, horses, and certain foodstuffs. But

Ottoman officials were even more lax in enforcing such restrictions than their Spanish counterparts. Bullion continued to drain out of the Ottoman Empire as it did out of Spain, while Western captains loaded cargoes as easily in the Levant ports as they did in the Spanish colonies.

After the sixteenth century the economic position of the Ottoman Empire grew worse. The Dutch forced their way to the East Indies in the first half of the seventeenth century and blocked the transit trade through the Ottoman lands much more effectively than had their Portuguese predecessors. At the same time the Venetians gradually were being squeezed out of the Levant trade. Their twenty-five-year war with the Turks (1645–1670) cost them so heavily in money and ships that they sank from a first- to a third-rate commercial power. This enabled the Westerners to dominate the foreign trade of the Ottoman Empire. Furthermore, they now brought in less bullion and more manufactured goods as their home industries grew stronger. They were able to sell these goods on the Ottoman market with virtually no hindrance because the treaty capitulations specifically limited import and export duties to between 3 and 5 per cent ad valorem. Thus Ottoman industries were left without protection and the empire steadily declined to a dependent status in its economic relations with the West. Like South America and the Far East, it served merely as a market for Western manufactures and a source of raw materials for Western industries.

In conclusion, it is apparent that the stagnant Ottoman economy experienced none of the revolutionary changes that were transforming the West. Ottoman merchants did not combine their resources to form joint-stock companies. One reason was the conservatism and individualism of a Moslem society that refused to countenance large-scale, impersonal business enterprises. Another reason was the tendency of Ottoman officials to regard any overly rich subject as fair game for extortion and confiscation. In any case the Ottoman merchants, who were almost invariably Armenians, Jews, and Greeks, confined themselves to individual operations within the borders of the empire.

Ottoman industry likewise remained at the handicraft stage in technology, and at the guild stage in organization. Whereas few guilds played an important role in the Western economy by the late seventeenth century, in the Ottoman Empire they continued to dominate both industry and commerce. The craftsmen and the merchants worked and trafficked in little shops built along narrow and crooked streets, and sometimes roofed over, street and all, to form the low rambling buildings known as bazaars. These were picturesque but scarcely a match for the new capitalism of the West. The inevitable outcome is depicted in the following observations of an English traveler in Constantinople in 1800:

> Suppose a stranger to arrive from a long journey, in want of clothes for his body; furniture for his lodgings; books or maps for his instruction and amusement; paper, pens, ink, cutlery, shoes, hats; in short those articles which are found in almost every city of the world; he will find few or none of them in Con-

stantinople; except of a quality so inferior as to render them incapable of answering any purpose for which they were intended. The few commodities exposed for sale are either exports from England, unfit for any other market, or, which is worse, German and Dutch imitations of English manufacture. . . . Let a foreigner visit the bazaars . . . he will see nothing but slippers, clumsy boots of bad leather, coarse muslins, pipes, tobacco, coffee, cooks' shops, drugs, flower-roots, second-hand pistols, poignards, and the worst manufactured wares in the world. . . . View the exterior of Constantinople, and it seems the most opulent and flourishing city in Europe; examine its interior, and its miseries and deficiencies are so striking that it must be considered the meanest and poorest metropolis of the world. The ships which crowd its ports have no connection with its welfare: they are for the most part French, Venetian, Ragusan, Sclavonian, and Grecian vessels, to or from the Mediterranean, exchanging the produce of their own countries for the rich harvests of Poland; the salt, honey, and butter of the Ukraine; the hides, tallow, hemp, furs, and metals of Russia and Siberia; the whole of which exchange is transacted in other ports without any interference on the part of Turkey. Never was there a people in possession of such advantages, who either knew or cared so little for their enjoyment. Under a wise government, the inhabitants of Constantinople might obtain the riches of all the empires of the earth. Situated as they are, it cannot be long before other nations, depriving them of such important sources of wealth, will convert to better purposes the advantages they have so long neglected.[9]

OTTOMAN AND WESTERN
MILITARY DEVELOPMENTS

The relative economic decline of the Ottoman Empire contributed to a corresponding military decline. During the fifteenth century the Ottoman armies had prevailed against the forces of Persia, Egypt, and the Balkan states because of two decisive advantages: their superior artillery and their incomparable janissary infantrymen. By the mid-sixteenth century these advantages no longer prevailed. In the place of the poorly disciplined feudal levies they had routed in the past, the Turks now encountered the veteran Spanish and Austrian foot soldiers serving under the Hapsburgs. After their long campaigns in Italy these men were better trained than the janissaries, particularly in large-scale and precise maneuvers. Also, they possessed more effective arms. Both side used the harquebus as a missile, but for an additional weapon the Turks clung to the saber while the Westerners were now using the pike. The superiority of the latter weapon already had been proved at the sieges of Rhodes and Malta, where the Hospitalers with their pikes repeatedly had cleared the janissaries out of the breaches. In the future the Hapsburg forces were to win repeated victories by answering the fire of the Turkish harquebuses and then advancing with their pikes.

The armament superiority of the Western armies became decisive with the development of firearms. The Turks from the outset had depended heavily on Western assistance for the forging and manning of their artillery. This assistance explains in large part their superiority in the field over the

Persians, the Mamelukes, and the Byzantines. But the Turks never were able to keep up with the Westerners. They were almost a century behind when they first used cannons in the mid-fifteenth century. This disparity increased as Western industry forged ahead of the Ottoman. The Turkish traveler, Evliya Chelebi, informs us that the Germans were "a race of strong, warlike, cunning, devilish, coarse infidels whom, excelling as they did in artillery, Sultan Suleyman endeavored to get equal with by recruiting gunners and artillerymen from all countries with the offer of rich rewards." [10]

The Turks also failed to make adequate use of even such weapons as were available to them. In 1548, for example, Suleiman attempted to persuade two hundred of the regular Turkish cavalry to use carbines and pistols in place of the traditional bow. The time was long overdue for the change; yet the cavalrymen were so mocked by their companions and so averse to trying new weapons that the experiment failed. It was not until the end of the century that the Turkish cavalry generally made use of small arms. Likewise, the janissaries stubbornly and successfully delayed the adoption of new weapons and tactics until they themselves were eliminated in 1826.

In the same manner that the backwardness of Ottoman industry contributed to the technological lag of the army, so the backwardness of the Ottoman merchant marine and shipyards contributed to the weakness of the navy. The Turks started out as a land people with no naval traditions. They established themselves in Asia Minor and overran the Balkans by relying exclusively on their armies. It was not until their defeat by the Venetians at Gallipoli in 1416 that they sensed the need for a fleet to protect and round out their conquests. The Ottoman navy was created for the specific purpose of defeating the Venetians. By the time of Mohammed II it had become a respectable force and contributed to the capture of Constantinople. Under Suleiman II it reached its height. With the leadership of Barbarossa and the support of North African sea power, the Ottoman navy made itself felt as far afield as the western Mediterranean, the Red Sea, the Indian Ocean, and the Persian Gulf.

Even during this glorious period the Ottoman navy was in a certain sense an artificial creation. It had, it is true, the great advantage of abundant mineral resources in the Balkan countries and an inexhaustible store of timber on the shores of the Black Sea. But this did not counterbalance the fatal lack of an Ottoman merchant marine. The basis of Western naval strength at this time was the rapidly growing number of merchantmen. These vessels kept the shipyards operating, provided an adequate number of trained seamen, and, in case of emergency, planted naval guns on their decks and served as men-of-war. But the Ottoman Empire had only small coastal ships, in no way comparable with the Spanish galleons that circled the globe to Manila or with the English merchantmen that were to be found on every ocean.

This mercantile deficiency explains to a great extent why the Ottoman navy remained an essentially non-Turkish organization without deep roots in the empire. Most of its ships were designed by Italian naval architects, built by Greek shipyard workers, and manned by heterogeneous and usually unreliable Christian crews. Likewise, the Ottoman navy failed to keep up with the West in the transition from the oar to the sail-propelled warship. Following a disastrous defeat at the hands of the Venetians in 1656, the Turks set about building sail warships of their own. But they lacked the experienced mariners needed to navigate and maneuver the new ships, and soon reverted to the traditional galleys. The foreseeable result was the loss of Morea to Venice in 1699 and the advance of the Russians around the Black Sea during the eighteenth century.

We may conclude that the Ottoman military decline was due to internal failings, such as the disorganization of the janissaries and the feudal spahis, as well as to the superior progress of the Western powers in developing new techniques and weapons in land and sea warfare.

OTTOMAN AND WESTERN POLITICAL EVOLUTION

The Ottoman Empire fell behind the West not only in the economic and military spheres but also in the political. With the advent of the Renaissance, Western Europe witnessed the rise of nationalism and the nation-state, the one stimulating and strengthening the other. The growth of absolutist monarchies, the appearance of a middle class desiring unity and order, the spread of literacy, and the development of new techniques for mass propaganda and indoctrination—all these contributed to the evolution of the modern nation-state. This state was the institutional form into which the idea of nationalism was infused, transforming former ducal subjects and feudal serfs and town burghers into the all-inclusive nation.

The Ottoman Empire never experienced such a political integration. It remained a congeries of peoples, religions, and conflicting loyalties. The average Ottoman subject thought of himself primarily as a member of a guild if he lived in a city, or as a member of a village community if he lived in the countryside. If he had any feeling of broader allegiance it was likely to be of a religious rather than a political character. It was likely to be directed to the head of his millet rather than to the person of the sultan. Thus the Ottoman Empire differed fundamentally from the Western nation-state. It was not a cohesive institution commanding the active loyalty and allegiance of all its subjects. Rather, it was a conglomeration of numerous disparate groups that were to a large degree self-centered and self-sufficient.

This looseness of organization weakened the resistance of the empire to foreign aggression. In the eighteenth century Austria and Russia were able to annex vast provinces north of the Danube with little difficulty. The reason, apart from military considerations, was that these provinces had few ties with Constantinople, and their populations felt no particular attachment to the central government. The empire was vulnerable not only to military aggression but also to intellectual aggression in the form of nationalist ideology. Since nationalism did not serve as a cement to hold the empire together, it functioned instead as a centrifugal force which eventually tore the empire apart. The absence of Ottoman nationalism left an ideological vacuum which was filled by the several Balkan, Arab, and even Turkish nationalisms. As a result World War I acted as a plunger that detonated with explosive force these nationalist sentiments and demolished the Ottoman imperial structure.

WESTERN SCIENCE AND OTTOMAN "EYES OF OXEN"

The Ottoman Empire lagged behind the West in economic development, military strength, and political cohesion; it also lagged behind in intellectual progress. This lag is often attributed to the stultifying influence of Islam. But the brilliant attainments of Moslem science and scholarship in the Middle Ages indicate that Islam cannot be equated with intellectual stagnation. The failure of the Ottomans to keep up with Western thought is to be explained not by the tenets of Islam but rather by its moribund state when the Turks adopted the faith. When the Ottomans were building their empire in the fourteenth and fifteenth centuries, Islam had degenerated to the point where it meant little more than a series of rituals to be performed and a Heaven-sent book to be memorized.

This had its effect on the Moslem colleges or medressehs. From the outset the Ottoman medressehs emphasized theology, jurisprudence, and rhetoric at the expense of astronomy, mathematics, and medicine. It is not surprising that the graduates of these schools showed no interest in the science and scholarship of the Greek and Arab worlds. They made no attempt to use the original manuscript sources to which they had easy access by virtue of their dominant position in the Near East. By contrast, Western Europe in the thirteenth and fourteenth centuries was producing men like Roger Bacon, Albertus Magnus, and Robert Grosseteste, who were the harbingers of the coming era of observational and experimental science.

Mohammed II in the mid-fifteenth century was a notable exception to the prevailing intellectual sterility. He was extraordinarily open-minded and curious. Contemporaries described him as "neither Moslem nor Christian." In addition to founding the unique Palace School for the training of slave administrators, he also reorganized the curriculum of the medressehs by placing greater emphasis on scientific subjects. He himself selected outstanding scholars from all the Moslem world to fill the chairs in medicine, astronomy, and mathematics. Both scholastic philosophy and Greek science were intensively studied during his reign. Symposiums were held to which the greatest native and foreign scholars were invited. Behind all this activity was an earnest effort to replace dogmatic by critical thought.

Unfortunately Mohammed's influence did not long survive his death. During the splendid reign of Suleiman the Magnificent there was an almost

abnormal interest in literature but very little in the sciences. The one exception was in the field of geography. Piri Reis, the outstanding Turkish cartog-
rapher of the sixteenth century, won international recognition for his geographical book on the Mediterranean Sea. This contains two hundred and
seven fine charts drawn by the author, as well as a considerable amount of
reliable scientific information. Another work by Piri Reis that has attracted
much attention recently is a large map of the world which he drew in 1513.
The one extant section of this map was discovered in Constantinople in 1929.
It depicts the Atlantic Ocean and the surrounding territories—Brittany, the
Iberian Peninsula, and the northwestern coast of Africa to the east, and the
Atlantic Coast of North and South America to the west. The accuracy and
scope of this map are remarkable if it is recalled that it was drawn only a
decade after the voyages of Columbus. This indicates how well informed the
Turks were of the western discoveries. In fact, Piri Reis explains on the margin of his map that he had in his possession various Portuguese maps and a
copy of the chart that Columbus compiled during his voyages.

The significance of Piri Reis's maps can be exaggerated. They indicate merely that the Turks were able to keep up for a while with the geographic discoveries of the West. But apart from this specialized field the
Turks were completely ignorant of the more basic advances of Western science. They knew nothing of the epoch-making achievements of Paracelsus in
medicine, Vesalius in anatomy, and Copernicus, Kepler, and Galileo in astronomy. At a time when Turkish armies were advancing into Central Europe, an intellectual iron curtain separated the Ottoman Empire from the
West.

The basic reason for this isolation was the dogmatic spirit which
reigned supreme in the lands of Islam. This is made clear in the writings of
Katib Chelebi, the famous Turkish bibliographer, encyclopedist, and historian
who lived in the first half of the seventeenth century. Coming from a poor
family, he was unable to obtain a formal higher education. This proved to
be a blessing in disguise. He was spared the superficial, hair-splitting special-
ization on Moslem sacred studies that characterized Ottoman education at
this time. The fact that he was self-taught explains in large part his open-
mindedness toward Western learning.

One of Chelebi's works was a short naval handbook which he compiled following the disastrous defeat of the Ottoman fleet by the Venetians in
1656. In the preface of this work Chelebi emphasized the need for mastering
the science of geography and map making, a field in which the Turks had
fallen sadly behind during the century that had elapsed since the days of Piri
Reis.

For men who are in charge of affairs of state, the science of geography
is a matter of which knowledge is necessary. They may not be familiar with
what the entire globe is like, but they ought at least to know the map of the
Ottoman State and of those states adjoining it. Then, when they have to send
forces on campaign, they can proceed on the basis of knowledge, and so the in-

vasion of the enemy's land and also the protection and defense of the frontiers becomes an easier task. Taking counsel with individuals who are ignorant of that science is no satisfactory substitute, not even when such men are local veterans. Most such veterans are entirely unable to sketch the map of their own home regions.

Sufficient and convincing proof of the necessity for learning this science is the fact that the heathen, by their application to and their esteem for those branches of learning, have discovered the New World and have over-run the markets of India.[11]

In his last work before his death in 1657, Chelebi courageously criticized the dogmatism of his contemporaries. After describing the splendid achievements of Moslem science and scholarship in the time of the Abbassids, he pointed out that philosophy and science had been ignored by the Ottoman medressehs after Suleiman's reign. As a result, warned Chelebi, "Henceforth people will be looking at the universe with the eyes of oxen." [12]

The significance of Chelebi is that he realized that the Ottoman Empire could not afford to remain self-satisfied and self-centered at a time when the West was forging ahead so rapidly. This may seem obvious, but to Chelebi's contemporaries it was incomprehensible. Ottoman officials and scholars looked down upon the West with contempt and arrogance. "Do I not know you," broke out the grand vizir to the French ambassador in 1666, "that you are a Giaour [non-believer], that you are a hogge, a dogge, a turde eater?" [13] As late as 1756, when the French ambassador announced the alliance between France and Austria that marked a turning point in the diplomatic history of Europe, he was curtly informed that the Ottoman government did not concern itself "about the union of one hog with another." [14] This attitude may explain a remarkable incident that occurred in 1770 when a Russian fleet sailed from the Baltic around Europe into the eastern Mediterranean and attacked the Turks. The latter, apparently having forgotten Piri Reis's maps, protested to the Venetians for permitting the Russians to sail from the Baltic into the Adriatic!

The military defeats and internal disorders of the seventeenth and eighteenth centuries forced intelligent men to admit that all was not well with the empire. Indeed, they acknowledged the need for reform and specifically advocated it in a long series of works known collectivey as the Nasibat literature. This literature consisted of books of "Good Counsels for Rulers." But the counsels they embodied invariably were based on the assumption that the troubles were purely domestic and had nothing to do with what was happening in the West. All these writers looked back with nostalgia to the glorious days of Suleiman the Magnificent. All were oblivious to the fact that the new capacities and techniques of Western Europe no longer could be ignored with impunity.

Not until the French Revolution and the landing of Napoleon in Egypt and Syria did reality force itself into the Ottoman mind. But even then the forces of reaction remained strong and unyielding. The medressehs still taught the old dogmas and the janissaries still dominated the armed forces and intimidated the government. In Russia, Peter the Great had been able to crush the mutinous Streltzi and to curb the hostile Orthodox Church at the end of the seventeenth century. But a hundred years later Selim III was deposed and strangled when he attempted to take similar measures. The curtain separating the Ottoman Empire from the West did not lift appreciably until the mid-nineteenth century. And it was not until the empire itself disappeared that Ataturk, like Peter, was able to launch his program of compulsory, forced-draft Westernization.

PLAGUE EPIDEMICS

One of the most appalling results of Turkish obscurantism was the persistence of the bubonic plague in the Ottoman Empire for over a century after it had petered out in the West. Following the Black Death of the mid-fourteenth century the plague continued to devastate Western Europe until the eighteenth century. Then it receded to the Eastern European lands, and until the mid-nineteenth century the Ottoman Empire suffered cruelly from the effects of this dread disease.

Travelers frequently reported that in Constantinople the plague was not considered to have reached major proportions unless it claimed a thousand victims a day. Epidemics broke out every few years with particularly devastating results in the cities. Forty thousand were killed in Constantinople in 1770. Bucharest and Belgrade lost one third of their total populations between 1812 and 1814. In particularly bad years, such as 1778 and 1812, the losses in the empire as a whole reached as high as 150,000 people.

Medical authorities do not agree as to the reasons for the persistence of the plague in the Ottoman Empire. It seems clear, however, that an important contributing factor was the refusal of Ottoman officials to adopt the preventive measures developed in the West. For the devout Moslem Turk an epidemic was an act of God. He was convinced that his days were numbered by Divine Providence. Accordingly, he regarded quarantine precautions as superfluous and even sinful. And in doing so he was neither stupid nor apathetic; he was simply religious.

Contemporary observers leave no doubt as to the paralyzing effect of the epidemics upon the commerce, agriculture, and population of the empire. The following comments are typical:

William Macmichael in 1817:

The number of its [Adrianople's] inhabitants, and the extent of its commerce have been greatly diminished by the plague of four years ago. . . . The two annual fairs which were held in the neighborhood, to which Russians with furs, and Germans with cloth, were in the habit of resorting, no longer exist. . . .[15]

William Hamilton in 1837:

At Beg-shehr [in Asia Minor] the plague was bad; at Kerali, which I reached the following day, still worse; and at Kara-Aghach three fourths of the population had died within the last three months, and the corn for many miles round the town remained uncut or uncarried. A more striking instance of the destroying character of this dreadful malady cannot be imagined, than this vast extent of uncut corn rotting on the ground, when you are told that not only there exists no one to claim it, but no one even to carry it away without a claim. . . . The very cattle have perished when tied up in the stables because, when the owners were dead, there was no one either to fed them or to release them.[16]

W. Eton, about 1800:

Without going further back than the memory of persons now living, it is easy to prove that *depopulation* has been in latter times, astonishingly rapid. . . . The great causes of this depopulation are the following:

1st. The plague, of which the empire is never entirely free.

2dly. Those terrible disorders which almost always follow it, at least in Asia.

3rdly. Epidemic and endemic maladies in Asia, which make as dreadful ravages as the plague itself and which frequently visit that part of the empire.

4thly. Famine, owing to the want of precaution in the government, when a crop of corn fails, and to the avarice and villainy of the pashas, who generally endeavor to profit by this dreadful calamity.

5th and lastly, the sicknesses which always follow a famine, and which occasion a much greater mortality. . . .

. . . a great part of European Turkey, except the countries towards the Adriatic and Hungary . . . [are] almost destitute of inhabitants. This state of the country is particularly striking on the road from Belgrade through Sophia, Phillippopolis, and Adrianople, to Constantinople.[17]

No systematic study has been made of the history and the precise influence of the plague in the Ottoman Empire. The evidence indicates, however, that it disrupted the economy and reduced the population, and this at a time when the external pressures upon the empire were the most severe. It is probably too much to say that the plague bears a causal relationship to Ottoman decline. We have seen that various other factors had set the empire on the downward path as early as the beginning of the seventeenth century. But it is quite clear that the devastating epidemics did accelerate the decline during the eighteenth and early nineteenth centuries.

OTTOMAN DECLINE IN RETROSPECT

The decline of the Ottoman Empire is an extremely complex phenomenon. If any pattern exists, it appears to center around the fact that the empire was essentially a military machine. It needed short, victorious wars to maintain its efficiency and prosperity. In the fourteenth and fifteenth centuries it was able to wage such wars because of the military weakness and social instability of the surrounding states. During those centuries the Turks went on from victory to victory—from Asia Minor to the Balkans, the Arab world, Egypt, and then across the Danube into Central Europe. With each conquest they gained strength and gathered momentum. To contemporary Westerners they appeared to be "a daily increasing flame, catching hold of whatsoever comes next, still to proceed further." [18]

The Turks might very well have proceeded farther if the states of Central and Western Europe had resembled those of the Balkans and the Near East. But they did not, thanks to the Renaissance, the discoveries, the Commercial Revolution, the scientific advances, and the rise of the absolutist monarchies. These developments transformed and strengthened immensely the Western world. The Ottoman Empire, in contrast, remained unaffected and unchanged. This explains in large measure why the Turks were halted at Vienna and soon afterward pushed back across the Hungarian plains.

For a military empire these reverses meant much more than merely the stabilization of the frontier along the Danube. This was noted and emphasized by Sir Paul Rycaut.

It hath been an ancient Custom, and Policy amongst the Turks, in the time of their prosperous Successes by which their Empire was enlarged, never to continue a War longer than for three Years, in which time they always advanced considerably, and would make no Peace with their Neighbors, until their Triumphs and Acquisitions would answer the expenses, and effusions of their Blood, and Treasures. . . . But these last Wars [culminating in the 1699 Treaty of Karlowitz] have quite put the Turks out of their Ancient Methods; for instead of maintaining a War no longer than Three Years, they have been forced to continue it for more than Twenty, to the great Ruin and Destruction of their Empire.[19]

Rycaut makes clear the fundamental contradiction facing the Ottoman Empire after the sixteenth century. It was organized for conquest and expansion but it now entered a period of defeat and contraction. The result was internal tension and dislocation. This increased the disparity between the empire and the West, which in turn led to more defeats, more contraction, more internal difficulties. And all this was compounded by the severe and frequent epidemics of the eighteenth and early nineteenth centuries. In short, the empire was caught in a vicious circle that persisted to the end. The only way out was a basic reorganization of the imperial institutions, but this proved incapable of realization. The failure of the Ottoman Empire was, in the broadest terms, a failure in adjustment, a failure to respond to the challenge of the new dynamic West.

9. Balkan Peninsula During Ottoman Decline

THE IMPOSITION of Ottoman rule upon the Balkan peoples was not an unmitigated misfortune as is often assumed. We have noted that the coming of the Turks was in certain respects a boon rather than a calamity. The new rulers forcefully established peace throughout the peninsula and put an end to the oppressive native nobility. In many regions the position of the peasantry improved substantially under the new regime.

This situation changed drastically when the Ottoman Empire began to decline. The imperial deterioration at once affected the Balkan peoples, as indeed it did also the Moslem subjects. We shall see that the effects of the decline upon the Balkan Peninsula were most far-reaching, extending into every field—political, economic, and cultural. The net result was the development of new conditions and institutions, which in turn created a new intellectual atmosphere characterized primarily by a growing sense of national consciousness. The historical role of this new Balkan nationalism was to end the preceding Age of Theocracy and to introduce the Age of Nationalism. During the course of the nineteenth century, nationalism gradually but steadily prevailed, culminating after World War I in the establishment throughout the peninsula of nation-states in place of the old imperial structure.

TERRITORIAL CHANGES

At the height of its power the Ottoman Empire embraced the entire Balkan Peninsula with the exception of Slovenia and western Croatia, which were held by the Hapsburgs. We noted earlier that the rule of the Ottoman sultans in the Balkans was comparable to that of the Chinese emperors in eastern Asia. The outlying Balkan and Danubian provinces—Moldavia, Wallachia, Transylvania, and Hungary—had an autonomous status comparable to that of the outlying Chinese provinces—Mongolia, Sinkiang, and Tibet. And in the same way that the Chinese provinces passed under British and

Russian influence when Peking became weak, so the border Balkan areas were annexed by neighboring great powers when Constantinople declined. We shall note that between the time of Suleiman the Magnificent and the beginning of the nineteenth century, the Turks lost Hungary, Transylvania, Croatia, Slavonia, Dalmatia, and the Banat of Temesvar to the Hapsburgs, and the northern shore of the Black Sea to the Pruth River to the Russians, while the Danubian Principalities possessed an antonomous status under Russia's aegis. Thus the Balkan peoples found themselves, as a result of Ottoman feebleness, divided among the three great empires of Eastern Europe.

The political effect of Austro-Russian expansion to the south was to make it much more difficult for the Balkan peoples to win their national independence. They now had to contend with three empires rather than one; furthermore, the Romanoffs and the Hapsburgs were more formidable adversaries than the Ottomans. Austro-Russian intrusion into the Balkans also had important economic and cultural repercussions. Those areas that came under Hapsburg rule reached a far higher level of economic and cultural development than those that remained under the Turks or that passed to the Russians. Schools, newspapers, factories, and railroads appeared much earlier to the north of the Sava-Danube line than they did to the south of it. When the Yugoslav state was organized after World War I it was noticeable that markedly higher economic and cultural levels prevailed in regions such as Slovenia, Croatia, and the Banat, than in Serbia, Montenegro, and Macedonia. Precisely the same discrepancy existed within Greater Rumania between Transylvania on the one hand and the old Provinces on the other.

It should also be noted that during the nineteenth century the more advanced peoples under Hapsburg rule aided their retarded brothers under the Turks to win their independence. The Hapsburg Serbs, especially, contributed greatly to the liberation of their fellow Serbs across the Danube, while they themselves remained under foreign rule for another century. Thus the division of the Balkan peoples between a relatively advanced and strong Hapsburg Empire and a weak and backward Ottoman Empire led to the paradox of the most retarded areas of the peninsula forming the first independent states.

TIMAR TO CHIFLIK

By far the most important effect of Ottoman decline upon the Balkan peoples, and one which vitally affected their everyday life, was the breakdown of the timar landholding system established at the time of the conquest, and its replacement with the infinitely more onerous chiflik system. We saw in Chapter 7 that when the Turks overran the peninsula they parceled out the most fertile plains areas as fiefs or timars to deserving warriors. These fief holders, or spahis, were strictly controlled by the central government. Their obligations were carefully defined, as were also the rights and privileges of the Christian peasants or rayas. The latter enjoyed hereditary use of their land and could not be evicted unless they failed to till it for three years. Their obligations—consisting of tithes to the spahi, taxes to the government, and limited *corvée* duty—were generally lighter than those borne at the time by the peasantry of Christian Europe. Furthermore, the rayas were protected against extortion by imperial laws or kanuns, which specified the taxes and services that could be exacted in each district. The spahis, on the other hand, were required to give military service in time of war in return for the revenue they derived from their timars. Unlike the rayas, they did not possess hereditary title to their fiefs and could be deprived of them if they failed to meet their military obligations.

This timar landholding system has been described by a Turkish historian as "a happy combination of the state's military needs and social security for the peasantry." [1] Indeed, its outstanding feature was strict control of the spahis so that they could neither exploit the rayas nor defy the state. During the early years of Ottoman rule, when this timar system was in its prime, the rayas enjoyed security and justice. But by the end of the sixteenth century the system began to break down, with most unfortunate repercussions for the Balkan peasantry.

One reason for the deterioration of the timar system was the progressive weakening of the central government. The spahis promptly took advantage of this development to violate the two regulations that they found the most objectionable, that is, the nonheritable nature of their fiefs, and the legal limits on the rayas' obligations. In other words, the spahis seized the opportunity to transform their fiefs into free and heritable property and to exploit their rayas as they pleased.

Another factor contributing to the degeneration of the timar system was the cessation of imperial territorial expansion after the mid-sixteenth century. We noted above that this caused serious trouble because it meant no more plunder and no more land for new fiefs. The difficulties increased as the empire began to lose its extensive trans-Danubian territories in the late seventeenth century. Large numbers of spahis and officials who had lived in those provinces now recrossed the Danube and tried to make a living in the Balkan lands by obtaining new fiefs or usurping the established ones. The increase in the number of spahis led to the division of the existing timars, which became increasingly smaller and inadequate to support the fief holders. The distress was accentuated by the accumulation of numerous timars by certain powerful individuals. This naturally produced pressure to abandon the limits set upon the rayas' obligations in order to increase the income of the spahis.

Still another factor explaining the breakdown of the timar system was the extension of the activities of the janissaries from the urban centers to the countryside. We noted above that the janissaries gradually had turned toward economic vocations, supplementing their meager military pay with earnings from commerce and the crafts. But this shift was paralleled by a general demographic decline. The population of the Ottoman cities fell after 1600, with the result that the urban markets shrank at the very moment when the number of janissary soldier-artisans was increasing. This disparity induced the janissaries to transfer their attention and their investments from urban enterprises to the land. In various legal and illegal ways—by foreclosing on mortgages, by offering "protection," or by simply taking advantage of the growing anarchy in order to dispossess rayas and spahis—the janissaries accumulated properties which they exploited as free personal holdings.

Finally, the timar system was undermined by the pressure of the constantly expanding economy of Western Europe. As stated above, the general European price inflation caused by the influx of New World bullion began to affect the Ottoman Empire about 1580. The resulting price dislocation disorganized the old economic system, including the land regime. Furthermore, urban population growth in Western Europe necessitated food imports and consequently stimulated maize cultivation throughout the Balkans. Likewise, the rise of cotton manufactures in the West stimulated cotton cultivation on the Macedonian plains. The spread and the significance of these new crops will be considered shortly in more detail. Suffice it to note here that the foreign demand for these new agricultural goods provided a powerful incentive to violate the timar system in order to obtain full control of the land and to exploit the peasants without hindrance for the production of export commodities.

These various factors explain the disintegration of the landholding system established at the time of the conquest and the replacement of the timars with chifliks. In some cases the spahis simply converted their timars into chifliks, while in others outside individuals—janissaries or powerful officials—usurped the estate or gave "protection" in return for perhaps a third of the produce. In the latter instance the outsider came between the spahi and the peasants, while the spahi continued to collect his traditional tenth. So far as the peasant mass was concerned, the main change was that the new chiflik owner now held the land as his full heritable property which he could dispose of as he wished. Consequently, he was free to evict the peasants if they refused to accept his tenancy terms. This was a far cry from the old timar in which the peasant had enjoyed hereditary rights to his plot while the spahi had been limited to certain specified revenue. It follows that rents on the chifliks were much higher than on the timars.

The precise arrangements varied considerably from region to region, but the following procedure was fairly widespread and illustrates the onerousness of the new regime. The total crop was assembled in the square of the chiflik village, where one tenth or one eighth was first taken as state tax. Then the necessary seed was subtracted, and the remainder was divided equally between the chiflik owner and the tenant. Frequently, however, the tenant received considerably less than one half because he was required to pay the state tax farmer and the chiflik manager for their services. Thus the tenant usually was left with about a third of his produce.

Furthermore, the tenant's freedom of movement was in practice severely restricted, though theoretically he was not tied to the land. His low share of the gross product commonly forced him to borrow from the *chiflik* owner in order to feed his family and to buy draft animals and tools. So long as he remained in debt he could not leave, and since he rarely could pay off the principal and the high interest, he was in effect bound to the estate. Thus the peasantry that worked on the chifliks were tenants in name but serfs in fact. As late as 1860 a British consul stationed in Saloniki reported that the Moslem peasants had grievances as well as the Christian, but that the latter were particularly oppressed by the onerous chiflik system.

> As the Mussulman peasantry are not as well off as they might be, the distinction between the condition of the Christians and that of the Musselmans in the villages is in some respects only relative. One point of difference consists in the fact that the irregularities of the tax and tithes collectors and the excesses of the police force, not to speak of the depredations of brigands, are practised to a larger extent and with more barefacedness on the Christian than on the Mussulman peasantry. . . . The Mussulman peasantry, nevertheless, suffer from the same causes as their fellow-labourers on the soil only to a smaller degree. There is, however, a positive difference, and a very important one, in the condition of the Christian peasants on the farms ("tchiftliks") held by Turkish proprietors. They are forcibly tied to the spot by means of a perpetual and even hereditary debt which their landlord contrives to fasten upon them. This has practically reduced many of the peasant families to a state of serfdom. As an illustration I may mention that when a tchiftlik is sold, the bonds of the peasantry are transferred with the stock to the new proprietor. In Thessaly there are Christians who own farms on the same conditions. Upon one occasion in which the landlord, who was a merchant, had become a bankrupt, I remember noticing that amongst the assets borne on his balance-sheet there figured the aggregate amount of the peasants' debts to him, and it formed a rather large item.[2]

The formation of the chifliks was never legally recognized but they were tolerated to such an extent that they eventually replaced the timars as the basis of Ottoman feudalism. The conversion process began in the late sixteenth and early seventeenth centuries and continued more rapidly during the following two centuries. The chifliks spread throughout the fertile plains areas, including the Peloponnesus, Thessaly, Macedonia, Thrace, the Maritsa Valley, Danubian Bulgaria, the Kosovo-Metahija basins, parts of Bosnia, and the coastal plains of Albania.

The oppressiveness of the chiflik system together with the disorder and brigandage arising from the deterioration of central authority led to widespread depopulation in the countryside. This reached such proportions that decrees were issued against the influx of peasants into Constantinople. Even so, European observers frequently reported the abandonment of holdings and the disappearance of villages. As early as 1675, Rev. John Covel wrote as follows: "I assure you this part of Thrace is very little inhabited and lesse cultivated. . . . I am confident, above 2 thirds of the land lyes unoccupied. . . . In many, many miles riding, we saw neither corn-field, nor pasture, nor flocks, nor herds, but onely wild neglected champion [uncultivated] ground." [3] By the beginning of the nineteenth century another British traveler observed,

> I should have mentioned a part of Bulgaria, and a great part of European Turkey, except the countries towards the Adriatic and Hungary, as almost destitute of inhabitants. This state of the country is particularly striking on the road from Belgrade through Sophia, Phillippopolis, and Adrianople, to Constantinople. . . . In taking a separate view of European Turkey, of Greece, and of Egypt, we shall find similar traces of that devastation, occasioned by the complicated evils under which this empire has so long groaned. [4]

GROWTH OF COMMERCE AND INDUSTRY

The period of Ottoman decline in the Balkan lands was characterized also by the rapid development of commerce and industry, with the attendant rise of a class of merchants, artisans, shipowners, and mariners. One reason for this economic trend was the shift to chifliks. This in turn led to the widespread cultivation of the new colonial products, cotton and maize, which were exported to Western Europe, where there was a steady and growing demand. Cotton first began to be grown in the Serres region of Eastern Macedonia in the late seventeenth century and then its cultivation spread westward to Saloniki and Thessaly. By the second half of the eighteenth century, cotton was by far the most important product of Macedonia and Thessaly. It was exported overland by way of the Danube to Budapest and Vienna, and also by sea through Trieste and Saloniki. Maize cultivation was also introduced in the seventeenth century. Unlike cotton, it was possible to grow maize in many parts of the peninsula. By the second half of the eighteenth century it was being exported from several regions, including the plains of Durazzo, the Epirote Plain of Arta, the coastal plains of Albania, the Danubian Principalities, and the Peloponnesus. In most cases the maize was grown for export purposes, the workers on the chifliks living on sorghum. It is significant that the geographic pattern of maize and cotton cultivation corresponded to the geographic pattern of the chiflik institution. The free mountain villages were the last to accept the new maize culture.

The development of the new crops for export in turn contributed to the growth of a class of native Balkan merchants and mariners. Foreign merchants and shipping handled much of the export business but a considerable proportion fell to the new entrepreneurs. The result was a rapid growth of the Ragusan, Dulcignote, and Greek merchant fleets, and also the enrichment of the Greek and Macedonian merchants who controlled much of the overland trade up the Danube Valley into Central Europe.

Another factor that contributed to the growth of Balkan commerce was the restoration of peace by the 1699 Karlowitz Treaty, which permitted the resumption of trade between the Balkan lands and the Hapsburg Empire and Venice. Equally important was the Russian expansion to the Black

Sea at the end of the eighteenth century. This made possible the exploitation of the Ukrainian plains, which in turn led to a lively commerce between the Russian Black Sea ports and the Balkan lands. Finally, the Anglo-French wars of the eighteenth and early nineteenth centuries disrupted commerce in the Mediterranean and ruined the Western merchants who had established themselves in various Balkan ports and had monopolized the overseas trade. Local merchants promptly took the place of the Westerners and exported Balkan products through overland trade channels into Central Europe.

These developments enormously increased the volume of Balkan commerce, both foreign and domestic. Trade was carried along transversal and longitudinal routes. The transversal routes began in the Adriatic ports of Dubrovnik (Ragusa), Split (Spalato), Durazzo, and Arta, and ended in Novi Bazar, Belgrade, Saloniki, Serres, Varna, and Constantinople. The longitudinal routes began in Budapest and Chernovtsy (Cernauti), and ended in Saloniki and Constantinople. At first the Greeks, Jews, and Vlachs controlled most of the trade, but gradually the Serbs and Bulgars also participated in it.

The expansion of trade in turn stimulated the demand and the output of handicraft products. Important manufacturing centers appeared in various parts of the peninsula, frequently in isolated mountain areas where the artisans could practice their crafts with a minimum of Turkish interference. In Bulgaria and Greece particularly, village artisans turned out substantial quantities of woolen and cotton thread and textiles, stockings, clothes, carpets, silks, and furs. Most of the output was marketed within the empire, but certain products were also exported to foreign countries, mostly in Central Europe. The degree of industrial expansion can be easily exaggerated. It never approached Western proportions for various reasons, including the lack of security, the competition of Western manufactured goods, the active opposition of Western consuls and the absence of a persistent mercantilist or cameralist policy on the part of the Ottoman government. Nevertheless, the fact remains that industrial output in the Balkans rose sharply during the course of the eighteenth century.

The rise of commerce and industry stimulated the growth of a merchant marine. The most important maritime centers were along the Dalmatian coast (Zadar, Kotor, Trogir, Split, and Ragusa, or Dubrovnik), the Albanian and Epirote coast (Durazzo and Arta) and the Greek littoral and islands (Hydra, Spetsai, Psara, Galaxidi, and Crete). The new merchant marine exported Balkan products such as cotton, maize and other grains, dyeing materials, wine, oil, and fruits, especially currants. In return they brought back mostly manufactured goods and colonial products, particularly spices, sugar, woolens, glass, watches, guns, and gunpowder.

POLITICAL DEVELOPMENTS

The developments in agriculture, commerce, and industry had far-reaching political repercussions. One was the appearance of a persistent and growing bandit movement. The bolder peasants, driven to desperation by the extortion and exploitation arising from the breakdown of order and the spread of chifliks, abandoned their plots and took to the mountains or forests, where they led the perilous but free lives of outlaws. In Greece these outlaws were known as klephts, in Serbia as haiduks, and in Bulgaria as haiduts. These men refused to accept any Turkish authority whatsoever. Instead, they organized themselves into small bands of twenty to a hundred men, though sometimes they numbered as many as two or three hundred. They robbed the Turks and sometimes the rich Christian oligarchs and the monks of the well-stocked monasteries, in preference to the poor peasants or the parish priests. They came to be regarded, therefore, not as ordinary brigands but rather as champions of the lowly and the downtrodden. Countless ballads glorified them as romantic Robin Hoods performing spectacular feats against the Turkish tyrant and against oppression in general.

Their chief historical significance is that they kept alive the idea of justice and freedom. They themselves had no political consciousness or ideology. Their ballads did not call on the Christians to create independent Balkan states. Instead, they glorified local skirmishes and extolled the fabulous exploits and magnificent trappings of individual guerrilla heroes. These warriors were almost invariably illiterate. They had no comprehension of the cultural and historical traditions of their respective peoples. A Greek scholar of this period relates that when he met the renowned guerrilla leader Nikotsaras, he acclaimed his prowess as equal to that of Achilles. Nikotsaras was deeply offended that he should be compared to an unknown. "What nonsense is this," he replied indignantly, "and who is this Achilles? Did the musket of Achilles kill many?" [5]

Despite their limitations, these outlaws did create a tradition of resistance that profoundly influenced the popular mind. And they also provided a ready-made fighting force when various factors which they dimly comprehended culminated in the series of national uprisings in the nineteenth century.

The spread of chifliks produced not only bands of outlaws but also periodic peasant revolts. The contrast was very sharp between the exploitative chiflik system and the original timar arrangement which had provided security and justice to the Christian peasantry. The peasants naturally resented their new degraded status in which they lost rights to their plots and lacked protection against excessive levies and *corvée* duties. The result was that peasant revolts became increasingly frequent as the chifliks, which first appeared in the late sixteenth and early seventeenth centuries, spread steadily during the eighteenth and nineteenth centuries. The significance of these revolts is that they provided the mass basis for the nationalist movements and insurrections that developed among all the Balkan peoples during the late eighteenth and nineteenth centuries.

The leadership of the nationalist movements was assumed to a considerable degree by the new middle-class elements created by the growth of commerce and industry. These groups, by their very nature, were dissatisfied with the Ottoman *status quo*. They had little use for a government that was unable to maintain roads, curb brigands, or prevent the open and never-ending extortions of its own officials. In this respect the following anonymous letter that appeared in the Moscow journal *Vestnik Evropy* [*Herald of Europe*] in January, 1805, is revealing:

> . . . the insecurity of life and property take away the stimulus to establish factories. Even the boyars in the Danubian Principalities consider this dangerous. . . . Not long ago a wealthy lord, Sandulati Sturza, the son-in-law of the present hospodar, Muruzi, started a woolen factory, but for safety's sake he built it in his village and not in town. . . . They have no understanding of promissory notes. . . . [Borrowers] have to pay 30 to 40 percent, which sum is subtracted at once from the loan. For transfer to Germany or to France, the banker charges 10 to 20 percent.[6]

The new middle-class groups also tended to be radically minded because of their contacts with the West. Merchants and seamen who journeyed to foreign lands could not help contrasting the security and enlightenment they witnessed abroad with the deplorable conditions at home. Very naturally they would conclude that their own future, and that of their fellow countrymen, depended upon the earliest possible removal of the Turkish incubus. It does not follow that every merchant and shipowner was an ardent revolutionary. We shall see later that when the Greek War of Independence began in 1821 some of the fabulously wealthy shipowning families hesitated to enter the struggle precisely because they had so much to lose. But they were exceptions. More typical of this group was the following lament of a Greek merchant, John Priggos, who had made his fortune in Amsterdam. While living in that city he had been impressed by the security and justice with which commercial operations could be conducted.

> But all this cannot exist under the Turk. He has neither order nor justice. And if the capital is one thousand he multiplies it tenfold so that he may loot and impoverish others, not realizing that the wealth of his subjects is the wealth of his kingdom. . . . he is altogether unjust, and he is not one for creating anything but only for destroying. May the Almighty ruin him so that Greece may become Christian, and justice may prevail, and governments may be created as in Europe where everyone has his own without fear of any injustice. . . .[7]

Merchants like Priggos made important contributions to Balkan national development not only because of their political activities but also because of their role as intermediaries between their native countries and the outside world. The Serbian merchants in southern Hungary, the Bulgarian merchants in southern Russia and in the Danubian Principalities, and the Greek merchants scattered widely in foreign cities such as Trieste, Venice, Vienna, Amsterdam, Budapest, Bucharest, and Odessa, all contributed greatly to the intellectual awakening of their fellow countrymen. They did so by bestowing upon their native towns and villages lavish gifts of books, equipment, and money. Frequently they financed the education of young men of their race in foreign universities. Also, they made possibile the publication of books and newspapers in their native languages. These books usually were printed in European cities and then shipped to the Balkan lands. It is striking and significant that the first Greek newspaper and the first Serbian newspaper were published in Vienna in 1790 and 1791, respectively; that for many years almost all Serbian and Bulgarian books in the Cyrillic script were printed by the Budapest University press; that the first Bulgarian book was published in Rimnik, Wallachia, in 1806; that the Philike Hetairia which planned the Greek War of Independence was organized in 1814 by Greek merchants in Odessa; that Bulgarian merchants in the same city were responsible for the first Bulgarian schools and the first Bulgarian textbooks used in their homeland; and that Novi Sad in southern Hungary was for long known as the "Serbian Athens" because of its contributions to the development of Serbian culture and national consciousness.

PASSING OF THE THEOCRATIC AGE

The various forces analyzed above created a new intellectual climate in the Balkan world. There was not only more education but a new type of education. It was no longer primarily religious. Instead, it was profoundly influenced by the current Enlightenment in Western Europe. The students who studied abroad returned with a firsthand knowledge of the new body of thought. A contemporary Protestant missionary complained:

> The educated portion of Greece, the elite of her gifted sons, are in the habit of sipping the poison of Voltaire and of Rousseau, whose writings have been put into modern Greek. I have met Greeks who have keenly defended the chilly theory of deism, and to meet their sophistries requires talent. . . . Can we wonder, therefore, if an impious, ignorant, lifeless [Greek] ministry produce a host of infidels? Is it at all surprising that young Greeks educated in Italy, Germany, France or England, should return to the classic land disciples of Alfieri, of Schiller, of Voltaire, of Lord Shaftesbury? [8]

As the missionary observed, the works of Voltaire and of Rousseau, and also of Locke, Descartes, Leibnitz, and others, were now being translated, usually into Greek first, and then into the other Balkan languages. The Greeks took the lead for various reasons. They had more contacts with the West because of their geographic position and extensive commerce; their merchants were more numerous and provided more funds for general educational purposes; moreover, their language and culture had been dominant for centuries and had prevailed in the church schools in their homeland and, indeed, throughout the peninsula. These advantages enabled the Greeks to take the lead in translating foreign authors as well as in transforming their educational system. They were the first to break clerical control of education and to establish secular schools with humanistic curricula. Hitherto most schools had been content to train the children to read the church service books, to write simple letters, and to do simple figuring. Now well-equipped new schools were built using new texts and offering new subjects, including modern languages and sciences.

This development was of importance for the Greeks and their neighbors. This was especially true in Rumania, where Greek administrators, merchants, and teachers occupied a prominent position. In fact, Bucharest society was essentially Greco-Rumanian in character, and it was directly and fully influenced by intellectual currents in the Greek world. Greek teachers taught at the Academy of Bucharest and at its counterpart in Jassy. Greek newspapers published in Vienna circulated widely throughout the Principalities. Greek translations of Western authors were common, and the French originals also could be read because of the new modern language instruction in the schools. Thus at a time when there was no direct contact between Bucharest and the Western capitals, Western ideas penetrated to the Principalities through Greek channels by way of Constantinople and Greece.

It is also noteworthy that a considerable number of Bulgarian pupils attended the new Greek schools. This is understandable in view of the fact that in 1750 only twenty-eight so-called cloister schools were to be found in Bulgaria, of which only two were located in towns and the remainder in villages. These cloister schools were of a very low level, offering only a little arithmetic, and reading and writing in the old Church Slavonic that was incomprehensible to the people. Consequently, Bulgarian students flocked to Greek schools in Athens, Chios, Yanina, Constantinople, Smyrna, Bucharest, Jassy, and elsewhere. The teaching naturally was in Greek but the significant point was its secular content. This had a dynamic effect upon the Bulgarian students who returned to their homeland and spread the new learning. They opened what were called "Greco-Slav" schools which represented a transition between the older cloister schools and the fully Bulgarian schools started in the 1830's with the support of Bulgarian merchants in Odessa.* Bulgarian scholars have recognized the contribution of Greek learning to their national awakening.

We should recognize, despite everything, that our renaissance owes much to the Greek schools. They gave instruction, education and progress to the Bulgarian people. . . . Several of our Bulgarian leaders received their education in Greek schools. . . . Greece, because of her favorable geographic position, came under the influence of Italy, and through the medium of Greece this influence also contributed to our renaissance.[9]

* See Chapter 19

Serbian students also attended Greek schools. Outstanding was Dimitrije Obradovich (c. 1743–1811), the founder of modern Serbian literature.* An important stage in his intellectual development was his attendance at a Greek school in Smyrna between October, 1765, and April, 1766. Obradovich himself relates that his teacher was

free from all superstition . . . a sworn foe and rebuker of monkish abuses, falsehoods and begging; of fraudulent ikons and relics; and of miracles wrought for money. Whenever anybody told him that such and such an ikon was miraculous, he would inquire: "Does it float in the air all by itself, or is it nailed or pasted on a wall or hung on a peg?" And when he heard that the first of these things was not true and the second was, he would say, "So you see that it is not miraculous." [10]

When Obradovich left Smyrna he was well on his way to becoming an eighteenth-century rationalist. His new ideas were crystallized and deepened when he journeyed to Vienna in 1771. Later, when he registered as a student at the university in Halle, he began, as he put it,

to publish a book on my own adventures, in which I had two primary purposes: first, to show the uselessness of monasteries for society; and second, to show the great need for sound learning, as the most effective method of freeing men from superstition and of guiding them to a true reverence for God, to rational piety, and to enlightened virtue, whereby a man gifted with reason enters on the true path of his temporal and eternal welfare. [11]

Obradovich was as ardent a nationalist as he was a rationalist. In his writings he addressed himself "to every person who understands our language. . . . I shall pay no heed whatever to what religion and faith any man belongs, nor is that a matter for consideration in the present enlightened age." [12]

Obradovich had many counterparts in Greece, outstanding being the revolutionary Rhigas Pheraios (1757–1798).† Rhigas likewise turned his back on religious distinctions. In his famous revolutionary song, "Thourios," he called on all enslaved peoples, Christian or Moslem, white or Negro, to rise simultaneously in revolt "from Bosnia to Arabia." His fiery slogans were the complete antithesis of Orthodox theocratic ideology: "Freedom of faith for all"; "Our hearts for our country"; "Draw the sword for liberty." [13]

Another prominent Greek exponent of the new ideology was the educator Adamantios Koraïs. Born in Smyrna, he came as a youth under the influence of a Dutch pastor who acquainted him with the Enlightenment. In 1782 he left for France to study medicine and never returned to his homeland. The impact upon him of Western society, and especially of the city of Paris, is reflected in the following letter he wrote to a friend:

I have been in the celebrated city of Paris since the 24th of May [1788], the home of arts and science, the Athens of today. Imagine a city, much larger

---

* For details concerning Obradovich, see Chapter 14.
† For more details concerning Rhigas, see Chapter 15.

than Constantinople, with 800,000 people, all sorts of academies, public libraries, where science and art have been developed to perfection, where learned men are to be seen all over the city, in boulevards, market places, cafes, etc. In the latter place you find political and literary newspapers written in German, English, and French, and in all other languages. . . . Such, my friends, is Paris. Anyone is bound to be astonished at these things, but for a Greek who knows that his ancestors had reached, two thousand years ago in Athens, an equal (if not higher) degree of learning, his surprise is mingled with melancholy. And when, moreover, he realizes that all these blessings exist no longer in Greece but have instead been replaced by myriad evils, that where once governed the wise laws of Solon (whose name, my friend, I have often heard mentioned with reverence by the learned men here) now reign ignorance, malice, force, wickedness, insolence, and shamelessness, that instead of a Miltiades and Themistocles, whom Europe still admires, we are governed by scoundrels and stupid men as well as by an ignorant clergy who are even worse than our foreign tyrants the Turks. When, I say, the unfortunate Greek is confronted with these things and recalls the past, then, my friend, his melancholy becomes sheer indignation and despair.[14]

In this manner the Balkan world was thoroughly transformed, so that by the beginning of the nineteenth century it was quite different from what it had been a century or two earlier. Ecclesiastics no longer were the sole spokesmen of the faithful; priests no longer were the sole teachers in the schools; and theological treatises no longer were the sole texts for instruction. The Age of Theocracy was giving way to a new Age of Nationalism— an age of secular ideas and leaders and aspirations.

ROLE OF THE ORTHODOX CHURCH

The Orthodox Church, as an institution, was generally hostile to the new currents of secularism and nationalism. Before considering the reasons for this situation it should be noted that the church contributed fundamentally to the preservation of the identity of the Balkan peoples. It is true that Christianity rested very lightly on the mass of the peasantry, which was illiterate and superstitious. Yet the fact remains that religion did serve as a barrier between the Moslem Turks and their Christian subjects, thereby forestalling the possibility of racial and cultural assimilation. Religion also represented a basic element in Balkan historical tradition and helped to keep alive memories of past independence and greatness. Furthermore, the church was the repository of the feeble remnants of literacy and culture during the centuries of darkness. Finally, the church served as a common and strengthening bond among the Balkan Christians until the advent of disruptive nationalism.

These factors were operative and significant during most of the period of Turkish rule. But by the eighteenth century a rift began to develop between the church and the new elements in Balkan society that were challenging the *status quo*. The explanation is to be found in the position that the church occupied in the Ottoman imperial framework. We saw in Chapter 4 that Mohammed II had granted the church extensive ecclesiastical and secular jurisdiction immediately after capturing Constantinople. But in the following centuries the church became corrupt and demoralized and incapable of independent action.

The main reason for this deterioration was the simony which permeated the entire ecclesiastical structure. This evil was partly a reflection of the corrupt Ottoman bureaucracy, but it was also a result of the rivalries of church factions that did not hesitate to intrigue and to bribe in order to obtain the coveted patriarchal throne. One of these factions succeeded as early as 1467 in deposing the incumbent patriarch by offering to pay one thousand gold pieces to the Ottoman government. This practice proceeded apace, with the Turks naturally encouraging it until it became the rule. Large sums were spent regularly as bribes to courtiers, eunuchs, janissaries, and female favorites of the sultans. The patriarchate came to resemble the medieval Papacy in the means employed to control elections. Of the 159 patriarchs who held office between the fifteenth and twentieth centuries, 105 were dethroned by the Turks; 27 abdicated, many of them involuntarily; 6 suffered violent deaths by hanging, poisoning, or drowning; and only 21 died natural deaths while in office. It is apparent that an institution functioning under such conditions was quite incapable of independent decision or action.

The church's freedom of action was further hampered by the fact that it was part and parcel of the Ottoman imperial machinery. The patriarch had the rank of vizir, and his bishops in the provinces worked together with the Turkish governors. The church's position in the empire certainly was not ideal, but it was recognized and established, and this inevitably led to a certain reluctance to challenge the *status quo.*

The church became further compromised in its relations with the Ottoman state when the Phanariotes gained a preponderant position in church councils. The origins and role of the Phanariotes will be examined in Chapter 15. Suffice it to note here that they were Greeks who entered the Ottoman service and gained great power and wealth as administrators, tax farmers, merchants, and contractors. The Phanariotes then infiltrated the Patriarchate, and with their wealth and government connections they were able by the end of the seventeenth century to dominate the church. At one point they were in a position to intervene decisively in the election of all church officials, including the patriarch himself. In view of the fact that the Phanariotes were Ottoman officials, their predominance in the church naturally committed that institution more than ever to the imperial *status quo.*

It does not follow from the above that the Orthodox prelates were at all times loyal to the sultan. In certain respects their position in the empire was ambivalent, which in turn made their own attitude and conduct ambivalent. Members of the Orthodox clergy, from the highest to the lowest, were subject to the caprice of the sultan and his ministers. Yet these same clergy exercised a civil authority over their Christian followers that they had never possessed in Byzantine times. Their church property was subject to pillage and confiscation, but in spiritual affairs the Moslem overlord, in contrast to his Byzantine predecessor, was indifferent and aloof. Thus the church was at once pampered and scorned, privileged and persecuted. Correspondingly, the church leaders wavered between loyalty and sedition toward the Ottoman master. As a rule they exhorted the faithful to respect the new emperor in Constantinople—to render unto Caesar such things as were Caesar's. Yet it was ever galling that the Caesar should be a Moslem sultan. And when this sultan became progressively weaker, and his rule progressively corrupt and tyrannical, some Orthodox leaders turned to another Caesar who was both Christian and Orthodox—the tsar of Russia.

A considerable number of patriarchs, bishops, and monks made the pilgrimage to Moscow to implore the aid of "our Tsar," "our Orthodox Tsar," "our sovereign of the True Faith." The petitioners came not only from Constantinople but also from the Serbian, Bulgarian, and Rumanian lands. The bishop of Transylvania presented to Tsar Alexis in 1668 a petition that was typical of others, both before and after.

> We will contribute willingly whatever will help to defeat the Turks, but nothing is possible without the help of other Christians and other sovereigns, and without the will and aid of God. . . . A large number of Orthodox Slavs live in these regions: Serbs, Bulgarians and Wallachians, and all these people wait only for the signal to be given to fall upon the vile Turk; since they groan in misery and oppression they would form, with the permission of God, a completely prepared army.[15]

Such appeals were natural and understandable, for they were made to the Tsar of Holy Russia, the Protector of the True Faith. But when the call for revolution came from Western-inspired leaders who wished to establish modern nation-states rather than to further the cause of Orthodoxy, the church leaders inevitably reacted violently. They did so not only for material reasons, not merely because of historic and advantageous commitments to the Ottoman regime. They were also repelled because of ideological considerations. The new doctrines from the West represented a challenge to the intellectual foundations of Balkan Orthodoxy. Throughout the centuries of Ottoman rule the Orthodox Church had been profoundly anti-Western. It had opposed the West because it was the home of Catholicism and Protestantism and because it was the birthplace of the Renaissance with its rationalism and secularism. Thus the church now regarded the French Revolution and its attendant ideology as the abominable culmination of this modern secular trend. It denounced the tenets of the Enlightenment and it opposed the agitation for revolution and for national independence. This opposition extended to all Balkan national movements—not merely to the South Slav and Rumanian, as is often assumed, but also to the Greek.

Thus we find the Constantinople Patriarchate prohibiting under penalty of excommunication the reading of those works of Rhigas Pheraios that related to the church. We find also the patriarch cooperating with the sultan in measures against the klephts. When the latter became dangerously strong in the Peloponnesus in the opening years of the nineteenth century, the patriarch, at the request of the sultan, issued a synodal excommunication directed against all Christians who refused to aid the authorities in the drive against the klephts. The most detailed exposition of the antinational attitude of the church hierarchy at this time is to be found in the pamphlet "Paternal Instructions," published in 1798 in Constantinople under the name of Anthimos, Patriarch of Jerusalem, though the actual author appears to have been the Patriarch of Constantinople, Gregory V. The pamphlet propounds the thesis that the Ottoman Empire is a divinely sanctioned institution established to ensure the religious liberty of the Orthodox and to protect them from the heresies of the West.

Behold, how our merciful and omniscient Lord has arranged things, to preserve again the integrity of the holy and Orthodox faith of us, the pious, and to redeem everybody; He raised from nothing this powerful kingdom of the Ottomans instead of our Roman [Byzantine] kingdom, which had somehow started to deviate in matters of our Christian orthodox spirit. And He raised that Ottoman kingdom above any other kingdom, to prove beyond doubt that this was according to His divine will . . . and to provide a great mystery, that is the salvation of His chosen people. . . .

The Devil devised another evil trick in the current century. . . . that is, the now much-talked-of system of liberty, which on the surface seems as if it were good. . . . But there is an enticement of the Devil and a destructive poison destined to cast people down into catastrophe and disorder.

Brethren, do not be cheated out of the way of salvation. . . . Close your ears and give no attention at all to those newly professed hopes of freedom. . . . Besides being contrary to the Holy Scriptures, they are professed deceitfully to cheat you and strip you of any heavenly and earthly wealth. Everywhere this illusory evil system of liberty has caused poverty, murders, losses, plunder. Deceitful, Christian brethren, are the teachings of those new apostles, and be careful.

> He [the Sultan] is, after God, their Lord,
> The depository of the goods and guardian of their life.
> Both divine and human laws command strongly,
> Call both young and old to faith and submission.
> And above all, the Scripture says, that we should pray
> For our king constantly. . . .
> And that he who opposes such authority
> Opposes the command of God himself.
> As we are indebted [to the Sultan] for all the charities
> We enjoy, both the old and young of us,
> Not only should we surrender every possession of ours
> But also detest every anarchy.[16]

A reply to this apologia for the *status quo* was published in the same year, 1798, in the form of a brochure by Koraïs entitled "Brotherly Instructions." Koraïs criticized the argument that the Turkish conquest was divinely ordained in order to shield Orthodox from Western heresies. He pointed out that this protection had never been extended to the more numerous Orthodox Christians in Russia, and he denounced Ottoman domination as an abomination rather than a divine blessing. The patriarch, added Koraïs, should have censured the corruption of the clergy who were fleecing their flocks. "It is readily understood," he wrote, "why the rapacious clergy fear the destruction of the Ottoman Empire and the attainment of liberty, because it will mark the beginning of their own misfortune." [17]

In the same year that this polemical exchange took place, the revolutionary Rhigas Pheraios was apprehended by the Turks and executed. As he was about to die he declared defiantly, "I have sown. Others will reap." History soon vindicated him and repudiated the patriarch. The reason was that the church no longer had the influence that it had enjoyed a century or two earlier. Its position had been undermined by the combination of forces described above. The Age of Theocracy was giving way, and with the coming of the nineteenth century one after another of the Balkan peoples took up arms to win the liberty that the patriarch had denounced and that Rhigas and Koraïs had acclaimed.

10. Defeat by Austria: Recession to the Danube: 1566–1699

THE CENTURY FOLLOWING the death of Suleiman in 1566 was generally one of decline and demoralization. Yet during this period the Ottoman Empire lost no territory. Its far-flung frontiers remained unbroken. The explanation is to be found in the fact that the neighboring states at this time were equally weak and disorganized. Persia experienced a revival under Abbas I but sank back into her usual anarchy following his death in 1629. The Hapsburgs offered no serious threat to Ottoman integrity during the long and ineffectual reign of Emperor Rudolf from 1576 to 1612. Six years later the outbreak of the Thirty Years' War provided the Turks with another long respite from foreign aggression. Thus a fortunate combination of historical accidents enabled the Ottoman Empire to reach the mid-seventeenth century intact if not unscathed.

During the second half of the seventeenth century the Ottoman Empire suffered devastating defeats and lost extensive territories. This occurred despite the fact that the empire at this time experienced a marked recovery under the leadership of the great Kiuprili grand viziers. The paradox is to be explained by new diplomatic and military developments. The Hapsburg emperor, Leopold I, organized an overwhelming anti-Turkish coalition including Poland, Venice, and Russia. He also commanded the services of three remarkable military leaders, the Duke of Lorraine, the Marquis of Baden, and Prince Eugene of Savoy. These men enjoyed the great advantage of new military techniques that had emerged from the Thirty Years' War but which had not yet been adopted by the Turks. The seventeenth century consequently closed with the epoch-making Treaty of Karlowitz in which for the first time "the ever-victorious frontier" shrank back from the walls of Vienna to the valley of the Danube.

SELIM II: 1566–1574

Selim II was a very different man from his distinguished father and predecessor, Suleiman the Magnificent. The latter owed his reputation in part to his impressive appearance and irreproachable character. The Hapsburg ambassador Busbecq describes him as "frugal and temperate," "a strict guardian of his religion and its ceremonies," "not indulging in wine," and of a "general physical appearance worthy of the ruler of so vast an empire." [1] Selim was the exact opposite in almost every respect—lazy, fat, dissipated, and so addicted to wine that he was known to his subjects as Selim the Sot. Yet he was not as degenerate as his disgraceful successors. He was not the puppet of harem intrigues. Although lacking the driving force and self-discipline of his father, he was intelligent, artistic, a fine poet, and capable of accepting good advice. He stands, in short, halfway between the great sultans who preceded him and the pathetic creatures that followed.

During Selim's reign additional territories were obtained at the expense of Venice in the west and Persia in the east. The acquisition of Venetian territory points up a notable shift in Ottoman foreign policy. Under Suleiman it had been directed against the Hapsburgs. Some of Selim's advisers favored the continuation of this policy. They wished particularly to strike against Emperor Charles's son, Philip II of Spain, who had hounded the Moors out of his country. Other advisers favored, instead, an attack upon the Venetian-held island of Cyprus, which was being used by Christian corsairs to prey upon Ottoman commerce and upon the pilgrim traffic to Mecca. The latter course was adopted, and in May, 1570, a fleet sailed from Constantinople for Cyprus.

The Venetians soon discovered that aid from other Christian states was not forthcoming. The only power in a position to give substantial assistance was Spain. It might be imagined that this country would welcome a Venetian alliance, given the constant threat of Ottoman aggression and the never-ending depredations of the Moslem North African corsairs. Yet Philip held back, fearing that the Venetians would use a Spanish alliance to make terms with the Turks and leave them free to attack him. Nor were his fears wholly unjustified. We know that the Signiory throughout this period conducted secret negotiations with Constantinople. Even the Venetians themselves were concerned lest an alliance with Spain should increase Spanish influence in Italy and threaten their own predominance in the Adriatic. Under these circumstances it is not surprising that the negotiations dragged on for over a year. The only disinterested figure on the scene was Pope Pius V, and it was largely due to his efforts that a Triple Alliance (Spain, Venice, and the Papacy) was concluded on May 20, 1571. By that date it was too late to save Cyprus.

The Turks had landed on the island on July 1, 1570. They laid siege to the capital, Nicosia, and captured it on August 8. Then they proceeded to invest Famagusta, the principal fortress of Cyprus. It was heroically defended by a mixed force of Italians and Greeks under the command of Bragadin, a gallant and experienced Venetian general. Hopes were raised at first by the news that an allied fleet of 187 ships was coming to the rescue. But the commander of the Spanish contingent had received secret instructions from Philip II to procrastinate and to avoid committing his ships in battle. These orders were carried out so effectively that the fleet did not reach Crete until September. It was then decided that it was too late in the season to proceed further. The expedition turned back, leaving the defenders of Famagusta to their fate.

The siege dragged on through the winter of 1570. It was not until August of the following year that the garrison surrendered, its provisions exhausted and only seven barrels of powder remaining. The Turks paid dearly for the victory, suffering some fifty thousand casualties. This heavy loss may account for the perfidious breach of the surrender terms. After promising to spare the lives of the defenders, the Turks executed Bragadin's immediate companions, tortured him to death, and made captives of the rest. But when the victors arrived in Constantinople with the prisoners and booty, they found the capital gloomy and depressed. News had just arrived of the great Christian naval victory at Lepanto on October 7, 1571.

The Christian allies had amassed a formidable fleet in the summer of 1571 for the relief of Famagusta. Profiting from the experience of the previous year when a similar fleet had accomplished nothing because of dissension among the commanders, the allies placed this fleet under the supreme command of Don John of Austria, the natural son of the late Emperor Charles V. Don John had at his disposal a total of 200 to 210 galleys, mostly Venetian and Spanish, together with 6 Venetian galleasses or supergalleys. This armada was at anchor off one of the Ionian Islands when news arrived early in October that Famagusta had fallen two months earlier. Some captains now urged retreat, but the majority, Don John among them, maintained that a defeat of the Turkish fleet would compensate to some extent for the loss of Cyprus even though it would not recover the island. Accordingly, the allied fleet crossed to Lepanto at the entrance of the Gulf of Corinth where the main Turkish fleet was reported to be gathered.

Meanwhile the Turks on their part were also divided on the advisability of engaging in battle. The top commander, Ali Pasha, was a young man with little naval experience. The veteran corsair, Uluch Ali, was the second in command, and a certain Perted Pasha commanded the troops. Both Uluch and Perted opposed an immediate battle on the ground that their men were inadequately trained. But Ali was able to show the sultan's definite orders to fight and thus silenced the opposition. On October 7 the two fleets met just inside the entrance of the Gulf of Lepanto. The Turkish galleys were decidedly superior in numbers, approximately 270 as against the slightly more than 200 under Don John. But the Christian vessels were larger and carried more soldiers, nearly 20,000 in contrast to the 16,000 Turks. Furthermore, the Christian soldiers wore more armor and carried more firearms than their opponents. Many of the latter had only bows and arrows and wore no armor whatsoever.

This Christian superiority in soldiers proved decisive, for the Lepanto battle was essentially a land battle on the water. The two fleets, drawn up in parallel lines, met in head-on collision. They became inextricably mixed, with several galleys frequently locked together and the soldiers battling to the finish on the decks. The melee went on for about three hours before the Turkish center and right wing began to give way. Uluch, in command of the Turkish left wing, succeeded in outmaneuvering the opposing Christian galleys, several of which he cut off and captured. When he became aware that the main Ottoman fleet was being defeated, he made a dash with forty of his galleys and succeeded in breaking through. These were the only Turkish ships that escaped. The remainder were sunk, driven ashore, or captured. In contrast, the allies lost only fifteen vessels. The casualties were approximately nine thousand Christians and thirty thousand Turks. It was an overwhelming defeat for the Ottoman Empire and the whole of Christendom received the news with tremendous enthusiasm and religious fervor.

With the Turkish high-seas fleet annihilated, it remained to be seen how the victors would exploit their triumph the following year. Various possibilities presented themselves—an expedition to recover Cyprus, a blow against the corsair nests in North Africa, or even an attempt at the Dardanelles, where the Turks were reported to be hastily rebuilding the entrance forts. The problem was to find a project agreeable to all the allies. This proved impossible. The Venetians were interested only in strengthening their position in the Levant. But the Spaniards did not wish to jeopardize their naval forces so far from home, especially since war with France was always possible. They preferred, instead, to strike against the North African pirates who were a constant scourge in the western Mediterranean. Finally, the death of Pope Pius V in May, 1572, deprived the allies of their only sincere and disinterested member and ended the possibility of resolute and effective united action.

Don John did bring the main Spanish fleet to Corfu, where the Venetians were waiting. But he did not arrive until September, 1572. And when the combined force set out to look for the Turks it received an unpleasant surprise. The Turks were waiting with a fleet fully as powerful as that which they had lost at Lepanto. Thanks to the energy and organizational ability of Grand Vizir Sokolli (Sokolovich), no less than one hundred and sixty galleys and eight galleasses had been built during the preceding winter. Uluch, the new captain pasha of the Ottoman fleet, decided not to risk battle with the Christians. The most serious loss suffered at Lepanto had been the skilled mariners, who were more difficult to replace than the lost galleys. Uluch now discovered that his crews had little experience in navigation or in warfare. Accordingly, he set out for the strongly fortified harbor of Modon on the west coast of Greece. When the allied fleet under Don John appeared before the harbor, Uluch refused to venture out. Don John landed soldiers in order to take Modon from the rear, but they were repulsed by strong Turkish reinforcements from the interior. By this time October had come, and with it the danger of storms. Don John decided to end the expedition and return to winter quarters. Uluch likewise returned to Constantinople and the operations were over for the year. The tardiness of King Philip together with the unexpected appearance of a new Ottoman fleet had prevented the allies from exploiting their victory at Lepanto.

The abortive 1572 expedition proved to be the last common effort of the Christian league. It was apparent to the Venetians by this time that the recovery of Cyprus was most unlikely. Furthermore, the war with Turkey had disrupted the Levantine trade and precipitated a serious economic crisis. These considerations led the Venetians to decide in favor of peace. Sokolli's terms were severe, for the shrewd Bosnian knew that he had the whip hand. On March 7, 1573, the Venetians signed a treaty in which they formally ceded Cyprus and also paid an indemnity of three hundred thousand ducats.

The terms could not have been worse if the battle of Lepanto had never been fought. This indicates that despite the rejoicing of the Christian world the battle was not decisive in the strategic sense. It did not alter the balance of power in the Mediterranean. By signing the peace treaty Venice tacitly accepted Ottoman naval supremacy in the eastern Mediterranean. Don John continued the war in the western part of the sea. In 1573 he captured Tunis but the following year the Turks recovered the base. From then on, naval operations were spasmodic and indecisive, consisting mostly of small-scale raids by each side. The reason was that both the Spaniards and the Turks now had more pressing problems elsewhere—the Spaniards in the Atlantic and the North Sea and the Turks along the Persian frontier.

During these years Persia was seriously weakened by incompetent rulers and by continual attacks from the Uzbeks to the east. The Turks seized the opportunity to launch an invasion from the west in 1578. They overran several provinces and retained them despite persistent Persian efforts. Finally, in 1590, they forced the Persians to accept a treaty ceding Georgia, Azerbaijan, and Shirwan. Thus the Turks extended their frontiers to the Caucasus Mountains and the Caspian Sea.

With these triumphs the Ottoman Empire reached its greatest extent. The island of Cyprus and the Persian provinces proved to be, with two exceptions, the last acquisitions of the Turks. The exceptions were the island of Crete and the province of Podolia, which were won from Venice and Poland in 1668 and 1676, respectively. But by that time the empire was being buffeted from all sides and was about to lose vast territories north of the Danube. We may conclude that the period from the death of Suleiman in 1566 to the Persian treaty of 1590 represents the crest of the wave of Ottoman expansion. In the following years the empire declined rapidly, and it continued to do so, with the exception of the short reign of Murad IV, until the accession of the great Kiuprili dynasty of grand viziers in 1656.

RULE OF THE SULTANAS

The predominance of the harem in the late sixteenth century was both a symptom and a cause of the empire's decline. Selim II, despite his vices and indolence, had not been altogether a puppet or a nonentity. But his son and successor, Murad III (1574–1595), devoted himself exclusively to the voluptuous life of the harem. He distinguished himself only by the number of his children, one hundred and three in all, of which forty-seven survived him. Since twenty of these were males, his successor, Mohammed III (1595–1603), began his reign by slaughtering his nineteen brothers. The next sultan, Ahmed I (1603–1617) left no sons of age and was succeeded by his lunatic brother Mustafa. After a few months Mustafa was deposed in favor of Osman II (1618–1622). The Ottoman traveler and chronicler, Evliya, notes in his journal that this unfortunate ruler "was removed by a rebellion of the Janissaries, and put to death in the Seven Towers, by the compression of the testicles; a mode of execution reserved by custom to the Ottoman Emperors." [2] The lunatic Mustafa was then reinstated on the throne for a fifteen-month period, probably the worst reign in Ottoman history. Out of this morass of degeneracy there now emerged unexpectedly and almost miraculously a ruler as forceful and capable as the early sultans. Murad IV (1623–1640) put an end to the anarchy and demoralization of the preceding years and inaugurated an exciting though short-lived period of recovery.

The reigns of the puppet rulers between Selim II and Murad IV might not have been so disastrous if capable grand viziers had been entrusted with the administration of the empire. But Sokolli (Sokolovich) unfortunately had been assassinated in 1578 and from then on the real rulers were harem favorites and self-seeking courtiers. Outstanding among these was Sultana Baffo, a Venetian noblewoman who had been captured by corsairs and sold to the harem of Murad III. She proved to be as clever and ambitious as she was beautiful. For three decades she dominated one ruler after another. After she lost her influence other favorites took her place. Although less famous, they played a similar role in the affairs of the empire. It was these women, together with their collaborators in the palace, who determined high policy, made and unmade grand viziers, profited from the sale of offices, and fomented janissary revolts when it suited their interests. Such was the state of the empire when it faced renewed war on the Danube and aggression in the east by a revived Persia.

WAR ON THE DANUBE

The Danubian basin had been relatively peaceful since the great invasions of Suleiman the Magnificent. But toward the end of the sixteenth century new factors upset the balance in that region and plunged it once more into a series of wars. The settlement in the various Danubian countries following Suleiman's conquests may be summarized as follows: Hungary was ruled directly by the Turks with the exception of a small strip in the north and west, which was left to the Hapsburgs; Transylvania was governed by the Zapolya princes, who recognized Turkish suzerainty; and the Danubian Principalities of Moldavia and Wallachia were under native Rumanian princes nominally elected by the nobility but actually selected by the dominant cliques in Constantinople.

This settlement was disturbed by the declining influence of the two great empires, the Ottoman and the Hapsburg. We have noted the type of rulers that succeeded Suleiman in Constantinople. Likewise in Vienna we find in place of Charles V the weak and ineffectual Rudolf II (1576–1611). This ruler was an unsociable eccentric and an uncompromising Catholic. In contrast to his tolerant father, Maximilian II, he strove earnestly to re-Catholicize the areas lost to Protestantism. This policy involved him in continued wrangles with the Protestants of Bohemia and Germany. It also weakened his influence in Hungary and Transylvania, where many of the numerous Calvinists and Lutherans preferred the tolerant government of the pasha of Buda to the bigotry and persecution of the Jesuit-ridden court of Vienna.

The decline of Hapsburg and Ottoman influence in the Danubian basin created a fluid situation which allowed local leaders to assert themselves and to extend their authority. In Transylvania, for example, the Zapolya princes had been, on the whole, docile subjects of the sultan. But this dynasty died out in 1570 and its place was taken by the Bathory princes, who showed much more independence. Stephen Bathory was even elected king of Poland and conducted a successful war against Ivan the Terrible of Russia. He was preparing far-reaching plans for a Central European coalition against the Turks when he died suddenly in 1586. His successor on the Transylvanian throne, Sigismund Bathory (1581–1602) was equally hostile to the Turks and collaborated with Emperor Rudolf against them. And in Wallachia Michael the Brave was elected prince in 1593. This intrepid ruler started out by massacring the imperial tax collectors who were ruining the principality with their extortions. Then he routed the Turkish forces sent against him and even made a winter raid across the Danube as far south as Adrianople.

This was the situation in the Danubian lands when Austria and Turkey drifted to war in 1593. During the two previous years both sides had carried on frontier raids. These culminated in the crushing defeat of the Turkish governor of Bosnia, who was killed together with almost all his men during an expedition into Croatia in June, 1593. Immediately full-scale fighting began and a number of border fortresses changed hands by the end of the year. In 1594 the Turks took to the field with a large army of one hundred thousand men. But the result was disappointing, only one city of any importance falling to the invaders. The old days, when a single campaign won a kingdom, obviously were over.

This fact encouraged Danubian rulers to form anti-Ottoman coalitions. In 1595 Sigismund Bathory concluded with Emperor Rudolf an offensive and defensive alliance aimed at Constantinople. In the same year Michael of Wallachia accepted Sigismund's suzerainty in return for aid against the Turks, who were still seeking to regain the principality. The aid actually materialized and Michael was able in 1595 to cross the Danube once more and to sack towns in Bulgaria. At the same time the combined Hapsburg-Transylvanian armies were winning important victories in Hungary.

This marked a low point in Ottoman fortunes. The prospect appeared so dark that the grand vizir insisted that the new sultan, Mohammed III, should take the field in person during the 1596 campaign. Mohammed did so, not too willingly, and after much maneuvering a decisive two-day battle was fought at Kerestes in northern Hungary. At first the allied forces were successful all along the line. Mohammed was ready to flee and his staff barely restrained him from doing so. At the last moment the tide was reversed by the cupidity of the Christian soldiers. Having burst into the sultan's camp, they broke ranks and scrambled around for plunder. At this point a large body of Turkish irregular cavalry which had been held in reserve bore down upon the disorganized enemy with irresistible force, carrying everything before them. Thousands of Germans and Hungarians fell in the rout and ninety-seven guns were abandoned on the field.

The Turkish victory was decisive in a negative sense. If the Turks had not won, all the lands north of the Danube would have fallen to the allies. But from the positive viewpoint the battle was of little significance. The Turks were unable to exploit their advantage. Indeed, a clear indication of Ottoman military decline is the fact that the great victory at Kerestes was followed by a series of defeats rather than territorial gains. By 1598 the Hapsburg generals reached Buda and laid siege to the capital. Only the approach of winter saved it from capitulation.

The war dragged on a few more years without decisive results. The Turks were distracted by a serious rebellion in Asia Minor and by an even more serious invasion from Persia. Emperor Rudolf also had his troubles. His attempt to reimpose Catholicism by force drove the Transylvanian nobles back into the Turkish fold. In 1599 they deposed the pro-Hapsburg Sigismund and elected in his place a succession of princes who accepted Turkish suzerainty and remained neutral in the war. Thus both the Austrians and the Turks were ready to end hostilities, and in November, 1606, they signed the Peace of Sitva-Torok. This treaty is significant for its form rather than its content. The frontiers remained virtually unchanged, and Transylvania was recognized once more as an Ottoman dependency. But the Hapsburgs no longer were required to pay tribute to Constantinople for the part of Hungary under their control. Nor were they compelled to accept the ignominious language of previous treaties which had been phrased as concessions granted to inferior princes. For the first time the Ottoman government negotiated with a Christian state a treaty drawn up as a settlement on equal terms between two sovereign powers.

Considering briefly Ottoman-Persian relations at this time, it should be noted first that Christian Europe owes a considerable debt to Persia for maintaining a second front against the Ottoman Empire and preventing it from turning full force upon the West. In this respect Persia played a role similar to that of Russia against Germany during the two world wars.

In the late sixteenth century, when the Ottoman Empire was declining, Persia experienced a spectacular though short-lived revival under one of its greatest rulers, Abbas the Great. When he came to the throne in 1587 he found the country in a deplorable state. Tribal chiefs were independent of the central government while the Turks were attacking from the west and the Uzbeks from the east. Abbas first concluded in 1590 an unfavorable peace with the Turks. He ceded various territories to them in order to be free to deal with the Uzbeks. Then he defeated the latter so decisively that Persia was freed of their depredations for many years to come.

Abbas turned next to domestic reorganization. He forced the unruly tribes to accept his authority and ruthlessly exterminated banditry. He started building projects throughout the country, especially roads and bridges. He organized the first infantry regiments to supplement the tribal cavalry which hitherto had been the mainstay of Persian armies. In recruiting his infantrymen Abbas imitated the Ottoman janissaries by using Christian Georgians and Armenians converted to Islam. In his military reforms Abbas had the assistance of two Englishmen, Anthony and Robert Sherley. These fabulous adventurers arrived in Persia in 1598 with twenty-six followers. Abbas employed them to organize regiments of infantry and batteries of artillery. He also sent the brothers on three diplomatic missions to Western Europe with instructions to obtain allies for a war against the Turks. Their adventures in the various European capitals attracted much attention at the time but came to no fruitful conclusion. The Western diplomats were unwilling to commit themselves, some for fear of jeopardizing the profitable Levantine trade and others because they had more pressing problems closer to home.

Despite the failure to find allies, Abbas began his long-planned war against the Turks in 1602. The time was well chosen. The Ottoman armies were involved in Hungary, and the Anatolian rebellion was still alive. Taking advantage of this situation Abbas fell upon the Turkish flank in Armenia and within a year won back all the territories he had ceded in 1590. Hostilities ceased in 1612 but were renewed in 1616. Two years later the Turks accepted a peace settlement by which they surrendered Azerbaijan and Georgia.

MURAD IV: 1623–1640

Meanwhile the Ottoman Empire was going headlong to ruin. The intrigues and corruption at the court and the recurring mutinies of the janissaries had produced a veritable state of anarchy. We have an authoritative account of this deplorable situation in the reports of the British ambassador, Sir Thomas Roe. He arrived in Constantinople in 1622 with instructions to obtain protection for British shipping from the depredations of the North African corsairs. He had little success in this matter. Ottoman officials promised redress but their instructions were simply ignored in Tunis and Algeria. Sir Thomas repeatedly stressed in his reports the helplessness of the central government and the manifold symptoms of decay.

> . . . this mighty monarchy hath no other walls to defend it, but the un-civill dissentions of christian princes. It never had but two pillars of any strength, the Janizaries and the gallies: These [latter] are rotten and decayed, and what are left, are unfitt for service, and the few fitt, without munition, and men to serve in them: The other [the janissaries] are corrupted from their antient disci-pline and institution, and have shaken off that reverence to their emperors . . . . and now they are neither souldiers, nor subjects. . . . they demand in troopes, at this court, all offices of gayne, to be stewards to the revenues of churches, which are great; to take the farmes of customes, and there commit those outrages that are insufferable. The viziers dare deny them nothing: they drink in the streetes without prohibition, contrary to their laws; and stand in companyes in the open day, and exact money without any punishment. . . . Complayne no man dares; or if he doe, to no purpose; the vizier answereth, That he cannot meddle with them; they have murthered their owne king, and all the bassaes [pashas]. . . .[3]

Sir Thomas sent this report in 1622. The following year Murad IV came to the throne. For the first time in half a century the empire had a sultan with sufficient intelligence and will power to end this ruinous anarchy. Since Murad was only eleven at the time of his accession, the janissaries were able to continue their seditious activities for another nine years. During this period they compelled no less than seven grand viziers to resign from office. By 1632 Murad felt strong enough to assert his prerogatives. He proceeded to do so with a ruthlessness that is said to have cost the lives of one hundred thousand of his subjects. The bloodletting proved effective. During the remaining eight years of his reign the empire experienced a revival that was soon felt both at home and abroad.

The Turkish traveler Evliya knew Murad intimately, having served under him as a page. The picture he has left of his hero is of a man strikingly reminiscent of Tsar Peter the Great—the same magnificent physique, the same will power and ruthlessness, and the same success in restoring order at home and winning victories abroad.

In short, Sultan Murad was a man who had the nature of a Dervish, but he was brave and intelligent. His fingers were thick, but well proportioned, and the strongest wrestler could not open his closed fist. He generally dressed in blue coloured silk, and liked to ride very fast. Neither the Ottoman nor any other dynasty of Moslem princes ever produced a prince so athletic, so well-made, so despotic, so much feared by his enemies, or so dignified as Sultan Murad. Though so cruel and bloodthirsty, he conversed with the rich and the poor without any mediator, made his rounds in disguise night and day to be informed of the state of the poor, and to ascertain the price of provisions, for which purpose he fre-quently went into cookshops and dined incognito. No monarch, however was guilty of so many violent deeds. On the march to Baghdad, when he left Caesarea, a wild goat was started in the mountains of Develi Kara Hisar. The emperor immediately gave chase, struck it with his spear, followed it up amongst the rocks, and divided his prey amongst his vizirs. The whole army was surprised to see him dismount and climb up the craggy mountain in pursuit of his game.[4]

Murad's interests were not limited to sports and to war. Evliya adds that he was also "a good poet," that he surrounded himself with dancers, musicians, poets, and divines, and that he met regularly with his ministers to consider matters of state. "In such a manner," concludes Evliya, "did he watch over the Ottoman states, that not even a bird could fly over them without his knowledge." [5]

Murad's chief aim was to reconquer the territories lost to the Persians. In preparing for war he pitilessly suppressed insubordination in the armed forces and obtained the necessary funds by drastic financial measures, including the confiscation of large fortunes. In contrast to his predecessors, Murad personally led his armies in two campaigns against the Persians. The latter as usual refused to fight pitched battles, so that the war consisted of a series of sieges. So long as Abbas was alive the Persians were able to hold their own. But the great shah died in 1629 and from then on Murad steadily gained the upper hand. Finally, in 1638, the Persians accepted a peace settlement providing for the cession of Baghdad and the surrounding territory to the Turks. Eighty years were to pass before another major war was fought between these traditional rivals.

When Murad returned to Constantinople he was greeted, according to Evliya, "with a splendour and magnificence which no tongue can describe." Enthusiastic multitudes crowded the streets shouting, "The blessing of God be upon thee O conqueror!" Murad was a fitting hero for such a welcome. "The emperor looked with dignity on both sides of him, like a lion who had seized his prey, and saluted the people as he went on, followed by three thousand pages clad in armour. The people shouted 'God be praised!' as he passed and threw themselves on their faces to the ground." [6]

Here was the ideal Turkish war lord, the idol of an adoring people, and the leader of an army that had recovered its ancient discipline and prowess. Western diplomats must have wondered anxiously where the conqueror would strike next. In fact, he openly voiced his ambition to crush his Western neighbors as he had the Persians. Furthermore, he began a complete overhauling of the whole military system. He held a census of the miltary fiefs and attempted to eliminate the abuses that had undermined the feudal forces. He abolished the child-tribute and reduced the janissary corps with the apparent aim of ultimately replacing it with a modern army of the Western type. But before these measures could take effect, Murad died in 1640, a victim of prodigiously hard work and equally hard drinking.

DECLINE CONTINUES: 1640–1656

Under Murad's successor, Ibrahim I (1640–1648), the old disorder and corruption immediately returned. This points up a basic difference between Murad and Peter the Great. As individuals the two men were extraordinarily alike. But as rulers, the tsar represented a turning point in the history of his country, whereas the sultan was a mere flash in the pan. An obvious reason for this difference is that Peter ruled for thirty-six years and Murad, in effect, for eight. If the latter had lived another two or three decades, Ottoman history in the seventeenth century undoubtedly would have been substantially different. On the other hand, there is little doubt that Murad never would have effected such far-reaching reforms as did Peter. One reason is that the opposition to Westernization was much stronger in Turkey than in Russia. Another is that the sultan was not a confirmed "Westerner," as was the tsar. Murad was ready to imitate Western armies but Peter was determined that his people should also master Western science and technology. Murad walked in disguise through the streets of his capital to apprehend lawbreakers, whereas Peter journeyed through Western Europe in order to learn what was unknown in his country. Most revealing, perhaps, is the spectacle of Murad's favorite, Evliya, returning from a trip through Northwestern Europe filled with contempt for the strange customs and manners of the Christian infidels. If anyone had suggested to him that he might have learned something beneficial in the Western lands he would have been completely dumfounded and undoubtedly would have rejected the notion as fantastic and sacrilegious. In contrast, half a century later Peter was forcing thousands of his subjects to go to school in the West and inviting Western teachers and craftsmen to Russia.

Whatever might have been the outcome had Murad lived longer, the fact remains that when Ibrahim became the sultan in 1648 the old evils immediately returned. Evliya, who witnessed the events of these years, relates that Ibrahim "fell into the hands of all the favourites and associates of the harem, the dwarfs, the mutes, the eunuchs, the women. . . ." and that together "they threw everything into confusion." [7]

Despite this decadence, Ibrahim involved the empire in a long and exhausting war with Venice. The immediate occasion was the capture of a Turkish galleon by Maltese corsairs. Among the captives was one of Ibrahim's wives and her young son. Ibrahim's first reaction was to send a fleet against Malta but his advisers wisely reminded him of Suleiman's failure to take that stronghold. They persuaded him instead to attack the more vulnerable island of Crete, at that time a Venetian possession. The fact that the corsairs had stopped at certain Cretan harbors on the way home provided a convenient pretext for the assault. An expedition of approximately one hundred vessels and fifty thousand men left Constantinople in April, 1645. With the help of the local Greek population, which detested Venetian rule, the Turks were able by August to capture the port of Canea at the western end of the island. The following year they took Retimo near the center of the northern coast, and in 1648 they began the memorable siege of the capital, Candia.

The siege dragged on a full twenty-five years. The reason for this unconscionably long ordeal was the inability of the Turks to protect their supply lines. A technological revolution had occurred in naval warfare since the days of Lepanto. That battle is memorable in naval history as the last major engagement fought by galleys. These vessels were encumbered with oars, benches, and rowers, and were too frail to carry heavy guns or to withstand their fire. In fact, they were essentially similar to the triremes and dromons of ancient times. Both in equipment and in tactics the battle of Lepanto had been a repetition of the battle of Actium sixteen centuries earlier. But now in the seventeenth century the Venetians began to use sail-propelled warships together with the traditional galleys. They had employed sailing-ships long before this date but only for commerce. In applying the sail to naval warfare the Venetians were following the example of the Northern Europeans, who had made the change earlier because of the impracticability of the galley in the stormy Atlantic.

The sail warship or galleon was an infinitely more efficient fighting machine than the galley. It was larger and more seaworthy; it carried heavy armaments on all sides; and it could undertake long voyages free from the limitations imposed by human muscles. Since the Turks were very slow in adopting the new warship, the Venetians usually had the advantage in the naval battles that accompanied the Cretan campaign. The climax came in the years 1654 to 1656, when the Venetians destroyed an Ottoman fleet in the Dardanelles, blockaded the Straits, and captured the nearby islands of Lemnos and Tenedos.

Meanwhile anarchy prevailed within the empire. The janissaries had deposed Ibrahim in 1648 and replaced him with his ten-year-old son, Mohammed IV. The government naturally remained in the hands of the harem. But the harem was divided by the struggle between two strong women, the mothers of the deposed ruler and of the new sultan. Both women had their supporters among the janissaries and the spahis, with the result that there were frequent disorders in the capital. Rycaut relates that all was in "a horrid and affrighting Confusion . . . and the whole City laid open to be pillaged and sacked by the licentiousness of an unbridled Souldiery. . . ." So desperate was the situation that the ruling oligarchy decided to accept the restraints of a strong hand in order to save the empire from complete destruction. Under these circumstances, Rycaut informs us, they

called for the Pasha of *Damascus* to receive the Dignity of the Great Vizier; for he being a person of eighty Years of Age, and of long Experience in Affairs, having managed the most weighty Charges of the Empire, was looked on by all as the most proper Person to compose and heal those great Distempers in the State; and this was that famous *Kuperlu.* . . .[8]

In this manner the great Kiuprili family made its entrance on the stage that it was to dominate for a full half-century.

KIUPRILI VIZIRS: 1656–1676

Mohammed Kiuprili, the founder of the remarkable dynasty of ministers, came from humble Albanian stock. His grandfather had migrated to Kiupril, a small town in Asia Minor, whence the family took its name. Mohammed began his career as a kitchen boy. He rose to be a cook, steward to the grand vizir, grand falconer, and then governor successively of Damascus, Tripoli, and Jerusalem. When he was offered the grand vizirate he refused to accept the post save under certain conditions: that his measures should be ratified without discussion or delay, and that he should have a free hand in the distribution of offices and honors. These conditions having been accepted, Mohammed entered upon the work of his high office.

The task he faced was staggering. Court intrigue and military insubordination reigned supreme in the capital at a time when the Venetians were in possession of the islands commanding the entrance to the Straits. Mohammed promptly proceeded to use his powers with the utmost severity. No delinquency, past or present, escaped his attention. He planted his spies in every province of the empire and ruthlessly rooted out the corrupt and the incompetent. The more fortunate were dismissed from office. The remainder were summarily executed. It is said that during his five years of office thirty-six thousand persons were put to death on his command. Since Mohammed had acquired a reputation for mildness and humanity as a governor, it may be assumed that this bloodletting was not without justification or purpose.

The beneficent results speedily became apparent throughout the empire. Corruption and injustice were stayed. Discipline was restored in the army and the naval strength of the empire revived. The Venetians were driven from the Lemnos and Tenedos islands, and revolts in Transylvania and Asia Minor were quelled. Ottoman authority was asserted even on the distant Don and Dnieper rivers, where new fortresses were built.

Mohammed died in 1661 and was succeeded by his son Ahmed. The new grand vizir proved to be one of the greatest of Ottoman statesmen, possessing the natural abilities of his father together with an excellent education and a thorough administrative training. Ahmed came to office the same year in which Louis XIV assumed the reins of government in France. To Western eyes the "Sun King" appears as the arbiter of his age. In actual fact, the Ottoman minister played a role fully as decisive and significant. His policies directed the course of events in Austria, Russia, Poland, and the Mediterranean.

In foreign affairs Ahmed wished to continue his father's policy of maintaining peace on the land frontier in order to press the Cretan war against Venice. He was diverted from this course by the aggressiveness of the Austrians, who had recovered from the effects of the Thirty Years' War and resumed their raids across the frontier. Full-scale war broke out in 1663 over the question of Transylvania. The local prince, George Rakoczy, aspired to make himself independent of Constantinople and attempted to win the support of the Moldavian and Wallachian princes. Ahmed promptly deposed Rakoczy and appointed in his place the compliant Prince Michael Apaffy. When the Hapsburg emperor, Leopold I, refused to recognize the new ruler, Ahmed declared war and marched north from Belgrade at the head of an army of a hundred and twenty thousand men. The Austrians were not prepared to meet such a force in pitched battle and withdrew behind their line of frontier fortresses. After capturing the important stronghold of Neuhäusel and several neighboring positions, Ahmed retired to winter quarters to prepare for more decisive action in the following year.

The spectacle of a Turkish army, comparable to that of Suleiman the Magnificent, advancing westward once more, after the interval of a century, made a profound impression in Europe. It aroused a faint echo of the old crusading ardor. Hungarian malcontents rallied to Emperor Leopold's banner, stimulated, no doubt, by the ravages of the Tatar horsemen. The Imperial Diet voted a levy of money and troops, and even Louis XIV provided a contingent of four thousand men to the common cause. This outside aid encouraged the Hapsburg commander, Count Montecuculi, to take the initiative. He recovered some of the forts lost the previous year and then entrenched himself behind the river Raab. On August 1, 1664, the two armies met near the convent of St. Gotthard, which gave its name to the memorable battle that ensued. Despite a substantial numerical superiority the Turks were decisively defeated. They fought with their usual courage and tenacity, but their arms and tactics were those of Suleiman's day. Their artillery was inferior to that of their opponents and they still used the scimitar at a time when the pike had become the supreme infantry weapon. The battle of St. Gotthard is significant as evidence of the passing of Turkish military superiority and as augury of the great Austrian victories a few decades later.

Ten days after their victory the Austrians surprised Europe by signing the unfavorable Treaty of Vasvar. They had lost too heavily at St. Gotthard to undertake the arduous task of clearing the Turks out of Hungary. The Austrians also were suspicious of French designs in the West and dared not commit themselves further in the east. The outbreak of the War of Devolution three years later proved their suspicions justified. These considerations explain the willingness of the Austrians to pay a financial indemnity, to surrender several frontier fortresses and districts, and to recognize Apaffy as the prince of Transylvania. Although defeated in battle, Ahmed had won the peace and had added to the empire of the sultan.

The grand vizir now turned his attention to Crete, where the war had dragged on without issue since 1645. He assumed personal command of the siege of Candia and pressed it relentlessly for three years. Despite the gallantry of the Venetian general, Francesco Morosini, and the assistance of a French fleet and of volunteers from all countries, the city was forced to capitulate in September, 1669. In the following peace treaty the Venetians surrendered the entire island, with the exception of three small ports which they retained for commercial purposes.

RUSSIA AND THE UKRAINE

The scene now shifts to the northern extremity of the empire where the wild no man's land known as the Ukraine was emerging from obscurity as the bloody battleground of three contending powers—Turkey, Russia, and Poland. This region was inhabited by two warlike and unruly frontier peoples, the Orthodox Cossacks and the Moslem Tatars. The latter controlled the entire Crimean Peninsula, together with the treeless steppes along the Black Sea shore from Bessarabia in the west to Circassia in the east. These Crimean Tatars, as they were collectively known, came under Ottoman suzerainty in the fifteenth century. The arrangement was mutually satisfactory and continued to the Russian conquest in the late eighteenth century. The Tatars could count on military aid from Constantinople when needed. In return they provided the Turkish armies with hordes of wild horsemen and also kept the imperial slave markets well stocked with the thousands of unfortunate victims that they rounded up during their incessant raids into Russia and Poland.

The Cossacks were the Christian counterparts of the Tatars. They resembled the American frontiersmen in that they were a sociological rather than an ethnic group. They hailed originally from Russia and Poland, whence they fled southward to the frontier lands to escape the bonds of serfdom that were being imposed upon the peasantry from the sixteenth century onward. By the early seventeenth century they had organized themselves into three separate Cossack "hosts," on the Don, Ural, and Dnieper rivers. The first two had come mostly from Russian lands and recognized in a vague and nominal fashion the suzerainty of the Muscovite tsar. The Dnieper Cossacks, having originated from Polish territories, accepted a corresponding connection with the king of Poland. All three hosts at this time were in fact independent. They fought, pillaged, and negotiated when and as they pleased, particularly with the Crimean Tatars and the Turks who controlled the river mouths to the south.

The main issue in the mid-seventeenth century was the Polish-Russian struggle for the control of the Cossack-occupied Ukraine. The conflict began in 1648 with the great Cossack revolt against the Poles, who had attempted to extend serfdom to the Ukraine. For six years the Cossacks fought under their famous hetman, Bogdan Khmelnitsky. Finally they concluded an agreement with Tsar Alexis placing themselves under the protection of Russia. Being Orthodox to a man, the Cossacks declared for "the Tsar who belongs to the Eastern Orthodox Faith," in preference to the Catholic king of Poland.

This fateful decision increased enormously the potential of Russian power and made inevitable the Polish-Russian War which immediately ensued. For thirteen more years the Ukraine was devastated by rival Cossack bands, Tatar raiding parties, and Polish and Russian armies. Finally the Treaty of Andrussovo (1667) divided the disputed land, Russia obtaining Kiev and the territory to the east of the Dnieper, and Poland the territory to the west.

One reason for this compromise settlement was the disquieting resurgence of Ottoman activity under Ahmed Kiuprili. The Turks hitherto had regarded the Ukraine as a buffer zone and had refrained from direct intervention. But the steady extension of Polish and Russian authority southward now led Ahmed to counter with a thrust northward. He found a useful ally in Peter Doroshenko, a Cossack chieftain who had won considerable following as the opponent of both the Polish and Russian regimes. In place of the partitioned Ukraine created by the Andrussovo settlement, Doroshenko demanded an autonomous and united state. He turned to Constantinople for support and was warmly welcomed by Ahmed. In December, 1668, an agreement was concluded whereby Doroshenko accepted Turkish suzerainty and agreed to pay annual tribute; in return the sultan recognized the autonomy of the Ukrainian lands and of the Ukrainian Orthodox Church, and also undertook to provide a force of six thousand men to uphold Doroshenko against his enemies. This arrangement was perfectly natural in the light of Ottoman administrative practice. The Ukraine was to occupy a position in the imperial framework similar to that of Moldavia, Wallachia, and Transylvania.

Ahmed had timed his intervention in Ukrainian affairs perfectly. The Cretan War was drawing to a close, the Poles were divided by their perennial dynastic succession difficulties, and the Russians were immobilized by Stenka Razin's formidable peasant revolt. Ahmed was fully informed of these developments, both through his own agents and through Doroshenko. In August, 1672, he crossed the Dniester River at the head of a powerful army composed of veterans of the Cretan campaign. He was joined by contingents of Crimean Tatars and by twelve thousand of Doroshenko's Cossacks. He quickly captured the important Polish city, Kameniec, and compelled the Polish king to sign the Treaty of Buczacz (1672) ceding the province of Podolia to Turkey and recognizing the western Ukraine as independent under Ottoman protection. The Polish Diet refused to ratify the treaty and the war was resumed. Under the able leadership of John Sobieski, and with some Russian assistance, the Poles won two important victories. But the superior resources of the Turks finally prevailed and in 1676 Sobieski accepted the Treaty of Zoravno. The Turks retained Podolia, but the western Ukraine was divided, the northern part remaining Polish and the southern passing to the Turkish sphere.

This treaty is significant in two respects. It marks the high-water point of Turkish advance into Eastern Europe and it also represents the beginning of direct Turkish-Russian contact and conflict. Having defeated the Poles in the western Ukraine, the Turks now faced the Russians along the Dnieper River. Hostilities began almost at once, the precipitating factor being the refusal of the Cossacks to accept Turkish rule. Even Doroshenko, who was bitterly disappointed by the provisions of the Zoravno Treaty, turned against his former Turkish allies and threw in his lot with the Russians. The Turks had no choice but to wage war with Russia in order to retain the territory they had won from the Poles.

For three years Turks and Tatars fought Russians and Cossacks. The countryside along the western bank of the lower Dnieper was completely devastated and its population fled eastward across the river. The inconclusive and exhaustive character of the war finally inclined both sides to peace. The Treaty of Radzin (1681)—also known as the Bakhchisarai Treaty after the khan's residence, where it was initially concluded—recognized Muscovite authority east of the Dnieper and in the Kiev enclave. It also provided that the Turks should withdraw from the southwestern Ukraine which they had wrested from the Poles, and that the Russians should not send troops or officials into this disputed region. Instead, it was to serve as a buffer zone separating the Russian-controlled Ukraine from the territory of the Crimean Tatars. In the light of later developments it is noteworthy that the treaty also allowed Russian subjects to trade in the Crimea and to journey to the Holy Land to worship.

SIEGE OF VIENNA: 1683

The Turks' willingness to surrender their foothold in the Ukraine was part of a grandiose plan formulated by a new grand vizir in Constantinople. Ahmed Kiuprili had died five years earlier and was succeeded by the sultan's son-in-law, Kara Mustafa. The new grand vizir was ruthless, energetic, and ambitious, but totally lacking in the sound judgment that had distinguished his predecessor. In all his actions he displayed a haughty contempt for the Christian infidels which would have been understandable a century earlier but which now had no relation to reality. His great aim was to declare war on Austria, capture Vienna, and make himself the viceroy of the ample provinces between the Danube and the Rhine. In preparation for this rash undertaking he accepted the unfavorable Radzin Treaty, hoping thereby to assure the neutrality of Russia during the coming war.

A rebellion in the Hapsburg portion of Hungary provided Mustafa with a convenient pretext for beginning hostilities. The rebels, led by Count Emeric Tekeli, appealed to Constantinople for aid against Emperor Leopold. Their appeal was strongly supported by the French government. Louis XIV had designs on the Rhineland which would be facilitated if the Hapsburgs were involved in a Turkish war. Accordingly, the French ambassador in Constantinople gave full assurances that no French troops would participate in the defense of Vienna. This was sufficient to cause Mustafa to reject the Hapsburg request for a renewal of the twenty-year Vasvar truce (1664) that was about to lapse.

In the spring of 1683 Mustafa set forth from Belgrade with an army of almost two hundred thousand men. The Austrians were poorly prepared, having spent precious time bickering over the command of the army and over such details as the salaries of the officers and the bread ration of the soldiers. The Duke of Lorraine, who commanded the Hapsburg forces, had no choice but to retreat. Mustafa marched quickly toward Vienna. A panic seized the capital. In great confusion the emperor, his court, and many of the wealthier citizens fled the city. Count Stahremberg was left to conduct the defense with a garrison of twenty-two thousand.

The siege began on July 17. The defenders repulsed six major assaults in as many weeks. At the end of that time both the besiegers and the besieged were suffering from lack of food. The latter were worse off, having lost six thousand men and exhausted virtually all their supplies. At this point the city was saved by the arrival of the Polish army under King John Sobieski.

Despite the opposition of French diplomacy, Emperor Leopold had concluded an anti-Turkish alliance with the Poles in March, 1683. Neither side was to conclude a separate peace, and provision was made for the adherence of other powers that wished to fight the Turks. After much delay Sobieski gathered an army of fifty-three thousand for the relief of Vienna. Thanks to the incompetence of Mustafa, he was able to effect a juncture with the Duke of Lorraine's twenty-seven thousand Austrians. On September 11 the combined force reached Mount Kahlenberg overlooking Vienna. Between the mountain and the Turkish encampment below were several valleys formed by streams running into the Danube. Mustafa had neglected to man these natural ramparts and the allied army advanced in a great semicircle upon the Turks. The Tatar irregulars and the Moldavian and Wallachian auxiliaries broke and fled, spreading confusion to the rest of the army. Sobieski led his best troops against the Turkish center and carried all before him. The janissaries, who had been left in the trenches before the city, were now attacked on two sides, by the relief army from the rear and by the Vienna garrison on the front. Terrible slaughter followed, and the whole of the Turkish camp, with immense booty, fell to the victorious allies.

The debris of the Ottoman army made its way to Buda. Mustafa continued to Belgrade, where he was put to death by order of the sultan. His successor made peace overtures to Emperor Leopold. The latter now had to make a critical decision. Louis XIV had invaded the Spanish Netherlands while Vienna was being besieged. He was willing to cease hostilities if Spain and Austria recognized his gains. The problem facing Leopold was whether he should accept a Turkish peace in order to force Louis to disgorge, or a French peace in order to follow up the Vienna victory. Leopold decided in favor of the latter, partly because of the popular clamor to deal once and for all with Islam, and partly because a Turkish campaign offered much more assurance of victory than did a French. This decision was a fateful one. It precipitated a war which continued to the end of the century and which finally freed Christendom from the Turkish menace and established Austria as the foremost power of Central Europe.

WAR OF THE HOLY LEAGUE: 1683–1699

Once the decision had been made for war against the Turks, attention was focused on the organization of a league of Christian powers. Leopold found an invaluable ally in Pope Innocent XI, who worked tirelessly to unite Christendom for another crusade. His exhortations, together with the victories of the Austrian generals who were trouncing the Turks in the upper Danube, induced the Venetians to join the existing Austrian-Polish alliance. The treaty, signed in March, 1684, defined the territorial interests of the three allies and called on the rest of Europe to support the great effort to drive the Turks back to Asia. Leopold was anxious to add Russia to the Holy League, as the anti-Turkish coalition was christened. After considerable diplomatic pressure he induced the Poles (April, 1686) to recognize Russian rule over Kiev and Smolensk, and in return the Russians agreed to send an army against the Crimea.

Meanwhile military developments had kept pace with the diplomatic. The eastern allies had little success. The Russian assaults on the Crimea (1687 and 1689) proved abortive, while Sobieski failed in his attempts to occupy the Danubian Principalities and to capture the Kameniec fortress that he had lost to the Turks in the previous war. But these campaigns were subsidiary. The decisive battles were being fought and won by the Austrians in Hungary and by the Venetians in the Peloponnesus.

The Austrians did not win spectacular victories during the first two years of the war, 1684 and 1685. But they did soften the Turkish defenses sufficiently to make possible the great successes that followed. In 1686, under the brilliant leadership of the Duke of Lorraine, they captured Buda, the capital of Turkish Hungary. The following year they won a great victory at Mohacs, on the very scene of Suleiman's triumph over the Hungarians a hundred and sixty years earlier. In 1688 the Austrians crowned their successes with the capture of the key city of Belgrade, thus opening the route into the Balkans.

The Venetians meanwhile had taken advantage of the concentration of the main Turkish forces in the Danube Valley to launch simultaneous attacks upon the Dalmatian Coast and upon southern Greece. In the latter area the command was entrusted to Francesco Morosini, the hero of the Cretan War. He was aided by galleys contributed by the pope, the Duke of Tuscany, and the Knights of Malta, as well as by an army of hired Hanoverian troops commanded by Count Königsmark. In 1685 Morosini established a beachhead in the Peloponnesus by taking the port of Coron on the western coast. The following year he overran the southern part of the peninsula. In 1687 he stormed Patras, entered the Isthmus of Corinth, and proceeded to Attica, where he laid siege to Athens. It was at this time that the Parthenon, which had survived so many centuries intact, was shattered by a bomb and reduced to the ruins that we now see. The surrender of Athens in September, 1687, marked the high point of the Venetian campaign.

The allied victories in Hungary and Greece created a panic in Constantinople. Sultan Mohammed paid for his fatal error in appointing Mustafa grand vizir by being deposed in 1687. The new sultan, Suleiman II, showed a certain courage and initiative that was surprising in view of his long incarceration in the imperial "Cage." After suppressing the mutinous janissaries in Constantinople he made peace overtures to the allies. But Louis XIV still wished to keep the Turks in the field against the Hapsburgs. To achieve this he began the War of the League of Augsburg in 1688. The Turks, as Louis anticipated, promptly raised their peace terms so high that Leopold rejected them.

All hopes for peace disappeared the following year with the appointment to the grand vizirate of Mustafa Kiuprili, brother of the great Ahmed. The new grand vizir acted with the energy and firmness typical of his family. He immediately broke off the peace negotiations and started a thorough housecleaning in preparation for a more vigorous conduct of the war. He was aided by the fact that the Austrians now were distracted by the war with the French in the west. In 1690 Mustafa began his counteroffensive.

The Austrians by this time had advanced from Belgrade through Serbia and deep into Macedonia. Some twenty thousand Serbs and Albanians joined the Hapsburg armies with the encouragement of their church leaders. Despite this defection Mustafa successfully drove the enemy out of the Balkans. He recovered in quick succession Nish, Smederevo, Vidin, and Belgrade, thus forcing the Austrians back across the Danube. The Austrian setback left the native insurgents in an impossible position. About thirty thousand Serbs followed the retreating Austrians into southern Hungary. We shall note in Chapter 14 that they settled there, establishing a flourishing community that was to make important contributions to the Serbian national renaissance in the Turkish lands. Mustafa's success, however, proved short-lived. The following year he advanced north of the Danube but was badly defeated in the battle of Salem Kemen, in which he was killed while trying desperately to turn the tide.

During the next several years the war subsided to minor and inconclusive engagements. The Austrians were becoming more deeply involved in the war with France, and the Turks gratefully welcomed the respite. The only significant event was the outburst of Russian activity under the new tsar, Peter the Great. Instead of attempting another attack on the Crimea, Peter turned eastward against the Turkish fortress at Azov commanding the mouth of the Don. His first assault in 1695 failed because he was unable to prevent the Turkish fleet from bringing in reinforcements. With typical persistence and energy, Peter built that winter a powerful flotilla at Voronezh, far up the Don, beyond the reach of the Tatars and near good forest supplies. Thanks to his new warships and to the aid of Austrian engineers, he captured Azov in 1696. Peter followed up his victory by founding a naval base near Azov and launching an ambitious building program under the supervision of Western experts. In fact, one of the main purposes of Peter's journey through

Western Europe in 1697–1698 was to find shipwrights and seamen for his Azov fleet. In this respect his trip was successful. By 1699 he had a strong fleet on the Azov Sea. He planned to use it to force his way through the Strait of Kerch and out into the Black Sea. But he was forestalled by decisive developments in the main theater of war.

The Treaty of Ryswick in 1697 had ended the War of the League of Augsburg. The Austrian army, now under the command of Prince Eugene of Savoy, one of the ablest generals of his time, returned to the Eastern front. Meanwhile, a new sultan, Mustafa II, had ascended the throne in Constantinople. Recognizing that the incapacity and slothfulness of his predecessors had contributed to the military disasters, he resolved to lead his armies in person after the manner of the early sultans. In 1697 he advanced northward from Belgrade toward the river Theiss. Eugene overtook Mustafa as he was crossing the river at Senta. Only two hours of daylight remained, but Eugene ordered an immediate attack. The vigor of the assault carried all before it. The Turks were so disorganized that a large body of janissaries mutinied on the field of battle and began to massacre their officers. By the time the sun had set, the Ottoman army had been annihilated. An immense booty fell to the victors, including all the Ottoman artillery and the sultan's treasure chest. This overwhelming disaster, together with the French desertion at Ryswick and the disturbing activities of Tsar Peter, decided the sultan to seek a peace settlement.

TREATY OF KARLOWITZ: 1699

The allies were divided on the question of the Turkish peace bid. Both the Russians and the Poles wished to continue the war, hoping thereby to win their respective objectives in the Black Sea and in the Ukraine. Some of Emperor Leopold's advisers, including Prince Eugene, also urged the continuation of the war until at least Belgrade might be recovered. The emperor, however, inclined toward peace, particularly because he correctly foresaw an early war with Louis XIV over the question of the Spanish succession. Both Britain and Holland also pressed strongly for peace, partly because their Levant trade had suffered severely during the war years and also because they were very anxious that Austria should be available as an ally in the approaching war with France.

The final decision rested with the emperor. Despite bitter Russian protests he decided to accept the mediation proposal of the British and Dutch diplomats. Late in 1698 the belligerents sent envoys to a congress held at Karlowitz (Sremski Karlovci), a village slightly to the north of Belgrade. After seventy-two days of negotiation, the momentous Treaty of Karlowitz was signed on January 26, 1699, at an hour fixed for astrological reasons by the Turks. With certain exceptions it was based on the *status quo* prevailing when hostilities ceased. Austria received Transylvania, Croatia, Slavonia, and all of Hungary except the Banat of Temesvar. Venice obtained the Peloponnesus and most of Dalmatia. Poland recovered the province of Podolia

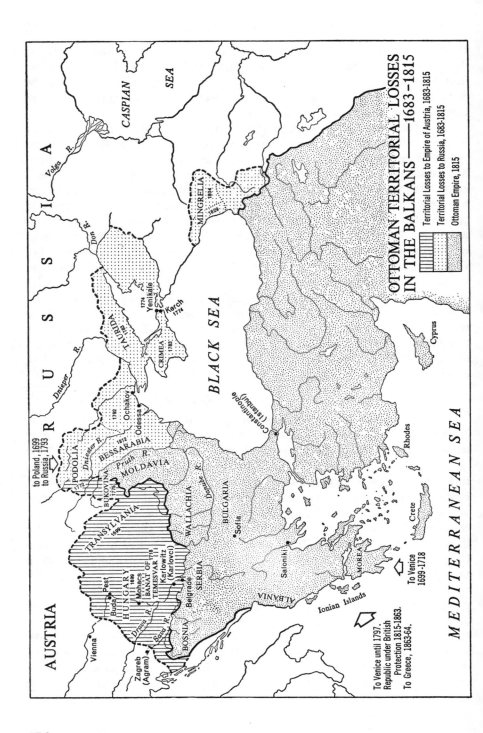

OTTOMAN TERRITORIAL LOSSES
IN THE BALKANS ——1683–1815

Territorial Losses to Empire of Austria, 1683-1815

Territorial Losses to Russia, 1683-1815

Ottoman Empire, 1815

CASPIAN SEA

Volga R.

R U S S I A

Don R.

Dnieper R.

MINGRELIA
1804
1829

TAURIDA
1774
Yenikale

Kerch
1774

CRIMEA
1783

BLACK SEA

Odessa
1792
Ochakov

to Poland, 1699
to Russia, 1793

PODOLIA

Dniester R.

BESSARABIA
1812

Prut R.

MOLDAVIA

BUKOVINA
1775

TRANSYLVANIA
1699

WALLACHIA

Danube R.

BULGARIA

Sofia

Constantinople (Istanbul)

Cyprus

Rhodes

MEDITERRANEAN SEA

AUSTRIA

Vienna

Buda
Pest

HUNGARY

Mohács
1699

BANAT OF
TEMESVAR
1718

Karlowitz
(Karlovci)

Belgrade

SERBIA

BOSNIA

Zagreb
(Agram)

Drava R.

Sava R.

Saloniki

MOREA

ALBANIA

Ionian Islands

Crete

To Venice
1699-1718

To Venice until 1797.
Republic under British
Protection 1815-1863.
To Greece, 1863-64.

176

lost in the previous war. The Russians, still determined to win Kerch, signed only a two-year truce by which they remained in occupation of Azov. The following year Peter willingly signed the Treaty of Constantinople in order to be free for the coming war with Sweden. The treaty formally ceded Azov to the Russians, granted them the right to permanent diplomatic representation at Constantinople, and acknowledged Peter's refusal to continue the annual tribute hitherto paid to the Crimean Tatars.

The Karlowitz settlement marks a turning point in the history of Southeastern Europe. Never before had the Turks surrendered such vast territories without any compensation. Austria had benefited the most, as befitted her primary role in the war. While Louis XIV was struggling to win a few square miles along the Rhine, she had conquered vast provinces and extended her borders to the summits of the Carpathians. She was now the dominant power in Central Europe and she overshadowed the Balkan Peninsula. Her frontiers paralled the Ottoman along the Drava, Sava, and Danube rivers. The Turkish tide unmistakably had begun to ebb. Never again was Europe threatened by the power which for almost three centuries had menaced its security.

Instead Europe henceforth faced precisely the opposite problem—the so-called Eastern Question created by the recession of Ottoman power. This recession produced a vacuum in the Near East, and one of the basic problems of European diplomacy until the end of World War I was how to fill this vacuum.

11. Defeat by Russia: Recession to the Dniester: 1699–1792

THE OTTOMAN EMPIRE enjoyed eleven years of peace after the Karlowitz Treaty. Then followed three decades of intermittent war culminating in the Belgrade Treaty of 1739. Thanks to great-power rivalries the empire survived this ordeal without territorial losses. Next came three decades of peace, during which Christian Europe was engrossed in the War of Austrian Succession and the Seven Years' War. The accession of Catherine the Great of Russia spelled the end of peace and the beginning of another series of wars (1769–1792) that were to prove as disastrous as those against the Holy League in the preceding century. Ruinous defeats followed one upon the other for a quarter of a century. When peace finally was restored by the Treaty of Jassy in 1792 the empire had lost the entire northern shore of the Black Sea. For the first time in centuries there was not only talk of expelling the Turk from Europe but also a distinct possibility that this goal might be realized.

The reason for this great setback was that the balance between Turkey and Russia had swung steeply in favor of the latter. Russia possessed a matchless instrument of military power in the brilliant Marshal Suvorov, and she also possessed a diplomat of consummate skill in her new sovereign, Catherine the Great. In an age that boasted such masters of the art of diplomacy as Empress Maria Theresa, Prince Kaunitz, and Frederick the Great, the new tsarina more than held her own. It is true that she appeared on the scene at an unusually propitious moment. Austria and Prussia were exhausted by the Seven Years' War; France under Louis XV and XVI was on the downgrade; and England was facing the revolt of the Thirteen Colonies. Yet it was Catherine's perception and resolute will that enabled her to exploit these advantages and to dower her adopted country, as she proudly boasted, "with Azov, the Crimea, and the Ukraine."

DEFEAT OF PETER THE GREAT

The exhaustion of the Ottoman Empire and the unwarlike character of Ahmed III explain the period of peace following the Karlowitz settlement. The Turks made no attempt to take advantage of the War of the Spanish Succession or the Northern War to try to recover the territories lost in the recent war. This policy of nonintervention saved Russia from serious trouble when she was invaded by Charles XII of Sweden in 1708. It also enabled Tsar Peter to defeat Charles at the battle of Poltava on July 8, 1709. The following year hostilities broke out again between Turkey and Russia. Oddly enough, it was Ahmed who declared war and Peter who tried to avoid it. Whatever his ultimate designs in the south might have been, Peter at this point wished to preserve peace with the Ottoman Empire. His failure was due not to lack of effort on his part but rather to the triumph of a war party in Constantinople.

Charles XII had fled to the Ottoman capital following his defeat in the Ukraine. Naturally he made every effort to enlist the Turks in his struggle against Peter. He had the active support of the French, who were unalterably opposed to Russian aggrandizement at the expense of their traditional anti-Hapsburg allies—Sweden, Poland, and Turkey. Perhaps most influential was the prowar attitude of the Crimean Tatars, who resented the cessation of Russian tribute following the 1700 Treaty of Constantinople. Also, they were alarmed by the Russian conquest of Azov and by the building of Russian forts on the lower Dnieper. These forts especially were thorns in their side. They hampered their raids, threatened their grazing and hunting grounds, and menaced their land communications with the Turkish fortresses on the Dnieper and with the Tatar tribes between the Bug and Dniester rivers. For these reasons the Crimean khan used his powerful influence in Constantinople for a campaign to beat back the advancing Russians. On November 16, 1710, the British minister in Constantinople reported to London: "The Tartar Han, who hath been all along bent upon a rupture [with Russia], displayed all his Eloquence to persuade the Ministers, the men of the Law, and the Soldiery of the Necessity thereof. . . ." Four days later the minister reported that the sultan had declared war, and added, "This great Turn of Affairs is wholly the Work of the Tartar Han." [1]

Peter postponed a formal declaration of war until March 11, 1711, in the hope of persuading the sultan to reconsider his decision. When it became clear that hostilities were unavoidable, he issued a proclamation to the Balkan peoples to arise against the Turks and to fight with the Russians "for faith and fatherland, for your honor and glory, for the freedom and liberty of yourself and your descendants." Thus would "the descendants of the heathen Mohammed be driven out into their old fatherland, the Arabian sands and steppes." [2]

Peter marched at the head of his army through the Polish Ukraine and into Moldavia, where he captured the capital, Jassy. For the first time since the days of Prince Sviatoslav, seven centuries earlier, Russian cavalry-men watered their horses in the Danube. But Peter's boldness proved his undoing. His army lost heavily from disease and lack of food. The Balkan Christians failed to give effective aid. The Turks crossed the Danube sooner than expected, and, reinforced by a large contingent of Tatars, they trapped Peter in a vulnerable position on the right bank of the Pruth. In order to save his army, Peter accepted the humiliating Treaty of Pruth (July 21, 1711). He surrendered all that he had gained in the previous war—Azov, Taganrog, the Dnieper forts, and the privilege of diplomatic representation in Constantinople.

The grand vizir, Baltadji, was dismissed a few months later on the charge of having neglected the opportunity of destroying or capturing the Russian army and the tsar himself. He was also accused of having accepted a huge bribe to conclude the treaty. This charge, which has been widely accepted, appears to be highly dubious. Baltadji was convinced, and with much justification, that in refusing to press the war further he was serving the interests of the sultan, if not those of the Tatar khan and the Swedish king. In fact, the British minister reported that the sultan had "no regard" for the interests of Charles of Sweden, and wished only to drive the Russians from the Black Sea "without any thoughts or even desire of extending his Territories far towards Muscovy." Thus the sultan, according to this well-informed envoy, was "exceedingly pleased with the Peace, and readily gave his ratification. . . ." [3]

A significant feature of this campaign was the failure of the Balkan Christians to respond effectively to Peter's appeal. Sporadic revolts did flare up in the mountainous areas of the western Balkans, particularly in Montenegro and in southern Herzegovina. The Montenegrin prince-bishop, Daniel Petrovich, concluded a treaty with a Russian agent in April, 1712. But there was no possibility of linking up with the Russians in distant Moldavia, and Peter's defeat doomed the uprisings to failure. Only the Rumanians of the Principalities were in a position to cooperate with the Russians. The hospodar of Moldavia, Demetrius Cantemir, secretly allied himself with Peter. He was unable, however, to give substantial aid, having only recently assumed his post and being at daggers drawn with the Wallachian hospodar, Constantine Brancoveanu. The latter had a sizable army and abundant supplies, and had maintained secret relations with Peter for some years. Yet he refused to commit himself during the crucial early days, and later, when the Turks crossed the Danube in force, he submitted to their demands.

The basic difficulty was that an effective Balkan uprising was impractical without a Russian invasion in force, and the latter in turn was impractical so long as Peter placed the Baltic first and the Balkans second. Russia was not yet strong enough to wage a two-front war. This had to wait until the time of Catherine at the end of the century. Hence it was Austria rather than Russia that had the commanding position during this period. Austrian rather than Russian generals assumed the role of liberators in the northern Balkans in 1690 and in 1716–1718. Nevertheless, Peter's campaign did have certain repercussions in the Balkans. It initiated close relations between Montenegro and Russia that were to continue for the next two centuries. It also led to the appointment of Greek administrators, known as Phanariotes, to the hospodarships of the Danubian Principalities. These men took the place of the Rumanian nobles who hitherto had filled the positions but who were now distrusted because of the defection of Cantemir and the vacillation of Brancoveanu. Phanariote rule in the Principalities continued until the Greek revolution of 1821 and, as we shall note in Chapter 13, contributed greatly to the ascendancy of Greek influence in the Ottoman Empire during the eighteenth and early nineteenth centuries.

RECONQUEST OF THE PELOPONNESUS

With the signing of the Pruth Treaty a struggle ensued in Constantinople between those who favored the formation of a Turkish-Swedish-Polish league in order to renew the war against Russia, and those who urged instead a war against Venice in order to recover the Peloponnesus lost in the Karlowitz settlement. The latter group prevailed because campaigns beyond the lower Danube were never popular in Turkey. Even if they ended successfully they did not bring many real advantages to compensate for the hardships and losses incurred in fighting in distant lands. Accordingly, the Turks consolidated their peace with Russia by concluding on June 27, 1713, the Adrianople Treaty reaffirming the terms of the Pruth Treaty.

The Turks then launched their long-planned war against Venice. In the summer of 1715 they sent an army under Grand Vizir Damad Ali to conquer the Peloponnesus. Everything favored the invaders. They outnumbered the eight thousand Venetian defenders several times. Their leader proved to be an energetic and skillful commander. They met with no resistance from the native Greeks, who were thoroughly dissatisfied after sixteen years of Venetian rule. Damad skillfully exploited this anti-Venetian sentiment by giving strict orders to his soldiers to respect the persons and property of the Greek peasants. The latter responded by welcoming the Turks and providing them with abundant provisions for which they received liberal compensation.

These circumstances enabled Damad to overrun the entire peninsula in one hundred days. First Corinth fell after a three-week siege. Then the Turks advanced southward in two divisions. No pitched battles were fought. The campaign consisted of a series of successful sieges until all the Venetian fortresses had been reduced. Meanwhile the Ottoman fleet, reinforced by ships from Egypt and the Barbary States, was driving the Venetians out of the Aegean Islands that they held. Before the end of the year Damad was preparing to follow up his success by attacking the Ionian Islands on the west coast of Greece and then proceeding against the Venetian possessions in Dalmatia.

At this point Austria intervened by concluding an alliance with

Venice early in 1716. The Divan in Constantinople debated whether the action should be considered a *casus belli*. Many Turks remembered the disasters of the previous Austrian war and counseled peace. But Damad, inspired by his victories and encouraged by his astrologers, persuaded the Divan to declare for war. In the summer of 1716 Damad marched north from Belgrade toward Peterwardein (Petrovaradin), where nemesis awaited him in the person of the Hapsburg general, Prince Eugene of Savoy.

WAR WITH AUSTRIA (PASSAROWITZ TREATY: 1718)

Since his great victories over the Turks in the previous war Prince Eugene had won many battles against the French and had earned a reputation equaled only by that of his companion-at-arms, the Duke of Marlborough. In the forthcoming campaign his brilliant generalship together with the superiority of his troops in training and armaments caused the Turks to suffer another series of disastrous defeats. The first engagement was fought before the Peterwardein fortress in August, 1716. Despite the numerical preponderance of the Ottoman army, Prince Eugene routed it and captured all its artillery. Grand Vizir Damad was killed in a desperate effort to turn the tide. Twenty days later Eugene was before Temesvar, the last great Turkish stronghold in Hungary. Its garrison capitulated after a siege of five weeks. This completed the campaign of 1716.

The following year Eugene took the initiative by besieging Belgrade. After three weeks a Turkish relief army appeared under the new Grand Vizir Khalil. Eugene was in a critical position. The Belgrade garrison was in front of him and Khalil's army, double the number of his own, threatened his rear. Eugene boldly attacked the Turkish army and again won a brilliant victory, inflicting twenty thousand casualties and suffering only two thousand of his own. The following day Belgrade's garrison of thirty thousand men surrendered.

Eugene followed up his victory by advancing southward from Belgrade and occupying a large part of Serbia and of western Wallachia. The Austrians appealed to the Serbians to join their armies as they had done during the previous War of the Holy League. But this time the response was negligible. The Serbians remembered the tragic fate of thousands of their compatriots who had taken up arms against the Turks and then were forced to flee their country following the Karlowitz Treaty. The passiveness of the Serbians did not affect the outcome of the war. By this time the Turks were ready to cease hostilities.

The peace negotiations that followed resemble closely those at the end of the War of the Holy League. Britain and Holland again pressed for peace because of the disruption of their Levant commerce. Venice favored the continuation of the war, as Poland and Russia had in the earlier conflict. The Venetians had beaten off a Turkish attack on Corfu in 1716. They had also received naval reinforcements from Spain, Portugal, and various Italian states, and were now in a position to recover some of the territories they had lost in the first year of the war. But Emperor Charles VI, like his predecessor, Leopold I, decided in favor of peace. And the reason again was a complication in the west—this time a Spanish attack upon Sardinia. Accordingly the emperor accepted the Treaty of Passarowitz (Pozarevac), July 21, 1718, based on the *status quo* at the end of hostilities. He gained the remainder of Hungary, most of Serbia, and part of Wallachia and Bosnia. The republic of Venice, in whose behalf Austria ostensibly had embarked on the war, fared badly by the treaty. It surrendered the Peloponnesus but retained the Ionian Islands and made a few gains in Dalmatia. This treaty raised Hapsburg prestige in the Balkans to new heights, in contrast to the sad decline of Venice and the military humiliation of the Ottoman Empire.

WAR WITH AUSTRIA AND RUSSIA (BELGRADE TREATY: 1739)

During the years following the Passarowitz Treaty the Turks were engaged in the east where, together with the Russians, they were annexing whole provinces at the expense of a weak and anarchical Persia. In 1723 Peter the Great acquired the entire western and southern seaboard of the Caspian Sea, and the following year the Turks gained the western provinces of Persia, including the cities of Tabriz, Hamadan, and Erivan. But neither the Russians nor the Turks were to keep their booty for long. There now appeared in Persia a great leader, Nadir Kuli, who organized a national revival and forced both Turkey and Russia by 1735 to return the lost provinces.

Russia had been willing to withdraw from the Caspian region in order to prepare for a move toward the Black Sea. The latter was more valuable both economically and strategically. Possession of the northern shore of the Black Sea offered Russia dazzling opportunities. It would finally rid her of the dreadful Tatar raids that had cost her so much in treasure and in human lives. It would open up vast new areas for settlement and exploitation. It would give her the great Crimean Peninsula which dominated the entire Black Sea. And it would enable her to control the outlets of five major rivers that drained her plains—the Dniester, the Bug, the Dnieper, the Don, and the Kuban.

All these prizes appeared at this time to be within the reach of Russian military power and diplomacy. Ivan Neplinev, the well-informed Russian ambassador at Constantinople, was reporting to his government that the Turkish defeats in Persia had left the Ottoman Empire ripe for plucking. The time has come, he urged, "to fall upon these barbarians." This advice is significant. For the first time Russia was in a position to consider seriously a drive to the Black Sea. Peter's expedition to the Pruth had not been part of a calculated offensive against the Ottoman Empire. His resources had not been sufficient to allow him to fight both the Turks and the Swedes, so he had concentrated against the latter. But Empress Anne now was in a more favorable situation. The Swedes had been subdued and the Poles had been forced to accept a pro-Russian king as a result of the War of the Polish Succession (1733–1735). Russia could turn to the south and engage the Tatars and the Turks without fear of diversion. Thus the Russo-Turkish War of 1736–1739 may be regarded as the beginning of Russia's systematic struggle to reach the Black Sea, a bloody and severe struggle that persisted until Catherine brought it to a successful conclusion at the end of the century. The Turks were not averse to a break with the Russians. They had been deeply disturbed by Russian aggression in Poland during the War of the Polish Succession. The French ambassador at Constantinople, Marquis de Villeneuve, had made every effort at that time to induce the sultan to declare war against the Russian empress. But his intrigues were neutralized by the crushing defeats that Nadir Kuli was then inflicting upon the Turks. Now, however, both the Turks and the Russians had concluded their Persian commitments, and having done so, they drifted almost inevitably to war, aided by the enthusiastic prodding of Villeneuve.

Two Russian armies advanced southward, one under Marshal Munnich against the Crimean Peninsula and the other under Marshal Lacy against the Turkish fortress of Azov. Munnich stormed and broke through the forttified lines stretching across the Isthmus of Perekop linking the peninsula to the mainland. He pressed forward, capturing the Crimean capital, Bakhchisarai, and overrunning and devastating the whole peninsula. His men, however, suffered so severely from disease and exhaustion that they revolted and compelled him to withdraw to the Ukraine before the winter. Meanwhile Lacy had met with obstinate resistance at Azov. The Turkish garrison had inflicted such heavy casualties that Lacy allowed it to march out with all the honors of war. Then, on hearing that Munnich had retreated to the Ukraine, he followed his example and abandoned the fortress.

This campaign of 1736 had cost the Russians dearly. Munnich alone had lost no less than thirty thousand of his fifty-seven thousand men, of which only two thousand had fallen in action. Empress Anne was encouraged, however, by the readiness of the Austrians to enter the war in order to garner a few more Turkish provinces. A secret treaty signed in January, 1737, provided that the two powers should wage war in concert against the Ottoman Empire. But the Austrians no longer had the incomparable Prince Eugene, while the Turkish forces showed some improvement in discipline and in maneuvering. Consequently the campaigns in 1737 and 1738 did not prove as decisive as expected. The Austrians barely held their own in the Balkans while the Russians overran the Crimea twice but were forced to withdraw each time because they could not support themselves in the devastated country. The only outstanding success was Munnich's capture of the Turkish fortress Ochakov, near the mouth of the Bug River.

Negotiations for peace had been held intermittently during the course of the war. A new attempt to end hostilities was made during the winter of

1738–1739. It failed, partly because the Turks were more demanding after their successes against the Austrians, and also because Marshal Munnich won the tsarina's support for his grandiose "Oriental project." Munnich proposed to cross the Danube, conquer the Danubian Principalities, and strike for Constantinople itself. He assured the tsarina that "all the Greeks regarded . . . [her] as their legitimate Sovereign . . . that it was desirable to seize this first moment of their hope and enthusiasm, and to march to Constantinople; and that such a frame of mind might never again be found." [4]

Munnich's optimism appeared to be justified. While his agents worked in Epirus and Thessaly for a Christian uprising, he advanced rapidly southward at the head of his army. Profiting from his experience in the previous campaign, he avoided the difficult country along the Black Sea coast and instead entered Moldavia through the Polish province of Podolia. On August 18, 1739, he routed a Turkish army before the fortress of Khotin, and a few days later captured the fortress itself. Then he entered the Moldavian capital, Jassy, without opposition, and thence wheeled into Bessarabia, intending to reduce the Turkish forts in that province before pushing on toward Constantinople.

At this point Munnich received the "miserable and crushing" news of the separate peace that the Austrians had concluded with the Turks. The Ottoman generals had followed a strategy that proved completely successful. They had concentrated their forces on the Danube, so that the Austrian generals found themselves outnumbered almost four to one. They suffered a decisive defeat in the open field and fell back upon Belgrade. This reverse was all the more serious in view of the Russian successes in the Principalities. The Austrians had no desire to continue a war that seemed likely to introduce a rival great power in the Balkans. This consideration—a recurring feature of Balkan politics to the present day—decided the Austrians to accept the mediation of Villeneuve and to sign the Treaty of Belgrade (September 18, 1739). They surrendered all that they had gained at Passarowitz—Bosnia, Wallachia, and Serbia, including the city of Belgrade.

The Austrian defection produced dismay and indignation in the Russian camp. But the consequences were unavoidable. Munnich could not continue his advance with a victorious Turkish army ready to fall on his flank. Reluctantly the Russians decided to conclude a peace on the best terms they could. By the Nissa Treaty of October 3, 1739, they surrendered their gains in Moldavia and in the Crimea, retaining only Azov on the condition that its fortifications be demolished and no fleet be maintained in its waters. The Russians did win the right to trade on the Sea of Azov and the Black Sea, provided, however, that their goods be carried in Turkish vessels.

The peace settlement was a humiliation for Austria, a success for the Turks, a triumph for the French, and a disappointment for the Russians. The latter, however, gained more benefits than appear to be the case at first glance. They had given the Crimean Tatars a taste of their own medicine and no longer had to suffer their devastating raids. The Russians also had raised greatly their military prestige in Europe, particularly in view of the contrast between the success of their armies and the failure of the Austrian. Indeed, the chief significance of the war is that it demonstrated Russia's growing strength and presaged what could be expected in the future. In 1711 Peter had suffered military defeat. A quarter of a century later Anne triumphed militarily but failed diplomatically. In another three decades Catherine was to win both the military and diplomatic battles, and to gain for Russia the long-coveted shores of the Black Sea.

THREE DECADES OF PEACE: 1739–1768

The Ottoman Empire enjoyed three decades of peace following the Belgrade and Nissa treaties. Persia was too exhausted after Nadir's ceaseless wars to cause any trouble along the eastern frontier. Austria and Russia were fully committed in the War of the Austrian Succession (1740–1748) and the Seven Years' War (1756–1763) and had no desire for further complications on another front. The Turks, on their part, did not wish to take advantage of the great European conflicts to attempt the recovery of their lost dominions north of the Danube. Sultan Mahmud preferred to keep the peace, and this policy was continued by his successors, Othman III (1754–1757) and Mustafa III (1757–1773).

It is noteworthy that Prussia emerged in the 1750's as an active participant in Near Eastern affairs. The explanation is to be found in Frederick the Great's search for allies against the enemies that surrounded him. His position had become perilous when the Austrian chancellor, Prince Kaunitz, engineered the famous Diplomatic Revolution and secured alliances with France and Russia. When the Seven Years' War began in 1756, Frederick faced this formidable combination without a single ally on the Continent. In anticipation of this encirclement he had sent an envoy to Constantinople in 1755 with a proposal for a commercial treaty and a military alliance. The Turks rejected this overture, deciding that it was to their advantage to remain neutral while the Austrians and the Russians weakened themselves fighting the Prussians.

Frederick persisted in his efforts. For several years he bombarded Sultan Mustafa with messages emphasizing the perils of neutrality and the possibilities of intervention. On three occasions the sultan and his ministers were influenced to the point of seriously considering intervention. But some incident always occurred to frustrate Frederick's design. In 1760 it was the refusal of the British government to sponsor the proposed Turkish-Prussian alliance. The following year it was the decision of Tsar Peter III to withdraw Russia from the war. Finally, the accession of Catherine the Great in 1762 led the Turks to hold back until the foreign policy of the new tsarina could be ascertained. In 1764 the Ottoman government received disquieting reports of a Russian-Prussian agreement for intervention in Polish affairs. An envoy was sent to Berlin to protest against foreign interference in the selection of the new Polish king. The reception accorded the envoy was an ominous portent of what was to come. Frederick affirmed his intention to intervene together with Catherine, and blandly asserted that the intervention would restore peace in Poland and would, therefore, be to the interest of all neighboring countries, including the Ottoman Empire.

This represented the beginning of a new era in Eastern European diplomacy. Russia and Prussia now took the place of Sweden, Poland, and Turkey as the leading powers of Eastern Europe. This shift set off a chain reaction that soon transformed the map of Europe between the Baltic and the Black seas. The intervention of Frederick and Catherine in Poland led to war between Russia and Turkey in 1768 and hence to the linking of the Polish and Turkish questions. By the end of the century Poland had ceased to exist as a nation while Turkey had lost the Crimean Peninsula and the whole of the Ukraine.

CATHERINE'S FIRST TURKISH WAR: 1768–1774

The primary factor behind Catherine's and Frederick's intervention in Poland was the sad decline of that country during the seventeenth and eighteenth centuries. For various reasons Poland had sunk to the point where foreign powers intervened openly in the election of her kings. When King Augustus III died in August, 1763, Catherine decided that his successor should be Stanislas Poniatowski, a Polish nobleman who formerly had been her paramour and who could be depended upon to do her bidding. To ensure his election Catherine signed a treaty with Frederick the Great in April, 1764, for common action in Poland. They agreed to secure the election of Poniatowski, to protect the religious rights of the Dissenters (Orthodox and Protestant Polish subjects), and to support each other if either were attacked. This diplomatic preparation, together with the judicious expenditure of money and the mobilization of Russian troops, persuaded the Polish Diet to vote as desired. But when Catherine continued to intervene blatantly in domestic Polish affairs, a group of Polish patriots formed the Confederation of Bar (in Podolia) to fight "for religion and for liberty." A bloody struggle ensued between these Confederates and the Russians.

France and Austria cordially supported the Confederates. They sent money, arms, and a few officers to their aid. In Constantinople the French ambassador pursued the customary strategy: goading the Turks to make a diversion on Russia's flank. The Turks were not loath to do so. They were alarmed by the increasing numbers of Russian agents operating throughout the Balkans. Indeed, a small insurrection had broken out in Montenegro in 1767 and threatened to spread to neighboring areas. The Crimean Tatars also favored war against Russia and exerted pressure in Constantinople toward that end. The breaking point came when Russian troops, pursuing a band of Confederates, violated the Ottoman frontier and burned a Turkish town. This act so inflamed Turkish public opinion that the Constantinople government was virtually forced to declare war suddenly in October, 1768. Catherine promptly appealed to Europe against "the common enemy of the Christian name." The Turks, not to be outdone, issued a manifesto declaring the Dissenters traitors to their church and religion. The war began on this comic note, the deist tsarina posing as the champion of Orthodoxy and Protestantism, and the Moslem sultan as the defender of Catholicism.

The superiority of the Russian armies was evident from the outset. But Frederick the Great was not impressed by their victories. With his customary tartness he remarked that the Russians were "ignorant of fortifications and tactics" and that "to form a clear idea of this war, one must imagine one-eyed men who have given blind men a thorough beating, and gained a complete ascendancy over them." [5] Frederick's observation was not altogether unjustified, but Catherine showed more sense of historical perspective in her reply to a similar disparagement by another critic: "Ignorance with the Russians is the ignorance of earliest youth; with the Turks it is that of dotage." [6]

Catherine began the war with her customary energy. She mobilized five armies, some to remain on the defensive in Russia and Poland, and others to take the offensive in the Balkans and the Caucasus. Prince Golitsyn on the Balkan front was the most successful. In the spring of 1769 he reached the Dniester River, defeated a Turkish army on its banks, and went on to occupy, first Jassy, the capital of Moldavia, and then Bucharest, the capital of Wallachia.

This was startling to Europe, but the following year unfolded still more unexpected events. The most dramatic was the appearance for the first time of a Russian fleet in the Mediterranean. Catherine had conceived the daring project of sending part of her Baltic fleet around Europe to the waters of the Levant. The objective was twofold: to foment a revolt in Greece, and to destroy the Ottoman fleet. In view of later developments it is worth noting that Britain not only tolerated but actively assisted this expedition. Both strategic and economic considerations explain this policy. Britain's great imperial rival at this time was France rather than Russia. Britain feared a French comeback in India where Clive had defeated Dupleix only seven years earlier. In contrast, she welcomed Russia's success over Sweden in the Baltic because it established an equilibrium in that area, and she also favored a Russian victory over France's ally Turkey because it would indirectly strengthen her own position in the Mediterranean. Finally, Britain faced stiff French commercial competition in the Levant, whereas Russia was an important market for her manufactured goods and an essential source of naval stores. According to an official French estimate, the total foreign trade (both imports and exports) of the Ottoman Empire in 1783 amounted to 110 million livres, of which trade with France accounted for 60 million. On the other hand, in the last quarter of the eighteenth century, no more than 27 British ships went to the Levant in any one year, against an average of 600 to 700 ships that went to Russia. [7] These considerations explain why Britain allowed the Russian fleet to stop for supplies and repairs at Hull, Gibraltar, and Port Mahon. They also explain why the British government repeatedly warned Paris and Madrid against taking any hostile action against the Russian fleet.

Advance units of the Russian expedition arrived off the western coast of Greece in February, 1770. From the first everything went wrong. Within a few months the Russian commander, Alexei Orlov, was reporting to Catherine, "The natives here are sycophantic, deceitful, impudent, fickle and cowardly, completely given over to money and to plunder." [8] The difficulty arose from mutual misunderstanding. Russian agents had sent glowing but exaggerated reports of a nation ready to spring to arms. In fact, the more sober Greek leaders had warned that large quantities of arms and at least ten thousand Russian troops were essential for a successful uprising. But now they saw only four ships, a few hundred soldiers, and forty boxes of arms. The Greeks naturally were disillusioned and held back, causing the Russians in turn to feel betrayed.

With the appearance of more Russian ships several thousand Greeks finally took up arms. But they were unable to coordinate their operations, either among themselves or with the Russians. The only notable success was the capture of Navarino in April, 1770. Other sieges failed because neither the Russians nor the Greeks possessed the necessary equipment and skills. Meanwhile, the local Ottoman governor had collected an overwhelming force of Albanians and was closing in on the Russians and their Greek allies. Orlov decided to abandon the ill-fated venture and sailed away in June. The unruly Albanians then ran wild, massacring the Greeks and pillaging the country-side until expelled forcefully by a Turkish army in 1779.

The Russians failed on land, but they won a resounding victory at sea. In this case Frederick's analogy of the one-eyed and the blind was fully justified. When a part of the Russian fleet put into English ports en route south, the British were astounded by the clumsiness and poor construction of the ships and by the inexperience of the crews—a fact which further explains why the British accepted so indifferently Russian intrusion in the Mediterranean. But the Ottoman fleet was worse. After thirty years of peace it was fit only to carry out its customary duty of collecting the revenue in the Aegean area.

The first engagement was fought in July, 1770, off the island of Chios near the coast of Asia Minor. Orlov, aided by some luck, and still more by the English officers under his command, won a decisive victory. The Turks fled to the nearby harbor of Chesmé. There a British lieutenant, under the cover of darkness, steered a fireship into the midst of the cooped-up Ottoman fleet. Night became day as the entire fleet went up in flames amid the ear-splitting roars of exploding magazines. The British officer, Admiral Elphinstone, favored an immediate attack upon Constantinople, but Orlov vetoed the project. To this day there is sharp conflict of opinion concerning the wisdom of Orlov's decision. Some authorities maintain that the veto was justified given the poor condition of the Russian ships and the almost complete lack of landing forces. Others claim that the Turks were so demoralized that an immediate attack upon Constantinople in all probability would have succeeded. In any case, Orlov spent the summer months occupying eighteen Aegean islands, which gave him control of the Levant waters until the end of the war.

Meanwhile, the Russians had been equally successful on land. A large army of Turkish soldiers and Tatar irregulars invaded Moldavia. They were decisively defeated at Karkal in August, 1770. The Turks fell back south of the Danube while the Tatars attempted to hold the line of fortresses in Bessarabia and the Dobruja. But one after another they fell to the victorious Russians—Kilia, Ackerman, Ismail, Bendery, and Braila. By the end of the year all the fortresses on the lower Danube were in Russian hands.

Two years earlier, when Choiseul, the French foreign minister, instructed Vergennes in Constantinople to incite the Turks against the Russians, he added cynically, "The rottenness of the Turks in every department might make this trial of strength fatal to them; that matters little to us, provided the object of an immediate explosion be attained." [9] Choiseul proved to be correct in his appraisal of the Turks, but not on the outcome of the war. The Turks lost the battles, but it was the Poles who lost their independence. The reason is to be found in the chain of events set off by the linking of the Polish and Eastern Questions.

The overwhelming Russian victories caused alarm both in Vienna and in Berlin. The Austrians regarded Russia's penetration to the Danube as a threat to their security. The more the Russians advanced the more likely the Austrians were to intervene and thus to precipitate a general European war. Frederick of Prussia was also unhappy about Russian aggrandizement at the expense of Turkey because it offered him no compensating gain. But he was equally unhappy at the prospect of a Russian-Austrian war because he would be involved and again with little likelihood of gain. The problem was to find some basis for a peaceful settlement acceptable to all three powers. Poland offered the way out. Since Poland had caused the Russo-Turkish war, Frederick remarked, she should also pay the "damages." Catherine could help herself in eastern Poland in return for renouncing her conquests on the Danube. Austria and Prussia could also find ample compensation in other parts of Poland. In this manner Ottoman intervention in behalf of Poland culminated paradoxically in the eventual disappearance of Poland.

Catherine was willing to end hostilities on the basis proposed by Frederick, particularly because of increasing difficulties at home. Maria Theresa, the Hapsburg empress, was far from enthusiastic, but the alternative she faced was a war in support of Turkey. This was out of the question, so Maria Theresa gave way and proceeded to bargain vigorously for her share of the booty. On August 5, 1772, the three powers signed, "in the Name of the Very Holy Trinity," the partition treaties by which Poland lost approximately one third of her territory and one half of her population. The following spring, Russian bayonets prodded the treaties through the Polish Diet and the partition became official.

The partition treaties provided that Austria should use her "good offices" to bring about peace between Russia and Turkey. Negotiations were conducted in Bucharest for several months. The Russians made reasonable demands, considering their military successes and their territorial conquests. The sultan and his ministers favored acceptance of the terms, but they were unable to win over the influential religious leaders. The war continued another two years. The 1773 campaign was inconclusive. The Russians won several victories in the open field but failed to capture the three Turkish fortresses south of the Danube—Varna, Silistria, and Shumla.

The following year the genius of Alexander Suvorov, the Russian marshal, forced the Turks to accept the terms they had previously rejected. Suvorov ranks with the great military captains of history. A slight, frail, and eccentric man, he was an accomplished scholar and linguist as well as a masterful strategist and a born leader of men. He was to win his most notable victories against the Turks in the next war a decade later. At this time he was stationed on the Danube where the grand vizir approached him with the main Turkish army. In accordance with his maxim of never allowing the enemy to strike first, Suvorov marched south and won a crushing victory at Kostliji. The Turks fell back upon Shumla, which Suvorov promptly surrounded and cut off from Constantinople. The grand vizir asked for an armistice. Suvorov refused but offered to discuss peace terms. The Divan in Constantinople accepted the offer. On July 16, 1774, after only seven hours of discussion, the plenipotentiaries signed the Treaty of Kuchuk Kainarji (The Little Fountain) in an obscure Bulgarian village of that name.

The treaty was suprisingly moderate in its territorial provisions. Yet it ranks with the Karlowitz pact in its significance for the future. The earlier treaty delivered Christian provinces from Turkish rule and marked the end of Ottoman expansion westward. The later treaty for the first time tore a Moslem province from the Ottoman Empire and, more important, established the diplomatic basis for future foreign intervention in the internal affairs of the empire. Thus a distinguished jurist has asserted that all the treaties executed by Turkey and Russia during the following half century were but commentaries on the Kuchuk Kainarji text.

For the sake of convenience the provisions of the treaty may be divided into three categories, territorial, commercial, and religious. The Russians won several strategic enclaves along the north shore of the Black Sea. To the east they gained the port of Azov, a part of the province of Kuban, and the Kerch Peninsula commanding the strait between the Azov and Black seas. To the west the Russians kept the great estuary formed by the Dnieper and Bug as they enter the sea, including the Kinburn fortress at the mouth of the former river. The Turks also surrendered the territories of the Crimean Khan, but these were to form an independent state. Both signatories agreed not to "interfere, under any pretext whatever, with the election of the said Khan, or in the domestic, political, civil, and internal affairs of the same. . . ." Finally, Russia restored the remaining territories she had conquered, including the Danubian Principalities. But in return Turkey guaranteed religious freedom and "humane and generous government for the future," and also agreed that "according as the circumstances of these two Principalities may require, the Ministers of the Imperial Court of Russia resident at Constantinople may remonstrate in their favor. . . ."

The commercial clauses of the treaty gave Russia the right to appoint consuls anywhere in the Ottoman lands, and allowed her subjects to navigate freely in the Black Sea and to trade in the Ottoman Empire "by land as well as by water and upon the Danube . . . with the same privileges and advantages as are enjoyed . . . by the most friendly nations, whom the Sublime Porte favors most in trade, such as the French and English. . . ."

Finally, the provisions pertaining to religion gave to Russia a preferential right to protect Ottoman Christians not conceded to any other foreign power. The crucial clause provided: "The Sublime Porte promises to protect constantly the Christian religion and its churches, and it also allows the Ministers of the Imperial Court of Russia to make representations. . . ." [10]

The results and implications of this treaty were far-reaching. Turkey had lost her former undisputed control of the Black Sea. Her frontier in the northeast was now the Bug River. It is true that the Russians had won only scattered outlets to the sea but these were all strategically important and provided a springboard for future advances. They also surrounded the new and nominally independent Crimean state which obviously could continue to exist only on Russian sufferance. More significant were the other provisions which made Russia the guarantor of Moldavian and Wallachian privileges and of the religious freedoms of the Ottoman Christians. These clauses gave Catherine and her successors a standing pretext for diplomatic intervention or for military aggression. It is not surprising that Baron Thugutt, the Austrian envoy in Constantinople, appraised the treaty as "a model of skill on the part of the Russian diplomatists, and a rare example of imbecility on the part of the Turkish negotiators." He added that "the Ottoman Empire becomes henceforth a kind of Russian province" and he warned his government that "events now passing in this empire will in the future exercise the greatest influence on the policy of all the other States, and will give rise to endless troubles." [11]

CATHERINE'S SECOND TURKISH WAR: 1787–1792

Within a few years the course of events fully justified the baron's gloomy prediction. The Turks were far from satisfied with the peace terms, resenting particularly the loss of the Crimean territories. More important was the attitude of Catherine. She regarded the settlement as the beginning rather than the consummation of Russian progress in Southeastern Europe. Under the influence of the masterful Prince Potemkin, who served her well as soldier, statesman, and lover, Catherine reverted to the "Oriental project" propounded half a century earlier by Marshal Munnich. Both she and her consort dreamed of expelling the Turks from Constantinople and of establishing in their place a revived Greek empire, oriented, naturally, toward St. Petersburg. It is not without significance that her second grandson, born in 1779, was christened Constantine, and that the medal struck to commemorate his birth showed on the one side the church of St. Sophia in Constantinople and on the other the Black Sea with a rising star above.

Catherine realized that she could not reach her goal without the support of another great power. She also realized that Prussia would never be that power. Frederick had made it clear during the preceding war that he had no intention of helping Catherine to expand in a region where he himself had no hope of compensation. Catherine therefore turned to Austria, encouraged by the death in 1780 of the old empress, Maria Theresa. The following year Catherine concluded an alliance with the new Hapsburg ruler, Joseph II. They agreed to aid one another in case of war and they also agreed that if either signatory acquired territory the other was entitled to corresponding compensation.

During the year 1782 Catherine set forth in her letters to Joseph the details of her "Grand Plan" against the Turks. Joseph was amenable, less out of enthusiasm for the plan than out of a compelling need to have Russia by his side against Prussia. Just as Maria Theresa had agreed reluctantly to the partition of Poland, so Joseph now reluctantly agreed to the partition of Turkey. By the end of the year the two rulers had settled the main points of their extraordinary project. Russia was to acquire the western Caucasus, the Crimea, and the lands to the Dniester River. Moldavia and Wallachia were to form the independent state of Dacia, designed to serve as a buffer between Russia and Austria. Joseph was to round out his empire by obtaining parts of Wallachia, Serbia, Bosnia, Herzegovina, and the Venetian provinces of Istria and Dalmatia. The remaining territory in the Balkans—that is, Bulgaria, Macedonia, and Greece—was to constitute the revived Greek empire with Constantinople as its capital and with Catherine's grandson Constantine as its emperor. To reassure Joseph, Catherine agreed that Constantine "should renounce all pretensions to the throne of Russia since the two crowns must not and should not be allowed to be placed on the same head." [12]

Fortified by the Austrian alliance, Catherine proceeded toward the realization of the Grand Plan. She began in the Crimea where, in complete violation of her pledges at Kuchuk Kainarji, she applied the same tactics that had proved successful in Poland. She encouraged a revolt against the reigning khan and installed in his place a pretender who faithfully executed her orders. When the Tatar population rose in protest she proclaimed the annexation of the country with professions of acting only to deliver its people from misgovernment. This highhanded robbery excited the greatest indignation in Constantinople. But the Turks received no support from any quarter. Even France advised acceptance of the *fait accompli*. The inevitable outcome was the Treaty of Constantinople (1783) ceding to Russia the Crimean Peninsula with the neighboring Kuban area and the Taman Peninsula.

Catherine appointed Potemkin the governor of the newly acquired territories. With an energy and vision reminiscent of Peter the Great, he threw himself into the task of colonization and fortification. He subdued the wilder elements among the Cossacks and Tatars and then brought in settlers from Germany and Austria as well as from the rest of Russia. With the assistance of numerous foreign experts, he founded cities, established industries, and built the great naval bases, Sebastopol and Nikolaev. By 1787 he was ready to display to his mistress and to the rest of the world the results of his work. Accompanied by a magnificent court, including the envoys of France, England, and Austria, Catherine embarked on the Dnieper. A fleet of galleys escorted her to Kherson, at the mouth, where she passed under a triumphal arch bearing the inscription "The Way to Byzantium." The climax came at Sebastopol when Catherine and Emperor Joseph were dining in a splendid new palace. At a signal from Potemkin the curtains were pulled back from the windows, revealing a magnificent view of the bay with a fleet of forty men-of-war in battle formation firing a roaring salute to Catherine.

The meaning of this display was not lost on the Turks. Sebastopol was within two days' sail of Constantinople. Russian agents were busy stirring up discontent throughout the Balkans and even in distant Egypt. The last straw was a new Russian ultimatum demanding the surrender of Georgia and Bessarabia and the appointment of hereditary governors in Moldavia and Wallachia. By this time the Western powers had abandoned their former indifference. With the encouragement of England and Prussia, the sultan presented a counterultimatum for the restitution of the Crimea and the evacuation of Georgia. On Catherine's refusal he declared war on August 15, 1787. Early the following year Joseph entered the war in accordance with his treaty obligation.

The allies had plannned to coordinate a Russian invasion of Moldavia with an Austrian offensive down the Danube. But an unexpected Swedish attack in the north prevented Catherine from fulfilling her engagement. At the same time Emperor Joseph foolishly assumed personal command of his army and proved so incompetent that he suffered a crushing defeat in 1788. The only notable allied victory that year was Suvorov's successful assault upon Ochakov, the key Turkish fortress near the mouth of the Bug River. In 1789 the allies finally hit their stride. A rejuvenated Austrian army under a new commander overran most of Bosnia and Serbia. Suvorov was equally successful in the Danubian Principalities. With some Austrian support he defeated two large Turkish armies in quick succession. Panic reigned in Constantinople. The Austrians were ready to cross the Danube into Bulgaria.

TREATY OF SISTOVA: 1791

The diplomatic situation at this point resembled that of 1771, when the Russian victories aroused the hostility of Austria and Prussia and culminated in the first Polish partition. The combined Austrian-Russian victories now caused equal apprehension in certain European capitals. France was unexpectedly indifferent. Her foreign minister, Vergennes, was so determined to aid commerce and to avoid war that he rationalized to his satisfaction the abondonment of the "Turkish barbarians." But Prussia still opposed Turkish partition as resolutely as in the time of Frederick the Great, and for the same reason. Partition would strengthen Russia and Austria enormously without compensation for herself. In 1788 Prussia joined Britain and Holland in a Triple Alliance which aimed primarily to keep France out of Belgium but which also sought to check Russia and Austria in the Balkans.

Such was the international situation when Joseph II died in February, 1790. His brother and successor, Leopold II, had no desire to continue the war against Turkey. He did, not trust Catherine; he faced a revolt in Hungary; and he feared a Prussian attack if his armies advanced closer to Constantinople. Accordingly, he concluded the Convention of Reichenbach with Prussia (July 27, 1790) by which he agreed to accept a peace with Turkey based on the prewar *status quo*. The peace was formalized a year later with the signing of the Treaty of Sistova on August 4, 1791. These developments had far-reaching consequences for Europe as well as for the Balkans. They not only eased the pressure on Turkey but they also ended the Austrian-Russian alliance and prepared the way for a new European coalition directed against Revolutionary France.

TREATY OF JASSY: 1792

The desertion of Austria was a serious blow for Catherine. She was left alone to carry on the war against Turkey and Sweden and to face the diplomatic maneuvering of the hostile Triple Alliance. Catherine rose to the occasion with courage and resourcefulness. First she persuaded Gustavus III of Sweden to accept the Wereloe Treaty (August 15, 1790) restoring the prewar frontiers. Then she turned full force against the Turks to win a decision before the other powers could intervene. Marshal Suvorov, as usual, presented her with the most telling arguments of diplomacy. In December, 1790, he successfully stormed Ismail, the strong Turkish fortress near the mouth of the Danube. At the same time the Greeks made a considerable diversion on the Turkish rear despite their unfortunate experience with Orlov during the previous war. They organized scattered revolts in the mountainous areas of their country and they also outfitted a fleet of privateers which operated actively in the Aegean throughout the war.

Fortified by these successes, Catherine haughtily ignored the demand of the Triple Alliance powers that she follow the example of Leopold and restore her conquests to the Turks. Instead, she informed the king of Prussia that she would make war and peace as she pleased and that she would not tolerate any interference in the conduct of her affairs. She also let it be known, however, that she would accept a settlement that left her in possession of the territory to the Dniester River.

This offer precipitated a significant and revealing debate in the British Parliament. During Catherine's first war with Turkey, Britain supported Russia because of certain economic and strategic factors already noted. Now the younger Pitt was in office, and he was the first British statesman to perceive and to state publicly that continued Russian expansion at the expense of Turkey was contrary to British interests. In order to check Catherine he proposed to cooperate closely with Prussia and to turn to Poland for the grain and timber supplies hitherto obtained from Russia. On March 27, 1791, he sent to Berlin the draft of a joint ultimatum to be presented to Catherine and demanding the restoration of the conquered territories. The following day he submitted to Parliament a bill for "some further augmentation" of the naval forces in view of the failure to "effect a pacification between Russia and the Porte." The bill passed both Houses by substantial majorities. But more significant was the tone of the debate and the reaction of public opinion.

The arguments presented on both sides were to be heard again and again throughout the nineteenth century as the clash of British and Russian imperial interests assumed world-wide proportions. Edmund Burke foreshadowed Gladstone in denouncing a policy that allied England with the "destructive savages" who had condemned "those charming countries which border upon the Danube, to devastation and pestilence." [13] Other speakers warned, in the manner of Disraeli, that the fall of Constantinople would be followed by that of Egypt, and "where [Russian] victories would afterwards end God alone could tell." [14] The debates, both in Parliament and in the country, indicated that public opinion was not prepared to sacrifice the flourishing Russian trade and to embark upon a hazardous war for the sake of a distant and dubious danger.

Pitt wisely decided that an aggressive foreign policy was impractical with the country so divided. He sent a special messenger to Berlin to forestall the presentation of the ultimatum. The sequel followed naturally and quickly. Without prospect of assistance from any quarter, the Turks were ready to come to terms. Catherine, on her part, was equally willing, especially since Poland required her attention. By the Treaty of Jassy (January 9, 1792) she retained the territory to the Dniester River and surrendered her conquests farther to the west.

It is not irrelevant to add that immediately after this settlement Catherine turned upon the unfortunate Poles. They had taken advantage of the Turkish war to conclude an anti-Russian pact with Prussia and to launch an impressive reform program for the rejuvenation of their country. But the course of international events doomed their efforts to failure. With the Turkish war ended and with the French Revolution engaging the attention of the other powers, Catherine was able to reassert her authority. The second and third partitions of 1793 and 1795 spelled the end of Poland as an independent state.

JASSY AND THE BALKANS

The Treaty of Jassy is a turning point in Near Eastern history. It marks the advent of Russia as a great Near Eastern power. When Catherine came to the throne the Black Sea was a Turkish lake. Before she died it had become a Russian-dominated lake. Its northern shore was ringed by great naval arsenals—Sebastopol, Kherson, and Nikolaev. Hitherto the issue had been whether Russia should enter the Black Sea. Henceforth it was whether she should advance to the Mediterranean.

The Treaty of Jassy is also a turning point in Balkan history. It signified that the Balkans were not to become another Poland. This assuredly would have been their fate if Catherine and Joseph had carried through their Grand Plan. Just as the three partitions divided Poland among Prussia, Russia, and Austria, so the Grand Plan would have divided the Balkan Peninsula between Russia and Austria.

Various factors explain Catherine's failure in the Balkans in contrast to her success in Poland. One was the role of geography. Russia and her allies could march directly and without hindrance into the heart of Poland. But in the case of Turkey they first had to overrun a vast and strongly fortified intermediate area—the Crimea, the southern Ukraine, and the Danubian Principalities—before reaching the Balkan ranges protecting Constantinople. Another factor was diplomatic. The partition of Poland was favored usually by Prussia and Russia and accepted by Austria. The partition of Turkey was favored usually by Russia alone and rarely accepted by either Austria or Prussia.

These factors help to explain the failure of the Grand Plan. The fact that it did fail determined the course of future Balkan history. Instead of facing the combined might of the Hapsburg and Tsarist empires, the Balkan peoples suffered only an ineffective and weakening Ottoman rule. One after another they won their independence during the nineteenth century, while the Poles remained shackled until World War I.

12. The Balkans, the French Revolution, and Napoleon: 1792–1815

T HE TURKS enjoyed six years of peace after their wars with Catherine. Russia and the other powers were too involved in the Polish partitions and in the problems created by the French Revolution to undertake new ventures in Southeastern Europe. This respite was fully appreciated by the harassed Turks. The following entry in the journal of Sultan Selim's privy secretary reflects the attitude of Ottoman officials at this time toward the turbulent events in Europe: "May God cause the upheaval in France to spread like syphilis to the enemies of the Empire, hurl them into prolonged conflict with one another, and thus accomplish results beneficial to the Empire, amen." [1]

The upheaval in France did spread as the Turks wished, but in the process they themselves were involved as well as their Balkan subjects. As early as 1797, by the Treaty of Campo Formio, the French acquired the Ionian Islands from Venice while the remaining Venetian possessions along the Adriatic coast went to Austria. This transfer of Balkan territory did not involve the Turks directly. But next year, in July, 1798, news arrived in Constantinople of Napoleon's descent upon Egypt. Now the period of peace was over. During the following years the Turks floundered around in a great side-eddy which changed according to the direction of the main current of the Continental wars. From 1798 until 1802 the Turks were allied with England and Russia against France. In the process the Russians replaced the French in the Ionian Islands and also gained a foothold in the Danubian Principalities. After 1802 the Turks enjoyed another four years of peace until Napoleon induced them to turn against their former allies. From 1806 until 1812 the Turks waged a desultory war against the English and the Russians. The Balkans now were affected directly because most of the fighting was conducted in the peninsula and in the Ionian Islands. When peace finally was restored by the 1812 Bucharest Treaty and by the 1815 Vienna settlement,

198

the great powers acquired certain outlying border territories. Dalmatia went to Austria, Bessarabia to Russia, and the Ionian Islands to Britain.

More important than the territorial change was the political and ideological impact of the French Revolution and of Napoleon upon the Balkans. The precise nature and extent of this impact cannot be measured, but there is no doubt that French Revolutionary ideology, the stirring events of the Revolution itself, the magnetic personality and tradition-shattering career of Napoleon, and the experiences of a considerable number of Balkan soldiers serving in foreign armies during these years—all these left a definite imprint upon the Balkan scene. Certainly the Balkan Peninsula of 1815 was quite different from that which had existed only a generation earlier when the Russian wars ended.

FRENCH RULE IN THE IONIAN ISLANDS

The first concrete impact of the French Revolution upon the Balkans came with the signing of the Campo Formio Treaty (1797) following Napoleon's Italian campaign. France and Austria divided the Venetian possessions, Austria obtaining Dalmatia, and France the Ionian Islands with the adjoining mainland. The French held the islands for only a few years—from 1797 to 1799 and then again from 1807 to 1814. Yet their rule had a convulsive effect upon the *ancien régime* type of society that prevailed. As we saw in Chapter 7, the Ionian Islands differed from the other Greek lands in that they did not fall under Turkish rule. Instead, they belonged to Venice for over four centuries, from 1386 to 1797. During this period they enjoyed a considerable degree of autonomy. Venice contented itself with the exercise of general control through its appointed agents: a governor general with a three-year term, a governor for each of the islands, a grand judge, and three "inquisitors" sent out periodically to investigate conditions and report on the conduct of all public officials. The actual rulers of the islands were the native aristocracy, whose lands and privileges had been recognized by Venice and who in turn supported Venetian rule. Thus Ionian society, unlike that of the Greek mainland, was highly stratified. In fact, the aristocratic families were registered in a Golden Book like that in which their counterparts in Venice were registered.

The French undermined this regime by introducing sweeping reforms in their customary manner. They burned the Golden Book, decreed the abolition of feudalism, democratized government, freed the peasantry from compulsory labor in the government salt works, reorganized civil and criminal justice, and extended educational facilities. The impact of these measures is reflected in the following report of the local English consul following the expulsion of the French:

I cannot but mention that the attempts of the French to poison the minds of the Peasants of Corfu, were not altogether unsuccessful. Indeed, so multifarious were the arts of the republicans, so great was the encouragement they gave to the description of people in question, that one cannot but feel that the Peasants must previously have had the strongest aversion to the French, not to have totally yielded to their seduction. . . . It affords me particular satisfaction to be able to close this account with a few words on the subject of the attachment of the highest orders of the inhabitants of all these Islands, to the English Nation. This attachment is the result of observation and enquiry; it is the more particularly flattering, as it is the more vigorous in the most wealthy, the most judicious, and the best informed.[2]

NAPOLEON INVADES EGYPT:
BALKAN REPERCUSSIONS

French rule in the Ionian Islands ended paradoxically as a consequence of Napoleon's invasion of Egypt. The Directory in Paris decided to strike at Egypt after deciding that a cross-channel invasion of Britain was too risky. It instructed Napoleon to take possession of Egypt, drive the English out of the Levant, cut a canal through the Isthmus of Suez, and at the same time maintain friendly relations with the Turks.

The fate of the expedition is well known. Napoleon set sail from Toulon, eluded Nelson's fleet through sheer luck, and landed at Alexandria late in June, 1798. A few weeks later he routed the Mameluke rulers of Egypt at the Battle of the Pyramids. But on August 1 Nelson discovered and destroyed the French fleet at Aboukir Bay. The expedition was doomed, regardless of how many victories Napoleon might win on land. To make matters worse, the Ottoman sultan, Selim III, the nominal sovereign of Egypt, was emboldened by Nelson's victory to declare war against France on September 1. Napoleon replied with customary audacity by invading Syria. He took by assault El Arish, Gaza, and Jaffa, and laid siege to Acre in March, 1799. With the assistance of an English fleet the defenders repulsed the French attacks. Napoleon reluctantly gave up his plan of taking Constantinople from the east and retreated to Egypt. There he defeated a Turkish army that had been transported by English ships. The victory was unavailing. So long as Nelson controlled the Mediterranean the French remained prisoners in Egypt.

News from France convinced Napoleon that his future lay in Paris rather than in the land of the Nile. With great secrecy he left Alexandria in a small sloop and successfully ran the English blockade, landing at Fréjus on October 9, 1799. Precisely a month later he was the first consul of France. And two years later the army that he had left behind in Egypt surrendered to the English.

Napoleon's expedition had lasting effects throughout the Near East despite its ultimate failure. In Egypt it weakened the position of the arrogant Mameluke warriors, who hitherto had mercilessly exploited the country. In their place appeared Mehemet Ali, an unscrupulous but extraordinarily capable Albanian adventurer. After making himself absolute master of Egypt he proceeded to extend his authority to the Sudan, Arabia, Crete, and Syria.

He built up his military establishment to the point where it far surpassed that of his nominal overlord in Constantinople. During the eighteen thirties, as we shall note in Chapter 16, Mehemet Ali was the central figure in a series of crises that convulsed the Near East and almost precipitated a general European war.

The Egyptian expedition also had repercussions in the Balkans. It enabled the Russians to strengthen their position in two strategic regions, the Ionian Islands and the Danubian Principalities. When Selim declared war on France in 1798, the Russians, together with the English, rallied to his support. The Russians first persuaded the sultan to sign the Treaty of Constantinople (January 3, 1799), permitting passage of their warships through the Straits. Then they sent a part of their Black Sea fleet to join the British at Alexandria, while the remainder proceeded with the Turkish fleet against the French-held Ionian Islands. By March, 1799, all these islands had passed under Russian-Turkish control, while the mainland dependencies, which had been lightly garrisoned by the French, had fallen to the attacks of the Albanian chieftain, Ali Pasha.

The Russian invaders were aided by the fact that the French occupation had lost its glamour with the local population. This was due partly to the anti-French propaganda of the aristocratic elements, which were aided in their efforts by the church. Also, it had become apparent that the French were more concerned with their own strategic interests than with the freedom of the islanders. These interests were stressed by Napoleon in a letter to the Directory: "The islands of Corfu, Zante and Cephalonia," he wrote, "are of more importance for us than all of Italy. . . . The Turkish Empire is crumbling day by day. The possession of the islands will enable us to support it [the Empire] as long as that proves possible, or to take our part of it." [3]

With the expulsion of the French, the Russians and the Turks signed a convention providing that the dependencies be ceded to Turkey and that the Ionian Islands proper be organized as the Septinsular Republic. This republic constituted the first autonomous Greek state of modern times. The transition from French to Russian rule was not without its complications. On October 3, 1799, the local British consul reported:

A disturbance lately took place at Zante in consequence of a change made in the internal Government of the Country by a Russian Officer who has been charged to organize the affairs of these Islands. The change in question was in favour of the nobility, who, since the expulsion of the French, had only had an equal share in the Government with those of the inferior Classes. As, then, this change throws all the Government into the hands of the nobility, those of the other Classes became tumultuous, but nothing material happened, and tranquillity was perfectly restored, by the imprisonment of three or four of the Leaders, one of whom has been sentenced to be shot. [4]

When the Russian troops departed, the islanders proceeded to draft a constitution that reflected the egalitarian impact of the few years of French rule. This constitution of 1801 proclaimed in its preamble that natural rights confer "perfect equality," and hence "equal right" to participate in preparing a "social contract" and electing representatives. The provisions of the constitution were somewhat less daring, apparently being designed to mollify the aristocracy. Universal suffrage was combined with indirect election, and eligibility to the Executive Council was restricted to the *aristoi* or landowners who had reached their thirtieth year. These concessions failed to win the cooperation of the aristocracy, with the result that the constitution remained a dead letter. A more conservative constitution was adopted in 1803. By various devices it limited participation and representation in government to a small percentage of the population. The oligarchical features of the Venetian regime were to a great extent revived, with the difference that privilege now was based on property rather than on birth qualifications. The constitution remained the law of the land until the French reoccupied the islands in 1807 in accordance with the terms of the Tilsit Agreement between Napoleon and Tsar Alexander. It is noteworthy that John Capodistrias, who later won fame as foreign minister of Russia and president of the new Greek state, played a prominent role in the drafting of this constitution.

Meanwhile, the Russians had also exploited their new friendship with the sultan to win important concessions in the Danubian Principalities. The Treaty of Kuchuk Kainarji (1774) had given the Russian ambassador in Constantinople the right to "remonstrate" in behalf of the Rumanian inhabitants of the Principalities. Now in 1802 the sultan granted more specific concessions. Henceforth no hospodar might be dispossessed without the express consent of Russia, and no Turks, unless they were merchants, which was extremely rare, were to be allowed to enter either principality. It is not surprising that future hospodars showed as much deference to the tsar as to their sultan. Russian inflence remained predominant in the Principalities during the next half century until it was smashed by force of arms during the Crimean War.

SELIM JOINS NAPOLEON: BALKAN REPERCUSSIONS

The next development that affected the Balkans in the great Continental struggle was the formation of the Third Coalition against Napoleon and the entry of Turkey into the war on the side of Napoleon. Britain and France had signed the Peace of Amiens in March, 1802, but hostilities between the two powers broke out again in May, 1803. Two years later Russia and Austria joined England to form the Third Coalition. The war now became continental in scope and the danger of Turkish involvement increased correspondingly.

The neutrality of the Ottoman Empire was menaced not only by the spreading conflict between Napoleon and the Third Coalition but also by a serious revolt among the Serbians of the Belgrade pashalik. Under the leadership of their formidable Karageorge or Black George, the Serbians rose in protest against the local janissaries, who insolently defied the sultan's authority and ruthlessly exploited Christians and Moslems alike. This Serbian revolt is of prime importance in the history of the South Slavs and of the entire Balkan Peninsula, and will be considered in detail in Chapter 14. At this point, however, we shall refer to it only insofar as it affected the international position of the Ottoman Empire.

During the course of their struggle the Serbian rebels appealed to Austria and to Russia for assistance. The two powers reacted according to the exigencies of the great war against Napoleon. Austria favored a speedy settlement of the Serbian insurrection because she was exhausted after the disastrous defeats at Ulm and Austerlitz (October and December, 1805) and dared not risk another war. England also opposed any assistance to the Serbian rebels for fear that it might drive the Turks into Napoleon's camp. She wished above all else to preserve the Russian-Turkish-British bloc that had proved successful against Napoleon when he invaded Egypt a few years earlier. Russia also favored the continuation of this bloc, but she had to take into account her interests in the Balkans that pulled her in the opposite direction. If she ignored the Serbian appeals for the sake of Turkish friendship she ran the risk of alienating the Serbians and forcing them to turn to Napoleon. This contradiction in Russia's position explains her ambivalent policy. She did not oppose the insurrection but neither did she support it outright. Instead, she secretly gave a little financial assistance and at the same time she urged the Ottoman government to reach some settlement with the Serbs.

This diplomatic situation changed drastically in the second half of 1806 under the impact of Napoleon's victories in Central Europe and his diplomatic offensive in Constantinople. After Ulm and Austerlitz, Napoleon compelled Austria to sign the Treaty of Pressburg (December 26, 1805), giving him Venetia, Istria, and Dalmatia. With these cessions Napoleon gained mastery of the Adriatic and a foothold in the Balkans. The next year he forced Prussia out of the war, following his victories at Jena and Auerstädt. Only England and Russia remained, and as a part of his campaign against them he set out to win Turkey to his side.

In the summer of 1806 he sent the capable and persuasive General Sébastiani to Constantinople with instructions to persuade the sultan to cancel the treaties granting special privileges to the Russians. The most important were the 1799 treaty permitting the Russians to send their warships through the Straits, and the 1802 treaty giving Russia a voice in the tenure of the Danubian hospodars. Napoleon also sent flattering personal letters to the sultan, addressing him as the "very high, very excellent, very powerful, very magnanimous, and invincible Prince, great Emperor of the Moslems, Sultan Selim." He assured the sultan that nothing was closer to his heart than the glory and the well-being of the Ottoman Empire. "I have the will to save it, and I put my victories at our common disposal." [5]

Selim was impressed by the dazzling prospect pictured by Napoleon and Sébastiani. Already Napoleon had undone part of Catherine's work by driving the Russians out of Poland. Might not the Ukraine and the Crimea also be recovered by victorious French and Turkish armies fighting side by side? With this vision before him Selim proceeded on the course urged by his new friends. He dismissed the pro-Russian hospodars in the Danubian Principalities; he reasserted his sovereignty over the Ionian Islands; and he closed the Straits to foreign warships—all these measures violating specific treaty obligations. Russia replied in November, 1806, by sending an army into the Danubian Principalities. The next month Selim declared war on Russia "to avenge the outraged national honor." At the same time he dispatched an emissary to Napoleon with instructions to conclude an alliance guaranteeing the recovery of the northern shore of the Black Sea. The alliance was never signed. During the following months the Turks learned to their cost the unreliability of great powers engaged in great wars.

Sultan Selim's decision to enter the war on the side of Napoleon produced an immediate reaction on the part of every great power involved in the Near East. Britain assaulted the Ottoman Empire from the south by sea, Russia attacked from the north by land, while Napoleon's envoys in Constantinople worked feverishly to bolster the decrepit Turkish defenses.

Britain used her navy to launch a two-pronged offensive—one against the vital Dardanelles passageway leading to Constantinople and the other against Egypt. This Dardanelles expedition of 1807 had many resemblances to that of 1915. Both expeditions were designed to aid the Russian ally and both eventually failed after coming within a hairbreadth of success. An important factor in the failure of this early expedition was the division of authority between the naval commander, Vice-Admiral Sir John Duckworth, and the diplomatic representative, Ambassador Charles Arbuthnot. On February 20, 1807, Duckworth appeared before Constantinople after fighting his way through the Dardanelles. The defenses of the city were in ruinous condition and the panicky Turks were disposed to accept almost any demands. But Duckworth had instructions to refer political questions to Ambassador Arbuthnot. The latter was in poor health and allowed the Turks to drag out the negotiations while French engineers under the direction of General Sébastiani hastily strengthened the defenses of the capital. Within a fortnight Duckworth's position had become militarily untenable. The surrounding Turkish fortifications increasingly threatened his ships and he lacked an adequate landing force to take decisive retaliatory action. Duckworth had no alternative but to withdraw. After sustaining considerable losses he repassed the Dardanelles on March 3, 1807.

A few weeks later General Mackenzie Frazer landed a force in Egypt and occupied the port of Alexandria. But Egypt was now in the capable hands of Mehemet Ali. By a combination of threats and promises he successfully kept in check the Mameluke chieftains, who inclined toward the English invaders. Frazer found himself isolated in Alexandria with his original small contingent of British troops. He failed twice to take nearby Rosetta, where he had hoped to find much-needed provisions. With supplies running short and with Turkish reinforcements pouring into Egypt, Frazer evacuated Alexandria in September, 1807, after considerable loss of both men and reputation. From then on the British-Turkish war remained unfought.

Meanwhile the Russians in the north had been preparing land operations. Their strategy was to organize an anti-Turkish front stretching from the Danubian Principalities to the Ionian Islands, both of which areas they still occupied. The vital link necessary to join the two extremities could be provided only by the Serbians, who already were in the field under Karageorge. Accordingly the Russians now became warmly cordial to the Serbians and proposed close military cooperation. But at the same time the Turks also began to woo the Serbs in order to keep them out of the Russian camp. Late in 1806 the Ottoman government announced that it was willing to concede political autonomy to its Serbian subjects.

Karageorge now had to choose between autonomy under the sultan and cooperation with the tsar. The latter alternative did not please him altogether. Certain aspects of the Russian offer smacked more of incorporation than cooperation. In the end, Karageorge sided with the Russians, partly because he feared a Franco-Turkish attack from Bosnia and partly because he suspected that his rival, Milosh Obrenovich, would welcome the Russians if he failed to do so. A formal agreement was signed on July 10, 1807. According to its terms the Serbian people solicited the protection of the tsar, who was to appoint a governor and certain high officials to organize an administrative system in the country. Russian garrisons were to occupy local fortresses, and Serbian troops were to be incorporated in the Russian armies and were to be used not only for local defense but also for operations against the Turks and the French in the Balkans. In return the Russians undertook to provide the Serbs with money, munitions, artillery, a medical staff, and a military mission.

The sultan countered the Russian strategy by seeking to enlist and to coordinate the forces of the powerful and virtually independent Balkan pashas—Ali in Albania, Krousseref Mehemet in Bosnia, and Osman Pasvan-Oglu, and Mustafa in northern Bulgaria. Napoleon aided the sultan by sending special agents and military advisers to each of these local potentates and by dispatching a force of five hundred artillerymen from Dalmatia to Constantinople. The pashas were willing to cooperate, not out of loyalty to the sultan, but rather because they saw possibilities of personal aggrandizement. Ali attacked the Russians in the Ionian Islands while Krousseref harassed the Serbians from the west. The regular Turkish army, supported by Mustafa, delivered the main attack against the Russians in the Principalities. The latter operation proceeded with considerable success. By June, 1807, the Russians had retreated to Bucharest and were preparing for a siege.

A month later news arrived that a revolution had broken out in Constantinople and that Sultan Selim III had been deposed.* This immediately paralyzed operations. The janissaries refused to continue the campaign. Mustafa and the other pashas were anxious about their relations with the new regime and retired to their respective domains. Thus the Turks abandoned the campaign at the moment when they appeared likely to drive the Russians out of the Principalities.

In the same month—July, 1807—another event occurred that was to have even greater repercussions than the revolution in Constantinople. Napoleon met Tsar Alexander at Tilsit and concluded an agreement that left the unfortunate Turks alone against the Russians.

FRENCH IN DALMATIA

Before considering the Tilsit agreement we turn to the Adriatic Coast, where French occupation was making a significant impression. Venice had been the dominant power in Dalmatia since the beginning of the fifteenth century, gaining possession of all the coastal cities except Ragusa or Dubrovnik. The latter city became Venice's chief competitor in the Adriatic and the Balkans. The Dalmatian hinterland was held at various times by Serbian, Bosnian, Croatian, and later Hungaro-Croatian rulers. A new era began with the Turkish conquest of Dalmatia, completed in 1537. In return for paying tribute, Ragusa remained unmolested during this period of Turkish rule. With the defeat of the Turks at the hands of the Holy League, Dalmatia passed to Venice by the terms of the Karlowitz Treaty of 1699. Dalmatia remained under Venice until Napoleon destroyed the Italian republic and divided its possessions with Austria (Campo Formio Treaty 1797). Dalmatia thus came under Hapsburg rule, which lasted until Napoleon intervened and established himself along the Adriatic Coast. By the Treaties of Pressburg (1804) and Schoenbrunn (1809), Napoleon acquired first Dalmatia (including the Ragusan Republic), and then Slovenia, Istria, and Trieste, and parts of Croatia. These territories were combined to form the Illyrian Provinces, which were incorporated as an integral part of the French Empire.

French policy was as revolutionary in the Illyrian Provinces as in the Ionian Islands, particularly since there was the same background of aristocratic Venetian rule in the two regions. The French administrators, headed by Marshal Marmont and V. Dandolo, freed the serfs and gave them the land that they had tilled. They introduced the Code Napoléon in place of the outworn medieval codes. They undertook reafforestation, land reclamation, and various public health measures. Also, they built splendid roads, reformed the old guild system, and enforced strict decrees against usury. "There is not a city," declared Marmont, "not a village which I have not visited, not a mountain whose name I do not know." [6]

* For domestic developments under Selim, see Chapter 13.

Despite these reforms, there was much dissatisfaction with French rule in the later years. One reason was the sweeping conscription measures that the French applied in order to obtain manpower for their armies. Also, the highly centralized administration antagonized the Dalmatians, who resented being managed from Paris as though they were Normans or Bretons. Finally, the trade of the area, which was vital for its well-being, suffered severely from the British cruisers during the long years of Anglo-French warfare. Thus there appears to have been little sorrow when Austrian troops in 1814 drove the French out of the Provinces.

It is worth noting that the ancient Republic of Ragusa disappeared during the French regime. Its existence was formally ended by French decree in January, 1808; thereafter Ragusa was first a part of the Illyrian Provinces and then passed, with the rest of Dalmatia, under Hapsburg rule. As important as the extinction of the republic was the inexorable and fatal decline of its trade. The departure of the French did not revive commerce, and Ragusa never recovered her former prosperity. The basic reason was that Balkan trade routes now were shifting, and leaving all the Dalmatian towns stranded on the periphery. Before the nineteenth century much of the trade between the Balkans and Central Europe flowed through the Dalmatian ports. But during the course of the nineteenth century new routes were opened with the building of roads, railroads, and river boats in the Balkan countries. Now goods could be transported back and forth along the new channels more economically and expeditiously than by sending them over the mountains to the Dalmatian Coast. Thus Dalmatia entered a period of decline that has persisted to the present day.

TILSIT, BUCHAREST, VIENNA

Meanwhile, the balance in the Balkans and throughout Europe had been drastically affected by the agreement reached by Napoleon and Alexander at Tilsit. Napoleon had persuaded Sultan Selim to come to his side only a few months earlier. But the French emperor from the outset had regarded his Turkish ally as a convenient and expendable pawn. A Turkish attack on the Russian rear might prove a useful diversion while he himself delivered the main thrust across the Polish plains. When he defeated the Russians decisively at Friedland on June 14, 1807, the Turks applauded enthusiastically. They imagined that the day was drawing close when the star and the crescent once more would be flying over the northern shores of the Black Sea. In reality Napoleon's victory at Friedland was a disaster for the Turks. Napoleon no longer had need for a diversion and hence no longer had need for the Turks. Tsar Alexander now was willing to negotiate for peace and Napoleon also was agreeable. If the tsar would abandon his English alliance the two emperors could divide the Continent between them. This was the essence of the treaty they concluded at Tilsit on July 7, 1807.

The provisions referring to the Near East stipulated that France should recover the Ionian Islands and the adjacent territory on the mainland.

This was immediately implemented, so that the French returned to the Ionian Islands in the summer of 1807. But this second French regime proved as brief as the first. British naval units captured five of the seven islands, leaving only two that remained French until the collapse of Napoleon's empire in 1814. The Tilsit pact also provided that France was to mediate a peace settlement between Russia and Turkey, and Russia likewise was to serve as mediator between France and England. If either or both of these projected mediations failed, the signatories were to render reciprocal military assistance. Finally, the treaty provided that if the Russo-Turkish war continued "the two powers will come to an arrangement with each other to detach from the yoke and vexations of the Turks all the provinces of the Ottoman Empire in Europe, the city of Constantinople and the province of Rumelia excepted." [7]

The reference to Ottoman partition was purposefully vague. Alexander urged a more precise commitment but Napoleon categorically refused. One reason that he gave was that if the empire were partitioned in time of war England would be free to seize a much larger share of the spoils than in time of peace. Another reason, and the one that probably weighed more heavily with Napoleon, was the problem of what to do with Constantinople. Alexander had aspirations to the Ottoman capital but Napoleon was unwilling to concede that prize. This is made clear in the testimony of De Meneval, one of Napoleon's private secretaries who participated in the conference. According to his account, the tsar and the emperor on one occasion returned from a walk still deeply engaged in conversation. Napoleon asked for a map of Turkey and then put his finger on Constantinople. As if in reply to a demand, and heedless of the fact that De Meneval was listening, he shouted heatedly to Alexander: "Constantinople, Constantinople, never! That is the empire of the world." [8]

The Tilsit Treaty strikingly resembles the 1939 German-Russian Nonagression Pact. Both agreements were aimed primarily against Britain; both divided the Continent between the signatories; and both proved to be of short duration. One of the principal factors contributing to the breakdown of the Tilsit Agreement was the problem of Ottoman partition. Napoleon sent Caulaincourt as ambassador to St. Petersburg with explicit instructions that French interests required "that the Ottoman Empire retain its existing integrity. . . ." [9] Alexander reminded Caulaincourt that the Tilsit Treaty included a reference to the liberation of the Balkans "from the yoke and vexations of the Turks." Caulaincourt refused to be drawn into a discussion of this matter. The basic difficulty was that the two emperors had quite different objectives in mind. Napoleon was interested primarily in obtaining Russian support against Britain. Alexander, in contrast, wanted Napoleon to approve and to support the partitioning of the Ottoman Empire.

At one point Napoleon concocted a rather fantastic scheme in an effort to work out a common plan of action. He authorized Caulaincourt to discuss Ottoman partition if Alexander would agree to a joint Franco-Russian expedition against the British in India. In a personal letter to the tsar, dated February 2, 1808, Napoleon painted a glowing picture of the possibilities of the proposed expedition. With the Russians on the Danube and the French in Dalmatia, a combined army could reach the Bosphorus in a month. And by the time it arrived at the Euphrates, he prophesied, "England would be trembling and on its knees before the continent." He admitted that the expedition was intended more to scare "the London merchants" to accept peace than actually to occupy India." [10]

Alexander accepted Napoleon's proposal, but when the division of the Ottoman lands was considered in detail, the conflicting views on the control of the Straits proved irreconcilable. Caulaincourt suggested a compromise. Russia could take Constantinople and the Bosphorus, but France must hold the Dardanelles entrance to the Mediterranean. The Russians refused this proposal. They demanded possession of both ends of the Straits, pointing out, logically enough, that "One without the other is nothing." [11]

In October, 1808, Napoleon and Alexander met at Erfurt and renewed the Tilsit alliance, with certain modifications necessitated by the actualities of the day. Alexander agreed to support French policy in the Germanies while Napoleon sanctioned Russia's annexation of Finland from Sweden. Napoleon also conceded Wallachia and Moldavia to Russia, and even recognized the transfer as taking effect "from this moment." For the sake of preserving French prestige at Constantinople, Alexander agreed to try to gain the Principalities first by diplomatic means.

The effects of the Erfurt Agreement were far-reaching. The Austrians were particularly alarmed by the prospect of Russian expansion to the Danube. The only other great power interested in forestalling this eventuality was Britain. Accordingly the Austrians used their influence to end the nominal state of war that still prevailed between Britain and Turkey. This was accomplished with the signing of the Treaty of Dardanelles on January 5, 1809, a treaty of particular interest in Near Eastern history because it contains the first formal assertion and acceptance of the principle that the Straits were to be closed to warships of foreign powers in time of peace. Britain undertook to respect "that ancient rule of the Ottoman Empire," and in so doing she anticipated the 1841 Straits Convention which committed also the other major powers to this rule.

Meanwhile the Russians had formally demanded the Danubian Principalities and had been indignantly rejected. In the war that ensued, the prospect for successful Turkish resistance appeared remote. Sébastiani had reported to Paris that the Russian army on the Danube would reach Constantinople in eighteen days. The estimate seemed reasonable. Anarchy had continued unabated in the Ottoman Empire since the deposition of Selim the previous year. Robert Adair, the British diplomat who had negotiated the Dardanelles Treaty, reported that disorders were rampant in the provinces; that the janissaries were the masters of Constantinople; and that "the Ottoman Empire may be said to be without a government." [12]

Despite these wretched conditions, the Turks withstood the Russian attacks surprisingly well. One reason was the inefficiency and unpreparedness of the Russian generals. Another was the deterioration of Franco-Russian relations, which forced Alexander to keep his best divisions along the western frontier. Thus the fighting swirled around the fortresses in the Danube Valley rather than in the Balkan mountains or in the environs of Constantinople.

The British government now sought to take advantage of the worsening Franco-Russian relations to promote peace between Russia and Turkey. The opportune moment arrived in the early months of 1812. By that time both belligerents were inclining toward peace. Russia was becoming increasingly apprehensive of Napoleon's designs, while Turkey was in no condition, financially or militarily, to pursue the war further. This situation afforded Stratford Canning, the young and daring successor to Adair at Constantinople, the first triumph of his long diplomatic career. It was Canning who established contact between sultan and tsar, and gradually overcame their mutual suspicions. Napoleon frantically attempted to prevent the *rapprochement*. He wrote to his ambassador in Constantinople: "If Sultan Mahmud will take the field with one-hundred thousand men, I will promise him Moldavia, Wallachia, and even the Crimea." [13] But the Turks, not as impressed by Napoleon's promises as they had been a few years earlier, accepted a compromise settlement with the Russians and signed the Treaty of Bucharest on May 28, 1812.

By this treaty the Russians gave up their claims to Moldavia and Wallachia but retained the province of Bessarabia. They also made a gesture in behalf of their Serbian allies by inserting a clause providing for amnesty and autonomy. But the Serbian fortresses were to be surrendered to the sultan and were to be occupied again by Turkish garrisons. This latter provision was the decisive one. The Serbs, for all practical purposes, had been left to their fate. We shall see in a later chapter that the Turks ignored their commitments and soon resumed their former practices in the Serbian lands.

The Ottoman Empire had no part in the stirring drama that unfolded during the years following the conclusion of the Bucharest Treaty. The disastrous invasion of Russia, the war of German liberation, the Hundred Days —none of these directly affected Southeastern Europe. Likewise, the diplomats at the Congress of Vienna concerned themselves with the problems of Poland, the Germanies, the Italian states, but scarcely at all with those of the Near East. The sultan did try to recover Bessarabia through the good offices of Austria, but he was informed that such a retrocession was out of the question. Likewise, Castlereagh proposed that the great powers sign a Treaty of Guarantee that would apply not only to the settlement in Central and Western Europe but also to the *status quo* in the Near East. Alexander replied that he did not consider the provisions of the Treaty of Bucharest as final. He had been willing to sign the treaty in 1812 under the threat of

Napoleon's invasion. But now that Russia was the dominant military power on the Continent he demanded additional concessions designed to establish Russian hegemony over the Black Sea and the Caspian. The sultan rejected a guarantee under such conditions, and Castlereagh's proposal was dropped.

Thus Balkan frontiers were not as much affected by the Vienna settlement as might have been expected after so many years of war and revolutionary upheaval. The Russians remained in Bessarabia, the Austrians acquired the original Venetian possessions along the Adriatic coast, while the Ionian Islands were to form, under British protection, an independent state to be known as "the United States of the Ionian Islands." The Russians and the Austrians retained their newly won Balkan provinces until World War I, but the British in 1863 ceded the Ionian Islands to the Greek kingdom established in the interval.

BALKAN AFTERMATH

More important than the shift in frontiers were the psychological and ideological impacts of the French Revolution and of Napoleon upon the Balkans. Despite the relative isolation of the peninsula, revolutionary ideas and literature did seep in through various channels. Merchants and mariners, steadily increasing in numbers during these years, were quick to absorb revolutionary doctrines while abroad, and usually spread their new ideas with zeal and enthusiasm among their discontented countrymen. Students were beginning to enroll in Western universities, and as a rule they returned home ardent admirers of Western institutions and ideologies. Important also were the French merchants, adventurers, secretaries, and tutors who were beginning to appear in appreciable numbers, especially in the Danubian Principalities. Finally, there was the systematic propaganda directed from Paris with the aim of undermining Ottoman authority. This was particularly intensive during the years of Franco-Turkish hostility. Needless to say, this propaganda was designed to utilize the local populations as pawns of French diplomacy. In the spring of 1797 Napoleon instructed his commander in the Ionian Isles to "flatter the inhabitants . . . and to speak of the Greece of Athens and of Sparta in the various proclamations which you will issue." [14]

Whatever the motives and the means of propagation, there can be no doubt about the very real influence of French Revolutionary ideology upon certain sections of the Balkan people. Masonic lodges and other secret organizations were established in the principal towns. Newspapers were founded dedicated to the spreading of revolutionary principles and to the overthrow of Turkish domination. The revolutionary ideology may not have been transferred intact from West to East, and the concepts of liberty, equality, and fraternity may have been but barely comprehended. Yet the uprisings in Paris and the exploits of Napoleon made the subject Balkan peoples more restless, more independent, and more determined to win their freedom. A contemporary Greek revolutionary testified: "The French Revolution in general awakened the minds of all men. . . . All the Christians of the Near East prayed to God that France should wage war against the Turks, and they believed that they would be freed. . . . But when Napoleon made no move, they began to take measures for freeing themselves." [15] Similar is the testimony of another Greek revolutionary, the colorful Theodore Koloko-trones, who after being a klepht in the Peloponnesus, served under the British in the Ionian Islands and then assumed a leading role in the Greek War of Independence:

According to my judgement, the French Revolution and the doings of Napoleon opened the eyes of the world. The nations knew nothing before, and the people thought that kings were gods upon the earth and that they were bound to say that whatever they did was well done. Through this present change it is more difficult to rule the people.[16]

The influence of France varied greatly from one Balkan region to another. It was quite marked in the Adriatic lands where French rule prevailed the longest. In fact, the creation of the Illyrian Provinces stimulated a few decades later an Illyrian or Yugoslav national movement of some importance. One reason for this development was that the French had encouraged the cultural as well as the economic development of the Provinces. They built a network of secondary, commercial, and agricultural schools. The national language was used in these schools and in the newspapers which now appeared. The French also subsidized the publication of grammars and dictionaries and encouraged the organization of a national theater. Thus although the name "Illyria" had no national meaning to Napoleon, it did possess that connotation in the Provinces. In a proclamation of March 10, 1810, Colonel Mangin announced to the people, "You are now a part of a large nation, confederated with a great and powerful empire; you have become Illyrians and you must make yourselves worthy of the protection of Napoleon, the savior of your country." [17]

It is noteworthy that French influence extended across the frontier among the South Slavs under Austrian and Ottoman rule. The leader of the Serbian revolt, Karageorge, sent a letter dated August 16, 1809, to Ledouix, French vice-consul at Bucharest, asking for the

powerful protection of the Great Napoleon. . . . The Serbians assure his Imperial and Royal Majesty that their compatriots, the inhabitants of Bosnia and of the duchy of Herzegovina, and those who live in the kingdom of Hungary, not excepting the Bulgarians who derive, so to speak, from the same branch, will follow their example at the first move which is made.[18]

The significance of the French interlude in the Adriatic is that for the first time it united Serbs, Croats, and Slovenes, and stimulated among them the idea of Illyrian or Yugoslav unity and independence. It was still only an idea. It could not be called a movement. It did not stir the masses. But it did provide a beginning—a tradition for the powerful Illyrian movement of the 1830's and 1840's, to be discussed in Chapter 14. This movement was to develop under the stimulus of Hapsburg repression after 1815 and of the writings of South Slav writers and scholars. In 1847 a French sociologist who had journeyed through the Balkans reported that, in creating the Illyrian Provinces, Napoleon "had truly touched the national fiber of the neighboring peoples of the Adriatic." They believed, he wrote, that having freed them from the Austrian yoke, Napoleon had planned to disrupt the Ottoman Empire and unify all Yugoslavs: "Even today it is still like a happy dream which their poets write about, and one cannot persuade them that the Illyria of the future never existed in Napoleon's mind." [19]

Finally it should be noted that during this period all the powers involved in the Balkans enrolled in their respective armies a considerable number of recruits from the local populations. This military service was quite significant, opening new horizons for the recruits as well as instructing them in military techniques. Before this time a considerable number of Serbians had served in the Austrian armies, and these veterans, Karageorge being prominent among them, played an important role in the 1804 Serbian uprising. Now, during the French Revolutionary and Napoleonic years, both Serbian and Rumanian recruits served in the Russian forces. It is noteworthy that Tudor Vladimirescu, who was to lead the Rumanian peasants in 1821, had fought with the Russians against the Turks in 1806 and had risen to the rank of lieutenant.

The Greeks also enrolled in foreign armies, many klephts crossing over from the mainland to the Ionian Islands for that purpose. The French organized these warlike recruits into the "Chausseurs d'Orient"; the Russians formed several companies with native commanders; and Sir Richard Church, a British officer, organized a regiment of the Duke of York's Greek Light Infantry. He reported on November 12, 1811, that he had been able to transform his men "from the most lawless of mankind, not only into good soldiers, but also into praiseworthy members of civilized society. . . . The number of recruits that flock to me from all parts of Greece is really extraordinary. . . . Should government wish for men, I will answer from my character alone in this country to raise 6000 or 8000 men in as many months." [20] With the end of the war the British government disbanded the Greek units, to the disgust of Sir Richard, who was an ardent philhellene and who saw the leaders of a future national uprising in the Greek soldiers he was training. His hopes were not in vain. The Greeks who served under him, as well as under the French and the Russians, provided much of the leadership in the Greek War of Independence that broke out only six years after the Vienna settlement.

1815-1878
Part IV. Age of Nationalism

13. *Dynamics of Balkan Politics: 1815–1878*

H AVING REACHED THE THRESHOLD of the nineteenth century we enter a new epoch of Balkan history. We call this the Age of Nationalism, and the reason for doing so is that during the course of the nineteenth century the burgeoning national consciousness of the Balkan peoples exploded into a series of revolutionary movements against Turkish rule. This national awakening, and the successful uprisings that followed, were responsible for the striking difference between the Balkan Peninsula of 1815 and that of 1878: the one ruled in its entirety by the Ottoman power and the other including three independent Balkan states and a fourth that was fully autonomous. It does not follow that nationalism was the only force at work in the Balkan world between 1815 and 1878. Indeed, the dynamics of Balkan politics during these decades may be defined as the interplay of three factors: the continued decline of the Ottoman Empire, the awakening of the subject nationalities, and the expanding interests and increasing rivalries of the various great powers. In this chapter we shall consider each of those factors in turn.

CONTINUED OTTOMAN DECLINE

From the purely territorial viewpoint the Ottoman Empire in the early nineteenth century was still a great world power. One of the largest states in Europe, it also sprawled over vast areas in Asia and Africa. In the latter continent it extended from Algiers to Egypt; in Asia it embraced Arabia, the Levant states, Mesopotamia, and Anatolia; in Europe it stretched from the Pruth River in the east to the Dalmatian coast in the west and to the tip of Greece in the south.

This façade of empire was impressive, but the substance behind the façade was very different. In earlier chapters we considered the causes and manifestations of Ottoman decline—the disintegration of the unique administrative system, the demoralization of the armed forces, and the heedless

215

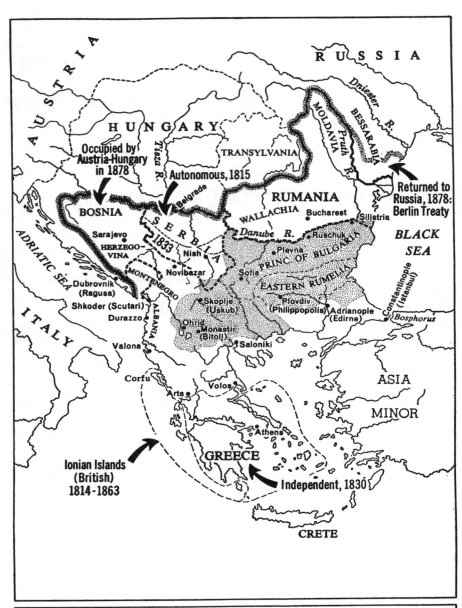

OTTOMAN TERRITORIAL LOSSES
IN THE BALKANS —— 1815–1878

—————— Boundary of Turkey in 1815	------- Boundaries in 1878: Treaty of Berlin
Boundaries in 1856: Treaty of Paris	Bulgaria as proposed by boundaries of San Stefano Treaty, 1878

216

exploitation of the peasantry. This downward trend continued unabated after the sixteenth century, with the exception of brief periods of superficial recovery. By the nineteenth century the results of this decline were plainly evident throughout the imperial structure.

The empire was divided into twenty-six provinces or eyalets, of which five were in the Balkan Peninsula. The bureaucracy that governed these territories bore little resemblance to the splendid organization of early times. The original slave administrator with his superb training and strict merit system of advancement had given way to the officeholder who normally bought his position and who regarded it as a private investment that should be made to yield as high a return as possible. This officeholder frequently was indebted to a wealthy Armenian or Greek banker who loaned the original capital and who added his exaction to that of the titular official. The same principle applied in taxation as in administration. A hierarchy of tax farmers bought and sold the tax collection concessions, each vendor pocketing a substantial profit. The net result was a system that combined maximum exploitation of subject with minimum benefit for government.

The one redeeming feature was that the sultan was unable to enforce this misgovernment throughout the empire. Most of the provinces had long since passed out of his control. The Barbary States of North Africa nominally recognized his suzerainty but, in fact, had been independent for centuries. In Egypt the imperial standard was permitted to fly over Cairo, but the real masters of that rich province were the Mameluke chieftains and, later, Mehemet Ali. Likewise, the governors of the great provinces of Syria and Mesopotamia ruled their domains with little or no regard for Constantinople. In the Arabian Peninsula not even the semblance of imperial authority remained. In that original home of Islam the fundamentalist Wahabite sect had arisen in protest against the corruption of the religion of the Prophet and had driven the Turks completely out of the peninsula. Even in Anatolia, the province closest to Constantinople, only two eyalets remained under the sultan's control.

Turning to the Balkan provinces of the empire, we find the situation basically similar. The fact that the population here was predominantly Christian was of no particular significance. Class distinctions in the Ottoman Empire were, in certain respects, more meaningful than those of religion. The ruling oligarchy in Constantinople included Christians and Jews as well as Moslems. Likewise, the peasant in the provinces was not exempt from exploitation simply because he happened to be a Moslem. Sometimes he was worse off than his Christian neighbor, who was more likely to have some measure of autonomy. On more than one occasion in the nineteenth century, Christians and Turks living in the Balkan provinces combined to rid themselves of the intolerable oppression of tyrannical pashas or of undisciplined janissaries.

Ottoman administration in the Balkan provinces was as chaotic as in the rest of the empire. Beginning with the islands, we find Crete full of janissaries who usually were able to defy the local pasha. Their depredations were so devastating that the island's trade and prosperity suffered severely. The Ionian Islands on the west coast of Greece had passed under British protection following the Napoleonic Wars. To the north of the Danube the Moldavian and Wallachian Principalities had an autonomous administration under hospodars or governors selected from the leading Greek phanariote families of Constantinople. Furthermore, Russia possessed special treaty concessions in the Principalities in regard to the establishment of consulates and the protection of all Greek Orthodox inhabitants. The Ottoman government also found it necessary to accept the *de facto* independence of certain mountainous and inaccessible parts of the peninsula—northern Albania, Montenegro, and a few regions in Greece. Finally, the Serbians of the Belgrade pashalik were in open revolt against janissary abuse from 1804 onward. Shortly after the conclusion of the Napoleonic Wars they were to win an autonomous status within the Ottoman Empire.

Two of the most prominent personalities in the Balkan Peninsula in the early nineteenth century were Ali Pasha and Osman Pasvan-Oglu, the *de facto* rulers of southern Albania and northern Bulgaria, respectively. In broad outline, their careers and policies were similar, and they are of significance for us in that they reflect the nature of Ottoman rule in the peninsula. Both men began their careers in areas where chaotic conditions prevailed and where the populace suffered from the depredations of bandits, local chieftains, and tax collectors. Both started out as brigands and gradually carved out personal domains by a combination of complete ruthlessness and unscrupulous exploitation of every opportunity. In both cases the imperial government attempted to check these powerful potentates but, finding this to be beyond its resources, ended by recognizing their authority.

Both men were able to assert and retain their authority because they satisfied local needs and won the support of the local population. It is true that they made liberal use of force and of outright terrorism. Such procedures as the murder of invited guests and the roasting of enemies on the spit were employed frequently and effectively by Ali and Pasvan-Oglu. But they are remembered not because of such lurid practices, which were common and accepted at the time, but rather because they were able to restore order, to protect the poor from the extortions of the beys and the tax collectors, and to provide security for their Christian subjects.

On this point the testimony of contemporary observers is emphatic and revealing. An English traveler, for example, reported that Pasvan-Oglu's capital, Vidin, "owes its rise chiefly to the emigration of poor families from Wallachia and Moldavia, who pass over the Danube, and take refuge in Bulgaria, to avoid the tyranny and extortion practised by Greek tax-gatherers, and their native boyars. . . ."[1] Likewise a British envoy in 1803 dispatched to his government the following appraisal of Ali and his administration.

He [Ali] is prompt in his measures, full of energy, and professes a very quick and nice discernment of Individual Character; but his want of education, and a life spent in arms, have rendered him in his Government cruel and despotic, because he found it to his advantage. He has however established the most perfect tranquility, and security of Persons and Property throughout his dominions, whose Inhabitants, Greeks and Turks, are richer, happier, more contented than in any other part of European Turkey.[2]

In conclusion, it is apparent that the Ottoman government in the early nineteenth century was a government in little more than name. Most of the empire it could not govern; the remainder it misgoverned. The need was still the same as it had been for over two centuries—a wholesale reorganization of the imperial structure with the aim of establishing the authority of the central government and also of improving the quality of its administration. At the turn of the century a sultan came to the throne with sufficient wit and sense of responsibility to appreciate this need.

Selim III ascended the Ottoman throne in 1789—a symbolically appropriate year, given the revolutionary nature of his ideas and aspirations. Selim was not the first sultan to recognize the need for reform in the empire. But he was the first to realize that the reform measures must look forward rather than backward. He was the first to consider reform in terms of borrowing from the West rather than returning to the days of Suleiman. His plans included the reorganization of administration, the revamping of education, and even the emancipation of women. But the prerequisite for these and other reforms was the abolition or the complete transformation of the janissary corps.

This body had become a degenerate and insubordinate Praetorian Guard, feared only by the people it was designed to defend. Its utter worthlessness had become apparent during the wars with Russia. Regiments showed up at the front with a total of five or six men. At the sight of the enemy the janissaries were likely to break and run, pausing only to plunder their own camp. Several sultans had attempted in the past to curb or destroy this pernicious body. They all failed because the ulema had sided with the janissaries to form a powerful coalition of religious and military vested interests. Also, important economic interests supported the *status quo* because of the revenue derived from speculation in janissary pay tickets. Each janissary had a document or sealed pay ticket which served as a passbook to receive pay. In 1740 permission was granted to buy and sell these pay tickets. They quickly became a type of stock certificate, eagerly bought up by officials and stock speculators in no way connected with the janissary corps. The scramble for tickets led inevitably to wholesale padding of the rolls. The names of dead janissaries were kept on the rolls and their tickets were bought and sold. Mustafa III attempted to abolish this glaring abuse in 1768. The janissary commander informed him that only half of the money paid out by the treasury actually reached the soldiers. And when he added that the other half found its way to the ulema, the palace officials, and the ministers of state, Mustafa discreetly decided to drop his plan.

Selim was more persistent than Mustafa, but in the end the combination of religious, military, and economic interests overwhelmed him. At the outset he was able to make some headway because of the popular revulsion against the scandalous showing of the janissaries during the wars with Russia. With the aid of a small group of like-minded ministers Selim began with peripheral measures designed to improve the imperial defenses. The Straits fortifications were repaired, new warships built, output of gunpowder increased, engineering and navigation schools reorganized under foreign direction, and Vauban's classic treatise, *The Assault and Defense of Fortified Positions,* was translated and published.

In 1793 Selim took the decisive step of establishing the *Nizamidjedid* or New Regulations Army. This was to be a Western type of army with common uniforms, specified enlistment and recruitment procedures, European methods of training, and modern armaments including the latest types of artillery, and the bayonet in place of the traditional scimitar. The plans called for an initial recruitment of 1,600 men and a gradual increase to 12,000. From the beginning the nizami demonstrated their worth. In 1798 they distinguished themselves at the siege of Acre, where they successfully held out against the great Napoleon himself. Likewise, in 1803 and 1804 they dispersed brigand bands that were ravaging the province of Rumelia in the Balkans.

Encouraged by this showing, Selim made three successive attempts, in 1805, 1806, and 1807, to bring the New Army up to full strength. On each occasion he was checked by the opposition of the janissaries and their allies. Finally, in May, 1808, he was forced to abdicate in favor of his nephew, Mustafa IV. The latter ruled less than three months before being ousted by the pasha of Ruschuk in Bulgaria. This local potentate, popularly known as Bairaktar, or Standard-Bearer, espoused Selim's reform program, largely because of the influence of an interesting group known as the Ruschuk Friends.

The Friends were mostly former ministers of Selim who, following the abdication of their master, had looked for support in order to resume their reform program. They turned to Bairaktar because he was known to be dissatisfied with the new regime in Constantinople and furthermore he had a standing army of thirty thousand men to do his bidding. Accordingly these reformers gathered in Ruschuk, where they made plans to overthrow Sultan Mustafa and restore Selim. They apparently enjoyed widespread support from patriotic elements because the very existence of European Turkey was now in jeopardy following the Tilsit Agreement between Napoleon and Tsar Alexander, discussed in Chapter 12.

In mid-July, 1808, Bairaktar marched upon Constantinople and seized the capital, but the unfortunate Selim was strangled before his rescuers could reach the palace. Bairaktar thereupon put on the throne Mahmud II, a nephew and also a pupil of Selim. Bairaktar assumed the posts of grand vizir and minister of war, while various members of the Ruschuk Friends comprised the cabinet. Having gained control of the empire, Bairaktar and his ministers dealt ruthlessly with the opposition and especially with the janissaries. They also proceeded to apply their reform program with more firmness and energy than Selim had ever displayed.

The janissaries and their supporters, as might be expected, were unalterably opposed to the new regime. Their opportunity came when Bairaktar was forced to send most of his men to Ruschuk to meet the attack of a neighboring pasha. The janissaries promptly rose in revolt on November 14, 1808, murdered Bairaktar, and for several days roamed the streets, hunting down the Ruschuk Friends and their supporters. Some five thousand homes were burned and eight to ten thousand persons were killed during the reign of terror.

Sultan Mahmud managed to survive the carnage. He had taken the precaution of strangling Mustafa a few days earlier and, because he was the last surviving member of the Ottoman house, the janissaries had no choice but to accept him. They did, however, compel Mahmud to renounce all that Selim and Bairaktar had tried to achieve. By the end of 1808 the Ottoman Empire seemed as unchanging as ever. The combination of economic, military, and religious vested interests appeared invincible.

Selim and Bairaktar had tried to do what Peter the Great of Russia had accomplished a century earlier. They failed in their attempt for various reasons. In the case of Selim, personal weakness and vacillation were involved. Certainly he lacked the vigor and firmness of Peter. But personal failings do not alone explain the course of events in Constantinople. Bairaktar gave abundant evidence of courage and decisiveness, but he also was ground down. It is necessary to take into account other factors, including the continued foreign wars which distracted Selim and Bairaktar and enabled their opponents to seize the initiative. Also, it should be recognized that the forces of reaction that Selim and Bairaktar had to cope with were much stronger than those that opposed Peter. The janissaries had a broader base in Ottoman society than the Streltzi in the Russian. Likewise, the Moslem ulema was more formidable than the Orthodox Russian clergy. It was firmly entrenched in the theocratic Ottoman Empire and usually could count on the unquestioning support of the devout population. It was a combination, then, of personal factors, foreign distractions, and the domestic balance of power that explains the doom of the first outstanding Ottoman reformers, Selim and Bairaktar.

The failure to reform the empire was of the utmost significance for the Balkan peoples. It assured the successful culmination of their national movements. With the triumph of the janissaries it became apparent that national aspirations could not be satisfied within the imperial framework. Henceforth the Balkan peoples could expect no relief from misgovernment, and they could presume some chance for victory if they made a bid for independence.

REVOLUTIONARY BALKAN NATIONALISM

The Balkan world during the early Ottoman period was static and theocratic. The Orthodox Church dominated education, written literature, and intellectual life in general. In the realm of politics, also, the leadership of the church was unchallenged. National policies and national objectives were virtually nonexistent. The Balkan world during these early centuries was a nonnational Orthodox world, and Balkan politics were conceived of and expressed in nonnational Orthodox terms. This Orthodox hegemony, as we noted in Chapter 9, was undermined by certain new forces that made their appearance long before the nineteenth century: the Age of Theocracy superseded by the Age of Nationalism as a result of the decline of the Ottoman Empire with the accompanying military and administrative deterioration; the rise of chifliks, which produced in certain regions a land-hungry and revolutionary peasantry; the growth of commerce and industry, which introduced to the Balkan scene new social elements with new ideas; and the great increase in the number of contacts with the rest of Europe, which led to a corresponding increase in the influence of foreign ideologies.

These new forces bore fruit when the various Balkan peoples during the course of the nineteenth century took up arms for liberation from Ottoman rule. We shall see in the following chapters that these nationalist movements were molded by varying combinations of the new forces. It does not follow, however, that Balkan nationalism was homogeneous or coordinated. The awakening of the Balkan peoples did not culminate in a united peninsular revolution against Ottoman rule. Instead, there occurred a series of independent uprisings spread over the whole of the nineteenth century. And in place of common effort there was continual rivalry and occasional open conflict.

One reason for this dissension was that the tempo of national revival varied greatly from people to people. The Greeks came first because of certain favorable circumstances: their numerous contacts with the West; their glorious classical heritage, which stimulated national pride; and their Greek Orthodox Church, which embodied and preserved national consciousness. After the Greeks came the Serbs. They led the other South Slavs because of the high degree of local self-government and because of the stimulating influence of the large Serbian settlements in southern Hungary. These advantages enjoyed by the Greeks and the Serbs suggest the reasons for the slower rate of national revival among the other Balkan peoples. The Bulgars had no direct ties with the West and were located near the Ottoman capital and the solid Turkish settlements in Thrace and eastern Macedonia. The Rumanians suffered from a sharp social stratification which was unique in the Balkan Peninsula and which produced a cultivated upper class and an inert peasant mass. Finally, the Albanians were the worst off with their primitive tribal organization and their division among three creeds, Orthodoxy, Catholicism, and Islam.

These factors explain why in place of a common Balkan revolution there occurred separate uprisings ranging from the early nineteenth century to the early twentieth. Another factor that contributed to Balkan disunity was an underlying and persistent hostility between the Greeks on the one hand and the Slavs and the Rumanians on the other. One reason for this hostility was the Greek domination of the Orthodox ecclesiastical machinery in the Balkans. We saw in Chapter 7 that the abolition of the Serbian Patriarchate of Ipek (Pec) in 1766, and of the Bulgarian Archbishopric of Ohrid in the following year, placed both Serbians and Bulgarians under the direct jurisdiction of the Greek patriarchs in Constantinople. This arrangement continued until 1831 when the Patriarchate recognized the autonomy of the Serbian church, and until 1870 when the Bulgarians obtained a firman from the sultan establishing their church as independent of the Ecumenical Patriarchate.* During the intervening decades Greek prelates filled virtually all the top church posts in the northern Balkans, while the Greek language was used in the church services and in the church schools.

This situation led to charges that the Greeks were conducting a deliberate Hellenization and denationalization campaign against the South Slavs. In actual fact, Greek cultural and ecclesiastical hegemony was more the product of historical tradition and contemporary reality. Neither the South Slavs nor the Rumanians had at the time the trained personnel necessary to fill ecclesiastical posts, or the literary languages and national literatures needed for educational purposes. The Rumanian historian Nicholas Iorga emphasized this point as follows:

> For many years a struggle has been conducted in my country against what is called "the Greek oppression." For forty years I have opposed this manifestly erroneous viewpoint. . . . If there was a Greek school [in Rumania], it was not a national school of contemporary Hellenism; it was for the whole world, like the Latin schools in the West. It provided a common bond with its use of one language and its propagation of one body of thought. . . . Common life under the Ottoman Empire, cooperation within the context of a civilization and one of the great languages of antiquity, made possible continual rapport [among the Balkan Christians].[3]

The fact remains, however, that with the first signs of national consciousness, the northern Balkan peoples naturally turned against the cultural and ecclesiastical domination of the Patriarchate. It did not matter that the Greek nationalists also found themselves at odds with the essentially antinational church hierarchy, to be discussed in Chapter 15. The South Slavs and the Rumanians understandably identified the Greek-dominated church with the Greek nationality, and became generally anti-Greek.

The northern Balkan peoples also had economic grievances against the Greeks. They heartily disliked the Greek financiers, who frequently were the local tax farmers and moneylenders. Underlying these specific considera-

* See Chapter 19.

tions were the traditional antipathy and distrust of the peasant for the man from the city. The overwhelming majority of the Greeks at this time were engaged in agriculture. But the type of Greek that the Rumanian and Slav peasants had dealings with was likely to be a merchant, a government official, a moneylender, a tax farmer, or an ecclesiastic. Hence the popular conception of the Greek as being well educated and intelligent, but also cunning, avaricious, and unscrupulous. A Serbian leader stated in 1810 that the Byzantine emperors had called in the Turks to destroy the Serbian empire, and that "from that period to the present day there has persisted, despite the religious tie, national enmity between the Serbians and the Greeks." [4] Likewise, a common saying of the Rumanian peasants is, "The Greek is a pernicious disease who penetrates to the bone." [5] The Greeks naturally reciprocated in kind. They tended to look down upon the other Balkan peoples as dull and ignorant country bumpkins. A contemporary observer relates:

> The Greeks despise the Sclavonians, calling them barbarians and "kondrokephalai" (wooden-heads), as they did even in the time of Michael Palaeologus, 1261: on the other hand the astute and wily spirit of the Greeks is utterly repugnant to the Sclavonians, who regard them with jealousy and distrust.[6]

The Balkan peoples were divided within themselves as well as among themselves. Merchants, mariners, and land-hungry peasants were likely to be dissatisfied with the imperial *status quo*. But the Balkan peoples had certain religious and secular leaders who were closely associated with the Ottoman imperial structure and who, therefore, were not so ready to turn against it. This was the case with the higher clergy who, as we saw in Chapter 9, opposed revolutionary agitation because of its rationalism, secularism, and Western origin, and also because it was a threat to their privileged position and their vested interests within the Ottoman framework.

Another important group that was lukewarm to change was the class of primates, known to the Greeks as kodjabashi, to the Bulgarians as chorbaji, and to the Serbs as knezes. The typical primate was a combination landowner, administrative agent, and tax collector. He collected taxes, tried civil cases, served as intermediary between the Turkish overlord and the Christian subject, and, in the more enlightened regions, concerned himself with public health, welfare, and education. He was elected by the local Christian population, yet he and his fellow primates constituted in most cases a self-perpetuating and all-powerful oligarchy. The average peasant, voting by show of hand, was practically forced to accept the leadership of the local landowners, who dominated the community by virtue of their wealth, their influence with the Ottoman authorities, and their power as tax collectors. In most regions the primates formed a provincial aristocracy with an almost exclusive and hereditary control over local government. At best these primates strove to wrest concessions from the Turkish officials, to dissuade them from undesirable actions, and to raise the health and educational standards of their constituents. At worst they used their authority to exploit their fellow Christians, who bitterly referred to them as "Christian Turks."

In either case the primates, by virtue of their function as intermediaries between rulers and ruled, had no choice but to maintain good relations with the Turkish officials. Their very existence as a class required acceptance and, if necessary, support of Ottoman rule. Thus the primates throughout the peninsula usually were opposed to revolution unless they could see their way clear to a successful outcome and to the preservation of their position and interests.

Contemporary travelers frequently reported that the Balkan peasants complained openly that they suffered more from the exactions of their own primates and clergy than of the Turkish officials. One English traveler, for example, relates that he encountered "a saying common among the Greeks, that the country labours under three curses, the priests, the cogia bashis and the Turks; always placing the plagues in this order." [7] This point should not be exaggerated, but neither should it be ignored. Ottoman administration, with its extreme decentralization, created certain native vested interests that inevitably were committed to the *status quo*. Lord Broughton was so impressed by this factor when he journeyed through the Greek lands in 1810 that he concluded that a national uprising was out of the question.

Any general revolution of the Greeks, independent of foreign aid, is quite impracticable; for notwithstanding the great mass of the people, as is the case in all insurrections, has feeling and spirit enough to make the attempt, yet most of the higher classes, and all the clergy . . . are apparently willing to acquiesce in their present condition.

The Patriarch and Princess of the Fanal [Phanariotes] are at the devotion of the Porte. The primates of the towns and the richer merchants would be cautious not to move, unless they might be certain of benefiting by the change; and of this backwardness in the chiefs of their nation, the Greeks are by no means insensible. They talk of it publicly, and make it the subject of their satire, revenging themselves, as is their constant practice by a song. . . . "We have found a Metropolitan, and a Bey of Wallachia, and a Merchant and a Primate, all friends to tyranny." [8]

Lord Broughton's pessimistic conclusion concerning the likelihood of a Greek revolt was not borne out by the course of events. Nevertheless, his observations, like those of other contemporary travelers, suggest why the Balkan nationalist awakening took the varying forms that it did. Their evidence indicates that Balkan nationalism was a complex movement with centrifugal as well as centripetal forces operating within and among the various peoples.

INTERVENTION BY THE GREAT POWERS

Balkan history during the nineteenth century was determined not only by continued Ottoman decline and by burgeoning nationalisms, but also by the increasing intervention of the great powers. This intervention represents the final phase in the history of the relations between the Ottoman Empire and the rest of Europe. At first it was the Turks who intervened in Europe. It was they who crossed the Straits, conquered the Balkans, overran Hungary, and, on two occasions, threatened Vienna and the whole of Central Europe. Christendom's first reaction to this Turkish onslaught was fairly consistently hostile. The Turk was an infidel as well as an invader. Hence the futile crusades of the fourteenth and fifteenth centuries.

By the sixteenth century Christendom's unity against the Turk had ended. It was not by chance that Pope Pius II died brokenhearted in 1464 waiting at Ancona for a Christian army that never materialized. By this time Christian diplomacy had become too secularized to allow for crusades. The new nation-states placed dynastic and commercial considerations before religious ones. The outstanding example of this new attitude was the Turkish alliance concluded in 1536 by the "most Christian" king of France against "the apostolic majesty" Charles V of the Holy Roman Empire.

The early sixteenth century marked the transition from uncompromising enmity to realistic accommodation in the relations between the Ottoman Empire and Europe. Two centuries later we come to another turning point. The Treaty of Karlowitz of 1699 represented the end of the Turkish offensive and the beginning of the European counteroffensive. Never again was Europe threatened by the power which for almost three centuries had menaced its security. Instead, Europe now faced precisely the opposite problem. Ottoman power receded so rapidly that a political vacuum was created in the Near East. One of the basic problems of European diplomacy henceforth was how to fill this vacuum. It is significant that at the time of the Karlowitz Treaty the French ambassador in Constantinople wrote to Louis XIV, "Providence probably has decided the end of the Turks in Europe." The ambassador went on to warn his master that he "could not dispense with taking measures . . . to avoid being a mere spectator to the division which the other powers made among them of the debris of that [Ottoman] Empire." [9] Thus the powers were confronted with the so-called Near Eastern Question—a question that was to run through European diplomacy like a red thread until the end of World War I.

Austria and Russia were the first powers to take advantage of the Ottoman decline. By the end of the eighteenth century they had conquered the vast territories across the Danube and along the northern shore of the Black Sea. At this time Britain viewed the Russian advance with equanimity. Britain was then in the midst of her prolonged struggle with France and could give little attention to the possible implications of Russian expansion. Furthermore, Britain had vital commercial interests in Russia. Following the 1734 Anglo-Russian commercial treaty, trade between the two countries had increased to the point where the British controlled 52 per cent of the total volume of commerce at St. Petersburg. Also, Empress Catherine had issued a ukase permitting British merchants in Russia to tap the Persian market. And Russian timber was essential to British naval power, particularly after the loss of the American colonies. These considerations explain why Britain in 1769 not only permitted Catherine's fleet to enter the Mediterranean but even notified Paris and Madrid that any action against this fleet would be considered a hostile act against herself.

In the early nineteenth century this commercial and political situation changed and British policy changed with it. Anglo-Russian trade suffered from various artificial restrictions. Britain curtailed her imports from Russia when she adopted the Corn Law in 1815 and granted heavy preference to imperial timber. Meanwhile, the English Levant Company was expanding its commercial operations in the Near East by leaps and bounds. The only Turkish levies on foreign trade were a small anchorage fee and a 3 per cent ad valorem duty on imports. Also, French commercial competition in the Levant had become negligible because of the effects of the Revolutionary wars and Napoleon's Continental System. More important was the growing industrial supremacy of England as a result of the Industrial Revolution. By the late eighteenth century English cotton goods were flooding the markets of the entire world. The effect upon the commerce of the Levant is evident in the following figures on the value of British exports to the Ottoman Empire: 1783—£88,065; 1816—£256,802; 1825—£1,079,671; 1835—£2,706,591; 1845—£7,620,140. By 1850 Turkey was a better customer of the United Kingdom than Italy, France, Russia, or Austria.[10]

At the same time that the commercial relations between England and Russia declined in relative importance, the political relations between the two countries became increasingly strained. Various conflicts developed in the process of the readjustment of power relationships following the defeat of Napoleon. The most serious was the crisis over the fate of Poland. Apprehension also began to be felt in England concerning Russia's designs upon Turkey, Persia, and India. Articles and books appeared depicting the Turks in a more favorable light and raising the bogy of the Russian colossus.

This combination of economic and political factors explains Britain's shift from a pro-Russian to a pro-Turkish policy. The Foreign Office came to regard further Russian expansion in the Near East as incompatible with British imperial interests. Specifically it feared that Russian control of the Straits would endanger Britain's Levantine trade, her naval power in the Mediterranean, and her position in India. It might even upset the balance of power in the whole of Europe. Thus British diplomacy throughout the nineteenth century worked unceasingly to preserve the integrity of the Ottoman Empire.

Britain's *status quo* policy conflicted with the more dynamic aims of three other great powers that were particularly interested in the Balkans and the Near East in the early nineteenth century: Russia, France, and Austria. Of these three, Russia was the most persistent opponent of Britain. After her spectacular territorial gains under Catherine and Alexander, Russia was not likely to halt her advance abruptly at the Dniester. She made this clear in a note that she circularized at the Vienna Congress in February, 1815. The note, after calling attention to the Turkish atrocities in Serbia, stated that the emperor of Russia was "the natural protector of the Orthodox Greek Christians under Ottoman domination," [11] in the same manner that the Austrian and French sovereigns were natural protectors of the Catholic Christians. Consequently, the note concluded, Tsar Alexander is obliged by his religion and by the voice of conscience to go to the aid of the oppressed Serbian people.

The significance of this note is obvious. It gave Russia grounds for intervention in Ottoman affairs whenever she so wished. But when she did try to intervene she met the resolute opposition of Britain. It is an oversimplification, however, to assert that Russia invariably strove to dismember the sultan's domains. We shall see that in 1829 she halted her armies outside Constantinople and deliberately decided to accept the existence of the moribund Ottoman Empire. Likewise, in the eighteen thirties she cooperated with Britain in supporting the sultan against the overly ambitious Mehemet Ali of Egypt. Despite these exceptions it remains true that Russian diplomacy was generally anti-Turkish while British diplomacy was usually pro-Turkish. Hence the frequent crises and periodic wars of the nineteenth century.

France also was vitally interested in Balkan and Near Eastern affairs. At one time her influence in the Ottoman court had been unrivaled. In 1536 she was the first Christian power to conclude an alliance and a commercial agreement with the Turks. From then on her diplomats worked unceasingly to bolster the Ottoman Empire because it was to the advantage of France to have a strong Turkish ally on Austria's rear. Napoleon's erratic diplomacy, however, undermined French influence in Constantinople. Furthermore, defeated France was forced to yield both Malta and the Ionian Islands to Britain. Thus France's position in the Near East in 1815 was at an all-time low. It is not surprising that in the eighteen thirties she sought to advance her position by supporting the insurgent Mehemet Ali of Egypt against the Constantinople government. But this strategy failed in the face of combined Anglo-Russian opposition. During the following decades France usually ranged herself on the side of Britain. The explanation is not that the two powers had no differences. Rather it was that they had an overriding common interest in blocking Russian expansion. Thus Britain and France fought together against Russia during the Crimean War and continued to cooperate on most crucial issues until World War I.

The other major power interested in the Balkans in the early nineteenth century was Austria. After her great triumph in the Karlowitz settlement she alternated between two contradictory policies toward the ancient Turkish foe. Sometimes she attacked him as a weak neighbor ripe for partition. At other times she supported him as a useful bulwark against the menacing advance of Russia. During the eighteenth century Austria followed both these policies at various times. Then in 1815 she acquired Dalmatia and other former Venetian possessions, which made her the dominant power in the Adriatic and in the western Balkans. During the rest of the nineteenth century Austria usually was on the side of Britain supporting the *status quo* in the Near East. She feared that a major rearrangement would strengthen primarily Russia, whom she considered particularly dangerous because of the many Slavic subjects in the Hapsburg Empire who might be attracted by Russian national and religious propaganda.

In conclusion, these four powers—Britain, Russia, France, and Austria—were the most involved in Balkan affairs in the early nineteenth century. They determined to a considerable degree the course of events throughout the Near Eastern world. Their conflicting interests and policies explain in large part why the moribund Ottoman Empire was able to survive until World War I despite its miserable showing against the Greek revolutionaries and Mehemet Ali in the opening decades of the nineteenth century.

14. The Serbian Revolution and the South Slavs to 1878

U NTIL RECENT TIMES the South Slavs have been the forgotten people of Europe. As late as the first quarter of the nineteenth century ethnographic maps of the Balkans depicted the peninsula as being inhabited predominantly by Greeks or Turks. The Slavs were either ignored altogether or else confused with the Illyrians of antiquity. This obscurity arose in part from the location of the Slavs in the interior of the Balkans, where they lacked the contacts and the opportunities enjoyed by the Greeks to the south. An equally important factor was the lack of unity among the South Slavs from the time of their first appearance in the Balkans in the sixth century to World War I in the twentieth century. This disunity prevented the Slavs from assuming a role commensurate with their numerical predominance in the peninsula. In the medieval period Stephen Dushan failed to incorporate in his empire all the Serbian people, let alone the other South Slavs. The Turks overran most of the Slavic territories in the Balkans, but they were finally checked by the Hapsburgs and were unable to extend their frontiers to include Slovenia and western Croatia. During the following centuries the South Slavs were divided between the Hapsburg and Ottoman empires, with the Hapsburg portion becoming increasingly larger as the Turks progressively weakened.

The South Slavs were divided in cultural as well as political matters. The Croatians and the Slovenes belonged to the Western world, being Catholics and under the influence of the Germans and the Italians. The Serbians and the Bulgarians, on the other hand, belonged to the Eastern world because of their Orthodox faith and their Byzantine-Ottoman background. This cultural and political heterogeneity of the Balkan Slavs explains in large part why they lagged behind the other Slavic peoples of Europe in the tempo of their national awakening. It also explains why their awakening, once it began, was a many-stranded affair. There was no common nationalist movement or common uprising for independence. Instead, the various South Slav peoples went their several ways, reacting individually to the various environments in which they lived.

The Serbs of the Belgrade region were the first to win autonomy because of a favorable combination of circumstances. In order to place their movement in its proper perspective we will first survey the position of the other South Slavs—Slovenes, Croatians, and Serbians—who lived under Hapsburg and Turkish rule. The Bulgarians will not be considered in this chapter because to the present day they have developed along sufficiently distinct lines to require separate treatment.

SOUTH SLAVS UNDER FOREIGN RULE

As noted in Chapter 2, the Slavs appeared in the Balkan Peninsula in the sixth and seventh centuries of the Christian Era and settled in a fairly solid belt from the Adriatic to the Black seas. This wide geographic dispersal brought them under a variety of foreign influences, so that gradually they evolved into four distinct peoples, Slovenes, Croatians, Serbians, and Bulgarians. At the beginning of the nineteenth century they were all under foreign domination, with the exception of a handful of mountaineers in Montenegro and a few merchants and mariners in the Dalmatian city-republic of Ragusa or Dubrovnik.

Slovenia. The westernmost of the South Slavs are the Slovenes who settled at the head of the Adriatic in a great arc around the city of Trieste. This location explains the distinctive character of the Slovenian language which is related both to the Serbo-Croatian spoken further east and to the Slovak spoken in the north. Thus the Slovenian language constitutes a connecting link between the southern and northern Slavic languages, and the same may be said of Slovenian culture in general. The location of the Slovenes also affected their religious development. Unlike the other South Slavs, they were profoundly affected by the Reformation. But the Counterreformation brought them back to the fold of the Catholic Church, so that the Slovenes today are overwhelmingly Catholic. Finally, the location of the Slovenes brought them into conflict with the Germans who surrounded them in the north and west. Conflict was inevitable because the Slovenes occupied strategic territory which denied the great German ethnic bloc access to the Mediterranean. Thus the Slovenes soon fell under German domination and for many centuries were subjected to a strong process of Germanization.

The Slovenes first appeared in their present homeland in the sixth century. After waging a long struggle against the Avars they succumbed to the Germans at the end of the eighth century. In the course of the fourteenth and fifteenth centuries they came under Hapsburg domination. Thus the Slovenes were never able to establish an independent state organization, living continuously under foreign domination until the creation of Yugoslavia at the end of World War I. But German rule was not altogether negative. It presented the constant danger of assimilation, but it also conferred very real benefits. German rule was responsible for the fact that the Slovenes were far ahead of the other South Slavs in cultural development, technological skills, and economic progress. Also, the Slovenes enjoyed comparative security, never experiencing the devastation and wholesale depopulation suffered by the other South Slavs. It is significant that almost all villages in Slovenia are centuries old, whereas in the other South Slav lands many of the villages are of recent origin and numerous traces may be found of destroyed or deserted villages.

The social structure in Slovenia, as in the rest of the Hapsburg Empire, was of a feudal nature before 1848. The native ruling class had been eliminated as early as the tenth century, so the nobility was German. Slovenia, like other countries of Central Europe, experienced a series of peasant revolts between the fifteenth and seventeenth centuries. It should be noted, however, that feudalism in Slovenia was not as onerous as in the other South Slav regions. An important reason for this was the mountainous character of the land, which did not make large estates as profitable as in the plains areas. It is also noteworthy that until the middle of the nineteenth century the urban population was predominantly German while the countryside was almost exclusively Slovenian.

Croatia.   To the southeast of the Slovenes are the Croatians. They profess the same Catholic faith but their language is quite different, being identical with that of the Serbians. Linguists refer to a common Serbo-Croatian language, though the Croatians, it should be noted, use the Latin alphabet whereas the more easterly Serbians use the Cyrillic.

The Croatians differ from the Slovenes not only in language but also in historical background. The Slovenes never established an independent state, whereas the Croatians developed in the medieval period an extensive and powerful kingdom. For some time after their arrival in the Balkans in the seventh century the Croatians were loosely organized on a tribal basis. In the ninth century they were subjected for brief periods to the Frankish and Byzantine empires but early in the tenth century they succeeded in establishing an independent state. By the following century this state had grown to be a formidable power, extending from the Drava River in the north to the Adriatic Sea in the south and including most of the Dalmatian coast line.

In 1089 King Zvonimir died without leaving heirs, and the country then passed under the control of Ladislaus I of Hungary, whose sister had married into the Croatian royal family. The establishment of Hungarian rule had important economic and political consequences. The Croatian nobles, who had invited Hungarian intervention, were allowed to keep their lands and feudal privileges, including tax exemption. Thus the native nobility survived under foreign rule in contrast to the other South Slav peoples, who lost their respective ruling classes and eventually emerged as exclusively peasant nations. The Catholic Church was also a powerful feudal force with its vast estates and its bishops holding high state offices. Croatia was thus ruled by a

combination of temporal and spiritual lords who also exercised all the prerogatives of the state over their serfs.

Croatia's relationship with Hungary was that of a dependency. Autonomy was granted in domestic affairs, but the Hungarian monarch exercised
control over foreign affairs and war, and also appointed a governor or *ban*
to represent him in the Croatian capital of Agram or Zagreb. This union
lasted to 1918, though with continual changes in the constitutional relations
as each party strove to improve its position.

The Hungarians were not always able to protect their Croatian dependency from foreign invaders. As a result, important Croatian lands were
lost to neighboring powers. Venice, for example, coveted the Dalmatian
Coast and gradually acquired it by conquest and by purchase. Dalamatia
remained a Venetian possession until Venice herself fell victim to Napoleon
in 1797. More serious was the loss of Croatian territory to the Turks. The
latter won most of Hungary following their great victory at Mohacs in 1526.
The following year the Croatian nobility swore allegiance to the Hapsburg
ruler, Ferdinand I, who had been elected king of Hungary. This did not deter
the Turks, who rapidly overran Croatia until only the western tip of the
country remained to the Hapsburgs. Thus most of Croatia passed under
Turkish rule and remained there until the treaties of Karlowitz (1699) and
Passarowitz (Pozarevac) (1718) established Hapsburg sovereignty over the
country.

This Turkish interlude of almost two centuries had important repercussions. Croatia was left devastated and depopulated because it had served
as a buffer zone into which the Turks had conducted raids and from which
the Hapsburgs had defended the remainder of their empire. Also, the composition of the noble class changed following the Turkish occupation. The
Hapsburgs granted the recovered Croatian lands mostly to foreign nobles—
Austrians, Hungarians, and others. Hence Croatia was ruled from the seventeenth century onward by a predominantly foreign nobility and by the princes
of the church.

The overwhelming mass of the Croatian people remained in servitude
to this ruling group, though not without periodic outbursts. A series of
peasant revolts wracked Croatia as well as other countries of Central Europe
in the sixteenth century. The most serious was the uprising led by Mathias
Gubec in 1573. It affected Slovenia as well as Croatia, and the demands included freedom and equality for all classes and a just apportionment of taxes
and of military service. Gubec wished to establish a government in Zagreb
responsible directly to the Hapsburg emperor, whom the peasants regarded
as their protector against the feudal lords. The uprising was speedily and
ruthlessly crushed, over six thousand serfs being killed and many villages
destroyed. But other revolts broke out periodically, attesting to the deep-
seated discontent of the peasants and to the impact that Gubec had made
upon their minds. In popular legend Gubec had not died. Instead, he and
his followers had been saved by the mountains which had closed over them

to shield them from their enemies. And now they sat behind a stone table and drank red wine and would continue to do so until Gubec's beard grew long enough to wind nine times around the table. Then the mountains would open once more and Gubec would march forth with his army to free the serfs from their oppressors.

An attempt to improve the lot of the serfs was made by Maria Theresa (1740–1780) and her son Joseph II (1780–1790), the Hapsburg rulers who were influenced by the ideas of the Enlightenment. A decree issued in 1785 proclaimed the serfs personally free and allowed them to move when they wished, to marry without the permission of the lord, to go to school, and to dispose freely of their movable property. Although this decree did not give the land to the serfs, it was still too much for the feudal lords to accept. And since they wielded enormous power they were able in large part to ignore this reform and others. A certain improvement in the position of the serfs did occur in the second half of the eighteenth century. But the fact remains that at the beginning of the nineteenth century the Croatian people were living under far from enviable conditions. A predominantly alien nobility held them in feudal bondage while a foreign power kept their country in a dependent status.

The Voivodina. The Slovenes and Croatians were almost all under Hapsburg rule, but the Serbians were much more divided. Some Serbians lived under the scepter of the Hapsburgs in southern Hungary. Others were in Bosnia-Herzegovina, where they were subject to the Turks until 1878, when these two provinces passed under Hapsburg control. Still others were to be found in the independent Montenegrin enclave within the Ottoman Empire. The remainder lived under direct Turkish rule to the south of the Danube. Each of these groups will be considered in turn.

The Serbs of southern Hungary lived between the Theiss and the Danube rivers, an area known as the Voivodina or Duchy. Most of them migrated to this region after the Hapsburgs recovered it during the campaigns of the late seventeenth century. Emperor Leopold I found the countryside almost depopulated by the years of warfare and adopted a systematic colonization policy. He preferred to keep the intractable Hungarians out of this strategic frontier territory, so he sent, instead, many German colonists who laid the basis for the large German minority that was to be found there until World War II. Leopold also encouraged the Serbians under Turkish rule to cross the Danube and some thirty thousand did migrate in 1690 under their patriarch. Leopold issued imperial charters on August 21, 1690, and August 20, 1691, assuring the immigrants full recognition as a nation and granting them freedom to practice their religion and customs and to control their own administration.

These privileges were not respected for long. The Jesuits were ill-disposed toward the Orthodox Serbs and used their influence at the imperial court against them. Also, the Magyars gradually gained control over the Voivodina and utilized their authority to try to Magyarize the Serbians. In the end, Leopold's charters became virtually dead letters and the Serbs were left with only an autonomous church organization.

The Serbs counterbalanced this setback with notable economic gains in the late eighteenth and early nineteenth centuries. Commerce expanded rapidly during those decades and the Serbs took advantage of the opportunity to gain control of most of the trade of southern Hungary. A new class of merchants appeared who had the same dynamic effect upon Serbian society as the Greek merchants at the same time were exercising in the Greek world. The city of Karlowitz (Sremski Karlovci) in the Voivodina became the true center of Serbian culture, extending its influence across the Danube to the lands still subject to the Turks. The first Serbian books and newspapers came from the wealthy and progressive Serbian communities in Karlowitz, Buda, and Vienna. When the Serbs of the Belgrade area rose in revolt in 1804 they received vital assistance from their brethren in the Voivodina, including money, volunteers, and trained officers and administrators. The significance of the Voivodina for the Serbian people is well summarized in a popular saying: "Montenegro with its doughty warriors saved the Serbians from despair; the Voivodina with its schools and presses saved them from ignorance."

Bosnia-Herzegovina. The distinguishing characteristic of Bosnia-Herzegovina, or Bosnia, as it is commonly called for convenience, is that it is a border area. Just as Alsace-Lorraine is the transition zone between the German and French ethnic blocs, so Bosnia is the transition zone between the Serbian and Croatian peoples and the Orthodox and Catholic religions. In addition, there is present a strong infusion of Islam dating from the period of the Turkish conquest. This ethnic and religious diversity explains much of the stormy history of the area, corresponding to the turbulent past of Alsace-Lorraine.

Bosnia began its independent statehood in the second half of the twelfth century. It expanded rapidly, acquiring lands from both the Serbians in the east and the Croatians in the west. Despite its imposing size, Bosnia from the beginning was afflicted with fatal weaknesses. One was the centrifugal effect of the turbulent nobility, who wielded inordinate power and left the central authority helpless and ineffectual. Another weakness was the lack of a common faith to bind the state together. Instead, there were the rival Orthodox and Catholic churches as well as the widespread Bogomil heresy. The latter emerged as a protest against the worldliness of the two churches and against the social injustices of the period. The political influence of Bogomilism was definitely disruptive, partly because of its uncompromising feud with the two churches and also because of its loose hierarchical organization, its otherworldliness, and its pacifism. Thus Bogomilism, as we noted in Chapter 4, contributed substantially to the collapse of the Bosnian state before the Turkish invaders in the fifteenth century.

Many Bosnian Bogomils, both nobles and serfs, became Moslems after the Turkish conquest. They had been persecuted by the Orthodox and

Catholic hierarchies and not unnaturally they now embraced Islam. Also, there were practical considerations. The feudal lord who became Moslem could keep at least some of his former lands and privileges, while the serf who accepted Islam became a free peasant. Thus the Moslem conquerors made more converts in Bosnia than in any other part of the Balkans. The population remains today almost one-third Moslem.

The beginning of the nineteenth century found Bosnia in the grip of a small group of Moslem feudal lords or beys. These proud nobles tolerated no interference from Constantinople. They did not permit the Turkish governor to reside in the Bosnian capital of Sarajevo, forcing him instead to live in the little town of Travnik. All the Christian peasants and a few of the Moslem ones were serfs, completely at the mercy of the beys. This feudal system represented a degeneration of the original arrangements made by the Turkish conquerors in the fifteenth century. At that time fiefs were granted in return for stipulated service of a military or administrative character. The fiefs were not hereditary and reverted to the central government if the required service was not forthcoming. Also, the peasants on the fiefs were protected by law. Their obligations were carefully defined and they had hereditary use of their plots so long as they tilled them and paid the stipulated dues.

This system worked well so long as the central government was able and willing to enforce it. From the seventeenth century onward the government was too weak to do so. The result was a complete transformation of Bosnian feudalism. A largely new nobility appeared, consisting of powerful officials, tax farmers, or miscellaneous adventurers, many of them former janissaries or spahis who had been chased out of Hungary and Croatia by the advancing Hapsburg armies. These individuals took advantage of the governmental breakdown in Bosnia to acquire fiefs in one manner or another. More important, they converted the former fiefs into private estates or agaliks, which meant that the peasants lost their former security and protection. The new beys increased the dues at will, maltreated their peasants if they wished, and even ousted them from the land which they had cultivated for generations. In short, the peasants had sunk to the status of serfs.

This development was not peculiar to Bosnia. We shall see that, with local variations, the same trend occurred in Serbia, Bulgaria, and Greece. In the latter areas the new private estates that were formed were known as chifliks rather than agaliks. A more significant difference was that the chiflik owners in the rest of the Balkans were mostly Moslem Turks, whereas the beys of Bosnia were mostly Moslem Slavs. This division of the Bosnian Slavs into a ruling Moslem class and a subject Christian mass explains in large part the slow development of a national movement in Bosnia. Another important factor was the division between the Orthodox Serbs and the Catholic Croats, the former outnumbering the latter by two to one.

The Bosnian beys were able to rule their province for centuries without serious challenge. They had the active support of the predominantly free Moslem peasantry, which constituted almost a third of the total population.

They could also count on religious-national rivalries to keep the remaining two thirds of the population divided. It was not until the masterful Sultan Mahmud II came to the throne that the beys finally were brought to order in the 1830's. And the beginning of the end became apparent at the turn of the century when Serbs and Croats began to identify themselves with the concept of an all-embracing Yugoslav nationalism.

Montenegro. The Montenegrins are a Serbian people whose country formed a part of the medieval Serbian Empire. When that empire fell to the Turks in 1389 the Montenegrins thereafter went their own way. In 1499 the Turks overran much of their country, retaining control of the towns, plains, and communication lines. At the same time the Venetians pressed in from the coast line, occupying the Kotor (or Cattaro) inlet and cutting off Montenegro from the sea. The Montenegrins now were hemmed in in their mountain fastnesses, where they were left pretty much to their own devices. Their country was so hopelessly poor that it was not worth while for the Turks to make the effort necessary to establish and maintain effective control.

In 1515 the bishop of Cetinje, under the title prince-bishop, established a theocracy which lasted over three centuries. The prince-bishop was elected from among the monks of the Cetinje monastery by the clergy and the populace. During the reign of Danilo Petrovich in the early eighteenth century the princely office was made hereditary in his family. This arrangement of a hereditary prince-bishop was continued until 1851, when the incumbent established himself as a secular ruler with the title Prince Danilo I. In the meantime an important treaty was concluded with Sultan Selim III in 1799 establishing the full independence of Montenegro.

Behind this façade of political and diplomatic developments Montenegro remained a loose association of tribes organized along patriarchal lines. The economy was utterly primitive. According to a rough census taken in 1855 the population was 80,000 and the arable land amounted to only one fourth of one hectare per person. The "national wealth" consisted mostly of livestock: 315,780 head of sheep and goats, 37,730 head of cattle, 6,000 pigs, 3,200 horses, and 19,300 beehives. The chief occupation, naturally, was animal husbandry. In fact, it was beneath the dignity of a Montenegrin male to do anything else than tend to his flocks and bear arms. The latter he did with relish and with skill born of constant practice. Other Serbians acknowledged that it was the Montenegrins that kept them from despair during the centuries of subjugation by keeping alight the fire of resistance. Even after the winning of independence Montenegro was in the forefront during the nineteenth-century wars against the Ottoman Empire. The role of Montenegro in South Slav and general Balkan affairs has been quite out of proportion to her ridiculously meager material resources.

Serbia. The Serbians living in Montenegro, Bosnia-Herzegovina, and the Voivodina represented the fringe of the Serbian ethnic bloc. The main body of the Serbian people was to be found in Serbia proper, the area to the south of the Danube and between Montenegro and Bosnia in the west and Bulgaria in the east. All this territory was an integral part of the Ottoman Empire and had been so since the fourteenth century. Turkish rule had long since become inefficient and corrupt, a heavy drag on any progress. This explains in part the fact that the Serbs to the south of the Danube lagged far behind their brothers under Hapsburg rule in cultural and economic attainments. On the other hand, they did enjoy certain advantages. The Turks were decadent but they were also feeble. A revolt against them had some chance for success. Against the more progressive and more efficient Hapsburgs there was no hope whatsoever. Thus it was the comparatively backward Turkish-ruled Serbs who first gained their freedom and who developed the nucleus for the Yugoslav state of the future. We will now consider the position of these Serbs in the Ottoman administrative system and the circumstances leading to their insurrection in 1804.

BELGRADE PASHALIK UNDER TURKISH RULE

The Belgrade pashalik, which was to become the core of the future Serbian state, comprised roughly the area bounded by the Danube and Sava rivers in the north, the Drina River in the west, and Bulgaria in the east. Its inhabitants were engaged mostly in raising livestock, particularly pigs, which grazed freely in the vast oak forests that covered much of the country. The livestock was marketed "on the hoof" across the Danube in the Hapsburg Empire. The pig trade alone brought about 130,000 pounds annually during the years around 1800. It is interesting to note that the two outstanding leaders of the Serbian revolution, Karageorge and Milosh Obrenovich, were both engaged in this trade. If an upper class may be said to have existed in the pashalik at this time it consisted of these enterprising pig dealers. Agriculture was definitely subsidiary to animal husbandry. Maize and wheat were grown in small clearings in the forest, but only enough to satisfy local needs. In fact, in some years grain had to be imported from the Hungarian plains.

The social organization of the Serbian peasantry was based on the zadruga or extended family group. This has been well defined by Professor Philip E. Mosely as "a household composed of two or more biological or small families closely related by blood or adoption, owning its means of production communally, producing and consuming its means of livelihood jointly, and regulating the control of its property, labor, and livelihood communally." [1] The zadruga flourished during these years for various reasons. It made possible more efficient production through division of labor. It afforded greater personal and economic security in turbulent periods. Also, it could meet with a minimum of disruption the frequent demands for labor from landlords and public officials. Thus the zadruga was an ideal form of social organization for an economic order in which the market and the use of money were of incidental importance. We shall see that it became an anachronism in later years when independence had been won, when order and security had been established, and when a money economy had replaced the earlier natural economy.

Turkish administration in the pashalik was headed by the sultan's representative, the pasha, who sat in Belgrade. Moslem judges or cadis resided in the towns and ruled on legal issues involving Moslem disputants. Janissary detachments were stationed in fortified places to defend the pashalik, which was situated on the northern frontier of the empire. Finally, there were about nine hundred spahis or feudal cavalrymen who held most of the arable land in the form of fiefs. The spahis did not actually own the land but were authorized to collect certain specified revenues from their fiefs.

The obligations of the Serbian peasant to his Turkish overlords were not onerous. To the spahi he paid one tenth of his grain crop, certain labor services, a head tax for each adult male in the family, and miscellaneous levies on watermills, orchards, vineyards, beehives, and the like. These revenues were collected by the spahi's agent, since the spahi almost invariably lived in Belgrade or some other town. The peasant also paid taxes to the sultan's treasury, the most important being the harach, a small levy on all male non-Moslems between seven and sixty years of age. This and other imperial taxes were collected with minimum friction by local village headmen, who transmitted the proceeds to the Turkish authorities.

The Turkish administrative system was based on the principle of indirect rule. In normal times it functioned satisfactorily. There was very little contact between the Serbian subjects and the Turkish officials. The towns were the centers of alien authority and consisted mostly of officials and soldiers who were Turks, and merchants and craftsmen who were mostly Turks, Greeks, and Jews. The countryside was purely Serbian and it had a well-developed system of local self-government. Each village elected a knez or lord, and each district an oborknez or grand knez. These leaders assessed and collected government taxes and exercised police and judicial functions of a local nature. The relations between the spahis and the peasants were normally harmonious. The dues that could be collected were regulated by law. Furthermore, the peasants were free to move so that the spahis found it expedient to treat them fairly.

Turkish rule as described above was far from burdensome. The Serbian peasants accepted it for centuries without serious questioning or opposition. When they rose in revolt in 1804 they did so not because of this governmental system but rather because of its disintegration. The imperial government had become so ineffectual that it was unable to supervise the administration of distant provinces, and anarchy and terrorism spread through the Belgrade pashalik. At the same time certain intellectual developments were broadening the horizon of at least a few Serbian leaders and making them disaffected with the deteriorating *status quo*. We shall now consider in turn the intellectual awakening and the administrative disintegration.

INTELLECTUAL AWAKENING

During the eighteenth century the Serbian world was transformed from an essentially theocratic community to one motivated by secular considerations and guided by secular leaders. The roots of this change go back to an earlier period when church and state were synonymous. In 1459 the Turks destroyed the medieval Serbian Empire and abolished the Serbian patriarchate located at Ipek (Pec). Almost a century later, in 1557, the famous grand vizir, Mohammed Sokolovich (Sokolli), a Serb by birth, used his influence to restore the patriarchate. During the following centuries this institution assumed the functions of the former Serbian government. It had its own law courts and administrative system. When the occasion arose, it conducted foreign policy and even provided military leadership. This was the case at the end of the seventeenth century when the Hapsburg armies had penetrated deeply into the Balkans. The Serbian patriarch, Arsenije III, responded by calling on all Christians to rise against the Moslem overlord. When the Austrians finally were defeated the same patriarch led his people in mass migration across the Danube.

Until the beginning of the eighteenth century the Serbian church was in fact the Serbian state. But by the end of the century it had lost its position of primacy. The explanation is to be found partly in certain divisive rivalries within the church and partly in the impact of Western secular thought upon Serbian intellectuals.

Two Serbian ecclesiastical centers existed following the migration to southern Hungary. One was the patriarchate whose seat still remained at Ipek (Pec) and the other was the metropolitanate, which was established at Karlowitz in 1713. Both of these centers declined in prestige and effectiveness during the course of the century. The Ipek patriarchate was abolished by the sultan in 1766 upon the urging of the Patriarch of Constantinople. The latter assumed direct jurisdiction over the Serbian dioceses and replaced the Serbian hierarchy with a predominantly Greek one. The change was strongly disliked by the Serbs, and the church thus lost its position as the accepted and unchallenged representative of the nation. Meanwhile, the Karlowitz metropolitanate had also fallen upon evil days. Factions within the institution fought bitterly against each other, and corruption and immorality were all too evident.

At the same time that the Serbian church was decaying the ideas of the Enlightenment were spreading among the Serbs of Austria. Students were beginning to turn away from the Orthodox schools of Russia and the Catholic institutions of Austria and to go instead to Protestant schools in Hungary and Germany. Most of them returned with the conviction that the future of their people rested with rationalism and the West rather than Orthodoxy and the East. They pointed to the imperfections of the Serbian church on both sides of the Danube to support their contention that national interest required the end of church domination and eventually the separation of church and state.

The outstanding exponents of this new secularism were Dimitrije Obradovich and Vuk Karajich, the two great leaders of the Serbian intellectual and literary renaissance. Obradovich was born in 1743 in the part of the Banat of Temesvar that is now Rumanian. As a boy he had a passion for reading, but he could find nothing written in his own language. At this time the Serbians had no newspapers and no literature of any sort in their spoken language. Only ecclesiastical literature in the artificial Church Slavonic was available. Obradovich devoured all that he could find, particularly the colorful lives of saints. These had the same effect upon him as dime novels had on American boys in the nineteenth century. Just as American lads ran away from home to fight Indians so Obradovich decided to become a saint like the heroes in his storybooks. He ran off to a monastery where he became a monk and stayed for three years. By the end of that time he had read and reread the monastery's meager stock of books. He became restless and in 1760 he set forth on travels that were to take him to all parts of Europe.

Obradovich lived many years in Germany and traveled widely in England, France, Russia and the Balkans. His observations and experiences turned him away from his earlier clerical ideals. From a Serbian monk with an intellectual outlook that was essentially Byzantine he became a man of the world and an enthusiastic champion of the current rationalism and enlightenment. He now found it intolerable that his own Serbian people should have no literature in their own language. So he proceeded to meet the need by creating both a modern Serbian literary language and a modern Serbian literature. His great contribution to the Serbian renaissance is that he was the first to write on secular topics in the unaffected spoken language of his countrymen. He narrated his own adventures, he expounded his new secular ideas, and he translated and adapted works from other languages. His purpose at all times was didactic. "Being a rational man," he wrote, "I have a God-given and natural authority to communicate my thoughts to my fellow men and to tell them whatever good and sensible things I have heard and learned from others." [2] The following passages from his works show that what Obradovich considered to be "good and sensible" was in reality intellectual dynamite for the clerical world from which he had originally emerged.

> I have learned to think and pass judgment in a better and more rational manner on my religious beliefs and my faith. The books of learned men have given me the means to distinguish orthodoxy from superstition and the pure teaching of the Gospels from all manner of human traditions and additions. . . . I am no longer deceived by any gay colors, by gilding and by external glitter: I recognize what is true and internal reverence and piety and what are external customs, ritual and ceremonies. . . .
>
> You ask me why I have rebelled against fasts, long prayers, and the great number of holidays; and wherein they offend me and make me take up arms against them. Read the Holy Gospel and you will see that the same things

offended our Savior, so that he cried out against them and on that account re-
buked the Pharisees, saying: "Woe unto you, scribes and Pharisees, hypocrites
who by fasting make pale and sad your faces and pray in the streets and byways,
that men may see you." The abuses that were committed in those times by those
acts are committed also today; and whoever receives, recognizes, and loves the
teaching of Christ must hate all that Christ hated and against which he cried out.
I have spent twenty-five years with various peoples of our faith in Greece, Albania, Bosnia, Herzegovina, Moldavia, and other regions: practically the entire
population are conscious of being Christians of the Eastern Church only through
its fasts and its holidays. And how do they fast? Ah, my brethren, God sees and
hears all things: we must tell the truth! No one fasts except such as are extremely
poor, people who live on sterile soil and who during several months of the year
would think that they sat at royal tables if they merely had bread of wheat or of
maize. These poor people fast the greater part of their lives, but by grim necessity.
But those who have various fasting foods, as we term them, including olive oil
and wine, never fast at any time whatever. (You should know that I do not
regard it as fasting when a man has no dinner but at supper eats enough for
both dinner and supper, nor when a man eats no meat but stuffs himself with
beans and sauerkraut till his belly rumbles and sweat comes out on his brow. . . .

Let us cast a brief glance at the enlightened nations of all Europe. At
the present time every one of those nations is striving to perfect its own dialect. This is
a very useful object, seeing that when learned men write their thoughts in the
general language of the whole nation, then the enlightenment of the intellect and
the light of learning are not confined to persons who understand the old literary
language, but are spread abroad and reach even the villagers, being taught to the
humblest peasants and to the shepherds, provided only that they know how to
read. And how easy it is to teach a child how to read his own language. . . .
I am aware that someone may reply to me that if we begin to write in the common dialect the old language will be neglected and will gradually disappear. I
answer: "What profit have we from a language which, taking our nation as a
whole, not one person in ten thousand understands properly and which is foreign
to my mother and my sisters?" . . . "Then let them learn it!" you may object.
That is easier said than done. How many people have the time and means to
learn the old literary language? Very few! But everybody knows the general,
common dialect; and in it all who can read may enlighten their minds, improve
their hearts, and adorn their manners. A language derives its value from the good
that it does. And what language can do more good than the general language of
the whole nation? The French and the Italians had no fears that the Latin language would perish if they began to write their own languages, and indeed it has
not perished. Nor will our old language perish because the learned men of our
nation will always know it. . . .[3]

Vuk Karajich continued the work begun by Obradovich. He was
born in 1787 in a small Serbian village near the Bosnian frontier. He was
able to get some education, and during the revolution that began in 1804 he
served as secretary to the illiterate Serbian commander of his district. When
the Turks temporarily reconquered the country he fled to Vienna. There he
met the young Slovene scholar Bartolomeus Kopitar, who encouraged him to

collect and study Serbian popular poetry and stories. His first collection published in 1814 was received enthusiastically in the West, where the Romantic movement then was at its height. Ten years later Karajich published a greatly enlarged edition in four volumes.

The purity of language and classic turn of phrase which Karajich found in the songs of the people impressed him profoundly. By this time he was an accomplished linguist, so he resolved to use his training to elevate the vernacular to the position of a literary language in place of the artificial ecclesiastical language. To this end he introduced phonetic reforms into the old Cyrillic alphabet, published his famous Serbian dictionary and grammar, selected the Herzegovinian dialect as the purest form of the Serbo-Croat language, and molded that dialect into the literary language of the Serbo-Croat people. His reforms, like those of Obradovich, were violently opposed by the church leaders, who feared that they endangered the national culture and religious character of the Serbian people. For some time his orthography was actually forbidden in Serbia and his works were not allowed to circulate. But before his death in 1864 he had won the support of the younger generation and his ideas had completely triumphed. Today, thanks to Karajich, the literary language of the Serbo-Croats probably is as close to the popular speech as that of any people in the world.

Obradovich and Karajich by no means thought alike. Obradovich was a rationalist and a cosmopolitan who wished to civilize his nation by spreading the ideas of the Enlightenment. Karajich was a Romantic and a nationalist who was interested primarily in the customs and folk literature of his people and who wished Serbia to develop independently of the West. Yet both were opposed to the church domination of the past. Both were on the same side on the basic issue of theocracy or secular nationalism. In fact, Karajich contributed enormously to the eventual political union of the Serbian and Croatian people by creating an acceptable Serbo-Croat literary language. And Obradovich specifically rejected religious distinctions for the concept of not merely Serbian but Yugoslav nationalism.

Who is ignorant of the fact that the inhabitants of Montenegro, Dalmatia, Herzegovina, Bosnia, Serbia, Croatia, Slavonia, Srem, Bačka, and the Banat (except for Rumanians), all speak the same language?

When I write of these peoples who live in these kingdoms and provinces, I mean the members both of the Greek and of the Latin Church, and do not exclude even the Turks [Moslems] of Bosnia and Herzegovina, inasmuch as religion and faith can be changed, but race and language can never be. . . . My book will be intended for every person who understands our language and who with a pure and honest heart desires to enlighten his mind and to improve his character. I shall pay no heed whatever to what religion and faith any man belongs, nor is that a matter for consideration in the present enlightened age.[4]

ROOTS OF REVOLT

The intellectual revolution among the Serbs was confined largely to those who lived in the Hapsburg Empire. For example, Obradovich was born in the Banat, and Karajich, although born in Serbia, spent most of his life in Vienna, where he won international fame as a scholar. However, Karajich's relatives had little appreciation of what he was accomplishing. The gulf between the Serbians on the two sides of the Danube is reflected in a letter which Karajich received in 1816 from his home village. He was informed that freedom from the Turks had brought economic prosperity and that one could make a comfortable living running a store or a tavern. "Our Obrad has come far selling liquor—you should look into his pocketbook! And Amidja wants to do the same as soon as he finishes the house. And you left for gay Vienna to waste your time. See that you finish those books as soon as you can. People are asking about them. And then come here to live." [5]

Nevertheless, it was these Serbs with such a limited horizon who first won freedom from foreign rule. And the reason was that they were driven to revolt by the breakdown of Ottoman administration. One manifestation of this breakdown was the rise of chifliks or private estates in place of the former fiefs. As imperial authority weakened, the spahis began to treat their fiefs as chifliks or to acquire chifliks in various illegal ways. As in the case of the agaliks in Bosnia, these chifliks worsened drastically the position of the Christian peasantry. No longer did they have the right to till a hereditary plot so long as they paid a defined and customary tithe. Now their obligations were sharply and arbitrarily increased and they had no choice but to pay or surrender their plots. Thus a major grievance of the Serbian peasantry was this chiflik system, which became particularly widespread in the late eighteenth century.

Another grievance which also derived from the decline of imperial authority was the lawlessness of the janissaries. These undisciplined troops were a curse for everyone in the pashalik, Serbs and Turks alike. They defied the pasha and victimized even the spahis, forcefully seizing their fiefs and converting them into personal chifliks. Partly because of this abuse many Serbs joined the Austrians when they penetrated into the Balkans during the war that began in 1788. But domestic complications and the specter of revolution in France caused the Austrians to accept the Sistova Treaty in 1791 and to withdraw beyond the Danube. The treaty did contain two provisions designed to protect the Serbians from reprisals. The janissaries were to be expelled from the Belgrade pashalik and the Serbian rebels were to be granted a general amnesty. These terms were strictly observed. The sultan was the reformer Selim III, who was continually at odds with the janissaries and who appointed enlightened pashas with instructions to enforce the treaty provisions.

One of these pashas, Hadji Mustafa, governed the pashalik so reasonably and benevolently that he was called "Mother of the Serbs." But his ultimate fate is revealing of the conditions then prevailing in the Ottoman Empire. Mustafa's predecessor had expelled the janissaries from the pashalik, forcing them to seek asylum with Pasvan-Oglu, the rebellious and separatist-minded pasha of Vidin. From there they conducted periodic forays against the Belgrade pashalik. Mustafa boldly armed the Serbians, allowed them to form voluntary corps under their own leaders, and with their support defeated Pasvan-Oglu and the janissaries in 1798. The spectacle of Christians routing Moslems with the approval of an Ottoman pasha shocked many Turks. Mustafa was ordered the following year to allow the janissaries to return to his pashalik.

This proved to be the beginning of the end for Mustafa, whose efforts to keep the janissaries in check were without success. In 1801 he was forced to send his Serbian levies once more against Pasvan-Oglu. The janissaries took advantage of their absence to attack Mustafa in the citadel and slay him before the Serbians could return. To Constantinople they reported, "Hadji Mustafa was a dog who sided with the rayas against true believers. He has received his just reward." [6]

The janissaries now were the masters of the pashalik. They instituted a reign of terror, plundering Turkish spahis as mercilessly as Serbian peasants. The spahis finally took up arms but they received little support from the Serbs and were brutally suppressed. The Serbians in desperation appealed to the sultan for relief. Selim responded by sending a sharp rebuke to the janissaries and warning them that he might send against them "an army not of your faith." The janissaries concluded that the threat referred to the Serbian levies used so effectively by Mustafa. So they began a preventive massacre of Serbian leaders or knezes.

Within a few days the heads of seventy-two victims graced the citadel walls at Belgrade. One of the knezes who was able to escape the roving bands of assassins was George Petrovich, known as Karageorge or Black George because of his swarthy complexion. A gigantic man, utterly fearless, and an outstanding leader, he quickly became the head of a desperate struggle for survival. As a prosperous hog dealer he appealed to the propertied elements, and as a former haiduk he attracted the traditionally anti-Turkish outlaws. Also, he had fought for the Austrians in the preceding war and had gained valuable experience which, combined with his great natural talents, made him a military commander of the first order.

The uprising was to prevail not only because of the qualities of its leader but also because it was supported by all segments of the Serbian population. The peasants wished to be rid of the oppressive chiflik system, while the more substantial elements—the priests, the knezes, and the pig dealers—were goaded on by the intolerable excesses of the janissaries. None of these groups was motivated at the outset by abstract ideals of independence and national unity. None took up arms against the rule of the sultan in Constantinople. Rather, they fought against those troublemakers who were flouting the sultan's authority and spreading disorder in the imperial administration. The Serbs wanted not a new order but a return to the old order of Hadji Mustafa. In this sense the Serbian insurrection of 1804 began as a fundamentally different movement from the Greek War of Independence of 1821.

COURSE OF THE REVOLT: 1804–1813

The Serbian revolt was characterized by unity in aim and diversity in method. Haiduk chiefs, village knezes, and warlike priests led their individual bands and pursued their own local objects. Karageorge operated in the central and wealthy Shumadia district. He had more followers and disposed of more money and arms than the other leaders. This advantage, together with his forceful personality and initial victories, enabled him to pull together what was essentially a scattered guerrilla movement.

The fighting began in February, 1804. Karageorge and the other leaders first attacked and overran small Turkish outposts. By the end of April they had forced the enemy into a few strong fortresses and begun regular siege operations. The surprised and outnumbered janissaries now sought a settlement and asked for the mediation of the Austrian commander at the frontier. A conference was held on May 10, 1804, in the Austrian border town of Semlin (Zemun). The Serbians professed their loyalty to the sultan but they also rejected mere promises of better treatment in the future. They insisted on guarantees, demanding that they should retain their arms and that the janissaries should be permanently expelled. These conditions were not acceptable and the conference broke up.

The Serbians had been receiving appreciable aid from the outside, particularly from their brothers across the Danube. At Semlin sixty workers were busy turning out munitions for the cause. The Serbian bishop of Novi Sad in south Hungary contributed a small cannon which proved very effective against the fortresses. Also, Serbian officers in the Austrian army deserted their posts and returned to their homeland in droves. It was on the advice of one of these officers that a delegation was sent to St. Petersburg in September, 1804, to secure Russian aid.

The Serbian deputies found Tsar Alexander ambivalent because of the conflicting pressures of the international situation. He had no dispute with Turkey at this time; instead, he was concerned about the danger of French expansion from Italy to the Balkans. Accordingly, he preferred that the sultan should not be weakened and that the Serbs should be reconciled to their sovereign as soon as possible. On the other hand, the tsar feared that if he rejected the Serbs altogether they might turn to France or Austria. This explains the equivocal advice that the Serbians received. They were warned to be "discreet and prudent" and to reach a peaceful settlement because Russian intervention was most improbable. But they were offered arms and officers and were promised diplomatic support in Constantinople.

Karageorge responded by sending a mission to the Ottoman capital.

It proved abortive because the sultan had already decided against concessions. He had tolerated the Serbian uprising so long as it was directed exclusively against the janissaries. But now the Serbians were demanding virtual autonomy and this the sultan refused to consider. The mufti in Constantinople issued a fetva proclaiming the Serbians enemies of all Moslems and a veritable Holy War was declared.

During the critical campaigns that followed, Karageorge demonstrated his talent as a strategist as well as a guerrilla leader. He depended on the local chiefs to harass the enemy on the advanced borders while he kept a strong reserve force in the center of Shumadia under his personal command. Thus he was able to reinforce any threatened point and to maintain a general control over operations. In 1805 he repulsed a Turkish army advancing up the Morava Valley from Nish. The next year he dispersed three armies attacking from the south, east, and west. In December, 1806, he captured Belgrade itself and by June, 1807, the last Turkish fortress in northern Serbia had fallen.

Meanwhile the international situation had changed drastically and had affected directly the Serbian cause. Sultan Selim had decided late in 1806 to throw in his lot with Napoleon. Immediately he was attacked on land by Russia and on sea by Britain. Selim naturally wished to be rid of the Serbian distraction, especially since the campaign had gone so badly. He offered to meet the Serbian demands, amounting to virtual autonomy for the principality. But at the same time the Russians also made advances to the Serbs, offering them money, arms, and close cooperation if they would continue fighting against the Turks. Thus the Serbian revolt became part and parcel of the great diplomatic and military struggle between Napoleon and the Allies for the control of Europe.

Karageorge had to choose between autonomy under the sultan and cooperation with the tsar. He chose the latter and signed an alliance with Russia on July 10, 1807. Serbian troops were to fight with the Russians, and in return Karageorge was to receive money, arms, and military, medical, and administrative missions.* This decision proved to be a turning point in the course of the Serbian revolt. By rejecting the offer of autonomy and concluding an alliance with Russia, the Serbs had converted what had begun as a protest against janissary oppression into a full-fledged war for independence. The Russian alliance was a turning point for another reason. International developments led Tsar Alexander to reverse his diplomatic policy and to desert his new Serbian allies, with ultimately disastrous results for them. In fact, three days before the Serbian-Russian alliance was signed Alexander had executed a sudden about-face and concluded the Tilsit Treaty, which temporarily resolved his differences with Napoleon. The tsar then withdrew his troops from Serbia and reached an armistice with Turkey on August 24,

* See Chapter 12.

1807. He attempted to include Serbia in the armistice agreement but the Turks flatly refused. Thus the Serbs were left alone to face the Turks, whose sizable armies were freed from the Russian front.

Karageorge desperately sought assistance from other quarters. He even went so far as to offer incorporation of the Belgrade pashalik into the Hapsburg Empire in return for Austrian aid. But the Vienna government was too greatly committed elsewhere to risk such involvement in the Balkan Peninsula. Karageorge also sent a letter to Paris on August 16, 1809, asking for the "powerful protection of the Great Napoleon" and assuring him that all the South Slavs were ready to follow his lead.[7] But Napoleon refused to make any move that might endanger his relations with Turkey.

Fortunately for the Serbians, the Turkish-Russian armistice did not lead to peace. The Turks refused to accept the Russian territorial demands and the war was renewed. But finally on May 28, 1812, the tsar hastily signed the Bucharest Treaty with the sultan in order to face the impending invasion by Napoleon's Grand Army. The tsar again made a gesture in behalf of his Serbian allies by inserting a clause calling for autonomy and "full amnesty." But these paper provisions proved worthless. While the Russians were engrossed in their great struggle against the French invaders, the Turks concentrated their armies in a three-pronged attack against the Serbians. This time Karageorge failed to rise to the occasion. At the height of the campaign he suddenly left his comrades and fled over the Danube. Apparently the strain of years of fighting together with the prospect of ultimate disaster proved too much even for his spirit. By the close of 1813 the Turks had reoccupied Belgrade and gained control of the entire country. In a war lasting nine years the Serbs had won their freedom and then lost it—though, as it turned out, only temporarily.

WINNING OF AUTONOMY: 1813–1830

A little more than a year after their defeat the Serbians again took up arms. The hero of this second uprising was a prominent knez, Milosh Obrenovich. He had not been one of the top leaders of the first revolt, perhaps because of his hatred for Karageorge, whom he believed to have poisoned his half brother. When Karageorge and other chiefs fled in 1813 Milosh chose to remain behind. The pasha in Belgrade, impressed by Milosh's local experience and by his enmity for Karageorge, decided to use him as an instrument to get the Serbians to submit. He appointed Milosh grand knez of three districts, thereby giving him control of most of the central Shumadia region.

Milosh was a much more complex character than Karageorge. He was an astute and inscrutable man, adept at hiding his feelings, capable of analyzing a situation objectively, willing to wait for developments to mature, and skillful in playing off one party or person against another. He did not altogether lack Karageorge's ability to deliver a hard blow in the field, but diplomacy came more naturally to him. It was as a diplomat rather than as soldier that he made his greatest contributions to his country.

Milosh at first made every effort to persuade his countrymen to submit to the Turks. Presumably he hoped that retribution might thereby be reduced to a minimum. But the returning Turks indulged in wholesale massacres and spoliation. They claimed and seized land and wealth which they had never before possessed. They systematically terrorized the countryside by planting garrisons of janissaries and wild Albanians in the fortresses and even in remote rural areas. In 1814 a revolt broke out in one of the districts assigned to Milosh. He dispersed some of the rebels and induced the rest to submit on a promise of amnesty from the pasha. The promise was broken and about two hundred rebels were executed, some impaled, the more fortunate beheaded. Finally, Milosh himself decided that collaboration was not feasible. On Palm Sunday, 1815, he unfurled the banner of revolt and the second insurrection began.

Milosh had better fortune than his predecessor. At first he had to fight hard against strong Turkish forces and he won four victories in quick succession. These established the insurrectionary movement as something more than a flash in the pan and served to attract timid souls that hitherto had been undecided. Thereafter Milosh never had to face the odds over which Karageorge several times had triumphed. The reason was partly the favorable international situation and partly Milosh's skillful diplomacy. By June, 1815, Napoleon had suffered final defeat at Waterloo and had been safely removed to St. Helena. Now Russia was not engaged in the West and was free to turn to the Balkans. The Turks therefore preferred a quick compromise with the Serbs to a protracted war that might end in Russian intervention. Milosh, on his part, was ready to accept minimal concessions and to wait patiently for opportunities to extract more.

An imperial decree in December, 1815, recognized Milosh as supreme knez of the pashalik and allowed the Serbs to retain their arms and to hold a national assembly or skupshtina. But pashas and spahis and Turkish garrisons were to remain as before, and taxes and tribute were to continue to be sent to Constantinople. This compromise arrangement represented the beginning of an eighteen-year struggle for self-government, at the end of which Milosh finally won for his country recognition as an autonomous principality.

Milosh had some solid basis for his diplomatic campaign. The Turks had troops in the country but he had his armed Serbs who would not be pushed around with impunity. Milosh also had a strong legal argument in Article VIII of the Treaty of Bucharest. It had been ignored hitherto by the Turks, but its stipulation was clear. It recognized Milosh as "Prince of the Serbian Nation" and authorized him "to administer the internal affairs of the country and to settle them in concert with the Council and Assembly of the Chiefs and Elders of the Nation." [8] Finally, Milosh had as his trump card the Turks' fear of Russia. He played this card discreetly, knowing full well that Russia would not move a finger unless it were to her own interest to do so. For this reason Milosh refused to entangle himself in anti-Turkish plots with neighboring peoples. In fact, it was over this issue that Milosh had his final and fatal difference with Karageorge. The latter returned to Serbia in 1817 with plans to arouse the country for a combined Serbian-Greek revolution against Ottoman rule. Milosh opposed him adamantly, being convinced that it was a foolish and ruinous move. Personal considerations also were undoubtedly involved, for Karageorge was a dangerous rival. In any case Milosh allowed, and perhaps inspired, a band of assassins to murder Karageorge in his sleep and to deliver his head to the pasha.

This terrible and tragic ending of the life of a great patriot precipitated the feud between the Karageorge and Obrenovich dynasties that was to wrack Serbian politics for a century and a half. Of the nine Serbian rulers between 1804 and 1945 four were assassinated and four were exiled. Supporters of Milosh could perhaps argue that in his case personal and national interest were one. For he did finally win autonomy for his country, and without further war and devastation.

The outbreak of the Greek War of Independence in 1821 gave Milosh an opportunity to extract concessions peacefully. Russian-Turkish relations were strained throughout the Greek war, so Milosh corresponded with the Russians, reminding them of Serbia's aspirations. But he refused to be drawn into the struggle despite Greek appeals for aid. On October 7, 1828, Tsar Nicholas forced the sultan to sign the Convention of Ackerman requiring the Turks to carry out immediately all provisions of the Bucharest Treaty, and specifically Article VIII pertaining to Serbia. The convention proved to be valueless. The Turks refused to honor it and finally the tsar declared war in the spring of 1828.

The Treaty of Adrianople (September 29, 1829) which ended the war required the Turks to fulfill all the stipulations of the Ackerman Convention. So far as Serbia was concerned, this was actually done the following year (August 28, 1830) when the sultan issued a decree recognizing Milosh as hereditary prince and granting autonomy to Serbia. Taxes henceforth were to be paid in a lump sum with the annual tribute; the spahis were to surrender their estates and their indemnity was to be included in the tribute payment; and the Turkish garrisons were to be restricted to the frontier fortresses.

There remained only the problem of delimiting Serbia's boundaries. The question had been raised in 1820 and again in 1826. Milosh claimed all the territory that had been occupied by Karageorge, but the Turks continued to hold certain outlying areas. Milosh characteristically bided his time. The Bosnian revolt of 1831 spread into the disputed areas and Milosh promptly occupied them "to restore order." Two years later, on May 25, 1833, the Turkish government, under pressure from Russia, acknowledged Serbia's jurisdiction. Thus Milosh at last reached his final goal. Serbia was an autonomous principality with definite boundaries and he was its recognized and hereditary ruler.

SERBIA UNDER MILOSH

When the famous French writer Alphonse Lamartine visited the Serbian principality in 1833 he found himself surrounded by an "ocean of forests" and he imagined that he was in the midst of the North American woodlands. His analogy was apt because Serbia in the early nineteenth century did in fact resemble an American frontier community of the same period. The winning of autonomy did not transform Milosh's Serbia into a modern state of the Western variety. Rather, it remained a poor and primitive pashalik with the physical appearance of an American frontier region and with cultural characteristics reflecting the past centuries of Ottoman rule.

The few roads that were cut through the forests could be traversed only on foot, on horseback, or by oxcart. Two roads alone were fit for carriage traveling, but this did not cause hardship because only two people boasted carriages, the pasha in Belgrade and Prince Milosh himself. The Serbian peasants regarded the surrounding forests as a nuisance to be rid of as soon as possible, and, like the American frontiersmen, they set fire to vast stands in order to scatter corn seed between the charred stumps. Also, the manner of everyday life in the Morava Valley closely resembled that in the Ohio Valley—the same log cabins, home-made furniture and clothes, plain food but plenty of it, plum brandy in place of rum, books and schools conspicuous by their scarcity, and an abundance of malaria and other diseases which were treated by a combination of home remedies, barbers, and quacks. In short, Milosh's Serbia was a typical, egalitarian, rough-and-ready frontier society knowing neither poor men nor rich. Foreign observers reacted to the Serbian peasants in very much the same way as they did to the frontiersmen in the New World. "They are a nation of shepherds and swineherds," reported the British consul from Belgrade, "and have no desire apparently to be anything else. . . . They prefer a life of sloth and intemperance in their native forests to the civilisation which might result from improved industry and intelligence." [9]

In the field of government the past centuries had left a deep imprint. Milosh remained essentially a pasha, albeit a Serbian one, and he ruled the principality as though it were his personal domain. The British consul sent to his superiors a description of Milosh's administration which reveals the degree to which the principality remained a pashalik.

No constitution exists in this country nor even any description of established laws, civil or criminal; the country is governed by the absolute will of the Prince: no contract is binding except by his power; no marriage can take place without his approval; no transfer of property can be effected except by his sanction, and no will of a deceased person is valid without the Prince's examination and approval. Again, criminals are tried by him and punishment awarded according to his decision, which in some instances is extremely rigorous. . . . The peasantry are forced to leave their own agricultural pursuits, and often at several days' distance from their home are assembled to work for the Prince, whose estates are cultivated in this manner: no sort of recompense . . . nor even any food or refreshment.[10]

Many foreigners and an increasing number of Serbians criticized Milosh for his autocratic administration. But his highhandedness was not due solely to his personal predilection for one-man rule. Existing conditions and historical traditions were such that personal freedoms and the Western type of representative institutions were out of the question. The war against the Turks had been fought by individual local chieftains, or voivodes, each of whom had his band of personal followers. These voivodes naturally tried to retain control over the areas which they had liberated. Only by arbitrary and ruthless measures was Milosh able to halt this trend toward a new and lawless military feudalism. Also, the Serbian peasants had a long tradition of village self-government, and they were unwilling to assume the obligations and burdens required by independent statehood. They imagined that having got rid of the Turks they would be free to sit under the shade of the village trees and drink plum brandy without any interference from the outside world. Again Milosh had to resort to forceful methods to combat this anarchical self-centeredness of the peasants, which was as dangerous as the disruptive aspirations of the voivodes. Thus a strong central authority was essential if the centrifugal forces that threatened Serbia's very existence were to be overcome.

These circumstances, together with Milosh's natural authoritarian tendencies, explain the extremely arbitrary rule described by the British consul. A skupshtina or national assembly did exist, but it met only when Milosh summoned it. Milosh retained full executive power, appointed all officials, and intervened in local affairs whenever he wished. This paternalism was tolerable so long as the Turks were at the gate. But after the Russo-Turkish War and the Treaty of Adrianople of 1829 the Serbians felt comparatively safe and refused to bow their heads any longer. An opposition group gradually crystallized, basing its demands upon the sultan's decree of 1830, the third clause of which stipulated that the prince should "administer the domestic affairs of the country in accord with the assembly of Serbian notables." [11] Milosh paid no attention to this provision and continued with his one-man rule. The extent of the opposition that developed is reflected in the following letter addressed to Milosh on April 18, 1832, by the famous Serbian linguist, Vuk Karajich.

No one is satisfied with you; some complain that there is no security for property or life; others accuse you of thinking more of yourself than of the public welfare. . . . You are capricious; even your confidants say that it is dangerous to live by your side. Merchants complain that you have ruined them; people of substance say that Karageorge treated them better. Even in your family there are disaffected—your brother Jevrem, your wife Ljubica. . . . You must make changes: give security to officials, end the *corvée*, train good officials, stop meddling in trade, buy no more property abroad, improve your private life, tolerate criticism of your acts. Otherwise there will be a revolt and no one will lift a finger for you. . . .[12]

Karajich's warning proved prophetic. A disturbance broke out in 1835 and Milosh hurriedly ordered his secretary to prepare a constitution to calm the agitation. The constitution was adopted but it was far too democratic for Milosh's liking. With the support of Turkey and Russia he abrogated it and returned to his old ways. This cleavage within Serbia led to the intervention of the European powers. Britain, oddly enough, supported Milosh while Russia demanded that he accept a constitutional regime. The explanation is not that the Russians had been won over to constitutional government but rather that they hoped thereby to secure a means of exerting influence in Serbia. So long as Milosh was the absolute autocrat he was likely to continue on his independent course. But if his authority were balanced by that of a senate, a constitutional conflict was likely to follow and the Russian consul then would have an opportunity to intervene decisively, "The intention of Russia," reported the British consul, "is to impose on Milosh a Senate or Council of her own agents in order to secure for herself ascendancy in Serbia. . . . The individuals thus attempted to be forced into the councils of the Prince Milosh are as despotic in their principles and as tyrannic in their dispositions as the Prince himself can possibly be." [13]

The final decision regarding constitutional arrangements in the principality lay with the sultan, who had issued in 1830 the original decree granting autonomous government. On December 24, 1838, the sultan decided in favor of the Russian position. He proclaimed a constitution which provided for a council of seventeen senators with very extensive rights, the most important being that they could not be removed without due cause. Milosh was compelled to appoint senators who were either openly or secretly hostile to him. These individuals promptly demanded that Milosh abdicate or face trial on various charges. Milosh chose to step down and on June 15, 1839, he crossed the Sava River to exile.

If Milosh had commanded widespread support within the country he might have been able to withstand the pressure of his political opponents even though they were backed by Russia. But his covetousness and irascibility had antagonized so many that his great contributions to his country were forgotten and his departure was generally applauded. Not many years were to elapse, however, before people were harking back to the good old days of Prince Milosh. And in the end he was called back to the throne in his seventy-eighth year amid popular acclaim and rejoicing.

ALEXANDER KARAGEORGEVICH: 1842–1858

Milosh abdicated in favor of his oldest son, Milan. The latter was mortally ill and died without being conscious of his elevation. His brother Michael succeeded him on July 8, 1839, but remained on the throne only three years. He was seventeen at the time of his accession; hence the Senate appointed regents to rule the country. The men selected were hostile to the Obrenovich dynasty. Furthermore, they had the backing of the Turkish and Russian governments. The odds were too great for the youthful Michael, and in August, 1842, he was forced to flee the country after a vain attempt to assert his independence.

The Skupshtina elected in his place Alexander Karageorgevich, a son of the great Karageorge. The new ruler was an upright and well-intentioned person but unfortunately he proved too weak to guide Serbia through the stormy waters that lay ahead. During the sixteen years of his reign the senators were the real rulers of the country. Their administration was marked by factionalism and corruption. Nevertheless, Serbia did progress appreciably beyond the primitive standards prevailing at the beginning of the century. By the end of the reign, 352 elementary schools were in operation, though almost all of these were located in the towns and cities. An Academy of Science was established in 1841 and the University of Belgrade in 1844. Foreign trade increased rapidly, particularly with the Hapsburg Empire. Western influences for the first time began to make an impression on the country. This process was hastened by the senators, who were mostly merchants and bureaucrats and who had little sympathy for the traditional paternalistic society of the past.

The result, in broad terms, was the spread of a money and credit economy and the growth of a Western type of state apparatus. Leaving the economic changes for later consideration and turning to the administrative innovations we find that, although they were generally necessary and inevitable, the immediate effects were frequently both unfortunate and unpopular. The government adopted in 1844 a civil code which was based on that of Austria and which hastened the spread of individualistic ideas and practices. Also, an elaborate judicial system was established, though it functioned poorly because of the shortage of trained personnel. Many of the judges were barely able to decipher the code, and the clerks were often incapable of keeping accurate records. Bribery was common and taken for granted. The police were popularly considered to be venal and brutal. A law in 1850 granted them authority to inflict fines, prison sentences, and even corporal punishment. Local self-government institutions which had flourished for centuries under the Turks now began to wither with the appearance of appointed officials. The latter frequently were Austrian Serbs, they being more likely to have the requisite education and training. But these prechani, as they were called (literally, "over the river"), were generally unpopular. They brought with them the autocratic attitudes and practices of the Hapsburg bureaucracy. These were foreign to the Serbian mentality, so that the average peasant regarded the prechani not as fellow Serbs but as Serbian-speaking Germans. These manifold changes were unavoidable manifestations of the breakup of the static and self-contained society of the past. But to the average peasant they were unsettling and uncomfortable, and he naturally looked back with nostalgia to the days of the "Old Lord" Milosh.

In foreign affairs the government was cautious and conservative. This was evident in 1848, when a series of revolutions swept over the Continent. The South Slavs under Hapsburg rule were directly affected by the upheaval. We shall note later in this chapter that both the Serbians and the Croatians took up arms against the intolerant Hungarian nationalists and that a strong movement developed for the unity and the independence of all South Slavs. The Serbian principality could not escape the repercussions of these stirring events across the Danube. Alexander and his chief minister, Ilya Garashanin, sympathized with the objectives of the insurgent Hapsburg Slavs. A few years earlier Garashanin had prepared a memorandum on foreign policy in which he declared that "the unification of Serbia with all the other subject peoples must be considered a fundamental law of the state." [14] This objective appeared to be within the realm of possibility with the outbreak of the 1848 revolutions. The Austrian consul in Belgrade reported much excitement, including the formation of "a club of pan-Slav and democratic tendencies." On the night of March 24, 1848, according to the consul, the club issued a proclamation calling on all South Slavs "to liberate themselves completely from the Ottoman Empire and to create, since Austria is in agony, a Yugoslav Kingdom under the banner of Prince Alexander Karageorgevich, consisting of Serbia, Bosnia, Bulgaria, Croatia, Slavonia, Syrmia, Dalmatia and Southern Hungary." [15]

But both Russia and Turkey were unalterably opposed to Serbian intervention in the revolutionary movement. Alexander and his ministers decided to remain safely neutral rather than risk the hazards of defying the two neighboring empires. Arms and volunteers continued to pour across the river to the embattled Hapsburg Slavs, but the Serbian government remained officially neutral. This policy cost Alexander much popularity. Many of his subjects believed that their unredeemed brothers under foreign yoke should have been helped regardless of the risk. Alexander's position was not strengthened when the Russian and Austrian governments sent him decorations for remaining neutral during the crisis.

The Crimean War further undermined Alexander's standing. Popular sentiment in Serbia was on the side of Russia, but Alexander again felt constrained to keep his people in check. So great was the clamor for joining Russia that Alexander admitted to the British consul that he dared not call the Skupshtina because of the "dynastic danger." But with Austrian and Turkish armies poised on his frontiers Alexander had no real alternative to neutrality. The Treaty of Paris, which ended the war in 1856, stipulated that "the rights and immunities of Serbia" be placed "under the collective guarantee of the signatory powers." This meant that henceforth no Turkish decision concerning Serbia would be valid without the concurrence of the signatory powers. To put it positively, Serbia now had a legal basis for appealing to the powers.

The average Serb did not appreciate this advantageous provision. He believed only that Alexander had deserted Russia during the war just as he had deserted the Hapsburg Slavs during the 1848 revolts. He also disliked the senators, regarding them with much justification as corrupt and self-seeking. A popular demand arose for a Skupshtina to settle existing grievances. When it met in December, 1858, it showed itself hostile to both Alexander and the Senate. It drew up a list of grievances and appointed a commission of seventeen members to "see to the welfare of the State." The commission at once called on Alexander to abdicate. Alexander refused at first, but since he was unwilling to call out the army he was finally forced to surrender the throne. Meanwhile, the Skupshtina had recalled the "Old Lord" Milosh with the enthusiastic endorsement of the people.

THE OBRENOVICHES TO 1878

Despite his age, Milosh showed the same energy, self-confidence, and highhandedness that had always distinguished him. He began by throwing into prison his old enemies who had forced his abdication years before. Then he successfully defied Austria when that power tried to interfere with the shipment of arms to Serbia. Finally, he sent a deputation to Constantinople with two demands: that the Turkish government should recognize his title as hereditary and that all Turks within Serbia should reside within the fortress bounds. Both these demands already had been granted in the sultan's edict of 1830 but they had not been respected in late years. Now the Turks responded to Milosh by resorting to their usual delaying tactics. Milosh settled the matter quickly by announcing to the Skupshtina on August 22, 1860, that, regardless of the sultan's suzerainty, the Serbian people thenceforth would consider the two disputed points as settled in their favor and having the force of law. The assembly approved this bold move enthusiastically. A month later the old patriarch, now in his eightieth year, was dead.

His son and successor, Prince Michael Obrenovich, proved to be the most successful ruler in the history of modern Serbia. Tall and gaunt, with a swarthy complexion and a heavy beard, Michael was a striking figure despite his frail health. Some contemporaries attributed his achievements to good fortune and to experienced advisers rather than to his own abilities. But all are agreed that he was strong-willed and upright, and that he had lofty ambitions for his country. Also, he was much better prepared for his duties than his illiterate father had been. He was highly educated and had visited the chief capitals of Europe. He realized that Serbia no longer could be governed in patriarchal fashion as a private domain. "The law is the supreme authority in Serbia"—his motto in government—Milosh would have found intolerable, and perhaps rightly so in his time.

Michael's goal was twofold: to complete the emancipation of Serbia by securing the withdrawal of Turkish troops from the fortresses, and to restore the ancient Serbian kingdom by bringing under his scepter the unredeemed brothers under Turkish rule. To reach this goal he first had to reorganize his administration and strengthen his armed forces. In 1861 he promulgated a new constitution which increased his prerogatives at the expense of the Skupshtina and especially of the Senate. Michael no longer was compelled to choose his ministers from the Senate or to share with it the direction of foreign affairs. He now was free to act quickly and authoritatively when the occasion arose. At the same time Michael built up the first regular Serbian army. Hitherto local chieftains had shown up with their personal followers in times of emergency and had not hesitated to depart when they so desired. Now Michael secured the services of a French officer, Lieutenant-Colonel Mondain, who organized a standing army of over fifty thousand men. This was supplemented by a Military Academy to train officers, a conscription act to provide recruits, and an income tax to furnish the necessary funds.

An opportunity to raise the question of the Turkish garrisons offered itself on June 15, 1862, when a Turkish officer killed a Serbian youth at a public function in Belgrade. Serbian police who intervened were fired upon by Turkish soldiers and killed. The Serbian population thereupon attacked the guardhouses and drove Turkish soldiers and civilians alike into the citadel. The next day, while feeling still ran high, the Turkish commander suddenly opened fire with his cannon and bombarded the open city for five hours. This insensate act proved a godsend for Michael. Although the damage was slight, he was able to demand a conference of the powers in order to end so intolerable a situation. The conference was held in Constantinople and on September 4 it was agreed that the Turks should evacuate all fortresses except those in Belgrade and three other cities. Also, all the Turkish civilians who still resided in Serbia were to leave, the Serbian government undertaking to compensate those who left property behind.

In 1866 Michael grasped another opportunity to complete the evacuation of the fortresses. The defeat of Austria by Prussia in that year weakened temporarily the power that was the most consistent champion of the *status quo* in the Balkans. In the same year a formidable revolt broke out in Crete, and Turkey found herself on the brink of war with Greece. Michael took this favorable occasion to suggest courteously that the sultan might surrender the perfectly nugatory right of maintaining garrisons in Serbia. Diplomatic pressure by friendly powers induced the sultan to give his consent. Early in 1867 the last Turkish soldiers left Serbian soil. No token remained of Ottoman suzerainty except the yearly tribute and the Turkish star and crescent waving over the Belgrade citadel beside the Serbian tricolor.

At the same time that he was winning these concessions Michael had been negotiating a series of agreements and alliances with neighboring Balkan countries. His aim was to create a Balkan League, drive the Turks back to Asia Minor, and unite under his rule the liberated South Slavs. His negotiations and pacts constitute an important chapter of Balkan diplomatic history and will be considered in Chapter 21. Suffice it to note here that Michael organized the first Balkan League between 1865 and 1868. But by the latter year the European diplomatic situation had changed so drastically that a combined assault upon Turkey no longer was feasible.

Before another favorable occasion could materialize Michael was assassinated on June 10, 1868. Public opinion accused the Karageorgevich family, though the responsibility for the crime remains a mystery to this day. For Serbia the murder represented a tragic and irreparable loss. An able leader was cut down at the height of his constructive activity and his successor proved utterly incapable of continuing his work.

If the assassins who murdered Michael hoped to secure the return of Karageorgevich they were speedily disillusioned. The ministry and the Senate met promptly in Belgrade, formed a provisional government, and summoned the Skupshtina. The latter body elected to the princely post Michael's cousin, Milan Obrenovich. Since Milan was only fourteen years old the Skupshtina appointed three regents to rule the country.

Milan had much to recommend him: a handsome appearance, outstanding intellectual ability, quick wit, ready eloquence, and a genial manner which endeared him to many of his subjects and made "Milan" so common a Christian name in Serbia. But these fine qualities were blighted by an unfortunate boyhood. A child of divorced parents, Milan grew up in Paris without affection or discipline. Brought to Belgrade in his adolescence, he was left isolated in the palace without brothers, sisters, or playmates. He was assigned a tutor who took his position to be a sinecure and allowed Milan to go his own way. The regents' contribution to the young prince's education was to provide him with a mistress while he was still in his teens. It is not surprising that Milan grew up to be utterly unfitted for his position. He was bored by the intrigues and squabbles of Serbian politics and he regarded existence in Belgrade as an intolerable exile from the gay life of Paris and Vienna. During a visit to the Austrian capital he referred to Serbia as "that damned country" which caused him nothing but grief. An English diplomat sized up Milan as a "third-class sovereign." But Milan in turn was not altogether unjustified when on one occasion he pointed to his regents and ministers and said "Whatever I am you are responsible."

During Milan's minority the regents promulgated a new constitution. This document, adopted on July 11, 1869, gave the illusion of providing democratic government but in reality it did not do so. The Skupshtina was elected on a liberal franchise but its powers were extremely limited. It did not have the right of initiative and it could not modify government bills, which were to be accepted or rejected en bloc. In the latter case the government could legislate provisionally without the Skupshtina and could even promulgate the budget by decree. Thus true ministerial responsibility was out of the question, and the Skupshtina came to be known as the "Chamber of Echoes."

After the adoption of the constitution the most important problem was foreign policy. Russia had strongly supported Prince Michael, providing equipment for his new army and giving diplomatic backing for his Balkan League. Upon his assassination Russia wished to see Prince Nicholas of Montenegro succeed to the Serbian throne. In view of the outstanding leadership qualities of Nicholas and his remarkable success as ruler of Montenegro between 1860 and 1918 there is little doubt that the selection of Milan was not the best choice. Furthermore, it antagonized the Russians, who turned their favors to the Montenegrins and the Bulgarians. In fact, the regents adopted the liberal-appearing constitution in the hope of winning popular support to withstand the Russian pressure. With the same end in mind the regents established close and cordial relations with Austria.

About 1870 relations between Serbia and Austria cooled, largely because of conflicting ambitions in the Turkish-held province of Bosnia-Herzegovina. Indicative of the new situation was Milan's visit to the Russian emperor in the fall of 1871. But Milan was not able to win Russian backing for Serbian territorial aspirations. The truth was that neither Austria nor Russia was willing to support or even tolerate any Serbian move that might jeopardize the *status quo* in the Balkans. The two powers, together with Germany, had concluded in 1872 the well-known *Dreikaiserbund* or Three Emperors' League.* By the terms of this pact Russia and Austria undertook to refrain from intervention in the Balkan Peninsula and to cooperate in maintaining existing frontiers.

Milan was perfectly willing to accept the *status quo* in return for Austro-Russian support for his dynasty. By this time his conduct and his extravagance had made him so unpopular that he needed outside support to assure his position on the throne. But the difficulty was that a *status quo* policy was unacceptable to most Serbians. They wanted their country to play the same role in the Balkan Peninsula that Piedmont had played in the Italian. They failed to see why Serbia should not be the nucleus of a new, unified, and independent South Slav state. The Liberal party, led by Jovan Ristich, favored such expansionism and for that reason enjoyed wide popular support. Milan, therefore, had to by-pass the Liberals and depend upon the Conservatives. Unfortunately for him the Liberals won a substantial majority in the Skupshtina in both the 1874 and 1875 elections. The outcome inevitably was friction between Milan and the Liberals.

Such was the situation in Serbia when a general European diplomatic crisis was precipitated by the outbreak of a revolt in Bosnia-Herzegovina in July, 1875. At once a clamor arose in Serbia for assistance to the embattled brethren across the border. Milan strove desperately to preserve neutrality in accordance with the wishes of Russia and Austria. Most Serbians regarded neutrality as almost treasonable at a time when fellow Serbians were fighting for their freedom. Agitation mounted to the point where Milan was faced with the alternative of war against the Turks or revolution at home. He

* See Chapter 21.

naturally chose the former and on June 30, 1876, Serbia declared war on Turkey.

Serbian history now merged with that of Europe during the years of crisis and war that culminated in the Treaty of Berlin of July 13, 1878. The details of the stirring events of those years are related in Chapter 21. So far as Serbia was concerned, she suffered quick defeat at the hands of the Turks. But the outcome was precisely what Ristich had expected and counted on. Russia could not stand by and accept the defeat of the Balkan Slavs. The pressure of public opinion forced her to intervene, and in the ensuing war the Turks were beaten back almost to Constantinople. Thus Serbia obtained considerable concessions at the peace conference despite her initial setback. The Berlin Treaty awarded her two hundred square miles of territory, including the strategic city of Nish, and also granted her recognition as a fully independent state. Thus the struggle begun by Karageorge in 1804 finally attained its fulfillment three quarters of a century later. The star and the crescent no longer flew over the fortress at Belgrade.

ECONOMIC DEVELOPMENT TO 1878

The most important economic change resulting from the Serbian revolution was in the system of land tenure. This was settled on the basis of the principle "The land belongs to those who till it." The peasants traditionally had clung to this notion even though they had been compelled to pay feudal dues to their spahi overlords. When the dues were increased arbitrarily with the spread of the chifliks the peasants reacted strongly. One of the main reasons they took up arms in 1804 was to rid themselves of landlord exploitation.

It was by no means a foregone conclusion that a successful revolt would mean deliverance from landlords. The wealthy peasants and livestock traders were more than ready to take the place of the spahis and the chiflik owners. The fact that they did not do so was due in large part to Milosh, who chose to base his rule on a free peasantry rather than on a landlord class. In 1815 Milosh abolished all chifliks, thus removing a major source of peasant grievance. The spahis continued to hold their fiefs and to collect their dues until in 1830 the Turkish government, under Russian pressure, abolished the spahlik system. For compensation the spahis were to receive a little over a third of the annual tribute received in Constantinople from Belgrade. This was a favorable arrangement for the peasants because they were not required to pay directly for the land, to which they now acquired full legal title. Indirectly, of course, they did pay. The tenth formerly collected by the spahis now went to the state as a regular tax. The proceeds were used to defray the expenses of the new state apparatus and also to provide for the tribute to Constantinople, which included the indemnity to the former spahis.

Milosh not only ended the feudal bondage of the peasants but also took positive measures to repair the depredations of the war and of Turkish misrule. The country was largely depopulated, and extensive areas lay un-cultivated. Milosh attracted new settlers by offering free land, temporary tax exemption, and security for life and property. A veritable land rush ensued, and, as usual, the most wealthy and influential obtained the choicest land. But in 1820 Milosh decreed that anyone possessing more land than he could work must surrender it for redistribution. It should be added that Milosh and a few of his cronies evaded the law by using forced labor on their estates. But with this exception, which is understandable in the Serbia of that period, the land settlement was definitely favorable for the peasantry.

The peasants were not always able to keep the land that they had obtained. In Serbia, as in other Balkan countries, the nineteenth century witnessed the growth of a money and credit economy with its manifold con-comitants—the appearance of the village merchant and usurer, increasing economic differentiation and peasant indebtedness, and eventually the dis-possession of peasant families. This trend induced legislation designed to prevent the pauperization of the Serbian peasantry. In 1836 Milosh decreed that a house, a certain amount of land, two oxen, and a cow were essential for every peasant family and could not be foreclosed for the payment of debts. This legal protection was not included in the civil code of 1844 and peasant indebtedness mounted rapidly. The economic crisis following the Crimean War worsened the situation drastically and aroused much popular agitation. Political freedom was declared a sham if the peasants were allowed to fall into the bondage of a new and more evil spahi, the usurer, who claimed not merely the tenth but the peasant's whole property.

This outcry produced new legislation for the protection of the peas-ant. Laws in 1860 and 1861 prohibited the foreclosure of certain farm implements, draft animals, and roughly one hectare of land. In 1873 an important bill increased the coverage generously to include enough land, buildings, livestock, and farm equipment to provide a reasonable living for a peasant family. The bill went further and forbade the peasant to sell his protected minimum of land and farm property, or to use it as collateral for credit. An exception was made only if the peasant abandoned farming for another profession. Supplementary laws prohibited foreclosure for nonpay-ment of taxes and also forbade the opening of commercial stores in rural areas.

This well-meaning legislation proved to be far from effective. One reason was that the government failed to provide adequate agricultural credit. The peasants consequently had to forgo legitimate loans, in which case their production was hampered, or else had to resort to various artifices in order to borrow from loansharks. No less than fourteen dodges were employed by both usurers and peasants to evade the laws. Also, the natural process of the évolution of an underdeveloped country could not be stopped by legal measures or by pious admonitions to preserve the traditional way of life. Finally, the rapid growth of population in the nineteenth century accelerated the trend toward the fragmentation of peasant property. All these factors combined to make Serbia a country of predominantly dwarf farms. The process was well on its way by 1878. It had become a serious problem by the end of the century and it remained serious and unsolved at the time of World War II.

The change in the land tenure system did not affect farming techniques. The peasants lacked the knowledge, the means, and the incentive to try new methods. For decades they continued to till the soil in the same manner as they had during the preceding centuries under the Turks. The growth of population created a need for more cropland. The peasants commonly met the need by burning down the forests. In the early years they farmed the cleared land for a while and then moved on to repeat the wasteful process after the manner of the American frontiersmen. The government did not adopt effective measures for conserving the forests until 1867.

The peasants commonly grew corn to feed themselves and their pigs, the latter being the most important "cash crop" until the end of the century. Each plot also had a few plum trees which the peasant needed to replenish his stock of shlivovitsa, a fiery plum brandy. Potato culture was new and not popular. Hoping to destroy the prejudice against them, Milosh decreed that each peasant should grow a patch of potatoes. But even by 1900 they had not become as popular in Serbia as to the east in Bulgaria. The practice of letting some land lie fallow was universal. Such rotation of crops as occurred was unscientific, and few peasants used manure as fertilizer. Sheep, not pigs, were the most common domestic livestock. Their meat, milk, and wool made them valuable for the peasants but there was no export market.

The winning of autonomy had little effect on Serbian commerce. Exports were shipped up the Danube to the markets of the Hapsburg Empire and consisted primarily of swine, cattle, and leeches. The latter were widely used for medical purposes at this time and were shipped as far as Paris. Imports included Austrian hardware, sugar, and cloth; Russian ecclesiastical articles; salt from Wallachia; and Turkish coffee. The important pig trade with Austria resulted in a favorable balance for Serbia and helped Milosh to pay the tribute to the sultan in cash.

Milosh hampered Serbian trade because of his monopolistic practices. Despite his many great contributions to his country he always regarded it as his pashalik. True, he was a Serbian rather than a Turkish pasha, and he certainly had the interest of his people at heart. Nevertheless, a pasha he remained to the end. He kept for his own use the former personal lands of the sultan. He used his authority and power to monopolize the salt imports from Wallachia and to control most of the pig trade with Austria. He made no distinction between the state treasury and his private purse, investing the Serbian treasury in Viennese banks in his own name. Part of his vast fortune he used to buy large estates in Wallachia as a hedge in case of future political setbacks.

When Milosh abdicated in 1839 the bureaucrats and merchants took over the direction of the state. They abolished the former monopolies and encouraged commerce and closer economic ties with the West. In 1844 they instituted a civil code based on the Austrian code which in turn followed the Code Napoléon. The new code paid little heed to Serbian customs and helped to spread individualistic ideas and to break up the traditional paternalistic society. The tempo of economic activity accelerated appreciably. Foreign trade increased from 13.5 million francs in 1842 to 68 million in 1868 and 86 million in 1879. But the national economy still remained comparatively primitive, as is illustrated by the fact that only foreign coins circulated in the country before 1868. In that year the first Serbian copper coins were minted, and in 1873 the first silver coins. Both, it should be added, were minted in Vienna.

Factory industry scarcely existed in Serbia before 1878. Various factors explain this, including the small domestic market, inadequate transportation, dearth of capital, lack of independent tariff authority, and the apathy of Serbian statesmen. Handicrafts flourished. The most prominent craftsmen were the smiths, tanners, furriers, shoemakers, masons, saddlers, and potters. According to the 1866 census they numbered 21,751, or 1.8 per cent of the total population. Shortly afterward they began to feel the competition of foreign products as imports increased. Also, a shift from Turkish to Western social customs affected Serbian artisans. Those who had made Turkish sofas or fezzes, for example, could not shift easily to a Western type of furniture or hats. Nor could they compete with the Austrian factories producing these Western commodities on a mass scale. Yet Serbian craftsmen did not disappear or even decline in numbers. By 1900 they had increased to 54,007, a rise proportionate to the growth of population. Certain types of craftsmen did suffer, generally those facing foreign competition or producing commodities which were becoming unfashionable. But others prospered and increased, particularly the building and service trades, which could fit into a more urban and Westernized society.

Social institutions also underwent change during the nineteenth century. The general trend of economic, political, and intellectual development undermined the traditional zadruga form of social organization. The revolutionary war took men away from their homes and exposed them to new ideas and customs. Also, the establishment of the Serbian state assured personal security and thus eliminated one of the reasons for the existence of the zadruga. The 1844 civil code was little more than a translation of the Austrian code, and as a result the zadruga appeared in it as an exceptional rather than an integral feature of Serbian society. In fact, the code prescribed the method by which the zadrugas might be dissolved. Finally, the spread of a money and market economy weakened the zadrugas. More specifically, the peasants were needing more money to pay the mounting state taxes and to buy the new commodities that were now available to them, such as textiles, clothing, footwear, jewelry, and household furniture and utensils. As a rule, the zadrugas were unable to increase production sufficiently and to market enough produce to meet the demand for more money. The members then were likely to agitate for the dissolution of the zadruga in the belief that thereby some of their economic problems might be solved. Thus by 1878 the zadrugas were on the way out and by 1914 they no longer were an important factor in the economy and the social life of the country.

HAPSBURG SLAVS TO 1878

Having traced the evolution of the Serbian principality from its origins under the Turks to the winning of full independence in 1878, we turn now to consider those South Slavs who were living under Hapsburg rule. The first major development to affect the Hapsburg Slavs was the establishment of Napoleon's Illyrian state in 1809. In Chapter 12 we saw that the administrative, economic, and cultural reforms of the French awakened the local population and provided a basis for the Illyrian movement of the 1830's and 1840's. The Hapsburgs, who inherited the Illyrian Provinces after Napoleon's downfall, stimulated the Illyrian movement by their repressive measures.

Immediately they erased, as with a great sponge, the reforms instituted during the French regime. Priests once more became schoolmasters and nobles again assumed their old titles and privileges. This restoration of a discredited past naturally led to the glorification of the brief Illyrian interlude. People forgot the conscription and the heavy taxes imposed by the French. They remembered only the prosperity and creative activity and free cultural expression. And with the passage of time they attributed these gains not to enlightened French rule but rather to the fact that under Napoleon they had been united for the first time in centuries. Thus the idea became deeply rooted that their fortunes in the future depended on their unification in a new Illyrian state. And the more reaction set in under the Hapsburgs the stronger became this Illyrian legend.

The legend was reinforced by the work of South Slav scholars and writers. Outstanding among these was Bartolomeus Kopitar, author of Slovene grammars and linguistic studies and creator of the Slovene literary language. Kopitar stimulated Vuk Karajich to undertake his studies which contributed so much to the creation of a uniform Serbo-Croatian literary language. Ljudevit Gaj, a Croatian, was not so distinguished as a scholar but he was much more effective as a journalist. He published a number of political and literary periodicals with such titles as *Croatian Gazette, Illyrian Gazette,* and *National Journal.* In these he carried on continual propaganda in favor of South Slav unity. How this unity was to be attained he was not certain. Sometimes he looked to Austria and at other times to Russia. In any case Gaj contributed greatly to an Illyrian movement which grew steadily in the eighteen thirties and forties.

Such was the situation among the Hapsburg Slavs when news arrived of the February, 1848 revolution in Paris. Repercussions were immediate and far-reaching, the most important being the abolition of serfdom in the

Hapsburg provinces in April, 1848. The step was taken with little hesitation because serfdom by this time had become economically and politically out-moded. Even the comparatively backward South Slav lands of the Hapsburg Empire had shifted from a predominantly natural economy to a money econ-omy producing for the market. In such a milieu agriculture had to become more productive and competitive, but it could not do so on the basis of serf labor. Also, the serfs were becoming increasingly unmanageable. With the news of the Paris revolt they simply refused to provide any longer the labor and other dues of the past. Thus the proclamation for the liberation of the serfs represented little more than official recognition of an accomplished fact.

Liberation did not mean distribution of all the land. The peasants kept the plots they formerly had tilled for themselves. The gentry received compensation from the state for these plots and they also kept all the re-maining land as well as most of the forest property. Thus the large estates and the political power of the landed aristocracy survived the 1848 revolu-tion. In fact, they survived in Croatia and the Voivodina until the Yugoslav agrarian reform of 1919, and in Hungary proper until the end of World War II.

The political developments among the Hapsburg Slavs in 1848 were spectacular and attracted wide attention. The Slavs tried to take advantage of the revolutionary upheavals to gain autonomy and unity. But they were forced finally by intolerant Hungarian nationalism to stand with the Haps-burgs on the side of reaction. When the Hungarian parliament passed laws in March, 1848, establishing a constitutional regime, it ignored completely the existence of Croats, Serbs, and all other non-Magyar people. Likewise, when the Hungarians proclaimed their independence on April 14 they over-looked the political aspirations of the Yugoslavs, even though they had been made abundantly clear by this time.

Both the Serbians and the Croatians reacted violently against this uncompromising pressure. Representatives of the Voivodina Serbs appeared before the Hungarian Diet in Pressburg (Bratislava) on April 8 and pre-sented their demands. They expressed sympathy with the Hungarian struggle for freedom but insisted on recognition of their own national rights. Louis Kossuth, the famous Hungarian orator and leader, replied that the Magyars would do their best to respect Serbian rights but insisted that only the Magyar language could bind the different nationalities together. "Then," the Serbs answered, "we must look for recognition elsewhere than at Pressburg." "In that case," replied Kossuth, "the sword must decide." "The Serbs," re-torted one of the deputation, "were never afraid of that." [16]

The following month, on May 13, 1848, the Serbians convened a national assembly at Karlowitz (Sremski Karlovci). It developed into a great demonstration of Yugoslav unity. Over fifteen thousand delegates gathered, including not only Serbs but also Croats, Bulgarians, and even Czechs and Poles. The original charters issued by Leopold I in 1690–1691 promising full autonomy to the Serbs were solemnly read aloud before the assembled

crowd. The assembly passed a series of resolutions declaring the Serbian nation "politically free and autonomous under the House of Austria and the
Crown of Hungary." The occasion was marked throughout by close Serbo-
Croat cooperation. "Byzantium and Rome," declared a Croatian spokesman,
"succeeded in separating the Serbs and the Croats, but the fraternal tie which
unites them is so strong that henceforth nothing in the world will be able to
sever it." [17]

Meanwhile, the Croatians were equally aggressive under the leadership of Baron Joseph Jellachich, who had been appointed governor of Croatia
by the emperor on March 23. The appointment proved to be of decisive importance because the baron rallied the South Slavs behind the Hapsburg
monarchy and thereby cut off the Magyars from the sea and from direct intercourse with liberal Europe. Jellachich immediately summoned a Croatian
assembly which met in Agram (Zagreb) in June, 1848. He welcomed the
delegates with an impassioned harangue. "The fraternal union of 800 years
[with Hungary] promises us a friendly solution of the prevailing dispute. But
should the Magyars assume the role of oppressors against us . . . we shall
prove to them with weapons in our hands, that the time is long past when
one nation can rule over another. Away, then, with the Magyar regime of
compulsion—we did not recognize it even before March 15, but after the
March Revolution we broke and annihilated it." [18] A Serbian deputation attended the meeting and both Jellachich and Gaj supported proposals for
Serbo-Croat unity. "We are only one nation," declared Gaj, "there are no
longer either Serbs or Croats." [19] The assembly declared all decisions of the
Hungarian government to be null and void insofar as they were at variance
with the rights of Croatia. Jellachich met later with Hungarian representatives
but no compromise could be reached.

By this time the imperial armies had crushed the revolution in Italy
and the Hapsburgs felt strong enough to take the offensive against the Magyars. In doing so they counted heavily on the Hungarian–South Slav rift. On
September 1, 1848, the Hapsburgs revoked the earlier concessions that they
had made to the Magyars. At the same time Jellachich crossed the Drava
and attacked the Hungarians at the head of a South Slav army. But now he
was fighting for Hapsburg interests rather than for Yugoslav unity and independence. Vienna had succeeded in turning the force of Serbo-Croat nationalism against the Hungarian revolution.

The Voivodina Serbs were likewise used for the preservation of the
Hapsburg Empire. Some of their younger and more radical leaders caused a
little difficulty because they wished to be rid of Austrian as well as Hungarian
rule. But Patriarch Rajachich, who was old and conservative, insisted on
keeping the Serbian movement within the imperial framework. With the support of Jellachich he was able to oust the young Serbian leaders from the top
posts and to replace them with Austrian officers. Thus the Serbs, like the
Croatians, fought for the defense of the empire.

The 1848 revolutions greatly stimulated the Hapsburg Slavs and evoked a popular Yugoslav movement. But powerful forces combined to prevent any significant modification of the *status quo*. Tsarist Russia was as opposed to disruption of the Hapsburg Empire by the South Slavs as she was to its disruption by the Magyars. As noted earlier in this chapter, the Serbian government was forced to remain neutral under Russian and Turkish pressure. Also, the intolerant nationalism of the Magyars blocked united action by the subject peoples that might have had some chance against the Hapsburgs. These factors, together with the conservative tendencies of Baron Jellachich and Patriarch Rajachich, induced these leaders to bring the powerful force of South Slav nationalism squarely on the side of the emperor.

Their decision contributed substantially to the final triumph of the Hapsburgs in 1849. But their reward was reversion to the prerevolutionary *status quo,* at least in regard to political arrangements. Hungarian rule in Croatia was ended only to be replaced by Austrian. Having suppressed the Magyar revolution, the Hapsburg ministers were unwilling to tolerate Croatian nationalism, which could become obstreperous in the future. So they violated without compunction the promises they had made to the Croats during the revolutionary period. They were not as apprehensive about the Voivodina Serbs, so they issued a decree on November 18, 1849, separating the Duchy from Hungary and granting it autonomy. But the concession was hollow because the autonomy was extremely restricted and the boundaries of the Duchy were so drawn as to include large numbers of Rumanians and Magyars as well as Serbs. The purpose, of course, was to employ the traditional Hapsburg tactic of divide and rule.

The next great development affecting the Hapsburg Slavs after the 1848 revolution was the Austro-Hungarian *Ausgleich* or Compromise of 1867. Defeats in Italy and Germany led the Vienna statesmen to seek a settlement with the most articulate and dangerous of the minorities. The result was the *Ausgleich,* which transformed the Hapsburg monarchy into the Austro-Hungarian or Dual Monarchy. The terms of the Compromise restored both Croatia and the Voivodina to Hungarian rule while Dalmatia remained under Austrian rule. The South Slavs naturally refused to accept this joint Austro-Hungarian domination. During the period from 1867 to 1914 they waged a steadily mounting campaign for autonomy. But the campaign was not coordinated. The various South Slav groups fought individual struggles which varied according to local conditions.

The Slovenes were the most conservative and unspectacular. They had remained quiet during the 1848 disturbances and they continued to be restrained during the following decades. One reason for this was that they had always been under Austrian domination rather than Hungarian, which was more intolerant and provocative. Another reason was that Slovenian politics were completely dominated by the Slovene People's party, a conservative Catholic organization which preferred peaceful tactics and piecemeal concessions to sweeping proclamations and revolutionary methods.

In the Hungarian part of the empire relations between the ruling

Magyars and the subject Serbs and Croatians became steadily worse. The Voivodina Serbs were left only with church autonomy and they steadily lost ground to the Hungarian and German elements in the Duchy. They also declined in importance in the Serbian world as a whole. At the beginning of the century Karlowitz (Sremski Karlovci) and Novi Sad were the great Serbian cultural centers, but in later decades these cities gave way to Belgrade and Sarajevo.

The Magyars were able to thwart the comparatively isolated Voivodina Serbs, but they had much more difficulty with the Croats. As soon as the *Ausgleich* was arranged, elections were held in December, 1867, for the Croatian Diet. The Magyars made liberal use of "oats and the whip" and secured a majority of unionist deputies who were amenable to Hungarian rule. This Diet accepted in 1868 a constitutional arrangement known as the Nagodba or Compromise, which defined the relations between Croatia and Hungary. It allowed for a considerable degree of self-government, more than was permitted in the Yugoslav state after World War I. Nevertheless, Croatia was an integral part of the Hungarian kingdom and this antagonized the nationalist leaders, who wanted either an independent Croatia or an independent Yugoslav state. In the elections of 1871 the antiunionists won a large majority and they went so far as to declare the Nagodba null and void. In the same year a minor insurrection broke out which had to be put down by military force. This opposition increased still more following the Hapsburg occupation of Bosnia-Herzegovina in 1878. By the end of the century the situation became alarming as Serbs and Croats joined forces and became increasingly militant in their struggle—a struggle that was to contribute substantially to the eventual dissolution of the Hapsburg Empire and to the establishment of the new state of Yugoslavia.

15. Greek Revolution and Independent Statehood to 1878

THE REVOLT OF THE GREEKS in 1821 followed that of the Serbs in time but not in importance. The Greek revolution was a much more significant affair for Europe as well as for the Balkan Peninsula. The Serbian revolution involved simply the control of a Balkan pashalik. But the Greek revolution, because of the strategic location of the Greek lands, raised basic questions of Near Eastern strategy and brought the great powers into sharp and open conflict. Likewise, the Serbian uprising was essentially a local movement with little effect on the rest of the empire. But the Greek insurrection had widespread and lasting repercussions, the reason being that the Greeks had played a much more important role in imperial affairs than had the Serbs.

It is true that the great majority of the Greeks, like the other rayas, were simple peasants. But there was also a small minority that was so extraordinarily active and highly placed that it might well be considered to have been almost as influential in the Turkish Empire as the Turks themselves. This minority controlled the larger part of the commerce of the Balkan Peninsula; dominated completely the Orthodox Church to which most of the Balkan Christians belonged; enjoyed a monopoly of educational and cultural institutions in the Balkan lands; and also filled some of the highest administrative and diplomatic posts in the Ottoman bureaucracy.

It follows that the Greek revolution was a complex movement involving more than an outbreak of desperate peasants. In order to grasp its complexity it is necessary to realize that, in effect, two Greek worlds existed within the Ottoman Empire—the one an imperial world of Phanariote administrators and Orthodox prelates with its headquarters in Constantinople, and the other a peasant world of illiterate and poverty-stricken rustics living in the Greek provinces. We shall now consider each of these worlds in turn.

269

GREEK IMPERIAL WORLD

The Greek Phanariote administrators and Orthodox prelates were at the height of their power in the eighteenth century. At that time they were by far the most influential of the various subject peoples of the empire. But this had not always been the case. In the sixteenth century the South Slavs rather than the Greeks had been especially prominent in imperial affairs. One reason for this was the Turkish conquest of Hungary (1526), which finally persuaded the South Slavs that Turkish rule was durable and that they had better accommodate themselves to it. Another reason was that, whereas few Greeks accepted Islam, a large proportion of the Slavic inhabitants of Bosnia-Herzegovina turned Moslem and thereby became eligible for high office. A large number did, in fact, attain the highest ranks. It was at this time that Sokolovich (Sokolli) became grand vizir and used his influence to secure the establishment of the Serbian patriarchate in 1557. Serbian troops were extensively used by the Turks to man the northern frontier, and the Serbian language was a common medium for diplomatic correspondence. In fact, a sixteenth-century observer wrote: "In our period the Ottoman rulers esteem so highly the Dalmatians that they appoint them Pashas of provinces and fleets and armies, and also Grand Vizirs who govern the whole Empire, and they give to them for wives the daughters, the sisters and the nieces of the Grand Turk [the Sultan]. . . . The Slavic nation rules the Ottoman Empire." [1]

If the Slavs ruled the empire in the sixteenth century, the Greeks had taken their place by the eighteenth. One reason for this was that the Slavs discredited themselves by supporting the Hapsburg armies whenever they crossed the Danube. Another reason was that from the mid-seventeenth century onward the Turks began to encounter formidable complications in the conduct of their foreign relations. No longer were they able to dictate terms to their neighbors. For the first time they had to carry on protracted and involved diplomatic negotiations. But they were not equipped to do this because hitherto they had regarded Western languages and cultures as being unworthy of their attention. Thus they found it necessary now to employ the services of those who had knowledge of foreign countries and foreign languages. It was under these circumstances that the so-called Phanariotes came to be attached as secretaries and interpreters to the staffs of Ottoman officials and officers.

The term "Phanariote" is derived from the extreme northwestern corner of Constantinople—the lighthouse or Phanar district. The Patriarch had established his headquarters there in 1601 after several moves following the loss of St. Sophia to the Turks. Gradually the district became the preserve of Greek merchants as well as of Greek clergy. These merchants, or Phanariotes, as they came to be called, prospered greatly. They became imperial tax farmers, they rented the salt monopoly, undertook contract works, became purveyors to the court, and gained control of the Black Sea wheat trade. These activities brought them into frequent contact with the Western world, and they acquired a firsthand knowledge of Western customs and languages.

Entering the Ottoman bureaucracy at the lower levels, they gradually rose to the topmost ranks. A certain Panayiotakis Nikousis was appointed the first Grand Dragoman of the Porte, a title that literally means Chief Interpreter but which, in practice, involved the functions of an under secretary for foreign affairs. Nikousis was succeeded by his protégé, Alexander Mavrokordatos, who was to win fame as the negotiator of the 1699 Karlowitz Treaty. Another high office regularly entrusted to the Phanariotes was that of Dragoman of the Fleet, or Under Secretary for the Navy.

From 1711 onward the Phanariotes also served as governors of the Moldavian and Wallachian Principalities with the title of hospodars or princes. Before this date the Principalities had paid tribute to the sultan in return for recognition of their complete autonomy, including the right of the Rumanian boyars or nobles to elect their own hospodars. This arrangement prevailed until Tsar Peter the Great invaded Moldavia, and the reigning hospodar, Demetrius Cantemir, went over to his side. This incident led the Ottoman government to strengthen its control over the Principalities, which were now assuming a new strategic importance as bulwarks against the expanding Russian and Hapsburg empires. Accordingly, Phanariote administrators were appointed regularly as hospodars of the Principalities from 1711 until the outbreak of the Greek revolution in 1821.

The Phanariotes not only controlled high and lucrative positions in the Ottoman bureaucracy but also infiltrated and to a large degree dominated the Constantinople Patriarchate itself. During the Byzantine period church offices, with almost no exception, had been closed to laymen. But now these offices were eagerly sought after by the wealthy Greek families of Constantinople because, under the conditions of Ottoman subjection, they offered the only means for attaining social status and a measure of security. In fact, the origin and development of the Phanariote aristocracy may be traced in part to its early associations with the Patriarchate. But having gained a foothold, the Phanariotes soon were able, with their wealth and government connections, to dominate the entire ecclesiastical structure. By the end of the seventeenth century these laymen filled all the important administrative offices of the church, which meant that they managed church properties and revenues, supervised the monasteries, safeguarded the valuable liturgical objects, and so forth.

Having gained control of the church administration, the Phanariote laymen then proceeded to intervene in the election of bishops, archbishops, and even patriarchs. By exerting pressure upon the Church Synod, which elected the Patriarch of Constantinople, they were able to influence decisively the selection of the head of the church. They were able to do this easily and effectively because of their commanding position within the church and their wealth and influence without. A contemporary observer remarked bitterly that the Phanariotes "who ought to aspire for the good of the Church, want to deprive it of the income of a see! and, moreover, in order to satisfy their conceit, they threaten to bring about the fall of the Patriarch. . . . Strange and reprehensible conduct against the spirit of Christianity; however, it is a fact now and will be repeated in the future. May God have mercy on all of us and on you." [2]

In self-defense against this Phanariote intervention the clergy secured a firman from the sultan in 1741 providing that the selection of the Patriarch be subject to the approval and recommendation of five specified metropolitans. This arrangement was adopted and continued to prevail until the second half of the nineteenth century. Thus the clergy curbed Phanariote encroachment by concentrating authority in a small body—the so-called System of the Elders. Patriarch Cyril V, the reforming churchman of the mid-eighteenth century, attempted to achieve the same end by establishing a "Committee of the Public," consisting of representatives of the Greek professional guilds of Constantinople and entrusted with the material affairs of the church. His strategy was to check the Phanariotes by democratizing the church administration. This was far too radical for the times and Cyril was eventually deposed and executed.

It should not be assumed that clear-cut issues ranged all the clergy against all the Phanariotes. In actual practice, most of the clergy had intimate connections with one or another of the Phanariote families, which probably explains Cyril's radical measure. Likewise, the Phanariotes were continually feuding among themselves, so that we find one or more of them actually supporting Cyril. In the end, a rough balance was reached whereby the clergy retained control of the strictly ecclesiastical affairs while the Phanariotes were left in charge of church administration.

Whatever the balance between the Phanariotes and the clergy may have been at given periods, the important point to note here is that by the beginning of the nineteenth century both groups occupied important positions in the Ottoman Empire and fulfilled essential functions. It is perhaps an exaggeration to state, as does Arnold Toynbee, that they were "the senior partners in the Ottoman firm," [3] but it is indisputable that they constituted one of the principal pillars of the Ottoman imperial structure.

GREEK PEASANT WORLD

We enter an entirely different world when we turn from Greek Phanariotes and churchmen to Greek peasants. During the years immediately following the Turkish conquest these peasants fared tolerably well under their new masters. Ottoman administration at that time was simple, efficient, and easy to bear. The conquerors divided the Greek lands into six sanjaks, later increased to ten when the Turks added Crete and the Aegean Islands to their possessions. The most desirable plains lands were distributed among deserving Turkish warriors in the form of large fiefs or ziamets and smaller fiefs or timars. The spahis who held these fiefs were required in time of war to present themselves for military service together with a number of armed retainers proportionate to the size of their fiefs. In the mid-seventeenth century the six mainland sanjaks mentioned above encompassed a total of 267 ziamets and 1,625 timars, which together furnished a force of 7,255 horsemen. Crete, after its conquest, was similarly parceled out into 17 ziamets and 2,550 timars, which produced 5,350 cavalrymen.

We noted in Chapter 7 that the Greek peasants living under this form of Ottoman feudalism were better off than their brothers under Venetian rule. Their church was allowed to function freely, their taxes were light, and they enjoyed a large degree of autonomy in a decentralized administrative system. Some villages and districts had more self-government than others. Certain towns, such as Yanina, received at the time of their conquest charters guaranteeing special administrative privileges. Many islands were left tax-free and unmolested in return for a specified number of recruits each year for the imperial navy. Also, certain regions designated permanent appanages of members of the royal family, of government officials, or of religious foundations were not subject to the common imperial administration and normally were left to their own devices. Finally, there were certain mountainous regions that were never completely subdued and were left unmolested so long as they paid a general tribute.

The only generalization that can be made about such a chaotic administrative system is that it allowed a large proportion of the Greek peasants to lead their lives without interference from Turkish authority. Apart from some areas in Thrace and Macedonia, where a large number of Turks actually settled and tilled the soil, the Greek population normally was free to select its own officials. These were variously designated as "elders," "archons," "primates," and "kodjabashis." In some communities they were elected in a democratic manner but in others they constituted a self-perpetuating oligarchy.

With the passage of time the Ottoman imperial structure deteriorated and the position of the subject Greeks worsened correspondingly. Embezzlement, corruption, and military defeats led inevitably to an increased tax burden. More serious was the transition from military fiefs to hereditary chifliks. The spahis originally had been granted only the right to collect certain specified revenues from their fiefs, and this right was revocable if they failed to perform their stipulated military duties. During the seventeenth and eighteenth centuries, however, the decline of central authority enabled the spahis to disregard their obligations and to become *de facto* hereditary owners of their fiefs. These fiefs were thus transformed in character and were known in Greece, as in the other Balkan lands, as chifliks. The tenants working on these chifliks no longer were protected by custom and law as they had been in the past. Their masters now were free to impose new burdens and dues, with the result that the position of the Greek tenants steadily deteriorated. Even the Greeks who lived in the free mountain areas were affected indirectly because the flight of population from the plains to the mountains produced overpopulation and economic distress in the latter regions.

The Greek population suffered also from the disruption of commerce during the Ottoman wars with Venice and Austria. Trade with Venice ceased from 1645 to 1699, and with Austria from 1663 to 1699. This ruined a rising class of Greek merchants, who had developed a profitable commerce by transporting Balkan raw materials to Central Europe and to Aegean and Adriatic ports, and then returning with sundry manufactured articles for which there was a strong demand. The Greek merchants were also adversely affected by the appearance of French, British, Dutch, and other Western merchants, who installed themselves in ports such as Saloniki, Patras, and Arta, and proceeded to funnel the import-export trade through their establishments. Their competition was particularly severe because, unlike the native Greek merchants, they enjoyed relative security and freedom from extortion.

The Greek people were hard hit also by the ravages of the Turkish-Venetian wars, which dragged on from 1645 to 1715. The Peloponnesus changed hands twice during the course of the fighting, and the local population suffered severely from property destruction, forced labor, and the other accompaniments of war. It was at this time that a considerable number of Greeks sought refuge by emigrating overseas, particularly to Italy and Corsica. In fact, the lowest point in the fortunes of the Greek people in modern times was reached during these decades in the late seventeenth and early eighteenth centuries. When the Venetians acquired the Peloponnesus by the Karlowitz Treaty in 1699 they found less than 90,000 inhabitants, a number smaller than that of any other period since prehistoric times.

The dire plight of the Greek peasantry during these years stands out in marked contrast to the power and affluence of Greek imperial circles in Constantinople. The Greek peasant world was waging a bitter struggle for survival at a time when Phanariote hospodars and merchant princes were at the height of their fortune. But during the course of the eighteenth century important changes occurred. The peasant world was gradually transformed by a combination of foreign and domestic forces that generated a remarkable revival in both the economic and cultural spheres. The final outcome was a national awakening or renaissance. This inevitably created cleavages and tensions within and between the two Greek worlds. But it also produced a heightened sense of national consciousness and a new feeling of power and confidence that were to culminate in 1821 in the beginning of the war for independence.

ECONOMIC REVIVAL

A fortunate combination of circumstances explains the great economic revival that transformed the Greek lands during the eighteenth century. The conclusion of the Karlowitz Treaty in 1699 made possible the resumption of trade with Venice and the Austrian Empire. Also, the British-French wars of the eighteenth century aided the Greeks by disrupting the operations of the Western merchants established in Saloniki, Patras, and other ports. The Greeks seized the opportunity to transport to Central Europe Balkan raw materials such as cereals, wool, cotton, and leather. In return they brought back various manufactured articles which hitherto had been imported directly by the Western merchants in the port cities. Before the end of the eighteenth century prosperous Greek trading communities had grown up in Vienna, Buda, Bucharest, Trieste, Venice, and other foreign cities.

The Greek economy was stimulated also by certain provisions of the Russo-Turkish treaties of Kuchuk Kainarji (1774) and Jassy (1792). They stipulated that the Black Sea and the Straits be opened to Russian and Austrian commerce, and that the Greek subjects of the sultan be allowed to fly the Russian flag on their ships. These provisions opened vast new fields to the energetic and commercially minded Greeks, who found a large and expanding market in the new provinces of southern Russia for such Greek products as fruit, wine, soap, and olive oil. They also reaped profits serving as the carriers of the rapidly growing Russian wheat trade. Since they now could fly the Russian flag they were able to sail back and forth through the Straits without fear of the customary Turkish extortions and restrictions. Thus the Greek merchant marine quickly rose to first place in Black Sea commerce and held that position for many years. At the same time, Greek communities were established and were soon flourishing in Russian ports such as Odessa, the Chersonese, and Taganrog. Russian historians have recognized the fact that "the Greeks were the chief middlemen in the whole of the southern trade . . . and that the success of the southern Russian trade depended to a very great degree on the freedom and safety of Greek navigation." [4]

The final and most spectacular factor in the Greek economic revival was the French Revolution and the Anglo-French wars that followed. During the course of these wars the British and the French virtually destroyed each other's merchant marine in the Mediterranean. Since they had previously controlled most of the carrying trade, an acute shipping shortage now prevailed. The Greeks at once seized the golden opportunity. Wherever profits were to be made, Greek mariners and merchants were present. They defied Napoleon's Continental blockade, ran the British blockade to Spanish and French ports, and sent caravans overland to France and to Germany to buy manufactured goods and colonial products. The merchants made vast profits while the shipowners multipled their fleets many times during these years. By 1813 the Greek merchant marine had increased to the phenomenal figure of 615 ships totaling 153,580 tons, equipped with 5,878 cannon, and manned by 37,526 seamen. The cannon, which were to prove useful in 1821, were standard equipment for merchant ships in the Mediterranean because of the ravages of the North African pirates.

The French Revolution not only stimulated the Greek merchant marine but also enabled Greek merchants to drive the Western merchants, and particularly the French, from the dominant position that they had hitherto held in Greek ports. On June 12, 1807, the Marseilles Chamber of Commerce informed the Minister of Interior: "We would be happy, Monseigneur, if we could, as you ask, send Your Excellency each month a bulletin on the state of French commerce in the Levant, but this commerce does not exist." [5] This meant, of course, that the wars with Britain had disrupted the commerce of Marseilles and had left the French merchants throughout the Levant stranded. Other European merchants in the eastern Mediterranean experienced the same misfortune to a greater or lesser degree. This naturally strengthened the position of the local Greek merchants. An English official reported that they were now able "to drive the Frank [Western] merchants from the fairs of Greece, to obtain a great part of the internal maritime commerce of Turkey, and at length to share very largely in the exchange of the corn, oil, silk and other products of Greece for the manufactured goods and colonial produce of the European nations." [6]

These commercial developments had their effect on Greek agriculture. They increased the demand and, therefore, the price of wheat, silk, cotton, grain, oil, and other Greek products. One authority has estimated that the general price level of Peloponnesian products increased between 1794 and 1815 in the proportion of 1 to 3.2.[7] It should be noted, however, that the rise in prices profited mostly the large Turkish landowners and those Greeks who also had big estates. The bulk of the Greek peasantry, which consisted of small farmers, tenants, and landless laborers, derived virtually no benefits.

On the other hand, many Greeks profited from the rapid expansion of handicraft industries, which they controlled almost exclusively. Their enterprises were located in the towns and in certain mountainous areas in Epirus, Thessaly, and western Macedonia. The latter regions produced woolen and cotton thread, stockings, cloths, ready-made clothes, carpets, silks, and furs. Most of these products were sold within the empire, but there was also an appreciable export to neighboring European countries. As a rule the domestic system prevailed, the goods being made in the homes of the craftsmen. In some areas the craftsmen organized cooperatives, of which the outstanding example was the Ambelakia enterprise on Mount Ossa in Thessaly. This was famous for its dyed yarns, which it marketed throughout Central Europe, competing successfully even with British-made products. One branch of the cooperative directed agricultural production while a second controlled the manufacturing, including the supply of raw materials and the marketing of the finished products. The cooperative distributed free corn to its poor members, and maintained schools, a hospital, and a relief fund. It was founded in 1795 with a capitalization of 100,000 francs, which had multiplied by 1810 to 20 million francs.

Such were the origins and the nature of the Greek economic revival in the eighteenth century. Its repercussions were far-reaching and varied. It created a new intellectual atmosphere and it generated new political forces that were to lead directly to the revolutionary outbreak of 1821.

NATIONAL AWAKENING

One of the significant results of the economic revival was the appearance of a new middle class, both in the Greek lands and in the Greek mercantile communities abroad. The emigrants to the overseas communities maintained close relations with their homeland. This was noted by Dr. Henry Holland, an English traveler who associated mostly with merchants while traveling in Greece in 1812:

The active spirit of the Greeks, deprived in great measure of political or national objects, has taken a general direction towards commerce. But, fettered in this respect also, by their condition on the continent of Greece, they emigrate in considerable numbers to the adjacent countries, where their activity can have more scope. . . . Some branches of the migrating families, however, are always left in Turkey, either from necessity, for the possession of property in the country, or from the convenience to both parties in a commercial point of view. Thus by far the greater part of the exterior trade of Turkey, in the exchange of commodities, is carried on by Greek houses, which have residents at home, and branches in various cities of Europe, mutually aiding each other, extending their concerns much more variously than could be done in Turkey alone.[8]

Dr. Holland also observed that there was interaction between the homeland and the overseas communities in cultural matters as well as in economic. When he visited the city of Yanina, in northwestern Greece, he was impressed by its flourishing schools and lively intellectual atmosphere.

The literature of this place is intimately connected with, and depending upon its commercial character. The wealth acquired by many of the inhabitants gives them the means of adopting such pursuits themselves, or encouraging them in others. Their connections in Germany and Italy, and frequent residence in these countries, tend further to create habits of this kind, and at the same time furnish those materials for literary progress, which would be wanting in their own country.[9]

The significance of Dr. Holland's observations is apparent. The Greek world had expanded. It had acquired a new dimension. It had established outposts in Vienna, in Venice, in Trieste and Odessa, and in many other European cities. The resulting interchange and interaction had a deep effect upon the homeland. This was particularly true because of the revolutionary temper and outlook of the new class of merchants and intellectuals. During their years of residence abroad they had become familiar with European countries and institutions. They had been impressed by the size and wealth of the great cities, by the unheard-of progress in science and learning, and, above all, by the rule of law and the safeguarding of individual rights. At home, under Turkish rule, everything was different. The progress that had been made during the past century had been made in spite of, rather than because of, Ottoman suzerainty. The merchant at home had no roads for the transportation of his goods. He lacked security and carried on his operations under the constant threat of extortion and outright confiscation. At times the weakness of the central government led to wholesale disaster. In 1769 the Moslem Albanians were permitted to wipe out completely the prosperous town of Moschopolis with a population of sixty thousand Greeks and Vlachs.

The contrast between the dazzling world of Europe and the wretched conditions at home naturally pointed to the conclusion that Turkish rule was an incubus that must be cast off as soon as possible. This explains why it was the merchants who organized the Philike Hetairia revolutionary society, who comprised the greater part of its membership, and who took the initiative in the conspiratorial work preparatory to the revolutionary outbreak.

The Greek national awakening was stimulated also by the exciting influence of the French Revolution and of Napoleon. As noted in Chapter 12, this influence, which was felt throughout the peninsula, was especially marked in the Greek lands. In January, 1798, the Austrian Ministry of Foreign Affairs complained that "the secret intrigues and exhortations of the French agents have turned the heads of the inhabitants of Morea and of Greece. . . . Thus the Greeks imagine that the moment is propitious for throwing off the Turkish yoke and recovering their former freedom." [10]

As will be recalled from Chapter 9, the two outstanding examples of the new intellectual climate in the Greek world were Rhigas Pheraios and Adamantios Koraïs. The latter was an educator who spent most of his life in Paris and became a disciple of the Enlightenment and the French Revolution. He contributed to the Greek cause most effectively by publishing the Greek classics with lengthy introductions written in a refined vernacular. These introductions served a twofold purpose. They provided a vehicle for thinly veiled political propaganda and they also contributed greatly to the movement for linguistic reform. Such reform was essential for the rejuvenation of the Greek people. Koraïs was distressed by the gap that existed between the vulgar patois of his illiterate countrymen and the language of ancient Greece. The latter was, for all practical purposes, a dead tongue, and so long as it remained so the Greeks would be unable to draw upon the splendid intellectual heritage of their greater past. Koraïs therefore set himself the task of reconstructing for his countrymen a literary language which should combine, as far as possible, the best elements of both the ancient and the modern tongues. His plan was to base his language on the common tongue but to remove from it all foreign accretions and restore all such ancient forms as had not become wholly obsolete. What Luther's Bible had done for Germany, Koraïs's editions of the classics, with their prefaces in modern Greek, were to do for Greece.

Rhigas was a very different person from Koraïs. He was a fiery and active revolutionary rather than a contemplative scholar. Entering the service of the Phanariote princes, he traveled throughout Central and Southeastern Europe and learned several European and Near Eastern languages. At the same time he absorbed the current revolutionary nationalist theories and, being the person that he was, promptly attempted to put them into practice. He joined secret lodges, organized new ones, and wrote and distributed various revolutionary tracts. His career was hectic but tragically brief. In 1796 Rhigas moved to Vienna where certain members of the large Greek community helped him to organize a conspiracy for the overthrow of the Turkish regime. The following year he left for his enslaved homeland but he was arrested by the Austrian police in Trieste, extradited to the Turkish authorities, and executed in Belgrade in June, 1798.

To the revolution which swept Greece twenty-three years later Rhigas bequeathed not only the memory of a martyr's death but also a collection of immensely popular national songs. Outstanding was his famous "War Hymn" ("Thourios"), still one of the most celebrated works of modern Greek literature. Its opening lines ring out its revolutionary message.

> How long, my heroes, shall we live in bondage,
> alone like lions on ridges, on peaks?
> Living in caves, seeing our children
> turned from the land to bitter enslavement?
> Losing our land, brothers, and parents,
> our friends, our children and all our relations?
> Better an hour of life that is free
> than forty years in slavery![11]

Rhigas blazoned forth this call to arms in the true language of the people rather than in the more refined but less comprehensible language of Koraïs. Very quickly the "War Hymn" became virtually a national anthem. "In a very short time," one contemporary relates, "Rhigas' song has spread throughout the entire country. Old and young, even women, sing it at banquets and meetings of all kinds. At first it was sung for pleasure, simply as a pleasant song, but little by little 'Thourios' has influenced their souls." [12]

EVE OF REVOLT

We cannot conclude from the above that by the early nineteenth century all Greeks were in a revolutionary frenzy and were waiting impatiently for an opportunity to rise. As a matter of fact, the opposite was the case. Greek society was deeply divided. Various groups had different and conflicting interests, and their attitudes and actions differed correspondingly. Certainly it cannot be said that the Greek revolution was a clear-cut bourgeois or class affair. In reality it was a much more complex movement. Perhaps the wealthiest element in the new middle class consisted of the shipowning families of Hydra and the other islands. But precisely because they had so much to lose, these families hesitated to support the revolution even after it had started on the mainland. They refused to move until they were forced to do so by rioting sailors led by revolutionary agitators. Likewise, it is difficult to ascribe the revolution in the Peloponnesus to the middle class because in that part of the country the landowners also controlled most of the trade.

Despite these reservations there is no doubt that the merchants and the intellectuals were more consistently opposed to the *status quo* than was any other group. Alongside them should be placed the peasantry, which could not provide leadership but did provide mass support. In the Peloponnesus, where the revolution was fought and won, the peasants were goaded to action by sheer land hunger as well as by less tangible yet very potent considerations of faith and nationality. It is estimated that the 40,000 Turks who lived in the Peloponnesus owned three million stremmata of good land (a stremma being roughly equal to a quarter of an acre), while the 360,000 Greeks were left with only one and a half million stremmata. Thus, on a per capita basis, the Turks had eighteen times as much land as the Greeks. Furthermore, most of the land left to the Greeks was in the hands of a small group of primates. Thus the bulk of the peasantry had the choice of working as laborers for either Greek or Turkish landowners. Under the circumstances many peasants supported the revolution as a means of getting land.

The primates, by contrast, were relatively ambivalent toward the revolution because they already enjoyed power, wealth, and status under Turkish rule. The increase in self-government during the eighteenth century had enhanced the authority of the primates who headed the local bodies. In the Peloponnesus, for example, each community elected two elders to a provincial body; then each of the twenty-four provincial bodies elected one delegate to a general Peloponnesian assembly, which in turn elected a two-man committee from its members. The general assembly and its committee had very extensive powers. They supervised the collection of taxes, and their consent had to be obtained before new taxes could be imposed. They represented the entire Christian population before the Turkish authorities, and they had the right to appeal directly to the sultan over the head of the Turkish governor.

This system of local government was aristocratic in character. As a rule, the members of the outstanding primate families were elected to the local and provincial offices. This was so because the primates were elected in their own districts where pressure was easy to exert and difficult to resist. Furthermore, in some cases the franchise was limited, and in others the primates were elected indirectly through electors. Thus a Greek ruling class existed which dominated local government, controlled the tax-collection apparatus, and owned most of the Christian-held land. The members of this class were regarded with a jaundiced eye by less prosperous Greeks, who referred to them as "uncircumcized Turks."

Some primates deserved this epithet. Others, however, used their influence to extract concessions from the Turkish authorities and to dissuade them from undesirable actions. Apart from individual cases it is apparent that the primates as a group were in a very different position from that of the merchants or the peasants. Far from being oppressed or financially ruined by Turkish rule, the primates owed to it their authority and their wealth. In fact, they themselves were an integral part of the Ottoman administrative system, and for this reason they were not likely to turn against it without much hesitation and reflection. When the agents of the Philike Hetairia began to prod for commitments and action, most primates refused to move unless they were certain that Russia was behind them and that they would be able to direct and maintain control of the revolution.

The Phanariotes were in somewhat the same position as the primates. They were also an integral part of the Ottoman administration and they also stood to lose rather than gain if they supported a revolution. Indeed, the Phanariotes were in a more precarious position than the primates because they lived not in the midst of the Greek population but rather in Constantinople and other administrative centers. It is not surprising that when the revolution began, the Phanariotes were sharply divided. Some turned their backs on their countrymen and remained loyal to the sultan. Others were convinced that the uprising was foolish and hopeless and believed that the only hope for deliverance lay with the great powers. A number of Phanariotes, however, supported the revolution and made important contributions both during the struggle and after the establishment of the independent Greek state.

The leaders of the Orthodox Church were perhaps the most skeptical about revolutionary ideology and revolutionary organizations. We saw in Chapter 9 that the top clergy generally believed that a revolution led by disciples of the Enlightenment would mean not only the destruction of an imperial structure in which the church had a definite place, but also the destruction of the intellectual foundations of Balkan Orthodoxy. On the other hand, the village priests as a rule had a very different attitude. Mostly illiterate, they lived on intimate terms with their congregations and tended to identify themselves with local aspirations and movements. This became apparent after 1821, when more than one village priest distinguished himself with rifle and sword. Indeed, one of the folk heroes of the revolution is Athanasios Diakos (the Deacon), who, in the popular poem, fought for three hours together with eighteen comrades against eighteen thousand Turks. He was finally taken prisoner, and when his captors pressed him to abandon his faith and become a Moslem, he replied scornfully in words that every Greek schoolboy knows:

> Go you and your faith, you filth, to hell with you!
> I was born a Greek, a Greek will I die.

The Greek people in the early nineteenth century were rent by deep cleavages, the product of revolutionary ideology from abroad and of economic and social differentiation at home. Despite those cleavages they were in a much stronger position than they had been a century earlier. They had increased in numbers to approximately three millions compared to half that number in 1715. They also had gained immeasurably in military strength.

They now possessed a large, well-armed, and skillfully manned merchant marine which was to give them command of the sea when the revolutionary struggle began. Likewise, on land they now had several thousand trained veterans who had gained experience fighting as mercenaries in Italy, in Egypt under Napoleon, and in the Ionian Islands under British, French and Russian auspices. Furthermore, the Greeks now commanded the capital resources necessary for a revolution, the chief sources being the shipowners of the islands and the merchants and bankers abroad.

Finally, and most important of all, the Greeks were intellectually and psychologically prepared for revolution. The experiences of the past century had broadened their horizon immeasurably. No longer did they live in a world consisting only of Turkish officials, Orthodox prelates, and local primates. No longer did they accept Ottoman rule as irresistible, nor did they consider deliverance to be feasible only if the Christian powers of Europe intervened in their behalf. Instead, the Greek rayas for the first time had enough self-confidence to think in terms of winning their independence by their own efforts. A decade before the outbreak of revolution Dr. Holland sensed this process of change that was taking place.

Of late years the Greeks, considering them in their whole extent as a people, have been making progress in population, in commerce, in education, and literature; and above all, as it would seem, in that independent consciousness of power which is necessary as a step to their future liberation.[13]

REVOLUTION AND STALEMATE: 1821–1824

The Greek revolution was planned by a secret organization that sought to disguise its true character by adopting the name "Philike Hetairia" or Society of Friends. To this day little reliable information is available concerning this body. We know that it was founded in 1814 at Odessa by Greek merchants. For the first three years of its existence it made little progress. Then it appears to have grown rapidly, though estimates as to its membership vary widely. The same cleavage between radical and conservative elements existed within the Philike Hetairia as in the Greek community as a whole. The conservatives prevailed in the matter of selecting a leader. They offered the post first to Count Capodistrias, a native of Corfu who had entered the Russian service and risen to the position of foreign minister. Capodistrias rejected their offer, so they turned next to Alexander Ypsilantis, who accepted it. Ypsilantis was of a well-known Phanariote family, and, like Capodistrias, had sought his fortune in Russia and had become a major general in the Russian army.

On the timing of the revolution the conservative Hetairists favored delay and careful preparation. But on this issue the radicals had their way. They insisted on immediate action, pointing out that the Turks were distracted by disturbances in Asia Minor, by friction with Persia, and by the revolt of Ali Pasha in Albania, and that the European powers also were faced with revolts in Spain and Italy. The radical Hetairists cleverly exploited Ypsilantis' Russian connections by claiming that the Russian government secretly supported them. This claim was quite unjustified, but it did serve the purpose of winning over certain vacillating primates in the Peloponnesus. The revolt began in the spring of 1821 after Ypsilantis hastily improvised plans for a diversionary blow in the Danubian Principalities and for a general uprising in the Peloponnesus and the islands.

The uprising in the Principalities was ill-fated from the outset. Ypsilantis had hoped for support from Russia, but Tsar Alexander immediately repudiated him and struck his name off the army list. Ypsilantis had also counted on some assistance from the Rumanian population of the Principalities, but again he was disappointed. The Rumanians knew the Greeks only as hospodars, tax collectors, and usurers. Consequently, liberation for them at this time meant liberation from the Greeks rather than from the Turks, with whom they had virtually no contact. Far from rising in behalf of Ypsilantis, the Rumanian peasants took up arms against "the reigning princes and the Greek and Rumanian boyars . . . who have robbed and pillaged us until there is left to us only our souls." [14]

Under the circumstances Ypsilantis did not have a chance even if he had been a capable military and political leader, which he was not. On March 6, 1821, he crossed the Pruth River into Moldavia at the head of the "Sacred Battalion," composed of young Greek patriots of the middle and upper classes. Three months later the battalion was cut to pieces by the Turks at Dragashani. Ypsilantis fled with two of his brothers to Austrian territory, but his followers fought on against overwhelming odds. At the end of June, less than four months after the beginning of the revolt, a few survivors of the "Sacred Battalion" swam across the Pruth back to Russian soil. We shall see in Chapter 18 that although Ypsilantis' campaign had little bearing on the Greek revolution, it did affect the Principalities decisively. It led to the abolition of Greek Phanariote rule in the two provinces and to the reintroduction of native Rumanian boyar princes.

Less than three weeks after Ypsilantis crossed the Pruth, the Greek revolution proper began in the Peloponnesus. The proclamation of independence came after a winter of tension and apprehension. The revolt of Ali Pasha and the increasing number of individual attacks upon Turks heightened the feeling of an impending outbreak. In February, 1821, the Peloponnesian primates met to discuss the explosive situation. They decided to postpone decision until they could determine how true were the rumors of Russian support. In March the Turkish authorities summoned the primates to Tripolitsa, the administrative center of the Peloponnesus. Guessing that the Turks' intention was to seize them as hostages, the primates resolved to ignore the summons. Instead, they went to the historic monastery of Aghia Lavra where, on March 25 (April 6), Bishop Germanos raised the standard of the cross as a signal of revolt.

The campaigns that followed were largely isolated and uncoordinated. One reason was the lack of unity among the Greeks. The revolution was by no means a national crusade in which all Greeks fought side by side for country and for faith. It was rather a complex movement in the course of which the Greeks fought not only against the Turks but also among themselves. Sectional differences ranged Peloponnesians against continentals, and islanders against both; ideological differences set cosmopolitan Phanariotes against guerrilla chieftains and high prelates against village priests; conflicting class interests separated wealthy shipowners from unemployed sailors and powerful primates from landless peasants.

The sporadic character of the war arose also from the mountainous terrain which divides the country into isolated compartments. This factor, however, operated against the Turks as well as the Greeks. Once the revolutionaries had gained control of the Peloponnesus, the Turks found it exceedingly difficult to plan a campaign for its reconquest. The sea approach was out of the question because of the Greek navy. The alternative was invasion from the north. But the only routes available were long, parallel, and vulnerable lines running down each side of the Pindus Range. Also, the winters in the mountainous interior were rigorous and long, so that open ground could not be held from early December to the end of March. This explains the repeated failure of the Turkish armies from the north. Each spring they set forth from their northern bases and marched down the parallel routes. Sometimes they were able to cross the Isthmus of Corinth and penetrate into the Peloponnesus itself. But they were not able to capture, within the time limit of one campaign season, the cities or forts necessary for winter quarters. So at the beginning of each winter the Turks trailed back north again, their mission uncompleted. The deadlock continued until 1825, when Mehemet Ali invaded the Peloponnesus by sea and almost snuffed out the uprising.

Turning from over-all strategy to individual campaigns, we find that during the first year the Greeks won control of the Peloponnesus and of numerous Aegean islands, the most important being the great maritime and naval centers—Hydra, Spetsai, and Psara. The Greek successes were stained by large-scale massacres of defenseless Turks—an inevitable accompaniment, perhaps, of a struggle that pitted, at one and the same time, Greek subjects against Turkish overlords, Greek peasants against Turkish landowners, and Greek Christians against Turkish Moslems.

By the summer of 1822 the revolutionaries had extended their rule north of the Isthmus of Corinth, capturing Missolonghi, Athens, and Thebes. But now the insurrection found its limits. To the north the Turks had speedily overwhelmed outbreaks in Thessaly, Macedonia, and Mt. Athos. In Constantinople they hanged the Patriarch, Gregory V, despite the fact that he had issued an encyclical condemning the revolution. On the island of Chios the Turks wreaked the most savage reprisals, massacring or selling into slavery most of the extensive population.

The Turks were able to stamp out the embers in the northern Balkans and in the islands, but the Greeks on their part were able to consolidate their position in the Peloponnesus. After defeating Ali Pasha in February, 1822, the Turks invaded the Peloponnesus with an army of 30,000 men. They failed to take the key fortress of Missolonghi, so they were obliged to retreat with the coming of winter. The campaigns the following year were essentially the same. Two Turkish armies advanced down the east and west flanks of the Pindus Range. Because neither one was able to cross the Corinth Gulf, before the end of the year both withdrew northward to their winter quarters.

The Greeks were unable to exploit their successes, owing to dissensions that were becoming increasingly acute and open. In January, 1822, a National Assembly had met at Epidauros and proclaimed "before God and man, the political existence and independence of the Greek nation." The representatives adopted an elaborate constitution and elected a Phanariote, Alexander Mavrokordatos, the first president of the Hellenic Republic. In actuality the new government was one in name only. No one with authority was willing to relinquish a particle of it, so that real power remained with Theodore Kolokotrones and the guerrillas, with Andrew Zaïmes and the primates, and with the Koundouriotes brothers and their fellow shipowners.

When the second National Assembly met in December, 1822, Kolokotrones was the virtual master of the country. He had just captured the port of Nauplion, but he refused to allow the Assembly to meet there even though it had been designated the national capital. The Assembly then gathered at nearby Astros, where it voted to deprive Kolokotrones of the supreme military command and to vest the office in a committee of three. Kolokotrones promptly retaliated by forcibly carrying off certain members of the government to Nauplion. The remainder fled to the island of Hydra, where they formed a new government headed by the wealthy shipowner, George Koundouriotes.

Two governments now existed, one on the mainland dominated by Kolokotrones and the other at Hydra led by Koundouriotes and including the Phanariote Mavrokordatos. Open civil war prevailed in 1824, when Kolokotrones was forced to surrender Nauplion and recognize the Koundouriotes government. Before the end of the year a second civil war had broken out. This time the Peloponnesians combined against a government which they considered to be unduly dominated by the islanders. Koundouriotes again prevailed, not because of his ability, which was mediocre, but because of an English loan, which he used to attract Rumeliote guerrillas to his side.

We may conclude that by the beginning of 1825 a stalemate had been reached in the Greco-Turkish war. The Turks had behind them an extensive empire and considerable resources, but they were unable to utilize them effectively because of corruption and inefficiency. On the other hand, the Greeks failed to take advantage of the Turkish weakness because of their meager resources and continual feuds. Liberated Peloponnesus was unable to carry the revolution further, but the Turks likewise were unable to reconquer the Peloponnesus.

FOREIGN INTERVENTION TO NAVARINO: 1825–1827

The balance between the Greeks and the Turks was ended in 1825 by outside intervention, first by the Egyptians, who tipped the scales in favor of the Turks, and then by the European powers, who rescued the Greeks from their perilous plight and finally won for them complete independence.

Mehemet Ali of Egypt intervened in the Greek war only after Sultan Mahmud had accepted his conditions. He was to receive the pashalik of Crete, and his son Ibrahim was to become governor of the reconquered Peloponnesus. The Egyptians had little trouble suppressing the Greek revolutionaries on the island of Crete, thanks to the dissensions that divided the Cretans fully as much as the mainland Greeks. Similarly, it was the indiscipline of the Greek sailors that enabled Ibrahim to ferry his army across the stretch of water to the Peloponnesus. Their pay being a month or two in arrears, the seamen insisted on returning to their islands. Thus on February 24, 1825, Ibrahim reached without interference the southern tip of the Peloponnesus with an army of 4,000 regular infantry and 500 cavalry. The transports went back to Crete and returned, again without opposition, with a second force of 6,000 infantry and 500 cavalry. The stalemate in the war was about to end.

The Greeks had paid little attention to the landing of the Egyptians, assuming that they could be scattered as easily as the Turks. Ibrahim soon dispelled this illusion. First he captured Navarino (Pylos), which became his naval base and supply center. Then he advanced through the Peloponnesus, "harrying, devastating, and slaughtering in all directions." The Greek forces, which had remained a conglomeration of virtually independent guerrilla bands, proved no match for Ibrahim's trained and disciplined veterans. In engagement after engagement the Greek guerrillas broke and fled before the unfaltering charges of bayonet-wielding Egyptian regulars. While Ibrahim advanced from the southwest, the Turks under Reshid Pasha renewed their attacks in the northwest. The two forces converged on Missolonghi, the key fortress guarding the entrance to the Gulf of Corinth. It was finally taken in April, 1826, after a full year's heroic defense. Ibrahim then returned to ravage the Peloponnesus while Reshid marched to Athens, where he forced the Greek garrison on the Acropolis to surrender on June 5, 1827. At this point, when the revolution appeared to be doomed, the situation changed overnight with the intervention of the European powers.

When the news of the Greek uprising was first received in the spring of 1821 the reaction of the European statesmen was uniformly hostile, for they faced a basic dilemma. They recognized the degeneration of the Ottoman Empire, but they could not answer the question of what should take its place.

This is the essence of what came to be known as "the Eastern Question." Countless books and articles were written on this question during the nineteenth century, and innumerable plans were advanced by way of solution. The difficulty was that the Turks ruled an empire so vast and strategic that the European balance of power would have been upset if their empire had been appropriated by any one of the powers. Likewise, the partition of the empire among several powers raised complications so dangerous that it was feared that a European war would almost inevitably ensue.

Was there no solution, then, that could reconcile Turkish disintegration with the requirements of European diplomacy? Today the answer seems obvious: liberate the subject peoples of the empire and erect a number of independent states on the ruins of the imperial structure. But this is viewing the past through the spectacles of the present, a practice that is as misleading as it is common. The fact is that most of the subject peoples of the Ottoman Empire were not nationally conscious to the point where independent existence would have been feasible. Also, the European statesmen were not then prepared to consider such a solution. It simply did not occur to them that free Balkan states might take the place of European Turkey. It is true that the Serbs already had won *de facto* independence, but they were little known in Western Europe. The inhabitants of the Danubian Principalities were not thought of as constituting a separate nationality. Even the Greeks, the descendants of a well-known and much-admired people of ancient times, were to a large degree forgotten. Koraïs describes an incident that occurred during the French Revolution when he applied for a *carte de securité* in Paris and identified himself as a Greek. Immediately, he relates, "the eyes of everyone present were fixed upon me, some approached me as if to convince themselves that a Greek was the same as any other human."[15]

Given this background it becomes understandable why the statesmen of Europe thought in terms of only two alternatives—the continued existence of the Ottoman Empire or else its partitioning among the great powers. And since the latter involved so many perils, the statesmen naturally preferred to prop up the Turk, decrepit and undeserving though he might be. It was not until decades later that there could be serious consideration of Gladstone's strategy of a barrier of free men against Russia.

Tsar Alexander shared this view concerning the necessity of preserving the *status quo* and the peace of Europe. For this reason he disapproved in principle of the Greek revolution. But in actual practice Alexander had to take into account certain special factors which placed him in an ambivalent position. He was the protector of the Orthodox Church and the hereditary enemy of the sultan. His subjects were deeply moved by the hanging of the Patriarch and the unhappy plight of their coreligionists. Furthermore, the Turks had continued to administer the Danubian Principalities by martial law in defiance of treaty obligations, and they had also interfered with Russian shipping in the Straits. The latter point was not insignificant, for it affected seriously the trade of the Russian Black Sea ports. Wheat exports from south

Russian ports in 1821 were 30 per cent less in quantity than those of 1820, and in 1822 they were 47 per cent below the 1820 level.

These factors explain why the tsar, after denouncing the Greek revolution, dispatched an ultimatum to Constantinople on July 27, 1821. His demands were concerned mostly with the protection of the Christian churches, freedom of Christian worship, and pacification of the Danubian Principalities. The Turks rejected the ultimatum and the Russians severed diplomatic relations. The prospect of war alarmed the European capitals. Lord Castlereagh and Prince Metternich persuaded the sultan to make certain concessions to the tsar. The danger of war passed for the moment, and Metternich happily expected that the bothersome revolt would, as he expressed it, "burn itself out beyond the pale of civilization."

Instead of burning out, the insurrection blazed on, and the longer it did so the more difficult it became to ignore it. Popular sentiment throughout Europe was rallying to the side of the Greeks. Philhellenic organizations in every country collected money and supplies and brought pressure to bear on their respective governments. Wide segments of the population that opposed revolution on principle supported the Greeks enthusiastically because they viewed them not as ordinary revolutionaries but rather as Christians fighting Moslems and as the descendants of Pericles and Aristotle struggling to free themselves from Turkish barbarism. Public opinion was particularly outraged by the rumor that Ibrahim planned to carry off into slavery all the Greeks whom he did not exterminate, and then to repeople the Peloponnesus with Egyptian fellaheen. A London newspaper wrote indignantly: "We would prefer Greece Russian to beholding a whole Christian people swept to the grave to make room for sanguinary hordes of Mohammedan negroes." [16]

This mounting popular agitation influenced George Canning, who had succeeded Castlereagh as British foreign minister in August, 1822. Although not a philhellene, he was convinced that a settlement could be postponed no longer. He feared especially that Russia might undertake unilateral action against Turkey. The Russians were at least as aroused as the Western Europeans, having the additional incitement of the Orthodox religious bond with the Greeks. When the vigorous Tsar Nicholas succeeded Alexander in December, 1825, Canning decided that immediate action was necessary. He sent the Duke of Wellington to Russia, and the outcome was the St. Petersburg Protocol of April 4, 1826. The two powers agreed to mediate between the Turks and the Greeks on the basis of complete autonomy for Greece under Turkish suzerainty.

This was an important step toward the settlement of the Greek question, but it did nothing to resolve the many outstanding questions between Turkey and Russia. In fact, the tsar already had sent an ultimatum to Constantinople (March 17, 1826) before he met with Wellington. The ultimatum demanded that the Principalities be evacuated immediately and that plenipotentiaries be sent to Russia to settle outstanding issues. Sultan Mahmud was not in a position to reject these demands because he was now making preparations for the extermination of his mutinous and useless janissaries—a long overdue project that he finally executed in June, 1826. Mahmud reluctantly agreed to send the plenipotentiaries and on October 7 signed the Convention of Ackerman, in which he accepted Russian demands concerning Serbia and the Principalities.

Meanwhile the fighting in Greece had been dragging on. The Greeks had formally applied for the mediation envisaged in the Petersburg Protocol. The Turks and Egyptians naturally were loath to stop with victory in sight. Canning therefore prepared for action by negotiating the Treaty of London (July 6, 1827) with France and Russia. This provided that the Allies should again offer mediation, and if the sultan rejected it they would "exert all the means which circumstances may suggest" to force the cessation of hostilities.

In August, 1827, the three powers offered mediation to the belligerents. The Greeks accepted and the Turks refused. The Allied fleets in the Levant were instructed to intercept supplies destined for Ibrahim's forces. In the process of doing so they sailed into Navarino Bay, where a squadron of Turkish and Egyptian ships was anchored. No hostilities were intended "unless the Turks should begin." Under the circumstances somebody was bound to begin. A shot was fired. Others were fired in reply. The battle became general, and before the day of October 20 was over the Turko-Egyptian fleet lay at the bottom of the bay.

The news of Navarino was received by most Europeans with unrestrained delight. The sultan denounced the affair as a "revolting outrage" and demanded compensation and apologies. Certain circles in Europe sympathized with him but the damage could not be undone. Navarino was as much a turning in the Greek revolution as the landing of Ibrahim had been two years earlier. The question henceforth was not whether the Greeks should be free, but rather, what precisely should be the extent of their freedom.

NAVARINO TO INDEPENDENCE

George Canning had died unexpectedly two months before Navarino. Had he lived he probably would have coerced the Ottoman government into granting Greek independence and would thus have forestalled the Russian declaration of war on Turkey. But his successor, the Duke of Wellington, followed precisely the opposite course. He publicly deplored Navarino as an "untoward event" and made clear his intention of bolstering Turkey against Russia. His aim was to preserve the independence and integrity of the Ottoman Empire. But no other course could have been more nicely calculated to defeat this object. Sultan Mahmud was emboldened by Wellington's support to continue hostilities in Greece and even to provoke Russia by denouncing the Convention of Ackerman. Russia responded in April, 1828, with a declaration of war. This was the denouement that the skillful Canning had been able to avoid but which Wellington had precipitated in a few months of blundering diplomacy.

The Russian army crossed the Danube but was stalled unexpectedly by the Turkish fortresses on the southern bank—Shumla, Silistria, and Varna. Britain and France took advantage of the respite to conclude an agreement with Mehemet Ali (August 9, 1828) providing for the evacuation of the Egyptian forces from Greece. This was carried out by a French expeditionary force under General Maison during the winter 1828–1829. The following spring the three Allied Powers concluded the London Protocol (March 28, 1829) by which Greece was to be an autonomous but tributary state, governed by a prince selected by the Allies.

Meanwhile the Russians had been able to break through the Danube barrier. They crossed the Balkan Mountains, marking the first time that a Russian army had advanced so far south. In August, 1829, the key city of Adrianople fell without firing a shot. The Russian cannon could be heard in Constantinople. The Ottoman Empire appeared to be approaching its end. In fact, the French foreign minister, Count Polignac, now brought forward a plan for a Franco-Russian alliance to effect the complete partition of the Ottoman Empire and to redraw most of the boundaries of Europe.

At this critical moment Tsar Nicholas appointed a "Special Committee on the Problems of Turkey" with instructions to consider the political complications arising from the war with Turkey. This committee made a decision of far-reaching significance. It concluded that a partition of the Ottoman Empire was contrary to Russian interests. One reason was that partition would create a "labyrinth of difficulties and complications" with the other great powers. Another was that partition would enable the other powers to seize various parts of the Balkan Peninsula and thus Russia "would be called on to meet dangerous enemies in southern Europe instead of indifferent Turks." These considerations led the Committee to agree unanimously

that the advantages of the maintenance of the Ottoman Empire in Europe are superior to the disadvantages which it presents; that its fall henceforth would be contrary to the true interests of Russia; that as a consequence it would be wise to try to prevent it, taking advantage of all opportunities which might yet present themselves to conclude an honourable peace.[17]

A week after this decision was reached, the news arrived in St. Petersburg that General Diebitsch had signed the Treaty of Adrianople with the Turks and that the terms, fortunately, were moderate and in keeping with the recommendations of the committee. Thus the work of the committee did not affect the peace settlement but it did determine Russia's Near Eastern policy during the following decades. In the following chapter we shall note that Russia consistently supported the sultan against the challenge of Egypt's Mehemet Ali. This policy is understandable only in the light of this committee's recommendations, which Tsar Nicholas unhesitatingly accepted.

By the Adrianople Treaty of September 14, 1829, Russia relinquished her conquests in the Balkans but advanced her frontier from the northern to the southern mouth of the Danube. She was to occupy the Danubian Principalities pending the payment of an indemnity of fifteen million ducats; the hospodars of Moldavia and Wallachia were to be appointed for life; and the Turks were to withdraw all Moslems and raze all fortresses in the two provinces. Thus the Principalities received practical autonomy under Russian protection. Finally, the Turks recognized Russia's title to Georgia and other Caucasian territories, and also agreed to accept the Treaty of London with respect to Greece.

The actual settlement of the affairs of Greece was relegated to a conference in London which concluded a new London Protocol (February 3, 1830), declaring Greece to be an independent and monarchical state under the guarantee of the three Allied Powers. Wellington's policy at this time was to protect the Ottoman Empire by restricting the area of the new Greek state as much as possible. Its northern frontier was pushed down almost to the Gulf of Corinth, leaving little more than the Peloponnesus and the Cyclades Islands.

The Greek question still was not quite settled. The powers offered the Greek crown to Prince Leopold of Saxe-Coburg, but he declined it on the grounds that the frontiers of the new state were inadequate. The Greeks themselves rejected the London Protocol because of the same frontier issue. Meanwhile the Greeks had elected, as President, Count John Capodistrias, a native of Corfu and at one time foreign minister of Russia. Unlike other Greek leaders of this period Capodistrias was incorruptible and patriotic. He suppressed piracy, organized a state apparatus, made provisions for public education, founded the first agricultural school, advocated the distribution of state lands among the war veterans, and disciplined the unruly primates, who were virtually independent potentates in the provinces. These statesmanlike measures won him many enemies. These included not only vested interests that were threatened by his measures but also other elements that were alienated by his sharp tongue and self-righteousness. The intellectuals he called "fools," the military chieftains "brigands," and the primates "Turks masquerading under Christian names." Thus he estranged the most powerful and articulate segments of the population. Furthermore, the British and French ministers discreetly encouraged the opposition groups because Capodistrias followed a pro-Russian foreign policy.

The end came suddenly on October 9, 1831, when Capodistrias was assassinated by two members of the powerful Mavromichalis clan, which he had tried to subject to his authority. The country now lapsed into utter anarchy. Meanwhile the three Allied Powers had offered the Greek crown to Prince Otho, a younger son of the king of Bavaria. By May, 1832, satisfactory terms had been arranged, including the extension of the frontier slightly northward to the Volo-Arta line. In July, 1832, the sultan recognized the independence of Greece in return for a cash indemnity. Finally, on February 6, 1833, Otho arrived in Athens and Greece began her existence as an independent state under a Bavarian dynasty.

Before considering the development of the new Greek state it should be noted that its establishment undermined the unique position that the Greeks had enjoyed in Ottoman bureaucratic and financial circles. A large number of Greeks still remained under Turkish rule, many more than were to be found in independent Greece. But after 1821 the Phanariote hospodars in the Danubian Principalities gave way to native Rumanian rulers. In Constantinople the Armenians took advantage of the difficult position of the Greeks to buy their property at reduced rates. During the following years the Armenians prospered to the point where they became an important element in banking. Likewise, the Bulgarians now took the place of the Greeks in government contracting, particularly in army equipment and provisions. The Greeks were far from being entirely excluded. They remained active in Ottoman economic affairs to the last days of the empire. But never again did they attain the position they had reached in the eighteenth century. The revolution ended their junior partnership in the Ottoman Empire.

POLITICAL DEVELOPMENTS TO 1878

The new Greece was born with more than its share of problems. Apart from those of an economic nature, which we shall consider in the following section, the foremost problem in the popular mind was irredentism. The northern frontier ran from the Gulf of Arta in the west to the Gulf of Volo in the east. This meant a population of about 800,000 in the new kingdom as against three times that number in the Turkish provinces and in the British-held Ionian Islands. Thus, thanks to the requirements of the European balance of power, Greece was born a rump state. During the following century—to the 1923 Lausanne Treaty—Greek energies were spent in pursuit of the Megale Idea, or Great Idea, the redemption of the enslaved compatriots abroad.

Another serious problem was the disruptive influence of the great powers. Their conflicting interests and policies, so apparent during the revolutionary war, continued unabated following the peace. Athens became the diplomatic cockpit of the three Allied Powers, and, inevitably, there appeared "French," "Russian," and "English" parties under the leadership of Kolettes, Kolokotrones, and Mavrokordatos respectively. Under these circumstances Greece, like other small states, was independent only in a nominal sense. A British minister in Athens once declared, with more frankness than discretion, that "a really independent Greece is an absurdity. Greece is either Russian or English and since she must not be Russian she must be English." [18]

The final problem was political. The decision of the three powers in favor of a monarchical regime ran contrary to the country's political tradition. The contending forces in the past had been the democrats versus the oligarchs. The latter had enjoyed both administrative and economic power in the autonomous communities of the Turkish period. Now their pre-eminence was challenged by the new monarchy, which was unrestrained by a constitution and which began its first proclamation with the words, "Otho, by the grace of God King of Greece." Thus it was the oligarchs who were in the forefront of the opposition movement that finally compelled Otho in 1843 to accept a constitution.

The political conflict was intensified by the unfitness of Otho's Bavarian regents for the task that faced them. Since Otho was only seventeen at the time of his accession, he was accompanied by three regents: Count von Armansperg, General von Heideck, and Dr. Maurer. Heedless of the actual conditions prevailing in the new Greece, these men devised an elaborate national system of education practicable only on paper, adopted a judicial code far too complicated for a primitive Balkan country, and imposed a highly centralized Western bureaucracy in the place of the ancient local institutions that had flourished under Ottoman rule. Their most serious error was in treating the Greeks as though they were primitive natives unfit to participate in their own government. A Council of Secretaries composed of Greek officials did exist, but these officials were only heads of departments. All important decisions were made by the Bavarian regents, whose attitude is revealed in the manner in which they organized a national army. They disbanded all Greek troops and imported in their place Bavarian volunteers, who were handsomely paid. Less than two thousand Greeks were allowed to enroll in the new army and *gendarmerie*. This arbitrary procedure left ten thousand uprooted Greek veterans without any means of support. Many of them turned to brigandage, which remained for decades an urgent problem.

Even the justifiable measures of the regents aroused the opposition of one faction or another. In 1833 they decreed the establishment of a national Orthodox Church independent of the Patriarchate. They also nationalized the lands of some of the superabundant monasteries. These measures were necessary for national and for economic reasons. Yet a clamor was raised by the Patriarch, by the dispossessed monks, and by the pro-Russian party, which objected to the king because he was Roman Catholic.

Otho, who had attained his majority in 1835, made a concession to public opinion by retaining only one Bavarian in his cabinet. Unfortunately, the king neutralized the effect of this gesture by acting as his own prime minister and presiding over the cabinet meetings. Thus popular criticism, which in the past had been directed against the regents, henceforth was focused on the person of the king. A series of untoward events in the following years added to the general discontent and culminated in the revolt of 1843.

The revolt was largely the work of the "English" and "Russian" parties. They were united in their desire to be rid of the king, though for different reasons. The British wanted the king to be constitutional and the Russians wanted him to be Orthodox. Both believed that he would abdicate rather than accept a constitution. But both were proved wrong. At midnight, on September 14, 1843, a certain Colonel Kallerges marched his troops to the palace and raised the cry "Long live the Constitution." After some vacillation Otho signed a proclamation dismissing from his service all foreigners except the old philhellenes who had fought in the Greek revolution, and undertaking to summon within thirty days a National Constituent Assembly. Thus the Bavarian Protectorate came to an end and Greece took her place among the constitutional states of Europe.

On March 30, 1844, King Otho took the oath to the constitution providing for a popularly elected Chamber and an appointed Senate. This step changed neither the king's views nor his policies. He soon rid himself of Metaxas and Mavrokordatos, the two politicians who had led the constitutional movement, and turned to Kolettes, the head of the "French" party. Kolettes organized a political machine similar to that which functioned in France at the time under Guizot. "The System," as it was popularly called, was based upon the highly centralized hierarchy of prefects, subprefects, demarchs, gendarmes, tax collectors, and judges. In every election the king nominated his own candidates and "The System" ensured their return.

Despite the corruption of this regime it did not provoke a widespread revolutionary movement, not even in 1848, when ancient dynasties were tottering. The reason was that the Government party, that is, Kolettes's "French party," was the very one the masses supported. This party had genuine democratic traditions dating back to the prerevolutionary period when those who were influenced by French Revolutionary ideology founded pro-French democratic groups. Kolettes held this popular following by theatrical protestations of love for the people and demagogic speeches on irredentism or the Megale Idea.

Kolette's tactics explain the paradoxical situation of an anticonstitutional regime supported by the masses and an opposition consisting of the naturally conservative sections of the population. It also explains the failure of a few local insurrections in 1847 led by rebels within the "French" party. These outbreaks reflected the grievances of the peasants; yet the government was never seriously threatened. This was due to the lack of a clear and consistent program and also to the fear of the conservative opposition parties that the revolts might get out of control. In other words, the "English" and "Russian" parties were opposed to the dynasty but were not willing to support a revolutionary movement for fear that it might go too far and threaten the existing order.

Kolettes's expansionist dreams, which were shared by Otho, led to repeated clashes with the British Foreign Office. Lord Palmerston had little patience with the tiny state that aspired to annex Turkish provinces and thus to disturb the balance of power in the Near East. "I am obliged to own," he declared on one occasion, "that one of the worst things I ever did was to consent to Otto's election and by that consent to place him on the throne." [19] In 1850 Palmerston ordered a blockade of Piraeus in order to force the Greek government to satisfy the claims of a certain Don Pacifico and several other British subjects. Anglo-Greek relations were further strained during the Crimean War, when Greek sympathies were on the side of Russia and against the Western powers supporting Turkey. Guerrilla bands invaded the Turkish provinces, Thessaly and Epirus, but their efforts were doomed from the outset. Britain and France could not tolerate disturbances on their rear and promptly sent a fleet which occupied Piraeus from May, 1854, to February, 1857. The Greeks had no choice but to recall their bands and forgo their territorial claims.

Otho reached the height of his popularity during the Crimean War by identifying himself with the nationalist aspirations. Six years later he was driven from the country and few regretted his departure. One reason for his expulsion was the Italian War of 1859, during which Otho openly favored Austria while the Greek people naturally sympathized with the Italians fighting for their freedom. Another reason was the problem of the succession. Otho was childless and no other Bavarian prince was eligible for the throne, since the 1844 Constitution provided that the successor "must profess the religion of the Orthodox Eastern Church." Otho was forced out also because there had appeared by this time a new and more democratic generation of political leaders who were the first products of the national university and whose political ambitions brought them into conflict with the king and his supporters. Finally, the three powers were indifferent, or worse, to the fate of the dynasty. Britain, especially, was cool to the king, who persisted in a foreign policy that ran contrary to imperial interests in the Mediterranean.

The revolution broke out in October, 1862, while Otho was on a tour of the Peloponnesus. Before he could return to Athens a provisional government was formed which proclaimed the deposition of the dynasty. On the advice of the foreign diplomats Otho accepted the *fait accompli* and embarked on board a British ship for the return to Bavaria.

The problem now was to find a new ruler acceptable to the various great powers. This proved to be an almost impossible task, and Palmerston was at his wit's end when he recalled "Prince (whatever his name is) of Denmark." He was referring to Prince William George of the Danish Glücksberg dynasty. Queen Victoria thought poorly of the proposal—"poor foolish boy Willy"—"a good but not overbright and very plain youth." [20] But the fact remained that he was the last resort. So Willy arrived in Athens on October 30, 1863, as "George I, King of the Hellenes." He brought with him, as his dynasty's dowry, the Ionian Islands, granted by Britain with the expectation that he would not encourage future insurrections against Turkey.

A year after his arrival George took the oath to the new constitution adopted by the National Assembly. It was a democratic document, providing for a unicameral parliament elected by manhood suffrage, and for strict limitations upon the royal prerogatives. Willingness to abide by these limitations explains why the new seventeen-year-old ruler remained on the throne to witness the great triumphs in the Balkan Wars of 1912–1913.

ECONOMIC DEVELOPMENTS TO 1878

The revolution of the 1820's had left the Greek land in a state of utter devastation. Over 200,000 people had lost their lives. Vineyards and olive orchards had been destroyed wholesale. Except for Nauplion it was rare to find a house with roof and walls intact. To add to the misery, many of the guerrillas at the end of the revolution took to brigandage for want of anything better to do. The coming of Otho and his Bavarian bureaucrats restored neither order nor prosperity. Ten years after the king's arrival an eyewitness reported that the peasants "distrust the population of the towns, and look on Bavarians, Fanariotes, and government officers, as a tribe of enemies embodying different degrees of rapacity under various names. They have as yet derived little benefit from the government of King Otho, for their taxes are greater now than they were under the Turks. . . ." [21] This description of the plight of the Greek peasants explains why travelers throughout the nineteenth century reported considerable emigration from the new kingdom to the Ottoman provinces. One traveler noted that "during the three years from 1834 to 1836, nearly 60,000 individuals quitted their fatherland to take up their abode in Turkey." Upon inquiry as to the reasons for the exodus he was told that "in the Christian villages of Turkey we find a greater amount of prosperity and comfort than in those of Greece." [22]

Independence did improve the position of the peasants in one important respect by making possible a more equitable distribution of land. We noted earlier in this chapter that before the revolution the Turks in the Peloponnesus owned eighteen times as much land per capita as did the Greeks. The disposition of their estates became a crucial issue following the winning of independence. During the course of the revolutionary struggle legislation had been passed converting Turkish property into national domain. This was of little significance because the national governments lacked authority to enforce their decrees. Instead, the primates, being the most powerful, helped themselves to the choicest Turkish estates. Thus the new state was born with a serious land problem. Much of the land that belonged theoretically to the public domain had actually passed into private hands. Titles and tenures were insecure and only one peasant in six had land of his own.

By the end of the century most of the land had been distributed and the great majority of the peasants had enough land to support their families. The process of distribution appears to have been gradual and largely unplanned. Legislation in the 1830's and 1840's provided for land grants to veterans and to settlers on the public domain. More effective was the appropriation of land through legal recognition of squatters' rights. Any person could gain title to land if he cultivated it without interruption for a period that varied from region to region from one to fifteen years. This appears to have been a widespread practice during the early years, when population was sparse and much of the land uncultivated. As late as 1861 an observer reported that "a landlord must walk over his estate daily like a gamekeeper in order to protect it from squatters." [23] Although this procedure gave rise to "interminable litigation and to deeds of fearful violence," it did effect a thoroughgoing distribution of land. By 1870 the average peasant owned a plot of thirteen to twenty-five acres, though the holdings were much smaller in the islands and in the overpopulated mountain areas.

Land distribution unfortunately was not accompanied by an improvement in agricultural techniques. The Greek peasant still used the wooden plow of ancient times. He rarely used manure as fertilizer and he scattered his seed wastefully by hand. He knew nothing about crop rotation, so that much of his land lay fallow each year. His livestock, lacking forage, were small and scrawny, with disproportionately low draft power.

Various factors explain this backwardness, which persisted through most of the country. One was the lack of adequate transportation facilities. Peasants had to limit their production to the needs of their own families and of their immediate neighbors. Coastal cities, such as Argos, imported their grain from Trieste and Alexandria while the fertile Tripolitsa region, only six miles away, had surplus supplies which were rotting because of the lack of roads. Another reason for the agricultural backwardness was the unfortunate manner in which the tithe was collected. The grain had to be carried from the fields to the threshing floor, where the tax farmer inspected the crop and collected his tenth. Since the peasants harvested at the same time the tax farmer was in great demand at this critical period. This offered an opportunity for extortion, which was almost invariably practiced. Peasants paid an extra 3 to 5 per cent rather than allow their grain to remain piled up on the threshing floor at least three months awaiting the tax farmer. After this transaction the grain needed for fodder had to be carried back to the fields. This naturally involved a great loss of grain and labor, as contemporary travelers invariably remarked.

The sheaves are trailed along the road on the backs of donkeys, which display unwanted gambols, and scatter the grain along the road, in order to steal from one another a mouthful. Innumerable birds of the air gather to the feast; the fowls and the pigeons of the whole district assemble at the threshing floor; the ox that treadeth out the grain is not muzzled; and the peasant who ought to keep him to his work sleeps during the heat of the day. The rats emigrate from the houses, and form colonies in the stacks of wheat, which remain piled up often for weeks until the farmers of the land-tax, who are more destructive than the rats, give the unfortunate peasant the permission to thresh out, measure, and house his crop.[24]

A third reason for the retarded state of Greek agriculture was the heavy burden of peasant indebtedness. The interest rate on mortgage loans ranged from 20 to 24 per cent, and on personal loans from 36 to 50 per cent. The government did little to aid the peasant by easing his debt load or by any other means. An authority on Greek agriculture has described its state in the early nineteenth century as follows:

Though the majority of the population depend for its existence upon the returns of the soil, nothing had been done by the state for the security, promotion, and development of agriculture. Communications with rural communities . . . agricultural credit and the clearing up of rural property titles were never accomplished. . . . Agricultural education was totally lacking and taxation was empirical, heavy, unjust. . . . Animal husbandry was neglected . . . and the communal lands were continually being reduced by state encroachment. In general the agrarian population had been entirely abandoned to its own fate. The vital powers of the state were consumed by internal factional strife in disputes between an autocratic ruler and political parties that owed allegiance to one person, in intrigues instigated by the powers, and in vain attempts at promoting an irredentist policy without military or economic strength.[25]

The most common crops were of the intensive variety which required much labor and little land—grapes, currants, olives, citrus fruits, and tobacco. Cereals were grown where the land permitted, but never in sufficient quantity to meet domestic needs. In fact, the basic problem of Greek agriculture to the present day has been to produce some exportable product in sufficient quantities to pay for the necessary grain imports. The problem was solved in the nineteenth century by the Corinth grape or currant, which literally paid for the bread of Greece. Even before the revolution most of the Patras Plain was planted in currants for the British market. After the middle of the century, production rose sharply as new markets were found in France, Italy, Austria and other Continental countries. When the phylloxera blight ruined French vineyards in 1878 Greek currant production shot up to meet the demands of French wine manufacturers. Thus currant exports mounted steadily through the years: 1821—6,000 tons; 1841—10,000 tons; 1861—42,800 tons; 1871—81,374 tons; 1878—100,700 tons.

The currant trade became the cornerstone of the entire Greek economy. The flourishing port of Patras was occupied solely with the export of currants and the import of cereals and manufactured goods. In 1887 it exported 18.3 million francs worth of goods, of which 17.8 millions were in currants. So long as the currant market held, the Greek economy was safe. We shall see later that before the end of the century the market collapsed, setting off a chain reaction in Greece, including government bankruptcy and mass migration to the New World. Precisely the same pattern is observable in Greek economic development in the twentieth century, but with tobacco taking the place of the currant.

The industrial development of Greece remained in the embryonic stage before 1878. We noted earlier in this chapter that various cooperative handicraft enterprises had flourished before the revolution. The one at Ambelakia, which manufactured and distributed dyed cotton thread, was the best known and the most prosperous. But as early as 1800 an English traveler, after describing enthusiastically the success and affluence of this cooperative, went on to predict an uncertain future because of English machine competition.

Murad IV. Portrait by an unknown seventeenth-century European artist.

Mohammed II. Portrait by Gentile Bellini, 1480.

A Janissary (Bildarchiv der Nationalbibliothek, Vienna).

A Spahi (Bildarchiv der Nationalbibliothek, Vienna).

Travnik in Bosnia reflects the Turkish influence on Balkan architecture (Yugoslav Information Center). Below is a Divan meeting, showing a Turkish interior (M. d'Ohsson, *Tableau General de l'Empire Othoman,* Paris, 1787–1790).

The title page of the first Bulgarian book, the *Kiriakodromion,* by Sofronii, Bishop of Bratsa. Printed in Rimnik, Wallachia, 1806 (Harvard College Library).

Below is a facsimile of the last page of the rules of the Serbian secret society "Union or Death," commonly known as the "Black Hand," which flourished a little over a century after the printing of the book shown above.

Karageorge Petrovich (Yugoslav Information Center).

Rhigas Pheraios inciting fellow-Greeks to
revolt (Peter von Hess, Munich Museum).

Athanasios Diakos, painted by Photis Kontoglou, contemporary painter
who blends folk patterns with the Byzantine tradition.

Charles I of Rumania, 1881–1914.

Ferdinand I of Bulgaria, 1908–1918.

Mustafa Kemal Ataturk (General Directorate of Publications, Propaganda, and Tourism, Ankara).

Paul I of Greece (*Greece,* Royal Greek Embassy Information Service, Washington, D.C.).

(Above) German poster offering reward of 100,000 Reichmarks for the capture of Tito, dead or alive (Yugoslav Information Center).

(Right) Stevan Filipovic, Unit Commander of Valjevo Partisan Detachment, calling on the people to resist the occupation troops before being hanged (Yugoslav Information Center).

Tito and Pijade jailed in Lepoglava Prison before World War II for Communist activities (Yugoslav Information Center).

(Left) Outstanding Greek resistance leader, Ares Velouchiotes, and (right) General Stephanos Saraphis, commander of ELAS resistance forces in Greece (D. Megalides, *Leykoma tou Agona,* Athens, 1946).

This Greek family was forced to make its home in a pigsty. Such abject poverty persisted in Greece long after the war (Courtesy of Foster Parents' Plan, Inc.).

The Stalin Dam in Bulgaria, providing electric power and irrigating the Sofia plain, contrasts markedly with the rose-picking in the Valley of Roses (both pictures from the Ministry of Foreign Affairs, Bulgarian Peoples Republic).

About this time the merchants of Ampelakia began to feel the effect of the preference given to English cotton-thread in the German markets; and it was a subject of their complaint. "They foresaw," they said, "that the superior skill of the English manufacturers, and their being enabled to undersell every other competitor upon the Continent, would ultimately prove the ruin of their establishment." This no doubt is owing to the improvement adopted in Great Britain of spinning cotton-thread in mills, by means of engines that are worked by steam, which has caused such a considerable reduction in its price;—all the thread made at Ampelakia being spun by manual labour.[26]

This gloomy forecast proved entirely justified. Those enterprises that survived the ravages of the revolutionary war petered out in almost every case during the following decades. The one exception was the shipping industry. Traditionally it had operated along cooperative lines, with carpenters, lumber merchants, seamen, and captains pooling their resources and sharing the profits. A large proportion of the ships were destroyed during the revolution, but island shipyards soon made up the losses. The rapid development of southern Russia proved a boon to Greek shipowners, who were particularly active in the Black Sea trade. The Greek merchant marine soon held first place in the eastern Mediterranean. But, as in the case of the currant industry, a crisis developed toward the end of the century. The reason, in this instance, was the competition of the new steam-powered ships which the Greek islanders could neither build nor afford to purchase. We shall see later that the problem was solved by the purchase and operation, though no longer along cooperative lines, of old steamships discarded by Western firms.

Industry proper cannot be said to have started in Greece before the abdication of Otho and the accession of George I in 1862. By 1878 a small number of modest enterprises existed in a few coastal towns, such as Patras, Syra, and Piraeus-Athens. These enterprises confined themselves exclusively to the production of consumers' goods, especially flour, textiles, olive oil, leather products, glass, and soap. By 1877 Greece had 136 plants employing 7,342 workers. It may be concluded that Greek industry did not really begin to develop until the advent of the Trikoupes administration in 1882. Premier Trikoupes was the first to undertake the systematic development of transportation facilities, the lack of which had hitherto shackled industrial growth.

We may conclude that the Greek economy in 1878 remained largely unaffected by the West's industrial dynamism. Apart from the currant growers of the Patras region and the Ionian Islands, the typical Greek peasant practiced subsistence farming. He could, in any case, produce only a small surplus on his tiny and crudely cultivated plot. This surplus sufficed for the purchase of the few commodities that he and his family could not grow or fabricate. The simplest of these commodities were supplied by the infant domestic industry and the remainder were imported from Western Europe.

16. Ottoman Reform and Near Eastern Crises: 1831–1852

T HE YEARS following the Greek revolution are of critical importance in Near Eastern history in two respects. In the first place, this was the period when the Turkish reform movement got under way in a positive sense. Selim had attempted reform at the turn of the century but without success. Mahmud, as we shall see, was to succeed where Selim had failed. He exterminated the janissaries, who hitherto had blocked reform, and asserted the authority of the central government to a degree unprecedented since the seventeenth century. In doing so, Mahmud paved the way for the positive reform measures of an outstanding minister, Reshid Mustafa Pasha, during the 1840's. With this beginning the reform movement was to continue its uneven course, sometimes appearing on the surface, at other times submerged by reaction, only to appear again, as it did most spectacularly with the Young Turk revolution of 1908 and the Kemalist revolution following World War I.

This was also the period when the so-called Eastern Question crystallized. The catalytic agent in this respect was the master of Egypt, Mehemet Ali. Twice he brought the Ottoman Empire to the verge of dissolution, and in doing so he forced the great powers to re-examine their Near Eastern policies and to take sides. The result was the crises of 1831 to 1833, and 1839 to 1841. These crises involved all the European powers and ended with treaty engagements to which they all subscribed. Henceforth the Eastern Question was to remain an ever-present factor in European diplomacy, and not infrequently the most important one.

MAHMUD AND THE JANISSARIES

Mahmud II ascended the throne at one of the gravest moments in Ottoman history. As will be recalled from Chapter 13, he was the third sultan to reign within fourteen months. Bloodshed and terror prevailed in

Constantinople to a degree unprecedented in that turbulent capital. The reaction of the European powers is suggested by the fact that they considered at least twelve specific plans for Ottoman partition during the first twenty-five years of Mahmud's reign.

Mahmud himself was young, untried, and unimpressive in appearance at the time of his accession in 1808. But he soon demonstrated that he was made of sterner stuff than his unfortunate predecessor, Selim III. He was not as attractive a personality as Selim. He was brutal, ruthless, and avaricious. His customary manner of replenishing his finances was to execute his wealthy subjects and confiscate their property. Yet his harshness was not capricious or senseless. "A drastic disease," he often said, "needs a drastic remedy." Furthermore, his aims were progressive and constructive. He stands out as one of the great reforming sultans of his dynasty. Mahmud was convinced that his empire must reform or perish, and he was aware that the janissaries were the principal obstacle to reform.

The janissaries were too strongly entrenched to be challenged at once, so Mahmud began by asserting his authority in the provinces. Imperial disintegration had reached the point where Mahmud effectively controlled only two provinces in Asia Minor at the time of his accession. During the following years he re-established imperial unity to a surprising degree. He did not hesitate to use both fair means and foul. His agents lured one of the great Smyrna notables onto a boat and poisoned him. In the case of the feudal chiefs of eastern Asia Minor, Mahmud dispatched an energetic pasha who built a road and brought up heavy artillery to smash the feudal castles. Likewise, the independent pasha of Baghdad was brought to terms by raising the Bedouin desert tribes against him. Where possible Mahmud used more diplomatic methods to gain his ends. He lured the sons of hereditary chieftains by offering them attractive posts elsewhere in the empire and then he placed his own men in the places of the chieftains when they died.

Mahmud encountered more serious resistance in the Balkans, where the octogenarian Ali Pasha had consolidated his position in northern Greece and Albania. For all practical purposes, Ali was an independent ruler with foreign consular representatives accredited to his fortified capital at Yanina. He overreached himself, however, when he sent agents to assassinate an enemy in Constantinople itself. The plot miscarried and one of the assassins was arrested and forced to confess. Mahmud deposed and outlawed Ali in March, 1820, and sent an army to destroy him. Ali, who was not called "the Lion" for nothing, resisted fiercely. Before his head was delivered to Mahmud in February, 1822, the Greeks had taken advantage of the opportunity to begin their war for independence.

The Greek revolution demonstrated once more the utter uselessness of the janissaries as a fighting force. They had been untried since their earlier fiasco during the Russian wars at the turn of the century. Now they proved incapable of putting down the uprising of a comparative handful of Greek guerrillas. At this point Mahmud decided to entrust the suppression of the

Greeks to his powerful Egyptian vassal, Mehemet Ali, while he made preparations to cut out the cancer that was threatening the life of the empire.

Mahmud was to prevail over the janissaries where Selim had failed. One reason was the difference between the two men. Selim allowed himself to be surrounded by untrustworthy advisers who feigned support while plotting against him. Mahmud, by contrast, selected his ministers carefully and placed dependable men in key positions. Typical was his appointment of a ferocious ex-janissary, Hussein the Black, as commander of the troops on the Asiatic side of the Straits. When the moment came, Hussein carried out Mahmud's orders and butchered his former comrades without qualm or mercy. Mahmud also carefully won over the ulema by promotions and favors. The grand mufti, or head of the learned jurists, issued a fetva testifying to all believers not only that Mahmud's proposed reform of the janissary corps was in accord with Islamic doctrine but also that its application was a sacred duty for all Moslems. Finally, Mahmud was fearless and decisive when the crisis came, in contrast to Selim, who repeatedly drew back and yielded before janissary threats.

Mahmud first presented his plan for the reorganization of the janissaries before an assembly of religious, military, and administrative leaders. The plan provided that about one third of the janissaries should be selected for training along Western lines. Discipline and morale were to be fostered by common uniforms, higher pay, improved rations, careful selection of officers, and elimination of bribery and favoritism. The assembly approved the plan and steps were taken to put it promptly into effect.

Mahmud now faced the same storm of protest and violence as did his ill-fated predecessors. The chief grievance appears to have been not the strange military drill or the new tight-fitting uniforms or any religious prejudice against imitating the infidel West. Rather, it was the threat to the substantial economic interests that manipulated the janissary pay tickets. We noted in Chapter 13 that these tickets were acquired in large numbers by wealthy individuals, who then drew the pay of janissaries theoretically in the service but usually long since deceased. By this time more than 135,000 pay tickets were extant and were being regularly honored by the treasury, though it is doubtful that even 5 per cent of this number represented live and active janissaries. Thus many important people were vitally interested in thwarting Mahmud and they now resorted to their customary intimidation and mob violence.

On the night of June 13–14, 1826, the janissaries overturned their soup kettles, the customary signal of revolt. But this time they met their master. Mahmud summoned Hussein the Black to cross the Bosphorus to Constantinople with a large body of troops and artillerymen. This show of force won the populace to Mahmud's side. The isolated janissaries had no cannon to defend themselves against Hussein's shell fire. Within a matter of hours their barracks were tumbling about their heads in blazing ruins. The British ambassador, who watched the smoke curling up from the wreckage, reported that 6,000 were killed in the holocaust and that another 18,000 were exiled to the Asiatic provinces during the following fortnight. Janissary garrisons in the provincial cities either submitted or were crushed with little difficulty. In this anticlimatic fashion disappeared a proud institution with half a millenium of history behind it.

Mahmud at last was the unchallenged master of his realm. Now he was free to build as he wished upon the ruins of the old. First and foremost he wished to organize a new and powerful army. He participated personally and enthusiastically in this task. He wore the new uniform, pored over drill books, and took part in maneuvers. Progress was slow in the face of innumerable difficulties—popular resistance to conscription, indolent and illiterate officers, and lack of adequate military academies. Most serious was the distraction of continual war, first with Russia in 1828–1829 and then with Mehmet Ali in 1832–1833 and 1839. Mahmud was not able to build up a first-class military machine comparable to that of the European powers or even of Mehemet Ali. But he did leave the Turkish army stronger than he had found it, although not strong enough to stand up to Ibrahim and his Egyptians.

It is often stated that Mahmud was not a true reformer and that his sole concern was to strengthen his army in order to subdue his enemies. There is some truth to this contention, in the sense that Mahmud was not a doctrinaire liberal like Selim. On the other hand, his interests ranged far beyond the military realm. Indeed, he attempted to change his subjects and his empire with a zeal reminiscent of Peter the Great. Just as the tsar had warred on beards and gowns, so Mahmud enveighed against turbans and slippers. More constructively, he built bridges and lighthouses, opened the Danube to steamer navigation, instituted the first official newspaper, the *Moniteur Ottomane,* and imposed sanitary measures to combat the plague despite the religious prejudices of his subjects. He also tried to improve administration and finances by raising salaries and paying them promptly, regularizing his diplomatic service, and adopting a new tariff in 1838 that eliminated an injurious system of monopolies in articles of commerce.

Finally, what was the significance of Mahmud's reforms for the Balkans? The answer is that his reforms had much less effect upon that region than might be imagined. Mahmud's great accomplishment had to do with imperial authority, which he asserted by crushing the janissaries and the semi-independent local potentates. This achievement did help the Balkan peoples by eliminating the open terrorism and anarchy that had driven the Serbs to revolt in 1804. Furthermore, Mahmud strove to improve specifically the position of his Christian subjects. Sometimes he was guilty of harsh measures, such as the hanging of the Greek Patriarch in 1821, but his motive always was political expediency rather than religious fanaticism. Thus in 1830 he ordered the release of all Greeks taken slaves during the Greek revolution, and compelled their masters to bear the expense of repatriating them to Greece. On his frequent tours he took specific measures to improve the lot of the Christians, and issued orders that "Turks and rayas be treated alike without distinction."

Despite these efforts the fact remains that the position of the Balkan Christians remained basically the same so far as everyday life was concerned. Janissary terrorism was gone, but the Ottoman officials remained, and they were as inefficient and corrupt as before. Appointments to provincial posts were still dependent on favoritism and bribery, and the salaries were still discouragingly low. Thus imperial administration remained a scourge for Moslem and Christian subjects alike. In fact, contemporary travelers frequently reported that conditions worsened when the bureaucrat from Constantinople replaced the former local lord. The latter had had a selfish interest in caring for the welfare of his subjects, whose prosperity would contribute to his own wealth and that of his successors. The government officials, by contrast, usually had paid for their appointments and thus found it necessary to exploit the citizenry to the limit before they were transferred.

Despite these qualifications, Mahmud stands out as one of the great constructive figures of Ottoman history. By destroying the janissaries and asserting the authority of the central government, he made possible the reform movement of the following decades.

NEAR EASTERN CRISIS: 1831–1833

Mahmud's life was to end tragically in the midst of defeat and humiliation. The person responsible for this misfortune was Mehemet Ali, the pasha of Egypt. For a full decade he kept the Near East in turmoil and repeatedly brought the European powers to the brink of war. Those who have studied the career of the masterful Mehemet Ali are not agreed as to his basic aim. Some believe that he sought to supplant the sultan and found a new dynasty in Constantinople. Others are of the opinion that he wished to gain control only of the Arab provinces and that he would have been content to share the empire on this basis. Whether he coveted the whole or only the part is not too important. Either objective was bound to lead to war, especially with the resolute Mahmud in Constantinople.

Mehemet Ali nominally was the governor of Egypt under the suzerainty of the sultan. But even before the Greek revolution Mehemet Ali had added the Sudan and a part of the Arabian Peninsula to his domains. Then he intervened against the Greek rebels after Mahmud had promised to hand over the pashaliks of Crete and the Peloponnesus. At Navarino Mehemet Ali lost his fleet, though he did gain Crete as payment for his assistance. When the sultan found himself at war with Russia in 1828 Mehemet Ali gave him only nominal aid. Instead, he concentrated his efforts on building a new fleet and improving his army. Thus in the early 1830's Mehemet Ali was stronger than his master and overshadowed him in almost every respect.

Mehemet Ali had the basic advantage of being the absolute master of his realm. He achieved this by ruthlessly eliminating the Mamelukes, who formerly had ruled the country. Mehemet Ali also completely controlled and freely exploited the resources of Egypt. He was able to draw into his own coffers a larger proportion of the national income than any other Eastern ruler. But Mehemet Ali was more than a superefficient Oriental despot. He was unique in that he began, like other pashas, by seeking to amass a fortune, and ended by attempting to develop and civilize his adopted country. He was also unique in realizing that the key to development and civilization was to be found in the West. He spent large sums in an attempt to establish modern industry in spite of the persistent and ultimately successful opposition of the British. He introduced cotton culture, which quickly became the mainstay of the national economy. He also developed a system of irrigation canals which extended the area under cultivation and made possible year-round farming. His most spectacular success was in the military field, where he made use of a corps of Western advisers, mostly Frenchmen, to build the first modern army and navy in the Near East. The contrast between the strength of pasha and sultan was revealed during the Greek war. It became more apparent during the following decade when Mehemet Ali made his bid for empire.

Following the Greek adventure Mehemet Ali turned his eyes eastward toward the rich and strategic pashalik of Syria. For a while he was diverted by a French proposal that he should expand with the support of France westward into Tunis, Algeria, and Morocco. The French, who had particularly close relations with Mehemet Ali, advised him that an advance into the Barbary States was less likely to meet with opposition from Constantinople and from the European powers than an invasion of Syria. The French, of course, had other and more selfish reasons, such as the desire to eliminate the Barbary pirates and to distract popular attention from pressing constitutional problems at home. Mehemet Ali decided to undertake the venture on the condition that the French cede outright four warships. While this was being considered, the European capitals got wind of what was afoot. The British protested vehemently. "France has no right," declared Wellington, "to appeal to Mehemet Ali because he is a subject of the Sultan. . . . The alliance of Mehemet Ali with France will be envisaged as a combination fatal for the Ottoman Empire."[1]

Faced with this opposition, the French dropped the notion of cooperation with Mehemet Ali. Instead, they began preparations for a purely French invasion of Algeria while Mehemet Ali again turned toward Syria. In the summer of 1830 a French expedition reached Algeria and quickly overran the country with little difficulty and with the diplomatic protests confined to London and Constantinople. But when Mehemet Ali invaded Syria in November, 1831, a full-fledged international crisis quickly developed.

The reason was that the great superiority of the Egyptian armies threatened the very existence of the Ottoman Empire. When that threat was made, European interests were involved and European powers intervened. Mehemet's son Ibrahim captured the Syrian cities and fortresses one after the other—Jaffa, Gaza, Jerusalem, Acre, and Damascus. He met and defeated a Turkish army near Alexandretta and advanced into Asia Minor without resistance. In December, 1832, he routed the main Turkish army led by the grand vizir in the battle of Konya. With no further opposition he pressed on to Brusa, within striking distance of the Straits and Constantinople.

Meanwhile Mahmud in the summer of 1832 had appealed to Britain for assistance. Foreign Minister Palmerston was in favor of telling Mehemet "forthwith to retire to Egypt and rest contented with that fertile country." [2] But his colleagues were engrossed in the question of parliamentary reform; furthermore, the navy at that time was engaged in operations off the coasts of Portugal and Holland. Accordingly the cabinet rejected Mahmud's request for aid. A few years later Palmerston expressed the opinion that "no British Cabinet at any period of the history of England ever made so great a mistake in regard to foreign affairs. . . . Our refusal at that time has been the cause of more danger to the peace of Europe, to the balance of power and to the interest of England than perhaps any one determination ever before produced." [3]

The French government was not concerned about the Egyptian victories since it was definitely partial to Mehemet Ali. Only the Russian government reacted strongly to Ibrahim's advance through Syria and Asia Minor. Its motivation was clear and simple. As in 1829, at the time of the Adrianople Treaty, so now the Russian government had no desire to see the weak Ottoman dynasty replaced by a new regime that was likely to be strong and aggressive. Accordingly, Tsar Nicholas sent General Muraviev on a special mission to Constantinople and Alexandria to promote a settlement. Muraviev arrived in Constantinople simultaneously with the news of the disaster at Konya. He offered Mahmud a naval squadron for the protection of Constantinople. The sultan hesitated, so Muraviev proceeded to Alexandria. The most that he could get out of Mehemet was that Ibrahim would not, for the moment, advance closer to Constantinople.

Meanwhile the sultan had decided that only outside aid could avert the ruin of his empire and formally requested the proffered Russian fleet. The British and French ministers in Constantinople protested strongly, but the Turkish foreign minister replied pointedly, "A drowning man will clutch at a serpent." [4]

On February 20, 1833, a powerful Russian squadron sailed into the Bosphorus and anchored before Constantinople. Both Britain and France were seriously alarmed and brought pressure upon the sultan to request its withdrawal. The tsar would not hear of this so long as Ibrahim remained in Asia Minor. And Ibrahim in turn refused to move until the sultan had met his demands, namely, the cession of Syria and the important town and district of Adana (Seghan) in southwestern Asia Minor. In March the sultan offered to cede Syria, but Mehemet Ali scornfully rejected the offer and instructed Ibrahim to march upon Constantinople if his demands were not fully satisfied.

Mahmud finally yielded and on April 8, 1833, signed the Convention of Kutahia, ceding both Syria and Adana to Mehemet Ali. Ibrahim began preparations for withdrawing his troops, but the sultan now gave signs of attempting to retain Adana despite his commitment. Ibrahim entrenched himself once more while the Russians brought additional warships to Constantinople and even landed fifteen thousand troops on the Asiatic side of the Bosphorus. The situation became too serious for the sultan to tarry longer, so on May 3 he formally recognized the cession of Adana.

Two days later, a special Russian envoy, Count Alexis Orlov, arrived in Constantinople. His instructions were to bolster the Turkish government until peace was concluded and to induce the sultan to look to Russia as the only hope of salvation. Since an agreement already had been reached, Orlov concentrated his attention on Mahmud. He was so conciliatory and charming that he completely won over the sultan and his court. They were already in a receptive mood because they suspected France of favoring Mehemet and resented England's original refusal of naval support. By contrast, the tsar appeared to be a generous and reliable friend. Orlov exploited this situation so skillfully that in the end it was Mahmud himself who proposed a Turkish-Russian alliance. The outcome was the Treaty of Unkiar-Skelessi signed on July 8, 1833.

The public articles proclaimed the existence of peace and friendship between the two emperors and provided that they should reach an understanding with each other upon all matters affecting their peace and security. They were also committed to "afford to each other mutually for this purpose substantial aid, and the most efficacious assistance." The real significance of the treaty, however, was contained in a secret article which released the sultan from any obligation to render such assistance to the tsar and provided that Turkey should instead "limit its action in favor of the Imperial Court of Russia to closing the Straits of the Dardanelles, that is, to not allowing any foreign vessels of war to enter them under any pretext whatsoever." [5]

The provisions of the secret article leaked out and caused an uproar, particularly in Britain. Palmerston charged that the sultan was bound to give the Russian fleet free access to the Straits and to the Mediterranean while the Western fleets, by contrast, would not be permitted to pass through to the Black Sea. The Russian foreign minister, Nesselrode, repeatedly denied this charge. He pointed out that the status of the Straits had been determined hitherto by the 1809 Anglo-Turkish treaty, which stipulated that it was at "all times forbidden for war vessels to enter the channel of Constantinople. . . ." Accordingly, he maintained, with full justification, that the secret article in the Unkiar-Skelessi Treaty "does not impose on the Porte any burdensome condition and does not cause it to contract any new engagement. It serves only to state the fact of the closure of the Dardanelles for the military flag of the foreign Powers; a system which the Porte has maintained at all times and from which, indeed, it could not depart without injuring its most direct interests." [6]

Palmerston's obvious rejoinder to Nesselrode was that "if this treaty did not bring you any advantages or new privileges, then who urged you to conclude it?" [7] The answer is to be found in the treaty's stipulation requiring the signatories "to come to agreement without reserve on all matters concerning their respective tranquillity and safety. . . ." In other words, Turkey was obligated, in case of trouble, to consult with Russia first and to depend upon Russia first in case assistance should be needed. Thus Russia had gained the right of prior consultation in Ottoman affairs. Palmerston perceived this when he pointed out that the "most objectionable part of the treaty is the mutual engagement between the two Powers to consult each other confidentially upon all their respective interests, and by which the Russian Ambassador becomes chief Cabinet Minister of the Sultan." [8]

Russia could not hope to reconcile Britain to the Unkiar-Skelessi Treaty and she did not try to do so. But she was bound by strategic considerations to reach some agreement with Austria concerning her Turkish policy. Land communications between Russia and Constantinople ran through the Danubian Principalities and Bulgaria. Austria was able, from her position in Transylvania, to sever those communications whenever she so wished. This explains why, two months after Unkiar-Skelessi, Russia concluded the Münchengrätz Agreement with Austria. By it Russia declared herself in favor of the maintenance of the Ottoman Empire and agreed that if partition became inevitable she would act only in concert with Austria.

During the following years Prince Metternich of Austria tried to extend the Münchengrätz Agreement to include Britain and France. But neither Britain nor Russia was willing. Tsar Nicholas had agreed to consult and to cooperate with Austria because of the exigencies of military strategy. But he absolutely refused to grant to the two Western powers a lever by which they could control his Turkish policy. Palmerston likewise rejected Metternich's proposal for a Four Power Pact. He plainly suspected that it was a trick and replied belligerently that the chief danger was "the active policy of the Russian Government [which] . . . for years has been directed systematically, perseveringly and with no small degree of success to the . . . annexation of large and important portions of the Turkish dominions. . . ." [9]

This suspicion of Russia is quite significant. In the light of later events it is clear that one of the chief and most ominous results of this Near Eastern crisis of 1831 to 1833 is precisely this Russophobia that it generated. Palmerston was not the only one affected. Wide sections of the British public shared his dislike and distrust of Russia. Various factors contributed to this deep-rooted feeling. In addition to the Near Eastern crisis there was the widespread resentment aroused by Russia's suppression of the Polish revolt of 1830. Very effective also was the propaganda and the deliberate provocations of a small group of dedicated Russophobes who labored zealously to promote the thesis that barbaric Asiatic Russia was about to swallow the entire Near East as she already had Poland. A leading role was played by a strange Scotsman named David Urquhart, a capable, energetic, and rather unbalanced mystic who in other circumstances might have been the messiah of a religious revival. The impact of these various factors is evident in the findings of a historian who carefully studied British public opinion at this time and concluded that "by the end of 1837 Russophobia was a major element in English opinion. . . ." [10] This should be kept in mind as one of the major antecedents of the Crimean War two decades later.

Palmerston was as much opposed to Mehemet Ali as he was to the Russians. "I hate Mehemet Ali," he declared frankly, "whom I consider as nothing but an ignorant barbarian, who by cunning and boldness and mother-wit, has been successful in rebellion; . . . I look upon his boasted civilization of Egypt as the arrantest humbug; and I believe that he is as great a tyrant and oppressor as ever made a people wretched."[11] This characteristic explosion is less than fair to Mehemet Ali. Palmerston undoubtedly would have been delighted if some of Mehemet Ali's many accomplishments, which he dismissed so airily, could have been effected in the provinces under the sultan's control. Palmerston obviously was prejudiced in this matter, and he was prejudiced because Mehemet's ambitions conflicted with British imperial interests.

The Near East at this time was beginning to assume a new significance as a short cut to India and the Far East. The Industrial Revolution was progressing in England with ever-increasing speed. The new factories required a constant flow of raw materials from overseas, while the manufactured goods likewise had to be transported to foreign markets. Steamships were now making their appearance and were proving speedier and more dependable than sailing ships. But for long voyages so much fuel and water were needed that little space was left for cargo. A shorter passage with frequent stops for supplies was indispensable. This meant a reversion to the old routes through the Near Eastern lands. During the 1830's several English surveyors and scientists conducted investigations. Their reports produced conflicting views in British official circles. Some favored a canal across the Suez Isthmus; others preferred a railway to a canal; and still others urged development of the Euphrates–Persian Gulf route.

The important point is that whichever route was considered, Mehemet Ali was found to be in the way. In Syria he blocked the route to the Euphrates and the Persian Gulf. In Egypt he controlled the vital Suez passageway. Furthermore, his armies were encircling the Red Sea by pushing down the west coast of the Arabian Peninsula. When they neared the strategic port of Aden in 1838 the British quickly intervened and annexed the port. Palmerston informed Mehemet that Aden was " a British possession" and "a hostile attack . . . will be dealt with accordingly." [12]

Palmerston explicitly acknowledged the strategic considerations underlying his difficulties with Egypt's ruler. Mehemet's "real design," he declared on one occasion, "is to establish an Arabian kingdom, including all the countries in which Arabic is the language. There might be no harm in such a thing in itself; but as it necessarily would imply the dismemberment of Turkey, we could not agree to it. Besides, Turkey is as good an occupier of the road to India as an active Arabian sovereign would be." The inference to be drawn from these assumptions is that Turkey should be supported to resist Mehemet. "We must try to help the Sultan," concluded Palmerston, "in organizing his army, navy, and finances; and if he can get those three departments into good order he may still hold his ground." [13]

The conclusion apparent from these remarks is that Palmerston was determined to protect the sultan against both the tsar and Mehemet Ali. During the crisis of 1839 to 1841 he cooperated with the tsar to end the Egyptian menace once and for all. A decade later he aligned himself with France and fought the Crimean War to remove what he considered to be the Russian threat to Ottoman independence.

NEAR EASTERN CRISIS: 1839–1841

The Near Eastern settlement of 1833 could not last indefinitely. Neither Mahmud nor Mehemet Ali was willing to accept the *status quo*. The sultan was determined to crush the upstart pasha and to recover his losses, whereas Mehemet Ali longed for more territory and for full independence. The great powers, suspicious though they were of each other's policies in the Near East, actively endeavored to keep the peace. At one time or another they all warned Mahmud and Mehemet Ali against renewing hostilities.

Mahmud broke the uneasy peace in April, 1839, and thereby precipitated a crisis that involved all the great powers and lasted to 1841. Mahmud had been encouraged by reports of widespread disaffection in Syria against Egyptian rule. Also, his army had been reorganized by a young Prussian officer, Helmuth von Moltke, destined to win fame in later years as the conqueror of Austria and France. It is true that Moltke warned the sultan that his army was not yet quite ready to be put to the test. But Mahmud by this time was far advanced in years and was resolved to delay no further his long-planned revenge. "The Sultan," reported Ponsonby, the British minister in Constantinople, "would rather die or be the vassal of Russia than not endeavour to destroy the rebel subject." [14]

The Ottoman armies gave a better account of themselves in this war than in the previous one. But the outcome was fully as disastrous—in fact, more so. On June 24, 1839, Ibrahim met the main Turkish army at Nezib (Nizip), just inside the Syrian frontier. The battle was hard-fought but ended with an overwhelming victory for Ibrahim. "The Turks threw down their arms," reported Moltke, "and abandoned their artillery and ammunition, flying in every direction." [15]

Before the news of disaster reached Constantinople the old sultan mercifully died, worn out by illness and excessive drinking. His successor, Abdul Mejid, was a boy of sixteen, lacking both ability and experience. At this critical moment another calamity befell the empire. The entire Turkish fleet, which had set sail from the Straits in search of the Egyptian navy, proceeded to Alexandria and surrendered to Mehemet Ali. It is not clear whether the Turkish admiral had been bribed to commit this extraordinary act or whether he had moved on the conviction that the war was lost and that it was preferable that the navy should fall to the Moslem Egyptians rather than to the infidel Russians. In any case, during the fateful week between June 24 and July 1 the empire lost an army, a navy, and a sultan.

Mehemet Ali now committed what proved to be a fatal blunder. He demanded not only that he should be recognized as hereditary ruler of Egypt and Syria but also that his bitter enemy, Grand Vizir Chosrew, should be dismissed from his post. The latter condition caused a delay which gave the great powers an opportunity to intervene under the aggressive leadership of Palmerston. Their intervention marked the virtual end of Mehmet Ali's career.

On July 27, 1839, the powers presented a collective note to the Ottoman government requesting it to suspend negotiations and to refrain from "any definitive resolution without their concurrence." The sultan welcomed the proposal and gladly accepted it. The surprising feature of this situation was the willingness of France to associate herself with the other powers. Palmerston repeatedly had declared that Mehemet Ali should be forced to surrender all his possessions except Egypt. The French from the outset were unwilling to support such a drastic proposal. Many Frenchmen regarded Mehemet as the disciple of Napoleon, almost as his apostolic successor in Egypt. Also, a strong Mehemet Ali in the eastern Mediterranean meant a correspondingly strong French influence in that vital region. Nevertheless, the French government maintained a discreet silence and refused to make an issue of these differences. It apparently assumed that, when the showdown came, Palmerston would decide to accept a compromise settlement with Mehemet Ali rather than risk another appearance of Russian warships and soldiers in the Straits.

This strategy was shrewd but it boomeranged against the French. The reason was that the Russians did the exact opposite of what was expected. They did not take aggressive measures in the Straits, as they could have on the basis of the Unkiar-Skelessi provisions. Instead, Nesselrode declared repeatedly that he would back up Palmerston in his support of the sultan. Nesselrode went further and sent Baron Brunnow as Envoy Extraordinary to London in September, 1839. The baron assured Palmerston that Tsar Nicholas agreed entirely with the British views concerning the Turkish-Egyptian question and would join in whatever measures might be necessary to put these views into effect. More specifically, he stated that Russia was willing to allow the Unkiar-Skelessi Treaty to lapse. He also declared that if it should prove necessary to send a Russian force to the Straits in order to coerce Mehemet Ali, the force would be sent only with the agreement and the consent of the other powers.

The significance of this Russian about-face is apparent. Russia was ready to surrender whatever special privileges she had obtained by the Unkiar-Skelessi Treaty. But in return she would obtain a close working agreement with Britain and she would also isolate France. In other words, Russia was exploiting the differences between Britain and France over Mehemet Ali in order to break up the Anglo-French entente. Palmerston was ready to accept this diplomatic revolution, but his colleagues and his sovereign were hesitant. They desired a more specific and secure agreement with Russia. They proposed that if it should prove necessary for Russian forces to enter the Bosphorus, allied forces should at the same time enter the other end of the Straits at the Dardanelles.

When Brunnow returned to St. Petersburg with this counterproposal, the tsar and his ministers were delighted. "If the plan of Lord Palmerston is adopted," declared Nesselrode, "the Anglo-French alliance is *ipso facto* dissolved and is replaced, in the affairs of the Orient, by an accord between the two Imperial Courts [Russia and Austria] and England. . . . For myself, I avow to you that I should like very much the plan of Lord Palmerston." [16] Brunnow returned to London in December, 1839, with an affirmative answer. Palmerston was as pleased as Nesselrode. "This will give us a pull upon France, and will enable us to carry our own views into execution about Turkey and Egypt; for Austria and Prussia will side with us and Russia;— and France if she stands aloof, will be left to herself." [17]

France indeed was isolated. At this critical stage the French government fell over a domestic issue and a new cabinet was formed headed by Adolphe Thiers. His strategy was to procrastinate and to cause delays in the hope that meanwhile the sultan and Mehemet Ali would reach an agreement between themselves. Given the strong sentiment in France in favor of Mehemet Ali, there was scarcely any other course that Thiers could follow. But the French minister in London, François Guizot, warned Thiers of the dangers of this policy of delay.

The more I observe, the more I satisfy myself that the British Cabinet considers the circumstances as favorable for settling the affairs of the East, and wishes seriously to take advantage of them. It would much prefer to act in concert with us; it is disposed to make concessions to establish that concert. Nevertheless, if, on our part, we do not decide on something positive, if we appear to desire only to adjourn and convert all difficulties into impossibilities, a moment may arrive, I think, when, . . . the British Cabinet would act without us and with others rather than not act at all.[18]

This astute analysis of the situation soon was proved fully justified. Palmerston now moved quickly and decisively, spurred on by two disturbing dispatches from the Levant. The one brought news of the dismissal of Grand Vizir Chosrew in Constantinople. Since he was a firm opponent of Mehemet Ali, the latter greeted the news joyfully and immediately sent an envoy to the sultan to seek a settlement. The other dispatch was from the British minister in Constantinople, who reported that a French journalist closely connected with Thiers was attempting to persuade the Turkish government to make a deal directly with Mehemet Ali.

Though conclusive proof is not available, it is almost certain that Thiers was cognizant of and had perhaps inspired this attempt to short-circuit the negotiations being conducted in London. Palmerston, at any rate, was convinced that such was the case. He was furious that Thiers should be acting independently in the Levant in contravention of the note of July 27, 1839, requiring collective action of the great powers. A direct Turkish-Egyptian settlement, Palmerston knew, would strengthen French influence in the Near East and set back the other powers there, particularly Britain. Palmerston thereupon secretly came to an understanding with the other three—Russia, Austria, and Prussia—concerning a common Near Eastern policy to which France would not be a party. Many members of the British cabinet were reluctant to break so sharply with their traditional French ally. Palmerston got his way by threatening to resign and by describing very effectively the dangers of inaction.

The immediate result of our declining to go on with the three Powers because France does not join us will be, that Russia will withdraw her offers to unite herself with the other Powers for a settlement of the affairs of Turkey, and she will again resume her separate and isolated position with respect to those affairs; and you will have the treaty of Unkiar-Skelessi renewed under some still more objectionable form. . . . The ultimate results of such a division will be the practical division of the Turkish empire into two separate and independent states, *whereof one will be the dependency of France, and the other a satellite of Russia; and in both of which our political influence will be annulled, and our commercial interests will be sacrificed;* and this dismemberment will inevitably give rise to local struggles and conflicts which will involve the Powers of Europe in most serious disputes.[19]

The "Convention for the Pacification of the Levant," as it was designated, was signed on July 15, 1840, by representatives of the four Allied Powers and an envoy of the sultan. The powers agreed to impose their terms upon Mehemet Ali and to support the sultan by armed force if necessary. Mehemet was to be offered Egypt as a hereditary possession and southern Syria for life, and in return was to return the Turkish fleet and give up northern Syria, Mecca, Medina, and Crete. Failure to accept these terms in ten days was to mean the withdrawal of the offer of southern Syria. Failure to accept the revised offer in another ten days would mean the withdrawal of the whole offer and freedom for the sultan to make other arrangements. Finally, the powers agreed that although in the existing emergency they might find it necessary to send forces to defend Constantinople, in the future they would conform to "the ancient rule of the Ottoman Empire" by virtue of which it had "in all times been prohibited for Ships of War of Foreign Powers to enter the Straits of the Dardanelles and of the Bosphorus."

Thus, almost a year after the powers had issued their collective note to the Turkish government, an arrangement for the solution of the Turkish-Egyptian question was concluded. The question now was whether Mehemet Ali would accept these terms, and, if not, whether France would dare assist him against a united Europe. Mehemet's answer was unequivocal. "I will rather perish than accept," he replied defiantly. He apparently calculated that he would be able to resist Allied pressure long enough for differences to develop between the British and the Russians. Thiers appears to have shared this hope. He believed that Mehemet Ali would be able to hold out against a naval blockade. A Russian land campaign would then be necessary, and this, he expected, would shatter Allied unity.

All these calculations were based on the assumption that Mehemet Ali was strong enough to hold his own against naval attacks and against small landing forces. Palmerston's strategy was based on the opposite assumption. His agents in the Levant had informed him that Ibrahim's position in Syria was precarious because of serious discontent against conscription and high taxes. These agents had encouraged the disaffection by judicious distribution of money and arms. Palmerston therefore was certain that Ibrahim could be ousted from Syria without large-scale land operations, and had specific plans for doing so. This explains his confidence and his refusal to give ground before the bluster and the war preparations of the French. On September 22, 1840, at the height of the crisis, he instructed his minister in Paris that "if Thiers should again hold out to you the language of menace, however indistinctly and vaguely shadowed out, pray retort . . . in the most friendly and inoffensive manner possible, that if France throws down the gauntlet we shall not refuse to pick it up; and that if she begins a war, she will to a certainty lose her ships, colonies, and commerce before she sees the end of it . . . and that Mehemet Ali will just be chucked into the Nile." [20]

Palmerston's confidence was justified. His estimate of the situation in Syria proved accurate and his strategy prevailed. British warships landed Turkish troops and Austrian and British marines. Also, twenty thousand muskets were delivered to Syrian rebels. These land forces operated under the command of Sir Charles Napier while the British fleet under Admiral Stopford bombarded coastal towns and military installations at will. Napier was able, with the support of naval artillery, to capture Beirut and Sidon in October, 1840, and the great fortress of Acre on November 3.

As it became clear that the Allies would have their way in the Levant, war fever mounted in Paris. Wild talk was heard of fighting the Austrians and Prussians on land and the British on sea. But the cautious king, Louis Philippe, refused to risk war any further. Ibrahim's unexpected collapse had ended his expectation that the Allies would be forced by military stalemate to accept a compromise settlement. Furthermore, the talk of war was accompanied by talk of revolution. The radical press was becoming increasingly outspoken, and on October 15 an attempt was made on the life of the king. Louis Philippe resolved to halt this dangerous trend. The opportunity came on October 20, when Thiers proposed that he deliver a particularly belligerent address at the opening session of the legislative chambers. Louis Philippe refused and Thiers immediately resigned. A new cabinet was formed with Guizot in charge of foreign affairs. The change in government clearly indicated that the king desired a peaceful ending to the crisis.

Meanwhile Mehemet Ali was being forced to accept the terms he had rejected several months earlier. The remnants of Ibrahim's shattered army were streaming into Egypt while a British squadron was anchored before Alexandria. On November 27, 1840, Mehemet reached an agreement with Napier by which he was to return the Turkish fleet and abandon his claims to Syria in return for being recognized as hereditary ruler of Egypt. This settlement was not formally concluded until the following summer. The Turkish government, feeling secure for the first time in years, was loathe to grant hereditary status to Mehemet. The British minister in Constantinople, Viscount Ponsonby, also delayed proceedings by his extreme partiality for Turkish interests. Finally, on June 1, 1841, the sultan issued a firman which, after acknowledging the "loyalty, devotion, and fidelity" of Mehemet Ali, solemnly conferred upon him the government of Egypt "with the additional privilege of hereditary succession."

With the Egyptian question settled, the cause for the European crisis was removed. France was invited to re-enter the European concert, which she did on July 13, 1841, by signing the Straits Convention together with Britain, Russia, Austria, and Prussia. This provided that the Straits be closed to the warships of all foreign powers in time of peace.

The ending of the Near Eastern crisis marks a high point in British prestige on the Continent. It was a great victory for England and an even greater personal triumph for Palmerston—perhaps the greatest of his career. Unkiar-Skelessi had been done away with, and the routes to India remained open and accessible. The principal beneficiary was the sultan, who was saved from the hostility of Mehemet Ali and the friendship of Russia. The loser was Mehemet Ali, much of his life's work in ruins and his active career ended. He lived on until 1849, when he died at the age of eighty. His grandson, Abbas I, succeeded him as khedive of Egypt, and for over a century his descendants were to follow one another on the throne. Although Mehemet Ali was prevented from becoming sultan or Arab emperor, he has come down in history as the founder of modern Egypt.

RESHID AND THE REFORM MOVEMENT:
1839–1852

On November 3, 1839, in the midst of the disasters of the Egyptian war, young Sultan Abdul Mejid issued a reform decree known as the Hatti Sherif of Gulhané. This decree stands out in Ottoman history as the beginning of the reform movement commonly referred to as the *Tanzimat,* as it is called in Turkish. This reform movement continued with varying effectiveness from 1839 until 1880, when Sultan Abdul Hamid established his autocratic regime which lasted to the eve of World War I.

The timing of the reform decree is paradoxical. The previous sultan,

Mahmud, had forced changes upon his unwilling subjects to the point of being called the *giaour,* or infidel sultan. But the final result was defeat so catastrophic that the very existence of the empire was threatened. Under the circumstances it would not have been surprising if the new sultan, Abdul Mejid, had turned back from the course followed by his predecessor. Far from doing so, he accepted a bold new reform program that marked the formal beginning of the *Tanzimat.* The person primarily responsible for this unexpected development was Reshid Mustafa Pasha, one of the outstanding reformers in Turkish history.

Reshid was born in 1802 in Constantinople, the son of a Turkish official. He early entered the government service, where his ability and leadership qualities advanced him rapidly to high office. His experience in various positions gave him valuable insight into the workings of the Ottoman imperial bureaucracy. In addition, he served as ambassador in London and Paris, where he became familiar with European affairs and was influenced by European institutions. Foreign officials with whom he dealt found him to be "a just, though severe man, . . . highly respected" and with "that kind of moral authority . . . which a leading man in any profession exercises over its inferior numbers." [21]

While in London Reshid presented to the Foreign Office on August 12, 1839, a long memorandum on the problem of Ottoman reform. The empire, he warned, is in "an extremely dangerous crisis. . . . But the Egyptian question," he added, "is only a symptom. It would not be enough to obtain . . . a solution for it. So long as there is no effective remedy for the real danger, for the ancient malady of the Sublime Porte, it will not be able to regenerate itself; furthermore a symptom may disappear but a thousand others might appear tomorrow." [22] This analysis is significant because it disproves the contention that the Gulhané reform edict, which Reshid persuaded the sultan to issue a few months later, was designed merely to win the support of the European powers against the Egyptian menace.

The provisions of the Gulhané decree were general in nature. They merely set forth the reforms which the government wished to effect. These were defined as follows: "1. Guarantees ensuring to our subjects perfect security for life, honor, and fortune. 2. A regular system of assessing and levying taxes. 3. An equally regular system for the levy of troops and the duration of their service." These objectives were somewhat elaborated upon, and then it was stipulated that they should "extend to all our subjects, of whatever religion or sect they may be; they shall enjoy them without exception." [23]

The implementation of this decree will be viewed from two vantage points, Constantinople and the Balkans. First, in regard to Constantinople, Reshid worked hard there to issue and to enforce the necessary edicts. His first edict, in December, 1839, provided that governors of provinces, cities, and towns were to be paid fixed salaries; that promotions were to be made on the basis of merit; and that governors should exact only the established imposts. In May, 1840, a new penal code established equality for all subjects, regardless of race or faith. It further stipulated that all trials terminating in capital punishment should be reviewed by the Supreme Council of Justice and that no capital sentence could be effected without the sultan's signature. These and other reforms alienated those whose interests had been affected. Reshid also made enemies by ousting powerful officials convicted of embezzlement. The opposition became so strong that Reshid resigned his position in March, 1841, and accepted the ambassadorship to Paris.

In 1845 Reshid returned to office, first as foreign minister and then as grand vizir. He was able again to promulgate some important reform measures. He established mixed tribunals in which the evidence of Christians had equal weight with that of Moslems. In the field of education a commission submitted a report in 1846 recommending sweeping changes. Some of these were adopted, including minimum salaries, improved textbooks, and new colleges for training civil servants and military, naval, and veterinary officers. An important measure for foreigners was the commercial code adopted in 1850 and based on French commercial laws. The code was supplemented by the establishment of mixed commercial tribunals which included Turkish and European representatives and which tried commercial cases between Turkish subjects and foreigners. This proved to be the last of Reshid's major reforms because a crisis in foreign relations was pushing the reform issue to the background.

Before turning to reform in the provinces it should be noted that although much of the above legislation did not pass beyond the paper stage, there did remain a residue of real progress. The whole tone of life in the empire changed appreciably. The change was most noticeable in the sphere of law and general security. Arbitrary confiscation of property was becoming a thing of the past, as was also the use of torture to force confessions. Pashas no longer could rob and kill with impunity. The principle was established that they would be brought to trial and punished for gross maladministration. Christians still were not allowed to serve in the army, but they probably were less concerned about this than were their champions in the West. Furthermore, they now were recognized as equals with Moslems before the law, and their testimony was accepted in all legal adjudications. Also, the advances in education were significant, though they concerned mostly the Moslem population.

At this same time that the various reform measures were promulgated in the capital, a serious effort was made to improve provincial administration, particularly in the Balkans, where the plight of the Christian population sporadically attracted the interest of the great powers. Three methods were employed by the Ottoman government in provincial affairs: it sent out commissioners on tours of inspection, it called delegates from the provinces to the capital, and it attached to each provincial governor a council representative to a slight degree of the people governed.

The first two procedures had been used before and did not yield startling results. The commissioners who toured the provinces submitted reports which do not seem to have had much effect. Similarly, the provincial delegates who met in Constantinople were not very articulate for fear of offending the ministers or the local authorities who had selected them for the mission to the capital. The third procedure, however, represented a real innovation. The council or mejliss, attached to each governor, consisted of a president and two secretaries appointed by Constantinople, of the defterdar or provincial treasurer, of the chief Jewish or Christian ecclesiastical authority, and of a few delegates from the Moslem and non-Moslem communities. The actions of the governor henceforth had to be accompanied by the masbatta, or written and sealed sanction of his mejliss. The theory was that the mejliss would represent and voice the needs of the governed, and would also serve as a brake against arbitrary acts by the governor.

The functioning of the mejliss varied from province to province but generally it was disappointing. Sometimes the mejliss became a mere rubber stamp for an avaricious governor, but more frequently it controlled the governor, having enough influence locally and in the capital to have its way. Whether the mejliss had a majority of Christians or of Moslems made little difference. The manner in which the Christian mejliss members were to be elected had never been specified, with the result that the wealthy primates naturally assumed the positions. This was particularly true because service in the mejliss carried no remuneration, so that only persons of means could accept appointment. Thus the Christian members usually represented local vested interests, and acted exactly like their Moslem colleagues. In fact, the mejliss, whether predominantly Christian or Moslem, almost invariably was found to be more retrograde than the governor from Constantinople. This tie-up between local vested interests and provincial administration explains why, in the period after the Crimean War, the reform of provincial administration with the vilayet law of 1864 was preceded by the reform of the millets or non-Moslem communal organizations, to be discussed in Chapter 20.

17. Crimean War: 1853–1856

IN THE 1770's Britain helped Russia to defeat Turkey and to gain access to the Black Sea. Likewise in 1827 Britain cooperated with Russia in behalf of the Greeks who wished to break away from the Ottoman Empire. But twenty-five years later Britain waged war against Russia in order to preserve the integrity of this same empire. In tracing the origins of this about-face we shall first analyze certain strategic and economic considerations which rarely came to the foreground but which nevertheless exerted substantial influence. Then we shall consider various other factors, including conflict of personalities, pressure of public opinion, and mutual suspicion and misunderstanding which together served to involve the European powers in a generally unwanted war. And finally we shall estimate the effect of the war upon the Balkans and, more important, upon the over-all European balance of power.

STRATEGIC AND COMMERCIAL BACKGROUND

The strategic considerations that contributed to the Crimean War were precisely the same as those that led Palmerston to support the sultan against Mehemet Ali. As in the 1840's, so now, a decade later, Britain was interested in the trade routes running through the Near East. Her interest, in fact, was greater because her trade with the Far East was increasing with the growing momentum of the Industrial Revolution. Furthermore, the trade was changing in character. In place of the spices and silks and calicoes of earlier centuries, Britain now was importing jute and other bulky raw materials for her industries. This created a transportation problem because the steamships now being introduced required so much coal and water for the long voyage around the Cape that little space was left for their cargoes. The solution was to return to the old Near Eastern routes that had been abandoned three centuries earlier. The distance from England to India by way of the Suez or the Euphrates was little more than one third of the Cape route. The precise

319

manner in which the Near Eastern lands were to be traversed—by canal or railway or river transportation—had not yet been decided. But regardless of the method, the prerequisite was that the routes should not pass under the control of a rival great power. Thus British imperial strategy required that the integrity of the Ottoman Empire be safeguarded against encroachment from any quarter.

British economic interests in the Near East also demanded that the Ottoman Empire be preserved intact. These were years when Britain's foreign trade was mounting steadily and steeply. In 1825 her imports and exports amounted respectively to £44,208,803 and £56,320,182. By 1853 the corresponding figures were £123,099,000 and £242,072,000. In little more than a quarter of a century imports had increased by 270 per cent, and exports by 432 per cent. It follows that Britain had to seek constantly for markets for her manufactured goods and for sources of raw materials and foodstuffs for her factories and her rising urban population. The Ottoman Empire satisfied both requirements admirably during this period.

As a market for manufactured goods the Ottoman Empire offered unique opportunities. Whereas the various Continental countries were raising their tariffs against British manufactures, the Turkish government was limited by the capitulatory treaties to a 3 per cent ad valorem duty on imports. An additional levy of 2 per cent on the consumer of foreign goods raised the tax to 5 per cent. This was insignificant compared to the high protective tariffs being adopted by Russia, France, Germany, and other Continental countries. It is true that British merchants complained against certain restrictions in Turkey, particularly excessive export duties, transshipment dues, and monopolies which raised the cost and decreased the consumption of various commodities. But most of these subsidiary charges and objectionable practices were dropped by the terms of the Balta Liman Convention signed by Britain and Turkey on August 16, 1838. The following figures reveal how British trade with Turkey flourished under these favorable circumstances.

Trade of the United Kingdom with Turkey, by Value, 1825–1852

Year	Exports from U. K. to Turkey	Imports to U. K. from Turkey
1825	£1,079,671	£1,207,172
1830	2,745,723	726,065
1835	2,706,591	879,089
1840	3,673,903	1,240,812
1845	7,620,140	1,465,972
1852	8,489,100	2,252,283

Source: F. E. Bailey, *British Policy and the Turkish Reform Movement* (Cambridge, Mass.: Harvard University Press, 1942), p. 74.

We see that between 1825 and 1852 British exports to Turkey increased eightfold while imports did not even double. This left a favorable trade balance amounting to over six million pounds each year during the decade before the Crimean War. Meanwhile protective tariffs were restricting trade with the Continent. Thus British exports to Turkey by the eve of the Crimean War surpassed the exports to Russia, Italy, France, or Austria.

The Ottoman Empire was also important to Britain as a source of foodstuffs and industrial raw materials. The most important of these commodities were madder root for textile dyeing, raw silk, raisins, and valonia, the latter being a by-product of acorns used for tanning purposes. Grains also began to be imported in increasing quantities following the repeal of the Corn Laws in 1846. By 1850 corn and wheat rated third and fourth respectively in value in the list of commodities imported by Britain from Turkey. Most of this grain came from the Danubian Principalities, which were becoming an important source of foodstuffs for Britain. This was reflected in the growing number of British ships that passed through the Straits each year. In 1842 only 250 used the passageway; in 1848 the number had increased to 1,397, and by 1852 to 1,741. By the latter year British vessels also accounted for one third of all shipping on the Danube River.

These figures illustrate the speed of British economic penetration in the Near East during this period. By 1851 Britain was obtaining as much grain from Turkey as from Russia, and in return was selling manufactured goods to Turkey of a value double that which she sold to Russia. Furthermore, Turkey had no modern industry or any plans to establish one in the future. Russia, in contrast, was deliberately fostering her infant industries behind high protective tariffs. In October, 1841, the British minister to St. Petersburg reported that these new industries were not competing with Britain but he warned that the time might come when they "may have a pernicious effect on British trade." [1]

These circumstances explain why Britain in the mid-nineteenth century valued her trade with Turkey as highly as she had her Russian trade a century earlier. In 1849 Palmerston declared to the House of Commons: "If in a political point of view the independence of Turkey is of great importance, in a commercial sense it is of no less importance to this country. It is quite true that with no country is our trade so liberally permitted and carried on as with Turkey." [2]

How far these new commercial relations affected diplomatic developments is difficult to measure. Documents rarely reveal explicit connections between trade and diplomacy. But it is not altogether coincidental that the period during which Britain adopted the policy of supporting Ottoman integrity was also the period when Britain developed her commerce with Turkey most rapidly and profitably.

DIPLOMATIC PRELIMINARIES

The roots of the Crimean War go back ultimately to the fact that although the Ottoman Empire had become the "Sick Man of Europe" it remained the owner of prized possessions coveted by others. Thus the essence of the Eastern Question, as Metternich aptly observed, was whether to turn the Sick Man over to the doctor or to his heirs. During the eighteenth century Russia favored the latter procedure, but in 1829 she changed her mind. The likelihood of squabbles among the heirs led her to adopt the new policy of tolerating the invalid while at the same time being ever-ready, in case of sudden death, to claim a full share of his estate. In accordance with this policy Nicholas cooperated with Palmerston in the 1840's to protect the Ottoman Empire against the attacks of Mehemet Ali. Nicholas cherished the new tie with England because it not only guaranteed the *status quo* in the Near East but also isolated France—the country of revolution which he feared and hated. For this reason he was anxious to establish a firmer relationship with Britain.

Late in December, 1840, the tsar asked the British ambassador in St. Petersburg whether "Her Majesty's government would object to record and establish by some act the alliance, which now happily existed between the Four Powers [Russia, England, Austria, and Prussia], to serve as a security against any efforts France might make to awaken revolutionary feeling in Europe." [3] The tsar added that if Parliament objected to such a commitment he would be satisfied with a verbal understanding between the two governments. Palmerston replied frankly that Parliament would not favor an agreement that bound England to take up arms in a contingency that was uncertain and unforeseeable. And as for a verbal agreement, he pointed out that without the approval of Parliament it would bind only the ministers who made it and could be disavowed by their successors. This reply not only ended the overture but also made a point concerning British constitutional practice that was quite significant in the light of later events.

In 1844 Nicholas made a second attempt to get a commitment from the British. He visited England and talked with Queen Victoria, the Duke of Wellington, Prime Minister Peel, and Foreign Secretary Aberdeen, all of whom he charmed with his graciousness and impressed with his frankness. The Russian foreign minister, Nesselrode, prepared a memorandum summarizing these conversations. According to this document the two powers agreed to preserve the Ottoman Empire as long as possible and, in case of impending dissolution, to consult with each other about what should be done. This memorandum was submitted to Aberdeen, who accepted it and exchanged letters testifying to "the accuracy of the statement."

This agreement was purely personal. It involved only Peel, Aberdeen, and Wellington on the one hand and Nicholas and Nesselrode on the other. The British cabinet knew nothing of it. It had no validity save that derived from the exchange of letters between Nesselrode and Aberdeen. But these letters were personal in character. They were never submitted to the British cabinet. Thus the point that Palmerston had made four years earlier—that personal engagements committed only the personalities involved—applied to this case perfectly. The British historian, Harold Temperley, rightly states, "If the Czar was deceived he had himself to blame for the deception." [4]

This self-deception, however, proved to be an important factor in the coming of the war. The tsar acted on the assumption that he could count on British support. By the time he realized that this assumption was unwarranted, compromise had become difficult.

Four years after this exchange the revolutions of 1848 broke out all over Europe. In an unexpected fashion these revolutions led to a crisis in British-Russian relations which in turn stimulated a wave of violent Russophobia in England. Palmerston, who was then foreign minister, tried not to provoke the tsar during this critical period. When Russian troops occupied the Wallachian Principality he assured the House that the occupation was temporary and that there was no cause for alarm. Likewise he made no protest when a Russian army crossed the Carpathians and helped the Hapsburgs crush the Hungarian revolution. The trouble did not begin until the fall of 1849, after the Hungarian uprising had been suppressed and the defeated revolutionaries had fled across the frontier into Ottoman territory.

The refugees consisted of 3,600 Hungarians and some 800 Poles, the latter being Russian subjects who had fought for Hungarian freedom. The Russian and Hapsburg emperors demanded the extradition of their fugitive subjects and intimated that they would use force to back up their demand. The Turks traditionally had warm feelings for both the Hungarians and the Poles. They also knew the fate that awaited the refugees if they delivered them across the frontier. Accordingly, the Turkish ministers, with the encouragement of the British and French ambassadors, voted to reject the extradition demand. They persisted in their refusal despite threats from Vienna and St. Petersburg. On September 17, 1849, Russia and Austria severed diplomatic relations with Constantinople. On October 7, Palmerston countered by announcing that Britain and France were resolved to support the Turkish government and that the British and French fleets were on their way to "the neighborhood of the Dardanelles."

This crisis passed away as quickly as it had risen. The tsar was alarmed by the vigorous reaction of the Western powers. On October 19 he took advantage of a personal appeal by a special Turkish envoy to announce that he was dropping his demand for extradition. But the damage had already been done. A wave of intense anti-Russian sentiment had swept over England. Palmerston wrote to Stratford in Constantinople that "there never was so strong and unanimous outburst of generous feeling, all men of all parties and opinions, politicians, soldiers, sailors, clergymen and Quakers. All newspapers, Tory, Whig and Radical have joined in chorus." [5] Despite the tsar's decision to back down, an enduring impression had been left on the minds of thousands of Englishmen. The tsar and the Hapsburg emperor were now "merciless tyrants" and the "hangmen of liberty." Not only had they crushed the liberation movements of the enslaved peoples of Europe but they also had attempted to wreak vengeance on helpless refugees. By an ironic twist of history Turkey now stood out in the public mind as the champion of European liberty against the brutal despotism of the two emperors. This popular impression was not without signifiance. A few years later, when another crisis developed, it greatly strengthened the position of Palmerston and others who favored strong measures against Russia.

HOLY PLACES DISPUTE

Less than a year after the settlement of the refugee crisis the dispute over the Holy Places began. After nearly four years of negotiations and blunders it culminated in the Crimean War. The Holy Places issue was in itself absurdly trivial. It has been described as a "churchwardens' quarrel" that could have been settled by any competent stage manager in half an hour. The question was whether Greek Orthodox or Roman Catholic monks should control certain shrines in the Holy Land. These included the great church of Bethlehem, the tomb of the Virgin at Gethsemane, the Holy Sepulcher, and the grotto of the Nativity. Traditionally Russia had supported the claims of the Orthodox monks and France the claims of the Catholic. Since the mid-eighteenth century, however, France had been too engrossed in the Enlightenment, the French Revolution, and the subsequent tumults to pay any attention to shrines in Palestine. The Greek monks, who continued to receive Russian backing, exploited this opportunity. By the mid-nineteenth century they had gained custody of numerous Holy Places originally held by the Latins.

At this point, when Catholic prestige was at its nadir, Louis Napoleon was elected president of the French Republic. He was determined to remain the head of France and immediately began preparations for a *coup d' état* to overthrow the republic and re-establish the empire. Since the radicals were hostile to him he turned to the powerful Catholic party. In order to win its support he aided in restoring Rome to the Papacy in 1849. For the same reason he sent an envoy to Constantinople in 1850 to demand the reinstatement of the Latins in the Holy Places. In this manner Napoleon hoped to use "the men in black" against "the men in red."

After heavy pressure upon the sultan, Napoleon won in 1852 several concessions for the Catholics. The most important was possession of the keys to both the inner and outer church of Bethlehem. About the same time Napoleon effected his coup in France and became emperor. He no longer needed to continue his risky game in Palestine. Accordingly, he sent an envoy directly to the tsar to negotiate an agreement on the Holy Places that would be mutually satisfactory. But by this time it was too late.

Various factors operated against a settlement at this early stage. Public opinion in Russia was genuinely aroused by the surrender of the keys to the hated Latin heretics. Also, there was personal enmity between Napoleon and Nicholas. The tsar looked down upon the French emperor as an *arriviste* who had obtained his throne by revolution and plebiscite. With studied contempt he addressed him as "bon ami" rather than as "mon frère," which was customary among sovereigns. Still another difficulty was that Napoleon's envoy arrived in St. Petersburg after Nicholas had sent

Prince Menshikov to Constantinople to negotiate directly with the Turks. Nicholas had been impressed by the success a few months earlier of an Austrian mission under Count Leiningen. The count had delivered an ultimatum regarding certain developments in Bosnia and Montenegro that concerned his government. The sultan accepted the ultimatum and took measures to settle affairs to the satisfaction of Austria. Tsar Nicholas noted Leiningen's success and sent out Prince Menshikov to settle the Holy Places dispute in a similar manner.

At the same time that he dispatched Menshikov to Constantinople the tsar conducted exploratory talks with the British ambassador, Sir Hamilton Seymour. His aim was the same as in 1840 and 1844, namely, to obtain an understanding with Britain that would isolate France and assure common action in the Near East. Nicholas was encouraged by the fact that a new British government had just been formed with the conciliatory Lord Aberdeen as prime minister and the bellicose Palmerston relegated to the humble post of home secretary.

The tsar had four conversations with Seymour in January and February of 1853. He asserted his views with typical frankness. He stated that he wished to maintain Turkey as long as possible. But he also expressed doubts as to the longevity of what he termed the "sick man" of Europe. Repeatedly he stated that Turkey was "gravely ill" and he urged that Britain and Russia agree beforehand concerning the disposition of the sick man's estate. So far as Russia's aims were concerned, the tsar specifically repudiated Empress Catherine's designs on Constantinople and the Balkans. He already had as much territory as he desired, the tsar declared, and he would be satisfied if Constantinople were made a free port. Serbia, Bulgaria, and the Danubian Principalities should be independent states under Russian protection. Finally, the tsar informed Seymour that he would have no objections if Britain acquired Crete and Egypt.

The British foreign secretary, Lord John Russell, replied that his government considered the fall of Turkey a remote contingency. Furthermore, the mere existence of a partition plan was likely to hasten the dismemberment of the Ottoman Empire and thus increase the danger of war rather than lessen it. This was a reaffirmation of traditional British policy and was not likely to please the tsar. But Russell went on to declare that Her Majesty's Government was "ready to promise that they will enter into no agreement to provide for the contingency of the fall of Turkey without previous communication with the Emperor of Russia." The tsar was delighted with this commitment. He wrote in the margin: "This is a precious assurance since it proves what perfect identity of intentions exists between England and Russia. . . ." [6]

Seymour was convinced that the tsar was a scheming hypocrite, seeking to destroy the Ottoman Empire by separating England from France and bribing her with a few Turkish provinces. This interpretation won popular acceptance with the outbreak of the Crimean War. But the evidence indicates clearly that the tsar sincerely wished to maintain the *status quo* in the Near East. Furthermore, he convinced the British cabinet that this was his intention. Lord Aberdeen and his ministers did not share Seymour's apprehension of Russian designs. They were not alarmed by the tsar's partition proposal even though they disagreed with him concerning the prospects of Turkish survival. In fact, the British were favorably impressed by the tsar's frankness and the conversations ended in an atmosphere of mutual good will.

Despite this favorable atmosphere the conversations did not contribute to the preservation of peace. It may well be that their final effect was precisely the opposite. The tsar was greatly encouraged by Russell's promise of "previous communication." He assumed that he could rely on Britain and that British cooperation with France was out of the question. But events had already occurred in Constantinople that were to demonstrate the fallacy of this assumption.

STEPS TO WAR

The diplomatic developments culminating in the Crimean War fall naturally into three phases: (I) the period of direct negotiation between Turkey and Russia, opening with the arrival of Prince Menshikov in Constantinople in March, 1853, and closing with the Russian occupation of the Principalities in July, 1853; (II) the period of neither war nor peace, marked by repeated attempts on the part of Britain, France, Austria, and Prussia to arrange a compromise settlement, and ended by Turkey's declaration of war on Russia on October 4, 1853; (III) the period of the Russo-Turkish War during which the four powers continued to seek a peaceful settlement until finally Britain and France declared war on Russia on March 28, 1854.

Phase I: The Menshikov mission to Constantinople started out with two handicaps. Menshikov himself was a rough and overbearing soldier, ill-suited for the delicate negotiations entrusted to him. The instructions he received were also unfortunate. He was charged not only to obtain full satisfaction in regard to the Holy Places but also to secure acknowledgment, embodied in a formal treaty, of the tsar's protectorate over all the Orthodox subjects of the sultan. If the Turks refused to sign such a treaty, Menshikov was to conclude a secret defensive alliance with Turkey to protect her from France. Thus the Russian envoy was expected not only to settle the problem of the moment but also to secure guarantees for the future.

Menshikov arrived in Constantinople with much fanfare on the last day of February, 1853. He began by insulting the Turkish foreign minister and forcing his resignation. The British and French ministers both happened to be absent from Constantinople at the time. But Menshikov moved too slowly to take advantage of this favorable opportunity to get what he wanted. The negotiations were still in progress when the masterful British ambassador, Stratford Canning, arrived upon the scene on April 5, 1853.

Stratford Canning, a cousin of George Canning, had left Constantinople less than a year before. His reappointment at this time had not been made without certain misgivings. He was known to be a strong man, given to independent thinking and actions, and holding pronounced anti-Russian views. This was a matter of some significance in these pre-wireless years when a dispatch from London required over two weeks to reach Constantinople. But the newspapers were clamoring for Stratford Canning's appointment, and the government itself was not anxious to keep him home where he was in the habit of asking awkward questions in Parliament. Thus Stratford Canning was sent back to the scene of his earlier triumphs. His instructions specifically forbade him to call the British Mediterranean fleet to the vicinity of the Dardanelles "without positive instructions from Her Majesty's government." [7]

Whatever Stratford Canning's failings may have been, he at least had influence with the Turks and he knew how to get things done in the capital. The Holy Places dispute had been dragging on for three years before his arrival. Within three weeks he was able to arrange a settlement acceptable to all parties concerned. Menshikov now proceeded, in accordance with his instructions, to demand a convention guaranteeing the ancient privileges of "the Orthodox Eastern religion, its clergy and possessions." Stratford Canning pointed out that the term "religion" covered the Orthodox lay subjects of the sultan—some twelve million in all. A convention with Russia concerning their privileges was, in his opinion, incompatible with "the desire of maintaining the Integrity and Independence of the Ottoman Empire. . . ." [8]

Stratford Canning expressed his views to the Turks, who felt sufficiently encouraged to reject Menshikov's demands. The Russian now offered to accept a Turkish diplomatic note instead of a convention. Stratford Canning advised the Turks that the new demand was essentially the same as the old, and that acceptance would mean "the introduction of Russian influence, to be exercised with the force of acknowledged right." The Turks again rebuffed Menshikov, who thereupon left Constantinople on May 21, 1853.

Menshikov's failure enraged the tsar: "I feel," he said, "the smart of the Sultan's fingers on my cheek." His first impulse was to declare war immediately. Nesselrode warned him that he might have to contend with the whole of Europe as well as Turkey. The tsar satisfied himself with a half measure. On May 31 he warned the Ottoman government that unless it accepted Menshikov's demands within eight days Russian troops would occupy the Principalities "by force, but without war." When the Turks replied with a polite refusal, the Russians crossed the Pruth River early in July.

Meanwhile in Britain the news of the stormy and ominous termination of Menshikov's mission also aroused agitation for action. The cabinet was divided, with Prime Minister Aberdeen and Gladstone favoring a pacific policy and Foreign Minister Russell and Palmerston demanding strong measures. Public opinion now began to make itself felt. Almost all newspapers clamored for positive measures against Russia. The factions in the cabinet finally agreed on a compromise policy. On May 31 they ordered the Mediterranean fleet to Besika Bay at the entrance of the Dardanelles, and they also authorized Stratford Canning to summon the fleet to Constantinople in case of emergency.

The Russian decision to occupy the Principalities and the British decision to send the fleet to Besika Bay were reached at the same time and independently of each other. The two decisions did not produce war but they certainly brought it nearer. A great-power fleet now kept watch over a great-power army. Also, the diplomats henceforth had to operate under the pressure of a time limit. The weather in the eastern Mediterranean broke in October. After that date the British fleet would not be able to remain in the exposed Besika Bay. The Russian army in the Principalities likewise would not be able to campaign once the rainy season began. This left the diplomats only three months—July, August, and September—in which to reach an agreement. In October, decisions would be inescapable.

Phase II: The task facing the diplomats was to find a formula that would assure the independence of Turkey, clear the Principalities of the Russians, and also save the face of the tsar. No less than eleven pacification projects were advanced during the second half of 1853. One of the obstacles in the way of settlement was the mounting war fever in Constantinople. The Turks had regarded the Russian occupation of the Principalities as a belligerent act. Only Stratford Canning's strong insistence had restrained them from beginning hostilities. During the following weeks the Turks strengthened the defenses of their capital. Also, they received assurances of aid from the bey of Tunis and the khedive of Egypt. Furthermore, the British fleet reached Besika Bay on June 13 and the French fleet followed the next day. The Turks had no reason to be conciliatory under such comfortable circumstances. Instead, they became more inflexible as national and religious feeling rose in Constantinople.

Under pressure from Stratford Canning the Turks accepted a compromise proposal which included this statement: "The ancient privileges of the religion professed by H. M. the Emperor of Russia, and by the greater part of his subjects, have been fully confirmed in perpetuity; the Sublime Porte hopes that the Russian Government will learn this with pleasure." [9] This proposal had two serious defects. It unfortunately was given the title "Turkish Ultimatum." Also, the guarantee concerning Orthodox privileges was not in the form of a bilateral pledge between Russia and Turkey as the tsar had demanded. Instead, it was a unilateral statement which the sultan could revoke whenever he so desired.

The "Turkish Ultimatum" was forwarded to the Conference of Ambassadors in Vienna for transmission to St. Petersburg. The ambassadors rejected the "Ultimatum" in favor of a counterproject which they were preparing and which they believed would be more acceptable to the tsar. This "Vienna Note," as it came to be called, reaffirmed the adherence of the Ottoman government to "the letter and spirit of the Treaties of Kainardji and Adrianople relative to the protection of the Christian religion." The "Note" also stipulated that "the existing state of things shall in no wise be modified without previous understanding with the Governments of France and Russia and without any prejudice to the different Christian communities." [10] The "Note" differed basically from the "Ultimatum" in that Russia and France were to be the legal guarantors of Turkey's good faith, thereby eliminating the possibility of unilateral revocation of privileges.

On August 5, 1853, the tsar accepted the Vienna Note. It was generally assumed that the crisis had passed. But on August 19 the grand vizir announced that Turkey would accept it only on condition that three amendments were incorporated. The tsar indignantly refused to permit any modification and so the deadlock continued more ominously than before.

Turkey's unexpected rejection of the Vienna Note was a major step toward war. Various factors explain the rejection. One was the inflamed state of public opinion in Constantinople. With great difficulty Stratford Canning had persuaded the sultan and his ministers to accept the "Ultimatum." Its rejection by the ambassadors in Vienna strengthened the position of the war party in Constantinople. It was further bolstered by the arrival of the Egyptian fleet and the presence of the Anglo-French squadron at the entrance to the Straits. The important question is whether Stratford Canning exerted himself fully to secure acceptance of the Vienna Note as he was instructed to do by his government. It is known that he officially supported the "Note." It is also known that he personally disapproved of it. The problem is whether he merely went through the motions of backing the "Note" while at the same time assuring its rejection by a private verbal message or by some other means.

This could very well have happened, but whether or not it did cannot be proven. Prime Minister Aberdeen spoke openly of Stratford Canning's "dishonesty." Other ministers felt that Stratford Canning had not used his influence fully in behalf of the "Note." Despite these misgivings the cabinet dared not remove him because of the pressure of public opinion. Such a step would have been popularly interpreted as appeasement of Russia and betrayal of Turkey. Also, Stratford Canning's position was strengthened by a letter from Nesselrode to the Russian minister at Berlin in which the Vienna Note was interpreted as granting Russia "the right of a protectorate over the Christian subjects of the Sultan." This so-called "violent interpretation" of the Vienna Note persuaded many that Stratford Canning had been right, though insubordinate, in failing to secure its acceptance.

The tsar now demonstrated his sincere desire for peace by substantially modifying his demands. He asked Austria to present a new proposal, known as the "Buol project" after the Austrian foreign minister. The proposal consisted of the original text of the Vienna Note but also included the explanation that the Russian government "will in no way exercise [for] itself the protection of a Christian cult inside the Ottoman Empire, and that the duty of protecting this cult and maintaining its religious immunity has devolved on the Sultan and that Russia only reserves to herself that of watching that the engagement contracted by the Ottoman Empire in the Treaty of

Kainardji be strictly executed." [11] This was obviously a serious peace gesture. Napoleon was impressed by it and favored its acceptance. So did Prime Minister Aberdeen, but he unfortunately was overruled by his cabinet. The latter went further and ordered Stratford Canning on October 8, 1853, to call the fleet from Besika Bay to Constantinople. This was an ill-advised move, to be attributed to the constant pressure of public opinion and to a deep-rooted distrust of Russia reinforced by Nesselrode's "violent interpretation" of the Vienna Note.

Meanwhile the war party in Constantinople had gained the upper hand. On the last day of August Stratford Canning wrote: "The Turks I think are bent on *war, unless their amendments are accepted,* and I fear they cannot help themselves with respect to their army and nation. . . ." [12] On October 4 the Turks issued an ultimatum demanding the evacuation of the Principalities within fifteen days. The Russians made no move, and on October 23 the first armed clash occurred when the Turks sent raiding parties across the Danube.

Phase III: Once Turkey and Russia were at war the question was whether the conflict could be prevented from spreading into a general European conflagration. Stratford Canning was able to persuade the Turkish ministers to suspend hostilties for ten or twelve days. Orders to this effect were issued but they reached the Danubian front too late. A few minor skirmishes were won by the Turks before the rains came in early November. These insignificant successes unfortunately inflamed the martial ardor of the Turkish naval officers, who rashly ventured into the Black Sea with a pitifully inadequate fleet. A powerful Russian squadron pounced upon them at Sinope, a harbor on the northern coast of Asia Minor. With the exception of a small steamer, every one of the Turkish ships was destroyed on that disastrous day of November 30.

The "Sinope massacre," as it came to be called, aroused passions to such heights that it made general war inevitable. There was no rational justification for the emotional outburst. The Turks had started hostilities on both the Danubian and Caucasian fronts. The Russian attack at Sinope was a perfectly natural and legitimate retaliation. There was no justifiable reason for calling it a massacre. But myth frequently triumphs over fact, and at this moment most Englishmen were little concerned with fact as they patriotically sang

> And did he say the Turk was sick
> And that the Turk should die?
> There's 50,000 Englishmen
> Will know the reason why! [13]

Even the hitherto moderate *Times* now gave way and informed its readers that peace was "no longer compatible with the honour and dignity of the country. . . . war has begun in earnest." [14]

The government was unable to ignore such a popular explosion. The pressure was heightened by the resignation of Palmerston a few days after the news of Sinope reached the country. The resignation was due to differences of opinion over the Reform Bill, but the press almost unanimously attributed it to Palmerston's disgust with the "un-English" foreign policy of the government. The cabinet also was under pressure from Napoleon, who demanded that the French and British fleets sail through the Straits and "sweep the Russian flag off the Black Sea." The government finally yielded. On December 24, 1853, it instructed Stratford Canning that the "Ottoman flag, as well as the Ottoman territory, should be protected by the combined fleets, and . . . all Russian vessels, other than merchant-men, met in the Black Sea, should be required to return to Sebastopol." The cabinet knew what this order signified. "Her Majesty's Government do not disguise from themselves that it may at no distant period involve England and France in war with Russia." [15]

War came soon enough. Russia retaliated on February 6, 1854, by breaking off relations with Britain and France. On February 27 an Anglo-French ultimatum to Russia demanded evacuation of the Principalities. The tsar did not even deign to reply to this, so on March 28 the two Western powers declared war.

With the exception of the Turks, the Crimean War was an unwanted war. Why, then, was it allowed to begin? Thomas Carlyle, laboring on the first volume of his *Frederick the Great,* sensed the influence of public opinion. With characteristic pungency he wrote in his diary:

> Russian war: soldiers marching off, etc. Never such enthusiasm among the population. Cold, I, as a very stone to all that: seems to me privately I have hardly seen a madder business. . . . A lazy, ugly, sensual, dark fanatic that Turk, whom we have now had for 400 years. I, for my part, would not buy the continuance of him there at the rate of sixpence a century. . . . It is the idle population of editors, etc., that have done all this in England. One perceives clearly the Ministers go forward in it against their will. Indeed, I have seen no rational person who is not privately very much inclined to be of my opinion: all fools and loose-spoken inexperienced persons being of the other opinions. Poor Souls! What could the Ministry *do* after all? [16]

Public opinion played a vital role, but that fact does not by itself explain the Crimean War. Equally important was the combination of blundering, incompetence, and misunderstanding demonstrated in the sending of Stratford Canning and Menshikov to Constantinople, the inability of the tsar to comprehend British constitutional procedure, and the failure of Aberdeen to control the aggressive elements in his cabinet—a failure that was doubly significant because the tsar acted on the assumption that the prime minister's pacific views would prevail. Finally, the roots of the war may be traced still further back to those strategic and economic factors whose influence cannot be measured but whose constant impress cannot be ignored.

WAR

The Crimean War was in many ways a strange war. It took longer to get itself declared than any other war in history. Once it began, the belligerents faced the very real problem of where they should fight. An encounter between landlocked Russia and the maritime West was akin to one between an elephant and a whale. And as soon as the fighting did begin, peace negotiations also began, and they continued from the beginning of the war in March, 1854, to its conclusion in March, 1856.

Britain and France could attack Russia only in two restricted areas, the Baltic and the Black Sea coasts. A combined fleet was sent into the Baltic Sea but it accomplished nothing. It could not lure the Russian fleet out from under the protecting guns of the Kronstadt fortress and it lacked the manpower needed for a land campaign. In the Black Sea the Allies sent a joint force to Varna with the intention of marching northward to relieve Silistria, the Turkish fortress on the Danube River. But on June 23 the Russians raised the siege of Silistria and the following month they began to evacuate the Principalities. By early August not a single Russian soldier remained on the Turkish side of the Pruth. Since the Allies had declared war in order to force the Russians back to their frontier, the object of their intervention appeared to have been attained. Yet the Allies now undertook a major operation by sending a joint expedition against the great Russian fortress of Sebastopol on the tip of the Crimea.

The explanation for the Russian withdrawal and the Allied thrust forward is to be found in the diplomacy of the great powers. Britain and France were allies, but their war aims were quite different. Napoleon wished to raise the prestige of his dynasty and to break up the alliance of Russia, Prussia, and Austria that had hemmed in France during the forty years since 1815. Britain, on the other hand, wished to further her economic and strategic interests in the Levant. She also claimed that Russian expansion since Peter the Great had upset the European balance of power and that Russia must be prevented from breaking into the Near East. This contention contained an element of truth and it was well suited for propaganda. The Western powers, therefore, proclaimed that they were fighting not for their own interests but for those of Europe. On this basis they sought to win allies and to found an anti-Russian "Concert of Europe" similar to the anti-French "Concert of Europe" at the end of the Napoleonic Wars.

The Western powers were not able to win over Prussia. Lack of immediate concern with the Near East, the traditional obsequiousness of the Hohenzollerns toward the tsars, and the prospect of great financial profit if Russia were blockaded all combined to persuade Frederick William that neutrality was the best policy. Austria was in a somewhat different position. She had direct interests in the Balkans and was therefore disturbed by Russia's occupation of the Principalities. On the other hand, she had no desire to join the Allies in driving Russia out. She remembered the four defeats she had sustained at the hands of the first Napoleon. She also realized that, unlike the Western powers, she had Russia as a neighbor. Austria's aim, therefore, was to abstain from hostilities but, at the same time, to keep Russia out of the Balkans and also to hasten the end of the war in order to reduce the danger of a general European conflagration. This aim explains the deviousness of Austrian diplomacy at this time. Austria made moves in the direction of the Allies but not with the purpose of actually joining them. Rather, she wished to use the Allies to check Russia in the Balkans and to force Russia to accept a peace settlement.

On June 3, 1854, Austria sent an ultimatum to St. Petersburg demanding that Russia should refrain from extending the war into the Balkans and also that she should set a date for the evacuation of the Principalities. Austria calculated that Russia would comply peacefully rather than add another major power to the ranks of her enemies. At the same time Austria opened negotiations with the Western powers in order to have assistance in case it should be needed. On August 8 Britain, France, and Austria agreed upon the so-called Vienna Four Points. These stipulated the conditions of peace: (1) Russian guarantee of Serbia and the Principalities replaced by a European guarantee; (2) free passage of the Danube mouth assured; (3) the 1841 Straits Convention revised in the interests of the European balance of power; and (4) Russia's claim to a protectorate over the Ottoman Christians abandoned and privileges secured for the Christians without impairing the independence of Turkey.

The Austrian calculations proved correct. Russia withdrew from the Principalities and on August 22 Austria occupied them for the duration of the war in accordance with an earlier understanding with Turkey. Austria's next move was to secure Russian acceptance of the Four Points in order to prepare the way for a peace conference. Russia at first refused indignantly, but when Austria mobilized on October 22 Russia accepted the Four Points. On December 2 Austria signed a tripartite treaty with the Western powers that was designed to put additional pressure on Russia to bring her to terms. The most important article provided that if peace on the basis of the Four Points were not obtained the signatories would consult on "the most efficacious means for attaining the object of their alliance."

The peace negotiations began in Vienna on March 15, 1855. The death of Tsar Nicholas a fortnight earlier raised hopes that the new tsar, Alexander II, would prove more conciliatory. In fact, the Russian envoys did make extensive concessions. They dropped the claims to special rights in Serbia and the Principalities. They agreed that a European commission henceforth should regulate the Danube. But they balked when the Allies insisted on limitation of Russian naval armaments in the Black Sea. The Austrian foreign minister, Count Buol, argued that since Russia was going to promise not to attack Turkey, she would not, in any case, need a Black Sea squadron. The reply of the Russians was significant. Sooner or later Turkey would crumble and Russia must have a fleet to get to Constantinople before the other powers. Equally significant was the position of the British. A few months before the conference Foreign Minister Lord Clarendon painted a black picture of what would happen if Russia were permitted to retain the Sebastopol fortress and to maintain her Black Sea navy. The Ottoman Empire, he warned, would be "held firmly in her grasp"; the Black Sea would become "really a Russian lake"; Circassia, Georgia, Persia, and Asia Minor "must at once fall under her dominion"; and Russian power "must extend over Greece, Thessaly, Albania, and the Danubian Principalities." Thus Russia, according to Clarendon, "would then be in a position to dictate the law to Europe; every evil that England and France hoped to avert by the war might occur. . . ." [17]

The negotiations broke down over this issue of naval limitation. Thus the Crimean War, which began ostensibly because of the Russian occupation of the Principalities, now was to be fought to the bitter end over the issue of Russian preponderance in the Black Sea.

Meanwhile the war was being fought in the environs of Sebastopol. On September 14, 1854, an Allied expeditionary force of approximately 60,000 disembarked in the Bay of Eupatoria to the north of Sebastopol. A few days later, while marching toward Sebastopol, the Allies fought and dispersed a small Russian force under General Menshikov. The latter fell back upon Sebastopol while the Allies marched around the fortress, occupied the harbor of Balaclava, and made preparations for a regular siege.

The slow and deliberate moves of the Allies gave the defenders an opportunity which they used to the full. Indeed, the campaign is outstanding in the annals of warfare only for the brilliant improvisation of a young Russian engineer, Colonel von Todleben. He cleared the largest Russian ships of guns and men and sank them at the entrance to the harbor. The remaining ships were kept inside the harbor to aid in the defense. By the time the Allies began their bombardment on October 17 the harbor was sealed and the defense works greatly strengthened.

The Allied bombardment had no perceptible effect on the fortress. Worse still, the Russians received reinforcements and captured and retained the heights above Balaclava. The besiegers had become the besieged. They were barely able to keep their precarious toe hold in Balaclava Bay until the arrival of reinforcements. On November 14, 1854, the Allies suffered a disastrous blow. A fierce hurricane accompanied by storms of rain and snow leveled installations on the shore and destroyed shipping in the harbor. Thirty vessels with their precious cargoes were lost.

This setback marked the beginning of the terrible "Crimean Winter" that has become a byword in military history. The effect of the storm was compounded by the breakdown of the supply and medical services. The lack of simple forage, for example, resulted in the wholesale death of transport animals. For a period, supplies distant only seven miles from the camps could not be made available to the troops. Many more men died from lack of drugs and of health facilities than from enemy bullets. Contrary to popular belief, the climate was not responsible for the misery and privations of the soldiers. The coastal area, in fact, traditionally has been a health resort in both summer and winter.

In May, 1855, the Allies assumed the offensive with an amphibious expedition through the Strait of Kerch. They captured all the shipping supplying the Russian armies and destroyed the main Russian supply depot at Taganrog. During the summer months the Allies repeatedly stormed Sebastopol but were repulsed by the gallant defenders. Finally, on September 8, the French captured the Malakov strong point in one of the most famous assaults of the century. The British failed in their simultaneous attack on the Redan outpost. But the French success proved sufficient. The Russians abandoned the fortress after blowing up the magazines and scuttling the fleet. On September 9, 1855, following a siege of 349 days, the Allies occupied the burning ruins of Sebastopol.

Meanwhile the Russians on their part had been besieging Kars, a key Turkish fortress in the Caucasus. Under the British General Fenwick Williams, the Turkish garrison held out heroically for six months against overwhelming odds. When a relief force failed to arrive in time, the garrison was starved out and forced to surrender on November 28, 1855.

TREATY OF PARIS

The victory at Sebastopol did not dispose the British toward peace. Palmerston was now the prime minister, having replaced Aberdeen early in 1855. Palmerston had maintained from the outset that the sword alone could force Russia to terms. Accordingly he made England's blade weighty and sharp. He added 30,000 men to the army, making 256,000 in all, and he strengthened the navy proportionately. England was fitter for war now than at the beginning. Furthermore, the failure of the British assault on the Redan meant that the fall of Sebastopol was viewed primarily as a French victory. Hence there was a general desire in Britain for another campaign in order to satisfy national honor and also to bring Russia really to her knees.

The attitude in France was quite different. Most Frenchmen felt that the war was being fought mainly for British interests. They could understand and support a war on the Rhine or a war to free Poland or Italy. But why should the fighting continue in the distant Crimea after Sebastopol had been taken? Napoleon shared this sentiment. He already had gotten what he wanted out of the war—prestige for his dynasty, glory for France, and the disruption of the Russian-Austrian-Prussian bloc.

Austria also was eager to end the war speedily, as indeed she had been from the very beginning. It was the French and Austrian diplomats, therefore, who now took the initiative for peace. They prepared tentative terms based on the Vienna Four Points. Palmerston fumed and fussed but had to go along. After lengthy negotiations the three powers agreed on terms which Austria then presented to Russia on December 28 in the form of an ultimatum. Austria threatened to intervene in the war unless Russia agreed to peace negotiations based on the Four Points plus the neutralization of the Black Sea and the cession of Bessarabia.

Austria calculated that Russia was exhausted and ready for peace and that she would therefore accept the ultimatum. This proved to be the case. Russia now faced not only Britain, France, and Turkey but also Sardinia, which had entered the war in January, 1855. Sweden, too, was veering toward the Allies. King Frederick William of Prussia urged Tsar Alexander to accept the terms and warned him that Austria was serious in her intervention threat. Alexander yielded to this pressure and the peace conference was held in Paris in February and March, 1856.

Palmerston was as bellicose during the conference as he had been before. He instructed his foreign minister, Lord Clarendon, that "Russia has brought . . . humiliation on herself and she must drink from the chalice which she herself has filled." [18] Napoleon had hopes of using the peace gathering to effect a general revision of the 1815 settlement, including the Polish and Italian problems. Palmerston refused to consider such wholesale change and drew closer to Austria in order to preserve the *status quo*. France thereupon sided with Russia on most controversial issues. In fact, the Paris Conference marked the beginning of a Franco-Russian *rapprochement* that was to result in close cooperation between the two powers during the following years. The French foreign minister, Count Walewski, who presided over the conference, was regarded as being "more Russian than the Russians."

The Treaty of Paris of March 30, 1856, included the following provisions:

1. The Ottoman Empire was formally admitted to the concert of Europe and the signatory powers engaged to respect and guarantee the empire's independence and territorial integrity.

2. The powers took appreciative cognizance of the reform edict, the *Hatti-Humayun,* issued by the sultan on February 18, 1856. This edict, which will be considered in detail in Chapter 20, promised religious equality before the law, reform of police and prisons, of coinage and taxation. But in recognizing the edict the powers expressly repudiated "the right to interfere, either collectively or separately," in the internal affairs of Turkey.

3. The Black Sea was neutralized. No fortifications, either Russian or Turkish, were to be maintained on its coasts. Its waters and ports were to be open to the mercantile marine of every nation but permanently closed to all warships.

4. The Danube was to be open to the ships of all nations and its navigation was to be under the control of an international commission.

5. Sebastopol was to be restored to Russia and Kars to the Turks.

6. Russia was to cede southern Bessarabia to Moldavia, thereby losing access to the Danube. The Principalities of Moldavia and Wallachia were to remain under the suzerainty of the Porte. Russia renounced her exclusive protection over them, and the signatory powers collectively guaranteed their

privileges. No agreement could be reached on the political organization of the Principalities, so this was left to an international commission which was to make recommendations after the wishes of the people had been expressed in popularly elected assemblies.

7. The liberties of Serbia were to be similarly guaranteed, though a Turkish garrison was to remain in that country.

Under a separate treaty concluded on April 15, Britain, France, and Austria agreed to regard any infringement of Turkish independence and integrity as a *causus belli* and to concert measures to meet it.

BALKAN AND EUROPEAN REPERCUSSIONS

Some twenty years after the Crimean War a British foreign minister declared that "England put her money on the wrong horse." Others have pronounced the war to have been both unnecessary and useless. Are these judgments justified in the light of history?

The answer depends on whether one is thinking in terms of Balkan or general European history. So far as the Balkans are concerned, the Crimean War had less impact than might be expected. Within a few years most of the provisions of the Paris Treaty had been violated. Russia repudiated the Black Sea clauses in 1870; Russia, Britain, and Austria encroached on Ottoman integrity in 1878; and Turkey failed to reform herself despite British expectations and her own *Hatti-Humayun*. On the other hand, it is sometimes argued that the Crimean War prevented Russia from engulfing the Balkan Peninsula and thus made possible the future independence of the Balkan states. This thesis has some basis in fact. The war did hasten the transformation of the Danubian Principalities into the united and independent Rumanian state. But to accept the thesis fully it is necessary to accept also its basic assumption that Russia wished to annex the Balkan lands and would have succeeded were it not for the Crimean War. This assumption is open to question. It is certainly true that Tsar Nicholas's constant preoccupation with Turkish partition came to be regarded in certain circles as evidence of a plot to subvert the sultan's empire. Yet the fact remains that a careful analysis of the tsar's statements and actions leads to the conclusion that he was prompted "not by any Machiavellian determination to encompass the Sultan's downfall as much as by a genuine and natural desire to safeguard Russia's vital interests and avoid the risk that Turkey's collapse might take the powers unawares and provoke a general war." [19]

The Crimean War had a greater impact on Europe than on the Near East. It marked a turning point in the course of European diplomacy. In the first place, it enhanced enormously the prestige of Napoleon and of France. The holding of the peace conference in Paris was symptomatic of the change in French fortunes. After 1856 France took the place of Austria as the leading power on the Continent.

More significant was the disruptive effect of the war upon the conservative, pro–*status quo* bloc of the three eastern Powers, Russia, Prussia, and Austria. The effectiveness of this bloc had been demonstrated in 1849 when Tsar Nicholas sent an army to help the Hapsburg emperor crush the Hungarian rebels. Only a few years later, in 1854, Austria repaid Russia by delivering an ultimatum and aligning herself with Russia's enemies. Nicholas gave vent to his fury by presenting his valet with a statuette of Francis Joseph which hitherto had adorned his study. This rupture between Russia and Austria was a diplomatic revolution of first-rate importance. The tripartite bloc no longer existed to maintain the *status quo.* Austria no longer could look to Russia or to Prussia for backing against the Western powers and against her own subject nationalities. Thus the Continent was unfrozen, and in little more than a decade Cavour unified Italy, Bismarck unified Germany, and Napoleon fell from the glory of the Malakov to the disaster of Sedan.

18. Making of Rumania to 1878

OSTENSIBLY THE CRIMEAN WAR was fought to maintain the integrity and independence of the Ottoman Empire. Yet the immediate effect of the war was the unification of the Moldavian and Wallachian Principalities into the autonomous kingdom of Rumania. This establishment of the Rumanian state cannot be explained entirely by the provisions of the Treaty of Paris and the diplomatic policies of the European powers. Account also must be taken of the Rumanian people themselves, who were by no means passive pawns. How did these people survive almost two millenia of barbarian invasions and foreign rule? Why were they now, in the mid-nineteenth century, beginning to awaken and to demand their place in the family of nations? Also, why were these people, unlike their Greek and South Slavic neighbors, divided into a small landowning class and a vast exploited peasant mass? Consideration of these questions will explain the creation of the Rumanian state and make its later history easier to understand.

HISTORICAL BACKGROUND

The Rumanians are the descendants of the original Dacian people, with additions of Roman, Slavic, and, to a much lesser degree, Tatar strains. These people occupy the lower Danubian lands on either side of the Transylvanian Alps. The "cisalpine" Rumanians live in the political entities of Moldavia, Wallachia, Bukovina, and Bessarabia, whereas the "transalpine" Rumanians occupy Transylvania and the Banat of Temesvar. By the mid-nineteenth century the Rumanians had fallen under the rule of three neighboring powers: Bessarabia belonging to Russia; Bukovina, Transylvania, and the Banat of Temesvar to Austria; Moldavia and Wallachia accepting the suzerainty of Turkey and the protectorate of Russia. It follows that a nationalist awakening among the Rumanian people was likely to be a matter of international rather than purely local concern.

We noted in Chapter 2 that the original Dacians were under Roman rule between A.D. 100 and 275. When the Romans retreated to the southern bank of the Danube the floodgates of invasion were left open. During the following centuries a host of barbarian invaders marched through the flat Rumanian valley lands on their way to the west and south. When this movement of peoples subsided, the Rumanians were able to organize two semi-independent states, Wallachia and Moldavia, in the thirteenth and fourteenth centuries, respectively. From the outset these states were in a precarious position, each being surrounded by powerful and aggressive neighbors. Wallachia had to contend with Turkey and Hungary, while Moldavia faced Turkey, Hungary, and Poland. When the Ottoman armies crushed all opposition in Southeastern Europe the Rumanians were forced to accept Turkish suzerainty. Wallachia became a Turkish dependency in the fifteenth century and Moldavia in the sixteenth. At one point an exceptionally capable Wallachian prince, Michael the Brave, was able to assert his independence and overrun Moldavia and Transylvania. In 1600 he proclaimed himself Prince of all Rumanians. But the following year he was killed and his purely personal empire disappeared with him. Ottoman domination then remained unchallenged in the Rumanian lands until the nineteenth century.

The Turks allowed their Rumanian subjects a large measure of autonomy. They exacted annual tribute and in return they agreed not to hold land in the Principalities. Also, the Rumanian nobles or boyars were free to elect their own princes, known as hospodars. The Turks continued to observe these terms but only in a nominal fashion. In actual practice Rumanian autonomy soon became meaningless. One reason was that the Turks used the right of pre-emption in the Rumanian markets to the point of economic spoliation. They normally paid for the large shipments of grain and sheep sent regularly to Constantinople, but they set the rates so low that they amounted, in effect, to additional tribute. Moreover, the Turks took advantage of quarrels among the boyars to influence directly and decisively the choice of hospodars. As noted in Chapter 7, aspirants to the princely office had to bribe the sultan's ministers for their support. Before long the Turks were appointing and removing the hospodars in rapid succession, for the quicker the turnover the greater the proceeds. The net result was a system of vicious economic exploitation and purely nominal political autonomy.

Those Rumanians who lived outside the two Principalities did not fare better. When the Ottoman Empire was at its height it encompassed all the Rumanian lands. But as it grew weaker it lost one province after another to the neighboring powers. The Hapsburgs obtained Transylvania by the Karlowitz Treaty in 1699, the Banat of Temesvar by the Passarowitz Treaty in 1718, and Bukovina in 1775. Likewise, Russia reached the Dniester River with the Jassy Treaty of 1792 and then annexed the province of Bessarabia by the Bucharest Treaty of 1812.

The Russians also steadily encroached on the sultan's authority in Moldavia and Wallachia. They began with the Kuchuk Kainarji Treaty of

1774, which gave them the right to protect the Christian religion and its churches throughout Turkey and which also allowed the Russian ambassador in Constantinople to intercede in behalf of the Principalities. From then on the Russians steadily extended their authority in the Principalities until finally they became virtually corulers with the Adrianople Treaty of 1829. This required that the sultan should accept the elected hospodars for life; he could not reject or dismiss them without Russia's concurrence; and he could not maintain any fortified place or any Moslem settlement anywhere in the Principalities. The sultan also agreed that the Russians should occupy the two provinces until the last installment of the war indemnity had been paid. Finally, he undertook to accept the new constitution for the Principalities which the Russian commander, General Kisselev, was preparing, and he even agreed that the Russian consuls in the Principalities should be specifically authorized to watch over the working of the constitution. This gave the consuls a major role in Moldavian and Wallachian affairs. Indeed, the sultan ordered the hospodars to comply with the wishes of the consuls as much as possible. And it is known that some hospodars were dismissed and others appointed on Russian insistence. Thus the Adrianople Treaty established a dual authority in the Principalities, and of the two powers Russia was clearly the senior partner.

We may conclude that in the early nineteenth century the outlook for the Rumanian people everywhere appeared dark and hopeless. Yet in 1848 they arose, together with the other subject nations of Europe, and they made clear their desire for national unity and for independence. The uprising was a manifestation of the slowly developing nationalist movement among the Rumanians. But this movement was a narrow and rather esoteric affair. It was nationalistic but not national. It did not include the vast peasant mass that constituted the overwhelming majority of the Rumanian nation. These peasants were quite unaware of nationalism or constitutionalism or any of the other isms of the period. They were concerned only with land, servile dues, labor obligations, and other such matters that affected their daily lives. The nationalist movement, therefore, cannot be placed in proper perspective unless the underlying peasant problem is first recognized and understood.

PEASANT PROBLEM

When the Wallachian and Moldavian Principalities were organized in the thirteenth and fourteenth centuries Rumanian society was rural and egalitarian. The peasants were free joint holders of the village lands and were required only to give the village headman one tenth of their produce and three days' labor each year. Land tenure rested on the principle that all the inhabitants had an equal right to the use of the soil.

With the founding of the two Principalities new social relationships developed which soon undermined the egalitarianism of Rumanian society. The appearance of a central authority dispensing justice and favors induced the village headmen to look more to the princes than to their own people. They began to leave the villages for court positions at Jassy and Bucharest. There they found opportunity for self-enrichment and social advancement. They also found a cultural pattern quite different from that of the village. As they adapted themselves to that pattern they drifted further away from the peasant mass. In this manner class differentiation gradually developed. The new noble or boyar class steadily gained in status and riches while the formerly free peasants declined into serfdom.

By the eighteenth century the boyars and the monasteries controlled a large proportion of the land to which the majority of the peasants were bound as serfs. Thus Rumanian serfdom, in its relatively late flowering, re-sembled that of Russia rather than that of Western Europe. Also, it should be noted that the peasants were subjugated not because of foreign invasion but rather because of the establishment of a central government with favors to bestow and needs to be fulfilled. It is significant that Michael the Brave, the most independent of the Rumanian princes, was the first legally to impose restrictions upon the peasantry. And he did so in order to ensure a settled population able to provide military supplies for his new standing army. Thus foreign domination does not explain the enslavement of the peasants, though it does account in part for the heavy tax burden that they had to bear. Not only did they supply the needs of the hospodars and the boyars, but in the final analysis it was they who also paid for the tributes, bribes, and other payments made to the Turks.

The Rumanian peasants had to contend with Greek as well as Turk-ish and native exploiters. Indeed, by the eighteenth century the Greek Phana-riotes had almost a strangle hold on the Rumanian economy. A native middle class did not exist between the boyars and the peasants, so the Greeks were able to move in as merchants, moneylenders, and tax farmers. As they be-came wealthier and won more influence in the Ottoman court they were able to make or break the Rumanian hospodars. The latter frequently were mere tools in the hands of the Phanariotes, dependent upon them for both finan-cial and political backing. In the early eighteenth century, as we noted in Chapter 13, the Phanariotes secured the office of hospodar for themselves. Until the Greek revolution of 1821 a succession of Phanariote hospodars followed one another in rapid succession at Jassy and Bucharest. Each paid lavish bribes for his office and naturally made every effort to recover his in-vestment and as much extra as feasible. The burden ultimately fell upon the back of the peasant. Thouvenel, the French ambassador in Constantinople, aptly observed that "the sultan weighed on the prince, the prince on the boyars, and the boyars on the peasants. . . ." [1] Likewise, a British consul reported in the early nineteenth century: "There does not, perhaps, exist a people labouring under a greater degree of oppression from the effect of despotic power and more heavily burthened with impositions and taxes than the peasants of Wallachia and Moldavia. . . ." [2]

The Phanariotes have been blamed for this unhappy state of affairs.

But the source of the trouble was institutional rather than personal. This is illustrated by the fact that exploitation prevailed before the Phanariotes appeared on the scene and continued after they had disappeared. Also, it was a Phanariote hospodar, Constantine Mavrokordatos, who issued decrees abolishing serfdom in Wallachia in 1746 and in Moldavia in 1749. These decrees relieved the serfs of personal bondage so that they no longer were tied to the land. But the position of the peasants did not show improvement. The reason was that Rumanian agriculture was beginning to be commercialized. It was beginning to produce for world rather than for local markets. This stimulated a drive for increased productivity which in turn led the boyars to impose new fetters upon the peasantry—fetters which were less obvious but fully as oppressive as the personal bondage of the past.

In the latter part of the eighteenth century increasing quantities of Rumanian grain were being shipped to Constantinople and other Turkish cities. Agricultural exports to other neighboring countries, and particularly Austria, also were mounting. But the great stimulus to the Rumanian economy was supplied by the Treaty of Adrianople. This abolished the Turkish right of pre-empting Rumanian products and declared that the trade of the Principalities should be freed from all Turkish restrictions. The immediate result was a rapid rise in the volume of exports. By the 1840's an average of 1,000 vessels totaling 200,000 tons called each year at Galatz and Braila, the shipping ports for Moldavia and Wallachia, respectively. An even greater volume of agricultural products was shipped overland or by river to Austria, Turkey, and Russia.

This economic flowering paradoxically contributed to the outbreak of the Crimean War. The Russians were chagrined that they should have unwittingly created competition for their own grain exports out of Odessa and Taganrog. Accordingly they used their position at the mouth of the Danube to obstruct by various ways the export of Rumanian grain. This drew loud protests from British merchants and led ultimately to the provision in the Paris Treaty for an international commission to control Danubian shipping.

So far as the Rumanian peasants were concerned, the immediate effect of the commercial expansion was detrimental. The boyars wanted more land and more labor to produce greater quantities of grain for export. In various ways, legal and extralegal, they increased tremendously the labor obligations of the peasants. Also, they reserved a steadily expanding proportion of the land for their own use and attempted to limit the peasants' right to pasture. Thus the peasant was deprived of both land and labor to the advantage of the boyar.

This trend was reinforced by the "Organic Statutes" introduced in 1831–1832 during the period of Russian occupation. These acts recognized the boyar for the first time as the legal proprietor of the land rather than as the leader of the village, which he originally had been. The peasants were granted use of land not in excess of two thirds of the estate, the remaining third being completely at the disposal of the boyar. In return the peasants were obliged to provide fifty-six to sixty days of service each year. Theoretically they were free to move if they were dissatisfied, but a network of regulations and restrictions effectively bound them to their villages. When a peasant died, the land he had tilled was not to pass to his sons as in the past. It reverted, instead, to the boyar, who was held responsible for providing newly married young cultivators with a holding.

General Kisselev was far from satisfied with these Organic Statutes, which were formulated primarily by boyar committees. It is true that they defined precisely the peasants' obligations and thus reduced the opportunity for arbitrary exactions. It is also true that Rumanian agriculture spurted forward during the following decades. The acreage in cereals nearly doubled during the thirty years between 1829 and 1859. But the peasants who constituted the backbone of the nation did not benefit from this expansion. They were definitely worse off than in the old days when they practiced a predominantly cattle economy and had access to as much land as their cattle needed. Now they found themselves involved, willy-nilly, in a commercial grain economy. They did not comprehend the circumstances that had produced this change. They knew only that their holdings had been reduced by more than one half and that their labor obligations had increased thirty times. Michael Eminescu, the famous Rumanian author, commented bitterly: "The country was but a big estate, administered like an estate—a complex of latifundia in which private law is public law, the inheritance of landed wealth the inheritance of power in the State." [3]

RISE OF NATIONALISM

The Rumanians constitute a single nationality but only recently did they unite under one flag. It was not until the collapse of the Russian and Hapsburg empires during World War I that they were able to establish their "Greater Rumania." Michael the Brave did bring all Rumanians under his scepter for a few years, but this cannot be interpreted as a triumph of Rumanian nationalism. Michael regarded his empire as a purely personal creation and possession. The Rumanians of Moldavia and Transylvania looked upon him at the time as a meddlesome usurper rather than as a liberator. His reputation as the father of his people is an unwarranted though understandable product of the national self-consciousness that manifested itself in the nineteenth century.

Rumanian nationalism appeared late and developed slowly. One reason was the foreign domination in every field—not only political and economic but also cultural. At first the main cultural influence was Slavonic. The old Church Slavonic was the official ecclesiastical and literary language among the Rumanians as well as among the Serbians and Bulgarians. Also, the Turkish invasion of Bulgaria in 1393 drove numerous Bulgarian priests and scholars across the Danube and strengthened the Slavonic tradition in the Rumanian lands. Greek influence began to supplant the Slavonic after the fall of Constantinople in 1453. By the following century Greek was taught in most monastic schools. The success of the Phanariotes in the political and economic spheres assured the predominance of Greek culture. By the beginning of the eighteenth century the Greek language was used in administration and learning, and the Greek liturgy in the churches.

The content of this imported Greek culture was at first Byzantine and ecclesiastical. But gradually Western secular thought penetrated the Greek world. This immediately affected the Rumanians because Bucharest and Jassy were, in the intellectual sense, as Greek as Athens and Yanina. A Phanariote hospodar first introduced the French language in the schools of Wallachia in 1776, and he was immediately imitated in Moldavia. The works of Voltaire, Rousseau, and the Encyclopedists were widely read in the Principalities, both in the original and in Greek translation. The French Revolution itself was followed eagerly in the columns of Greek newspapers published in Vienna. The famous Greek revolutionary, Rhigas Pheraios, was the moving spirit in a literary and political organization in Bucharest. In short, a highly cultured and politically conscious Greco-Rumanian society was active in Bucharest and Jassy in the latter part of the eighteenth century.

This explains why Alexander Ypsilantis, who was of a Phanariote hospodar family, decided to launch the Greek revolution in 1821 with an uprising in the Principalities. He soon learned that the gulf between a cosmopolitan drawing-room society and an inert peasant mass was too great to be bridged by political slogans. When Ypsilantis crossed the Pruth River with his small force of Greek revolutionaries on March 16, 1821, as described in Chapter 15, his only hope of success was to arouse the peasants and win them to his side. But the few peasants that were armed and organized at this time were led by a certain Tudor Vladimirescu, who was not disposed to follow Greek leadership blindly. Vladimirescu was not an uninformed rustic, as is usually assumed. He was of peasant origin but he had amassed considerable wealth and had gained experience fighting with the Russians during the 1806 Russo-Turkish War. He rose to the rank of lieutenant in the Russian army and later served the Russian consul in Bucharest in various capacities.

Vladimirescu had been in contact with the Greek revolutionaries before they entered the Principalities, and had indicated his willingness to cooperate with them. But in doing so, his aim was to further the Rumanian cause rather than the Greek. In taking up arms at this time, he issued proclamations demanding tax reform, a national army, a national assembly representative of all classes of the population, and native hospodars in place of the Greek Phanariotes. When the tsar repudiated Ypsilantis, Vladimirescu decided that the Greeks were doomed and that nothing would be gained by fighting with them. "We will help Ypsilantis," declared Vladimirescu, "to recross the Danube so that he might liberate his own fatherland." [4] Vladimirescu now had to find other allies, so he tried to establish a working arrangement with the boyars. On August 23, 1821, he called on his followers to support a boyar government that had been established in Bucharest. This move proved to be a fatal miscalculation. It alienated his peasant following and failed to win over the boyars, who preferred the re-establishment of Turkish rule to the perils of an unpredictable uprising. Thus Vladimirescu found himself largely deserted, and soon afterward he fell into the hands of the Greeks and was executed.

These events in 1821 are significant because they represent the prelude to the large-scale peasant uprisings of the following decades, and also because they mark the beginning of the end of Greek influence in the Principalities. The Ottoman government reacted to the Greek revolution by henceforth appointing Rumanian boyars in place of the Phanariotes as hospodars of Moldavia and Wallachia. At the same time that the Greeks were losing their official positions in the Principalities they were also declining in their cultural influence. The new currents that were gaining predominance were the so-called Latinist movement and, above all, the ideology and culture of France.

Latinism began in the late eighteenth century, when a number of Transylvanian Rumanians were sent to Jesuit institutions in Rome. The young students were inspired by the monuments of antiquity that they saw about them. The most exciting was the famous column of Trajan, the emperor who had made their own homeland, ancient Dacia, a part of the Roman Empire. It is not surprising that these young men, the representatives of a people who had suffered under foreign rule for centuries, responded enthusiastically to this association with a glorious past. They developed and popularized the theory that they were the direct descendants of the noble Romans. They claimed that the Rumanians were a chosen people, an outpost of Latin culture in the surrounding sea of Slavic and Teutonic barbarism. The chief work of these champions of Latinism was in the linguistic field. They replaced the Slavonic alphabet with the Latin. They purged the Rumanian language of Slavic, Greek, and other non-Latin words. They gradually secured the use of Rumanian as the language of instruction in place of Greek. These reforms helped to create a uniform literary language and thereby provided the essential basis for the development of Rumanian culture.

The influence of France was much greater than that of the shadowy Roman Empire. We have seen that French ideas reached the Rumanians indirectly by way of the Greeks. Another medium of French culture was the Russian army during the years of occupation. Russian officers spoke French, affected Western manners, and taught the ladies how to dance *à la française.* Rumanian students who attended French universities also contributed to the propagation of French language and culture. Not all of them obtained their degrees, but they all returned ardent admirers of the great Latin sister nation. Their proudest boast was that their own Bucharest was the "Paris of the Balkans." Finally, the French Revolution and the exploits of Napoleon made a deep impression on politically minded Rumanians. The French viceconsul at Jassy reported: "For the small portion of the boyars who know how to reason, the French Revolution is not without attraction. They like to be told about it and cannot help showing a certain approval and at least admiring its prodigious accomplishments." [5]

An early political manifestation of this intellectual ferment was the organization of the Philharmonic Society in 1833. Its stated purpose was to encourage literature and the arts. But the younger and more radical members drew up a program of their own that reflected clearly the influence of France. They wanted the unification of the two Principalities, a constitutional regime, freedom of the press, free education, and equality for all Rumanians before the law. The bolder spirits among them tried to take advantage of the Near Eastern crisis of 1839–1841 to realize their aims. They staged scattered outbreaks but were easily suppressed.

The year 1848 was a year of revolution in the Principalities as well as in Central and Western Europe. The leaders were the students who had studied abroad. The great majority of them had gone to Paris, where they were profoundly affected by the liberal doctrines expounded at the Collège de France. They heard Jules Michelet lecture on his philosophy of history. They identified themselves with Adam Mickiewicz, Edgar Quinet, and others who depicted the sad plight of the Italians and the Poles and raised hopes for future revolutions that would liberate all the enslaved nations of Europe. Under such tutelage the young Rumanian students became strongly nationalistic and also anti-Russian. They regarded the tsar as the hateful gendarme of Europe. Some of them published articles and pamphlets in Paris with the aim of bringing the Rumanian problem to the attention of the West. Their principal argument was that a free and united Rumania would serve as "an insuperable barrier against the encroachments of the Tsar." [6]

With such ideas and aspirations the Rumanian students were quick to take up arms when the 1848 revolutions swept over Europe. Some of them took part in the February uprising in Paris and hoisted the Rumanian flag at the Hôtel de Ville, where it flew with the French, Polish, and Italian flags. Thus was symbolized the union of the oppressed peoples of Europe against international reaction. The Rumanian students then hurried home full of plans for the liberation of their countrymen and the establishment of the millenium.

The ground had been prepared at home by the cultural and propaganda work of various literary societies and by the activities of a secret revolutionary organization, the Fratia or Brotherhood. The uprising in Jassy proved a fiasco. It was poorly organized and the reigning hospodar was able to crush it quickly and easily. In Wallachia the revolutionaries were more successful. They presented several petitions for reform to the hospodar, George Bibescu, who rejected them at the insistence of the Russian consul. Disturbances then broke out in the streets and, after vain efforts to curb them, Bibescu lost his nerve and accepted on June 23 a revolutionary cabinet and a constitution. Two days later he abdicated and a provisional government was established.

The new government issued decrees abolishing ranks and establishing freedom of speech, assembly, and the press. It also declared itself for the unification of the Rumanian people. "All lands inhabited by Rumanians should be called Rumania and form one state. . . . the Rumanian nation demands that it be one and indivisible." [7]

This dream of national unity was soon dispelled. It was apparent from the outset that Russia was determined to stamp out this conflagration near her border. The revolutionaries were aware of this and tried to win the Turks over to their side. The Turks were rather pleased to have an avowedly anti-Russian government in Wallachia. One of the sultan's officials declared gleefully, "There is only one thing still wanting—the union of the two Principalities. That would be a stake in the entrails of Russia." [8] But the decisive factor determining Turkish policy was, as usual, the attitude of the powers. Russia demanded that the revolutionary regime be destroyed and the Western powers refused to offer support against this pressure. Accordingly, the sultan bowed to the will of the tsar. He sent an army across the Danube and after a brief skirmish the provincial government collapsed and its leaders scattered in all directions.

The 1848 revolutions in the Principalities had an *opéra bouffe* quality about them. They were doomed from the outset, partly because of the hands-off policy of London and Paris, but also because of the narrow outlook of the leaders. The fundamental problem in the provinces was agrarian. But most of the revolutionaries, with their midde-class viewpoint, failed to grasp the significance of this fact. They did establish a commission to investigate the problem. It held meetings long enough for some peasant spokesmen to give passionate expression to their grievances.

If the Ciocoi [a grasping parvenu or exploiter of the peasants] could have laid his hand on the sun, he would have seized it and sold to the peasant for money the light and the heat of God. Your lands would bring you nothing if we were not there to fill your granaries with produce and your houses with gold and silver. These riches are not the fruit of the work of your arms, they are made by the sweat of our brow, under the blows of your whip and that of your Government.[9]

A few of the leaders of the provisional government sympathized with the viewpoint of the peasants. Nicholas Balcescu, for example, stated: "The *boyar* has no love for the land; he does not live on it and work it. . . . He looks upon the land as a penal settlement in which to keep the peasant so as to exploit him. . . . The peasant represents the *boyar's* capital." [10] Few members of the government were willing to go so far. Most of them wanted political reform, not social revolution. Nor did they wish to add the boyars to the list of their enemies. So they dissolved the commmission and did nothing about the agrarian problem. The grievances of the peasants remained unsatisfied and the revolutionaries thus forfeited whatever chance they may have had of winning mass support against their external foes.

The only significance of the revolution is that it demonstrated that a nationalist spirit existed—the embryo of the "Greater Rumania" of the future. But this spirit should not be exaggerated. It was still only an embryo. It cannot be dignified with the name of a nationalist movement. Only an infinitesimally small proportion of the population held national ideals. And even this small group was divided into conservative and radical wings. The conservatives wished to unite the Principalities, get rid of the Russians, and assume power and office themselves. The radicals wanted to go further. They wished to remake Rumanian society in accordance with the liberal principles they had imbibed in Paris. The fact that these had little relevance or meaning for the millions of peasants they scarcely perceived.

WINNING OF UNITY: 1856–1859

After the failure of the insurrection in Wallachia many of the nationalist leaders fled to Paris. There they sided with the republicans against Napoleon. One of the Rumanians, Dimitrie Bratianu, was arrested and jailed for participating in a plot. While in prison he gave vent to his feelings in a letter in which he execrated Napoleon as "a bastard, a miserable wretch, without country and without family." [11] A few years later the same Bratianu gratefully hailed Napoleon as the founder of the Rumanian state. This tribute was fully deserved. Without Napoleon's support the Principalities would not have been united when they were.

Why did Napoleon champion the cause of a little-known nationality in Eastern Europe? One theory holds that Napoleon wished to unite the Principalities in order to protect Turkey against Russian encroachment. This seems plausible until it is recalled that Russia herself favored the unification of the Principalities, and that Napoleon during these years sought friendship, and perhaps an alliance, with the Russia which he allegedly wished to block. More convincing than this barrier theory is the nationality theory. It attributes Napoleon's Rumanian policy to his espousal of the nationality principle in general, of which the unification of the Principalities was but one manifestation. Napoleon had good reasons, both as a Bonaparte and as the head of the French state, for opposing the 1815 settlement with its wholesale disregard of Europe's nationalities. Perhaps the explanation for Napoleon's support of the Rumanians is to be found in Lord Clarendon's report of what Napoleon told him at the Paris Congress.

He [Napoleon] said that the great fault of the Congress of Vienna was that the interests of the sovereigns were only consulted, while the interests of their subjects were wholly neglected, and that the present congress [of Paris] should not fall into a similar error.[12]

Napoleon consistently and ardently urged that the Principalities be united under a foreign prince. His firmest opponent was Austria, partly because she had plans for the economic exploitation of the Rumanian lands, but primarily because she feared the attraction that a united Rumania would hold for her own Rumanian subjects in Transylvania and Bukovina. Turkey also opposed union, considering it with much justification as a long step toward full independence. Britain wavered from lukewarm acceptance of unification at the beginning to strong opposition before the end. Her traditional distrust of Russia explains the shift. Britain wanted to strengthen Turkey, and she feared that unification would soon deprive Turkey of her two strategic provinces across the Danube. The powers that backed Napoleon were Sardinia, who naturally favored the nationality principle, and Prussia, who desired to weaken her Austrian rival. But Napoleon's chief ally, paradoxically enough, was Russia. By favoring unification Russia hoped to win the good will of the Rumanian people and also to widen the rift between Britain and France.

These differences among the powers made a final settlement at the Paris Conference impossible. The treaty provided that the wishes of the Rumanian people should be ascertained through freely elected assemblies representative of all classes in each Principality. A commission, composed of representatives of the powers, was to meet in the Principalities, determine the views of the assemblies, and report them to a future great-power conference that was to make the final decision. This procedure for consulting the people concerned was unimpeachably democratic. But in a land with mass illiteracy and despotic traditions it led to wholesale fraud and intimidation. And the representatives of the powers became deeply involved as they desperately strove to further the interests of their respective governments.

The first election was held in Moldavia on July 19, 1857. An antiunionist majority was returned, but only through the most blatant chicanery on the part of the Turkish-appointed officials. This precipitated an unseemly brawl among the representatives of the powers with Stratford Canning and the French ambassador, Thouvenel, in the forefront. Thouvenel, supported by the Russian, Prussian, and Sardinian representatives, presented to the Ottoman government what was in effect an ultimatum demanding the annulment of the election. Stratford Canning bristled and warned the Turks that if they did not stand firm the French ambassador "will ride roughshod over us." Thouvenel retorted that Stratford Canning "is not an ambassador but a sovereign," an opinion that even the Austrian representative seems to have shared when he remarked that Stratford Canning acted like "the sixth Great Power of Europe." [13] In any case the Turks refused to satisfy Thouvenel, who thereupon embarked dramatically on a French warship. The other three ministers broke off diplomatic relations at the same time.

The danger of war became real, and Palmerston increased it by informing the French ambassador in London that "the English were ready for any eventualities, however painful they may be." [14] Fortunately for the cause of peace, British public opinion was concentrated on the Indian Mutiny. This distraction left the more temperate elements in the cabinet free to restrain the bellicose Palmerston. By great good luck an official visit of Napoleon III and Empress Eugénie to Queen Victoria and Prince Albert had been arranged for August 6 at Osborne on the Isle of Wight. Long conversations between the sovereigns and their chief ministers finally produced a compromise. The elections were to be annulled, but in return Napoleon agreed that the Principalities should not be united. Instead, they were to receive "similar organic institutions" and "a common system in all things civil and military."

New elections were held in both Principalities in September, 1857. The assemblies met in Jassy and Bucharest the following month. They voted overwhelmingly that the Principalities be united into a single state, subject to the suzerainty of the sultan, and under the constitutional government of a foreign prince. This was contrary to the terms of the agreement reached at Osborne. What were the powers to do? After months of deliberation they decided in the Paris Convention of August, 1858, that the Principalities should remain separate, that each should have its own prince and its own parliament to be elected by itself, and that affairs common to both should be entrusted to a joint Central Commission of sixteen members consisting of an equal number of deputies from each parliament.

This arrangement was artificial and clumsy, and failed to satisfy the aspirations of the Rumanian nationalists. But at least it placed them well along the road to unity. And their good fortune held out so that they quickly reached the end of the road. War clouds now were gathering over Europe. Events were under way that soon were to culminate in the Franco-Austrian war over Italy. While the powers were distracted by this crisis the Rumanians boldly cut the Gordian knot tied by the powers. The two parliaments met in their respective capitals in January and February, 1859. Both unanimously elected as their prince the same man, a native boyar, Colonel Alexander Cuza.

Napoleon recognized Cuza at once. Austria and Turkey expressed strong opposition. Britain fortunately came forward with a face-saving formula that was accepted. Turkey recognized Cuza as prince with the understanding that this was an exceptional case and that the two separate parliaments should continue. Thus the "illegitimate offspring of the two Principalities," as a British consul called Cuza, was legitimatized. For all practical purposes a united and autonomous Rumanian state existed.

ECONOMIC DEVELOPMENTS TO 1878

When Cuza was elected prince the foreign consuls described him in their reports as a card player who "preferred Jamaica rum to public affairs." Like so many other Rumanians of his class, Cuza was easygoing, self-indulgent, and dissolute. But he had one quality that made up for his failings. Unlike most of his fellow boyars, he had some sense of social responsibility. Rumania for him was not simply the ruling class to which he belonged. He recognized the plight of the peasants, sympathized with them, and endeavored to help them. He was fortunate enough to have as chief minister Michael Kogalniceanu, an energetic Moldavian reformer who declared that his aim in public life was "to level up society, to lower the highly placed and to raise the humble." [15]

The humble of Rumania did need raising at this time. These were years of peasant reform throughout Europe. Serfdom had been abolished in Austria in 1841 and in Prussia in 1850. In Russia the emancipation of 1861 was being prepared. Only in the Rumanian provinces were the landlords still strong enough to block reform. As a result the Rumanian peasants under Russian and Austrian rule were substantially better off than those in the two Principalities. The representatives of the great powers were aware of this situation. Accordingly they stipulated in the 1856 Paris Treaty that the assemblies that were to be elected in each Principality should represent "the interests of all the social classes." A few peasants were permitted in the assemblies, and they voiced their grievances passionately. "We want to buy our freedom that we may no longer belong to anybody, but only to the soil, so that we, too, should have a fatherland. . . . We do not want to trespass upon anyone's rights, but neither do we wish our own rights to be forgotten." [16] The boyars angrily denounced these "communistic tendencies" and nothing was done.

The powers still persisted, and the Paris Convention of 1858 which dealt with the future organization of the Principalities contained this stipulation: "All the privileges, exemptions and monopolies which certain classes still enjoy shall be abrogated, and the laws which regulate the relations of landlords and peasants shall be revised without delay, with a view to improving the conditions of the peasantry." [17]

Cuza complied enthusiastically with this directive for reform. He began by expropriating the so-called "Dedicated Monasteries," a measure that was generally popular because it did not affect native interests. The monasteries had been lavishly endowed by princes and boyars so that they might perform necessary social functions such as maintaining schools, hospitals and orphanges, distributing alms in time of famine, and providing hospitality and asylum to travelers in distress. In order to protect these endowments the practice had grown up of placing the monasteries under the protection of the Holy Places in Jerusalem, Sinai, Athos, or one of the great patriarchates of the Levant. Then as Greek Phanariote influence became dominant in both church and state, the "Dedicated Monasteries" passed more and more into the control of foreign monks, who diverted the revenues abroad. Because the monasteries had accumulated over the years about one fourth of the arable land in Wallachia and one third of that in Moldavia, it is apparent that the disposal of the revenues was a major issue that affected the welfare of the population and the income of the state. In September, 1863, the Assembly voted to expropriate the monasteries with a certain amount of compensation. The Patriarch and monks refused to negotiate, hoping to gain more by foreign support. In the end they received nothing, and thus what were probably the richest ecclesiastical properties in Christendom passed under state control.

Kogalniceanu next introduced a bill giving the peasants clear title to the land they were working. This affected the boyars who indignantly rejected the bill. They had no difficulty doing so since they dominated the Assembly elected by 3,796 voters. The boyars then passed a bill of their own which freed the peasants of all dues and restrictions but failed to provide them with any land. This would have created a landless rural proletariat that would have constituted a cheap and dependent labor supply for the landlords. Cuza now decided that the land question could not be settled without forceful measures. He vetoed the boyars' bill, dissolved the Assembly, and, in imitation of Napoleon III, appealed to the people through a plebiscite. The peasants, he confided to the French consul, "are the state's active force. The rest do not matter, and the day an effort is made to overthrow me, I shall have three million peasants with me." [18]

Cuza fatally overestimated the responsiveness of his peasants. They were certainly the most numerous element in Rumanian society but they were scattered and unorganized. When the showdown came they may have been for him but they were not beside him. The plebiscite was held on May 14, 1864. The people were asked to vote yes or no on two proposals: a new electoral law that established virtually universal suffrage, and a new constitution that greatly strengthened the position of the prince. The returns were favorable by 682,621 to 1,307. Cuza then promulgated his famous Agrarian Reform Law of August 25, 1864. It freed the peasants of all restrictions on their movements and abolished all dues in labor and in kind. In return the landlords received compensation in state bonds which were to be paid for by the peasants over a period of fifteen years. The peasants also were given holdings which varied according to the number of cattle they possessed. Up to two thirds of a boyar's land could be used for this purpose, and in regions where this did not suffice the state lands were to be used.

Despite the good intentions of its authors, this act did not solve the agrarian problem in Rumania. Indeed, the general welfare of the peasants probably deteriorated during the following decades. One reason was that the boyars, who controlled local administration, twisted the provisions of the law to their advantage. They kept the best land for themselves, used false measuring standards, and so divided the holdings that the individual peasant either spent much of his time walking from one small lot to another or was unable to reach his property without paying a toll. The law provided that the peasants should receive the land they had used before the reform but actually they received less land and of lower quality.

Not only was the law unjustly enforced but certain of its provisions were shortsighted and proved most unfortunate in practice. The peasants could not obtain more than two thirds of the lord's estate, but in those lightly populated regions where the peasants required less than the two-thirds portion the lord was permitted to retain as his absolute property all that remained. Thus it is estimated that by fair means or foul, the boyars ultimately kept over one half the total land, while the state reserves were used to provide plots for the peasants from thickly populated areas. Also, the Organic Statutes of 1831–1832 had held the boyar responsible for providing each newly married peasant with a holding, but the new act made no provision for subsequent generations. Since the population rose rapidly and the peasants invariably divided their plots equally among their sons, the result was the progressive fragmentation of peasant property. The original holdings in many cases had not been large enough to support a family. After fragmentation had occurred, the land-hungry peasants had no choice but to work the lord's land on almost any terms he stipulated.

The plight of the peasantry was worsened by certain developments in the latter part of the nineteenth century. One was the growth of population, which increased 54 per cent between 1859 and 1899. Another was the passage of laws on agricultural contracts in 1866 and 1872. These laws gave the landowners sweeping powers in enforcing labor contracts, even to the point of using military units to drive the peasants to work. In fact, the army customarily "loaned" soldiers to the landowners during busy seasons, 26,538 soldiers being used in this manner in 1912. Also, the peasants' theoretical freedom of movement rarely existed in fact because of their chronic indebtedness to their landowners or to the tax collectors. "I have known sober, hard-working peasants," one landlord admitted, "who laboured fifteen years to pay off a debt they contracted in the winter 1866–7 for maize which they had borrowed to feed their families." [19]

Finally, social friction in the countryside was increased by the growing prevalence of absenteeism on the great estates. The effects were particularly unfortunate because the landowners, who spent their time in Bucharest or in foreign capitals, commonly leased their properties not to individual peasants but to entrepreneurs. The latter were essentially speculators who merely sublet the land to the peasants for as high rents as possible in order to get a big return on their investment. Because of the population pressure they were able to impose fantastically unjust terms on the land-hungry peasants, who responded with a bitter hatred that periodically burst out into open revolt.

The 1864 reform failed completely to create the small peasant proprietor class that Cuza and Kogalniceanu had in mind. Instead, the great majority of the peasants found themselves with totally inadequate holdings and were forced into a position of complete economic subservience to the great landowners. Their plight has been well summarized by an authority as follows:

. . . the agrarian system fell into a peculiar compound of serfdom and capitalism; from it landlords and their tenants secured all the advantages of both while the peasants were saddled with all the burdens of both. From serfdom the landlords had all the facilities of servile labour without any of the feudal obligations towards it; while from capitalism they had the freedom to bargain with labour without the restraint of a free labour market. The peasants, however, were subjected to servile labour without its counterpart in land rights; and from capitalism they had all the trials of wage earners without being really free to trade their labours where they willed. One class, says M. Gherea, had achieved for itself "roses without thorns, while the thorns—and the thorns alone—were left for the peasants." [20]

This unhealthy imbalance in Rumanian society stood out in marked contrast to the conditions in the other Balkan countries. Direct Ottoman rule over the Greeks and the South Slavs had eliminated the native nobilities and had left comparatively egalitarian peasant nations. To find a parallel to Rumania's economic and social structure one must look east of the Pruth rather than south of the Danube. Russia and Rumania emancipated their peasantry in 1861 and 1864, respectively. But the outcome in both countries was a land-hungry, depressed, and dissatisfied peasant mass. It is not surprising that the political repercussions were correspondingly similar—sporadic peasant outbreaks in both countries in the late nineteenth century, violent revolution in Russia in 1905 and in Rumania in 1907, and the great Russian Revolution of 1917 which stimulated directly the Rumanian agrarian reforms of 1917–1921.

POLITICAL DEVELOPMENTS TO 1878

Cuza ruled as prince of Rumania from 1859 to 1866. During those seven years he passed from one crisis to another. His regime never took on the appearance of stability. It always seemed a temporary stopgap affair, as, indeed, it turned out to be. Perhaps the basic reason for this was the irreconcilable opposition of the boyars, the only organized and articulate element in Rumanian society. Another important factor was the character of Cuza himself. He was a poor administrator, so that many of his reforms remained only paper measures. Also, he lacked completely the arts of the demagogue. He disliked public spectacles and participated in them rarely and diffidently. Thus he was incapable of rallying his subjects and popularizing his leadership.

Despite these failings, Cuza accomplished much, in the political field as well as in the economic. When he was first elected he had the almost impossible task of serving as prince of two principalities with two assemblies, two cabinets, and a central commission. He found it necessary to spend half his time traveling back and forth between Bucharest and Jassy. In October, 1860, Cuza paid a visit to Constantinople, where he pleaded very effectively for a real instead of a personal union of the Principalities, and in the following year the sultan issued a firman granting his assent. Finally, on December 23, 1861, the union of the Principalities was formally proclaimed. The new united and autonomous, though not independent, state was christened Rumania, and Bucharest was designated the capital, to the mortification of Jassy.

Cuza now let loose a torrent of reform measures. The most outstanding was the 1864 agrarian law noted above. In the same year he issued a decree on public instruction. This provided for free and obligatory education.

New primary and secondary schools were established, as well as the universities of Jassy and Bucharest. Also, scholarships were made available for poor students of merit wishing to continue from their village school to a secondary school. Many provisions of this law remained unenforced because of the inadequate number of schools. But the law did set forth certain principles and goals upon which future progress was based.

Cuza and his ministers were responsible for many other measures. They established a conservatory of music and a school of fine arts, adopted the Napoleonic Code with slight modifications, improved the judicial system, introduced trial by jury in a limited form, established government monopolies in salt and tobacco, and improved the tax-collecting system.

This program of improvement justified the benevolent dictatorship that Cuza established following his *coup d' état* of 1864. But the coup and the agrarian reform that followed it won him the irreconcilable enmity of the boyars. And since Cuza lacked the qualities necessary to attract an enthusiastic and organized mass following, he had little chance of remaining indefinitely on the throne. Moreover, Cuza played into the hands of his enemies in various ways. He treated in a scandalous fashion his wife, who was of the powerful Rosetti family. He erred in dismissing his reform minister, Kogalniceanu. The latter had become increasingly ambitious and domineering, yet he had provided an indomitable driving power that Cuza sadly lacked. Also, the peasants were confused and wavering because the agrarian reform was enforced tardily and in many cases most unjustly. Finally, financial difficulties had their effect because the treasury was bankrupt and government employees, including army officers, were left unpaid for months.

The end came on the night of February 23, 1866. A number of army officers broke into the palace and roused Cuza from his bed. After he had been forced to sign abdication papers he was permitted to dress, as was also his mistress, who had hid behind some draperies. A regency was established while Cuza crossed the frontier on his way to Vienna. When he reached the Austrian capital the French ambassador talked with him. Cuza showed no rancor. He merely expressed his gratitude to Napoleon for supporting the Rumanian cause and begged that he should continue to do so. Whatever his faults, Cuza put country before self to the end.

Cuza's successor was the Hohenzollern Prince Charles, a cousin of the King of Prussia. It is said that Charles had never heard of Rumania when the offer reached him. After locating the country in an atlas he was impressed by its strategic location. "That is a country with a future," he remarked, and promptly decided to accept the crown.[21] Bismarck also had something to do with Charles's decision. The Prussian chancellor, who was about to plunge into war with Austria, perceived the advantage of enthroning a Hohenzollern dynasty in Bucharest. When Charles departed for his kingdom on May 11, 1866, Austria was already mobilizing against Prussia. It was a hazardous moment for a Prussian to set foot on Austrian soil. So Charles journeyed in disguise southeastward on a Danube steamer. His passport was made out for a certain Herr Hettingen bound for Odessa. When the steamer reached the first Rumanian port, Turnu-Severin, Charles prepared to go ashore. The captain asked why he was leaving when his destination was Odessa. Charles replied he wished to stretch his legs for a few minutes. As he stepped off the gangplank he heard the captain exclaim, "By God, that must be the Prince of Hohenzollern." [22]

A few days later Charles arrived in Bucharest. His regal bearing and urbanity impressed his new subjects, being a decided contrast to Cuza's aloofness and slovenliness. Charles was a young man of twenty-seven at this time, and he remained on the throne until his death in 1914. He was not a person of exceptional attainments. He lacked Cuza's social perceptiveness and fertility of ideas. He accepted existing institutions and thus enjoyed the support, by and large, of the landowning class. But his patience, tenacity, and a strong sense of duty perhaps made up for his lack of brilliance. In contrast to the ruinous conduct of Milan and Alexander Obrenovich in Serbia, he provided his adopted country with dignified and stable leadership for forty-eight years.

The most serious crisis that Charles faced during his reign occurred during the Franco-Prussian War. Public sentiment in Rumania was overwhelmingly pro-French. Charles's position was particularly delicate because it was his own brother Leopold whose candidacy for the Spanish throne had precipitated the war. "We cannot go to France to fight the Germans," the demagogues shouted, "but we will do it here." [23] In August, 1870, a revolt broke out in the town of Ploesti. The army remained loyal and suppressed the uprising easily. But the jury's acquittal of the conspirators reflected the state of public opinion. The following spring a Bucharest mob broke the windows of a hall in which the German colony was celebrating the victories against France. The police made no move to curb the rioters. Charles's position was so difficult that he submitted his abdication, and withdrew it only after the Conservative party promised full support in the future.

Rumanian politics during these decades revolved around the Conservative and Liberal parties. The constitution, which was adopted on Charles's arrival, was based on that of Belgium, and the legal system was taken from the Napoleonic Code. Thus Rumania had all the trappings of a Western parliamentary democracy, but the substance underneath was very different. The Conservative party represented primarily the landowners, and the Liberals the middle class. The peasants were inarticulate and ignored. A system of electoral colleges, rather like that of Prussia before 1918, assured the political preponderance of the landowners and the wealthy urban groups, and left the peasants unrepresented. Much estimable legislation was passed by men who had studied law in the West and who imitated Western models. But most of it was inadequately enforced or forgotten altogether. Likewise, in other fields—public finance, civil rights, and the press—the same dualism existed between appearance and substance. And the dualism persisted unchallenged until the great peasant revolt of 1907.

TRANSYLVANIA, BUKOVINA, AND
BESSARABIA TO 1878

With the decline of the Ottoman Empire various outlying Rumanian lands passed under the control of neighboring great powers. Austria acquired Transylvania in 1699 and Bukovina in 1775, while Russia obtained Bessarabia in 1812. Developments in these provinces during the period prior to 1878 had considerable bearing on the history of the Rumanian people as a whole. This was particularly true of the Transylvanian Rumanians, who, despite their double Hapsburg-Hungarian yoke, exerted a considerable leavening influence on their compatriots in the Principalities.

The outstanding feature of Transylvania's history in modern times has been the uncompromising struggle between the Rumanians and the Hungarians for control of the province. Both claimants have drawn upon history to buttress their positions. The Rumanians contend that they are the descendants of Trajan's colonists, that Transylvania is the cradle of their race, that they have lived continuously in that province since Roman times, and that the Magyars consequently are mere interlopers from Asia. The Hungarians, on the other hand, claim that Transylvania was left abandoned when the Romans withdrew in A.D. 271, that they found no Rumanians in the province when they conquered it early in the eleventh century, that the Rumanians did not recross the Danube into the Principalities until the thirteenth century, and that only after that date did the Rumanians gradually overflow into Transylvania in response to the welcome extended by the Hungarian rulers to foreign settlers. Rumanian and Hungarian historians have waged polemics over this issue for generations, although with no perceptible practical results. Even if the historians had discovered evidence deciding the issue definitely and indisputably in favor of either side, this obviously would not have affected in the slightest degree Magyar predominance in Transylvania before World War I nor would it have affected Rumanian predominance since the war.

The Hungarians conquered Transylvania early in the eleventh century and proceeded to invite colonists from various countries to settle in their sparsely populated province. In time four distinct ethnic groups comprised the bulk of the population: Rumanians, Germans, Magyars, and Szeklers, the latter believed to be the descendants of an Avarian tribe that settled down and adopted the Magyar language. When Sultan Suleiman destroyed the Hungarian kingdom at Mohacs in 1526 Transylvania became a part of the Ottoman Empire. The Turks granted full autonomy to their new province, requiring only payment of tribute and recognition of their suzerainty. On the whole, Transylvania fared well under the Turks, being spared both foreign invasions and the horrors of the religious wars that were devastating the West at the time.

The failure of the Turks to take Vienna in 1683 was followed by the great Hapsburg victories in Hungary and eventually by the 1699 Karlowitz Treaty which ended Ottoman rule in Transylvania. The Hapsburg emperor had already issued in 1691 the so-called "Leopoldine Diploma," defining the status of Transylvania within his empire. The province technically became a part of Hungary but in practice it was controlled by the emperor who, in his Diploma, confirmed all existing laws, rights, and privileges, both civil and religious. For several decades Transylvania led an existence of peaceful obscurity under the Hapsburgs.

Until the late eighteenth century the principal issues were of an ecclesiastical character, though they acquired in time definite social and political overtones. Ecclesiastical questions came to the fore with the establishment of Hapsburg rule because powerful Catholic interests engineered a schism among the Orthodox Rumanians of Transylvania. Numerous material inducements persuaded the Orthodox hierarchy to accept papal supremacy and to establish a new Uniate Church in 1698. The aim of those who sponsored the new church was to promote Catholicism in the Orthodox East and at the same time to contribute to the cohesiveness of the Hapsburg Empire. But the final outcome was quite different from these expectations. The Uniate Church stimulated rather than extinguished Rumanian national feeling. It raised standards of education, financed seminaries and printing presses, and established connections between the Rumanian people and the West. These developments had a strong catalytic influence upon the hitherto neglected and dormant Rumanian people.

The first outstanding champion of the Rumanian cause in Transylvania was Bishop John Innocent Micu, better known by his germanized name of Klein. As the head of the Uniate Church between 1729 and 1751 he regarded himself as the representative not only of his church but also of all his fellow Rumanians. He fought courageously and uncompromisingly against both the Hungarians who strove to Magyrize his people and against the Jesuits who wished to control his church. "Our nation," he proudly asserted, "is not inferior to any in Transylvania, either in virtue, in knowledge or in judgement of affairs." He appealed repeatedly to the imperial authorities to end the policy of "holding the clergy and nation of the Wallachs [Rumanians] in Egyptian bondage under the bloody whip." [24]

Eventually the bishop was forced by overwhelming pressures to surrender his post and to spend his last years as an exile in Rome. But his valiant struggle did not prove to be in vain. He aroused his long-suffering people to such a degree that many of them now left the Uniate Church for their original Orthodox faith. In fact, the imperial government felt constrained in 1762 to issue a patent providing an organization for the Orthodox Rumanians in Transylvania. The Orthodox community, of course, had a status inferior to that of the Uniate Church, and the latter in turn ranked below the four traditional and privileged churches of Transylvania: the Catholic, Calvinist, Lutheran, and Unitarian. Nevertheless, both the Uniate and the Orthodox churches performed an invaluable service for the Transylvanian Rumanians by providing cultural tradition, intellectual leadership, and organizational strength.

In the later years of the eighteenth century, issues in Transylvania became more overtly political and social. The reforming emperor, Joseph II, was partly responsible for this trend. He toured the province in 1773 and was moved to action by the appalling conditions he observed. He found the Rumanians to be the chief victims of an exceptionally extortionate feudal system. They were required to work from three to five days a week for their landowners, who were usually Magyars. They also had to pay a tithe on the produce of their fields and their wives had to spin a certain amount of flax for the lords. They had no civil rights, could not plead in court, could not own land, and were always at the mercy of the lash. Those who escaped with the regulation "five and twenty" considered themselves fortunate. Some wretches did not survive the ordeal, in which case the responsible noble was required at the most to pay a slight fine.

In 1783 and 1784 Emperor Joseph issued several decrees to alleviate the plight of the Rumanian serfs. He declared that they were no longer tied to the soil and he allowed them to marry, to practice a trade, and to dispose of their property without the sanction of their lords. These and other measures proved abortive because Joseph's reform program was wrecked by unfavorable domestic and foreign developments. But the liberal emperor left behind him a legacy of idealism and effort, and the Rumanian peasants, although they remained serfs, were not altogether unaffected by "our emperor," as they fondly termed Joseph.

The Transylvanian Rumanians were also stirred by increasing contact with the West. The Uniate Church made an important contribution in this respect because of its associations with Rome. The three pioneers of the Rumanian cultural awakening in Transylvania—George Sincai, Peter Maior, and Samuel Klein, the latter a nephew of the great bishop—began their careers as theological students in Uniate seminaries. Continuing their studies in Vienna and Rome, they were inspired in the latter city by the monuments of antiquity. They popularized enthusiastically, though uncritically, the theory that they were the direct descendants of the noble Romans. This vision of past greatness spurred these young apostles to begin the work of cultural regeneration which throughout Eastern Europe has been the prelude to national awakening and eventual political independence.

In 1780 they produced the first modern Rumanian grammar, *Elements of the Daco-Roman or Wallach Language*. In 1812 they published the first national history by Rumanian authors, *History of the Origin of the Rumanians in Dacia*. At the same time they did essential work in the linguistic field, replacing the Slavonic alphabet with the Latin and purging the Rumanian language of Slavic, Greek, and other non-Latin words that had been adopted through the centuries. These achievements were comparable to those of Obradovich and Karajich among the Serbians. And just as the influence of Obradovich and Karajich extended beyond the Danube to the Belgrade pashalik, so these Rumanian reformers in Transylvania, as noted earlier in this chapter, exerted great influence on their compatriots across the Carpathians in the Principalities.

The first great test for the Transylvanian Rumanians came during the 1848 revolution. At this time the Hungarians took up arms against the Hapsburgs in the name of liberty and nationality. On March 15, 1848, the Hungarian Parliament adopted its famous reform program which boldly swept away the old feudal order with all its special privileges and exemptions. In its place the Hungarians decreed annual parliaments, responsible ministerial government, direct franchise, liberty of the press, religious equality, and trial by jury. They also voted that Transylvania be united with Hungary, and at the same time they affirmed their readiness to maintain "all those special laws and liberties of Transylvania which, without hindering complete union, are favorable to national liberty and unity." [25]

The key phrase in the Hungarian pronouncement was "without hindering complete union." This was in reality a euphemism for the Magyarization of the non-Hungarian peoples of Transylvania. Louis Kossuth, the Hungarian leader, stated outright in his personal newspaper that "we must hasten to Magyarise the Croats, Roumanians and Saxons, for otherwise we shall perish." [26]

The Rumanians had no intention of accepting this type of "complete union." Forty thousand of them gathered on May 15, 1848, in a memorable meeting held in the "Field of Liberty," a meadow near the small town of Blaj. They passed resolutions approving the liberal reforms which the Hungarians had decreed but adding certain demands of their own. They claimed that the Rumanian nation henceforth should be represented in proportion to its numbers in political, legal, and military offices. They also demanded that the Uniate and Orthodox churches should enjoy equal rights with the other churches, and, above all, they insisted that there should be no union of Transylvania and Hungary without their prior consultation and approval.

Kossuth rejected these demands of the Rumanians just as he rejected those of the South Slavs. The outcome was a race war made doubly savage by the fact that it was at the same time a social conflict between Magyar landowners and Rumanian serfs. Thus the Transylvanian Rumanians, like the Serbians further west, it will be recalled from Chapter 14, helped the Hapsburgs put down the Magyar revolution. When Tsar Nicholas sent an army into Transylvania to attack the Hungarians in the rear, the Rumanian peasants gave invaluable help to the army. The following report by the Russian general, Lüders, throws much light on the status and role of the Transylvanian Rumanians at this time.

There is a profound hatred between the Austrians and the Hungarians and the latter are equally detested by the other races in Hungarian territory, the Saxons, Serbs, Croats and Wallachians [i.e., Rumanians]. The Wallachians especially have the status of pariahs and are the most miserable people in Transylvania, it is they who have, since the beginning of the insurrection, supported the Austrian army and have cooperated in supplying provisions to the Russians. Since the beginning, the union of the Wallachians with Hungary would have given a different turn to the insurrection. Without the provisions which I have found in the Principalities and without Yanco, the leader of the Wallachians in Transylvania, I could not have succeeded.[27]

After the Rumanians had made their vital contribution to the defeat of the Hungarians, the Hapsburgs treated them in the same cavalier fashion as they did the South Slavs. First there was a decade of extreme centralization and subservience to Vienna. Then came the 1867 *Ausgleich* or Compromise which the imperial government concluded with the Magyars at the expense of the Rumanians. Since the Magyars were becoming increasingly difficult to keep under control, the Hapsburgs agreed to share their empire with them in equal partnership. This meant that the Magyars now were the unchallenged masters of the Hungarian part of the new Austro-Hungarian Dual Monarchy, and Transylvania was included in their part. Thus the Rumanians were left to the mercy of the Magyars under the most unfavorable circumstances. So long as Transylvania remained a separate unit the Rumanians could hold some hope for the future because they constituted a majority of the population—1,397,282 Rumanians in 1900 as against 814,994 Hungarians and Szeklers combined, and 233,019 Germans. But after being incorporated into Hungary the Rumanians were reduced to a powerless minority of 15 per cent facing a master race still bent upon Magyarization.

The Rumanians in Bukovina and Bessarabia were not faring better than their brothers in Transylvania. In Bukovina Austrian rule at first represented a substantial improvement over the old state of affairs. When the Austrians took over the province in 1775 they found the population in miserable straits. Not a single doctor practiced in the whole country. There were no bridges, scarcely any roads, and only five schools. Most of the land belonged to the monasteries, which were shockingly mismanaged by alien monks.

Perhaps the most important measure of the Austrians was their reform and supervision of the monasteries. Sufficient funds were thereby made available for church schools, clerical stipends, and episcopal endowments. The Austrians also organized an education system, establishing in the first decade a seminary, three normal schools, and nine state schools.

Despite these gains the Rumanians steadily lost ground in Bukovina during the nineteenth century because of heavy Ruthenian immigration from the east. When the province first came under Austrian rule there were only a few Ruthenians in the eastern countries. By 1848 they numbered 108,000 as against 209,000 Rumanians. The proportions were reversed by 1880, when the Ruthenians outnumbered the Rumanians by 239,690 to 190,005. The 1910 census showed 305,101 Ruthenians as against 273,254 Rumanians. The same census revealed that the principal elements other than the Rumanians and the Ruthenians were the Jews and the Germans, who numbered 102,000 and 66,000, respectively.[28]

The Rumanians of Bessarabia were subjected to a combination of blatant misgovernment and severe Russification. When Tsar Alexander acquired the province in 1812 he issued instructions to his officials that reflected his well-known liberal sentiments.

Let the inhabitants feel the advantage of a fatherly and liberal administration. Draw the attention of neighboring peoples to this province by making it happy. The last war had aroused great hopes among the Christian peoples: now that our army has been called away to another field, one must take care to preserve that devotion towards us and to withdraw them from the influence of our enemies. The Bulgars, the Moldavians, the Wallachians, the Serbs, seek a fatherland: you can contribute towards finding one for them.[29]

This lofty goal was never realized. The Russian officials, both military and civil, were hopelessly incompetent and corrupt. They were concerned less with the welfare of the local population than with the acquisition of princely estates. Within a few decades most of the land had fallen to a small group of foreign Russian proprietors. With the accession of Tsar Nicholas in 1825 Russification became the order of the day. The courts were reorganized after the Russian pattern, Russian became the exclusive language of administration, and power was concentrated in the hands of a military governor who was directly dependent on the governor-general in Odessa.

Even the introduction of the zemstvo system of local government in 1869, which elsewhere in the Russian Empire marked the first faint dawn of liberalism, served only to worsen the situation in Bessarabia because the most reactionary elements gained control of the councils. The 1905 Russian revolution led to a slight improvement of the situation, but within two years the old restrictions had been reimposed. Yet the Rumanian peasants retained their identity through the decades of exploitation and Russification. According to the census of 1908 the 2,345,000 inhabitants of Bessarabia were 54 per cent Rumanian compared to 28 per cent Russian, the remainder being mostly Jews, Germans, Bulgars, and Turco-Tatars. "Father is Russian and mother is Russian," a revealing local proverb relates, "but Ivan is Moldavian."

In conclusion it is apparent that the outlook for the Rumanians of Transylvania, Bukovina, and Bessarabia was indeed dark in 1878. The Rumanian motherland was as weak as the Hapsburg and Russian empires appeared to be invincible and everlasting. The ferocious denationalization measures of the Magyars and the Russians seemed destined to continue indefinitely and to achieve their purpose ultimately. Certainly no one in 1878 could have foreseen that within four decades all Rumanians would be united for the first time in their history within the frontiers of a great Rumanian state.

19. Bulgarian Awakening to 1878

THE BULGARIANS were the first of the Balkan peoples to succumb to the Turkish invaders. They were also the last to regain their independence, with the exception of the Albanians, who were held back by certain exceptional factors. In the mid-nineteenth century the Bulgarians experienced a cultural awakening which was largely the work of certain pioneer teachers and writers, who in turn were subsidized by a rising new class of wealthy merchants and artisans. The cultural awakening was followed, as in the case of the other Balkan peoples, by political activity that was partly revolutionary and partly reformist. The revolutionary bands were not able to accomplish anything concrete despite periodic insurrections. The most important achievement before the Russo-Turkish War of 1877–1878 was the establishment in 1870 of the autocephalous Bulgarian Exarchate church— an event of major significance for the entire peninsula as well as for Bulgaria.

TURKISH RULE

The late awakening of the Bulgarian people can be explained in large part by their location close to the center of Turkish power in Constantinople. One result of this location was that more Turks and other Moslem peoples settled in the Bulgarian lands than in the more distant Greek and Serbian provinces. Another result was that Turkish forces were able to reach the Bulgarian lands easily and quickly along the roads leading north and west from Constantinople. Finally, the location of the Bulgarians in the eastern part of the Balkans isolated them from the countries of Central and Western Europe. Unlike the Greeks, Serbians, and Rumanians, they did not have direct contact with any of the major powers of Europe. Thus the Bulgarians not only were subject more directly to Turkish power but also were deprived of the stimulating effects of Western contacts. Accordingly, they remained subject to Turkish domination longer than the other Balkan peoples who inhabited the more peripheral regions of the empire.

364

The Bulgarians were not at all times oppressed during the centuries of Turkish rule. At first they were better off than they had been under their own nobles with their never-ending rivalries and internecine wars. In fact, the Turks were able to overrun Bulgaria as rapidly as they did because they were widely welcomed as deliverers who would end the anarchy and establish order. The Turks at the outset fulfilled this expectation reasonably well. After they defeated the Christian crusading army at the battle of Varna in 1444 they were able to consolidate their hold over the Balkan Peninsula and to regularize their administration.

The Turks ruled the Bulgarians in essentially the same manner that they did the Serbians and the Greeks. They divided the country into five sanjaks and applied their usual laissez-faire principles in matters of religion, language, and local administration. They also followed their customary practice of encouraging certain towns, villages, and professions by granting varying degrees of tax exemption or complete self-government or both. They favored in this manner the localities that supplied frontier and mountain guards, military police, falconers, and grooms for the sultan's horses. They likewise favored certain industries that they regarded important, including cattle raising, mining, rice cultivation, and charcoal burning.

In general, Turkish rule in Bulgaria was the same as in the rest of the peninsula, with the important exception that it was more direct and controlling. There were no counterparts in Bulgaria to such self-governing regions as Montenegro or as Mane in Greece. The real core of the Turkish Empire in Europe lay southeast of a line drawn from Vidin on the Danube through Nish and Prizren. All the Bulgarian lands were located within this core.

Close Turkish rule was not a handicap during the period immediately following the conquest. Rights and privileges were respected, roads were maintained, and commerce prospered. But gradually conditions deteriorated in Bulgaria as they did in other parts of the empire. And here also a manifestation of the worsening state of affairs was the increasing frequency of revolts. It is true that some uprisings were provoked by outside stimulation. One example of this was the disturbance in 1598 inspired by Michael the Brave's successful defiance of the Turks. Similar outbreaks accompanied the Austrian invasion of the Balkans in 1689. There is no doubt, however, that the basic factor behind Bulgarian unrest was the steady deterioration of Ottoman institutions which affected directly the everyday life of the peasantry.

The decline in the discipline and morale of the Turkish armies was a serious matter for the Bulgarians, whose lands were located on the routes northward to the Danubian front. During the long wars with Austria the Turkish soldiers ravaged the Bulgarian countryside through which they passed. In earlier times observers reported that disciplined Ottoman armies scrupulously respected private property and paid fair prices for all provisions requisitioned. But by the eighteenth century the typical Turkish soldier was as undisciplined as he was ineffective, and he wreaked more damage upon the unfortunate peasantry who lived near the routes of march than he did upon the enemy.

The general breakdown of Ottoman administration also affected the Bulgarians. The weakening of central authority left the provinces subject to extortion and open violence. In the late eighteenth and early nineteenth centuries the Bulgarian lands were particularly hard hit by the depredations of the kirjalis, armed bandits who roamed the countryside looting and devastating. Pasvan-Oglu (see Chapter 13) succeeded in organizing a popular and virtually independent regime at Vidin in the late eighteenth century precisely because he was strong enough to curb the depredations of both the kirjalis and of the rapacious government officials.

Finally, the peasants in Bulgaria, as elsewhere in the Balkans, suffered from the rise of chifliks. We saw in Chapter 9 that with the decline of imperial authority the timar landholding system established at the time of the conquest gave way to the much more onerous chiflik system. Peasants frequently reacted against the new bonds by revolting or by fleeing to the free mountain areas. In Bulgaria the chiflik owners not infrequently used the kirjalis to guard their estates and to replenish their labor supply by conducting impressment raids into the countryside.

A British traveler who journeyed through the Balkans in 1802 discovered that "the *Pashas* throughout all *Thrace* and *Macedonia* were in a state of warfare; either among themselves or with the Turkish government; and there was no road entirely free from the danger either of the insurgents, or of those bands of plunderers, who, profiting from the distracted state of the country, poured down from the mountains upon the plains." Later in the same year this traveler set out from Constantinople in the train of a Turkish ambassador who was proceeding in great state to his post in Paris. As they made their way through the Bulgarian lands the Englishman noted:

> The dread of being pillaged by the Turkish grandees, cause the people everywhere to fly at their approach. We had therefore choice enough of lodgings; for every place of habitation was deserted. . . . If the Grand Signior [Sultan] should choose to travel through his dominions, he would not find an inhabitant in any of the towns to receive him: for no sooner does the news arrive of the coming of Turks of distinction, than the people betake themselves to flight; and the stillness of death prevails in all the streets.[1]

GREEK PRELATES

The Bulgarians had to contend with Greek bishops and teachers as well as Turkish officials and kirjali marauders. We saw in Chapter 3 that the Bulgarian patriarchate came to an end with the fall of Tirnovo to the Turks in 1393. During the succeeding centuries a Bulgarian archbishopric survived at Ohrid with a certain though steadily diminishing degree of autonomy. But this also was abolished in 1767, a year after the elimination of the Serbian patriarchate at Ipek (Pec). Thus the Patriarch of Constantinople became the direct and supreme religious leader of all Orthodox South Slavs.

Bulgarian nationalists have criticized bitterly what they term the economic exploitation and cultural oppression of the Greek prelates during this period. They have charged specifically that the Greeks monopolized all high church offices; that these offices were regularly sold to the highest bidders; and that the sums expended were recovered by systematic fleecing of the Bulgarian peasantry. They have also maintained that the Greeks practiced cultural imperialism by making Greek the language of instruction in the schools, by using the Greek liturgy in the churches, and by deliberately destroying the old Bulgarian manuscripts, images, and testaments.

Some of these charges are true and regrettably so; others are true but unavoidably and naturally so; while still others are altogether false. The charge that the Greeks destroyed manuscripts and other symbols of Bulgaria's glorious past is now rejected by most Bulgarian historians as a legend created during the process of national awakening and self-assertion. On the other hand, the Greek clergy did monopolize the higher posts and they did collect a multitude of taxes to support themselves and the Patriarchate in Constantinople. It may be argued in their defense that simony in the church was part and parcel of the corruption that permeated the entire Ottoman imperial structure. But this argument, despite its validity, was not likely to satisfy the ardent and indignant Bulgarian nationalists.

The charge of Greek domination in schools, churches, and culture, in general, is largely justified. But this domination was to a considerable degree unavoidable because of the cultural disparity between Greeks and Bulgarians. A later generation of Bulgarian nationalists keenly resented the use of Greek in schools and churches and they assumed that their forebears had felt the same resentment. This assumption is unjustified and is a good example of the common error of interpreting the past in terms of the present. The fact is that in the eighteenth and early nineteenth centuries the ideas "Greek" and "culture" were identified one with another. An educated Bulgarian was one who spoke Greek, and if he could not do so he at least adorned his speech with Greek phrases. Commercial and private correspondence also was carried on in Greek or in Bulgarian written in Greek script. As late as the 1840's a French traveler noted that throughout the Balkans "the best commercial houses . . . the best schools are held by the Greeks. The Greek is the *mens agitans molem* [leavening intellect] of all the East: where he is not, there is barbarism." [2]

Viewed in this historical context the cultural domination of the Greeks becomes understandable. This domination was acceptable so long as the Bulgarians remained an illiterate peasant people wishing only to be left alone to earn their livelihood from the land and caring nothing for either their past or their future. But as soon as some of them experienced a sense of national consciousness they were bound to challenge the Greek hegemony. Bulgarian national regeneration inevitably was as much anti-Greek as it was anti-Turkish. The French traveler who found that the Greeks were the intellectual leaders of the Near East also reported:

The enlightened men of the country realize fully that the clergy of Bulgaria, as it exists, is the greatest obstacle to emancipation; it is almost impossible for a Bulgarian nationality to arise before there is a national clergy. One might object that all the lower clergy and the monks are indigenous; yes, but episcopal thunderbolts threaten the Bulgarian priests who dare to show their patriotism too clearly.[3]

REGENERATIVE FORCES

The low point in Bulgarian fortunes was reached in the late eighteenth and early nineteenth centuries—the time when the Greeks and the Serbs were successfully struggling for freedom. The Bulgarians lagged behind their neighbors by several decades. Toward the middle of the nineteenth century they began to show significant signs of awakening national consciousness. Various factors explain this regeneration. One was the illiteracy of the overwhelming mass of the population. The peasants continued to speak their Bulgarian language and remained unaffected by the Greek literate culture that Hellenized so many of the educated Bulgarians. If illiteracy saved the Bulgarians from the Greeks, religion saved them from the Turks. Their Orthodox faith served effectively as a barrier between themselves and their Moslem masters. Only a few Bulgarians accepted Islam; their descendants, known as Pomaks, still live in southern Bulgaria.

Language and religion prevented the Bulgarians from becoming Greeks or Turks; the rapid growth of commerce and handicrafts in the early nineteenth century helped to make them actively aware of the fact that they were Bulgarians. As in the case of the Greeks, the economic revival of the Bulgarians owed much to the success of the colonies established abroad. The greatest of these was in Constantinople where, by the 1870's, some thirty or forty thousand Bulgarians worked and prospered as tailors, gardeners, and tradesmen. A few of them became immensely wealthy as contractors supplying cloth, foodstuffs, and other provisions to the Ottoman army and palace. Many Bulgarians also made their fortunes in Bucharest, Odessa, and other cities in Russia and the Danubian Principalities. Within Bulgaria itself handicrafts flourished in centers such as Gabrovo, Tirnovo, and Kotel. These, it should be noted, were all small and out-of-the-way mountain towns. They were preferred to large cities such as Sofia, Varna, and Ruschuk, which were located on the main routes and vulnerable to the disorders of the time.

This economic revival of the Bulgarians had cultural and political repercussions as far-reaching as that of the Greeks. The new class of merchants and moneyed men exerted a dynamic influence on Bulgarian society. Their contacts with the outside world had given them new ideas while their wealth enabled them to act. They were particularly effective because of their organization into guilds. In these guilds they learned self-discipline and collective action. Each guild had its treasury, supported by dues, fines, and a profit tax. The large sums thus collected were used not only to meet the needs of the guild members but also to finance the work of national regeneration. It was the guilds that provided the new schools and books that were Bulgarian rather than Greek. It was their members who formed the bulk of the reading public which bought the books, newspapers, and journals. It was the guilds, also, that furnished most of the leaders of the nationalist movement. The Bulgarian national revival was to a very considerable degree the work of the Bulgarian guilds.

Foreign countries also contributed to the Bulgarian awakening. Serbia, by virtue of her proximity and her racial, linguistic, and religious affinity, exerted much influence in western Bulgaria. Bulgarian students attended Serbian schools in Belgrade. Bulgarian books were printed by the Serbian government's official press. Certain Bulgarian leaders came under the influence of Obradovich and Karajich and through them became familiar with Germano-Slavic currents emanating from Vienna and Prague. In general Serbia served as a channel through which Central European and Russian influences eventually reached isolated Bulgaria.

Greece left a deeper imprint upon Bulgaria than did Serbia. Until the mid-nineteenth century the great majority of educated Bulgarians had attended Greek schools in Smyrna, Athens, Saloniki, and Yanina, and in the various Aegean Islands. The teaching they received in these schools was generally secular and enlightened, thanks to the intellectual revolution that had occurred in the Greek world during earlier decades. Thus liberal Western ideas reached the Bulgarians indirectly through the Greeks. Eventually the Bulgarians realized that the nationality principle was applicable to themselves as well as to the Greeks. When they grasped this point they turned upon their former teachers in much the same way as Indian nationalists a century later quoted John Stuart Mill against their British teachers.

Of all foreign countries Russia had the greatest influence on the Bulgarian national revival. Before the nineteenth century Russo-Bulgarian ties were restricted largely to the sphere of religion. Churchmen exchanged visits and Russian ecclesiastics sent printed literature to Bulgaria. The next stage in the relationships between the two countries was reached when large numbers of Bulgarians settled in Russian towns, particularly along the Black Sea. Many of these emigrants became wealthy and employed their fortunes to help and to arouse their compatriots at home. The Odessa community played an especially important role in the Bulgarian renaissance.

Russian influence in Bulgaria became more strong and direct when the Russians began to take an interest in their Slavic Bulgarian brothers following the Crimean War. Up to that time Tsar Nicholas and his ministers had no sympathy for any revolutionary nationalist cause. In 1858, however, the Slavonic Benevolent Committee was established in Moscow for the purpose of aiding the South Slavs. In practice this society concentrated its attention on the Bulgars. Between 1856 and 1876 some five hundred Bulgarian students received scholarships for study in Russia. This served to increase Russian influence in Bulgaria enormously, but the nature of the influence proved to be quite different from that which had been planned. The aim had been to indoctrinate the Bulgarian students with Pan-Slav, Orthodox ideas. We shall see shortly that many of them came under the influence of the Russian revolutionaries and returned home implacable opponents of tsarist autocracy. But regardless of the precise nature of Russia's influence, it surpassed that of Greece after the mid-nineteenth century.

The domestic and external forces noted above explain the Bulgarian revival in the nineteenth century. We shall now consider the various stages of this revival—the initial cultural phase, the struggle for the exarchate which ended in victory in 1870, and the revolutionary movement that culminated in the "Bulgarian Horrors" of 1876.

CULTURAL AWAKENING

The lonely pioneer of the Bulgarian renaissance was Father Paisi, a monk in a monastery at Mt. Athos. In 1762 he wrote a history of Bulgaria in which he tried to make his long-subjugated people aware of their illustrious past. His work, considered as history, was of no scientific value. It was naïve and uncritical, and was written in a clumsy and artificial idiom, half Church Slavonic and half modern Bulgarian. But it was alive with nationalist fervor, and it had a dynamic effect in the limited circles in which it was read. It remained in manuscript form for eighty years, but was copied so frequently that forty manuscript copies are extant today. The following passage illustrates the author's fervent nationalism:

I have seen many Bulgarians adopt a foreign language and customs and scorn their own language; I have written for their instruction. O senseless people, why are you ashamed to call yourselves Bulgarians and why don't you think and read in your own language? Didn't the Bulgarians in former times have a great empire? Why be ashamed of your race and adopt a foreign tongue? One will say: the Greeks are a wiser and more cultivated race. The Bulgarians are stupid and have no refined language. It is therefore better for them to stay with the Greeks. But think well! There was a time when the Bulgarians were famous throughout the world; many times they have imposed tribute upon the strong Romans and the wise Greeks; they have given in marriage the daughters of our kings to the sovereigns of these peoples; of all the Slav peoples the Bulgarians have been the most illustrious. They were the first to receive baptism, the first to have a patriarch, the ones who made the most conquests, the first Slav saints were of our race. . . .[4]

Bishop Sofronii of Vratsa carried on Paisi's work. For twenty years he taught at Kotel and raised a generation of patriots. In 1803 he fled to Bucharest because of the unsettled conditions in his homeland. He enjoyed his new-found security but he was conscience-stricken for having deserted his flock. To make amends he spent the rest of his life writing "night and day," as he put it, so that at least he could be read if not heard. He copied Paisi's manuscript and wrote a delightfully naïve autobiography which he called *The Life and Sufferings of Sinful Sofronii*. The only one of his works published in his lifetime was the *Kiriakodromion* or *Sunday Book*. This collection of sermons proved very popular, serving as the family bible in many Bulgarian homes. Ten editions in all were published, the first in 1806 and the latest in 1914. The views that the indefatigable bishop expressed in his sermons were very advanced. With a passion reminiscent of Paisi he called on his people to read and to support schools and to educate their children so that they would not remain "dumb animals."

The Bulgarian communities abroad now began to make their contribution to the national cause. In 1829 a Ukrainian historian, Yurii Venelin, published his book entitled *The Bulgarians Ancient and Modern*. It was the first attempt at a comprehensive history of the Bulgarian people. Two years after its appearance it was read by Vasili Aprilov, a wealthy Bulgarian merchant in Odessa. Aprilov himself relates that up to this time he had identified himself with the Greeks, even to the point of joining and contributing heavily to the revolutionary Greek organization, the Philike Hetairia. But after reading Venelin he was "born anew," as he put it. He was thrilled by the story of Bulgaria's past greatness. He dropped his earlier philhellenism and devoted his life and fortune to the cause of his people.

He sensibly realized that their greatest need was for education. Hitherto the Bulgarians had available only two types of educational institutions, the church schools with their narrow and sterile ecclesiastical curriculum, and the famous Greek schools which were secular in their outlook and progressive in their methods. The latter were unacceptable to the Bulgarian nationalists because, although they provided a good education, it was naturally a Greek education. Some of the Bulgarian students who attended these schools became so Hellenized that they were lost to their race. Aprilov therefore decided to use the techniques of the Greek schools but for Bulgarian purposes.

He secured the assistance of other Bulgarian merchants in Russia and the Danubian Principalities and in 1835 he opened in Gabrovo, his native town, the first modern Bulgarian school. It was the first one conducted by and for Bulgarians and using the Bulgarian language and Bulgarian textbooks and wall charts. Because of the shortage of teachers and funds the Lancaster-Bell system of instruction was employed. By making use of the most advanced pupils as assistants and monitors, a single teacher could instruct or supervise the instruction of as many as one thousand pupils. Not only did students flock to Gabrovo from all over Bulgaria, but teachers also came to learn the new methods and to obtain the new texts. A rapidly growing number of schools organized after the Gabrovo model appeared throughout the country. Thus the establishment of the Gabrovo school marked the beginning of the end of Greek cultural hegemony. It represents an important milestone in the development of Bulgarian nationalism.

BULGARIAN EXARCHATE

The first great victory for Bulgarian nationalism was the establishment in 1870 of a national church known as the exarchate. The origins of the movement for a national church go back to the 1820's, when occasional demands were made for the rectification of financial abuses and for the appointment of Bulgarian bishops to head Bulgarian dioceses. Such demands were made periodically until the period of the Crimean War when the Turkish government issued its reform edict, the *Hatti-Humayun*, on February 18, 1856.* The edict contained an article specifically providing for the reorganization of the non-Moslem communities, or millets. The Bulgarians hailed this stipulation because reform of their Orthodox millet offered hope that some of their grievances, and perhaps even some of their nationalist aspirations, might be satisfied.

The patriarch did summon a council of bishops and laymen which, between 1860 and 1862, passed legislation for lay participation in the election of the patriarch and the administration of the secular affairs of the church. These measures failed to satisfy the Bulgarians. Of the seven bishops and thirty-eight representatives who had comprised the council, only four representatives were Bulgarians. And when these four requested that church taxes be fixed and that Bulgarians be allowed to select their own bishops, they were turned down on the ground that the canons of the church did not recognize national distinctions.

The Bulgarian community in Constantinople now took the lead in the movement for a national church by announcing early in March, 1860, that the Bulgarians henceforth would not recognize the jurisdiction of the patriarch and of the Greek bishops. On Easter Sunday, April 15, 1860, the Bulgarian church in Constantinople substituted in its services the sultan's name in place of the patriarch's. This was repeated in some thirty churches throughout Bulgaria, and was followed by the selection of a Bulgarian prelate, Ilarion Stoyanovich, to be the head of the Bulgarian church.

These measures were of obvious significance. The Bulgarians no longer were content with demanding financial reforms and native bishops. Their aim henceforth was the establishment of a Bulgarian national church. This precipitated a bitter and prolonged conflict with the Greeks. It is important to note that this conflict was political rather than religious in nature. It represented a clash of rival Greek and Bulgarian nationalisms rather than a dispute over religious doctrine. On both sides there were radical and moderate elements. Some Bulgarians were willing to accept an improved status under the Patriarch of Constantinople while others insisted on a separate national church. Similarly, among the Greeks some prelates were willing to make wide concessions for the sake of maintaining the unity of the church. Paradoxically enough, they were hampered in their efforts because the ecclesiastical reorganization effected following the *Hatti-Humayun* increased the power of the lay elements which tended to be less conciliatory toward the Bulgarians. Greek laymen were concerned about the political implications of Bulgarian ecclesiastical independence, seeing in it a threat to the future of Hellenism. Thus the decade of the 1860's witnessed an all-out struggle between Greek and Bulgarian nationalism fought under the guise of an ecclesiastical issue.

* To be discussed in the next chapter.

Foreign powers were involved in the conflict, partly because the Bulgarians turned to them for support and partly because some of the powers themselves intervened to further their own interests. The Bulgarians were not backed by Russia as solidly as is often assumed. Russia was generally sympathetic with the Bulgarian aspirations but at the same time she wished to avoid a schism and to avoid alienating the Patriarchate and the Greeks. The result was an ambivalence which the Russian ambassador in Constantinople, Count Nicholas Ignatiev, described as follows:

Our situation is very delicate. We cannot recognize the creation of a Bulgarian synod in Constantinople nor enter into communication with an autocephalous Bulgarian church before it is recognized by the Patriarchate. Otherwise we shall alienate not only the Ecumenical patriarch, but all the other patriarchs of the Orient as well as all the other Greeks. If, however, we do not recognize the Bulgarian hierarchy, the Slavs will see in us enemies making common cause with the Greeks; furthermore, the Bulgarians perhaps would be tempted to follow suggestions from the Western powers and the Turks and accept union with Rome.[5]

Ignatiev's concern about Catholic penetration was not altogether fanciful. France and Austria actively supported Catholic propaganda in the Balkans with the approval of the Porte, which hoped thereby to counter Orthodox Russian influence. By promising to champion Bulgarian nationalist aspirations the Catholics converted a few Bulgarians in Constantinople and a few more in the homeland itself. In 1861 a Uniate Bulgarian Church was organized which recognized the supremacy of the Pope but retained Orthodox dogma and ritual. Despite abundant financial backing and the approval of the Porte, the Uniate Church never amounted to anything. The great majority of Bulgarians wanted a church of their own rather than the Pope in the place of the Patriarch. Not infrequently those Bulgarians who turned to Catholicism did so in order to frighten the Russians into supporting their cause.

The Protestant missionaries in Bulgaria were as unsuccessful as the Catholics, especially because the Protestant powers were unwilling to back the Bulgarian demand for a national church. Sir Henry Bulwer, the British ambassador in Constantinople, erroneously identified the Bulgarian agitation with Russian Pan-Slavism and refused to lend his support. Furthermore, most of the Bulgarians were as unwilling to embrace Protestantism as Catholicism. One of the Protestant missionaries, after an interview with some Bulgarians in Constantinople, wrote: "The few leaders who would be ready to take the Bible as their foundation care more for keeping a united Bulgarian people than for obedience to Christ's teachings." [6] Thus the overwhelming proportion of Bulgarians rejected the foreign creeds and strove instead to win a national Orthodox Church.

The first major concession to the Bulgarians was offered by Patriarch Joachim in July, 1860, when he proposed the use of Bulgarian in churches and schools, and the appointment of Bulgarians to a few bishoprics. Ilarion promptly replied that nothing short of a national church would now suffice.

The next significant offer came in 1867, when a new Patriarch, Gregory VI, conceded the establishment of an autonomous Bulgarian church whose jurisdiction was to be limited to the territory between the Danube and the Balkan Mountains. "I am building with my hands," the Patriarch told Ignatiev, "a bridge to the political independence of the Bulgarians." [7] Ignatiev appreciated the significance of the Patriarch's offer and urged the Bulgarians to accept it. Instead, they rejected it because of the territorial limitation.

The issue separating the Greeks and the Bulgarians was fundamental and pointed up the essentially political nature of the whole controversy. Once the principle of an autonomous Bulgarian church had been conceded there arose at once the problem of the church's territorial limits. The Greeks were afraid of losing Macedonia and therefore insisted on setting a limit at the Balkan Mountains. The Bulgarians, on the other hand, despite pressure from Ignatiev, demanded that populations of all the dioceses should themselves decide to which church they should belong. The Turks secretly encouraged the Bulgarians in their firm stand. The island of Crete was about to break out in one of its periodic revolts and the Turks wished to make certain that the Bulgarians would not line up with the Greeks when the trouble began.

In an effort to obtain some sort of compromise Ignatiev induced the Porte to set up a commission of three Greeks and three Bulgarians to study the problem. With the aid of Turkish officials and Ignatiev, the commission evolved a plan acceptable to both sides. A national Bulgarian church was to be established and the dioceses were to be divided as follows: thirty-seven to the Patriarchate, twenty-five to the Bulgarian church, four to the Serbian, and eight to be divided between the Patriarchate and the Bulgarian church. Everything seemed settled and only the consent of the Patriarch was needed. But he insisted that some Bulgarian clergymen who had come to Constantinople without his permission should first admit in writing that they had violated the canons. On this trivial disciplinary issue the whole plan foundered.

This proved to be the Patriarch's last chance of coming to an agreement with the Bulgars. The Turks now ended the dispute by issuing on March 11, 1870, a firman establishing an autonomous Bulgarian church or exarchate. The church was to be headed by an exarch elected by a synod. The jurisdiction of the new church was to extend over seventeen dioceses, in contrast to the twenty-five specified in the earlier plan of the sultan's mixed commission. This difference was more than made up by the all-important Article X of the firman, which stated that new dioceses could be added to the Bulgarian exarchate upon the vote of two thirds of the inhabitants. This cleared the way for the expansion of the exarchate into any area inhabited by Bulgarians.

Ignatiev, upon informing his government of the new church, stated that the Turks, "speculating solely on the rivalry which the bitter struggle had sown between the Greeks and the Bulgarians, calculated that it would be worth while for the Porte to recogninize the Bulgarians and detach them from Turkey, and by so doing break the unity of the Christian nationalities of Turkey and alienate at least one of them [the Greeks] from Russia." [8] The repercussions of the establishment of the exarchate did, in fact, correspond to the aims that Ignatiev attributed to the Turks. When the exarchate was actually created in February, 1872, the Patriarchate declared the new church heretical and excommunicated the exarch and his bishops. At the same time crowds of Greeks shouted in the streets of Constantinople: "Long live the schism. We won't be absorbed by the Slavs; we won't let our children be bulgarized." [9] An anti-Slav journal, now founded in Athens, accused Russia "of exploiting the Greek element in favor of the purely Slav interests." The journal warned its readers "not to let yourselves be caught in snares disguised by apparent religious affinities," and it recommended common action with the Moslem element "which would be less dangerous for the expansion of the Greek spirit than is Slavism." [10]

This dissension among the Balkan peoples was not a passing storm. During the following decades, when the exarchate expanded steadily with the progressive application of Article X of the firman, the Bulgarians and the Greeks became locked in a desperate struggle for Macedonia. Eventually even the Serbs were alarmed by the growth of the exarchate and turned against their Bulgarian fellow Slavs. Thus the establishment of the exarchate had a direct and decisive effect on the vexed Macedonian question* that was to dominate Balkan diplomacy in the coming decades.

So far as the Bulgarian national revival was concerned, the establishment of the exarchate was a victory of incalculable importance. Patriarch Gregory VI had stated in 1867 that a Bulgarian church confined to the area north of the Balkan Mountains represented "a bridge to the political independence of the Bulgarians." Obviously a church that was free to expand anywhere it received a two-thirds majority was much more than a bridge. It was, in fact, a solid foundation for the independent Bulgarian state that now obviously could not be long forestalled.

REVOLUTIONARY MOVEMENT

The struggle against Greek ecclesiastical domination was paralleled by a struggle against Turkish political subjugation. At first the Bulgarian revolutionaries did not feel strong enough to make an independent bid for freedom. Instead, they supported other Balkan peoples when they rose in revolt. Many Bulgarians fought with the Serbs under Karageorge and Milosh Obrenovich. Many more joined the Philike Hetairia and fought in the Greek War of Independence. Bulgarian volunteers also joined the Russian armies when they entered the Balkans in 1806, in 1811, and in 1829.

With the 1830's the Bulgarian revolutionaries began to act for the liberation of their own country. As in the case of the other Balkan peoples, the attitudes of the various classes of the Bulgarian population toward revolution varied a good deal. In the mountains there were the haiduk outlaws, the Bulgarian equivalent of the Greek klephts. They kept the spirit of resistance alive with their daring exploits but they were few, unorganized, and ingenuous.

* See Chapter 28.

Quite different were the chorbajis, corresponding to the Greek kodjabashis. They were wealthy and frequently served as moneylenders and tax collectors. In these capacities they aroused the antagonism of many of their fellow countrymen, so that the term "chorbaji" came to have an antinational connotation. This was by no means always justified, for many chorbajis generously supported schools and churches and opposed the most flagrant injustices of Turkish rule. Yet the fact remains that the chorbajis were closely associated with, and dependent upon, the Ottoman administrative system. The more public-spirited of them supported peaceful reform but almost unanimously they opposed revolutionary measures.

The peasants were generally inert, though not without certain exceptions. These can be explained by the spread of chifliks, which was most pronounced in the second quarter of the nineteenth century in the northwestern part of the country. It is significant that a number of revolts broke out in that region at precisely that period. The Ottoman government was aware of the relationship between Bulgarian unrest and the inequitable land system. It made several attempts to improve conditions, including a decree in January, 1851, which provided for the distribution of the chiflik lands to the peasants. Nothing came of this act, which was opposed not only by the lords but also by the peasants, who objected because they would not have received clear title to the land. Thus agrarian unrest contributed to the revolutionary movement in certain sections of Bulgaria.

The most politically active elements in Bulgarian society came from the new class of craftsmen and merchants, including the teachers and writers who were dependent on them. These people were divided into two factions, the reformers who wanted improved status within the framework of the Ottoman system and the revolutionaries who demanded nothing less than full independence. The reformists were strengthened by the vigorous and enlightened administration of Midhat Pasha. Between 1864 and 1867 Midhat transformed his vilayet, which included most of the Bulgarian lands, into a model province. We shall note in the following chapter that he ruthlessly crushed every revolutionary manifestation but at the same time he established agrarian banks and built roads, bridges, and schools. The Bulgarian communities abroad, which participated actively in the liberation movement, were also divided between revolution and reform. The large colony in Constantinople was predominantly reformist, and naturally so, since it was directly dependent upon the Turkish government for its privileges and prosperity. By contrast, the Bulgarian colony in Bucharest was largely, though by no means exclusively, revolutionary. The Rumanian capital was beyond the reach of the Turkish police, yet close enough for easy communication across the Danube. Thus it served as the headquarters for innumerable revolutionary groups which collected arms, hatched innumerable plots, and occasionally effected an actual revolt.

In 1834 a revolt occurred at Tirnovo, and the following year another uprising broke out along the Serbian frontier. In 1841 simultaneous insurrections occurred in Nish on the Serbian frontier, in Kirk-Kilissa near Adrianople, and at Shimla west of Varna. The revolutionaries expected help from the powers, especially from France, who claimed to be the protector of the Christians in Turkey. The Serbian cabinet alone made an official protest against the excesses of the Turks in suppressing the disturbances. The French government did send an economist, Jerome Blanqui, to Bulgaria to investigate conditions. After extensive travels he wrote an official report and also published a bitter attack against the Turkish administration. He described it as "an outrage to the dignity of human nature. . . . A single word would suffice to put an end to this scandal: When will Europe say this word?" [11] No power responded to Blanqui's plea, but his writings, together with those of other publicists, made Western public opinion for the first time aware of the existence of the Bulgarians and of their plight under the Turks.

In 1849 and 1850 new revolts broke out in the northwestern Vidin region. The rebels numbered at least 10,000, indicative of the mass agrarian unrest in that area. In 1853 still another uprising occurred, and the following year a considerable number of Bulgarians flocked to the Russian colors to fight against the Turks during the Crimean War. Among the participants in the 1841 insurrections and in the Crimean War was a young man named George Rakovski. He was the first of a series of famous revolutionary leaders who now appeared successively to incite their countrymen to action. These men accomplished nothing of a concrete nature but their heroic and self-sacrificing efforts captured the popular imagination much more than did the reformers. To this day Rakovski—and after him Lyuben Karavelov, Vasil Levski, and Khristo Botev—are reverently referred to as the martyrs and the apostles.

Rakovski joined the revolutionary movement at the age of sixteen. With the failure of the 1841 revolt he fled to Marseilles, then returned to Constantinople and later fought in the Crimean War with the Russians. In 1863 he went on a tour of the Greek, Montenegrin, and Serbian capitals to enlist support for the Bulgarian cause. He was disillusioned by what he considered to be the cynical selfishness of his Balkan neighbors and the indifference of the great powers. When he was in Athens he remarked: "There is nothing to be done here. . . . The Greeks only think of finding a European princelet who would deign to command them [following the overthrow of King Otho which occurred at this time]. . . . Italy has abandoned us. France does not concern herself with us, as if the keys to the Balkans were not in our hands. Europe does not recognize us. . . . However the Bulgarians are honest and brave! . . . I must address myself there, where there is at least a glimmer of hope." [12] Rakovski did turn to his beloved Bulgarians and feverishly published newspapers, wrote poetry and hatched plans until tuberculosis burned out his life in 1867 at the age of forty-nine.

The wealthy and relatively conservative Bulgarian merchants of Bucharest had disapproved of Rakovski because of his violent methods and his radical political and social tenets. Now they espoused three successive schemes designed to secure Bulgarian freedom with outside aid. The first of these involved a group of Bulgarians and Rumanians who, in March, 1866, drew up an "Act of Union between the Bulgarians and Rumanians." This provided that the two peoples should make preparations for a common revolt which should include, if possible, also the Serbs. The Rumanians lost interest, however, when the domestic crisis that they had faced following the abdication of Prince Cuza was ended by the election to the throne of Prince Charles on May 10, 1866.

The second scheme called for a dual Turko-Bulgarian state in which the sultan was to be crowned tsar of the Bulgars as well as sultan of the Turks. A petition presenting the details of this plan was sent to Sultan Abdul Aziz early in 1867 by a Bulgarian committee in Bucharest. The plan appears to have been inspired partly by the Austro-Hungarian *Ausgleich* of the same year and partly by the Greco-Bulgarian feud that was raging at the time over the church question. The Turks ignored the petition with the result that the revolutionary committee sponsoring it petered out.

The third scheme that appeared at this time seemed to have more chance of success. It consisted of an agreement concluded on May 22, 1867, by the Serbian government and a Bulgarian committee in Bucharest. The agreement provided for the creation of a Yugoslav kingdom consisting of Serbia and Bulgaria and headed by Prince Michael of Serbia. The Serbian government obligated itself to "render all material and moral assistance for the attainment of the common end. . . ." [13] This understanding, like several other inter-Balkan pacts concluded at this time, depended on the ambitious Prince Michael of Serbia, who organized a Balkan League * in order to drive the Turks out of Europe. When Michael was assassinated on June 10, 1868, the League collapsed and the Serbian-Bulgarian agreement was forgotten.

Meanwhile, the true revolutionaries had had no traffic with these plans for collaboration with the Rumanians, the Turks, and the Serbs. Since the death of Rakovski new leaders had appeared who continued his work of preparing for revolution. Outstanding among these were Lyuben Karavelov and Vasil Levski. The latter was a young deacon who in 1862 ran away from his monastery to join the revolutionary movement to which he devoted and sacrificed his life. Karavelov spent nine years as a student in Moscow, where he came under the influence of Russian radical thought. He returned to Belgrade in 1867 and in the next year settled in Bucharest, whence he conducted his revolutionary activities. In 1871 these two men established a new revolutionary committee in Bucharest and organized an underground network in Bulgaria. They also established communication with Serbian and Russian agents, and by the end of 1872 everything was supposed to be ready for a coordinated rising. But the whole movement was brought to an end by an adventurer who was caught robbing a Turkish transport and forced into divulging the secret plans. Soon afterward Levski was apprehended and executed, and thus the revolutionists' hopes were once more dashed.

Two new leaders now appeared, Khristo Botev and Stephen Stambulov. Both men had absorbed nihilist doctrines during school days in Russia and then

* See Chapter 21.

had gone to Bucharest, where together they published a volume of patriotic poems and plunged into the work of revolutionary organization. Stambulov, though only a lad of twenty, was given the task of resuming Levski's underground work in Bulgaria. Disguised as a book peddler, he wandered through the countryside, reviving and extending Levski's secret groups. One of the members betrayed him to the Turks, forcing him to flee to Bucharest. He arrived there in the spring of 1875, and a few months later news arrived of the July revolt in neighboring Herzegovina.

The Bulgarian leaders had no way of knowing that this revolt was to persist and to spread until it culminated in a general South Slav revolt and a Russo-Turkish war. At this point they knew only that the Herzegovinian uprising provided them with a favorable opportunity to proceed with their own plans. Botev wrote enthusiastically at this time: "Herzegovina is fighting; Montenegro is spreading over its mountains and coming with help; Serbia is ready to put its forces on the move; Greece is about to declare war; Rumania will not remain neutral. . . . Is there any doubt that death is hanging over Turkey?" [14] In accordance with this overoptimistic interpretation, the revolutionaries made preparations for another uprising. The Turks intercepted their messages and forced them to take up arms on September 16, 1875. Stambulov had been assured that several thousand impatient patriots were waiting for the signal to rise, but when the showdown came only twenty-three souls met on a hilltop. Without doing anything more violent than singing a revolutionary hymn, the crestfallen would-be rebels fled to the mountains with the Turks in pursuit. Another chapter in the story of revolution in Bulgaria came to its dismal end.

Botev's committee broke up at this point following a controversy involving misappropriation of funds. A new body now appeared dominated by an impatient young revolutionary, George Benkovski. Plans were made for an uprising on May 13, 1876. Because of treachery and arrests the revolt began instead on May 2 in the town of Panagyurishte in central Bulgaria. The rebels issued a proclamation that ended with these words: "From today on, we make known in the name of the Bulgarian people before all the world that we demand: Freedom or death to the people! Forward, forward, Brother, God is with us." [15] A young woman teacher, who had learned the art of needlework in an American missionary school, prepared a flag showing a savage yellow lion with his paw on a crescent and, with it, the motto "Liberty or Death." The excited populace assembled in the square, sang revolutionary songs, heard flaming speeches by Benkovski, and then scattered to kill peaceable Turks wherever they could be found.

Retribution was not long in coming. The enthusiastic rebels made several fatal mistakes from the outset. They allowed some Turks to escape and sound the alarm. They failed to cut telegraph lines and burn bridges. Worst of all, instead of concentrating their forces, they remained isolated and scattered in their various villages. Thus the Turks were able without opposition to amass their troops and overwhelm the villages one by one. The Turks, who were alarmed by the violence of the outbreak, collected some 5,000 regulars and also a considerable number of irregular bashi-bazouks recruited from the local population. Towns and villages fell one after another to these forces. The bashi-bazouks were particularly savage because of the earlier killings of their Moslem fellow villagers. When the looting and burning and killing finally ended, thousands of bodies lay scattered amid the smoldering ruins. An official Turkish estimate set the casualties at 3,100 Christians and 400 Moslems. A British consular agent estimated the dead at 12,000, while an American investigator set the figure at 15,000. Subsequent Bulgarian historians claimed losses of 30,000 to 60,000.

More important than the precise number of dead was the international reaction to this bloodshed. In Russia and in Western Europe, and especially in Great Britain, there was a general revulsion against the "Bulgarian Horrors," as they were promptly dubbed. The patriots had failed miserably as they had so frequently in the past. But their sacrifices this time were not again in vain. The "Bulgarian Horrors" contributed appreciably to the combination of pressures that finally culminated in the intervention of the powers, in the Russo-Turkish War, and finally in the liberation of Bulgaria.*

* See Chapter 21.

20. Reform and Revolution in the Ottoman Empire: 1856–1877

AT THREE O'CLOCK in the afternoon of February 18, 1856, a crowd of several thousands gathered in Constantinople to hear the solemn reading of the reform edict known as the *Hatti-Humayun*. A week later the representatives of the great powers signed the Treaty of Paris in which they recognized "the high value" of the edict and guaranteed the independence and the integrity of the Ottoman Empire. In this manner the Turks were given, at least in theory, an opportunity to reform their empire without interference from the outside. The many obstacles that they were to meet on the path of reform were foreshadowed symbolically by the unexpected ending of a banquet given by the sultan to celebrate the Treaty of Paris.

A minute or two after the Sultan had retired we were startled by two frightful claps of thunder followed by a storm of wind and hail. The whole building seemed to shake, and in a moment the gas went out and we were in total darkness. The band dropped their instruments with a clash and fled. For some moments no one spoke, and then a thin, shrill voice was heard in French saying, "It wants but the handwriting on the wall and the words 'Mene, Mene, Tekel, Upharsin' to make this a second feast of Belshazzar." [1]

This incident was indeed a portent of the difficulties that lay ahead. The first part of the *Hatti-Humayun* was devoted to the non-Moslem minorities, promising them equal rights in matters of taxation, justice, military service, education, public office, and social respect. The degree to which this promise was implemented will be the subject of this chapter. Other sections of the *Hatti-Humayun* prescribed legislation for the reform of the whole empire, but the discussion here will be confined to the crucial question of whether the Ottoman rulers were capable of changing institutions and conditions sufficiently to arrest the disruptive tide of nationalism among their Christian subjects.

As for the Turks themselves, this was a period of intellectual and literary renaissance. A new group of critically thinking individuals turned

381

against the artificial, Persian-dominated culture of the past and looked to the West for both political and cultural guidance. These were also years of increasing economic difficulties and increasing subservience to the West in financial as well as commercial matters. The combination of economic distress and intellectual ferment led to revolution in 1876—the year of the three sultans. The last of these rulers, Abdul Hamid, ruthlessly crushed the bid for a constitutional regime. Thus the year 1877 marked the end of the period of reform and revolution and the beginning of the new period of Hamidian autocracy that was to last to 1908.

NATURE OF REFORM PROBLEM
AND OF BALKAN POLITICS

The problem of reform in the Ottoman Empire was quite different in the middle of the nineteenth century from what it had been at the beginning. In the earlier period, reform could not even be considered until the central government was able to assert its authority over the janissaries in the capital and the local lords in the provinces. When Mahmud II finally destroyed these impediments to imperial authority he and his successors were able to deal directly with the problem of improving administration.

This problem was formidable, involving as it did the ignorance, apathy, and almost ingrained corruption of the Ottoman bureaucrats. These individuals were, on the whole, an unlovely lot. They were known popularly as Stambul effendis, meaning, literally, learned gentlemen of Istanbul. Most of them were graduates of the translation bureau attached to the foreign office. This bureau had been established by Mahmud II at the time of the Greek revolution in order to train interpreters to take the place of the Greek officials, who no longer were acceptable. The students inevitably became familiar with Western culture as well as Western languages. Some of them rose to high office and served the empire intelligently and faithfully. These were the best of the Stambul effendis. But the majority acquired only a veneer of Occidental manners. Some also acquired contempt for their own country. An Englishman who lived in Asia Minor at this time described these superficially Westernized bureaucrats in unflattering terms: ". . . the same black frock coat, black trousers, generally unbuttoned where European ideas would most rigorously exact buttoning, the same padded underclothes, shiny boots, and slight red cap, the same sallow puffy features, indicative of an unhealthy regimen, the same shuffling gait and lack-lustre eye, characterize every man of the tribe." [2]

The chief obstacle in the way of reform was not so much the personality of those bureaucrats as it was the system in which they worked. As a rule, they had to bribe in order to obtain their posts. Tenure was uncertain and usually short. Under these circumstances they were almost driven to extortion and embezzlement in order to repay their debts and provide for an uncertain future. "I have no inducement to be honest," a pasha told an American missionary. "If I attempt to rule justly all of the other pashas will combine against me and I shall soon be turned out of my place, and unless I take bribes I shall be too poor to purchase another." [3]

It is apparent that the problem of reform in the Ottoman Empire was not merely one of redressing the grievances of the subject Christian peoples. Naturally this was a part of the reform problem, but only one part. Oppression in the empire was not confined to the Christians. Contemporary travelers almost invariably reported that the Moslem peasantry was as badly off as the Christian. They also reported that the Christians were maltreated fully as much by fellow Christians as by Turks. This latter point needs to be emphasized for an understanding of the plight of the Balkan Christians under Turkish rule. It is commonly assumed that their troubles arose from the misgovernment and tyranny of the Turks. But the fact is that the Christian peoples complained as much against the rapacity of their own ecclesiastical and civil leaders as against that of the Turks. On June 11, 1860, the British ambassador in Constantinople circularized a questionnaire among his numerous consuls throughout the Ottoman Empire. One of his questions was: "Are many of the grievances of which the Christian population complains owing to the conduct of their own authorities?" [4] The replies invariably were in the affirmative. The following reports from three of these consuls reveal the realities of Balkan affairs and the true nature of the problem of reform in the Ottoman Empire.

Consul Charles J. Calvert in Saloniki, July 23, 1860:

The Christian authorities—by which I mean their Spiritual chiefs and their Primates ("Cojabashis")—are even more rapacious and tyrannical in their small sphere than the Turkish authorities are in a larger sphere. The Bishops and Metropolitans are guilty of many acts of oppression and cupidity towards their flocks, which, if committed by Turks, would rouse a storm of indignation on the part of the Christian sympathisers. Only a few days ago, the Bishop of Vodena, being in want of money, sent to a small hamlet of only forty families in his diocese and extorted 1000 piastres. The assessed taxes are collected by the Cojabashis, who resort to the harshest measures in order to exact more than is justly due, so as to enable them to appropriate the surplus. In the village accounts, which are kept by the Cojabashis, the expenditure for extras is frequently exorbitant; and a large amount is generally charged for "presents" (i.e., bribes), the greater part of which has not, probably, ever been disbursed.[5]

Consul A. Cathcart in Prevesa, July 20, 1860:

A vast deal of the discontent among the Christians arises from the petty exactions and tyranny of their own ecclesiastics, who exercise an almost unbounded authority, recognized by the Porte, over them. Here, as everywhere else in Turkey, every sort of injustice, malversation of funds, bribery, and corruption is openly attributed by the Christians to their clergy. The lower grades of priests who are miserably poor, are obliged to labor manually, and to dig and delve in the fields, like any other peasant, for a living, and are usually grossly ignorant; while the upper ranks roll in riches obtained from the vast unaudited funds of the Church, and are generally mixed up in every intrigue by which any money, influence, or position is to be obtained.[6]

Vice Consul Blunt in Adrianople, April 4, 1867:

These notables, be they Turks, Christians, or Jews, are, generally speaking, very despotic, and they take care to force the poorer classes, to pay much more than the richer, or to exact more than the legal amount. The assessment of the "verghi," or tax on property, may serve as an example. A Tchorbadji (Christian) or a Bey, owning a farm of about 250 acres, pays in proportion much less than a peasant who holds 30 acres. The former may pay about £7, while the latter would pay £2 10s. The Greek Primates in this city levy a great deal more than the legal quota; the surplus falling almost exclusively on the poorer class. What they do with this surplus is a secret. They pretend that they employ it in support of the schools in this place. If this is true, Adrianople should have a greater number of schools and pupils than the other cities in the Vilayet, which is not the case. . . .

The same abuses and arbitrary acts committed by the Greek Primates in assessing and collecting the taxes are more or less experienced by all the other communities. Turkish Beys, Armenian Elders, and Rabbis and Hahambashis are equally hard and unjust to their respective correligionists. The arbitrary assessment of the taxes has more sway in the district towns and villages. When a village, Christian or Turkish, is very slow in paying the taxes, the Tchorbadjies and Muhtars call in the police to enforce the payment of the amount due, and something more besides. The police generally perform this duty with little lenity, and frequently with unjustifiable severity. This is done at the instigation and with the sanction of the Tchorbadjies or Muhtars.[7]

This basic feature of Balkan politics and of the Ottoman reform question has been well analyzed by Professor R. H. Davison. After a careful study of available materials he has concluded: "The Turk was no worse than the Christian. The true distinction between oppressor and oppressed is not to be drawn on religious lines. . . . chiefly it was a matter of ruling class against those under its control." The evidence he presents in support of this conclusion is revealing:

The chief form of oppression to be corrected was that of the Armenian and Greek hierachies over their own people. Their rule over the Christians was similar to that of the *effendis* over the Turks. Simony was usual, and to recoup themselves the bishops and lower clergy squeezed their flocks. . . .

Religion had become essentially politics and business. In pursuit of this policy the people were kept as ignorant as possible. It was the ordinary peasant or artisan in the Greek *millet* who suffered from clerical misgovernment. The primates and *hodja-bashis* of a village, themselves not clerics, were part of the system. In Patmos the Greek people found the Turkish sub-governor much more just than the Greek primates and the archbishop. In Salonica the clergy and primates were more rapacious than the Turks, extorting money by overtaxation and falsifying the village accounts. In Smyrna "the Christian population have far more reason to complain of grievances emanating from their own clergy and primates than from the Turks."

Bulgaria constituted a special case. European travellers and residents there likened the Greek clergy to clerical tax-farmers, bent only on monetary gain, in order to make a substantial profit on the presents they paid to their superiors for investiture. It was not unknown for Greek clergy to lend the Bulgarian peasants money at sixty per cent interest. Villages tried to avoid having a resident priest because of the expense entailed by this spiritual luxury. . . .

In the Gregorian Armenian *millet* the situation was as bad. . . . The Armenian *sarrafs,* or moneylenders, were in league with the *effendis* of the capital to cheat the government. . . . In the provinces conditions were not different. There the Armenian notables were in league with the Turkish officials to oppress the people. . . . At Bandirza the [Armenian] *hodja-bashis* formed "an unholy league with the Turkish governors, judges, and authorities of the neighboring places, and the Armenian bishop, whoever he might be. . . . All in office, ecclesiastical and civil, of all religions, unite in one object and in one only, to oppress and fleece the people and cheat the government." [8]

FAILURE OF REFORM IN THE BALKANS

The significance of the above testimony is that it demonstrates that reform was needed within the millets as well as in the empire as a whole. Reform decrees in Constantinople would have meant little for the Christian peoples so long as their relations with their own ruling class remained unchanged. This fact was recognized in the *Hatti-Humayun* of 1856. It specifically provided for the reorganization of the millets as well as for the protection of the rights of Christians and the reform of various branches of the administration.

Two Ottoman statesmen, Aali Pasha and Fuad, attempted persistently and sincerely to fulfill the reform prescriptions of the *Hatti-Humayun*. With few interruptions they controlled the affairs of the empire until 1871. They tried to help the Balkan Christians in three ways: by enforcing the existing legislation and supplementing it with new decrees and with inspection tours; by reforming the Orthodox millet, and by issuing the 1864 vilayet law reorganizing provincial administration.

Appreciable progress was made toward enforcing existing laws, though the record remained far from perfect. Also, beginning in May, 1858, Christian delegates were appointed, in questions of general interest, to sit on the Grand Council composed of the ministers and dignitaries. Most of the value of this innovation was nullified by the fact that the Christian representatives were selected from among those families whose interests were closely identified with those of the effendi class. One of the first issues facing the Council was the perennial problem of Christian military service. In the belief that this would be an advantage for the Christians, European pressure had forced the inclusion in the *Hatti-Humayun* of a provision for Christian military service. In actual fact, most Christians preferred to continue under the old arrangement by which they paid a modest tax in lieu of military service. The Council decided, probably as a gesture to European opinion, to prepare a census of all non-Moslems eligible for military service. When this was done, it was found that some two million Christians were eligible for service. But popular opposition to the measure was obvious, and the whole matter was eventually buried, to the satisfaction of both Christians and Moslems.

In contrast to this shadowboxing, definite results were derived from the promulgation of a new penal code in 1858. It was based on the 1810 French code and was gradually enforced throughout the empire. Within the next few years other codes having to do with the regulation of commerce were adopted, though they were not as important as the penal code.

Another device employed for the benefit of the Balkan Christians was periodic tours of inspection. Outstanding was that of a new grand vizir, Mehmet Kibrisli Pasha, who personally toured Macedonia and Bulgaria in 1860. One reason for the trip was the marked discontent in those areas after the Crimean War. Another was the pressure of the great powers, which were demanding fulfillment of the promises made in the *Hatti-Humayun*. Kibrisli and his entourage, which was half Christian in composition, spent four months in the provinces. The grand vizir received many petitions in person and, like Harun al-Rashid, dispensed justice himself on the spot. Among the conclusions reached by the investigators were that the system of tax farming was unjust and generally unsatisfactory; that a number of the Turkish officials were corrupt; that the evidence of Christians was frequently rejected in lawsuits; that there was no systematic oppression of Christians by Moslems, either officially or unofficially; and that the Greek Orthodox hierarchy was often tyrannical and extortionate. Kibrisli's tour was followed by others in later years, particularly because the investigations were very popular with the peasantry. Commissions visited Bulgaria again in 1861, 1862, and 1863, while others investigated Bosnia in 1861 and 1863. These tours did not produce fundamental reform but they did correct certain abuses, they stimulated the local authorities to improve conditions, and they provided the central government with a mass of information which formed the basis for reform measures.

One of the most important of these reform measures affecting the Balkan peoples was the reorganization of the Orthodox millet. A total of six millets existed in the Ottoman Empire. In order of numerical importance they were the Greek Orthodox, Gregorian Armenian, Jewish, Roman Armenian, Roman Catholic, and Protestant. Only the first three were reorganized, the remainder being comparatively small, of recent origin, and therefore not requiring outside ministrations. One reason for the millet reform was that the *Hatti-Humayun* had stated specifically that the millets were to be reorganized to suit "the progress and enlightenment of the times." Also, Kibrisli's tour had revealed the existence of Greek Orthodox corruption in Bulgaria. However, millet reform was by no means imposed exclusively from above by the Turkish government. Lay elements within each millet were also agitating for reorganization to end the traditional domination by ecclesiastical prelates. The Turks took advantage of this cleavage to force the adoption of new and more democratic constitutions by the three millets.

The Orthodox millet, which concerned the Balkan peoples most, had fallen to a considerable degree under the control of five metropolitans who selected the Patriarch of Constantinople.* Under Turkish prodding, a series of changes were effected between 1860 and 1862 which provided for lay participation in the election of the patriarch and the administration of the secular affairs of the church. Changes of a similar nature were adopted by the Armenian and Jewish millets in 1863 and 1865, respectively.

The Turks had hoped that these reforms, by minimizing clerical control, might lower the barriers separating religious groups and encourage them to think of themselves as fellow Ottoman citizens rather than as Jews or as Christians of various denominations. This change in attitude did not occur because of the rising nationalist sentiments that were separating rather than bringing together the peoples of the empire. The Jews, who had no national aspirations, constituted the only exception. As for the Greeks, the strengthening of the lay element in the Orthodox Church made that institution more susceptible to Greek nationalist influence. This made it correspondingly more difficult for Greek and Bulgarian nationalism to reach a compromise within the structure of the church, and thus led eventually to the establishment of the separate Bulgarian exarchate, as described in Chapter 19.

Provincial administration was reorganized by the vilayet law of 1864. This divided the empire into vilayets or provinces, which in turn were subdivided into sanjaks and other still smaller administrative units. These were to be administered on the principle of greater decentralization and greater popular participation. The vilayets were larger in area than the former provincial units or eyalets, and the governors of the vilayets were given considerable authority. Also, they were assisted by advisory bodies known as mejlisses, whose members were partly appointed and partly elected by a complex indirect procedure. Similar advisory bodies functioned in the smaller administrative units.

One vilayet was set up in 1864 to test the new law. It consisted of three former eyalets and covered a large part of the central Balkans, including most of the Bulgarian lands. Midhat Pasha was appointed governor and he proved to be extraordinarily successful. He himself was of a Pomak or Moslem Bulgarian family. With characteristic energy and uncompromising honesty he transformed his vilayet into a showplace and won the support of both Christians and Moslems. As noted in Chapter 19, he built bridges, roads, schools, and public buildings. He established agrarian banks to lend to the peasants at low interest rates, and curbed brigandage to a large degree. But at the same time he ruthlessly crushed all revolutionary tendencies in the country.

From his Balkan province Midhat was transferred to Baghdad, where his efforts proved equally fruitful. Midhat's success encouraged the government to apply the vilayet law throughout the empire. But the results were not as favorable everywhere as in Midhat's province. The working of any administrative system depends on the administrators. And since they were of poor caliber in the empire, government in the vilayets remained correspondingly poor. The Baghdad vilayet, for example, did not again receive a governor approaching

* See Chapter 15.

Midhat's stature until 1911. When an honest and energetic official did appear he was likely to be frustrated by the government's policy of shifting officials frequently. This lack of capable and conscientious administrators was particularly serious because an essential feature of the vilayet law was the increased authority and responsibility entrusted to the governors. Thus Professor Davison has reached the following negative conclusion concerning the vilayet law:

> The existing [vilayet] law, though it could be improved in many respects, was fundamentally sound. Two conditions were necessary for its successful fulfillment. The first was an enlightened and patriotic ministry in the captital which should have power to curb the caprices of the Sultan. The second was a group of administrators with enough education, patriotism, and enthusiasm for progressive measures to make them truly devoted to hard work in the public service. Until such men could be developed, . . . a system of Westernized offices and councils filled only by the typical *effendis* would be far worse than government by fewer, more tyrannical *derebeys* [literally "lords of the valleys," or insubordinate local lords who had been crushed by Mahmud II] who were nevertheless sincerely interested in efficient rule.[9]

This judgment outlines the reasons for the eventual doom of the Ottoman Empire. The essential failure of Ottoman reform efforts in the Balkans meant that the imperial *status quo* could have no attraction to counteract the centrifugal force of Balkan nationalism. Neither millet reform nor vilayet reorganization had succeeded in inducing among the subject Balkan peoples a sense of loyalty to Constantinople strong enough to neutralize their growing feeling of national consciousness.

REVOLUTION AND REACTION IN THE EMPIRE

The awakening of the Christian peoples of the Ottoman Empire has attracted considerable attention. But the Turks themselves experienced a similar awakening beginning in the 1860's. The reason for this development is that the Western world at this time was undermining on all fronts the Ottoman old order. The Suez Canal was completed in 1869. Railroads were being built in Asia Minor and in the Balkans. Foreign-owned banks were appearing in the principal cities. The Ottoman government itself was becoming dependent on foreign loans and rapidly coming under Western financial control.

Even in the field of religion the West was impinging upon the Moslem Near East. Missionaries were preaching and founding schools throughout the empire. Also, the Turks themselves by this time had established several institutions of higher learning, including the School of Medicine (1867), the Imperial Lycée (1868), the University of Constantinople (1869), the School of Law (1870), and the School of Political Science (1878). The Turkish press, too, was developing rapidly during these years. In 1859 there were only one official and one semiofficial weekly in the empire. By 1872 there were three daily papers and several weeklies. In addition, six French dailies appeared in cities such as Constantinople, Smyrna, and Alexandria, and were read by educated Turks.

The effect of all these developments cannot be measured precisely. But there can be no doubt that they gradually cracked the hitherto impregnable and monolithic Islamic structure. Canals, railways, banks, missionaries, schools, and newspapers constitute the background and also the explanation for the literary and intellectual awakening of the Turks.

The best-known leaders of this awakening were Ibrahim Shinassi, Namik Kemal, and Abdul Hamid Ziya. These men did not agree on all issues, but they did have certain common experiences and they did share certain fundamental principles. All had lived in Western Europe and all had been tremendously impressed by the thought and literature as well as the material achievements of the West. They returned to Constantinople determined to sweep away what they now considered to be the deadweight of their classical literary and intellectual heritage. In other words, these men wished to do for their people what Obradovich had done for the Serbians, Koraïs for the Greeks, and Aprilov for the Bulgarians.

These pioneers of the Turkish renaissance differed as to the degree to which the West should be imitated. But they were agreed that Western ideas and institutions could not be ignored and that they could be reconciled with Islam. These early reformers did not organize a political party. The only real parties in the Ottoman Empire at this time were the "ins" and the "outs" gathered about individual political leaders. But by 1865 a fairly well-defined group of young Western-minded writers had formed about the newspaper *Mushbir*, or *Herald of Glad Tidings*. The paper championed Turkish literature and language against the traditional Persian-dominated Ottoman culture; favored the introduction of some form of constitutional representative government; and also advanced the concept of a Turkish nation and Turkish nationalism as distinct from the Ottoman dynasty and empire. The latter concept owed a good deal to the new European science of Turkology, which threw light on the historical role of the Turkish peoples scattered from Central Asia to Central Europe.

The articles published in *Mushbir* proved too militant for the government, and the paper was suppressed in 1867. The editor and his supporters fled abroad, where, after the manner of the Russian exiles, they continued their journalistic attacks from London and Paris. While they were in the foreign capitals they acquired the name "Young Turks." It was coined by Western writers, partly because the Turkish reformers were predominantly young and partly to distinguish them from the older and more conservative Turkish leaders. The name persisted and it was used thereafter in a rather loose fashion to refer to any antigovernment Turkish groups.

While these exiles were issuing their challenges from abroad, the government at home was sinking into reaction and bankruptcy. When Aali Pasha, the reform statesman, died in 1871, Abdul Aziz declared that at last he was a free man. After years of obscurity he now took the reigns of government into his own hands. The results were unfortunate because the sultan was an eccentric given to strange and unpredictable acts. Within fourteen months after Aali's death twenty-three vilayets received seventy-two governors, or, on an average, a governor every three and a half months. The sultan was especially fond of Mahmud Nedim, whom he made his grand vizir. Opponents accused the new chief minister of excessive partiality toward the Russians and gave him the nickname "Mahmudov." They also attacked the reckless expenditure of money and the mounting government debts. It is significant that these criticisms were directed not at the ministers, as in the past, but at the sultan, who now was held personally responsible.

The 1870's were also years of widespread economic distress and increasing financial difficulties culminating in outright bankruptcy. One reason for this is to be found in the basic economic structure of the empire, which was primitive and unsound. The chronic financial difficulties of the Ottoman government were accentuated by the cost of the Crimean War. The Turks contracted their first foreign loan in 1854. They discovered that borrowing on the international money market was easy. They lavishly spent the money that came so easily and borrowed more. Being inexperienced in the ways of high finance, the Turks paid little attention to the problem of how they were going to repay these sums. The international bankers not only failed to caution the Turks but in some instances brought pressure to bear upon them to borrow more. The net result was that by 1875 the Ottoman government had contracted fourteen loans of various kinds with a nominal capital of about £200,000,000 sterling. This required some £12,000,000 sterling a year to meet annuities, interest, and sinking fund, a sum which amounted to a little more than half the total annual revenues of the empire.

Such was the situation when the government suffered three serious economic setbacks, one after the other. The first was widespread drought and famine in Asia Minor in 1873–1874, for the relief of which the government did next to nothing. At the same time the international financial panic of 1873 affected Constantinople, breaking several banks and making money scarce. Then the revolt that broke out in Bosnia-Herzegovina in July, 1875, spread to the other Slavic provinces and added to the burdens of the imperial treasury. By November, 1875, soldiers, sailors, and civil officials had not been paid for eight months, and had to cash the government's promissory notes at a twenty-five per cent discount in order to eat. When the government tried to raise additional revenue from the peasantry it met fierce resistance. The traditionally compliant Turkish peasants of Asia Minor had been alienated by the triple burden of drought, heavy taxation, and conscription for the Balkan front. They were particularly incensed because the sultan was continuing his reckless expenditures during this crisis, including the erection of a costly mosque.

Thus the personal regime of Abdul Aziz lost support at home as well as abroad. When revolt came in 1876 most foreigners were surprised and interpreted it as a staged affair designed to forestall European intervention.

Actually, it was the natural outcome of widespread unrest and reflected the sentiments of a large proportion of the population.

The natural leader of the revolt was Midhat Pasha. He had the support of progressives who recalled his model administration in Bulgaria and Iraq, of conservatives who knew him as the scourge of the Bulgarian revolutionaries, and also of unpaid army men and officials who hoped for a more efficient and solvent government. On May 11, 1876, Abdul Aziz yielded to the clamor and dismissed Mahmud. But the agitation continued unabated. For some weeks Midhat had been planning a coup with the cooperation of the minister of war and high military officers. They had the support of the Sheik-ul-Islam, who issued a favorable fetva or legal pronouncement. Armed with this fetva the conspirators struck on May 29 late at night. By four the next morning a cannonade from the warships announced to the sleeping populace that the empire had a new sultan, Murad V.

Murad remained on the throne only three months before his mental instability compelled Midhat to replace him with his younger brother, Abdul Hamid II. This was a critical time for the empire because Turkish troops had suppressed the Bulgarian uprising with wholesale atrocities, and public opinion in Europe was deeply stirred. Midhat, who had been a model governor in Bulgaria, was the person to mollify the indignant Europeans. Abdul Hamid appointed him grand vizir on November 25, 1876. The following month the representatives of the European powers met in Constantinople to arrange a settlement of the Balkan crisis that was threatening to develop into a general European war.* When the first plenary session opened on December 23 the deliberations of the delegates were interrupted by the booming of cannon. The Turkish foreign minister, who was present, immediately rose and declared, "Gentlemen, the cannon that you hear notifies the commencement of the promulgation by His Majesty the Sultan of a Constitution guaranteeing equal rights and constitutional liberties to all the subjects of the Empire alike; and in the presence of this great event I think our labors become superfluous." [10]

The very first article of the new constitution stipulated that the Ottoman Empire formed "an indivisible whole" and that no part could be detached "for any reason whatsoever." This was a defiant answer to those diplomats who were urging autonomy or independence for certain provinces. The constitution also provided for an elected parliament, a bill of rights, an independent judiciary, and considerable provincial decentralization. Midhat was largely responsible for this document, though he had been forced against his will to leave much power in the Sultan's hands. Abdul Hamid retained authority to appoint ministers, convoke and prorogue Parliament, exile any individual he considered to be dangerous to the state, and prevent any bill from becoming law by withholding his signature.

Despite these provisions Abdul Hamid refused to abide by the con-

* See Chapter 21.

stitution. The basic reason is that he was determined to be master in the empire. Midhat, on the other hand, believed strongly that a representative assembly was needed to check the sultan's power now that the traditional janissary and derebey counterweights no longer existed. Obviously this viewpoint could not be reconciled with that of the sultan. Furthermore, Midhat was notoriously brusque and even dictatorial in his manner. He regarded the constitution as his handiwork and was resolved to put it completely into effect. On January 30, 1877, he sent a letter to Abdul Hamid in which he set forth his constitutional principles in an extraordinarily undiplomatic manner. Abdul Hamid replied by dismissing Midhat and banishing him from Constantinople. The only signs of protest were a few placards on the walls. Mass discontent had made the revolution possible, but more than discontent was needed to preserve the constitution.

There was still the hope that the Parliament, which met on March 9, 1877, might survive Midhat's downfall. It was the first representative assembly in Turkish history and many bizarre scenes occurred. The presiding officer was an arbitrary old Turk who was impatient of parliamentary niceties and who on one occasion abruptly stopped a long-winded deputy with the stentorian shout *"Sus eshek!"*—"Shut up, you donkey!" [11] Despite such incidents, the representatives conducted their work with surprising courage and intelligence. They did not split along racial or religious lines but considered each issue on its merits. They uncovered much evidence of governmental corruption and voted to summon certain ministers for questioning. Such earnestness was too much for the sultan. Using the outbreak of war with Russia as a pretext, he adjourned Parliament and unceremoniously packed off the deputies to their respective constituencies. It was typical of Abdul Hamid that he never formally abolished the constitution. He even had it published regularly each year in the *Government Year Book*. But Parliament did not meet again until the revolution of 1908.

21. Balkan Crisis and the Treaty of Berlin: 1878

T HE BALKAN CRISIS concluded by the Berlin Treaty of 1878 represents a milestone in both European and Balkan history. For Europe it marked the disintegration of the newly formed Three Emperors' League of Germany, Austria, and Russia. This in turn meant the renewal and intensification of the Austro-Russian rivalry in the Balkans which started with the Crimean War. It also meant the re-emergence of Britain as an active force in European affairs after years of splendid isolation under Gladstone.

For the Balkans the Berlin settlement involved major changes in frontiers and in political status. Bulgaria became autonomous, and Serbia, Montenegro, and Rumania gained complete independence and additional territory. The European powers also helped themselves to portions of European Turkey. After this reshuffling, the map of the Balkans was to remain virtually unchanged until the Balkan Wars of 1912–1913 completed the process of liberation from Turkish rule.

EUROPEAN BACKGROUND: THREE EMPERORS' LEAGUE

The Ottoman Empire was left in a very comfortable position at the end of the Crimean War. The Treaty of Paris admitted the empire into the European concert of nations and explicitly guaranteed its integrity and independence. But this favorable situation did not last long. The protective diplomatic wall was demolished by a series of explosions that followed one another in quick succession. These explosions were the four wars that broke out in Europe in little more than a decade—the French-Austrian War over Italy in 1859, the Austrian-Prussian attack upon Denmark in 1864, the unexpected Prussian victory over Austria in 1866, and the still more unexpected Prussian victory over France in 1870.

These wars disrupted the Crimean bloc of nations that had guaranteed Ottoman integrity in 1856. In fact, they completely demolished the Euro-

393

pean balance of power. For centuries France and Austria had struggled for Continental supremacy with Central Europe as their battleground. The events of 1859 to 1871 abruptly ended this struggle and created an entirely new setting. Austria no longer was the dominant power in Italy and Germany, while France was left shorn of Alsace-Lorraine and burdened with an indemnity and military occupation. England under Gladstone was engrossed in domestic affairs and anxious to avoid Continental entanglements. This left the new German Empire under Bismarck the first power on the Continent. "Europe," as someone put it, "had lost a mistress and gained a master." [1]

Bismarck after 1871 had every reason to be satisfied with his accomplishments. He now wished only to preserve the *status quo*. France with her *revanche* policy was the most dangerous disruptive force on the Continent. Accordingly, he sought to isolate France and to keep her powerless. His instrument for accomplishing this was the Three Emperors' League, or *Dreikaiserbund*. The bloc of eastern empires, Russia, Prussia, and Austria, had preserved the Treaty of Vienna for over a generation. Bismarck now endeavored to perpetuate his own achievements by reviving this bloc. The heads of the three empires met in 1872 and 1873 and agreed to cooperate in the preservation of peace. In case war threatened, they were to consult together "in order to determine a common course of action." As for the Balkans, the two countries directly interested were Russia and Austria-Hungary. Both emphatically denied any intention of expansion into the peninsula and both undertook to refrain from any intervention and to maintain the existing situation.

The significance of these commitments is apparent. The bitterness that had characterized Austro-Russian relations since the Crimean War at last had given way to reconciliation. But the agreement to freeze the *status quo* in the Balkans was easier to undertake than to enforce. Bismarck soon discovered that the Balkans were the "Achilles heel" of his League. A revolt broke out in Herzegovina in 1875 and, despite the efforts of the League members, it spread and created international complications until eventually it disrupted the *Dreikaiserbund* and brought Europe to the brink of war.

BALKAN BACKGROUND: FIRST
BALKAN ALLIANCE SYSTEM

The Balkan states came of age during the years following the Crimean War. For the first time they joined in a series of bilateral pacts to free themselves from Turkish rule. At the center of this alliance system was the prince of Serbia, Michael Obrenovich. Michael was not as forceful a personality as his patriarchal sire, Milosh, whom he succeeded in 1860. But he was better fitted to meet the current needs of his country. Milosh had accomplished much, but he belonged to the past. Serbia no longer could be governed as a private pashalik. A more modern state administration was needed and Michael was well suited for the task. He had a good education, was familiar with Western institutions, and possessed the drive and strength of character necessary for leadership.

When Michael ascended the throne he found the South Slavs thoroughly aroused by the events in Italy. Just as the Italians were uniting into one nation, so the Yugoslavs dreamed of freeing themselves from Austrian and Turkish rule and uniting to form a great, independent, South Slav state. Prince Michael shared these aspirations. His ambition was to make Serbia the Piedmont of the Balkans. But since Serbia was too weak to act alone, Michael devoted himself to the task of bringing the Balkan states together for a war of liberation.

The Greeks to the south were ready to cooperate. They also had been aroused by the success of the Italians. They followed avidly the victories of Garibaldi in Sicily and Naples, and imagined themselves sweeping in similar fashion through Epirus and Macedonia. In fact, a revolution did break out in the summer of 1866 on the island of Crete. The islanders convoked a general assembly and proclaimed their union with Mother Greece. Immediately Greco-Turkish relations became strained and the Greeks eagerly sought an alliance with their Serbian neighbors.

The European diplomatic situation in the 1860's was also favorable for close Balkan ties. Austria was the great opponent of revolution and change in the Balkans, but her defeats in Italy and Germany temporarily reduced her influence. On the other hand, Napoleon, the champion of the nationality principle, actively favored the liberation of the Balkans. Tsar Alexander II took the same position, in part for dynastic reasons because he wished to arrange a marriage between King George of Greece and the Russian Princess Olga. Accordingly he supported Greece on the Cretan question and urged the Balkan states to band together for common action against Turkey.

This combination of favorable domestic and international conditions made possible the series of alliances that Prince Michael concluded with Rumania (May 26, 1865, and January, 1868), with Montenegro (September 23, 1866), with a Bulgarian revolutionary society (May 22, 1867), and with Greece (August 26, 1867). The most important was the Serbian-Greek pact which allocated Thessaly and Epirus to Greece and Bosnia-Herzegovina to Serbia. The signatories undertook to propagandize and arm the Christians of European Turkey and also to oppose any great power that sought to annex Balkan territory. A coordinated Balkan revolt against the Turks was planned for March, 1868.

These ambitious plans came to nought for various reasons. One was that the pacts were concluded too late. The logical moment to strike was in 1866, when the war with Prussia had tied Austria's hand and the Cretan insurrection had distracted the Turks. But the Balkan countries were not ready for action then. By the time they had increased their armaments and negotiated their alliances the opportunity had passed. The Austro-Prussian

War lasted only seven weeks; after that, Austria was free once more to watch the Balkans. Also, the Turks had been able to pacify Crete before the signing of the Greek-Serbian pact. In fact, the Greeks were becoming increasingly anti-Slav because of Russia's support for a Bulgarian church independent of the Patriarchate. An anti-Slav society was organized in Athens in 1869 for the purpose of blocking the expansion of the Slavs in the Balkans. It will be recalled from Chapter 19 that when the Bulgarian Exarchate church was established on March 11, 1870, the Greeks reacted violently. Many advocated *rapprochement* with the Turks, whom they considered to be "less dangerous for the expansion of the Greek spirit than is Slavism." [2]

The final blow to the plans for a coordinated revolt was the assassination of Prince Michael on June 10, 1868. This was a tragic setback, particularly because his cousin and successor, Prince Milan, was utterly incapable of taking his place. Although highly intelligent, Milan had been thoroughly debauched in an unsavory family environment and had become a frivolous and unprincipled neurasthenic.

Thus the first Balkan alliance system disintegrated almost overnight. This became apparent during the Franco-Prussian War, when the Balkan peoples once more had an opportunity to strike without fear of intervention. But by this time united action was out of the question. The Russian ambassador in Constantinople, Count Nicholas Ignatiev, described the state of inter-Balkan relations in 1870 as follows:

> If the Franco-Prussian conflict had started immediately after Sadowa, during the Cretan insurrection, the Greeks and the Serbs probably would not have hesitated to march against the Turks and to accomplish this gathering of the Christian shields which they so often dreamed of and discussed. Undoubtedly the very existence of the Ottoman Empire would have been in question. In 1870 the situation was drastically changed and one did not need to be a prophet to see that the complications of this period would not exercise the same fascination on the minds of the Eastern peoples. . . .[3]

REVOLT IN BOSNIA AND HERZEGOVINA

Despite the apathy and disorganization of the Balkan peoples in 1870, the revolt in Bosnia and Herzegovina only five years later found immediate response and spread from the Adriatic to the Black Sea. The explanation is to be found in the local conditions prevailing in Bosnia-Herzegovina and also in the effect of certain ideologies and foreign propaganda upon the South Slavic people.

Bosnia-Herzegovina, the two westernmost provinces of the Ottoman Empire, were held in a state of semifeudal serfdom by a unique Moslem Serbian landowning class. At the time of the Turkish invasion four centuries earlier, the native Serbian nobility accepted Islam and retained their lands. But the bulk of the population remained Christian, of both Catholic and Orthodox varieties. At the time of the revolt, out of a total population of

1.2 million in the two provinces, 40 per cent were Moslem, 42 per cent Orthodox, and 18 per cent Catholic.

Only a handful of the Moslems were large landowners, the remainder being peasants who were exploited in the same manner as their Christian counterparts. But the Christians were more susceptible to foreign influences and were more dissatisfied with their lot. In practice, though not in law, they were bound to the estates of the Moslem landowners. They had the right to own landed property but the difficulties in the way of acquiring land were so formidable that few were able to surmount them. Peasants paid one third to one half of their crop to the landowner and also one eighth to the tax farmer. The latter also collected petty taxes on animals and on specific produce. In fact, as elsewhere, these tax farmers were a grievous burden because they paid a cash sum for the privilege of collecting the taxes and then proceeded to fleece the peasants mercilessly in order to secure a large return on their investment. It made no difference to them if the crops were poor and the peasants were in difficulty. Indeed, the immediate cause for the 1875 revolt was the crop failure of the previous year and the unrelenting pressure of the tax farmers.

These conditions had existed in Bosnia-Herzegovina for centuries. By themselves they do not explain the wide ramifications of the 1875 uprising. It is necessary to take also into account certain currents of thought and foreign influences. The most important of these were Pan-Serbism, Pan-Slavism, and Hapsburg expansionism.

Pan-Serbism persisted despite the assassination of Prince Michael. It is true that Milan had little sympathy for revolutionary movements. He looked to Vienna for support and followed the Austrian policy of opposing agitation among the South Slavs under foreign rule. But the popular sentiment for liberation and national unity was too deep-rooted to be banished by disapproval from above. Baron von Kállay, the Austrian diplomatic representative in Belgrade, warned his government in 1873 that "the mistaken notion that Serbia is called upon to play the role of Piedmont among the Slavs of Turkey is so strongly rooted that the Serbs no longer can understand that the Slavs of the different Turkish frontiers should seek aid and protection from any state except Serbia." [4] The following year the Serbian national assembly, or Skupshtina, voiced the national aspiration as follows in its address to the throne: "To direct the scattered forces of our people toward a serious and common action, to reach an understanding with and to draw closer to our fellow peoples who have the same objectives, the same interests, and the same dangers, that is the road on which the national Skupshtina ardently wishes to see always its illustrious sovereign." [5] Thus Pan-Serb agitation continued despite the opposition of Milan. There can be little doubt that it had significant influence on the unredeemed brothers across the frontier in Bosnia-Herzegovina.

Pan-Slavism was also a major factor in Balkan affairs during these years. Its origins go back to the Slavophil cultural movement which stressed the intrinsic value of Russian as against Western European culture. Political overtones soon appeared and Slavophilism gradually was transformed into Pan-Slavism. The emphasis now was on the unity of all Slavs under the aegis of Russia. In 1858 the Slavic Welfare Society was established in Moscow, where a Slavic Ethnographic Congress was held in 1867. The cause was also furthered by the extremely popular books published by two prominent Pan-Slav leaders, General Rotislav Fadeev (*Opinion on the Eastern Question,* 1870) and Nicholas Danilevski (*Russia and Europe,* 1871). The general thesis advanced was that the Slavs were young and vigorous in contrast to the decadent Western Europeans, and that with the aid of Russia they should free themselves from Turkish and Austrian domination and unite in a great confederation of which Russia would be the leader and Constantinople the capital.

Of particular importance for the Balkans was the well-known Pan-Slav diplomat, Count Nicholas Ignatiev, who represented Russia at Constantinople between 1864 and 1877. Ignatiev believed firmly in the principle of Slavic unity, which was to take the form of common action against the arch enemy, Austria-Hungary. "The Austrian and Turkish Slavs must be our allies, the weapons of our policy against the Germans." These views, it should be noted, were quite different from those of Ignatiev's superiors in St. Petersburg. The contrast was particularly noticeable regarding the future of Bosnia-Herzegovina. The Russian foreign minister, Prince Alexander Gorchakov, was of the opinion that "the Turkish Slavs can be made happy at the hands of the Government of Vienna, that Russian interests will not suffer from the annexation of Bosnia and Herzegovina by Austria." Ignatiev, on the other hand, considered it preferable to "postpone all thoughts of solving the Eastern Question, of liberating Bosnia and Herzegovina from Turkish domination, rather than surrender these provinces to Austro-Hungarian rule and sacrifice the future of the Serbian nation." [6] Being the person that he was, Ignatiev had no compunction about working toward his Pan-Slav goal despite the official policy laid down by his superiors in Petrograd.

It is impossible to estimate how much influence Pan-Slav doctrines had on the Balkan peoples. A French expert reported in 1876: "I have visited the Turkish Empire several times. I have had occasion to see Slavic, Serbian, Montenegrin and Bulgarian patriots on the Danube or on the Adriatic. I always found them very dissatisfied with the Ottoman regime but determined not to substitute Russian domination for it." [7] This and other evidence of a similar nature suggest that the "Mother Russia" approach of the Pan-Slavs was not too popular in the Balkans. On the other hand, Pan-Slavism cannot be ignored, especially during the thirteen years when Ignatiev was in Constantinople. He was undoubtedly the best-informed ambassador in the Balkan Peninsula, and, after 1870, he was so influential in Turkish government circles that he became known as the vice-sultan.

The Pan-Serbs and the Pan-Slavs were not alone responsible for the 1875 crisis. Certain elements in Austria-Hungary also were involved. It is true that only a few years earlier Count Julius Andrassy, the Hapsburg foreign minister, had promised his Russian counterpart, Prince Alexander Gorchakov, that Austria would refrain from intervening in Balkan affairs. This commitment accorded with Andrassy's personal inclination as a Magyar. The Slavs already constituted the largest ethnic bloc in the Hapsburg Empire and he did not wish to increase their preponderance by annexing any part of European Turkey. On the other hand, he was determined that Serbia should not take over Bosnia-Herzegovina and he was ready to have Austria take over the two provinces herself rather than see them absorbed in a large South Slav state.

Certain groups in Austria-Hungary disagreed with Andrassy and favored a more aggressive policy. Many South Slavs who were already under Hapsburg rule wished to include all their fellow Slavs in the empire, which was then to be transformed from a dual Austro-Hungarian state into a triune Austrian-Hungarian-Slavic state. But the most influential exponents of expansion into the Balkans were the military men. Their argument was that possession of Bosnia-Herzegovina was essential for the defense of Dalmatia, the narrow province stretching down the length of the Adriatic coast. These military leaders persuaded Emperor Francis Joseph to spend a month traveling in Dalmatia in the spring of 1875. During his journey the emperor received many petitions from the Christians of Bosnia-Herzegovina complaining of Turkish oppression and asking him for protection. The avowed object of the trip was to stimulate unrest in the Turkish provinces and in this it was successful. Francis Joseph's tour was to a considerable degree responsible for the conflagration that began in Herzegovina in July, 1875. The emperor, on his part, was convinced by the end of his tour that the occupation of Bosnia-Herzegovina could not be long delayed. In fact, orders were issued to the imperial forces in Dalmatia to be prepared for a march across the frontier.

We may conclude that several factors explain the outbreak and the course of the revolt in Bosnia-Herzegovina. In the background were the centuries-old religious conflict and economic oppression. A more immediate impulse was provided by the extortionate tax farmers and by Francis Joseph's tour in Dalmatia. Once the revolt began, it was sustained by Austrian and Russian officials, who sought to exploit it for their own purposes. Hapsburg officials in Dalmatia, many of whom were Serbo-Croats by race, gave aid and comfort to the rebels and provided asylum for the refugees. Similarly, the Russian consul in Ragusa, the ardent Pan-Slav Alexander Ionin, frankly admitted: "I did not create the situation but I profited by it. It began as a small stream, which might have been lost for want of direction; so I put up a stone here, and a stone there, and kept the water together." [8]

FAILURE OF MEDIATION

In mid-July, 1875, Andrassy and Gorchakov received reports that the Christian peasants of Herzegovina had risen in revolt. Neither statesman was pleased by the news. Both were anxious to preserve the *Dreikaiserbund* and both knew that trouble in the Balkans could easily create a rift between their countries. For this reason they took the initiative, together with their partner, Bismarck, in dealing with the disturbance. They persuaded the Turks to send a commissioner to Herzegovina to investigate the situation and at the same time they instructed their consuls to attempt mediation. These efforts came to nothing. The Turks were lavish with promises of reform but the rebels were not impressed by promises that had always proved valueless in the past. They demanded either autonomy under a Christian prince or occupation by foreign powers until their grievances had been redressed. So the insurrection continued and it spread rapidly throughout Herzegovina and into Bosnia.

Andrassy now prepared a reform program which provided for complete religious freedom, abolition of tax farming, agrarian improvements, a guarantee that provincial revenues should be spent on provincial needs, and the establishment of a mixed Moslem-Christian commission to supervise the working of these reforms. This Andrassy Note, as it was called, was approved by the other powers and accepted by the Turks early in February, 1876. But the rebels again frustrated the attempt at mediation. They rejected the concessions on the ground that they were useless without a firm guarantee by the powers.

Meanwhile the fighting had become more widespread and savage. By March, 1876, approximately 156,000 refugees from Bosnia and Herzegovina had crossed the frontiers into Serbia, Montenegro, and Austria-Hungary. Public opinion in Serbia and Montenegro was demanding intervention in behalf of the unfortunate fellow Slavs. Prince Milan in Belgrade and Prince Nicholas in Cetinje were both anxious to keep the peace. They were not prepared for serious campaigning and they had received strong warnings from Vienna and St. Petersburg to remain neutral. But the popular clamor was becoming so insistent that there was danger of a general Balkan conflagration.

Faced with this critical situation, the foreign ministers of the *Dreikaiserbund* met in Berlin in May, 1876. They prepared a new reform program, the so-called Berlin Memorandum, which was an extension of the earlier Andrassy Note. The Turkish government was to provide funds to settle the refugees in their homes, the Christians were to retain their arms for the time being, and the consuls of the powers were to supervise the application of the reforms and the repatriation of the refugees. The Memorandum was submitted to the French, Italian, and British governments for approval. The first two sent positive replies. But the British refused to follow the others, and in doing so they ended the possibility of an early and peaceful settlement of the crisis.

To understand the British action it is necessary to recall that a Conservative government under Disraeli had come to power in 1874. Disraeli had long criticized the "splendid isolation" policy of his predecessor Gladstone. At the time when Prussia was overwhelming the Second French Empire he had delivered a famous speech warning Parliament of the far-reaching repercussions of the war.

> This war represents the German Revolution, a greater political event than the French Revolution of last century. . . . Not a single principle in the management of our foreign affairs, accepted by all statesmen for guidance up to six months ago, any longer exists. There is not a diplomatic tradition which has not been swept away. You have a new world, new influences at work, new and unknown objects and dangers with which to cope. . . . The balance of power has been entirely destroyed, and the country which suffers most, and feels the effects of this great change most, is England.[9]

Soon after assuming office, Disraeli demonstrated the new spirit behind British foreign policy. In 1875 he purchased the Suez Canal shares of the khedive of Egypt. The following year he arranged a series of magnificent celebrations in India, culminating in the proclamation of Queen Victoria as Empress of India. It was in keeping, then, that Disraeli should bristle when the *Dreikaiserbund* confronted him with the Berlin Memorandum. He objected to specific provisions, but above all he balked at the highhanded manner in which the Memorandum had been handled. It had been prepared without Britain's being consulted and now it was presented for approval with the request for a reply in two days. Disraeli sarcastically observed that Britain was being treated as though she were Montenegro or Bosnia. This he refused to tolerate, and he rejected the proferred Memorandum.

Disraeli's action proved a decisive turning point in the development of the crisis. During the same month of May events of far-reaching significance were occurring in the Balkans. On May 10 the Turkish reformer, Midhat Pasha, assumed office in Constantinople. On May 30 Abdul Aziz was deposed in favor of Murad V. And in the same month the Bulgarians rose in revolt and were immediately suppressed with barbarous brutality by Turkish irregular troops. We shall see that the "Bulgarian Horrors," as they were called at the time, aroused a wave of indignation in Europe and helped to magnify a Balkan disturbance into a European crisis. It was at this critical juncture that Disraeli rejected the Berlin Memorandum and temporarily disrupted the efforts at collective mediation.

WAR IN THE BALKANS

While the struggle raged on in Bosnia-Herzegovina, Milan and Nicholas were slowly giving way to the growing clamor for war. On August 16, 1875, elections were held in Serbia. The opposition Liberal party headed by Yovan Ristich won a substantial victory over the Conservatives. This represented a popular vote in favor of war. "I regret to have to report to Your Lordship," wrote the British consul in Belgrade, "that the affairs of Servia have assumed a much more critical aspect. . . . Whenever a decided advocate of a Revolutionary War against Turkey was confronted by a doubtful candidate, the preference was given by the electors to the former one. . . ." [10]

Milan fought hard to restrain his bellicose subjects. A coalition cabinet was formed, and when it showed signs of yielding to the popular clamor he summarily dismissed it. The succeeding ministry failed to stand more firmly. "I find very little difference amongst public men here, whether Radical or Conservative," the British consul reported; "of whatever shade of opinion, all are equally imbued with the desire to see Servian aggrandizement accomplished. . . ." [11] Milan's insistence on neutrality made him increasingly unpopular in the country. Hostile demonstrations convinced him that if he did not accept war he would face revolution. Furthermore, the Russian consul, who was an ardent Pan-Slav, officially transmitted his government's demands for peace but unofficially advised Milan to go to war. Finally, on May 5, 1876, Milan gave way and accepted a new ministry including Ristich.

Ristich was by no means an irresponsible firebrand. He was fully aware of Serbia's limited resources and of the real possibility of defeat. But he calculated that the combination of Pan-Slav pressure and Russian interests in the Balkans would force the tsar eventually to wage war on Turkey. His calculation proved correct, but he failed to foresee the diplomatic difficulties that Russia would have to overcome before being allowed to take up arms. He did not anticipate that Russia would be obliged to concede Bosnia-Herzegovina to Austria-Hungary, and that Serbia consequently was about to undertake a futile struggle irrespective of the outcome of battle.

Not being able to foresee these complexities of great-power diplomacy, Ristich finally decided to risk intervention. On June 30, 1876, Milan proclaimed war against Turkey. He was immediately followed by Nicholas of Montenegro. The two rulers were rivals for the leadership of the South Slavs; hence one could not remain inactive after the other had entered the fray. So Nicholas also declared war, and on July 2, 1876, his troops invaded Herzegovina while the Serbs crossed over into Bosnia.

Ristich made every effort to win the support of Rumania and Greece and thus to present a united Balkan front against the Turks. He sent representatives to Bucharest and Athens and made repeated appeals. But the Rumanians and the Greeks had no interests directly involved in Bosnia-Herzegovina and refused to abandon their neutrality. The British consul in Belgrade sent a report which threw revealing light on the extent to which Michael's Balkan alliance system had disintegrated by this time.

My Greek Colleague has often spoken to me of the way in which the Servians had kept aloof from all participation during the Cretan Insurrection and he has frequently repeated to me that the lesson of 1867 [in Crete] has not been lost on his Government, which had no reason to disturb their good relations with the Porte, and would certainly discourage by every means, any disturbance in Turkish Provinces largely inhabited by Greeks, unless they saw first the Slavs fairly committed and the conflagration assuming a general character and one presenting a reasonable chance of success.[12]

Despite the lack of allies, the Serbians and Montenegrins began the war with wild enthusiasm. "The idea which animates everyone," wrote the Rumanian representative in Belgrade, "is to free from Turkish domination their Yugoslav brothers inhabiting the Balkan Peninsula. Their aim is re-union, temporarily under two sceptres and eventually under one. . . . This is a war to the death between the South Slavs and the Turks. It is a war of race and of religion." [13] But the Turks were also excited and determined. More volunteers flocked into Constantinople than the army could use. They, too, regarded the war as one of "race and religion." The outcome of the struggle was a crushing defeat for the Serbs. Not only did they receive no aid from the Greeks and the Rumanians, but the Montenegrins insisted on fighting only in Herzegovina, where the Turkish forces were negligible. Thus the Montenegrins were able to advance some distance, but on the decisive Bosnian front the Serbs were defeated with heavy losses. Before the fighting ended Serbia mobilized one sixth of her total population, of which one tenth were killed or wounded.

CONSTANTINOPLE CONFERENCE

The spreading of the war in the Balkans increased the complexity of the problem facing the great powers. No longer was it merely a question of arranging a satisfactory settlement in Bosnia-Herzegovina. Now Serbia and Montenegro were belligerents, while in Bulgaria the large-scale atrocities had so aroused European public opinion that the restoration of Turkish rule no longer was feasible. The English were particularly sensitive to the "Bulgarian Horrors" because they had fought the Crimean War to preserve the Ottoman Empire. In June, 1876, the first reports began to reach England of the depredations of the bashi-bazouks, the Turkish irregulars who had destroyed dozens of villages and massacred rebels and innocent alike. Disraeli at first summarily rejected the charges because his diplomatic representatives were slow in sending reports. But a mass of detailed information began pouring in from various trustworthy sources, including British correspondents, the American consul-general, Eugene Schuyler, President George Washburn of Robert College, and several American missionaries. It became clear that well over ten thousand Bulgarians had been massacred and several dozen villages destroyed.

A great storm of moral indignation swept over England. The high point was Gladstone's passionate indictment of Turkish rule in his pamphlet, "Bulgarian Horrors and the Question of the East," of which it is said fifty thousand copies were sold in a few days. Gladstone did not call for outright partitioning of European Turkey. Rather, he demanded autonomy for the subject Christians so that they might be freed from the oppression of Turkish administrators and soldiers. "Let the Turks now carry away their abuses in the only possible manner, namely by carrying off themselves. Their Zaptiehs and their Mudirs, their Bimbashis and their Yuzbachis, their Kaimakams and their Pashas, one and all, bag and baggage, shall, I hope, clear out from the province they have desolated and profaned." [14]

So great was the furor that one of the cabinet members, Lord Salisbury, wrote to Disraeli that concessions would have to be made to public opinion.

It is clear enough that the traditional Palmerstonian policy is at an end. We have not the power, even if we have the wish, to give back any of the revolted districts to the *discretionary* government of the Porte. . . . I should like to submit for your consideration whether the opportunity should not be taken to exact some security for the good government of the Christians generally throughout the Turkish Empire. The Govt. of 1856 was satisfied with promises. . . . We must have something more than promises. . . . [15]

This statement is quite significant. It suggested the possibility of fundamental changes in European Turkey. Russia could be counted on to press for "something more than promises." Bismarck from the beginning had urged wholesale partitioning of the Ottoman Empire as a means of satisfying both the Balkan peoples and the great powers. But Disraeli refused to consider any drastic measures. He was convinced that the agitation in England was a momentary aberration and that the country soon would come to its senses. Also, he was determined, for reasons of prestige, to pursue an independent policy rather than follow behind the *Dreikaiserbund*. The result was that now, as in the time of the Crimean War, Britain emerged as the defender of the Ottoman Empire. The Balkan crisis became more and more a duel between Britain, the supporter of the *status quo,* and Russia, the self-appointed champion of Balkan liberation.

The remainder of the year 1876 was characterized by intense diplomatic activity. The most important consequences were the Reichstadt Agreement reached by Russia and Austria on July 8, the Russian ultimatum to Turkey which resulted in an armistice on October 31, and the international conference held in Constantinople in December, 1876, and January, 1877.

The background of the Reichstadt Agreement was the mounting Pan-Slav agitation in Russia for assistance to the embattled Balkan Slavs. This agitation reached such proportions that the Russian diplomats had to consider the possibility of intervention even against the wishes of the government. In that eventuality a prior agreement with Austria would be essential. Otherwise the Russian army would run the risk of being ordered out of the Balkans, as had happened during the Crimean War. So Andrassy and Gorchakov met at Reichstadt and agreed that the prewar *status quo* should be restored if Serbia and Montenegro were defeated. But if the two Balkan states were victorious, Austria and Russia were to cooperate to regulate the territorial changes. They agreed that no large Slavic state should be set up in the Balkans, but misunderstanding existed from the start regarding the details of the new frontiers. Gorchakov understood that in case of victory Serbia and Montenegro would annex the larger part of Bosnia-Herzegovina and that Austria would receive only a small part of Bosnia. Andrassy, on the other hand, thought that the larger part of Bosnia-Herzegovina would fall to the Hapsburg Empire. This misunderstanding was to cause difficulties between the two powers before the crisis was resolved.

Meanwhile, it was the Turks who were winning over the Serbs and drawing closer to Belgrade. The Pan-Slavs redoubled their agitation and whipped up popular indignation in Russia. Finally, the tsar took action and dispatched a forty-eight-hour ultimatum to Constantinople demanding an armistice of six weeks for the Serbs. The Turks yielded and accepted the armistice on October 31, 1876. This was the last opportunity for a peaceful settlement. The powers agreed to send representatives to a conference in Constantinople to work out terms.

The conference opened on December 12. The British delegate was Lord Salisbury, one of the ministers who had less fear of Russia and more sympathy for the Balkan Christians than did Disraeli. Salisbury got along well with Ignatiev and the conference quickly reached a compromise agreement. The main provisions were that Bulgaria should be divided into an eastern and western province, Bosnia-Herzegovina united into one province, and each of the three provinces to have a considerable degree of autonomy, including a provincial assembly and a local police force. Also, Serbia was to lose no territory and Montenegro was to be allowed to keep the areas she had overrun in Herzegovina and northern Albania.

These terms were presented as the "irreducible minimum" which the powers would accept. The Turks nevertheless rejected them. This was the celebrated occasion, described in the last chapter, when the sultan promulgated the constitution which provided for reforms and which stipulated that Ottoman territory was inalienable. Under the circumstances the work of the conference became irrelevant and the delegates were so informed. The latter tried to salvage something from the wreckage by reducing their demands from the original "irreducible minimum" to what they now described as the "quintessence." [16] But the Turks remained adamant in their refusal to grant concessions to the rebels.

The Turks took such a strong stand because they knew they had strong popular backing. Public opinion was aroused and articulate in Constantinople as well as in London and St. Petersburg. Also, there is little doubt that the Turks were encouraged to stand firm by the British ambassador, Sir Henry Elliot, who effectively undermined Lord Salisbury in Constantinople. Elliot considered the terms laid down by the conference as "impossible demands." He criticized them severely to his government and apparently he did not hide his views from the Turks. Salisbury asked that Elliot be removed from Constantinople. The request was denied because both Disraeli and Foreign Minister Lord Derby shared Elliot's views. In fact, Lord Derby had informed the Turkish ambassador the day before the conference opened that England would not "assent to, or assist in coercive measures against Turkey." [17] Likewise, Disraeli was criticizing Salisbury severely for conceding too much to Ignatiev. "Sal. seems most prejudiced," he wrote to Lord Derby on December 30, "and not to be aware, that his principal object, in being sent to Const., is to keep the Russians out of Turkey, not to create an ideal existence for Turkish Xtians. He is more Russian than Ignatieff. . . ." [18] The Turks were aware of these views in high places in England and therefore expected substantial assistance in case of war with Russia. Under these circumstances they naturally refused to make serious concessions.

Russia had anticipated the failure of the Constantinople Conference and had opened negotiations with Austria beforehand in order to clear the way for action against Turkey. Russia had no choice in this matter because she could not wage a campaign in the Balkans without the consent of Austria. On January 15, 1877, the two powers signed the so-called Budapest Convention. This provided that if the Constantinople Conference failed and war ensued between Russia and Turkey, Austria would remain benevolently neutral and in return could annex Bosnia-Herzegovina. Russia was to regain the Bessarabian area lost in 1856. Like the Reichstadt Agreement, this convention stipulated that no large state should be created in the Balkans.

These terms meant that in case of war Russia would do the fighting and Austria would derive most of the advantage. Russia therefore made a final effort for a peaceful settlement. She persuaded the powers to sign the London Convention (March 31, 1877), which merely asked Turkey to introduce those reforms which she herself had already proposed. The powers were to watch the operation of the reforms, and if conditions remained unsatisfactory they reserved the right "to declare that such a state of things would be incompatible with their interests and those of Europe in general." The "irreducible minimum" had been reduced virtually to the vanishing point. But the Turks felt themselves in a strong position and rejected the proposal on the grounds that it violated the Treaty of Paris. Finally, on April 24, 1877, after nearly two years of futile negotiations, Russia declared war upon Turkey.

RUSSO-TURKISH WAR

Russia began the war against Turkey under exceptionally favorable diplomatic circumstances. Both Austria and Germany were benevolently neutral while France and Italy were noncommittal and reserved. This left only Britain, but that country was distinctly unfriendly. Disraeli was convinced that the Russians would be in Constantinople in nine weeks and that "it would take nearly that time for us to reach and entrench ourselves in the Dardanelles." [19] Accordingly, he proposed that Britain should occupy Gallipoli for the duration of the war. The cabinet rejected the proposal, fearing that it would lead to an alliance with Turkey and to speedy involvement in the war. Instead, a note was issued warning Russia against attacking or occupying Constantinople, the Straits, the Suez Canal, or Egypt.

Meanwhile, the Russians were making spectacular progress into the Balkans. They had traversed Rumania at a leisurely pace, not crossing the Danube until June 23. But then they pushed rapidly southward to the Balkan Mountains. On June 19 they occupied the Shipka Pass, opening the way to southern Bulgaria. The further the Russians advanced the higher the tension mounted in Britain. Bismarck was gravely concerned with the danger of a general conflagration and again advanced his favorite scheme for a wholesale partition of the Ottoman Empire. But Disraeli distrusted the German chancellor and refused to consider his proposal. Instead, he persuaded his cabinet to vote on July 21 that war should be declared if the Russians occupied Constantinople and did not make arrangements to retire immediately.

The gathering tension subsided for some time when the Russians met an unexpected reverse at Plevna, a Turkish fortress located close to the Russian bridge over the Danube. The Russians made repeated attempts to take the fortress but were repulsed with heavy losses. Finally, General Todleben, the hero of Sebastopol, arrived upon the scene and established a complete blockade. But a regular siege required time, and in the meanwhile the Russian wings could not advance farther. This stalemate allowed the summer of 1877 to pass without incident.

The unexpected reversal in Russian fortunes produced an amusing shift in the relations between Russia and the Balkan states. When the Russians were forging ahead all the Balkan countries eagerly offered their services in order to be eligible for a share of the booty. Russia rejected the offers because she assumed she would not need assistance and because she feared that, if all the Balkan peoples intervened, the war would take on the appearance of a general Balkan revolutionary movement and would antagonize Britain and Austria-Hungary. Then, after the setback at Plevna, the Russians urged the Balkan states to enter the war at once. But the latter now held back, discouraged by the unexpected resistance of the Turkish forces. Only Rumania entered, and that country, it should be noted, had already been half involved because its territory was being used by the Russians for transit purposes. In taking up arms the Rumanians had no illusions regarding the future. They were quite aware that a victorious Russia would demand the cession of southern Bessarabia lost in 1856. But they calculated that by intervening they would get some compensation elsewhere. And besides, intervention for them was not as risky as for the other Balkan states located to the south of the Danube.

Plevna finally was starved out and forced to surrender on December 10. The Russians resumed their advance and by January 4, 1878, reached Sofia. The Turks appealed to England to mediate. The tsar refused mediation and referred the Turks to the Russian commander in the field. Armistice negotiations began on January 19. By that time the Turkish defenses were crumbling. Reports reached London that Adrianople could not be held and that the road to Constantinople was wide open. Disraeli again fumed and stormed while Queen Victoria swamped him with a deluge of almost hysterical letters demanding immediate action. "There is not a moment to be lost or the whole of our policy of centuries, of our honour as a great European Power, will have received an irreparable blow! . . . Oh, if the Queen were a man, she would like to go and give those Russians, whose word one cannot believe, such a beating! We shall never be friends again till we have it out. This the Queen feels sure of." Even Disraeli was moved to remark, "It is something to serve such a sovereign." [20]

Disraeli tried to prod the Austrians to mobilize but they were committed by the Budapest Convention and refused to move unless the Russians actually violated its provisions. Disraeli finally persuaded the cabinet on January 23 to order the fleet to Constantinople, though the foreign minister, Lord Derby, resigned in protest. Then, in anticlimactic fashion, the order was recalled upon the receipt of reassuring reports, which later proved to be completely erroneous.

Meanwhile the Turks and Russians concluded an armistice agreement on January 31. The terms provided that the Russian forces should occupy Turkish territory almost to the outskirts of Constantinople. The British were not informed of this provision, so that war fever mounted once more as the Russians drew closer to the capital. By this time the "Bulgarian Horrors" and the bashi-bazouks had been forgotten, and, instead, the crowds in England enthusiastically sang,

> We don't want to fight,
> But, by Jingo! if we do,
> We've got the ships,
> We've got the men,
> We've got the money too!

On February 12 Disraeli again ordered the fleet to steam to Constantinople. This time the orders were carried out, though, on the request of the sultan, the ships anchored on the Asiatic side of the Sea of Marmora. Thus Russian soldiers were quartered at San Stefano, ten miles from Constantinople, while British warships rode at anchor across the Straits less than fifty miles away. Peace hung in the balance in this precarious manner until finally the Turks and the Russians signed the Treaty of San Stefano on March 3, 1878.

TREATY OF SAN STEFANO

The Treaty of San Stefano provided that Bosnia-Herzegovina be granted the reforms proposed by the Constantinople Conference, though with some modifications. Serbia and Montenegro were to be made independent and somewhat enlarged. Rumania was also granted full independence and was to receive part of the Dobruja in return for southern Bessarabia, which went to Russia. Russia was to acquire, in lieu of the greater part of the financial indemnity which she claimed, Batum, Kars, Ardahan, and Bayazid in eastern Asia Minor. Bulgaria was to be established as an autonomous principality with an elected prince. The most significant provision of the treaty had to do with the territorial extent of the new principality. With the exception of Constantinople, Adrianople, and Saloniki, it included virtually all the territory between the Danube in the north, the Black Sea in the east, the Aegean Sea in the south, and Lake Ohrid and beyond in the west. Thus a greater Bulgaria was created and European Turkey virtually annihilated.

Leaving aside for the moment the volcanic question of Macedonian ethnology, it is clear that from the diplomatic viewpoint the San Stefano Treaty was bound to arouse opposition in all quarters. Austria complained with justification that the new Bulgarian principality violated the stipulation in the Budapest Treaty that no large Balkan state was to be established. Disraeli was convinced that the principality would be merely a Russian outpost and that it would give Russia access to the Aegean and virtual control over Constantinople. He also feared that Russia's acquisitions in Asia Minor would culminate eventually in a Russian base on the Gulf of Alexandretta.

Both the Greeks and the Serbs also were opposed to San Stefano. The Greeks had attempted to enter the war after the fall of Plevna but, being vulnerable to sea power, they were forced to remain neutral by the threat of a British blockade. Naturally they were bitter when the war ended with Bulgaria becoming the largest state in the Balkans while they received nothing. The Serbs found San Stefano equally distasteful. They had re-entered the war two days after the surrender of Plevna. Austria warned them to strike south toward Macedonia rather than west into Bosnia. They heeded the warning and occupied a considerable area while the Turks were fleeing before the Russians. But now all this territory was to be incorporated in the Bulgarian principality. The Serbians protested to St. Petersburg, but were informed bluntly that Russia's interests came first, Bulgaria's second, and Serbia's last. The Belgrade government naturally was indignant and decided to hold the land it occupied, even to the point of resisting the Russians by force.

The Russians undoubtedly expected this opposition. Probably they took more than they expected to keep in order to have some surplus for bargaining. They had long recognized the right of the other powers to pass upon such articles as infringed upon the 1856 settlement. They now agreed to attend a congress in Berlin to reconsider these articles. But they did not anticipate the degree to which San Stefano would be mutilated before a settlement could be arranged that was satisfactory to all the great powers.

Before the congress met, much diplomatic activity occurred. Britain and Russia tried to win the support of Austria-Hungary but both failed to pin down the evasive Andrassy. So the new British foreign minister, Lord Salisbury, approached the Russians directly for a preliminary agreement before the congress. The Russians were ready to compromise because their army was in no condition for more fighting and the revolutionary movement at home was becoming serious. On May 30 the two powers signed an agreement covering the general lines of settlement. The most important modification of San Stefano was the splitting of Bulgaria into two parts divided by the Balkan Mountains. The Austrians were now afraid that they would be isolated at the congress; hence on June 6 they also concluded an agreement with the British. They undertook to support Britain on various points concerning Bulgaria, and the British in turn were to back any proposal regarding Bosnia-Herzegovina that Austria might present. After these preliminaries the congress convened at Berlin on June 13.

TREATY OF BERLIN

An impressive galaxy of diplomats gathered in Berlin to reconsider the San Stefano Treaty. Bismarck was elected president in accordance with customary practice. By this time he had lost some of his old vigor, and according to his own account he downed a tumbler of port every few hours to keep going. Yet he dominated the congress, and time and again his energy and decisiveness kept it from breaking up. Disraeli was another outstanding personality. He suffered from asthma and gout and hobbled around on a stick. But Bismarck was sufficiently impressed by him to remark, "The old Jew, he is the man." Disraeli's associates were on tenterhooks lest he address the congress in his barbarous French. They coped with the delicate situation by informing him that the entire gathering eagerly waited to hear a speech from "the greatest living master of English oratory." No one ever quite knew whether Disraeli took the hint or accepted the compliment. The Russian foreign minister, Prince Gorchakov, could not resist attending, though he was eighty and had to be carried upstairs to the chamber. He did not contribute much to the work of the congress with his artificial graces, inordinate vanity, and passion for bon mots.

In addition to these and other diplomats representing the great powers, there were delegates from Turkey and from the Balkan states. The latter were at least politely heard before being ignored. But the Turks were both ignored and insulted. "If you think the Congress has met for Turkey," Bismarck bluntly told them, "disabuse yourselves. San Stefano would have remained unaltered, if it had not touched certain European interests." [21] Even the British, who supposedly were the champions of the Turks, gave them orders and suffered no back talk. The British ambassador in Constantinople, Sir Henry Layard, assured Salisbury that he had made certain of the cooperation of the chief Turkish delegate, Caratheodory Pasha. "I have given Caratheodory to understand that if I find him playing false I will leave no stone unturned to break his neck, and as he knows I can do it, it is to his interest to keep well with us." [22]

The congress was not a meaningless rubber-stamp affair. It is true that agreements had been reached beforehand but these were of a general nature. On several occasions the congress almost foundered over specific issues, such as the amount of territory that Russia should obtain in eastern Asia Minor and the degree of control that Turkey should keep over the southern Bulgarian province. Finally satisfactory terms were arranged and the treaty signed on July 13, 1878.

The essential difference between the Treaty of Berlin and that of San Stefano has to do with Bulgaria. The large autonomous principality originally established now was divided into three parts: Bulgaria proper, north of the Balkan Mountains, to be autonomous with its own elected prince, though tributary to Constantinople; Eastern Rumelia, south of the Balkan Mountains, to be under a Christian governor appointed by Constantinople but approved by the powers; and Macedonia, which was to remain under direct Turkish administration. Thus the Bulgaria of Berlin was only one third that of San Stefano and was completely cut off from the Aegean.

Serbia and Montenegro were declared independent and given additional territory, though not as much as stipulated at San Stefano. Rumania also became independent and acquired part of the Dobruja, though, as expected, she was forced to surrender southern Bessarabia to Russia. Bosnia and Herzegovina, where the crisis originated, were handed over to Austria to occupy and administer though not to annex. Austria was also authorized to garrison the strategic Sanjak of Novi Bazar located between Serbia and Montenegro. This provision was designed to forestall a development that Austria always feared—a large, united Yugoslav state that might attract the South Slavs under Hapsburg rule. Greece claimed Crete, Thessaly, Epirus, and a part of Macedonia, but received nothing. The powers had so many other interests to promote that they evaded the Greek case by inviting the Turkish government to come to terms with Greece concerning the rectification of frontiers. Bismarck remarked cynically that with thousands of years of history behind them the Greeks could afford to wait a few more to fulfill their ambitions.

Russia received Batum, Kars, and Ardahan in addition to southern Bessarabia. The British had prepared for this Russian advance in Asia Minor by concluding earlier, on June 4, the Cyprus Convention with the Turks. This committed the British to resist any further Russian expansion in Asia Minor; in return they were to occupy and administer the island of Cyprus for as long as the Russians retained Kars and Batum. When the French demurred at this new British foothold in the eastern Mediterranean, Bismarck told them, "Why do you not go to Carthage?"—a hint that the French acted upon three years later by occupying Tunis.[23]

This Berlin settlement aroused strong reactions from the outset. Upon returning to London Disraeli boasted that he brought with him "Peace with Honor." The phrase was adopted and repeated by his admirers. But many at the time bitterly criticized "the peace that passeth all understanding and the honour that is common among thieves." [24]

Any estimate of the Berlin Treaty depends in the final analysis upon one's viewpoint. If it is considered purely within the context of European diplomacy, then Disraeli's boast is fully justified. The Berlin Treaty was indeed a resounding triumph for Britain. Russia had fought a costly war, but other powers won most of the prizes. Britain now was entrenched in Cyprus, and Austria in Bosnia, Herzegovina, and the Sanjak. Bulgaria was cut down and partitioned and most of European Turkey was preserved. Russia naturally was humiliated and indignant, and she turned against her *Dreikaiserbund* partners for failing to support her. This breakup of the *Dreikaiserbund* represented another great victory for Britain. She no longer was faced with the massive coalition of the three eastern empires that hitherto had dominated the Continent. "Next to making a tolerable settlement for the Porte," Disraeli justifiably boasted a few years later, "our great object was to break up and permanently prevent the alliance of the three Empires, and I maintain there never was a great diplomatic result more completely effected." [25]

If the peace settlement is considered from the Balkan viewpoint, then one must emphasize the disregard of ethnic and nationalist considerations. Disraeli from the beginning made it clear that he was interested in checking Russia, and not, as he put it, in creating "an ideal existence for Turkish Xtians." As a result, every one of the Balkan peoples was left thoroughly dissatisfied. The Bulgarians were embittered by the partition of their country, the Serbians by the advance of Austria into Bosnia-Herzegovina, the Rumanians by the loss of southern Bessarabia, and the Greeks by their failure to obtain any territorial compensation. This situation was particularly unfortunate because it provoked dissension and strife among the Balkan peoples. The establishment of the exarchate church had pitted Greek against Bulgar in Macedonia. Now, with Bosnia-Herzegovina in the hands of the Austrians, the Serbs also were forced to turn southward to Macedonia. The result was a suicidal three-cornered conflict which poisoned inter-Balkan relations and fomented anarchy and bloodshed in Macedonia until World War I and even later.

For the Balkan peoples, then, the Berlin Treaty meant not peace with honor but rather frustration of national aspirations and future wars. The direct and logical outcome of the Berlin settlement was the Serbian-Bulgarian War of 1885, the Bosnian crisis of 1908, the two Balkan wars of 1912–1913, and the murder of Archduke Francis Ferdinand in 1914.

Part V. Age of Imperialism and Capitalism

22. *Dynamics of Balkan Politics: 1878–1914*

THE FIRST THREE QUARTERS of the nineteenth century constituted the revolutionary age of nationalism during which all the Balkan peoples, with the exception of the Albanians, gained their independence or autonomy. The period from 1878 to 1914 proved to be an equally revolutionary age—the age of imperialism and capitalism which, so far as the everyday life of the Balkan peoples was concerned, had deeper and more far-reaching repercussions than the age of nationalism.

We saw in Chapter 13 that the three most important factors determining the course of events in the Balkans during the age of nationalism were the continued decline of the Ottoman Empire, the awakening of the subject nationalities, and the increasing intervention of the great powers. These factors continued to operate during the years after 1878, but the emphasis shifted from the awakening of the nationalities to the rapidly increasing activity of the great powers. This activity manifested itself not only in the usual diplomatic channels but also, and most dramatically, in the economic realm. During these years at the turn of the century the dynamic and expanding civilization of Western Europe impinged upon the Balkan Peninsula and undermined the latter's self-sufficient natural economy. This traditional economy gave way to a money or capitalist economy, which in turn led to fundamental changes in the social organization and daily life of the Balkan peoples. These manifold changes warrant the use of the term "the age of imperialism and capitalism" for these decades between 1878 and World War I.

It does not follow that other forces at work at this time were no longer of consequence. The state of the Ottoman Empire was still a prime factor, though not quite as central as in the past. The Ottoman Empire after 1878 did not control as much of the Balkans as it did early in the nineteenth century. Also, nothing of great significance occurred within the empire because, as we shall see, Abdul Hamid was the autocratic ruler until 1908 and he tolerated no opposition. Similarly, Balkan nationalism was still a potent force in the peninsula and its influence was to spread into areas hitherto unaffected, such as Albania, Macedonia, and the South Slavic provinces of the Hapsburg Empire.* But this did not represent something new. It was simply the continuation and completion of a movement that had begun a century earlier. By contrast, the impact of the dynamic West upon the Balkan Peninsula was unprecedented in nature and revolutionary in effect. Accordingly, in this chapter we shall examine this new imperialism of the West which was impinging on the Balkan world, as well as the new capitalist order which was developing within the peninsula with a greater disruptive effect than the winning of national independence in the preceding decades.

THE NEW IMPERIALISM

Imperialism has been defined in a recent study as "the rule or control, political or economic, direct or indirect, of one state, nation or people over other similar groups. . . ." [1] Taken in this sense, imperialism obviously has been practiced by the great powers in the Balkans and throughout the Near East for centuries. One can begin with the medieval period, when the Crusaders invaded the Holy Land, and trace imperialist activities down to modern times, when Catherine the Great attempted to win for her grandson an imperial throne in Constantinople, and when Britain acquired Egypt, Cyprus, and the Ionian Islands.

Although imperialism has been a constant factor in Balkan affairs, it is generally agreed that it changed in character decisively at the end of the nineteenth century. It became more dynamic and more pervasive. It produced sharper and more frequent conflicts among the imperialist powers themselves. And it had a far greater impact on the territories subject to its influence, whether in the Balkans or anywhere else in the world. This change in character was sufficiently marked to warrant the use of the term "new imperialism."

The roots of this new imperialism go back to certain economic developments that occurred in Western Europe earlier in the century. During the first three quarters of the nineteenth century Britain was the unchallenged "workshop of the world." The entire globe was an open market for her manufactured goods. This was also the period when free trade was in its heyday and when colonies were regarded as expensive nuisances—as "ripe fruit" that would drop off sooner or later.

This situation changed abruptly during the last quarter of the nineteenth century, when the Continental countries in turn became industrialized. At the same time these countries began to adopt protective tariffs in order to safeguard their "infant industries." Thus the Continental markets were closed to British manufactured goods at the same time that European manufactures

* See Chapters 24, 27, 28.

were beginning to invade British markets overseas and even the British home market itself.

The leading European powers competed with one another not only in selling the output of their factories but also in finding markets for their rapidly accumulating capital. The more capital piled up at home the lower the returns fell and the greater the need for more profitable investment markets abroad. Vast amounts of capital were, in fact, invested in foreign countries, especially by Britain, France, and Germany. Britain, for example, had invested by 1914 4 billion pounds abroad, a sum amounting to one fourth of her total national wealth. By the same date France had invested 45 billion francs, or one sixth of her national wealth. Germany, a late-comer who was using most of her capital for domestic industrial expansion, had invested overseas between 22 and 25 billion marks, or one fifteenth of her national wealth. Thus Europe by 1914 had become the banker as well as the workshop of the world.

The tremendous outpouring of capital and of manufactured goods was inevitably accompanied by a sharp struggle for foreign markets. This in turn led to a race for empire because colonies were considered to be the most secure of all possible markets. In fact, many European statesmen at this time believed that Britain's economic primacy was derived from her vast colonial possessions. So they set out to acquire colonies for their own countries, and this in turn induced the British to prize more highly their own empire and even to add to it when possible. These economic factors leading to expansion gained effectiveness from other sources, particularly the current vogue for social Darwinism, with its doctrines of struggle for existence and survival of the fittest. These led naturally to ideas of race superiority and of the white man's destiny to rule over the "inferior" colored peoples of the earth.

The net result of these economic and intellectual-psychological factors was the greatest land-grab in the history of the world, unequaled even by the conquests of Genghis Khan. The table on page 416 illustrates the fantastic territorial expansion of the Western European states by 1914. It should be noted that well over one half of the colonial possessions listed below were acquired after 1878.

The influence of the dynamic Western European states was not confined to the colonial territories that they owned outright. It also extended to other areas which were economically and militarily weak but which, for one reason or another, were not actually annexed. This was the case with the Ottoman Empire, whose central core remained intact because the great powers could not agree upon the details of partition. But even though the sultan's lands did not suffer dismemberment, they did experience, nevertheless, the disruptive impact of the new imperialism. Both the Ottoman Empire and the new Balkan states were subjected to intensive Western economic penetration, the principal manifestations being government loans, which caused financial

Colonial Empires of the World in 1914

Countries having colonial or non-contiguous territory	Number of colonies, etc.	AREA (SQUARE MILES) Mother country	AREA (SQUARE MILES) Colonies and other non-contiguous territory	POPULATION Mother country	POPULATION Colonies and other non-contiguous territory
United Kingdom	55	120,953	12,043,806	46,052,741	391,582,528
France	29	207,076	4,110,409	39,602,258	62,350,000
Germany	10	208,830	1,230,989	64,925,993	13,074,950
Belgium	1	11,373	910,000	7,571,387	15,000,000
Portugal	8	35,500	804,440	5,960,056	9,680,000
Netherlands	8	12,761	762,863	6,102,399	37,410,000
Italy	4	110,623	591,250	35,238,997	1,396,176
Total	115	707,116	20,453,757	205,453,831	530,493,654

Source: Compiled from *Encyclopedia Americana*, 1943 ed., VII, 297. Statistics concerning the colonies acquired between 1876 and 1900 are given in F. Sternberg, *Capitalism and Socialism on Trial* (New York, 1951), p. 57.

dependency, and railway building, which increased the foreign indebtedness and also led directly to an influx of Western machine-made goods.

Government loans, railway building, and all the other modes of Western economic penetration in the Balkans started as early as the mid-nineteenth century at the time of the Crimean War. But in the late nineteenth century, under the pressure of the new imperialism, this penetration changed significantly in degree and in character. It changed in degree because it became much more forceful and pervasive. Not only British and French but also Italian, Austrian, and especially German financiers appeared on the scene, eager to gain a return on their money in excess of the 2 or 3 per cent procurable at home. They invested their capital in unprecedented amounts, most of it being expended on military establishments and on railways, but some also being used to transform the Balkan scene with roads, ports, docks, tramways, irrigation works, and lighting and power plants. This was a far cry from the beginning of the century, when economic intercourse with the West was virtually limited to foreign ships calling at the seaports.

Western economic penetration changed not only in degree but also in character, the reason being the growing tendency to identify private and national interests abroad. This meant in practice that private investors felt free to call on their governments to protect their foreign investments or to bring pressure to bear to make foreign investments possible. Conversely the European governments encouraged loans to states considered friendly and discouraged loans to states deemed hostile. This development created a much more tense situation because considerations of national prestige now were introduced in a field hitherto regarded as beyond the realm of government concern. The appearance of this new imperialism, according to one authority, transformed the Balkans and the Middle East "from what had been regarded

as a profitable field for investment and speculation into a cockpit of international rivalry." [2]

In the following chapters we shall note the operation and the effect
of the new imperialism in each of the Balkan countries and in Turkey. At
this point a brief over-all survey of railway building and of government loans
will give a general impression of the new imperialism in practice. Railway
building started in the Balkans after the Crimean War, when British interests
built two lines from Constantsa and Varna on the Black Sea to Cernavoda
and Ruschuk respectively, on the Danube. These were only local lines designed to enable the British to tap the commerce of the Danube Valley.

Preparations for large-scale construction began when Sultan Abdul
Aziz in 1868 gave a concession for the building of a main stem to run from
Constantinople through Adrianople, Philippopolis, Sofia, Nish, Sarajevo and
on to the Austrian border to connect with the Austrian southern railways
and so with Vienna. The concession was given to a certain Baron Hirsch,
who was influential with the southern Austrian system. Construction did not
begin till 1872, and by 1875, when the Near Eastern crisis intervened, the
project was far from completed. Only two lines had been built: one from
Saloniki to Üsküb and Mitrovitza, and the other from Constantinople to
Adrianople and Sarambey in Eastern Rumelia, with a branch connecting this
line with Dedeagach on the Aegean.

All these lines ran from the coastal ports into the Balkan interior,
thus giving British commerce an opportunity to penetrate the peninsula. For
this reason the Austrian government was anxious to connect the Balkan railways with its own network. Specifically, it wished to see the Constantinople-
Sarambey and Saloniki-Üsküb lines continued to Nish, whence Serbian lines
could be built to Belgrade and on to Semlin on the Austrian border. For
this reason the Berlin Treaty included provisions requiring Bulgaria and
Serbia to build the necessary connecting links running through their territories. This was done after many delays, and on August 12, 1888, the first
through train rumbled over the tracks from Vienna to Constantinople.

During the following decades numerous proposals were advanced for
additional railway construction. Very few went beyond the planning stage
because of the conflicting political interests that were involved. Several chan-
celleries scrutinized carefully every proposal for new track and did not hesitate to oppose it vigorously if their respective interests were not safeguarded.
A good example was the proposed seventy-mile line connecting Saloniki with
the Greek network to the south. The Turkish government vetoed the proposal, presumably for strategic reasons. As a result, the Greek railways were
kept isolated from the rest of Europe until the eve of World War I.

A more significant example was the rivalry between the Austrian interests that favored a north-south line through Bosnia and Novi Bazar to
Saloniki, and the Serbian-Russian interests that wanted an east-west line
between the Danube and the Adriatic. Proposals for such trans-Balkan lines
were advanced periodically from the 1870's on. But Austria was determined

to prevent Serbia and Russia from gaining access to the Adriatic through an east-west line, while Serbia in turn opposed a north-south line that would compete with her own railways and give Austria free access to the Aegean through purely Turkish territory. The net result was that neither one of these trans-Balkan lines had been even started by the beginning of World War I. Similarly, in Asiatic Turkey the European powers competed with each other for railway contracts, the most spectacular manifestation of this competition being the "Berlin to Baghdad" railway concession granted to German interests in 1903. This concession at once became an international football until 1913–1914, when the great powers adjusted their claims and literally divided Asiatic Turkey into spheres of economic influence.

Government loans were closely related to railway building as a means of Western economic penetration in the Balkans and in the rest of the Near East. Government loans, in fact, were necessitated by the heavy cost of railways as well as of other construction, such as roads and ports. Also, the burgeoning military establishments contributed substantially to the growing indebtedness of the various governments. When the latter turned to the money markets for loans, the reception they received depended largely on political considerations, especially by the turn of the century. Bulgaria provides a good example of the manner in which foreign offices intervened in international financial transactions.

On March 13, 1912, Bulgaria signed an alliance with Serbia which became the cornerstone of the Russian-sponsored Balkan alliance system. Immediately thereafter Bulgaria turned to the Paris market for a substantial loan. An earlier application in 1909 had been turned down, but Bulgaria now had the backing of Russia. "You know," the Russian minister in Paris wrote to his government on June 7, 1912, "he [France's Premier Poincaré] said to me that the French Government is disposed to facilitate the Bulgarian loan in Paris only because the Russian Government declared to it that Bulgaria, after forming a secret agreement with Serbia, had firmly decided to ally itself with the Entente." [3]

Poincaré, who had opposed the original Bulgarian application for a loan, now reversed his position and gave his agreement in principle. But a few weeks later he returned to his earlier opposition because Ferdinand meanwhile had visited Vienna and Berlin, where he was received with conspicuous honors. When the Balkan Wars ended in 1913 Bulgaria again sought a loan on the Paris market. The French government was still opposed, suspecting with justification that Ferdinand was drifting toward the Central Powers. But when Ferdinand received some advances from Vienna banks, the French government became concerned and offered to support a loan if the Radoslavov cabinet were replaced by one less favorable to Germany. Now Germany in turn offered a loan on condition that a tobacco export monopoly be established under her control as security for the loan. France countered by dropping the condition concerning the Radoslavov cabinet, whereupon Germany waived her demand for loan security. Ferdinand finally accepted the German offer in 1914, a step that contributed to his decision the following year to join the Central Powers. Throughout this episode financial considerations were subordinated to political, and the loan was used as a pawn to attain diplomatic objectives.

Under these circumstances the Balkan and Turkish governments borrowed heavily on the European markets. The Balkan states, which had negligible debts in 1878, were all in serious financial difficulties by 1914. In the latter year the Bulgarian public debt amouted to 850 million francs, the Serbian 903 million francs, the Greek 1.25 billion francs, and the Rumanian 1.7 billion francs. Bulgaria was better off financially than most of her neighbors, yet by 1914 30 per cent of her total government revenues was needed to service her debts. The Turkish debt in 1914 amounted to 3.9 billion francs, of which 2.4 billions were held by French interests, 900 million by German, and 600 million by British. Finally, it should be noted that the Turkish government and all the Balkan governments, with the exception of the Rumanian, had to accept arrangements whereby their creditors were given a measure of control over the revenues pledged to the payment of the bonds they held. In each case this foreign control was accepted to avoid bankruptcy or as a consequence of it.

The impact of the new imperialism upon the Balkans was much more profound than this brief survey would suggest. Thus far we have observed Western economic penetration from the outside. We have analyzed it in terms of loans and railways provided by the West. Now we shall reverse our procedure and look at the process from the inside out. We shall examine the specific effects of Western economic penetration upon institutions and practices and everyday living within the peninsula. We shall note that the dynamic civilization of the West affected the Balkan peoples in myriad ways and operated as a powerful catalyst in stimulating the new capitalist order that was now appearing and which we shall next examine.

THE NEW CAPITALISM

The Balkan peasants in the late nineteenth century were experiencing uncomfortably rapid change in virtually every field of life. Subsistence farming was giving way to commercial farming. Traditional customs were changing as communications between neighboring towns became more common. New political institutions were emerging with the rise of modern state structures of the Western type. What were the roots of these far-reaching changes and what was the general pattern of the new Balkans that finally took form?

One source of change was the winning of political independence by many of the Balkan peoples during the first three quarters of the nineteenth century. Those peasants who had been in feudal bondage now won their freedom, while many who had been landless were able to acquire plots. In general, political liberation created a more fluid social structure that was more susceptible to outside forces and to innovation. Political liberation also led to the appearance of the modern state, which took the place of the old feudal lord. The state was not as arbitrary as the lord had been, but it was fully as exacting, if not more so. The state rapidly created a large bureaucracy and army, which in turn involved heavy expenditures and a rising public debt. For the peasant this meant heavy taxes, burdensome service in the army, and periodic forced labor on roads and fortifications. In return for these burdens the peasant received very little from the state. Little wonder that he regarded this new impersonal master as something foreign and fearful. The hatred that he formerly held for the feudal lord he now turned against the bureaucrat, the tax collector, and the gendarme.

As significant as the appearance of modern state structures was the unprecedented increase of population in the Balkans during the nineteenth century. Greater security probably explains the growth of population in the early part of the century. The more rapid rate of increase after 1878 was caused by a fall in the death rate, usually explained by spreading medical knowledge and improved hygienic conditions. Thus the population of Serbia rose from 1.7 million in 1878 to 3.02 million in 1914, while that of Bulgaria, including Eastern Rumelia, increased from 2.82 million in 1881 to 4.33 million in 1911. Over a longer period the population of Moldavia and Wallachia rose from 1.5 million in 1815 to 7.2 million in 1912, and that of Greece increased from 750,000 in 1829 to 2.75 million in 1912. Since the area of Greece during those years grew only slightly from 18,346 to 24,558 square miles, it follows that the population per square mile jumped from 41 to 114. This represents an almost threefold increase in less than a century.

The rapid growth of population had many important consequences. First, it compelled the Balkan peasantry to shift from a predominantly pastoral economy to an agricultural economy in order to increase their productivity. Instead of raising livestock, the average peasant now grew corn, grains, and potatoes in the interior of the peninsula, and currants, tobacco, citrus fruit, olives, and grapes in the coastal Mediterranean areas. This shift to agriculture made possible the support of a much larger population than heretofore. Yet by the end of the century the soaring birth rate created a serious problem of agricultural overpopulation at the existing technological level. In Serbia the census of 1897 showed that over 11 per cent of all rural households were landless. And this was in a country which had suffered from depopulation at the beginning of the century and which never had had large estates in any appreciable numbers. In Rumania, where land distribution was less equitable, 60 per cent of the peasants at the turn of the century either had no land at all or else owned less than seven acres.

This overpopulation had unhappy consequences for the Balkan peasants. The majority were landless or else owned tiny plots incapable of supporting their families. The situation steadily deteriorated because the constantly growing population led to progressive fragmentation of peasant properties. This land hunger in turn forced the prices of agricultural land to rise ever higher. In some areas the mounting pressures were relieved by large-scale emigration overseas. It is noteworthy that the heaviest emigration was from regions with poor soil, such as certain parts of Greece, or from regions where much of the land was held in large estates, such as Slavonia and the Voivodina. By contrast, there was comparatively light emigration from Serbia and Bulgaria, where land distribution was more equitable. Those regions that lost a large proportion of their young men do not seem to have experienced a labor shortage—an indication of the degree of their overpopulation. Rather, these regions experienced unprecedented prosperity because of the remittances of the industrious and thrifty emigrants. Greece, as we shall note in Chapter 25, represented the extreme case of a country whose entire national economy rested heavily on the golden flow of remittances from fabulous America.

The Balkan peasants were affected not only by the increase in their numbers but also by the steady, inexorable shift from the traditional natural economy to a money economy. Money had been used in the earlier economy but only in a peripheral manner. Production had been carried on by the peasant households primarily to satisfy family needs. A few commodities were sold in the local market, but not with the purpose of making profit. Rather the aim was to secure enough money to meet taxes and other obligations, as well as to buy a few essentials such as salt, a little iron, and perhaps a few pieces of cloth. In the latter part of the century this pattern changed radically. An increasing number of peasants began to produce primarily for the market in order to make a profit. In doing so they became dependent upon the growing market economy and fell subject to its all-pervading dynamics.

What persuaded the peasant to abandon his traditional manner of earning a livelihood? The truth is that he had little choice in the matter. The new economy was the product of forces which he could not control and which he probably did not comprehend. One was the building of railways, which had two direct effects. The money spent in the process of construction undermined the traditional self-sufficient economy of the regions immediately affected. Moreover, the railways, when completed, made possible the importation of large quantities of foreign machine-made goods. These goods were cheap and were bought to an increasing degree by the peasants, who thereby became correspondingly less self-sufficient.

Another factor responsible for the new money economy was the growing European demand for Balkan agricultural products such as Rumanian grain, Serbian livestock, and Greek currants and tobacco. Railway and steamship transportation now enabled the Balkan peasant to produce for the European market, and he did so to an increasing extent as the century progressed. If he had any hesitation about availing himself of the opportunity, he was soon forced to bestir himself by the growing demands of the tax collector. The new state apparatus, with its mushrooming bureaucracy and army, everywhere caused taxes to soar. This tax burden, together with the cost of the new manufactured goods now made available, compelled the peasant to earn a money income by increasing his production or by getting outside work or both.

This spread of the money economy had far-reaching social consequences, many of them uncomfortable and unsettling for the peasants. The manner of everyday living changed considerably. Tea, coffee, sugar, and similar commodities passed out of the class of luxury goods into more common use. Town-made lamps replaced the home-molded candles, and the more prosperous peasants also bought furniture and household utensils. Iron and steel plows became more common, though the poorer peasants still used the home-made ironshod variety. A few households bought some ready-made clothing but the majority wove their garments from purchased yarn. In some peasant homes even a few books began to appear that were not exclusively religious. The number of purchased articles may appear insignificant by urban standards, but they represented, nevertheless, a radical departure from the self-sufficiency of earlier decades.

The diffusion of the money economy also increased village contacts with the outside world and thereby affected the traditional pattern of village life. The peasant sensed that literacy was essential under the new order if he were to be able to deal with the townsmen. Hence he readily accepted elementary schooling for his children whenever it was made available. Once reading and writing became reasonably common, new ideas and ethics, new tastes and ways of living, began to alter the age-old peasant traditions. The younger generation was soon questioning the assumptions and attitudes upon which peasant life had been based. Age no longer was regarded as sacrosanct. A new spirit of individualism and a desire for self-advancement and for personally owned possessions undermined the solidarity of village life and even of the family.

Village solidarity was also shattered by the development of economic stratification. The peasant was frequently unable to meet his obligations because he lacked the knowledge and the capital to increase his productivity and because opportunities for outside employment were scarce. As his debts mounted he was forced to turn to a new figure in the village—the well-to-do peasant who was turning merchant and moneylender. Being unfamiliar with money matters, the peasant frequently overburdened himself with debts at usurious rates ranging from 10 to over 100 per cent. Peasant indebtedness early became a serious problem in each of the Balkan countries. The governments made some efforts to free the peasants from the usurers by providing credit at low rates. But the peasants usually were unable to provide the required security or else found the formalities and legal expenses excessive for the small sums they needed. Thus it was the usurers who borrowed the government funds at around 6 per cent and reloaned them to the peasants at double, triple, or several times that rate.

Finally, the spread of the money economy made the Balkan peasants subject to the vagaries of the national, and even the international, market and credit mechanism. No sooner did they begin to produce for the European market than they felt the crushing competition of overseas agricultural products. The Balkan peasants by no means escaped the effects of the long depression which all European agriculture experienced from 1873 to the mid-nineties.

Purely national factors also affected the economic well-being of the Balkan peasants. Here too, they felt helpless before something they could not control. That something they symbolized as the city. It was the city that was the center of political, commercial, industrial, and financial power. Try as they might, the peasants were unable to insulate themselves from its influence and control. The railway, the local usurer and storekeeper, the government-appointed teacher, tax-collector, and gendarme—all subjected the peasants to the new urban centers with inseverable bonds. The peasant reacted by turning against the omnipotent city and all that it stood for. "The natural consequence of this situation," states one authority, "was an increasing political and, especially, economic antagonism between the urban and the rural populations. It replaced the centuries-old antagonism between the peasantry and the feudal class. The struggle between the town and the village has remained the chief characteristic of the whole political, social and economic life in the South Slav lands up to the present day." [4] Precisely the same point was made by a Bulgarian novelist writing in 1892:

> The peasant has but the vaguest idea of our transition from servitude to independent life; for him it matters little whether he pays tax to Akhmed or Ivan. In fact, Ivan is often more distasteful to him than Akhmed, for Akhmed could be more easily fooled or bribed; Akhmed did not take his son off as a soldier whereas Ivan does; Akhmed was naïve and spoke Turkish, while Ivan is to all appearance a Christian like him, speaks Bulgarian, yet exacts more from him than did Akhmed. The meaning of state, rights, and duties for the peasant add up to tax-payment and sending his son off as a soldier. His attitude to nature, life and livelihood are still those of fifty years ago. [5]

In conclusion, what pattern emerges from this survey of the rise of a market economy in the Balkan countries? We have seen that the transition from a natural to a money economy occurred because of the operation of domestic factors such as population increase and political change, and also because of the intrusion of the new imperialism with its loans and railways and machine-made goods and markets for Balkan raw materials. The end result was the emergence in the peninsula of what may be termed a new money economy or capitalist economy. This capitalism, needless to say, was quite different from the advanced industrial variety that prevailed in Western Europe. All the Balkan countries still remained overwhelmingly agrarian. Industries were few and were usually financed and operated by foreigners. Nevertheless, the new capitalism in the Balkans represented a fundamental break with the past. It affected profoundly not only the economies of the Balkan countries but also their political institutions and their traditional social patterns. Such disruptive change inevitably created a host of new problems—rural overpopulation, fragmentation of peasant properties, peasant indebtedness, and strife between the city and the village. These problems persisted not only to World War I but also to World War II and even to the present day. Thus the late nineteenth century is a particularly significant period because it is the seedtime of the basic problems that still beset the Balkans, and, indeed, the underdeveloped regions of the world in general.

23. Making of Bulgaria: 1878–1914

IN 1878, after five centuries of Turkish domination, an autonomous Bulgarian state was established. Its domestic development during the decades up to World War I was basically similar to that of the other Balkan countries. Western political institutions were adopted, but these did not prove altogether successful, as indicated by the political instability, fragmentation of parties, low political morality, and recurring conflict between the foreign-born rulers and the elected assemblies. The economic development of the country also corresponded to what was happening in the peninsula as a whole. The national economy grew rapidly, but at the cost of painful dislocation and re-adjustment. For the traditional, agrarian, self-contained economy gradually gave way to a market economy under the impact of the industrialized and constantly expanding Western world.

The foreign relations of Bulgaria were dominated by two all-important issues, relations with Russia and the Macedonian problem. Russia had been primarily responsible for the winning of Bulgarian autonomy. To this day the outstanding landmark in Sofia is the monument to Tsar Alexander II, the liberator of Bulgaria. Yet obligation and gratitude did not lead to dependence and servility. For almost two decades the most popular political party in Bulgaria battled against Russian intervention and looked to the Western powers for support. And when World War I broke out, Bulgaria was to be the only Balkan country to ally itself with the enemies of Russia.

Bulgaria also had a pressing irredentist problem, so that the Bulgarians, like the Greeks, Serbians, and Rumanians, devoted much of their wealth and energy to liberating their unredeemed brothers remaining under Turkish rule. In 1885 they successfully incorporated Eastern Rumelia. But when they pressed on to Macedonia they collided not only with the Turks but also with the Greeks and the Serbians, who also had aspirations in that area. Thus the question of what was to be done with Macedonia provoked a furious conflict which involved all the Balkan states and, ultimately, the European powers.

DYNAMICS OF BULGARIAN POLITICS

One of Disraeli's proudest boasts was that he had disrupted the *Dreikaiserbund* at the Berlin Congress. This claim was indeed justified. Tsar Alexander II referred wrathfully to the congress as a "European coalition against Russia under the leadership of Prince Bismarck." So disgruntled were the Russians that it seemed quite possible at one point that they might ally themselves with the French. This aroused Bismarck's old fears of a Continental coalition against Germany similar to that which had almost overwhelmed Frederick the Great. In order to forestall this menace Bismarck concluded on October 7, 1879, his epoch-making alliance with Austria. This proved to be the beginning of an expanding and self-perpetuating system of alliances and counteralliances which ultimately culminated in World War I.

Tsar Alexander was jolted by the Austro-German alliance. He was not ready to go so far as actually to conclude an alliance with republican France as a counterweight. But neither did he wish to remain isolated in Eastern Europe. The only alternative was to revive the *Dreikaiserbund*, and this was done, largely on Alexander's initiative, on June 18, 1881. So far as the Balkans were concerned the renewed alliance provided that Austria should be free to annex Bosnia-Herzegovina whenever she chose and that the unification of Eastern Rumelia and Bulgaria should not be opposed when produced by force of circumstances. The alliance also stipulated that modifications of the territorial *status quo* in the Balkans should be preceded by consultation and agreement among the signatories.

This pact regulated the relations between Austria and Russia in the Balkans but it did not eliminate their rivalry. It was essentially a truce while the two powers watched each other suspiciously and sought to strengthen their respective positions in the Balkans. In this contest Austria was by far the more successful. She concluded alliances with Serbia and Rumania in 1881 and 1883. Russia counted heavily on Bulgaria, expecting that her influence in that country would be accepted and unchallenged. But the Bulgarians took their newfound independence seriously and reacted strongly against outside interference. Within a few years they had broken openly with Russia and were looking to the West for support.

The failure of the Russians is surprising because Tsar Alexander sincerely wished to help the country which his armies had liberated. The Berlin Treaty had provided that before a prince was elected, an Assembly of Notables was to meet "under the superintendence of a Russian imperial commissioner" in order to prepare a constitution. The tsar selected Prince Alexander Dondukov-Korsakov to go to Bulgaria. He was a competent administrator with liberal inclinations and was well liked by the Bulgarians. On February 22, 1879, Dondukov officially opened the Assembly of Notables at Tirnovo. Of the 231 deputies, 21 were appointed by Dondukov, 89 were elected, and the remaining 121 came ex officio as members of the church hierarchy, the Moslem and Hebrew faiths, and the provincial and district councils.

Dondukov presented a draft constitution to the Assembly with the explanation that it was designed only to facilitate their work. "The final decisive word," he assured the gathering, "belongs to you and to you alone." [1] This affirmation was scarcely needed. Disraeli had assumed all along that the liberated Bulgarians would become the tools of the Russians. But now the British consul who was observing the proceedings at Tirnovo reported to London that there did not "exist any Pan-Slavistic tendency, or even sympathy, among the Bulgarians, whether leaders or mass. Their tendencies are remarkably, I might almost say unamiably, exclusive; and may not incorrectly be defined as Pan-Bulgarian; nothing more. As to their Servian and Russian cousins, they make no secret of their hearty dislike of the former, and of their wish, gratitude apart, to be well rid of the latter." [2]

As soon as the Assembly began discussion a rift manifested itself and soon crystallized into the Liberal and Conservative parties. This represented a continuation of the differences that had divided the Bulgarians under Turkish rule. During the struggle for ecclesiastical independence the conservative Bulgarians had favored compromise with the Patriarchate while the radicals had demanded a complete break and an autonomous church. Similarly, in the struggle against Turkish rule the conservatives had wanted reform while the radicals worked for revolution and independence. Now that the country had been liberated this cleavage persisted. Many of the Conservative party leaders had been educated in the West, were convinced that their illiterate countrymen were not ready for democratic self-government, and believed that political power should be entrusted to substantial citizens through an indirect system of voting or through a judiciously selected upper house. Also, they were inclined to look favorably toward Russia as the champion of conservative principles. By contrast, many Liberal leaders had received their education in Russia but returned with an assortment of nihilist-revolutionary doctrines and with a strong dislike for the tsarist autocracy. In domestic affairs they insisted on full popular sovereignty and opposed any artifice which limited the participation of citizens in government. The British consul, William Palgrave, defined the issues separating the two parties as follows: "The so-called Conservative has in view the extension of the Administrative or Executive Power, and, though covertly, of the Princely Prerogative; the so-called Liberal, that of the Legislative or Representative authority. . . . Personal motives, love of power or place, and the like, have doubtless much to do in the struggle now commencing; but below all these there is a real divergency of principles at work, and it is likely to widen as time goes on. The general feeling of the country is certainly with the Liberals." [3]

The Liberals not only commanded popular support, as Palgrave reported, but also dominated the Assembly of Notables. Consequently, the constitution which was adopted on April 29, 1879, was an extremely liberal document. It guaranteed civil liberties and delegated large powers to an assembly elected by universal suffrage. An attempt by the Conservatives to create an upper house was easily defeated. Alexander of Battenberg was elected Prince of Bulgaria the day after the constitution was adopted. He was an ideal choice so far as background was concerned. He was a German prince, he was related by marriage to the English royal family, he was a favorite nephew of the tsar, and he had fought as a volunteer in the Russian army against the Turks. Furthermore, he was an attractive young man, tall and imposing, of military bearing, and with a pleasant personality. But it soon became evident that Alexander not only was inexperienced but lacked discernment and statesmanship. He repeatedly misjudged the diplomatic situation; moreover, he persisted in trying to transform his primitive peasant country into a strong military and aristocratic state of the type that he was familiar with in Germany. His family background and military training led him to regard the Tirnovo constitution as "ridiculously liberal." This attitude was bound to end in conflict with the Liberal leaders, who refused to compromise on their principle that "the National Assembly makes the laws, the Prince proclaims them." [4]

The Russian representatives in Bulgaria were another disruptive force. Some followed their foreign office policy of maintaining good relations with England and Austria and adhering strictly to the Berlin Treaty. Others were ardent Pan-Slavs who thoroughly despised the treaty and openly disregarded it. Still others followed the orders of the Russian war ministry, which wanted to train a strong and dependable Bulgarian army and to build a strategic railway from the Danube to Sofia. In order to attain these ends the war ministry was prepared to support and to work through the majority Liberal party.

The turbulence that characterized the early years of the new Bulgarian state is comprehensible in the light of these conflicting forces: a people who were generally suspicious of all foreigners and resolved to govern themselves; a popular party that had adopted an ultraliberal constitution and was determined to enforce it; a likable but inexperienced and tactless prince who knew little of his adopted country except that he could not abide its constitution; and a great power with supervisory authority but with no clearly defined and generally accepted policy.

RUSSIA FAILS IN BULGARIA: 1878–1885

Prince Alexander arrived in Bulgaria early in June, 1879. The elections for the Assembly, or Sobranie, were held on October 12, 1879, and the Liberals won a large majority. A deadlock ensued because Alexander had appointed a Conservative prime minister who now faced a preponderantly Liberal Assembly. Alexander finally ordered new elections for January 25, 1880, but again the Liberals won an overwhelming victory. The prince's position appeared to be hopeless. The Liberals dominated the Assembly while a Russian general, Peter Parensov, commanded the army and, in accordance with the war ministry's instructions, was supporting the Liberals on the constitutional issue.

The only way out for Alexander was to appeal to the tsar, with whom he had cordial personal relations. An opportunity presented itself when he visited St. Petersburg in February, 1880, for the celebration of the twenty-fifth anniversary of Alexander II's reign. The tsar agreed to replace General Parensov, but he refused to approve the immediate suspension of the Tirnovo constitution. He insisted instead that the Liberals be allowed to hold office in order to determine whether or not the constitution was a practical instrument of government. Prince Alexander accepted this decision with satisfaction because he had no doubt about the outcome. "It is impossible," he declared in St. Petersburg, "to rule with the absurd Bulgarian constitution, for it makes no difference whether the Conservative or the Liberal party is in power, as both are equally democratic and unreliable." [5]

The Liberals formed a ministry on April 5, 1880, and remained in office one year. Their record was, on the whole, creditable. They passed constructive legislation and were restrained and correct in their relations with Alexander. But in retrospect it is clear that there never existed a real possibility that the constitution would remain in force and the Liberal party would remain in power. The reason is that Alexander had convinced himself that, regardless of election returns, the Liberal party did not represent the people. He was certain that his subjects looked to him rather than to the Liberal politicians, and that it was his duty to abolish the constitution which stood between himself and his people.

I have travelled through Bulgaria this year, and have again been able to satisfy myself how good, diligent, and thoroughly loyal my people are, and how slightly the idea of the Constitution has made its way among the real body of the people. They address themselves directly to me in the most trivial matters, and by so doing express their distrust of the Ministers, and at the same time their conviction that I both ought to and can help them directly. . . . This very last session has again clearly proved to me that the present Constitution is not suited to the country. It places the person of the Ruler in continual opposition to the National Assembly, and this must constantly become more acute, and culminate in time in open enmity. Besides this the people lack the most elementary requisites for constitutional life. The nation suffers under it, and only a few aspiring commonplace men profit by it. I wish, above all things, for an organization that will allow me the possibility of guiding and interfering in a lawful and effective manner, and, at the same time, bestow on me the necessary authoritative powers for preventing measures and deeds that run counter to the interests of the State, and so enable me to fulfil my duty towards my new country. . . . I do not see how I am to comply with Russia's demands and wishes in the face of the anti-Russian current in my nation and the army. . . . [6]

The assassination of Tsar Alexander II in March, 1881, gave Prince Alexander the opportunity to have his way. The new tsar, Alexander III, was a strong opponent of liberalism and constitutionalism. Also, he was preoccupied with the domestic crisis and unlikely to concern himself with what might happen in Bulgaria. Prince Alexander took advantage of this situation to execute his coup on May 9, 1881. He dismissed the Liberal ministry and demanded, upon the threat of abdication, that he be given extraordinary powers for a period of seven years and that at the end of that period the constitution be amended in the light of the experience acquired in the interim. The outcome of this bold move depended upon the tsar's reaction. This proved to be favorable. The tsar was presented with reports depicting the Liberal party as the Bulgarian counterpart of the Russian nihilists and terrorists. When he received a telegram from the Liberal leaders requesting support, he wrote on the margin: "I will not consider any telegram from revolutionaries, and these Liberals are nothing other than socialists. The Bulgarian people will, I am sure, support the prince—for these are only a band of rowdies and cowards." [7]

Alexander now proceeded to hold elections under conditions which, as the British consul reported, made the outcome a "foregone conclusion." The Liberal press was muzzled and uniformed officers at the polls openly questioned and intimidated the voters. When the Assembly met on July 31, 1881, it voted unanimously to accept all of Alexander's demands. The Austrian diplomatic representative reported to his government that Bulgaria now had "a dictatorship but not a dictator." [8] This shrewd analysis suggests why Alexander's troubles henceforth increased rather than lessened. The basic difficulty was that neither Alexander nor the Conservatives had enough popular backing to rule the country without leaning upon Russia. Yet they were not willing to pay the price for this support. Russian contractors wanted to build a railway from the Danube to Sofia while Russian speculators and concession-hunters regarded Bulgaria almost as a new imperial province opened for exploitation. But the Conservative leaders were unwilling to accept this semicolonial status and reserved lucrative investment openings for themselves and their friends. Thus Alexander and his associates were asking for both Russian protection and for full independence—two mutually exclusive conditions.

The outcome was a deadlock between the Russians on the one hand and Alexander and the Conservatives on the other. Relations became embittered as Russian officials disregarded Alexander and declared publicly that they were taking their orders from the tsar. In fact, Bulgarians of all political complexions reacted against these foreign taskmasters and wished above all else to be rid of them. Finally, after much negotiating and jockeying, Alexander and the two political parties of Bulgaria formed what was in effect a national front against the Russians. A new Liberal-Conservative coalition government took office and, on the insistence of the Liberals, the Tirnovo constitution was restored with the understanding that it would remain in force for three years before any amendments were considered. "The real common basis of this compromise," reported the Austrian consul, "is the prodigious hatred that has developed . . . of the Russian yoke which is becoming increasingly intolerable. . . . The program of the government may be summarized quite simply in the Italian formula: *La Bulgaria fara da se* ["Bulgaria will do it herself"].[9]

UNIFICATION OF BULGARIA: 1885–1886

Alexander took a momentous step in deciding to break with Russia. Apparently he assumed that the other powers would give him enough support to maintain his independent position. The assumption proved unjustified. England was unwilling to involve herself in the northern Balkans, while Bismarck told Alexander with brutal frankness that he need not look to Germany. Bismarck went further and actively opposed Alexander's courting of Princess Victoria, daughter of the German Crown Prince Frederick. The German chancellor acted as he did because of diplomatic considerations. When Prince Alexander visited Berlin in May, 1884, Bismarck told him frankly, "Germany has no interest in Bulgaria, our interest is: Peace with Russia." Bismarck explained that he could not allow the match with Princess Victoria because St. Petersburg would interpret it as meaning that Germany was opposing Russia in the Balkans. The original *Dreikaiserbund* had been disrupted in 1878 because of a crisis in the Balkans and Bismarck was determined that the revived League should not founder from the same cause. Finally, Bismarck warned Alexander, prophetically as it turned out, that if he continued to act independently of Russia he would eventually be forced to abdicate. "But if you wish to remain in Bulgaria, then give yourself up to Russia unconditionally. . . . In St. Petersburg they know our view. So I advise you to seize any opportunity to restore good relations with Russia." [10]

Alexander apparently took Bismarck's lecture to heart. In August, 1885, he met the Russian foreign minister, Nicholas Giers, and discussed at length the possibility of reconciliation. But nothing came of this because the following month an insurrection broke out in Eastern Rumelia which was to provide Alexander with his greatest triumphs and also to force his abdication.

The revolution occurred suddenly on September 18, 1885. The rebels had no difficulty in arresting the governor, Gavril Pasha, who was a Christian in accordance with the provisions of the Berlin Treaty. Gavril offered no resistance, declaring, "I am a Bulgarian and shall not call in the Turks. I wish happiness to the Bulgarian people." [11] The rebels formed a provisional government and issued a grandiloquent manifesto proclaiming the union of Eastern Rumelia with the principality of Bulgaria.

It had been common knowledge that the people of Eastern Rumelia had wanted unification and that plots with this end in view had existed. Even the members of the *Dreikaiserbund* had recognized this situation and had agreed that they would not oppose unification. Nevertheless, Prince Alexander was seriously embarrassed by the timing of the revolution because he had just assured Giers that there would be no disturbance in Eastern Rumelia. Thus if Alexander now accepted union he would almost certainly alienate the Russians irrevocably, but if he refused to accept union he would alienate his own subjects and make his position in Bulgaria impossible. Alexander was urged by Stephen Stambulov, a rising young Bulgarian politician, to throw in his lot with his people. "Sire," he said, "the Union is made—the revolt is an accomplished fact, past recall, and the time for hesitation is gone by. Two roads lie before your Highness: the one to Philippopolis, and as far further as God may lead; the other to Sistova, the Danube, and Darmstadt. I counsel you to take the crown the nation offers you." After a little reflection Alexander answered, "I choose the road to Philippopolis." [12]

The question now was how the powers would react to this violation of the Berlin Treaty. The tsar made his position unmistakably clear by recalling all Russian officers serving in Bulgaria. This virtually decapitated the Bulgarian army, whose officers above the rank of lieutenant had been Russians. Tsar Alexander revealed the reason for his opposition when, in reply to a Bulgarian petition, he stated: "There can be no question whatever of dissolving the Union, but as long as you keep your present Government, expect from me nothing, nothing, nothing!" When Stambulov heard of this response he requested the Russian consul for clarification. If by "present Government" the tsar referred to the Bulgarian ministry, then it was ready to resign immediately. The consul replied that the phrase referred to Prince Alexander, and that so long as he remained in Bulgaria Russia would do nothing for her.[13] Thus Russian policy may be described as being opposed not to unification per se but to unification under Alexander.

Britain, by contrast, now favored unification, so that Britain and Russia had completely reversed their positions on Bulgarian unity between 1878 and 1885. The reason for the British reversal was that Eastern Rumelia had not proven the anti-Russian barrier that had been planned at Berlin. The Turks had not garrisoned the passes in the Balkan Mountains; in any case, Bulgaria had Sofia and Varna, which outflanked the Balkan passes. Under these circumstances Britain decided that an unfortified and disaffected Eastern Rumelia was not likely to be as effective a barrier against Russia as a united Bulgaria, particularly in view of the strong anti-Russian sentiments that the Bulgarians had manifested.

Bismarck, as usual, was interested only in preserving the *Dreikaiserbund*. For this reason he wished to settle the unification issue as speedily as possible and was ready to support any arrangement that was acceptable to Austria and Russia. Austria found herself in a difficult position because she preferred to remain on the side lines but could not do so because of her commitments to Serbia. Her 1881 alliance with Serbia committed her to support that state if it attempted to expand to the south. The sudden enlargement of Bulgaria had provoked a public clamor in Serbia for expansion. Prince Milan felt impelled to heed this clamor for fear of losing his throne. In fact, his scandalous private life and his complete unconcern for the welfare of his country had made him so unpopular that he was almost overthrown by a revolt in 1883. Accordingly, Milan now decided to make some move, he cared not where, as long as it allayed the agitation. The Austrians reluctantly advised him to march, if he must, against Bulgaria rather than against Turkey, because they wished to keep open the route from Austria to the Aegean.

Meanwhile, Russia had proposed an informal conference of ambassadors in Constantinople. This was held in November, 1885, but a deadlock ensued because Britain favored acceptance of unification while the *Dreikaiserbund* powers, on the insistence of Russia, were opposed. At this point Milan laid violent hands on the course of events. He decided that the impasse in Constantinople ended any possibility of obtaining territorial compensation through diplomatic means. Accordingly, he declared war on Bulgaria on November 13, 1885.

A quick Serbian victory was generally expected. Not only had the Bulgarians lost their officers; their main forces were concentrated along the Turkish frontier. Only weak detachments had been left to guard Sofia, but these were able to hold off the Serbians until Alexander came up from Rumelia in a series of forced marches. The decisive engagement was a three-day battle fought at Slivnitza, twenty-five miles from Sofia, on November 17–19. The Serbians were routed, and by November 26 Alexander had entered Serbian territory. The triumphant Bulgars won further victories until the road to Nish and Belgrade lay open before them. The Austrians now intervened, warning Alexander that if he advanced farther he would be confronted with Austrian troops. Alexander naturally accepted an armistice, and on March 3, 1886, the Treaty of Bucharest was signed restoring the prewar *status quo.*

The victory of the Bulgarians ensured that the union of Eastern Rumelia and the Bulgarian Principality would not be undone. Even Russia recognized this fact and accepted a compromise arrangement providing for the personal union of the two areas. Because of Russia's insistence, Prince Alexander was not mentioned by name. Instead, the agreement reached on April 5, 1886, stipulated that the prince of Bulgaria be named governor of Eastern Rumelia for five years. Thus the violation of the Berlin Treaty was concealed by this legal fig leaf.

ABDICATION OF ALEXANDER: 1886

The Russians had insisted that Alexander should not be specifically named the new governor of Eastern Rumelia because they were as determined as ever to drive him out of Bulgaria. On August 20, 1886, their wish was suddenly fulfilled when Alexander was melodramatically kidnapped in his palace and hustled across the border. The deed was not the work of a few hired miscreants, as is often claimed. The fact is that half of the regimental commanders and many higher officers participated in the plot. Some had decided that the unrelenting hostility of the tsar required that Alexander be removed for the good of the country. Others had personal grievances against Alexander involving promotions and discipline. Still others were dissatisfied with the terms of the personal union by which Alexander's legal status was virtually that of a Turkish pasha.

In any case, a band of conspirators burst into the palace in the dead of night and demanded, with loaded pistols in hand, that Alexander abdicate. A captain tore a page out of the visitors' book which lay in the hall and sat down to draw up the deed of abdication. Drink and excitement prevented him from scrawling more than a few unintelligible words, so a young cadet took the pen and completed the document. Alexander signed it on the back of a stooping officer and added the words "God protect Bulgaria." He was then conducted under guard to the Danube, put aboard his yacht, and landed several days later on Russian soil, where he was released.

The leaders of the revolt did not have definite plans as to what to do after Alexander had been removed. A provisional government was formed under the Russophil church leader, Metropolitan Clement. But it soon became apparent that the public by no means approved of the coup. This gave Stambulov his chance, and he rose to the occasion brilliantly. He declared the members of the provisional government to be outlaws and organized a counterrevolution. Within a few days the provisional government had collapsed and Stambulov was master of the country. The next step was to find Alexander. After sending telegrams all over Europe he was finally located at Lemberg, Austria. Stambulov sent him a telegram imploring him to return and assuring him that all Bulgaria awaited him. Alexander promptly accepted and started back.

When he arrived at Ruschuk he was met by the Russian consul, who made clear the uncompromising opposition of his government. Deciding on a direct appeal to the tsar, Alexander sent an abject telegram placing himself at his mercy: "Russia gave me my crown: I am ready to return it into the hands of her sovereign." Alexander hoped to win over the tsar by his humbleness, but he was soon disillusioned. "Cannot approve your return to Bulgaria," Tsar Alexander replied, "foreseeing disastrous consequences to country already so severely tried. . . . Your Highness will judge what is your proper course." [14] The ultimatum was perhaps veiled but ultimatum it was nonetheless. Stambulov attempted to persuade Alexander to ignore the tsar's threats and to remain on the throne. But the prince was overwhelmed by the tsar's relentless enmity as well as by the defection of his army officers. The odds seemed to him impossible, so on September 7 he formally abdicated and left Bulgaria.

Alexander failed partly because he did not heed Bismarck's advice to "give yourself up to Russia unconditionally." Instead, he vacillated back and forth between defiance and obsequiousness. Also, his inflated notion of royal prerogative antagonized a good many of his own subjects. Thus lacking solid support within his country, openly rejected by Bismarck, and receiving only moral backing from England, Alexander was doomed to succumb to the weight of Russian pressure.

FERDINAND AND STAMBULOV: 1887–1894

When Alexander departed from Bulgaria the tsar announced that he was sending General Nicholas Kaulbars as special commissioner to help the Bulgars elect a new prince. Immediately upon his arrival Kaulbars began giving "advice" on all matters. But the real leader of the Bulgarians now was Stambulov. He had engineered Alexander's return after the kidnapping and he had done his utmost to persuade Alexander to remain on the throne. After these events Stambulov was in no mood to listen to any "advice" from the Russians. Kaulbars insisted that the election of a new Assembly be postponed, but Stambulov paid no attention and held the election as scheduled on October 10, 1886. Despite the brazen intervention of Kaulbars, who toured the country urging the peasants to boycott the elections, the returns gave Stambulov's National party an overwhelming majority.

The Assembly, or Sobranie, met and voted to offer the crown to Waldemar of Denmark. The tsar's opposition caused Waldemar to reject the offer. The Sobranie then named a commission of three to search the European courts for a ruler. Serious consideration was given for a while to a proposal for the personal union of Bulgaria and Rumania under King Charles. But Russia again intervened successfully by threatening to sever relations with Rumania if Charles accepted the Bulgarian throne. This hostility of Russia, together with the fresh memory of what happened to Alexander, sufficed to scare off potential candidates. For six months the crown of Bulgaria went a-begging.

When the three commissioners reached Vienna one of them spent an evening drinking beer at Ronacher's well-known circus. Here, at one of the marble-topped tables, he met a gentleman who professed to know the very man they were looking for. The delighted commissioner told his colleagues, and next day all three waited upon Prince Ferdinand of Saxe-Coburg and offered him the throne. At first he stipulated that all the powers approve his candidacy. But he was too anxious for the post to insist on this condition. When the Sobranie elected him unanimously he accepted the throne and was crowned on August 14, 1887. He estimated that he had a sporting chance to keep the crown on his head. "After all," he remarked, "if I am only the flea in the ear of the [Russian] bear, the experience ought to be none the less amusing." [15]

Stambulov was the natural choice to serve as premier under the new ruler. The ministry which he formed remained in office from September 1, 1887, to May 31, 1894. Bulgarian history during those seven years revolved around the two men, Prince Ferdinand and Premier Stambulov. At the outset there was no doubt that the prince had the junior status. He was young, inexperienced, and ignorant of his country. He possessed none of Alexander's charm and dash. He had no taste for military affairs and he never assumed command at maneuvers. It is not surprising that his subjects did not respond to him as they had to his predecessor.

Stambulov, on the other hand, had already earned and established his reputation. Born the son of an innkeeper, he had behind him by this time, at the age of thirty-three, an extraordinary career as a revolutionary leader during the Turkish period, a brilliant statesman under Alexander, and a successful lawyer in Sofia. For sheer ability and force of character he towered above his contemporaries. More than once he demonstrated his courage and decisiveness under trying circumstances. Not without reason was he referred to as the Bulgarian Bismarck and considered to be one of the two or three really "strong men" of Europe. But with all his great gifts Stambulov also had great faults. He believed that the end justified the means, and he never hesitated to employ force and even brutality in order to have his way. In his personal relations he remained a peasant—rough, impatient, and offensively blunt. Not only did he dominate Ferdinand in the early years but he treated him like a puppet. On one occasion he revived the plan that had been proposed earlier for a personal union of Bulgaria and Rumania. He pointed out the advantages of the union to a Rumanian diplomat, who replied by asking what he proposed to do with

Ferdinand. Stambulov laughingly said, "I will see to it that he is packed out of Bulgaria within fifteen days." [16]

Stambulov grossly underestimated his adversary. Ferdinand was perhaps unimpressive in appearance, but he had a highly developed capacity for political and personal intrigue as well as a consuming ambition. He was determined to be undisputed master in his country and to make his country the dominant power in the Balkans. Numerous stories have been told of incidents illustrating his ambition. On one occasion the French consul, Maurice Paléologue, was kept waiting for ten minutes in a room in which was hung a panoramic painting of Constantinople, the Bosphorus, and the Asiatic shores, all of which were overshadowed by a majestic mounted figure designated as "Tsar Ferdinand." [17] Paléologue had many other opportunities to observe the complex character of the Bulgarian ruler, and in 1907 he dispatched to Paris a brilliant pen portrait which explains better than any other document the vicissitudes that later befell the Bulgarian nation.

Refined to excess, enamored of art and given to whim, very proud of his origins, as disdainfully aristocratic as a prince of ancient German blood can be, he has come to live in a primitive and rough country without tradition and without culture. After twenty years of rule he has become attached neither to the people nor to the country. In private he calls his subjects "my Bulgarian wolves." He has made some of them his servants and others his adherents but not one of them is his friend. His court is empty; he never receives. . . . He detests Sofia and was not embarrassed to tell me so. He does not live in his capital more than three or four months a year. The rest of the time he shuts himself in his beautiful Euxinograd villa on the shores of the Black Sea, or in his Ebenthal castle near Vienna, or else wanders between Paris, London, Carlsbad, Coburg; he moves about ceaselessly.

He does not like the army, he ignores financial matters, and he has little taste for administration. In domestic affairs he concentrates all his attention and skill upon dominating the political parties and keeping his ministers divided and insecure.

His pride suffers continually from everything that reminds him of his status as vassal of the Sublime Porte; he disagreeably tolerates the presence of an imperial Turkish Commissioner at Sofia; he is humiliated by the title, "general aide de camp of the Sultan," which the Gotha Almanac includes in the list of his titles. None of the courts he visits renders him sovereign honors. . . .

What is particularly discouraging for him is that his ambition is not shared by the nation. The Bulgarians do not care to form a kingdom. Ottoman sovereignty does not weigh upon them; in fact, they enjoy complete autonomy and since they are very realistic souls they are satisfied with this regime. . . . They are also profoundly egalitarian and democratic; they know that a sovereign court would cost them dearly, and they are not at all impressed by monarchial trapping. This is one more contrast, and not the least curious, between the Prince and his people.[18]

Despite his aspirations Ferdinand had no choice but to lean upon Stambulov at the outset. The two could not possibly establish a congenial relationship, given the aspirations of the aristocratic Ferdinand and the intolerance and imperiousness of the plebeian Stambulov. But Ferdinand bided his time and meanwhile exploited Stambulov's talents to the full. Stambulov's greatest service was in repulsing the Russian attempts to unseat Ferdinand and to set up a Russophil regime. At first the Russians employed diplomatic pressure, though without success because Stambulov was supported by Britain and to a lesser extent by Austria. Finally, Tsar Alexander III decided to adopt a policy of nonintervention in Bulgaria, though he was resolved not to recognize Ferdinand under any condition. The other powers followed the tsar's lead, and Ferdinand remained unrecognized.

Despite the tsar's decision against further intervention, various Russian diplomatic officials with Pan-Slav tendencies attempted to foster revolts in Bulgaria. Invariably the conspiracies were unearthed and the ringleaders summarily executed on orders from Stambulov. The Russian agents and their accomplices next tried assassination. They killed a number of government officials, but their principal intended victims, Ferdinand and Stambulov, escaped unharmed. Stambulov resorted to measures as ruthless as those of his opponents. He rounded up suspects and used torture to extract information. His critics accused him of instituting a reign of terror but he did succeed in stamping out the conspiracies.

At the same time Stambulov countered Russia's diplomatic boycott by effecting a *rapprochement* with Turkey. This paid handsome dividends because the sultan reciprocated by granting several bishoprics in Macedonia to the Bulgarian exarchate church. This and other concessions enabled the Bulgarians to achieve an extensive peaceful penetration of Macedonia. Neighboring countries that also had designs upon this area reacted vigorously to Stambulov's success, and the result was the bitter struggle for Macedonia which was to dominate Balkan politics to World War I and beyond.*

Ferdinand's position in Bulgaria was also strengthened by his marriage to Princess Marie Louise of Parma (April 20, 1893) and by the birth of a son and heir. Complications were encountered at first because the princess was Catholic and the children were to be raised as Catholics, whereas the Bulgarian constitution provided that the heir to the throne should belong to the Orthodox Church. Stambulov demonstrated his strength in the country by passing through the Sobranie the necessary constitutional amendment despite strong opposition from Russia and from certain Russophil ecclesiastical functionaries within Bulgaria. Stambulov now was at the height of his power, as was made clear when the elections held in the fall of 1893 returned only 15 or 16 Opposition deputies in a house of 160.

A few months later, on May 31, 1894, the world learned with surprise that Ferdinand had dismissed his Bulgarian Bismarck. And the following year, on July 15, 1895, Stambulov was assassinated, the victim of a foul and tragic murder. The factors behind this sudden downfall are clear. Ferdinand had al-

* See Chapter 28.

ways disliked his overbearing minister and had wanted to be the actual as well as the titular ruler of the country. Now for the first time he felt that he could dispense with Stambulov's services, partly because he had acquired experience and personal followers during the past years and also because his marriage had strengthened his position. Furthermore, Ferdinand was desperately anxious to secure recognition from Russia in order to assure the future of his dynasty. But Stambulov was the leader of the anti-Russian forces in Bulgaria and as long as he remained in office a *rapprochement* with Russia was out of the question. These considerations led Ferdinand to decide to dismiss Stambulov.

Having reached this decision, Ferdinand now revealed the dark side of his character. He deemed it prudent not to dismiss Stambulov outright, so he resorted to petty intrigues and annoyances to force his resignation. Then, after Stambulov had resigned, mobs were allowed to gather about his house shouting threats and imprecations. The police played their part by keeping him under what almost amounted to house arrest. This torment had continued for three months when the correspondent of the *Frankfurter Zeitung* called upon him on August 14, 1894. Stambulov unbosomed himself in a violent diatribe in which he held Ferdinand up to contempt by relating various incidents of a personal nature.

Hitherto Ferdinand had been content with petty persecution. Now he was bent upon complete destruction. He instituted legal proceedings for defamation and dismissed Stambulov's adherents from every public post. A law was enacted "for the prosecution of government officials who appear to possess more wealth than they ought." Another law abolished the existing pension system and reduced the families of former ministers to beggary. Most of Stambulov's property was sequestered, and he was even refused a passport to go abroad to recover his health. The end came one evening when three assassins fell upon Stambulov in the street and mutilated him fearfully in the face, head, and arms. The police in the vicinity appeared unconcerned. Three days later, on July 18, 1895, Stambulov breathed his last. The veteran London *Times* Balkan correspondent, James Bourchier, reported these tragic events to his paper as follows:

A heavy responsibility rests with those who refused Stambulov permission to leave the country, and who, detaining him here like a prisoner, neglected the measures necessary to ensure his safety. . . . Stambulov was a thorough Bulgarian —a thorough Oriental perhaps—with the virtues and failings of his kind. With little of the veneer of civilization, with little distinction or refinement of manner, he concealed beneath a rough exterior a natural tenderness and delicacy of feeling which only those who knew him intimately could appreciate. There was nothing of humbug or affectation about him; he was a man—a great man. Whatever his defects may have been, of his patriotism and devotion to his country there could never be any doubt.[19]

BULGARIA UNDER FERDINAND: 1894–1914

Ferdinand at last was the unchallenged master of his country. He remained the master throughout his long reign until his abdication in 1918. His success was based on two maxims: "Divide and rule" and "Every man has his price." In order to forestall the rise of another Stambulov, Ferdinand purposefully set political leaders against each other and disrupted political parties into warring factions. As a result, Bulgaria soon had more political parties than any other country in the Balkans. Ferdinand also gained effective control over the small class of educated and politically active people by developing a highly organized system of "spoils." R. W. Seton-Watson, the British historian, who witnessed the system in operation, described it as follows:

"Enrichissez-vous" became the scarcely veiled invitation to every public man. . . . The secret of Ferdinand's power has lain in his skill in calculating the psychological moment for driving each batch of swine away from the trough of power, and, still more, in his policy—pursued with a relentless and uncanny mastery of detail—of supervising their diet. In other words, he has made it his business to pry into the personal activities of his ministers, and his dossier of compromising documents is the envy of every criminal investigation department in Europe. . . . Ferdinand set himself to create a system by which the individual might grow rich and prosper exceedingly, so long as he remained the faithful servitor of the throne, but risked immediate disgrace and ruin if he ventured to assert his independence. Thus there was always a waiting list for the post of Premier, and whenever Ferdinand had had enough of one politician and his following, he merely had to turn to a rival group and entrust it with the "making" of an election and a majority.[20]

Under these circumstances the identity and the party label of the politicians that were allowed to hold office at various times are not as significant as might ordinarily be expected. When Stambulov resigned, Constantine Stoilov formed a cabinet which included all the elements formerly in opposition. The cabinet remained in power to 1899, when it fell, partly because of Ferdinand's intrigues among the ministers. The next cabinet worthy of notice was headed by Vasil Radoslavov, and lasted from 1899 to 1901. Its only claim to fame is that it provoked the organization of the Agrarian party when it attempted to reintroduce the tithe in 1900. The peasants had suffered heavily from a series of bad harvests during the preceding years. They refused to pay the new levy and resorted to armed resistance in several districts. The disorders which ensued not only forced the government to resign but also stimulated the peasants to form their own Agrarian party. This grew slowly but steadily until World War I discredited the other parties and enabled the Agrarians to assume office in 1919.

Two elections were held in 1901 and the outcome was a ministry under Stoyan Danev. Its chief characteristic was its extreme Russophilism. Danev is reputed to have declared, "We have no secrets from Russia." [21] In the fall of 1902 Grand Duke Nicholas and numerous Russian officers attended the consecration of a Russian church and monastery in the Shipka Pass, the occasion being the twenty-fifth anniversary of the taking of the pass by Russian troops.

No basic issues or principles distinguished the various ministries that held office during the years 1894–1914. Only on the question of relations with Russia were there meaningful differences, so that the cabinets that passed in kaleidoscopic succession may be classified as being either Russophil or, as the other school was termed, Stambulovist. The Russophil Danev cabinet lost popularity because of the failure of Russia to support Bulgaria actively in Macedonia. In May, 1903, it gave way to a Stambulovist government, which remained in office under various leaders until 1908. During these years international relations impinged more and more upon domestic affairs. The Stambulovist ministry concentrated much of its attention on the 1903 insurrection in Macedonia and the complications that followed. Similarly, the succeeding governments concerned themselves with the Young Turk Revolution, the proclamation of Bulgaria as a fully independent kingdom, and the negotiations leading to the Balkan League of 1912.

Turning to these international relations of Bulgaria, we find that two issues stand out above all others: relations with Russia, and the problem of Macedonia. As noted above, one of Ferdinand's motives in dismissing Stambulov in May, 1894, was to clear the way for a *rapprochement* with Russia. This was made easier by the death of Alexander III later in the same year. Ferdinand sent condolences to the new tsar, Nicholas II. In July, 1895, he dispatched to St. Petersburg a deputation headed by the metropolitan of Tirnovo to place a gold wreath on the tomb of Alexander III. Ferdinand went so far in his reconciliation campaign as to rebaptize his son, Crown Prince Boris, in the Orthodox faith. Tsar Nicholas responded by standing as the godfather of the crown prince and sending a special envoy to represent him in the ceremonies held in February, 1896. The tsar went further and took the initiative in procuring for Ferdinand the recognition of the great powers. The reconciliation between Russia and Bulgaria was complete, and Ferdinand at last had secured the recognition he so long had desired.

During the following years the relations between Russia and Bulgaria were not always close and cordial. The high point of friendship was reached with the secret military convention concluded between the two countries in 1902. This was directed against an Austrian-Rumanian pact of the previous year and provided that Russia should aid Bulgaria in case of attack by Rumania. Despite these close ties the Bulgarians were not altogether satisfied. Russia extended her favors to Serbia as well, and at times this affected Bulgarian interests. Russia displayed interest in Serbia particularly after the Austrophil King Alexander Obrenovich was overthrown in June, 1903, and replaced by Peter Karageorgevich. Also, Russia refused to support actively Bulgarian aspirations in Macedonia because she wished to avoid another Balkan crisis. This desire was understandable at a time when Russia was busily engaged in the Far East. Nevertheless, Bulgarian ambitions in Macedonia remained unsatisfied and many held Russia responsible. For these reasons Russian-Bulgarian relations were by no means uniformly close, and in the end Bulgaria was to be the only Balkan state to align itself against Russia during World War I.

Turning to the Macedonian question, we find that here also Stambulov's downfall led to a basic shift in Bulgarian policy. Stambulov's strategy had been to cultivate friendship with the Turks in return for concessions and peaceful penetration in Macedonia. This had proved highly profitable; yet certain elements remained dissatisfied and demanded more aggressive measures. They received the green light when Stambulov was removed. Ferdinand was resolved that Macedonia should follow the path of Eastern Rumelia. He was careful to deplore publicly the activities of the secret committees that fomented revolution and created anarchy and bloodshed in Macedonia. In actual practice the committees carried on their work with little interference. One reason was that tens of thousands of Macedonians had settled in Bulgaria as immigrants or refugees and Ferdinand dared not antagonize them for fear of an antidynastic movement or even assassination. Also, there was the fact that Ferdinand and his subjects did want Macedonia and were not willing to make a serious effort to curb the committees unless the diplomatic situation at a given moment called for such a gesture. The details of the Macedonian problem and its effect on Bulgarian and general Balkan diplomacy will be considered in Chapter 28. Suffice it to note here the following excerpt from the report of the British consul in Sofia reviewing the events during the period from 1897 to 1907:

During the decade under review each successive Government was confronted by the issues raised by the Macedonian question. . . . The attitude of successive Bulgarian Governments towards the insurrectionary movement differed only in degree. While condemning the criminal practices of the Committees, they one and all sympathized with their aims and were powerless to suppress them altogether. Measures were, indeed, from time to time taken to prevent the passage of bands and the sale of arms, but the wooded hills near the frontier always remained the centre of the recruiting operations of the bands, while rifles were occasionally abstracted from the military stores.[22]

ECONOMIC DEVELOPMENT TO 1914

Bulgaria was almost exclusively agrarian under the Turks and it remained overwhelmingly so between the winning of independence and the outbreak of World War I. Toward the end of the Turkish period the peasants were granted the right to own land and some of them did buy plots from the Turkish landholders and from the state. But the great majority remained landless and in a state of feudal or semifeudal dependence on the Turkish lords. This dependence varied from region to region, the most onerous being in the western part of the country, which could not be supervised adequately from Constantinople. Here the lords collected a heavy stipulated rent rather than a tithe, and they had complete authority over the villages, including the right to sell them when they wished. In other areas the peasants were much better off, being provided with houses, seed grain, and fodder, and sharing the crops equally with the landowner.

Tax payments to the state also varied greatly. Tax farming prevailed to the end, with the exception of brief interludes when the government tried unsuccessfully to collect taxes directly. The tithe of 10 to 15 per cent on grain was collected in kind and the taxes on other produce usually in money. The grain tax in Bulgaria, as in other Balkan countries,* was collected in such a manner that the peasants were left vulnerable to extortion by the tax farmers. In the years just before liberation the Bulgarian lands north of the Balkan Mountains paid the equivalent of 36 to 37 million francs yearly in taxes, and an additional 3 million in customs duties. Of this total, 32 million francs were sent to Constantinople. Thus the Turks drained the wealth of the country through their tax levies in addition to the dues collected by the Turkish landowners from the peasants.

The Turkish feudal system began to disintegrate in June, 1877, as the Turks fled south before the advancing Russian armies. The exodus had two important results: it left the peasants freed of the personal dependence and obligations of the past, and it enabled them to seize the Turkish-owned lands which they previously had worked. When the peace settlement was arranged in Berlin in 1878 a provision was included recognizing the property rights of the Turkish landowners. Legally they now had the right to return to Bulgaria and take possession of their estates, but in practice they were effectively prevented from doing so.

The Russians had no desire to see the Turks return, fearing that British influence would return with them. Accordingly, the Russians issued a directive on August 2, 1878, stating that any returning Turks charged with crimes of murder, robbery, arson, rape, or destruction of villages would be immediately tried before a military court. Two landowners who did return were in fact tried and sentenced to death, though the tsar commuted their sentence to exile from Bulgaria. Other Turks who might have wished to return now decided otherwise.

The Turkish landowners were not able to take physical possession of their estates but they were given financial compensation. The funds were obtained from the Bulgarian peasants, who were forced to pay for the lands they had seized. Some had to go into debt to do so while others were obliged to sell their stock. Despite this burden, the fact remains that a significant agricultural revolution occurred in Bulgaria in 1877–1878. Feudalism was abolished and so were the large estates. Bulgaria became a country of small peasant proprietors.

One of the main problems in the following years, as elsewhere in the Balkans, was the continual fragmentation of the peasant plots. One reason for this was the rapid increase of the population from about 2,825,000 in 1881 (in both Bulgaria and Eastern Rumelia) to about 4,330,000 in 1911.

* See Chapter 15.

Moreover, the inheritance law adopted in 1890 provided for the equal distribution of land among the children in contrast to the previous Turkish law which favored the sons over the daughters. These factors explain the following landholding statistics for the year 1908 (a decare equals approximately a fourth of an acre):

Size of holding	Percentage of total number of landholders	Percentage of area of private holdings
Very small (less than 20 decares)	45.52	6.9
Small (20 to 100 decares)	41.44	42.3
Medium (100 to 300 decares)	11.96	36.5
Large (300 to 1,000 decares)	0.98	8.8
Very large (over 1,000 decares)	0.10	5.5

Source: L. Pasvolsky, *Bulgaria's Economic Position* (Washington, D. C., 1929), p. 25.

Holdings under twenty decares or five acres were considered below the minimum necessary to provide a livelihood, yet 45 per cent of all landholders were in this category. This was so despite the fact that, in contrast to Rumania, very few large estates existed. Thus the land hunger of the Bulgarian peasant arose not from maldistribution of land but rather from the growth of population and the dependence of 80 per cent of that population upon the soil for livelihood.

The revolutionary changes in landholding and in land tenure did not produce a corresponding change in agricultural techniques. The reason was that feudalism was abolished not by the operation of economic forces, as had occurred in England, but rather by political developments. These developments did not uproot the peasants, who, in most cases, continued to till the same soil as in the past and in the same manner. As late as 1911 agricultural machinery was used only on a few large estates and even the common plows were mostly made of wood. In the whole of Bulgaria at that time there were 114,000 iron plows as against 420,000 wooden ones.

The peasants grew wheat as their cash crop and maize for home consumption. Before World War I Bulgaria had a greater per capita acreage in wheat than any other European country. Consequently, exports depended on the wheat crop and the welfare of the peasants depended on the world wheat markets. In the late nineteenth century the peasants began to feel the competition of the wheat that was beginning to reach Europe from the New World and from Australia. They were ill-prepared to meet this competition because their productivity was almost the lowest in Europe: 11.8 quintals per hectare in 1911, compared to 13.5 in Rumania, 14 in Hungary, 22.2 in England, and 38.1 in Denmark.[23] Wheat obviously offered no future, so the peasants began to specialize during the years before 1914. Increased exports of poultry, eggs, attar of roses, and tobacco reflected this trend. After World War I tobacco production rose until it became by far the most valuable export.

Finally, it should be noted that throughout this pre-1914 period Bulgaria remained overwhelmingly agrarian. It is estimated that in 1911 agriculture and livestock accounted for 65 per cent of the total national income, compared to 14 per cent for industry and handicrafts.

Industry and handicrafts were of some significance during the Turkish period. They were concentrated mostly in mountain villages, where streams provided power and where the livestock formed the basis for the woolen and leather crafts. Textiles were the chief product, Bulgarian woolens clothing most of the Turkish army. Water power was used for flour mills, iron forges, sawmills, and some machine spinning. These crafts flourished so long as they operated within a large free-trade empire. Independence brought dislocation and in some cases extinction.

Some of the handicrafts had declined even before liberation. Improvements in Danubian navigation in the 1840's had led to increased imports of Austrian manufactured goods, though the poor land transportation facilities still provided some protection against this influx. But the building of railways from the 1860's on left the country open to Austrian, British, and other manufacturers. This competition was ruinous in many fields, and nothing could be done to curb it because the Berlin Treaty forbade import tariffs above 8 per cent ad valorem. Thus in Sofia there were 20 soap factories in 1876, but twenty years later there were only 5 left even though the population had increased greatly in the meantime. In Stara Zagora, 2,500 looms had woven woolen cloth before independence, but by 1913 only 30 remained. In 1876 Pirdop had 700–800 spindles, by 1896 only 20–30 were left. During the same period the knife makers of Kazanlik dropped from 25 to 3, and the saddlers of Panagyurishte from 100 to 5 or 6.[24]

It should be noted that the handicrafts which were going under were those that faced direct competition from the West. But other trades flourished as the national economy became more complex and required more auxiliary services. This was the case with blacksmithing, tinsmithing, locksmithing, and construction work. The proportion of people engaged in artisan industry probably did not decline, the number totaling about 150,000 in 1911.

Factory industry was very slow in developing in Bulgaria because of the restricted import tariff. With the fall of Stambulov in 1894 the government adopted a new and more aggressive economic policy. Legislation in 1894 and 1897 raised import tariffs to 25 per cent ad valorem. Large industries were given positive encouragement in the form of tax exemptions, freedom from duties on certain imported machinery, lower rates on Bulgarian railroads, and guaranteed state purchases even if their prices were higher than for imported articles. The earliest factory industries were in textiles, tanning, flour milling, and food and agricultural processing. Later came factories for chemicals, ceramics, metals, paper, wood, and sugar refining. All these, of course, were on a small scale. Both handicraft and factory industries, as we noted above, accounted for only 14 per cent of the national income in 1911, as compared to 65 per cent from agriculture and livestock.

The building of railroads profoundly affected the economic development of Bulgaria. Railroads were primarily responsible for the Western economic penetration of the country and for the transformation of the subsistence economy which traditionally had prevailed there. Before liberation the only railroads were the Ruschuk-Varna built by an English company in the 1860's to speed traffic down the Danube to Constantinople, and the 697 kilometers of the main Vienna-Constantinople line which had been constructed on Bulgarian soil. In 1885 legislation was passed requiring that all railroads should be state-owned. The government then bought these lines and proceeded to build others with the assistance of borrowed foreign capital. One reason for this new construction was the provision in the Berlin Treaty requiring both Bulgaria and Serbia to complete the sections of the Vienna-Constantinople line running through their territories.

By 1912 Bulgaria had 1,948 kilometers in operation. This construction was an immense burden on government finances. As in the western United States, these lines were built ahead of the traffic, hoping thereby to stimulate it. But this did not occur in Bulgaria. One reason was the poor layout of the network, pork-barrel motives having determined some of the construction. But more important was the fact that the Bulgarian economy was too poor and insufficiently specialized to warrant a complex grid of railroads. Thus the return from the lines was never enough to cover the interest on the capital invested, the return in 1911 being 3.56 per cent in contrast to the interest charge of 7 per cent.

In the field of public finance the central fact was the chronic and increasing indebtedness of the government, due to the heavy expenditures on the army and on internal improvements, such as port development and railroad construction. Unfortunately, the growth of the country's productive capacity did not keep pace with its mounting debt obligations. The percentage of the state budget allocated for payments on the public debt increased from 4.3 in 1887 to 19.7 in 1911. The result, as in other Balkan countries, was a certain degree of foreign control over national finances. In 1902, for example, the government gave its creditors control over the revenue from a special tobacco tax in order to secure a consolidation loan.[25]

The general pattern that emerges from this survey of Bulgarian economic development is typical of what was to be found throughout the peninsula at this time. The traditional agrarian subsistence economy was disintegrating under the impact of the dynamic industrial economy of the West. The repercussions of this impact were varied and ever-expanding until they affected virtually every phase of the national economy. Change produced still more change in a never-ending chain reaction. Western loans made possible the building of railroads; railroads led to the importation of Western machine-made goods; these goods undermined many traditional handicraft industries; Western loans also created a rising national debt and heavier public taxes; and, finally, at the base of the pyramid, were the peasants who were forced to shift from their traditional subsistence farming to commercial farming in order to pay the new taxes and to buy the new Western manufactured goods.

Change was not limited to the economic sphere. The everyday life of the peasants was also affected in innumerable ways. Improved transport facilities made the villages more susceptible to the influence of the neighboring towns. The new state education system left its imprint throughout the country. Moreover, the new national army was a potent leavening force, broadening the horizon of the peasant recruits and giving them new ideas on food, clothing, and sanitation.

Political institutions underwent corresponding changes and the results were by no means always positive. The pashas, the agas, the bashibazouks, and the other representatives of Ottoman authority that Gladstone had excoriated were now gone. With them went the inefficiency, the arbitrariness, and the extortion that characterized Turkish administration at this time. In its place was established a Western type of state structure with the usual bureaucracy, centralized administration, and party system of government. This did not fit well with the historical traditions and existing institutions of the country. The communal self-government allowed by the Turks withered under the centralism of the modern nation-state. The peasants regarded the new political structure with the same suspicion that they had learned to look upon all governmental authority. Their attitude did not change with time because they generally felt that they received little in return for the military service and the mounting taxes which they paid.

Thus the cleavage between rulers and ruled that characterized the Turkish period persisted after independence to a considerable degree. The new rulers were Bulgarian bureaucrats rather than Turkish pashas or Greek prelates. They usually were peasants by origin and yet they frequently tended to look down upon their illiterate countrymen and to have little rapport with them. The peasants reciprocated by regarding the cities with mingled fear, aversion, and contempt. Their attitude toward Sofia illustrates this point. Under the Turks Sofia was a squalid little provincial town with a predominantly alien population—Turkish, Greek, Jewish, and Armenian. Bulgarians did not feel at home there and kept away. After liberation Sofia became the capital of the country. It grew rapidly in size and became overwhelmingly Bulgarian in population. Yet for many peasants Sofia remained something alien and to be feared—a symbol of the exploitation and injustice under which they felt they suffered. Alexander Stambuliski, leader of the Agrarian party and prime minister after World War I, voiced this antiurbanism of the peasants when he referred to Sofia as "Sodom and Gomorrah." The famous Bulgarian poet-philosopher, Stoyan Mihailovsky, expressed the same sentiment through one of his characters:

Do you see this pretty, coquettish Bulgarian capital? It is built out of plunder and robbery! Do you recollect what a dirty village it used to be some twenty-five years ago? Now it shines, it attracts like a Parisienne. . . . Well, to me, it is a thousand times filthier, filthy in the purity of its atmosphere, foul in the cleanliness of its streets and courtyards, foul because it is a living proof that the history of young Bulgaria has begun by spoliation.[26]

24. Serbia and the South Slavs: 1878–1914

THE STRUGGLE between Russia and Austria for control of Serbia determined to a considerable degree the development of that country throughout the nineteenth century. Not only Serbian foreign relations but also Serbian domestic politics were influenced profoundly. Political leaders were classified as being Austrophil or Russophil. The former usually were admirers of Western culture, regarding Russia as an Asiatic and semi-barbarous state. Accordingly, they were convinced that Serbian national interest demanded close relations with Austria. The Progressive party was the most important in the Austrophil camp and after 1878 it was supported strongly by Prince Milan.

The Russophils, on the other hand, were to be found mostly in the Radical party. It also derived its ideology from the West but its leaders were strongly influenced by the Russian exiles in Switzerland, ranging from the anarchist Bakunin to socialists of every complexion. As time passed, the Radical party leaders dropped their socialism and republicanism for nationalism and monarchism, and thereby became more acceptable to the conservative Serbian peasantry. In foreign affairs, the Radicals, in contrast to the Progressives, regarded Russia as the leader of the Slavic world and the protector of the Slavic peoples against their traditional enemies, the Germans and the Turks. This position appealed to many Serbs and constituted the basis for the strong popular following of the Radical party.

Until Milan's abdication in 1889 Serbia was firmly committed to a pro-Austrian course. Milan's hapless son and successor, Alexander, vacillated between Austria and Russia in a futile effort to find support for himself and his unpopular queen. The murder of both Alexander and his queen in 1903 led to a change of dynasty and to a change in general national policy. Subservience to Vienna gave way to a more independent and nationalistic course. One repercussion was the so-called Pig War, an economic conflict with strong political overtones. The political component became more pro-

448

nounced as the new regime in Belgrade made Serbia increasingly attractive to the South Slavs under Hapsburg rule. The struggle came out into the open with Austria's annexation of Bosnia-Herzegovina in 1908. Thenceforth Austria was the mortal enemy of the South Slavs, and Serbia an intolerable menace to the Hapsburg Empire. Sarajevo and World War I were the logical outcome of these decades of irrepressible conflict.

AUSTRIA'S TUNIS

The outstanding factor in the history of Serbia after 1878 was the subservience of that country to Austria-Hungary. This relationship was due in part to Russian policy. Serbia was rebuffed at the Berlin Conference by Russia, who showered her favors instead upon her new Bulgarian protégés. Serbia's representative, Jovan Ristich, had no alternative but to seek the support of Austria's foreign minister, Count Andrassy. The latter took advantage of Serbia's predicament to drive a hard bargain. He backed up Ristich at the conference and enabled him to gain certain territories as well as full independence for Serbia. But in return Andrassy required Ristich to sign an agreement on July 8, 1878, promising certain railway construction in Serbia to link up with Austrian lines, and promising also to conclude a tariff treaty with Austria with the ultimate aim of a customs union between the two countries.

Ristich was not an Austrophil and apparently had no intention of fulfilling these commitments. He repeatedly postponed negotiations for the proposed tariff treaty and he turned the Skupshtina against a customs union by pointing out its dangers for Serbia's independence. But Austria was able to have her way by making use of Milan. Not only was the prince bitter against the Russians and the Bulgarians because of the experiences during the recent war; he needed Austrian financial and diplomatic support in order to assure his position on the throne. Accordingly, Milan was ready to oblige the Austrians by discharging Ristich in October, 1880, and replacing him with a Progressive ministry headed by Milan Pirochanats and Milutin Garashanin.

On April 24, 1881, the new government negotiated a trade treaty providing for such low duties on Austro-Serbian trade that it came close to being a customs union. This was favorable for the Serbian peasants, who were provided with an almost limitless market in the Hapsburg Empire. On the other hand, no protection could be afforded to Serbian industry against the competition of Austrian manufacturers. Also, the entire Serbian economy now became dangerously dependent upon Austria. Between 1884 and 1892 approximately 87 per cent of Serbia's export trade and 66 per cent of her import trade was with her northern neighbor.

Much more serious than the trade treaty was the political pact which Milan concluded on his own authority while visiting in Vienna in June, 1881. When he brought the document back to Belgrade, Pirochanats and Garashanin threatened to resign in protest against its terms. And well they might, for the text required Serbia to prevent intrigues on her territory against Austria (including the Slav provinces of Bosnia, Herzegovina, and the Sanjak of Novi Bazar) and to conclude no treaties with foreign countries without Austria's permission. In return for these extraordinary commitments Austria undertook to recognize Milan as king if he decided to assume that title, and also to support Serbia if she attempted to expand southward, excepting into the Sanjak of Novi Bazar. Upon reading the text of this pact Pirochanats commented that "by such a convention Serbia would stand in the same relation to Austria-Hungary as Tunis to France." [1]

In order to appease his ministers Milan returned to Vienna to secure modifications of the terms. He was able to get a statement on October 30, 1881, providing that the treaty "cannot impair the right of Serbia to negotiate and conclude treaties, even of a political nature, with another government. It implies for Serbia no other engagement than that of not negotiating and of not concluding any political treaty which would be contrary to the spirit and the tenor of the said secret treaty." [2] This forthright statement satisfied the Serbian ministers and the political crisis passed. But in actual fact the statement was worthless. In order to obtain it Milan had secretly signed a letter a week earlier, on October 24, in which he recognized the full validity of the original treaty. "I hereby assume the formal engagement on my honour, and in my quality as Prince of Serbia, not to enter into any negotiations whatsoever relative to any kind of political treaty between Serbia and a third state without communication with and previous consent of Austria-Hungary." [3] In this manner Milan double-crossed his ministers and relegated his country to the role of Austria's Tunis.

The assurance of Austrian support did not solve Milan's problems. In fact, his position became increasingly precarious because of mounting opposition to his rule. One reason for his unpopularity was his pro-Austrian policy, which necessitated acceptance of what most Serbians considered to be an utterly unacceptable *status quo* in Bosnia-Herzegovina and in the Turkish-held provinces to the south. Another reason was his treatment of his queen, Nathalie, the daughter of a Russian colonel. Milan was anything but a faithful husband, and since Nathalie was beautiful and spirited, public sympathy was on her side. Furthermore, she was naturally pro-Russian, which increased her popularity in the country. Thus the royal estrangement assumed a political aspect, with Milan being definitely the unpopular party in the dispute. More and more frequently talk was heard that Serbia would be better off if Milan were replaced by Prince Nicholas of Montenegro or by Peter Karageorgevich, who was living quietly in Geneva.

On March 6, 1882, Milan assumed the title of king and raised Serbia to the dignity of a kingdom. But the glamour of the new title did not make Milan popular. In fact, a local peasant insurrection broke out the following year with the rebels threatening to massacre all government officials. About the same time the opposition Radical party won a majority of the seats in the Skupshtina. This party was by far the best organized in the country, with committees functioning in each district and a national committee in Belgrade providing over-all leadership. The effectiveness and popularity of the Radicals made Milan's position correspondingly more difficult since he was forced, because of his foreign policy, to rely upon the Austrophil Progressive party.

The last blow came when Milan declared war on Bulgaria on November 14, 1885. Bulgaria had just incorporated Eastern Rumelia, and Milan decided that it was essential for his personal prestige to obtain corresponding compensation for Serbia. At first he thought of attacking Turkey and expanding to the south. But he feared that the Turks might repeat their victory of 1876, so he turned against the Bulgars. Instead of winning an easy victory, Milan suffered the series of humiliating defeats described in the preceding chapter. The Bulgarians were marching triumphantly on the road to Belgrade when the Austrians intervened and forced the victors to accept a peace restoring the *status quo ante bellum*. Defeat at the hands of the Bulgarians was shameful enough for the Serbians. But the fact that the Austrians rescued them from their ignoble plight was unbearably mortifying.

Milan's position had become impossible. He appears to have been aware of this, for he now sought to gain public approval by adopting on January 2, 1889, a new and liberal constitution to replace that of 1869. This gesture failed; hence two months later, on March 6, he made the supreme sacrifice in behalf of his dynasty by abdicating in favor of his son, Alexander. Milan still was only thirty-five years old, although he had been on the throne twenty-one years. He was a man of far above average ability who had squandered his talents and opportunities. His departure was greeted generally with a sigh of relief despite the lingering affection of some of his subjects for their genial monarch.

THE LAST OBRENOVICH

If Milan's reign was depressing, that of Alexander was pathetically tragic. The only son of his father, and without near relatives, Alexander was the last hope of the house of Obrenovich. His childhood had been spent in an unhappy atmosphere of domestic strife. When he came to the throne at the age of thirteen he was a quiet, introspective, and melancholy boy, a lonely and pitiful figure in his exalted position. His divorced parents continued to keep the capital in a ferment with their unceasing bickering. On one occasion a mob of townspeople and students clashed with the police when the latter attempted to expel Nathalie from Belgrade. At length the royal parents agreed to live abroad in order not to damage the prestige of the dynasty further. But Alexander completed the destructive work they had begun. In his search for the affection and security denied him in his boyhood Alexander contracted a marriage which was violently opposed by his subjects and which was to prove fatal to himself, to his queen, and to his dynasty.

Whatever his failings, Alexander early demonstrated that he had a will of his own. On April 13, 1893, when he was still only seventeen, he got rid of his regents and took power into his own hands. This move was generally acclaimed because the regents were unpopular. But Alexander soon came into conflict with the predominantly Radical Skupshtina. On the advice of his father, who now returned from Paris, he abrogated the liberal constitution of 1889 and restored that of 1869. Milan ensconced himself in the palace and became commander in chief of the army. In that capacity he did excellent work, devoting his time and talents to a complete overhauling of the armed services. But the press was bitterly hostile, so Milan retaliated by promoting legislation restricting the press and the right of association. In July, 1899, an attempt made on Milan's life led to more repressive measures, particularly against the Radical party.

Meanwhile, Alexander was being urged from all sides to find a wife and assure the future of his dynasty. He expressed willingness to accommodate, but set very high conditions. His bride, he declared, must be "young, beautiful, and lovely. . . . politically well connected . . . at least have family relations with one of the first-class Courts of Europe; further, she ought to be a highly cultured and gifted woman; and, last but not least, very wealthy." Count Goluchowski, the Austrian foreign minister, who was naturally concerned about the future of the Obrenovich dynasty, considered Alexander's expectations to be excessive. "Please tell the King," he said to a Serbian diplomat, "that a Princess who possesses all these conditions could do better than marry King Alexander of Servia and spend her life in Belgrade! Therefore he ought to be satisfied if we succeed in finding for him a Princess who possesses some of his stipulations. . . . I think we are in a position to recommend to him one of the most charming and most cultured Princesses in Europe." [4]

The princess in question was of a minor princely German family. Alexander admitted that she looked attractive in photographs shown to him. "Certainly by the end of the year, if not sooner," he promised his father, "you will see me a married man." [5] But Alexander did not have the German princess in mind when he made this pledge. Unknown to his parents, to his ministers, and to everyone else, he had already found his true love and future queen. She was Madame Draga Mashin, widow of a Bohemian engineer and former lady-in-waiting to his mother. When Alexander announced his intention to marry her a major crisis broke out. His entire cabinet resigned. The press made clear the public indignation. Milan warned his son prophetically that "the dynasty would never recover from the impossible marriage for which you have decided." [6]

But Alexander would not be dissuaded. He was unmoved by the weighty arguments that Draga was considerably older than he, that she was probably sterile, and that her past was not above reproach. His reply to all this is revealing of the inner forces that impelled him to sacrifice himself and his dynasty:

I have had neither childhood nor youth like other men. The eternal quarrel between my parents made my life bitter, undermined my health in general, and my nerves more especially. Such a life killed in me every sentiment. . . . In the whole world there is only one woman who can make me forget the bitterness of my past life, and make me feel happy. . . . There is no power on earth which could prevent my marrying Draga, whatever the consequences may be. . . . If I cannot marry Draga as King, I will leave Servia for ever, and marry her as a private individual.[7]

Alexander might have found the happiness he was seeking if he had carried out his threat to abdicate before marrying Draga. Instead, he remained on the throne and made her his queen on July 23, 1900. From then on life was almost a continuous nightmare for the unfortunate Alexander. Draga, according to the Austrian minister, "revealed herself as ambitious, avaricious, greedy; and persecuted unmercifully any who did not at once hurry to Court to do her homage or who did not believe in her ability to bear children." [8] Alexander tried frantically to have Draga accepted, even to the point of naming regiments, schools, and villages after her, and designating her birthday a state holiday. But many Serbians continued to look down upon her as the disreputable widow of an obscure foreign engineer. Equally galling was the social ostracism of the European courts, which refused to receive the royal couple.

The crowning humiliation was the fantastic "false expectancy." In August, 1900, only a month after the wedding, the government announced that the queen was an expectant mother. Alexander was overjoyed and ordered the news to be made public despite the obvious inference of premarital relations. He hoped thereby to arouse sympathy for Draga and to check the widespread rumors of her sterility. Gifts were beginning to shower the court when the news broke that the queen was not pregnant at all. The Russian government had been dubious of the reported pregnancy and had sent three obstetricians to examine the queen. They discovered that she was not pregnant and signed a protocol to that effect. The "false expectancy" as it was called, aroused widespread popular resentment. Many believed, and not without justification, that Draga had been deliberately deceitful and that she had planned to adopt the child of her sister, who was pregnant at the time. It also appears that this was not her first "false expectancy," and that she had feigned others before her marriage in order to inveigle the naïve Alexander.

Alexander was now in an even worse position than his father had been after the disastrous Bulgarian adventure. The opposition movement grew rapidly to revolutionary proportions. In the elections of July 22, 1901, the Radical party won a substantial majority of the seats in the Skupshtina. Propaganda literature in favor of the Karageorgevich dynasty began to circulate in all parts of the country. On March 23, 1903, students demonstrated in Belgrade and were dispersed only after police had killed several participants and arrested over a hundred. Alexander met the gathering storm with severe restrictions on the press and on civil liberties. On May 19, 1903, he held new elections but under such intimidation and police terror that the

Radicals refused to participate. The Skupshtina that was elected was properly subservient but as inconsequential as it was unrepresentative.

Such was the situation in Serbia when a group of army officers organized a conspiracy to murder Alexander. The plotters enlarged their circle to include various political leaders. But the conspiracy remained essentially apolitical, the aim being simply to get rid of Alexander. Participants included not only Karageorgevich supporters but also traditional Obrenovich adherents and even a number of republicans. The government got wind of what was afoot and began to make arrests. The conspirators decided to strike at once before it was too late.

On June 10, 1903, at two o'clock in the morning a group of twenty-eight officers forced their way into the palace. Someone turned off the electricity and the conspirators rushed through the palace hallways in confusion. They dynamited door after door in their search for Alexander and his queen. Finally they found the royal chamber, only to discover their quarry gone. The officers knew that they were hiding somewhere in the building, so in desperation they prepared to raze the palace to the ground with dynamite and artillery. Finally one of the conspirators stumbled on to a door concealed behind draperies and leading to a secret alcove where Alexander and Draga were hiding. In a moment the king was riddled by thirty bullets and the queen by eighteen. Then the two corpses were put to the saber.

At 3:50 A.M. the jubilant officers rushed out on the palace balcony shouting, "The Tyrant is no more!" "Long live Peter Karageorgevich!" Troops lined up below on the palace grounds responded enthusiastically, roaring for Peter and shooting their revolvers in the air. Bullets rained everywhere and general pandemonium ensued. In the midst of the din two young officers hurled the bodies of the king and queen out of a palace window into the garden below. Before the bloody night was over the queen's two brothers were also killed, as well as the prime minister, the minister of interior, and several officers who had remained loyal to Alexander.

Twenty-four hours after the carnage a provisional government was formed consisting of four conspirators and six representatives of the political parties. This government summoned the Skupshtina of 1901 rather than that which had been elected two weeks before the royal tragedy. The Skupshtina voted to restore the liberal constitution of 1889 and then elected Peter Karageorgevich king of Serbia. Some of the younger conspirators favored a republic, but it was realized that such a form of government would not have been recognized or even tolerated by the European powers. On June 24, 1903, Peter returned to Belgrade after forty-five years of exile.

REVOLUTION AND REVIVAL

Peter was sixty years of age at the time of his accession. During his long sojourn abroad he had attended the military school at Saint-Cyr, fought in the Franco-Prussian War of 1870–1871, and been decorated with the Cross of the Legion of Honor. In 1877, on the outbreak of the revolt in Herzegovina, he had organized a band of volunteers and fought against the Turks. Though a soldier by training and inclination, he was also a man of scholarly taste and achievement, having translated into the Serbian language John Stuart Mill's *Essay on Liberty*. This rich background more than balanced his lack of experience with Serbian affairs. Furthermore, his queen was a daughter of Nicholas of Montenegro and most Serbians welcomed this dynastic tie with the neighboring sister state.

The first problem facing the new regime was to secure recognition from the foreign powers. There was no question about the regime's popularity and control of the country. Only a week after the murder the British minister ruefully reported that "Belgrade had resumed its ordinary life and not only forgotten, but apparently rejoiced in, the murderous extinction of the royal family." [9] Yet regardless of the popular reaction, the chancellories of Europe were profoundly shocked and were most reluctant to accept the regicides. Oddly enough, the first powers to recognize Peter were Russia and Austria. The explanation given by the Russian foreign minister is revealing: ". . . the risk of seeing a republic proclaimed could not be incurred." [10] The example of the eastern empires was followed by other states, including France and Germany. But Britain refused recognition unless all the regicides were ousted from official positions. Because of the unsettled international situation the Serbian government finally decided to accept this condition. On the third anniversary of the palace murders, diplomatic relations between Serbia and Britain were renewed and the new regime in Belgrade thus gained general international recognition.

Meanwhile, elections had been held on September 8, 1903. The overwhelming majority of the seats were won by the Radicals, who were divided into two factions which alternately split off and joined together. The most durable cabinets were led by Nikola Pashich, who later was to become the political boss of the new Yugoslav state. The outstanding characteristic of Serbian political life during the years after 1903 was the consolidation of civil liberties and of democratic freedoms. Irregularities did occur during elections and at other times, but the king and the politicial leaders generally kept within the bounds of the law. For the first time Serbia enjoyed true constitutional government, and the relations between government and people became much healthier than in the past.

In its foreign relations the new regime faced two major problems: the struggle for Macedonia, which will be considered in Chapter 28, and the so-called Pig War, which was fought with Austria. The basic cause of the "Pig War" was Austria's attempt to continue her economic and political domination over Serbia. We have seen that on April 24, 1881, Serbia was constrained to sign a tariff agreement with Austria which established a virtual customs union. Serbian agricultural goods and Austrian manufactures were to be exchanged with very low custom duties or none at all. Thus Serbian industry continued to be stifled while Serbian agriculture remained dependent on the Hapsburg markets.

This tariff agreement was renewed in 1892 on essentially the same terms, with the result that Austria continued to dominate Serbia's commerce. For the five-year period preceding 1906, Austria-Hungary supplied 53.35 per cent of Serbia's imports and absorbed 83.66 per cent of Serbia's exports. This economic dependence was especially irksome for the Serbians because it also meant political dependence. Austria could, and did, bring political pressure to bear whenever she wished by closing her border to Serbian livestock on the pretext that it was diseased.

With the accession of the new dynasty, Serbian policy became markedly nationalistic and anti-Austrian. This manifested itself when the Austrian-Serbian trade treaty expired in 1905. It was extended to March, 1906, with the understanding that a new treaty would be concluded during the interim. But the negotiations bogged down, partly because the Serbians wanted more independence but also because Hungarian agricultural interests were demanding protection against Serbian products. An impasse ensued; whereupon the Serbians concluded a far-reaching economic pact with Bulgaria. It established virtual free trade between the two countries; it allowed citizens of one country to work and live in the territory of the other; and it foresaw the establishment of a customs union on March 1, 1917. It was speculated at the time that the pact might lead eventually to a united Serbo-Bulgarian state that would be strong enough to block Austrian influence in the Balkans.

Austria countered by demanding that the Bulgarian treaty be voided. Serbia refused, so Austria "discovered" that the Serbian livestock was diseased and closed her border to further imports. In this manner the "Pig War" began between the Serbian David and the Austrian Goliath. The Vienna press warned Serbia that she was economically dependent on the Hapsburg Empire and predicted that she would "suffocate in her own swine-fat." [11]

The question of tariffs was now complicated by that of armaments. Serbia had bought military equipment earlier from the Austrian Skoda works and had found it to be unsatisfactory. Now she began negotiations for French arms, but Austria again objected. The Austrian foreign minister informed the Serbian ambassador in Vienna that "we shall certainly determine the extent of the concessions under the new commercial treaty by the extent to which the state contracts now under discussion are given to Austria-Hungary." [12] Serbia ignored this pressure; indeed, she could scarcely do otherwise. If she had placed her order with the Skoda works the Austrian government would have obtained valuable information about Serbian armaments and also would have had control over munition supplies in the future. On November 7, 1906, Serbia gave her arms contract to the French firm of Schneider-Creusot.

Having crossed the Rubicon, Serbia looked desperately for new markets. Her search was surprisingly successful. From Turkey she obtained railway transit and a loading zone in Saloniki. In Egypt she discovered a large market for her cattle. Also, she concluded trade agreements with numerous European countries, including Germany, France, Britain, Russia, and Italy. The net result was that Serbia did succeed in lessening her economic subservience to Austria. The two countries finally signed a customs pact on July 27, 1910. But whereas Serbia before the "Pig War" had shipped about 90 per cent of her exports to Austria, henceforth she sent only about 30 per cent. Also, Serbia was now beginning to process her agricultural products because of the greater distance to her new markets. In place of cereals, for example, she now exported flour, and in place of cattle she shipped fresh and salt meats and animal products of various types. Serbia also had substantially increased the import duties on certain manufactured goods, thus giving protection to her industries for the first time. Finally, the Serbian army was now provided with French rather than Austrian artillery, a change that was to prove of the greatest importance less than a decade later.

We may conclude that during the years following the accession of the new dynasty Serbia experienced a marked recovery. The political atmosphere was healthier, the national economy was sounder, and the international prestige of the country rose immeasurably from the dark days of the Bulgarian war and the Draga buffoonery. The revival came none too soon, for Serbia now was faced with a series of life-and-death tests—the Bosnian crisis of 1908, the Balkan wars of 1912–1913, and the Sarajevo murder of 1914, which precipitated World War I. These great events constitute a part of Balkan and general European diplomacy and will be considered later in that context.*

ECONOMIC DEVELOPMENT

Serbia remained an overwhelmingly agricultural country during the period from 1878 to 1914. By the latter year 84 per cent of the population was engaged in agriculture, 7 per cent in industry, 5 per cent in government employ or in the professions, and 4 per cent in trade. Belgrade, the capital, had a population of only 90,000 in 1910, and the next largest city, Nish, had 25,000.

Conditions in the countryside were changing rapidly during these decades. One reason was the sharp increase in population from 1.7 million in 1878 to 2.9 million in 1910, a growth of 71.3 per cent in 32 years. Serbian industry did not expand rapidly enough to absorb this population increase. Also, Serbia did not have an emigration safety valve as did areas like Croatia and the Voivodina, the reason probably being that latifundia did not exist in Serbia and consequently there was not as much pressure upon the Serbian peasants to emigrate. The net result was a mounting population pressure upon the land which led to increased fragmentation of peasant property. This is revealed in the following statistics on the size of farms in Serbia in 1897. Since 7 to 8 hectares of land were needed to support a family of

* See Chapters 28 and 29.

five, by the end of the nineteenth century about 60 per cent of the Serbian peasants did not have sufficient land to support their families.

Distribution of Farms by Size in Serbia, 1897

Size in hectares	Number	Percent of total
Rural households without land	34,952	11.34
0 to 1 hectare	19,173	6.22
1 - 2	31,368	10.18
2 - 5	93,627	30.39
5 - 20	117,939	38.29
20 - 50	10,277	3.33
50 - 100	710	0.23
100 - 200	68	0.02
Above 200	6	0.00
Total	308,120	100.00

Source: J. Tomasevich, *Peasants, Politics and Economic Change in Yugoslavia* (Stanford, Calif., 1955), p. 206.

Another important change in the Serbian countryside was the shift from livestock raising to cereal cultivation. The shift occurred because the population increase forced the peasants to put more land under cultivation, leaving insufficient land for pasture. Also, the demand for grain rose with the growth of population. As a result, the number of livestock per thousand inhabitants fell from 1,498 head in 1859 to 695 in 1895. The drop in the number of pigs was even more sharp, from 1,061 per thousand inhabitants in 1866 to 416 in 1890.

Serbia had a more varied agricultural production at the beginning of the twentieth century than either Rumania or Bulgaria. The peasants grew mostly corn, eating it themselves and also feeding it to their pigs. They grew less wheat but consumed little of it, about a quarter to a third of the crop being exported. The peasants also grew barley for the cattle, for the beer industry, and for export. Tobacco crops were limited by the state but enough was grown to meet domestic needs. Sugar beets were introduced about 1900 and a German concern established a refinery. About 1850 the Serbs began to dry plums into prunes for foreign markets. The government controlled the quality carefully and a lucrative export trade resulted.

The most important development affecting Serbia's economic progress at the turn of the century was the "Pig War" with Austria, which began in 1906. We noted above that as a result of the war Serbia found new outlets for her agricultural goods in Western Europe and elsewhere, thereby reducing her dependence on the Austrian market. The "Pig War" also aided Serbian industry. A protective tariff was adopted in 1906, and by 1910 Serbia had 470 factories with a production valued at 74.4 million francs in contrast to 270 factories in 1905 with a production worth 29.4 million francs. Milling was the most important industry, accounting for a third of the total value of the industrial output. Other important branches were meat packing, sugar refining, brewing, woolen textiles, and mining. Serbian industry, like that of the other Balkan countries, was devoted almost entirely to the processing of local raw materials and agricultural products. Despite the increased industrial production in the early twentieth century, only 7 per cent of the population were engaged in industry on the eve of World War I.

The growth of industry was also helped by the improvement of transportation facilities. The first stage was road building, which got under way intensively in the 1860's. Railroads followed about two decades later. In this, as in other respects, Serbia lagged far behind the South Slav provinces under Hapsburg rule. From 1846 onward, railroads were being built from Austria and Hungary through Slavonia and Croatia to the ports of Trieste and Fiume. By contrast, no railroads were built on Serbian territory before 1878. The Ottoman government had let contracts a few years earlier for a main line from Constantinople to Zemun on the Austrian border. Sections had been built running northward into the Balkan interior from Constantinople, Dedeagach, and Saloniki. But none had reached the Serbian frontier by 1878.

The Berlin Treaty stipulated that Austria, Turkey, and Serbia make the necessary arrangements for constructing the gaps on Serbian territory. The three countries reached agreements in 1880 and 1883, and the first through train from Vienna to Constantinople passed through Serbia in 1888. The Serbian section of the Orient Express, as the main line was called, had been built by a French firm and was 461 kilometers in length. The Serbian government was dissatisfied with the service provided by the French company and bought it out between 1889 and 1892. By 1912 the government had built another 400 kilometers of railroad, mostly narrow gauge. The government also organized the Royal Serbian Shipping Company in 1890 to challenge the foreign monopoly of shipping on the Danube. By 1913 the company had thirteen river steamers in operation but the foreign companies were still in control of most shipping on the Danube.

One of the most significant features of Serbian economic development in the late nineteenth century was the rapid rise in government expenditures and debts. This reflected the growth of a money and credit economy as well as the mounting cost of the state bureaucracy and the armed forces. Government expenditures rose from 12.5 million francs in 1869 to 46.2 million in 1890, to 76.3 million in 1900, and to 120.1 million in 1911. Increasing expenditures meant increasing debts. The first foreign loan came from Russia in 1867 for military equipment. Later borrowings were made in Austria, Germany, and, after the "Pig War," in France. Thus the public debt rose from 2.3 million francs in 1867 to 16.5 million in 1880, to 414.0 million in 1895, and to 903.8 million in 1914. Increasing indebtedness was accompanied by increasing foreign control over national finances. Debt payments were guaranteed by the Monopolies Administration comprising two representatives each from the Serbian finance ministry, the Serbian National Bank, and the foreign bondholders. This body was given control over the revenue from the taxes on such commodities as tobacco, salt, petroleum, and liquor.

Reviewing the economic development of Serbia during the nineteenth century, we find the pattern similar to that in other Balkan countries. The peasant had freed himself from Turkish landlords and feudal obligations but he had then to contend with usurers and merchants and to support an expensive state bureaucracy and army. He found that he needed money to pay taxes and to buy the manufactured goods that now were made available to him. This compelled him to produce more and to sell his output on the market. Thus he became dependent on the domestic and international market and, all too frequently, on the village usurer.

These far-reaching economic developments were paralleled by equally far-reaching social changes, and the connection between the two was intimate. We noted in Chapter 14 that the zadruga was giving way to the individual family unit. Another social trend was the continuation of the gulf between the city and the country. The cleavage was understandable during the Turkish period, when the cities consisted of Turkish officials and soldiers and of assorted foreign merchants and artisans. But it persisted for some time after independence had been won. One reason was the rise of a bureaucratic class which was not very efficient, which was frequently corrupt, and which was generally regarded by the peasants as an expensive and dispensable luxury. Indeed, a common peasant attitude was that independence should mean at least no more interference and exactions from the city.

The rift between city and country existed also because of the cultural difference between the two. The countryside was largely illiterate. Three fourths of Serbian peasant children in the early twentieth century did not attend school. On the other hand, the bureaucrats who were in contact with the peasants had an academic training and tended to despise illiterates and to regard themselves as being superior.

The final social development to be noted is the growing class stratification within the village itself. The successful peasant who turned moneylender and merchant made his appearance in the mid-nineteenth century. It was he who borrowed money from government institutions at a low rate while most peasants were unable to do so because they could not provide security. Thus the moneylender borrowed at 6 per cent and lent to the peasants at 12 per cent, 36 per cent, even 120 per cent. The wealthy peasant-usurer could send his sons to secondary school, perhaps even to the university. Then the doors were open to a career in the army and to positions of authority in the city. This naturally reflected prestige upon the family in the village. But the poor peasant families found it almost impossible to achieve such distinction. This class differentiation caused considerable tension in the villages. The usurer-merchants tended to be shrewd and ruthless, and were generally hated by the poorer villagers. "Our own lice eat us," was the latter's grim commentary.

In conclusion, these economic and social developments were typical of the Balkan countries during these decades. Serbia, like the rest, was changing from a closed and static natural economy to a dynamic money and market economy. Most peasants found the change uncomfortable and incomprehensible.

We live in a time of wonders.
Wise people tell me that carts roll without horses to pull them,
That proud ships sail fast as an arrow without sail or wind,
That wonder-doctors can cut off legs or hands and one feels no pain or utters any cry,
That, on a wire stretched across the earth, news can travel around the world faster than one counts to three,
That, of itself, the scythe mows, the spinning wheel runs, and the plow cuts a furrow,
And still the hunger for bread is among us as it has ever been.[13]

HAPSBURG SLAVS

The most important development among the Hapsburg Slavs between 1878 and 1914 was the increasing cooperation between the Serbs and the Croatians and the growing tendency for them to look to Belgrade rather than to Vienna or Budapest. But this occurred only in the later years. During the period immediately following the 1867 *Ausgleich* the South Slavs were divided among various leaders and parties, and the Austro-Hungarian authorities carefully fostered these divisions in order to strengthen their rule.

One of the outstanding personalities among the South Slavs throughout the second half of the nineteenth century was the Catholic bishop, Joseph George Strossmayer. Though of German ancestry, he early became a champion of Croat national rights. His aim was to establish within the Hapsburg framework an autonomous Croatia which would serve as the nucleus of an all-inclusive Yugoslav state. Although the Croats and Slovenes and the Serbs and Bulgarians were divided by religion and culture, he considered them all to be of one nationality. His efforts in behalf of South Slav culture were as significant as his work for South Slav unity. Strossmayer subsidized scholars, built schools, and established in Agram (Zagreb) a seminary, an art gallery, a national university, and a learned academy.

Quite different from Strossmayer's genuine Yugoslavism was the program of the Party of the Right, an extremist nationalist group led by Ante Starchevich. On his death in 1896 the party split into two factions, the larger one being led by Joseph Frank and known as the Party of Pure Right. Its program was Pan-Croatian rather than Yugoslav and its aim was Croatian hegemony rather than union on equal terms with the other South Slavs. It was a Catholic-oriented party which tended to regard Serbians as being degenerated Croats who had adopted the Orthodox religion and Byzantine culture. In fact the word "Right" in the party's title stood not for conservative leanings but for the avowed righteousness of its claims for the creation of a Greater Croatia.

Hungarian officials exploited this situation by pitting Croatians against Serbians. The kingdom of Croatia, according to the 1910 census, included 1,630,354 Croats and 644,955 Serbs, together constituting 90 per cent of the total population. Khuen-Hedervary, governor of Croatia from 1883 to 1903, fostered the latent antagonism between the two people by granting special concessions to the Serbian minority. He opened Serbian schools, appointed Serbs to public office, and granted privileges to the Serbian Orthodox Church. The tactic proved quite successful, physical clashes between Croatian and Serbian patriots being very common in the eighteen nineties.

The situation began to change with the turn of the century. In 1903 Khuen-Hedervary left Croatia to become premier of Hungary. His successor lacked finesse and resorted to naked force, which drove the Serbs and Croats to cooperation in self-defense. In the same year the new Karageorgevich dynasty succeeded to the Serbian throne. It was anti-Austrian and it encouraged the Hapsburg Slavs, with considerable success, to look to Belgrade as their hope for the future. Also, a younger political generation of Serbian leaders in Croatia now began to see that periodic support of their claims by the Magyars was designed to serve Hungarian rather than Serbian interests. Finally, the outright annexation of Bosnia-Herzegovina by the Hapsburgs in 1908 greatly accelerated the trend toward Serbo-Croatian cooperation.

The Hapsburgs had first occupied Bosnia-Herzegovina in 1878 in accordance with the terms of the Berlin Treaty. The population of the provinces at the time comprised 43 per cent Orthodox Serbs, 39 per cent Moslems, and 18 per cent Catholic Croatians. The Moslems were the privileged group. Six to seven thousand Moslem begs owned the large estates and wielded political power. This ruling class exploited 85,000 serf families of which 60,000 were Serbian, 23,000 Croatian, and 2,000 Moslem. In addition, there were 77,000 free peasant families which were almost exclusively Moslem.

The Hapsburgs decided not to challenge the Moslem ruling class and allowed the existing feudal system to continue. The serfs were permitted to buy their freedom but comparatively few were able to do so by 1914. The Austrians did make important contributions in certain fields. They organized an efficient administrative system, built railways, conducted reforestation and agricultural research, and established flourishing mining, timber, and chemical industries. But their failure to change the feudal land tenure system held back agriculture in which the great majority of the population were engaged. The large domains of the begs were not cultivated efficiently as single units after the manner of English and Prussian estates. Rather, a multitude of serfs tilled small individual plots, using the traditional implements and techniques. The result was not only low productivity but also agrarian unrest. The fact that an exceptionally strong revolutionary movement existed in

Bosnia-Herzegovina before World War I is to be explained by the combination of this agrarian unrest with the religious cleavage between Moslem overlords and Christian tenants, and the political conflict between the imperial authority and the growing Serbo-Croatian nationalist movement.

All these factors account for the almost continual crisis in Croatia and Bosnia-Herzegovina during the decade before 1914. Disorders in Croatia in 1903 forced the authorities to proclaim a state of siege and to arrest hundreds of demonstrators. In 1905 a group of Croat politicians adopted the historic Fiume Resolutions, asserting the right of every people "to decide its own life and destinies freely and independently," and demanding franchise reform, free elections, and civil liberties. Later in the same year Serbian politicians from Croatia met in Zara (Zadar), endorsed the Fiume Resolutions, and appealed for Serbo-Croat cooperation throughout the empire. During the winter of 1905 most of the opposition parties combined to form the Serbo-Croat Coalition. The only important parties that abstained were Joseph Frank's Party of Pure Right and a new Peasant party headed by Stjepan and Antun Radich. The Serbo-Croat Coalition demonstrated its popularity by winning a plurality of the seats in the Croatian Diet in the 1906 elections.

In January, 1908, the Hungarian government appointed a new viceroy, Baron Paul Rauch, to tame Croatia and its Diet. Rauch was greeted in Agram (Zagreb) with catcalls and a shower of rotten eggs. He dissolved the Diet and held new elections in February of the same year. Although the Croatian franchise was extremely restricted, not a single delegate was elected who could be relied upon to support Rauch. The Diet was again dissolved and Rauch governed by decree for two years.

The Hapsburg annexation of Bosnia-Herzegovina in October, 1908, heightened the crisis. South Slav nationalists regarded the two provinces as the Alsace-Lorraine of the Balkans and vowed to recover them at any cost. This was the atmosphere in which the notorious treason trials were conducted at Agram in 1909. Rauch arrested some fifty Croatians and Serbians on vague charges that they were conspiring to unite Croatia and Bosnia-Herzegovina with Serbia. Although no conclusive proof of treasonable activities was presented, the court found over thirty of the defendants guilty and sentenced them to prison at hard labor. The condemned men appealed their case to a higher tribunal, which annulled the sentences on the ground that the evidence was inadequate. The entire Slav press denounced the affair as a case of judicial persecution and this charge received wide circulation and acceptance abroad.

Before the Agram trial had closed, another *cause célèbre,* the Friedjung affair, had crowded to the fore. Heinrich Friedjung, an eminent historian and patriotic Hapsburger, published an article accusing certain Croatian and Serbian politicians of seditious relations with the Serbian government. The accused individuals brought libel suits and a sensational trial ensued. Before it was over Friedjung was forced to acknowledge that his "incriminating documents" were forgeries. The affair seriously damaged the reputation of the Austrian government because it was obvious that Friedjung had received the documents from official sources. As for the politically conscious among Hapsburg Serbs and Croats, the Friedjung suit, coming as it did on the heels of the Agram trial, intensified discontent with the existing scheme of things.

New elections were held in Croatia in 1912. Again the Serbo-Croat Coalition won a majority and again the Diet was dissolved and the country ruled by decree. The University of Agram, which was a hotbed of anti-Magyar agitation, was bolted and barred. A Bosnian student, Tukich, who had attended the university, attempted to assassinate the viceroy. In the trial that followed it was shown that Tukich was a member of the notorious "Black Hand" society of Belgrade, a city he had visited a month before the crime. The evidence did not disturb Serbian patriots, who hailed Tukich as a martyr to the cause of Greater Serbia. "We have ten million Tukiches now," a Belgrade newspaper exulted. "We are firmly convinced that through his prison window he will see the final shot for freedom." [14] The boast did not appear farfetched at the time. When the Balkan war broke out in 1912 Croatian youths streamed across the border to fight in the Serbian army. And when they were reviewed by King Peter they shouted enthusiastically, "Long live our King!"

This discontent in Croatia had its counterpart in Bosnia-Herzegovina. We have seen that a combination of factors made the situation there particularly explosive, including the deep-seated agrarian problem, the Moslem-Christian conflict, and the growing nationalist sentiment for Yugoslav unity. At the turn of the century the situation became steadily worse because of the influence and activities of a new generation of Serbian intellectuals in Bosnia-Herzegovina. Hitherto the Serbian intellectuals had been very limited in numbers and had originated from a small middle class of lawyers, doctors, and officials. But now there appeared a new generation of intellectuals, many of them the product of a cultural society known as the Prosveta, or "Enlightenment." This organization was established in 1902 for the purpose of enabling peasant and lower middle-class children to get an education. Thus Serbian intellectuals of a new type made their appearance. They derived from the "small and insignificant classes"—from peasants, teachers, journeymen, and village priests. They were usually penniless and unemployed because of the traditional preference in bureaucratic circles for Croats over Serbs. Also, they were very radical in their views, partly because they had no vested interest in the *status quo* and partly because they knew at firsthand the plight of the mass of the people. When Archduke Francis Ferdinand was struck down in Sarajevo in 1914, his assassin, the student Gavrilo Princip, declared defiantly in court, "I have seen our people being steadily ruined. I am a peasant's son and know what goes on in the villages. That is why I meant to take my revenge and I regret nothing." [15]

The new generation constituted the backbone of the Mlada Bosna, or "Young Bosnia." This was an amorphous nationalist movement rather than a definite political organization. Its adherents were not gathered in one body, being scattered in various groups such as agricultural cooperatives, choral societies, and numerous student associations. They shared a common aspiration for liberation from Hapsburg rule and for social reform. But they were not agreed as to just how these objectives were to be attained. Most of them were inspired by Russian revolutionaries in whose works they read widely— revolutionaries like Kropotkin, Herzen, Bakunin, Stepniak, Gorky, Chernishevsky, and Plekhanov. With such tutelage the young Bosnian radicals naturally reacted enthusiastically to the great Russian Revolution of 1905. They tended more and more to think in terms of revolution rather than of reform within the existing framework. They turned their backs on the old political leaders who were satisfied with slow change by "legal" methods. Instead, they developed the "cult of the individual deed." Only by acts of terrorism, they believed, would they be able to rid themselves of Hapsburg rule and set up their own nation-state.

The first notable expression of this new cult was the "deed" of Bogdan Zerajich, a Serbian from Herzegovina. On June 15, 1910, he attempted to assassinate the governor, General Vareshanin, at the opening of the Bosnian Parliament. Zerajich failed and committed suicide on the spot. In doing so he became a national hero, the "first martyr" of the Serbian cause. The Bosnian youth were inflamed by the oft-repeated story of the general scornfully spurning with his foot Zerajich's body as it lay sprinkled with mud and blood upon the bridge at Sarajevo.

Zerajich's exploit was glorified by a pamphlet entitled "The Death of a Hero" and written in 1912 by Vladimir Gachinovich, the son of a Herzegovinian priest. The pamphlet quotes Zerajich's own phrase, "I leave it to Serbdom to avenge me," and concludes with the pointed question, "Young Serbs, you who are rising from the ruins and foulness of to-day, will you produce such men?" [16] Gachinovich then went to Belgrade, where he joined a new secret revolutionary organization, the Ujedinjenje ili Smrt, or Union or Death, better known as the Black Hand. This was the society which engineered the murder of Archduke Francis Ferdinand in 1914. Before that date Gachinovich exploited his prestige among the Bosnian youth to organize many terrorist groups which were directed by the Black Hand in Belgrade. Little wonder that the Hapsburg officials cracked down hard on this revolutionary agitation. Between 1909 and 1914 they tried 166 persons in Bosnia for treason or espionage, and convicted the majority. A Serbian diplomat stationed in Vienna at this time testified: "The year 1913 in Bosnia was the year of revolutionary organization. . . . 'Action, action, enough of words' was the cry on all lips. The young dreamed of nothing but bombs, assassinations, explosives to blow up and destroy everything." [17] An Austrian diplomat similarly described the atmosphere on the eve of the war:

> All who knew the country had the impression that an explosion was imminent. Especially in the schools Pan-Serb propaganda had created such chaotic

conditions that a regular continuance of instruction hardly seemed to be any longer possible. . . . Not only in Serbia itself but also in the Austro-Hungarian territories inhabited by Southern Slavs, the conviction took root that the collapse of Austria-Hungary was near at hand.[18]

25. Greece: 1878–1914

GREEK ENERGIES in the first half of the nineteenth century were largely dissipated in squabbles over the prerogatives of the autocratically minded Bavarian monarch. With the revolution of 1862 the Greeks acquired a new king and a democratic constitution. Now they were masters in their own house, at least as much as any small nation could be. But it was still a house from which the majority of the national family was excluded. This fact determined the course of Greek history for the next fifty years—years of frustration during which domestic progress was sacrificed to largely futile efforts to extend the frontiers. The low point was reached at the end of the century with national bankruptcy in 1893, humiliating defeat by the Turks in 1897, and imposition of foreign financial control in 1898. Recovery began with the revolt of the Military League in 1909, which ended the domination of the inadequate political oligarchy. This enabled a young Cretan politician, Eleutherios Venizelos, to rise to power and to effect sweeping reforms in the administration and in the armed forces. Thus Greece was prepared for the decisive events that began in 1912 with the outbreak of the Balkan Wars.

PURSUIT OF IRREDENTISM

Irredentist goals were foremost in the public mind and were universally referred to as the "Megale Idea" or "Great Idea." This national mania is natural and understandable. The islands and the provinces to the north were in fact Greek lands, and the aspiration of the Greek people to incorporate them in the motherland differed in no respect from the similar aspiration of the German and Italian people during this period. Theodore Deligiannes was the great spokesman of this irredentism, in contrast to his rival, Charilaos Trikoupes, who was more interested in domestic reform and reconstruction. These two men might be compared to John Kolettes and Alexander Mavrokordatos of the previous generation.

Although the Megale Idea was understandable and inevitable, it was not an unmixed blessing for Greece. In some circles it was extended and distorted into a program for the restoration of the Byzantine Empire. In this form it was avowedly imperialistic, involving, implicitly or explicitly, the subjugation of other Balkan peoples to Hellenism. Irredentism was also unrealistic because of the fantastic disproportion between national strength and national ambitions. Furthermore, the Megale Idea too often was exploited in a demagogic manner to distract attention from domestic problems. At a time when bankrupt Peloponnesian peasants were uprooting their currant bushes, when tens of thousands of young men were leaving their homeland in search of a livelihood overseas, and when control of the country's finances was passing into foreign hands, Greek politicians, with their eyes fixed upon Constantinople, delivered themselves of speeches on how to "take the City."

Greece could expand in two directions, southward over the islands and northward into Thessaly, Epirus, and Macedonia. The most concern was felt for Macedonia because, whereas the other areas were indubitably Greek and could be counted upon to pass to Greece sooner or later, Macedonia was a region of mixed ethnography to which Bulgaria and Serbia, as well as Greece, were laying claim.

The first blow to Greek aspirations in Macedonia was the sultan's firman of March 11, 1870, establishing the Bulgarian exarchate church, discussed in Chapter 19. Article X of this act stated that new dioceses could be added to the exarchate upon the vote of two thirds of the inhabitants. This opened the way to the indefinite expansion of the exarchate in Macedonia. The Greeks reacted sharply to the setback. An anti-Slav society was organized in Athens, while Greek crowds shouted in the streets of Constantinople, "We won't be absorbed by the Slavs; we won't let our children be bulgarized." [1]

The next blow to Greek hopes occurred during the Near Eastern crisis of 1875–1878. The original Bosnian uprising of 1875 had spread to include the Bulgarians, Serbians, and Montenegrins, and finally had culminated in the armed intervention of Russia. The spectacle of the Balkan Slavs fighting for their liberation with Russian support naturally caused much excitement in Greece. At first a coalition government with Trikoupes as foreign minister was strong enough to keep the hotheads in check. But when the Russian armies neared Adrianople the clamor for war became irresistible. A new government with Deligiannes as foreign minister took office and announced its intention of "occupying provisionally" the Greek provinces of Turkey. But before the Greek army could move, the Russo-Turkish armistice was signed and the war ended.

The Treaty of San Stefano of March 3, 1878, shocked the Greeks with its provisions for a "Greater Bulgaria" including almost the whole of Macedonia. The Western powers also found this unacceptable, so a new settlement was negotiated at Berlin later in the same year. But the Greeks were still far from being satisfied. The other Balkan nationalities gained additional territory together with independence or autonomy. Britain was authorized to occupy the Greek-populated island of Cyprus. But the Greek claims, by contrast, were passed over with merely an "invitation" to Turkey to cede parts of Thessaly and Epirus to Greece. This was all that Greece received at Berlin, beyond the gratuitous advice from Disraeli to the effect that Greece was a country of such antiquity that she could afford to wait for a few more years to satisfy her territorial aspirations.

The Turks naturally did not rush to accept the invitation to surrender their territory. Instead, their military experts argued that the new Greco-Turkish frontier proposed at Berlin was not a defensible line. Also, the Albanians now gave signs of national consciousness for the first time in centuries, and they organized an "Albanian League" to contest the Greek claims to Epirus. Under these circumstances the Greeks were unable to persuade the Turks to accept any frontier adjustment. Two international conferences also proved futile because the powers were unable to agree on measures of coercion. At length a settlement was reached in 1881 at a conference in Constantinople between representatives of Turkey and the great powers. Greece was not represented, and although Britain supported the cessions originally proposed in Berlin, the final award was substantially less. Greece obtained nearly the whole of Thessaly but in Epirus she received only the district of Arta. These acquisitions represented the sum total of Greek expansion to 1912.

Greece made another attempt to extend her frontier northward in 1885, when Bulgaria absorbed Eastern Rumelia. The Athens government at that time unfortunately was headed by the jingoist Deligiannes. His custom was to pander to the nationalism of his people without considering whether there was adequate supporting force. Deligiannes now began mobilization, arguing, not without reason, that if Bulgaria was to be allowed to keep Eastern Rumelia, then Greece should at least receive the Epirus territory proposed at Berlin. The powers peremptorily demanded that the mobilization cease. When Deligiannes refused, they blockaded the Greek coast on May 8, 1886. Deligiannes then resigned and Trikoupes returned to office and withdrew the troops from the border. The powers thereupon lifted the blockade, which had been in force nearly a month. The crisis thus passed, but Greece was left with a large deficit and nothing to show for it.

Only eleven years later Deligiannes was to repeat this folly, and with consequences far graver for his country. The occasion was one of the interminable crises between Greece and Turkey over the island of Crete. Throughout the nineteenth century the attention of the Greeks had been diverted periodically from Macedonia to Crete, where recurring revolts attested to the strong feeling for *enosis* or union with Greece. The root of the trouble went back to the War of Independence, when Britain, for strategic reasons, refused to allow the inclusion of Crete in the new Greek kingdom. Instead, the island was ruled from 1824 to 1840 by Mehemet Ali of Egypt and then reverted to the sultan.

The situation within Crete was roughly comparable to that in Bosnia. At the end of the nineteenth century one out of every four or five inhabitants was a Moslem. These Moslems were almost all Greeks who had apostatized to Islam and who had therby gained material advantages, including control of the fertile plain lands. Thus the revolutionary movement in Crete, as in Bosnia, was fed from several sources: from the nationalist aspiration of the Greek majority for *enosis* with the mother country; from the antagonism of the Christian majority against the renegade Moslem minority; and from the conflict between a small landlord class controlling the fertile plains and the remainder of the population left with hillside plots or none at all.

The inevitable result was recurring insurrection—in 1841, 1858, and 1866–1868. By the "Organic Statute" of 1868 the Porte gave the Cretan Christians a share in the government and lightened their tax burden. During the 1875–1878 crisis the Cretans again revolted and again were given additional concessions by the so-called Halepa Pact of October, 1878. This pact provided for the election of an annual general assembly in which the Christians held the majority of the seats. Despite this favorable arrangement new disturbances broke out in 1889. This time the sultan issued a new firman which rescinded many of the concessions embodied in the Halepa Pact. During the following years Crete was ruled by a succession of Moslem governors who did not even bother to summon the general assembly.

Moslem-Christian relations deteriorated to the point of large-scale clashes in February, 1896. Faced with the prospect of another full-scale Cretan revolt, the powers persuaded the sultan to grant very extensive concessions which went considerably beyond those of the Halepa Pact. The Cretan leaders at first accepted these terms, but a lasting settlement depended as much upon public opinion in Greece as upon developments in Crete. Unfortunately, the propaganda of nationalistic organizations in Athens had created an atmosphere in which almost any arrangement short of *enosis* was regarded as a national betrayal. Also, the premier at this moment was Deligiannes, who was not likely to restrain the mounting passions of his people despite the complete unpreparedness of the country for any serious trouble.

In February, 1897, lurid reports reached Athens of Turkish soldiers massacring Cretan civilians. Huge mobs gathered in the streets shouting for immediate intervention. Any government that attempted to stem the tide would quickly have been swept away. On February 6 the insurgents in Crete decreed union with Greece. A week later an expeditionary force of fifteen hundred men reached Crete from the mainland. Now only the European powers could have halted the drift to war by imposing a naval blockade upon Greece. This might even have been welcomed by the king and by Deligiannes, for it would have enabled them to back down before *force majeure* without loss of prestige. But strong anti-Turkish public opinion at home prevented the British government from accepting a blockade. So the drift to war continued even though the unpreparedness of Greece was apparent to all. Deligiannes ordered mobilization on March 15, 1897. Greek irregulars crossed the border on April 10 and attacked Turkish outposts in Thessaly. A week later Greek regulars also crossed over and war began.

The Thirty Days' War that ensued was a war in name only. The Turkish army, which had been recently reorganized by a German mission, was incomparably superior in training, in equipment, and in leadership. Moreover, warned by Russia and Austria against intervention and conciliated by the Porte with timely concessions, Bulgaria and Serbia remained neutral. Thus the Greeks were left alone, and within two weeks their army was scattered and demoralized. Prince Constantine abandoned Larissa without attempting resistance. Two further setbacks on the plains of Thessaly left the road to Athens open to the victorious Turkish armies.

The powers now intervened, if for no other reason than to save the Greek dynasty, which was under heavy fire in Athens. An armistice was signed on May 20, 1897, and a peace treaty on December 4. The Turks returned Thessaly except for a few strategic points and a single village. But the Greeks had to pay an indemnity to the victors and the powers established an International Financial Commission of Control over Greek finances. The nature of this foreign financial control will be considered later in this chapter.

The paradox of the war is that the Cretans gained the substance of their demands despite the ignominious defeat of Greece. The powers, who had occupied the island in February, 1897, sought a governor to organize an autonomous regime. The sultan maintained that this official should be an Ottoman subject chosen by the Ottoman government with the approval of the powers. But Russia and Britain proposed for this post the second son of the Greek king, Prince George. The sultan finally had to give way and in November, 1898, Prince George was named commissioner of Crete with a mandate from the powers to organize an autonomous regime.

From the viewpoint of international law, this settlement was patently absurd. Professor William Langer has aptly observed: "After the exchange of thousands of despatches and notes between the powers, after the most flagrant breach of international law by the Greeks, after the intervention of Europe and a crisis that threatened a general conflagration in the Balkans and possibly a European war, the Greeks, totally defeated on the field of battle, secured what they had started out to get." [2] A Greek nationalist undoubtedly would reply that this inconsistency of the great powers in 1898 was merely the inevitable consequence of their original inconsistency at the beginning of the century when they refused to allow the Cretans to join the motherland.

CRISIS AT HOME

Despite the favorable settlement in Crete, the prestige of Greece was at low ebb at the turn of the century. In addition to the crushing defeat at the hands of the Turks, the domestic situation was dreary and unpromising. Charilaos Trikoupes, the only political leader of stature during these years, was continually undermined by electoral reverses and financial crises. In contrast to the romanticists of irredentism, Trikoupes strove to lessen corruption in political life and to develop the country's resources by means of extensive public projects. More specifically, he reorganized the police system, raised civil service standards, strictly enforced the law concerning irremovability of judges, and in general freed administrative officials from the more brazen political pressures. His most lasting work was the building of roads, railroads, and harbors on a scale unprecedented in Greece. This construction, which will be discussed later in the chapter, broke the transportation bottleneck which hitherto had retarded the development of agriculture and industry.

Despite these achievements, Trikoupes was not a favorite of the populace. He was reserved by temperament, being commonly called "the Englishman." In contrast, his rival Deligiannes was a consummate politician who played upon the popular irredentist aspirations to win elections. Thus Trikoupes was defeated in the 1885 election after having been in office since 1882. The following year he returned to power, but in the interval the financial situation had deteriorated dangerously because of Deligiannes's mobilization measures. From now on, Trikoupes was plagued by financial difficulties which eventually proved his undoing.

The basic trouble was that Greece was borrowing heavily on the international money market during these years, obtaining no less than six loans between 1879 and 1890. The sums borrowed totaled 630,000,000 gold francs. But the price of issue ranged from 25 to 30 per cent below par, so Greece received only 458,622,000 francs. And of this amount only about 100,000,000 gold francs actually reached the country, the remainder being spent abroad to purchase armaments and to meet the charges on the rapidly mounting national indebtedness. Furthermore, most of the 100,000,000 francs that did reach Greece were used to cover the recurring budgetary deficits. Thus a quite insignificant portion of the borrowed money went for productive enterprises within the country.

Under these circumstances the national debt rose sharply despite mounting taxes. In 1875, the per capita tax burden was 15.16 drachmas and the per capita debt burden was 102.75 drachmas. In 1893, the corresponding figures were 37.63 and 363.20. Thus in less than two decades taxes had more than doubled; yet the national debt had more than tripled. By 1893, Greece's foreign indebtedness was consuming 33 per cent of her budgetary receipts.

Such was the situation when the international market for Greek currants collapsed. The circumstances of this catastrophe will be noted later in this chapter. Suffice it to note there that currants, which hitherto had far surpassed in value all other Greek exports combined, dropped in price 70 per cent during the year 1893. The effect of this blow may be gauged from the fact that Greece had always suffered from an unfavorable balance of trade. The value of exports during the 1880's had run between two thirds and three fourths of the value of imports. Now with currant prices falling precipitously and remaining at a depressed level, the Greek economy became hopelessly bankrupt.

Faced with this emergency, Trikoupes temporarily reduced interest payments on loans by 70 per cent. This caused an uproar in foreign financial circles and diplomatic representatives in Athens protested officially. Negotiations followed between representatives of the foreign bondholders and of the Greek government. The talks failed but were resumed when Deligiannes replaced Trikoupes in January, 1895. After protracted bargaining, a satisfactory compromise was reached in February, 1897. But unfortunately for Greece, the war with Turkey intervened before the agreement could be officially ratified. The creditors then took advantage of the helpless position of Greece following her defeat and imposed terms much more severe than those they had just accepted.

The Greeks found themselves in a desperate economic position at the end of the war. International trade was at a low ebb while the treasury was again beggared by the expenses incurred during the military operations and by the burden of crowds of destitute refugees. On top of this, the Turks were demanding a large indemnity in lieu of territorial claims. The representatives of the great powers, whom Greece had entrusted with the negotiation of peace, became concerned lest a heavy indemnity force the Greeks to cease further payments to the foreign bondholders. Because of this complication the debt question was now tied to the peace settlement. Greece was required to pay four million pounds as indemnity to the Turks and also to accept an International Financial Commission of Control.

This commission was authorized to collect certain specified taxes and to use the revenue to service past debts as well as to service a new "Indemnity Loan" which Greece was to receive in order to pay the Turks. When a bill legalizing this commission was presented to the Greek parliament it was bitterly criticized by all parties as a disgraceful and unjust measure which violated the independence of the country. But there was no alternative, and Greece was forced to accept foreign financial control on top of humiliating military defeat.

The decade following the Turkish war was one of demoralization and petty party strife. Trikoupes had retired from public life in 1895. He was succeeded by George Theotokes, who continued the duel with Deligiannes. Cabinets fell frequently during these years and on the most frivolous pretexts. In 1905 Deligiannes was killed by an assassin and his party split into two factions led by Demetrios Rhalles and Kyriakoules Mavromichales. Neither of them was particularly distinguished; nor was Theotokes, for that matter. In fact, none of these party chiefs was capable of providing the country with the leadership it sorely needed. Furthermore, the dynasty was under a cloud at this time because of the failure of Prince Constantine during the war. All in all, the turn of the century was one of the most depressing periods since the winning of independence.

RECOVERY UNDER VENIZELOS

In August, 1909, a military revolt in Athens broke the grip of the old political leaders and cleared the ground for the remarkable national recovery under the leadership of the outstanding statesman of modern Greece, Eleutherios Venizelos. The insurrection was preceded by a significant literature of criticism and revolt, the targets of which were the parliamentary system, the old politicos, and the dynasty itself. Various factors explain this deep-seated and widespread discontent. One was the patent failure of Greece in both her international relations and in her domestic progress. Another factor was the aspiration for political power on the part of the rising middle class. It is significant that the intellectual and political ferment was confined largely to the cities. When the revolt occurred it was supported most strongly by the trade guilds, the more advanced intelligentsia, and the mercantile and professional classes. And the effect of the revolt was to bring to the top a younger generation of mostly middle-class politicians who replaced the former political oligarchy that had depended on local clan control.

The immediate origins of the revolt can be traced to the Young Turk revolt and to the international repercussions that followed it. The Young Turks won power in July, 1908. On October 5 the Bulgarians took advantage of the resulting confusion to proclaim their full independence. The next day Austria announced the annexation of Bosnia-Herzegovina. Two days later, on October 8, the Cretans proclaimed their union with Greece and appointed a committee to conduct affairs in the name of King George. If the Athens government under Theotokes had responded immediately and presented the Turks with a *fait accompli*, the long-sought *enosis* probably would have been attained. The British ambassador in Constantinople reported on October 13 that "the Cretan question does not touch the Turks very closely . . . and if they could get a nice sum down for it that would satisfy them." [3] But the memory of the disastrous 1897 war was still fresh in Athens, and Theotokes made no move.

The showdown came when the European powers withdrew their remaining troops from Crete on July 26, 1909. Three days later the Cretans hoisted the blue-and-white flag of Greece. By this time the Young Turks were in a stronger position than that of the year before, so they demanded from the Greek government "a written disavowal of the Cretan agitation for union." Premier Rhalles, who had just assumed office, had no choice but to submit to the ultimatum and to give the required assurance. But the Turkish government was not satisfied. A fortnight later it demanded immediate disavowal of the activities of Greek officers who allegedly were fomenting rebellion in Macedonia. Again Rhalles submitted and assured the Turks that Greece would refrain from any move prejudicial to Turkish sovereignty. In addition to this humiliating experience, the Greeks suffered severely from an economic boycott which the Young Turks organized and continued even after the assurances had been received from Athens. And in the meantime the powers had sent to Crete a detachment of marines who solemnly cut down the offending Greek flag.

These simultaneous blows to the national pocketbook and the national pride aroused the Greeks as much as the loss of Bosnia-Herzegovina did the Serbs. The general indignation found expression in the *coup d'état* of a Military League which had been organized by younger army officers in May, 1909. Under the leadership of a Colonel N. K. Zorbas, these officers made a show of force outside Athens and compelled Premier Rhalles to resign. His place was taken by the docile Mavromichales while the League ruled.

The League's officers wanted to reorganize drastically the army and the political system. But they lacked the necessary experience and did not know how to attain these ends. In a moment of inspiration they decided to obtain the counsel of a rising young politician in Crete by the name of Venizelos. Some of the officers had met him earlier and had been impressed by his ability and character. George Clemenceau also had made his acquaintance during a visit in Crete and on his return to France he told a friend: "In Crete I have discovered a phenomenon much more interesting than the excavations. It is a young advocate, Mr. Venezuelos—Mr. Venizelos? Frankly, I cannot quite recall his name, but the whole of Europe will be speaking of him in a few years." [4]

Venizelos, who was born in Crete in 1864, was prophetically given the name of Eleutherios, signifying freedom. He studied law at the University of Athens, whence he returned to his native island where he soon made his name at the bar. He took an active part in the 1896 revolt against Turkey; when Crete gained autonomy, he was elected to the assembly and quickly rose to be minister of justice. When Prince George, who had been appointed commissioner of Crete by the powers, began to take too much power into his own hands, Venizelos boldly defied him by establishing a rival provisional government and proclaiming the union of Crete with Greece. Prince George was finally obliged to resign and was succeeded as commissioner in 1906 by a conservative Greek politician, Alexander Zaïmes. Under the latter's regime Venizelos became the leading statesman of Crete and the idol of his fellow countrymen. This career on his native island prepared him admirably for the larger political stage on the mainland, where he played the leading role for many years.

Venizelos accepted the invitation of the Military League to serve as its political adviser and arrived in Athens on January 23, 1910. He perceived at once the anomalous state of affairs in which the army had deprived the old political leaders of any real power but had failed to set up a new political system in their place. He proposed, therefore, that a national assembly be summoned to revise the constitution. His advice was followed and the Assembly convened on September 14. Among those elected was Venizelos himself, who was able to take his seat because he was technically a Greek subject. When he returned to Athens he was wildly acclaimed by huge crowds as a national hero. This surprising reception reveals the political vacuum that existed in Greece at this time. Venizelos' past deeds and writings were noteworthy but certainly not so dazzling as to warrant such a fervent welcome. The explanation is that he appeared at a moment when the Greek people, disgusted by the ineffectiveness of the old politicos and by the humiliations of the past decade, were psychologically ready to accept unreservedly a fresh political figure who had confidence in himself and in his country.

The Assembly that was elected mirrored the cleavages within the country and the deep-seated problems that had to be faced. Forty-five Agrarian deputies arrived from Thessaly pledged to work for the expropriation of the feudal estates in that province, to be discussed later in this chapter. Ten socialist deputies appeared for the first time, with their usual program for social reorganization. There was also a body of eighty independent deputies representing the extreme wing of the Military League. They were strongly antidynasty, and their chief demand, significantly enough, was that the Assembly should be constituent rather than revisionist.

This issue dominated the proceedings of the Assembly from the beginning and was decided largely by Venizelos. He had proposed originally that the Assembly be revisionist and he insisted on this after he became premier on October 18, 1910. Many of his admirers were disappointed, having expected the Cretan revolutionary to lead the fight against the Danish dynasty, which had become unpopular in many quarters. But Venizelos persisted in his revisionist position and was able to have his way. The result was that he diverted a potentially violent movement into constructive channels. He led the way to reform and reconstruction and avoided a feud over the dynasty question which would have fatally divided the nation.

Venizelos did not assume command without opposition. The old party leaders naturally resented the rise of this outsider from Crete. They resorted to the old trick of boycotting the Assembly and thus preventing a quorum. Venizelos countered this obstructionism by submitting his resignation to the king. Immediately the trade guilds and the university students organized great protest meetings in Athens, shouting against the old politicians and demanding that Venizelos be retained. King George bowed to this pressure and kept Venizelos in office. The latter, perceiving that the party leaders had discredited themselves, dissolved the Assembly and set new elections for December 24, 1910. The returns represented an overwhelming personal triumph for Venizelos, 300 of the 364 new deputies being members of his Liberal party.

The way was now clear for the work of national regeneration. The Assembly passed fifty-four amendments to the Constitution of 1864 and adopted the revised constitution on June 11, 1911. These amendments, together with the legislation passed during the following year, affected every phase of national life. The quorum for the Assembly was reduced to one third of its members in order to check obstructionism. Elementary education was made free and compulsory. Military men, mayors, and other public servants were declared ineligible for election to the Assembly. Security of tenure was enjoined for government officials in place of the spoils system, which hitherto had plagued public administration. A ministry of agriculture was established, and plans were made to disseminate modern agricultural techniques through model farms under foreign experts. Expropriation was defined in the constitution in order to prepare the way for the division of the large Thessalian estates. And, finally, foreign officers were made eligible for state service.

The purpose of the last provision was to legalize the calling of foreign missions to reorganize the Greek military establishment. A British mission was engaged for the navy and a French mission for the army. This military revival came none too soon; a year later Greece, together with her allies in the Balkan League, was involved in war against Turkey. The story of the formation of the League and of the ensuing campaigns constitutes a part of general Balkan diplomatic and military history and will be considered later in Chapter 28 in that context.

ECONOMIC DEVELOPMENTS

The period from 1878 to 1914 was one of steady economic growth in Greece. The progress made was certainly unimpressive in comparison with that of Western Europe at the same time. Yet the Greek economy by 1914 had reached a level far above that of the mid-nineteenth century. One of the most important achievements was the development of a land transportation system where virtually nothing had existed before. The first paved road worthy of the name was built in 1852 and was 100 miles in length. By 1867 only another 150 miles had been completed. But great spurts forward came in the 1880's under Trikoupes and under Venizelos on the eve of World War I. By 1914 Greece had a network of 3,500 miles of paved roads. Railroad building followed the same pattern of growth. The first line was built in 1870 between Athens and Piraeus, a distance of 7 miles. By 1914 several other lines had been completed, totaling 1,000 miles. Another important achievement in transportation was the completion in 1893 of the Corinth Canal between the Peloponnesian Peninsula and the mainland. Thousands of small craft use the canal each year to avoid the treacherous journey around the peninsula.

The improvement of transportation facilities helped agriculture by making it possible for the peasants to ship their produce to urban centers. Agriculture was also helped by the abolition in 1880 of the tithe, which, as noted in Chapter 15, had hitherto seriously retarded productivity. As for the types of crops grown, the emphasis continued to be on currants, grapes, olives, citrus fruits, and tobacco. Also, there was the same dependence on large-scale imports of grain. Until the end of the century the cost of the imported grain was met by currant exports. When the phylloxera blight ruined French vineyards in 1878 there was a great demand for Greek currants to meet the needs of French wine manufacturers. The value of currant exports exceeded by far the value of all other Greek exports combined. But eventually the blight was brought under control and in 1892 the French government adopted a high protective tariff against Greek currants. Exports to France dropped off from a maximum of 70,000 tons in 1889 to 3,500 in 1893.

The effect of this blow may be gauged from the fact that the French market in the past had absorbed one third of Greek currant exports. Thus the French tariff now caused a disastrous price slump, the price quotation in the

London produce market tumbling during the year 1893 from twenty-one shillings per hundredweight to six shillings. The growers increased their output in order to make up for the drop in price. The effect, of course, was to widen the gap between supply and demand and to depress the price level further. The government tried to help with various measures, such as setting a minimum price, prohibiting new acreage in currants, and subsidizing growers who shifted to other crops. These devices alleviated the distress slightly, but the fact remained that currants no longer could be depended upon to pay for the bread of the nation.

Fortunately for Greece, tobacco exports began to mount at the same time that currant exports were declining. Land devoted to tobacco cultivation increased from 6,500 acres in 1860 to 10,000 in 1875, 16,000 in 1889, and 38,750 in 1911. The great jump in tobacco exports came after World War I, when Greece was able to exploit the rich tobacco-growing regions of Macedonia and Thrace which had been newly acquired. Thus during the period between the two world wars tobacco took the place of currants as the breadwinner for Greece.

The acquisition of Thessaly in 1881 raised the hope that the burden of grain imports would be eased somewhat because the chief products of the fertile Thessalian plains were wheat, barley, and maize. But the hope was not realized, the reason being that the land tenure system curtailed production. Most of the land in Thessaly was held in large estates or chifliks owned by Moslem landlords and by a few wealthy Greek families. The Moslems left when Thessaly passed to Greece, and their chifliks were bought by local Greek families and by wealthy Greeks in Constantinople, Smyrna, Alexandria, and other foreign centers. Thus the chiflik system remained unchanged, particularly in the plains areas.

The chifliks varied in size from the small ones, averaging 250 acres, to the medium estates, averaging 750 acres, and to the large ones, running as high as 10,000 acres. Tenancy arrangements differed greatly, depending upon the locality and upon the number of oxen owned by the tenant. But the important point to note is that the proprietor received a stipulated percentage of the crop, usually from a third to a half. This arrangement did not encourage the tenant to increase his output because the landowner continued to receive his full share of the crop; hence the cost of any improvements made was hard to recover. Also, it should be noted that only a third of the cultivable land of Thessaly was cropped each year. The explanation for this is to be found partly in the primitive fallow system of farming and partly in the preference of the landowners, especially those in hilly areas, to lease their property to nomadic shepherds who descended from the Pindus Mountains each autumn as they had done for centuries past.

This chiflik system generated much agrarian unrest, particularly because in the rest of Greece most large estates had disappeared by this time. Before World War I a certain amount of progress was made in dividing the Thessalian chifliks. In 1881, out of 658 villages in Thessaly, 466 were chiflik villages and only 198 were *kephalochoria*, or free villages. By 1918 the number of chiflik villages had been reduced by a third, the decrease being due to land purchases made by the peasants and by the Agricultural Bank of Thessaly. The latter was established by the government in 1907 under the pressure of rising peasant unrest. It is apparent that the land problem in Thessaly was still far from solution when it was compounded by the acquisition of the new provinces of Macedonia, Epirus, and Thrace following the Balkan Wars and World War I. The choicest lands in these new territories were held as chifliks, so the Greek government found it necessary to adopt the sweeping land reform measures during and following World War I to be discussed in Chapter 34.

Turning from agriculture to industry, we find that the industrial development of Greece did not really get under way until the last quarter of the nineteenth century. In 1877 Greece had 136 industrial establishments with 7,342 workers. By 1917 these had increased to 2,213 establishments and 36,124 workers, of which 622 establishments and 9,227 workers were to be found in the newly acquired provinces in the north. The big spurt in industrial growth came in the 1880's under the stimulus of tariff protection, the influx of considerable foreign long-term capital, and Trikoupes's railroad building and public works program. In the 1890's industry was slowed down by the bankruptcy of the government and by the defeat inflicted by Turkey. But rapid progress was made after 1900 and was accelerated by the Balkan Wars and World War I, which added greatly to the resources of Greece.

The industries were largely of the consumer goods variety. By far the most important were flour milling and textiles, the latter including cotton, wool, and silk. Other industries were pottery, glass, shipbuilding, tanning, soap making, and the processing of olives and grapes. Most industries were located in the Athens-Piraeus metropolitan area, the remainder being in provincial towns like Volos, Patras, Kalamata, and, after 1913, Saloniki.

Despite the growth at the turn of the century, Greek industry remained primitive in comparison with that of Western Europe. One reason for this backwardness was the scarcity of coal, iron, and other essential raw materials. Also, the supply of motive power was inadequate. Furthermore, the typical Greek capitalist preferred to invest his money in a business that was safe, that required little capital, and that he could personally manage. This led him to the consumer goods industries rather than to heavy industries, which involved more risk and required technical managerial skills and a heavy capital outlay. Foreign capital did not go into Greek industry, preferring mining and railway construction, which offered higher returns.

The country did possess an abundance of labor, but it was unskilled and averse to industrial employment. The prevalence of small landholdings held potential industrial workers to the soil, particularly because going to the city and becoming a day laborer was regarded as a step down in the social scale. When Greek peasants were forced by overpopulation and by the currant crisis to leave their ancestral villages, they sought their fortune in glamorous America rather than in a nearby city.

Shipping was an industry in which these limiting factors did not operate and which therefore has always flourished in Greece. The numerous islands provided an abundant supply of skilled seamen, while Greek craftsmen constructed sailing ships that were widely admired for their seaworthiness and trim lines. The merchant marine consequently was an important element in the national economy both before and after the Greek War of Independence. Most of the sailing vessels were run cooperatively, with the carpenters, lumber merchants, seamen, and captains all pooling their skills and capital to construct and operate the ships.

The advent of steam navigation seriously affected the Greek merchant marine. Neither the skills nor the funds were available for the construction or purchase of the new steamships. The shipping industry declined so drastically that the islands lost much of their population. The crisis was overcome when wealthy overseas Greeks began to purchase old steamships in England and to lease them to captains in Greece. Large profits were made during the South African War, and the capital was used to buy still more steamships. Thus the merchant marine experienced a renaissance and for the first time the blue-and-white flag of Greece was carried all over the world by tramp steamers owned and operated by Greeks. The following figures make clear the decline of the sailing fleet and the advent of the steamships:

	SAILING SHIPS		STEAMSHIPS	
Year	Number	Tonnage	Number	Tonnage
1834	2,891	. . .	. . .	. . .
1845	3,581	164,103	. . .	. . .
1875	5,410	253,781	37	1,241
1895	1,059	246,196	107	144,975
1915	884	107,466	475	893,650

Source: Ch. Evelpides, *Oikonomike kai koinonike istoria tes Ellados* [*Economic and Social History of Greece*] (Athens, 1950), p. 96.

One of the most important and spectacular developments affecting the Greek economy at the turn of the century was the large-scale emigration overseas. Overpopulation was the basic factor behind this emigration, as was the case in the other Balkan countries. Between 1829 and 1912 the area of Greece increased from 18,346 square miles to only 24,558 square miles, whereas the population jumped from 750,000 to 2,750,000. The population per square mile consequently rose from approximately 41 to 114, an increase of almost three times in less than a century. The modest expansion of industry during that period was quite insufficient to absorb the growing population.

Since ancient times the pressure of population has driven Greeks to seek their livelihood in foreign lands. In the eighteenth and nineteenth centuries many emigrated to neighboring countries such as Russia, Rumania, and Egypt. At the end of the nineteenth century the tide of emigration rose immeasurably and shifted its direction to the United States. The character and the role of the emigrants also changed fundamentally at this time. Those who had emigrated in the previous decades to neighboring countries were usually superior in business capacity to the native population and were able to make fortunes out of Egyptian cotton and Russian and Rumanian grain. In contrast, those who went to the United States found themselves at first in an inferior status in regard to education and capital. The great majority were virtually illiterate and possessed less than fifty dollars upon their arrival. Accordingly, instead of employing native unskilled labor as did the Greek immigrants in Egypt, Russia, and other Eastern countries, they themselves constituted an unskilled labor force.

But the United States was vast and rich, and the Greek immigrant who shined shoes or sold flowers, or worked in a factory or in a railroad gang, was able to earn sums that appeared to him to be fabulous. He sent back to his village glowing accounts of the Eldorado of the West. The money which he enclosed in his letters spoke even more eloquently of the opportunities awaiting in the New World. Thus the exodus started, and the currant crisis of the 1890's swelled it to startling proportions. According to American immigration statistics, 3,773 Greek immigrants arrived in 1900 and 12,144 in 1905. Then between 1906 and 1914 a total of 283,851 immigrants poured in, or an average of 31,000 a year. During the war years emigration fell sharply because of the recruiting of young men for military service. And then, before the exodus could reach its former proportions, the American immigration restriction laws adopted in 1921 abruptly set a quota of only one hundred Greek immigrants a year.

The flood tide of emigration during the pre-1914 period left many Greek villages with almost no able-bodied young males. But in return Greece received a golden stream of remittances from her thrifty emigrant sons. The high point occurred in 1921, when the remittances totaled no less than 121 million dollars. The flow of dollars from America rectified the extremely unfavorable balance of trade that followed the collapse of the currant market. This in turn strengthened the position of the drachma, which rose to parity by the time of the Balkan Wars. The remittances also enabled many peasants to pay off their debts, so that whole districts were freed from mortgage encumbrances. As early as 1906 a Greek government commission investigating the effects of the emigration reported: "No one can deny that it is to them [the emigrants] in great measure . . . that we owe the rise in the value of our paper currency almost to par. . . . Everyone mentions . . . that in these provinces, particularly in Peloponnesus, which are the oldest and most prolific sources of emigration to the United States, there has been a striking fall in the rate of interest and a proportionate rise in the value of agricultural real estate. . . ."[5]

There remains the question concerning the influence of the emigrants who returned to their homeland. Many did return for a variety of reasons, including economic pressure during slump periods in the United States, desire to resume family ties or to marry and raise a family in the native land, and also preference for the more familiar and easygoing life of the mother country. It is estimated that of the more than half million Greeks admitted into the United

States by 1931, about 40 per cent, or 197,000, went back as repatriates. Upon their return many of them found adjustment difficult. They were oppressed by the poverty and the slow tempo of life. They found that, apart from their money, they had gained little social prestige by their stay in America. A popular saying was, "He left as a young donkey and returned as an older one." Also, the repatriates were usually besieged by poverty-stricken relatives and sometimes fleeced in shady business deals. On the other hand, many repatriates were able to settle down in towns and villages and contribute to their communities out of the new skills and experiences that they had acquired in America. At the time of World War I Arnold Toynbee foresaw the leavening influence of these repatriates:

> It is a strange experience to spend a night in some remote mountain-village of Greece, and see Americanism and Hellenism face to face. Hellenism is represented by the village schoolmaster. He wears a black coat, talks a little French, and can probably read Homer; but his longest journey has been to the normal school at Athens, and it has not altered his belief that the ikon in the neighbouring monastery was made by St. Luke and the Bulgar beyond the mountains by the Devil. On the other side of you sits the returned emigrant, chatting irrepressibly in his queer version of the "American language," and showing you the newspapers which are mailed to him every fortnight from the States. . . . His greatest gift to his country will be his American point of view.[6]

Following World War II a systematic study was made of the effect of the repatriates upon their homeland. The findings are particularly significant because they are probably also applicable to the other Balkan countries which likewise received a stream of returning emigrants:

> The repatriates who returned from the United States could not help . . . bring to Greece some of both the material and the intangible qualities of American life. In going from an advanced to a retarded social economy, they took with them money, higher standards of living, a spirit of optimism, reformist attitudes, and pronounced pro-American sentiments. They had come into contact with a different language, with different customs and attitudes. They could hardly have failed to acquire new skills and techniques; their tempo of life had quickened; they had seen people worship in different churches; for better or for worse, they were exposed to the American press, periodicals and literature; they had seen women treated differently; and they had sensed the pulsating effects of living in a strong and wealthy country. What they brought back often filtered down into the poverty-stricken areas of the country, and many of the services they and the expatriated rendered were of a character normally furnished by local governments in America. Even though their names failed to appear on the façades of the libraries, museums, and schools of Athens, their contributions were nevertheless genuine. Their devotion to Greece was more altruistic than that of their voluble critics or of the Athenians who flocked to the sidewalk cafes.[7]

26. Rumania: 1878–1914

IN 1906 an exhibition was held in Rumania to celebrate the fortieth anniversary of the arrival of King Charles in his adopted country. Visitors saw many signs of the impressive progress that had been made during the preceding four decades. Rumania had acquired all the external attributes of Western civilization. Two thousand miles of railroads facilitated travel where, at Charles's coming, there had not been a single train. The Iron Gates had been blasted, opening the Danube River to large steamers. Also, a splendid bridge spanned the Danube at Cernavoda, connecting the Dobruja to the rest of the kingdom. Rapidly mounting oil production was modifying the purely agricultural character of the economy. The Rumanian government commanded such confidence in international financial circles that it was able to borrow at a trifle over 4 per cent.

Despite this substantial progress, the more perceptive visitors in 1906 might have noted that the foundations of political and economic life were far from secure. Eighty per cent of the population depended on the land for its livelihood, but half of this land belonged to a handful of large proprietors. The great bulk of the Rumanian peasants existed at an appallingly depressed standard of living. The peasants were also effectively excluded from parliamentary representation by a complicated and artificial electoral system. Rumanian politics consisted to a large degree of barren squabbles between "Liberals" and "Conservatives"—meaningless party labels without underlying principles.

These realities behind the façade of material progress explain the paradoxical history of Rumania in the late nineteenth and early twentieth centuries —a richly endowed country that was making notable advances in many fields but which was rent by social fissures that undermined the national edifice and finally precipitated a veritable *jacquerie* in 1907.

AFTERMATH OF 1878: THE 1883
SECRET ALLIANCE

The Rumanians fought on Russia's side in the Balkan War of 1877–1878. During the critical days of the siege of Plevna they gave valuable assistance to the hard-pressed Russian army. Their reward was the loss of southern Bessarabia, which Russia recovered by the terms of the Berlin Treaty, discussed in Chapter 21. As compensation the Rumanians were given the Dobruja, an exchange which they considered to be far from equitable. The Russians added insult to injury by informing the Rumanian delegates at Berlin that the cession of the Dobruja was "an act of generosity on the part of Russia." The Russians further alienated Rumania by supporting Bulgaria on the question of the Dobruja frontiers. Rumania demanded the inclusion of the key fortress of Silistria on the grounds that it was essential for the defense of the province. But Russian diplomacy at this time strongly favored Bulgaria on the assumption that the new Balkan state would serve as a complacent tool in the future. Thus Silistria, on Russia's insistence, was awarded to Bulgaria in June, 1880.

The unhappy Rumanians were further antagonized by the intervention of the great powers on the issue of Jewish disabilities. Since the beginning of the nineteenth century many Jews had migrated to Rumania from Russia and Russian-held Poland. At the outset they settled mostly in northern Moldavia, so that in 1859 there were 118,000 Jews in Moldavia but only 9,200 in Wallachia. Gradually they increased in numbers and spread southward, until by 1900 they numbered 201,000 in Moldavia and 68,000 in Wallachia.

A quarter of a million Jews in a country with a total population of five millions would not appear to be a cause for alarm and discriminatory legislation. But these Jews were concentrated almost exclusively in the cities, and since the total urban population in 1900 amounted to only 700,000, the Jews comprised about two fifths of all the urban inhabitants. Moreover, the Jews had developed financial and commercial skills to a high degree, and, it should also be noted, were more industrious and thrifty than the native Rumanians. As a result they gained control over much of the trade, industry, and finance. In time they even acquired a foothold in agriculture by leasing the large estates of absentee landlords and extending loans to improvident landowners.

The growing economic power of the Jews explains in large part Article VII of the 1866 constitution denying them the privilege of naturalization: ". . . only foreigners belonging to a Christian confession can obtain naturalization." This inability to gain citizenship meant also inability to participate in political affairs and to hold public office. These disabilities became an international issue after 1878 because of Article XLIV of the Berlin Treaty, which provided: "In Rumania the difference of religious creeds and confessions shall not be alleged against any person as a ground for exclusion or incapacity in matters relating to the enjoyment of civil and political rights, admission to public employments, functions, and honors, or the exercise of the various professions and industries in any locality whatsoever." [1]

This provision aroused widespread indignation in Rumania. The assembly refused to repeal the discriminatory article of the constitution despite strong pressure from the powers. Finally, on October 18, 1879, the assembly decreed that naturalization could be obtained "without distinction of religion." But it also stipulated that a special act of parliament was required for each individual case of naturalization, and a formal petition and ten years' domicile were demanded in all save exceptional cases. Furthermore, it expressly provided that only Rumanian citizens could own land, though lack of citizenship did not carry with it exemption from military service. These provisions were designed as a gesture to appease the powers which were withholding recognition of Rumania as an independent state pending settlement of the Jewish issue. The powers pointed out that the assembly's legislation fell far short of their original requirements. But they were anxious to settle the protracted dispute, so in February, 1880, they extended recognition to Rumania as a full sovereign state. The following year Prince Charles was crowned King of Rumania in the cathedral at Bucharest.

In the light of Rumania's experiences during and after the Russo-Turkish War it is understandable that there should have been considerable resentment against the great powers and particularly against Russia. The Rumanians felt that Russia had used them for the realization of her aspirations in the Balkans, and that after they had made their contribution at Plevna they were forgotten and ignored. It would have been natural, therefore, for the Rumanians to turn to Austria after 1878. But various obstacles stood in the way of a *rapprochement* with the Dual Monarchy. One was the large bloc of unredeemed Rumanians in Transylvania. Another was the economic domination of Austria over Rumania. Between 1875 and 1882 over 50 per cent of Rumanian imports came from Austria-Hungary, and about 32 per cent of her exports went to the same country. Very naturally there was in Rumania, as in Serbia, much concern over this economic subservience to a foreign power.

Being repelled by both Russia and Austria-Hungary, the Rumanian statesmen attempted after 1878 to draw closer to Germany. Bismarck did not encourage them at first because he did not consider a Rumanian alliance worth the risk of alienating Russia. It will be recalled from Chapter 23 that it was not until the summer of 1883, when the situation in Bulgaria had deteriorated to the point where Russian military intervention was a real possibility, that Bismarck opened serious discussions with the Rumanians. He explained to them that Germany and her ally, Austria, were anxious to avoid a conflict with Russia. Accordingly, he proposed that Rumania first conclude a purely defensive pact with Austria, which Germany then would be ready to join. The Rumanians agreed, and on October 30, 1883, they signed an alliance with Vienna to which Germany acceded on the same day.

The alliance provided that the two contracting parties should not enter into alliances directed against one another, that Austria-Hungary should come to the assistance of Rumania if the latter were attacked without provocation, and that Rumania in return should aid Austria if she were attacked without provocation in a portion of her states bordering on Rumania. This last phrase was a circumlocution inserted because of the German emperor, who insisted that Russia should not be specifically named as the country against which the alliance was directed. The treaty was to be in effect for five years and was to be kept strictly secret. It was renewed several times and remained effective until the outbreak of World War I. Secrecy was so well maintained that during the entire period to 1914 only a few party leaders in Rumania were even aware of its existence. The pact greatly strengthened Rumania's international position. Two great powers guaranteed her against aggression, and a third was added with the participation of Italy in 1888.

POLITICAL EVOLUTION

The political institutions of Rumania resembled those of the Western European countries in form but not in substance. The 1866 constitution, which remained in force with minor changes until World War I, was based on the Belgian Charter of 1831. The legal system, taken from the Napoleonic Code, specified certain abstract principles, such as liberty of conscience, of instruction, of the press, and of assembly. Also, the two-party system of government prevailed, with the Conservatives and Liberals alternating in office.

Rumania had all the trappings of a Western parliamentary democracy. But the reality beneath the surface was very different. The franchise rested upon a complicated and artificial system of electoral colleges which assured the political preponderance of the landowners and wealthy urban elements. The two parties tended to be coteries grouped about prominent political personalities or families. The constant factionalism usually reflected personal rivalries rather than public issues. Both parties depended primarily upon the landowners and virtually ignored the peasants, who constituted four fifths of the total population. The only significant difference between the two parties was that the Conservatives were the more explicit spokesmen of the landed interests, whereas the Liberals were becoming increasingly interested in commercial and industrial expansion and occupied the leading positions in the growing financial institutions.

The influence of King Charles on Rumanian politics should not be overlooked. He played a role comparable to that of King Ferdinand in Bulgaria. He appears to have been more likable as an individual and more popular as a ruler than the Bulgarian king. But his political goal and methods were very much the same. He kept a firm grip on the political balance of power by making full use of his constitutional authority of appointing and dismissing ministers. The party ministers generally were dependent upon him and could be persuaded by one means or another to do his bidding. A British authority has described Charles's receipe for ruling the country as "the old panacea of Government by 'Ins' and 'Outs,' retaining in his own hand the power to drive each successive drove from the trough of office when its appetite seemed to him sufficiently appeased." [2] For all practical purposes this represented government by and for an entrenched oligarchy. Bismarck, who was scarcely liberal in his political views, warned on one occasion that Charles "is making a false calculation. . . . in seeking the friendship of the aristocracy instead of winning the devotion of the peasantry. . . ." [3]

During the decade following 1878 Rumanian politics were dominated by Ion Bratianu, the leader of the Liberal party. Bratianu started his career as a revolutionary, having participated in the events of 1848. Later he played a leading role in the selection of Charles as the successor to Prince Cuza. Bratianu and Charles were able to work together closly because both agreed upon an anti-Russian orientation in foreign affairs. They did so for different reasons, Charles because of his Hohenzollern family ties and Bratianu because of his revolutionary background. Nevertheless, both looked toward the Central Powers and both were responsible for the 1883 secret alliance which determined Rumanian foreign policy until World War I.

Bratianu's close partnership with Charles is also explained by the fact that he modified his earlier revolutionary views and adjusted to the realities of Rumanian political life. He was generally regarded as being a man of principle and character in his own personal affairs. But in building up his party machine he did not hesitate to accept and practice the spoils system. The rapid expansion of the Rumanian economy at the turn of the century offered many opportunities for the accumulation of private fortunes, and Bratianu never inquired too closely how these fortunes were acquired. His main concern was to make sure of the election returns, and in this he left little to chance. In the 1883 elections, for example, only 12 opposition deputies were elected to face 134 Bratianu Liberals. But Bratianu, it should be noted, had no monopoly on political opportunism. It was almost a principle of Rumanian political life that election returns depended more upon which party conducted the elections than upon the views of the voters. But in this respect Rumania differed from the other Balkan countries only in degree.

In March, 1888, Bratianu resigned his office and withdrew from public life despite the fact that the elections in the previous year had returned the usual government majority. Bratianu retired partly because of advancing age and partly because of charges of malversation brought against high army officers—a scandal that particularly concerned the military-minded Charles. After several months of frequent cabinet changes a stable Conservative government was formed in January, 1889, and remained in office until 1895. This government, which was headed by Lascar Catargiu, passed a number of important measures. It adopted the gold standard, improved the currency, negotiated several commercial treaties, and established the irremovability of judges, a measure which erased a dark blot on Rumanian public life. Generally speaking, the domestic record of the Conservative government was a creditable one.

In the field of foreign affairs the advent of the Conservative government created a serious dilemma. The 1883 alliance had been kept so secret that only King Charles and a few of the former Liberal ministers were aware of its existence. Charles now hesitated to inform the new ministers of the pact because he was uncertain what their reaction might be and because he did not expect them to remain long in office. Thus a fantastic situation prevailed in which responsible government officials pledged themselves publicly and in good faith to a policy of neutrality, without any inkling of the fact that their predecessors had already concluded a full alliance with the Central Powers. In fact, only one copy of the treaty existed in Rumania and that was in the king's private safe. No copy was to be found in the archives of the Rumanian foreign office.

This anomalous situation became serious as the time approached for the expiration of the pact. Finally, in March, 1892, Charles informed the foreign minister of the existence of the alliance and, two months later, he took Premier Catargiu into his confidence. Now it was possible to renew the treaty, and this was done in July, 1892. With the leaders of both parties informed of the commitment, the treaty was renewed without difficulty on later occasions— in 1896, 1902, and 1913. But to the very end it was kept a secret from the parliament and the public.

During the years at the beginning of the century Rumanian politics proceeded in the customary manner of the "Ins" and the "Outs." The German foreign minister observed caustically that the king acted on the maxim "To the most vicious dog the juiciest morsel." [4] In accordance with this principle the parties took their turn in office at appropriate intervals. The Liberals followed the Conservatives in 1895 and remained in power until 1899, their leader at the time being Demeter Sturza. Then came the Conservatives from 1899 to 1901, the Liberals from 1901 to 1904, and finally the Conservatives from 1904 until 1907, when the great storm of the Peasant Revolt broke in upon this half-unreal world of the Bucharest politicians.

THE PEASANT REVOLT

The great Peasant Revolt of March, 1907, was indeed a thunderbolt out of a clear blue sky. The government was caught by surprise, even though well-informed Rumanians had repeatedly made ominous predictions of the future: "a volcano is trembling under our feet," "a day will come when fire will devour the palaces, the granaries and all the property of those who exploit the peasantry," "if no reforms are introduced the Agrarian question will be solved by a dreadful jacquerie." [5] Despite these warnings, little attention was paid by responsible officials to the plight of the peasantry and the explosion was a rude awakening for them.

The insurrection began in northern Moldavia near the Rumanian frontier. At first it appears to have been partly anti-Semitic in character, the peasants sacking Jewish houses and stores. But the movement quickly developed into a full-scale agrarian revolt. All large tenant farmers and absentee landowners became the objects of peasant fury. Troops were called out, but the conflagration spread rapidly southward, reaching all the way to the Danube River. The peasants not only demanded an adjustment of their contracts with the landowners but in some districts seized land and organized revolutionary bands.

The Conservative government in office was unable to cope with the crisis, so the Liberal leader, Sturza, took over on March 25. He adopted the policy of the carrot and the stick. On the one hand, the king promised various reforms—the abolition of middlemen on the state lands, extension of small holdings, and restriction of agricultural leases to a maximum of eight thousand acres. On the other hand, the minister of war, General Alexander Averescu, launched regular military operations to crush the uprising. Flying columns with mounted artillery were dispatched to the affected areas. Ruthless measures were employed wherever the peasants refused to lay down their arms. Certain villages were bombarded and completely destroyed. By the end of April the uprising had been quelled by a force of 120,000 troops. At least 10,000 peasants were killed in the process. The full facts of the revolt will never be known because the official dossiers in the ministries of war and the interior have been removed and presumably destroyed.

Although the revolt was crushed within a month, it was nevertheless a sobering experience. The government made allusions to foreign agitators, but the fact remained that the movement was a purely Rumanian affair reflecting the unhealthy state of Rumanian society. Its roots were to be found in the agrarian history of Rumania during the preceding century, as described in Chapter 18: in the failure of Prince Cuza's land reform measure of 1864 and, more generally, in the disruptive impact of the Western European market economy upon a formerly self-sufficient natural economy. By the time of the revolt the inequality of land distribution was probably more pronounced in Rumania than in any other European country, not excluding Russia. About 85 per cent of the Rumanian peasants either had no land at all or had so little that they were forced to work part time for the landlords to support their families. By contrast, five thousand large estates covered about half of all the arable land.

The Peasant Revolt induced the Rumanian parliament to pass in December, 1907, four decrees designed to curb the exploitation of the peasantry. The first regulated agricultural contracts; the second created a state-supported Rural Office to promote the transfer of land to the peasants; the third limited the size of leases to 4,000 hectares of cultivable land; and the fourth established cooperatives for renting land. This last measure proved to be the most successful, the amount of land rented by cooperatives increasing from 133,000 to 410,000 hectares between 1908 and 1916. But taken as a whole, these decrees merely scratched the surface. The plight of the peasantry remained almost as desperate as ever. The basic reason appears to have been that the application of the reforms was entrusted to those who stood to lose the most if they were actually enforced. The net result under such circumstances was understandably negligible. An authority on Rumanian agriculture has concluded:

> The men who were to interpret and apply them [the reform decrees] remained the same, and, beyond a passing flush, the temper and habits of Rumanian public life were hardly affected by the peasants' show of despair. . . . In a peculiarly agrarian and peasant country the last issue that seemed capable of enlisting political zeal was the problem of the peasants' fate. How strange it

is, e.g., that the wise King Carol (1866–1915), who had the welfare of the people truly at heart, should not have used his great influence to bring about a solution of the rural problem; unless it be that he knew that, like Cuza, he would be faced with the ruthless opposition of all political factions.[6]

Such was the position of the Rumanian peasants when their eyes were opened by the course of events during the Balkan Wars. Peasant recruits observed that across the Danube River, in Bulgaria, peasants had their own small holdings with no great landowners or extortionate middlemen. Only a tenth of 1 per cent of the arable land in Bulgaria was in estates of 500 hectares or larger, as compared with 40 per cent in Rumania. The Rumanian peasant soldiers also observed that the Bulgarian villages were better built and the fields more successfully tilled than at home. This revelation of what existed across the Danube impelled the Liberal leader, Ionel Bratianu (eldest son of the first Bratianu), to advocate in 1913 expropriation of large estates. This was a significant step, since both parties hitherto had declared themselves strongly against such a drastic procedure. When the elections were held in February, 1914, the Liberals gained a majority of the seats. The new assembly voted in favor of the principle of revising the 1866 constitution to permit expropriation of private property. But World War I broke out before anything concrete could be accomplished. During the course of that war revolutionary forces were unleashed which far surpassed those of 1907 and which were to culminate at last in the long-awaited distribution of land.

ECONOMIC DEVELOPMENT

Turning from agriculture to industry, we find that Rumania was as underdeveloped in this field as the other Balkan countries. It is estimated that in 1914 only 1.5 per cent of the national wealth was invested in industry. Similarly, Rumanian exports comprised 75.7 per cent of agricultural products and only 3 per cent of industrial goods. The usual factors lay behind this backwardness—lack of local capital and shortage of skilled labor and trained management.

At an early date the government endeavored to stimulate industrial growth. In 1887 it decreed that anyone founding an industrial establishment with a capital of at least 2,000 pounds or employing at least 25 workmen (of whom two thirds should be Rumanians), would be granted 12 acres of state land, exemption for a term of years from all direct taxes, freedom from customs dues for machinery and raw material imported, reduction in cost of transporting materials on the state railroads, and preferential rights in supplying manufactured articles to the state. Despite this encouragement Rumanian industry remained feeble and was confined largely to the processing of local raw materials. The principal industries were oil refineries, iron foundries, distilleries, flour mills, sugar refineries, sawmills, paper mills, chemical and glass factories, and soap and candle works.

Apart from grains, the only other exports of any significance before

1914 were lumber and oil. Both these commodities were produced largely by foreign-financed and foreign-operated enterprises. The forests of Rumania were long either neglected or exploited in the most reckless fashion. Nevertheless, in 1910 there were 2,760,000 acres under forests, chiefly in the mountains of northwestern Moldavia. More than 1,000,000 acres were state property. The lumber was floated down the rivers of the Carpathian watershed to the Danube and thence exported to Turkey and Bulgaria. Also, casks, shaped planks, and petroleum drums were sold to Austria and Russia. King Charles, who was an ardent forester, halted the destruction of forest resources by signing a law in 1886 making private wooded properties liable to state control.

The oil industry developed around the Ploesti fields to the north of Bucharest. As early as the sixteenth century the peasants used the crude oil as lubricant and medicine and the boyars burned it for fuel. In 1844 the first concession was granted to a Russian firm, and by 1857 the first refinery had been built in Ploesti. Production rose steeply at the turn of the century, jumping from 50,000 tons in 1890 to 1,885,000 tons in 1913. In the latter year investment in the oil industry totaled 77,200,000 dollars. Only about 1 per cent of this sum was Rumanian capital, the remainder being German, British, Dutch, American, French, and Belgian. In 1917 British engineers blew up the oil wells to prevent their falling to the Central Powers. Production did not reach prewar levels again until 1921.

The first railroad in Rumania was built in 1869, running from the capital to Giurgiu, its port on the Danube. Other lines followed rapidly, some built by private enterprise and others by the state, which in 1888 bought the entire system. By 1914 the total mileage amounted to approximately 2,500. The main line ran from Bukovina south through the whole length of Moldavia and then turned westward through Wallachia to the Hungarian frontier. Branch lines extended on one side up the lateral valleys of the Carpathians and on the other to Jassy and to the principal Danube and Black Sea ports.

Rapidly increasing emigration to the New World was occurring in Rumania as well as in the other Balkan countries at the turn of the century. By 1910 a total of 70,217 had left Moldavia and Wallachia, but of these, 67,301 were Jews and only 2,916 Gentiles. Discrimination against the Jews as well as the greater mobility of the Jewish urban dweller presumably explains these figures. On the other hand, the Rumanians in Transylvania did not hesitate to emigrate; in that province they were the victims of exploitation by Hungarian landowners and of Magyarization by the state. Thus, 76,755 Transylvanian Rumanians had migrated to the United States by 1910.

Rumania, like her Balkan neighbors, borrowed heavily in the last quarter of the nineteenth century in order to support her army and to build railways and other public projects. At first she had difficulty in meeting payments for interest and amortization because her imports consistently exceeded her exports. But the balance of trade became favorable in 1900 and remained so until 1913. Thus the credit of the Rumanian government on the eve of World War I was higher than that of any other Balkan government, and no foreign control was exerted over Rumanian revenues. In 1914 Rumania's external debt was about 1.7 billion francs, of which 52 per cent was held in Germany, 32 per cent in France, 5 per cent in Belgium, and 11 per cent in Rumania.

IRREDENTISM AND FOREIGN POLICY

The position of the Rumanian minorities in Austria-Hungary and Russia was becoming increasingly difficult in the late nineteenth century. This was especially true of the Transylvanian Rumanians, who were subjected to severe and unrelenting Magyarization following the *Ausgleich* of 1867. As discussed in Chapter 18, that agreement had transformed the Hapsburg Empire into the Dual Monarchy and left Transylvania under Hungarian domination. The new masters were determined to Magyarize the various peoples of the province. When certain Rumanian leaders demanded autonomy for Transylvania, a Hungarian spokesman replied arrogantly: "Don't provoke us to employ towards the other nations the methods of total extermination employed by the Anglo-Saxons towards the Red Indians of North America." Other Rumanian objectors were met with such answers as "Be silent and pay," "Go to Bucharest." [7]

Theoretically, minority groups in Hungary, such as the Rumanians, Serbians, and Slovaks, were represented in the Hungarian parliament. But in practice they were effectively barred by the Electoral Law of 1874, which ensured the return of government-approved candidates through such time-honored procedures as gerrymandering, unequal distribution, a highly complicated franchise, public voting, and inadequate legal checks upon corruption. All this enabled Koloman Tisza's Liberal party to acquire an almost automatic control of the 250 constituencies in the non-Magyar districts. Paradoxically enough, the Liberal party was the most intolerant toward the minorities, so that, in effect, the non-Magyar constituencies were being utilized to enforce a program of Magyarization.

Some Rumanians wished to resist actively this campaign of denationalization. But they were overridden by Andrew Shaguna, metropolitan of the Orthodox Church of Transylvania and the outstanding leader of the Transylvanian Rumanians in the second half of the nineteenth century. Shaguna had played a leading role in the struggle against the Hungarians in 1848. Yet now, after the 1867 *Ausgleich,* he opposed agitation and violence. He believed that the Austro-Hungarian partnership was too strong to be challenged openly and directly. Instead, he developed his church organization to such a point that it became a highly effective instrument for national representation and national defense. He used his influence to secure from the Hungarian parliament in June, 1868, a church constitution which was to become an important bulwark of Rumanian nationality during the next half century. The constitution emphasized democratic elections and lay representation at all levels, from the metropolitan at the top to the village priests at the base. This made it possible for the clergy and the laymen to work together intimately and harmoniously for the interests of the nation.

Shaguna also made essential contributions in education and learning. He established a printing press, issued liturgies and religious books, reorganized the theological seminary, and, above all, founded numerous primary and secondary schools. By the time he died in 1873 his strategy of peaceful and constructive work had been thoroughly vindicated. His services to the Rumanian national cause were no less outstanding than those of his great contemporary, Bishop Strossmayer (discussed in Chapter 24), to the cause of Yugoslav culture and unity.

The first important development after Shaguna's death was the organization of the Rumanian National party in 1881. Its aim was reform within the empire rather than union with Rumania. The party's program included the restoration of Transylvania's autonomy, revision of the electoral law, autonomy for the Rumanian churches, and the use of the Rumanian language in the administration of Rumanian districts. The Rumanian National party lasted until 1894, when it was dissolved in the aftermath to the spectacular "Memorandum Trial." This trial arose out of a memorandum which the Rumanians prepared, listing their grievances and presenting their demands. When Emperor Francis Joseph refused to receive the document, the Rumanians made it public and circulated it widely. The Hungarian government thereupon arrested the entire committee of the Rumanian National party on the charge of "incitement against the Magyar nationality."

The Rumanians took advantage of the trial to appeal for world support:

> What is under discussion here is the very existence of the Rumanian people, and *the national existence of a people is not discussed, but affirmed.* . . . There can be no question of judgement: you can condemn us as individuals, but not as the representatives of our people. . . . But though you are not competent to judge us, there is none the less another tribunal, larger, more enlightened, and assuredly more impartial—the tribunal of the civilised world, which will condemn you yet more severely than it has hitherto done. By your spirit of medieval intolerance, by a racial fanaticism which has not its equal in Europe, you will, if you condemn us, simply succeed in proving to the world that the Magyars are a discordant note in the concert of European nations.[8]

Under such circumstances the outcome of the trial was a foregone conclusion. The defendants were given jail sentences and the Rumanian National party was ordered dissolved. But the most important result of the trial was that it attracted international attention to the Rumanian question in the same manner that the Agram (Zagreb) treason trial was to publicize the Croatian question fifteen years later.*

The Rumanians hoped for some improvement in their position when the Hungarian Liberal party was defeated in the elections of 1905. But the new government continued the policy of Magyarization as zealously as did the old. It passed an education bill in 1907 that established state control

* See Chapter 24.

over the Rumanian denominational school system and attempted to Magyarize this major stronghold of Rumanian nationalism. In the 1910 elections the Liberal party, now known as the Party of National Work, came back to power in Budapest. Its new leader was Count Khuen-Hedervary who had governed Croatia with an iron hand for two decades. Now, as premier, he stated publicly that "our non-Magyar fellow-citizens must first of all reconcile themselves to the fact that they here belong to a national state, which is not a conglomerate of different races, but which one nation has conquered and founded, upon which one nation has stamped the ineradicable impress of its individuality." The premier specifically warned the Rumanians not to form parties on the basis of nationality, for "in that moment they are already denying the political unity of the Magyar nation. With this shade of opinion there can be no negotiations: it must be fought, and if we conquer, we must destroy it." [9]

The reaction in Rumania to this unceasing campaign against the Transylvanian Rumanians was not as vigorous as might be expected. Certainly it did not approach the intensity and violence of the Serbian reaction against Hapsburg rule in Bosnia-Herzegovina. One reason for this difference is that the Serbians could count on Russian support against Austria-Hungary, whereas the Rumanians had strained relations with Russia and could not turn to any other great power for assistance against the Dual Monarchy. Furthermore, the Rumanian government was bound to Vienna by a secret alliance which precluded any serious or protracted campaign in behalf of the Transylvanian Rumanians. It is true that there were certain manifestations in Rumania in support of the hard-pressed brethren in Transylvania. Most important was the organization of the Rumanian Cultural League in 1891 by a group of teachers and students in the two universities at Bucharest and Jassy. The League carried on propaganda work to enlist public support within Rumania and also abroad. The fact remains, however, that public opinion in Rumania was not as agitated over the irredentist issue as that in Serbia.

Similarly, the Rumanian government at the turn of the century was much more concerned with the growing strength of Bulgaria than with the Rumanians in Transylvania. Premier Ionel Bratianu stated repeatedly during these years that his principal aim was to prevent Bulgaria from expanding into Macedonia and upsetting the balance of power in the Balkans. The concern of the Rumanians with what was happening to the south of the Danube is evident in the extravagant interest they showed in the fate of the Vlachs. They claimed as kinsmen this race of shepherds and traders scattered through the central Balkans.* Each year the Rumanians spent considerable sums subsidizing Vlach schools, the amounts reaching half a million francs by 1900 and one million by 1912. Needless to say, no one in Bucharest was so naïve as to imagine that the Vlachs could ever be incorporated into Rumania. They were regarded rather as a sort of speculative investment to be used for

---

* See Chapter 1.

bargaining purposes whenever an opportunity presented itself. When the Austrian foreign minister inquired in Bucharest, "Of what use is a Rumanian group in the Pindus Mountains?" he was told, "The time will come when it will serve as a device for compensation." [10] The point to note here is that the Rumanian government lavished more official attention upon the comparative handful of Vlachs than it did upon the massive bloc of Transylvanian Rumanians. The explanation was the secret alliance with Vienna and the strength of the Dual Monarchy compared to the flabbiness of European Turkey.

And on the other side of the Carpathians the leaders of the Transylvanian Rumanians did not look to Bucharest for delivery. Rather, they looked to Budapest and Vienna for reform. They tended to be anti-Magyar rather than anti-Hapsburg. As late as 1913 a leading spokesman for the Transylvanian Rumanians denounced the notion of an all-inclusive Rumanian state as a "beer-table fantasy." Many Rumanians had high hopes in Archduke Francis Ferdinand, who was known to be anti-Magyar and sympathetic to the minorities. But these hopes were dashed by the Sarajevo crime, which removed the archduke and released forces that brought into being precisely that state which a few years earlier had been regarded as a fantasy.

27. *Albanian Awakening to 1914*

ALBANIA IS THE SMALLEST COUNTRY in the Balkan Peninsula, being approximately the same size as the state of Massachusetts. It is a country with meager resources, consisting merely of a small strip of the mountainous western coast of the peninsula. This probably explains why the Albanians cannot look back to an earlier period of glory and greatness. Their homeland has been too poor and restricted to enable them to expand and to found an empire comparable with those of the medieval Byzantine, Serbian, and Bulgarian emperors. At the time of the Turkish invasion in the fifteenth century the Albanians did attract attention momentarily because of their gallant resistance under their famous leader Skanderbeg. But during the following centuries of Turkish rule they lived in uneventful obscurity in their remote mountains. Even after neighboring Balkan peoples began to awaken in the eighteenth and early nineteenth centuries, the Albanians slept on, oblivious to what was happening about them. Only in the late nineteenth century did they begin to stir, prodded by a new sense of national consciousness as well as by the increasing pressure of acquisitive neighboring powers. With the opening of the twentieth century Albania ceased to be merely a geographic expression and came to be recognized as the homeland of a distinct people with specific claims and aspirations, and resolved to take their place in the family of Balkan nations.

ALBANIA UNDER THE TURKS

The Albanians are generally considered to be the most ancient ethnic group in Southeastern Europe. They are the descendants of pre-Hellenic stock that was pushed back into the mountains of the western Balkans by the Hellenes and the Slavs. In this respect the Albanians may be compared to the Celts of the British Isles who were forced into the mountains of Wales, Scotland, and Ireland by the Anglo-Saxon invaders. The Albanian language is organically distinct from the neighboring Slavic and Greek languages in

496

the same manner that the Celtic language is different from the Germanic. It should be noted, however, that the Albanians use a considerable number of words that are of foreign origin—Latin, Italian, Turkish, Greek, and Slav. This linguistic borrowing represents the cultural residue of a long series of invaders—Romans, Goths, Slavs, Normans, Venetians, and, finally, Turks. The latter conquered Albania only after a bitter struggle. For once the Albanian chieftains rallied behind a single leader, the celebrated George Kastriotis, who so distinguished himself that he acquired the name Skanderbeg after Alexander the Great. During the years 1444 to 1466 he fought thirteen campaigns against the Turks and successfully held them at bay while Christian Europe applauded. After his death the Turks were finally able to prevail and to impose their rule, which was to last for four and a half centuries.

The Turks never governed Albania as closely as did the Romans. This was particularly true in the north, where the Turks doubtlessly calculated that the wild and rugged countryside would never repay the cost of thorough subjugation. But Turkish rule was prolonged, even though superficial, and in the course of the centuries it effected a number of fundamental changes. In the first place, it caused many Albanians to emigrate to foreign countries. Even before the appearance of the Turks there had been a considerable Albanian exodus southward into Greece because of Serbian pressure in the north. These Albanians settled in many parts of Greece, both mainland and islands, and some of them played leading roles in the Greek War of Independence. With the Turkish invasions more Albanians left their country, many of them crossing over to southern Italy and Sicily. Franceso Crispi, twice premier of Italy, was a descendant of these emigrants. The Italian census of 1901 reported a little over 200,000 Albanian-speaking citizens in the country. These Albanian colonies in Italy were more advanced culturally than the homeland under Turkish rule and therefore were able to contribute substantially to the national awakening in the late nineteenth and early twentieth centuries.

In addition to stimulating emigration, the Turks accentuated and perpetuated religious and social differences among the Albanians. These differences existed before the appearance of the Turks. Traditionally there has been the division between the Ghegs in the north and the Tosks in the south, the Shkumbi River being the line of demarcation. The two peoples speak dialects that differ as much as those of northern and southern Italy. The Ghegs are typical mountaineers—tall, rough, and warlike, and preferring, until recent times at least, to pass their days shining their guns or using them in their interminable feuds. The Tosks are shorter, more sober, somewhat mellowed by centuries of contact with Byzantine culture, and more amenable to discipline, perhaps because their physical environment is not as wild and as conducive to defiance of central authority as that in the north.

Religious differences also existed before the coming of the Turks. Originally all Albanians had belonged to the Eastern Orthodox Church, to which they had been attached at the time of the schism between the church of Rome and that of Constantinople. Then the Ghegs in the north adopted Catholicism, apparently in order better to resist the pressure of the Orthodox Serbs. Thus the Albanians were divided between the Catholic and Orthodox churches before the time of the Turkish invasion. Finally, it should be noted that feudalism prevailed in Albania when the Turks appeared, particularly in the regions along the coast.

The first and most important effect of the Turkish conquest was the conversion of the majority of the population to Islam. Many of the Catholics in the north embraced the new religion, the reason apparently being their fear and hatred of the Slavs. By becoming Moslems they became the allies and the equals of the Turks and thereby obtained security against the neighboring Christian Slavs. In southern Albania, where Turkish rule was more of a reality, the ruling Albanian families apostatized in order to retain their lands. Most of the common people soon followed their example. Islam also spread in the center of the country, where the most solid Moslem bloc now is to be found. As a result of these mass conversions Albania today is the only European country that is predominantly Moslem, approximately 70 per cent of the population being Moslem, 20 per cent Orthodox, and 10 per cent Catholic.

Another effect of the Turkish conquest was the freezing of social divisions. The Albanian feudal lords accepted Islam and the suzerainty of the sultan and thus retained their lands and their authority. In northern Albania the tribal chiefs were the *de facto* rulers of the country. The Turkish governor could do little without their consent and cooperation. Within each tribe the chief was assisted by a council of elders and, on special occasions, by a general assembly to which every family sent a delegate. In southern Albania the countryside was dominated by large landowners or beys, rather than by tribal chiefs. Members of this landowning class were also prominent in the Turkish service, thereby buttressing their economic position with political power.

Whatever the titles or the forms, Albania during the Turkish period was ruled by a handful of feudal families. Some produced outstanding statesmen who made notable contributions to their country. Outstanding among these was Ismail Kemal Bey, who began a distinguished career in the Ottoman service in 1860 and remained to contribute substantially to the winning of Albanian independence during the Balkan Wars and World War I. But on the whole, the Albanian lords were shiftless, unprogressive, and extortionate. This was especially true in the south, where tribal egalitarianism was lacking. Instead, the beys owned most of the fertile land, and the peasants, who constituted 95 per cent of the population, were dependent upon them as tenants or as agricultural laborers. The following accounts bring out the contrast between the lives of peasants and of landlords at the end of the nineteenth century. The first account describes daily existence in the villages of southern

Albania; the second, from the memoirs of Ismail Kemel Bey, recounts his life as the son of a landlord.

The peasant was haunted by a nagging fear that his supply of the principal staple of diet, a coarse bread made of corn mixed with rye and wheat, would not suffice for his needs. . . . To supplement the corn bread the peasant might occasionally use barley, ordinarily reserved for horses and mules; and, if times were good, his table might display beans, rice, or green vegetables. Meat, like fish, which was consumed chiefly by the Christians, was reserved for feast days. Although some butter, cheese, and olive oil were usually stored away for winter use, dairy products, including milk, were considered luxuries. Malnutrition and filth brought about a high mortality; consumption, bone diseases, and malaria were rampant. . . . Several families often lived in two or three rooms. The usual house, one- or two-storied and constructed of rough stone, had rooms reserved for married couples and for entertaining guests, and a large *ashef,* or kitchen, which served as living room, dining room, and sleeping quarters for the unmarried members of the family. The fireplace, center of family life, provided all the heat that was available either for cooking or for fighting the damp chill of the roughly floored house. In winter, the unglassed windows were filled with old rags, straw, or wooden slabs, in the hope that the bitter wind might be kept out. Sewage systems were unknown; although a house occasionally boasted its own well, the peasants generally carried their water in earthenware or copper kettles from streams or troughs. Most houses had several of these kettles, and perhaps a few wooden spoons and copper plates. A wooden chest set against the wall indicated that the woman of the family had some homespun garments to treasure, or a few trinkets garnered from her wedding celebration. No one had beds. They used home-made mats of wool, cotton, or straw, covered with coarse blankets. In the daytime they were piled in a corner; too few for cleanliness, the blankets were often infested with lice. It was an evening ritual in many of the houses for members of the family to congregate at the fireplace before going to bed, each one solemnly shaking out his blanket to kill a few of the pests. The Mohammedans, poorer than the Christians and even less solicitous about cleanliness, were easy prey for vermin. Directly adjacent to the house were the quarters reserved for horses, mules, donkeys, cows, sheep, and goats. Such were the better homes. In the poorer huts only a scant partition divided the one long room into a house and a barn.[1]

The chief elements in the education of a young Albanian of the period were horse-riding, shooting, and hunting. At each of the four seasons I was sent to make a horseback tour in the interior of the country, accompanied by my two tutors and by young companions of my age, and with a numerous suite. On these occasions I visited the various villages and was the guest of the notables, and there were all kinds of festivities, especially the performance of the national dances, which formed a part of youthful education. In the hunting season I frequently rode to hounds, every man in comfortable circumstances in those days keeping a pack of dogs. Hare-hunting was carried on, especially with a view to exercise in horsemanship. Our principal sport with the gun was shooting wild duck and woodcock. Another sport was carried on in the month of May, when we went up in the mountains to catch partridges with nets. . . . My suite consisted of young men of the household service and professional hunters. There were no paid upper servants. Young men from the families of the notables were attached to the service of the chief family in the country in an entirely honorary capacity as a part of their education or apprenticeship. This practice enabled them to take part in the events of the day, to learn manners and good breeding, and to get an acquaintance with public affairs. . . . All these young men were dressed in the national costume of rich embroidered cloth or velvet, and armed with pistols and yataghans in silver-gilt, which they carried in embroidered leather belts. Most of them possessed their own saddle horses, and the Beys at fetes and on other occasions made gifts to them of arms and similar objects.[2]

The significance of this social stratification should not be exaggerated. It did not have political repercussions before the twentieth century. Up to that time the peasant accepted his lot as a part of the natural order of things. When he took up arms it was not against the landowning beys but rather under their leadership and at their instigation. As a rule he fought not for social reform, which was beyond his ken, but in order to pillage neighboring Christians or to resist sultans who tried to impose conscription or to levy taxes or to curb the power of those same beys or chieftains that the peasant unquestioningly followed.

The religious divisions in Albania were also not as significant as might be assumed. The Albanians never have been fanatics in religious matters. Most Moslem Albanians belonged to the bektashi sect, an extremely unorthodox and tolerant order that preached a pantheistic universalist creed. Moslem and Christian Albanians lived side by side for centuries, and, although quarrels between tribes and individuals were only too common, religion was rarely the issue in dispute. Tolerance went so far that members of the same family not infrequently professed different religions. More than one traveler reported that infants were both baptized as Christians and circumcised as Moslems, and that adults who had begun life in that fashion used two names, one Christian and the other Moslem, depending upon the circle in which they happened to be moving at the time.

Even though the Albanians did not take any religion too seriously, the fact remains that three religious communities did exist in their country. This meant that whereas religion was a unifying force amongst other Balkan peoples, with the Albanians it was a disruptive factor, even though mildly so. Moslem Albanians felt a genuine reverence for the sultan in Constantinople, a sentiment that their Christian brothers could not share. In education and general culture the divisive influence of the three religions was most apparent and most serious. It is true that throughout the country, schools were conspicuous mostly by their absence. Only in 1860 did the imperial government begin to open schools but these were reserved for Moslems and used Turkish as the language of instruction. In addition there were a considerable number of Orthodox church schools in the south, which used the Greek language in their teaching and were pro-Greek in their orientation. Only a handful of

Catholic and Protestant schools used the Albanian language, and they were able to do so only because they were under foreign protection.

The Ottoman government used its authority to suppress the Albanian language wherever possible. It forbade the publication of any works in Albanian and it also forbade the use of Albanian for instruction. This was contrary to the usual practice of the Turks, who normally did not concern themselves with schools and languages. The explanation for this deviation is that the Albanians, divided as they were by religion, had only their language in common. Only the Albanian language could unite Moslem, Orthodox, and Catholic Albanians. And a common language could lead, as it had with the other Balkan peoples, to a common literature, to the discovery of a common historical past, and, eventually, to the growth of an active and all-embracing national consciousness.

The Turks naturally wished to forestall this development, particularly because the Albanians traditionally had constituted the backbone of their fighting forces in Europe. The Greek ecclesiastical authorities also opposed the rise of Albanian national consciousness because it would interfere with the Hellenizing work of Greek schools and Greek churches. Thus the Ottoman government and the Greek church officials purposefully exploited the religious divisions among the Albanians to foment discord and to prevent the growth of a unifying national sentiment.

Albanian leaders were well aware of the separatist influence of the three religions. "Awake, Albanians, Awake!" exhorted the pioneer nationalist, Vassa Pasha. "Let not mosque and churches divide you. The true religion of the Albanian is his national ideal." [3] But this appeal evoked no response for many decades. Albania remained only a geographic expression until the late nineteenth century. The Albanians followed far behind the other Balkan peoples in their national awakening.

The reasons for this lag were many and weighty. The Albanians had no schools of their own, no national church, and no national literature. They were not even oppressed by the Turks or goaded to revolt by real or fancied grievances. On the contrary, the position of the Albanians in the Ottoman Empire was comfortable and advantageous. Most of them were of the same faith as their Turkish overlords. They all enjoyed a large degree of autonomy. And those who wished for a career had opportunities open to them in the imperial army and bureaucracy which far surpassed anything available in their poverty-stricken homeland.

Many Albanians did take advantage of these opportunities in the imperial service. Out of forty-nine grand vizirs in the period 1453 to 1623, eleven were Albanians, eleven were South Slavs, only five were Turks, one each were Italian, Georgian, Armenian, and Circassian, and the remaining ten are of undetermined origin. Likewise, in the late nineteenth century Abdul Hamid depended to a great extent upon the Albanians, whom he trusted above his other subjects. The Palace Guard and the First Army Corps, which garrisoned the capital, consisted largely of Albanians. The grand vizir for many years was the Albanian Ferid Pasha. Other Albanian leaders also received favors and high posts from Abdul Hamid. This advantageous position of the Albanians in the Ottoman Empire, together with their lack of means for defending and fostering their national culture, explains why for centuries they accepted Ottoman rule without question and remained oblivious to the appeal of nationalism that was arousing their Balkan neighbors.

ALBANIAN LEAGUE

The first manifestations of Albanian nationalism appeared not within Albania itself but rather in the Albanian colonies abroad, where the restraints of Turkish officials and Greek prelates did not prevail. Conditions were particularly favorable in Italy, where a large number of Albanians lived in separate communities with full freedom to conduct their own schools and to preserve their own language and traditions. The two great pioneers of Albanian nationalist literature both hailed from these settlements in Italy. One was Demeario Camarda, who published in 1864 a scientific study of the Albanian language demonstrating its antiquity. The other was Girolamo de Rada, whose poem "Skanderbeg" (1872) extolled the struggle of the Albanian people against the Turkish invader. In other works De Rada sought to revive memories of past achievements and glory and thereby to stimulate national consciousness and pride.

Meanwhile the Albanians at home remained asleep until awakened by a shock from the outside. This took the form of the San Stefano and Berlin treaties concluded at the end of the Russo-Turkish War of 1877–1878. The San Stefano Treaty gave extensive lands to Serbia, Montenegro, and Bulgaria which Albanian nationalists regarded as their own. As described in Chapter 21, the Western powers were not satisfied with the terms of San Stefano and they called the Berlin Congress (June 13–July 13, 1878) to consider a new settlement. The Albanian leaders of the period, being apprehensive of the decisions that might be made, organized on July 1 the "Albanian League for the Defense of the Rights of the Albanian Nation." The aim of the League was twofold, to "resist until death" any attempt to annex Albanian territory, and to obtain an autonomous status within the Ottoman Empire.

The Porte encouraged the Albanian League, hoping that it might be successful in checking the expansionism of the Slavic Balkan states. The League did resist the Slavs valiantly and with considerable success. But its true significance is that it represents the beginning of the Albanian national movement. In fostering the League the Turks unleashed a force which, within three decades, was to grow beyond their power to control.

The Berlin Congress assigned much less territory to the Balkan Slav states than they had received at San Stefano. But the leaders of the League were still dissatisfied, claiming that Albanian territory in the north was being handed over to the Slavs. The League sent a resolution to the powers at Berlin protesting against the new frontiers and proclaiming the unity of all

Albanians regardless of religious differences. Bismarck, as usual concerned only with the power relationships of the great states, commented curtly, "There is no Albanian nationality."

But the Albanians, now aroused and organized for the first time, were not to be dismissed so lightly. They decided to go beyond protests and to take up arms in defense of what they considered to be their homeland. They could do nothing about the lands assigned to the Serbs because the latter had already occupied them. But when the Montenegrins tried to take over the towns of Podgorica and Antivari (Bar) and the surrounding areas, the Albanians resisted fiercely and successfully. The Montenegrins, having been repulsed, appealed to the great powers. A compromise settlement proposed by the Italian Count Corti was accepted by the Porte in April, 1880. But the Albanians refused to consider any territorial cessions to Montenegro and defied both the powers and the Porte. The latter gladly exploited this Albanian resistance as a means of stalling on the cession of territory. But the powers finally decided to intervene decisively in order to settle the dangerously prolonged controversy. Hence they brought sufficient pressure to bear in Constantinople to force the sultan to take adequate measures against his obstinate subjects. In November, 1880, a Turkish army dispersed the Albanian forces and delivered the disputed territories to the Montenegrins.

The Albanian League opposed not only the Montenegrins in the north but also the Greeks in the south. The latter were demanding the provinces of Thessaly and Epirus to balance the expansion of the South Slavs. The Albanians claimed Epirus as their own and mustered a considerable force to stop any Greek advance. In the negotiations that followed between the Greek and Turkish representatives, the latter argued that Epirus could not be ceded because of the armed opposition of the Albanian League. Finally, after protracted negotiations, Greece was given most of Thessaly but only the Arta region of Epirus.

With the frontier question settled, the Albanian League turned to its other objective, that is, an autonomous status within the empire. It is significant that at no time did the Albanian leaders demand full independence. The reason was that they knew that the Albanian people were not ready for independent statehood and they feared that if European Turkey were partitioned, the Albanian lands would be divided along with the rest. Thus the Albanians, unlike the other Balkan peoples, favored the continuation of Ottoman rule in the Balkans and preferred the security of autonomy to the dangers of independence.

The League demanded specifically that the four vilayets—Yanina, Monastir (Bitolj), Üsküb (Skoplje), and Shkodra (Scutari)—which it considered to be Albanian, should be united into one province; that the Turkish governor of the province should be advised by an Albanian Council elected by universal suffrage; that a national militia should be organized with Turkish officers; and that Albanian should be made the language of administration. The Turks had favored the League to this point, but now they rejected its demands. Autonomy invariably had been the prelude to independence in the rest of the Balkans, and the Turks did not care to risk a repetition. The Albanians, with their customary boldness, forced the issue by ousting Turkish officials in various parts of the country and assuming full control. The Turks responded by sending an army which dispersed the League's forces and asserted the sultan's authority throughout Albania.

In conclusion, the significance of the League should not be exaggerated. It by no means had a united and informed people behind it. The League's program had been largely the work of southern leaders who had held posts in the imperial service and who thereby had acquired sufficient background and perspective to think in terms of the nation as a whole. By contrast, most northern leaders hitherto had been isolated and engrossed in purely local affairs. Consequently, they were more interested in autonomy as a means of getting exemption from taxes and from military service than as a step toward national unity and ultimate independence.

Nevertheless, the League did accomplish a good deal. Its determined stand undoubtedly saved certain territories from foreign rule. Also, it gave the Albanian people their first national organization and national program. Finally, it compelled the great powers to take note that Albanians did exist and that they could not be ignored with impunity. The following significant dispatch sent by the British ambassador in Constantinople on July 26, 1880, would never have been written were it not for the League and its work.

I venture to submit to your Lordship, as I have done before, that the Albanian excitement cannot be passed over as a mere manoeuvre conducted by the Turks in order to mislead Europe and evade its will. Nor can it be denied that the Albanian movement is perfectly natural. . . . the Albanian nationality is an element which ought not to be overlooked in any future political combinations. . . . I would recommend that the formation of a united Albanian province should at least always be kept in view.[4]

NATIONAL AWAKENING

The years following the collapse of the Albanian League witnesesed a steady growth of Albanian national culture and consciousness. When the League was formed in 1878 the Turks expressed their approval and support by removing the ban which they had previously imposed on Albanian schools and on printing in the Albanian language. For some reason they did not reimpose the ban when they suppressed the League in 1881. It was not until 1886 that the old restrictions were again put into force. During the interval Albanian nationalists eagerly seized the opportunity to found schools and to print the books and newspapers necessary to arouse the people from their centuries' long slumber.

Hitherto almost all Albanians had been illiterate. On the rare occasions when they wished to send written messages they had turned to Turkish professional letter writers or to Greek Orthodox priests. These scribes wrote the messages in Arabic or Greek characters. Albanian youths who aspired for education had a choice of Orthodox Church schools, where instruction was in Greek, or Ottoman government schools where instruction was in Turkish. Only a handful of Catholic and Protestant schools used the Albanian language, but these schools could not even be considered by the majority of Albanians, who were Moslems.

A decisive step forward in the growth of national culture was taken in 1879 in Constantinople, where a group of Albanian intellectuals organized the "Society for the Development of the Albanian Language." The aim of the society was to publish readers and other educational texts in the Albanian language. The first task was to prepare a standardized alphabet that would be generally acceptable. This was accomplished by three members of the Society—a Moslem, an Orthodox Christian, and a Roman Catholic—who worked out an alphabet consisting of Latin and a few Greek letters. The first book published by the Society was the *Abetare* or ABC of the Albanian language. The Society also issued a literary journal, the *Drita* or *Light*. In addition to its work in Constantinople the Society conducted schools and promoted literary work within Albania and also in foreign centers, such as Bucharest and Sofia, where Albanian colonies were to be found.

The Moslem Frasheri family was especially prominent in this cultural activity, its members publishing patriotic poems and histories of the Albanian people. Naim Frasheri, the apostle-poet of Albanjan nationalism, wrote in his *Notebook of the Bektashis* (he himself belonging to this Moslem pantheistic sect): "The Bektashis are brothers not only among themselves but with all humanity as well. They love the rest of the Moslems and the Christians as their soul and they get along well with all men. But above all they love their fatherland and their countrymen, this being the highest of all virtues." [5]

Both the Turks and the Greek Patriarch became alarmed at the rapid tempo of this Albanian cultural revival. Particularly disturbing was the breakdown of religious barriers, Albanians of all three creeds participating enthusiastically in the educational and literary work. Accordingly, in 1886, the Ottoman government reimposed its ban upon Albanian publications and schools. The Patriarch strengthened the ban by threatening with excommunication anyone convicted of reading or writing in the Albanian language. These measures retarded seriously the growth of a national culture within Albania. But activity did not cease in the Albanian communties outside the homeland. By 1908 more than thirty Albanian newspapers and periodicals were being published abroad, including seven in Bulgaria, seven in Italy, four in Egypt, four in Rumania, three in Belgium, and one each in Austria-Hungary, Greece, England, and the United States.

The most active community abroad was that in Italy. It consisted of Albanians who had emigrated to Sicily and southern Italy from the fifteenth century onward. They settled in distinct communities and preserved their language and customs. In the middle of the nineteenth century they began to publish linguistic and other studies demonstrating the existence of the Albanian nationality. By the 1890's they had organized an extensive nationalist movement centered around the Albanian National Society with branches in all Italo-Albanian colonies. The Society had issued more than two hundred publications by 1900, and in that year the Italian government founded a chair of Albanian language and literature at the Instituto Orientale of Naples.

The Albanian colony in the United States was the youngest but the most rapidly growing. After 1900 a considerable number of Albanians emigrated to the United States, where they settled along the eastern seaboard. In their new surroundings, and with a variety of foreign nationalities living about them, the Albanian immigrants for the first time became fully conscious of their national identity. In their native villages they had been much more absorbed by family ties and family feuds than by any conception of Albanian nationality. But now the bewildered and homesick immigrants thought nostalgically of their homeland as they worked long hours in stifling textile mills and dingy shoe factories. In this alien and forbidding environment they felt keenly that they were different from others and they experienced a new sense of pride in their native country.

The establishment of the weekly *Kombi* or *Nation* in Boston in June, 1906, laid the cornerstone of the Albanian nationalist movement in the United States. Most of the Albanian immigrants were illiterate, but usually a "learned one" could be found to read the *Kombi* to the others as well as to read letters from home and to write letters in return. As important as the *Kombi* was the Albanian Autocephalous Orthodox Church founded in 1908 under the leadership of the Reverend Fan S. Noli. Before this time the immigrants, who were almost all Orthodox Christians from southern Albania, had attended Greek churches, where the services were naturally conducted in Greek and where the atmosphere was far from friendly to Albanian nationalism. In the new church the services were held in the native tongue, while Fan Noli ardently preached nationalistic sermons from his pulpit.

Another important step was taken in April, 1912, when various Albanian societies in the United States combined to form the Pan-Albanian Federation, Vatra (The Hearth). Vatra published various books and sponsored activities designed to foster the national spirit. In this manner the Albanians in the United States, who numbered perhaps five thousand by 1912, entered the stream of the Albanian nationalist movement. They were well prepared for the important role which they were to assume during the Balkan Wars and World War I, when the future of their country was being decided.

STRUGGLE FOR AUTONOMY

While Albanian nationalism was being nurtured in the scattered colonies abroad, the homeland, which for so many centuries had languished in obscurity, was beginning to show signs of national consciousness and activity.

A fairly clear pattern is noticeable in this movement, which began in the late nineteenth century and gained momentum thereafter. Most of the revolutionary activity originated in the north because the Moslems of the Kosovo area and the Catholic mountaineers of Scutari and Mirdita had enjoyed autonomy for centuries and were ready to fight against the centralizing reforms of Constantinople. In southern Albania political activity was more common than armed resistance. One reason was that the means of communication were better developed in the south than in the mountainous north, thereby facilitating control by the state. Also, education was more widespread among the southern Albanians, who consequently tended to think more in terms of the over-all national cause than of purely local privileges. Between the north and the south was the bloc of Moslems in the central lowlands. Politically they were the most backward of all Albanians, not participating in the nationalist movement until the 1912 revolt which brought about the overthrow of the Young Turk regime. Various factors explain the inertness of these people. They were mostly peasants completely dominated by the feudal landowners. Also, they were fanatic Sunnis, in contrast to the liberal Bektashis of the south. And because they were located in the center of the country they were not goaded into national organization for self-protection as were the northerners by Slavic pressure and the southerners by Greek pressure.

One of the main tasks of the nationalist leaders was to serve as a link between these disparate and isolated regions of their country. Another task was to counter the increasing interest of the great powers in Albania. The two powers most directly concerned with Albania were Austria-Hungary and Italy. Each was determined to prevent the other from gaining a dominant position in Albania because of that country's strategic position at the entrance to the Adriatic Sea. The neighboring Balkan states were also interested in Albania. Greece had territorial aspirations in the southern part of the country and Montenegro and Serbia in the north. Fortunately for Albania, some of these external pressures neutralized each other. The Austrians resolutely opposed Montenegrin and Serbian expansion in order to forestall a solid wedge of Slavic territory across the Balkans. The Italians likewise did not wish to see Greece becoming large and strong at the expense of Albania.

Faced with these external dangers, the Albanian leaders decided that the safest course was to accept and support Turkish rule in the Balkans. They calculated that the Albanian people were not ready for an independent existence and that, consequently, if European Turkey were partitioned, all or most of Albania would suffer the same fate. Accordingly, they strove not to overthrow Turkish rule but rather to obtain reforms and autonomy under its aegis. A. Lorecchio, a prominent Italo-Albanian author, wrote in 1904, "Reforms are the only and continuous goal of this people. There is no memorandum . . . sent to the Sultan or the Powers, there is is no newspaper or review . . . there is no committee, congress, assembly, or any other collective manifestation of Albanian will in which the highest and dominant note is not one and the same: reforms, administrative autonomy to the people of Albania." [6]

This strategy explains why the Albanians supported Turkey during the 1897 war with Greece. It also explains why many Albanians joined the Young Turks, hoping that the energy and decisiveness of these reformers would forestall the partitioning of European Turkey which seemed at the time to be imminent. The successful revolt of the Young Turks in 1908 and the constitution that they immediately put into effect * were both hailed enthusiastically in Albania, though few understood precisely what a constitution was or what it signified.

The Young Turks not only established a constitutional regime but also proclaimed liberty and equality for all nationalities within the empire. This unleashed the nationalist forces in Albania and led to a great outburst of educational and organizational activities. Within ten months the Albanians established 24 night schools with 1,753 pupils, 34 day schools with 1,850 pupils, and a normal school with 145 pupils and 14 teachers. These schools were supported by 66 national clubs with 10,000 members and were directed by a National Board of Education established at a National Congress held at Elbasan in August, 1909. At the same time the Albanians founded 4 printing presses and 17 newspapers, as well as several literary and musical societies.

The Young Turk leaders were alarmed by the magnitude of this Albanian awakening. They had strong centralist tendencies, wishing to transform the various subjects of the empire into loyal Ottoman citizens. Accordingly, they disapproved of further fragmentation along national lines, particularly in the case of the Albanians, who for so long had been the chief pillar of Turkish rule in the Balkans. The Albanians, on their part, were no more willing to accept Ottomanization by the Young Turks than they had been willing to accept it from the sultans. In fact, many Albanians now began to turn against the new regime in Constantinople. This was especially true of the conservative Moslem peasants, who found it hard to abandon their traditional loyalty to the sultan and who became increasingly distrustful of the Young Turk leaders with their Western ways and their insistence on uniformity and centralization. These same considerations alienated the numerous Albanian soldiers in Constantinople who comprised the majority of the capital's garrison. Even liberal-minded Albanian leaders turned against the Young Turks, the outstanding example being Ismail Kemal Bey. This well-known statesman, who had served the empire in various capacities since 1860, now joined the Liberal Union in opposition to the dominant Committee of Union and Progress.

When the counterrevolution against the Young Turks broke out in

* See Chapter 28.

April, 1909,* it was largely the work of the disaffected Albanian regiments supported by the Liberal Union and by Moslem religious leaders. The Young Turks promptly suppressed the revolt and then proceeded to enforce vigorously their Ottomanization program. They required Turkish to be the language of instruction in Albanian schools and they imposed compulsory military service and regular taxation upon Albanian tribesmen, who had never been subjected to such exactions. The minister of interior went so far as to deny in the Ottoman assembly the very existence of an Albanian nationality but he was immediately challenged by the Albanian deputies present who shouted, "Var, Effendim, var!" ("There is, Sir, there is!")

The mountaineers of the Kosovo area took up arms in March, 1910, against these Ottomanization measures. The Turks speedily crushed the revolt and then closed the Albanian schools throughout the country, suppressed the Albanian newspapers, arrested hundreds of prominent nationalists, and even forbade the printing of the words "Albania" and "Albanians." The country was treated as conquered territory. Never before had the traditional customs and practices been flouted in this manner. Twelve thousand refugees were living under miserable conditions in neighboring Montenegro as the aftermath of the abortive uprising.

Another revolt broke out in March, 1911, among the Catholic highlanders in the north. Nicholas of Montenegro instigated the uprising, hoping thereby to satisfy his territorial aspirations in that area. The Turks were again able to suppress the rebels, but in June, 1911, the Catholic Albanians once more took up arms. This time they were more successful and by August, 1911, the Turks felt constrained to grant substantial concessions. They undertook to grant an amnesty, to open Albanian schools, to recognize the right of Albanians to carry weapons, and to require Albanian recruits to serve only in the European part of the empire. The Turks abided by these terms, one reason undoubtedly being that the outbreak of war with Italy on September 29, 1911, made it essential that further troubles in Albania be avoided.

The defeats sustained by Turkey during the Italian war created an extremely dangerous situation for the Albanians. The Balkan nations, emboldened by the plight of Turkey, concluded a series of alliances in the spring of 1912. It was an open secret that their aim was to strike at the preoccupied Turks and drive them out of Europe. This raised for the Albanians the old nightmare of partition among their acquisitive neighbors. To forestall this fate they decided upon a full-scale insurrection in order to establish definitely and indisputably their autonomous position. Then if Turkish rule in the Balkans collapsed, the Albanians at least would have a viable base upon which to stand and face the victorious Balkan allies.

The Kosovo mountaineers took the lead, starting hostilities in June, 1912. Revolts followed quickly in other parts of the country. The Turks

* See Chapter 28.

were unable to bring in reinforcements, and the movement was soon completely out of control. In many cases Turkish troops joined the insurgents. By mid-July of 1912 the rebels were the masters of the entire country. With an army of fifty thousand at their disposal they peremptorily demanded on July 30, 1912, that the Ottoman parliament be dissolved within forty-eight hours, and that a new government replace the existing one, which was dominated by the centralist-minded Committee of Union and Progress. The Turks had no choice but to comply, whereupon the Albanians presented their specific demands for autonomy: the four vilayets of Scutari, Kosovo, Yanina, and Monastir to be united into one province; Albanian soldiers to serve only in that province; Albanian to be the language of administration and instruction; local revenues to be expended locally; all Albanians to have the right to bear arms; and certain politicians in Constantinople to be impeached for their past measures against the Albanians. The Ottoman government held back only on the demands for impeachment and limited military service, but the Albanians insisted on acceptance of all their terms. Before these differences could be resolved the Balkan allies one after the other declared war upon Turkey during October, 1912.

The beginning of the Balkan War created an entirely new situation for the Albanians. Hitherto they had chosen to remain under the aegis of the sultan in order to checkmate the expansionist tendencies of their neighbors. But now the rapid succession of allied victories abruptly ended Turkish rule in the Balkans and compelled the Albanians to abandon the sinking ship in order to safeguard their own national security. Thus they were forced to give up their traditional autonomist strategy and to strike out for full independence.

A national congress assembled in Valona consisted of eighty-three Moslem and Christian delegates from all parts of the country. On November 28, 1912, the delegates proclaimed the independence of Albania and hoisted the flag of Skanderbeg for the first time in 445 years. They elected a cabinet of seven Christian and Moslem ministers, with Ismail Bey as president. They also sent a telegram to Constantinople and to the great powers announcing the "political independence of Albania" and requesting protection "against all attacks on their national existence and against any dismemberment of their country." [7]

But the establishment of a new Albanian state required more than mere resolutions and proclamations. Serbia and Greece naturally preferred to divide the Albanian lands between themselves. Nikola Pashich, the Serbian premier, declared that "an independent Albania was neither desirable nor possible," while the Greek press announced that "to allow the barbarous Albanians an independent existence amidst Greek civilization was inconceivable." [8] The great powers also were by no means agreed on this matter. Austria-Hungary and Italy favored Albanian independence because they feared Serbian expansion to the Adriatic. Conversely, France and Russia, precisely because they wanted a strong Serbia, opposed Albanian aspirations.

Only Britain and Germany dealt with the Albanian issue with any degree of objectivity. Given these conflicting forces, it is understandable that the new Albania for several years should have led a precarious existence amid diplomatic intrigue and armed assault.

WILLIAM OF WIED

As will·be seen in Chapter 28, the Treaty of London terminating the first Balkan war left the status of Albania to the decision of the great powers. The latter entrusted the problem to the British foreign minister and the ambassadors in London of the other five powers. On December 20, 1912, this Conference of Ambassadors announced their decision in favor of an independent Albania. The Conference then appointed two commissions to delimit the new state's frontiers with Greece in the south and Serbia and Montenegro in the north. Neither frontier had been definitely settled, at least in regard to details, by the time World War I began.

In addition to delimiting the frontiers of the new state, the Conference of Ambassadors undertook to define its political institutions. On July 29, 1913, the Conference decided that Albania should be "an independent, sovereign Principality," [9] and that the powers should guarantee her neutrality and select her prince. In accordance with this arrangement, the powers, after a long delay, chose William of Wied, a thirty-five-year-old German army captain, to be the ruler of Albania. Prince William, who was the nephew of Queen Elizabeth of Rumania, was tall and impressive in appearance but lacked the political experience and forcefulness necessary for the position he had assumed. On March 7, 1914, he landed at Durazzo (Durrës), where he was enthusiastically welcomed as the successor to Skanderbeg. Only six months later he was to flee the country after vain efforts to assert his authority.

The chief reason for William's failure was the dissension among the great powers and especially between Italy and Austria-Hungary. These two countries, desirous of keeping the Slavs from the Adriatic, had been largely responsible for the original decision to establish an independent Albania. But now they drifted apart because Italy considered Prince William to be pro-Austrian and pro-German. Italy therefore decided to checkmate the new prince by supporting Essad Pasha Toptani, an ambitious and unscrupulous feudal lord who aspired to become the ruler of the country. Prince William also failed because of his personal shortcomings. His past experience as an officer of the German army had been narrowly military. He was naïve in diplomatic matters and completely ignorant of the country he had come to rule. Consequently, he made many errors, but when they were pointed out to him he usually lacked the decisiveness to take prompt corrective measures.

William's first mistake was to accept a cabinet that had little popular support. Essad held the ministries of war and interior, a dangerous concentration of power in a person so covetous. Most of the remaining ministers had been absent from the country for many years and were representatives of the small class of large landowners. The peasants were keenly disappointed that the prince had surrounded himself with feudal landlords, especially because they had naïvely expected that the new regime would perform miracles and deliver them from their age-old bondage. Now their disappointment, combined with their ignorance, made them readily susceptible to propaganda. And there were many who were conducting propaganda against the new government. Essad himself, with Italian support, secretly distributed arms to his followers and incited the people against the German prince. Agents of Serbia, Montenegro, and Greece fomented trouble in order to prevent the new state from becoming stable. Finally, Moslem religious leaders and Turkish agents feared that the new regime would discriminate against the Moslem majority. Accordingly they worked to restore Ottoman rule or else to obtain a Turkish or an Egyptian prince in place of William.

Under these circumstances it is not surprising that William lasted only half a year. He did take action against Essad when proof was furnished of his machinations. On May 19 Essad was forced to leave the country and embarked on an Italian vessel. But three days later a revolt broke out in the Durazzo region, apparently with Italian backing. The government proved incapable of suppressing the rebels. In fact, it controlled little more than the city of Durazzo itself, the rest of the country now coming under the control of various local armed groups.

At this point the outbreak of World War I ended what little chance William still had of pulling through. Foreign warships began to leave Albanian waters. German and Austrian volunteers left to join their respective armies. A Dutch military mission which had been attempting to organize a *gendarmerie* was recalled to Holland. Even food was running short in beleaguered Durazzo. By August 13 the treasury was completely empty and the great powers were too distracted to consider the loan that they had promised to William when he assumed the throne.

The foreign diplomats unanimously urged William to leave the country. He refused to do so, hoping that assistance would come from some source. But his hopes evaporated as the powers one by one became involved in the war. Finally, on September 3, 1914, Prince William left the country, though he did not formally abdicate. Instead, he explained in his proclamation that, because of complications arising from the war, "it is more useful if for some time I go to the west." [10] William never was to have an opportunity to return. An Albanian leader aptly observed that "Prince William can be criticized only for being unable to perform miracles." [11]

28. Diplomatic Developments: 1878–1914

THE CONGRESS OF BERLIN of 1878 represented a turning point in both European and Balkan diplomacy. In Europe it had been preceded by thirty years of revolution and constant warfare. It was followed by thirty-four years of almost unbroken peace. The only violence during those thirty-four years occurred in the Balkan Peninsula with the 1885 Serbo-Bulgarian War and the 1897 Greco-Turkish War. These two exceptions point up the fact that, however much the Berlin settlement satisfied the ambitions of certain great powers, it certainly did not contribute to peace and stability in the Balkans. By giving Bosnia-Herzegovina to Austria it poisoned Serbian-Austrian relations and led directly to the 1908 Bosnian crisis and the 1914 Sarajevo murder. Furthermore, the loss of Bosnia-Herzegovina forced the Serbians to look southward toward Macedonia, where they came into conflict with the Bulgarians and the Greeks, who had also been disappointed by the 1878 settlement. Thus the fruits of the Berlin Treaty, so far as the Balkans were concerned, were the Austro-Serbian duel over Bosnia-Herzegovina and the suicidal Bulgarian-Greek-Serbian struggle for Macedonia.

To this disquiet should be added the unsettling influence of great-power diplomacy. Austria and Russia were particularly disruptive as they competed with each other in the Balkans for spheres of influence. A good example of this activity was Austria's violent opposition to the Bulgarian-Serbian *rapprochement* of 1904, an opposition that was carried even to the point of embargo and trade war.

This combination of disruptive forces operating within and without the peninsula explains the series of crises and wars that punctuated Balkan history with such tragic frequency between 1878 and 1914.

OTTOMAN TERRITORIAL LOSSES
IN THE BALKANS ———— 1878-1913

1	To Greece, 1881	——— Boundaries in 1878: Treaty of Berlin
2	To Bulgaria, 1885	░░░ Boundaries in 1913: Treaty of Bucharest
*	Full independence, 1908	▨ Contested regions in second Balkan War

AFTERMATH OF THE BERLIN CONGRESS

The two powers most interested in the Balkans after 1878 were Austria and Russia. By contrast, France was busy in North Africa, Bismarck was interested in the Balkan Peninsula only insofar as it affected relations among the great powers, while Britain was more concerned with Asia Minor and Egypt. Austria and Russia, however, were vitally interested in developments in the Balkan Peninsula. In fact, Austro-Russian rivalry during the Balkan crisis of 1875–1878 had broken up the Three Emperors' League or *Dreikaiserbund* of Austria, Russia, and Germany. Because Bismarck despaired of being able to persuade his two partners to cooperate more smoothly in the future, in 1879 he selected Austria as his ally and concluded with her the Dual Alliance that remained in effect to World War I.

But Bismarck always took care to maintain some tie with St. Petersburg; hence, he encouraged the renewal of the *Dreikaiserbund,* which was accomplished on June 18, 1881. The treaty gave Austria the right to annex Bosnia-Herzegovina whenever she wished, and in return Austria agreed not to oppose the eventual unification of Bulgaria and Eastern Rumelia. Also, the three signatories agreed that modifications of the territorial *status quo* in Turkey should take place only after agreement among themselves, and if any of them should feel compelled to go to war with Turkey, it should consult its allies in advance as to the eventual results.

This arrangement regulated the relations between Austria and Russia in the Balkans but it did not eliminate their rivalry. The agreement was regarded primarily as a truce while the two empires watched each other suspiciously and sought to strengthen their respective positions. Fortunately for the Balkan states, neither one of the powers was interested in territorial expansion. Rather, their aim was to extend their political and economic influence. Austria, for example, could have annexed Bosnia-Herzegovina at this time without any resistance. But she refrained from doing so because of Magyar opposition to any further acquisition of Slavic territory. Accordingly, Austria confined herself to pacific penetration.

She was most successful in Serbia, where she concluded a commercial treaty on May 6, 1881, and a secret alliance on June 28, 1881. It was noted in Chapter 24 that the commercial agreement made Serbia economically dependent upon the Dual Monarchy, and that the alliance made her a virtual Hapsburg protectorate. The alliance provided that if Serbia expanded southward, "Austria-Hungary will not oppose herself thereto and will use her influence with the other powers for the purpose of winning them over to an attitude favorable to Serbia." In return Serbia promised to prevent intrigues on her territory against Austria and to enter into no treaties with other foreign countries without Austria's permission.[1] The significance of this remarkable treaty is obvious. Austria had obtained full control over Serbian foreign policy and had blocked Serbian expansion westward and diverted it expressly toward Macedonia. Only four years were to elapse before the unfortunate effect of this alliance upon Balkan politics was to be demonstrated by the Serbian attack upon Bulgaria.

In addition to this hegemony over Serbia, Austria concluded an alliance with Rumania on October 30, 1883. We saw in Chapter 26 that this pact required Austria to go to the aid of Rumania if the latter were attacked without provocation, and Rumania to go to the aid of Austria if the latter were attacked by Russia. In addition to the Serbian and Rumanian alliances, Austria during these years enjoyed close relations with Greece. On June 13, 1885, for example, the Greek premier wrote to his ambassador in Constantinople that the Dual Monarch "is our most sincere and natural ally in all questions which might arise in the Ottoman Empire." [2] Thus Austria established herself firmly in the Balkan Peninsula with her Serbian and Rumanian alliances, with her friendly relations with Greece, and with her occupation of Bosnia-Herzegovina and the Sanjak of Novi Bazar.

In the meantime Russia had staked everything on the Bulgarians, whom she expected to control and use for her purposes. Chapter 23 described the manner in which this policy back-fired unexpectedly. The Bulgarians elected Alexander of Battenberg as their prince and made clear their intention of being their own masters. The showdown came in September, 1885, when the Bulgarians of Eastern Rumelia revolted against Turkish rule and proclaimed their union with their brethren to the north. Being a violation of the Berlin Treaty, this move precipitated a European crisis. The Russians turned against their unruly protégés and opposed their unification. The British and the Austrians then reversed the position that they had taken a few years earlier at Berlin and supported the union of the two Bulgarias. After long negotiations a compromise was reached whereby the prince of Bulgaria was appointed governor of Eastern Rumelia by the sultan for a period of five years. By this means the union was effected *de facto* while nominally the Berlin Treaty was respected.

Meanwhile Prince Milan of Serbia had declared war on Bulgaria in an effort to gain territorial compensation to balance Bulgaria's expansion. Serbia was unexpectedly defeated in a fortnight of fighting, after which the Bucharest Treaty of March 3, 1886, restored the prewar *status quo*. In this manner the unification of the two Bulgarias was successfully effected despite all obstacles. But Prince Alexander did not enjoy his triumph for long. Unrelenting Russian hostility finally compelled him to abdicate on September 7, 1886. The following year Ferdinand of Coburg was elected prince in his place.

Thus the Bulgarian crisis ended with far-reaching effects on both European and Balkan diplomacy. By pitting Russia against Austria over the question of unification it disrupted the renewed *Dreikaiserbund* just as the 1875–1878 crisis had disrupted the original *Dreikaiserbund*. The Bulgarian crisis was also responsible for the first armed conflict between the young Balkan states. And it was ominous for the future that the ruler who now ascended the Bulgarian throne was inordinately ambitious. An English journalist who was granted an interview by Ferdinand, found him standing before a window in a Napoleonic posture with one hand thrust in the breast of his tunic. "Do you see those mountains?" asked the prince, pointing to the south. "They are the key to Macedonia, and it is I who holds that key!" [3] Ferdinand's melodramatic statement was not an empty one. After the Bulgarian crisis Macedonia became increasingly the vortex of Balkan and also of great-power diplomacy.

MACEDONIAN PROBLEM

Macedonia may be defined as the area around Saloniki consisting roughly of the three Turkish vilayets of Saloniki, Monastir (Bitolj), and Kosovo. No other area in the Balkans has been the subject of so much dispute and the cause of so much bloodshed. To a very considerable degree Balkan diplomacy since 1878 has revolved around the explosive question of how Macedonia should be divided among the three neighboring countries, Bulgaria, Greece, and Serbia.

One reason for the ruthless struggle for Macedonia is the strategic and economic value of the area. It commands the great corridor route which leads from Central Europe to the Mediterranean along the Morava and Vardar valleys, a route which has invited countless invaders, Roman, Gothic, Hun, Slav, and Turkish. Macedonia is also desirable because it includes the great port of Saloniki as well as the fertile plains much coveted in the mountainous Balkan Peninsula. As important as these strategic and economic considerations in explaining the struggle for Macedonia is the ethnic complexity of the area. This provides all the neighboring countries a basis for their aspirations and claims. Macedonia is a border zone where several ethnic blocs meet and overlap. It cannot be called a melting pot because intermarriage between the several ethnic elements has been rare. Individual villages and even various groups within a single village have retained their identity over periods of centuries. This freezing of ethnic strains explains the extraordinary assortment of peoples that have survived to the present day in an area about half the size of the state of New York.

Population statistics for Macedonia are virtually meaningless. Turkish authorities rarely bothered with a census, and when they did the returns were computed on the basis of religious affiliation rather than language or nationality. A 1905 census of the three Macedonian vilayets produced the following figures concerning the non-Moslem peoples:

Greeks (Rum Millet)	648,962
Bulgars (Bulgar Millet)	557,734
Serbs (Serb Millet)	167,601
Miscellaneous (Jews and others)	77,386

These figures are meaningful only for religious affiliation. Under the heading "Greeks" were included all those who attended patriarchist schools or churches, regardless of whether their speech was Greek, Slav, Albanian, or Vlach. Similarly, the "Bulgars" comprised all those who attended Bulgarian churches and schools, and the same held for the "Serbs." It is apparent that so far as national allegiance was concerned, these figures are of little use. In practice they obscured the issue because each party juggled the figures to support its case. The Greeks, for example, claimed all those listed under "Rum Millet," but this was strenuously contested by the other Balkan peoples, who argued that an Albanian, Vlach, or Slav-speaking individual did not necessarily become a Greek simply because he attended a patriarchist school or church.

Only a few general conclusions may be safely drawn from the available evidence. Those inhabitants of Macedonia who lived close to the Greek, Bulgarian, and Serbian frontiers could be classified as being mostly Greek, Bulgarian, and Serbian, respectively. The remainder of the population, with the exception of such distinct minorities as Turks, Vlachs, Jews, and Albanians, may be considered as being distinctively Macedonian. These Macedonians had a dialect and certain cultural characteristics which justify their being classified as a distinct South Slav group.

The important point about these Macedonians, so far as Balkan politics were concerned, was that they lagged behind their neighbors in developing a sense of national consciousness. Accordingly, they were claimed by the Serbians, the Bulgarians, and the Greeks. The Serbians pointed to certain characteristics of their grammar and to their "slava" festival as proofs of their Serbian origin. The Bulgarians argued that physiologically the Macedonians were closer to them than to the Serbs and that the Macedonian language was in reality a Bulgarian dialect. Finally, the Greeks emphasized the fact that the Macedonians were Orthodox Christians and that many of them were under the jurisdiction of the Patriarch of Constantinople. They also claimed that many Slav-speaking Macedonians considered themselves to be Greeks and therefore they referred to them as Slavophone Greeks.

At the outset the Greeks had no competition in Macedonia. The abolition of the Ipek (Pec) patriarchate (Serbian) and the Ohrid archbishopric (Bulgarian) in 1766 and 1767, respectively,* left all of Macedonia under the jurisdiction of the Patriarch of Constantinople. This meant Greek education in the schools, Greek liturgy in the churches, and Greek prelates in all the higher ecclesiastical posts. Thus the Macedonians were subjected to an unchallenged process of Hellenization. In fact, they might well have become completely Hellenized were it not for the fact that they were almost all illiterate. The few who did acquire a formal education became Greeks to a greater or lesser extent. But the peasant masses of Macedonia were largely untouched by Greek culture in the academic sense and they continued to speak their Slavic dialects.

This is significant because so long as they retained their dialects and their customs they possessed the prerequisites for a national awakening in

* See Chapters 7, 19.

the future. It is true that language was not of great consequence during the prenationalist period. Religious affiliation was then the all-important consideration. The Macedonian peasant did not think of himself as being a Serb or a Bulgarian because he spoke a Slavic language. Rather, he identified himself with his village. And if he thought in broader terms he would style himself as an Orthodox Christian in order to set himself apart from his Catholic or Moslem neighbors.

This situation changed drastically when the concept of nationalism reached the Balkans from the West and the newly established Balkan nation-states began to look covetously toward Macedonia. The Bulgarians, the first to challenge the hegemony of the Greeks in Macedonia, were to a large degree successful. Their instrument was the exarchate church established by Turkish firman in 1870.* Under the terms of the firman the exarchate was limited almost entirely to the Bulgarian lands between the Danube and the Balkan Mountains. But Article X of the firman provided that additional territories might adhere to the new church if two thirds or more of the population so voted. This provided an entering wedge. By 1912 seven bishoprics in Macedonia had come under the jurisdiction of the exarchate. The Serbians claimed that this did not signify that the inhabitants were Bulgarians but rather that they were Slavs who disliked the Greek prelates and the incomprehensible Greek service. Whatever the reasons, the fact remains that the expanding exarchate provided an instrument for Bulgarian propaganda in Macedonia just as the Patriarchate earlier had served as a means for Greek propaganda. By 1895 the Bulgarians had, according to their own figures, some 600 to 700 schools in Macedonia with 25,000 to 30,000 pupils. The majority of contemporary observers agreed that most Macedonians considered themselves to be Bulgarians.

The fall of Stambulov in 1894 produced a change in Bulgarian tactics in Macedonia. Stambulov had followed a policy of peaceful penetration by cooperating with the Turks and receiving concessions in return. This procedure, though very effective, was too slow and undramatic for the Macedonian Bulgarians, thousands of whom had emigrated to Bulgaria proper. They insistently clamored for a more aggressive campaign to liberate their brothers under Turkish rule. In fact, certain disreputable elements among these Macedonian immigrants appeared to have been employed for the murder of Stambulov in 1895.

Even before Stambulov's downfall a number of Bulgarian Macedonians had gathered in the little Macedonian town of Resna in 1893 and established a secret revolutionary body known as the Internal Macedonian Revolutionary Organization, or IMRO. Its aim was to prepare the people of Macedonia for a great uprising against the Turks in order to gain autonomy. It opposed the partitioning of Macedonia; instead, it favored a South Slav federation in which the Macedonians, together with the Bulgarians and Ser-

* See Chapter 19.

bians, would participate. The IMRO was ably led and spread throughout Macedonia within a few years. Arms were gathered, men were trained, and plans made for a mass uprising.

In April, 1895, a rival organization was established to foment revolution in Macedonia. This was known as the External Organization because it was founded outside Macedonia, in Sofia, and ostensibly represented the Macedonian immigrants in Bulgaria. It was organized under the auspices of the Bulgarian crown and was essentially a Bulgarian instrument, in contrast to the IMRO which, at the outset at least, was a Macedonian movement. The IMRO's slogan was "Macedonia for the Macedonians" but the External Organization wanted Macedonia for Bulgaria. The former body had more popular support within Macedonia, while the latter naturally was more favored in Sofia and received more backing there. The IMRO concentrated on organizing the population for a mass revolt and refrained from armed action until 1897, when it was forced to strike back after Turkish authorities uncovered a part of its underground network. The External Organization, on the other hand, resorted to violent measures from the outset, these usually taking the form of assassination or raiding parties across the frontier. Its first major act of violence was in 1895, when a band, which included several former officers of the Bulgarian army, seized the town of Melnik and held it for some time against the Turks before being obliged to flee back to Bulgaria.

These Bulgarian inroads into Macedonia naturally aroused both the Serbians and the Greeks. Before 1878 the Serbians had concentrated their attention on Bosnia-Herzegovina. But when Austria took over the two provinces the Serbs were forced to turn to Macedonia. The Austrians encouraged them to do so by undertaking in the Austrian-Serbian alliance of 1881 to help the Serbs expand southward. But it was not until the Serbs were defeated by the Bulgars in 1885 that they fully realized that Macedonia might follow the example of Eastern Rumelia and become a part of Bulgaria. The Serbs then took action and organized the Society of Saint Sava in 1886 with the purpose of stimulating nationalism in all Serbian lands and particularly in Macedonia. The Society trained teachers, printed books, and conducted propaganda activities. Its work was taken over first by the minister of education and in 1889 by the minister for foreign affairs. The Turks welcomed the appearance of the Serbs in Macedonia and granted them various concessions in order to create a counterweight to the Bulgarians. By the mid-1890's the Serbs had established, according to their account, over 100 schools in the Kosovo vilayet with at least 5,000 pupils. Serbia had become a force in the Macedonian embroglio.

The Greeks also took energetic measures to counter the Bulgarians in Macedonia. In November, 1894, they founded in Athens a secret organization known as the Ethnike Hetairia, or National Society. It was supported by three quarters of the officers of the Greek army and by many wealthy and influential Greeks at home and abroad. Its ultimate aim was to liberate all Greeks under Turkish domination, but its immediate efforts were directed against the Bulgarian challenge. It subsidized Greek schools in Macedonia, and by 1895 these schools numbered, according to Greek statistics, over 1,400 with 80,000 pupils. The magnitude of this effort is indicated by the fact that the Greeks spent more money in proportion to population on schools in the so-called unredeemed territory than they did in Greece proper. The National Society also carried on propaganda work of a general nature and organized armed bands to make forays across the frontier. In all these activities it was assisted by the Greek consuls in Saloniki, Monastir, and other Macedonian cities. In fact, the Serbian and Bulgarian as well as the Greek consuls were all busily engaged in propaganda activities and in extending, when feasible, surreptitious aid to their respective bands.

The Serbians, Bulgarians, and Greeks were the main contestants for Macedonia, but the Rumanians also attempted to stake out a claim. As noted in Chapter 26, they based their case on the Vlachs, shepherds and traders who were widely scattered in Macedonia, Epirus, and Thessaly, and who spoke a language akin to Rumanian. In 1879 the Rumanian budget included an appropriation of 14,000 francs for the support of schools for the Vlachs. By 1912 1,000,000 francs a year were being spent for these schools, which reputedly numbered over 30 with an enrollment of some 2,000 pupils. Since the Vlachs were scattered over wide areas to the south of the Danube the Rumanians obviously did not expect to incorporate them within their state. Rather, they made use of the Vlachs as a sort of speculative investment which perhaps could be used profitably for bargaining purposes some time in the future.

The over-all effect of this struggle for Macedonia was catastrophic, and the victims were the Macedonians themselves. This explains why the IMRO attracted so much popular support with its slogan of "Macedonia for the Macedonians." The miserable peasants were torn this way and that, and retribution was sure to follow whatever decision they made. If they declared for the exarchate they could expect a visit from the Greek bands. If they remained under the Patriarchate they were hounded by the Bulgarians as traitors. And the Turkish troops that marched back and forth were almost as great a curse as the bands that they pursued but never banished.

MACEDONIA, THE BALKAN STATES, AND THE GREAT POWERS

One of the most discouraging features of the struggle for Macedonia was that it was self-perpetuating. It set one Balkan state against another and made it impossible for them to band together and to attempt a decisive settlement of the Macedonian problem in the manner envisaged by Prince Michael in the 1860's, namely, by driving out the Turks. Between 1889 and 1891 both the Serbs and the Greeks proposed to the Bulgarians an alliance based on a delimitation of claims in Macedonia and a combined attack on Turkey. But Stambulov was then in office and, in accordance with his Turkcophil policy, he betrayed these proposals to the Turks and received in return additional concessions in Macedonia. The dismissal of Stambulov in 1894 did not brighten the prospect for common Balkan action because Ferdinand had equally ambitious designs on Macedonia.

The Bulgarians were by no means solely responsible for the rivalry and disunity. In 1892 the Serbs and the Greeks tried to reach an agreement between themselves. Their purpose was to combat Bulgarian propaganda and, in their words, to "propagate the idea that there exist in Macedonia only Serbs and Greeks." [4] But when they attempted to delimit their respective claims they discovered that they overlapped so extensively that an agreement was not feasible. Greece and Serbia made another attempt in 1899 to reach an agreement concerning Macedonia but again they failed to reconcile their differences. This discord among the Balkan states was fully demonstrated during the Greco-Turkish War, which began in April, 1897, over the Cretan question. The Bulgarians and the Serbians stood by unconcerned while the Greeks were quickly and decisively defeated.

The attitude of Austria and Russia at the time was of the utmost importance for the entire peninsula. The two powers concluded on May 8, 1897, the Goluchowski-Muraviev agreement with the professed purpose of "eliminating the danger of a rivalry disastrous to the peace of Europe on the seething soil of the Balkan Peninsula." The agreement provided that the *status quo* in the Balkans should be maintained as long as possible and that, if it could not be upheld, the two parties should cooperate to prevent any other power from acquiring territory in the peninsula. Austria's special interests in Bosnia-Herzegovina and in Albania were recognized with reservations by Russia, and the question of Constantinople and the Straits was declared to be of an "eminently European character." [5] The significance of this agreement is apparent. The Austrians were concerned with domestic problems while the Russians wished to be free to turn to the Far East. So they joined forces to "keep the Balkans on ice."

The determination of the neighboring great powers to freeze the *status quo* and the inability of the Balkan states to join for common action ensured the continuation of anarchy and bloodshed in Macedonia. In fact, the situation became steadily worse, particularly after November, 1897, when the Turks uncovered a part of the IMRO underground organization. Up to that point the IMRO had concentrated on gathering arms and perfecting its organization. Now it was forced in self-defense to violent measures. These were reported by the British consul in Sofia as follows:

> The period of secret preparation, at which they [the IMRO] had worked for five years, was brought to an abrupt close and a period of action inaugurated. The Committee was now transformed into a terroristic organization, whose decisions were executed by the bands. Every year which followed witnessed fresh excesses on the part of the Turks and fresh reprisals on the part of the Committee. Assassination was the only weapon which the latter possessed, and they did not hesitate to have recourse to it. . . . Forced contributions, whether in

money or in kind, were exacted from all persons within reach of the bands, and all villages were expected to shelter and protect them. Those Bulgarian villages which still acknowledged the jurisdiction of the Patriarch were the greatest sufferers. If they showed any inclination to join the Exarchate, they were liable to be denounced to the Turks by Greek priests and to lose the immunity from attack by the troops which their Greek patrons secured for them; if, on the contrary, they refused to do so, they were exposed to the vengeance of the Komitajis [IMRO bands]. Though the policy of the bands was to act on the defensive, they had between 1898 and the commencement of 1903 no less than 130 engagements with the Turkish troops.[6]

This wave of terrorism and violence culminated in the IMRO uprising of August, 1903. The rebels seized most of the Monastir vilayet, where they organized a revolutionary council and attempted to liberate the rest of Macedonia. Bands crossed over from Bulgaria and joined the insurgents. The Bulgarian government was taken by surprise and was far from pleased because it was not prepared for war. Yet it dared not close the border to the bands because popular sympathy for the insurgents was so strong that it feared an antidynastic movement. This was by no means farfetched because nearly half the population of Sofia at this time consisted of Macedonian refugees or immigrants. The Turks meanwhile were bringing up troops which, in customary fashion, indiscriminately harried the Macedonian peasantry with fire and sword. It is stated that some 200 villages and 12,000 houses were burned and 70,000 persons left homeless.

The revolt was quickly suppressed, but it did serve to goad the great powers to action. Austria and Russia, the two powers most immediately concerned, prepared the so-called Mürzsteg reform program of October, 1903. It provided that a Russian and an Austrian civil agent should accompany the Turkish Inspector-General on his tours and report on conditions. The *gendarmerie* was to be reorganized and put under the command of a foreign general and a staff of foreign officers. Also, the judicial system was to be reorganized and financial provisions made for the return of the refugees and for the rebuilding of houses and churches destroyed during the insurrection.

The other powers approved this reform plan, and the sultan thus felt constrained to accept it. But it contributed little to the pacification of Macedonia. In fact, it probably worsened the situation. A clause in the Mürzsteg program provided that when order was restored a new delimitation of administrative districts should be made along ethnic lines. This stimulated more propaganda and more violence as each side redoubled its efforts in order to improve its position in preparation for the day when the administrative boundaries were redrawn. More than ever before the Balkan states were deadlocked in their furious struggle for the control of Macedonia.

For a brief while it appeared that the murder of the Serbian king, Alexander, in June, 1903, and the accession of Peter Karageorgevich might lessen Balkan tensions and lead to an agreement over Macedonia. The new Serbian dynasty was not acceptable to Vienna and it could not expect support from Russia because that country was drifting to war with Japan in the Far East. The alternative left to the Serbians was to turn to Bulgaria, and they signed two treaties with that country. The first was a military alliance, concluded on April 12, 1904, and providing for mutual aid in case of attack from any quarter. This pact was kept strictly secret and remained unknown until 1929, when its provisions were published. The other treaty, signed on June 22, 1905, established virtual free trade between the two countries and foresaw the establishment of a customs union on March 1, 1917. In fact, it was widely speculated at the time that this commercial cooperation might lead eventually to a united Serbo-Bulgarian state that would be strong enough to block Austrian influence in the Balkans.

We saw in Chapter 24 that Austria violently opposed this Serbo-Bulgarian *rapprochement*, even to the point of closing her frontiers to Serbian livestock and thus precipitating the famous "Pig War" that dragged on until 1910. This Serbian-Austrian estrangement did not lead to durable friendship between Serbia and Bulgaria. The Bulgarian government that negotiated the alliance with Serbia fell from office in 1907. The succeeding ministries were soon engaged in the usual polemics with Belgrade, the reason being the perennial Macedonian problem. This was emphasized in a report written on April 2, 1908, by the British representative in Belgrade.

To sum up the whole situation as regards the relations between Servia and Bulgaria, it is clear that they can never be cordial and stable until the competition between the two nationalities for an eventual acquisition of the Slav countries still under Turkish rule comes to an end. M. Pashitch was in favour of cooperating with Bulgaria for common aims, and of deferring the discussion of the rights of the two nations to the expected inheritance until it should actually fall due, but his intentions were frustrated by the uncompromising claim of the Bulgarians to the whole of the territory awarded to them by the Treaty of San Stefano.[7]

Such was the situation in the Balkans in 1908 when a totally unexpected event, the Young Turk revolt, suddenly changed the outlook completely.

YOUNG TURK REVOLT

Abdul Hamid became the autocratic ruler of the Ottoman Empire following his dismissal of the first Turkish parliament in 1877. At first he was generally praised for being industrious and sober in contrast to many of his predecessors. This favorable attitude gradually changed with the Armenian massacres of the 1890's and the chronic anarchy and bloodshed in Macedonia. By the turn of the century Abdul Hamid had become "Abdul the Damned" and the "Great Assassin." Whether villain or hero, Abdul Hamid was the master of the Ottoman Empire for three decades.

In his relations with the great powers Abdul Hamid's policy was simply divide and rule, or more accurately, divide and survive. He acquired a reputation as a consummate diplomat in pursuing this policy, though it is doubtful that much skill was required to persuade the British to oppose Russian ambitions in the Near East. In domestic affairs Abdul Hamid strove to safeguard his absolutist rule against the disruptive forces of nationalism and constitutionalism. To this end he discouraged travel and study abroad, maintained a great army of informers, and enforced a strict censorship of the press.

Three trouble spots in the empire gave Abdul Hamid the most trouble. One was Armenia, where a nationalist awakening similar to that of the Balkan peoples manifested itself in the second half of the nineteenth century. Another was the island of Crete, where the predominantly Christian Greek population took up arms on every promising occasion in order to attain their cherished *enosis,* or union with Mother Greece. The third area of trouble was Macedonia, the tinder box of the Balkans, to which Greeks, Serbians and Bulgarians laid claim. In the end Abdul Hamid was overthrown not by Armenian or Greek or Macedonian revolutionaries, but rather by his own Turkish subjects. And the successful revolutionaries were not the Young Turks in exile who had attracted international attention as the opponents of the sultan, but rather a completely unknown group of conspirators within the empire.

We noted in Chapter 20 that from the time of the reign of Abdul Aziz in the 1860's critics of the Ottoman dynasty fled abroad, where they continued their defiance and where they came to be known collectively as the Young Turks. Their numbers increased markedly during the decades of Abdul Hamid's autocracy. Not only discontented Turks, but also revolutionary leaders of the subject peoples, Moslem as well as Christian, sought refuge in foreign capitals and especially in Paris. All these Ottoman exiles—Turks, Arabs, Greeks, Armenians, Albanians, Kurds, and Jews—held a congress in Paris in February, 1902, with the aim of organizing a common front against Abdul Hamid. But they quickly discovered that they agreed on nothing except that they all disliked the sultan. One group, led by a veteran Young Turk, Ahmet Riza, stood for Turkish predominance and centralized rule, while another group led by one of Abdul Hamid's relatives, Prince Sabaheddin, favored a decentralized empire in which the subject people should have full autonomy.

While the exiled intellectuals were quarreling in Paris, Turkish army officers were taking decisive measures in Saloniki. One of the earliest leaders of these army officers was Mustafa Kemal, who was to win lasting fame after World War I as the founder of the Turkish Republic. In 1905 Kemal organized in Damascus the secret military society, Vatan, or Fatherland. This was later absorbed by another secret military organization, the Ottoman Society of Liberty, with headquarters in Saloniki. This organization spread throughout the empire very rapidly. Army officers were the backbone of the Society of Liberty, though they were greatly aided by other groups, and particularly by the Jews, who were the most numerous and wealthy element in Saloniki.

The Society of Liberty was organized into cells of five so that no one knew more than four fellow members. A new recruit had to be sponsored by a regular member and was observed closely during a probationary period. For the purpose of communication each cell contained a "guide" who received the orders of the top central committee from the "guide" of another cell, and who was required to pass on the orders without delay. The activities of the Society have been described as follows:

> To meet the expenses each member was compelled to contribute a fixed percentage of his income to the Committee chest, while rich members, in addition to this tax, made generous donations when funds were required. Arms and ammunition were secretly purchased. A considerable sum was set apart annually to provide for the families of members who lost life or liberty while working for the cause. Their several duties were apportioned to the members. There were the messengers who, disguised in various ways, went to and fro over the Empire carrying verbal reports and instructions. . . . There were the men who had to assassinate those whom the Committee had condemned to death—Government officials who were working against the movement with a dangerous zeal, and Palace spies who were getting on the scent. Other members were sent out to act as spies in the interest of the cause, and the *contre espionage* became at last so thorough that it baffled the espionage of the Palace. . . . The first and most important task . . . was, of course, that of bringing round to the cause the Macedonian garrison—the Third Army Corps. . . . By degrees a number of the young officers were affiliated and received instructions to win over the rank and file. . . . At last the whole Macedonian army was won over to the cause of the Young Turks. . . .[8]

This account brings out the glaring contrast between the rootless intellectuals arguing with each other in Paris and the practical revolutionaries quietly building up their underground organization within the empire. The latter group staged its revolt in July, 1908, partly because the sultan's agents were beginning to penetrate its organization and also because the powers were openly considering intervention in Macedonia. The British foreign minister, Sir Edward Grey, proposed in March, 1908, an autonomous regime for Macedonia. A little later it was announced that the British and Russian monarchs would meet at Reval on June 10 to discuss reforms for Macedonia. The Saloniki conspirators, fearing that the end result would be Ottoman partition, decided to act at once.

Events now moved quickly and according to plan. The Saloniki group telegraphed an ultimatum to the sultan threatening to march upon Constantinople unless the 1876 constitution was restored within twenty-four hours. The Third Army Corps solidly backed its revolutionary leaders. In Constantinople the State Council advised Abdul Hamid to comply with the ultimatum. Also, the Sheik-ul-Islam refused to issue a fetva authorizing suppression of the rebels. On July 24 Abdul Hamid proclaimed the restoration of the constitution.

The news of the sultan's capitulation was greeted with wild rejoicing. The long reign of repression was at an end. Christians and Turks embraced one another in the streets. The Young Turk leader, Enver Pasha, exclaimed: "There are no longer Bulgars, Greeks, Rumans, Jews, Mussulmans. We are all brothers beneath the same blue sky. We are all equal, we glory in being Ottoman."[9] This euphoric atmosphere did not last long. The issues that had divided the exiles in Paris now had to be faced as urgent issues of policy rather than differences in theory. Three political groupings began to emerge at this point.

The dominant one comprised the Saloniki leaders, now popularly known as the Young Turks. In general they adopted the position supported by Riza in Paris. They were ready to grant political representation and religious freedom to all peoples of the empire. But in return they required that these peoples should support the imperial structure and accept Turkish predominance. They frequently stated that they wished all citizens of the empire to become Ottomans in the same manner that all citizens of France were Frenchmen. But this analogy was unrealistic. It failed to take into account the very different historical background and ethnic composition of Western Europe and the Near East. Genuine Ottoman nationality might have existed by the twentieth century if during the preceding centuries the Turks had not administered their empire on the millet principle, and if, instead, they had coerced their subject peoples into becoming Moslems. But they had not taken these measures, and as a result their empire remained from beginning to end an aggregate of self-governing communities. Now it was too late to attempt to fuse them into a homogeneous nation. Nationalist sentiment already had made each one of these communities self-conscious and desirous of an independent existence. The Young Turk program was adopted at least a century too late to have had any hope of success.

The second political group that existed at this time was the Liberal Union headed by Prince Sabaheddin. This organization did not agree that centralization and Turkish hegemony were necessary to preserve the empire. Instead, it held that only through local autonomy and full development of communal life could the empire retain the support of its peoples and thus survive. There is no way of knowing whether this proposition was sound because it was never put into practice. It is worth recalling, however, that in the hectic early days of the revolution many Greeks in Smyrna unfurled the blue-and-white flag of the Hellenic Kingdom rather than the star and crescent of their own empire. In any case, the Liberal Unionists never had a chance to assume office. Many Turks suspected them because of the strong backing they received from the Greeks and other nationalities. More important was the military power which the Young Turks commanded and which Sabaheddin and his followers lacked completely. Thus the Liberal Union was condemned to the role of an impotent opposition party.

The third political group was the League of Mohammed. It professed to support the constitution but was most vocal in demanding strict enforcement of the Sheri, or Sacred Law. It opposed the Saloniki Young Turks, claiming that their leaders were Jews, freethinkers, or Westernized Turks who did not observe the precepts of the Koran and who set a bad example with their irreligious ways. This argument was effective with the devout Moslem population, as the brief counterrevolution of 1909 was to demonstrate dramatically.

On April 12, 1909, a counterrevolution in Constantinople broke the hold of the Young Turks from Saloniki and left the capital in the hands of conservative Moslem forces. The Saloniki leaders immediately assumed that Abdul

Hamid was behind the counterrevolution. Acting on this assumption they deposed him later in the year when they regained power. But conclusive proof that the sultan inspired the counterrevolution is lacking. In fact, circumstantial evidence suggests that he was not involved. He remained passive throughout the struggle and made no attempt to guide the unorganized and leaderless rebels. In any case, the Young Turks gathered their forces in Macedonia, marched upon the capital, captured it after only a few hours' fighting, and then compelled Abdul Hamid to abdicate on April 27. The new sultan, Mohammed V, had spent his entire life in strict palace confinement and, according to his own account, had not been allowed to read a newspaper for ten years. The Young Turks therefore expected him to be a compliant figurehead, but to make doubly certain they revised the constitution in August, 1909. The sultan henceforth was to name the grand vizir, who in turn selected the other ministers. Also, the sultan was deprived of the power to dissolve parliament and the cabinet was made responsible to the parliament rather than to the sultan.

The Young Turks now were the unchallenged masters of the empire. With the exception of a few months they remained masters until World War I. All opposition having been crushed, they proceeded with their policy of centralization and Turkish hegemony. But the more they persisted in this policy the more opposition they created. Neither Turkish nationalism nor Ottoman nationalism could exorcise the inexorable awakening of Albanians, Arabs, Greeks, Bulgarians, and other subject peoples. Thus the result was a vicious circle of repression and resistance. Young Turk nationalism, as noted in the previous chapter, was responsible for the Albanian revolt of 1910. And, of more concern at this point, is the fact that the Young Turk revolt affected Balkan diplomatic development in two respects: it encouraged the Austrian and Russian foreign ministers to fish in the troubled Balkan waters, thereby precipitating the grave Bosnian crisis; and it stimulated the Balkan countries to form the Balkan League and, at long last, to drive the Turks almost completely out of Europe.

BOSNIAN CRISIS

When Count Alois Aehrenthal, the Austrian foreign minister, received the news of the Young Turk revolt, he turned to his wife and exclaimed, "Now I must bear the odium of doing what all my predecessors shrank from doing." [10] Aehrenthal was not as reluctant to take the action he contemplated as his statement implied. In fact, he welcomed the Young Turk revolt because it offered him the opportunity to realize his long-cherished plan for annexing Bosnia-Herzegovina.

Aehrenthal had assumed office in 1906 as the successor to the cautious Count Goluchowski, who for years had cooperated with the Russians in "keeping the Balkans on ice." But Aehrenthal was a very different person from Goluchowski. He was an able and well-informed diplomat, but he was also arrogant, vain, impatient, extremely ambitious, and none too scrupulous. His aim was to score a personal triumph by annexing Bosnia-Herzegovina and thereby ending once and for all Serbian expansionist dreams. At times Aehrenthal even talked of partitioning Serbia with Bulgaria. "We would then," he maintained, "have an independent Albania under our aegis, a Montenegro dependent upon our good will, and a Greater Bulgaria bound to us by gratitude." [11]

In the same year that Aehrenthal assumed office in Vienna, a new foreign minister, Alexander Izvolsky, took over in St. Petersburg. Like his Austrian counterpart, Izvolsky was capable, industrious, widely read, and also inordinately ambitious. Itching for some dramatic personal success, he proposed to the council of ministers on February 3, 1908, an Anglo-Russian military action against Turkey which, he said, "might lead to dazzling results." Since Russia had not yet recovered from the losses of the Japanese war, his colleagues emphatically rejected his plan. Undaunted, Izvolsky turned his attention to getting the Straits open to Russian warships. On July 2, 1908, he sent a note to Aehrenthal offering to support the annexation of Bosnia-Herzegovina by Austria if she in return would support Russian designs on the Straits.

Aehrenthal naturally welcomed Izvolsky's proposal. A few weeks later news arrived of the revolution in Turkey. The moment obviously had come to proceed with the annexation of the two provinces. There remained only the question of time and procedure. This question Aehrenthal discussed at length with Izvolsky at a meeting at Buchlau. On September 16, 1908, the two men agreed that Russia would not oppose the annexation of Bosnia-Herzegovina by Austria, and in return Austria would not oppose the opening of the Straits to Russian warships. Unfortunately, a verbatim account of the precise details of this Buchlau Agreement was not drawn up at the time. As a result, it was followed by a noisy and serious diplomatic controversy.

The difficulty originated from the failure of Izvolsky and Aehrenthal to set an exact date for the annexation of the two provinces. Izvolsky assumed that nothing would be done immediately, so he went first to Bavaria for a vacation. Then he began a leisurely tour of European capitals for the purpose of obtaining the consent of the powers to changes in the Straits regulations. Meanwhile Aehrenthal was busy making the necessary arrangements for the annexation. In order to be sure that Bulgaria would be on his side he encouraged that country also to violate the Berlin Treaty by proclaiming its independence from Turkey. When Prince Ferdinand visited Budapest on September 23, a week after the Buchlau meeting, Aehrenthal told him that Bulgaria should not hesitate to realize her legitimate desires. The ambitious Ferdinand, who for years had been chafing under the limitations of Ottoman sovereignty, did not need any further prompting. On October 5 he proclaimed the independence of Bulgaria and assumed the proud title of tsar after the manner of the medieval Bulgarian kings. The next day, apparently by prearrangement, Aehrenthal announced the annexation of Bosnia-Herzegovina by Austria.

These moves aroused a storm that brought Europe to the brink of war. The Serbians reacted perhaps the most violently against the incorporation of the two South Slav provinces into the Hapsburg Empire. Traditionally they had regarded Bosnia-Herzegovina as their rightful heritage. Now they refused to accept the Austrian annexation as final and they raised the cry for revenge and restitution as the French had done after 1871. In fact, the Serbians regarded Bosnia-Herzegovina henceforth as the Alsace-Lorraine of the Balkans. The foreign minister, Milovanovich, went so far as to say to the British minister in Belgrade that many Serbians "now were of the opinion that a warlike adventure, even with the certainty of defeat, would not place the country in any worse position, from the national point of view, than it would be if finally deprived of all hope of development." [12]

In Russia also there was a strong popular reaction against the sacrifice of Slavic territory to the Hapsburgs. This feeling extended to the government, particularly because Izvolsky had not consulted his colleagues before concluding the Buchlau Agreement. The Russian cabinet now repudiated the unfortunate Izvolsky, the prime minister going so far as to declare that they should "dismiss Izvolsky and announce publicly that he had acted without the permission of his government." [13] Faced with this painful situation Izvolsky tried to save himself by gaining some concessions at the Straits. But neither his French nor British allies would support him on this matter. So Izvolsky was forced to change his tactics and to demand that the annexation of Bosnia-Herzegovina be submitted to a conference. Aehrenthal retorted that the annexation was a part of the Buchlau bargain and refused to accept a conference unless it met for the purpose of merely registering rather than discussing the annexation.

This controversy dragged on into the following year, with the Austrian and Russian foreign ministers accusing each other of lying about the agreement reached at Buchlau. The situation was complicated by the demand of the Serbians that they should be given a portion of the disputed provinces as compensation. Izvolsky was compelled by Russian public opinion to support this demand, particularly because he had not been able to win any concessions at the Straits. When Aehrenthal refused to hear of compensation, a complete deadlock ensued between Austria on the one side and Serbia and Russia on the other.

The outcome of the crisis was determined by the working of the European alliance system. Germany backed her Austrian partner through thick and thin. The chief of the German general staff exchanged letters with his Austrian counterpart in which he agreed that Russian intervention "would create the *casus foederis* for Germany. . . . At the same moment that Russia mobilizes, Germany will also mobilize and will mobilize her entire army." [14] Izvolsky, on his part, was unable to obtain any such firm support from France or Britain. Thus his position became increasingly untenable and dangerous. The Serbs were continuing their agitation against Austria, and the latter country, assured of German backing, was preparing an invasion of Serbia. Izvolsky could not continue to stand by Serbia without support from another power, and this support was not forthcoming.

Such was Izvolsky's dilemma when, on March 21, 1909, he received a threatening dispatch from Germany demanding that he make clear whether or not he would accept the annexation. "We expect a precise answer—yes or no; we shall have to consider any evasive, conditional or unclear answer as a *refusal*. We should then draw back and let matters take their course; the responsibility for all subsequent events would then fall exclusively on M. Izvolsky." [15] The Russian foreign minister was terrified by this communication and promptly gave the affirmative answer demanded. Serbia now was left alone and had no alternative to backing down. On March 31 she addressed a note to the powers (not to Austria alone) in which she stated that "her rights have not been affected by the *fait accompli* brought about in Bosnia-Herzegovina." Serbia also undertook "to refrain from an attitude of protest and opposition in the question of Bosnia-Herzegovina and in addition . . . to change the direction of her policy towards Austria-Hungary in order to live henceforth on terms of good neighborliness with the latter." [16]

Meanwhile the Turks, who theoretically were most directly affected by the annexation and by the Bulgarian declaration of independence, had been largely forgotten amid the tension of the crisis. There was strong popular feeling in the empire against the loss of further territory, and this feeling expressed itself in a very effective economic boycott against Austria. But the Ottoman government knew full well that it could not hope to defy the decisions of the European powers. So it salvaged what it could, accepting financial indemnities from Austria and Bulgaria on February 26 and April 9, 1909, respectively.

It is clear in retrospect that the Bosnian crisis had most unfortunate consequences in the Balkans. It poisoned Austro-Serbian relations to the point where a peaceful settlement became virtually impossible. The Austrian minister in Belgrade reported as early as April 3, 1909, that "the Serbian government will be cautious for some time. But the hatred against us and 'Russian hypnotism' . . . are too strong for me to have any great hopes for a real change of attitude by Serbia and for a satisfactory development of her relations with us. Everyone here thinks of revenge, which is to be realized only with the help of the Russians. . . ." [17]

The crisis also ended the Austro-Russian cooperation, which for some years had preserved a measure of balance in the Balkans. In place of cooperation the two powers henceforth engaged in what proved to be a mortal duel for influence in the peninsula. Russian diplomats worked energetically to organize a Balkan League which would serve as a barrier against Austria. Such a league was in fact founded in the spring of 1912. Thus the Balkan League and the Balkan Wars that followed may be said to stem directly from the crisis over Bosnia-Herzegovina. On October 2, 1912, when the Balkan Wars were about to begin, Count Berchtold, the Austrian foreign minister who succeeded Aehrenthal, wrote, "We delude ourselves if we do not face the fact that our procedure in annexing Bosnia and Herzegovina gave the first impetus to the Balkan League. . . ." [18]

BALKAN LEAGUE

The first Balkan League was organized in the 1860's as a result of the efforts of Prince Michael of Serbia, discussed in Chapter 21. The second Balkan League was largely the handiwork of Russian diplomacy. Another factor, however, contributed significantly to the formation of the second alliance system. That was the Turkification policy pursued by the Young Turks after they seized power in 1908. We saw earlier in the chapter that the Young Turks, as disciples of Western nationalism, attempted to enforce centralization and Turkish hegemony upon their polyglot empire. But it was too late in the day to forestall or to suppress the national awakening of Albanians, Arabs, Greeks, Bulgarians, and other subject peoples. The outcome of Turkification was not unity but rather discontent and revolt. The Young Turks antagonized the Balkan peoples and drove them to combine for self-protection. James Bourchier, the London *Times* correspondent and well-known Balkan authority, reported in December, 1909, that "the question of nationalities in Turkey, which the Young Turks are not approaching in the right way, will prove an insuperable obstacle to the realization of their programme." On October 4, 1912, after the Balkan League had been formed, Bourchier wrote that it was the direct result of "the insensate efforts of the Young Turks to stifle national sentiment among the various races of the Empire." [19]

The principal factor contributing to the establishment of the 1912 Balkan alliance system was the reaction in Serbia and Russia to the Bosnian affair. In both countries it was felt that a Balkan bloc of some sort was needed to keep Austria in check. This feeling was shared by Russia's Western allies, Britain and France. As early as December 25, 1908, Izvolsky made a speech in the Duma in which he openly favored the creation of a Balkan bloc. Sir Edward Grey immediately wrote that he considered Izvolsky's speech "very satisfactory," and he added: "I am glad he emphasized the need for community of feeling between the Balkan States and the combination of all three of them with Turkey for defence of common interests. I am quite in favour of this and will encourage it, whenever I can." [20]

The league did not materialize until four years after the Bosnian crisis. One reason for the delay was the ever-present Macedonian problem. Serbian-Bulgarian negotiations in 1909 for an alliance foundered on this issue. Another reason for the delay was that Russia's diplomats did not all have the same objective in the Balkans. Some wanted primarily to open the Straits; others wished to organize a Balkan League including Turkey; while still others preferred to exclude Turkey. A strong stimulus to Balkan unity was provided by the outbreak of the Italo-Turkish War in September, 1911, following the Italian invasion of Tripoli. This development encouraged the Balkan statesmen to conclude alliance pacts in the hope of being able to take advantage of Turkey's preoccupation.

Negotiations for a Serbian-Bulgarian alliance were pressed seriously after October, 1911, with the energetic encouragement of the Russian minister in Belgrade, Nicholas Hartvig. A stalemate was reached at one point because the Bulgarians insisted that the alliance be directed against Turkey rather than Austria, and that Macedonia should receive autonomy. Finally the differences were ironed out and on March 13, 1912, the Serbian-Bulgarian alliance was signed. The two states agreed to aid each other in case either was attacked, and to take joint action against any great power which tried to occupy any Balkan territory under Turkish suzerainty even though only one of the signatories considered the attempt injurious to its interests. This was aimed obviously at Austria.

A secret annex of the treaty stipulated that all territory won by the allies was to be administered at first by a condominium but was to be liquidated according to the arrangements of the treaty within three months after the conclusion of peace. The territorial claims were defined as follows: the territory north and west of the Shar Mountains, that is, Old Serbia and the Sanjak of Novi Bazar, was to go to Serbia; the territory east of the Rhodope Mountains and the Struma River to Bulgaria; the intermediate regions of Macedonia "lying between the Shar Mountains and the Rhodope Mountains, the Archipelago, and the lake of Ohrid" were, if possible, to be formed into the autonomous province long desired by Bulgaria. But if such an organization of this territory appeared to the two parties to be impossible it was to be divided into three zones: Bulgaria was to have the region around Ohrid; Serbia was to get an additional strip in northern Macedonia; and the unassigned portion was to be subject to the arbitration of the Russian tsar.

Two months later, on May 29, 1912, Greece and Bulgaria also concluded an alliance. This was due primarily to the initiative of the Greek premier, Eleutherios Venizelos, who first proposed a pact in the spring of 1911. The alliance did not delimit Greco-Bulgarian claims in Macedonia, doubtless because both countries aspired to Saloniki. The main provision stipulated that if either of the signatories were attacked by Turkey the other would give full aid.

The last of these Balkan pacts were the alliances of Montenegro with Bulgaria and Serbia concluded in late September and on October 6, 1912, respectively. By this time the Balkan allies were definitely planning to attack Turkey; hence these Montenegrin pacts were avowedly offensive in character. The Bulgarian-Montenegrin alliance required the signatories to begin hostilities against Turkey, Montenegro not later than September 20 and Bulgaria not later than one month after the Montenegrin action. The text of the Serbian-Montenegrin Treaty has never been published, but its provisions apparently were similar to those of the Bulgarian-Montenegrin pact. Montenegro also probably reached an agreement with Greece, but it appears to have been of a defensive and oral nature.

With these Montenegrin agreements the second Balkan alliance system was completed. Once before, in the 1860's, the Balkan states had succeeded in banding together, but at that time circumstances had prevented them from taking action. On this occasion circumstances were more favorable. In the first place, the Balkan states were now much more powerful than in the 1860's, while the Ottoman Empire was relatively weaker. At the time of the first Balkan League the Bulgarian state had not yet been formed, the very existence of Rumania was threatened by internal dissension, and Greece and Serbia had no armed forces worthy of the name. By 1912 the Balkan states had built up fairly efficient military establishments; moreover, political and military conditions within Turkey were exceptionally chaotic. The empire was torn by the Albanian revolt within and the Italian attacks from without. Elections were held in April, 1912, and by dint of coercion and bribery the Young Turks, or Committee of Union and Progress, obtained 215 of the 222 seats. But this majority proved valueless. The Albanians, antagonized by the arbitrary measures employed during the election and emboldened by clandestine Montenegrin aid, revolted once more in May, 1912. This time they were successful, even to the point of forcing the Young Turk government to resign. But the new cabinet was not able to accomplish much because of unrelenting Young Turk opposition. Moreover, the strength and morale of the Turkish army were seriously undermined by these political squabbles. In an effort to get rid of unreliable elements the government conducted a wholesale purge which left about fifty thousand untrained recruits in the army. All these circumstances provided the Balkan countries with a rare opportunity which they now lost no time in exploiting to the full.

Another advantage which the Balkan allies enjoyed during this period was their favorable position vis-à-vis the great powers of Europe. In the 1860's the opposition of a great power, such as Austria, to change in the Balkan *status quo* was sufficient to check any concerted anti-Turkish action. But by 1912 the diplomatic situation was completely altered. Austria was still opposed to the partitioning of European Turkey and was still capable, militarily speaking, of keeping the Balkan states in check. But the division of Europe into two hostile camps meant that any intervention in Balkan affairs was bound to have Continent-wide repercussions. It now was necessary for every great power to consult its allies and usually the members of the opposing camp before making any move.

This immobilization of the great powers became evident at this time, when they tried to prevent the Balkan allies from attacking Turkey. The Austrian foreign minister, Count Leopold Berchtold, proposed on August 13, 1912, that an attempt be made to secure reforms from Turkey and to restrain the Balkan states. But it was October 7 before a program and a statement could be worked out that was satisfactory to all the powers. On the next day Austria and Russia issued the agreed warning to the Balkan states to the effect that even if they defeated Turkey they would not be allowed to annex any territory. The warning came too late. On the same day Montenegro declared war on Turkey. Ten days later she was joined by her allies—Greece, Serbia, and Bulgaria. They all knew that the great powers would never be able to cooperate long enough and closely enough to enforce their threat of no annexations.

Thus Russia lost control of the Balkan League, which she had sponsored in order to use for her purposes. Instead of following the lead of their Russian patron, the Balkan statesmen struck out on their own and turned against the weakened Ottoman Empire. The French premier, Raymond Poincaré, described the situation aptly when on October 15, 1912, a week after the outbreak of war, he remarked that "it is too late to wipe out the movement which she [Russia] has called forth . . . she is trying to put on the brakes, but it is she who started the motor." [21]

A half century earlier, when the first Balkan League was formed, the Russian ambassador in Constantinople, Nicholas Ignatiev, commented as follows:

> But we must not have any illusions about the sincerity and stability of the entente. It is inevitable that once the struggle with the Turks is ended, race rivalries will reappear and nothing stable will be built in the Balkan Peninsula until many years have elapsed. But sufficient unto the day is the evil thereof.[22]

Ignatiev's analysis was amply justified during the following decades of continued strife over Macedonia. And now the second Balkan League was about to prove that Ignatiev indeed had been a prophet. The Balkan states had been able to unite in 1912 only because of the pressure of Russian diplomacy, the shortsighted policies of the Young Turks, and the encouragment provided by the Italo-Turkish War. Mutual trust or any conception of lasting inter-Balkan organization never entered into the picture. In fact, when the Serbo-Bulgarian Treaty was about to be ratified, the Serbian premier, Nikola Pashich, confided to his colleagues that he had no faith in King Ferdinand and that, despite the provisions of the alliance, he did not believe that Bulgaria would come to the aid of Serbia in case of an attack by Austria. Nor had the allies definitely settled their divergent claims in Macedonia. Serbia and Bulgaria had left certain areas for arbitration by the Russian tsar, while Greece and Bulgaria did not even attempt to delimit their respective claims. It is not surprising that once the Turks were defeated and the fighting ended, there was nothing left to hold the league together. It quickly disintegrated, as Ignatiev had foreseen, and the second Balkan War followed closely upon the first.

FIRST BALKAN WAR

Western military experts generally believed that the Turks would be more than a match for the Balkan allies. But the latter from the beginning were victorious on all fronts. One reason for this was the numerical superiority of the allied armies, which totaled about 715,000 men. By contrast, the Turks probably did not muster more than 320,000 in the first few weeks, and such reinforcements as arrived thereafter from Asia failed to compensate for the heavy losses at the front. The Turks dared not weaken their forces in Asia for fear of Russian intervention in the Caucasus or an Arab revolt in the south. Also, they could not transport troops freely to Balkan ports because the Greeks throughout the war had command of the sea.

In addition to their numerical advantage, the allies proved to have slightly superior arms and equipment and better organized staffs. The Turks were thoroughly disorganized by the change in officers and dismissal of trained troops that had accompanied the political convulsions of the preceding year. An Austrian attaché with the Turkish forces reported that their means of communication were inferior to those they had employed a century earlier. No telegraphic system existed, so that it took seven to eight hours for the generals to agree on an order and to get it to the troops. Turkish commanders sat on their horses, sending out couriers with orders and waiting for others to come in with news, after the manner of Napoleon at Waterloo.

The Bulgarians bore the brunt of the fighting because of their position near Constantinople. In fact, they faced from the outset an insoluble dilemma. Their political objective was Macedonia and Saloniki, but military considerations forced them to send the bulk of their army eastward against Adrianople and Constantinople. And while they were thus engaging the main Turkish forces, the Greeks and the Serbians were advancing into Macedonia and occupying that prized region. This was to have tragic consequences later, though at the beginning the division of fronts among the allies produced splendid results.

The Bulgarians won their first great victory on October 22 at Kirk-Kilissa, forcing the Turks to withdraw to the Lüle Burgas line. After a week of hard fighting the Bulgarians overran this position also and advanced to the Chatalja lines before Constantinople. After only a month of fighting the inhabitants of the Ottoman capital could hear the Bulgarian guns thundering before the Chatalja fortifications. Adrianople and Constantinople alone continued to hold out against the victorious Bulgarians.

Meanwhile the Greeks and the Serbians were winning similar triumphs to the west. On October 19 the Serbs crossed the frontier into Macedonia and five days later they scored a decisive victory at Kumanovo. Then they sent a part of their forces to help the Bulgarians before Adrianople and another part to occupy the Sanjak of Novi Bazar together with Montenegrin detachments. The main Serbian army continued southward, routing the Turks at Prilep, advancing on to Monastir (Bitolj) and Ohrid, and driving the fleeing Turks into the guns of the Greeks pushing northward. Having cleared Old Serbia, western Macedonia and the Sanjak of Novi Bazar, the Serbs now turned westward and, with the aid of the Montenegrins, occupied Durazzo on the Adriatic and laid siege to Scutari.

The Greeks in the meantime had advanced northward against comparatively light resistance. They occupied Grevena on October 31, Preveza on November 3, and the great prize, Saloniki, on November 8. A Bulgarian detachment had also raced for the Aegean port but arrived there one day after the Greeks. The latter, after some demur, allowed their allies to enter the city. But from the outset the Greeks made it clear that they had come to Saloniki to stay and they refused to share their authority with the Bulgarians. Meanwhile smaller Greek contingents had invaded Epirus and began the siege of Yanina on November 10. The major contribution of the Greeks to the allied cause was at sea, where they established complete supremacy and prevented the transportation of Turkish troops from Asia. The Greeks also used their fleet to occupy numerous islands in the Aegean which they had long coveted.

The Turks lost in a few months all their European territories except four cities: Constantinople, Adrianople, Scutari, and Yanina. On December 3 Turkey concluded an armistice with Serbia and Bulgaria, the Greeks refusing to join because they wished to continue the siege of Yanina and the blockade of the Ottoman coasts. Peace negotiations opened in London on December 16. At first a deadlock ensued because the Turks insisted on retaining all four cities that were still holding out. But by January 22 they had given way and agreed to relinquish all territory west of a line from Midye (Midia) on the Black Sea to Enez (Enos) at the mouth of the Maritsa on the Aegean. In other words, the Turks were to keep only Constantinople and a narrow strip of territory along the Straits.

At this point a *coup d'état* occurred in Constantinople. Premier Kiamil Pasha was forced to resign in favor of Enver Bey, leader of the extreme nationalist Young Turks who refused to accept the loss of most of European Turkey. On January 30, 1913, fighting was resumed on all fronts. The Young Turks proved incapable of redeeming the military situation. It was indeed beyond redemption. On March 6 Yanina fell to the Greeks and on March 26 Adrianople to the Bulgarians. There remained to the Turks, outside the walls of Constantinople, nothing but Scutari in Albania.

This town now became an international issue. The reason was that the European powers insisted that it be reserved for an autonomous Albanian state that was to be created from the wreckage of European Turkey. Furthermore, Austria and Italy wished to make the new Albania as large as possible in order to counterbalance the Serbians and block them from the Adriatic. But the Montenegrins defied the European powers, continued their siege of Scutari, and finally starved out the defenders on April 23, 1913. Austria immediately issued an ultimatum to the Montenegrins to evacuate the town or suffer the consequences. The Montenegrins finally yielded and Scutari was taken over by an international force from warships in the Adriatic.

Meanwhile an armistice had been concluded between Turkey and the Balkan allies on April 16, 1913. Peace negotiations were reopened in London on May 20, and ten days later the Treaty of London was signed terminating the first Balkan War. Turkey ceded all territory west of the Enez-Midye line and also relinquished her title to Crete. The status of Albania and that of the Aegean Islands were left to the decision of the powers.

SECOND BALKAN WAR

With the Turks practically ousted from Europe, dissension now developed among the allies. The problem was how to divide the spoils. A part of the territory which in the original Serbo-Bulgarian Treaty had been assigned to Serbia was now reserved for the new Albania. The Serbs accordingly demanded a larger share of Macedonia and this the Bulgarians indignantly refused. Similarly, the treaty between Greece and Bulgaria had said nothing of Macedonia and both states now were laying claim to the Saloniki area. Moreover, Rumania, as recompense for her neutrality, demanded a part of the Dobruja which had remained in the hands of Bulgaria after the Congress of Berlin. This question was arbitrated by a conference of the great powers and a very small boundary rectification finally was granted. Rumanian statesmen blamed Austria for the failure to obtain greater compensation and they continued their hostility to Bulgaria.

The situation was further complicated by the conflicting policies of the powers. Russia, anxious to preserve the unity of the league, was concerned by the differences among the allies. The Belgrade and Sofia governments were reminded of the stipulation in the Serbo-Bulgarian Treaty providing for Russian arbitration in case of failure to attain agreement by direct negotiation. In contrast, Austria strove to disrupt the Balkan League by bringing Bulgaria and Rumania together. This proved unsuccessful, for the Bulgarian government believed that its differences with Serbia and Greece could be settled peacefully and therefore refused further concessions to Rumania. Actually, the relations between the allies deteriorated rapidly, with the result that Serbia and Greece drew closer together. Under pressure of repeated reports of skirmishes with Bulgarian forces in Macedonia, the two countries on June 1, 1913, signed a treaty of alliance. They agreed that they would not conclude a separate treaty with Bulgaria concerning the division of the newly won lands, and also that they would have a common frontier in the area west of the Vardar River. If there should be disagreement with Sofia over the delimitation of frontiers, the two powers engaged to ask for the mediation or arbitration of the Triple Entente or of other European powers. Should Bulgaria refuse and war thereupon ensue, the two states were to aid each other with all their forces. Not only did the Serbs and the Greeks negotiate an alliance between themselves, but they also set out in realistic fashion to win the support of the other Balkan states. Rumania refused to commit herself in advance, but the Montenegrin foreign minister announced on June 27 that in case of war between Bulgaria and Serbia, Montenegro would join Serbia in accordance with alliance obligations entered upon in the previous year. Even Turkey was approached and, although no definite agreement was reached, the way was paved for Turkish intervention at a later date.

The stage was now set for the fratricidal war. Venizelos did begin short-lived negotiations with the Bulgarian minister at Athens, but he was restricted by the signed agreement with Serbia. Moreover, he found it necessary to transfer Greek troops as rapidly as possible to Macedonia, where frequent clashes were occurring with Bulgarian forces that were being shifted from the Chatalja lines. Some Bulgarian statesmen now began to demand the whole of Macedonia—a claim that antagonized the Serbians as much as it did the Greeks. The tension became so acute that on June 8 the tsar sent a personal telegram to the Bulgarian and Serbian governments advising them to ask for the arbitration foreseen by the alliance treaty. The replies were evasive, but the Russian foreign minister, Sergei Sazonov, invited the premiers of Bulgaria, Serbia, and Greece to come to St. Petersburg to settle their disputes.

The Bulgarian government now was pressed by its general staff which, because of the growing restlessness of the army, demanded either action or demobilization within ten days. Accordingly, the Bulgarian premier, Stoyan Danev, sent a wire to St. Petersburg requesting that a decision be reached within seven days. Because of a misunderstanding Sazonov did not take cognizance of this request. Danev thereupon dispatched a rash and fateful telegram withdrawing from the negotiations. Sazonov, who was reported to be suffering from a "severe gastric attack complicated by kidney troubles," was so incensed by this injudicious action that he washed his hands of Bulgaria. "Now, after your declaration I communicate ours to you! Do not expect anything from us, and forget the existence of any of our engagements from 1902 until today." [23]

Danev was greatly upset by this communication and attempted to mollify Sazonov. But events now had gone too far. Public opinion in Bulgaria was strongly for war. The Macedonian groups even threatened Danev and King Ferdinand with assassination if they accepted arbitration at St. Petersburg. The general staff assured the government that the army was ready for action. On June 28 King Ferdinand, with the knowledge and apparent approval of Danev, ordered General Savov to attack the Serbian and Greek lines in Macedonia. The attack, which took place on the night of June 29–30, seems to have been intended as a means of strengthening Bulgaria's position in the settlement which was to come through the mediation of Russia. In other words, the advance was considered a political demonstration rather than a military measure. But the Serbians and the Greeks seized the opportunity and answered the Bulgarian "demonstration" with a declaration of war. Sazonov refused to make any move and thus left Bulgaria to her fate.

Montenegro immediately joined Serbia against Bulgaria. On July 10 Rumania also declared war on Bulgaria. Two days later Turkey followed suit. Attacked from all sides, Bulgaria was incapable of putting up serious resistance. Both Serbs and Greeks won easy victories. Enver Bey re-entered Adrianople and the Rumanians occupied the Dobruja. On July 31 an armistice was concluded and on August 10 peace was signed by the Balkan states at Bucharest. Greece received Saloniki, Kavalla, and the greater part of the coast of Macedonia; Serbia was granted north and central Macedonia, including the city of Monastir or Bitolj; Rumania was allowed to keep a generous slice of the Dobruja; Montenegro extended her frontiers slightly until they touched Serbia; and Bulgaria retained only a small portion of Macedonia as the reward for her efforts during the first war. On September 29 Bulgaria and Turkey signed the Treaty of Constantinople by which Turkey regained the greater part of Thrace, including both Adrianople and Kirk-Kilissa. The territorial balance sheet at the end of the two Balkan wars is summarized in the following table.

Area and Population of the Balkan States before and after the Balkan Wars

	AREA (SQUARE MILES)		Per Cent	ESTIMATED POPULATION		Per Cent
	Before	After	Change	Before	After	Change
Albania	...	11,317		...	850,000	
Bulgaria	33,647	43,310	+29	4,337,516	4,467,006	+ 3
Greece	25,014	41,933	+68	2,666,000	4,363,000	+67
Montenegro	3,474	5,603	+62	250,000	500,000	+100
Rumania	50,720	53,489	+ 5	7,230,418	7,516,418	+ 4
Serbia	18,650	33,891	+82	2,911,701	4,527,992	+55
Turkey in Europe	65,350	10,882	−83	6,130,200	1,891,000	−69

Source: *Report of the International Commission to Inquire into the Causes and Conduct of the Balkan Wars* (Washington, D. C., 1914), p. 418.

The effect of the treaty of Bucharest on inter-Balkan relations is not difficult to surmise. Viscount Grey summarized the results as follows:

It left Bulgaria sore, injured, and despoiled of what she believed belonged to her. Any future Balkan peace was impossible so long as the treaty of Bucharest remained. Turkey, of course, was also sore and despoiled. Thus when the great war came a year later, there were two Powers, Bulgaria and Turkey, hungering for a *revanche* and ready to take whichever side would give them a prospect of obtaining it. This naturally was the side of Austria and Germany. For Serbia was at war with Austria, while Greece and Roumania were sympathetic to Serbia or to the Western Powers.[24]

Such was the stormy history of the second Balkan League. It had enabled the Balkan states to put an end, finally, to Turkish rule in Europe. But, aside from that, nothing constructive had been accomplished. Instead, the second Balkan War had so embittered relations between the former allies that conditions in the peninsula were more chaotic and more explosive in 1913 and 1914 than in the preceding years.

ON THE EVE

For a few months in 1912 the Balkan states had been able to present a united front and to adopt and pursue a policy of their own in spite of the opposition of the great powers. After the Treaty of Bucharest the situation was completely different. The Balkan League was smashed. Bulgaria refused to accept the peace settlement as final. Greece, Serbia, and Rumania were equally determined to maintain the *status quo*. This disunity was heightened by the great powers and especially by Austria and Russia, who pulled the Balkan states this way and that in their scramble for allies. Furthermore, the questions of Albania and the Aegean Islands, which had been left unresolved by the London and Bucharest treaties, remained unsettled and a perennial source of friction and war danger. Thus the Balkan Peninsula in 1913 and 1914 was a veritable powder keg which in the end blew up with disastrous consequences for Europe and the entire world.

The Treaty of London at the end of the first Balkan War had left the status of Albania and the Aegean Islands to the decision of the great powers. The latter had settled neither problem by the outbreak of World War I. In the case of Albania the London Conference of Ambassadors announced on December 20, 1912, that the country should become an independent state. The Conference then appointed two commissions to delimit the northern frontier with Montenegro and Serbia and the southern frontier with Greece. In the case of the northern frontier, clashes broke out between the Albanians and the Serbians; whereupon the latter occupied territory which the Conference of Ambassadors had already assigned to Albania. Despite repeated warnings, the Serbians continued to hold the territories until forced to get out by an Austrian ultimatum on October 18, 1913. The frontier commission then resumed its labors in the north but it had not yet completed its task when World War I intervened.

The commission sent to the southern frontier proved equally unsuccessful. The Conference itself already had defined the main course of the frontier, assigning to Albania Koritsa (Korcë) and Argyrokastron (Gjinokastër), the two chief towns in dispute. The commission's task, therefore, was limited to settling the details of the frontier line. This it did in its so-called Protocol of Florence, which it issued on December 19, 1913. The question now was whether the Greeks would accept the loss of Koritsa and Argyrokastron, especially since their forces were occupying all the territory in question. With much justification they wished to link the Albanian question with that of the islands, hoping thereby that their claims would be satisfied either in one area or the other. The London Conference accepted the Greek position and announced on February 13, 1914, that Greece should withdraw all her troops from the territory assigned to Albania by March 13, 1914, after which she was to obtain all the Aegean Islands save three that were close to the Straits.

This decision settled nothing because neither the Greeks nor the Turks accepted it. On February 28, 1914, the Greeks of southern Albania (or northern Epirus, as the Greeks called that area) declared their independence under the leadership of G. Ch. Zographos, former foreign minister of Greece. This move, as a British observer reported, "could not have been adopted without the knowledge and connivance of the Greek occupation authorities. . . ." [25] The new Greek-dominated state of Epirus naturally was unacceptable to the Albanians, who viewed it as an unofficial Greek occupation. Meanwhile Turkey also refused to accept the Conference decision on the Aegean Islands, insisting that the two large islands of Chios and Mytilene should be returned to Turkey along with the three islands near the Straits.

To strengthen her position Turkey bought a British warship, but Greece countered by buying two American warships. Thus the two countries were drifting to war over the islands issue when the news from Sarajevo took precedence over all.

The Balkan Peninsula was in turmoil in 1913 and 1914 not only because of the unsettled Albanian and islands questions but also because the two Balkan Wars had left the Balkan states embittered and divided, while the rivalries of the great powers added to the confusion and discord. In Bulgaria, for example, Austria was successful in pulling that country away from Russia and closer to the Central Powers. Russian diplomacy during the Balkan Wars, and especially Russia's consent to the Rumanian intervention, had strained Russo-Bulgarian relations and culminated in the establishment of the Austrophil Radoslavov government. The latter promptly proposed an alliance with the Dual Monarchy and Berchtold accepted the proposal in principle. But the alliance was not actually concluded because Berchtold insisted that Bulgaria should first patch up her differences with Rumania. Another indication of Bulgaria's new orientation was King Ferdinand's autumn visit to Vienna and his acceptance of a German loan in preference to one offered by French bankers.

Rumania, by contrast, was drifting toward the Entente Powers. The traditional Austro-Rumanian alliance of 1883 had been weakened by Austria's support of Bulgaria during the Balkan Wars and by the perennial Transylvanian problem. In the spring and summer of 1914 the Rumanian and Russian royal families exchanged visits, and on June 24, 1914, Sazonov reported to the tsar that in case of war Rumania would not automatically side with Austria but would instead "take the side which will be strongest and which will be in a position to promise her the greatest gains." [26]

Greece at this time was being urged by both Austria and Germany to reach an understanding with Turkey. King Constantine, whose queen was the kaiser's sister, apparently favored such an entente as part of a Balkan bloc under German tutelage. But this project failed because of the Aegean Islands dispute, which was dragging the two countries toward war.

Serbia's foreign relations were relatively simple after the events of 1908 and 1913. She remained at odds with Austria and Bulgaria but she had close ties with Greece, Rumania, and Montenegro. Serbia also was strongly backed by the Entente Powers. In January, 1914, she received a loan of 250 million francs from France and at the same time was negotiating for war materials from Russia. These developments naturally increased Austria's apprehension of Serbia and further strained the relations between the two countries.

In conclusion it is apparent that the Bucharest Treaty settled nothing. It merely papered over the cracks for the time being. The period between August 10, 1913, and June 28, 1914, proved to be but a breathing spell during which the Balkan states jockeyed for position in preparation for future developments. Thus when World War I broke out there was no possibility of a united Balkan front. Rather, each state stood ready to throw in its lot with whatever side seemed most likely to satisfy its national ambitions. From the Balkan viewpoint the war was essentially a continuation of the Balkan Wars.

1914—

Part VI. Age of War and Crisis

29. Sarajevo and War: 1914–1918

On June 28, 1914, Archduke Francis Ferdinand, the heir to the Hapsburg throne, was assassinated at Sarajevo, the capital of Bosnia. The teen-age perpetrators of the crime wished to demonstrate their opposition to Hapsburg rule and their desire for South Slav independence and unity. Certainly they did not foresee that their act would lead directly to a world-wide war with terrible consequences. They could not have foreseen such an outcome because the war was not merely the product of the murder. Why should the whole world have taken up arms because of an assassination in an obscure Balkan town? Obviously other factors, such as imperialism, nationalism, and the clash of rival alliance systems, were in the background.

We shall not concern ourselves with these background factors, which are of a general European rather than Balkan character. Instead, we shall attempt in this chapter to determine the responsibility for the Sarajevo murder and to trace the events which led from the murder to the war. This is not a simple undertaking. Since that fatal day in June, 1914, many thousands of pages have been written about the assassination of the archduke. The question of responsibility is far from academic, in view of the article in the Versailles Treaty holding Germany and her allies responsible for the war. A deluge of documentary materials has poured forth since 1914, totaling in all over sixty thousand documents. Despite this overwhelming flood of evidence, there is still considerable difference of opinion on certain details of the Sarajevo murder and the beginning of the war. Yet we do know much more about those events today than did the diplomats in 1914 and the peacemakers in 1919. And the one fact which emerges indisputably from this knowledge is that war guilt is something nebulous which cannot be isolated and which spreads widely over many frontiers.

THE MURDER

Archduke Francis Ferdinand, the victim of the Sarajevo murder, is one of the outstanding tragic figures of history. He was the nephew of Emperor Francis Joseph and the heir to the thrones of Austria and Hungary. Unlike his uncle, he was a man of very considerable intellectual powers and wide interests. He had a keen artistic appreciation, he was a famous collector of antiques, he was an ardent sportsman and gardener, and he possessed an acute political sense which gave him much more insight into the real state of the empire than the emperor himself ever enjoyed.

At the same time there was a certain lack of stability and of proportion in his character. "He was unbalanced in everything," one of his close friends observed; "he did nothing like other people." [1] He was overbearing and hot-tempered, and was subject to fits of ungovernable rage. At shooting parties he would sometimes blaze away at everything within range, terrorizing all his companions. He is known on one occasion to have drawn his sword and hacked furiously at the upholstery in his railroad compartment because of some incident that displeased him. Certainly there was much speculation in court circles concerning his mental health, particularly because of the history of insanity in his family.

Francis Ferdinand's relations with the emperor were always strained. One reason was his morganatic marriage with the Countess Sophie Chotek, who was from an ancient but impoverished Bohemian family. More important was the marked difference in the two men's temperaments and political views. Francis Ferdinand was impulsive and aggressive and preferred to settle problems quickly and decisively. Emperor Francis Joseph, on the other hand, was by nature a procrastinator who avoided decisions as long as possible and who, if forced to act, preferred compromise measures. More specifically, the emperor was a staunch supporter of the 1867 settlement which had transformed the Austrian Empire into the Dual Monarchy. Francis Ferdinand took the opposite position on this basic issue. He perceived the fatal flaw of a system which established the hegemony of the Austrians and Hungarians and left the more numerous Slavic citizens in a permanently subordinate position. He knew that the Hungarians were unalterably opposed to a revision of the Dual System and for that reason he was extremely critical of them. On one occasion, when it was pointed out to him that the Hungarians would block constitutional revision, he remarked, "Very well, Hungary will have to be conquered once again at the point of the sword. I do not see how it would be possible to escape from this necessity." [2] On another occasion he expressed his hostility to the Hungarians with the remark, "It was bad taste on their part ever to come to Europe." [3]

Francis Ferdinand never elaborated specifically his ideas on imperial reorganization. It is known, however, that he favored the formation within the empire of a third state, consisting of the territories inhabited by the Croats, Slovenes, and Serbs. Such a state, he believed, would satisfy the nationalist aspirations of the South Slavs and effectively neutralize the Pan-Serb propaganda emanating from Belgrade. In proposing this plan the arch-duke met with the uncompromising opposition not only of the Magyars but also of the South Slav nationalists, who saw in it a dangerous threat to their own dream of an independent Yugoslav state. We shall see that this threat was uppermost in the thoughts of the Bosnian nationalists who plotted the murder of Francis Ferdinand. Indeed, this was the great irony of his career—that he was killed by South Slav nationalists precisely because he wished to raise the status of the South Slavs.

In June, 1914, Francis Ferdinand attended army maneuvers in Bosnia in his capacity as inspector general of the army. Since he was in the vicinity of Sarajevo it was decided that it would be politic for him to pay an official visit to the Bosnian capital. The day selected was Vidovdan or St. Vitus's Day, commemorating the battle of Kosovo, which in 1389 rang the death knell of the medieval Serbian empire. The decision was unpardonably shortsighted, for this was a day when Serbian nationalist sentiment was bound to be inflamed. It was particularly shortsighted in view of the tense situation that had prevailed in Bosnia in recent years * and the repeated attempts that had been made on the lives of Hapsburg officials.

On St. Vitus's Day, June 28, the archduke and his duchess made their official visit to Sarajevo. It was a radiant Sunday, and, by bitter coincidence, the anniversary of their marriage. At ten in the morning the procession of four cars entered the capital, proceeding in the direction of the city hall. No less than six assassins were waiting along the route, armed with hand bombs and revolvers. Most of them lost their nerve at the critical moment or else were unable to act because the cars sped by too fast. But one of the assassins, Nedeljko Chabrinovich, hurled a bomb which fell on the folded hood of the archduke's car. Thence it rolled off and exploded under the following car, wounding the archduke's adjutant.

The procession resumed its way, reduced to three cars. After the ceremonies at the city hall Francis Ferdinand insisted on visiting his adjutant at the hospital. This involved a change of route but the chauffeurs were not informed. The archduke's car consequently made a wrong turn. General Potiorek, the Governor of Bosnia, who was in the back seat with the royal pair, leaned forward and ordered the chauffeur to stop, back up, and turn to the right. This proved to be a fatal move. At that very corner was another revolutionary, Gavrilo Princip. He had let the car go past but now that it had backed up in front of him he drew his revolver and fired two shots, one at Francis Ferdinand and the other at Potiorek. The second shot went wild and hit the duchess instead. Before medical aid arrived both the archduke and his wife were dead.

There is little doubt that the murder would not have occurred if the chauffeur had been given proper instructions and had not made the wrong

* See Chapter 24.

turn. There is also little doubt that the assassins would not have been able to line up in the streets of Sarajevo in broad daylight if even elementary security precautions had been taken. When the emperor visited Sarajevo in 1910 the street along which he passed was lined with a double cordon of troops while hundreds of suspected individuals were forbidden to leave their homes. During the archduke's visit, in contrast, six individuals who were known to the police as dangerous revolutionaries were permitted to move about in the streets with impunity. So gross was the negligence that it has even been suggested that enemies of the archduke deliberately neglected to provide adequate protection in order to be rid of him. The fact that General Potiorek sat beside the archduke and escaped the assassin's bullet only by accident indicates that this theory is unfounded. Rather, it appears that strained relations between the civilian and military authorities of Bosnia were responsible for the lack of proper security measures.

The royal couple was buried in a memorial chapel which Francis Ferdinand had built in the country at Artstetten, his wife being too lowborn to rest in the Hapsburg vaults in Vienna. The very elements seemed to conspire to mark the tragedy of the occasion. At the moment when the funeral procession was about to start up the hilly road to Artstetten, a deafening thunderstorm broke over the Danube. Torrential rain threw everything into confusion. The coffins were carried hastily into a tiny railroad station and everyone crowded in to wait for the storm to pass. The heavens had given warning of the furies to come.

THE CONSPIRACY

The Vienna government responded to the murder by sending a legal expert to Sarajevo to collect evidence in order to prepare a tight case. In July, 1914, five of the assassins were placed on trial, the sixth one having managed to escape to Serbia. The defendants consisted of Princip, who committed the murder, Chabrinovich, who threw the bomb, and three of their accomplices. The most resolute and defiant was Princip, who boldly stated his beliefs and motives. "I have no regret," he said, "because I am convinced that I have destroyed a scourge and done a good deed. . . . I have seen our people going steadily downhill. I am a peasant's son and know what is happening in the villages. . . . All this had its influence on me and also the fact of knowing that he [the archduke] was a German, an enemy of the Slavs. . . . As future Sovereign he would have prevented our union and carried out certain reforms which would have been clearly against our interests." [4]

After protracted hearings the court found the defendants guilty. Under Austrian law they could not be sentenced to death because none of them had completed their twentieth year. So Princip and Chabrinovich received sentences of twenty years' imprisonment and the remainder from thirteen to twenty years. The verdict of the court read as follows:

The Court regards it as proved by the evidence that both the *Narodna Odbrana* and military circles in the Kingdom of Serbia in charge of the espionage service, collaborated in the outrage. . . . There is no doubt that both the *Narodna Odbrana* and military circles on the active list in the Kingdom of Serbia knew of the aims of the outrage and were prodigal of all possible assistance and all possible protection to the perpetrators for whom they actually procured the means of carrying out the assassination.[5]

The Narodna Odbrana, or National Defense Society, which the court held responsible for the crime, had been organized in 1908 immediately following the annexation of Bosnia-Herzegovina. Its objectives were avowedly revolutionary and anti-Austrian, including "encouragement and promotion of national feeling; enrollment and recruitment of volunteers; formation of volunteer units and their training for armed activity." [6] The Narodna Odbrana enrolled recruits not only in Serbia but also in Bosnia-Herzegovina and Croatia. It transformed itself into a cultural society in 1909, when Serbia was forced to promise that she would live "on good neighborly terms" with Austria. But the change was more one of form than of substance. A pamphlet published in Belgrade in 1911 stated: "While the *Narodna Odbrana,* evolving with time, has adjusted itself to the changes in the situation, it continues to maintain the links formed at the moment of the annexation and remains the same as it then was. . . . Today demands quiet work, fanatical, indefatigable, and incessant, on the tasks and duties needful as preliminary preparation for the fight with rifles and heavy guns." [7]

Under these circumstances the Austrian authorities had no trouble finding abundant evidence of Narodna Odbrana activity in Bosnia. Hence they concluded that the Society was responsible for the murder and made this charge in the court verdict. Since then, however, much new evidence has been collected which indicates clearly that the Narodna Odbrana was not responsible for the crime. Rather, it was a secret Serbian organization which had infiltrated the Narodna Odbrana and used it for its purposes. This secret organization was the Ujedinjenje ili Smrt or Union or Death, more popularly known as the Black Hand. The Austrian court came closer to the facts when it included certain "military circles in Belgrade" in its indictment. But the court did not know of the Black Hand which these "military circles" had organized and which was directly responsible for the murder.

The Black Hand was founded in Belgrade in 1911 with the aim of realizing "the national ideal: the union of all Serbs." As described in Chapter 24, the organizers of the Society were mostly army men who had participated in the 1903 revolution which had placed Peter Karageorgevich on the Serbian throne. After that bloody episode they had remained in contact with each other and had kept a watch over the new dynasty and its governments. Being men of action and fanatically nationalistic, they became increasingly impatient with what they considered to be the dilatory tactics of the Serbian government and of the Narodna Odbrana. Accordingly, they organized the

Black Hand in order to redeem their Serbian brothers under Hapsburg and Turkish rule by more violent and speedy measures. "This organization," the bylaws stated, "prefers terrorist action to intellectual propaganda, and for this reason must be kept absolutely secret from non-members." [8]

Certain features of the Black Hand appear almost adolescent to the outsider. The initiation of a new member took place in a darkened room, lighted only by a wax candle, before a small table covered with a black cloth on which lay a crucifix, a dagger, and a revolver. The Society's seal bore a skull and crossbones, dagger, bomb, and bottle of poison, with the inscription *Ujedinjenje ili Smrt.* These extravagances reflected the fanatical earnestness and single-mindedness of the members, and especially of the leader, Colonel Dragutin Dimitrijevich. He had been one of the ringleaders of the 1903 conspiracy and had been appointed in 1913 head of the Intelligence Service of the Serbian General Staff. He was an utterly selfless and dedicated man with great charm as well as proved courage and passionate patriotism. He commanded the complete devotion of his followers, who regarded him as a Mazzini and Garibaldi rolled into one.

Before the Balkan Wars the Black Hand had fought for the Serbian cause in Macedonia by conducting propaganda and organizing armed bands. It had been also active in Bosnia, where it had operated through the Narodna Odbrana and through the Bosnian nationalist society, the Mlada Bosna, or Young Bosnia, described in Chapter 24. Vladimir Gachinovich, a prominent leader in both the Narodna Odbrana and the Mlada Bosna, was also a member of the Black Hand. On the model of the Black Hand Gachinovich organized in Bosnia a network of revolutionary cells which were controlled by the Central Committee in Belgrade. Thus the Black Hand infiltrated the older organizations, utilizing them very effectively to organize an underground revolutionary apparatus and to carry on agitation. This work was so effective that contemporaries described Bosnia as a volcano that was about to erupt.

It is important to note that the Serbian government was not involved in this revolutionary activity. In fact, its relations with the Black Hand were anything but cordial. One reason was that the Belgrade government feared that the unceasing agitation might provoke Austria to attack Serbia. Another reason was that Premier Pashich and his Radical party were more interested in Pan-Serbism than in the Yugoslav ideal which animated the Bosnian revolutionaries and the Black Hand. Furthermore, a sharp conflict had developed between the Serbian civilian and military authorities after the Balkan Wars over the administration of the newly won territories in Macedonia. The Black Hand took the side of the military and the situation became so acute that the Austrian minister in Belgrade reported on May 8, 1914:

> The conflict between the Government and the conspirator party (Black Hand) . . . has become so aggravated in the last few weeks that a violent clash

between the two rivals for power seems not impossible. . . . The Black Hand being probably none too fastidious in its choice of means to gain its ends, I regard the possibility of violent eruptions, even of an overthrow of the Government or a *coup d'état,* as not entirely inconceivable developments. . . .[9]

Thus the Black Hand operated almost as a state within a state. Certainly Premier Pashich feared this secret organization and dared not oppose it too openly for fear that the same thing might happen to him as did to Alexander Obrenovich in 1903. Indeed, the army paper, *Piemont,* at this time was making none too subtle references to "the memory of 29 May 1903."

Such was the situation in Serbia and Bosnia when the announcement was made that Archduke Francis Ferdinand was to visit Sarajevo on St. Vitus's Day. The effect on the young firebrands in Bosnia may be imagined. Two of them, Gavrilo Princip and Nedeljko Chabrinovich, decided they would attempt to assassinate the archduke. It is significant that they did not go to the Narodna Odbrana for arms, money, and other assistance. They were Black Hand members and they got in touch with leaders of the secret society who approved their plot and gave them full assistance. It is almost certain that Colonel Dimitrijevich was consulted about such a major undertaking, especially since he made all important decisions. In any case, the young assassins were provided with four Brownings from the Serbian state arsenal, six bombs, 150 dinars, a map of Bosnia, and cyanide of potassium to be taken immediately after the deed so that they would not be captured alive. They were also given a letter addressed to the officer of the frontier guards instructing him to allow the bearers to pass. Thus Princip and Chabrinovich were able to reach Sarajevo, where they joined forces with other conspirators and went into hiding until the day of the royal visit.

At this point there arises the much-discussed question of whether Premier Pashich was in any way implicated in the plot. In view of the relations between him and the Black Hand it appears certain that he was not. On the other hand, the evidence indicates quite clearly that he had heard of the plot and that, after some hesitation for fear of assassination by the Black Hand, he made two attempts to prevent the murder. He sent orders to the frontier guards to stop the assassins and he also instructed his minister in Vienna to warn the Austrian government.

Unfortunately, neither of these moves proved effective. The frontier guards, who were members of the Black Hand, professed that the orders arrived too late. And the Serbian minister in Vienna was on bad terms with the Austrian Foreign Minister, so he spoke instead to the Minister in Charge of Bosnian Affairs. He did not make his warning very specific or urgent; hence, the minister did not pass on the information to the archduke. The latter thus proceeded with his trip to Bosnia, which, as we have seen, was to end in tragedy because of the criminal laxity of the officials in Sarajevo. It is evident, in conclusion, that both the Austrian and Serbian governments were guilty of negligence and blundering and hence must be held partly responsible for the assassination of Francis Ferdinand.

We may end this story of murder with the question of motive. Why did Colonel Dimitrijevich approve of the plot and arrange for its execution? The colonel's nephew, Dr. Milan Zivanovich, has given this revealing answer:

> The motive of the Sarajevo crime is to be sought in the Slavophil policy of Francis Ferdinand. The Archduke fell a victim of his political views favourable to trialism. If he had succeeded in carrying through this design, Serbia would have ended by gravitating towards Austria-Hungary. Apis [Dimitrijevich's pseudonym], an acute political thinker, had grasped all the danger of the Archduke's plan. Austria meant to bring about Southern Slav union within the framework of the Danubian Monarchy. Dimitrijevich, who had been for several months at the Serbian Legation in Berlin, must have been seriously perturbed by what he learnt of the political intentions of the Austrian Heir Apparent and the information, continually brought to him by Serbs and Croats from the Monarchy, of the growing sympathy which that programme roused among the Slav subjects of Austria. That is why he decided to seize the first occasion to eliminate Francis Ferdinand.[10]

WAR

Just as blundering was largely responsible for the murder of the archduke, so now it contributed greatly to the outbreak of World War I. The first miscalculation was made by certain members of the Austrian government, who assumed that they could employ forceful measures to punish Serbia without international complications. The foreign minister, Count Berchtold, and the chief of staff, General Conrad von Hötzendorf, both insisted that "Austria must draw the sword." On the other hand, Emperor Francis Joseph, the Austrian premier, Count Stürgkh, and the Hungarian premier, Count Tisza, all wished to wait until the crime could be investigated and the attitude of Germany ascertained. Berchtold thereupon sent a special emissary, Count Hoyos, to Berlin to explain Austria-Hungary's position.

Hoyos took with him a memorandum on the Balkan situation that had been completed by the Foreign Office on June 28. To it was added a postscript stating that the "ruthless assassination" afforded "unmistakable evidence of the insuperability of the antagonism between the Monarchy and Serbia" and demonstrated "the necessity for the Monarchy to destroy with a determined hand the net which its enemies are attempting to throw about its head." Hoyos also took a letter from Francis Joseph to the kaiser stating that "a reconciliation" with Serbia "is no longer to be thought of" and that "the pacific policy of all European monarchs will be threatened so long as this center of criminal agitation in Belgrade is not subjected to punishment." [11]

Both the kaiser and his chancellor, Bethmann-Hollweg, responded to these statements with promises of full support. The Austrian ambassador in Berlin telegraphed to his government on July 6, 1914, that "the German

Government is of the opinion that we must judge what is to be done to clear up the situation; whatever we may decide upon, we can always be sure that we shall find Germany at our side, as the ally and friend of the Monarchy." [12] This unqualified assurance of support constitutes the famous "blank check" which proved to be another big step toward war. The Germans, it should be emphasized, did not give the "blank check" because they wanted war. Rather, it was because they assumed that Russia would not dare support Serbia against both Germany and Austria, and that she would therefore back down as she had done in 1908.* It was not long before this assumption was proved to be a fatal miscalculation.

Meanwhile in Vienna Berchtold was strengthened by the assurances from Berlin and by reports from Sarajevo that evidence had been found proving that the crime had been planned in Belgrade with the assistance of Serbian officials. This enabled Berchtold to win over the emperor and the Austrian and Hungarian premiers to his position. On July 14 they all agreed that a drastic ultimatum should be issued, which it was expected—and hoped —that Serbia would reject. The ultimatum was presented in Belgrade on July 23 with a time limit of forty-eight hours. It made ten specific demands upon the Serbian government: (1) that it suppress anti-Austrian newspapers; (2) that it dissolve the Narodna Odbrana; (3) that it remove anti-Austrian teachers from the schools, and (4) anti-Austrian officers from the army; (5) that it accept Austrian collaboration in conducting the inquiry regarding responsibility for the crime; (6) that it institute proceedings against those accessory to the plot, Austrian representatives participating in the investigation; (7) that it arrest two Serbian officials known to have been involved in the plot; (8) that it dismiss and punish certain frontier guards; (9) that it explain the utterances of certain high officials; and (10) that it notify the Austrian government of the execution of these measures.

At first glance the Serbian reply appeared very conciliatory. It seemed to concede all the Austrian demands except the sixth, and it offered to submit the whole matter to the Hague Court or to the powers of Europe for settlement. But these concessions were so hedged about with qualifications as to be evasive and of questionable value. The Austrian minister in Belgrade declared the reply unsatisfactory and broke off diplomatic relations, leaving the country within half an hour. Even before presenting their reply the Serbs ordered the mobilization of their army in the afternoon of July 25. That evening Austria replied by mobilizing eight army corps against Serbia.

In the next few days the Austrian-German assumption that the Serbian affair could be localized was proved to be a terrible miscalculation. The basic reason was that Russia was in a much more favorable position at this time than she had been in 1908. Her army was reorganized and stronger than in 1908, when it had not yet recovered from its defeat in the Far East. Also, Russia now had firm support from France, in contrast to 1908, when France

* See Chapter 28.

expressly declared her unwillingness to risk war over Bosnia. It happened that President Poincaré and Premier Viviani of France were paying an official visit to St. Petersburg between July 20 and 23. Poincaré, a native of Alsace, had always favored a tough policy against Germany. Now he apparently disregarded the intrinsic merits of the Serbian-Austrian dispute and looked upon it as a test of Entente solidarity against the Triple Alliance. Accordingly, he urged the Russians to stand firm and assured them of France's support.

The Russians from the beginning took the position that the Serbian-Austrian crisis was of general European rather than purely local concern. When the Austrians dispatched their ultimatum, the Russian foreign minister, Sergei Sazonov, declared heatedly that he would not allow Austria to attack and "devour" Serbia. Even before Serbia gave her reply Russia began military preparations. Thus the stage was set for the great catastrophe. Austria was determined to use force against Serbia; Russia was equally determined to prevent such force; and Germany and France had committed themselves to support their respective allies.

Many proposals were made for preserving the peace. Germany urged that pressure be put on the Russians to restrain them. France, on the other hand, wanted pressure on Vienna to force the Austrians to modify their demands. Italy, with a foot in each camp, sincerely desired an equitable settlement but her proposals received scant consideration. Earl Grey in London issued without success three successive plans for maintaining peace. Berchtold feared that all these mediation proposals might interfere with his plans for a final and forceful settlement of the Serbian menace. So on July 28 he declared war on Serbia.

The chancellories of Europe now became feverishly active in their search for a means of forestalling a general conflagration. Bethmann-Hollweg had realized by this time that his assumption that the dispute could be localized was no longer tenable. Accordingly, he recommended to Berchtold that the Austrian forces should not advance beyond Belgrade. He hoped that in this way a European war might be averted, while at the same time Austria would be able to use the Serbian capital as a pawn in conducting negotiations for a settlement. When Berchtold did not reply to this "Halt in Belgrade" proposal, the German chancellor repeated it twice more, gaining British support in the meantime.

Berchtold now felt constrained to call a meeting of the council of ministers for July 31 to formulate a reply. But the day before, Russia ordered full mobilization; whereupon the German chief of staff, Helmuth von Moltke, telegraphed to his counterpart in Vienna, Conrad von Hötzendorf, to follow suit with the assurance of full German support. When the council of ministers met it naturally decided under these circumstances to return a polite but evasive reply to the German-British proposals. In this manner Bethmann-Hollweg's frantic efforts to check Austria were brought to nought by Russia's mobilization.

The mobilization of Russia proved to be the final move that made war inevitable. Sazonov decided to make this move because of the prodding of his military advisers and the repeated assurances of support from Paris. When Austria declared war on Serbia, the French ambassador, Paléologue, gave Sazonov a formal declaration promising French support. Sazonov decided that the time for action had come, so he asked for partial mobilization against Austria alone. The Russian military leaders opposed partial mobilization for fear that if general war broke out it would prove impossible to shift to full mobilization against both Austria and Germany. Sazonov gave way to the military men and also persuaded the tsar to accept general mobilization.

At this point the tsar received a personal telegram from the kaiser stating that a direct understanding between Russia and Austria was both possible and desirable, and urging that no military measures be taken. Nicholas was sincerely devoted to peace and acted upon the kaiser's request. He countermanded the plans for general mobilization and ordered partial mobilization instead. The military men now were in a panic and Sazonov with them. They feared that the drift to war could not be stopped despite the personal wishes of the tsar and the kaiser. Hence they envisaged a nightmarish situation in which Russia would be obliged to fight against both Austria and Germany but would be unable to do so because partial mobilization would be under way and the troops and war material already en route to the Austrian front.

Sazonov and the military pleaded with the tsar to change his mind, which he finally did with great reluctance. In the afternoon of July 30 he signed the order for general mobilization which made war virtually inevitable. Germany retaliated the next day with a twelve-hour ultimatum to Russia demanding that the mobilization be stopped. When no reply was received, Germany declared war against Russia on August 1. German war plans, prepared years earlier by Count Schlieffen, called for an immediate and overwhelming attack against France with the aim of defeating her quickly and then turning against the slower-moving Russians. In accordance with this strategy, Germany demanded on July 31 that France make clear her position in the case of a Russian-German conflict. France replied that she would be guided by her own interests. Germany then cleared the way for the implementation of the Schlieffen plan by declaring war on France on August 3 on the flimsy pretext of frontier violations. The next day England entered the war on the side of France and thus the great powers of Europe were at each others' throats five weeks after the murder at Sarajevo.

When the tsar reluctantly signed the order for general mobilization he said to Sazonov, "Think of the responsibility which you are advising me to take! Think of the thousands and thousands of men who will be sent to their death!"[13] The tsar could not foresee that he was also signing the death warrant for himself and for his entire family. Nor did he realize that he was unleashing forces that were to transform completely the Balkan Peninsula and to create that great South Slav state for which Princip and other Bosnian youth had sacrificed themselves.

SERBIA'S TRIUMPH

The first round of fighting in the Balkan Peninsula proved to be a bitter disappointment for Austria and a glorious triumph for Serbia. The reason for this unexpected outcome was that the Austrian army was paralyzed by precisely that confusion of conflicting mobilizations which the Russian generals had feared and had avoided by persuading the tsar to proceed with general mobilization.

The origin of the confusion was the Austrian assumption that the war could be confined to the Balkans. In accordance with this assumption the Austrians on July 25 ordered the implementation of their Mobilization Plan B, which was designed for a purely Balkan war against Serbia. It soon became evident that the war could not be localized; hence on July 21 the Austrians switched to Mobilization Plan R, which required that most of the troops be sent to the Russian front. This switch created fearful anarchy because the bulk of the Austrian army already was en route to the Danube. There was nothing to do but to allow the divisions to proceed southward and then, upon their arrival at the Serbian front, to start northward for Galicia, where the Russians were advancing. They arrived there so far behind schedule that the Russians were able to overrun the whole of the province of Galicia in the first month of the war.

The Austrians suffered not only a serious defeat in the north but also a humiliating setback in the south. They left only 250,000 men under General Potiorek along the Danube front. The Serbian army numbered over 350,000 men, 90 per cent of whom were seasoned veterans of the Balkan Wars. Nevertheless, Potiorek, who had barely escaped Princip's bullet in Sarajevo, was eager to charge ahead and was certain that he could destroy "the viper's nest." On August 12 he crossed the Drina River and began the invasion of Serbia. At first he had some success because the Serbians had expected the attack at Belgrade rather than further west, where it came. The Serbian commander, General Putnik, rushed reinforcements to the threatened sector. Some of the troops marched sixty miles in forty-eight hours and then plunged into battle without rest. By August 24 the Austrians had been pushed back across the Drina River into Bosnia with a loss of a third of their forces.

On September 8 Potiorek returned to the attack, invading Serbia once more from Bosnia. After hard fighting and heavy losses he was able to take Belgrade on December 2. On the same day Putnik ordered a counteroffensive, which he began without artillery preparation because of the extreme shortage of ammunition. The undaunted Serbian soldiers attacked with such spirit that they broke through the Austrian positions. They kept pressing forward, giving the Austrians no chance to re-form their lines. On December 15 Serbian cavalrymen galloped into Belgrade while the Austrians once more fell back across the river to their own territory. Potiorek retired to a sanitarium while Putnik announced to the world: "On the territory of the Kingdom of Serbia there remains not one free enemy soldier." [14]

The Serbians had paid heavily for their victory, their casualties totaling over 100,000. And their ordeal had only begun. As soon as the fighting ended a devastating typhus epidemic began. The crowding in the cities and the generally unsanitary conditions resulting from the war made the epidemic exceptionally virulent. Despite the aid of medical missions from Allied countries it raged on until June, 1915, causing at least 150,000 deaths. And then a few months later came still another blow. Bulgaria joined the Central Powers in a coordinated attack upon Serbia from all sides. Before considering this new campaign we shall turn to the ill-fated Dardanelles expedition which had far-reaching consequences in the Balkans and throughout Europe.

DARDANELLES AND GALLIPOLI

The Allies attacked the Dardanelles because Turkey joined the Central Powers on November 2, 1914. The Turkish government leaders intervened as early as they did because they were certain that they had picked the winning side and they hoped that as a result they would recover the territory they had lost in the Balkan Wars. On July 27, before hostilities had started, the Turkish grand vizir offered to the German ambassador a secret offensive and defensive alliance against Russia. The ambassador was cool to the proposal because he considered the Turkish army to be of little value. But the kaiser intervened energetically, stating: "It is now a question of getting hold of every gun which is ready in the Balkans to let go *for* Austria against the Slavs. . . ." [15]

The ambassador hurriedly dropped his objections and concluded a treaty of alliance on August 2. The two parties agreed to observe neutrality in the conflict between Austria and Serbia, but Turkey promised to enter the war in case Russia intervened—which she already had done when the treaty was signed. The Germans now discovered that it was one thing to secure an alliance with the Turks and quite another to persuade them to fight. The Turks delayed intervention on the grounds that they wished first to complete their mobilization, an operation for which they required several weeks. During that period the Turks amused themselves by pretending to conduct serious negotiations with the Allied ambassadors. They swore that they were not committed and even offered to join the Allies if a sufficiently lucrative offer were made. The Allied representatives, completely taken in, pursued these negotiations earnestly and hopefully.

The Turks enjoyed this game until it was rudely interrupted on August 11 by the arrival in Constantinople of two German cruisers, the *Breslau* and the *Göben*. These ships had been sailing in the Mediterranean when the war began. Since the Allies controlled the Suez and Gibraltar exits the German admirals sought a refuge in the Straits. The Allies protested to

Constantinople because the entry of non-Turkish warships into the Straits was a violation of long-standing treaty stipulations. The Turks replied blandly that they had purchased the ships in question and that they should be considered henceforth as Turkish. The citizens of Constantinople now witnessed the strange spectacle of blond and blue-eyed German sailors wearing red fezzes and enjoying the sights of the capital while on shore leave.

Needless to say, the German admirals retained control over their ships and paid no attention to Turkish naval officials. In fact, it was these admirals who finally forced the Turks into the war. On October 29 they steamed into the Black Sea, apparently without the consent or knowledge of the Turkish government, and shelled Odessa and Sebastopol and sank Allied shipping. Russia responded by declaring war on November 4 and Britain and France followed suit the next day.

With Turkey on the side of the Central Powers the Straits were completely closed to the Allies. This was a particularly serious blow for the Russians, who, short of war matériel, depended on their Western allies to make up the deficit. But now that the Straits were blocked it was extremely difficult for the Russians to obtain the needed supplies. The only ports that could be reached by Allied shipping were on the Arctic and Pacific coasts, both far removed from the front lines.

A group of Allied strategists led by Winston Churchill proposed to meet this dilemma by sending an expedition to force the Dardanelles and take Constantinople. In this way, they argued, Turkey would be put out of the war, the route to Russia would be opened, Western factories would be able to supply Russia's inexhaustible manpower with weapons, and the war would thus be won in short order. Most professional soldiers opposed this plan on the ground that victory could be gained only on the western front by a direct assault upon the German lines.

Churchill eventually persuaded the cabinet to try his strategy. But because the high command of the army remained hostile, he had to rely only on naval forces. On March 18, 1915, a squadron of fourteen British and four French battleships steamed into the Straits with guns blazing. The principal obstacle was the multitude of mines rather than the shore fortifications. On the first day three ships were sunk and two others badly damaged. The British admiral in command of the operation decided that the losses were prohibitive and withdrew the squadron. In doing so he allowed one of the greatest opportunities of the war to pass. It is known now that the Turks had used up most of their ammunition and that the Allied ships probably would have reached Constantinople without much difficulty if the attack had been resumed the next day.

On that night the chief German officer at the Straits, General Mertens, declared, "We expect that the British will come back early tomorrow morning, and if they do, we may be able to hold out for a few hours." [16] It is also known that the Ottoman capital was deeply demoralized and divided and would not have offered serious resistance. The American ambassador in Constantinople, Henry Morgenthau, reported that "the whole Ottoman state, on that eighteenth day of March, 1915, when the Allied fleet abandoned the attack, was on the brink of dissolution. . . . Among the subject races the spirit of revolt was rapidly spreading. . . . The Turks themselves were praying that the British and French would take their city, for this would relieve them of the controlling gang [Young Turk government], emancipate them from the hated Germans, bring about peace, and end their miseries." [17]

It is quite understandable that the British admiral should have decided to withdraw; nevertheless, it is fascinating to speculate how different the course of European and even of world history might have been if his decision had been otherwise. Constantinople probably would have been taken, in which case Turkey would have been forced out of the war, Russia would have received the supplies she needed so desperately, her armies would have fared better than they did, and quite possibly the Bolshevik revolution of 1917 might have been averted.

With the failure of the Dardanelles expedition the Allies decided to try to take the Gallipoli Peninsula by land and thus open the Straits to their fleets. They were able to scrape together only five divisions of British, Australian, New Zealand, and French troops, only one of these being well trained. Landings were made on the Gallipoli beaches on April 25 but only shallow footholds could be secured in the face of withering machine gun fire. Both sides brought up reinforcements, dug trenches, and consolidated their lines. But the Turks commanded the heights and could look down on the beaches on which every man and every box of ammunition had to be landed. The Allies did not have sufficient reserves to overrun the peninsula; yet they hesitated to withdraw once more because of prestige considerations. Finally, they were forced to face facts and in January, 1916, they extricated their forces in the only successful operation of the campaign.

An obvious reason for the failure of the Allies at the Straits was that their strength never reached more than half of the 800,000 men in the Turkish lines. Equally important was the dissension among the Allies, which prevented them from utilizing to the full their potential resources. Much of the dissension arose from Russian suspicion concerning the objectives of her Western allies in the Straits. This was paradoxical in view of the fact that one of the aims of the Dardanelles and Gallipoli campaigns was to open a sea route to Russia. Nevertheless, the Russians could not be certain that, if the British were able to take such a glittering prize as Constantinople, they would then be willing to relinquish it. Furthermore, the Russians were suspicious of Premier Venizelos of Greece who, on March 5, 1915, offered his country's land and sea forces for the assault on the Straits. The Russians were well aware of the centuries-old Greek aspiration for Constantinople and they knew that this aspiration was still very strong. Accordingly Sazonov stated outright that Greek participation in the Straits campaigns was unacceptable to Russia. It is not altogether certain that Venizelos in any case would have been able to persuade his king to commit the Greek forces. But he might have succeeded if Russia's attitude had been different. And the addition of Greek manpower to that of the Allies might then have spelled the difference between defeat and victory.

The Russians not only vetoed Greek participation but also pressed Britain and France to recognize legally their claims to Constantinople and the Straits. On March 4, 1915, Sazonov issued his famous memorandum in which he claimed the city of Constantinople, the Asiatic side of the Bosphorus to the Sakaria River, and the entire European shore of the Straits together with Thrace to the Enez-Midye line. Britain and France reluctantly accepted these demands on March 12 and April 10, respectively. At the same time the Western Allies reserved the right to define at a later date their claims in Asiatic Turkey. They did stake their claims in secret treaties in 1915, 1916, and 1917. And at the end of the war they secured these claims in the form of the Palestine, Iraq, and Syria mandates. But Russia, having gone Bolshevik in 1917, was unable to gain the great prize which her allies had conceded in 1915.*

BULGARIA'S INTERVENTION

The failure of the Dardanelles and Gallipoli expeditions affected not only the position of Russia but also the situation in the Balkans. If the expeditions had succeeded there is little doubt that the Balkan states sooner or later would have joined the Entente. As it was, the failure at the Straits contributed substantially to Bulgaria's decision in the fall of 1915 to intervene on the side of the Central Powers.

Bulgaria, by virtue of her strategic location, was the pivot of the Balkan theater of war. To the Central Powers she offered a safe overland route to Constantinople and an essential ally for defeating Serbia. Contrariwise, she was important to the Allies for the security of Serbia and the isolation of Turkey. Thus from the beginning of the war both sides ardently wooed Bulgaria. The Allies labored under a distinct disadvantage because the Central Powers could promise Bulgaria territory at the expense of Serbia, whereas they could find little to offer as compensation. They persuaded Pashich to offer a few bits of Macedonia in exchange for the territory that Serbia would gain from Austria. But these concessions, far short of what Bulgaria had lost in the second Balkan War, did not impress Ferdinand. The Allies also suggested that Greece give up something in return for compensation in Asia Minor. The Greeks did not respond, preferring the sparrow in the hand to the pigeon in the air.

When Turkey entered the war at the end of October the Allies made a serious effort to win over Bulgaria. On November 13 they offered Ferdinand both Thrace and Macedonia as well as financial aid if he would attack Turkey. Thrace was to be taken from Turkey but Macedonia was being offered against the will of its current owners—neutral Greece and Serbia—the

* See Chapter 30.

latter, of course, being the state for whose integrity the world had just been plunged into war. The Austrians easily overbid their opponents by offering Ferdinand a larger share of Serbia. The Bulgarian king listened to all these offers, asked for more, and refused to commit himself until it became clearer which side was likely to win.

In 1915 Ferdinand decided that the Central Powers would be the victors. He reached this conclusion because of the failure of the Allies at the Straits and also because of the overwhelming defeats sustained that year by the Russians. Having made his decision Ferdinand soon reached an agreement with the Central Powers despite frantic last-minute offers by the Allies. The Germans smoothed the way by persuading the Turks on July 22 to hand over immediately to Bulgaria a part of Thrace. The next month the German and Austrian governments gave Bulgaria a loan of 200 million francs. Finally, on September 6, 1915, Ferdinand signed an alliance and a military convention providing for mutual aid against a neighboring state, for a German-Austrian campaign against Serbia within thirty days, and for Bulgarian participation five days later. In return Bulgaria was to receive the Macedonian boundaries of 1912 as well as the Dobruja if Rumania joined the Allies, and the Kavalla region if Greece did likewise.

Ferdinand did not have much popular support in pursuing the policy he did. Considerations of race, religion, and historical traditions made the Bulgarian people much more sympathetic to Russia than to the German powers. This is borne out by the experiences of the Russian ambassador at Sofia.

. . . as far as the people were concerned I can certify that in spite of all the mistakes made by the Russian Government during about forty years, the nation had preserved intact its feeling of gratitude to her deliverers. Indeed, as soon as the war had broken out, I began receiving pile upon pile of letters, one more touching than the other, coming from the most obscure and remote parts of the country, wishing success to the Slavic cause and containing donations to be forwarded to the sons of the heroes of the emancipation war of 1877–78.[18]

Despite this popular sentiment Ferdinand was able to have his way without serious trouble because the premier in office at the time was Vasil Radoslavov, leader of the traditionally anti-Russian Liberal party. Radoslavov had assumed office in 1913 following the disastrous outcome of the second Balkan War. His appointment reflected the tendency in Bulgarian court circles to blame Russia for the misfortunes of the second Balkan War.

Despite the authority of both king and premier, considerable resistance was organized against the alliance with the Central Powers. On September 17, 1915, the leaders of the opposition parties secured an audience with Ferdinand and expressed their disapproval of the impending attack upon Serbia. The leader of the young Agrarian party, Alexander Stambuliski, was particularly outspoken in his comments, warning the king that if he intervened in the war he would lose his throne. Ferdinand replied that if Stambuliski were not more careful he would lose his head. In fact, Stambuliski was arrested and sent to prison for *lèse-majesté*. But within three years he was completely vindicated as Ferdinand fled to Germany before the victorious Allied armies.

OCCUPATION OF SERBIA

Bulgaria's intervention spelled Serbia's doom. An overwhelming number of German, Austrian, and Bulgarian divisions were gathered for a simultaneous attack upon Serbia from three sides. On September 22 Bulgaria ordered general mobilization. The Serbs, suspecting the worst, favored an immediate preventive attack on the Bulgars. But the Allies vetoed this proposal, still cherishing the illusion that they would be able to keep Bulgaria neutral.

Serbia then appealed to Greece for assistance under the terms of their alliance of May, 1913. But no assistance was forthcoming from that quarter either. We will consider later the political deadlock that developed in Greece during World War I and which was to convulse that country for many years. Suffice it to note here that King Constantine, who had married the kaiser's sister, insisted on neutrality, while Premier Venizelos ardently urged intervention on the side of the Allies. This split, which manifested itself when Serbia asked for aid on the eve of the Bulgarian attack, will be discussed later in this chapter. The 1913 alliance had provided that Serbia should supply 150,000 men in a joint war, a condition that she manifestly was now incapable of fulfilling. So Venizelos notified the Entente Powers on September 22 that if they would supply the 150,000 men Greece would enter the war. The Allies accepted and on October 3 British and French troops began to disembark at Saloniki.

This development appeared promising for the Serbians, but in the end nothing came of it. King Constantine insisted that Greece remain neutral and Venizelos resigned in protest on October 5 when the Allied troops were still landing in Saloniki. The king had strong arguments to justify his stand. Britain and France had failed at the Straits, Russia was battered to helplessness, Bulgaria was about to join the Central Powers, while Mackensen was poised along the Danube with a powerful army. Under these circumstances, Constantine argued, any policy other than neutrality was sheer suicide.

Regardless of the merits of the king's action, the fact remains that it made effective aid to the Serbians almost impossible. The Allies had counted heavily on the Greek army to reinforce their own army that they had planned to send forth from Saloniki to rescue the Serbs. Now the Greeks were unavailable and the rescue plan unfeasible.

To make matters worse, the Allies were divided as to whether the Saloniki foothold should be maintained. The French strongly favored it while the British just as strongly wished to give it up on the ground that it was too late to give effective aid to the Serbians. As is usual in such cases, the outcome was an ineffectual and worthless compromise. The Saloniki front was maintained but not enough troops were provided to bolster the Serbians.

On October 5 news of the Saloniki landings reached General Mackensen, commander of the Austro-German army gathered along the Danube. The next day he gave the order to advance. The position of the defending Serbs was quite untenable. Because of the Bulgarian threat on their flank they had stretched out their forces thinly along a six-hundred-mile line on their northern and eastern frontiers. The Serbians nevertheless fought gallantly in the vain hope that help would come from Saloniki if they slowed down the enemy's advance. They resisted fiercely in Belgrade, fighting the invaders street by street for three days before surrendering the capital. Then the Bulgarians attacked from the east on October 14. Advancing rapidly in the southern sector, they cut the all-important Belgrade-Saloniki railroad and severed Serbia from her newly acquired Macedonian territories. General Sarrail, who commanded the Allied forces at Saloniki, attempted to come to the rescue. But he had only twenty thousand men available at this time, so the Bulgars were able to stop him and to push him back into Greek territory.

The Serbians now were alone, outnumbered in manpower and outweighed in artillery. Germans, Austrians, and Bulgarians moved forward simultaneously for the kill. The Serbians fought desperate delaying actions, always managing to escape encirclement and to continue the struggle. On November 5 the Bulgarians took Nish and effected a junction with Mackensen's troops. But the Serbs again slipped out and retreated toward Kosovo, where, in 1389, their medieval empire had been destroyed by the Turks. After more than five hundred years the Serbians once more were fighting for national existence on the same historic Kosovo field.

As the enemy armies were drawing in, the Serbians had to decide upon one of three possible courses that were open to them: they could surrender and sign a separate peace; they could fight on defiantly to the end, as their ancestors had done before them; or they could attempt a retreat through the mountains of Montenegro and Albania to the Adriatic coast, where Allied shipping could rescue the survivors. The third course was chosen; whereupon ensued one of the great epics of World War I.

The Serbian retreat to the Adriatic coast has been compared to the famous marches of Xenophon and Napoleon. Preceded by thousands of refugees and with winter closing in, the Serbian army plunged into the mountains that separated them from the Adriatic ports. Enemy bombing planes attacked from above and hostile Albanians harassed those detachments that struggled through their lands. But the worst enemy was hunger. Starvation, together with cold, disease, and enemy action, took a toll of twenty thousand soldiers and countless refugees.

The miserable survivors reached Scutari, fled on to Durazzo with the Austrians on their heels, and finally reached safety at Valona. From there a fleet of Allied ships transported them to Corfu. By April 15, 1916, the retreat was over. And by July of the same year a Serbian army of 125,000 rested and re-equipped veterans was ready to return to the front. The homeland was under enemy occupation but the Serbian cause was not lost.

RUMANIAN INTERVENTION

The outstanding event in the Balkans in 1916 was the intervention of Rumania on the side of the Entente. Rumania had been allied with Germany and Austria since the secret treaty of 1883. But the plight of the three million Rumanians in Transylvania had aroused such strong feeling against the Dual Monarchy that it was no surprise when the Rumanian government proclaimed its neutrality on August 3, 1914. Indeed, the Austrian minister in Bucharest reported that there were only two parties left in Rumania—those who believed in immediate war against Austria and those ("our friends") who favored delay because the Monarchy had not yet been beaten.

After her declaration of neutrality Rumania was courted by both sides. The Allies offered Transylvania while the Central Powers promised Bessarabia. The Rumanian premier Ionel Bratianu, preferred to remain neutral until the outcome of the war became more certain. In the meantime his country sold vast quantities of food to the Central Powers at handsome profits. In the spring of 1915 Bratianu almost joined the Allies, having extracted a high price—Bukovina, Transylvania, and the Banat of Temesvar. He was about to follow the example of Italy and abandon his neutrality when news arrived of the catastrophic Russian defeats in Galicia. Bratianu had not committed himself as far as the Italians, so he was able to draw back and remain on the side lines.

The following year Bratianu was impressed by the failure of the Germans to take Verdun and by the unexpected Russian victories in Bukovina. He decided that the right moment had come, so on August 18, 1916, he joined the Allies with the same territories pledged to him as had been in the year before. "Today it is given to us," proclaimed King Ferdinand to his people, "to assure unshakeably and in its fulness the work momentarily realized by Michael the Brave—the union of the Rumanians on both sides of the Carpathians." [19]

From the military viewpoint the Rumanians should have acted in June when the Russian offensive was still under way. But they decided to wait until their harvest had been gathered. Even then they proved to be very inadequately prepared for serious war. At the outset they enjoyed a victorious march into Transylvania, which was lightly defended. But this advance turned out to be a serious strategic blunder. The Central Powers decided to make Rumania an object lesson for other neutrals who might be contemplating throwing in their lot with the Allies. Austro-German forces counterattacked in Transylvania while German, Bulgarian, and Turkish forces under Mackensen pushed up from the Dobruja.

Meanwhile the Allied army at Saloniki was too weak to make a serious diversion from that quarter, while the Russian offensive in Bukovina had petered out. Thus the Central Powers were left free to strike down the hapless Rumanians from all sides. Within three months the Rumanian armies were crushed. On December 6, 1916, Bucharest fell to the enemy. By mid-January two thirds of Rumania was occupied, including the important wheat- and oil-producing areas.

Meanwhile, the defeat of Russia and the outbreak of revolution in that country had left Rumania completely isolated from her Western allies. Thus when the Bolsheviks were forced to sign the Brest-Litovsk Treaty with the Central Powers on March 3, 1918, the Rumanians had no alternative but to follow suit and accept the Treaty of Bucharest on May 7 of the same year. By its terms they ceded the Dobruja to Bulgaria and the Carpathian passes to Austria-Hungary. Also, they undertook to pay the expenses of an enemy army of occupation, to grant rights of military transport through their territory, and to lease their oil wells to the Germans for ninety years.

By one of the strangest quirks of the war, the Rumanians were able to gain immediate compensation for the losses and humiliations imposed by the Bucharest Treaty. The compensation consisted of the province of Bessarabia, which had been a part of the Russian Empire since the earlier Bucharest Treaty of 1812. The circumstances of this territorial shift remain a controversial issue to the present. Bessarabia had fallen into a state of anarchy following the collapse of the tsarist regime in February, 1917. By the middle of the year the peasants began to seize land and by the end of the year they had taken over about two thirds of the landed property. Meanwhile, two political currents had emerged, a nationalist Moldavian that looked to Bucharest, and an agrarian-revolutionary that was hostile to Rumania as a land dominated by boyars. The separatism of the Moldavians was accentuated by the advent of the Bolshevik regime, with its revolutionary doctrines and centralized administration. The Moldavians convoked a national council or Sfat, which announced on December 2, 1917, the formation of a Democratic Moldavian Republic as a self-governing unit in the Federative Democratic Russian Republic.

It soon became apparent that the new republic was incapable of standing on its own feet, menaced as it was by the Ukrainian Republic recently formed under German auspices, and by Bolsheviks of both the Russian and native varieties. In fact, soviets were established in several cities and were effectively challenging the Sfat's authority. Under these circumstances the Sfat on April 9, 1918, voted—86 to 3, with 36 delegates abstaining—in favor of union with Rumania. The controversy concerning the annexation of Bessarabia by Rumania has centered on this vote of the Sfat. The Soviet thesis is that the Sfat was not representative, that its vote did not reflect the wishes of the people, and that it was merely the tool of the big landlords who used it against the soviets, which truly represented the peasant masses. The high number of abstentions does suggest that the vote was scarcely an ideal referendum, especially in view of the presence of Rumanian troops, which had entered the province in January at the request of the Sfat. In any case, Rumania acquired Bessarabia, thus presenting the altogether unique case of a country, overwhelmingly defeated in war, extending her territory at the expense of one of her own allies. The Soviet government refused to recognize the loss of Bessarabia, and the province became a critical issue between Russia and Rumania during the entire period between the two world wars.

GREEK INTERVENTION

Meanwhile, Greece was being forced to take up arms by blatant Allied pressure. Since the beginning of the war the question of neutrality or intervention had been a burning issue in that country. During the last days of July, 1914, when it seemed that the war would be localized, King Constantine and Premier Venizelos agreed that Greece should remain neutral. The 1913 alliance with Serbia had provided for mutual aid only in the case of unprovoked aggression. The Greek leaders were agreed that Serbia had been guilty of "provocative conduct" and that there was no obligation to give aid. They let it be known, however, that if Bulgaria attacked Serbia, Greece would go to the assistance of her ally.

Once the war became general, the kaiser brought strong pressure on King Constantine to join the Central Powers. He appealed to him "as a comrade, as a German marshal . . . and as a brother-in-law, to march together, hand in hand, against the common enemy, Slavism." The kaiser went so far as to threaten that if Greece did not do this, "then there will be a complete break between Greece and the [German] Empire." In his reply of August 7 Constantine explained and defended his neutrality position to which he adhered throughout the war. "The Emperor knows that my personal sympathies and my political views draw me to his side. . . . After mature reflection, however, it is impossible for me to see how I could be useful to him, if I mobilized my army immediately. The Mediterranean is at the mercy of the united fleets of England and France. . . . Without being able to be useful to him in anything, we should be wiped off the map. I am compelled to think that neutrality is forced upon us. . . ." [20]

Greece was also courted by the Entente Powers, which had the enthusiastic backing of Premier Venizelos. The latter was convinced that the Allies would win the war in a short time. As early as August 18 he prophesied to his cabinet that the Allies would crush the Central Powers within three weeks and that Greece should act immediately if she wished to profit from the war. Although the cabinet was divided, Venizelos called on the Allied ministers that very afternoon and offered them Greek aid without asking for any compensations. This unprecedented generosity led the Allies to suspect that Venizelos' motive was to gain their support for an attack upon Turkey. And since the Allies at this date had hopes of keeping Turkey neutral, they turned down the Greek premier.

Venizelos next tried to embroil Greece during the Dardanelles expedition. The thunder of Allied cannon at the Straits revived the age-old dream of a new Greek empire based upon St. Sophia and Constantinople. Venizelos persuaded the crown council to give him a free hand in negotiating with the Entente. But the Greek general staff was strongly opposed to intervention on the grounds that an attack upon the Straits or Constantinople would leave Greece vulnerable to a flank attack by Bulgaria. Venizelos nevertheless offered on March 5, 1915, to provide Greek military units for use in the Dardanelles campaign. He added that "without having any political views on Constantinople and the Straits, we have such interests of a moral and commercial order there that we could not be disinterested in their fate." [21]

Venizelos' effort at intervention was again frustrated. As noted earlier in the chapter, Russia categorically refused to allow the Greeks to participate in the action against Constantinople and the Straits because she would brook no competition in that region. Furthermore, King Constantine now repudiated Venizelos' offer, having been swayed apparently by the arguments of his military advisers and by the representations of the Russian minister. Venizelos had no choice but to resign (March 6), and a new government that was less favorable to the Entente took office.

Later in the year, when Bulgaria's intervention was imminent, Serbia appealed to Greece for aid. We saw earlier in this chapter that Venizelos, who had resumed the premiership in the interval, wished to respond to their appeal. He invited the Allies to land troops at Saloniki but he was unable to persuade the king to go as far as actual intervention. So on October 5, 1916, Venizelos once more resigned and Greece continued to remain neutral.

By this time the relations between king and premier had become embittered, particularly because Venizelos had the support of the majority in the chamber for his foreign policy. He accused the king of authoritarianism and constitutional irresponsibility, and he refused to participate in the election of December 19, 1916. This decision allowed the Royalist party supporting Constantine to win a majority. But more important than this, Venizelos' boycott drove his Liberal party into extraparliamentary opposition and thereby exacerbated the constitutional conflict into a veritable revolutionary situation.

Meanwhile the British and French governments had come to the conclusion that the security of their forces in the Saloniki area required a new regime in Athens. Two actions of the royalist cabinet goaded the Allies to take extreme measures. One was its refusal to permit the Serbian army, which had re-formed in Corfu after its great retreat, to cross Greek territory to the Saloniki front. The other was its surrender to the Bulgarians, without any attempt at resistance, of the strategic Fort Rupel commanding the entrance to the Struma Valley. The Allies retaliated by demanding on June 21 that the chamber be dissolved, that a new cabinet be formed, that the Greek army be reduced to a peace footing, and that certain obnoxious police officials be removed. Rarely had an independent country been subjected to such humiliating treatment. And this was only the beginning. Greece, as a contemporary observer remarked, had become a "public place," in which each side felt free to act as it wished.

In September, 1916, a German-Bulgarian force occupied Kavalla and sent its garrison of eight thousand Greek soldiers to Germany for internment. This convinced Venizelos that nothing short of a revolution could force a change in Greek policy. On September 25 he went to his native Crete, where he proclaimed, amid wild enthusiasm, a revolutionary movement to bring Greece into the war. From Crete he made a triumphal tour of the islands, which joined his cause wholeheartedly. On October 9 he landed at Saloniki where, with popular acclaim, he established his provisional government.

The Allies recognized the new government and took various high-handed measures to eliminate the king. The climax came on November 30, when they landed troops in Piraeus to compel the king to surrender certain arms. These troops were fired upon by Greek forces as they were marching on the capital and were forced to return to their ships. The Allies retaliated by imposing a blockade and forcing Constantine to withdraw his army to the Peloponnesus. Then the entry of the United States into the war in April, 1917, left the Allies free to take the final steps. Hitherto they had held back because of concern for American public opinion. But now that the United States was in the same camp, the Allies felt free to present an ultimatum on June 11, 1917. They gave Constantine the alternative of abdication within twenty-four hours or bombardment of Athens. He chose abdication and left for Switzerland, leaving as his successor his second son, Alexander. On June 27 Venizelos became premier and on July 2 he formally brought Greece into the war on the Allied side.

But the cost was a country divided by a bitter feud whose evil effects were to be felt until World War II and beyond. The intensity of the emotions aroused is illustrated by an event that occurred in Athens on December 26, 1916. On that day the Archbishop of Athens, standing on a cairn of stones, performed the medieval rite of excommunication. Eight bishops standing around him, representing royalist Greece, chanted: "Cursed be Eleutherios Venizelos who imprisons priests and who plots against his king and his country." Each participant cried, "Cursed be he," and cast a stone upon the cairn. Sixty thousand Athenians took part in this ceremony, each bringing his stone and his curse.

ALLIED VICTORY

In September, 1918, a year after Greece's entry into the war, the Allies began their long-awaited offensive from their Saloniki base. The commander, Franchet d'Esperey, had at his disposal a cosmopolitan army of twenty-eight divisions: nine Greek, eight French, six Serbian, four British, and one Italian. The Bulgarians were of about equal strength in men and guns but they were outnumbered in the air. More important, they were thoroughly demoralized by this time. Bad harvests and insufficient food had undermined civilian morale, while the soldiers hated the Germans, who had taken over the key posts and who were better fed and clothed than they. In fact, thousands of Bulgarian soldiers had deserted in the summer of 1918 and could not be forced back to the colors.

The Allied offensive began on September 15. The Serbian army and a French division spearheaded the attack, overrunning strong enemy positions west of the Vardar River. The Serbs fought savagely, wreaking vengeance for what they had suffered in 1915. They pierced three enemy defense lines and rolled back German reinforcements that were hurried to the front. On September 18 British and Greek divisions attacked further to the east and broke through after stubborn fighting. On September 21 the Allies launched still another offensive, this time in the west in the Monastir (Bitolj) region. The Bulgarian and German troops now were in full retreat, with British air units inflicting heavy losses in the Vardar and Struma valleys.

The Bulgarians now realized that defeat was inevitable sooner or later. Being desperately anxious to avoid invasion of their home territory by Serbs and Greeks, the Bulgarians decided to surrender at once. After brief negotiations they signed an armistice with Franchet d'Esperey on September 29. The Bulgarian collapse had a decisive effect on the course of the whole war because Germany and Austria-Hungary no longer had the reserves needed to organize a new defense line on the Danube. Thus Ludendorff and Hindenburg officially notified the German civilian authorities on October 3 that "as a result of the collapse of the Macedonian front, and of the weakening of our reserves in the West, which this has necessitated . . . there appears to be now no possibility, to the best of human judgement, of winning peace from our enemies by force of arms. . . . in these circumstances the only right course is to bring the war to a close. . . ." [22]

The Serbs exploited to the full the strategic opportunities afforded by Bulgaria's downfall. They pressed onward tirelessly, pursuing the Germans and Austrians northward. On October 12 they recaptured Nish and on November 1 they entered Belgrade. Within six weeks they had swept the country clear of its enemies from border to border.

Austria-Hungary was now being battered from all sides—in the west by the Italians, in the south by the Serbians, and in the east by the Rumanians, who re-entered the war on November 10. At the same time the various subject peoples were taking matters into their own hands, proclaiming their independence from Hapsburg rule. Finally, on November 3 Austria-Hungary concluded an armistice with the Italians, and on November 13 Hungary alone signed a separate armistice with Serbian and French commanders on the Danube. In this manner the historic enemy of the South Slavs was humbled and torn apart.

Meanwhile, the other great empires of Eastern Europe were also disintegrating. In Russia the Romanovs were gone and the country was torn by civil war and intervention. The Ottoman Empire was crumbling before attacks in Mesopotamia and Palestine by British, Indian, Australian, New Zealand,

and Arab forces. Thus in these last months of 1918 whole centuries of past history were being reversed. The conquests of Mohammed and Suvorov and Prince Eugene were being undone irresistibly and irrevocably. At long last there was being realized the visionary slogan, "The Balkans for the People of the Balkans." Out of the ruins of the old empires arose the sturdy forms of new states: Yugoslavia—the home of the South Slavs; Greater Rumania— greater even than Michael the Brave's short-lived creation; a new Albania— for the first time since Skanderbeg; a larger Greece—though not measuring up to the fantasy of the Megale Idea; and finally Bulgaria—the black sheep, shorn once more, and left embittered and revisionist.

30. Peace Settlement: 1918–1923

WHEN WORLD WAR I had ended and the armistice agreements had been concluded, there arose the problem of how to proceed with the peace settlement. After long deliberation the Allied leaders decided in favor of separate treaties with the enemy states rather than one general agreement. But a considerable time elapsed before any of the treaties could be concluded. The reason was that the war had been extraordinarily destructive of state structures and of power relationships. This was especially true in Central and Eastern Europe, where four great empires had disappeared— the German, the Austro-Hungarian, the Russian, and the Turkish.

Amid such wreckage it proved extremely difficult to restore some semblance of order and to draw new frontiers. The war nominally ended in 1918 but hostilities continued to flare up sporadically throughout the Continent during the next five years. In the Balkans alone, the Yugoslavs clashed with the Austrians over Carinthia and with the Italians over Fiume; the Rumanians occupied Bessarabia and beat back the Russians and the Ukrainians; and Greeks and Turks fought a full-scale war in Asia Minor for three years. Eventually the fighting ceased and peace treaties were negotiated— the Versailles Treaty with Germany (June 28, 1919), the Saint-Germain Treaty with Austria (September 10, 1919), the Trianon Treaty with Hungary (March 22, 1919), the Neuilly Treaty with Bulgaria (November 27, 1919), and the Sèvres Treaty with Turkey (August 20, 1920).

The last treaty proved to be the only one that could not be enforced. Oddly enough, Turkey alone of the Central Powers was able to repudiate the terms imposed by the victorious Allies. She defeated a Greek army in Asia Minor, successfully defied the war-weary Western powers, and in the end won a more favorable settlement—the Lausanne Treaty of July 24, 1923. It was not until that date, then, that World War I came to a close in the Balkans. And it should be remembered that the war had begun in the peninsula, for all practical purposes, in 1912 with the outbreak of the first Balkan War.

571

Thus the Balkan states were engaged in hostilities almost continuously for over a decade. And the outcome, as we shall see, was a peninsula that was altogether different in 1923 from what it had been in 1912 or 1914.

THE OLD ORDER PASSES

The downfall of ancient empires during the course of World War I made possible the establishment of a new order in the Balkan Peninsula. The collapse of the tsarist regime enabled Rumania to acquire the province of Bessarabia. Similarly, the disintegration of the Ottoman Empire led the new Turkish Republic to accept as final the loss of most of European Turkey. But most important, so far as the Balkan states were concerned, was the disappearance of the Hapsburg Empire. This great event released vast territories to the north of the Danube and made possible the formation of Greater Rumania and the new state of the South Slavs—the Kingdom of the Serbs, Croats, and Slovenes, in 1929 renamed Yugoslavia, the name by which this country is now known and the name which will be generally used henceforth in this text.

The partitioning of the Hapsburg Empire has frequently been criticized as a grave error that brought only grief and peril to the Continent of Europe. Winston Churchill expressed this viewpoint in his usual forceful manner.

The . . . cardinal tragedy was the complete break-up of the Austro-Hungarian Empire by the Treaties of St.-Germain and Trianon. For centuries this surviving embodiment of the Holy Roman Empire had afforded a common life, with advantages in trade and security, to a large number of peoples, none of whom in our own time had the strength or vitality to stand by themselves in the face of pressure from a revivified Germany or Russia. All these races wished to break away from the federal or imperial structure, and to encourage their desires was deemed a liberal policy. The Balkanization of Southeastern Europe proceeded apace, with the consequent relative aggrandisement of Prussia and the German Reich, which, though tired and war-scarred, was intact and locally overwhelming. There is not one of the peoples or provinces that constituted the Empire of the Hapsburgs to whom gaining their independence has not brought the tortures which ancient poets and theologians had reserved for the damned.[1]

Churchill is certainly justified in pointing out that the principle of self-determination of peoples did not usher in the millenium that some idealists had naïvely expected. But he is quite unjustified in attributing the breakup of the Austro-Hungarian Empire to the diplomats who negotiated the Saint-Germain and Trianon treaties. The fact is that the empire had dissolved long before the diplomats began their deliberations. They merely gave legal recognition to a *fait accompli* and also delineated frontiers whose main course had been determined many months earlier by revolutionary upheavals.

It might be argued that the peacemakers should have resisted rather than accepted the desire of the former Hapsburg subjects for national independence. But Central and Eastern Europe were so devastated and exhausted, and so infected with the virus of Bolshevism, that it never occurred to the diplomats to undertake so hazardous a task as to combat both revolutionary nationalism and revolutionary Bolshevism. And if they had been so rash as to assume this task there is no reason to assume that they would have been more successful in curbing South Slav or Rumanian nationalism than they were with Turkish nationalism.

A review of the developments in Central and Eastern Europe during these years will demonstrate that the diplomats at Saint-Germain and Trianon had little to do with the breakup of the Hapsburg Empire or with the formation of the new Yugoslavia and Rumania. The natural starting point from which to trace the unfolding of these momentous developments is the death of Emperor Francis Joseph on November 21, 1916. This marked the beginning of the end of the empire over which Francis Joseph had ruled since the revolutions of 1848. His successor was Emperor Charles, a young man of high character and ideals, but lacking in balance and experience. Even without these failings the new ruler would have had little chance of coping with the overwhelming odds that he faced. His foreign minister, Count Ottokar Czernin, informed him early in April, 1917, that "another winter campaign would be absolutely out of the question: in other words, that in the summer or late autumn an end must be put to the war at all costs." [2]

Charles attempted to meet the growing crisis by calling a meeting of the Austrian parliament for May 30, 1917. When the representatives of the South Slavs and Czechs and other nationalities met in Vienna they expressed not their loyalty to the monarchy but rather their determination to win full independence. And in Hungary the resignation of the strong-man premier, Count Stephen Tisza, reflected the crumbling of the old imperial order.

During the following year Count Czernin's prophecy of impending disaster was dramatically fulfilled. The empire began to crumble under the combined pressures of military defeat, economic distress, and national separatism. On October 7, 1918, the Austro-Hungarian leaders applied for an armistice on the basis of Wilson's Fourteen Points. While awaiting the answer, Emperor Charles issued a manifesto on October 16 transforming Austria into a federative state. The representatives of each national group in the Austrian Reichstag were to withdraw and form national councils.

This far-reaching concession failed to halt the process of disintegration in Austria. The national leaders in the Reichstag wanted independence rather than federation. Accordingly, they formed national councils and then took a step further and severed the ties with Vienna. The Czechs proclaimed their independence in Prague, the Germans did likewise in Vienna, while the South Slavs in the Austrian part of the empire joined with their brothers under Hungarian rule in declaring for union with Belgrade.

The same development occurred in the Hungarian part of the empire. The liberal aristocrat, Count Michael Karolyi, took office on October 31, 1918, with the hope of preserving Hungary as a federative state. He appointed as minister of nationalities Professor Oscar Jaszi, a well-known champion of the subject peoples. Jaszi offered the nationalities full autonomy as the basis for a new Danubian confederation of free peoples. But this offer, which would have been gratefully accepted five years earlier, was now unhesitatingly rejected. The Rumanians of Transylvania declared for independence and then union with Bucharest. Likewise, the Croatian Diet passed a resolution on October 29 that "Dalmatia, Croatia and Slavonia with Fiume are . . . a State completely independent of Hungary and Austria and . . . join the common national and sovereign State of the Slovenes, Croats and Serbs. . . ." [3] No one offered resistance to the national groups, and thus the Hapsburg Empire passed into history quietly and anticlimactically.

This sequence of events shows that the subject nationalities rejected both the old Hapsburg Empire and the new democratic federation proposed by Austrian and Hungarian liberals. However desirable it might have been for the Hapsburg Empire to have been preserved in one form or another, the fact remains that it completely lacked any popular support upon which it could have been based. It follows inescapably that the Hapsburg Empire was the victim not of shortsighted diplomats but rather of triumphant nationalism which now was coming into its own throughout Central and Eastern Europe.

SAINT-GERMAIN TREATY

The Saint-German Treaty was signed on September 10, 1919, after serious conflicts that threatened at one point to wreck the Peace Conference. The conflicts arose among the Allied Powers themselves over the question of how the Austrian possessions should be divided. The sharpest clash was that between Italy on the one hand, and Serbia and the Hapsburg South Slavs on the other. The origins of this clash go back to the secret Treaty of London of April 26, 1915, by which Italy, in return for entering the war, was promised the Trentino, Istria, Dalmatia, the Adriatic islands, and lands or spheres of influence in Albania, Asia Minor, and Africa. These territories included at least 250,000 Germans and 500,000 South Slavs.

The implementation of this treaty was obstructed by certain developments that occurred during the course of the war. The most important of these was the Yugoslav movement among the South Slavs in the Hapsburg Empire. Several leaders of these South Slavs fled to Rome soon after the beginning of the war and organized themselves as the Yugoslav Committee, with a Dalmatian, Dr. Ante Trumbich, as their president. The Italians were openly hostile to the Committee, fearing that it would lead to the establishment of a strong Slavic power in the Adriatic. Accordingly, the Committee moved its headquarters to London, where it carried on propaganda in behalf of a postwar federal South Slav state.

We shall see in Chapter 32 that Premier Pashich of Serbia was not altogether happy about this Yugoslav movement. He and other Serbian leaders were undecided whether to strive for a greater Serbia or a Yugoslav state. This fundamental question remained unresolved during the war period despite official proclamations and agreements. It persisted into the postwar years, wracking the new state throughout its existence.

Pashich finally decided to cooperate with the Yugoslav Committee, at least for the time being. One reason for his decision was the fall of the tsarist regime, which had supported him strongly in the past. Another reason was the intervention of the United States, which generally favored the Yugoslav idea. Accordingly, Pashich and the leaders of the Yugoslav Committee on July 20, 1917, signed the Declaration of Corfu. This document stated that all the South Slavs were one people and that, in accordance with the principle of self-determination, they wished to be united at the end of the war into one state. This state, to be called the Kingdom of the Serbs, Croats, and Slovenes, was to be a constitutional monarchy under the Karageorgevich dynasty. Freedom of religion would be guaranteed, the Cyrillic and Latin alphabets would be equally acceptable, and all citizens would be equal before the law. But on the crucial question of centralism versus federalism (or Pan-Serbism versus Yugoslavism), the declaration was deliberately vague because no agreement had proved possible. Nevertheless, the Declaration served its purpose of presenting a solid front to the outside world, and particularly to the Italians.

The latter were also now willing to cooperate, at least formally, with the Yugoslavs. They were persuaded in part by the same factors that had influenced Pashich. The Italians also hoped that a gesture toward Yugoslavism would soften the Croatian regiments which were still fighting stoutly in the Alps under the Hapsburg flag. Accordingly, the unofficial Congress of Oppressed Nationalities was allowed to meet in Rome and to proclaim the unofficial Pact of Rome in April, 1918. This document asserted the right of subject peoples, and particularly of Italians and Yugoslavs, to national unity and independence on the basis of self-determination. More binding was an official Italian government statement (September 8, 1918) to the effect that "Italy considers that the movement of the Yugoslav people for independence and for the constitution of a free state corresponds to the principles for which the Allies are fighting and to the aims of a just and lasting peace." [4] These Italian commitments, together with similar ones by the Western powers, contributed substantially to the revolutionary Yugoslav movement within the Hapsburg Empire. The climax came, as we have seen, on October 29 when the Croatian Diet adopted the resolution for incorporation in a unified South Slav state.

In the light of these wartime developments it is understandable that serious trouble should have ensued when the Italians at the Peace Conference demanded not only what they had been promised by the London Treaty but even more. They demanded the port of Fiume in addition to the other Adriatic territories listed in the Treaty of London. The Yugoslavs vehemently opposed the cession of Fiume. They claimed that the disputed territory was overwhelmingly Yugoslav in population and pointed out that if it was given to Italy they would be deprived of the only economic outlet available to them on the Adriatic. Thus Italy and the new Yugoslavia collided squarely on the issue of Fiume.

When the question was discussed at the Paris Peace Conference, President Wilson strongly supported the Yugoslavs. His Fourteen Points had stipulated that the Italian frontiers should be drawn "along clearly recognizable lines of nationality." Wilson, under pressure from the British and French, waived this principle in the case of the 250,000 Germans in the Tyrol. He also agreed to allot Trieste to Italy but he resolutely refused to do likewise with Fiume. A deadlock ensued, whereupon Wilson made his famous appeal to the Italian people over the head of their representative, Vittorio Orlando. The Italian chamber gave Orlando a ten-to-one vote of confidence and the deadlock continued. Finally, it was agreed that both the Saint-Germain and the Trianon treaties should include clauses assigning all the disputed territories to the Allies to be allotted at a later date.

When Italy and Yugoslavia resumed negotiations, the latter country was more inclined to yield because of the repudiation of Wilson's policies in the November, 1920, presidential election. Finally, on the twelfth of that month the Treaty of Rapallo was signed. It awarded to Italy more islands and a larger portion of Istria than Wilson had been willing to concede. In return Italy renounced her claims to Dalmatia, and Fiume was made an independent state. The latter provision was never enforced because the flamboyant D'Annunzio made his famous coup in Fiume on September 12, 1919, and established himself as dictator of the city. He was later forced to leave Fiume, but Italian troops took his place and remained the *de facto* occupants while negotiations dragged on year after year. At length a new Italo-Yugoslav Treaty of January 27, 1924, ceded Fiume to Italy but its suburb, Susak (Porto Barros), to Yugoslavia. This settlement proved to be economically absurd. Yugoslavia spent large sums to develop the naturally inferior Susak, while Fiume, with its superior facilities, suffered a disastrous decline.

In conclusion, the Saint-Germain Treaty and the later agreements left Austria with only a little over one quarter of her prewar territory. The remainder was divided among several states. In the north, Galicia and a part of Silesia went to Poland, and Bohemia and Moravia to Czechoslovakia. As for the Balkan territories of Austria, they were distributed as follows: Bukovina to Rumania; the Tyrol, a part of Istria, and bits of other provinces to Italy; and the remainder of Istria, Carinthia, Carniola, Dalmatia, and a part of Styria to Yugoslavia. The Trianon Treaty, to which we now turn, changed the map of the Balkans much more radically because Hungary's Balkan possessions were far more extensive than those of Austria.

TRIANON TREATY

In Hungary the liberal Count Michael Karolyi had taken office on October 31, 1918. His aim was to preserve the country's integrity by reorganizing it along democratic federal lines. But he was frustrated by the uncompromising demand of the subject nationalities for complete independence. And behind the nationalities stood the new Yugoslav and Rumanian states determined to annex as large portions of Hungary as possible. The Serbian army crossed the Danube and occupied a large section of southern Hungary. The Rumanians, who had been forced to sign a separate treaty in 1917, now re-entered the war on November 9, 1918. Their forces poured into Transylvania, and the Peace Conference supported them by ordering Hungary to withdraw her troops from the territories claimed by the Rumanians. At the same time the Czechoslovak army was advancing into Hungarian territory from the north.

Karolyi at this point resigned in despair and turned over the government to a coalition of Socialists and Communists headed by Bela Kun. The new regime represented partly a social revolution and partly a nationalist Hungarian protest against foreign invasion. Bela Kun not only appointed People's Commissars and proclaimed a Soviet Republic, but also sent forces to stop the advancing Rumanian and Czechoslovak armies. The attempt failed and the victorious Rumanians entered Budapest and occupied and looted the capital between August 8 and November 14, 1919. When they evacuated the city a new government was formed representing the old conservative elements and headed by Admiral Horthy.

With the danger of communism on the Danube ended, the Allies invited the Horthy regime on December 1, 1919, to send delegates to Paris to conclude a peace. The delegates tried to minimize the loss of territory by demanding plebiscites in all disputed regions. The Allies replied on May 6, 1920, that plebiscites were superfluous because they "would not give results substantially different from those at which they had arrived after a minute study of the ethnographic conditions and national aspirations. The wish of the peoples was expressed in October and November 1918 when the Dual Monarchy disappeared under the blows inflicted by the Powers, and when long-oppressed populations welcomed their Rumanian, Yugo-slav, and Czecho-Slovak brethren." [5]

The Hungarians had no alternative but to submit, and on June 4, 1920, they signed the Trianon Treaty. In the north they ceded the provinces of Slovakia and Ruthenia to the new Czechoslovak state. In the Balkans they surrendered extensive territories to both Yugoslavia and Rumania. Yugoslavia received Croatia and Slavonia without any dispute. This transfer had been prepared by the activities of the Yugoslav Committee during the war and by the vote of the Croatian Diet on October 29, 1918.*

Yugoslavia also received from Hungary a triangular piece of the Hungarian plain to the north of the Danube. This consisted of three districts— Baranja, Bachka, and the Banat—and was given the title of the Voivodina, or Duchy, after being incorporated in Yugoslavia. The frontiers of the Voivodina were drawn further to the north than the ethnic distribution of the Serbs warranted. As a result, about 200,000 Magyars found themselves under Yugoslav rule. The explanation is to be found in strategic considerations. A strictly ethnic line would have run so close to Belgrade that it would have left the capital almost as vulnerable as it had been before the war.

In the eastern portion of the Voivodina, that is, in the Banat, the Serbi-

* See Chapter 32.

ans came into conflict with the Rumanians. The latter had been promised the entire Banat in the secret 1916 treaty under which they entered the war. But the Allies now maintained that the treaty had become invalid because Rumania had signed a separate peace with the Central Powers in 1917. Furthermore, the Serbians claimed the western part of the Banat on justifiable ethnic grounds. As a matter of fact, the area was populated by such a mixture of Serbs, Magyars, Germans, and Rumanians that it was impossible to draw a frontier line that would not leave considerable minorities on either side. In the end, the frontier was adjusted in such a way as to balance the number of Serbians awarded to Rumania against the number of Rumanians awarded to Yugoslavia. The result was that the western third of the Banat went to Yugoslavia and the remainder to Rumania.

Rumania acquired from Hungary the province of Transylvania as well as a portion of the Banat. There was no serious question about Transylvania because the Rumanians of that province had rejected all offers of autonomy and had declared in favor of union with Bucharest. Furthermore, Rumanian troops had already occupied Transylvania, so that the Trianon Treaty merely gave legal recognition to a *fait accompli*. In addition to the acquisition of these territories from Hungary, as noted earlier, Rumania also obtained Bukovina from Austria and Bessarabia from Russia.

The net result of the Trianon Treaty was that Hungary was left with 28.6 per cent of her former territory. The remainder had been divided as follows: 31.5 per cent to Rumania (Transylvania and two thirds of the Banat); 19.6 per cent to Yugoslavia (Croatia, Slavonia, and one third of the Banat); and 18.9 per cent to Czechoslovakia (Slovakia and Ruthenia). The remaining 1.4 per cent consisted of miniscule cessions to Austria, Poland, and Italy, the latter being the Fiume city area.

NEUILLY TREATY

Military defeat forced far-reaching changes upon Bulgaria as well as upon the other Central Powers. We saw in the last chapter that King Ferdinand and Premier Radoslavov did not have enthusiastic popular backing when they took the country into the war. As the fighting dragged on, discontent spread widely, particularly because of the conduct of the German allies. The latter had between 16,000 and 18,000 men stationed on the Bulgarian front, but by various means they drew rations for over 100,000 men, thus stripping the country of foodstuffs. Furthermore, the Germans refused to allow Bulgaria to occupy northern Dobruja in 1916, when it was taken from Rumania, and set up instead a condominium. Consequently, popular antipathy grew against the Central Powers and against Ferdinand and Radoslavov, who had ranged the country on their side.

In 1918 Bulgaria began to suffer military reverses for the first time after the easy victories following intervention. Public unrest reached such proportions that Ferdinand felt constrained to make some concessions. On June 21, 1918, he dismissed the Radoslavov ministry and appointed in its place a coalition cabinet of Democrats and Liberals headed by Alexander Malinov, head of the former party. As described in Chapter 29, the crisis came in mid-September, 1918, when the front crumbled and the demoralized troops began deserting. On September 29 Premier Malinov accepted an armistice. Four days earlier Ferdinand had released the Agrarian party leader, Alexander Stambuliski, from prison, where he had been sent in 1915 because of his opposition to intervention. Ferdinand hoped that Stambuliski would use his influence to calm the mutinous troops and check the disintegration of the army. Instead, Stambuliski proclaimed a republic on September 27 and marched on Sofia at the head of the disaffected soldiers. He was defeated by combined loyalist and German forces and compelled to go into hiding.

Nevertheless Ferdinand's position by this time had become patently untenable. The national catastrophe had completely discredited both him and his policies. On the insistence of the party leaders he abdicated on October 4 and made his way to Germany, where he was soon joined by Radoslavov. Ferdinand was succeeded by his twenty-four-year-old son, who ascended the throne as Boris III. Thus ended the reign of an able but utterly unscrupulous and inordinately ambitious ruler who sought to make Bulgaria great in order to satisfy his own megalomania but who instead brought disaster upon himself and upon his country.

On November 19, 1918, the Malinov cabinet gave way to a coalition government including the comparatively radical Agrarians and Socialists as well as the traditional party leaders. Elections held on August 17, 1919, reflected the drastic changes in the political balance that had occurred during the course of the war. The Agrarians received one third of the total votes, the traditional parties about two fifths, and the Communists one fifth. Since the Agrarians were the strongest, Stambuliski organized a new coalition government on October 6 with the support of two of the traditional parties. Shortly afterward he headed a delegation to Paris to negotiate the peace settlement.

The Bulgarians, like the Hungarians, demanded plebiscites in disputed areas in order to reduce the loss of territory. The Allies paid no attention, for in drawing the new frontiers they were motivated by strategic rather than ethnic considerations. Their aim was to deprive Bulgaria of certain key areas that would make it difficult for her to launch another offensive war. Accordingly, the Neuilly Treaty (November 27, 1919) restored the Dobruja to Rumania and gave Yugoslavia four small but strategic salients totaling 975 square miles. These salients left the Yugoslavs in control of certain passes and also pushed the Bulgarian frontier away from the vital Belgrade-Saloniki railroad.

The treaty also required Bulgaria to cede Western Thrace to Greece. Nor did ethnic considerations enter into this decision, for the population of the province was extremely mixed. The most numerous were the Greeks, Bulgarians, and Turks, but none of them constituted a majority. Thus the motive of the Allies again was strategic—to interpose a barrier between Bulgaria and the Straits. Nevertheless, the Bulgarians resented this loss most of all because it left them without any outlet to the Aegean, whereas Greece already had gained the prize ports of Saloniki and Kavalla during the Balkan Wars. Greece did offer to make available a trade outlet at a suitable Aegean port with appropriate harbor and rail facilities and with duty-free handling of commodities. These terms would have secured for Bulgaria virtually the same advantages as if the port had belonged to her. But there remained the intangible yet powerful factor of prestige. Furthermore, the Bulgarians did not wish to weaken their territorial claim by accepting the proffered trade outlet. Hence they rejected the Greek offer, and the issue of an outlet to the Aegean remained a bone of contention between the two countries throughout the postwar years.

In addition to these territorial losses Bulgaria was compelled to renounce compulsory military service, to limit her army to 33,000 men, and to pay an indemnity of 450 million dollars over a period of thirty-eight years. All in all, these terms were generally considered by most Bulgarians to be unjustifiably severe. They felt this the more strongly because they maintained that Ferdinand and his ministers had been primarily responsible for the intervention on the side of the Central Powers. But now that Ferdinand was gone, why should the new Bulgaria be compelled to pay for the sins of the old? Why should Bulgarians be compelled to live under Greek and Rumanian and Yugoslav rule, in blatant disregard of the principle of self-determination? These grievances were exaggerated and kept alive by some 250,000 Bulgarian-speaking refugees who had come from the neighboring countries between 1913 and 1925. Thus revisionism became in the postwar years a political football within Bulgaria and a perennial source of friction between her and her neighbors.

SÈVRES TREATY

The arrangement of a peace settlement with Turkey was complicated by the fact that during the war the Allies had concluded four secret treaties for the dismemberment of that country. Two of these have already been mentioned: the Treaty of Constantinople of April 10, 1915, giving Constantinople and the Straits to Russia, and the Treaty of London of April 26, 1915, assigning southwestern Asia Minor to Italy as her zone of influence. In addition, there were the Sykes-Picot Treaty of May 16, 1916, defining the manner in which Britain and France would divide the Arab provinces of Turkey between themselves, and finally the Saint-Jean-de-Maurienne Treaty of April 21, 1917, allotting to Italy a larger share of Asia Minor. Thus the effect of these secret treaties was to leave to the Turks only north-central Asia Minor. Furthermore, the Greeks also had large ambitions in Asia Minor, especially in the Smyrna region, where Greek settlements had existed since antiquity.

The 1917 revolution in Russia raised certain obstacles in the way of the secret treaties. The Bolsheviks not only repudiated the treaties but also published the texts, thereby arousing considerable opposition to their provisions in certain Allied circles. The intervention of the United States also created difficulties because of the glaring contradiction between the secret treaties and the Fourteen Points. The latter provided that purely Turkish territory should remain independent and that the non-Turkish parts of the Ottoman Empire should be assured "an absolutely unmolested opportunity of autonomous development." But when it came to the actual definition of the Turkish peace treaty, the United States was not able to exert much influence. Thus the Sèvres Treaty of August 10, 1920, incorporated most of the provisions of the secret treaties.

The articles concerning the Asiatic part of the empire need not detain us, except to note that Britain and France, in accordance with the terms of the secret treaties, received Palestine, Syria, and Mesopotamia as mandates. Russia, struggling with civil war and Allied intervention, and having repudiated the secret treaties, did not obtain Constantinople and the Straits. Instead, the treaty provided that this strategic region should be left under Turkish sovereignty, though the Straits were to be demilitarized and placed under international control. The Dodecanese Islands were ceded to Italy, who had occupied them since her war against Turkey in 1911–1912. Finally, the treaty provided for important concessions to Greece which were to have far-reaching consequences for the Balkan Peninsula.

The Greek premier, Eleutherios Venizelos, had proved to be extraordinarily persuasive and successful at the Peace Conference. One reason was his diplomatic skill and his personal prestige as a champion of the Allies from the very first days. Another reason was that Venizelos kept the Greek army intact, and even increased it, at a time when the Allied powers were rapidly demobilizing. Thus Venizelos was able to counter and overcome Italian opposition to his claims in Asia Minor. One of his main objectives was to acquire Smyrna and the hinterland, but the Italians were strongly opposed because this region had been allotted to them by the Saint-Jean-de-Maurienne Treaty. When Orlando boycotted the Peace Conference during the Fiume crisis, Venizelos took advantage of his absence to secure the Supreme Council's permission to occupy Smyrna. Greek troops landed at the city on May 15, 1919, and occupied the hinterland. Having the advantage of actual possession, Venizelos was able to secure a clause in the Sèvres Treaty providing that Smyrna and its environs should be administered by Greece for five years, and that the final disposition of the territory should then be decided by a plebiscite. The Sèvres Treaty also allotted to the Greeks Eastern Thrace, which, together with Western Thrace obtained from Bulgaria, gave them control of the entire Aegean coast to the gates of Constantinople. Finally, the treaty also gave Greece many of the islands in the Aegean, including Imbros and Tenedos at the entrance to the Straits.

The two powers which had gained the most by the Sèvres Treaty were Britain and Greece. The latter country had obtained all that it wanted in the Balkans from Bulgaria, and in the Aegean Sea and Asia Minor from Turkey. But the lion's share went to Britain, who strengthened her position in the eastern Mediterranean to an unprecedented degree. She had obtained Palestine and Mesopotamia as mandates; she had legalized her hold over Cyprus and Egypt; she had consolidated her primacy in the Arabian Peninsula; and, through the demilitarization of the Straits, she had become the mistress of Constantinople and the Black Sea, with all that that implied for Russia as well as for Turkey.

This Draconian treaty was based on the assumption that Turkey was powerless and had no choice but to accept the loss, not only of the Arab provinces, but also of the Smyrna enclave and Eastern Thrace. At this time this assumption appeared reasonable. The population was war-weary, having fought almost continuously since 1911 against the Italians, the Balkan League, and the Allies. When the war ended, some of the educated Turks believed that the only hope was for their country to become an American mandate. In Constantinople Sultan Mohammed VI had succeeded his brother, Mohammed V, on July 4, 1918. But he was the helpless and pliant tool of the Allies and did as he was told. The American representative in Constantinople reported on January 4, 1919: "At the present time ordinary government activities of country are badly organized. Tewfick Pasha cabinet contains no prominent or really able men and has no real hold on country. . . . Orders issued by Constantinople therefore often receive but scant consideration in the provinces and public safety is very poor throughout Asia Minor. . . . General attitude among Turks is one of hopelessness, waiting the outcome of the Peace Conference." [6]

Out of this apathy and demoralization developed a powerful nationalist movement. The Allies themselves provided the impetus when they landed Italian troops in southwestern Asia Minor in April, 1919, and Greek troops in Smyrna a month later. These infringements upon the Turkish homeland provoked a nationalist reaction which was superbly led by Mustafa Kemal. At the same time that the Turks were experiencing this revival the Greeks were undergoing a profound crisis which weakened their army in Asia Minor. And since the enforcement of the Sèvres Treaty depended largely upon this army, the Turks were able to accomplish what none of the other Central Powers had dared even to try. They repudiated the treaty, defied the Allies, drove the Greeks into the Aegean, and emerged triumphantly with a more favorable peace settlement and with a new republic in place of the old and discredited Ottoman Empire.

TURKISH REVIVAL

The George Washington of modern Turkey is Mustafa Kemal, later known as Ataturk, or Foremost Turk. Kemal had participated in the Young Turk revolt of 1908, though not as one of the top leaders. During World War I he distinguished himself as a military leader in the Dardanelles and at Syria. But again he did not rise to the highest posts, being at odds with the Young Turk clique that had embroiled Turkey in the war. His opportunity came at the end of the war, when his country lay helpless before the victorious Allies. He recognized the necessity for surrendering the non-Turkish parts of the empire but he refused to accept the Allied plans for partitioning Anatolia. Having made himself obnoxious in Constantinople with his defiant nationalism, he was sent to eastern Asia Minor as inspector of the Third Army. This appointment proved to be the genesis of the Turkish nationalist movement.

During his tour of inspection in the heart of Asia Minor Kemal saw more clearly than ever before that the future of the nation required the repudiation of the imperial regime in Constantinople. His aim, in his own words, was to organize and lead the people "against the Ottoman regime, against the Ottoman Sultan, against the Caliph, and against everything Mohammedan. The whole Turkish nation and the whole Turkish army had to be won over to the idea of revolution." [7] Accordingly, Kemal traveled about the country in the summer of 1919, organizing popular support for his nationalist movement. Everywhere he met with enthusiastic response, especially because of the intense national reaction to the landing of Greek troops in Smyrna a few months earlier in the spring of that year.

By September, 1919, Kemal was able to summon a nationalist congress which adopted the National Pact. This document enunciated six principles, including self-determination, abolition of capitulations, security for Constantinople, and a new Straits regime. The success of Kemal's efforts was demonstrated when his followers won a majority in the October, 1919, elections. Parliament met in Constantinople in January, 1920, and immediately adopted the National Pact.

The Allies retaliated by occupying Constantinople on March 16 in order to check the spread of the nationalist agitation. But this move stimulated the nationalist cause as much as the landing of Greek troops had done in the previous year. Kemal now made the final break with the Allies and with the old imperial order. He summoned the nationalist deputies to meet in April, 1920, in Ankara, a town in central Anatolia. There they convened as the Grand National Assembly and on April 23, 1920, they denounced the Constantinople regime and established a provisional government with Mustafa Kemal as president. This was the government which henceforth commanded the loyalty and support of most of the Turkish people. With Kemal at the head, it organized and led to a successful conclusion the national struggle against foreign intervention.

The final victory was due not only to the national awakening but also to a remarkably successful diplomatic campaign which strengthened immensely the position of the nationalists and made feasible their self-appointed task. In essence, Kemal exploited the serious differences among the Allies to conclude separate treaties with them, thereby isolating the Greeks and paving the way for their defeat. Kemal signed the first pact with the Italians, who were the most dissatisfied with the terms of the Sèvres Treaty. They had not obtained any mandates, as had Britain and France. Worse still, they had lost the rich Smyrna area to the Greeks, even though it had been promised to them by the Saint-Jean-de-Maurienne Treaty. It is not surprising, then, that Italy should have struck back at her rivals by reaching an accord with the Turks on March 13, 1921. In return for certain economic concessions in southeastern Asia Minor, Italy agreed to withdraw her forces from that area and to give diplomatic support to the Turks in their efforts to regain Smyrna and Eastern Thrace.

The French soon followed the Italian example. They were motivated partly by the desire to protect their precarious position in Syria and partly by resentment against the British, who had seized the lion's share of the booty in the Near East. On October 20, 1921, the French signed a pact with the Turks defining the frontier between Syria and Turkey and settling various railroad and other economic issues. This agreement was particularly significant because it revealed a definite split in the Levant policies of the two leading Allied powers, Britain and France.

Meanwhile, the Turks had also been negotiating with the Russians. The relations between the two at this time were quite different from what they had usually been in the past. Instead of being opposed to each other, they now were almost forced to cooperate because they had a common enemy, Great Britain. Britain occupied Constantinople and the Straits and supported the Greeks in Asia Minor. Britain also had been a leading interventionist power against Bolshevik Russia and she still threatened southern Russia by virtue of her control of the Straits and the Black Sea. It was only natural, therefore, for Turkey and Russia to sign a treaty of friendship and virtual alliance on March 16, 1921.

Both parties pledged themselves not to recognize any treaty imposed on either by force. They defined their common frontier in the Caucasus, Batum going to Russia and Kars and Ardahan to Turkey. They also agreed to entrust to a special conference, composed of delegates from all the riverain* states, the drafting of the international status of the Black Sea and the Straits. After the signing of the treaty, Russia began to furnish arms and money to the Turkish nationalists. She calculated that Turkey thereby might go Bolshevik. And even if that did not happen, Turkey at least would be able to fight more effectively against the common enemy. The Turks, on their part, accepted the Russian aid as a necessity but took care to check any communist infiltration. Emissaries from Russia who sought to propagate the new proletarian gospel mysteriously disappeared on their arrival in Turkey.

This series of treaties effected a veritable diplomatic revolution in the Near East. Turkey and Russia now presented a united front, while the Allies were irrevocably divided. Only Britain and Greece were left to enforce the terms of the Sèvres Treaty. And Britain, because of her world-wide commitments and the state of public opinion at home, could do no more than maintain her position in Constantinople and the Straits. In other words, the Greeks now were left alone to face the growing Turkish nationalist upsurge in Asia Minor. And this at a time when they were being steadily weakened by political dissension and by the strain of a decade of continual warfare.

GREEK CRISIS

While the Turks were staging their remarkable comeback the Greeks were floundering in a crisis which led almost inexorably to catastrophe. The taproot of their difficulty was Venizelos' original decision in favor of an Anato-

---

* Because this would exclude the Western powers that both Russia and Turkey opposed.

lian adventure which his country could not possibly see through to a successful conclusion. Greece lacked the resources needed for such an undertaking and the Greek colonies in Asia Minor were not strong enough to turn the balance. Venizelos himself at the beginning of World War I considered any claims upon Asia Minor territory to be visionary. "The Greeks in Turkey are so scattered," he pointed out on November 27, 1914, "that we cannot expect any compensation from that quarter." [8]

Only six weeks later the same Venizelos had completely changed his mind. One reason was that he had learned in the interval that plans for Ottoman partition were being discussed and that Italy was claiming the Smyrna region, where many Greeks had lived since antiquity. Another reason was that Sir Edward Grey on January 23, 1915, made Greece his famous offer of "important territorial concessions on the coast of Asia Minor." [9] In return Grey proposed that Greece should cede some parts of Macedonia to Bulgaria in order to keep that country from joining the Central Powers. These developments proved sufficient to induce Venizelos to change his mind. On January 24, 1915, he prepared a historic memorandum for the king in which he formulated for the first time the new policy of expansion in Asia Minor. "I would not hesitate," he wrote, "to recommend . . . the sacrifice of Kavalla, if only to save the Ottoman Greeks [of Asia Minor] and so ensure the foundation of a really big Greece. . . ." [10]

Having adopted this policy, Venizelos pursued it with his customary skill and success. He brought Greece into the war on the Allied side despite the opposition of the king. He landed a Greek army in Smyrna in the face of bitter Italian opposition. And in the peace settlement he got not only Smyrna but also the two Thraces. Venizelos apparently had attained his aim of "a really big Greece."

But in 1915, when Greece's intervention in the war was being debated, Venizelos had received two memoranda (January 27 and 31) which clearly pointed out the fatal flaw in his new policy. The author of these documents was Colonel John Metaxas, at that time acting chief of the general staff, and later to attract international attention as dictator of Greece in the 1930's. Metaxas presented a brilliant analysis of the insuperable difficulties in the way of successful intervention in Asia Minor. He noted that out of Asia Minor's total population of ten million, less than two million were Greeks, and they were so scattered along the seaboard that they did not constitute a majority in any one district. Hence an attempt to annex any portion of Asia Minor would require a long and arduous campaign in a population that would be predominantly hostile. Moreover, the physical obstacles would be immense, given the series of mountain ranges running north and south, and the lack of roads and other means of communication.

Metaxas therefore warned that a Greek army might have the advantage at the outset but that, because of the necessity of guarding its flanks and lines of communication, its strength would dwindle as it advanced farther into the interior. Inevitably a point would be reached when the equilibrium would tip over to the advantage of the Turks fighting on interior lines in their own country. Thus Metaxas foresaw a repetition of Napoleon's experience in Russia. In fact, the distances in Russia and Asia Minor were on a similar scale. It was approximately 600 miles from the Niemen to Moscow compared to 400 miles from Smyrna to Ankara and 1,000 miles from Smyrna to the eastern frontier of Turkey.

In view of these factors Metaxas concluded that an expedition in Asia Minor would have no chance of success except under the following two conditions: first, that the Allies should participate in the intervention with forces sufficient to ensure success; and second, that Anatolia should be partitioned among the Allies, or that the portion left under Turkish sovereignty should be so restricted as no longer to constitute a serious menace to the Greek position in Smyrna.

We have seen that neither of these conditions prevailed when the Greek army landed in Smyrna. In fact, the situation was exactly the opposite to that which Metaxas had stipulated. The Russians were aiding the Turks openly, while the French and Italians were doing so covertly. Only the British and the Greeks were left to resist the Turkish nationalists. And since the British, because of domestic political considerations, could do no more than hold their ground in Constantinople and the Straits, the Greeks now had to face alone the rising wave of Turkish nationalism. Under these circumstances it was not long before Metaxas' gloomy prophecy was tragically fulfilled.

At the same time that Greece was facing insuperable odds in Asia Minor she was also being weakened by growing dissension at home. As noted in the last chapter, the country had been left divided by the forced abdication of King Constantine in June, 1917, and the intervention in the war the following month. These developments had divided most Greeks into two bitterly hostile factions, the Venizelists and the Royalists. The intensity of feeling was demonstrated when two Greek naval officers attempted to assassinate Venizelos in Paris two days after he had signed the Sèvres Treaty.

When Venizelos returned to Athens in the fall of 1920 after a two-year absence abroad, party strife flared up again in full violence. The precipitating event was the unfortunate death of King Alexander on October 25, 1920, from the bite of a monkey. The country at the time was in the midst of hectic campaigning for elections scheduled for November 14. The death of the king immediately raised the delicate question of the succession to the throne. The crown was offered to Prince Paul, Constantine's third son, but was refused on the ground that his father and elder brother had never renounced their rights to the throne. Thus it became clear that the main issue in the forthcoming elections would be the question of Constantine's return. A monkey's bite had brought the feud once more to a head by pitting the old adversaries against each other— Constantine versus Venizelos.

The election results surprised everyone—even the most sanguine royalists. Venizelos himself was unseated, and only 120 of his Liberals were returned to a house of 370. Venizelos did gain 52 per cent of the total vote, which, under proportional representation, would have given him about 200 seats. Even so, the returns represented a stinging defeat for a man who had just won spectacular triumphs at the Peace Conference. On November 17, 1920, only three months after he had signed the Sèvres Treaty, he boarded a British private yacht and went into exile.

Venizelos' defeat was as stunning as that of Winston Churchill in 1945. One explanation is to be found in his long absence from the Greek political scene. Another was the inefficiency and corruption of some of the deputies he had left behind. But most important was the war-weariness of a country whose army had been mobilized almost continuously since the beginning of the first Balkan War in 1912. Undoubtedly many Greeks voted against Venizelos not because they preferred Constantine but because they wanted the soldiers to return.

On December 19, 1920, Constantine returned to Athens amid popular acclaim. The chief question facing the new regime was whether or not to continue the intervention in Asia Minor. When the royalists had been in opposition they had denounced Venizelos' foreign policy as foolhardy and adventurous. But now they chose to pursue the same policy, apparently mesmerized, as Venizelos had been, by the vision of a Greater Greece in the eastern Mediterranean. The final outcome, as Metaxas had warned, was a national disaster of the first magnitude.

GRECO-TURKISH WAR

The operations in Asia Minor began at the end of March, 1921. The Greek army appeared to have all the advantages at the outset, but serious weaknesses soon became manifest. It was poorly equipped, it lacked munitions, and there were no funds in the treasury to remedy these deficiencies. Also, the officer corps was badly divided because the new regime had appointed royalist sympathizers to top posts even though many had no training in the latest military techniques.

At first the Greeks met little resistance because the Turkish forces were still little more than guerrilla bands. But, as Metaxas had foreseen, the farther the Greeks advanced the stiffer became the opposition. Only a single railroad was available to bring supplies from Smyrna. And the distances were so great and the population so hostile that fully two thirds of Greek manpower had to be used to guard lines and to provide transportation.

Kemal allowed the Greeks to advance until they reached a battleground of his own choosing—the line of the Sakarya River where the heights of the farther bank formed an ideal defense position. The Greek commanders instructed their troops to "annihilate" the enemy and to "advance to Ankara." The Greek soldiers were in no position to do anything of the kind. They were exhausted by a long march through desert country. They were short of every kind of food except meat, which could not be cooked for lack of fuel. They were also low on gasoline and ammunition, and their horses were weak because of lack of forage. By contrast, the Turkish army was entrenched in a strong position, not far from its base, and was inspired with enthusiasm for the nationalist cause.

The Greeks began their attack across the river on August 24, 1921. For fourteen consecutive days they kept on attacking despite the scorching sun and the constant raids on their communication lines. The Turks, who were about equal in men and equipment, held their ground grimly. The casualties on both sides mounted to almost 50 per cent of the effectives. Neither the Greeks nor the Turks could claim victory on the battlefield. But so far as the campaign was concerned, the fact that the Turks were able to stop the Greek advance represented the decisive turning point of the war. The Greeks, as Metaxas had foreseen, were now in an untenable position. They had failed to smash the Turkish defense and they could not hope to winter on the Sakarya line because of communication difficulties. There was no alternative but to retreat to more defensible positions.

Retreat brought demoralization to the Greek ranks. They were aware of the fact that their allies had in effect deserted them. They hung on to their new positions, but their fighting spirit was gone. The number of deserters increased alarmingly. Kemal held back his counteroffensive to allow the demoralization to proceed apace. Finally, on August 26, 1922, a full year after the Sakarya battle, he gave the order to attack. The following day the Greek lines were cut in two. The northern section, after a skillful retreat, reached the Sea of Marmora and embarked almost intact for Greece. The southern section broke and ran in a wild stampede. Soldiers and civilian refugees flocked into Smyrna. The bulk of the army was evacuated to the adjoining islands before Kemal, on September 9, triumphantly rode into the city. The great victory of Turkish nationalism was celebrated by setting fire to Smyrna, the hateful stronghold of Hellenism.

The Athens government was staggered by the extent of the calamity. In the space of a fortnight it had lost what had taken three years to conquer. The temper of the troops was such that the government issued orders for demobilization. This left the frontiers undefended, but it was hoped that demobilization would avert a revolution and save the dynasty. However, the disaster was too great to pass without convulsions in Athens.

A Revolutionary Committee was organized by Colonel Nicholas Plastiras and a large number of officers who had fled to the island of Chios off Asia Minor. On September 26, 1922, the committee sent an ultimatum to Athens calling for the abdication of the king. The following day the king complied, leaving his eldest son on the throne as George II. The reaction to the catastrophe was not yet completed. The committee appointed a Commission of Inquiry to determine the responsibility for the Asia Minor debacle. The commission indicted eight of Constantine's principal ministers and military advisers, who were brought to trial before an extraordinary court-martial of eleven officers. All the accused were found guilty of sacrificing the interests of the country to party considerations. Six of the eight were sentenced to death and immediately executed. Thus fuel was added to the flames of party strife at a time when Greece faced the desperate problems of negotiating a peace with the victorious Turks and salvaging the million and a half homeless refugees from Asia Minor.

LAUSANNE TREATY

Following their great victory in Asia Minor the Turks demanded that the Greeks evacuate Eastern Thrace at once. To back up their demand they began to advance into the Straits zone. There they were confronted with British troops, and for a few days an Anglo-Turkish war seemed imminent. In the end the Mudanya Armistice was concluded on October 11, 1922, and in the following month peace negotiations began at Lausanne.

The Lausanne Conference developed into a duel between the British representative, Lord Curzon, and the Turkish representative, Ismet Pasha. Curzon endeavored with his forceful personality and debating skill to browbeat the conference into accepting his position. Ismet, who was a military man, was unable to cope directly with the Englishman's brilliant rhetoric. Yet he held his ground stubbornly, resorting to delaying tactics when he needed time to think and to formulate replies. His aim was to attain to as great a degree as possible the objectives set forth in the National Pact. More specifically, he wanted territorial integrity and full independence—meaning thereby the restoration of Eastern Thrace and the Straits, and the abolition of all foreign control over Turkish finances, minorities, justice, or anything else. These goals were not easily reached. In fact, the conference, after beginning on November 20, 1922, broke up on February 4, 1923, because no agreement could be reached. The sittings were resumed on April 23, and finally, on July 24, the marathon sessions ended and the Lausanne Treaty was signed.

So far as the Balkan Peninsula was concerned, Eastern Thrace, including Adrianople, returned to Turkey and the Imbros and Tenedos Islands near the Straits also reverted to Turkey, though the remaining Aegean Islands went to Greece. Italy retained the Dodecanese Islands, and England, Cyprus. The capitulations were abolished in return for a promise of judicial reforms, and Turkey was not required to pay reparations though she did accept treaties for the protection of minorities.

On the crucial question of the Straits, the principal conflict had been between Russia and the Western powers. Russia wanted the Straits to be closed to all warships, whereas the Western powers wished to be free to send a limited number of warships into the Black Sea at the price of giving Russia similar access to the Mediterranean. Turkey accepted the Western position in return for the restoration of Eastern Thrace. As a result, the agreement reached on the Straits represented a balance between Western and Turkish interests at the expense of Russia. The provisions were as follows: (1) Freedom of passage was established for merchant vessels in peace and war. (2) Freedom of passage was allowed to all warships in time of peace, though no power might send a fleet into the Black Sea larger than the largest fleet of a littoral power. This provision, it should be noted, prevented a single fleet larger than that of the Soviets from passing the Straits, but a combination of hostile fleets was still permissible. (3) An international Straits Commission was established to see that the provisions concerning the passage of warships was carried out. (4) The shores of the Dardanelles and the Bosphorus were demilitarized but, in contrast to the Sèvres Treaty, the Sea of Marmora was exempted from this demilitarization stipulation. This safeguarded Turkish security, as did also the provision allowing Turkey to close the Straits to enemy ships in a war in which she herself was belligerent. Furthermore, the freedom of the Straits and the security of the demilitarized zones were guaranteed jointly by Britain, France, Italy, and Japan. This regime for the Straits was to last until 1936, when it was replaced by the Montreux Convention, which was more favorable to Turkey and Russia.*

A separate agreement also reached at Lausanne on January 30, 1923, provided for the compulsory exchange of Greek and Turkish minorities. This undertaking is of considerable significance because it altered substantially the ethnographic map of the Balkans and especially of Macedonia. It should be noted that the migrations following the Lausanne agreement were but the culmination of a series of Balkan population shifts that began with the Balkan Wars.

The first occurred in 1912, when about 100,000 Turks fled before the successful armies of the Balkan League. Then with the second Balkan War and the Bucharest Treaty that concluded it, other mass migrations occurred, involving approximately 50,000 Turks, 60,000 Bulgarians, and 70,-000 Greeks. During 1914 the population movements continued as many people found themselves on the wrong side of the newly created frontiers. About 115,000 Moslems left Greece, another 135,000 left the other Balkan countries, and 115,000 Greeks departed from Turkish Eastern Thrace. During World War I the migratory movements ceased, though the Bulgarians expelled about 36,000 Greeks from Eastern Macedonia in 1916 when they occupied that region. With the end of the war the migrations resumed, the largest being the voluntary exchange of Greek and Bulgarian minorities provided for under the Neuilly Treaty, and the compulsory exchange of Greek and Turkish minorities required by the agreement reached at Lausanne. It is estimated that 53,000 Bulgarians emigrated from Greece and 30,000 Greeks left Bulgaria. The Greco-Turkish exchange was of an altogether different magnitude, involving some 400,000 Turks and 1,300,000 Greeks.

Population shifts of such dimensions involved a tremendous amount of dislocation and suffering. Ancient communities were uprooted in the name of nationalism and resettled in strange and frequently barren and inhospitable surroundings. The Asia Minor Greeks had perhaps the most difficult time in adjusting, partly because of their numbers but also because there were fewer opportunities in poor and overcrowded Greece than in Turkey, where they had dominated economic life.

* See Chapter 37.

On the other hand, the population transfers did reduce the size of minority groups in the Balkans and thereby removed a leading source of friction. Very few Greeks were left in Turkey, with the exception of Constantinople, where the compulsory exchange had not been applicable. Similarly, in Bulgaria the Greek settlements were reduced to negiligible proportions. In Western Thrace the Turks still constituted about 30 per cent of the total population, having been allowed to remain in return for the similar privilege extended to the Constantinople Greeks. The greatest change occurred in Macedonia, where there now was much greater ethnic homogeneity than at any time in the past. This was particularly true because many of the Asia Minor Greeks settled in sections of Greek Macedonia evacuated by Turks and Bulgars. According to an ethnographic map of the League of Nations Refugees' Settlement Commission, whereas in 1912 the population of the portion of Macedonia now belonging to Greece was 42.6 per cent Greek, 39.4 per cent Moslem, 9.9 per cent Bulgarian, and 8.1 per cent miscellaneous (including the Saloniki Jews), by 1926 it had become 88.8 per cent Greek, 0.1 per cent Moslem, 5.1 per cent Bulgarian, and 6 per cent miscellaneous (again including the Saloniki Jews).

In conclusion, the Lausanne Treaty obviously represented a great victory for Turkish nationalism. With the exception of the Straits provisions, Ismet had gained almost all the points set forth in the National Pact. Greece had suffered a disastrous and presumably final setback to her Megale Idea. But she did come out with a net gain consisting of Western Thrace and the Aegean Islands. And if Hellenism had been extirpated in Asia Minor it had thereby been consolidated in Macedonia. As for great-power interests in the Balkans, Britain had won a victory in securing the demilitarization of the Straits and the right to send her warships through that waterway. The strongest opponents that the British encountered on this issue had been the Russians, who, for obvious reasons, wanted the Straits closed to all foreign warships. Consequently, in the postwar years they were as opposed to the new Straits regime as were the Turks.

THE NEW BALKANS

The territorial changes effected in the Balkans by the various treaties may be summarized as follows:

State	Territory in square miles 1914	Territory in square miles 1923	Population in thousands 1914	Population in thousands 1923
Bulgaria	43,305	39,841	4,753	4,910
Greece	41,933	50,146	4,363	5,537
Rumania	53,489	122,282	7,516	17,594
Turkey	1,950,000	296,107 [a]	34,740	13,357
Yugoslavia	33,891	96,134	4,548	12,017

[a] Of the total area of postwar Turkey, only about 9,000 sq. mi. are in Europe, the remainder comprising Asia Minor.

Source: J. A. Lukacs, *The Great Powers & Eastern Europe* (New York: American Book Co., 1953), pp. 32–33.

Apart from Turkey, Rumania remained the largest Balkan state after the war, as she had been before. She more than doubled in territory and population as a result of her acquisitions from Russia, Austria-Hungary, and Bulgaria. But Rumania faced the problem of sizable minorities amounting to 27 per cent of the total population. Furthermore, her extraordinary gains had been made possible because of the power vacuum that prevailed with the disappearance of the German, Russian, and Austro-Hungarian empires. When Russia and Germany revived in the 1930's under new regimes Rumania's position became untenable. Thus she lost most of her newly acquired territory at the beginning of World War II and regained only a portion at the end of that war.

Serbia gained the most on a percentage basis, almost tripling in area and population. But Yugoslavia also faced serious problems as a result of her expansion, outstanding being the conflict with Italy in the Adriatic and the friction between the Serbs and the Croats over the question of the form of government. Greece also gained substantially, finally realizing her irredentist aspirations with the exception of the Dodecanese Islands and Cyprus and her claims to Southern Albania.

Turkey lost the most so far as territories were concerned. But in the end she gained because of the homogeneity and unity following her transformation from a multinational empire to a nation-state. Furthermore, the relations between Turkey and the Balkan states changed basically in character because Turkey now definitely gave up any thoughts of regaining her former European provinces. She was satisfied to have retained the Straits and surrounding area, and she now concentrated her energies on developing her Anatolian heartland.

Bulgaria was left as the sole revisionist power in the Balkans, having fallen from second to last place in the Balkan hierarchy. The influx of refugees from Macedonia and the activities of their IMRO organization made irredentism a prime issue in the interwar years. Just as the defeat in the second Balkan War had driven Bulgaria into the camp of the Central Powers in 1915, so now the defeat in World War I was to lead Bulgaria to the side of the Axis Powers in 1941.

Having examined the various treaties that concluded World War I we will analyze in the following chapter the new political, economic, and social factors that determined the course of Balkan history during the interwar period.

31. The Dynamics of Balkan Politics: 1918–1939

THE BALKAN COUNTRIES began the postwar era with every promise of a bright future. Millions of Rumanian and South Slav peasants had been freed from foreign imperial rule. It is true that new minorities appeared, consisting now of the defeated Bulgarians and Hungarians. But these were of minor significance compared with the massive blocs of subject peoples in the prewar multinational empires. The Balkan frontiers conformed to the principle of the self-determination of peoples to a greater degree than at any time in the past.

The war years and those immediately following also witnessed land distribution on an unprecedented scale. In every Balkan country the large estates, which comprised a substantial proportion of the total arable land, were divided among the landless and dwarf peasants. The only exception was Bulgaria, where small holdings already prevailed. But even there the few large estates were broken up. Thus the Balkan peasants, who had freed themselves from serfdom and coercive labor during the nineteenth century, now gained possession of the land they worked.

In this manner two revolutionary principles were to a large degree realized: "The self-determination of peoples" and "Land to those who till it." It was naturally expected that these developments would promote political harmony and social stability. In actual fact, the outcome was political crisis and social conflict. In this chapter we shall analyze the factors determining Balkan politics in the period between wars and accounting for the unhappy denouement.

ECONOMIC TRENDS

Land Distribution. The Balkan countries during the interwar years remained overwhelmingly agricultural, and their populations remained correspondingly agrarian. The outstanding experience of these peasant masses during the years immediately following World War I was the acquisition of

593

private plots as a result of sweeping land reforms. Various factors were responsible for the radical land distribution. One was the nationalistic urge to divide among the long-oppressed Rumanian and South Slav peasants the estates of foreign landowners, such as the Magyars in Transylvania and the Russians in Bessarabia. Another factor was the widespread feeling that social justice for the peasants was long overdue. They had borne the brunt of the war and they now deserved to be given an equitable share of the national wealth. Economic necessity was also involved in the case of the land given to the destitute refugees who flocked into Bulgaria and Greece. But the overriding motivation behind land reform was undoubtedly the fear of revolution. After six years of almost continual fighting the Balkan peoples were war-weary and disaffected. The great upheaval in Russia and the spread of Bolshevism to Hungary and other parts of Central Europe raised the specter of a vast revolutionary wave sweeping over the Balkan Peninsula. This induced the landowners and the ruling political circles to enact land reform in the hope that it would function as a lightning conductor during the revolutionary storms.

The above factors explained the thoroughgoing manner in which land was expropriated and divided. In Yugoslavia one out of every four peasants received some land. Even in Bulgaria, where large estates were a rarity, some 6 per cent of the arable land was distributed. In Rumania the percentage mounted to 21 and in Greece to 38. The high figure in the case of Greece presumably arose from the mass exodus of Turkish landowners from the newly acquired provinces.*

This drastic distribution of land among the Balkan peasants has been criticized on the grounds that it reduced productivity and was economically unsound. This criticism is irrelevant because the reforms were politically motivated and politically inevitable. Economic considerations could not and did not enter into the picture.

Population Pressure. The breakup of the large estates did not solve the problems of the Balkan peasantry. Agriculture remained in a precarious state during the interwar years. One of the basic reasons was the pressure of a rapidly increasing population. The Balkans today are passing through the same phase of great population growth that Western Europe experienced during the eighteenth and nineteenth centuries. Originally Western Europe had the same demographic pattern as the rest of the world, that is, a high birth rate and a correspondingly high death rate, leaving a stationary or only slightly expanding population. In the eighteenth century this traditional pattern suddenly changed. The death rate dropped sharply because of medical advances, hygienic measures, and improved nutrition. After a considerable interval the birth rate also dropped down to approximately the new death rate, apparently because of conscious social restriction. The lag be-

---

* Details of land distribution in each Balkan country are given in the relevant chapters below.

tween the fall in the death rate and the subsequent fall in the birth rate produced the unprecedented growth of population in Western Europe during the
eighteenth and nineteenth centuries.

In the Balkan Peninsula, and throughout Eastern Europe, the decline in the death rate occurred in the latter half of the nineteenth century.
But a corresponding drop in the birth rate has not yet developed. Consequently, the Balkan countries today far exceed Western Europe in rate of
population growth. Despite this fact, Western Europe still has a denser population in relation to area than do the Balkan countries. On the other hand,
a much larger percentage of the Balkan peoples are dependent upon agriculture than is the case with the populations of the industrialized West.
The net result is that more people subsist on each unit of arable land in the
Balkans than in Western Europe.

The table on page 596 shows that population pressure per unit of
arable land was much greater in the Balkans than in most Western European
countries. This pressure, which was continually increasing because of the
persistently high birth rates, fundamentally affected the character of Balkan
agriculture. It caused the small peasant plots to be divided and redivided
among the numerous sons to the point where the majority of holdings in
each Balkan country became too small to support a family. The difficulty
was aggravated by the fact that each peasant commonly held several widely
scattered parcels of land rather than one plot. This parcelization wasted much
land in the form of boundaries and paths, and also made impossible the introduction of rational productive methods. Thus the average Balkan peasant,
if he had not been obliged by economic pressure to give up his land, owned
several parcels, each a fraction of a hectare in area and the total quite inadequate for his family needs.

This meant that every Balkan country in the interwar period suffered
from rural overpopulation. More people were engaged in agriculture than
were needed for the prevailing type of cultivation. It has been estimated that
in 1930 no less than 61.5 per cent of the rural population in Yugoslavia was
"surplus," 53 per cent in Bulgaria, 51.4 per cent in Rumania, and 50.3 per
cent in Greece.[1] These appallingly high figures, it should be noted, were
chronic. They did not represent passing unemployment as in the case of the
Western countries during the depression years. In other words, the majority
of the people in the Balkan villages were not needed. In fact, they were an
outright burden. If perchance they had disappeared overnight the remaining
minority would have been able to carry on the work and would have had
more left to eat. Such was the tragic plight and bleak future of most of the
Balkan peasantry.

Low Productivity. Heavy population pressure on the land is not
necessarily incompatible with agricultural prosperity. The Netherlands, for
example, had 81.7 people dependent upon agriculture per square kilometer
of "arable-equivalent" land in 1930 compared to 79.7 in the case of Ru-

Demographic and Economic Indices of Balkan and
Selected Western European States in the Interwar Period

Country	Average Annual Interwar Population Growth in % [a]	Population Density per square Kilometer [b]	Per Cent of Population Dependent on Agriculture [c] ca. 1938	Density of Population Dependent upon Agriculture per Square Kilometer of "arable-equivalent" Agricultural Land,[d] ca. 1930 [e]
Greece	1.93	48	60	86.7
Yugoslavia	1.43	56	75	100.1
Bulgaria	1.30	59	80	95.4
Rumania	1.27	61	78	79.7
Italy	0.85	133	44	53.4
Germany	0.67	139	20	52.1
England and Wales	0.49	264	5	33.8
France	0.44	76	29	28.8

[a] D. Kirk, *Europe's Population in the Interwar Years* (Geneva, 1946), pp. 263 ff.

[b] *Ibid.*

[c] Based on W. E. Moore, *Economic Demography of Eastern and Southern Europe* (Geneva, 1945) p. 26; H. L. Roberts, *Rumania: Political Problems of an Agrarian State* (New Haven, Conn., 1951) pp. 355 ff.; J. Tomasevich, *Peasants, Politics and Economic Change in Yugoslavia* (Stanford, Calif., 1955); S. D. Zagoroff, *The Agricultural Economy of the Danubian Countries 1935–45* (Stanford, Calif., 1955), p. 11; *Economic Development in S. E. Europe* (London, 1945); *South-Eastern Europe: A Political and Economic Survey* (London, 1939), pp. 125, 139, 156, 167. Although the above sources give different figures concerning population percentages dependent on agriculture, all give much higher percentages for the Balkan states than for the others.

[d] "Arable-equivalent" is a statistical device to achieve a rough comparability between different types of land (arable, pasture, vineyards, etc.) used for agricultural purposes. This is necessary for meaningful comparison because a sq. km. of pasture obviously is not equivalent to a sq. km. of arable.

[e] Moore, *op. cit.,* pp. 197 ff. Different figures on density of population dependent on each unit of arable land are given in Tomasevich, *op. cit.,* p. 309; *Economic Development in S. E. Europe,* p. 26; A. Pepelasis, "Socio-Cultural Barriers to the Economic Development of Greece" (University of California, Berkeley, unpublished doctoral dissertation, 1955), p. 34, and *Report of the FAO Mission for Greece* (Washington, D.C., March, 1947), p. 134. But again all sources agree that population pressure per unit of arable land is greater in the Balkans than in most Western European countries.

mania. Yet the income and the living standards of the Dutch farmers were infinitely higher than those of the Rumanian. The explanation is to be found in the much higher productivity of the Dutch farmers. Thus agricultural prosperity depends upon productivity as well as population pressure. But the peasants of every Balkan country operate at a very low level of productivity. In general, one Balkan peasant grows food sufficient for one and a half persons, whereas the ratio of the Western European farmer is one to four. The contrast between Balkan and Western European agricultural productivity is revealed more specifically in the following table.

Indices of Agricultural Production in Balkan and Selected
Western European Countries, 1931–1935 Average
(Europe = 100)

Countries	Per Person Dependent on Agriculture	Per Hectare of Agricultural Land
Albania	22	70
Yugoslavia	38	69
Bulgaria	47	80
Rumania	48	69
Greece	50	77
Italy	73	69
France	174	109
Germany	195	181
Netherlands	259	377
England and Wales	319	193

Source: Moore, *op. cit.,* p. 35.

We may conclude that the basic problem facing Balkan agriculture is the combination of low productivity and mounting population pressure. This constitutes a truly vicious circle because rural overpopulation perpetuates low productivity. It does so because low income means poor nutrition and health which impair the efficiency of labor. Low income also leaves no surplus for investment and thus blocks economic development. And rural overpopulation leads to fragmentation of plots, which makes efficient cultivation impossible.

Thus the Balkan peasants, like those of other underdeveloped regions, found themselves on a treadmill during the interwar years. They could not emigrate in large numbers because of the barriers raised by the United States and the British dominions. They could not move to their own cities because industry was not sufficiently developed to absorb a large influx from the country. The alternative was to increase productivity as the Western farmers had done during the preceding two centuries. But this required capital and technical knowledge, neither of which the Balkan peasantry possessed.

External Pressures. In addition to these difficulties arising from domestic conditions, the Balkan states had to contend with severe economic pressures from without. One was the agricultural protectionism adopted by most of the European industrial states during the interwar years. This reduced substantially the market for Balkan agricultural products. Another external pressure was that of the overseas cereal exporters who, with their vast land resources and mechanized techniques, were able easily to undersell the Balkan peasants. Finally the world depression that began in 1929 hurt the Balkan economies especially severely because the prices of raw materials dropped much more than those of manufactured goods. This created a price scissors which is evident in the table on page 598.

Price per Metric Ton of Exports and Imports
(In Swiss francs)

	RUMANIA		GREECE		BULGARIA	
	Export	*Import*	*Export*	*Import*	*Export*	*Import*
Average 1922–1930	121.3	815.8	577.9	315.6	531.6	617.0
1931	68.5	853.9	472.4	231.9	288.9	591.4
1932	57.0	823.4	385.3	142.5	215.4	498.0
1933	49.3	768.5	224.4	129.6	241.1	346.5
1934	46.5	629.6	205.4	128.2	222.1	329.1
1935	49.4	547.0	234.6	128.4	369.1	401.6
Percentage fall between 1922–1930 average and lowest point 1931–1935	62	33	64	59[a]	60	47

[a] The price scissors was slight in Greece because that country imported much grain which fell in price almost as much as the tobacco that Greece exported.

Source: The Balkan States: I. Economic (London, 1936), p. 65.

Role of Governments. The Balkan governments did little to relieve the plight of the peasants during the interwar years. They apparently assumed that since the peasants had been given land they could now be left to their own devices. This assumption was quite unjustified although understandable. In actual fact the Balkan peasants urgently needed government aid in various fields. They needed credit facilities to improve their plots and equipment, but the government credit agencies set such security requirements that only the small minority of medium and wealthy peasants could qualify. The remainder were forced to turn to the village usurers, who charged rates as high as 200 per cent and more. This was one of the reasons why the Balkan peasantry sank progressively deeper into debt during these years.

The peasants also needed instruction in modern farming methods in order to exploit their plots efficiently. Many of them were too bound by tradition to accept such instruction. But those who were not could turn to few agencies for guidance. None of the agricultural ministries of the various Balkan countries received adequate funds to provide the necessary services. In Yugoslavia, for example, the ministry of agriculture received only 1.06 per cent of the total government appropriations for the fiscal year 1929–1930. That year, it should be noted, was the most prosperous of the entire interwar period. Two years later the ministry received only 0.76 per cent of the government appropriations. The situation was very similar in the remainder of the peninsula. And this in a region where about three fourths of the population depended on agriculture for its livelihood.

The Balkan governments failed in various other fields to give the peasants a proper return for the taxes they paid. Most important were education, public health, and transportation. In fact, an analysis of Balkan tax systems shows that peasants, whose per capita income was far below that of the city dwellers, were forced to bear most of the tax load. This was done by levying light taxes on incomes and heavy taxes on mass consumption articles. Income taxes in the various Balkan countries provided 19 to 28 per cent of total tax revenues while taxes on commodities supplied 55 to 65 per cent. It is estimated that at least 50 per cent of the cash disbursement of the Balkan peasants was taken by indirect taxes on necessities such as clothing, boots, salt, sugar, matches, tobacco, fertilizers, agricultural implements, and petroleum. In Yugoslavia, for example, agricultural machinery cost three times more than in Central and Western Europe, and fertilizers two and a half times more. The natural result was that the use of both machinery and fertilizers decreased as being "unprofitable." Thus it can be seen that the discriminatory taxation prevalent in the Balkans had far-reaching repercussions. It contributed strongly to widespread malnutrition, primitive agricultural methods, low consumption of manufactured goods, and slow development of local industry.[2]

Failure of Industrialization. The Balkan governments did follow one policy consistently and energetically, that is, industrialization. They employed various methods to develop their industries, including tariff protection, tax exemption, special railway rates, lucrative concessions to foreign investors, and state investment in industry and transportation. It was hoped that industrial expansion would provide work for the surplus rural population, provide manufactured goods and fertilizers for the peasants, and furnish a large market for agricultural foodstuffs and industrial crops.

None of these objectives was realized to a significant degree. One reason was that foreign investments, which financed much of the industrial growth, were definitely a mixed blessing. Extremely high profits indicated excessively generous concessions and led to the siphoning of much capital to outside shareholders. Equally serious was the unsystematic development of natural resources. Foreign investors pursued the most profitable and least risky enterprises, regardless of how they affected the general development of the local economies. They concentrated on the production of raw materials and semifinished products, and were reluctant to invest their profits for the production of finished products. This retarded and distorted the economic development of the Balkan countries, perpetuating a semicolonial relationship between them and the industrial West. Domestic investors were equally at variance with national economic interests. They concentrated on those industries which showed the most promise of gaining a monopolistic position through tariffs and import regulations or through positive state support.

Balkan industry did expand considerably during the interwar period in spite of the methods and effects on the various countries. But the expansion was far from adequate to absorb the surplus rural population. In Yugoslavia, for example, the number of industrial workers rose from 200,000 in 1919 to 385,000 in 1938. But in the same period the population of the country rose from 11.6 to 15.6 millions, an increase of 4 millions, of whom about one half were of working age.[3] The same disproportion prevailed in the other Balkan countries between industrial employment and population increase.

Balkan industries not only failed to meet the basic population problem but aggravated the plight of the peasants by imposing on them the cost of industrialization by such means as high import duties on manufactured goods and high export duties on agricultural products. Rumanian economists, for example, estimate that the burden of their industry was such that it depressed rather than raised the living standards of the peasants. "It is certain," one of these economists stated, "that the position of quasi-monopoly created by the system of protection of the national industry is the principal cause of the state of inferiority into which agriculture in general and peasant agriculture in particular have been driven." [4]

German Domination.   During the late 1930's Germany gained control of the lion's share of Balkan trade. Germany's advance was partly at the expense of Italy, who lost ground especially after the imposition of sanctions during the Italo-Ethiopian War. Germany also advanced abruptly after she annexed Austria and Czechoslovakia, countries which had traded extensively with the Balkans. But the basic reason for Germany's gains was her willingness to buy Balkan products like tobacco and cereals which could not be sold anywhere else. Germany paid high prices for these products and bought them in large quantities. Balances in blocked marks accumulated to the credit of her Balkan suppliers. The latter had to buy German goods in order to get paid. The effect upon Balkan trade is evident in the following figures.[5]

Share of Greater Germany (including Austria and Czechoslovakia) in Balkan Foreign Trade (1938)

Country	Imports from Greater Germany	Exports to Greater Germany
Bulgaria	57.9%	63.6%
Greece	31.1	43.2
Yugoslavia	50.0	49.9
Rumania	48.5	35.9

The Balkan countries found themselves in a weak bargaining position because they could find no other market for their products. Under the circumstances Germany could have raised the prices of her manufactured goods, which the Balkan countries would have had to accept in order to liquidate their clearing balances. Germany also might have supplied only certain types of goods that she wished to unload. In practice, however, Germany did not exploit her strangle hold on the Balkan economy. She charged competitive prices and did not restrict the types of goods she sold. Reports that Germany supplied only aspirin, cameras, mouth organs, and such trifles were quite unfounded. In fact, Germany's treatment of her Balkan customers was more generous than was necessary in the given circumstances. This suggests that considerations other than purely economic ones were involved. Germany was apparently seeking to develop in the Balkans a source of vegetable and mineral raw materials that was secure from blockade. Whatever the reasons, the fact remains that Germany already dominated the Balkan countries economically before she occupied them militarily during World War II.

Conclusion. We may conclude that the Balkan countries made no significant economic progress between the two wars, in the sense that the basic economic problems remained largely unresolved. Agricultural productivity remained low and industrial growth was inadequate from the viewpoint of the needs of the Balkan economies. This created a vicious circle because the weakness of industry restricted the market for agricultural products and limited the jobs available for the surplus rural population, while the poverty of agriculture restricted the domestic market available to industry. For obvious reasons, the Balkan armament industries were booming on the eve of the war. But most of the consumers' goods industries were operating at 40 to 60 per cent of capacity because of the lack of domestic purchasing power. In fact, it is a question whether the real income of the Balkan peoples declined during the interwar period. Certainly their living standards were far below those prevailing in the rest of Europe.

Estimates of National Income in Selected Countries (1925–1930)

Country	Income per Head of Working Population in International Units[a]
Rumania	243
Bulgaria	284
Yugoslavia	330
Greece	397
Czechoslovakia	455
Austria	572
Great Britain	1,069
United States	1,368

[a] An "international unit" represents the amount of goods and services that could be purchased for $1 in the United States over the average of the decade 1925–1934.

Source: Colin Clark, *The Conditions of Economic Progress* (London, Macmillan & Co. Ltd. and St. Martin's Press, Inc., 1940), pp. 40, 132. Estimates of Balkan national incomes and productivity are given by the Greek agricultural economist, Ch. Evelpidi, "Le revenu national des pays balkaniques," *Metron,* XIV (June 15, 1940), 167; and his *Les états balkaniques* (Paris, 1930), p. 341. His estimates differ from those of Colin Clark in detail, but both are agreed concerning the discrepancy between Balkan and general European incomes.

SOCIAL AND CULTURAL TRENDS

Variations. The low income of the Balkan peoples produced social conditions typical of underdeveloped areas. Malnutrition was rampant in the prewar years, housing was substandard, and health conditions were far below those prevailing in Central and Western Europe. This does not mean that unrelieved misery prevailed throughout the peninsula. The city dwellers generally were better off, their per capita income in every Balkan country being at least double that of the peasants. Rumania had 4.6 doctors per 10,000 inhabitants but only 1.1 in the rural districts. Contrary to widespread belief, the diet of the majority of peasants who owned small plots or none at all was poorer than that of industrial workers.[6]

Wide variation in living standards existed between regions as well as between social groups. In the Banat of Temesvar the peasants tilled their fertile plots efficiently and enjoyed relatively good incomes. In central Serbia a happy balance prevailed between cereal growing and livestock raising. In the foothills of the Carpathians fruit farmers organized selling cooperatives and lived comfortably. But in other sections of the peninsula the peasants lived miserably amid poverty and squalor. This was especially true of poorly endowed areas such as the "karst" region of western Yugoslavia and the barren mountain areas of Epirus in Greece and western Transylvania in Rumania. Apart from these local variations it is correct to say that social and cultural standards in general were far lower than elsewhere on the Continent.

Food and Housing. Travelers in the Balkans praise the tasty national dishes of grilled meats and numerous meat-and-vegetable stews. These dishes are national in the sense that they are specific to particular regions or countries. But they definitely are not national in terms of consumption. The great majority of the peasants taste meat only several times a year during certain holidays. The rest of the time they can afford only poor bread, cheese, onions, fruits and vegetables if they are in season, and olive oil and olives if they live in a Mediterranean area. The table on page 603 shows how low income in the Balkans has affected nutrition.

The salient feature of the nutrition standards reflected in these figures is the excess of grains, which are cheap, and the deficiency of animal proteins, which are expensive. The Balkan countries export large quantities of protective foods such as meat, eggs, butter, and cheese. But this reflects a lack of domestic purchasing power rather than a real surplus. In fact, if the "desirable diet" prevailed in the Balkans it would be necessary to import rather than export foodstuffs. A Yugoslav rural health worker has noted and analyzed this paradox of food exports from malnutrition areas.

A survey undertaken in several rural countries on the nutritional status of the population showed that there exists undernourishment among a large number of the rural population, and that agricultural products are exported from rural countries without consideration of the nutritional requirements of the people. The reasons are purely commercial. The industrial products imported into the rural countries in exchange serve merely the urban population and industrial establishments from which the farming population derives comparatively small benefit. To cover their money requirements, the farmers owning small holdings are usually compelled to sell the best products of their farms to the town people. Thus they are helping the cities and industries, themselves remaining far in the rear in regard to sanitation, housing, health, and general education.[7]

Estimated Consumption of the Main Foodstuffs
per Head of Population Kilos per Year
(Figures in brackets are conjectural)

	Desirable Diet[a]	Rumania	Yugoslavia	Greece	Bulgaria
Wheat, rye, and maize	104	240	227	168	195
Potatoes	82	48	60	15	16
Sugar	16	5	5	9	3
Meat (all kinds)	41	17	16	16	21
Milk and cheese	217	[70]	[75]	[75]	[85]
Butter, animal fats, and vegetable oils	23	11	9	16	8
Eggs (in numbers)	228	90	75	76	80
Vegetables and fruits	137	[60]	[60]	[60]	[75]

[a] Recommended by the U.S. National Research Council.

Source: Economic Development in S. E. Europe, p. 21.

Housing conditions in most parts of the Balkans are extremely bad. A large percentage of peasant dwellings are of one story and have floors of packed earth. In the most primitive regions, such as sections of Bosnia, the livestock are sheltered in the same room as the family. More commonly there is a wooden or stone partition, or else the livestock take the first floor and the family the second. Living conditions are further depressed by the custom of setting aside a "parlor" for the entertainment of guests. Social prestige demands that this be done, though it usually means crowding the entire family into one other room. Hygenic conditions are deplorable, as much from ignorance as from poverty. The findings of a survey made in 1939 of the Drina region of Yugoslavia are reasonably representative of the Balkans as a whole. Out of 219,279 households, 46.4 per cent had no beds, 54.3 per cent had no latrines of any sort, and 51.6 per cent had no wooden flooring, having to do with packed earth.

Health. Health conditions in the Balkans during the interwar years reflected the low income and poor food and housing. The death rate had declined substantially since the Ottoman period, yet the incidence of deficiency diseases, especially in the poorer districts, remained much higher than in Central and Western Europe. Pellagra and anemia were widespread in Rumania. Malaria was prevalent in Greece and rickets in Bulgaria. Scurvy, rickets, night blindness, and anemia were common in Yugoslavia. And everywhere tuberculosis and infant mortality decimated the peasant masses. Comparative statistics are available for infant mortality and they show that the rate in the Balkans was double and even triple that of Western Europe. In 1938, deaths under one year per 1,000 live births amounted to 183 in Rumania, 144 in Yugoslavia and Bulgaria, 106 in Italy, 99 in Greece, 66 in France, 60 in Germany, 55 in England and Wales, and 37 in the Netherlands.[8]

Various factors contributed to the bad health conditions, including lack of hygenic information and excessive and wasteful feasting on special occasions such as Christmas, Easter, weddings, and baptisms. But the basic factor was the overwhelming poverty which left the great majority of the Balkan peoples ill-clad, ill-housed, and ill-fed. This is made clear in the following passage by Professor Jozo Tomasevich which refers specifically to Yugoslavia but which is equally valid in a general sense for the rest of the peninsula.

Deficient nutrition is not only responsible for the greater incidence of typical nutritional deficiency diseases, but by weakening the bodily strength it makes people less resistant to practically all diseases, especially such diseases as tuberculosis and malaria. . . .

A general characteristic of the dietary pattern of the rural population in Yugoslavia is that its adequacy and variety are basically influenced by the seasonal factors in the local production of food. As a rule, nutrition is at its best in the fall and early winter months. Cereals, potatoes, onions, and in some areas turnips, from the current harvest, last into these months in most families; some types of cabbage are available in fresh form, as are some types of fruit. Legumes and some fruits are available in dried form, and some vegetables are pickled. Among the preserved vegetables, by far the most important is sauerkraut. The supply of fresh and dried meat, animal fats and oils, and cheese is most plentiful at that time. These foods of vegetable and animal origin are the "winter reserves" (zimnica) that every family tries to secure for the months when there is little or nothing in the fields.

On the other hand, the nature and amount of work to be performed in the months when the food is best and most plentiful are limited, the days are short, and the length of time available for sleeping and leisure is much longer. That is also the period of most frequent feasting because of many holidays, while the number of fasting days is limited.

But in the spring, in some households beginning in January or February, nutrition in the villages suffers. A large portion of rural families have by that time used up their home-produced cereals and practically all other winter reserves of food, and have to start buying much of what they need for subsistence. Of course, the medium and wealthier peasants have sufficient cereals to last them the whole crop year, and their winter reserves of other foods last usually well into the spring. The very fact that some peasants have to start buying food contributes to quantitative and qualitative worsening of the diet. Generally speaking, the peasant diet during the spring months is limited to cereals, home produced or bought, dried beans, some potatoes, and what the family is able to afford of such products as rice and pastes (both cereal foods), and such vegetables as onions.

The intake of meats, dairy products, and fats and oils is reduced much below that of the previous months, and so is the intake of wine in areas in which wine is produced. Until the late spring there are no vegetables and fruits in the fields and gardens. The supply of milk and eggs begins at this time to be larger, but practically all of such products have to be sold in order to buy the high calory foods.

On the other hand, field work becomes progressively heavier with the advance of spring and summer, the days become longer, and the time available for sleeping and leisure is drastically cut. It is in these months that, owing to poorer nutrition and greatly intensified physical exertion, a great portion of the peasants become dangerously less resistant to the ravages of disease. It is during these months that most of them lose weight, their faces become drawn, their skin acquires a parchment-like color, their eyes become dull. In these months the appearance of most of the rural people is in profound contrast to the budding spring around them. Only when the summer finally arrives is there bread from the field and a more plentiful and more varied supply of vegetables and fruits. . . .

Now, while this rhythm in nutrition in rural areas could be called a natural one because it reminds us of a similar pattern (though at other seasons) in the case of wild animals and also of most of the livestock herds in Yugoslavia, it is certainly nothing in which one could find any comfort when it applies either to people or to domestic animals. Was not one of the foremost objectives of mankind from the dawn of civilization to secure life against the vagaries of nature, including the rhythm in nature's production? Abundance and variety of production of food, high income, well-organized trade, development of storage facilities and food-preservation technology have almost completely eliminated the influence of seasonality of food production on the pattern of nutrition in advanced countries. Underdeveloped areas, on the contrary, are very far behind indeed from this goal.*

Emigration.   Life had been difficult in the Balkans long before 1914. But it had been possible in the prewar years to leave for the New World where the emigrants usually were able to support not only themselves but also several relatives back home. Emigrant remittances had played an extremely important role in the economies of Greece, as we noted in Chapter 25, and of certain parts of Yugoslavia. But the immigration restrictions adopted by the United States and certain British Dominions after the war reduced Balkan emigration to a trickle. This meant the loss of what hitherto had served as an important safety valve. The extent of the emigration drop in indicated in the table on p. 606.

Education.   The Balkan countries suffered from the combination of mass illiteracy and unemployment in the professions that was common to underdeveloped regions. The governments did try to provide schooling for all, but only with modest success because of the shortage of funds and the reluctance of some hard-pressed parents to dispense with the labor of their

* Reprinted from *Peasants, Politics, and Economic Change in Yugoslavia*, by Jozo Tomasevich, with the permission of the publishers, Stanford University Press. Copyright 1955 by the Board of Trustees of Leland Stanford Junior University.

Balkan Emigration Overseas

Country	Yearly Average 1901–10	Yearly Average 1921–30	Yearly Average 1931–37
Bulgaria	7,000	5,000	400
Greece	25,000	12,000	3,100
Rumania	Negligible [a]	10,900	1,700
Yugoslavia	15,000 [b]	13,600	1,500

[a] For old kingdom only.
[b] For Serbia and Montenegro only.

Source: Economic Development in S. E. Europe, p. 128.

children. The percentage of illiteracy at the age of ten and over on the eve of World War II amounted to 27 in Greece, 32 in Bulgaria, over 40 in Yugoslavia, nearly 50 in Rumania, and about 85 in Albania. The nature of the teaching in the lower schools left much to be desired. The teachers usually were poorly trained and the classrooms were overcrowded because of the lack of funds with which to provide more schools. As a result, the pupils rarely received more than a grounding in the "three R's," together with a healthy dose of nationalistic indoctrination. They were taught to look back to their respective periods of glory and greatness during the medieval ages and to regard the neighboring peoples as inferior in culture, morals, and military prowess. The Serbian pupils learned about their Dushan the Great, the Bulgarian about Tsars Simeon and Samuel, the Rumanian about Michael the Brave, and finally the Greek pupils reveled in the exploits of Byzantine emperors such as Basil the Bulgar-Slayer.

Some of these pupils were able to continue beyond their village elementary school to the secondary school in the nearest town and a few even to the university in the national capital or to some foreign institution. Most of these aspiring students were bright and ambitious but desperately poor. Through the difficult years of training they struggled and starved in the attics of Paris, Berlin, Munich, Vienna, or their own capitals. After many sacrifices, by their families as well as by themselves, they finally graduated, splendidly equipped for careers in their chosen professions. But all too frequently no positions were available, even though their countries needed more doctors and engineers and teachers. Thus the young intellectuals were left in limbo, unable to find work for which they were trained and yet unfitted and unwilling to take up the manual work which had been the lot of their peasant fathers and grandfathers.

It is true that too many of these students selected law as their profession. But it is also true that not all those who became agronomists or some other type of scientist were able to find employment despite the need for their services. The explanation is to be found in the underdeveloped state of the Balkan societies. An agronomist, for example, could not hope to be employed privately by the poverty-stricken peasantry of his country. His only chance lay in obtaining a position in the ministry of agriculture. We have seen that these positions were few because of the scanty funds that were appropriated. Thus the trained agronomist was left with the unfortunate choice of seeking employment of any sort in another branch of the government bureaucracy or accepting a position in a foreign country where he would be able to use his training and talents. Agronomists were not alone in this predicament. It has often been observed that doctors crowded together in a few Balkan cities while the countryside remained neglected. But it is not generally realized that the doctors did so not only for social reasons but also because the peasants could not afford medical care. This explains why an appreciable number of scientists and professional men of Balkan origin were to be found practicing in Western Europe and the United States despite the fact that their own countries urgently needed their services. It also explains why the unemployed intellectuals who stayed at home became frustrated and rootless and were prone to join such organizations as the Communist parties, the Peasant parties, and the fascist *Ustashi* of Croatia, and Iron Guards of Rumania, which had one thing, at least, in common—all were opposed to the *status quo*.

   State Administration. Balkan bureaucracies were proverbially overgrown, inefficient, and corrupt. The reasons were partly historical and partly economic. State structures developed in the West naturally and harmoniously with the growth of economic life. But in the Balkans the machinery of government was copied from the West and was superimposed with all its elaborateness and costliness upon an underdeveloped agrarian economy. At the same time the pressure of the unemployed university graduates for government positions also tended to swell the ranks of the civil servants. The result was that all the Balkan bureaucracies became grotesquely overstaffed. Many more officials per capita were to be found in the Balkan states than in the Western, despite the weakness of the Balkan economies. The load was borne only by reducing salaries to ridiculously low levels. In Rumania, for example, a study undertaken in May, 1941, revealed that a group of state employees in the Central Institute of Statistics were obliged to devote 62.3 per cent of their personal budgets to food alone, 13 per cent to housing and 11 per cent to clothing.[10] Inevitably such conditions led to inefficiency and corruption. The harrassed civil servant worked at other jobs on the side in order to make ends meet, and when the opportunity arose he was understandably tempted to accept the traditional bakshish.

   Corruption was not limited to the petty operations of poverty-stricken clerks. It permeated to the highest levels of government for the simple reason that in the Balkans, as in other economically underdeveloped regions, the greatest fortunes were made in politics rather than in commerce or industry. Ministers received handsome rewards, for example, in return for granting generous concessions to foreign companies, awarding monopolies to domestic syndicates, raising high tariffs in favor of some industry, or allowing favorable railway rates to certain companies. Occasionally scandals of a particularly revolting nature came to light. In the early thirties it was discovered in Greece that the state quinine monopoly had been dispensing a worthless powder in place of the drug with which it had been entrusted. And this in a country where a fifth of the population suffered from malaria. In Bulgaria most outgoing governments voted an amnesty commuting or completely abrogating such sentences as had been passed against their supporters for infringements of the law. The minister of justice pointed out on December 29, 1931, that thirty-five such amnesties had been voted since 1881.[11] The following passage captures the atmosphere that prevailed in Balkan government bureaus and illuminates the gulf that separated the rulers and the ruled.

The Balkan official regards himself as immeasurably superior to the peasants among whom he lives and from whose ranks he has sprung. To be an official is the fondest dream of every able young son of a peasant. The Balkan official does not like to work. He considers himself so fine a fellow that the State and the public should be proud to support him for life, and should not ask him to make efforts that will tax his intellect or character. A visitor to a Balkan Ministry or Police Headquarters in the middle of the morning will find the rooms filled with good-natured fellows comfortably enjoying a cup of Turkish coffee and a chat with their friends. The papers lie on their desks. Outside stand, sit and squat patient queues of peasants awaiting their various permits and receipts. Foreigners and citizens with "protekcija" * obtain swift and polite attention, but the people can afford to wait. They have waited many hundreds of years already for justice, and a few more hours will not make much difference.[12]

POLITICAL TRENDS

Pattern.   A consistent pattern is noticeable in Balkan political developments during the interwar period. At first a revolutionary atmosphere prevailed, with the left-wing Socialist, Communist, and Agrarian parties commanding a large following. In Greece the dynasty was overthrown and a republic established. In Bulgaria, King Ferdinand was forced to flee and, although his son Boris succeeded him on the throne, the country was dominated by an agrarian government under Alexander Stambuliski. In Rumania the National Peasant party led by Iuliu Maniu successfully challenged the entrenched Liberal party and assumed office in 1928. Finally, in Yugoslavia the Peasant party organized by the Radich brothers retained the support of the great majority of Croatians throughout the interwar period in defiance of the centralist governments in Belgrade.

Despite this initial radical upsurge, the left-wing parties in each Balkan country eventually were suppressed and dictatorial governments established. Stambuliski was murdered in 1923 and a rightist regime followed, end-

---

* This is the Serbian form of a word used, with different terminations, in all the languages and countries of Eastern Europe, to denote "special protection," "connections," "graft," or "pull." It is indispensable for the making of a career.

ing ultimately in a royal dictatorship. Similarly in Yugoslavia, Stjepàn Radich was assassinated in 1928 and King Alexander established a personal dictatorship the following year. Maniu did not suffer the fate of the other Agrarian leaders but he also was forced to give way in 1930 to King Carol, who soon established a corporatist regime. In Greece the monarchy was restored in 1935 and the following year a full-fledged dictatorship was imposed by General John Metaxas. Thus the interwar period, which began with a sweeping revolutionary wave, ended with dictatorial regimes in every Balkan country. The question arises what forces were operating in the background to produce this common pattern.

The reasons for the revolutionary atmosphere following World War I are clear enough. During the war years the peasants gained greatly in self-confidence because they realized that they were essential to the national economy as producers of foodstuffs and raw materials. At the same time the millions of peasant recruits widened their horizon immeasurably as a result of their war experiences. They observed not only the differences between city and village life but also the differences between various countries in regard to living standards and social institutions. The peasants were also strongly influenced by the Russian Revolution, the collapse of the Austro-Hungarian Empire, and the spread of Bolshevism into Central Europe. Finally, the unprecedented destruction and suffering during the long years of war aggravated the revolutionary situation. This was especially true of the countries that suffered defeat, and explains the abdication of both Ferdinand and Constantine.

The precise political manifestation of this revolutionary ferment varied from country to country according to local circumstances. The Communist parties did not play an outstanding role because they were outlawed everywhere as soon as they appeared to be dangerous. This happened in Yugoslavia and Rumania in 1921, in Bulgaria in 1923, and in Greece in 1936. This left the Agrarian parties as the only legal opposition organizations of any significance. Thus the Agrarian parties bulked large in Balkan politics during the 1920's, though they were by no means predominant throughout the peninsula. The most successful, durable, and best-organized Balkan Peasant party was that in Croatia organized by the Radich brothers. It retained the support of the great majority of Croatians during the interwar years not only because it concerned itself with the needs of the peasant majority but also because it assumed the leadership of Croatian nationalism against Serbian hegemony. The Agrarian Union in Bulgaria was also strong and influential, primarily because two disastrous wars in succession discredited the dynasty and the old parties. In Rumania the National Peasant party attracted a wide following because of the difficult position of the peasants and the identification of the hitherto dominant Liberal party with the urban interests.

On the other hand, Agrarianism did not make appreciable progress in Serbia or Greece. One reason was that peasant proprietorship traditionally had prevailed in both countries. Another reason was that both Nikola Pashich, who headed the Serbian Radical party, and Eleutherios Venizelos, who headed the

Greek Liberal party, enjoyed such prestige and following that no Agrarian program could compete seriously with them. Finally, important political issues in
each country diverted public attention from agrarian problems—the Venizelos-
Royalist feud being the overshadowing issue in Greece, and the centralism-
federalism dilemma in Serbia.

Agrarianism. The appearance of organized Peasant parties in Balkan
politics was an unprecedented development. Similar Peasant parties became
prominent at the same time elsewhere in Eastern Europe, particularly in
Czechoslovakia and Poland. All these Agrarian movements had certain common general objectives. In regard to agriculture, they wished to distribute the
land to those who tilled it and to substitute cooperatives for the ubiquitous
middlemen. They were fundamentally hostile toward industrialization because
it was incompatible with the rural type of society they cherished. Where industry was inescapable they preferred either public or cooperative ownership. They
also favored light industry that processed local agricultural products rather than
heavy industry that required much capital and transformed the entire economy.

In the field of government the Peasant parties were strongly egalitarian.
They wanted representative government based on universal franchise and also
full local self-government. They favored popular referendum and the people's
initiative in such matters as dismissal of public officials and convocation and
dissolution of parliament. Cheap and prompt justice was another prominent
feature of Agrarian programs, including the establishment of arbitration courts
for the settlement of the perennial peasant disputes. On the question of monarchy or republic, the Peasant parties were divided. The National Peasants of
Rumania accepted monarchism, whereas the Croatian and Bulgarian parties
both favored republicanism in their platforms, though in practice they found it
necessary to accept their respective dynasties.

In international affairs the Peasant parties had marked pacifist leanings. They advocated reduction of armaments, reliance on militia forces rather
than large standing armies, and promotion of policies designed to further international peace and understanding. A very common attitude throughout the
Agrarian parties was that war was an unmitigated evil, in support of which the
peasants were forced to pay high taxes and provide the cannon fodder. Accordingly, various Peasant leaders, and especially Stambuliski of Bulgaria, conceived
the idea of an international Peasant organization to end the traditional national
rivalries. This "Green International," as it was commonly called, was to offset
the "Red International" of revolutionary Bolsheviks and the "White International" of reactionary monarchs and landlords. The first step was the establishment in Prague of the International Agrarian Bureau designed to serve as an
information center. Dr. Milan Hodza, the head of a Czechoslovak Agrarian
party, described the purpose of the bureau in 1925 as follows: "We know that
agrarian democracy . . . is a strong bond which will bring the peoples together in an international unity—a formal, organic and spiritual unity against
which all attacks whether from the imperialist Right or the Bolshevik Left will
shatter themselves." [13] The bureau held annual congresses but they were

gradually dropped with the oncoming of the world depression and the accompanying political storms.

This unprecedented upsurge of peasant political consciousness and activity aroused great expectations. Many were dazzled by the vision of one hundred million peasants on the march in Eastern Europe for the first time in history. "The Green Rising is a thing like the Great War," wrote G. K. Chesterton in the early twenties. "It is a huge historical hinge and turning point, like the conversion of Constantine or the French Revolution. . . . What has happened in Europe since the war has been a vast victory for the peasants, and therefore a vast defeat both for the Communists and the capitalists. . . . In a sort of awful silence the peasantries have fought one vast and voiceless pitched battle with Bolshevism and its twin brother which is Big Business, and the peasantries have won." [14]

Chesterton's acclaim of a historic peasant victory was decidedly premature. Agrarianism proved a failure so far as immediate concrete results were concerned. Few Peasant parties came to power and none retained power long enough to test the practicability of their program. In country after country they were suppressed and dictatorships established. One reason for the failure of the Peasant parties in practical politics was their pacifism and distaste for violence. This left them vulnerable to the entrenched military and bureaucratic elements which did not hesitate to use force in order to seize and retain power.

Another reason for the failure of Agrarianism was that it tended to deceive itself with the romantic illusion of village cohesiveness and peasant unity. In actual fact no such solidarity existed. A few peasants were well off but the great majority were miserably poor. A few ate well but most did not. Some could afford to hire help while the majority were forced to accept outside employment to make ends meet. Some wealthy peasants loaned money which their less fortunate neighbors borrowed at extortionate rates. Thus the peasantry was by no means as cohesive a class group as Agrarian ideologists commonly assumed.

It should also be noted that the Peasant parties came increasingly under the control of lawyers and urban intellectuals, who were attracted by the initial electoral successes of the new Agrarianism. This influx of nonpeasant elements created an ever-widening gulf between the peasants and their leaders. Furthermore, the Agrarian parties usually represented the interests of the wealthy peasants and ignored the small-holder class. This accentuated the differences between the party leaders and the mass of poor peasants.

Perhaps the greatest weakness of the Peasant parties was their idealization of agriculture as "a way of life" as well as a means of livelihood. Consequently, they looked upon industry as a necessary evil that should be strictly limited and controlled. A Peasant spokesman has expressed this attitude as follows:

According to the program of the Peasant Movements, industrialization is only an auxiliary measure in the scheme of improvement of the peasant economy, and should not be regarded as an economic goal in itself. . . . The Peasant Movement opposes the establishment of substantial heavy industry because it leads to conglomerates of industrial population, which means in practice a considerable change in the social structure of the country. . . . Most of the finished products of heavy industry such as war matériel (e.g., tanks, guns, tractors and trucks) are either not needed in a peasant country or if needed can always be acquired under more favorable conditions from the industrialized West in exchange for the agricultural products that can be produced at home.[15]

This attitude was in reality quite impractical. The experience of all the peasant countries during the interwar years demonstrated that the exchange of agricultural products for manufactured goods was by no means as simple and satisfactory as pictured above. The industrial countries resorted increasingly to agricultural protectionism, which reduced the market for agricultural products. Furthermore, there was the competition of overseas foodstuffs which were produced on a much larger scale and were correspondingly cheaper. Consequently, all the Balkan countries found it difficult to market their exports and were forced to accept unfavorable terms for what they did sell. This in turn meant a low income for the Balkan peasant peoples. In fact, we noted above that the predominantly agrarian economies of the peninsula were quite incapable of supporting their respective populations, and that the resulting "surplus" population had nowhere to go precisely because of the absence of a well-developed industry.

"The solution of the problem of agriculture and peasantry," one authority has observed, "could not be found within agriculture itself but rather in a policy directed toward rapid development of industry and modernization of agriculture." [16] According to another authority, "The brutal truth is that the Peasant States can only become prosperous and healthy when they cease to be Peasant States." [17] This conclusion, inescapable though it is, naturally could not be considered or accepted by the peasant parties. Indeed, it represented the Achilles heel of the Agrarian movement in the Balkans and elsewhere.

Dictatorships. Whatever the failings of the peasant parties may have been, they cannot be held solely responsible for the triumph of absolutism in the Balkans. Dictatorial regimes prevailed not only in the northern Balkans but also in Greece, where agrarianism was virtually nonexistent. Thus the origins of the dictatorships cannot be attributed merely to various defects of the agrarian movement. It is certainly necessary to take into account the world depression, which hurt Venizelos' Liberal government in Greece as well as Maniu's Peasant government in Rumania, and which paved the way for the dictatorship of Metaxas in Greece as it did that of Carol in Rumania. It is also necessary to note the wide gap that separated the rulers from the ruled. Such a gap exists in all societies, but it was especially pronounced in the Balkans, where the average peasant was unable to exercise his rights and duties as a citizen. One reason was that he was usually illiterate and ignorant, and lacked any tradition of democratic self-government. Another reason was that his economic role as a relatively self-sufficient producer restricted his interests and activities to his village. His economic and social life did not extend into the numerous fields that comprised the necessary activities of modern government. Consequently there was much less rapport between citizen and official in the Balkans than in Western Europe.

It is true that many Balkan political leaders were educated in the West and that they faithfully initiated Western political institutions, such as written constitutions and political parties with traditional names such as Liberal, Conservative, and Radical. But all this was a thin veneer. Indeed, the attempt to graft Western institutions on a native stock produced serious maladjustments. The following indictment of Rumanian institutions by a citizen of that country is equally applicable to the entire peninsula.

Unfortunately our glorious urban institutions, for all their liberal-democratic techniques, are pure falsehoods. . . . we have introduced universal suffrage, but with ballot stuffing; we have ruined rural households in order to increase credit institutions, but have not permitted free competition among these institutions, but have favored some—those belonging to us—and have attacked others—those belonging to our adversaries; we have encouraged national industry, but not for the benefit of the rural population, as would have been right, since they made the sacrifices, but for the benefit of politicians who are pensioners of this national industry; we have centralized the administration of the country, but not in the hands of a trained bureaucracy but in the hands of the party and its partisans; in a word we have aped the European bourgeoisie in form, but at bottom we have persisted in the sycophantic habits of the past. In this way we have transformed political life into a hopeless turmoil.[18]

Such a combination of political, economic, and historical factors explains the appearance of dictatorships in all the Balkan countries. These regimes, however, were very different from the contemporary authoritarian governments in Fascist Italy and Nazi Germany. The main difference is that the Balkan regimes lacked mass support. They did not possess an ideology that caught the imagination of the masses. Nor did they have the efficiency and technical facilities necessary to indoctrinate the masses even if they had possessed an effective ideology. Thus the great bulk of the population remained unaffected by the heroics of Balkan fuehrers like Carol, Metaxas, and Stoyadinovich. "The eastern dictatorships," one authority has concluded, "never rested on the support of strong sections of the masses. The villagers especially looked with bland peasant skepticism on the uniforms and parades and oratorical antics of these would-be tribunes. The eastern dictatorships were never anything but bureaucratic and military regimes, as brittle as they were inefficient and oppressive." [19]

Communism. In view of the unprecedented developments following World War II it is worth noting at this point the position and role of the Balkan Communist parties during the interwar period.* The Communist parties in the Balkans, as in other parts of the world, emerged from the split that occurred in the prewar Socialist parties following the Russian Revolution. The right-wing

* The individual Balkan Communist parties are considered in Chapters 32–35.

elements remained Socialist and continued to be affiliated with the Second (Socialist) International, while the left-wing elements constituted the new Communist parties and affiliated with the Third (Communist) International or Comintern. In January, 1920, delegates of the Bulgarian, Yugoslav, and Greek parties met in Sofia and formed the Balkan Communist Federation in order to coordinate and strengthen their activities. At that time the Bulgarian and Yugoslav parties each claimed to have 30,000 members. The Greek party claimed only 1,300, while the Rumanian party probably was at about the same low level.

The activities and influence of the Communist parties are difficult to assess because they were all soon outlawed and forced to operate underground. Under this circumstance they conducted their work with two objectives in mind. One was to recruit and train disciplined cadres in order to keep the movement alive despite severe repression. The other was to carry on propaganda based on directives from the Comintern and designed to win sympathizers and create a mass movement. The Communists were most successful with urban workers, disaffected intellectuals, minority groups such as the Jews and Hungarians in Rumania, and uprooted groups such as the Asia Minor refugees in Greece and the Macedonians in Bulgaria.

The Communists were not able to accomplish much during the interwar years because of the many handicaps under which they operated. One was the repression from above which forced them to work underground and hampered their propaganda activities. Another was the fear that devout peasants had for godless communism, a fear that was particularly strong in Catholic areas such as Slovenia and Croatia. Fear of Slavic Russia was also an important factor in non-Slavic countries, such as Rumania and Greece. Finally, and perhaps most important, the Balkan Communists labored under the great disadvantage of being required to accept and to carry out orders from the Comintern. These orders proved to be a constant source of embarrassment and hindrance for the Communist cause in the Balkans.

This was especially true in regard to the national question on which the Comintern took an extreme position based on the principle of the self-determination of peoples. Thus the Fifth World Congress of the Communist International held in the summer of 1924 stated that the Versailles Treaty had created a number of small imperialist states in Eastern Europe to serve as a *cordon sanitaire* against the Soviet Union. These states had been formed by the annexation of large areas with foreign populations. Accordingly the Congress proclaimed "the right of every nation to self-determination, even to the extent of separation," and called for "the political separation of oppressed peoples from Poland, Rumania, Czechoslovakia, Yugoslavia, and Greece."

More specifically the Congress declared itself in favor of stripping Macedonia and Thrace from Greece; Macedonia, Croatia, and Slovenia from Yugoslavia; and Transylvania, Dobruja, Bessarabia, and Bukovina from Rumania. All these territories were to become independent political units in a Balkan Communist Federation, with the exception of Bessarabia and Bukovina, which were slated for incorporation in the Soviet Union.

It is apparent that parties committed to the wholesale dismemberment of their own countries had little chance of gaining widespread support. In fact, the Comintern directives not only isolated the Balkan parties from the people but also fomented dissension within the communist movement. Both the Yugoslav and the Greek parties protested strenuously against the establishment of an independent Macedonia while the Bulgarian party favored this policy. The Comintern denounced all opposition as opportunism and betrayal of the proletariat. In June, 1925, Stalin replied to Sima Markovich, head of the Yugoslav party, as follows: ". . . he has not grasped the fact that the national question must be considered not in isolation, but in inseparable connection with the question of the victory of the revolution, as a part of the general question of revolution." [20] The Comintern was able to keep most of its followers in line in the Balkans as elsewhere in the world. But a few refused to accept the argument that the international revolutionary cause required acceptance of dictation from Moscow. Pouliopoulos, a Greek leader who later became a prominent Trotskyite, challenged the very principle of Comintern domination. "It is inadmissible that any international commando should autocratically decree that other Communist Parties should promulgate principles incompatible with the objective conditions of their countries." [21]

It should not be assumed, however, that the position of the Communist parties was wholly unfavorable. They did have certain unique advantages that enabled them eventually to play a leading and dramatic role in Balkan affairs. One was their propaganda, which was simple and effective. It was based essentilly on two ideas—social justice and revolution. Simple Balkan peasants who knew little about Marxist ideology could grasp and appreciate these ideas. Social justice was bound to have appeal where social injustice was the rule. Revolution also found fertile soil in the Balkans because of the tradition of violence and direct action. In fact, this explains to a large degree why the socialist parties, with their emphasis on legal action and parliamentary procedures, were never able to compete successfully with their communist rivals in the Balkans.

Another advantage of the Communists was their militancy and their dogged underground activity despite fierce repression. The Socialists tended to give up the struggle as hopeless when the various dictatorships were established. They either compromised with existing authority or else waited in the hope that international events would affect the domestic situation. The Communists, by contrast, continued their opposition underground, fortified, as the Socialists could not be, by the belief that a great power was on their side. This characteristic of the Communists proved to be of basic importance because, when the Axis armies overran the peninsula in 1940–1941, only the Communist parties possessed trained and trusted cadres for underground resistance. Thus they were able to lead and dominate the resistance movements during the occupation years. And their connection with the Soviet Union gave them another and decisive advantage during the postwar years when Russian armies controlled the northern Balkans.

32. Yugoslavia: 1918–1939

By ALL ODDS the most serious problem facing the new state of Yugoslavia was that of centralism versus federalism. This was scarcely surprising in view of the disparate origins and composition of the state. It consisted of Slovenia and Dalmatia—former territories of Austria; Croatia-Slavonia—formerly a quasi-autonomous province of Hungary; the Voivodina—formerly an integral portion of Hungary; Bosnia-Herzegovina—formerly an Austro-Hungarian condominium administered by their joint ministry of finance; and finally Montenegro and Serbia—former independent kingdoms. Furthermore, it should be noted that Serbia and Montenegro included portions of Macedonia and the Sanjak of Novi Bazar, which had been Turkish territories until 1912.

Given this complex background, it becomes understandable why the leaders of Yugoslavia met with so much difficulty in their attempts to construct a viable state. Their efforts eventually failed, as is indicated by the stormy course of Yugoslav politics during the interwar years. The reason for their failure is to be found in the fact that from the beginning—indeed, even before the new state was born—there were two diametrically opposed viewpoints concerning the political organization of the South Slav peoples, the Greater Serbian and the Yugoslav.

SEEDS OF DISUNITY:
CENTRALISM VERSUS FEDERALISM

The Greater Serbia idea, held by the Belgrade politicians led by Nikola Pashich, had as its principal goal the addition to Serbia of all lands inhabited primarily by Serbs. This involved specifically the annexation of Bosnia-Herzegovina with an outlet to the Adriatic. The bonds holding together the new Greater Serbia were to be the common Orthodox religion and Serbian nationality of its inhabitants. Other South Slav lands, such as Slovenia, Croatia, Dalmatia, and the Voivodina, might also be acquired sometime in the future,

616

TERRITORIAL GROWTH OF YUGOSLAVIA

- 1815 Formation of Principality of Serbia
- 1833 Turks recognize Serbian control of border regions
- 1878 Nish-Pirot region ceded by Turkey
- 1913 Part of Macedonia ceded by Turkey
- 1918-1919 Kingdom of Yugoslavia formed by unification of Montenegro with Serbia, and acquisitions of Bosnia-Herzegovina, Dalmatia, and Slovenia from Austria ; Croatia, Slavonia, the Voivodina, and part of the Banat from Hungary ; and Strumitsa, Bosiligrad, Caribrod (Tsaribrod) and Timok enclaves from Bulgaria
- 1947 Istria and the Lastovo (Lagosta) and Palagruza (Pelagosa) Islands ceded by Italy

but their acquisition was not considered indispensable. Whatever the area it embraced, the state was to be strongly centralized, Serbian-dominated, and ruled by the Orthodox Karageorgevich dynasty.

The Hapsburg South Slavs, who were the chief supporters of the Yugo-slav idea, opposed every aspect of this Greater Serbia program. In place of a Greater Serbia they wanted an all-inclusive South Slav state. In place of a Serbian-dominated realm they wanted a federal political structure in which each group would be able to preserve its unique political, cultural, and religious characteristics. And as for the Karageorgevich dynasty, they were willing to accept it on the condition that its members considered themselves to be Yugo-slav rather than purely Serbian rulers.

This divergence in views came to the fore as soon as World War I began. On July 29, 1914, the day after Austria declared war on Serbia, the Pashich government issued a manifesto calling upon the Serbs to defend their homeland. Not until four months later, after considerable pressure from groups sympathetic to Yugoslavism, did Pashich announce that the aim of his government was the liberation and unification of all South Slavs. Meanwhile a number of Hapsburg South Slav leaders had fled abroad and established the Yugoslav Committee headed by a Dalmatian, Dr. Ante Trumbich. The stated purpose of the committee was to conduct propaganda directed toward "the deliverance of all Yugoslavs from the Austrian yoke, and union with our free brothers in Serbia and Montenegro in one united state." [1] In April, 1916, Dr. Trumbich met with the Serbian Crown Prince Alexander in Paris and told him that the Serbo-Croat-Slovene nation in Austria-Hungary "has come to the firm conviction that it cannot expect life and freedom in that monarchy, and thus our people asks to be freed from foreign domination and to be united with their brothers in Serbia under the glorious dynasty of the Karageorgevich." [2]

This campaign in behalf of Yugoslavism was one-sided until July 20, 1917, when Pashich and Trumbich signed the Corfu Pact, calling for the establishment of a Yugoslav state at the end of the war. One reason why Pashich signed the document was that Serbia at the time was occupied by enemy forces and consequently he was not in a position to be intransigent concerning postwar political organization. Also, the tsarist regime, which had strongly supported Great Serbism, had fallen in March, 1917, and the American government, which was inclined to be pro-Yugoslav, entered the war the following month. Under these circumstances Pashich felt constrained to accept an agreement providing for a constitutional, democratic, and parliamentary monarchy under the Karageorgevich dynasty. The state was to include all the South Slav peoples and its constitution was to be prepared by a constituent assembly elected after the war by universal suffrage and secret ballot.

Despite this agreement the relations between the Yugoslav Committee and the Serbian government continued to be strained. The committee complained because Serbia's ambassadors, on instructions from Belgrade, continued to work for purely Serbian interests rather than for the new Yugoslav program. It also resented Pashich's refusal to support plans for a large, all-Yugoslav congress in Paris to publicize the Yugoslav cause. In spite of this mutual suspicion and hostility, both sides were forced to work together by the headlong course of events attendant upon the collapse of the Hapsburg Empire.

In August, 1918, the Hapsburg South Slavs held a congress in Ljubljana and established the Yugoslav National Council under the leadership of Father Koroshetz, head of the Catholic Slovenian Populist party. It was to this body that the Austrian military authorities handed over their power on October 28. The following day the council proclaimed the independence of the South Slav provinces from Hapsburg sovereignty. The Austrians and the Hungarians had no choice but to recognize the authority of the council. But the Allies refused to do so at this time, and the Italians seized the opportunity to move their troops into territories claimed by the council. Meanwhile the peasants were seizing land and rumors were spreading of the growing danger of Bolshevism.

This critical situation compelled all parties to act swiftly. On November 11 the Declaration of Geneva was signed by Koroshetz for the National Council, by Trumbich for the Yugoslav Committee, and by Pashich for the Serbian government. The Declaration called for "one state, formed of Serbs, Croats and Slovenes," though with the proviso that the former Hapsburg provinces were to have full autonomy until a National Constituent Assembly met to decide the form of government of the new state. On November 26 an assembly met at Podgorica in Montenegro, formally deposed King Nicholas and his dynasty, and proclaimed the union of Montenegro with Serbia. Finally, on December 1, 1918, representatives of all the South Slav lands met in Belgrade and formally proclaimed the new Kingdom of the Serbs, Croats, and Slovenes.* At last all the South Slavs were gathered under one flag. But the conflicting viewpoints which had been expressed during the war still remained to be resolved. And a portent of the trouble ahead was the little-noticed fact that Stjepan Radich, leader of the Croatian Peasant party, had refused to recognize the transfer of power to Prince Alexander, demanding, instead, an independent peasant Croatian republic.

LAND REFORM

The first Yugoslav government was formed in January, 1919. It represented all groups, the premier being the Serbian statesman Stojan Protich, the vice-premier the Slovene Koroshetz, and the minister of foreign affairs the Dalmatian Trumbich. A provisional National Assembly was also formed, comprising delegates from the Serbian Skupshtina and the Yugoslav National Council together with representatives of Montenegro and the Voivodina. The cabinet and the assembly addressed themselves to pressing problems such as the negotiation of the peace treaties and the reconstruction of devastated Serbia. But the outstanding problem, in the view of most Yugoslavs, was that of land reform.

In view of the fact that much criticism has been levied against the drastic land distribution that took place in Yugoslavia, it is well to recall that this was quite unavoidable at that time. Repeated promises of land reform had been made during the course of the war by both the Serbian government and the Yugoslav National Council. Also, nationalist considerations were involved in the demand for land distribution: in the northern areas five out of every six landlords were foreigners, mostly Austrians and Hungarians. It was unthinkable after four years of war that landless Yugoslav peasants should continue to work the estates of enemy nationals. In the south, religious considerations entered, most of the landowners in Macedonia and Bosnia-Herzegovina being Moslems. Another factor that entered into the picture was the contrast between the small peasant plots that prevailed in Serbia and the large estates that dominated the former Hapsburg provinces. The perpetuation of this contrast was

* The name of the new state was changed in 1929 to Yugoslavia. This name has been employed here for all periods, in accordance with common usage.

politically impossible now that the Hapsburg power had been broken. Also, it should be recalled that the peasants were in a revolutionary frame of mind in 1918 and that for this reason the landlords accepted land reform uncomplainingly at the beginning for fear of more radical developments. In fact, in many areas the peasants were overrunning and dividing the estates without waiting for government action. Thus the land reform legislation that was eventually passed simply gave legal recognition to a *fait accompli* and defined precisely the terms of expropriation.

The basic land bill was the "Interim Decree" of February 25, 1919. This set forth three general principles that were to govern land distribution: abolition of all feudal and quasi-feudal institutions, expropriation of a portion of the large estates above a certain minimum, and payment of indemnity to the former landowners. The weakness of this bill was its preliminary character, merely defining the general lines of reform. Because of the very different conditions prevailing in the various provinces it was necessary to prepare specific legislation for each area. But the delay gave the landlords time to organize opposition and to fight against terms which they would have gladly accepted in 1919. With the passage of time, land reform unfortunately became a political football. The most flagrant case was that of the Moslem landowners, who controlled a bloc of seats in the Skupshtina representing the sizable Moslem minority in Macedonia and Bosnia-Herzegovina. We shall see that Pashich needed these Moslem votes to get his centralist constitution through the Constituent Assembly. So he struck a bargain by which he gave very generous terms to the Moslem landowners when their estates were divided, and in return he received their votes and thus passed his constitution.

Under these conditions a large number of land bills were passed during the following years. Because of the complexity of the problem and the opposition of the landlords, a full legal settlement had not been reached in certain regions even by the 1930's. In fact, a few cases remained unresolved when World War II began. Despite this vacillation and delay, the fact remains that a tremendous amount of land changed hands throughout the country, with the exception of Serbia and Montenegro, where it was felt that land reform was not needed. Well over 2,000,000 hectares were distributed, not counting forest land. The land distributed represented over a quarter of all the arable land. And the beneficiaries were 500,000 peasant families, or more than one out of every four.

TRIUMPH OF CENTRALISM:
1921 CONSTITUTION

The Constituent Assembly was elected on November 28, 1920. The election itself was eminently fair, a quality that was not to be characteristic of later elections. See the table on the following page.

Party	Deputies elected
Democrats (Davidovich and Pribichevich)	92
Radicals (Pashich)	91
Communists	58
Croatian Peasant party (Radich)	50
Agrarians	39
Slovene People's party (Koroshetz)	27
Moslems (Spaho)	32
Socialists	10
Miscellaneous	20
Total	419

Source: Charles A. Beard and G. Radin, *The Balkan Pivot: Yugoslavia* (New York, 1929), p. 41.

In the light of the events of the interwar years, the most important of these parties were the Radical and the Croatian Peasant. The Radical party was founded in 1881 by Nikola Pashich, the outstanding figure in Serbian politics before the rise of Tito. White-bearded, grave, and taciturn, Pashich was an anomalous figure among his voluble and explosive countrymen. He resembled most closely a Tammany Hall chieftain in the party machine that he organized, in his political shrewdness, and in his capacity to foresee trends and to adjust his policies accordingly. His party at first lived up to its name, fighting vigorously for local self-government and improved agricultural credit, and supporting parliament as against the crown and the bureaucracy. It also gained great prestige by leading the struggle against the Obrenovich dynasty and its pro-Austrian foreign policy. With the accession of the Karageorgevich dynasty in 1903 the Radical party came to power and remained in power almost without interruption until Pashich's death in 1926. But with its change in status the party soon also changed in character. Its leaders dropped their radical phrases and lost their former interest in political liberties and peasant welfare. Gradually it became the main party of the rising Serbian bourgeoisie.

This process was greatly accelerated after 1918. The possibilities for money-making were far bigger in the new Yugoslavia than in the parochial prewar Serbia. The small shopkeepers and tradesmen of the pre-1914 period grew to the proportions of big businessmen. And since political power was the quickest road to business success, big business had good reason to consolidate its hold on the Radical party. The party became correspondingly conservative; yet it managed to retain its hold over the Serbian peasantry. The reason was partly Pashich's great prestige and partly the efficient party machine which dispensed patronage and made loans. Thus the Radical party remained to the end the strongest party in Serbia. It also remained strongly nationalist, the formidable bulwark of Great Serbism.

The Croatian Peasant party was the antithesis of the Radical party in almost every respect. It was organized in 1905 by the Radich brothers, two intellectuals of peasant stock. Antun was the original thinker who evolved the party ideology, while Stjepan was the political organizer and brilliant demagogue who moved the multitudes. Before the war the party had no chance because of the extremely limited franchise which allowed less than 1 per cent of the peasants to vote. But in the 1921 elections, held under universal suffrage, the party showed that it had the support of the overwhelming majority of the Croatian voters. This gave rise to serious complications because at the end of the war Stjepan Radich had voted against the union of Croatia with Serbia. At the time little attention was paid to him, but now he was the master of Croatia. He was to remain the master until his assassination in 1928. And after that his party continued to receive the support of the great majority of Croatians until the German invasion in 1941.

The party owed its success to the fact that it voiced perfectly the grievances and aspirations of the Croatian peasants. They were heartily sick of war, and a main plank in the party's platform was pacifism and antimilitarism. They were determined not to submit again to rule from a distant capital, so the party called for an independent peasant republic. After the creation of Yugoslavia it dropped its republican plank, but it demanded instead a federal state structure with full local government. In economic matters as well as political the party was strongly egalitarian. It glorified the peasant and viewed the growing big business clique in Belgrade with the traditional distrust of the countryside. Specifically, it demanded land to the peasants and a drastic reduction of military, bureaucratic, and other state expenses in order to ease the tax burden on the rural population. Obviously there was bound to be serious trouble given this conflict on every crucial point between the leading Serbian and Croatian parties. Unfortunately, Stjepan Radich's character and temperament increased the friction. He was a man of great talents, generous impulses, and deep social conscience, but he was also a fuzzy thinker and completely unpredictable. He never knew clearly what he wanted or what strategy he should pursue. Pashich and the other Serbian leaders were alienated by his erratic behavior apart from any question of ideology. It was a great misfortune for Croatia and Yugoslavia that his clear-headed brother died in 1919.

The Communist party, to which we now turn, arose out of the prewar Social Democratic parties that had existed in Serbia, Croatia, Slovenia, the Voivodina, and Bosnia-Herzegovina. With the triumph of the Bolsheviks in Russia these parties split, the right-wing elements uniting to form the Socialist party of Yugoslavia and the left-wing groups to form the Communist party of Yugoslavia. A few months before the 1920 elections the Communist party proclaimed its goal to be the establishment of a Yugoslav Soviet Republic which would unite "with all neighboring peoples for the establishment of a Soviet federation of Balkan-Danubian countries, which will be an integral part of the international federation of Soviet Republics." [3] To everyone's surprise the party won 58 seats in the elections that followed. In the light of developments during World War II it is significant that most of the votes came not from the small industrial proletariat but rather from an illiterate peasantry suffering hardships and demanding land.

The Belgrade authorities were shocked by the strength of the Communists. They took advantage of the murder of the minister of interior by a young Communist in 1921 to suppress the party. By a majority vote of the assembly the party and its press were declared illegal and the party deputies were unseated. During the entire period to World War II the party remained outlawed, its members being forced to operate underground. As will be recalled from Chapter 31, their effectiveness was undermined, however, by the Comintern resolutions concerning national self-determination which called for the partitioning of Yugoslavia into several independent republics. But with the outbreak of World War II and the occupation of the country by Axis forces, the Yugoslav Communists, thanks to their underground experience, were able to rise to the top.

Of the other parties in the 1920 elections, the Democratic was by far the largest with 92 seats. It was organized in 1919 and comprised two groups: the Hapsburg Serbs led by Svetozar Pribichevich, and the Independent Radicals who, under the leadership of Ljuba Davidovich, seceded at the beginning of the century from the Radical party when the latter became conservative. The Democratic party later split and never again approached the Radical and Croatian Peasant parties in parliamentary strength. The Agrarian party, which won 39 seats in the 1920 elections, declined to insignificance thereafter. The reason was partly the land reforms which tempered peasant radicalism, and partly the ability of the Radicals to retain the support of the Serbian peasants. Since the Croatian peasants were loyal to Radich there remained only the Slovenes. But they in turn were attached to the Catholic Slovene People's party led by Father Anton Koroshetz. This party served its supporters well, organizing an efficient system of cooperatives and pressing for social legislation. In the political field Koroshetz was interested primarily in winning autonomy for Slovenia. When he failed to achieve this by opposing the Belgrade centralists, he switched his tactics and in the 1930's struck a bargain with them which gave him what he wanted. In addition to the Socialists who, like their opposite numbers in the other Balkan countries, were never able to challenge the Communists effectively, there remains the Moslem party. Its strength lay in Bosnia and its leaders were opportunists who before 1914 had supported the Austrian regime and who now supported most of the Belgrade governments. In return they obtained material advantages for their coreligionists, especially positions on the state railroads. Indeed, so many Belgrade cabinets were able to remain in office because of Moslem and Slovene votes that a popular saying appeared to the effect that the Moslems and the Slovenes together ruled Yugoslavia.

This proved to be justified in the case of the 1921 constitution, which was passed only with the aid of Moslem votes. Pashich was determined to secure a centralist constitution based on that of Serbia with some modifications to meet the needs of the new enlarged state. Radich was unalterably opposed to such a constitution but, since he boycotted the assembly, Pashich did not have to contend with the 50 Croatian votes. Pashich was also rid of the 58 Communist votes after the party had been outlawed. Thus he was able to push through the constitution by 223 out of the 419 votes in parliament. It is significant that the great bulk of the positive votes were Serbian—the Radicals (91) and the Democrats (92). The remaining votes that were needed were virtually bought—Moslems (32), and Slovene Peasant (8). It is also noteworthy that the parties which supported and passed the constitution represented less than half of the popular vote cast for the members of parliament.

The "Vidovdan Constitution," named after St. Vitus's Day, the Serbian national holiday on which it was voted and on which Francis Ferdinand was murdered in 1914, was based on the prewar Serbian constitution. It provided for a one-chamber parliament and a highly centralized administrative system. The king controlled the army and chose the premiers in accordance with the balance of votes in parliament. In practice this gave him wide choice because proportional representation created a large number of parties. The prewar constitution had accorded the Orthodox Church a privileged status, but the new document granted equality and toleration to all religions. Although more liberal in matters of religion, the new constitution placed more restrictions on freedom of press, speech, and public meetings. In fact, despite the customary phrases of Western liberalism incorporated in the constitution, the police power of the government was without practical limits. And so it proved to be in practice during the following years. The constitution did include a long section on social reform, but this proved to be meaningless with the exception of the agrarian reform which was already under way. In short, the new constitution was a reproduction of that of 1903 with such modifications as were needed to adjust to the new conditions.

POLITICAL PATTERN

Political developments during the two decades between the adoption of the constitution in 1921 and the German invasion of 1941 may be divided, for the sake of convenience, into three periods. The first, from 1921 to 1928, was characterized by political deadlock between the supporters of centralism and of federalism. The second period, from 1929 to 1934, was one of dictatorship, which was established by King Alexander in the hope of ending the political crisis. The assassination of Alexander in 1934 inaugurated the third period, rule by the regency, which lasted until the Axis occupation in 1941.

The outstanding feature of Yugoslav politics during these two decades was the domination of the entire state apparatus by the Belgrade centralists. This domination is clearly revealed by a statistical analysis of the individuals who filled the top posts in the various branches of government. During the parliamentary era from December, 1918, to January, 1929—a period of 121 months—Serbians held the premiership for 117 months, ministry of the army and navy for 121 months, ministry of the interior (which controlled the police) for 111 months, ministry of foreign affairs for 100 months, ministry of finance for 118 months, ministry of education for 110 months, and the ministry of justice for 105 months. Likewise in the era of dictatorship, from January, 1929, to March, 1941—a period of 147 months—Serbians held the premiership, the ministry of the army and navy, and the ministry of foreign affairs for 147 months, the ministry of the interior for 129 months, the ministry of finance for 98 months, the ministry of education for 126 months, and the ministry of justice for 132 months.

In addition to controlling the main ministries, the Serbians also controlled the armed forces. Of the 165 generals in active service in 1938, 161 were Serbs, 2 were Croats, and 2 Slovenes. Also, all the important diplomatic posts, such as the ambassadorships to Paris, Rome, London, and Berlin, were always in the charge of Serb diplomats. Likewise, the four tremendously important state financial institutions—the National Bank (the central bank), the State Mortgage Bank, the Postal Savings System, and the Chartered Agricultural Bank—were always headed by Serbs. Finally, it should be noted that the Serbians, in controlling these focal power positions, also controlled a vast amount of patronage which they utilized effectively as a political weapon.[4]

There arises at this point the basic question of how the Serbs were able to maintain their hegemony in view of the fact that the centralist constitution was supported by parties that received a minority of the popular vote in the 1920 elections. One of the important factors undoubtedly was Alexander's complete control of the army. This control dated from the extremely controversial "Saloniki Affair" of June, 1917. At that time Alexander brought to trial before a court in Saloniki the leaders of the Black Hand, including Colonel Dimitrijevich himself. It will be recalled from Chapter 29 that in the immediate prewar years the Black Hand under the leadership of the redoubtable colonel had dominated the army, terrorized government officials and even the court, planned the assassination of Francis Ferdinand, and generally functioned as a state within the state. Prince Alexander, who was more strong-willed than his father, was determined to destroy this rival power before the time came to return to liberated Serbia. Accordingly, the Black Hand leaders were found guilty at the Saloniki trial of various crimes that apparently were trumped up, such as negotiating secretly with the Germans and planning to assassinate Alexander. Dimitrijevich and two others were executed, and about two hundred other officers were imprisoned or sent to Africa for internment. Having wiped out the Black Hand, Alexander then organized the so-called White Hand, comprising loyal and trusted officers. He showered favors upon this group during the interwar period, and in return he was assured of full military support at all times.

Another factor explaining Serbian hegemony in the Yugoslav state was the inability of the opposition to act in concert. Radich must bear a good deal of the blame for this situation. He undoubtedly erred in boycotting the assembly when the constitution was being debated. And in the following years he confused friends and foes alike by his erratic behavior, now defying the government and going to jail, now joining the government and accepting office. Also, small minority groups like the Slovenes and the Moslems made it possible for many cabinets to remain in power by supporting them in return for various concessions.

A final factor explaining Serbian hegemony in Yugoslavia was the diligent use of all the various legal and extralegal devices that governments everywhere, and especially in the Balkans, have utilized to remain in power. These included patronage, bribery, gerrymandering, rigged elections, unfair electoral laws, and, when necessary, the use of the police and *gendarmerie*. One specific example might be mentioned. Every politician was eligible for a lifelong pension after having served as a minister or an undersecretary for one year. A very large number fell into this category, and they all felt strongly constrained to forbear from voicing any opposition to the royal dictatorship established in 1929.

All these facts suggest that Radich was not unjustified when he complained that few non-Serbs were permitted to hold high office, and even these few were "not in the government but attached to the government." [5]

POLITICAL DEADLOCK: 1921–1928

Following the adoption of the constitution, the country was ruled for a short while by the same coalition of Radicals, Democrats, and Moslems that had put through the document. On March 18, 1923, new parliamentary elections were held with the following results: Radicals, 108 seats; Croatian Peasants, 70; Democrats, 51; Slovenes, 21; Bosnian Moslems, 18; Macedonian Moslems, 14; Agrarians, 10; miscellaneous, 20. Both the Radicals and the Croatian Peasants had increased their representation at the expense of the Agrarians, who were almost wiped out, and the Democrats, who lost heavily. Pashich was able to remain in office because Radich again decided to boycott parliament. He did so because the Serbians rejected his plan for a new constitution which he had proposed in May, 1923. The rejection is not surprising in view of the fact that he demanded that Yugoslavia should be transformed into a loose confederation in which Croatia should have full autonomy, including her own constitution and army.

Such an arrangement was out of the question for Pashich, who continued to rule the country with the aid of the Moslem deputies. But in March, 1924, all the opposition groups in the assembly reached an agreement to cooperate for the overthrow of the Pashich cabinet. They included the Croatians, who decided to return to parliament to vote, and the Davidovich faction of the Democrats, which was becoming disillusioned with Pashich's centralist rule. Pashich could not retain office against such opposition, so he ordered new elections for February 8, 1925.

In order to ensure favorable returns Pashich took legal action against the Croatian party leadership. Radich had visited Moscow during the course of a European tour and had established friendly relations with the Communist International. Undoubtedly this was more in the nature of blackmail against Belgrade than a serious alliance with the Bolsheviks. Radich's egalitarian peasant philosophy was poles apart from communist materialism, as he himself made clear on his return. Nevertheless, the Belgrade government ordered the dissolution of the Croatian Peasant party on the ground that it had placed itself under the orders of an alien subversive organization. All meetings and publications of the party were prohibited, and Radich himself was imprisoned. Despite this action, the Croatian Peasant party demonstrated its continued hold on its followers by winning 67 seats. However, the elections did give the government parties (the Radicals and the Independent Democrats under Pribichevich) a majority of 162 seats against 153 for the opposition parties.

At this point Radich made one of his unpredictable turnabouts. On July 14, 1925, he reached an agreement with Pashich by which he left his jail cell and became minister of education. By the terms of the agreement the Croats were to accept the dynasty and the centralized state, and in return the Serbs were to grant autonomy at the district level and equalize taxation throughout the country. This coalition regime lasted less than a year. Before long the erratic Radich was denouncing the government of which he was a member. In April, 1926, the cabinet was re-formed without the inclusion of Radich, and the old feud was resumed.

Later in the year, in December, 1926, Pashich died. His Radical party now lost some of its cohesiveness, giving Alexander more opportunity to intervene in party politics. In February, 1927, another important political development occurred when the Slovene leader, Koroshetz, joined the government. Hitherto he had opposed the Belgrade centralists but had gained nothing for his efforts. Now he joined them and in return his party was given control over the nomination of administrative officials in Slovenia. This, of course, did not solve the perennial Croatian problem. Rather, it hardened the lines because the Belgrade government now could count on a large bloc of Slovene as well as Moslem votes. Such was the situation when on June 20, 1928, the political tension culminated in a wild crime in the Skupshtina. A Montenegrin deputy of the Radical party pulled a revolver and killed two Croatian deputies and wounded three others. One of the wounded was Radich, who died a few weeks later. The Croatian cause now had a martyr.

ALEXANDER'S DICTATORSHIP: 1929–1934

The Croatian peasants responded to the death of their beloved leader by rioting and demanding "a free Croatia." Their representatives in Belgrade returned home, vowing to have nothing to do with the "bloody Skupshtina" until a new federal Yugoslavia was created. On January 4 and 5, 1929, Alexander granted audiences to Radich's successor, Vladimir Machek. The latter demanded a new constitution reorganizing the state into five federal units. Each unit was to have its own constitution and assembly, and the authority of the federal government was to be limited to such essentials as the army, foreign affairs, customs duties, and currency. Alexander asked the Serbian party leaders whether they were willing to accept such a drastic reorganization. When they replied in the negative Alexander issued a decree on January 6, 1929, abolishing the 1921 constitution and dissolving the Skupshtina. Later in the month he suppressed all parties and established his personal dictatorship.

The dictatorship nominally ended on September 3, 1931, when Alexander issued a constitution. This document, which remained in force to the 1941 German invasion, was merely a legal fig leaf for the royal dictatorship, which continued as before. In comparison with the 1921 constitution, it reduced sharply the powers of the Skupshtina, violated the independence of the judiciary, and established a police state with strict censorship, serious abridgment of individual liberties, and severe penalties for actions furthering separatism. Electoral laws issued a few weeks after the constitution abolished proportional representation and stipulated that the party receiving the plurality in a national election should receive two thirds of the seats. As a result, the government party in the 1935 elections received 303 seats with 1,746,982 votes, while the opposition received only 67 seats with 1,076,345 votes. In the 1938 elections the disparity was even greater—306 seats with 1,643,783 votes as against 67 seats with 1,364,524 votes.

In establishing authoritarian rule in this fashion Alexander doubtless was moved by patriotic motives. The party squabbles and political deadlock of the preceding years had disgusted him. By temperament and by training he was intolerant of such proceedings. Brought up at the court of St. Petersburg, he had no real understanding of constitutional government. The Russian Revolution enhanced his intolerance of political opposition, which he came to equate with sedition and Bolshevism. Thus in establishing his dictatorship he was sincerely convinced that he was thereby benefiting his country and his people.

Alexander hoped that he would be able to create by force a Yugoslav nationalism to replace the particularism of the past. With this aim in mind he changed the name of his country from the Kingdom of the Serbs, Croats, and Slovenes to the Kingdom of Yugoslavia. But neither the new title nor the new constitution created the desired national unity. The Croats remained faithful to the memory of Radich and continued to vote for their Peasant party despite electoral shenanigans and police intimidation. The result was that the national dictatorship that Alexander had planned became in practice an anti-Croatian dictatorship.

It did not follow that all Serbians supported Alexander's dictatorship. It is true that members of various Serbian parties served Alexander and thereby gained wealth and high office. But this was true also of ambitious members of the other parties, including the Croatian. The parties themselves, however, remained opposed to the dictatorship. Even the Radical party announced in January, 1933: "The internal organization of the State should be established by agreement between the Serbs, Croats, and Slovenians. . . . through freely elected representatives of the people who alone have the right to decide the organization of the country." [6] All the other major parties, including the Slovenes and Moslems, issued statements along the same lines. In other words, Alexander, like Carol in Rumania and Boris in Bulgaria, was able to attract individual leaders from the various parties. But these persons represented only themselves, and their adhesion to the regime did not add to its strength.

Alexander was aware of the fact that his dictatorship had proved a failure. Yugoslav nationalism remained only a phrase. Serbian-Croatian enmity was as sharp as ever. The king, according to several sources, decided to end his dictatorship and replace it with a more democratic and decentralized arrangement. If such was his intention, he did not have the opportunity to put it into effect. On October 9, 1934, he was murdered at Marseilles, together with the French foreign minister, Louis Barthou, by a Macedonian terrorist aided by Italian and Hungarian authorities.

REGENCY: 1934–1941

The crime united the Yugoslavs in an unexpected manner. The Serbs were incensed that their own Karageorgevich dynasty should have been victimized. The Croats had no special love for Alexander, but they did not miss the significance of Italian involvement in the murder in view of Italy's well-known aspirations to the Dalmatian coast. This explains the impressive processions that greeted the royal coffin during its passage through the country to Belgrade. The brief moment of national solidarity afforded a chance for some conciliatory gesture to the Croats, but unfortunately the opportunity was allowed to pass.

Alexander had provided in his will for a three-man regency to rule in the name of his young son, Peter. Prince Paul, Alexander's cousin, was the first regent, and in practice he ruled the country from the beginning. He was ill-suited for his task, being a dilettante and more interested in his art collection than in Yugoslav politics. He began auspiciously, however, by releasing Machek from prison and pursuing a conciliatory policy in the hope of furthering a settlement. But a compromise was becoming increasingly difficult because extremist elements were appearing in both the Serbian and Croatian camps. Among the Serbs it was the fascist Yugoslav National party consisting of various generals and politicians who opposed any weakening of the 1931 constitution and any concessions to the Croats. At the other extreme was a group of Croatian terrorists led by Ante Pavelich and known as the Ustashi. (The word means "insurgent," and in Serbo-Croat it is spelled "Ustasha" for the singular and "Ustashi" for the plural.) This organization had been outlawed for some time and its leaders lived in Italy and Hungary where, among other things, they participated in the planning of Alexander's murder.

The new regime began by holding elections in May, 1935. We have seen that the electoral law enabled the government to obtain 303 seats to the opposition's 67, even though it received only 1,746,982 votes as against 1,076,345 for the other side. Machek therefore decided to continue the boycott of parliament. Paul attempted to break the deadlock by dismissing the cabinet and appointing a banker, Milan Stoyadinovich, as premier. Liberal circles hoped that this portended a relaxation of the dictatorship, especially since Stoyadinovich earlier had written a pamphlet advocating recognition of the Soviet Union. But these hopes were soon to be dashed.

Stoyadinovich's foreign policy, which we shall examine in Chapter 37, involved a shift toward the Axis and away from Yugoslavia's traditional pro-West orientation. Prince Paul may have been primarily responsible for this shift since he was uninterested in domestic politics and concentrated his attention on foreign affairs. In the domestic field Stoyadinovich did make certain concessions. He granted amnesty to ten thousand political prisoners, slightly relaxed the police pressure, and tolerated the activities of the Croatian Peasant party. But these moves were really superficial. Stoyadinovich did not seriously attempt to reach a settlement of the basic constitutional question. And the reason was that he was able to organize a new political party that had sufficient votes to keep him in office. This was the Yugoslav Radical Union, which comprised three elements—a section of the Radical party led by Stoyadinovich, the Moslem party of Bosnia led by Spaho, and the Catholic Slovene People's party led by Koroshetz.

Koroshetz, as a Catholic, was anxious to settle the Croatian problem. He encouraged Stoyadinovich to negotiate a concordat with the Vatican in 1937 giving the Catholic Church a number of privileges. It was hoped that this would appeal to the more conservative Croats and induce them to accept a settlement that would not necessitate the introduction of a democratic system. Stoyadinovich defended the concordat by pointing out that in 1919 all religions had been promised full equality. During the intervening years both the Orthodox Christians and the Moslems had received statutory definition of their legal position. Accordingly, he presented the concordat as an overdue application of the principle of equality conceded in 1919. But the Orthodox Church leaders bitterly attacked the settlement, maintaining that certain concessions went beyond equality and bestowed exclusive privileges on the Catholics.

The outcome of the struggle between the defenders and the opponents of the concordat sheds a revealing light on the political balance in Yugoslavia at this time. The fascist Yugoslav National Union tried to mobilize the outburst of Orthodox religious feeling against Stoyadinovich by representing the concordat as a betrayal of the Serbs to the Italians. The response was hardly what they expected. Violent demonstrations occurred in Belgrade, but the crowds shouted not for a dictator but for a return to democratic institutions. Even in Catholic Croatia, where Stoyadinovich had hoped for a favorable reaction, there was general indifference. Many Croatians interpreted the concordat as an attempt to drive a wedge between the peasants and their clergy and thereby to break the unity of the Croat opposition. Machek washed his hands of the affair by announcing that the Croatians were interested in political rather than religious reform. The lack of interest in Croatia, together with the furious opposition in Serbia, led Stoyadinovich to announce early in 1938 that he would not attempt to pass the concordat through parliament.

EVE OF WAR

Out of the storm over the concordat arose an important political development. In October, 1937, a united opposition bloc was formed comprising the Croatian Peasant party, the Agrarian and Democratic parties, and the Serbian Radical. The latter consisted of those elements that had refused to join Stoyadinovich in the Yugoslav Radical Union. These parties signed a manifesto setting forth the basis of their collaboration. They agreed that the constitutions of 1921 and 1931 had no validity because they were made without the full consent of the sovereign people. Thus the existing government was held to be without legal status. The opposition bloc therefore demanded that a new and fully democratic electoral law be enacted preparatory to free elections for a constituent assembly. This assembly would then seize the nettle of federalism versus centralism and determine the form of government with the authority of an unquestioned popular mandate.

Stoyadinovich's reply to the opposition program was that constituent elections and a new constitution would divide the country at a time when the international situation was critical. Point was given to his argument in March, 1938, when Hitler annexed Austria and Nazi divisions reached Yugoslavia's northern frontier. The mutilation of Czechoslavakia at Munich in September, 1938, further strengthened the premier's position. In order to test public opinion he ordered elections for December 11, 1938. A unique feature of the campaign was Stoyadinovich's adoption of fascist "leadership" techniques. He was accompanied on his electoral tours by uniformed green-shirted youths who greeted him with cries of *Vodja! Vodja!* ("Leader! Leader!").

The returns were significant in several respects. The opposition increased its vote from 1,076,345 in 1935 to 1,364,524, or to 41 per cent of the total vote. The 1931 electoral law, however, was still in force, and it gave the government party 303 seats to the opposition's 67. The regional distribution of the vote was also instructive. Stoyadinovich received 70 per cent of the votes in Serbia and Machek 80 per cent in Croatia and Dalmatia. This was impressive evidence of the deep gulf between Serb and Croat which three years of the Stoyadinovich regime had failed to bridge.

The continued discord in Yugoslavia caused much concern because of Hitler's success in using the Sudeten Germans to disrupt Czechoslovakia. The Croatian Ustashi were only too willing to be used in a similar manner, and the presence of German divisions along the frontier removed the Czechoslovak-Yugoslav analogy out of the realm of theory. This situation led Prince Paul to replace Stoyadinovich in February, 1939, with Dragisha Tsvetkovich, a Radical party boss. Tsvetkovich was a man of limited intelligence but ready to carry out Paul's orders. In April, 1939, Paul did order him to begin negotiations with Machek. The complete disappearance of Czechoslovakia a month earlier apparently convinced Paul that there was no more time to lose.

Two procedures were open for dealing with the Croatian problem.

One was to form a coalition cabinet in which representatives of the Croats and of all the Serbian parties would sit together and work out a solution. This would mean that Stoyadinovich's Yugoslav Radical Union, which still was the basis of the government in Belgrade, would have to abandon its monopolistic position, and that more democratic electoral procedures and governmental practices would be demanded for Serbia as well as for Croatia. The second procedure was to open direct discussion between the Belgrade government and Machek to define the powers and territorial extent of an autonomous Croatia. This involved the danger of widening Serbo-Croat differences, but it also gave the government an opportunity to drive a wedge between the Serbian and the Croatian parties in the opposition bloc. The government chose the second method, and after some hesitation Machek agreed to accept negotiations on this basis, which implied betrayal of his allies He did so because of the impatience of his own followers, the pressure of the rapidly deteriorating international situation, and the obvious unwillingness of Prince Paul to consider the demands of the Serbian opposition parties.

After weeks of negotiations Tsvetkovich and Machek concluded their Sporazum, or Agreement, on August 26, 1939. It defined the frontiers of the new autonomous Croatia, allotting to it 27 per cent of the territory of Yugoslavia and 29 per cent of the population. Croatia was given full autonomy in internal administration and finances, including the right to elect her own assembly. In return Machek agreed to enter the Belgrade government as vice-premier.

World War II began a week after the Agreement was signed. Prince Paul congratulated himself for having handled the old problem so neatly. But the situation in reality was little improved. The opposition Serbian parties were bitter at having been ignored, and accused Machek of having betrayed the cause of democracy in Yugoslavia. On the other hand, extremist elements in Croatia complained that Machek should have demanded more territory and more autonomy. Furthermore, the Slovenes and the Moslems immediately began pressing for autonomy rights comparable to those won by the Croats. Thus Yugoslavia was in a state of flux when German armies invaded the country on April 6, 1941 The pressure of the international crisis had contributed much toward breaking the old log jam of centralism versus federalism. But now war and occupation ended what chance there may have existed for a peaceful settlement of Yugoslavia's problems.

ECONOMIC DEVELOPMENT

Serbia emerged from World War I greatly enlarged but also terribly devastated. It is estimated that her battle casualties, on a per capita basis, were two and a half times those of France and three times those of Britain and Italy. In addition, both her army and civilian population suffered heavily from the typhus and other epidemics connected with the war. The death toll appears to have been especially high among the better educated, who had served as officers in the army and who had functioned in civilian life as teachers, doctors, lawyers, and so on. This decimation of the flower of Serbia's manhood began not in 1914 but in 1912 with the first Balkan War. The South Slavs who had been under Hapsburg rule had been required to serve in the imperial army, so they also suffered war losses, though not comparable with those of the Serbians. There is no doubt that Yugoslavia, like other European countries, was held back a good deal in the postwar years by the loss of such a large portion of her intelligentsia. In fact, many observers attribute the shortcomings of Yugoslav public life in large part to the holocaust of the war years.

The toll in treasure was comparable to the toll in blood. "World War I," a Serbian economist wrote, "brought about a great evenness in the distribution of wealth. Everybody became more or less a beggar." [7] The loss of livestock is typical, the number of cattle declining by 27.4 per cent, horses by 35.1 per cent, pigs by 46.6 per cent, and sheep by 54.6 per cent. Agriculture suffered a reduction of its productive capacity because of the shortage of manpower and draft power, the lack of manure and commercial fertilizers, and the destruction or deterioration of housing and of farm implements. Transportation facilities also declined drastically during the war years. Roads were not properly maintained, many railroad tracks and bridges were blown up, and some of the rolling stock was carried away by the invaders.

Yugoslavia began the postwar period with a problem of integration as well as of reconstruction. During the preceding centuries, the various provinces of the enlarged state had advanced to varying economic levels and developed different economic institutions. The former Hapsburg provinces of Slovenia, Croatia, and the Voivodina were much further ahead in both industry and agriculture than the former Turkish territories of Macedonia, Montenegro, and Serbia. On the other hand, Serbia, with its small peasant plots, had a more equitable social structure than the Hapsburg provinces with their large estates and predominantly foreign landowners. We have seen that this disparity in social organization contributed greatly to the pressure for land reform at the end of the war. Yugoslavia also faced the task of integrating several fiscal systems and transportation networks. The latter posed a particularly difficult problem because the Austrian authorities had deliberately sought to isolate Serbia from the Hapsburg Slavs. Consequently, no adequate link existed between the Serbian and Austro-Hungarian railway systems with the exception of the Orient Express trunk line stretching on to Istanbul. Yugoslavia thus found that she possessed a disconnected railway system built with three different gauges.

Turning from the aftermath of war to postwar developments, we find that agriculture remained the principal source of livelihood in Yugoslavia during the interwar years. In 1921, 79 per cent of the population was engaged in this occupation, and in 1938 the percentage had fallen only to 75. By all odds the outstanding development in agriculture following World War I was the division of the large estates among the peasantry. We noted early in this chapter that approximately one fourth of all the cultivated land was distributed after 1918 and that one out of every four peasant families benefited from the reform. The difficulties of the Yugoslav peasants were by no means permanently solved by this drastic upheaval. In fact, the peasants were at least as badly off by the eve of the second world war as they had been on the eve of the first.

The leading factors explaining the plight of the peasantry were the rapid increase in population, the apathy of the government, the operation of the "price scissors," the lack of credit, and the heavy burden of taxation. The population problem in Yugoslavia was similar to that which prevailed throughout the Balkans. The total population increased rapidly from 11,985,-000 in 1921 to 15,973,000 in 1941, a growth of 3,988,000 or 33⅓ per cent in two decades. Emigration did not offer a way out, as it did before 1914, because of the barriers erected by the United States and the British Dominions. Between 1930 and 1938 the emigrants exceeded the returnees by only 57,237. At the same time industry expanded so modestly that it was able to absorb only an insignificant percentage of the annual population increase. Consequently, the growing population had no place to go, and it piled up, year after year, in the already overpopulated villages. In Yugoslavia, as in the other Balkan countries, a much larger number of peasants were forced to eke out a living from each unit of arable land than in the Western European countries.* It is estimated that in 1930 fully 61.5 per cent of the rural population was "surplus," in the sense that it was not needed for the performance of the agricultural work. The population pressure was particularly disastrous in its effects because of the low productivity of Yugoslav agriculture compared to that of the West.†

This combination of a constantly increasing population and a persistently low productivity created a vicious circle that paralyzed the entire Yugoslav economy. The peasants were unable to save a portion of their income for investment to increase productivity. Since increased investment is a prerequisite for economic progress it becomes apparent why rural overpopulation brought Yugoslav agriculture to a standstill. And this in turn affected the rest of the economy, since an impoverished peasantry that constituted three fourths of the total population obviously offered no basis for industrial and commercial expansion.

Another factor explaining the plight of the peasantry was the government's tendency, after the land had been distributed, to leave the peasants to their lot. In 1929, for example, as noted in Chapter 31, the ministry of agriculture was allotted 1.06 per cent of the total budget funds, and in 1931 the percentage fell to a mere 0.76 per cent. This restricted correspondingly the amount of agricultural education that the ministry could conduct. The government also failed to take adequate measures to cope with the peasants' chronic shortage of capital. It did establish certain institutions to provide

* † Statistics in Chapter 31.

agricultural credit, but only a small minority of rich peasants possessed the required security to avail themselves of the opportunity. A survey made in 1932 revealed that 35.7 per cent of all rural households were in debt and that many of the remainder needed credit but were unable to obtain it. The total peasant indebtedness amounted to between 80 and 90 per cent of the total cash income of agriculture in 1931. And it was also discovered that 45 per cent of these peasant debts were from usurious individual lenders and country storekeepers who commonly charged between 100 and 200 per cent per annum.

The government not only failed to take adequate measures to help the peasants but also imposed upon them a disproportionate share of the tax load. In the fiscal year 1931–1932 indirect taxes (stamp duties, customs duties, monopoly taxes, turnover tax, and the like), which bore most heavily on those least able to pay, provided 76.3 per cent of the total revenue from taxes. It is estimated that in the same year the total tax load on the peasants amounted to at least 40 per cent of their total cash income and more probably about 50 per cent. This was an extremely heavy tax burden in relation to the low aggregate income of the agricultural population.

The government did concern itself with the plight of the peasantry to a certain degree, particularly during the depression years. It declared a moratorium on peasant debts in 1932 and later drastically reduced these debts. Also, it helped the peasants by importing fine livestock for breeding purposes, by distributing select seeds and grapevines, and by providing at cost various drugs for the control of livestock diseases such as hog cholera. These and other measures undoubtedly helped the peasants to a certain degree.

But the fact that they were inadequate to cope with the basic ailments of Yugoslav agriculture was evidenced by the growing pauperization of the countryside. It was indicated by the unhappy position of the 43 per cent of the peasants who were "surplus." It was also demonstrated by the increasing number of peasants who lost their land or who were unable to obtain any when they came of age. Five hectares were considered necessary in most regions to support a family. But by 1931, 16.8 per cent of the peasants had one hectare or less; 17 per cent had between one and two hectares; and 34 per cent between two and five hectares. Thus 67.8 per cent of the peasants had five hectares or less. The state of Yugoslav agriculture was also reflected by the chronic indebtedness of the peasants. In fact there existed not only the disparity between poor and rich peasants, but also that between poor peasants and those nonpeasants who flourished in the villages as country storekeepers, tavern keepers, lawyers, and usurers. Frequently these people did not keep the land that they acquired because of nonpayment of debts. They found it more profitable to sell the land and use the proceeds again in usury or in trade. Sometimes they preferred to invest their capital in some urban enterprise, a procedure that further aggravated the acute shortage of capital in the villages. A peasant spokesman graphically described his plight and that of his fellow villagers as follows:

Our population is 2,500. We have 400 *gospodarstva* (families or homes which exist as independent economic units). We have 2,000 acres of soil, of which 300 are not cultivated because occupied by buildings or otherwise unavailable. That leaves us 1,700 acres, or about four acres per family. Which is not enough. To live at all, even according to our standards, a family of five or six should have at least eight acres to cultivate. But since some of us have anywhere from twenty to forty acres, most of the families have not even four, and a great many, aside from the ground their shacks stand on, have no soil whatever. . . . In other words, in this village of 2,000 souls and 1,700 fertile acres, two-thirds of us don't belong, economically speaking. Two-thirds of us are not really peasants, but village proletariat who barely exist—paupers dependent on the resources, the charity of others. . . . Once upon a time one could go to America and with one's earnings there support from five to ten persons back here. Now America can't take us any more. Our emigrants are returning to share our misery. We are as caught in a trap.[8]

The most serious problem confronting Yugoslav statesmen in the interwar years was to find some way out of this agricultural impasse. Since emigration no longer was feasible, and since little additional arable land was available, the only remaining course open was to attempt to increase the productivity of the soil already tilled. This effort met with little success. One reason was the inertia of the tradition-bound, backward-looking peasantry. Even more important was the fact that modern agricultural methods were economically unfeasible under the existing structure of Yugoslav agriculture. The overwhelming majority of the peasants were unable to save enough to finance technological innovations or to incur the risks connected with them. Also, the small size of their farms made the use of machinery unjustifiable for both physical and financial reasons. Furthermore, the price relationship between agricultural equipment and agricultural produce was so unfavorable to the latter that it discouraged additional capital investment. And if credit was needed to finance any innovations, the exorbitant interest rates greatly increased their cost. There were, of course, certain exceptions to this general picture. In the areas north of the Sava and Danube rivers agriculture was considerably specialized and commercialized, and techniques were relatively advanced. But the overwhelming majority of Yugoslav farm households were primarily subsistence units rather than agricultural business enterprises, and their farming methods were correspondingly primitive.

The quagmire in which Yugoslav agriculture found itself led many economists and political leaders to the conclusion that the solution was to be found not in agriculture itself but rather in industry. Accordingly, the government sought to stimulate industry in various ways. It invested heavily in transportation and in certain industries, so that by World War II the government owned and operated all railroads, all telegraph and telephone lines and radio stations, most of the banks, most of river shipping and harbor storage facilities, some large lumber mills, numerous coal mines, iron mines, and steel plants, several sugar factories, and all processing facilities for tobacco and salt. The government also sought to aid industry by raising high protective tariffs. In fact, the tariff system introduced in June, 1925, was among the highest in Europe. Finally, the government encouraged industrial development by granting extremely favorable concessions to foreign investors. Most of the industrial expansion in the interwar years was financed by foreign capital. In 1937, 33 per cent of private corporation financial resources were foreign-owned.

These measures stimulated considerable industrial development during the years between the two world wars. The most important, as in all Balkan countries, were the agricultural industries—milling, sugar, alcohol, jam, chocolate, and vegetable-oil refining. Next in importance came the textile industry, and then timber and woodworking, metallurgy, and the chemical industry. The over-all development is reflected in the following figures:

Year	Number of Factories	Number of Workers	Value of Investment
1918	100.0	100.0	100.0
1923	135.1	137.9	125.5
1928	163.7	159.2	135.9
1933	191.7	176.9	149.5
1938	213.1	188.6	154.9

Source: J. Tomasevich, *Peasants, Politics and Economic Change in Yugoslavia* (Stanford, Calif., 1955), p. 638.

So far as the economic health of Yugoslavia is concerned, the significance of the above figures is that the number of industrial workers increased from about 200,000 in 1918 to 385,000 in 1938, but the population of the country increased in the same period from 11,600,000 to 15,600,000, or by 4,000,000, of whom about one half were of working age. In other words, industry, despite the government's efforts, was able to absorb only 19 per cent of the new labor force that entered the market during these two decades. Equally disturbing is the fact that in 1938 the flour-milling and sugar industries were operating at only half capacity, beer brewing at one seventh, and industrial alcohol at one fourth. This low rate of production was due to the lack of purchasing power at home and to the vigorous agricultural protectionism in the important Central European markets. But whatever the cause, the inability of the agricultural industries to operate at anywhere near capacity challenges a favorite thesis of Peasant parties in Yugoslavia and elsewhere—that the problem of rural overpopulation can be solved by establishing industries to process agricultural products.

In addition to her industries, Yugoslavia was a rather important producer of minerals—much more so than any other Balkan country. Many deposits were exploited during the interwar years, the most important being the Bor copper mines and the Trepca lead and zinc mines. Other deposits included bauxite, iron, chrome, antimony, gold, and silver. In many regions the opportunity to work in mines made it possible for poor peasants to supplement their meager farm income and to support their families. On the other hand, the mining industry did not begin to meet the problem of agrarian overpopulation, only 27,000 persons being employed in 1931 in the entire industry.

Turning to foreign trade we find that 50 to 60 per cent of the country's exports in terms of value during the interwar period consisted of agricultural and livestock products. This composition reflected, of course, the predominantly agricultural character of the Yugoslav economy. More specifically, Yugoslavia's exports in order of importance in the late 1930's were timber, hogs, copper, wheat and flour, corn, meat, hemp, and lead and zinc concentrates. Imports in order of importance in the same period were cotton yarn and cotton products, iron and steel and products, machinery and tools, woolen yarn and products, raw cotton, transportation equipment, and electrotechnical products.

Yugoslavia's chief markets before 1930 were, in order of importance, Italy, Austria, and Germany. This created a conflict between Yugoslavia's economic and diplomatic ties. France, with her balanced economy, had little need for Yugoslavia's raw materials. Likewise, the neighboring Balkan countries had economies similar to that of Yugoslavia and therefore exchanged few products. The only significant exceptions were Yugoslav food products to Greece and Rumanian oil to Yugoslavia. Thus Yugoslavia in 1930 sent 57.7 per cent of her exports to three revisionist powers—Italy, Germany, and Austria.

In the same year, 1930, Yugoslavia began to feel the impact of the world depression. The value of her foreign trade fell by 1932 to 38.7 per cent of the 1929 value. The wholesale price indices of agricultural products fell from 100.0 in 1926 and 118.6 in 1929 to 89.3 in 1930, 74.3 in 1931, 67.5 in 1932, and 57.2 in 1933. This unprecedent slump undermined the entire economy because the level of agricultural prices determined the purchasing power of the great majority of the population. Furthermore, Yugoslavia found it exceptionally difficult to recover from this setback because the industrialized countries of Central and Western Europe were compelled for financial reasons to reduce their imports of raw materials and foodstuffs from Southeastern Europe. It was at this point that a resurgent Nazi Germany stepped in and established her economic hegemony in Yugoslavia and throughout the Balkans.

Yugoslavia originally had had a consistently unfavorable trade balance with Germany. Germany then redressed the balance by buying large amounts of corn, wheat, lard, and meat, part of which it sold on the world market for free exchange. Thus the Yugoslav trade balance with Germany became favorable in 1933 and in the following years the clearing balance shifted more and more to the credit of Yugoslavia.

One reason for this change, as noted in Chapter 31, was the Nazi commercial policy of accumulating blocked balances throughout Southeastern

Europe and thereby forcing those countries to become economically dependent upon Germany. The Yugoslavs tried to break out of the German economic orbit but without success. The fact was that they had to depend upon Germany as their chief market because the Western powers were unable or unwilling to buy more Yugoslav products. This dependence upon Germany increased when Yugoslavia applied economic sanctions against Italy from November, 1935, to September, 1936, because of the Ethiopian affair. Trade with Italy dropped from an average of 1,193.3 million dinars between 1933 and 1935 to 238.9 million dinars in 1936, while trade with Germany jumped during the same period from 1,098.1 million dinars to 2,126.7.

Thus Germany took first place in Yugoslav trade in 1936, and in the following years she increased her lead tremendously. In 1937 the German share in Yugoslav exports was 36 per cent and in imports 32.5 per cent, but in 1938, with the German annexation of Austria, it advanced to 42 per cent and 39.5 per cent respectively. Then with the dismemberment of Czechoslovakia in September, 1938, and March, 1939, Germany took more than 50 per cent of Yugoslav exports and supplied about 50 per cent of Yugoslav imports. At the same time it should be noted that Germany took over all Austrian and Czechoslovak investments in Yugoslavia, thereby extending greatly her hold over the national economy. With the outbreak of World War II in September, 1939, Yugoslavia came more completely under German economic domination. In October, 1939, she found it necessary to grant new trade concessions to Germany, especially greater quotas of metals and foods. In fact, the Yugoslav government had to curtail domestic consumption of meat, fats, and other foodstuffs in order to meet the export quotas to Germany and to Italy. The final step in this penetration of the national economy came with the German victories in Western Europe in the spring of 1940. Germany was thereby able to gain control of a large portion of the French, Belgian, and Dutch holdings in Yugoslavia. In this manner Yugoslavia had fallen under German economic domination by April, 1941, when Hitler ordered his troops to march into the country.

SOCIAL AND CULTURAL DEVELOPMENT

The social trends that we noted in Serbia before 1914 * continued to manifest themselves in Yugoslavia in the interwar period. Class differentiation in the villages proceeded apace, not only between poor and rich peasants, but also between poor peasants and nonpeasants who flourished in the villages as country storekeepers, tavern keepers, lawyers, and usurers. Another trend that persisted during these decades was the increasing penetration of the money and market economy into the countryside. It is true that most Yugoslav peasant households practiced an essentially subsistence type of agriculture. On the other hand they all had to sell a portion of their produce on

* See Chapter 24.

the market in order to obtain money for taxes and for essential commodities such as salt, matches, kerosene, and a few household items and agricultural implements. With the passage of time the peasants became accustomed to buying more and more commodities and their financial obligations increased correspondingly. The degree to which the peasants became dependent upon the market was demonstrated by the devastating effect of the depression and by the need for government action to reduce debts and declare moratoria.

Another trend that continued through the interwar period was the friction between peasant and government or, more broadly speaking, between village and city. The factors behind this friction were the same as those before 1914, though they became more acute as time passed. There was the same opposition to conscription, especially in Croatia, where strong pacifist sentiment was articulated by the Croatian Peasant movement. There was also the same resentment against the high tariffs and government monopolies which raised the prices of necessities such as matches, sugar, tobacco, and farm implements. Finally, the peasants continued to begrudge the expenditure of vast sums on the army and bureaucracy while they, who paid most of the taxes, received virtually nothing in return. Nor was their sentiment altogether unjustified in view of the fact that during the fiscal year 1931–1932 the ministry of war spent 2,188 million dinars and the ministry of interior 590 million dinars, compared with 178 million by the ministry of public health and 56 million by the ministry of agriculture.

Considering next the actual social conditions prevailing during the interwar period, we find that they were uniformly poor, reflecting the underdeveloped economy of the country. Yugoslavia exported considerable quantities of foodstuffs, but this was made possible by the low domestic purchasing power rather than by a true surplus. A study of food consumption in the late 1930's revealed a rather high average per capita caloric intake of about 3,000 calories a day. But about 77 per cent of the caloric supply was derived from cereals and 41 per cent from corn alone. In some rural areas corn supplied 85 to 90 per cent of all calories. This diet, deficient in fats and in protective foods of animal origin, resulted in widespread malnutrition and contributed to a high incidence of disease. Housing was also definitely substandard. A 1938 survey in the Zagreb region, which was by no means the poorest in the country, showed that 73.2 per cent of all peasant houses had only one room for living and sleeping, that in 63.4 per cent of all peasant households there were five or more persons living and sleeping in one room, and that 48.7 per cent of all houses lacked latrines of any kind. Housing was as poor or even poorer in the cities for the low-income groups, which constituted the majority of the urban population. Families of four to six persons frequently lived in one damp basement room which served for living, cooking, and sleeping. One of the most appalling facts established by a survey in 1934 was that 86 per cent of all people suffering from tuberculosis in Belgrade were sleeping in the same rooms with noninfected people, and that 42.6 per cent of them slept in the same bed with noninfected people.[9]

Home and personal cleanliness also left much to be desired, partly because of custom but primarily because of poverty. Soap, after all, was an expensive commodity which could be afforded only when the need for more essential goods had been satisfied. Surveys in certain Bosnian villages disclosed that no soap at all was used in washing clothes and little if any in washing the person. Clothes were usually washed with the help of a detergent derived from wood ashes by passing warm water through them. The clothes were soaked in this water for several hours, the length of time depending on whether the owners possessed another change. The process was then completed by taking the clothes to a nearby stream where they were beaten and rinsed.

The combination of bad nutrition, poor housing, and unsanitary surroundings contributed to the high incidence of disease. In 1937 Yugoslavia had a higher death rate from pulmonary tuberculosis than any other country in Europe: 19.9 persons per 10,000, followed by Rumania with 17.8, and Hungary with 15.2. It is estimated that in the mid-1930's between 400,000 and 500,000 were suffering from tuberculosis out of a total population of 15,000,000. The incidence of malaria was even higher—between 500,000 and 600,000 people, or 4 to 5 per cent of the total population. Syphilis was also extremely widespread, about 100,000 being infected in 1939 in Bosnia alone. The disease was transmitted not so much by sexual contact as by the use of the same eating and drinking utensils by all members of the family. As a result a large percentage of the infected were children. Other diseases that were common included trachoma, typhoid fever, dysentery, scarlet fever, diphtheria, chicken pox, and whooping cough. The public health service combated these conditions as vigorously as possible by improving the water supply in rural areas and by spreading health education, including information concerning nutrition. But many obstacles stood in the way of effective control, including shortage of funds and of trained personnel, the concentration of physicians in a few cities, the widespread ignorance and superstition, and, above all, the debilitating poverty of the great majority of the population.

Education standards in Yugoslavia were also generally low, though great differences prevailed from region to region. The 1921 census showed a national illiteracy rate of 51.5 per cent. But the regional percentages varied from 8.8 per cent in Slovenia to 23.3 per cent in the Voivodina, 32.2 in Croatia, 49.5 in Dalmatia, 65.4 in Serbia, 67.0 in Montenegro, 80.5 in Bosnia-Herzegovina, and 83.8 in Macedonia. These figures show that in cultural matters as well as economic the former Hapsburg provinces in the north were far ahead of the former Turkish territories in the south.

The Yugoslav government attempted to reduce the illiteracy rate during the interwar years. Between 1919 and 1940 the number of elementary schools increased from 5,600 to 9,169, the number of pupils from 650,000 to 1,493,000, and the number of teachers from 11,000 to 31,000. Impressive as this increase was, there still were in 1940 about 250,000 children who attended no school. In some cases they were held back by their parents who needed their labor, but in most cases the explanation was the lack of schools in inaccessible areas. Consequently the illiteracy rate in 1940 still remained at slightly above 40 per cent.

The educational system, like most other institutions, was firmly controlled from Belgrade. The ministry of education appointed, promoted, and dismissed all teachers, who had no right of appeal. It was no secret that many of the numerous education ministers used their authority to promote relatives and political supporters. This unhealthy situation, together with the glaring social and economic injustices in Yugoslav society, alienated a considerable proportion of the teachers.

The more conscientious teachers observed numerous cases of inefficiency in the administration, but their efforts to have the law enforced were hamstrung because the central government too often supported those responsible locally for the mismanagement. In *Uchiteljska Iskra,* a Left-wing Serbian teachers' periodical, there are innumerable letters from teachers who had struggled with Commune presidents, etc., to have village schools put in proper repair, kept clean and supplied with heating. But so long as the latter continued to give political support to the politicians in power, nothing was done to punish them. On the contrary, the teachers themselves found that they were labelled as trouble-makers, with disastrous effect upon their hope of promotion. After 1929, even the little safety-valves offered by papers such as *Uchiteljska Iskra* were denied them.

Out of the conflict in which many teachers found themselves involved between loyalty to the ideals of their profession and the crude interpretation of the claims of the state insisted upon by part of the government circles, there naturally tended to arise in teachers' minds the idea that education could never play its proper role until changes had been made in the state. In the case of Croat teachers, this often took the form of attaching them to the extreme Croat nationalists and so gave the Yugoslav government an excuse for disciplining them. Other teachers were attracted by socialist ideas as the one hope for effecting the reforms they desired, just as the peasant students looked to Socialism and Communism to relieve the distress caused by social and economic inequalities.[10]

The universities were not controlled from the capital as were the lower schools. Although financed by the education ministry, they elected their rectors and deans and appointed their professors through their senates, subject only to confirmation by the minister. The university students also enjoyed a considerable degree of independence through their corporate bodies, even during the most strict years of the dictatorship. Yet curiously enough the universities were outstanding centers of radicalism. The following explanation of this significant phenomenon is worth noting.

Many of the students were sons of poor peasant families. By great efforts their parents had scraped together the small sums necessary to transport them to the capital and to pay their entrance fees. Having once obtained admission to the university the students kept themselves alive by earning a few pence as tram-drivers, waiters and window cleaners. Undernourished and weak in health, worn out by the double strain of physical and intellectual labour, they grew up to hate the system which caused their sufferings. Familiarised by their teachers with the old principles of Liberty, Equality and Fraternity, they saw around them nothing but injustice, repression and silence. Protests against abuses brought down on their heads the persecution of the apparatus of the Dictatorship. They were driven to the conclusion that only revolutionary methods and solutions could improve the lot of the Serbian people and make Jugoslavia a decent country. . . .

Like the Russian intellectuals of the seventies who set themselves to "return to the people," the Serbian students devoted themselves to the service of the people. The movement suffered, perhaps, from a certain naïve and exalted romanticism, but it had a serious effect on the life of the Serbian people. Its followers gave many proofs of resolution, courage and sincerity. In a country where learning and knowledge enjoy immense prestige, where the peasant's son who has a university degree is regarded as a prophet in his own village, the movement was bound to have a powerful influence. . . .

None of these tendencies were reflected on the surface of political life, in the manoeuvres of the official political parties, in which the younger generation had no say. But beneath the waters new forces were being created.[11]

In retrospect it may be said that a fitting epitaph on the tomb of the Kingdom of Yugoslavia would be the following three phrases: federalism versus centralism, rural overpopulation, and the alienation of the intelligentsia.

33. Bulgaria: 1918–1939

BULGARIAN HISTORY during the interwar years was more stormy than that of any other Balkan country. Bulgaria was the first to establish an agrarian regime and the first to experience an agrarian reform program. Bulgaria was also the first to witness the violent overthrow of a duly elected government and the brutal murder of the leader of that government. There then followed years of repression and terrorism, highlighted by such events as the blowing up of the Sofia Cathedral and the establishment of a military dictatorship and then a royal dictatorship.

The violent swing of the pendulum from radical agrarianism to extreme reaction appears paradoxical in view of the fact that Bulgarian society was more egalitarian than that of the neighboring countries. The gap between the rich and the poor was not so wide or glaring as in most parts of the Balkans. Sofia itself was sober, clean, and unimpressive, with its straight orderly streets and rows of modest houses. It had none of the garishness of Bucharest and Belgrade with their new skyscrapers towering incongruously over low, red-tiled Turkish hovels. Thus the turbulence of Bulgarian politics is to be explained not so much by the social and economic institutions of the country as by its unfortunate political history.

Ferdinand had discredited his dynasty by engaging in two disastrous wars in 1913 and 1915. The widespread popular reaction compelled him to abdicate in favor of his son Boris. Public feeling was so strong that the dynasty might have been eliminated altogether were it not for Allied disapproval of republicanism in the Balkans. In any case, the old prewar order was even more discredited in Bulgaria than in most of the peninsula. This enabled the Agrarian leader, Alexander Stambuliski, to establish his regime and to push through a fairly comprehensive program of social reform. Because of the revolutionary atmosphere of these years, Boris had no alternative but to accept the changes. The bureaucratic-military oligarchy that had ruled the country before the war, however, had no intention of surrendering

TERRITORIAL GROWTH OF BULGARIA

▇ Principality of Bulgaria	▦ Western Thrace
▤ Eastern Rumelia	▦ Southern Dobruja
▥ Northeast Macedonia, South Bulgarian Territories, and Akhtopol Enclave	▦ Western Enclaves ceded to Yugoslavia

1878	Formation of Principality of Bulgaria by Berlin Treaty
1885	Annexation of Eastern Rumelia
1913	Western Thrace, Northeast Macedonia, South Bulgarian Territories, and Akhtopol Enclave ceded by Turkey to Bulgaria

1919	Western Thrace ceded to Greece, and Strumitza, Bosiligrad, Tsaribrod, and Timok Enclaves ceded to Yugoslavia
1940	South Dobruja ceded by Rumania to Bulgaria

its prerogatives permanently. After the peak of the postwar revolutionary wave had passed, it organized a coup against Stambuliski and successfully executed it in June, 1923, with the aid of disgruntled IMRO terrorists. The following years were characterized by reaction and terrorism calculated to put the peasants back in their place. But the opposition was not all stamped out, as was evidenced in various elections in which, despite severe restrictions, both the Agrarians and the Communists showed considerable strength. Nevertheless, the combination of the dynasty, the army, and the bureaucracy was able without difficulty to maintain the *status quo* until the outbreak of World War II.

STAMBULISKI'S REGIME: 1918–1923

Stambuliski formed a government on October 6, 1919, and signed the Neuilly Peace Treaty the following month, on November 27.* Upon his return to Sofia he ordered elections for March 28, 1920. The following results demonstrated strikingly the new political climate prevailing in the country.

Party	Votes	Seats
Agrarians	346,949	109
Communists	181,525	50
Democrats	97,581	24
Populists	60,992	14
Socialists	55,017	9
Progressives	52,733	9
Radicals	41,770	8
Guenadievists	26,181	4
Liberals	23,537	2
	886,285	229

These figures show that the Communists alone offered any significant opposition to Stambuliski. The roots of the Bulgarian Communist party go back to 1891, when the Bulgarian Social Democratic party was founded. The Socialists gained steadily in strength though they were hampered by that perennial question which has plagued working-class parties throughout the world, namely, collaboration or noncollaboration with the progressive bourgeois parties. The final result was a split into the orthodox, radical, "Narrow" Socialist party led by Dimitar Blagoev, and the moderate "Broad" Socialist party led by Yanko Sakuzov. It is interesting to note that the split occurred in 1903—the year when the Russian Social Democratic party also divided into Bolshevik and Menshevik groupings. In fact, the issues that rent the two parties were roughly similar, Blagoev insisting, like Lenin, upon a highly centralized and disciplined elite party.

Before 1914 the "Broad" Socialists had the larger popular following. But during World War I they lost ground because they supported Ferdinand's intervention in the war in contrast to the "Narrows," who took the same position on the war question as did the Bolsheviks. At the end of the war the "Narrows" were able to capitalize on the war-weariness and on the prestige of the Bolshevik revolution. In 1919 they re-formed themselves into the Communist party of Bulgaria, and at the elections of that year they won a quarter of all the votes and four times as many seats as the Socialists headed by Sakuzov. In December, 1919, the Communists challenged Stambuliski by leading a railway strike that paralyzed transportation and threatened to end in revolution. The Allies, preferring the Agrarians to the Communists, helped Stambuliski to break the strike. We have seen that in the elections that fol-

* See Chapter 30.

lowed in March, 1920, the Communists were by far the strongest group in the country next to the Agrarians. In fact, Stambuliski perceived that, although his party by itself did not quite command a majority in the chamber, his party together with the Communist controlled 70 per cent of the seats. Stambuliski therefore reached an agreement with the Communists whereby he allowed them to function as freely as the other parties, and in return they supported him in parliament.

This arrangement enabled Stambuliski to remain in office and to put his party's program into effect. The Bulgarian Agrarian party had been founded in 1900 by Dimitar Dragiev. Its platform called for curtailment of the growing powers of the crown, economy in administrative expenditures, disbandment of the regular army in favor of a militia, and adoption of a peaceful foreign policy. Accordingly, the party strongly opposed Ferdinand's role during the Balkan Wars and World War I. Meanwhile, Stambuliski had entered parliament in 1908 and had become the head of the party in 1911. He was of humble peasant stock but had been helped financially by his teacher to study agronomy in Switzerland. Upon his return he married his benefactor and plunged into politics with enormous success. Stambuliski was virtually the personification of the Bulgarian peasantry—a huge man with fierce upturned mustaches, great personal courage, strongly held convictions, and blunt and forthright manner.

One of Stambuliski's reforms was the distribution of land among the peasants. Bulgaria was already a country of small landholders, a farm of over thirty hectares being considered a large estate. Nevertheless, some of the peasants owned no land at all, and a larger number had only dwarf plots. Stambulisky passed a land reform law in 1920 distributing arable state lands, unused forest and grazing land in dispute between communes, and all privately owned arable land over thirty hectares in extent. The beneficiaries, in order of preference, were landless peasants, owners of dwarf plots, and Bulgarian refugees from regions under foreign rule. As a result of this reform 80.6 per cent of the peasants by 1926 owned the land they tilled; 16.8 per cent owned their plots but found it necessary to rent more; and only 2.6 per cent rented all the land they worked. Thus Bulgaria, both before and after World War I, had a healthier property structure in agriculture than any other Balkan state.

Another important Stambuliski measure was the introduction of compulsory labor service to take the place of the compulsory military training forbidden by the terms of the Neuilly Treaty. The purpose of the labor plan was not only to provide the state with services that it could not pay for, but also to instill in the conscripts a sense of duty to the community and a liking for manual work and open-air living which most Balkan intellectuals considered to be beneath their dignity. The labor law required all men between twenty and forty to serve eight months in the labor corps. Conscripts could purchase exemption from all or part of their labor service by paying a special tax varying from 25 to 350 dollars, depending on the wealth of the conscript and the amount of time from which he wished to be exempted. The great majority of the recruits chose to work out their obligation, and over the years they built many highways and bridges, repaired old roads and railways, and worked without pay in government factories and forest preserves. Their achievements were considerable, although much manpower was wasted because of the lack of sufficient engineers to direct the work.

Stambuliski also reformed the legal system, making justice cheaper and more accessible to the people. Another reform that was popular with the peasantry was revision of the tax system in order to distribute the tax burden more equitably. Meanwhile, in foreign affairs Stambuliski followed the type of foreign policy traditionally desired by peasants—international cooperation, avoidance of war, reduction of army expenditures, and diminution of the role of military men in national affairs. More specifically, Stambuliski hoped to unite all the European Agrarian parties into a "Green International." Early in 1921 he visited Prague, Warsaw, and Bucharest to mobilize support for his scheme. On his return he stated that the purpose of his "Green International" was to unite the peasants of Central and Eastern Europe in order to offset the White International of the reactionaries, who wished to restore the monarchs and landlords, and also the Red International of the Bolsheviks, who were attempting to destroy all government and individual initiative. "I have no doubt," he added, "that our 'Green International' will ultimately free Russia from the Soviets. At least, it is destined to free farmers elsewhere from the unjust restrictions placed upon them by the manufacturers and capitalists, who know nothing about farming, and make both realize that the farmer is just as necessary to the life of a country as the workers on the roads, in the factories, or employed in transportation." [1]

So far as his Balkan neighbors were concerned, Stambuliski wished first to establish friendly relations with them all. Then, if possible, he favored a South Slav federation including Yugoslavia and Bulgaria, and even a peninsula-wide federation of all the Balkan states. Article VII of his Agrarian party program, which he formulated while in prison during the war, stated: "The Agrarian Union favors durable and peaceful relations between Bulgaria and her neighbors. . . . It seeks to strengthen these good relations by uniting Bulgaria with the other Balkan states on a federative basis." [2] Although Stambuliski was far from satisfied with the terms of the Neuilly Treaty, immediately after its signature he sent letters to the premiers of Greece, Rumania, and Bulgaria urging that the past be forgotten and that all Balkan governments collaborate for common security and economic welfare.

In addition to these gestures Stambuliski took concrete measures to effect a *rapproachment* with Yugoslavia. The great obstacle was the Internal Macedonian Revolutionary Organization, or IMRO, discussed in Chapter 28. This body, which at the turn of the century voiced the aspirations of the Macedonian people and fought with their support against Turkish misrule, had now degenerated into a band of unprincipled adventurers. After the first Balkan War it ceased to be a truly Macedonian organization and became, in effect, an instrument of the Bulgarian government. During World War I it fought with the Bulgarian army and was given the administration of Serbian Macedonia. In this task it distinguished itself by its irresponsible violence and terrorism. The debacle of 1918 seemed to discredit the Organization completely. The great majority of Bulgarians and Macedonians were alienated by its unprincipled and disastrous behavior, while the Stambuliski government was strongly hostile to it.

Despite these unfavorable circumstances, the IMRO continued to exert a pernicious influence on Balkan affairs during the postwar years. One reason was the harsh terms of the Neuilly Treaty, which gave the IMRO the opportunity to pose as the champion of Bulgarian national rights. Another reason was the severe Serbification policy followed by the Yugoslav government in its newly acquired Macedonian territories. Petrovs and Popovs were required to become Petroviches and Popoviches. The Organization again was able to capitalize on outraged Bulgarian national sentiment. In addition, the Italian government secretly gave monetary and other aid to the IMRO, considering it justifiably as a useful tool for keeping Yugoslavia and Bulgaria apart. In fact, the Italians twice proposed to Stambuliski that he should join them in a pact directed against Yugoslavia. On his refusal they backed the IMRO in order to keep the Balkan states at loggerheads. And the IMRO repaid them by conducting raids into Yugoslavia and Greece and keeping inter-Balkan relations in a constant turmoil.

Stambuliski did his best to curb the IMRO, though with indifferent results because the top army leaders did not wish to see it eliminated. Stambuliski also negotiated in April, 1923, the Nish Treaty with Yugoslavia providing for better supervision of the frontier. All trees and undergrowth were to be cleared for one hundred meters on each side of the frontier, and suspected IMRO sympathizers were to be banned from the frontier zones.

Stambuliski's relations with Greece were not so cordial because of the unresolved issue of an outlet to the Aegean. The peace settlement had stipulated that Bulgaria should have freedom of transit through Western Thrace and a lease in perpetuity in the port of Dedeagach (Alexandroupolis). This failed to satisfy Stambuliski, and at the Lausanne Conference he presented his case. He declared that it was unacceptable that Bulgaria's outlet to the Aegean should be across Greek or Turkish territory and demanded that Western Thrace be transformed into a neutral zone in which Bulgaria could build railways and ports. Stambuliski refused a Greek offer to establish a Bulgarian free zone in Saloniki similar to that provided for Yugoslavia. Finally, the Allies decided at Lausanne to leave the solution of the question to direct negotiations between Greece and Bulgaria. Two years later, in October, 1925, the Greek government voluntarily established a free zone in Saloniki for the use of all Balkan states, including, of course, Bulgaria. But the latter rejected this as inadequate for her needs, and the question of an Aegean outlet remained between the two countries throughout the interwar period.

1923 COUP

Stambuliski's policies met with overwhelming popular approval. In the April, 1923, elections his Agrarian party won 212 seats compared with 16 for the Communists, 2 for the Socialists, and 15 for all the remaining parties that had dominated Bulgarian politics in the prewar years. Confronted with this landslide, the opposition groups despaired of ever unseating Stambuliski by constitutional means. So they resorted to the only alternative available and made plans for an armed coup.

Of the various elements participating in the preparation of the coup, the IMRO was prominent, hating Stambuliski as it did for his *rapproachment* with Yugoslavia. Leaders of the old political parties also participated, hoping to be rid of the bold parvenu who had ousted them from their traditional positions. The army leaders also came out against Stambuliski, their professional interests having suffered at the hands of the antimilitaristic Agrarians. But not all the conspirators were moved by selfish motives. Many sincere liberals turned against Stambuliski because of his overbearing and tactless manner. He had dealt roughly with his opponents, shutting down the university and abolishing freedom of the press. Also, many of his lieutenants were uncouth peasants, made dizzy by unexpected power and abusing it wildly. This does not mean that the Agrarian regime was worse than, or as bad as, the governments that preceded and followed it. Nevertheless, it did have certain glaring faults that drove well-intentioned men into the enemy ranks. Whether or not the king was privy to the plot remains a controversial question, though there is no question that Boris heartily detested his premier and was delighted to see him go.

The leaders who actually planned the coup were Professor Alexander Tsankov, who started his political career as a Socialist and ended as an avowed follower of Hitler; General Volkov and Colonel Damian Velchev of the Officers' League, and Ivan Mihailov, assistant to the IMRO leader, Todor Alexandrov. These men used the Sofia garrison to seize control of the capital on June 9, 1923. Then they presented themselves at the palace and persuaded Boris to recognize them as the government. Meanwhile Stambuliski, who was at his country home, led a few unorganized and poorly armed peasant bands in hopeless resistance. Within a few days they were overcome and Stambuliski was taken prisoner. He was handed over to the IMRO terrorists, who sadistically led him back to his home, multilated and tortured him, made him dig his own grave, and finally finished him off. Before the operations were completed some thousands of peasants were massacred.

During these fateful days the Communists remained quiet, calculating that they would be able to profit later from the turmoil. The Communist International severely criticized this strategy and called upon the Bulgarian Communists to support the Agrarians. The Communists did stage a revolt in September, 1923, but after stiff fighting were put down. Terrorist bands of the IMRO committed their customary barbarities, slaughtering peasants and

Rumeli Hissar or Castle of Europe, on the Bosphorus, built by Mohammed II in preparation for the siege of Constantinople (General Directorate of Publications, Propaganda and Tourism, Ankara).

Mykonos Island, Greece. The mill is for grinding grain (Peter Buckley).

Turkish influence in Balkan architecture is shown in this mosque in Constantza, Rumania (Institutul Remin Pentru Relatile Culturale cu Strainatatea), and a street with mosque in Novi Bazar, Bosnia (Yugoslav Information Center).

Rumanian peasant house.

Fishermen's houses, Missolonghi, Greece (Royal Greek Embassy, Information Service).

Bulgarian peasant.

Cretan peasant.

Albanian peasant woman spinning.

Shepherd in southern Serbia.

Lower part of woman's folk costume, south-western Bulgaria (Ministry of Foreign Affairs, Bulgarian Peoples Republic).

Painted Rumanian Easter eggs.

The typical Byzantine mosaics in Hagia Sophia make an interesting comparison with the mosaics of the St. Clement Basilica; the latter are noteworthy for their approach to the Renaissance and abandonment of the formalism of the Byzantine.

(Left) an interesting example of Slovenian folk art, St. Catharine painted on glass. (Right) the romanesque Cathedral of Zadar, in the Adriatic; (below) the Byzantine-Serbian Basilica of St. Clement in Ohrid, Macedonia. These two thirteenth-century cathedrals represent eastern and western church architecture in the Balkans.

The old and the new in Istanbul: Suleymaniye Mosque and the Hilton Hotel.

workers in large numbers. In this manner Bulgaria's first and only Agrarian government was overthrown and Tsankov replaced Stambuliski as premier.

REACTION: 1923–1934

The decade following the 1923 coup was characterized by disorders and outrages that gave Bulgaria an unenviable notoriety. One reason was the free hand enjoyed during these years by the IMRO. It completely dominated the Petrich district, or Bulgarian Macedonia. There it functioned as a state within a state. The unfortunate inhabitants were required to pay two sets of taxes, one for the Sofia treasury and the other for the IMRO. The basis of the IMRO's strength was the large number of Macedonian refugees in Bulgaria. Some were assimilated but many remained uprooted and embittered. They provided a reservoir of manpower on which the IMRO could draw for its terrorist cadres. Specifically, the IMRO not only conducted raids into Yugoslavia and Greece but also operated in Sofia, where it assassinated scores of Bulgarian leaders who advocated friendship with neighboring countries or some other policy that was contrary to the IMRO's tenets. The organization was able to commit these outrages with impunity because it was favored in high places. Tsankov's war minister, General Volkov, regarded the IMRO as a useful instrument for keeping revisionism alive and for getting rid of bothersome political opponents.

But the IMRO proved to be a difficult instrument to control. It broke into several warring factions that earnestly endeavored to liquidate each other. The main issue was that between the Federalists, who wanted a united and autonomous Macedonia, and the Centralists, who wished to have Macedonia annexed by Bulgaria. Sofia naturally supported the Centralists, or Mihailovists, as they were called after their leader Ivan Mihailov. For years the Federalists and the Mihailovists shot each other almost daily in the streets of Sofia, while the authorities refrained from intervening because of orders from above.

The first elections following the coup were held in November, 1923. The results were very different from those of the April, 1923, elections. The traditional parties grouped around Tsankov won 185 seats compared with the 15 they had gained in April. Contrariwise, the Communists and Agrarians together won 62 seats compared with 212 in April. The huge government majority did not bring peace to the country. The opposition deputies attended parliament at the risk of their lives. Some fell victims to IMRO assassins. On April 16, 1925, a bomb exploded in Sofia Cathedral at a service which Boris was to have attended. He was detained and thus saved, but over a hundred persons were killed in the crowded building. Two Communists were found to be responsible for the crime, though they appear to have acted without party orders. Again there were mass executions, mostly by the Macedonian bands and some by the official police. The next shock was the Greek invasion of southern Bulgaria in October, 1925, following a series of border disturbances. The League of Nations intervened in this case and compelled the Greeks to withdraw and to pay an indemnity.*

The Tsankov government was replaced on January 4, 1926, by a new one headed by Andrew Liapchev. The shift did not produce any significant change within Bulgaria. In fact, Liapchev was himself a Macedonian and he allowed the IMRO even greater freedom than it had enjoyed before. His government was never popular, so that in the 1927 elections it received 495,000 votes against 556,000 given to the opposition parties. Yet he obtained 163 of the 249 seats, thanks to the disunity of the opposition and the majority system of voting. During the depression years discontent in the country mounted, culminating in a clear-cut victory for the opposition parties in the elections of June 21, 1931. The Liberal, Democratic, and Progressive parties combined with a faction of the Agrarian party to form a united front against the government forces led by Liapchev and Tsankov. With the triumph of the opposition bloc, a new government was formed by the Democratic leader, Alexander Malinov, on June 29. He was succeeded on October 12 by another Democratic premier, Nikola Mushanov.

The new regime did not bring about significant changes. The parties within the coalition government quarreled over such issues as protectionism versus freer trade. Also, there was wrangling among the political leaders for spoils and influence. Meanwhile the IMRO still ruled unchallenged in the Petrich district and the army refrained from taking any measures against it. The government tolerated the IMRO and the latter reciprocated by tolerating the government. The popular revulsion against this inactivity was manifested in the Sofia municipal elections of September 25, 1932, in which the Communists won 19 of the 35 seats. They were not allowed to take office, but the returns did reflect the public's growing exasperation. Furthermore, as will be discussed in Chapter 37, the banding of Bulgaria's neighbors into the Balkan Entente in February, 1934, left Bulgaria diplomatically isolated. This convinced many that a radical change in foreign policy was needed. But this was out of the question so long as the IMRO was allowed the free hand it had hitherto enjoyed. Such was the situation in Bulgaria when a group of army officers intervened and imposed a military dictatorship.

MILITARY AND ROYAL DICTATORSHIP: 1934–1939

Colonel Velchev was the leader of the military coup of May 19, 1934. Velchev had been one of the organizers of the revolt that had overthrown Stambuliski in 1923. Since then he had been increasingly alienated by the terrorism, inefficiency, and instability that had marked Bulgarian political life. He also became convinced that the political parties were incapable of cleaning house and that the army's high command was unwilling to do anything

* See Chapter 34.

against the IMRO terrorists. Accordingly, he organized in 1930 the Military League, which included a large proportion of the army officers. Velchev was also connected with the Zveno, a small group of political reformers whose leader was his friend and collaborator in the 1923 coup, Colonel Kimon Georgiev. This civil group, also founded in 1930, had the same general objectives as the Military League. Both organizations wished to abolish political parties and establish a government free from the influence of the high command and capable of suppressing the terrorists and coping with the political and economic crisis.

Meanwhile King Boris, Professor Tsankov, and the high command were also planning to establish a military dictatorship. Velchev and his colleagues got wind of what was afoot and decided to strike on May 19, 1934. They gained control of the capital and the leading cities without difficulty. Boris reluctantly accepted the *fait accompli* and Georgiev formed a government while Velchev remained in the background as "adviser"

The new government was dictatorial but not fascist. It did not introduce the ideological or demagogic trappings inseparable from fascism. It did dismiss parliament, dissolve all parties, and impose an official censorship on the press. But if political freedom was for the moment suppressed, so also was the IMRO. One of the most impressive achievements of the new regime was its liquidation of the entire IMRO apparatus within a few days. The ridiculous ease with which this was accomplished revealed that the organization had completely lost any popular support that it once may have possessed. It also revealed that the previous governments, despite their frequent protestations, had lacked the will rather than the means of eliminating the IMRO. The new government also reduced peasant debts, reorganized the credit system, and created a new state bank. It attempted to reorganize education, placing greater emphasis upon technical and scientific branches. Doctors were encouraged to practice in the villages, where the peasants badly needed medical attention, rather than concentrating in the towns as they had in the past.

In its foreign policy the government made two changes that proved popular with most Bulgarians. It restored diplomatic relations with the Soviet Union and it sought reconciliation with Yugoslavia. The suppression of the IMRO convinced Belgrade of the sincerity of the Bulgarian overtures. In September, 1934, King Alexander and his queen paid a ceremonial visit to Sofia, where they were warmly received. But a few weeks later Alexander was assassinated in Marseilles by an IMRO member who was assisted by the Croatian Ustashi and by Italian and Hungarian officials. Despite this tragedy, relations between Yugoslavia and Bulgaria continued to remain friendly.

The Georgiev government did not remain long in office because of the hostility of the king. The relations between Boris and Velchev had long been strained. In 1928 Boris had dismissed Velchev from his post as commandant of the Military Academy because he had opposed the policies of General Volkov, the war minister. Rumors now were spread that Velchev was using his special influence in the government to arrange for the deposition of the king and the establishment of a republic. This does not appear to have been true, though the government did wish to strip the king of such powers as disposing of all promotions and appointments in the army and nominating the war minister

In any case, Boris obviously was ill-pleased with a government over which he had no influence whatsoever, so he skillfully undermined it by winning over royalist-minded officers on the issue of the alleged republican plot. Thus Boris was able to foment a cleavage between Velchev and Georgiev on the one hand and the royalist officers on the other. Finally, Velchev withdrew from politics and Georgiev resigned the premiership. His place was taken by General Petko Zlatev until April 18, 1935, when a purely civilian government was formed by Andrew Toshev. Both of these men were close to Boris and could be depended upon to do his bidding. But Boris's closest friend was George Kiosseivanov, who became premier on November 23, 1935, and remained in office until World War II.

On April 21, 1935, Boris issued a manifesto that symbolized the reestablishment of his authority. On the one hand he declared that there would be "no going back," which was intended as a promise to the army that there would be no return to party politics. On the other hand he undertook to issue a new constitution in the near future to satisfy the popular demand for some form of representative government. In other words, Boris planned to allow a certain degree of popular participation in government but with no real authority. On October 21, 1937, he issued an electoral law giving the vote to men and married women but forbidding candidates to run as the representatives of parties. In fact, all parties remained prohibited. Elections were held in March, 1938, and, despite much intimidation, about 56 of the 160 deputies elected were in the opposition camp. Yet there was not much that they could do because parliament had only consultative powers. During the following years Bulgaria was controlled effectively by a royal dictatorship. Boris sent the army back to the barracks and ordered it to forget about politics. He governed the country through individuals chosen by himself and supported by the police and administrative apparatus. This arrangement prevailed until the begnning of World War II and thereafter until the death of Boris on August 28, 1943.

ECONOMIC DEVELOPMENT

Bulgaria's economic development received a serious setback as a result of World War I. Bulgaria lost certain territories that left wide gaps in her economy. One was Southern Dobruja, the most important grain-producing province in the country. In contrast to the rest of Bulgaria, Southern Dobruja was a region of large farms in which relatively efficient agricultural techniques were practiced. As a result it produced 20 per cent of the national grain output, although it constituted only 8 per cent of the area of prewar Bulgaria. The loss of Dobruja would have been counterbalanced if Bulgaria had been able to keep Western Thrace, with its rich tobacco fields and Aegean ports. But the Neuilly Treaty awarded that territory to Greece. It is true that the treaty stipulated that Bulgaria should be afforded facilities in one of the Thracian ports. These ports, however, had not as yet been developed and were of little value without extensive improvement and coordination with railway facilties. As a result, Bulgaria preferred to concentrate her efforts on the development of her own Black Sea ports.

The war also retarded Bulgaria by producing enormous budgetary deficits which were covered partly by foreign borrowing and partly by monetary inflation. The latter progressively deteriorated the exchange value of the currency. Furthermore, the Neuilly Treaty saddled Bulgaria with reparations totaling 2,250 million gold francs, an absurdly large sum representing approximately 22.5 per cent of her entire national wealth. In the end Bulgaria paid very little of this sum, though she did negotiate and fulfill separate settlements with Greece and Yugoslavia.

Another deleterious effect of the war was the influx of some 200,000 refugees. Some were provided with plots made available by the land reform legislation. But the majority remained uprooted and embittered, becoming easy prey for IMRO propaganda. In 1926 Bulgaria received a League of Nations loan of 2,250,000 pounds to finance the settlement of the refugees. The latter not only caused financial problems but, more seriously, increased the already severe population pressure upon the land.

Bulgaria's mountainous terrain leaves only 35 per cent of her area available for cultivation. But her population has mounted rapidly since the beginning of the century, partly because of the refugee influx but primarily because of the high birth rate. Starting with 3.7 million in 1901, Bulgaria's population rose to 4.3 million in 1911, 4.8 in 1921, 5.7 in 1929, and 6.3 in 1937.[3] At the same time Bulgaria lost the provinces of Southern Dobruja and Western Thrace. This combination of increasing population and decreasing land reduced the average size of peasant holdings from a little over 6 hectares at the end of World War I to 4.9 in 1934 and 4.3 in 1946. The inadequate size of the plots was aggravated, as in the other Balkan countries, by the excessive parcelization of individual holdings. The average farm in 1934, which amounted to 4.9 hectares, consisted of 13.4 plots, and the average size of each plot was 0.37 hectares.[4] This parcelization wasted much land on roads and boundaries and also hampered the peasant by requiring him to trudge from one strip to another and by making improvement of agricultural methods more difficult. The net result was that by 1930 Bulgaria had a degree of agrarian overpopulation estimated at 53 per cent.

Various measures were taken to cope with this situation. One was land distribution, which we noted earlier in the chapter. This helped only to a very limited extent because of the modest amount of available land. Another measure was to bring under cultivation land formerly used for grazing and other purposes. As a result, the area devoted to cereals, which averaged 2.5 million hectares between 1908 and 1912, increased to 2.6 million hectares by 1933 despite the loss of Southern Dobruja. Owing, however, to the increased population, the per capita production of cereals diminished substantially. The amount of cereals available for export dropped from 609,169 tons in 1914 to 120,000 tons in 1934. The peasants also tried to meet the land shortage by shifting to intensive crops. The most important of these were tobacco, sunflower seeds, soya beans, cotton, hemp, flax, table grapes, and strawberries. Before 1914 the percentage of tilled land sown with cereals was 76, with fodder crops 17, and with intensive crops 7. By the eve of World War II the percentages had changed to 70, 18, and 12, respectively.[5]

Despite these measures the position of the Bulgarian peasants remained precarious during the interwar years. The average income of rural families was less than one third that of urban families. A careful study made in 1934 revealed that only peasants with five or more hectares of land were able to make ends meet. The remainder fell increasingly into debt each year. The significance of this figure is that 45.9 per cent of all peasant families fell below the 5 hectare minimum.[6] Although agriculture offered such scanty rewards, about 80 per cent of the population remained dependent upon it for their livelihood. The overwhelmingly agrarian character of Bulgaria's economy is evident in the fact that in 1935, 53.5 per cent of the national income was derived from agriculture, compared with 7.6 per cent from handicrafts and 6.3 per cent from industry.[7]

The above figures are also significant in showing that handicrafts (tailoring, shoemaking, carpentering, coopering, and building) produced a greater value than industry. Bulgarian industry, like that of other Balkan countries, was held back by lack of capital, of skilled labor, and of trained management. It also suffered from poor natural resources, the only ones of any consequence being lignite and coal. As a result, industry employed only 43,000 persons in 1933. Almost half worked in textile factories, and most of the remainder produced consumers' goods such as leather and rubber shoes, cigarettes, beer, and soap. Foreign capital played an important role in the economy of Bulgaria as of the neighboring countries. In 1936 foreign investments comprised 31 per cent of total capital in banks, 49 per cent in industry, and 55 per cent in transportation.

In international trade the most important development in the interwar years was the decline of cereal exports in favor of fruits and vegetables, tobacco, animals and animal products, and especially tobacco. The latter was the most important export, followed in order of value by animals and animal products, cereals, and fruits and vegetables. These agricultural commodities together accounted for more than 90 per cent of exports, while machinery, metal goods, textiles, chemical products, and railroad cars and motor vehicles together accounted for more than 80 per cent of imports.

Before 1914 Britain and Belgium were prominent in Bulgarian trade because they imported wheat. After the war they gave way to Germany, Austria, Italy, and Czechoslovakia, which took the growing tobacco exports of Bulgaria. In the 1930's Bulgaria became increasingly dependent upon Germany for both her exports and imports. In fact, her dependency was more marked than that of any other Balkan country. Germany's share in Bulgaria's exports rose from 10 per cent in 1921 to 30 per cent in 1929, 48 in 1935, and 68 in 1939. Likewise, Germany's share in Bulgaria's imports rose from 17 per cent in 1921 to 22 per cent in 1929, 54 in 1935, and 66 in 1939.[8] This commercial relationship was somewhat similar to that between Mexico and the United States. At the same time Germany acquired control of an increasing proportion of foreign investments in Bulgaria when she overran Austria, Czechoslovakia, France, and the Low Countries. Thus Germany effectively dominated Bulgaria's economy even before her troops began to cross the Danube from Rumania in January, 1941.

SOCIAL AND CULTURAL DEVELOPMENT

Bulgarian peasant families in the interwar years continued to be largely self-sufficient. They lived off their own land, owning a few sheep, cows, goats, pigs, oxen or water buffaloes, horses or donkeys, and poultry. They purchased only a few items such as salt, soda, shoes, sugar (when honey was not used), and coffee to flavor the home-roasted wheat or barley substitute. Peasants in isolated villages bought kerosene for their lamps, but an increasing percentage of those living near towns or near central electric stations in the mountains used electricity. It was not only more convenient but also cheaper because the peasants never used more than one small bulb hanging from the center of the ceiling of each room. The women usually made soap at home with soda and the fat of their own sheep or cows. They also dried herbs, smoked meat and bacon, made jam and put down cabbages in great vats of salt and water. The men presided over wine making and the distillation of a fiery spirit, raki, from various fruits.

The houses usually were built of sun-baked mud bricks, covered with a plaster of mud and cow dung mixed with chaff, which, when dry, was white- or color-washed inside and out. The rich peasants had houses like those in town, consisting of several rooms and furnished with table, chairs, and beds. But the poorer peasants still sat on low, wooden, homemade stools around a wooden table about fifteen inches high. At night they spread their sheepskins or woven reed or maize mats on the ground, the whole family often sleeping in the same room.

Health conditions continued to be far below Western standards. The reasons were the traditional ones—ignorance, superstition, and poverty. This is clearly illustrated in the following account of health practices in a village near Sofia.

If a child became sick, "the first thing was to warm him, for he might have caught cold." Then he was given some home remedies prescribed by the *babi* [old women or midwives]. If the child did not then recover, the parents tried everything they knew, hoping that after some time "everything bad would pass away." In case the child grew worse, they called some of the neighbors or some old woman to come to see him. Only in very serious cases, when the peasants became convinced that nothing could help the child, would they carry him to the doctor. The reason for taking the child to the doctor was to save the extra fee charged for a home visit. Finally, "if God has given the child some more days to live, then the child will recover; if not, then his days are finished and God wants to take the child." [9]

This account explains why 123 out of every 1,000 infants born in 1941 died during their first year of life—a rate of infant mortality more than two-and-one-half times that prevailing in the United States. Figures were correspondingly high for tuberculosis, malaria, and other diseases requiring adequate nutrition and control measures to bring them down to Western rates of incidence. Educational standards were also low in Bulgaria, though not quite as low as in the other Balkan countries. The 1934 census showed 20.4 per cent of the males and 42.8 per cent of the females to be illiterate. The law provided for free and compulsory education between the ages of seven and fourteen. About 8 per cent of the children failed to attend school, either because their villages were remote or because their parents objected. The latter was frequently the case among the Moslem population (about 10 per cent of total population), 26 per cent of whose children did not attend school.

As in all the Balkan countries, the educational system was badly neglected so far as financial appropriations were concerned. Not enough schools were available, necessitating two shifts of pupils a day. According to a report in parliament in 1924, only 39 per cent of the school buildings were adequate. The teachers were miserably paid and were obliged to pay commissions to various political intermediaries to obtain their posts. Then with every change of government they ran the risk of losing their positions. Under such circumstances it is not surprising that an appreciable proportion of Bulgarian teachers turned to communism as a panacea.

Widespread unemployment in the professions also drove some Bulgarian intellectuals to communism. The pattern was one that was common to the whole peninsula. The country needed many more teachers and doctors and engineers, but it lacked the means to support even those that it possessed. On December 1, 1935, 555 university graduates were registered as being without work in the city of Sofia alone, 313 of them being under thirty. Since only 792 students graduated from institutions of higher learning in 1934, the figure of the unemployed in Sofia is impressive. An official report in 1935 described the situation as follows:

The need for university-trained persons is so great that the annual supply of graduates could not satisfy it for many years to come. . . . While exact statistical data are not available, there are many symptoms indicating that all the careers for which the institutions of higher learning prepare are saturated. The universities in Bulgaria and in other countries where Bulgarians study produce more university-trained people than can be absorbed in public offices or by private enterprises. . . . It is therefore evident that the unemployment of intellectual workers in Bulgaria is above all and fundamentally due to the economic crisis. . . .[10]

Since many university graduates could not find employment in the fields for which they had been trained, they naturally tried to find some post in the bureaucracy. As a result the government offices were cluttered with many more employees than were needed, and the salaries were correspondingly low. This in turn led to open nepotism and corruption. A government deputy stated artlessly in parliament on September 8, 1926: "What God gives is for all, but the blessings which the State may confer are first for our kin. That is how we understand democracy. So it was yesterday, is today and will be tomorrow." [11]

Such conditions help to explain why the Bulgarian Communist party probably was the largest and most effective in the Balkans. On the other hand, Bulgaria definitely was not a country of Communists or of intellectuals. A sociological study of Dragalevtsy, a village near Sofia, reveals in fascinating detail how the 80 per cent of the population that tilled the soil continued to live in the traditional pattern.

The sense of belonging to a large mass of kindred spirits, who shared the agrarian point of view, dressed in village clothes, and abided to a great degree by tradition, gave each peasant a "consciousness of kind" which in our [American] society has to find its substitutes in the Farmers' Union, the Farm Bureau, the National Grange, and a host of other organizations devoted to serving those who farm. This self-identification with a mass of other peasants of course nourished conservatism and made the Dragalevtsy farmer of 1937 feel so secure that he had little incentive to rise above his present lot. . . . Thus Dragalevtsy proved an interesting illustration of the paradox that a traditional society, while deadly from the standpoint of scientific, material, or intellectual progress, nevertheless accentuated those traits which made for contentment and for developing a perspective toward death and time which helped keep life on an even keel. There individual maladjustment was at a minimum, for each conforming individual had the backing of all other guardians of tradition.[12]

The Bulgarian peasant definitely preferred to live in his village and to continue with his accustomed and satisfying work. But he was also well aware of the obstacles that were arising, especially the growing land shortage as the tiny plots were divided and subdivided among the many children. This is why he sought to educate at least one of his sons in order to attain security and social prestige. As one Dragalevtsy father said to his son upon sending him to school: "If you don't study you will plow, sow, and work in the fields, and where will you get then?" [13] But all too often the son studied, and even graduated with honors, yet found himself not only unemployed but also unfitted and unwilling to take up the plow again.

Thus Bulgarian society was deeply ambivalent. One part of it wanted only to be left alone to continue living as in the past. Another part had concluded from experience that change was necessary and inevitable. This ambivalence is significant for the period after World War II. It explains the reception accorded to the Communist plans for the reorganization of society. Some of the younger elements accepted and even supported these plans. But the bulk of the peasant mass remained suspicious and hostile to the upsetting intrusion from the outside world.

34. Greece: 1918–1939

G REECE EMERGED FROM WORLD WAR I under circumstances that were far from happy. Her armies had been routed in Asia Minor, her economy was strained by the great deluge of destitute refugees, her political life was embittered by the conviction and execution of six of King Constantine's ministers and generals who were held responsible for the Asia Minor disaster.* But the dark clouds did have their silver linings. The Lausanne Treaty and the exchange of minorities virtually settled the traditional irredentist problem with the exception of less pressing claims to southern Albania, British-held Cyprus, and the Italian-held Dodecanese. Also we shall see that land was distributed on a large scale to the peasants during and after the war years. These significant developments presumably should have contributed substantially to political and economic tranquillity in the postwar years. Instead, Greece was to experience economic distress, political strife, and frequent revolution.

One reason was the unresolved question of the form of government. Venizelos preferred a constitutional monarchy to a republic, but the violent conflict of the war years and the partisan activities of Constantine I and George II combined to force most of the supporters of the Liberal party into a doctrinaire republican position. On the other hand, the monarchical cause still had many ardent supporters, particularly in the Peloponnesus. Thus the political question remained a source of dissension until the outbreak of World War II and even thereafter.

The issue of the form of government was aggravated by the readiness of military officers to enter the political arena by exerting pressure behind the scenes or resorting to armed force. This occurred much more frequently in Greece than in the other Balkan countries. The explanation appears to be that in the other countries the dynasties controlled or had working arrangements with the military establishments, and therefore were able to cooperate

* See Chapter 30.

661

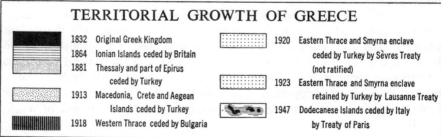

TERRITORIAL GROWTH OF GREECE

1832	Original Greek Kingdom	1920	Eastern Thrace and Smyrna enclave
1864	Ionian Islands ceded by Britain		ceded by Turkey by Sèvres Treaty
1881	Thessaly and part of Epirus		(not ratified)
	ceded by Turkey	1923	Eastern Thrace and Smyrna enclave
1913	Macedonia, Crete and Aegean		retained by Turkey by Lausanne Treaty
	Islands ceded by Turkey	1947	Dodecanese Islands ceded by Italy
1918	Western Thrace ceded by Bulgaria		by Treaty of Paris

with them in maintaining the *status quo*. In Greece, on the other hand, republican officers gained predominance in the armed forces as a result of the Asia Minor debacle. They forced Constantine to abdicate in 1922 and they executed further coups in behalf of the republican cause in 1925, 1926, 1933, and 1935. When the royalists regained political power they naturally purged the army of its republican officers and used it to keep themselves in power. Thereafter the court and the armed forces were on the same side and no more was heard of military coups.

The final principal cause for instability was the deterioration of the national economy. We shall see that in this respect the plight of Greece was basically similar to that of the other Balkan countries. The high birth rate, the low agricultural productivity, the inability of industry to absorb the population surplus, and the lack of a domestic market adequate to support industrial expansion—all these condemned the peasants and the urban workers to a low living standard with no hope for the future. Such conditions inevitably provoked political repercussions. To a much greater degree than in the past, Greek politics now reflected the underlying economic difficulties and social cleavages. It was not accidental that the outbreak of World War II found Greece under a full-fledged dictatorship.

REPUBLIC ESTABLISHED: 1923–1928

The revolutionary regime established by Colonel Plastiras and other republican officers following the Asia Minor defeat held elections on December 16, 1923, as a step toward the return to constitutional government. The royalist Populist party abstained, so that the seats were divided among 200 Venizelists, 120 avowed republicans, and 6 Agrarians. King George was persuaded to leave the country while the assembly considered the question of the form of government. The Venizelists preferred to decide the question by a plebiscite, but the republicans insisted on the immediate explusion of the dynasty and the establishment of a republic by vote of the assembly. The latter had their way, securing a majority vote in the assembly in favor of a republic. A confirmatory plebiscite, held on April 13, 1924, returned 758,742 votes for the republic and 325,322 for the king.

A constitution for the republic was now needed. But a series of incidents with neighboring countries distracted the republican cabinets and postponed the adoption of a constitution. The most serious affair occurred the previous year, on August 27, 1923, when Italian members of a Greek-Albanian frontier commission were murdered on Greek soil. Although the responsibility for the crime was never established, Mussolini sent a drastic ultimatum to Athens. When it was not accepted unconditionally he bombarded and occupied the island of Corfu. Greece appealed to the League of Nations but Mussolini rejected the "intervention" of the international organization. Nevertheless, the public opinion of Europe expressed itself so strongly through the League that Mussolini found it advisable to evacuate Corfu on September 27. His susceptibilities were saved by the Conference of Ambassadors in Paris, which awarded an indemnity to Italy on the ground that there had been negligence on the part of the Greek authorities.

Greece was also involved in a series of frontier incidents with Bulgaria, the most serious occurring in October, 1925, when a Greek soldier and a Greek officer were killed. In retaliation the Greek army crossed the border in force, occupying a considerable portion of Bulgarian territory. Bulgaria appealed to the League and the latter found, following a report by an investigatory commission, that there was no premeditation on either side. The League therefore ordered that Greece should pay an indemnity of 45,000 pounds for violating Bulgarian territory, and that Bulgaria in turn should pay damages for the shooting of the Greek army men.

Greece was also engaged in protracted disputes with Yugoslavia and Turkey. The issue with Yugoslavia concerned an outlet to the Aegean. On May 10, 1923, the two countries had signed a convention providing that an area of 94,000 square meters in the port of Saloniki should be under Yugoslav customs administration (but under Greek law and police administration), and that goods passing between the free zone and the Yugoslav frontier should be exempt from Greek taxes. The Yugoslavs found this arrangement unsatisfactory, complaining that the zone was too small for their needs and that railway service between Saloniki and the Yugoslav frontier was too slow and expensive. They demanded that the zone be enlarged and that they be allowed virtually to own the zone and the railway leading to it. The Greeks rejected this demand and the issue remained unresolved until a settlement was finally reached in 1929.

The differences between Greece and Turkey involved the position of the Patriarchate and of the Greek minority in Constantinople. At the time of the exchange of the minorities it had been agreed that the Greek inhabitants of Constantinople who had been "established" before October 30, 1918, should be exempted from the exchange. The Turks interpreted the term "established" narrowly and sought to expel most of the Greek population. They actually ousted the Patriarch as an "exchangeable Greek." The dispute was referred to the Permanent Court at the Hague, which decided against the Turkish interpretation and allowed most of the Greeks who were still residing in Constantinople to remain there. The position of the Patriarch was also settled by arranging for the election of Greeks who were of the "established" status and who thus could not be expelled. There still remained, however, several outstanding issues between the two countries, including the disposal of properties left behind by emigrants from Greece and Turkey, and the return to Constantinople of Greeks in possession of Turkish passports. These and other questions remained unsettled until the Greco-Turkish *rapprochement* in 1930.

Meanwhile there had been a good deal of political instability and corruption in Athens. The two leading parties were the Liberal headed by Themistocles Sophoules in the absence of Venizelos, who was abroad, and the Populist or royalist headed by Panayiotes Tsaldares. In addition there were several other small parties led by ambitious politicians such as the ultraroyalist General Metaxas at the one extreme, and the outright republican Alexander Papanastassiou at the other. Under the circumstances cabinets rose and fell until January 3, 1926, when a doughty republican general, Theodore Pangalos, effected a coup. The general proclaimed a dictatorship with the avowed object of restoring political peace and reviving the economy. As a dictator he was a curious phenomenon. He had no new political doctrine to advance. He did not repudiate democracy as outmoded or impractical. Rather, he was determined to end the bickering of the numerous parties and to curb the press, which he accused with justification of fostering the bickering. He acted with the arbitrariness of a Turkish pasha, imposing a rigid censorship, seizing newspapers, banishing political leaders, and even holding courts-martial. Yet there was a purpose and a benevolence about his ferocity that made it hard to condemn him except, as the liberals did, on principle. A typical measure that aroused the most interest abroad was his decree forbidding women to wear their skirts more than fourteen inches above the ground.

After half a year of furious activity Pangalos was ousted by his own Republican Guard on August 22, 1926. New elections were held on November 7 and this time the Populists participated. The republican parties received a majority of only 34 seats in a chamber of 286. Accordingly, it was decided that a coalition cabinet of all parties should prepare the long-delayed constitution. The cabinet was formed but, like most coalitions, it proved a cumbersome instrument of government. In fact, it already was in process of disintegration when Venizelos returned from abroad and assumed the premiership on July 3, 1928. He dissolved the chamber, abolished proportional representation by presidential decree, and held a general election on August 19. He received a majority over all other parties and governed Greece for the next four years.

VENIZELIST RULE: 1928–1933

Venizelos had lived abroad since 1920 with the exception of a few months early in 1924, when he tried without success to persuade the chamber not to depose King George before a plebiscite had been held. Now in 1928 he returned to Athens partly because representatives of all parties had repeatedly requested him to do so in order to end the political instability. Another reason was the ambition of his wife, a wealthy London-born Greek whom he had married in 1921 while abroad. The name Venizelos still had irresistible prestige, so that he was able to assume at once the office of premier as well as the leadership of the Liberal party.

On the other hand, the Venizelos of 1928 was not the Venizelos of 1910 who had arrived from Crete to resurrect his mother country. He was now sixty-four years old. The years of living abroad, together with the acquisition of wealth, had blunted his keenness and crusading ardor. He tended to accept things as they were and to overlook corruption and inefficiency. The fact is that he had lost interest in the hurly-burly of everyday Greek political life. Instead, he turned his attention to foreign affairs, where he was as successful as usual.

Venizelos' general aim in formulating his foreign policy was to avoid dependence on any great power. The most likely way of achieving this, he believed, was to establish friendly relations with the neighboring countries and with those powers especially interested in the Mediterranean. Accordingly, Venizelos first signed a treaty of friendship and arbitration with Italy (September 23, 1928) settling all outstanding questions between the two countries. He thought it unwise at that juncture to challenge the status of the Dodecanese

Islands, which were Greek in population but which had been occupied by the Italians in 1912 during their Tripolitan War with Turkey. Venizelos next settled the troublesome Saloniki Free Zone dispute with Yugoslavia on March 17, 1929. The zone was to remain under Greek sovereignty but Yugoslavia received more privileges in its use. With this issue removed, Venizelos concluded later in the month a friendship and arbitration treaty with Yugoslavia. He attempted to conciliate the Bulgarians by offering them a Free Port in Saloniki or at Alexandroupolis (Dedeagach). The Bulgarians refused, being still hopeful that they would eventually gain full possession of a strip to the Aegean. Thus Venizelos was only able to arrange for full diplomatic relations with Bulgaria.

His greatest diplomatic triumph was the establishment of cordial relations with Turkey. Despite baiting by nationalistic elements, he assured the Turks privately and publicly that Greece had no aspirations to their territory and that he wished to settle outstanding issues. After prolonged discussions, during which many concessions were made by both sides, an agreement was reached on June 10, 1930. Greece paid 425,000 pounds in settlement of the claims of the Turks who had left Greek territory, and Turkey in return agreed to accept the Constantinople Greeks as permanent residents. A few months later Venizelos went to Ankara where, on October 30, he signed treaties of friendship and commerce. This diplomatic *rapprochement* was accompanied by a remarkable change of public feeling between the two countries. Venizelos was warmly welcomed in Ankara, and the Turkish foreign minister received enthusiastic public acclaim when he visited Athens the following year.

These diplomatic achievements strengthened Greece's international position and prepared the ground for the Balkan pact that Venizelos' successors were to negotiate a few years later. Meanwhile Venizelos was losing ground at home. One reason was that the republican ranks were far from closed. Many of the republican leaders, resenting Venizelos' return, which automatically relegated them to second place, frequently cooperated with the royalists against their own leader. Another reason for Venizelos' decline in popularity was the incompetence and corruption of some of his subordinates, whom he defended instead of dismissing. But by far the heaviest blow to Venizelos' regime was the depression which devastated Greece's sickly economy. The products that Greece normally exported were luxury agricultural items—tobacco, currants, wine, olives, and olive oil. The demand and the price of such goods naturally dropped sharply during the depression years. Between 1929 and 1934 the gross trade of Greece declined 21.5 per cent in quantity and 70.5 per cent in value, and in the latter year the value of imports totaled 587.78 million gold francs as against exports of only 279.87 million gold francs. In normal years such import surpluses were largely offset by revenues from tourists, from the large Greek merchant marine, and from the remittances of Greek emigrants. But the depression drastically reduced the income from all three of these sources.

Venizelos was ill-equipped to meet the emergency. He was a typical nineteenth-century romantic nationalist who never really understood the new world of depression, unemployment, agrarian indebtedness, and crop surpluses.

The difficulty was that Venizelos and his Liberal party had undergone the same process of ossification as Pashich and his Radicals, or the Bratianus and their Liberals. Before World War I Venizelos' party had led the reform movement. It divided the large estates and reorganized the schools, the administration, and the army. It represented the rising, progressive middle class of merchants, manufacturers, bankers, and shipowners. But by the 1930's the ideas of this middle class had changed. It had arrived. It wanted to preserve and retain rather than to change and discard. It viewed with alarm the agitation for reform bred by the depression.

The other major political force, the Populist or royalist party, was not any more inclined to adopt a comprehensive reform program in keeping with the seriousness of the situation. But the royalists had the great advantage of being out of office and thus being able to blame all the trouble on the Liberals. The Populist leader, Tsaldares, exploited this favorable situation to the full by stating unequivocally that he and his party accepted the republic and would work within its framework. Thus he was able to attract the votes of citizens who wished to vote against the government in office but not against the republic.

The change in the political climate was revealed by the results of the elections on September 25, 1932. Venizelos lost his majority, the Liberal party securing 102 seats against 96 for the Populists and 52 for assorted republican and royalist groups. These returns required a coalition government but Tsaldares refused to associate with the Liberals. Venizelos allowed him to form a royalist cabinet including General Metaxas. When the new government could muster only 103 votes in the assembly it was forced to exist on the sufferance of the opposition. This anomalous arrangement lasted until January, 1933, when Venizelos attacked the government's financial policy and compelled Tsaldares to resign. Venizelos resumed the premiership, dissolved the chamber, and decreed a new election in order to end the stalemate.

The outcome of the election, held on March 5, 1933, showed that he had misread the trend of public sentiment as disastrously as he had in November, 1920. His Liberal party declined from 102 to 96 members while the Populist party gained a clear majority with 135 seats. Despite this, the total royalist vote comprised only 40.33 per cent of the 1,141,331 votes cast. Furthermore, Tsaldares' reiterated pledges of loyalty to the republic undoubtedly attracted many who were dissatisfied with four years of Venizelist rule but who did not necessarily wish to see the king return. Thus the 1933 election cannot be interpreted as registering a preponderant shift toward the dynasty.

This interpretation, which prevailed among republican politicians, was not shared by the republican officers headed by General Plastiras. They were seriously concerned about the future of the republic, being convinced that Metaxas and other royalist generals were intriguing behind Tsaldares to secure the return of the king. Also, they had no faith in Venizelos as a defender of the republic, considering him too weak and inclined to appeasement. Accordingly, these republican officers staged two revolts—in 1933 and 1935—"in order to save the republic." The revolts failed dismally and served merely to hasten the outcome that they were designed to prevent. The blundering republican officers contributed substantially to the failure of the Greek republic.

FALL OF THE REPUBLIC: 1933–1935

On the morning following the election of March 5, 1933, the Athenians were awakened by the booming of artillery in the suburbs. General Plastiras, on learning of the election returns, declared himself dictator in a flamboyant declaration announcing that he was intervening by the will of God to save the nation. He received so little support that within twelve hours he was forced to abandon the attempt and to flee. Nevertheless the ill-advised venture revived party passions, particularly because Plastiras had been the head of the 1922 revolutionary government which had tried and executed the six royalist leaders. The die-hard royalists now became more bold in their campaign to overthrow the republic. General Metaxas introduced a motion in the chamber to impeach Venizelos on the ground of complicity in the coup—a charge that was without any foundation. In the midst of the political storm aroused by this motion a brazen attempt was made on the life of Venizelos. On the night of June 6, 1933, when he was returning with his wife from a dinner party in a suburb, a car full of assassins pursued his car for three miles, riddling it with machine-gun bullets. Venizelos escaped unscathed but his bodyguard was killed and his wife and chauffeur were wounded. The car used in the attempt was found abandoned next day; it belonged to the brother of the chief of police of Athens!

The outrage caused the smoldering Venizelist-royalist feud to flare up with renewed violence. The various republican leaders were moved to effect a reconciliation with Venizelos, forming a united republican front. They demanded the apprehension and speedy trial of those implicated in the assassination attempt. The evidence indicated plainly that the police were the organizers of the crime and that certain unidentified ultraroyalist politicians were the instigators. The government refused to press its investigation seriously despite bitter protests from the opposition. Finally, on October 3, 1934, Venizelos' private police arrested a notorious brigand suspected of having participated in the attempted murder. The government now felt constrained to take action and opened the long-deferred trial early in 1935. Before it could be completed another republican revolt rescued the royalists from their uncomfortable position and undermined the foundations of the republic.

The revolt was organized by republican officers who had been placed on the retired list since the 1933 Plastiras coup. They were joined by other officers who were apprehensive because the government had passed a bill providing for radical revision of the cadres of the army, navy, and air force. These men were convinced that the government was planning a wholesale purge of the armed forces preparatory to the restoration of the monarchy. Thus they identified their professional interests with the republican cause and, far from regarding themselves as rebels against constituted authority, they felt that they were the true defenders of the republic against the machinations of a crypto-royalist administration.

The insurgents seized the Military College and some barracks in Athens. Units of the fleet put to sea and summoned the garrisons of the provinces by telegraph to join the movement. The only response from the mainland came from Macedonia, where rebel officers seized several towns, though not Saloniki. Both in Macedonia and in Athens the revolt was quickly and easily crushed. Not only was it poorly planned but everywhere it failed to win popular support. The people were tired of these perpetual coups, and were not at all convinced that their liberties would be best safeguarded by the militarists.

Meanwhile, the rebel naval officers had arrived with their ships in Crete, where they persuaded Venizelos to assume the leadership of the movement. Venizelos, by his own admission, had known of the preparations for the revolt and had withdrawn his objections to such action in December, 1934, though he had advised his followers to wait "until they [the government] attempted to restore the monarchy." [1] Possibly the revolt might never have been attempted if he had not committed himself by implication. Now Venizelos felt that he had no honorable alternative to throwing in his lot with the insurgents. But the failure of the movement in the capital and on the mainland left the rebel naval units stranded. The officers fled to the Italian-held Dodecanese Islands, where Venizelos also arrived on March 13. The net result of the ill-fated coup was that it accelerated the process it was designed to check. Within eight months the republic had collapsed and the king was back in Athens.

The royalists quickly took advantage of the anti-Venizelist sentiment engendered by the revolt to purge the entire state apparatus, including the armed forces, the bureaucracy, and the judiciary. Then they hurriedly ordered an election for June 9, 1935. The republicans abstained, claiming that the continuance of martial law, press censorship, and other repressive measures made a free contest impossible. As a result, the election became a test between the moderate Tsaldares, who headed the Populist party, and the extremist General Metaxas, who headed the Royalist Union. The returns gave Tsaldares 1,074,479 votes and 287 seats, as against 147,245 votes and 7 seats for Metaxas. Tsaldares now made arrangements for a plebiscite which would give the people an opportunity to vote directly on the question of whether or not the king should return. But the royalist generals, who now controlled the army, were not at all certain of the outcome of such a plebiscite. So General Kondyles, an estranged Venizelist who had become an ultraroyalist and who had suppressed the revolt of the republican officers, by a show of force compelled Tsaldares to resign. Assuming the premiership, Kondyles summoned parliament, of which only a rump of about 100 appeared. The majority, although royalist, supported Tsaldares and refused to work with Kondyles. The latter nevertheless passed decrees through the rump parliament abolishing the republic and ordering a plebiscite for November 3, 1935. The outcome of the plebiscite was startling. The official figures showed a 97 per cent majority for the monarchy. Even Crete, which was a solid Venizelist stronghold, was reported to have voted 50,655 to 1,214 in favor of the king. Herbert Low epitomized the plebiscite in a celebrated cartoon showing a bewildered peasant entering the polling station. He is confronted by three fierce-looking men, one with fixed bayonet and two behind a machine-gun covering the booth of the "Nays." The inscription reads, "These Greeks do their polling business so much better than we do. Instead of having to vote to get something, you get something you have to vote for."

MONARCHY TO DICTATORSHIP: 1935–1936

King George II arrived in Athens on November 25, 1935. As already noted, he had previously occupied the throne for a brief period from September, 1922, to December, 1923. The following years he had spent in exile in London. Despite this experience he began his reign with a statesmanlike policy of conciliation. He announced that he wished to forget the past and to rule justly as the King of all Hellenes. He showed that he was in earnest by demanding a general amnesty for all who participated in the March, 1935 revolt. When General Kondyles demurred, the king paradoxically forced the kingmaker to resign the premiership. He appointed in his place Constantine Demerdjes, professor of civil law at the University of Athens. Demerdjes organized a nonparty government and proceeded to liquidate the Kondyles dictatorship.

He granted a full amnesty and also reinstated republican civil servants, judges, and university professors who had been deposed by the preceding governments. Demerdjes then held a general election on January 26, 1936, that was noteworthy for its fairness. One surprise of the election was the recovery of the Liberal party, which won 126 seats. Another was the strong showing of the Communists, with their 15 seats. The net result was a deadlock, the various royalist and republican parties having 143 and 142 seats, respectively. Thus the Communists found themselves holding the balance of power. The election of the Communists marked the advent of a new force on the Greek political scene, a force that was to play an important role henceforth, and especially during the occupation years of World War II.

The Communist party of Greece had been organized in 1918 but had remained a negligible factor in Greek politics until the 1930's. The landowning peasantry found little in Marxism to attract them, while the small urban working class was too close to its village origins to abandon its traditional peasant frame of mind. Also, the party was continually undermined by Comintern resolutions calling for an independent Macedonian state.* Most Greeks were naturally repelled by a party committed to a policy of mutilating the state. It was not until the advent of the depression that the party began to attract many converts. Most of the recruits were students and professional men who saw no future in the prevailing social order, but many were refugees who were crowded

* See Chapter 31.

in the urban centers and who, unable to attain the prosperity they had enjoyed in Asia Minor, turned to communism in their frustration.

After the 1936 elections, the Communists launched a campaign for a Popular Front with the republican parties. They won their greatest success when they concluded on February 19, 1936, a secret political deal with the Liberal party leader, Themistocles Sophoules, successor to Venizelos. This deal provided that the Communists should vote with the Liberals in order to elect Sophoules president of the chamber. In return the Liberals undertook to pass, within a month after forming a government, various reforms, including reduction of the price of bread, moratorium for small proprietors, amnesty for political prisoners, and dissolution of the recently formed special security police.

On March 6, Sophoules was duly elected president of the chamber with the aid of the Communist deputies. But under pressure from the king and from royalist military officers, who threatened that they could not remain indifferent to the formation of a government dependent on Communist support, Sophoules failed to authorize a Liberal government. Instead, he permitted Professor Demerdjes to form a "nonparliamentary" government on March 14, 1936. General Metaxas was included in the government as vice-president of the council and minister of war, despite the fact that his royalist group had won only seven seats in the elections.

On April 13 Professor Demerdjes died and on the same day the king appointed Metaxas premier without consulting any party leaders. The Communists urged that the Metaxas government be overthrown by passing a lack of confidence resolution. Sophoules refused on the ground that this might antagonize the royalist officers and precipitate a coup. Instead, Sophoules facilitated the passage of a resolution adjourning parliament for five months and allowing Metaxas to govern by decree, subject to a parliamentary committee of forty members. The delegation of so much power to Metaxas proved to be the death knell of Greek democracy.

Metaxas quickly arrested and deported labor leaders; dissolved the most militant trade unions and seized their funds; enacted a Compulsory Arbitration Act which declared strikes illegal; and prepared the army for the coup. The Communists retaliated by signing a pact of cooperation with a small Socialist-Agrarian party and by effecting the unification of the rival Unitary (Communist) and General (Reformist) Confederations of Labor. Numerous strikes were organized, demanding higher wages, release of political prisoners, and withdrawal of the recently enacted antilabor legislation. A general strike in Saloniki on May 9 resulted in the killing of thirty workers and the wounding of four hundred. With the unification of the rival labor confederations, orders were issued for a nation-wide general strike on August 5.

Sophoules now concluded an agreement with the royalist leader, John Theotokes (whose party held sixty seats), to form a coalition government to replace that of Metaxas. On August 3 Sophoules and Theotokes called on the king to inform him that they were ready to form a government that would have majority support. By this time the king had come under Metaxas' influence and had accepted his contention that drastic, extraparliamentary methods were needed to govern the country. It is not known why the king shifted so sharply from his earlier policy of conciliation and cooperation with the moderate elements in both camps. Perhaps he was impressed by resurgence of the Communists and the threatening events in Saloniki, and thus made susceptible to the arguments of the brilliant and forceful Metaxas. In any case, the king did not act upon the offer of Sophoules and Theotokes to form a majority cabinet. Instead, twenty-four hours later, on August 4, 1936, he signed decrees that inaugurated the Metaxas dictatorship. The decrees declared a state of emergency, dissolved parliament without setting a date for new elections, and suspended the provisions of the constitution guaranteeing personal liberties.

Metaxas followed up by proclaiming martial law, arresting about four hundred opposition leaders throughout the country, and mobilizing state employees and workers in the most important branches of industry. Street demonstrations were speedily crushed by the overwhelming force of police and military which had been marshaled beforehand. The official justification for these measures was that the impending general strike was designed to "overthrow the legal, political and social system of the country." In this manner was established the "Fourth of August Regime," as the dictatorship officially was named. Metaxas made clear the nature of his regime in the following statement:

I took the minimum of power necessary to face the Communist danger, but I am not going to relinquish it until the country is cleared of Communism and the social order made unshakable. The Greek press as well as all the Greeks will have to abide by national discipline. . . . For the time being there is no question of new elections being held. . . . Those of you who in the past have belonged to parties are now under the obligation of forgetting them utterly; there are no more parties in Greece. . . . The old parliamentary system has vanished for ever. . . .[2]

METAXAS DICTATORSHIP: 1936–1941

Metaxas faced a difficult task when he became the archigos or fuehrer of Greece. He had gained power by means of a coup rather than a popularly supported revolution. He had no mass following behind him as did Hitler in Germany. He had no historical tradition to bolster him—no roots in Greek society or civilization. So he appointed a journalist, Theologos Nikoloudes, to the post of undersecretary of press and tourism, with instructions to propound and publicize an official ideology. The outcome was a novel thesis to the effect that the history of Greece experienced three periods of national greatness and all three, maintained Nikoloudes, were under authoritarian regimes. The first was the Golden Age of the fifth century B.C., when Pericles ruled as a virtual dictator behind a democratic façade. The second was the Byzantine period, when the Greeks flourished for a thousand years under an imperial autocracy. The third period of national greatness was the dictatorship of Metaxas—the Regime of the Fourth of August.[3]

Nikoloudes did not depend upon exhortations alone. He muzzled the press with regulations forbidding the publication of information on a long list of topics that might embarrass the government. Education was also strictly controlled. On orders from Athens the following provincial order was made general for all Greece: [4]

Protocol No. 534   Yanina, February 26, 1937
TO THE PRINCIPALS OF THE 12TH EDUCATIONAL DISTRICT
Taking into consideration that controversies arising from the teaching of material, for which the students are not sufficiently mature, may create among them unfortunate misconceptions at the expense of the attainment of our educational goal, we order:
A) That during the teaching of the course on natural history, do not include the Darwinian theory or that material connected with the appearance of man on earth at the end of the Tritogene geological period. This, not because the scientific consciousness should be chained, nor because scientific deductions disprove religion, for, in the words of Bacon, "Little science combats religion and great science elevates it," but because apparent conflicts between science and faith might be understood as fundamental conflicts at the formative age of youth, and thus undermine the prestige of science or of religion, and
B) In the teaching of ancient Greek in the 6th High School grade, omit the funeral oration of Pericles, substituting this with some Platonic dialogue, because the funeral oration, truthfully grand of democratic ideas, may be misunderstood by the students as indirect criticism of the vigorous governmental policy and, in general, of the trend of the present State. We say misunderstood, because the National Government in reality is furthering democratic ideas and properly conceived liberty by striking at demagogic tendencies and sources of decay. Because, however, adolescence does not have the ability for induction and for the tiresome search for truth, and is prone to the formation of beliefs based only upon emotions, it is advisable that the brilliant pages of Thucydides be left for those years when the Greek youth, sufficiently mature, may hear from university professors an analysis of the beauty of the ancient texts. Otherwise, there exists the probability that these pages will produce the same ruinous and disintegrating results that they did during the period of the Peloponnesian War, when they were recited to the unstable populace of Athens by the great Pericles, who presented so brilliantly the victories of democracy to the intellectually unprepared Athenian rabble, that it overestimated its strength and destroyed with its anarchistic arrogance the wonderful works which democratic ideas had created in a more suitable period.

While ordering adherence to the above instructions, we beg our colleagues not to interpret them as motivated by a reactionary spirit, but rather by the desire to further the genuine interests of the students and the wider and higher interests of our country.

THE GENERAL SUPERINTENDENT OF THE 12TH DISTRICT
D. PAPOULIAS

The most ambitious attempt of Metaxas to control the Greek youth was the establishment of the National Youth Organization, or EON. This was created in 1937 and was modeled after the German and Italian youth bodies.

Its members were provided with uniforms, were given some training by army and navy officers, and were required to present the fascist stiff-arm salute. On the occasion of the first Congress of the Regional Commanders of the EON, held in January, 1939, Metaxas delivered a speech which was reported in the newspapers as follows:

> What are the aims of the organization? King! (*Tempest of applause, acclamations and manifestations of all types.*) King! Country! Religion! Family! Rebirth of Greece and the Fourth of August Regime! (*Prolonged applause and acclamations.*) This latter point, the fourth of August regime, I underline, because it is the security, the vigilant safeguard of the others. When we did not have it, when we did not have the Fourth of August Regime, you saw to what depths fell monarchy, religion, country, family, and all.

Concerning the reception accorded to the EON Metaxas stated:

> The schools, at the outset were hesitant. Only the primary schools joined with a great, a magnificent enthusiasm. The secondary schools hesitated at first to aid us. . . . The reason for this is that at the national Ministry of Education there was originally a defiance which gradually disappeared, but the tone was set. But the Youth [of the EON], little by little, without threats or violence, and only by persuasion, managed to win over and conquer the secondary schools almost entirely, teachers and pupils alike. . . . In the Universities we encountered at the outset much resistance . . . as much from the students as from a large proportion of the teaching personnel. Did you know this? Of all those who fought and who gave us our liberty in 1821, not one was an intellectual leader. I do not wish by this to belittle the value of intellectual work. But allow me to say that I consider it a secondary question in comparison with the importance of character. (*Applause.*) As for the teaching personnel, I admit that I found a certain resistance, not on the part of all, but of some. But since I assumed the portfolio of Public Instruction, I have found a greater comprehension and conviction, and even enthusiasm, so that I am certain that all will go well.[5]

An important person in the Metaxas regime, in addition to Nikoloudes, was the minister of interior, Constantine Maniadakes. As the head of the ubiquitous security forces he came to represent the most hated aspects of the dictatorship. His police were free to break into any house and search it at any time of the day or night, and to arrest any suspected citizen without a warrant. The prisoners were taken to a "security committee" which existed in every prefecture and which consisted of the prefect, the chief of the *gendarmerie*, and the attorney. This commitee could condemn prisoners to exile merely on grounds of suspicion. The prisoner had the right of appeal, but in the interval he was shipped to an exile island whence his appeal could be made—and almost invariably rejected. There were two principal types of political prisoner—working-class members of the underground who were usually Communists, and prominent members of the opposition parties. The latter, as a rule, were middle-class liberals, republicans, sometimes even royalists who were antagonized by the excesses of the dictatorship, even though it had the blessing of the king.

The dictatorship was not all regimentation and repression. Metaxas worked hard to cope with the problems of his country. There is no doubt about the vigor and sincerity of his efforts, as even his critics will concede. The controversy arises concerning the effectiveness of his efforts. In the field of labor legislation, for example, he established a minimum daily wage rate of 55 drachmas (about 50 cents at the time), and he gave all workers two weeks' annual vacation with pay, or two weeks' double pay in place of the vacation. This meant a substantial improvement for the lowest-paid unskilled laborers. Collective agreements were signed with the various labor groups, such as railwaymen, clerks, civil servants, bank employees, and factory workers. These agreements defined the length of the working day, the wages of the various categories of workers, the length of the vacation, and similar matters. A Compulsory Arbitration Act declared all strikes illegal and provided for the arbitration of all labor disputes by ministry of labor representatives. According to official statistics, 44,217 such disputes were settled during the first two years of the regime. In addition, the workers were provided with medical clinics and working mothers were assured medical care and monetary compensation at childbirth.

Critics of the dictatorship argued that most of this legislation was stillborn because of the absence of free trade unions. This made it easy for the employers to ignore or evade the law. They paid wages below minimum level to their employees and threatened to denounce them to the secret police as Communists if they made trouble. They forced their employees to sign receipts for wages higher than those actually received. They classified workers in a lower wage category than that to which they really belonged by virtue of their skills.

The opposition further charged that the public health legislation was also largely futile because the government failed to provide the funds necessary to put it into practice. The best case for the dictatorship probably can be made on the basis of its extensive public works program, including roads, government buildings, and fortifications. The program increased the debt sharply and brought on a marked inflation. But it did provide much-needed employment and it also strengthened the defenses of the country.

In conclusion there is little doubt that the dictatorship was never popular. Metaxas himself had none of the politician's gifts. He was a brilliant officer, as he demonstrated during the Balkan Wars and World War I. But when he attempted to build up a royalist party of his own he attracted very little support. He had only six followers in the chamber when he assumed power. In fact, his predisposition for authoritarian rule may stem in large degree from his disillusioning experiences with party politics as well as from his temperament and military training.

It is difficult to gauge the attitude of the inarticulate mass of peasants and urban workers toward the Metaxas regime. But there is no doubt of the deep hostility of the intellectuals, the politicians, the professional people, and the class-conscious workers led by the Communists. The question arises how Metaxas contrived to retain power until his death in 1941 despite the opposition of such important elements of Greek society. One reason was that most of the old political leaders happened to die within the space of a few months—General Kondyles on January 31, 1936; Venizelos on March 18; Demerdjes on April 13; and Tsaldares on May 16. Thus Metaxas was fortuitously rid of the outstanding politicians who might have led the opposition against him. Another reason was the lack of unity among the opposition forces. On the one hand were the Communists, who operated underground, organizing strikes and demonstrations, and who continued to favor a Popular Front as they did in the pre-Metaxas period. On the other hand were the old-line party leaders and republican military officers who did not wish to associate with the Communists and who were divided among themselves as to whether they should direct their efforts against Metaxas alone, or against both Metaxas and the king.

The final and most important reason for Metaxas' success in retaining power was the unswerving support he received from the king. The army was the source of power in Greece, and the army with its royalist officers took orders not from Metaxas but from the king. The latter was not dependent upon Metaxas as Victor Emmanuel was upon Mussolini. King George could have rid himself of Metaxas whenever he had so wished. But he did not choose to do so, apparently regarding the dictatorship as preferable to any political arrangement that might have taken its place.

In the light of later developments two features of this situation in Greece on the eve of World War II are worth noting. One is that the Communists alone operated effectively in the underground and that this experience was to enable them to organize and lead a national resistance movement during the occupation period. The other is that the king's consistent support of Metaxas later enabled the Communists to discredit the dynasty by identifying it with fascism and dictatorship.

ECONOMIC DEVELOPMENT

World War I was responsible for two developments that profoundly affected the economy of Greece—the influx of refugees and the distribution of land among the peasants. Approximately 1.5 million refugees inundated a country with a population at the time of only 5.5 million. These refugees came partly from Asia Minor as a result of the 1922 military disaster, partly from Bulgaria by virtue of the Neuilly Treaty, and partly from Russia following the 1917 revolutions. Thus Greece, exhausted by three wars, and after having given hospitality to refugees following the Cretan revolts of 1867 and 1897 and the Balkan Wars of 1912–1913, now found herself faced by the problem of supporting and settling a mass of immigrants equal to a quarter of her own population.

In these circumstances the League of Nations came to the aid of Greece. The Geneva Protocol, signed on September 29, 1923, established the Refugees' Settlement Commission consisting of two foreign members nominated by the Council of the League, and of two Greeks appointed by the Greek government. The League also sponsored two loans totaling thirteen million pounds to Greece to finance the work of settlement. The bulk of the refugees settled in rural areas, mostly in the newly acquired territories of Macedonia and Thrace. They formed small rural colonies totaling 1,954, of which 1,047 were in Macedonia, 574 in Thrace, and 333 in other districts. A considerable number of the refugees chose to start afresh in urban centers, especially in the Athens-Piraeus region, where overnight great new suburbs appeared bearing nostalgic names such as "New Smyrna" and "New Ionia." The refugees contributed substantially to the economic development of the country. They increased tremendously the cultivated area in the north, they developed flourishing market gardens near urban communities, and they introduced a number of new industries, such as carpet weaving and specialized pottery manufacturing. Generally speaking, however, the refugee influx probably aggravated Greece's chronic economic difficulties arising partly from too many people and too few resources.

The other important economic development following World War I was the distribution of land. This was hastened and extended by the deluge of destitute refugees. We saw in Chapter 25 that by the end of the nineteenth century peasant proprietorship predominated in "old" Greece. The province of Thessaly acquired in 1881 was dominated by Moslem landlords with their large estates or chifliks. By 1914 the number of chifliks had been somewhat reduced, though not by more than a third. Then with the addition of Macedonia and Epirus (1913) and Western Thrace (1919), the land problem became acute because chifliks were prominent in these former Turkish territories. It is estimated that in 1920 a total of 2,259 chifliks existed in Greece, distributed as follows: Macedonia, 818; Thessaly, 584; Epirus, 410; "old" Greece, 363; Thrace, 84.[6]

With the coming of the refugees, land distribution became essential in order to provide them with a means of livelihood. The legal basis for land reform had been provided by the national assembly, which had revised the constitution in 1911, giving the government the right to expropriate land for public purposes. The first series of land distribution acts had been passed in 1917. They authorized the government to expropriate state and church lands for division among the peasants. If these properties proved insufficient to meet local needs, the government could purchase estates above certain stipulated acreages. Under the terms of this law the government distributed 53,700 hectares of state land and 48,000 hectares of church land. Then with the coming of the refugees more legislation was passed regulating the disposition of various properties available in the new provinces. As a result, an additional 1,142,000 hectares were divided, of which 592,130 were vacated by departing Turks and Bulgars; the remainder consisted of former church, state, and private holdings. The magnitude of the reform is indicated by the fact that the lands distributed constituted 38 per cent of the total cultivated area of Greece.[7]

Despite this extensive land distribution, Greek agriculture, like that of all the Balkan countries, was in an unsatisfactory state during the interwar period. The reasons were basically the same in Greece as in the other countries. Rural overpopulation stood out in its usual prominence. The total population rose steeply from 2.6 million in 1907 to 5.5 in 1920, 6.2 in 1928, and 7.6 in 1951. This increase was due mostly to the influx of refugees. But it should be noted that the population will continue to grow rapidly in the future because of the extremely high birth rate which leaves a net annual increase ranging from 1.3 to 1.5 per cent. Since the Greek population falls in the category of so-called young populations, the ratio of productive age groups (fifteen to sixty years) to total population is constantly rising. The ratio stood at 57.4 per cent in 1940. It was estimated at 61.4 per cent in 1950, with the prospect of reaching 63.3 per cent in 1960 and 64.5 in 1970.

Increasing population with limited land resources has resulted in a very dense rural population. The number of people dependent on agriculture per unit of arable land is in Greece, as in the other Balkan countries, much higher than in the West.* Consequently much of the village population is "surplus," the percentage being estimated at between 40 and 50. This situation is especially serious because Greek agriculture has remained stagnant—the same crops, the same methods, and the same low productivity.

About 60 per cent of the population on the eve of World War II depended on agriculture for its livelihood. Most of the arable land—about 74 per cent—was used for the cultivation of grains—wheat, corn, barley, oats, and rye. Nevertheless, Greece imported an average of half her grain requirements —a major cause for her chronically unfavorable trade balance. The principal commercial crops continued to be tobacco, currants, olives, and olive products. In 1938 they accounted for 68 per cent of the value of all exports. These crops were particularly suitable for Greece because they required heavy labor investment. Whereas 25 man-days per hectare were needed for grains, 328 man-days were needed for tobacco, including local processing. Considerably greater quantities of these commodities could have been grown, but the demand was restricted and highly variable. Because of their luxury character they were the first to be eliminated in foreign markets in case of economic trouble, as Greece discovered to her cost during the depression.

The over-all productivity of Greek agriculture, like that of the other Balkan countries, is much lower than Western levels.† One reason is the natural environment—poor soils and inadequate rainfall. Another reason is the small size of the plots which excludes the introduction of more efficient capital-using methods of production. According to the 1950 census, the average size for all Greece is about 8.1 acres. This figure does not mean much because the amount of land needed to support a family varies tremendously according to the nature of the crop. The highest average is in the wheat plains of Thessaly and Macedonia, where it reaches 13 acres. The lowest is in the tobacco regions of Macedonia and Thrace, where the average family farm is 3/4 to 1 1/2 acres. In between are the olive- and currant-growing areas of Crete, the Peloponnesus, and the Ionian Islands, where the average family farm is from 2 1/2 to 5 acres. Taking into account the essential factor of the type of crop grown, it has been estimated on the basis of the 1929 census that 37.6 per cent of the Greek farmers in that year had insufficient land to support their families at a locally accepted standard of living.[8]

* † Statistics in Chapter 31.

The deleterious effects of the small size of peasants' plots are accentuated by the parcelization of individual holdings. The agricultural census of 1929 recorded 5,356,819 separate land parcels of an average size of 0.75 to 1 acre.[9] The average farm consisted of 5.6 different holdings. This dispersion of plots increased the distance between village and fields and made for waste of manpower and draft-animal power. Also, precious land was wasted because of the innumerable footpaths and markers between the various parcels.

Finally, agricultural productivity was kept down by the extremely low level of technology. Only 1,700 tractors were to be found in the entire country on the eve of World War II. This represented 218 agricultural workers per tractor, compared to 122 in Bulgaria, 8 in Denmark, 5 in Sweden, and 3 in Britain.[10] Likewise, 3.3 pounds of fertilizer were used per acre, compared to 19.4 in Italy, 27.5 in France, and 249.4 in Holland.[11] Similar backwardness was evident in irrigation, drainage, soil research, and use of seeds.

It is important to note here, as elsewhere in the Balkans, the close relationship between rural overpopulation and low productivity. The consolidation of land parcels would be a step forward from the technological viewpoint because it would save labor and make worth while the use of a certain amount of machinery. But given the prevailing overpopulation, these measures merely would further increase the percentage of "surplus" population and add to the strains on the social structure of the country.

Turning to industry, we find that it expanded substantially during the interwar period. One reason was the refugee influx, which provided a greatly enlarged market as well as abundant cheap labor. More important was the high protective tariff adopted in the mid-1920's and extended and intensified during the 1930's. As a result, the index of industrial output rose as follows: 1913, 100; 1921, 260.7; 1925, 322.1; 1929, 359.6; 1932, 342.2; 1935, 477.3; 1938, 537.1.[12] The industries continued to be concentrated in the Athens-Piraeus and Saloniki regions, which are accessible and have a relatively large market and labor reservoir. The most important prewar industries, on the basis of the number of persons employed, power used, and the value of total production, were (1) the food industry, processing domestic agricultural products (flour milling, olive oil and wine pressing, canning, confectionery and edible pastes, alcohol); (2) textiles, especially the cotton industry, which used mainly Greek cotton; and (3) the chemical industry, processing mostly local raw materials and producing fertilizers, paints and varnishes, dyestuffs, soap, resin, turpentine, and various chemicals and drugs. With the exception of a few textile, chemical, paper, cigarette, and building material factories, employing a considerable number of workers and equipped with up-to-date machinery, most of the prewar Greek factories (92 per cent of the total) were no more than small workshops, employing from one to five men and using little or no power.

The growth of industry had its negative as well as positive aspects. Greece, like the other Balkan countries, paid dearly for the increased number of factories because of the high tariff protection (20 to 150 per cent ad valorem), which meant for the consumer high prices and usually inferior quality. The most important point, however, is that Greek industry, like that in the rest of the peninsula, did not begin to absorb the annual population increase. The urban population in 1928 was 33 per cent of the total, and in 1940 it was 33.73 per cent. Thus most of the farm population increase between 1928 and 1940 was forced to remain in the already overpopulated countryside.

Greek foreign trade remained essentially the same after World War I as before. The one exception was that Greece, like the other Balkan countries, became increasingly dependent on the German market in the late 1930's. The proportion of Greek exports taken by Germany rose from below 20 per cent between 1929 and 1933, to 43 per cent in 1938. Likewise, the percentage of Greek imports from Germany rose from about 10 between 1929 and 1933 to 31 in 1938. Apart from this trend there was the traditional dependence on a few "luxury" types of export commodities. Tobacco took the place of currants as the main export, accounting in 1938 for 45.5 per cent of the value of all exports. The other principal exports in 1938 were currants, 12.4 per cent; olives and olive oil, 9.8 per cent; and wine, 2.9 per cent.[13]

In the same year, 1938, Greece imported three fourths of the raw materials used by her industry, one third of the cereals she consumed, and substantial quantities of machinery and other manufactured goods. As a result, Greece continued to suffer from the traditionally unfavorable balance of her trade. In the past the deficit had been largely covered by invisible receipts, the most important being emigrant remittances and income from shipping services. The latter remained important, but emigrant remittances fell off sharply with the depression. In 1934 they amounted to less than one quarter of what they had been in 1930.

In addition to an unfavorable balance of trade, Greece also faced the problem of a crushing debt and corresponding interest payments. As noted in Chapter 25, following the Greco-Turkish war of 1897 the great powers imposed on Greece an international control commission with extensive authority over the national economy. This continued to function during the interwar years. Nevertheless, the debt load of Greece became ever heavier, being increased by the debts incurred during World War I, by the high cost of refugee settlement, and by the sharp drop in national income during the depression. By 1929 the per capita public debt was about 100 dollars, which was somewhat more than the average per capita income in that year. By March 31, 1940, the public debt amounted to $630 million, and the claim of the foreign debt on the national income was 9.25 per cent for Greece, as against 2.98 per cent for Bulgaria, 2.32 per cent for Rumania, and 1.68 per cent for Yugoslavia.[14]

The combination of limited foreign markets, low productivity in agriculture and industry, and an extremely heavy debt load meant a continuation of the low per capita income. In fact, the income probably decreased because it is estimated that during the twelve years preceding World War II the average annual rate of income growth was about 1.2 per cent while the average annual rate of population increase was 1.3 per cent. As a result, the national income per capita in 1939 is estimated to have been $75, compared to $125 for Bulgaria, $140 for Italy, $283 for France, and $469 for the United Kingdom.[15] The plight of the poor in Greece was actually worse than these figures indicate because of the unequal tax burden. Indirect taxes during the interwar years contributed between 75 and 82 per cent of all tax proceeds. Thus a large proportion of the income of the poorer classes was taken away in the form of levies on necessities.

In conclusion, it is worth noting that although Greece's natural resources are scanty compared to those of some other countries, nevertheless they are adequate to support the existing population at a considerably higher standard of living than that prevailing during the decade before or after World War II. The political and economic crisis that developed in Greece after World War II stimulated studies of the ailing Greek economy by several foreign missions. All agreed that Greece has the natural and human resources for a much higher standard of living than has ever prevailed.

Typical is the work of the UNRRA Committee on the Development of the Productive Resources of Greece. The Subcommittee on Mineral Resources published a 250-page study on the *Mineral Wealth of Greece*. Its findings open new horizons for the economic future of the country. For example, the Supreme Financial Council in 1933 estimated the available deposits of lignite as 5 million tons certain, 27 million tons probable, and 156 million tons possible. It is known today that the basin of Ptolemaïs alone holds 1 billion tons of this fuel. The committee concluded that Greece has abundant supplies of bauxite, chromite, magnesite, and that geologic indications suggest substantial deposits of high-grade iron ore, lead, zinc, and other minerals.

The UNRRA scientists pointed out the significance of those findings:

> We believe that the arbitrary and superficial views about the poverty of the country in mineral resources are quite incorrect, and we hope that they will be discarded entirely after systematic research to discover the real natural endowment of the nation. . . . Research should be extended to all branches. . . . The hydroelectric resources, the fisheries, and even agriculture, are mostly *terra incognita*. . . . The State has never attempted to plan a systematic program for the mineral resources. Individual initiative is likewise responsible. . . . Natural resources exist for substantial industrialization. . . . The industrialization of the country on the basis of the mineral wealth and the hydroelectric resources promises to correct to a significant degree the three basic weaknesses of the pre-war economy, that is, the low national income, the chronic unemployment of labor, and the nightmare of balancing imports and exports.[16]

These are not the dreams of starry-eyed idealists. The most comprehensive study of the economic potentialities of Greece has been made by the Food and Agriculture Organization of the United Nations. Its mission to Greece found just what the UNRRA Committee found:

> Greece has resources and people capable of sustaining far higher productive levels than those so far attained. The country can very materially increase

its per caput production and national income, probably to double or triple its present level within two or three decades. This can be done by effective development and use of water potentialities for irrigation and hydroelectricity, by the education of its citizens in modern technologies, by the development and use of improved agricultural methods, and by the expansion of industry to use unemployed labor effectively.[17]

These reports suggest that Greece is not necessarily doomed to poverty and social unrest and political instability because of her dense population and comparatively meager resources. The roots of Greece's economic difficulties are to be found in the use, or misuse, of her natural resources. The following analysis by Professor Adam Pepelasis, an expert on Greek economic development, points up the retarding and distorting influence of politics upon economics in Greece:

It is not difficult to explain why Greece has not succeeded in raising the level of living of its people. A careful survey of the economic history of Greece for the period 1830–1940 reveals clearly two facts—lack of a systematic and consistent economic policy, however defined—and administrative inability to implement those few measures initiated by progressive politicians.

With reference to agriculture, there was no coherent policy until 1917 when the Ministry of Agriculture was established. During this whole period Greece was faced with two great agrarian questions. The first was that of the "national lands" formerly owned by Turks which became the property of the State. This problem was solved in the worst fashion as the lands were sold at auction to city people with no knowledge of farming. The other problem was the distribution of latifundia. Although the question came into prominence in 1882, it was not effectively answered until after World War I. With the establishment of the Ministry of Agriculture and under the strong impact of the modernizing policy of Venizelos appeared the beginnings of some consistent agricultural policy. But the consequent military and political upheavals prevented it from becoming effective or a permanent part of Greek political life. Professor Sideres wrote in 1934, "After a century of free national life our agricultural policy is again where it started." Before the war no public service attempted a survey of the agricultural resources and potentialities of Greece, a predominantly agricultural country. Such a survey was undertaken only after the last war by FAO. The fisheries were neglected for a hundred years. In the early 1920's the legislation concerning fisheries was the same as in 1830, and this in spite of the fact that fresh fish are an important source of protein in the Greek diet. The FAO Mission to Greece reported, "There is no record of any scientific research (on fisheries) having been undertaken, and it is evident from clauses of legislative enactments that existing regulations were not based on scientific findings." Similarly, there was no systematic study on the part of the public administration of the mineral wealth and the hydroelectric potentialities of the country. Whatever attempts were made were on paper or by private individuals. UNRRA surveyed these resources in 1947.

Industrial policy began with the establishment of the Ministry of National Economy in 1911 and was intensified during the interwar period. This field of economic policy has been characterized by bureaucratic rigidity and short-sightedness. In the 1920's and 1930's protectionism was the general theme of Greek industrial policy. As a result, all sorts of industries came into existence under protectionist measures taken offhand, with no consideration as to the advisability of the establishments or to the future world economic situation.

It is not an exaggeration to say that by trade policy Greek officials always understood a mess of detailed regulations concerning imports and exports rather than the laying down of general principles in promoting exports, regulating imports to the best advantage of the domestic economy and coordinating foreign trade policies with other domestic policies.

The inadequacy of the Greek administrative service is also revealed in the field of taxation. The taxation system is unequal, emphasizes indirect taxes, and is very complex in its structure. Thus, for example, as reported by the FAO Mission, twelve different taxes were collected on cotton at various stages in the manufacture and shipment of cotton between Thessaly and the factory at Volos (a distance of about twenty-five miles).

Generally, Greek economic policy and social legislation have been whimsical, fickle, self-contradictory, and unplanned.[18]

SOCIAL AND CULTURAL DEVELOPMENT

Low national income meant low living standards. Food consumption in Greece on the eve of World War II is estimated to have been between 2,300 and 2,500 calories daily per capita. This placed Greece at the bottom of the scale for Europe together with Albania and Portugal. Not only was the quantity of food extremely low; the quality was very poor. Only one fifth of the protein came from animal sources as compared with one third to one half in Western Europe. Consumption of dairy products and meat was low even for the Balkans. The following figures on food consumption in Greece and the United States in 1948 are relevant, at least for purposes of general comparison, for the prewar period.

Annual Consumption (Pounds per Capita per Year) in Major Food Categories in Greece and the United States, 1948

Food Group	Greece	United States
Cereals	348	172
Potatoes	68	108
Sugar, honey, etc.	20	103
Pulses and nuts	33	15
Vegetables and fruits	265	447
Meat, fish and eggs	51	222
Dairy products	77	420
Oils and fats	33	45
Total	895	1,532

Source: L. G. Allbaugh, *Crete: A Case Study of an Underdeveloped Area* (Princeton, N. J.: Princeton University Press, 1953), p. 131.

Health conditions inevitably reflected the low income and poor nutrition. Infant mortality rates in Greece, as in the other Balkan countries, were more than double those in Western Europe. Malaria was one of the most terrible scourges, the incidence in the interwar years being approximately 30 per cent of the population. In certain years the quantity of quinine imported into Greece was reported as amounting to 5 per cent of the world's production. Malariologists estimated that about 30 million man-days per year were lost because of this disease. Thus malaria represented a serious drain upon both the health and the wealth of the Greek people.[19] Great progress has been made against the scourge by the Near East Foundation, the Rockefeller Foundation, and UNRRA. Mass DDT-spraying throughout the country after World War II reduced the disease to insignificant proportions—a truly epoch-making accomplishment for malaria-ridden Greece.

No such success has attended the campaign against tuberculosis, the prime killer in Greece. Some 25,000 died of it each year, establishing a death rate almost ten times as high as that in the United States. This figure is revealing because tuberculosis, probably more than any other ailment, is a gauge of a country's housing and nutrition. Other common diseases are amoebic dysentery, typhoid, and trachoma. The over-all death rate in the interwar years averaged about 15 per 1,000. If we compare this with the American rate of 10.6 in 1938 we see that Greece had a mortality rate more than 40 per cent higher.

In the field of education Greece in modern times has had one of the highest rates of illiteracy in Europe. The 1928 census showed 40.9 per cent of the population over eight years of age as illiterate. For women and girls the record was far worse: 58 per cent could not read or write as compared with 23.5 per cent of the males. After 1928 illiteracy decreased rapidly, falling by 1940 to an estimated 27 per cent. The figure undoubtedly rose during the chaotic years of World War II and immediately thereafter. In Greece, as in other underdeveloped countries, there was a large discrepancy between the number who started acquiring an education and those who proceeded far with it. In 1936–1937, for example, 967,588 children attended the elementary schools, 90,709 the secondary schools, and 10,561 the universities.

Education in Greece has been poor in quality as well as inadequate in quantity. The chief defect has been the inordinate emphasis on the classical period and classical subjects. This can be explained partly as the natural reaction of a small, poor country with a past of towering greatness. Another factor is the extremely centralized character of the educational system. The organization of the schools, the curriculum, the courses, and their content are prescribed by the Higher Educational Council in Athens, which works with the minister of education and his staff. The eighteen members of the council are usually eminent classical scholars and their interests are naturally reflected in the educational system they devise for the elementary and secondary schools. The study of the classical period consists too frequently of sterile note learning of historical facts and of ancient grammar, etymology, and syntax. Insufficient effort is made to understand the philosophical, ethical, and social systems of the ancients as products of the times, or to analyze what the significance of those systems might be for present-day society. Such a curriculum, needless to say, has little relevance to the life and problems of the graduating students.

A similar disparity between educational practice and social needs exists in higher education. Of the university graduates of 1938, 45 per cent became lawyers and 33 per cent doctors; most of the remainder trained in science and the humanities. A realistic catalogue of the trained men that the country needed would have shown very different percentages. But this at once raises fundamental questions of social and economic organization. Greece certainly needed more doctors, especially in the rural areas. Greek doctors, like those of other Balkan countries, tended to congregate in a few large cities. They did so for economic as well as for obvious social and cultural reasons. The impoverished peasantry simply lacked the financial resources to support doctors in their respective localities. The same holds true in the fields of agronomy and other sciences. The schools of Theology and Philosophy of the University of Saloniki had two and a half times as many students as the Agriculture and Forestry School, while the School of Law had eleven times as many students as the Veterinary Department. Certainly the proportions should have been different, given the objective needs of the country. But if two or three or four times as many agronomists and veterinarians had been trained there arises the question of how they could have found employment within the framework of the prevailing agricultural system. The government's department of agriculture offered almost the only opportunity for employment, and its meager budget could afford few agronomists and veterinarians. Thus in Greece, as in the rest of the Balkans, the country needed more scientists than it trained, but actually it could not utilize the few that it possessed. This explains why a number of the most distinguished Greek agronomists and other scientists accepted positions in the United States during the interwar years. There is no doubt that Greek students have shunned vocational education and scientific careers because of the traditional prejudice against manual work and preference for a white-collar job. On the other hand, it is also true that, given the existing structure of Greek society, the government is the main source of jobs, and a lawyer's education is the most acceptable qualification for such jobs. Since no business representatives scour Greek universities, as they do the American for trained scientists, the students understandably study law in the hope of filling some miserably paid government position.

Another problem arising from the classics-oriented system of education is that of language. Greece has been cursed in modern times by the unresolved issue of whether to use the vernacular or a rather artificial literary language that is close to classical Greek. The issue has persisted because for various reasons, discussed in Chapter 7, classical Greek has not followed the same course as classical Latin. Whereas Latin gave way to several Romance languages, ancient Greek has survived, or rather has been revived, in a corrupted form known as the katharevousa, or purist language. But during the centuries of Turkish rule, a demotike, or vernacular language, developed with simplified grammatical constructions and with a limited number of Slavic, Albanian, Turkish, and Italian words. The vernacular differs as much from the purist language as modern English does from that of the time of Chaucer. This has created serious problems because the average citizen who has attended school only a few years or not at all simply cannot understand a speech or read a book couched in the purist. Nevertheless, the purist was established by government decision in 1849 as the official language. Henceforth it was used in the administration, the schools, and the newspapers. The Higher Educational Council, consisting largely of classical scholars, naturally has supported the purist. The church also has backed it, and that institution has been an extremely important factor in education because the ministry of education and religion are one and the same. In its own ministrations the church continues to use, untranslated, a fourth-century liturgy and a first-century scripture.

In the last two decades of the nineteenth century a group of outstanding poets and authors began to champion the vernacular as the people's living language in contrast to the artificial and sterile purist. Thereafter most of the outstanding literary figures took this position. As a result, the language question became a lively political issue in which the liberal-minded generally favored the vernacular and the traditionalists the purist. It is easy in retrospect to mock the traditionalists as impractical archaizers who have been out of touch with reality. Yet their effort to "purify" the language is understandable if not fitting. After Greece won her independence it seemed intolerable to many patriots that they should be constantly reminded, through the presence of foreign words in their vocabulary, of the black days of national servitude. So they set out to eradicate linguistic traces of foreign domination and to create a renascent language that would serve as the symbol of a renascent nation. In addition to this nationalist factor there was also a very practical consideration behind the purist drive. The centuries of domination by different foreign rulers had promoted linguistic differentiation to the point where the various dialects had become almost incomprehensible to all except their respective users. Furthermore, when the country was liberated it was discovered that among the babel of dialects no single one was sufficiently prominent to afford a basis for a national language. Thus the educated class, with its classicist tradition and preference, naturally decided that it was necessary to manufacture a national language on the basis of classical and ecclesiastical Greek.

After more than a century of rivalry the purist and vernacular languages have reached a fairly clear division of fields. The purist is used in all government work, in business correspondence, nonfictional books and treatises, law courts, and formal conversation. The vernacular is the language of conversation, of trade, of popular periodicals and song, and most literary works. In the schools the two are mixed in the lower grades, making it difficult for the pupils to understand either. The higher one progresses in the educational system the more the purist predominates. In conclusion, it is apparent that the combination of factors responsible for the understandable yet misguided effort to revive an ancient language has resulted in much wasted effort in the schools, in an onerous ambivalence in literature, and in a serious discord between the language of the people and that of their government.

35. Rumania: 1918–1939

A<small>T THE END</small> of World War I Rumania appeared to be on the threshold of a dazzling future. New provinces had been acquired which more than doubled the population and area of the country. These provinces possessed industries and natural resources that raised Rumania's economic status tremendously. Also, a thorough land reform program was effected in the immediate postwar years, giving rise to hopes for a prosperous peasantry and social stability.

These rosy prospects failed to materialize. Indeed, the history of Rumania in the interwar years was in certain respects more dismal than that of the other Balkan countries. Only Rumania nurtured a genuine mass fascist movement with all the paraphernalia of virulent anti-Semitism and demagogic trappings. Also, Rumania was the only Balkan country that was mutilated at the beginning of World War II without any resistance from within or assistance from without.

Various factors explain this melancholy outcome. In the field of economics Rumania experienced the same impasse as the other Balkan countries —low agricultural productivity, rural overpopulation, and a weak industry incapable of absorbing the surplus population and raising the national income. In politics there was the usual gulf between the rulers and the ruled, but it was complicated by King Carol's ambitions and machinations, which ended in outright dictatorship. Finally, in international affairs Rumania was in a peculiarly hazardous position. She had been able to realize all her territorial aspirations at the end of World War I because of the power vacuum that existed at that moment in Eastern Europe. But the vacuum was filled in during the 1930's by the revival of Germany and the Soviet Union. As a result, Rumania was subject to overwhelming pressures which culminated in the partitioning of the country and in its domination first by Germany and then by the Soviet Union.

TERRITORIAL GROWTH OF RUMANIA

⋯⋯⋯	Rumanian frontier: 1861	———	Rumanian frontier: 1947

Bessarabia

Southern Bessarabia

Bukovina

Northern Transylvania

Transylvania

Northern Dobruja

Southern Dobruja

1861 Formation of Principality of Rumania
1878 Northern Dobruja ceded by Turkey;
    Southern Bessarabia ceded to Russia
1913 Southern Dobruja ceded by Bulgaria
1919 Transylvania and part of Banat of Temesvar
    ceded by Hungary; Bukovina ceded by
    Austria; Bessarabia ceded by Russia

1940 Bessarabia and northern Bukovina ceded
    to Russia; southern Dobruja ceded
    to Bulgaria; Northern Transylvania
    ceded to Hungary
1947 Northern Transylvania
    regained from Hungary

LAND REFORM: 1918–1921

A drastic land reform program was effected in Rumania in the immediate postwar years. Although there was much controversy concerning the amount of land to be distributed, it was universally agreed that some reform was inevitable because of the revolutionary situation that prevailed at the time. Rumanian troops on the Moldavian front were in close contact with Russian soldiers who were organizing soviets under Bolshevik influence. At the same time the government had suffered disastrous military defeat and the country had been occupied by the Central Powers. Under these circumstances the old order in Rumania had been discredited as well as shattered. "This is the state of mind in the country," declared a Rumanian professor on May 27, 1917, "disbelief in the government, disbelief in Parliament, disbelief in the constituted authority. . . . Today as yesterday revolution appears to the Rumanian peasant the only possible means for him to resolve the great case between him and the proprietors of estates." [1]

King Ferdinand met the crisis by visiting the front in April, 1917, and making the following declaration to the troops:

> Sons of peasants, who, with your own hands, have defended the soil on which you were born, on which your lives have been passed, I, your King, tell you that besides the great recompense of victory which will assure for every one of you the nation's gratitude, you have earned the right of being masters, in a larger measure, of that soil upon which you fought.
> Land will be given you. I, your King, am the first to set the example; and you will also take a large part in public affairs. [2]

After the armistice had been signed Ferdinand issued a new proclamation on November 12, 1918, reaffirming his pledge of 1917. The following month, on December 15, he signed a decree defining the terms of land reform in the Old Kingdom. All arable crown, foreign, and absentee properties were to be completely expropriated. Another 2 million hectares were to be expropriated on a sliding scale from private properties of over 100 hectares. Expropriation was to be based on properties rather than on proprietorship, to the advantage of the landowner with multiple holdings. Compensation was to be based on a number of factors but was not to exceed twenty times the regional rental rate. Payments to proprietors were to be made by 5 per cent state bonds redeemable in fifty years, the state contributing up to 35 per cent of the cost.

These terms were modified by a later reform law passed on July 17, 1921. The political background of the new law was as follows. The Liberal leader, Ion Bratianu, who had succeeded the Germanophil Premier Alexander Marghiloman in November, 1918, found it necessary to resign on September 27, 1919, as a protest against the terms of the Paris Peace Conference. A transition government held elections on November 8, 1919, which were conducted fairly and which, as a result, produced surprising returns. The Liberals lost almost all of their seats to two new parties—the National party of Transylvania headed by Alexander Vaida-Voevod and the recently formed Peasant party of the Old Kingdom headed by Ion Mihalache. These two parties formed a coalition government and introduced a new and more radical land reform bill. The old parties and the king opposed the measure vehemently. Ferdinand finally dismissed the government despite the fact that it held a substantial parliamentary majority. The war hero, General Alexander Averescu, was selected to be the new premier. He immediately held new elections and won a majority for his People's party, thanks to the usual control techniques as well as to his own great personal popularity. Averescu then passed the new reform law of July 17, 1921, mentioned above. It was a more carefully drafted law than that of 1918, and it introduced several changes, such as basing expropriation on proprietors rather than on properties. The net result of these two land measures was that a total of 2.8 million hectares changed hands in the Old Kingdom.

Land reform was also effected in each of the newly acquired provinces through individual laws that took into account local geographical factors, previous agrarian conditions, and political circumstances. These laws were on the whole more radical than that pertaining to the Old Kingdom. One reason was the more revolutionary atmosphere in the provinces. In fact, both Transylvania and Bessarabia had voted for union with Rumania on the explicit condition of thorough land reform. Also, the fact that most of the landowners were foreigners further encouraged radical land distribution.

The total amount of land expropriated throughout Rumania amounted to about 6,000,000 hectares, of which about 3,900,000 hectares were distributed to some 1,393,000 peasants. The remaining 2,100,000 hectares were used for communal grazing lands and woodlands as well as for the creation of a land reserve from which public needs such as the building of roads, model farms, and town extensions could be satisfied. The most important immediate effect of this land distribution was that it stopped the wave of revolutionary Bolshevism at the Dniester River. The peasants now had land and no longer were interested in challenging the *status quo.*

The Peasant leader, Mihalache, acknowledged this effect of the reforms when he declared: "The ruling class has made only such concessions as were necessary to assure its own existence. The reforms have been a kind of safety valve." [3] They did indeed serve effectively as a safety valve. Even in the later years communism never won the following in Rumania that it did in the other Balkan countries. The reason was not only the land distribution but also the traditional antipathy of the Rumanians for everything Russian. The Rumanian Communist party labored under the additional disadvantage of being obliged to support the Comintern line calling for the detachment of Transylvania, Bessarabia, the Dobruja, and Bukovina on the grounds of national self-determination. Thus communism and treason came to be regarded in Rumania as completely synonymous. The party was still further weakened in public esteem by the fact that many of its leaders belonged to the minority groups—Hungarians, Bulgarians, and Jews. Finally, the Communist party was fiercely repressed from the beginning and was outlawed in 1924. The net result was that communism never had the popular support and the tight organization in Rumania that it did to the south of the Danube.

Land reform proved successful politically but not economically. It failed to solve the basic and long-standing problems of Rumanian agriculture. It is true that the reform laws were politically motivated and therefore were not formulated with these economic problems in mind. Yet their failure in the economic field was to have far-reaching consequences on all aspects of Rumania's development during the interwar period.

LIBERAL RULE: 1922–1928

Rumania's political institutions were patterned after those of the West. The constitution adopted in 1866 was a modified translation of the Belgian constitution, while the two prewar parties bore the time-honored labels of Conservative and Liberal. But in actuality there was little relationship between the theory and practice of Rumanian politics. Elections were held periodically but in almost all cases signified very little. It is not unfair to say that in both the prewar and postwar periods the country was ruled by a few for their own benefit. This was true to a greater or lesser degree of all the Balkan countries. But the gap between form and content, between the oligarchy and the mass, was perhaps greatest in Rumania.

Politics, which retained a distinctly Phanariot flavor, was the art of taking advantage of the amorphous character of the peasantry. Rumanian elections were notorious for their corruption, ballot stuffing, and general unreliability as measures of public sentiment. Perhaps only two elections in the entire [interwar] period were at all free and fair, and both produced a marked upset in political life. In most cases elections were "made" in advance. Many governments were in power through no popular mandate whatsoever but merely through political arrangements; dismissals were equally arbitrary and only occasionally resulted from the loss of popular confidence. It would be futile and misleading to attempt to explain the course of Rumanian politics by an analysis of the elections.[4]

The outstanding change in the political pattern in the years immediately following World War I were the disappearance of the Conservative party and the rise of the National Peasant party. The Conservative party, which was based primarily on landowning interests, suffered because of its Germanophil position during the war and because of the breakup of the estates following the war. As a result, the first phase of postwar politics, from 1922 to 1928, was dominated by the Liberals. This was followed by a brief interlude of Peasant rule from 1928 to 1930. The third period, 1930 to 1938, was marked by the disintegration of all the parties and the triumph of King Carol. The fourth and final period was that of royal dictatorship culminating in Carol's ignominious flight in 1940.

The Liberals dominated Rumanian politics until 1928 because they had supported the victorious Allies during the war and because they enjoyed the confidence and support of King Ferdinand. They received an unpleasant shock from the 1919 elections, but Ferdinand saved the situation by dismissing the Vaida-Mihalache government and installing General Averescu as premier. The Liberals did not object to this appointment because the popular general served as a useful lightning conductor. They gladly allowed him to handle the explosive land reform problem and to crush a general strike that developed in October, 1920. Then, after the storm and strife had passed, the Liberals withdrew their support from the general and forced him to resign.

On January 19, 1922, they assumed office under Ion Bratianu, son of the prewar Liberal leader.

The Liberals remained in office until November, 1928, with the exception of one interlude from March, 1926, to June, 1927, when General Averescu was premier for a second time. But again he was dependent upon the Liberals for a majority and again the Liberals ousted him after he had served their purpose. Their long tenure in office did not mean that they enjoyed general support in the country. In fact, it is extremely doubtful that they did so, for they had few followers in the new provinces and they had to contend with the strong opposition of the Peasant party in the Old Kingdom. The Liberals were able to hold power as long as they did because the king backed them, because the opposition was divided, and because they resorted to crude electoral manipulations and to repressive police measures, usually in conjunction with staged Communist scares.

The most noteworthy policies pursued by the Liberals were industrialization and administrative centralization. The techniques and results of industrialization will be considered later in this chapter. Centralization was effected in a manner reminiscent of Premier Pashich in Yugoslavia. The Liberals held elections in March, 1922, and won by a landslide, gaining 260 seats as against 17 in the 1920 elections. The fact that the Liberals conducted the elections was not unrelated to their phenomenal turn of fortune. Indeed, the opposition parties challenged the validity of the election and withdrew from parliament. Bratianu seized the opportunity to pass hurriedly a new constitution in March, 1923. The key article was the first one, which stated, "The Kingdom of Rumania is a unitary and indivisible state." This made clear the basically centralist character of the constitution. As in the case of Yugoslavia, the newly acquired provinces protested violently and demanded autonomy.

The strongest opposition came from Transylvania. The inhabitants of that province resented the efforts of Bucharest banks to gain control of their industries. They were equally hostile to the hordes of officials sent from the Old Kingdom to govern them. With justification the Transylvanians compared these officials unfavorably, in terms of honesty and efficiency, with the Hapsburg bureaucrats of the prewar years. The struggle against the centralist constitution stimulated the organization of the National Peasant party in 1926, which was a fusion of the National party of Transylvania and the Peasant party of the Old Kingdom. The Transylvanian leader, Dr. Iuliu Maniu, soon became the head of the new party.

So long as Ferdinand was alive the National Peasants had no hope of coming to power. But Ferdinand's death in July, 1927, was followed in November of the same year by that of Ion Bratianu. Ferdinand's son, Prince Carol, had renounced his right to the crown some two years earlier because of a liaison with Mme Lupescu disapproved by the court and government. Consequently, a regency was now appointed to rule during the minority of Carol's young son, King Michael. These changes at the top encouraged hopes that a new government at last would be tolerated. The National Peasant party increased its pressure, sending thousands of peasants on a demonstrative "march on Bucharest." Reluctantly the regency finally yielded, entrusting Maniu with the formation of a government and the holding of elections. The latter were held on December 12, 1928, and are generally considered to have been the freest of the whole interwar period. The National Peasants won an overwhelming victory, gaining 333 seats as against 13 for the Liberals. It was hoped that this represented the beginning of a new era.

PEASANT RULE: 1928–1930

The Maniu government failed dismally to meet the expectations of its supporters. Its failure was one of the most depressing features of Rumania's history between the wars. It also proved to be a fateful turning point in the country's political course. The advent of the Peasant government in November, 1928, represented the culmination of a political struggle that had begun at the end of World War I. Accordingly the government took office on a wave of national enthusiasm and optimism. Its failure to relieve the agrarian problem and to maintain its political power produced widespread disillusionment. When the government resigned in October, 1930, Rumania began the long descent culminating in the disasters of 1940 and 1941. Thus the failure of the Maniu government ended the possibility of a peasant democracy.

Maniu did try to help the peasants with several measures. The Liberals had imposed very heavy export duties on cereals in order to finance their industrialization program. Maniu now repealed these duties, which the peasants had resented keenly as a discriminatory tax burden. Maniu also attempted to raise agricultural prices, to encourage cooperatives, and to introduce more rational agricultural methods. Another measure was a law passed in 1929 abolishing the restrictions on the right of peasants to sell plots that they had received through the land reforms. The reasoning was that free sale of land would lead to concentration of holdings and thus create a solid peasant middle class. A number of peasants did accumulate medium-sized holdings, but a much larger number sank down and became a rural proletariat of landless or dwarf peasants. In fact, a fatal weakness of the government's agrarian program was that it benefited only the minority of well-to-do and wealthy peasants. It did nothing for the rural proletariat, which comprised 75 per cent of the peasantry in 1930 and certainly a higher percentage a decade later. Also, the world depression ruined the government's efforts by undermining the drive to raise agricultural prices and by making it difficult to finance projects for rural education and aid to cooperatives.

Much more important than its agrarian program was the National Peasant government's decision to throw the country open to foreign capital. The Liberals had followed a nationalistic economic policy, seeking to develop Rumania's resources with Rumanian capital. For this reason they had raised high protective tariffs and imposed heavy export duties. To the peasants this meant high prices for the manufactured goods they bought and low prices for the agricultural produce they sold. In effect they were being forced to pay the cost of industrialization. Accordingly, Maniu now adjusted the tariff structure to protect only those industries that showed some promise of growth. Also, he eased the restrictions on the investment of foreign capital, with the result that large sums were invested during his brief tenure in office. These investments eased the economic situation, even if only for a short time and at the cost of creating new problems. But politically the influx of foreign capital proved an embarrassment for Maniu because a number of his lieutenants were involved in shady deals with Western businessmen.

Another major economic measure was the negotiation of a loan of 72 million dollars for currency stabilization and railway construction. The loan was floated in Washington, London, and Paris in February, 1929. Again the government was doomed to disappointment because the onslaught of the depression before the end of the year blasted the hopes for prosperity and stability. In fact, the government was dogged steadily by ill fortune in the economic field. The 1927 and 1928 crops failed badly. The 1929 crop was excellent but the market was already shrinking. In the following years exports dropped catastrophically in both quantity and value. And the government could do nothing in the face of the world-wide crash.

At this critical juncture, when the National Peasants were experiencing a perceptible decline in popularity, Carol dramatically returned to Rumania on June 6, 1930, and reclaimed his throne. Maniu had sanctioned his return for a variety of reasons. One was the desire to avoid the disadvantages inherent in the regency, which still had many years to go before Michael reached his majority. Another was Carol's obvious popularity in Rumania, which the National Peasants hoped to exploit to their own advantage. Perhaps they also expected that Carol would express his gratitude by favoring them in the coming years just as Ferdinand had backed the Liberals in the 1920's. But Carol, instead, showed his gratitude by turning upon his benefactors and forcing them out of power.

As mentioned above, Carol had become attached to an adventuress, named Magda Wolff Lupescu. He had promised Maniu that he would sever this connection, but no sooner had he regained the throne than he brought her to Bucharest. Maniu resigned in protest in October, 1930. This proved to be his second fatal error. The first was his decision to allow Carol to return. And now he chose to force a showdown with Carol over an issue that was insignificant and unpopular. "Bourgeois sexual morality," it has been pointed out, "is probably less esteemed in Rumania than anywhere else on the Continent. It was not the right issue on which to base the whole conflict between Democracy and Dictatorship." [5]

Maniu's resignation marked the end of Rumania's brief experiment with true constitutional government. There arises the question why the experiment ended so feebly and anticlimactically. The most important single factor probably was the shattering impact of the world depression. The National Peasants had lowered the tariffs in order to stimulate international trade but instead the depression dried up the channels of world commerce. Exports dropped in volume and even more in value. The national income fell off correspondingly and the government in office was inevitably held responsible. If it is recalled that the world crash wreaked political havoc in democracies of long standing, it becomes understandable that the new Peasant government in Rumania should have gone under.

Another factor explaining the fate of the Maniu government was the peculiar origin and nature of the National Peasant party itself. We have seen that it was a fusion of the National party of Transylvania and the Peasant party of the Old Kingdom. The latter represented a radical agrarian movement, at least in its earlier phase. But the National party had arisen in the prewar years as a defender of the Rumanian peasants against the Magyar overlords and thus was inclined to be more national than peasant in its outlook. The Peasant party had denounced the Liberals as the spokesmen of the ruling classes and financial interests, whereas the National party had opposed the Liberals primarily because they were the advocates of administrative centralism. In other words, the Peasant party was essentially a horizontal organization while the National was vertical. The fusion of two such disparate bodies inevitably produced ambiguity and vacillation.

The downfall of the National Peasant government was due also to certain failings in Maniu's leadership. Maniu was a man of conviction and utter incorruptibility. His strength of character stood out in the laxness and opportunism of Rumanian public life and gave him an influence which is otherwise difficult to explain. On the other hand, there was a strong negative and passive streak in Maniu's character that prevented him from giving adequate leadership. Certainly he was no match for the forceful and opportunistic monarch that he allowed to return to Bucharest. Maniu's tendency to withdraw on occasions when positive action was needed is illustrated in the following speech he delivered in February, 1932:

> Today the nation is deprived of its constitutional rights; we are on the threshold of bankruptcy, both economic and moral; we see anarchy enthroned in men's souls and hatred fomented in the provinces, and in the murmur of this growing dissolution one hardly hears the voice of national conscience, one and undivided. . . . In such solemn moments you ask for my guidance. I shall offer you none. You have both intelligence and conscience. I pray you to revere the memory of the sufferings which brought about the consummation of the national unity.[6]

CAROL'S TRIUMPH: 1930–1938

The following analysis of Carol's character helps to explain why the National Peasants were eclipsed and why Rumanian politics during the 1930's were so turbulent and unhealthy.

Superficially brilliant and basically ignorant, gifted with enormous energy and unlimited lust for power, a lover of demagogy, melodrama and bombastic speeches, he was determined to be a Great Man, the Saviour and Regenerator of his country. His impressionistic mind was filled with admiration of Mussolini, then still the most picturesque figure on the European political stage, and he set himself to imitate him. In his untiring work, which lasted for ten years, he combined a little of the terrorist methods of the Duce with much of the well-tried Balkan procedure of corruption and intrigue. . . . For a decade the history of Roumania consisted of this man's flamboyant gestures and cunning manoeuvres, set against a drab background of peasant misery and police oppression.[7]

Carol's shrewdness and will-to-power are seen in the fact that he started as a barely tolerated monarch and ended as the undisputed master of his country. He climbed to power by fomenting dissension within the political parties and breaking them one by one. He won over the more ambitious politicians with favors and flattery and set them against the old leaders. His first success was with his former tutor, Professor Nicholas Iorga, a historian of international reputation who was also prominent in the National Peasant party. By playing upon his immense vanity Carol persuaded Iorga to break with his party and to form a government on April 18, 1931. By June 6 of the following year Iorga had outlived his usefulness and was forced to resign.

Carol replaced Iorga with Vaida, another Peasant leader whom he had successfully embroiled with Maniu. Vaida held elections on July 17, 1932, and won 45 per cent of the votes compared with the 80 per cent the party won in 1928. Nevertheless, he received a majority of the seats in accordance with the provisions of the electoral law. But a Peasant majority by this time had little significance because the party was hopelessly divided. Carol had won over a number of promising young Peasant leaders and irrevocably estranged them from Maniu.

Carol conducted his intrigues against the Liberals as well as the National Peasants. Ion Bratianu, who had died in 1927, was succeeded as head of the party by his brother Constantin. The latter was hostile to the king and consequently received the same treatment as Maniu. Carol enticed a number of Liberal politicians to his camp, including George Tatarescu, whom he allowed to form a government. Tatarescu held elections on December 20, 1933, and won the majority customarily obtained by the party in power. He remained in office for four years but this did not mean that this was a period of Liberal dominance comparable with that of the 1920's. There was a growing cleavage between Tatarescu, the head of the government, and Constantin Bratianu, the head of the party. Furthermore, Carol by this time held the leading strings of political power regardless of who filled the position of premier.

During the four years of Liberal rule the fascist Iron Guard gained ground rapidly. This was a novel development in the Balkan Peninsula, where no other fascist movement has ever won a genuine mass following. The Iron Guard's success was due partly to a strong ethnic nationalism arising from the old feeling of isolation in a surrounding sea of Slavs. This was aggravated by the traditional fear of the neighboring and ever-threatening Russian colossus. Also, anti-Semitism, which has been endemic in Rumania since the winning of independence, provided a congenial atmosphere for a native fascist movement. The depression had the same effect, causing many Rumanians to turn in despair from the old parties to the crusading Iron Guardists. Finally, Carol contributed a good deal to the rise of the Iron Guard by providing it indirectly with funds, presumably with the aim of using the organization to further his own designs.

The founder and leader of the Iron Guards was Corneliu Codreanu, a tall, handsome, and impressive young man with powerful and compelling features. As a student Codreanu gained nation-wide notoriety by shooting the police chief of Jassy for trying to stop his anti-Semitic activities. In 1927 he organized the League of the Archangel Michael, which in 1930 he renamed the Iron Guard. His efforts were not taken seriously until Carol began to subsidize him and until the depression provided a favorable environment for proselytism. By the 1930's many Rumanians had become disillusioned by both the Liberals and the Peasants and were ready to try something new. Codreanu now came forth with promises of ending the misrule of professional politicians, wiping out administrative corruption, eliminating the unpopular Jewish middlemen, and distributing land to all the peasants. Many Rumanian voters, impressed by the contrast between the old politicians on the one hand and the crusading young Iron Guardists on the other, accepted these promises at face value. In this manner an extremist student organization grew to the proportions of a fascist mass movement.

The change in the political climate was revealed with the elections of December 21, 1937. The Tatarescu government received only 36 per cent of the votes, falling below the 40 per cent required to obtain the majority of seats. The National Peasants polled 21 per cent of the votes (compared to 45 per cent in 1932), the Iron Guards 16 per cent (1.2 per cent in 1932), and another fascist party, the National Christians led by Octavian Goga and Alexander Cuza, received 9 per cent of the votes. If account is taken of the great advantage enjoyed by the party in office, the elections clearly reflected a growing lack of confidence in the Tatarescu government. The alternative was to call again upon the Peasants, but Carol refused to do this because of his dislike for Maniu. Instead, he turned to Goga as the least dangerous of the fascist leaders.

Goga proceeded to act upon his anti-Semitic principles in flamboyant fashion. Jews all over the country were hounded and beaten and driven out of business. Economic life was disrupted to such a degree that the British and French ministers protested. Carol intervened on February 10, 1938, ending the farce by dismissing Goga. Then he announced that parliamentary rule had proved impossible and that he was compelled in the interests of the country to establish a dictatorship. Thus, after eight years of patient endeavor,

Carol rid himself of the political parties and became the undisputed master of the country.

ROYAL DICTATORSHIP: 1938–1940

Carol acted quickly to establish his personal regime after he dismissed Goga. He abolished the 1923 constitution and promulgated in its place a corporatist constitution on February 20, 1938. The new document greatly increased his prerogatives and allowed no role for the political parties. Carol then turned against the Iron Guard, which had served as a useful weapon against the parties but which now was no longer needed. In fact, it was a potential threat to the royal dictatorship. So Carol ruthlessly and violently attacked it, outlawing it, and imprisoning Codreanu in April, 1938. In November of the same year Codreanu and thirteen of his followers were shot "while attempting to escape." Carol now was supreme. In December, 1938, he launched his own organization, the Front of National Rebirth, to take the place of the disbanded parties.

Carol was by no means the international playboy he is frequently depicted. He considered himself to be "the first peasant, the first laborer and the first public servant" of his realm. He worked furiously to fulfill the duties of his self-imposed roles. But there was no meaning or direction to his efforts. Now that he finally had supreme power he was at a loss what to do with it. He made speeches exhorting his subjects to work together in a disinterested spirit for the welfare of the country. But no one took him or his speeches seriously. He was surrounded by incapable and unprincipled politicians who operated in the traditional manner behind the façade of the royal dictatorship.

Despite the hollowness of his regime, Carol was secure because the parties were gone and he could rely on the army and the police. But he had nothing solid with which to resist an attack from the outside. The tragedy of his dictatorship is that it left Rumania with no leadership worthy of the name. Carol had no trustworthy advisers at a time when the international situation was becoming increasingly dangerous. As for the masses, they had become thoroughly disillusioned and apathetic after witnessing the fate of the Liberals, the National Peasants, and finally the Iron Guardists. Thus Rumania, like Yugoslavia, lacked spirit and cohesiveness when the national crisis came in 1940. Just as Yugoslavia crumpled with little resistance before the German onslaught, so Rumania without a struggle yielded Bessarabia and northern Bukovina to Russia (June 27), northern Transylvania to Hungary (August 30), and southern Dobruja to Bulgaria (September 7).* The climax came on September 6, when Carol and Mme Lupescu fled the country in Wild West fashion with revengeful Iron Guardists in pursuit. When the pair crossed the frontier their railway train was pock-marked with bullet holes. In this ignominious manner the shining prospects with which Rumania began the interwar era faded away.

* See Chapter 37.

ECONOMIC DEVELOPMENT

Prior to World War I Rumania's economy was limited to agriculture, lumbering, and petroleum production. The provinces acquired at the end of the war brought new resources and new industries. Greater Rumania now had textile, sugar, chemical, and metallurgical industries as well as fairly extensive natural resources, including petroleum, lignite, iron, lead, zinc, salt, and rich forest lands. The first task was to integrate the economies of the several provinces into a cohesive national unit. The various currencies that were in circulation—the Rumanian leu, the Austro-Hungarian crown, and the Russian ruble—had to be consolidated into a single currency. The railway lines needed to be rerouted, having been designed originally to serve the Austro-Hungarian and Russian economies. New links were built to center the railway system upon Bucharest, and the various gauges that existed in the provinces were converted to the standard gauge prevailing in the Old Kingdom. The whole complex of commercial and financial relationships, disorganized by the war and by the transfer of territories, had to be reoriented and placed upon a functioning basis.

The first major economic measure undertaken by the Bucharest government was the distribution of land. We have seen that this was carried out on a tremendous scale involving 6,000,000 hectares of land and 1,393,000 peasant beneficiaries. But land reform did not solve the agricultural problem in Rumania any more than it did in the other Balkan countries. The difficulties arose from the usual twin dilemma of rural overpopulation and low productivity.

Rumania's population was just over 18 million at the time of the 1930 census and probably about 20 million when World War II began. This represented a population density of 61 per square kilometer, which was less than that of most Western European countries. But a much larger percentage of the population lived off the land (78 per cent) than was the case in Western Europe. As a result, substantially more people were dependent upon each unit of arable land in Rumania than in most Western European countries.* This heavy population pressure upon the land led to severe fragmentation of private properties. In 1941 over 58 per cent of the plots were less than 3 hectares. Another result of the population pressure was a high degree of rural underemployment. A survey made by Rumanian economists in 1933 revealed that only 43.66 per cent of the potential energy of agricultural labor was being used in farm work. Another investigation of 200 farms of less than 3 hectares and of 100 farms between 3 and 5 hectares showed that on farms under 3 hectares only 38 per cent of the available labor was being utilized; and on farms between 3 and 5 hectares, only 60 per cent.[8]

The large number of dwarf properties arose in part from the unequal

* Statistics in Chapter 31.

distribution of land. It appears that the land reforms of 1918 to 1920 were not enforced as thoroughly as had been assumed. Also, a good deal of land that had been distributed during the reforms had since been sold by poor peasants who were unable to make ends meet. By 1941 properties of over 100 hectares comprised 16 per cent of the privately owned land. On the other hand, if all holdings over 100 hectares had been divided among the peasants owning less than 5 hectares, the average size of their plots would have risen from the 2 hectares shown by the 1941 census to only 2.7 hectares. This indicates that in Rumania, as in the other Balkan countries, the solution to the agricultural problem lay in increased productivity rather than in more land distribution. This is borne out by the experience of Holland, where a slightly higher number of people lived off each unit of arable land. But agricultural productivity in Holland was much greater than in Rumania, with the result that the Dutch farmer enjoyed a standard of living far above that of the Rumanian peasant.

Most of Rumania's farm lands continued to be devoted largely to grain cultivation. A slight shift did occur toward industrial plants such as sunflower and soybean. But the percentage of arable land under cereals dropped only from 87 to 82 during the interwar years. Rumania's wheat yield during the four-year period 1928–1932 was below that of any Balkan state except Greece, averaging 9.5 quintals per hectare, as contrasted with a French yield of 14.8 and a Danish yield of 29.4 quintals per hectare during the same years. The reasons for the low productivity included limited use of fertilizers, a primitive crop-rotation system, low quality of livestock, shortage of agricultural equipment, prevalence of strip farming, and lack of moisture-conservation measures necessary in a country with rich soil but uneven rainfall.

During the depression years the Rumanian peasants suffered severely because the prices of the agricultural products they sold dropped far more than the cost of the manufactured goods they bought. This price scissors, which operated in all the Balkan countries, affected the Rumanian peasants as follows:

	Wholesale Agricultural Prices	*Prices of Industrial Products Required by Agriculture*
1929	100.0	100.0
1930	68.2	98.0
1931	50.8	86.6
1932	47.7	80.9
1933	44.9	81.1
1934	44.1	82.6
1935	48.4	90.2

Source: Cited by H. L. Roberts, *Rumania: Political Problems of an Agrarian State* (New Haven, Conn.: Yale University Press, 1951), p. 177.

The deleterious impact of this "price scissors" was aggravated by the failure of the government to provide adequate credit facilities for agriculture. A national bank existed to aid commerce and a Society for Industrial Credit to aid industry, but there were no provisions for agricultural credit on a similar scale. As a result, the peasants paid dearly for the money they borrowed. In 1931 a League of Nations investigation of agricultural credit in Eastern Europe found that in Rumania the banks of agricultural credits charged 9 to 13 per cent, private banks 12 to 15 per cent plus a quarterly commission of 1 to 3 per cent, and private lenders from 12 to 30 per cent.[9]

The Rumanian peasants also suffered from the discriminatory nature of the national tax system. Most of the revenue came from indirect taxes on consumption goods rather than from income levies. In 1935–1936, income and other direct taxes provided 22.8 per cent of the total revenue compared with 44.9 per cent from consumption taxes, 12.3 per cent from taxes on property transactions, 12.1 per cent from turnover taxes, and 7.9 per cent from customs duties.[10] The net result of this situation was that the Rumanian peasantry sank progressively deeper into debt. In 1938 the interest charge on debts equaled 10 to 11 per cent of the average gross income on 6,000 farms. By 1931 this rose to 35 per cent.

The position of Rumanian agriculture during the interwar years cannot be analyzed adequately in a vacuum. To understand the reasons for its difficulties it is necessary to examine its relationship with other branches of the national economy, and particularly with industry. All Rumanian governments, with the exception of the short-lived National Peasant administration, took strong measures to stimulate industrial growth. The Liberals began during the 1920's with a nationalistic economic policy, seeking to develop Rumania's resources with Rumanian capital. They passed four laws in 1924 regulating a wide range of industrial activities—hydroelectric power, natural gas, petroleum, mines, railroads, river navigation, postal services, telephones and telegraphs, and government monopolies. The laws stipulated that foreign capital in these enterprises could not exceed 40 per cent and that at least three fourths of the personnel and two thirds of the boards of directors were to be Rumanians. Since the subsoil had been nationalized under the constitution, all mines and oil wells were in the form of concessions which would ultimately revert without indemnity to the state, although existing enterprises were to be guaranteed their holdings for a period of fifty years.

These regulations discouraged foreign investors and compelled the Liberals to attempt to build up industry with little outside aid. They adopted a protective tariff system in 1921, and increased the duties in 1924, 1926, and 1927 until Rumania had one of the highest tariff walls in Europe. The Liberals also imposed heavy export duties on agricultural products, sometimes equaling 50 per cent of the value of the commodity. The prime purpose of these export duties was to provide revenue for industrialization purposes. They were successful in this respect, yielding in certain years more revenue than the import duties.

Both the export and the import duties bore heavily on the peasants. The latter were, in effect, shouldered with the cost of the industrialization program. Consequently, one of the first and most important measures of the National Peasants when they came to office was to reverse the Liberal economic policies. They repealed the export duties, threw open the doors to foreign capital, and restricted import duties to those fields in which domestic industry showed some promise. But the National Peasants held power for only two years. The governments that followed reverted to the policy of forced industrialization. One reason was the spread of agrarian protectionism among the industrial states during the depression years. This undermined the international grain market and stimulated Rumania, as well as the other Balkan countries, to develop her own industries. Another reason was the growing international tension in the 1930's, which created a desire for a strong armament industry at home.

Industrialization during the 1930's was encouraged not only by protective tariffs but also by import quotas and restrictions, tax exemptions, state subsidies, special transport rates, obligatory use of certain locally produced goods, and monopolies granted to industries considered nationally desirable. These measures were successful in raising industrial productivity, especially in heavy industry. Between 1927 and 1937 the output in quantity of capital goods increased by 57.4 per cent compared to a 45 per cent increase in consumer goods. Steel production, which hit a high of 143,511 metric tons in 1928, and dropped to a low of 103,046 in 1932, rose to 276,-532 in 1938. The general index of manufacturing production rose from 100 in 1913 to 136.9 in 1929, then dropped to a low of 111.9 in 1932, and thereafter rose steadily to 167.8 in 1934, 175 in 1936, and 177.9 in 1938.[11]

In terms of capital investment, the chief industries in order of importance were chemical (chiefly petroleum), food processing, metallurgical, and textile. In terms of value of output, the order was food processing, textile, chemical, and metallurgical. The petroleum industry was noteworthy because of its strategic and economic significance. The Rumanian oil fields were the only ones of any size to be found in Europe outside the Soviet Union. Less than 25,000 workers were employed in the oil fields and refineries in 1938. But their output accounted for 46 per cent of the value of all Rumanian exports, 22 per cent of total railway receipts, and 15 per cent of total budget receipts. Approximately 90 per cent of the oil was extracted by foreign firms. The high point of Rumanian oil production came in 1934, with 8.5 million tons of crude oil, or 4.05 per cent of total world output. By 1938 production had fallen to 6.6 million tons or 2.41 per cent of world output.[12] The decline was due to the fact that the existing oil fields were being exhausted and exploration for new fields was discouraged by restrictions on foreign prospectors and the lack of domestic capital and technical knowledge.

Rumania also possessed sizable mining and lumber industries. The chief minerals were lignite, salt, iron, gold, silver, and copper. Rich timber resources were available in Transylvania and Bukovina, lumber comprising 11.7 per cent of the value of all exports in 1938. The mineral resources were far from adequately surveyed and exploited; on the other hand, the forests were wastefully lumbered, young trees as well as old being felled.

The Rumanian economy, like that of the rest of the Balkans, came increasingly under German control in the late 1930's. During the early depression years Rumania was able to hold her own against Germany because of her oil exports, which she was able to market at a time when cereals were a glut. As late as 1937 the German share in Rumanian trade was no greater than it had been in 1929. Then the situation changed drastically with Germany's annexation of Austria and Czechoslovakia. Germany now dominated all Southeastern Europe, and Rumania gravitated toward Germany for political as well as economic reasons. Whereas Germany in 1937 had provided 28.9 per cent of Rumanian imports and taken 22.3 per cent of Rumanian exports, the figures in the next year had risen to 40 and 26.5 per cent, respectively.[13]

Then on March 23, 1939, Germany imposed on Rumania a treaty that definitely subordinated Rumania's economy to that of the Reich. The principal aim of this treaty, which was to run for five years, was to expand and diversify Rumanian agricultural production. Germany was to aid in promoting the cultivation of agricultural products of interest to its economy, especially foodstuffs, oilseeds, and textile plants. Germany also undertook to aid industries for processing agricultural products and to supply machinery for exploiting mineral and petroleum resources. These and other provisions were designed to develop Rumania into a producer of vegetable and mineral raw materials for the German industrial economy. This was advantageous to Germany because it gave her more security from blockade. On the other hand, it reduced Rumania to a semicolonial status vis-à-vis Germany. Indeed, German economists specifically stated that Rumania should concentrate on raising her output of foodstuffs and raw materials, and should restrict her industrial activities to the processing of agricultural products.

In conclusion it should be noted that Rumania remained an overwhelmingly agrarian country despite the strenuous government efforts to promote industry. The 1930 census showed 78 per cent of the population engaged in agriculture and forestry. Industry did little to aid this large majority of the population. In fact, the tax structure compelled the peasantry to bear a large proportion of the cost of industrialization. In return, industry was not able to absorb the excess labor force that was accumulating in agriculture in the absence of a more intensive cultivation. Between 1929 and 1939, personnel employed in manufacturing industries increased by 90,000, or by about 10,000 a year. By contrast, the annual excess population in the countryside has been estimated at between 100,000 and 200,000. Industry also failed to aid agriculture by providing it with the facilities for increasing productivity. A Rumanian economist has made this point as follows:

> With all the accelerated rhythm of the process of industrialization, the cultivation of the soil and the raising of livestock have not received any stimulus

toward intensification; food industries based upon agricultural produce have not developed; the textile industry, while well advanced, has neglected native textile plants—flax and hemp—it has stimulated the cultivation of cotton only in the last years, and has provided no incentive for improving the quality of wool; the oil industry has been unable to cause an increase in the production of oleaginous plants, and the introduction of the soy bean in recent years is the result solely of the influence of foreign commercial relations. Finally, the rudimentary and insufficient technical investment in agriculture and the minimal importance of chemical fertilizers illustrate the absence of any positive influence in this direction by the metallurgical and chemical industries.[14]

Thus the growth of Rumanian industry did not help the peasants, either by intensifying agriculture or by absorbing the surplus rural population. Dr. Henry Roberts, an authority on Rumania's economic development, has reached the following negative conclusion concerning this interwar period:

Despite the agrarian reforms of 1918–21, an independent small peasantry was not established; instead, dwarf holdings, insufficient to sustain a peasant family, predominated. So long as there was no alternative field of employment for peasants driven below the margin of subsistence, the appearance of a larger class of medium peasants by no means compensated for the increasing fragmentation and subdivision of the majority of peasant holdings. On the other hand, industry, which was regarded as a means of raising the level of productivity and of draining off surplus agrarian population, seems to have had the effect of reducing purchasing power and of aggravating the difficulties of the countryside. In general, one receives the impression that the Rumanian economy in attempting to lift itself by its bootstraps had merely driven the feet through the soles.[15]

SOCIAL AND CULTURAL DEVELOPMENT

Greater Rumania was not an ethnically homogeneous state. The census of 1912 showed that the Old Kingdom had a population of 7.2 million, of which over 92 per cent was Rumanian. With the territorial expansion at the end of World War I the proportion greatly changed. The 1930 census reported a population of almost 18 million, of which only 73 per cent was Rumanian. The largest minority was the Hungarian, amounting to almost 8 per cent of the population. Then came the Jews, Ukrainians, and Germans, each comprising between 4 and 5 per cent. Turks, Bulgarians, gypsies, and Russians made up most of the remainder.

In 1919 Rumania signed a minorities treaty only after the Allies had presented as an alternative the surrender of some of her recent territorial gains. Despite the provisions of the treaty the minorities were on the whole poorly treated. The Jews suffered from the traditional anti-Semitism which became especially virulent with the rise of the fascist movements in the late 1930's. The Hungarians were the most disaffected and outspoken, partly because of the manner in which the Hungarian estates in Transylvania were divided, but also because the Hungarians had traditionally looked down upon the Rumanians, who now were the overlords. The Ukrainians and other minorities in Bessarabia justifiably complained of the wretched Rumanian administration. In fact, Bessarabia has been described as "perhaps the most mis-governed province in Europe." [16] The Germans, who lived mostly in the former Hapsburg provinces, came increasingly under the sway of National Socialism during the thirties. Finally, the Bulgarians in southern Dobruja resented the settlement of Rumanian colonists in their midst. Thus the minorities remained an unassimilated and divisive element in Greater Rumania. The majority of them probably welcomed the partitioning of the country in 1940.

Class stratification and inequality probably were more marked in Rumania than in any other Balkan country. "The unmistakable signs of luxury spending—palatial villas and flats in the residential sections, large automobiles, yachting clubs, and Parisian fashions—were in startling contrast to the conditions in the countryside. . . . The colorful costumes and picturesque folk dances of the Rumanian peasantry should not obscure the fact that in 1930 nearly half the population was illiterate and in 1938 one child in five died before it was a year old." [17] Scientific investigations of village life were conducted during the 1930's by the distinguished Rumanian sociologist, Professor Dimitrie Gusti, and his students. Their valuable studies brought to light the true plight of the peasantry and served to narrow the gulf between city and village. Gusti had an opportunity to ameliorate the conditions he studied after being appointed director of a public Cultural Foundation by King Carol in 1934. He sent teams of doctors, veterinarians, and farm experts to various villages with the aim of combating illiteracy and improving public health and village life in general. The effort attracted international attention. An American scholar reported the campaign as follows:

> All treatment and medicine are free. . . . Home industries and cooperatives are encouraged. The team, however, imposes no ready-made plan; it merely assists the village to plan and carry out some short and practicable step in the long path which leads out of its present blind-alley. The team organizes libraries, peasant schools, singing circles, and evening meetings, mingling instruction with amusement after the manner of the itinerant American Chatauqua. The village intelligentsia and more energetic peasants soon begin to run their own meetings and lectures, and continue them after the team leaves. . . . The cultural work in the villages has one unexpected side: the enlightenment of the urban population. . . . Through literature, lectures, films, and expositions the Institute is trying to give the city a true picture of village life. Perhaps its most powerful weapon is the direct contact of the teams with the peasants. These enthusiastic and high-minded young men and women carry away from their summer's work a new understanding of the moral and artistic wealth of the Rumanian village, as well as a deeper sympathy for its economic and social needs.[18]

Gusti's work, remarkable though it was, did not begin to scratch the surface so far as the peasants were concerned. The teams visited only a handful of Rumania's 15,000 villages. Furthermore, they could do little about the background economic factors that were largely responsible for the deplorable social conditions. According to League of Nations estimates, the average per capita income in 1937 was between 60 and 70 dollars a year. This inevitably led to serious dietary deficiencies. Food consumption and living standards appear to have improved appreciably during the immediate postwar years. Between 1913 and 1927 annual per capita consumption (in kilograms) of sugar rose from 4.59 to 5.94; of cotton goods, from 2.26 to 2.82; of paper, from 1.41 to 2.50; and of soap, from 0.20 to 0.41.[19] But during the depression years living standards again fell markedly. A number of surveys made during these years showed that the caloric content of the peasant diet was adequate but its quality very poor. The principal food was maize in the form of corn meal. Meat, eggs, milk, and other protective foods could rarely be afforded. An indication of the inadequacy of the national diet was the reappearance of pellagra on a scale reminiscent of the prewar years.

Low income and faulty diet led to poor health conditions. Rumania had the highest infant mortality rate in Europe and was second only to Yugoslavia in the death rate from pulmonary tuberculosis. There was the usual concentration of medical facilities in the cities to the neglect of the countryside. In 1938 Rumania had 4.6 doctors per 10,000 inhabitants, but only 1.1 in the rural districts. The latter figure, it is interesting to note, is the same as that for India.[20]

In the field of education Rumania faced the same problems as the other Balkan countries. Illiteracy was high and the professions were overcrowded. Before 1914 the illiteracy rates were approximately 40 per cent in Transylvania, 60 per cent in Bukovina and the Old Kingdom, and 94 per cent in Bessarabia. The Rumanian government spent considerable sums on education following the war; yet the 1930 census showed that almost 50 per cent of the population remained illiterate. The great majority of the students who were able to continue to higher educational institutions avoided the technical and agricultural schools. They chose, instead, the traditional classical type of education in order to prepare themselves for a white-collar position, preferably in a government office.

The sons of peasants, that is all the coming life-blood of our nation, fall over each other in their anxiety to get into the secondary schools. The majority, of course, are left on the way and fail to reach the University. What becomes of these young men? Do they return to the village? No. Do they take up some trade? Never. They come to the town to swell the pitiful mass of applicants for official posts. . . . The pupil of a technical school, if he discovers in himself a gift for study, will pass to a theoretical school [*lycée*], but the unsuccessful pupil of a *lycée* will abandon it but never enter a technical school. He becomes an official.[21]

The validity of the above statement is indicated by the fact that in 1925 the United Kingdom had 10.7 university students per 10,000 people and Rumania 6.8, but by 1932 the proportion had changed to 12.1 and 19.7.[22] At first the graduates poured forth by the *lycées* and universities were able to find government posts because of the great need for officials in the new Greater Rumania. But before long the supply exceeded the demand. Some were left unemployed but a large number managed to enter government service. The result was that both the civil and military bureaucracies were badly overcrowded and were extended far beyond the financial means of the state. This in turn meant very low salaries for public servants. A study undertaken in May, 1941, of a group of state employees in the Central Institute of Statistics revealed that on the average 62.3 per cent of the personal budgets of employees were devoted to food, 13 per cent to housing, and 11 per cent to clothing. It is understandable that civil servants living under such conditions should have been susceptible to bakshish. Thus we see that Rumania suffered from the same vicious circle common to all underdeveloped regions—a weak economy, an overcrowded bureaucracy, low salaries, and widespread corruption.

36. Albania: 1918–1939

ALBANIA BECAME INDEPENDENT when the Conference of Ambassadors decided on December 20, 1912, in favor of a new Albanian state.* Soon afterward World War I intervened and Albania almost disappeared during the ensuing years of chaos and occupation. But in 1920 Albania was admitted to the League of Nations as a sovereign state. Independence, however, proved to be largely illusory because of unavoidable dependence upon Italy for economic aid. The history of Albania between the two wars demonstrates graphically that a country that is not economically viable has no chance of surviving unless it receives disinterested assistance from some international organization. The Albanians repeatedly applied to the League of Nations for economic aid but were rejected. They had no choice but to turn to Mussolini, who provided them with financial and technical help. Mussolini naturally expected compensation, which he obtained in the form of increasing control over the economy and armed forces of Albania. The logical next step was the outright occupation of Albania, which Mussolini effected in April, 1939. Thus Albania came under foreign occupation on the eve of World War II. Her neighbors were to suffer the same fate only two years later.

OCCUPATION: 1914–1918

As noted in Chapter 27, Albania sank into a state of anarchy following the departure of Prince William in September, 1914. Not even a nominal central authority existed any longer. Each region became absorbed in its own local problems. In the south the main concern was to resist Greek territorial aspirations. The north, with its Catholic population, tended to look to Austria-Hungary for support against the surrounding South Slavs. In the central part of the country, which was overwhelmingly Moslem, there was considerable feeling in favor of the restoration of Ottoman rule. Under these circumstances

* See Chapter 27.

709

it is not surprising that the great powers were able to do as they wished in Albania during the war years. Within a short time the country was occupied by at least seven foreign armies—Italian, Austrian, French, Greek, Serbian, Montenegrin, and Bulgarian.

During the first year of the war the attitude of both the Allies and the Central Powers toward Albania was determined mainly by their anxiety to win Italy and Greece to their respective sides. This consideration prompted the Allies in October, 1914, to allow Greece to occupy southern Albania on condition that the occupation be temporary, that Greece should withdraw whenever the powers requested her to do so, and that she should agree to an Italian occupation of Valona (Vlona). In October and November, 1914, Greek troops occupied southern Albania, including the towns of Koritsa (Korcë) and Argyrokastron (Gjinokastër), which had been awarded to Albania by the 1913 Protocol of Florence.* From the beginning the Greeks paid no attention to the conditions stipulated by the Allies. In January, 1916, they allowed deputies from southern Albania (or northern Epirus as they called the region) to sit in the Greek chamber. In April, 1916, a royal decree announced the incorporation of the territory with Greece. The Allies protested and were able to secure the exclusion of the "Epirote" deputies from the chamber. But the disputed area remained under full Greek control.

The Serbians and Montenegrins occupied adjacent Albanian territory in June, 1915, without prior arrangements with the Allies. Using border incidents as pretexts, the Montenegrins entered Scutari (Shkodër) in the north, while the Serbians occupied central Albania, including Elbasan and Tirana (Tiranë). The Serbians did not extend their zone to Durazzo (Durrës) on the coast, contenting themselves with a strategic line commanding the coastal plains.

Meanwhile, the Italians also had taken steps to safeguard their interests in Albania. Their main concern was to obtain the magnificent harbor of Valona, situated only sixty miles from the Italian coast and controlling the entrance to the Adriatic. On October 30, 1914, they occupied Saseno Island commanding the entrance to Valona. On December 16 they occupied the harbor itself. The Italians strengthened their foothold in Albania by the terms of the secret Treaty of London (April 26, 1915) under which they entered the war. The treaty gave to Italy "full sovereignty over Valona, the island of Saseno and surrounding territory of sufficient extent to assure defence of these points. . . ." The treaty also stipulated that if Italy received all the other territories assigned to her in the Alps and the Adriatic, then she would "not oppose the division of Northern and Southern Albania between Montenegro, Serbia and Greece, should France, Great Britain and Russia so desire." Finally, central Albania was to become a "small autonomous neutralized State," and was to be represented by Italy in its foreign relations.[1] Thus the powers, which in 1912 had guaranteed the independence and neutrality of Albania, in 1915 agreed to the partitioning of the entire country.

* See Chapter 28.

The Allies did not have their way altogether in Albania. Bulgaria's intervention in September, 1915, enabled the Central Powers to overwhelm the Serbians and Montenegrins and to take their places in central and northern Albania. By February, 1916, the Austrians were ensconced in Scutari and Durazzo while the Italians held on in Valona. Later in the year the Allies decided to force the Greeks out of southern Albania because they distrusted the royalist regime in Athens. Accordingly, the Italians took over Argyrokastron and even Yanina in Greece proper, while the French General Sarrail, who commanded the Saloniki front, extended his positions eastward until he occupied Koritsa and effected a junction with the Italians.

Thus by the end of 1916 northern and central Albania were under the Austrians, the Valona and Argyrokastron regions were under the Italians, and the Koritsa region was under the French. All the occupation authorities granted a certain measure of self-rule in order to ease the burden of administration and to conciliate the local population. On June 3, 1917, the Italian commander went so far as to issue a proclamation calling for a united and independent Albania "under the shield and protection of Italy." Apart from the question of how far the "shield and protection" would extend, this proclamation reflected a shift in Italian policy. When Italy negotiated the 1915 London Treaty she was prepared to divide Albania with Serbia, Montenegro, and Greece. But now, in 1917, she was no longer willing to do so. And the reason was that she was becoming alarmed by the specter of a large South Slav state which threatened to take the place of Austria-Hungary as a rival in the Adriatic. Accordingly, Italy now was determined to check the Slav menace by getting as much of the Adriatic Coast as possible for herself, and by setting up a large Albania between the Slavs and the sea.

The surrender of Bulgaria in September, 1918, forced the Austrians to evacuate Albania. French, Serbian, and Italian forces followed on the heels of the retreating Austrians, reaching Scutari on November 5. When the war ended on November 11 the Italians were in possession of most of Albania, with the French in Koritsa, and the Serbs on the left bank of the Drin River. The Allies decided to continue this occupation arrangement until the Peace Conference settled the fate of Albania.

INDEPENDENCE REGAINED: 1918–1920

The Albanians had been too disorganized to play a decisive role during the war years. But now that hostilities had ceased, they took measures to safeguard their interests. On December 25, 1918, forty-eight delegates from all parts of Albania met in Durazzo and established a provisional government. This government sent a delegation to the Paris Peace Conference, where there also appeared delegations from Albanian colonies in the United States, Constantinople, and Rumania.

The chief aim of the Albanians was to regain the frontiers drawn in rough form in 1913 by the Conference of Ambassadors. But the Albanians found themselves in a difficult position when the negotiations began. Austria-

Hungary, their chief defender in the prewar years, no longer existed. The Greeks, Serbians, and Montenegrins were pressing their claims as vigorously as in the past. And Italy wavered erratically from the position she had taken in 1917 in favor of a large Albania. One reason for Italy's vacillation was that she was having difficulty realizing all her claims in the Adriatic because of President Wilson's opposition, and therefore she wished to obtain compensation in Albania. Another reason was that Italy was weakened at the end of the war by widespread Bolshevism and war-weariness. This led her to seek a quick settlement with Albania's neighbors rather than hold out for the 1913 frontiers of Albania.

These considerations explain the secret Venizelos-Tittoni agreement of July 29, 1919, by which Italy was to support Greek claims in southern Albania and the two Thraces, and Greece to support Italian claims to sovereignty in the Valona area and to a mandate for the remainder of Albania. Britain and France were willing to accept this bargain in order to facilitate territorial settlements elsewhere. In fact, on January 14, 1920, Lloyd George, Clemenceau, and Nitti agreed that Italy should have all of Istria and Fiume, that Yugoslavia in return should get northern Albania, while the rest of the country should be divided as stipulated in the Venizelos-Tittoni agreement.

This plan was defeated by the vigorous representations of the Albanian delegation and by the firm opposition of President Wilson. The Albanians worked hard countering the Greek argument that race and language did not count and that the decisive consideration was national consciousness. They replied that the population of southern Albania was overwhelmingly Albanian precisely in national consciousness as well as in race and language. They argued that the Greek statistics were based on the erroneous assumption that all who belonged to the Orthodox Church were necessarily Greeks, whereas the great majority were Albanians in every respect. Most impartial experts since then have taken the position that the disputed area is, in fact, predominantly Albanian. An American scholar has concluded:

> Albanian nationalism had always been suppressed under Turkish misrule and Greece had been given the upper hand with every opportunity to Hellenize the population by means of the Greek Orthodox Church and Greek schools teaching the Greek language. . . . Given freedom to develop naturally without restrictions, saving only those that would safeguard as far as possible the rights of minorities, there can be little doubt that a few years' time would see "Northern Epirus" thoroughly Albanized. Inclusion of the district in Greece, on the contrary, would probably be opposed by a far stronger Albanian sentiment among the population than had been supposed to exist, and seems contrary to the principle of the independence of small nationalities. On the whole, then, judging the matter solely on the merits of the case, the Albanian argument seems by far the stronger, and is upheld by the reports of an investigating committee sent out later by the League of Nations. . . .[2]

More effective than the arguments of the Albanian delegates was Wilson's unyielding stand against the partitioning of Albania. On March 6, 1920, he flatly opposed giving Albanian lands to Yugoslavia as compensation for Fiume and other Adriatic territories that Yugoslavia would relinquish to Italy. "Albanian questions should not be included in the proposed joint discussion of Italy and Yugoslavia . . . the President must re-affirm that he cannot possibly approve any plan which assigns to Yugoslavia in the northern districts of Albania territorial compensation for what she is deprived of elsewhere." [3] Wilson's unequivocal position caused the British-French-Italian plan for the partitioning of Albania to be shelved. No other agreement was concluded before the conference disbanded. Thus by default Albania escaped partitioning.

Although Albania had been rescued at the Peace Conference she was still occupied by foreign armies. The nationalist leaders now undertook the work of political organization and military preparedness necessary to liberate the country. They convened a National Congress at Lushnja on January 28, 1920, and decided to hold a general election. The deputies that were elected met in Tirana on March 27, 1920, as a National Legislative Assembly. Thus began the parliamentary life of Albania.

During the following months various measures were taken to prepare the country for independent statehood. Tirana was selected as the capital, its inland and central position protecting it from both the Italian fleet and the neighboring Balkan countries. A government loan was floated to which Albanians at home and abroad generously subscribed. The delegates also debated the question whether the country should remain a principality or declare itself a republic. They decided to postpone decision until territorial integrity was assured and foreign influence eliminated. In the meantime Albania was still nominally a principality, because Prince William had not formally abdicated. Accordingly, the assembly elected a High Council of Regency consisting of one representative of each of the four religions—Bektashi Moslem, Sunni Moslem, Roman Catholic, and Orthodox. Finally, the assembly established a Committee of National Defense to organize the armed forces.

Meanwhile, the Italians were finding it increasingly difficult to maintain their position in Albania because of war-weariness and disaffection at home. The communists and socialists, who were at the height of their strength during these immediate postwar years, staged strikes to prevent the sending of soldiers and war materials to Albania. By May, 1920, the Italians had found it necessary to evacuate all Albania except Valona. The following month the Albanian Committee of National Defense sent an ultimatum to the Italian commander to withdraw his troops immediately from Valona. Upon refusal the Albanians attacked and were repulsed only with the greatest difficulty. In reply to appeals for reinforcements the Italian minister for war confessed, "Internal conditions of country [Italy] do not permit sending of troops to Albania. Attempt to do so would provoke general strikes, popular demonstrations, gravely injurious to solidarity of Army, which must not be exposed to such hard tests." [4]

Italy obviously was in no condition to maintain her hold on Valona. On August 2, 1920, she accepted the inevitable by signing an agreement for the evacuation of the port, though she was to keep her forces on Saseno Island. A month later, on September 2, the last Italian troops left Albania.

The year 1920 marked a turning point for modern Albania because of the departure of the Italians and also because in that year Albania was admitted into the League of Nations as a sovereign and independent state. When the League Assembly debated the question of Albania's membership, France supported the Greek and Serbian protests that Albania was not a well-defined political entity. But England strongly backed the Albanian application and secured its acceptance. On December 17, 1920, Albania became a full member of the League of Nations.

This recognition did not settle the vexed question of frontiers. In fact, Yugoslav troops made a new sortie into Albania in October, 1921. Finally, on November 9, 1921, the Conference of Ambassadors voted for the reaffirmation of the 1913 frontiers. By 1922, all Yugoslav and Greek troops were withdrawn from Albania, though it was not until July 30, 1926, that Greece and Yugoslavia, together with Britain, France, and Italy, signed a final agreement fixing Albania's frontiers.

The League of Nations Council eased the way for the new state by appointing in 1921 a commission with instructions to check on the withdrawal of foreign troops in Albania and to report any foreign intervention in domestic Albanian affairs. This commission submitted on May 12, 1922, a report which may be taken as the birth certificate of the new Albania.

. . . the argument is still put forward that the Albanians are not inherently a nation, that they will always be unable to exist as an independent modern State and that sooner or later the country is certain to be divided up among its neighbors. This argument in itself constitutes a serious menace to the independence of the country. The Commission, after thorough study of the whole Albanian question, was led to the conclusion not only that an Albanian nation exists, but that its existence is a necessity. . . .

They are united by common customs, age-long traditions and even language, the difference between the Gheg and the Tosk languages being at bottom nothing more than a difference of dialect. Although differences in religion occasionally have some effect upon the politics of the country, the fanatical manifestations so frequent in other countries which are divided in religion are very rare in Albania. . . . Moreover, the sufferings endured in common during the Balkan wars and the world war, in all of which Albania was a theatre of operations, gave a new impulse to Albanian nationalism which has extended to all the classes of the population. . . .

Albania possesses not only the nationalist feeling, which is a factor in the formation of an independent nation, but also the material resources which are essential to its economic existence. . . .

To sum up, it seems clear that the essential elements of a prosperous Albania exist [and] that this little country possesses all the conditions necessary for the formation of a politically and economically independent State. . . .[5]

PROBLEMS OF INDEPENDENCE

The League commission testified to Albania's potentiality as an "economically and politically independent state." But it also emphasized that the potentiality was still far from realization. "We must not delude ourselves so far as to believe that this result is already achieved. On the contrary, the country is still in a similar situation to that of several of the Balkan countries immediately after their liberation from Turkish domination. Its social and political organization is, indeed, only beginning." [6]

Albania did, in fact, face a host of basic problems at this time, and one of the most serious was her appalling poverty and general lack of development. She had no railways whatsoever and only a few roads connecting the chief towns. Industry was almost exclusively of the handicraft variety. The mineral resources lay unexploited and unsurveyed. Agricultural techniques were rudimentary and wasteful. Much fertile soil lay untilled because of malarial swamps that could not be drained because of lack of funds. The value of all the exports in 1921 amounted to 420,000 dollars, and the budget in the same year totaled 3.6 million dollars.

General economic development was obviously needed, both to raise living standards and to provide the economic base necessary for modern statehood. The League commission warned that stagnation at the prevailing level "would be the greatest danger to the maintenance of the independence of the country. Albania is geographically in and of Europe. She must partake of its economic current. If her present rulers prove unfitted for the task, some other regime would inevitably replace them—such is the teaching of history." [7]

We shall see that Albania was to find it difficult to make her way into the "economic current." Instead, she was caught helplessly in a whirlpool. Economic development required capital, but Albania was unable to produce capital precisely because she was underdeveloped. In other words, she faced the same dilemma that confronted all underdeveloped countries, including her own Balkan neighbors.

Another problem facing Albania at this time was her cultural backwardness. No educational system existed because of the ban on Albanian schools during the centuries of Turkish rule. Even the language was inadequate for literary and educational purposes. The vocabulary was retarded and the different dialects spoken in the north and south needed to be fused into a national language. The small percentage of the population that was educated had attended foreign schools—Greek in the south, Italian along the Adriatic, and Austrian in the north.

Deep-rooted political problems also plagued the new state. Centuries of Turkish misrule had bred a general distrust of all government. Most Albanians wished only to be left alone. This was especially true of the mountaineers of the north and east whose social organization resembled that of the Scottish highlanders of earlier times. Even in the rest of the country conditions were singularly unsuitable for modern parliamentary government, given the widespread illiteracy and the unlimited power of the local feudal lords.

Furthermore, the question of the form of government was of immediate concern because the National Congress that had met at Lushnja in January, 1920, had adopted only a provisional political arrangement. Consequently, a permanent constitution had to be adopted sooner or later, and this raised the controversial question of which form of government was most suitable for the country. Some favored a republic and others a monarchy. The League commission warned that "the task of the Constituent Assembly will be an extremely difficult one, and it is quite possible that an effective solution may not be found immediately. The result will be an indefinite period of instability. . . ." [8] This warning proved prophetic. Albania was to experience political turmoil for five years until a "strong man" arose in the person of Ahmed Zog to impose his authority by forceful means.

Finally, the new Albania had to face basic social problems, particularly that of land reform. This was especially acute in the south, where the Moslem beys owned large estates worked by Orthodox Christian tenants. Thus the land issue was complicated by the religious factor. Furthermore, many of the Orthodox Albanians spoke Greek, which added the further complication of Greek irredentist claims to the agrarian and religious problems. This explains why the question of southern Albania has been so complex and why it has constituted a perennial issue between Greece and Albania.

Fortunately there are available the valuable reports of Professor J. J. Sederholm of Finland who, as a member of the League commission, traveled in all parts of Albania between 1921 and 1923. Sederholm estimated that the Moslems and the Orthodox Christians were about equal in numbers in southern Albania. The Moslems spoke Albanian but many of the Christians spoke both Albanian and Greek. In such cases he considered the language spoken at home to be the mother tongue. Sederholm estimated that those who spoke Greek at home—the Grecophones—constituted at the most 17 per cent or one sixth of the total population of southern Albania. For this reason he concluded that "the decision taken by the Powers in fixing the southern frontiers of Albania was on the whole a just and wise one." [9]

Yet Sederholm noted considerable friction between Moslem and Christian Albanophones. The cause for the strife, he reported, was to be found in economic and social considerations rather than in the difference in religion. More specifically, a few Moslem families during the Turkish period had acquired the best lands and had filled the top government posts. The Christian Albanians resented this discrimination and were emboldened by the fact that across the border, in nearby Greece, the situation was reversed. The Christians were also strengthened by the considerable emigration to the United States after 1900. Almost all the emigrants were Christians, and many returned with radically new democratic ideas concerning political institutions and social relationships. In fact, these emigrants played a significant role in the winning of Albanian independence. And once they had shaken off Turkish domination they naturally looked forward to sweeping changes. They particularly wanted agrarian reform in order to divide the estates of the Moslem beys, and they also wanted political reform in order to gain a voice in the government of their country. But radical changes did not occur overnight in Albania any more than they did in Greece, Serbia, and the other Balkan countries when they gained their independence in the previous century.

Many of the Orthodox Albanians inevitably became disillusioned and discontented, and they directed their resentment against Ahmed Zog, the Moslem bey who seized power and ruled the country as Zog I until World War II. Despite this disaffection Sederholm concluded that the Albanophone Christians, as distinct from the Grecophones, were too nationalistically minded to turn from Tirana to Athens. "It seems to me certain that no revolutionary movement is now being prepared within Southern Albania. The Christian population is pacific, and its feelings for Greece are not those of an irredenta, but only those for a country which has been the source of their culture and the enemy of the hated Turkish regime." [10]

POLITICAL INSTABILITY: 1920–1924

The cleavages in the new Albanian state were reflected in the political parties that appeared in parliament in 1921. One was the Progressive party led by Shevket Verlazi of central Albania, the largest landowner in the country. This group was unalterably opposed to land reform and, in general, wished to preserve as much as possible of the older order bequeathed by the Turks.

The other party was the Popular or reform party. The returned emigrants from the United States were particularly influential in this body and imbued it with their philosophy of immediate and radical change. The outstanding leader of these reformers was Bishop Fan S. Noli, who first rose to prominence among the Albanians in the United States. Noli was born in 1882 in an Albanian village in Eastern Thrace. He was educated in a Greek elementary school and in a Greek gymnasium. For a time he lived in Athens; in 1903 he moved to Egypt, where he taught in a Greek school. While in Egypt he first became aware of the Albanian nationalist movement through resident Albanian merchants. It was these compatriots who persuaded him to sail to the United States and provided him with passage money.

In the United States Noli quickly became the leader of his illiterate fellow countrymen. His greatest contribution was the organization in 1908 of the Albanian Autocephalous Orthodox Church with himself as the first head. Never before, not even in the mother country, had the Albanians had the opportunity to worship in their own church with the service conducted in their own language rather than in Greek. When an independent Albania was established in 1920 the American Albanians were allowed to elect one of their number to the national assembly. The person that they selected was their Bishop Noli, who had in the meanwhile found time to graduate from Harvard University. Noli returned to Albania with many of his countrymen, all determined, after their heady experiences in America, to uproot the old order with its backwardness and corruption and exploitation. The radical philosophy impelling these men was set forth frankly in the columns of *Dielli*, the newspaper of the American-Albanian nationalist organization, Vatra.

> The Albanians in America and their organization, *Vatra,* are men who have tasted enough freedom to enable them to understand the real reason for the sufferings of the people, and it is they who are leading the people's struggle. . . . *Vatra* has now opened warfare against Albania's internal enemies, against those who are enemies of freedom. . . . Albania has fallen into bad hands, into the hands of those who have never wished for her welfare, who always fought against the national cause under the Turks. The majority of those who now fill government positions were formerly tools of Turkey and have always tried to skin the poor. *Vatra* is not going to surrender its struggle until it wipes away the injustices committed in Albania against the people. *Vatra* is going to strive, as it has always done, for a civilized and cultured Albania.[11]

Another leader of the Popular party at this time was Ahmed Zog, who had an entirely different background and outlook from Bishop Noli's. Zog was born in 1895, the son of the chieftain of the Mati district in central Albania. Both his father and grandfather had been pashas in the Turkish service, and one of his ancestors had risen to be grand vizir. Zog attended military schools in Monastir and Constantinople. When the first Balkan War began, he hurried home from Constantinople to defend his ancestral lands, though still only seventeen years old. From then on Zog was seldom in the background. He possessed precisely the qualities necessary for a public career in the Albania of his time —daring, decisiveness, sober realism, and utter ruthlessness. He was active during World War I until interned in Vienna by the Austrians. In the first Albanian government formed after the war he headed the key ministry of interior. He used this office to strengthen his personal position and to prepare the way for the climb to the top. In family background, in education, and in experience, Zog was precisely the opposite of Noli. In contrast to the thoroughly democratic and socially conscious Orthodox bishop, Zog was interested primarily in power for himself. This did not mean that Zog did not have the interests of his country at heart. But the fact remains that he was a ruthless *Realpolitiker* in contrast to the idealistic and rather impractical bishop. Zog's single-minded pursuit of power, together with his undoubted ability, enabled him to realize his ambitions and to rule Albania during most of the interwar period.

The Popular party formed a government on December 14, 1921, in which Noli served as foreign minister and Zog again occupied the ministry of interior. Although still under thirty years of age Zog resolved to disarm all civilians in the lowlands, a dangerous and unpopular task, given the traditions of the country. Zog also antagonized the highlanders in the northeast because he refused to support their irredentist aspirations to the Kosovo area in Yugoslavia which was predominantly Albanian. These factors contributed to the outbreak of a revolt in March, 1922. Noli took the opportunity to resign because he already had clashed frequently with Zog and wished to dissociate himself from his policies. Other ministers also resigned but Zog remained in the menaced capital. His bravery and presence of mind, together with the assistance of the British minister, who negotiated with the rebels, enabled Zog to ride out the storm.

Zog's prestige was greatly enhanced by this affair, and on December 2, 1922, he became premier in name as well as in fact. In his speech to parliament he declared his intention of founding "a fully civilized Western state" and of following democratic procedures.[12] His opponents derided his statement, pointing out that he was already exercising power dictatorially. They also noted his engagement to the daughter of Shevket Verlazi and forecast that he would be more interested in safeguarding existing vested interests than in transforming Albania into "a Western state."

Accordingly, Noli and other reformers left the Popular party and organized an opposition bloc which attracted many disparate groups that were against Zog for one reason or another. Noli was the leader of this bloc, and the most articulate element in it were the Orthodox Christians from the south. These people were becoming increasingly disillusioned because independence had failed to materialize their aspirations. They still did not have the role in government that they felt they deserved. The estates of the Moslem beys were still intact despite the talk of agrarian reform. And they paid the larger share of the taxes since their part of the country was the most developed; yet they received little in return because most of the national revenue was spent in Tirana on the army and the bureaucracy. Thus Professor Sederholm reported early in 1923 that "there is at present a strong discontent among the Christian population in Southern Albania. While we noted it last year, mainly among the people who had been educated in Greece, it must now be stated that the discontent has spread also to the nationalists [Albanophones] in the Koritza region." [13]

Despite this disaffection in the country and the criticism of the opposition in parliament, Zog did make some progress during his premiership. He disarmed a large part of the population and established order in many regions where brigandage traditionally had been an accepted form of livelihood. This assertion of government authority obviously was essential for independent statehood. But it did not satisfy those elements of the population that were more interested in social change than in state power. Accordingly, Zog failed to win a majority in the elections of January, 1924. Noli's followers won 35 of the 95 seats, while Zog had the support of two groups which together won 40 seats. Zog resigned the following month and was succeeded by the landowner Shevket Verlazi.

The opposition, needless to say, considered this change quite insignificant and continued to agitate for a new government. The opportunity came with the murder on May 5, 1924, of Avni Rustem, a reform leader who had organized the liberal Union of Young Albanians. The opposition deputies accused Zog of being involved, directly or indirectly, in the crime. They boycotted the chamber, leaving it without a quorum, and issued a proclamation stating that Zog still dominated the government and demanding that he leave the country. The reformers were joined by various disaffected groups, including some army leaders and northern chieftains. The movement reached such proportions that the government fell and Zog fled to Yugoslavia.

On June 17, 1924, Noli formed a cabinet and issued an ambitious nineteen-point reform program. The following selections indicate its scope and temper: "4. To uproot feudalism, free the people, and establish democracy definitely in Albania; 5. To introduce radical reforms in all branches of the administration both civil and military; 9. To balance the budget by radical economies; 11. To ameliorate the condition of the farmers so as to ensure their economic independence; 15. To introduce judicial reforms; 18. To organize the department of education on modern and practical lines so that the schools should produce capable citizens, good patriots and able workers. . . ." [14]

This program remained almost wholly on paper. One reason was that Noli was able to stay in office only five months. Another was that Noli's cabinet was by no means united behind him. Some of the members had supported him because of their dislike for Zog, but now that they were in office they were unwilling to go along with him on many of his proposed reforms. Thus Noli was able to accomplish little more than balance the budget. He erred fatally in not reorganizing the armed forces into a dependable instrument. And he supplied the opposition with effective ammunition when he extended diplomatic recognition to the Soviet Union, even though he was merely following the example of Britain's Labor government.

While Noli was floundering in Tirana, Zog was in Belgrade preparing his comeback. He secured the assistance of the Yugoslav government, which presumably assumed that henceforth he would do their bidding. On December 13, 1924, Zog crossed the frontier at the head of a force which included, in addition to his Albanian followers, 1,000 volunteer soldiers and 16 officers from the Yugoslav regular army, 800 soldiers and 40 officers from General Wrangel's White Russian refugee army that had found asylum in Yugoslavia, as well as artillery and machine guns from the Yugoslav government arsenal. The first attack was made by Yugoslav frontier forces with the intention of opening a path for Zog. Thus the loyal Albanian units were overwhelmed and Zog was able to proceed to Tirana with little resistance. On Christmas Eve he entered the capital as Noli fled to Italy. On January 22, 1925, the rump of the National Assembly proclaimed Albania a republic, and on January 31 it elected Zog president of the republic for a seven-year period.

In retrospect it is clear that Noli's radical reform program was bound to arouse last-ditch opposition from the powerful vested interests. It might have had some chance only if an organized and militant mass movement had existed to push it through against all opposition. But such a movement did not exist when Noli came to office. Nor was he a sufficiently experienced politician to stimulate such a movement by immediate and far-reaching changes. Noli himself later perceived this flaw in his strategy: ". . . by insisting on the agrarian reforms I aroused the wrath of the landed aristocracy; by failing to carry them out I lost the support of the peasant masses." [15]

PRESIDENT ZOG: 1925–1928

Having advanced himself to the presidency of the republic, Zog then took steps to assure his permanent occupancy of the position. At home he crushed all opposition by the usual punitive measures. He outlawed Noli and his followers who had fled abroad; he imprisoned or executed the opposition leaders who remained behind; and he placed his own men in command of the army and *gendarmerie*. Zog also secured a constitution (March 7, 1925) which concentrated state power into his own hands. As president he could appoint and dismiss ministers, veto bills passed by parliament, decree fresh elections, initiate changes in the constitution, and control all appointments to top posts in the army and bureaucracy.

Having consolidated his position within Albania, Zog looked abroad for economic assistance in order to develop his country and, incidentally, to buttress his regime. Previous governments had also sought foreign economic aid. The League of Nations had sent an expert to Albania in 1922 to study the economic and financial condition of the country. He prepared a program of development and recommended a foreign loan of twenty-two million dollars to finance it. The Albanian government requested League assistance in raising the loan, offering to submit to any control the League wished to impose. The League failed to undertake the task, partly because of the unsettled financial state of Europe at that time and also because of the opposition of certain powers.

In retrospect it is clear that disinterested financing of Albania through the League would have been a profitable investment in Balkan peace. But repeated appeals for financial aid brought no response. When Noli was premier he personally attended the League Assembly and asked:

> But do tell me, Mr. Secretary-General, why you refuse to give Albania a loan to enable her to get on her feet. . . . The answer is very easy to give. You will find it in Shakespeare: "Words, words, words!" and that is to say, in plain English, hot air, that's all. Oh! "It is a tale told by an idiot, full of sound and fury, signifying nothing." [16]

A month later Zog was in office. Realistically he looked elsewhere for the assistance the League had refused. Although Yugoslavia had backed him in his rise to power, he now turned instead to Italy. One reason was that Italy appeared at the time to be a less dangerous power to lean upon than Yugoslavia. The Serbs traditionally wanted a small Albania, while the Italians, in the face of the new Yugoslav state, normally would prefer as large and as strong an Albania as possible. Furthermore, Albania's natural economic ties were with Italy, two thirds of her trade being with that country. Thus Zog on March 15, 1925, concluded with an Italian financial group an agreement that had far-reaching consequences.

The agreement provided that the Italian group should establish the National Bank of Albania which was to have the exclusive right of issuing paper currency, coining metal money, and negotiating government and municipal loans. The bank was to have its administrative seat in Tirana but in practice its operations were directed from Rome. Within a month after the bank began operations it was to organize the Company for the Economic Development of Albania, commonly known as SVEA. This company undertook to procure a loan of ten million dollars for Albania, to be used exclusively for public works —roads, swamp drainage, agricultural development, and construction of ports. The repayment of capital and interest was to be guaranteed by a lien on the Albanian customs duties and on the state monopolies of salt, cigarettes, and matches.

The capital invested in both SVEA and the bank was almost entirely Italian. Albanians and foreigners were free to participate, but very few availed themselves of the opportunity. The Italians themselves did not regard this venture as a normal business enterprise that could be justified on economic grounds. Rather, they regarded their investments in Albania as an instrument of Italian diplomacy. Speaking to a meeting of stockholders, the president of SVEA declared:

> Due to the special character of our company, springing from and living in the orbit of a happy and much vaster political conception of the relations between Italy and Albania, our attainments unfold themselves in a sphere so superior and so foreign to the internal results of a balance sheet that it is a legitimate wish on your part to prefer to hear what our activities have contributed to the development of the program of Italo-Albanian collaboration.[17]

There is no doubt that Albania profited economically from these arrangements with Italy. For the first time the country had a national currency in place of the dozen different foreign currencies which had previously circulated. Also, the interest burden proved in practice to be light because the Italians were not strict about repayment schedules. Instead, they granted still more loans to Albania, some on ludicrously easy terms. In 1931, for example, Italy agreed to provide a series of annual loans extending over a period of ten years and limited to a maximum of two million dollars in any one year. The loans were to draw no interest, and the date and manner of repayment were to depend on the financial condition of Albania! But Italy made it clear that the annual payments to Albania would depend on "the continuation of full and sincere technical and political collaboration between the two governments." [18]

Obviously, Italian economic aid to Albania was politically inspired. The generous loans were to be used as an entering wedge to gain control of a country that Italian policy makers considered to be necessary for their national security. As early as June, 1926, only fifteen months after the first economic agreement, Italy apparently began to impinge upon Albania's sovereignty. Reports from Tirana alleged that Italy demanded, in virtual ultimatum form, that she be given control of Albania's economy, armed forces, and foreign relations. The details of this episode remain obscure, though it does appear that Italy did make certain demands and then drew back in the face of British representations. Whether or not Italy presented these alleged demands at this time, the fact remains that she soon won all these concessions.

Before the end of the year, on November 27, 1926, Zog felt constrained to sign the Tirana Pact with Italy. This was a "friendship and security" treaty in which the signatories agreed to cooperate to maintain "the political, juridical and territorial *status quo* in Albania" and also undertook "not to conclude with other powers, political and military agreements to the prejudice of the other party. . . ." [19] Yugoslavia reacted strongly against this pact, regarding it as a long step toward an Italian protectorate over Albania. She severed relations with Albania for a month and exchanged bitter recriminations with Italy despite a friendship treaty that she had concluded with that country in 1924. The basic difficulty was that the Tirana Pact brought to the surface the ever-present rivalry between Yugoslavia and Italy in the Adriatic. Because of this rivalry the Albanian policy that Italy considered to be necessary for her security was regarded on the other hand by Yugoslavia as a menace to herself and to peace in the Balkans.

Italy proceeded on her chosen course, concluding a year later, on November 22, 1927, a twenty-year defensive military alliance with Albania. This was followed by increasing Italian control over Albania's armed forces. Italian arms and ammunition were introduced. A military mission under General Pariani reorganized the Albanian army. Albanian officers went to Italy for advanced training. Fascist instructors arrived to organize Albanian youth and to give it premilitary training on the fascist model. The public works financed by Italian loans consisted largely of strategic roads and bridges. Likewise, the port of Durazzo was modernized and enlarged to make it suitable for large-scale landing. Thus Albania became Italy's bridgehead in the Balkans.

These developments consolidated Zog's position, at least on the surface. He now commanded sizable armed forces, while Italy was committed to supporting the "political *status quo*" in Albania. Zog took the final step upward in 1928 when he elevated himself to kingship. Although his term as president had run little more than half its appointed course, he held elections for a constitutional assembly in July, 1928. On September 1 this body unanimously proclaimed Albania "a democratic, parliamentary and hereditary kingdom," bestowing the title "Zog I, King of Albanians," on the former president. Three months later, on December 1, 1928, a monarchical constitution was adopted which again left most state power to Zog. He had authority to appoint and dismiss premiers, command the armed forces, veto parliament bills, suspend legal procedures for political crimes, conclude agreements with other nations, and proclaim war in case of aggression.

KING ZOG: 1928–1939

Zog ruled from September 1, 1928, until April 7, 1939, when he was compelled to flee before an Italian invasion. During this eleven-year period he introduced many reforms, though they proved more impressive on paper than in practice. For example, his Agrarian Reform Law of April 17, 1930, provided for the expropriation, with compensation, of one third of each bey's estate. The lands thus acquired were to be resold on easy terms to the peasants. The operation of this law was reported as follows:

> It seems, however, that too long a time has elapsed between mooting this reform, passing the law, and putting it into 'execution. The other day Government officials went down to Fier in Myzeqe to expropriate certain lands, and found that the owner had so sub-divided it among the various members of his numerous family by ante-dated deeds of sale or gift that there was nothing left to expropriate. The same thing has happened near Tirana also. At Elbasan, too, a certain youthful Bey received early information that grazing lands were to be exempt from expropriation, then evicted his tenants at almost a moment's notice, burned their houses, and turned down to grass all the land they had formerly cultivated.[20]

Zog also reorganized completely the laws of the land, adopting a penal code based on the Italian model (1928), a civil code patterned after the Napoleonic Code (1929), and a commercial code modeled on French and Italian examples (1932). But again there was considerable discrepancy between law and practice. Even Zog himself continued to practice traditional Turkish government customs, such as direct interference with the courts of justice and personal discrimination in selecting and promoting officials. Parliamentary elections were held regularly, but signified little because of the apathy and ignorance of the electorate and the intimidating power of the local beys and gendarmes. The following descriptions of the functioning of parliamentary government in Albania demonstrated how skin-deep Zog's reforms proved to be:

> The calm in which these elections [1932] are being conducted is very striking, particularly to those who have known the heat and fever of a Greek contest. The townspeople are so uninterested that for days on end the newspapers appear without referring to the elections, and most of the country people are voting only because the local gendarmes have ordered them to go and do so. The fact is that for the populace Parliament is not an instrument of government, and a deputy is only an important man to whom the King has granted a large salary, as he has granted small salaries to smaller men all over the country for doing nothing but keep the peace.[21]

> As was confidently expected by all observers, the Parliamentary elections held in Albania on January 31 [1937] ended in a sweeping victory for the Government, which succeeded in winning 100 per cent of seats. The youngest of the Balkan States, having spent its infancy amid falling democracies and diverse experiments in corporate and other forms of dictatorial government, has evolved a system which conserves all the names of democracy—parliament, elections, candidates, voters—but which has excluded all uncertainty and all chance that Opposition candidates may be elected. One of the first results of such a system is the complete apathy of the people. In the election of voters, for each district elects a number of representatives who go to vote in the name of the whole district, there were districts in which only 18 men out of 187 cast their votes. A number of intelligent and educated young men put up as Opposition candidates,

but the machinery is such that it is well known in advance that not one of them would be elected. The 58 Government candidates elected are mostly men who have been deputies before, and who belong to the parties supporting the Government in practically the same proportion as those who made up the last parliament.[22]

In foreign affairs Zog attempted to keep Italian influence under control as much as possible. In 1932 he rejected a proposal for a customs union with Italy and later concluded trade agreements with Yugoslavia and Greece in order to loosen Italy's economic strangle hold. The next year he dismissed some of his Italian military advisers and, by nationalizing education, closed the Italian schools in Albanian towns. Rome reacted by sending a squadron that suddenly appeared before Durazzo on June 23, 1934. The Albanian government agreed to open negotiations, and in the end accepted more Italian aid and also the control that went with it. During the following years Italian influence in the army and the national economy steadily increased, reaching the point where Italian settlers were allowed to colonize certain areas in Albania.

Zog was caught in the contradiction of his own strategy. On the one hand, he was unable to curb the Italians, upon whom he had leaned for so many years. On the other hand, the tightening Italian strangle hold increasingly turned his own nationalistic subjects against his rule. Disaffection spread among all segments of the population—particularly the youth, but also among army officers, Roman Catholics, and conservative Moslem landowners. A plot against the regime was uncovered in 1932, and a revolt broke out in 1935. Zog married a Hungarian countess, Geraldine Apponyi, on April 27, 1938, hoping that an heir would strengthen his position. The best man at the wedding was the Italian foreign minister, Count Ciano. The day after the ceremony Ciano wrote in his diary: "I leave Albania more firmly convinced than ever of the need for a radical solution." [23] Zog's reign, despite his marriage, was drawing to a close.

ITALIAN OCCUPATION

When Ciano returned to Rome he presented his plan for a "radical solution" to Mussolini. The latter agreed enthusiastically, especially because he was becoming increasingly jealous of Hitler's victories in Central Europe. A month earlier the Fuehrer had annexed Austria but now Mussolini looked forward to scoring his own triumph in Albania.

Ciano at once began preparations for taking over Albania. He bribed the chiefs so that they would be on his side when the moment came. For a while he considered arranging for the assassination of Zog, having found an Albanian who was ready to perform the deed for ten million lire. Zog got wind of these preparations and sent a pathetic message to Ciano on October 13, 1938. "Albania now is in Italy's hands, for Italy controls every sector of the national activity. The King is devoted. The people are grateful. Why do you want anything more?" [24]

This plea fell on deaf ears. Hitler's annexation of Bohemia and Moravia on March 15, 1939, spurred the Italians to seek solace in Albania. "It is useless," wrote Ciano, "to deny that all this concerns and humiliates the Italian people. It is necessary to give them a satisfaction and compensation: Albania." [25] Mussolini and Ciano agreed to present an ultimatum to Zog, demanding that he accept an Italian protectorate. "It seems probable that King Zog will give in," wrote Ciano. "There is, above all, a fact on which I am counting: the coming birth of Zog's child. . . . I cannot imagine Geraldine running around fighting through the mountains of Unthi or of Mirdizu in her ninth month of pregnancy." [26]

On March 25, Zog received the ultimatum to sign a "treaty" transforming Albania into an Italian protectorate. He tried to stall for time but the British envoy told him that he could expect no aid. Britain did not wish to mar her relations with Italy. Nevertheless, Zog continued to stall. On April 2 he asked for time to call the council of ministers to reach a decision. Mussolini refused and gave orders for the invasion.

On Good Friday, April 7, Italian warships began bombarding the coast, and landings were made at several points. Two days earlier the queen had given birth to a boy, who was named Prince Leka or Skender, after Albania's national hero. Ciano observed cynically, "How long will he be an heir to the Albanian throne?" [27] The Italian armored columns gave the answer as they entered Tirana the day after the landings. Zog and his family fled over the mountains to Greece. The Italians encountered no resistance, either military or diplomatically. Their total casualties were twelve killed and fifty-three wounded. On April 10, Ciano wrote exultantly in his diary: "Reaction abroad begins to lessen. It is clear above all that the British protests are more for domestic consumption than anything else. News from Albania is good; military occupation is carried out according to plan and without obstacles." [28]

Ciano went to Tirana on April 12 to make arrangements for the administration of the new Italian possession. He convened the Albanian assembly, which obediently voted to abolish the 1928 constitution and to offer the crown to King Victor Emmanuel III. The latter now assumed the title King of Italy and Albania and Emperor of Ethiopia. Albania henceforth was ruled by an Italian viceroy functioning in the name of the king. Ciano's notes on his reception in Tirana are not without significance. "The crowd receives me triumphantly; there is a certain amount of coolness, especially among the high school students. I see that they dislike raising their arms for the Roman salute, and there are some who openly refuse to do it even when their companions urge them. . . . I see the eyes of some patriots flaming with anger and tears running down their faces. Independent Albania is no more." [29]

ECONOMIC DEVELOPMENT

Albania developed substantially during her two decades of independent existence between the world wars. Yet even in 1939 she still remained by far the most backward state in Europe. Albania was less touched by Western civilization and more remote from the general life of the Continent than any other country. Her retardation was evident in every aspect of her economic and social life.

Agriculture was the principle economic activity, occupying at least 80 per cent of the population. Much of the best land was held in large estates by great landowners, which included the Moslem beys, the Christian churches, and the Moslem religious orders. This left about 40 per cent of the peasant families landless. Zog attempted to correct the situation with his land reform of 1930, but, as noted above, the law was not effectively enforced. Farming techniques changed little in the course of centuries. An iron plow was used in southern Albania, but a wooden ox-drawn plow was the most common in the rest of the country. The same crop was resown in the same field year after year. When the yield began to fail, the land was left fallow, a procedure which put about 20 per cent of the land out of cultivation. The principal crops, in order of importance, were corn, which was the mainstay of the peasant diet, wheat, oats, and barley. Fruits were grown in sheltered places, but only what was surplus for home requirements found its way to local markets. The olive tree was extensively cultivated along the coast and was found as much as fifty miles inland. Vines were cultivated in the south, much of the produce being used to produce the popular and fiery wine spirit known as raki. The Albanian peasant was far less productive than his Balkan neighbors, who in turn were among the least productive in Europe.

The following analysis by an Italian authority explains the reasons for the backwardness of Albanian agriculture and the obstacles in the way of progress.

Albania is a country endowed with resources that have not been sufficiently utilized. With modern methods of cultivation it could support normally a population considerably larger than the actual population, and there are probably no inconsiderable riches in the subsoil. But it is also true that to bring agriculture up to the level it has reached in other civilized countries, in addition to enterprise and technical capacity, a very large capital would be needed for machinery and supplies. There is not enough of this. Even if there were, the products thus obtained would not be marketable because of the lack of roads. Hence if we are to think of a productive Albania, at the very beginning the problem of means of communication must be solved. Furthermore, for the extension of cultivation a radical solution would unquestionably call for control over the waters which today are quite without rule and curb. There exist, it is true, very fertile plains like the Muzakija, but they are cursed with malaria and are uninhabitable. To make them sanitary would involve heavy expense, with long preparation and skill and method in carrying out the work.

An obstacle to the development of modern agriculture lies in the areas occupied by *latifundia,* particularly numerous on the plains of the center and the south. . . . These large estates remaining undivided from generation to generation are ill utilized and give poor yields. On the other hand the condition of agriculture is much better in the southeast region in the basin of Koritsa where landed property is closely subdivided and whither emigrants come back enriched from America.[30]

Stock raising is a traditional and important occupation in Albania, as is evident in the fact that in 1938 about 31 per cent of the country's area was in pasture compared to 11 per cent in arable and orchard land. For the little cash that he needed, the average Albanian peasant looked more to his livestock than to his fields. He grew corn to feed his family, but his animals supplied him not only with draft power and a little meat, but also with wool, mohair, and hides. In fact, live animals and animal produce comprise the largest percentage of the total value of Albanian exports. In 1937 the livestock, cheese, hides, and wool exports totaled 5,159,000 gold francs, compared to 1,726,000 gold francs from agricultural products (chiefly eggs, beans, olives, olive oil, tobacco, and cigarettes), and 1,695,000 from asphalt and petroleum. Despite this prominence, stock-breeding methods were as primitive as those of agriculture. The cattle were small and poor, largely because of the starvation diet during the winter months. Probably more than half the cattle were draft animals, milk cows being of less value in the prevailing economy. The peasants obtained their milk supply from their goats, while cow's milk usually was sold in the towns.

The potential value of Albanian forests is considerable, 36 per cent of the country being woodland, compared to 31 per cent pasture and 11 per cent arable. But there was no systematic exploitation of this resource before World War II because of the problem of transportation. The rivers, rushing through precipitous gorges, were unsuitable for floating timber, while the best woodland areas had neither roads nor railways. Consequently, very little lumber was produced.

The mining industry likewise was in its infancy prior to World War II. Here again the lack of transportation was a basic handicap; moreover, no extensive surveys had been made. The only resources that were exploited to an appreciable degree were asphalt and petroleum. The latter was controlled completely by an Italian company subsidized by Rome. The company spent large sums drilling in the modest Albanian oil fields, presumably because the domestic Italian resources were quite inadequate and the Albanian fields were close enough to be securely available in case of war. Finally, the Italians discovered two fields, one near Berat and the other near Valona. They built a forty-four-mile, eight-inch pipeline to Valona and thence shipped the crude oil to refineries in Trieste, Leghorn (Livorno), and Bari. Annual production rose from 7,000 barrels in 1926 to 273,000 in 1936, 752,000 in 1938 and 1,659,000 in 1940.

No large industrial establishments existed in Albania prior to World

War II. Instead, there were mostly cottage industries supplementary to agriculture or stock raising, and catering mainly to the needs of the household. Each of the half-dozen leading towns had a flour mill and three or four additional factories, including dairies, cigarette factories, distilleries, brickworks, breweries, fish canneries, wagon works, and soap factories utilizing olive oil.

Transportation facilities were as underdeveloped as industry. On the eve of World War II Albania possessed no railways with the exception of two narrow-gauge lines each less than twenty miles in length. Road building in the modern sense was introduced by Austrian and Italian occupation troops during World War II. The Italians continued the work after the war by providing money and technical help. The road system they developed was designed with strategic as well as economic aims in mind. The main line ran along the coast through Scutari, Durazzo, Tirana, Valona, and Argyrokastron. Also, two lines of good road crossed the country east to west: one in the north from Scutari to Prizren and the other in the center from Tirana to Koritsa. Altogether a total of approximately 500 miles of surfaced road existed by the eve of World War II.

Because of the backwardness of the national economy, Albania's imports consisted largely of manufactured goods. But since agriculture also was at a low level of productivity, it was necessary to import appreciable quanties of wheat, corn, and rice in order to meet the food requirements of the country. In addition, miscellaneous colonial products, such as coffee, sugar, and spices, were imported. Apart from these commodities the imports consisted of manufactured goods, such as machinery, metals, textiles, ceramics, oil products, vehicles, dyestuffs, explosives, chemicals, and paper. These were paid for by the exportation of raw materials—hides, wool, crude oil, asphalt, lumber, livestock, cheese, eggs, olives, and olive oil. Italy far outranked all other countries in Albanian trade, absorbing in 1939 about 65 per cent of Albania's exports and providing about 40 per cent of her imports. Albania's total commerce was extremely low, even when calculated on a per capita basis. This reflected the low productivity and low living standards of the population. In 1936, the sum total of exports and imports divided by the population—in other words, the volume of trade per head of the population—was 2½ times as great in Bulgaria, 1¾ times in Yugoslavia, 7½ times in Greece, and 31 times in Great Britain.

SOCIAL AND CULTURAL DEVELOPMENT

Social conditions and institutions reflected their primitive economic background. The simplest peasant huts comprised a single room with a central hearth and with walls of stone, wood, or earth. Construction differed in various parts of the country, with thick-walled, fortresslike houses prevailing in the north, and lighter houses with more windows in the south. Sleeping bunks and couches were built into the walls and a low ceiling under the gable roof served as a floor to a loft, with access by a ladder. Home industries included basketry, woodwork, spinning, knitting, and weaving of rough cloth. Transportation was by donkeys, mules, and a few horses with wooden pack saddles for goods and travelers alike.

The towns were few and poorly developed, being retarded by the lack of transportation facilties. Consequently they were little more than bazaars for the surrounding countryside. As noted above, they had a few essential industries for the processing of local materials. They also had tanners, potters, coppersmiths, and tinsmiths who met the needs of the local peasantry. The town shops held the reserves of foodstuffs, wool, leather, and manufactured imports. Very important were the guesthouses, cafes, and barber shops, which served as the centers of social life. The outstanding buildings were the mosques, churches, baths, and the private dwellings of officials, merchants, and landowners.

No drainage facilties were available, and water supply was limited to private wells and cisterns and a few public fountains. Only Tirana, Durazzo, and Valona boasted residential suburbs of European layout. The other towns were distinctly Oriental in appearance, with their mosques and bazaars and narrow winding streets, ill-paved and ill-kept. The following population figures of the six largest towns illustrate the retardation of Albania's urban centers.

Town	Population in 1916	Population in 1939
Tirana	1,200	35,000
Scutari	. . .	30,000
Koritsa	10,000	22,500
Elbasan	12,000	14,000
Berat	8,500	11,000
Valona	6,500	10,000
Durazzo	600	9,000

Living standards corresponded to the level of the national economy. Maize bread, cheese, cucumbers, melons, and onions were the staple foods. Meat, eggs, milk, and butter were rarely eaten by the peasants or by the poor in the towns. Such expensive foods could be afforded only by the wealthy few, and what they did not consume was exported abroad to pay for the coffee, sugar, and manufactured goods that were imported.

The poor diet, together with the almost complete lack of public health services, left the population very vulnerable to diseases. The greatest scourge was malaria, which probably was more widespread and devastating than anywhere else in Europe. Tuberculosis, influenza, and syphilis were the other most common diseases. No reliable statistics are available on causes of death because deaths were not always reported and ailments frequently were incorrectly diagnosed.

Education was in a rudimentary state, 85 per cent of the population being illiterate on the eve of World War II. No university existed, so that the few students who could afford higher education were obliged to continue their studies abroad. Albania did not produce a national encyclopedia, a national dictionary, or a translation of the Bible into the native language. Albania, in short, was by all odds the most backward state of Europe, having remained largely outside the streams of Contintental developments and progress.

37. Diplomatic Developments: 1918–1941

The Balkan Peninsula, because of its location at the crossroads of three continents, has oscillated back and forth between foreign domination and varying degrees of independence. For almost five centuries the peninsula was under the rule of the Ottoman Turks. With the decline of Ottoman strength it appeared that Russia and Austria would divide the Balkan lands as they did Poland. This fate was avoided because of various factors, including Austro-Russian rivalry, Western intervention, and Balkan nationalism. Consequently the nineteenth century witnessed the appearance of several Balkan states, some independent and others autonomous. These states, however, were surrounded by the Austrian and Russian empires, which dominated the entire peninsula and owned outright large portions of it, such as Dalmatia, Croatia, Slovenia, Bosnia-Herzegovina, Transylvania, Bukovina, and Bessarabia. Thus millions of South Slav and Rumanian peasants were subjects of the Romanov and Hapsburg dynasties rather than citizens of the small, independent Balkan states.

This half-free, half-subject status of the Balkan peoples changed overnight with the disintegration of the Austrian, Russian, and Ottoman empires during World War I. Out of the imperial ruins emerged Greater Rumania, an enlarged Greece, and the new Yugoslav state. For the first time in history, Balkan frontiers were drawn on the basis of the principle of the self-determination of peoples. The triumph of this revolutionary principle proved possible because of the power vacuum that developed in Southeastern Europe with the collapse of the prewar imperial structures. In other words, the large new Balkan states owed their existence to an unprecedented power vacuum that, by its very nature, was bound to be transitory. It follows that the inevitable revival of Germany and Russia sometime in the future would inexorably undermine the foundations of the new Balkan states.

Theoretically, this Damocles sword could have been banished by the unification of the new states into a bloc sufficiently strong to resist any out-
732

side pressure. In fact, this was precisely the aim of the Little Entente formed by Czechoslovakia, Yugoslavia, and Rumania, and of the Balkan Entente comprising Yugoslavia, Rumania, Greece, and Turkey. President Benes defined the Little Entente as "an organization of Central Europe in which our liberated countries have been their own masters, without the predominating influence or domination of any Great Power." [1] Likewise, the Rumanian foreign minister, Nicholas Titulescu, declared that "thanks to the Balkan Entente the Great Powers would not be able to pit one of us against the other and thus plunge this part of the world into a war which means a greater conflagration than that of 1914." [2]

These expectations that an aggregation of small states would be able to function with the strength and cohesion of a great power proved to be illusory. The Little and Balkan Ententes never withstood the strains for which they were devised. The centrifugal pull of the great powers was too strong. At each critical juncture one or the other of the small states gave preference to its great-power relationships over its relations with its putative allies. Consequently, the decisive aspects of interwar Balkan diplomacy were the Balkan policies of the great powers rather than the relations among the Balkan states. Hence the organization of this chapter, which concerns itself first with the French and Italian alliance systems in Eastern Europe and then, after the fruitless interlude of the Balkan Conferences and Balkan Entente, traces the ascendancy of Germany to the outbreak of World War II and to the occupation of the entire peninsula by the Axis.

FRENCH ALLIANCE SYSTEM: 1920–1927

During the years following the peace settlement France was by far the strongest power on the Continent. No state could challenge her primacy, Germany having been humbled, Italy being torn by domestic strife, Soviet Russia fighting for survival, and Britain remaining aloof. Under these circumstances France now, like Bismarckian Germany after 1870, sought to build up an alliance system to preserve the favorable *status quo*. Renewal of the prewar Russian alliance being out of the question, the only feasible alternative was to link up with the new succession states in Central and Eastern Europe. The latter were as interested as France in preventing both the resurgence of Germany and the spread of Bolshevism.

The succession states did not wait for French initiative before taking steps to preserve the peace settlement. In 1920–1921 Yugoslavia, Rumania, and Czechoslovakia banded together to form the Little Entente, the basic purpose of which was to prevent the Hungarians from upsetting the Trianon Treaty or restoring the Hapsburg dynasty.

The first alliance that France concluded with the new succession states was with Poland in 1921. This remained a key link in the chain of French alliances because Poland was almost twice as large as any other succession state and was indispensable as a barrier to Russia and a counterpoise to Germany. Poland in turn formed an alliance with Rumania in the same year. The two countries were natural allies because both had taken extensive territories from Russia at the end of the war and both were therefore apprehensive of a Russian comeback in the future. Since Poland and Rumania had a common frontier and together stretched from the Baltic to the Black seas, the two countries were holding the neck of Europe against Russian intrusion from the East.

In addition to the tie with Poland, France linked herself with the Little Entente by signing a treaty of friendship and alliance with Czechoslovakia in 1924. France then completed her connections with the Little Entente by concluding alliances with Rumania in 1926 and Yugoslavia in 1927. This series of treaties marked the high point of French ascendancy in the Balkans and Eastern Europe. Henceforth the French alliance system was subjected to steady Italian undermining which unwittingly proved to be the entering wedge for German expansion a decade later.

ITALIAN ALLIANCE SYSTEM: 1926–1930

Italy emerged victorious but embittered from World War I. Turkish nationalism in Asia Minor and President Wilson's opposition in Paris prevented her from acquiring the extensive territories promised in the secret Treaty of London of 1915. During the immediate postwar years, Italy was unable to do much toward satisfying her territorial ambitions because of serious unrest at home. The advent of Mussolini to power in October, 1922, made possible a more vigorous foreign policy. Mussolini silenced all opposition at home and then turned to expansion abroad. Four months after assuming office he declared: "It is necessary to have the courage to say that Italy cannot remain for ever shut up in one sea, even if that sea be the Adriatic. Besides the Adriatic there is the Mediterranean, and there are other seas that may interest us. . . . I need not repeat that Treaties are transactions which represent agreements, points of equilibrium. No Treaty is eternal. . . ." [3]

It will be recalled from Chapter 34 that in September, 1923, Mussolini demonstrated that he was to be taken seriously by bombarding and occupying Corfu island off the west coast of Greece. Although he evacuated the island a month later, his debut in international affairs was not forgotten in Athens, Belgrade, and other Balkan capitals. In fact, it was eastward toward the Balkan Peninsula that Mussolini was looking covetously at this time. "Now Italy can only move in an easterly direction," he declared after the 1924 Fiume Agreement, "the fact being that on the west there are national states which have taken national form and to which we can send nothing except our labour. . . . Therefore the lines for the pacific expansion of Italy lie towards the east." [4]

In seeking to expand eastward Mussolini came into conflict first with Yugoslavia, the large new state across the Adriatic, and ultimately with France, the protectress of the general Continental *status quo*. He combated this opposition by gaining complete domination over Albania and by backing the revisionist states—Austria, Hungary, and Bulgaria. He also resorted to secret subsidizing of fascist and terrorist groups in other countries. In the Balkans he aided the Ustashi in Croatia and the IMRO in Macedonia. As noted in Chapter 33, the latter organization served Mussolini well by conducting raids into Yugoslav and Greek territory and thus eliminating any possibility of Balkan unity that would have blocked his penetration.

In 1929 the leader of the Ustashi, Dr. Ante Pavelich, fled from Yugoslavia to Italy, whence he continued to direct his operations with the cooperation of the IMRO. It was this conspiratorial gang that was responsible for the murder of King Alexander of Yugoslavia in 1934. In the final analysis Mussolini did not have sufficient strength to attain the ambitious goals he set forth in his grandiloquent speeches. Thus his gunrunning and subsidizing of terrorists served only to widen the fissures within and among the Balkan countries, and to contribute substantially to the turbulence of Balkan politics during the interwar period.

Mussolini's diplomacy became overt in 1926, when he rejected a French and Yugoslav proposal for a tripartite treaty to stabilize the Balkans. As noted in Chapter 36, in November of the same year he concluded a treaty with Albania committing the signatories to "mutual support and cordial collaboration," and expressing their common interest in the preservation of the political, juridical, and territorial *status quo* in Albania. The signatories also undertook to refrain from any political or military agreement with a third power prejudicial to the interests of the other. Yugoslavia reacted violently against this pact, pointing out that the guarantee of the political *status quo* gave Italy a basis for complete control over Albania. In June, 1927, Yugoslavia broke off diplomatic relations with Albania and rumors spread of impending war. Five months later, on November 11, 1927, Yugoslavia announced her treaty of friendship with France. Within two months Mussolini countered with the announcement of a new twenty-year military alliance with Albania. Its terms converted Albania into a virtual Italian protectorate and provided Mussolini with a jumping-off place in the Balkan Peninsula.

Italy had considerable influence in Bulgaria as well as in Albania. In August, 1928, Italy sharply refused to join Britain and France in urging the Bulgarian government to curb IMRO activities. In July, 1929, an Italian naval and air squadron paid a visit to Bulgaria, in the course of which General Italo Balbo made a speech encouraging Bulgaria to press her claims to Yugoslav Macedonia. In the spring of 1930 Bulgaria granted Italy a free harbor at Varna and a virtual monopoly of the automobile trade in all of Bulgaria. The high point of this *rapprochement* came in October, 1930, with the marriage of King Boris of Bulgaria with Princess Giovanna of Italy.

It should be noted that Mussolini effected a tie not only with revisionist Bulgaria in the Balkans but also with revisionist Austria and Hungary in Central Europe. The details of Italian diplomacy in the latter region lie outside the scope of this study. Suffice it to note here that the peak of

Italian influence in Central Europe was reached with the signing in 1934 of the Rome Protocols with Austria and Hungary providing for economic cooperation and for consultation on political matters.

Italy completed her diplomatic incursion into the Balkans by negotiating friendship and arbitration treaties with Rumania (September 16, 1926), Turkey (May 10, 1928), and Greece (September 23, 1928). Mussolini had hoped that the last two agreements would lead to a tripartite Italian-Greek-Turkish bloc that would strengthen his position in the eastern Mediterranean. But both Greece and Turkey were wary of the Italian dictator. In fact, Greece used her new tie with Italy to press Yugoslavia into settling the long-standing dispute over the free zone in Saloniki. On March 18, 1929, Greece and Yugoslavia reached an agreement concerning the administration and operation of the free zone. This settlement was not a source of pleasure for Mussolini, who was interested in isolating Yugoslavia from her neighbors. He was also disappointed by the outcome of the Greco-Turkish Treaty of Friendship, Neutrality, and Arbitration signed in October, 1930. This treaty settled several issues that had arisen as a result of the exchange of minorities several years earlier.* Mussolini had encouraged the Greco-Turkish *rapprochment* in order to complete his eastern Mediterranean triangle. But the Greco-Turkish tie, once achieved, proved to be one of the strongest bulwarks of the *status quo* in the Balkans. Neither Greece nor Turkey was willing to allow herself to become the pawn of Mussolini's expansionist strategy.

BALKAN CONFERENCES: 1930–1933

In the early 1930's the outstanding diplomatic development in the Balkans was the attempt to organize a bloc strong enough to resist the pulls and pressures of the great powers. The attempt was made at that time because the agreements reached by Greece, Yugoslavia, and Turkey in 1929 and 1930 had removed major sources of discord. This did not mean that all Balkan problems had been solved. Bulgaria and Greece were still divided over the issue of an outlet to the Aegean. Bulgaria and Rumania were at odds over the treatment of Bulgarians in the Dobruja. Yugoslavia still regarded Albania suspiciously, while France and Italy backed their respective protégés in the peninsula. Nevertheless, inter-Balkan relations were better at the end of 1929 than they had been in years, and this improvement was a factor in the calling of the Balkan conferences.

Another factor was the world-wide economic depression that descended in 1929. We saw in Chapter 31 and later chapters that the Balkan countries, being predominantly agricultural, were particularly hard hit by the disproportionate drop in agricultural prices during the depression. In addition to the drop in prices there was a considerable decline in the quantity of exports. This was due partly to lack of purchasing power and partly to agrarian

* See Chapter 34.

protectionism in Central and Western Europe. Wheat production in France, Germany, Czechoslovakia, and Britain together increased by some 15 per cent between 1925–1929 and 1930–1934, while that of the agrarian countries in Eastern Europe fell appreciably. This situation drove home the lesson that purely national measures were incapable of coping with an international economic crisis. Accordingly eight Eastern European agrarian states—including Bulgaria, Yugoslavia, and Rumania—held two conferences in August and October, 1930 in Warsaw and Bucharest. The aim was to form a customs union that would be able to bargain on equal terms with the industrialized states of Western Europe. A few more conferences were held, but gradually the meetings merged with those of the League of Nations Commission of Inquiry for European Union. Nevertheless, the mere holding of these conferences pointed the way to similar action in the political field.

These circumstances led Alexander Papanastassiou, leader of a small agrarian party and former premier of Greece, to propose a semiofficial conference to consider the possibilities of a Balkan federation. He gained the support of the International Bureau of Peace at Geneva, and the first Balkan Conference met in Athens October 5–13, 1930. The best description of this conference, and of those following, has been given by Papanastassiou.

> Though based on the national groups, composed of politicians, representatives of peace organizations, universities, and professional organizations, and though its decisions do not obligate the governments, this organization has nevertheless an official character, not only because the governments of the six countries support the activities of the national groups, but also because the delegations of each country to the Conferences are chosen after consultation with the government, and these governments are represented at each Conference by their diplomatic officials (who follow the deliberations in the capacity of observers) in the country in which the Conference meets.[5]

A total of four conferences were held, the first, as we have seen, in Athens, the second in Istanbul (October 20–26, 1931), the third in Bucharest (October 22–29, 1932), and the fourth in Saloniki (November 5–11, 1933). The results of these conferences were very similar to those of the League of Nations in Geneva. A number of commissions were established during the conferences to deal with nonpolitical matters such as Communications, Economic Affairs, Intellectual Cooperation, and Social and Health Problems. These commissions prepared a number of valuable and constructive projects, some of which were put into operation. These included the exchange of university professors and students, the establishment of a Balkan Historical Institute and a Balkan Chamber of Commerce and Industry, and the adoption of plans for a Balkan Labor Office and a Postal Union.

In regard to political issues, however, the Balkan Conferences were no more successful than the League of Nations. From the outset the Commission on Political Relations was faced with the task of reconciling sharply conflicting interests and viewpoints. It prepared a Balkan Pact of Nonaggression, but little progress was made toward its adoption. The Bulgarian representatives persistently refused to consider any proposals that involved formal acceptance of the existing frontiers and demanded that the Bulgarian-speaking populations of Greek and Yugoslav Macedonia be granted the minority rights they claimed. Attempts to reconcile the Bulgarians by modifying the provisions of the Nonaggression Pact met with no success. The Bulgarians described their attitude to the pact in the following note to the United States Secretary of State, Cordell Hull:

> In spite of the pressure which has been brought to bear on her, Bulgaria has been unable to see her way to signing a pact which would crystallize for all time the actual *status quo* in the Balkans which has been established mainly at her expense. Bulgaria could see no reason to accord voluntary endorsement to penalties imposed upon her by a dictated peace treaty, and further to aggravate her position by renouncing, without even a hint of compensation, the hope deeply imbedded in the nation's heart for a revision of the Treaty, though by peaceful means.[6]

The basic difficulty was that Bulgaria refused to accept the Neuilly Treaty as final and therefore rejected any pact that involved recognition of the *status quo*. This attitude caused considerable concern to Bulgaria's neighbors. An isolated Bulgaria obviously was no threat, but as long as she refused to accept a nonaggression pact so long she would continue to offer a foothold to any great power desirous of interventing in the Balkans. Nor was this merely a hypothetical danger by 1933. Italy still was very much interested in revisionist Bulgaria. In fact, she had been largely responsible for Bulgaria's negative position at the Balkan Conferences. When Bulgaria celebrated the twenty-fifth anniversary of her independence in October, 1933, Italian spokesmen used the occasion to proclaim their continued support for Bulgaria. Moreover, the rise of Hitler to power and his bellicose statements regarding the Versailles settlement and the need for *Lebensraum* stimulated the revisionist movement throughout Europe and aroused the apprehension of Bulgaria's neighbors. Accordingly, they sought to counter the increased danger by strengthening the ties among themselves.

BALKAN ENTENTE: 1934

Bulgaria's neighbors decided to come to an agreement among themselves in the hope that Bulgaria would join them later to form a Balkan-wide bloc. After negotiations carried on in Geneva and Belgrade, a four-power Balkan Pact—Greece, Yugoslavia, Rumania, and Turkey—was initiated at Belgrade on February 4, 1934, and signed at Athens five days later. The signatories bound themselves to guarantee mutually the security of the existing Balkan frontiers and to consult with one another in case they were threatened. They also undertook not to embark upon any political action in relation to any other Balkan state without the consent of the other signatories. The pact was declared open to any other Balkan countries whose adherence would be "the object of favorable examination by the contracting parties." An additional protocol, the terms of which were not made public for some weeks after signature, declared that the pact was not directed against any power. Its object was to guarantee Balkan frontiers against aggression by a Balkan state, but it would also come into operation against a Balkan state which joined another power in an act of aggression against a signatory.

In October, 1934, the foreign ministers of the four states met at Ankara, where they prepared and adopted the Statutes of the Balkan Entente. They provided for regular meetings of the Permanent Council of the Entente, consisting of the foreign ministers of the member states. They also made plans for economic collaboration, for the establishment of a Balkan Bank, and for integration of legislative activities. The Entente thus was designed to carry on much the same type of work as the Balkan Conferences had in the past, with the important difference that the Permanent Council would be able to make decisions and take action where the Conferences had been only able to make recommendations. This overlapping led to the cancellation of the fifth Balkan Conference, which was to have been held in Istanbul. The Balkan Entente had replaced the Balkan Conference.

The two, however, were not similar. Indeed, the differences between them were fundamental. The Balkan Conference had striven to bring all the Balkan states together on some program, limited though it might be, in the hope that it would be expanded gradually as outstanding issues were settled. The Balkan Entente was more restricted, having been organized for the purpose of maintaining the *status quo* and therefore automatically directed against revisionist Balkan states. Even in regard to this objective the Entente was limited. The Soviet ambassador in Ankara drew attention to the possibility that in the event of hostilities between the Soviet Union and Rumania, Bulgaria might be drawn in on the Russian side, in which case Turkey, by the terms of the pact, would be obliged to support Rumania against Bulgaria and therefore against Russia. Such action on Turkey's part would contravene the Turko-Russian treaty of neutrality of 1925. In order to avoid this difficulty the Rumanian government issued a written declaration to the effect that it would expect no aid from Turkey in the event of a conflict with the Soviet Union. When the terms of the pact were made public, the opposition in Greece, led by Venizelos, attacked the government on the ground that it should have taken similar precautions to ensure that Greece would not become involved in war with Italy as a result of the obligations which she had undertaken in regard to the protection of Yugoslavia's frontiers. In these circumstances the Greek government asked for and received assurances from the other three governments that under no condition would the application of the pact involve Greece in hostilities with a great power. The significance of these reservations lies in the fact that they narrowed the pact to a purely anti-Bulgarian instrument. So long as Bulgaria remained isolated and the great powers refrained from military or diplomatic intervention in the Balkans, the Entente could operate effectively. To state these conditions is to reveal the futility of the pact. The Entente was to prove as short-lived as the first Balkan alliance of the 1860's and the second of 1912–1913.*

BALKAN ENTENTE UNDERMINED: 1934–1937

The Entente began to show signs of cracking almost as soon as it was organized. The principal reason was the pressure of resurgent Germany. Hitler's success in rearming Germany, first clandestinely and later in open defiance of the treaties, was the first shock for the Balkan allies. More serious was the reoccupation and refortification of the Rhineland in 1936, which effectively isolated both the Balkan and Little Ententes from France. At the same time Germany was rapidly extending her economic influence throughout Southeastern Europe. The percentage of Hungarian, Yugoslav, Rumanian, Bulgarian, and Greek imports from Germany rose from 19.5 in 1933 to 35 in 1937, while the percentage of their exports to Germany increased during the same period from 16 to 27. Moreover, the exports of these countries to Germany were considerably greater than their imports, so they found themselves tied by a double bond to Germany—as the principal market for their products and as a debtor who would liquidate his debts only with exports. This German economic hegemony, which became increasingly pronounced during the late 1930's, inevitably had diplomatic repercussions. The Balkan countries could not afford to antagonize their principal customer because, as noted in Chapter 31, there was none other able or willing to purchase their goods.

These developments altered fundamentally the balance of forces in Central and Eastern Europe and thereby undermined both the Balkan and Little Ententes. The new situation has been analyzed aptly as follows:

The five South-East European anti-revisionist states, in their relations with one another, were now faced with the question whether a pair of ententes which had originally been made mainly with an eye to Hungary and Bulgaria should be built into a larger structure of alliances covering Europe as a whole and involving the risk of a collision not only with Hungary and Bulgaria but also with Italy and Germany, or whether the original arrangements would cease to be operative, even within their narrow regional limits, now that the two local vortices of post-war political disturbances round Hungary and round Bulgaria were being caught up into a maelstrom of European dimensions.[7]

It was the latter course which was adopted, particularly when it became apparent that the Western powers were unwilling or unable to oppose effectively German and Italian aggression. As each crisis arose, one after another of the Balkan states hastened to loosen their ties with the threatened country, and thereby, as events were to prove, ensured their own ultimate destruction.

The first blow was the assassination of King Alexander of Yugo-

* See Chapters 21 and 28.

slavia at Marseilles on October 9, 1934. It was quickly established that the assassins were members of the IMRO and of the fascist Croatian Ustashi organization. For years they had been subsidized by the Italian and Hungarian governments. In fact, two of those implicated in the crime sought refuge in Italy, where the fascist government refused their extradition. Feeling ran high in Yugoslavia, but the French government, wishing at all costs to reach an agreement with Italy against the rising German menace, put pressure on Yugoslavia to adopt a conciliatory attitude. Thus the affair was glossed over in the League Council, to which it was referred. Nevertheless, the death of Alexander was a serious setback for the Balkan and Little Ententes and for the entire French alliance system, which the Yugoslav king had consistently supported.

The next blow suffered by the Balkan Entente was Mussolini's conquest of Ethiopia in 1935–1936 despite League of Nations sanctions. All the members of the Entente applied the sanctions and suffered heavy economic losses in the process, particularly Yugoslavia and Rumania. Furthermore, the Entente members, together with France, entered into a reciprocal undertaking with Britain providing for mutual aid in case any signatory were attacked by Italy because of the application of sanctions. Despite these sacrifices and commitments, Mussolini had his way in Ethiopia and the League was forced to drop the sanctions in the early summer of 1936.

The Ethiopian fiasco had important consequences in the Balkan Peninsula. It demonstrated to the Entente members that they could not rely upon the League of Nations for security against aggression. It also revealed the weakness and vacillation of Britain and France, who had been primarily responsible for the failure to impose adequate sanctions against Italy. Finally, the Ethiopian War weakened the ties between France and her allies in Central and Eastern Europe because Hitler took advantage of the general preoccupation with Ethiopia to reoccupy the demilitarized Rhineland on March 7, 1936. The Western powers again failed to take action, so Hitler proceeded to fortify the Rhineland by constructing the Siegfried Line. This development altered fundamentally the European balance of power. Heretofore the Little and Balkan Ententes had calculated that if the Reichswehr struck to the southeast, its right flank would be exposed to a French counterattack across the Rhineland and southern Germany. Now, however, the German armies could operate with impunity behind the protecting Siegfried Line. What this meant for Central Europe and the Balkans was stated frankly at the time by the French foreign minister, Pierre-Étienne Flandin: "French alliance with the Little Entente was now valueless. In the future France could not hope to give effective assistance to Poland, Czechoslovakia, Yugoslavia or Rumania, in the event of German aggression. . . . In my opinion, the last chance of saving central and eastern Europe from German domination has been thrown away." [8]

The proceedings of the Balkan Entente Conference held in Belgrade May 4–6, 1936, reflected the new international situation. The main concern of the Entente members now was to make certain that their obligations would not involve them in a war with a great power. General Metaxas was particularly insistent on this point because the problem of obligations under the pact had become a political issue in Greece. The opposition was charging that Greece had been secretly committed to action in case of an Italian attack upon Yugoslavia, a contingency which at the time did not seem at all improbable. Consequently Metaxas, with the support of the Turkish representatives, sought to limit the obligations of the Entente members as much as possible. Despite strong opposition from Yugoslavia and Rumania, the Greco-Turkish viewpoint prevailed. It was agreed that the liability for mutual defense should be limited to purely Balkan exigencies and that in all other cases the obligations of the Entente members should be restricted to the action required by the League Covenant. When the conference ended, Metaxas significantly remarked that "the Entente has now become more diplomatic than military." [9]

The reoccupation of the Rhineland in March, 1936, had further repercussions in the Balkans. Only four months later, in July, 1936, Turkey secured the right to fortify her Straits. Turkey had raised this demand regularly since 1933, and now she had her way by the provisions of the Montreux Convention, which replaced the Lausanne Treaty of 1923.* The Montreux Conference, like the earlier one at Lausanne, developed into a conflict of interests between Russia and Britain, but with the difference that France now was on the Russian side. Russia wanted egress from the Straits for the purpose of securing her communications with her French ally. Britain wished to obtain compensation for permission to Russia to send her fleet into the Mediterranean, which would affect the balance of power in that sea. But Britain was isolated at Montreux; hence the resulting convention represented a balance between the national security of Turkey and the power interests of Russia. The new provisions laid down by the Montreux Convention were these: (1) The principle of freedom of passage for merchant vessels through the Straits was reaffirmed. (2) Non–Black Sea powers might send only light surface vessels into the Black Sea, with a limitation on their aggregate tonnage; but Black Sea powers might send capital ships of any size into the Mediterranean. (3) The International Straits Commission was abolished and its functions were transfered to Turkey. (4) Turkey was allowed to close the Straits in time of war or of an imminent threat of war. (5) Turkey was given permission to remilitarize the Straits immediately.

The resurgence of Germany and the discrediting of the League principle of collective security affected Central Europe as well as the Balkans. The first indication was the dismissal of the veteran Rumanian foreign minister, Nicholas Titulescu, on August 29, 1936, long known as an ardent Francophile and as a supporter of the League and of the two Ententes. His dismissal foreshadowed a fundamental shift in Rumanian foreign policy.

* See Chapter 30.

Rumania at this time was torn between two possible courses of action. The first, dictated by the needs of the Little Entente and the German threats to Czechoslovakia, involved an alliance with Russia, the powerful ally of the French and the Czechs. This was the policy advocated and pursued by Titulescu. The alternative course was a conciliatory attitude toward Germany and Italy, and a closer relationship with Poland, the latter country having drifted away from France and followed an independent course since concluding a nonaggression pact with Germany in January, 1934. Arguments for this alternative policy included the fear of Russian designs upon Bessarabia and the danger of becoming a corridor for Russian armies marching to the relief of Czechoslovakia. The dismissal of Titulescu and the appointment of Victor Antonescu to his position was a clear indication that Rumania had selected the latter course.

Antonescu, it is true, emphasized that Rumanian policy would not be altered. But more significant than his assurances was the marked strengthening of Polish-Rumanian ties. During the autumn of 1936 a number of visits were exchanged between political and military leaders, and agreements were signed for technical and cultural cooperation and for "close military collaboration" between the two countries. In view of the Polish-German Nonaggression Pact and the well-known hostility between Poland and Czechoslovakia, the *rapprochement* of Rumania and Poland naturaly raised doubts regarding Rumania's position in the Little Entente and her commitments to Czechoslovakia. Certainly by the end of 1936 Rumania's position had shifted considerably from the days when Titulescu had so actively espoused the principle of the "indivisibility of peace."

The slackening of the Little Entente ties was manifested at the Bratislava Conference of the Entente Council held on May 7–8, 1936. The council announced that greater elasticity had been agreed upon in relation to extra-Danubian affairs. Unable to reconcile the divergent attitudes of its members, the council decided that Czechoslovakia's treaty with the Soviet Union should involve no obligation upon Rumania and Yugoslavia, and that the latter countries should be free to assume any attitude they wished toward Germany and Italy. The final step in the disintegration of the Little Entente was reached at the conference held in Belgrade in April, 1937. Czechoslovakia, in mortal danger from Germany, proposed enlarging the military clauses of the pact to include a guarantee of full military assistance in case of aggression from any quarter. Rumania and Yugoslavia rejected this proposal and thereby sealed the fate of the Little Entente.

The shift of Rumanian foreign policy under Antonescu was paralleled by a more marked shift of Yugoslav foreign policy under Milan Stoyadinovich. More than any other Balkan country, Yugoslavia feared Italy's ambitions in the Balkans, especially after the Ethiopian affair. Yet the decisions of the Belgrade Conference of the Balkan Entente in May, 1936, eliminated any likelihood of aid for Yugoslavia in case of an Italian attack. Accordingly, Premier Stoyadinovich, in the face of strong popular opposition, abandoned the traditional pro-French policy, which had been followed by Alexander, and came to terms with Bulgaria and Italy. On January 24, 1937, he signed the pact with Bulgaria which provided simply that "there shall be inviolable peace and perpetual friendship between Bulgaria and Yugoslavia." Nothing at all was said either about renunciation of territorial demands or about Bulgarian entry into the Balkan Entente.

Much more disturbing was the Italo-Yugoslav agreement of March 25, 1937. Czechoslovakia and the members of the Balkan Entente had been informed as to the general conditions, but under Italian pressure the treaty had been rushed through before its final text could be communicated to Yugoslavia's allies in accordance with the procedure laid down in the statutes of the Little and Balkan Ententes. Both countries agreed not to attack each other, to remain neutral in case of unprovoked attack by a third power, and to consult on matters affecting their common interests. Italy made substantial commercial concessions, extending to Yugoslavia the tariff proferences hitherto reserved for Austria and Hungary under the Rome protocols, and doubling the Yugoslav export quota. It also promised to ameliorate the lot of the Croat-Slovene minority in Italian Istria and to refrain from encouraging the Croat terrorist Ustashi. In return, Yugoslavia recognized the Ethiopian Empire, made a reciprocal pledge to prevent anti-Italian activities within its borders, agreed to increase imports of Italian goods, and promised to respect the existing frontiers of Albania.

These terms were favorable to Yugoslavia. Yet Stoyadinovich encountered much opposition from his compatriots and from his allies in the two Ententes. Yugoslav democratic elements viewed the treaty as a short-sighted desertion of the Western liberal camp for the sake of immediate temporary gains. Likewise, the Belgrade Conference of the Little Entente (April, 1937) criticized Stoyadinovich for concluding the pact without previous consultation and for starting a system of bilateral accords that were contrary to the spirit of the two Ententes. In retrospect it does appear that the Italo-Yugoslav treaty is significant as a symptom of a general European trend from collective security to bilateral pacts. Indeed, it may be said that it reflected the general decline of Western democratic prestige. This is startlingly evident in the following explanation that Stoyadinovich gave to Ciano concerning his new foreign policy:

> We do not and have not received anything from France. Economically she is a zero for Yugoslavia. We have contracted several debts in France and we are repaying them at a usurious rate. Militarily she, together with Czechoslovakia, has been our principal supplier of armaments. But she has not given us a single bayonet as a gift. We have paid for what we have received. . . .
>
> I should add that the cultural and moral influence that France has exercised in our country has been truly pernicious and divisive. Their press and literature are expressions of the Jewish, Masonic, and communistic mentality of Blum's France. . . .
>
> Should Germany attack Czechoslovakia we would, with weak and uncer-

tain help from Rumania, be obliged to invade Hungary in order to help the Czechs. Even if we could occupy Hungary completely (and I consider this highly difficult), we would arrive at the Czech borders only in time to meet with the remnants of the defeated Czech armies. Behind us would be Hungary, occupied but hostile. Before us the victorious German armies. A most unpleasant situation, this, and a risk that we cannot inflict upon the Yugoslav people. . . . While relations between Yugoslavia and Rumania will remain unchanged—that is, loyal and cordial, those between these two and Czechoslovakia will be reduced to the level of an empty formality. . . .

I do not have any regard for the League of Nations. I am a member and must continue to be a member, more because of public opinion and inertia than because of my personal conviction. . . . The pact that I signed with you . . . is most assuredly a pact outside and perhaps even against the League of Nations, and constitutes proof of my scant sympathy for Geneva.[10]

GERMAN ASCENDANCY: 1938–1939

During the year 1938 both the Balkan and the Little Ententes were crippled by the German annexation of Austria and of the Sudetan regions of Czechoslovakia. Only a few years earlier Yugoslavia had warned that if any power intervened in Austria she would do likewise. But now, in March, 1938, Austria disappeared completely from the map of Europe without a single protest from any of the great powers. Under the circumstances the Yugoslav government felt constrained to announce that it "held the point of view that the Austrian question was an internal German affair." [11] Despite this formal disavowal of interest, the fact remained that the *Anschluss* altered drastically the strategic situation in Central and Southeastern Europe. Hitler now was in a position to isolate Czechoslovakia and to dominate the Danube Valley. Mastery of Vienna gave him control of the main communication routes to the Balkan Peninsula and brought him to the frontiers of Italy, Hungary, and Yugoslavia.

The significance of these facts could not be overlooked by the Balkan states. They tried to cope with the rising tide of revisionism by coming to terms with Bulgaria. On July 31, 1938, the president of the Entente Council signed a Treaty of Friendship and Nonaggression with the Bulgarian foreign minister by which the allies recognized Bulgaria's right to rearm and agreed that the clauses of the Lausanne Convention providing for the demilitarization of the frontiers between Bulgaria, Greece, and Turkey should be allowed to lapse. In return, Bulgaria agreed not to attempt to change her existing frontiers by force and to submit all disputes with her neighbors to arbitration or judicial settlement. It is interesting to note that the agreement said nothing about the permanence of the territorial *status quo* or about Bulgarian membership in the Entente.

The partitioning of Czechoslovakia in the fall of 1938 disrupted the Little Entente and threatened the Balkan Entente. The members of the latter organization held conferences in November, 1938, and February, 1939, but could think of nothing to do. They realized that some move was necessary to appease Bulgarian revisionism, but they were afraid to make any concession lest the situation pass beyond their control. King Carol, for example, contended that if he satisfied Bulgaria's demands for Dobruja he would leave his country open to similar demands from Hungary and Russia. The truth of the matter, however, is that the basic issue no longer was Bulgaria. Rather, it was the struggle between the great powers, which rapidly was involving the entire Continent. It is conceivable, though improbable, that a genuine Balkan agreement of the type envisaged by the Balkan Conference, including all the Balkan states and based on the principle of the Balkans for the Balkan peoples, might have succeeded in keeping the peninsula out of the maelstrom. Certainly this could not have been accomplished by the Balkan Entente as it was constituted in 1939. Thus in the last few months before the outbreak of World War II the decisive factor was the battle for influence in the Balkans waged by Germany and Italy on the one hand and Britain and France on the other.

First Germany followed up the partitioning of Czechoslovakia in November, 1938, by taking over the entire country on March 15, 1939. Several days later, on March 23, Germany imposed on Rumania a treaty that subordinated Rumania's economy to that of the Reich. As described in Chapter 36, within another fortnight, on April 7, Mussolini sent his legions into Albania, completing his hold over the country that he had dominated for more than a decade. Britain and France retaliated on April 13 with unilateral guarantees of the independence of Rumania and Greece. On May 12 a joint declaration was issued in London and Ankara that, pending the conclusion of a formal agreement, the British and Turkish governments would aid each other in case of an act of aggression leading to war in the Mediterranean area. A similar Franco-Turkish declaration was issued on June 24. These preliminary arrangements were replaced on October 19 by a fifteen-year mutual-aid pact signed by Britain, France, and Turkey.

Meanwhile Hitler had concluded his nonaggression pact with Stalin on August 23. On September 1 he invaded Poland and thereby precipitated World War II. The extent to which the Balkan states were helpless victims in the face of these unfolding events is dramatically revealed in the following extemporaneous address that Hitler delivered to his generals when he was about to sign the pact with Stalin.

> I have decided to go with Stalin. On the whole there are only three great statesmen in the world: Stalin, myself and Mussolini. Mussolini, the weakest, has not been able to break either the power of the crown or that of the church. Stalin and I are the only ones who see only the future. So I shall shake hands with Stalin within a few weeks on the common German-Russian border and undertake with him a new distribution of the world.[12]

BALKAN ENTENTE DESTROYED: 1939–1940

That the Balkan states managed to remain out of the world war for several months after it began was due not to their strength or skill but rather to the fortunate accident that it did not suit the interests of any of the belligerents at this time to extend hostilities to the peninsula. The German-Russian Nonaggression Pact, however, contained the seeds of future conflict over the Balkans. The pact required the signatories to refrain from aggression against each other, either individually or in alliance with other powers. It also stipulated that each party remain neutral in case the other were attacked by a third power. Issues arising between the two signatories were to be settled by arbitration and the treaty was to remain in force for ten years.

These were the terms made public to the world. But on the same day, August 23, 1939, Molotov and Ribbentrop signed a "Secret Additional Protocol" defining spheres of influence "in the event of a territorial and political rearrangement" in Eastern Europe. Russia was to have Finland, Estonia, Latvia, eastern Poland, and the Rumanian province of Bessarabia. To Germany fell Lithuania and the rest of Poland.

The significance of this demarcation line dividing Eastern Europe between Germany and Russia is that it stopped at the Danube. It was not carried beyond into the Balkan Peninsula because neither Germany nor Russia wished at this time to be involved in that region. Furthermore, Italy now declared her neutrality because of her military unpreparedness. This left no one to molest the Balkan states, which thus gained a reprieve of several months.

During this period of peace there was considerable diplomatic activity in the Balkans. Italy was concerned about the possibility of Russian penetration across the Danube and tried to organize Hungary, Rumania, and Yugoslavia into a defensive bloc. Likewise, Turkey tried to combine with Greece, Bulgaria, and Rumania to form a group under Allied auspices. Neither of these efforts succeeded and they were abandoned when Russia turned her back upon the Balkans in December, 1939, to wage war against Finland.

A few months later, on February 2–4, 1940, the Balkan Entente held a meeting in Belgrade. The delegates confined themselves to platitudinous remarks about their desire for neutrality and peace. More significant was their failure to reach an agreement for effective mutual aid in case of attack from without. Accordingly, it was tacitly agreed that it was up to the various members to deal individually with the great powers in order to preserve their neutrality. The Balkan Entente had become a paper organization lacking unity, independence, and effectiveness.

This was demonstrated all too clearly when the Soviet Union and Italy intervened in the Balkans in the summer and fall of 1940. The Soviet Union moved first, impelled by the spectacular German conquest of France in May and June, 1940. The Russians had already exploited their pact with Germany to acquire eastern Poland, the Baltic states, and strategic bits of

Finnish territory. Now the Russians set out to strengthen their position in the Balkans as a counterweight to the German successes in the West. On June 24, 1940, they resumed diplomatic relations with Yugoslavia after a lapse of over twenty years, thereby emphasizing their interest in Balkan affairs. A day earlier Molotov informed the German ambassador of his intention to take not only Bessarabia, already assigned to Russia by the 1939 treaty, but also Bukovina, a province which had never belonged to Russia. The German government expressed surprise at this additional claim, but an agreement was reached when Molotov decided to demand only the northern part of the province which was inhabited predominantly by Ukrainians. On June 26 the Soviet government addressed a twenty-four-hour ultimatum to Bucharest demanding the surrender of Bessarabia and of northern Bukovina. King Carol's advisers were divided in the face of this emergency. Professor Iorga, for example, urged resistance, while Iuliu Maniu favored compliance in order to be free to face Hungarian demands for his native Transylvania. When Germany and Italy both advised acceptance of the ultimatum, Carol decided to surrender. Thus the Russians gained considerable territory, pushed the frontier a safe distance away from Odessa, and also gained access to the Danube River.

The loss of Bessarabia and nothern Bukovina started the dismemberment of Rumania. Hungary demanded Transylvania and Bulgaria the Dobruja. Meanwhile Rumania had reacted to her loss of territory by turning to Germany. A new pro-Nazi government had withdrawn from the League of Nations, expressed sympathy for the ideals of the Nazi-dominated "New Europe," and dismissed British managers and engineers from the Rumanian oil fields. These developments posed a serious dilemma for Germany. She approved of the new Rumanian government and highly prized Rumania's resources. She therefore wished to spare Rumania as far as possible. On the other hand, she also had to give some support to Bulgaria and Hungary in order to assure their loyalty to the Axis. Germany and Italy at first encouraged the three Balkan governments to negotiate an agreement by themselves. The ensuing talks failed and rising nationalist feeling in Rumania opposed the cession of more territory. The Axis was alarmed at the prospect of a Balkan war that could end in the destruction of the valuable Rumanian oil fields. To forestall such a disaster the Axis intervened and dictated its Vienna Award on August 30, 1940. This partitioned Transylvania along an east-west line, the northern part going to Hungary. About one million Hungarians and over a million Rumanians came under Hungarian rule, while over half a million Hungarians were left in Rumania. A week later, on September 7, Rumania was obliged to cede to Bulgaria southern Dobruja, a province with a predominantly Bulgarian population of 400,000.

In two months Rumania had lost more than a third of her territory and some three million Rumanians as well as about two million subjects of non-Rumanian national origin. This wholesale dismemberment provoked a violent reaction within the country. King Carol abdicated in favor of his son

Michael and fled the country ignominiously on September 6. An authoritarian regime was established under General Ion Antonescu, who became the Rumanian Duce or "Conducator." The fascist Iron Guard now became the only legal political organization in the country.

These developments in Rumania put an end to the Balkan Entente for all practical purposes. Rumania had received no support from her Balkan allies in the same manner that Czechoslovakia earlier had been abandoned by her Little Entente partners. Rumania now turned her back on her Balkan neighbors and entered the Axis camp. When the Axis Powers issued the Vienna Award they agreed at the same time to guarantee the integrity of Rumanian territory. General Antonescu accepted this guarantee and made it clear against whom it was directed when, on September 6, 1940, he defined Rumanian policy as follows: "Rumania, on her own initiative, has entered the political sphere of Germany and Italy. Consequently it is not permissible to attack the Axis Powers in any way. With regard to the Western Powers an attitude of reserve must be maintained, with the limits of objective information." [13]

HITLER'S FATEFUL DECISION: JULY 31, 1940

The developments in Rumania not only marked the end of the Balkan League; much more important, they reflected a fateful decision made by Hitler a few months earlier on July 31, 1940. On that date the Fuehrer held a conference with his top army and navy commanders. He was advised that a successful invasion of Britain that fall was highly improbable. Hitler then made his momentous decision to invade Russia the following spring. He reached his decision through the following reasoning:

In the event that invasion [of England] does not take place, our action must be directed to eliminate all factors that let England hope for a change in the situation. . . . *Britain's hope lies in Russia and the United States.* If Russia drops out of the picture America, too, is lost for Britain, because elimination of Russia would tremendously increase *Japan's power* in the Far East. . . . *Russia is the factor on which Britain is relying the most.* . . . *With Russia smashed, Britain's last hope will be shattered.* Germany then will be master of Europe and the Balkans.

Decision: Russia's destruction must therefore be made a part of this struggle. Spring 1941.

The sooner Russia is crushed, the better. Attack achieves its purpose only if Russian state can be shattered to its roots with one blow. . . . If we start in May 41, we would have five months to finish the job in.[14]

The decision to invade Russia had important consequences for the Balkan countries. It is frequently asserted that Russian-German differences in the Balkans brought the two countries to war in 1941. The sequence appears to have been precisely the opposite. First Hitler decided to attack Russia because a cross-Channel invasion appeared too hazardous. Then in preparing for the campaign in the east he took various steps in the Balkans that antagonized the Russians. One of these steps was the Vienna Award and the Axis guarantee of Rumania's integrity. The Soviet government complained that it should have been informed about the Vienna negotiations and that the guarantee to Rumania was unnecessary. More serious for the Russians was the dispatch of German troops to Rumania in October, 1940. Berlin informed Moscow that these were "training troops" being sent to "instruct" the Rumanian army. But at the same time a secret German order stated that the "real task" of the troops was to prepare the Rumanian army to participate in the forthcoming invasion of the Soviet Union.

At this point, when Hitler was occupying Rumania, Mussolini launched his blundering invasion of Greece. This ill-fated move was to force Hitler to undertake a Balkan campaign and thus to postpone his attack on Russia from the spring to the summer of 1941.

ITALIAN-GREEK WAR: 1940–1941

On October 28, 1940, the Italian ambassador in Athens demanded of Premier Metaxas that Italian troops be allowed to occupy "certain strategic points on Greek territory." He warned that any resistance would be "crushed by force of arms." [15] Metaxas rejected the ultimatum and the Italo-Greek War began.

Only four months earlier, when Mussolini had attacked France on June 10, 1940, he had proclaimed to the world: "I declare categorically that Italy has not the slightest desire to draw into the conflict any other nation. . . . Let Switzerland, Yugoslavia, Greece, Turkey and Egypt mark my words." [16] Various factors explain why Mussolini forgot so quickly this assurance of peace and declared war against Greece. One was his disappointing experience in France. He had hoped to win glory and territory at the expense of that country but Hitler had vetoed his demands. The Fuehrer wished to use the French colonies and the French navy against the British and he feared that if he allowed Mussolini a free hand the colonies and the navy might go over to the Free French forces of General de Gaulle. In addition to this frustration, Mussolini had been alienated by Hitler's sweeping successes and highhanded methods. Although they were supposedly allies, Hitler had gone on from triumph to triumph without consulting or notifying his Italian partner. The latest case had been the occupation of Rumania early in October, 1940. "Hitler always faces me with a *fait accompli,*" complained Mussolini to Ciano. "This time I am going to pay him back in his own coin. He will find out from the papers that I have occupied Greece. In this way the equilibrium will be reestablished." Ciano commented in his diary: "The Duce seems determined to act now. In fact, I believe that the miltary operation will be useful and easy." [17]

The Italians thus undertook their Greek adventure with the hope that it would offer a way out of their difficulties. In Greece they expected to save face, to regain prestige, and also to acquire valuable bases that would make

Britain's position in the eastern Mediterranean very difficult. Furthermore, Mussolini's advisers assured him that there would be no serious opposition. General Visconti Frasca reported: "We should be able to take care of the Greek forces . . . and complete the occupation of the region [Epirus] in ten days or two weeks." When Mussolini asked him, "What do you know about the morale of the Greek army?" the general replied, "They don't like to fight. We've planned our operation so as to impress them with the fact that we can crush them within the space of a few days." [18]

Thus assured, the Italians began to manufacture incidents, going so far as to bomb and torpedo Greek warships in Greek ports. Since Athens refused to be provoked, there followed the ultimatum and the declaration of war on October 28, 1940. From the outset Mussolini's Greek adventure proved to be ill-fated. His troops expected a triumphal procession to Athens but experienced a very different reception. After pushing some distance across the Greek-Albanian frontier they suffered a decisive defeat at the battle of Metsovo on November 11. The crack Italian Alpine "Iulia" division, counting on its tanks and supporting air force, had advanced along the valleys toward Metsovo without bothering to occupy some higher positions on their rear. Greek mountain regiments made a forced night march and occupied the heights overlooking the Italians in the valleys. At dawn they swooped down and, after some hard fighting, the Italians broke and fled.

The Metsovo battle served as the model for future Greek victories. Taking advantage of the difficulties of the ponderous Italian armored divisions in the mountains of Epirus, the Greeks invariably made for the high ground and from there cut off and surrounded the enemy below. By mid-November they had driven the Italians back across the frontier into Albania. On November 22 the Greeks captured Koritsa, the third largest town in Albania and defended by six Italian divisions totaling seventy-two thousand men. The Greeks also took Argyrokastron, the fortified base of the Italian Eleventh Army, as well as the port and naval base of Santi Quaranta, which in happier times the Italians had renamed Porto Edda, in honor of Mussolini's daughter, Countess Ciano.

Mussolini suffered not only humiliating military defeat but also diplomatic failure. Before beginning the invasion Mussolini had tried to reach an agreement with Yugoslavia and Bulgaria for the partitioning of Greece. Yugoslavia and Bulgaria had no desire to be surrounded by Fascist Italy, so they rejected the overture and warned Athens of what was afoot. After the defeat of the Italians in Greece Hitler revived the plan for a joint partitioning of Greece. "Yugoslavia should have Salonica," the Fuehrer told Ciano, "Bulgaria, her outlet to the Aegean, and Italy the rest of Greece." [19] But the South Slavs were even less disposed to accept this scheme now that Italy had been driven back into Albania. Instead of attacking Greece, Yugoslavia concluded a nonaggression and friendship treaty with Hungary on December 12, 1940. The signatories of this pact hoped to extend it later into a neutral bloc including Bulgaria, Turkey, and possibly Greece if the Italo-Greek War ended in a negotiated peace.

Not only did Mussolini and Hitler fail to unite the Balkans against Greece; they saw their archenemy, Britain, gain a foothold in the peninsula. Britain had guaranteed the independence of Greece on April 13, 1939, at the time that Italy invaded Albania. Consequently, Churchill promised full support to Greece when Metaxas appealed for aid following the Italian invasion. As a matter of fact, the British strengthened their position in the eastern Mediterranean substantially by securing permission to land forces on the strategic Greek islands of Crete and Lemnos. In return, the British sent to Greece five squadrons of bomber and fighter planes which bombarded Albanian ports and Italian communications.

Mussolini found humiliating defeat in Greece in place of the glory he had expected. Amid these disasters Mussolini instructed his ambassador in Berlin, Dino Alfieri, to report to Rome. Alfieri has left a vivid description of Mussolini as he saw him early in December, 1940:

> I found the Duce plunged in the depths of depression. I had never before seen him looking so dispirited. His face was pale and drawn, his eyes swollen and tired, his expression sad and preoccupied. He looked all the more dejected inasmuch as he was wearing a shirt with a grotesquely large turn-down collar, and he had not shaved for at least two days.[20]

OPERATIONS MARITA AND BARBAROSSA: DECEMBER, 1940

Mussolini had called Alfieri to discuss the advisibility of requesting Germany to mediate between Italy and Greece. Hitler, however, did not need to be asked to intervene in the Balkans. He was being forced to do so as a result of his decision in July, 1940, to invade Russia. He had sent troops to Rumania in October, 1940, in preparation for the invasion. Now he could not sit back and allow Britain to consolidate her foothold in Greece. To have done so would have created an intolerable threat to his right flank when his armies marched eastward. He would have been risking a repetition of the 1918 Allied offensive from Saloniki. This, then, was one reason why Hitler decided to send his armies into the Balkans in the spring of 1941 before undertaking the Russian campaign. Certainly he was not motivated by sentiments of loyalty to Mussolini. According to Field Marshal Wilhelm Keitel, "Hitler was extremely angry about . . . the dragging of the Balkans into the war and only the fact that Italy was an ally prevented a break with Mussolini." [21]

Hitler was also impelled to intervene in the Balkans because of increasing friction with the Soviet Union over that region. This was manifested during Molotov's visit to Berlin on November 12, 1940. The Germans had invited Molotov in order to assuage the Soviets, who had reacted frigidly to the signing of the German-Italian-Japanese Tripartite Pact on September 27,

1940. Hitler did not expect his conversations with Molotov to affect his plans to attack Russia. On the eve of Molotov's arrival he ordered that "regardless of what outcome these conversations will have, all preparations for the East already orally ordered, are to be continued." [22]

Hitler did not expect anything from Molotov's visit nor did he make any serious effort to reach an agreement with the Soviet foreign minister. Churchill has noted and emphasized this point clearly. "The Berlin conversations made no difference to Hitler's deep resolve. . . . Hitler's heart was set on destroying the Bolsheviks, for whom his hatred was mortal. He believed that he had the force to gain his main life-aim. . . . He must have known . . . that the proposals which he made [to Molotov] fell far short of Russian ambitions." [23]

Hitler proposed to Molotov that Russia join the Tripartite Pact of Germany, Italy, and Japan for the purpose of partitioning the British Empire—"a gigantic world-wide estate in bankruptcy of 40 million square kilometers." Molotov replied that Russia had no objection in principle to associating herself with such an undertaking but first "there were issues to be clarified regarding Russia's Balkan and Black Sea interests with respect to Bulgaria, Rumania and Turkey." [24] On November 25 Moscow submitted proposals that defined precisely Russia's claims. So far as the Balkans were concerned, Moscow demanded "the establishment of a base for land and naval forces of the U.S.S.R. within range of the Bosporus and the Dardanelles by means of a long-term lease." Moscow also required that Germany and Italy should recognize that "Bulgaria is geographically located inside the security zone of the Black Sea boundaries of the Soviet Union and that it is therefore a political necessity that a mutual assistance pact be concluded between the Soviet Union and Bulgaria which in no way shall affect the internal regime of Bulgaria, her sovereignty or independence." [25]

Hitler made no effort to negotiate on the basis of the Moscow proposals. As Churchill has observed, "No effective answer was returned to this document. No attempt was made by Hitler to split the difference. Issues so grave as these might well justify a prolonged and careful study in a friendly spirit by both sides. The Soviets certainly expected and awaited an answer." [26] No answer was forthcoming, the basic reason being that Hitler had in mind not a compromise settlement but rather his July decision to invade Russia. Preparations for the invasion had been continued uninterruptedly, and now, in December, 1940, a month after Molotov's departure, he issued directives for the invasion of the Balkans and then of Russia.

Since the issuance of the directives followed the failure of the Molotov negotiations it appears superficially that a causal relationship exists between the two events. It would be more correct, however, to say that both the failure of the negotiations and the issuance of the directives were the direct and logical result of Hitler's original decision to turn from the English Channel to the Russian plains. Hitler's resolve to carry through his decision was fortified by his apprehension concerning Britain's foothold in Greece and by his suspicion, after Molotov's demands, that the Kremlin intended to establish control of Bulgaria and Turkey and then, perhaps, to join forces with the British to encircle the Reich. Under these circumstances Hitler issued his directives for Operation Marita and Operation Barbarossa—directives that were to prove so fateful not only for the Balkans but also for Europe and indeed, the whole world.

December 13, 1940. Directive No. 20. Operation Marita. Because of a dangerous situation in Albania it is doubly necessary that the British endeavor be foiled to create air bases under the protection of a Balkan front, which would be dangerous above all to Italy as well as to the Rumanian oil fields.

My plan, therefore, is (a) to form a slowly increasing task force in Southern Rumania within the next months. (b) after the setting in of favorable weather, probably in March, to send the task force for the occupation of the Aegean North coast by way of Bulgaria, and if necessary to occupy the entire Greek mainland.[27]

December 18, 1940. Directive No. 21. Operation Barbarossa. The German Armed Forces must be prepared *to crush Soviet Russia in a quick campaign* even before the conclusion of the war against England. . . . Preparations are to be completed by May 15, 1941.[28]

HITLER INTERVENES: APRIL 6, 1941

The period between December, 1940, when Hitler decided to strike eastward, and April, 1941, when he invaded Yugoslavia and Greece, was characterized by a triangular diplomatic tug of war among Germany, Britain, and the Soviet Union for the support of the Balkan states. Germany won this contest because she was able to back her arguments with superior force.

The Soviets proposed a treaty of mutual assistance to the Bulgarians on November 25, 1940, but were turned down, for the Bulgarians by this time were too involved in the German war plans to be able to shift their orientation. Likewise, General Sir Archibald Wavell met with failure when he went to Athens and Ankara in mid-January, 1941, to consult about organizing resistance against the expected German invasion. In both capitals he was turned down because the help he could offer was insignificant compared to what was needed to meet the Germans. The Greeks stated that they would need nine British divisions, together with large-scale air forces, in order to hold their lines. Wavell could offer only one artillery regiment, one antitank regiment, and about sixty tanks. The Greeks naturally concluded that if they accepted British aid they would merely provoke the Germans with no possibility of successful resistance.

By contrast, Hitler was able to force Bulgaria to his side because of the German divisions that he had massed across the Danube on Rumanian soil. On January 3 Bulgaria agreed to the entry of German troops; on January 10 the troops began to cross the Danube from Rumania; and on March 1 Bulgaria formally adhered to the Tripartite Pact. Russia, who already had made clear her interest in Bulgaria, protested strongly against the German advance into the heart of the Balkans. But by this time Hitler had enough divisions lined up along the Russian frontier to feel free to ignore the protests from Moscow. Hitler also tried to draw Turkey and Yugoslavia into the Tripartite Pact but without success. The adhesion of Bulgaria, however, sufficed for his purposes, since it opened the route to the Greek frontier.

With the appearance of German troops across the Danube the Greeks appealed to the British on February 8 for aid against the impending invasion. Two weeks later a British mission arrived in Athens headed by Foreign Secretary Anthony Eden. It was quickly determined that the Greeks would resist the Germans at all cost and that the British would give all possible aid. But differences and misunderstanding developed on the question of strategy. The British understood that only covering detachments would be left in the Metaxas Line along the Bulgarian frontier, and that the main British and Greek forces would be concentrated at the Aliakmon Line running along the hills west of the Vardar River. On the other hand, the Greek commanding officer, General Alexander Papagos, maintained that this arrangement was contingent upon Yugoslav aid against the Germans. Since this was not forthcoming, Papagos insisted on keeping three of his six available divisions in the Metaxas Line. He also held that it was unfeasible to withdraw any troops from the Albanian front because an Italian offensive was expected and adequate transportation facilities were lacking.

Prime Minister Churchill and his cabinet were so discouraged by this situation that for a moment they inclined toward leaving the Greeks to their fate. But Eden and his military advisers, who were on the spot in Athens, recommended that they stand by the Greeks regardless of the consequences. "No doubt," Eden reported, "our prestige will suffer if we are ignominiously ejected, but in any event to have fought and suffered in Greece would be less damaging to us than to have left Greece to her fate." [29] Churchill accepted this recommendation and in early March British reinforcements began to arrive in Greece.

Meanwhile, the Yugoslavs had been pressed on the one hand by the British to join Greece and Turkey in a Balkan front, and on the other by the Germans to accept the Tripartite Pact. The Yugoslavs had little choice because, with German troops in Bulgaria, they were surrounded on three sides. They tried to appease the Fuehrer by offering a nonaggression pact but were rejected. In the end they capitulated to a virtual ultimatum and on March 25, 1941, Premier Dragisha Tsvetkovich and Foreign Minister Tsintsar-Markovich signed the Tripartite Pact in Vienna. The terms were favorable to the Yugoslavs: no German troops would pass through their country and no territorial cessions would be demanded. On the contrary, Hitler promised that eventually the Yugoslavs could have Saloniki. The explanation for these generous conditions is that Yugoslav neutrality was important for both Operation Marita and Operation Barbarossa.

Premier Tsvetkovich and his foreign minister returned on March 26 to a hostile capital. That midnight a group of army and air force officers executed a lightning coup. Within an hour and a half they seized all government buildings, the radio center, and the barracks. Early in the dawn Prince Paul resigned as regent and young Peter was proclaimed King Peter II of Yugoslavia. A military government took office under General Dushan Simovich, the chief of the air force who had led the coup. Public opinion was known to have been strongly opposed to the capitulation to the Axis Powers. Yet the world was surprised by this sudden revolt and by the tumultuous enthusiasm of Belgrade's populace. The Allied ministers were cheered wherever they appeared, while enthusiastic crowds paraded in the streets shouting "Better War than the Pact." Less than a fortnight later war did come in the form of a devastating aerial bombardment of the capital.

The new Yugoslav government did its best to avoid a showdown with Hitler. It assumed a correct position of neutrality and declared that it would adhere to all previous pacts. As a token of friendly disposition to the Axis the government rejected British proposals for consultation following the coup. These gestures and asurances failed to protect Yugoslavia from German retribution. Equally futile was a pact of friendship and nonaggression which the new government concluded with the Soviet Union on the night of April 5–6, 1941. A few hours later, at six in the morning of April 6, the German blitz began.

The assurances of the Simovich government to Berlin had been wasted effort from the outset. Hitler had decided to destroy Yugoslavia almost as soon as he learned of the coup. He felt that he had made great concessions to bring Yugoslavia into the Axis camp. The Belgrade revolt demonstrated that they had been in vain and that the country could not be trusted. An unreliable and basically hostile Yugoslavia he regarded as an intolerable threat to his communications during the forthcoming campaigns against Greece and Russia. Accordingly, he called his generals together the day following the Belgrade coup and gave orders for a simultaneous invasion of Greece and Yugoslavia.

> The Fuehrer is determined, without waiting for possible loyalty declarations of the new government, to make all preparations in order to destroy Yugoslavia militarily and as a national unit. No diplomatic inquiries will be made nor ultimatums presented. Assurances of the Yugoslav government, which cannot be trusted anyhow, in the future will be taken note of. The army will attack as soon as the means and troops suitable for it are ready. . . . The war against Yugoslavia should be very popular in Italy, Hungary, and Bulgaria, as acquisition of territory can be promised to these states, namely the Adriatic coast to Italy, the Banat to Hungary, and Macedonia to Bulgaria.[30]

SWASTIKA OVER THE BALKANS

The German invasion of Greece and Yugoslavia proved to be an irresistible blitz. In less than three weeks Hitler's *Luftwaffe* and *Panzer* divisions overwhelmed all resistance and reached the southern capes of Greece.

One reason for this outcome was the gross discrepancy between the forces that Hitler had massed for the invasion and those that the British were able to spare from the North African front. Junior British officers had foreseen this gap and submitted to General Wavell a paper drawing attention to the dangers of the proposed campaign. Wavell returned the paper with a short note written across the top in his own hand. It read: " 'War is an option of difficulties,' Wolfe. A.P.W." [31] The officers were impressed more by the spirit than the judgment of their chief, and secretly proceeded to prepare plans for evacuation before the expeditionary force had even landed.

The German invasion was also facilitated by the failure to coordinate the Greek and Yugoslav defense plans. Not until April 3 was a meeting held in northern Greece between British, Greek, and Yugoslav military representatives. The conversations proved to be fruitless. They revealed that the Yugoslavs had a greatly exaggerated idea of the strength of the British forces in Greece and had made no serious preparations to meet a German attack. Three days later the German invasion began and no further contact with the Yugoslav army was effected.

The Balkan campaign opened with the furious air bombardment of Belgrade in the early morning of April 6. The *Luftwaffe* disregarded Belgrade's status as an "open city" and inflicted casualties estimated at 15,000 to 25,000. Simultaneously, the *Luftwaffe* swept without resistance over the whole of Yugoslavia and Greece. The key port of Piraeus was reduced to a shambles. Railway centers were devastated, crippling transportation facilities. The Yugoslavs were particularly hard hit by these air blows because their army was not fully mobilized and most of it was concentrated in the north. Meanwhile the British air force was too weak to counter the *Luftwaffe* or to conduct effective tactical operations against German ground units. Instead, it bombed Sofia by night, an operation which had some psychological repercussions but which left the invaders unharmed.

The German command of the air cleared the way for swift and decisive operations by the motorized divisions. They converged on the four Yugoslav army corps in the north, supported by Hungarian troops which crossed the Danube and by German and Italian forces advancing toward Zagreb. The main Yugoslav forces thus were driven in confusion southward, allowing the Germans to enter Belgrade on April 13. Meanwhile, other German divisions were advancing even more rapidly through the lightly defended passes of southern Yugoslavia. Starting from Bulgaria, they struck across to the Vardar Valley and down the Vardar Pass toward Saloniki. This thrust separated the Yugoslavs from the Greeks and turned the Metaxas Line, which was cut off from the rest of Greece. Even more serious was the advance of other German units from the Vardar Valley southwest across Yugoslav Macedonia to Prilep, Monastir, and into Greece near Florina, many miles behind the Anglo-Greek forces holding positions to the west of Saloniki. The Germans had outflanked the Aliakmon Line as well as the Metaxas Line. To complete the rout, other German units struck south from Bulgaria and, after hard fighting, pierced the Metaxas Line and raced for Saloniki.

In this manner the battle for the Balkans was decided in the first seventy-two hours of the campaign. The Germans speeded their victory by conducting political as well as armed warfare. In Yugoslavia they shrewdly exploited the rift between the Serbians and the Croatians. They spared the Croat cities from the air raids and conducted radio propaganda presenting the Axis forces as the "liberators" of the Croat nation. Also, they incited the Croat regiments to revolt against their leadership, which was almost exclusively Serbian. Scattered mutinies did occur, and the Yugoslav fleet, manned by Croat seamen, was slowly paralyzed. When the Germans reached Zagreb on April 9, the leader of the fascist Croatian Ustashi, Ante Pavelich, entered the city amid the roar of German tanks and established a "Croatian National Government." On April 16 General Simovich authorized the remaining Yugoslav army groups to surrender, and the following day King Peter fled the country in a British plane.

No counterpart existed in Greece to the Serbo-Croatian schism and to the Ustashi movement. But there did appear a certain amount of defeatism and fifth-columnist activity among a few top military and civilian leaders. These men had served loyally against the Italian invaders, but they considered resistance against the Germans as well as the Italians to be a futile sacrifice. This was especially true of the generals commanding the armies in Epirus and western Macedonia. Headed by General George Tsolakoglou, they opened armistice negotiations with the Germans despite explicit orders to the contrary from Athens. The national government at this time was led by Alexander Koryzes, who had become premier when Metaxas died on January 29, 1941, during the Italian War. Koryzes now committed suicide on April 18, goaded to the act by the disasters at the front as well as by the discovery of treason within his own cabinet. He was succeeded by Emmanuel Tsouderos, who gave orders that resistance be continued. Tsolakoglou and his fellow officers again disregarded instructions and on April 20 concluded an armistice with the Germans. Tsolakoglou later was rewarded by being made the first quisling premier of Greece.

Foreign observers have testified to the crippling effect of this vacillation and treason in high places. The London *Times* correspondent reported at the time:

> The masses of the nation were always united and had no thought but of victory, cost what it might. When Germany attacked them they did not falter— they could "take" it. Not so their Government, whose conduct of the war became definitely vacillating. There were several quislings in the Cabinet, and many provincial governors and senior officers and officials were pro-German. Defeatist tendencies became only too apparent in the administration, but the Greek people remained lion hearted until the end.[32]

Likewise, Field Marshal Lord Wilson, the British commander in chief in the Middle East, wrote some years later:

> Towards the Germans I sensed the feeling to be lukewarm. Under the Metaxas dictatorship certain Nazi ideas had been adopted. . . . Our position in Greece in 1941 was really a paradox in that in our struggle against totalitarianism we should be supporting one Fascist government against another. It is to this that most of the subsequent troubles of the Greek Government can be traceable as it started the war, to use a military cliché, "on the wrong foot." [33]

Tsolakoglou's surrender did not end the fighting in Greece. Anglo-Greece forces were still in the field in the northeast. But their efforts to stem the German tide were of no avail. The Greek units in the Metaxas Lines were cut off and isolated beyond hope of re-establishing contact. The British and Greek divisions along the Aliakmon Line were also outflanked but at least were able to retreat southward. First they fell back upon a Mt. Olympus Line. When they were not able to hold out there, on April 20 they retreated further south to a Thermopylae Line. Next day General Wavell and King George agreed that further resistance was futile and that evacuation should be started.

Evacuation proved to be difficult because in Greece the British lacked the air cover they had enjoyed at Dunkirk. Detachments of Anzac troops held a thirty-mile line from Thermopylae to the Gulf of Corinth against six enemy divisions while their comrades retreated southward. The chief port of Piraeus had been rendered unusable by repeated bombings; hence the British troops crossed the Corinth Canal and reached the ports along the southern tip of Greece. A lucky series of moonless nights (April 24–31, 1941) aided the evacuation operations. In all a little over 50,000 men were taken out safely, representing about 80 per cent of the forces originally sent into Greece.

The Germans did not stop in Greece. Less than a month later they launched their spectacular air-borne invasion of Crete and captured the island in a fortnight of furious fighting. British units had been located in Crete for several months but had not anticipated an air attack because Greece was 180 miles to the north. Their defense arrangements were designed only to secure Suda Bay as a refueling base for the British navy. Following the evacuation of Greece, 27,000 Imperial troops were landed in Crete, but most of their antiaircraft artillery had been lost. Hurricane fighters in Africa, 350 miles to the south, were too far away to give support.

The first German parachutists landed in Crete on May 20. Their losses were very heavy during the early days but nothing could stop the steady stream of glider trains and troop-carrier planes once airfields had been seized for their landing. The British navy retained control of the sea and prevented German convoys from reaching the island, though in doing so it suffered heavily from *Luftwaffe* attacks. The Germans were not stopped by the failure of their sea-borne reinforcements to reach the island. They continued to pour in troops by air and by May 25 were able to capture the strategic airfield commanding Suda Bay. British garrisons at other airfields stood their ground but were isolated from each other as German parachutists cut their communications along the northern coastal road. As more German reinforcements arrived the pockets of resistance were overcome one by one, and by June 2 organized resistance ceased.

The evacuation of Crete proved more difficult than those of Dunkirk and Greece. The survivors climbed over the mountain ranges of the interior to the southern coast. By day they hid in caves until the night when they were able to board destroyers which carried them to Alexandria under a rain of enemy bombs. A total of 16,500 men were brought safely back to Egypt but 13,000 were lost in Crete in addition to 2,000 during the evacuation.

Hitler now had a golden opportunity in the Mediterranean which he might have exploited with every chance of success and with the prospect of overrunning the entire Middle East. In addition to the triumph in the Balkans his armies had won an equally impressive victory in North Africa under the able and energetic General Erwin Rommel. Wavell had gained the initial success in North Africa when, between December, 1940, and February, 1941, he pushed the Italians back from the Egyptian frontier to Tripolitania. Immediately thereafter the British forces were weakened by the withdrawals for the Greek campaign. At the same time the Germans rushed reinforcements to North Africa to bolster their Italian allies. British intelligence underestimated the strength of these reinforcements, so that when Rommel attacked on March 31, 1941, he was able to sweep all before him. In less than a month he captured Benghazi, Bardia, and all of Cyrenaica.

The victories in the Balkans and in North Africa presented Hitler with the opportunity to execute a gigantic pincer operation upon the Suez through Libya and Egypt on the one side and Turkey and Syria on the other. But the Fuehrer allowed this opportunity to pass because, as a German diplomat observed, Hitler was moving "along a mental one-way street against Russia." [34] Instead of exploiting the promising situation in the Middle East, he moved his divisions from the Balkans to the eastern front. So hurriedly did he make this transfer that he did not allow his soldiers enough time to do a thorough job of "mopping up" in Yugoslavia—an oversight for which he was to pay dearly later.

When the German *Panzer* divisions finally crashed across the Soviet frontier on June 22, 1941, the entire Balkan Peninsula was under Axis rule. The swastika fluttering over the Acropolis was the symbol of the "new order" that now prevailed. This "new order" was to last until the fall of 1944, a period of almost four years during which Greece and Yugoslavia suffered the trials and exactions of enemy occupation while the other Balkan countries continued to serve as Axis satellites.

38. Occupation, Resistance, and Liberation: 1941–1945

$\mathbf{B}$ALKAN FRONTIERS changed only slightly as a result of World War II. The map of the Balkan Peninsula after World War II closely resembled that following World War I. And yet the later war had such a tremendous impact upon all the Balkan countries that it represents a major turning point in the history of the entire peninsula. Its influence, however, was exerted on the structure of domestic institutions rather than upon the configuration of national frontiers. The great aftermath of World War II was social revolution in contrast to the national revolution that characterized the earlier conflict.

The origins of the social revolution that accompanied World War II are manifold. One was the shattering effect of the Axis occupation which discredited the old regimes in the satellite countries (Rumania and Bulgaria) and completely destroyed those of the occupied countries (Yugoslavia, Greece, and Albania). Another was those resistance movements which flared up under predominant Communist leadership in the occupied countries and which reached such proportions and commanded such fierce loyalties that they soon overshadowed the governments-in-exile led by the prewar politicians. A final factor was the massive intrusion of the Red Army which dealt the final blow to hopes for the restoration of prewar institutions and regimes. Only in Greece was British influence strong enough to check this formidable combination of revolutionary forces. In the rest of the peninsula the national regimes that had been set up only a generation earlier were replaced by radically new creations.

In this chapter we shall consider the nature and influence of the first two of these revolutionary forces—the occupation and the resistance movements—leaving to the following chapter the strife between Russia and the West and the peace settlement that finally ensued therefrom.

761

PATTERN OF OCCUPATION AND RESISTANCE

One significant feature of Axis rule over the Balkans was the substantial difference between the position of the satellite countries, Rumania and Bulgaria, and that of the occupied countries, Yugoslavia, Greece, and Albania. It is true that the satellites were ruthlessly exploited for both human and material resources. Nevertheless, they did have their own governments and they did succeed in escaping the worst consequences of foreign domination. In Rumania, for example, Marshal Antonescu permitted the Peasant leader, Iuliu Maniu, to express his opposition to governmental policy throughout the war period. King Boris in Bulgaria allowed a similar latitude to the heads of the moderate opposition groups, and, more important, he refused to involve his country in the war against Russia despite heavy pressure from Berlin. The situation was quite different in the occupied countries, where the Axis authorities were free to do as they wished with no one to say them nay. They set up puppet regimes to camouflage their rule, but these proved to be of little significance. They were known to be the creations of the foreign masters, so they commanded little respect or support. By contrast, both Boris and Antonescu had considerable popular backing, at least until the fortunes of the Axis began to take the downgrade.

Another characteristic of the war years was the great difference among the Balkan peoples in the degree of their resistance to foreign rule. For various reasons the satellite nations offered the least resistance. They had escaped the excesses of full occupation and thus were not goaded to resistance by sheer despair as was the case with the Greeks and the Yugoslavs. Also, many nationalistically minded citizens in the satellites swung over to the Axis camp because of the extensive territories that their countries were allowed to acquire during the early days of the war. It is true that a certain amount of resistance was to be found in the satellites, but it was mostly of a nonviolent and rather ineffective variety emanating from Anglophile court circles and from certain political parties that were sufficiently moderate to be tolerated in parliament. Open armed resistance was rare in Rumania and, if not so rare, still far from common, in Bulgaria.

The situation prevailing in the occupied states was altogether different. The governments of these countries were obviously of the quisling variety and were thoroughly disliked by the mass of the people. Resistance under these circumstances was a natural and patriotic manifestation of defiance against the foreign rulers and their hirelings. Resistance was also stimulated by the rigors and excesses of the enemy occupation and by the loss of extensive national territories. The latter factor was especially important in Greece and Yugoslavia because of the wholesale mutilation of those countries. These various considerations explain why resistance was more extensive and more violent in the occupied portions of the peninsula. On the other hand, it should be noted that throughout the Balkans, and, indeed, in the whole of Europe, resistance was a discordant movement that was seriously weakened by deep-rooted dissension.

The dissension arose basically because some wished to resist in order to expel the enemy and restore the prewar *status quo,* and others in order to expel the enemy and create a new postwar society. This division represented essentially a continuation of prewar political struggles. Those who had supported the prewar dynasties and regimes wished to restore them after the occupation, while those who had opposed them now seized the opportunity to work enthusiastically for a new postwar society. This division naturally had an economic basis. In general, the "haves" wanted resistance and the old *status quo* while the "have-nots" wanted resistance and social revolution. There were, of course, certain exceptions to this generalization, particularly among the younger generation. A good many sons and daughters of the "haves" were alienated by what they considered to be the injustices of their society and devoted themselves to the cause of revolution and social reorganization.

The "haves" and the "have-nots" differed not only as to postwar objectives but also as to the immediate strategy to be employed against the enemy. The "haves" tended to be more passive because they had more to lose and were more vulnerable to reprisals. Accordingly, they wished to limit resistance primarily to organization and preparation, and opposed large-scale armed uprising until it could be coordinated with an Allied invasion from the outside. This, generally speaking, was the position taken by all the anti-Communist resistance leaders, including Iuliu Maniu in Rumania, Nikola Petkov in Bulgaria, Drazha Mihailovich in Yugoslavia, John Zevgos in Greece, and Abas Kupi in Albania.

The "have-nots," by contrast, having nothing to lose and everything to gain, preached and practiced all-out resistance against the enemy. This gave them an important advantage over their more cautious and conservative rivals. Furthermore, they were led by the Communists, who were by far the most experienced and effective in underground work. As a result, the radical, Communist-led resistance organizations soon attracted many more followers than the so-called "national" groups, which were discovering to their cost that it was much more difficult to maintain guerilla armies by waiting than by fighting.

This development serves to explain a phenomenon which otherwise seems inexplicable, namely, the collaboration of sincerely patriotic citizens with quislings and with occupationists. The more the "have-nots" assumed the leadership of the resistance struggles, the more likely it became that the postwar regimes would be of a revolutionary and Communist-dominated character. This prospect drove many members of the "nationalist" organizations to choose collaboration as the lesser of two evils. This may appear extreme and unwarranted at first glance, but it becomes perfectly understandable upon further consideration. A "nationalist" about to embark upon the course of collaboration would have defended his conduct somewhat as follows:

The liberation of our country will be determined by the strength of Britain, the Soviet Union and the United States. If they win, our country will be freed. If they lose, our country will remain under the Germans. There is nothing we can do which will affect the outcome appreciably one way or the other. So why shouldn't we concentrate on our own problem—the menace of the Communist-controlled resistance organization? We must fight it in order to prevent it from controlling our country after liberation. Our natural allies in this fight are the Germans and their quisling government. Why should we not join forces with them? This will not delay or hasten liberation. Rather it will ensure a sensible, non-Communist, postwar regime.

This reasoning and this course of action were followed by certain "nationalist" leaders in each of the occupied Balkan countries. Typical was the case of Stylianos Gonatas, who before the war had been prominent in the Liberal party of Greece. During the occupation, however, he was so appalled by the threat of the Communist-controlled resistance that he supported the collaborationist Security Battalions. These were Greek troops that were organized by the quisling government in Athens, armed by the Germans, and utilized to assist the Axis forces in their campaigns against the resistance bands. In a letter that Gonatas sent to the premier of the government-in-exile in the spring of 1944 he admitted that the Security Battalions were armed by the Germans. But then he asked:

Where else could they obtain arms if not from the Germans? . . . Most people do not regard the Germans as a threat to the future of Greece, especially after the war has been decided in favor of the Allies, but they do foresee a terrible danger for the country in even a temporary post-liberation Communist domination, and they prefer to ally themselves even with the devil in order to exclude the possibility of such domination. The arms which these people [Security Battalionists] have received from the Germans will not be used against the Allies. Everyone may be absolutely certain that this will never happen.[1]

The "devil" that Gonatas was ready to ally himself with was fully aware of this unbridgeable rift in the ranks of the resistance. A German report analyzing the political situation in Greece between September 1 and October 3, 1943, described the Communists as

the most dangerous because they represent the most active group, and because they have considerable forces available and are very well organized. The other political parties are slowly permeated with the thought that a further development of the Communist Party signifies the greatest danger. In this connection it is significant to note that it is the so-called Anglophiles who are the most persistent in demanding that the Germans take action against the Communists.[2]

SATELLITE RUMANIA

Rumania's course during World War II was as turbulent and erratic as it had ben during the first holocaust. In 1916 she had joined the Allies, then concluded a separate treaty with the Central Powers, and finally emerged as the new Greater Rumania with rich provinces gained from both her enemies and her allies. Now, during World War II, Rumania was the first Balkan state to be partitioned, the first to throw in her lot with the Axis, the first in the magnitude of her war effort in behalf of the Axis cause, and finally the first to change sides and to throw open the door into the Balkans and Central Europe for the advancing Red Army.

We saw in Chapter 37 that King Carol was forced to abdicate on September 6, 1940, after having yielded without a struggle Bessarabia and northern Bukovina to Russia, northern Transylvania to Hungary, and southern Dobruja to Bulgaria. Carol's young son, Michael, succeeded to the throne, but the real ruler of the country now was Ion Antonescu, a talented and ambitious general of the regular army. Antonescu established a government that represented a compromise between the old ruling class and the revolutionary fascist Iron Guard.* His deputy premier was Horia Sima, the new leader of the Guard following the execution of Codreanu in November, 1938. But the relations between the two elements in the government were never close. The Guardists did not trust Antonescu, nor did he them. The basic difficulty was that Antonescu wanted to establish an efficient, army-dominated regime while the various elements in the unruly Iron Guard worked at cross-purposes for such objectives as social revolution, division of the land, elimination of the Jews, ending of corruption, and revenge on those who had massacred their leaders in 1938. The Guardists broke loose repeatedly, inciting bloody Jewish pogroms, massacring political prisoners, and assassinating public personalities whom they disliked for one reason or another. In November, 1940, they murdered two distinguished professors who had been prominent in politics, the historian Nicholas Iorga and the economist Virgil Madgearu.

Antonescu was finally forced to take measures to restore order. The Guardists had counted on the support of the German troops that had been arriving in the country since October, 1940. But this support did not materialize despite the ideological affinity between the Guardists and the Nazis. The explanation is to be found in the fact that Germany needed for her purposes a disciplined Rumanian army and a productive Rumanian economy. These were more likely to be attained by Antonescu's military dictatorship than by the Guardist terror squads. Hence the paradox of Nazi approval for the suppression of one of Europe's earliest fascist movements.

Antonescu now established a dictatorship that left the army and the Germans in complete control of the country. The old bureaucracy continued to conduct the administration while military men moved into the cabinet posts. Antonescu enjoyed the confidence and trust of Hitler probably more than any other head of a satellite state. He was far from servile or obsequious to the German dictator. In fact, he was one of the few who dared to stand up to the Fuehrer's harangues. This independence appears to have impressed Hitler, as did also Antonescu's enthusiastic anti-Slavism. When Hitler con-

* For details on the Iron Guard, see Chapter 35.

fided his plans for invading Russia, Antonescu exclaimed, "Of course I shall be with you from the very first day. . . . You can always count upon Rumania for fighting the Slavs." [3] When the invasion began on June 22, 1941, Antonescu promptly sent his troops marching into Bessarabia after issuing a bombastic proclamation.

It is difficult to gauge Rumanian public reaction to this attack upon Russia because all political parties had been abolished on February 15, 1941. The only resolute opponents to the war were the Communists, but they were inconsequential because they were a mere handful and almost all imprisoned. The former political leaders naturally disliked Antonescu's dictatorship but they approved of the intervention because it offered an opportunity to regain Bessarabia and northern Bukovina. Some Rumanians also hoped that if they fought loyally beside the Germans they might be rewarded with the return of northern Transylvania from Hungary. These considerations presumably explain why the Liberal party leader, Constantin Bratianu, and the Peasant party leader, Iuliu Maniu, both publicly supported the intervention against Russia. The thinking of the peasant masses cannot be surmised but there is little doubt that the war received substantial support from the articulate elements of the population.

Rumania's war effort was considerable, both in the economic and military realms. She exported to Germany invaluable oil supplies, large quantities of grains and other foodstuffs, and the output of her sizable munitions industry. She also sent about thirty divisions to the front in 1941. At first these troops met with little resistance, overrunning Bessarabia easily and capturing the large port of Odessa. In the enthusiasm of the moment Antonescu promoted himself to the rank of marshal and ordered Odessa to be renamed Antonescu!

At this point began a new and sadder phase of the war. The conquest of the Crimea and the storming of the great Sebastopol fortress were largely the work of the Rumanians. But they paid for these victories with extremely heavy casualties. In the summer of 1942 some fifteen Rumanian divisions participated in the offensive toward Stalingrad. The catastrophic defeat that ensued was as much a Rumanian disaster as it was German.

Meanwhile disaffection was spreading within Rumania. One reason was the appalling bloodletting and the growing realization that it was destined to be in vain. Another was the unceasing drain of the country's wealth as the Germans continued to take out foodstuffs, oil, and munitions. Also, some of the opposition leaders, including Maniu and Bratianu, had turned against the war as soon as it was extended beyond Bessarabia into Russian territory. These men had naïvely assumed that it would be possible to wage only a "little war" to regain the lost provinces and then to retire from the scene. When Antonescu persisted in remaining by Hitler's side they made repeated but futile protests to Antonescu, demanding that Rumania should regain Transylvania from Hungary rather than squander her strength on the Russian steppes:

The country is suffering a long and continuous haemorrhage. . . . Have you any document in writing such as Ion Bratianu took care to obtain before entering the [first] World War beside France, England, and Russia, which assures us the return of lost Transylvania? . . . Continuation of the war in present conditions cannot lead to the reintegration of the country, but only to the complete extinction of the country, exposed to the Hungarian peril. In consequence, while there is still time, Germany must be informed that you have already done everything which Rumania can do, without exposing herself to grave disasters; that Rumania has made sacrifices which Hungary and Bulgaria have not made.

Therefore withdraw troops from Russia! . . .[4]

Despite this disaffection no mass resistance movement developed in Rumania as in Yugoslavia, Greece, and Albania. The Rumanian Communists organized a Patriotic Front in the summer of 1943, but it lacked the popular appeal of similar Communist-led organizations in other Balkan countries. One reason was Maniu's refusal to participate because of conflict over the question of Bessarabia. Maniu insisted that Rumania should keep the "liberated" province, while the Communists, as might be expected, demanded that it be "restored" to the Soviet Union. Maniu's stand does not by itself explain the weakness of the Patriotic Front. Machek in Croatia also refused to join the Partisans, but it did not prevent the latter from becoming the major force in their country. It is necessary to take into account, therefore, other important factors that were operating in Rumania.

One was the status of Rumania as a satellite country. This confronted would-be resistance leaders with the prospect of combating a Rumanian government and a Rumanian army as well as German forces. Also, many Rumanians were strongly anti-Communist and anti-Russian because for them Russia was the country that coveted Bessarabia, whereas for the Yugoslavs Russia was the great Slav country that would bring liberation. Finally, the Rumanian Communists were generally regarded as un-Rumanian and antinational, not only because they were mostly Jews but also because they had supported the Soviet seizure of the Rumanian provinces in 1940 and because they now favored the "restoration" of those provinces to the Soviet Union.

These various factors serve to explain the lack of popular support for Rumania's Patriotic Front. The few guerrilla bands that did operate in scattered localities were of negligible significance. Even Soviet accounts concede that "the struggle against Antonescu did not attain the stage of a mass national uprising." [5] Likewise, an American who traveled through Rumania in 1944 at the time of liberation reported that "there was a good deal of vague talk about their deeds of derring-do, but I could never obtain any specific examples." [6] The significance of this situation is that it allowed the course of events to be decided from above and from the outside rather than from below. When the Red Army neared the Danube in the fall of 1944 many dramatic repercussions ensued in Rumania. But the initiative came not from mass organizations within the country but rather from the court in Bucharest and from the Allied Powers that began to compete for the waning predominance of Germany.

SATELLITE BULGARIA

Bulgaria during World War II played a comfortably modest role, being spared the exhausting resistance struggles of her occupied neighbors and the equally exhausting war effort of Rumania. The fact that Bulgaria did not have a common frontier with either Germany or the Soviet Union helped her to remain aloof from the great campaigns that convulsed the Continent. Also, the traditional Russophile sentiment in Bulgaria was so strong that no serious effort was made to align the country with Germany against the Soviet Union. Furthermore, Boris, who was neither intimidated nor intoxicated by Hitler, exploited these advantages to the full in order to limit as far as possible his commitments to the Axis.

We saw in Chapter 37 that Boris had found it necessary to join the Axis on March 1, 1941. German troops then poured into the country and used it as a base for their attack upon Yugoslavia and Greece on April 6. The role of the Bulgarian army in these operations was unimportant. With the subjugation of the peninsula, Bulgaria was allowed to take from Yugoslavia her Macedonian lands and from Greece the eastern part of Macedonia and the province of Western Thrace. Bulgarian troops also occupied a part of Serbia, where they performed garrison duties for the Axis overlords. In the later stages of the war, when German troops were needed on other fronts, the Bulgarians were forced to extend their garrison commitments to additional parts of Greek Macedonia and Serbia.

The Bulgarian government made every effort to absorb the Greek and Yugoslav territory it had annexed. In Yugoslav Macedonia it opened some eight hundred schools and sent teachers and priests to Bulgarize the inhabitants. The city of Skoplje was endowed with a national theater, a library, a museum, and an institution of higher learning named King Boris University. The general policy of the Bulgarian occupation authorities was to win over the inhabitants of the former Yugoslav lands with generous treatment. This apparently proved unsuccessful because, by the end of 1943, Macedonian partisans under Tito's leadership were offering armed resistance. The Bulgarian occupation forces retaliated with harsh measures which served only to fan the flames of revolt.

Bulgarian policy from the outset was much more ruthless in the former Greek lands. Since there were few Slavs in these regions, the Bulgarians here sought not to convert the local population but to eliminate it in one way or another and to replace it with Bulgarian colonists. Greek citizens were conscripted, deported, deprived of their property, and in various other ways hounded until they sought refuge in flight. These measures explain why popular feeling in Greece during the occupation was much more bitter against the Bulgarians than against the Germans or the Italians.

The early years of the war were comparatively uneventful for Bulgaria. The only significant development in 1942 was the organization of the Fatherland Front in the middle of the year. The Communist leader, Georgi Dimitrov, who had gained international fame by defying the Nazis during the Reichstag fire trial, had urged the establishment of a "Front" organization during his broadcasts from Moscow, where he spent the war years. This Communist strategy proved more successful in Bulgaria than in Rumania, where the Patriotic Front had attracted little support. One reason was that the Communist party of Bulgaria had always been much stronger and better organized than its counterpart in Rumania. Also, the Bulgarian Communists did not have to face the opprobrium of favoring the cession of national territory as did the Rumanian Communists in the case of Bessarabia and Bukovina. These factors explain why the Communists were able to organize the Fatherland Front, together with the Social Democrats, the left-wing Agrarians led by Nikola Petkov, and the *Zveno* group led by Kimon Georgiev. The latter group consisted of intellectuals and military men who were associated with the review *Zveno* and who had close relations with the army. The Fatherland Front adopted a twelve-point program including the breaking of relations between Bulgaria and the Axis, the re-establishment of civil liberties, and the suppression of fascist organizations. It should be noted that some opposition groups existed outside the Fatherland Front, the most prominent being the Democratic party led by Nikola Mushanov and the right-wing Agrarians led by Dimiter Gichev. These parties were overshadowed, however, by the Fatherland Front, which was more active and which was strongly supported in Soviet radio broadcasts.

By the summer of 1943 guerrilla or Partisan bands began to offer armed resistance in the mountainous areas. The bands failed to grow to the proportions of a mass national resistance movement comparable to those that developed in the occupied Balkan countries. The main reason was that most Bulgarians suffered very little from the war and hence saw no point in assuming the great risks of resistance. In fact, the peasants, who constituted the majority of the population, prospered during the war because they were paid high prices as an incentive to increase production. In one village near Sofia it was found that the number of radios had risen from three or four in 1937 to over one hundred by the end of the war. Furthermore, only a few thousand German troops were stationed in the country and they behaved most correctly. Under these circumstances not many young men felt impelled to join the Partisans in the mountains. Those that did found themselves fighting not the Germans but the Bulgarian army and *gendarmerie,* which was a much less popular thing to do. The Bulgarian forces were extremely efficient and ruthless, so that the Partisans were reduced to hit-and-run tactics. They usually raided a village, shot the mayor, the policeman, and other functionaries if they were particularly obnoxious, destroyed the village land register and other records, looted the village dairy, made a few propaganda speeches to the villagers, and then fled to the safety of the nearby mountains.

On August 28, 1943, King Boris suddenly died in Sofia under circumstances that remain a mystery to this day. It was widely assumed at the time that the Germans were responsible for his death because only three days earlier Boris had had a particular stormy session with Hitler. On the other hand, German records made available after the war do not substantiate this assumption. Rather, they show that the Germans themselves tried to investigate the death of the Bulgarian king. In any case the removal of Boris from the scene aided the Partisan cause. Boris was succeeded by his son, Simeon, who was only six years old, so the country was ruled by a regency headed by Boris's brother, Prince Cyril. The latter was strongly pro-German, with the result that the subservience of Sofia to Berlin now became much more marked than in the past.

The new political course aroused considerable opposition and thus created an atmosphere that was more favorable for Partisan activity. Allied air raids, which began to punish Sofia in 1943, also aided the Partisan cause. In October, 1943, the Central Committee of the Fatherland Front began to circulate news bulletins. About the same time a trickle of British arms began to reach the Bulgarian bands. They were dropped by parachute to the British liaison officers within Serbia and then transferred to the Bulgarian Partisans. In a few cases the British officers remained with the Bulgarians and participated in their operations. The bands were nominally under the orders of the Fatherland Front but in practice they were dominated by the Communists. The leaders of the bands were usually Communists and the entire resistance struggle depended largely on the Communist underground apparatus for its functioning.

During 1944 the position of the Sofia government became increasingly difficult as the Red Army neared the Balkans and as the Anglo-American air raids became more severe. In May, 1944, a new government was formed under a former Agrarian, Ivan Bagrianov. It was markedly less subservient to the Axis than its predecessor. It released fifteen thousand political prisoners, set free relatives of Partisans who had been held as hostages, and relaxed the anti-Jewish measures. On August 22 the foreign minister declared that he would seek peace with the Western powers and that he would evacuate Serbian and Greek territory occupied by Bulgarian troops, but he added that Macedonia and Thrace were "Bulgarian by right."

The following day Marshal Antonescu was overthrown in Bucharest. This changed the situation in the Balkans overnight and made inconsequential the Bulgarian reservations concerning Macedonia and Thrace. The all-important fact now was that the advancing Red Army had an open path into the Balkan Peninsula. This presented the Fatherland Front and the Communist-led Partisan bands with an opportunity hitherto denied to them. The approach of the Red Army also suddenly brought to the fore the hitherto muted issue of postwar power relationships in the Balkans. Was the waning hegemony of Germany to be replaced by that of the Soviet Union or of the Western powers?

OCCUPIED YUGOSLAVIA

Partition. The Axis Powers, having overrun Yugoslavia in April, 1941, set about dismembering the state. Slovenia was divided into two parts, the northern two thirds going to Germany and the southern third to Italy. The Germans followed a policy of denationalization in their zone. They deported Slovene intellectuals and professionals and brought in German settlers from Bessarabia, Bosnia, and Austria. Also, they proscribed the Slovene language in the schools and the administration, and called up the young men to serve in the German army. Because the Italians were not so severe in their zone, a considerable number of Slovenes fled southward for security.

The Voivodina was also divided by the Axis, the western part going to Hungary and the eastern (the Banat) being placed under a special administration dominated by the local German minority. Macedonia, as we saw earlier in this chapter, was taken over by the Bulgarians, who proceeded to apply a Bulgarization program. Western Macedonia and the province of Kosovo in southwestern Serbia went to Italian Albania, their populations being in fact largely Albanian. Montenegro was taken over by the Italians, who attempted to set up an autonomous administration. The Italians also annexed large parts of Bosnia, Herzegovina, and Dalmatia which, together with Albania, gave them full control of the Adriatic Sea.

There remained of the old Yugoslavia only two rump states with puppet status—Serbia and Croatia. Ante Pavelich, the leader of the Ustashi, the terrorist organization, was installed as the Fuehrer, or Poglavnik, of Croatia. The frontiers of this new "independent" state were extended to the east to include most of Bosnia-Herzegovina at the expense of the Serbs. But at the same time Croatia was deprived of the larger part of Dalmatia, which was taken by Italy. In May, 1941, Croatia was proclaimed an independent kingdom and the throne was offered to the Duke of Spoleto, a member of the Italian house of Savoy. The duke accepted the offer, but he found the pleasures of Rome too attractive to renounce, so he never assumed his royal office. "The King," wrote the Italian foreign minister, Count Ciano, in his diary on November 17, 1941, "wants the Duke of Spoleto to leave Rome. . . . In fact, the behavior of this young man is quite absurd. He is living with a well-known society girl and takes her about in his private car. He frequents restaurants and bars and gets tight. . . . He is a fine man to be a King!" [7] Croatia thus remained a kingdom without a king. Throughout its brief existence it was an "independent" state with no real independence. Its most strategic territories were occupied by Axis forces and the remainder soon fell to Chetnik and Partisan units.

Serbia was even more closely controlled than Croatia. It was subject to the authority of the local German commander and its frontiers were reduced to those that had prevailed before the Balkan Wars. When resistance began to manifest itself, the Germans attempted to enlist some popular support for themselves by persuading General Milan Nedich to form a "Government of National Salvation." Nedich, who had been chief of staff of the pre-war Yugoslav army, now played a role akin to that of Pétain in France. He did not have ideological ties to the Axis as did Pavelich in Croatia. Rather, he considered himself the temporary representative of the exiled King Peter until the war was over. The Germans allowed him to form a small military force called the Serbian State Guard. They were careful, however, to retain full control over the country because of its importance in Balkan strategy. They maintained garrisons in the cities and the communications routes and they kept close watch over the actions of the Nedich regime.

Not only was Yugoslavia partitioned but its peoples were persecuted and their traditional feuds were purposefully exacerbated to the point of mass fratricidal butchery. Yugoslav Albanians, organized in their fascist-led Skanderbeg Division, conducted an indiscriminate massacre of Serbians. Like-wise, the Hungarians and the Germans of the Voivodina killed thousands of Serbs in that area. The Bulgars in Macedonia did not shed so much blood, but they did use every pressure to convince or compel the local inhabitants to regard themselves as Bulgarians.

The worst situation prevailed in Croatia, where the slogan of the Pavelich regime was "Za dom spremni" or "Ready for the Fatherland." By this was meant that there was no room for Serbians in the new Croatian state. The *Ustashi* accordingly set out to exterminate one portion of the Serbian population and to force the remainder to become Croatians. There followed a series of St. Bartholomew's Nights against the Orthodox Serbians and also against the Jews. Some members of the Croatian Catholic hierarchy endorsed the butchery and participated in the forcible conversion of Serbians to Cathol-icism. The Moslems joined in the massacres, so that Yugoslavia was rent by a virtual religious war with Catholics and Moslems allied against the Orthodox and the Jews. In 1942 Pavelich boasted that "Great deeds were done by Ger-mans and Croats together. We can proudly say that we succeeded in breaking the Serb nation, which, after the English, is the most thick-headed, the most stubborn and the most stupid." [8] The Serbians, needless to say, retaliated wherever they could, and they exacted bloody vengeance, especially in Bosnia-Herzegovina and the neighboring Sanjak.

Yugoslavia's future appeared hopeless indeed. Not only was the country mutilated and the people driven to wholesale massacres, but the pre-war leaders had failed in their responsibility to provide guidance. This was especially true of Vladimir Machek, whose Peasant party still commanded the support of most of the Croatian peasants. Yet Machek withdrew from politics after advising his followers to obey the regime of the Ustashi. Yugo-slavia thus became a hell of blood and torment and destructive hatreds. Out of this hell emerged the searing yet purifying fires of the resistance.

First Resistance. During the first days of the occupation the Yugo-slavs were in a state of shock and bewilderment. Their army had been de-stroyed, their king had fled abroad, and their state had been torn to pieces brutally and, apparently, irrevocably. The occupation, however, proved to be less solid than appeared on the surface. The Germans turned against Russia immediately after their Balkan campaign. They did not have time to disarm thoroughly the scattered Yugoslav army units. Nor could they afford to leave strong garrisons behind them when they smashed across the Russian frontier on June 22, 1941. Thus it proved possible for a few bold leaders to begin the resistance struggle within a few weeks after the occupation.

One of these resistance leaders was a regular army officer, Colonel Drazha Mihailovich, who in the early summer made his way from Herzegovina to central Serbia. His followers came to be known popularly as Chetniks, a Serbian term with revered historical associations. A Chetnik was literally a member of a Cheta or a military detachment that had fought against the Turks in the nineteenth century. The first Chetnik bands were now organized in Bosnia, where the Serbians were forced to defend themselves against the murderous attacks of the Ustashi. Apart from this primary aim of self-preservation the Chetniks generally tended to be strongly nationalistic, or, in other words, anti-Croatian and anti-Communist. Under the stress of the national emergency, Chetnik bands were organized in traditional fashion by local leaders in various parts of the country. The most disciplined groups were those under the direct supervision of Mihailovich in Serbia proper. Other bands in Montenegro, Bosnia, Herzegovina, and Dalmatia operated virtually independently and had little in common with one another apart from a general ideological affinity. This loose organization and the lack of discipline were to be important factors in Mihailovich's failure to build up an efficient army.

The other resistance leader was the secretary-general of the Communist party, Josip Broz, usually known as Tito. A Croatian by birth and a machinist by trade, he had served in the Austro-Hungarian army during World War I and had been taken prisoner by the Russians. During the Bolshevik Revolution he sided with the Communists and received a thorough training in Communist tactics. On his return to Yugoslavia he played a prominent role in the Communist underground, eventually rising to head his party. He worked mostly from Zagreb, but with the establishment of the Ustashi regime in Croatia he transferred his headquarters to Belgrade early in May, 1941. His activity during the two months' period between the occupation of Yugoslavia and the invasion of Russia has remained a matter of dispute to the present. His enemies accuse him of complete inactivity, while his lieutenant, the journalist Vladimir Dedijer, claims in his diary to have received a party leaflet on April 12 calling "on all its best sons to defend their country against Hitler."

With the German attack upon the Soviet Union, a wave of emotion engulfed the Yugoslavs, whether Communists or not. The intensity of feeling was comparable with that which had brought about the Belgrade coup three months earlier. With the brother Russians on their side, the Yugoslavs arose in July in a series of unorganized revolts. The Serbians were the most prominent in this spontaneous and incoherent movement. Many of them joined the

Chetnik bands, but the Communists, with their superior organization, were also able to exploit the mass enthusiasm to strengthen their forces. The Germans, surprised by this spontaneous upheaval, were soon confined in Serbia to the Belgrade region and the Morava Valley.

Tito now sought to apply the official Comintern policy of a People's Front of all patriotic forces against the foreign invaders. Between September and November, 1941, he held several conversations with Mihailovich and reached vague agreements for common action. But instead of cooperating, the Chetnik and Communist Partisan bands were soon at each other's throats. Their tragic feud was to be a major factor determining the course of events in Yugoslavia until the triumph of the Partisans and the establishment of the Communist Tito regime at the end of the war.

Certain clear-cut issues explained the bitter struggle between the two camps. One was their basic incompatibility in political outlook. Mihailovich, the royalist army officer, regarded the Communists as lawless and atheistic criminals. The Communists, in turn, looked upon Mihailovich as the representative of the reactionary prewar regime they had fought for years. Thus the interwar struggle between the monarchist government and its opponents was now continued by the Chetniks and the Partisans. And the stake at issue was the nature of the postwar regime—whether it should be the monarchy restored or a radical new government of Communist complexion.

Another fundamental difference between the Chetniks and the Partisans concerned the strategy to be employed against the Axis. Mihailovich, an orthodox military man, opposed large-scale armed resistance because the enemy was overwhelmingly strong and the end result could only be merciless reprisals upon the defenseless civilian population. He believed that the bands should lie low and husband their resources until a propitious moment arrived, such as an Allied invasion from the outside. By contrast, the Partisans preached, and practiced, uncompromising and continual resistance. Their slogan was, "Attack the enemy wherever and however you can." The Germans retaliated with savage reprisals—the burning of villages and the shooting of ten, fifty, and even a hundred inhabitants for every German casualty. Mihailovich was appalled by the bloodshed, especially because the Serbians usually were the victims.

By November, 1941, the Chetniks and the Partisans were irreconcilable enemies and openly at war with each other. At the same time the Axis forces counterattacked on a large scale, using armor and aircraft. By the end of the year both the Chetnik and Partisan bands had been scattered. The Germans then massacred thousands of Serbians and imprisoned or deported to forced labor other thousands. In the industrial town of Kragujevac they shot eight thousand people, including several hundred school children. This bloodshed appeared to vindicate Mihailovich, who now lapsed into comparative inactivity in accordance with his strategy. The Partisans continued their relentless resistance, though they withdrew from the Serbian plains to the protecting mountains of Montenegro, Bosnia, and Herzegovina. There they established a firm base for their resistance movement, which was to make them the masters of Yugoslavia within three years.

Tito's Partisans. The Partisans gained two important advantages when they moved their base of operations to the central mountain massif of Bosnia, Herzegovina, and Montenegro. One was the ruggedness of the terrain, which gave them protection against the enemy and an opportunity to employ their hit-and-run tactics. Another was the poverty of this region, which made it unattractive to the enemy and unworthy of his attention. The Germans were interested primarily in three sections of Yugoslavia: the Dalmatian coast as a possible objective for an Allied landing; the northern Danubian plains with their cities and food surplus; and the Morava-Vardar Valleys as the main route from the Balkans to Central Europe. Between these three regions lay the mountain strongholds of the Partisans.

The Partisans gradually mastered the art of guerrilla warfare through the bloody process of trial and error. Beginning with small arms and limited ammunition, they learned that positional warfare was impossible against a well-trained and well-armed enemy supported by armor, artillery, and aircraft. The only alternative was to hit and run—to strike at the enemy where he was the most vulnerable and then to escape to the mountains or woods. All gains had to be regarded as temporary. Villages and small towns captured by sudden attacks were abandoned when the enemy counterattacked in force. Villages and towns changed hands repeatedly, each time becoming more battered and losing more inhabitants.

The Axis authorities retaliated with savage reprisals against the populace for supporting the Partisans. These tactics boomeranged, engendering such hatred and bitterness that multitudes flocked into the ranks of the resistance. Also, many were reduced to the position where they literally had nothing to lose but their lives by taking up arms. With their houses burned, their orchards destroyed, and their animals and crops confiscated, they were driven to adopt the Partisan thesis that only implacable resistance held hope of individual and national survival.

This bloodshed and devastation, together with the national and religious hatreds depicted above, constitute the background out of which emerged the extraordinarily effective resistance movement led by Tito and his Communists. The success of the Communists becomes more impressive if it is recalled that at the time of the Axis invasion their party had 11,879 full members and 14,873 Communist Youth members—a total of less than 27,000. One reason why this handful of Communists was able to dominate the resistance movement was their organization and discipline. Their party had been badly split during much of the interwar period, but Tito had reorganized and tightened it when he became secretary-general in 1937. The new men that he appointed to positions of responsibility now proved their worth in the resistance struggle. Brigadier Fitzroy Maclean, the head of the British Mission to Tito's headquarters, was greatly impressed by the spirit and discipline of the Partisans:

Living as we did among the Partisans, we came to know them well, from Tito and the other leaders to the dozen or so rank and file who acted as our bodyguard and provided for our daily needs. All had one thing in common: an intense pride in their Movement and in its achievements. For them the outside world did not seem of immediate interest or importance. What mattered was *their* War of National Liberation, *their* struggle against the invader, *their* victories, *their* sacrifices. . . .

With this pride went a spirit of dedication, hard not to admire. The life of every one of them was ruled by rigid self-discipline, complete austerity; no drinking, no looting, no love-making. It was as though each one of them were bound by a vow, a vow part ideological and part military, for, in the conditions under which they were fighting, any relaxation of discipline would have been disastrous. . . .[9]

Another factor explaining the effectiveness of the Communists was their strategy in organizing a national rather than a Communist resistance movement. They invited to the Partisan ranks all who were willing to fight against the enemy. Their slogan was "Death to Fascism, Freedom to the People"—sentiments to which no patriotic Yugoslav could take exception. In this manner the Communists were able to attract to their side many who were nationalists rather than Communists. At the same time the Communists did not lose sight of their ultimate revolutionary goal. A united national effort was needed against the foreign occupationists, but after that would come the long-awaited social revolution. The Communists realized full well that a resistance struggle, especially if Communist-led, would in itself clear the way for postwar social change. Maclean was told this by Tito himself when the two men first met in September, 1943:

We talked of politics in general. I said that I was a Conservative; he, that he was a Communist. We discussed the theory and practice of modern Communism. His theme in its broad lines was that the end justified the means. He developed it with great frankness. I asked him whether it was his ultimate aim to establish a Communist State in Jugoslavia. He said that it was, but that it might have to be a gradual process. For the moment, for instance, the Movement was based politically on a "popular front" and not on a strictly one-party system. At the same time, the occupation and the war were rapidly undermining the foundations of the old political and economic institutions, so that, when the dust cleared away very little would be left, and the way would be clear for a new system. In a sense the revolution was already in progress.[10]

A third factor that helped the Communists to rise to the top was their adoption of the principle of self-determination for all nationalities. When the war began, the Communists were by no means prepared to deal with the nationality problem. The Comintern during the interwar years had insisted on the principle of self-determination, including the right of separation. This formula involved or implied the disintegration of Yugoslavia, or, at the very least, the separation of Yugoslav Macedonia and its inclusion in an independent Macedonian state. This was in line with Soviet policy which sought dur-

ing those years to revise the Versailles settlement. It was unacceptable, however, to the Yugoslav Communists, who split into "right" and "left" wings on
this issue. Thus the party had not defined its position on the nationality problem when the war began.

The occupation, and the subsequent outburst of national and religious hatred deliberately fanned by the enemy, compelled the Communists to
reconsider the entire nationality problem. The outcome was Tito's article,
"The National Problem in the Light of the National Liberation War," first
published in September, 1942, and later frequently reprinted in several languages. Tito stated that the liberation war and the national question were
"inseparably joined" and that the several Yugoslav nations had the right of
self-determination, even to the point of separation. Although this article was
only a statement of general principles, it attracted many to the Partisan camp.
All the other Yugoslav parties were organized in practice, if not in theory, on
exclusive national or religious lines. Only the Partisans now had an all-Yugoslav organization and program based on national toleration. Thus many
Yugoslavs accepted Communist leadership as the only alternative to the destruction of the Yugoslav state and the mutual extermination of the Yugoslav
nationalities.

The fourth and final factor explaining Communist success was their
adoption of local National Liberation Committees as natural and extremely
effective instruments for expansion and administration. The precise nature
of the Partisan administrative system will be analyzed later. Suffice it to note
here that the first National Liberation Committees were organized spontaneously in Serbia by the peasants during their uprising in the summer of
1941. Before the end of the year they were wiped out by the Germans, but
the Communists recognized the potentiality of such popularly elected committees and initiated them wherever they went. The committees continued to
function even in areas that the Partisans were forced to evacuate before
enemy offensives. Thus a network of National Liberation Committees spread
over most of the country, whether liberated or occupied, and formed the organizational basis for resistance and administration. In the same manner that
the Russian Bolsheviks adopted the soviets that had been organized spontaneously by the workers during the 1905 revolution and utilized them to conduct the 1917 revolution, so the Yugoslav Communists adopted the National
Liberation Committees that had also been organized spontaneously by the
peasants, and utilized them as the basis for resistance and administration.

The strength of the Partisans varied a good deal from region to
region. For reasons noted above they were always strongest in the mountains
of Bosnia, Herzegovina, and Montenegro. They were least influential in Serbia and the Voivodina because of the flat terrain, the local Chetnik tradition,
and the large German and Hungarian forces assigned to control these
strategic areas. Resistance was also difficult in Slovenia, for this region
was physically separated from the Partisan strongholds and it was carefully watched by both the Germans and the Italians because of its strategic

location on the routes to the Mediterranean. Nevertheless, a considerable Slovenian Partisan movement developed, especially in the Italian zone. In July, 1942, the Italians launched an offensive against the Slovene Partisans but without lasting results. Thereafter the Partisans grew steadily in strength under the leadership of Boris Kidrich and Edward Kardelj, who maintained a precarious liaison with Tito's headquarters.

In Macedonia the local population at first welcomed the Bulgarian occupation forces. But before long Bulgarian rule had become as unpopular as the Serbian had been before the war. A curious contest now developed between the Yugoslav and Bulgarian Communist parties as to which one should lead the resistance struggle in Macedonia. The two parties betrayed a chauvinism regarding Macedonia not unlike that of their respective governments. In August, 1941, the Comintern decided in favor of the Yugoslav party, apparently because the Bulgarian comrades were considered too passive toward the Russo-German struggle. Tito sent one of his trusted lieutenants, the Montenegrin Svetozar Vukmanovich, to organize the Macedonian resistance. He won considerable support with the Partisan program of a federal Yugoslavia in which the "Macedonian nation" would enjoy full equality with other peoples. By the summer of 1943 Partisan bands were in the field and Vukmanovich had established liaison with the Partisan bands in Albania, Greece, and Bulgaria.

In Croatia the Partisans met with more success than anywhere else outside the mountain areas. The Partisan principle of self-determination and federalism appeared to offer the only alternative to the Serbian hegemony of the past and the Serb-Croat massacres of the present. Mihailovich, with his Great Serb ideology, was naturally repugnant to the Croatians. Even the venerable Machek, the head of the Croatian Peasant party, had remained passive and had withdrawn from politics. Pavelich, who had been installed by the Axis as the Poglavnik, or fuehrer, of Croatia, had been discredited by his failure to resist the Italian annexation of Dalmatia. Thus the younger generation in Croatia turned to Tito's Partisans in increasing numbers. Pavelich's "Independent Croatia" shrank steadily until it included only a few cities and railway lines. Partisan bands sometimes held the suburbs of Zagreb for days at a time. When Pavelich visited Hitler in April, 1943, the German officials remarked that a mayor had never been received by the head of a state with so much ceremony. The Germans knew that their Poglavnik controlled little more than the city of Zagreb.

Mihailovich's Chetniks.　　While the Partisans had been organizing their resistance movement, the royal Yugoslav exile government had promoted Mihailovich to the rank of general and appointed him in January, 1942, to the position of minister of war. These honors did not enable Mihailovich to hold his own against the Partisans. Not only did he fall far behind his Communist rivals, but he ended by collaborating with the enemy occupation forces. This does not mean that Mihailovich was a fascist-minded traitor like Pavelich. In fact, he had associated before the war with liberal, anti-

German political elements. It is said that his promotion in the military hierarchy had been retarded because of his opposition to what he considered to be his government's pro-Axis foreign policy. Thus the explanation for Mihailovich's course during the occupation period is not to be found in any ideological predilection for fascism. Rather, the explanation lies in his political and military preconceptions which proved totally inadequate for dealing with the problems of occupied Yugoslavia and which led him almost inexorably toward disaster.

Mihailovich was above all else an ardent Serbian nationalist in his political outlook. He believed that one of the main reasons for Yugoslavia's military collapse had been the fifth-columnist activties of the Croatians, who had betrayed their country. He felt strongly that the Serbs should dominate the Yugoslavia of the future. More specifically, he wanted postwar Serbia to be greatly enlarged by the addition of Macedonia, Montenegro, Bosnia-Herzegovina, and a large part of Croatia. This Greater Serbia would then be in a position to overshadow Croatia and Slovenia and thus control the Yugoslav state. It is scarcely necessary to add that this Pan-Serbism had little chance of competing successfully with Tito's slogans for federalism and self-determination of peoples.

Mihailovich was handicapped by his conservative social views as well as by his Great Serbism. He wanted to restore the prewar social order and the Karageorgevich dynasty, to which he was devoted. He hated the Communist-dominated Partisans because he feared, with justification, that their aim was to establish a Communist Yugoslavia and to abolish the dynasty. The fate of the dynasty was almost an obsession with Mihailovich. His loyalty to King Peter was probably as deep-rooted as his Serbian nationalism. He was aware that the king's popularity was steadily declining during the occupation years but this served only to intensify his devotion to the crown. This marked quixotic streak in Mihailovich's character further decreased his chances against the realistic Tito.

Finally, Mihailovich was also hampered by his cautious military strategy. He was appalled by the torrents of Serbian blood that had been shed in the two world wars. He feared that this decimation would weaken the position of the Serbs vis-à-vis the other Yugoslav peoples. He wished to stop the bloodletting, and for this reason he opposed indecisive and costly skirmishes with a superior enemy. Instead, he decided to remain quiet and husband his resources until the day the Allies landed in Yugoslavia. Then he would muster five hundred thousand men and drive the Germans out of the country in one great campaign. This strategy proved to be impractical for two reasons. One was that the Allies wanted action against the enemy and distributed their arms on the basis of deeds accomplished. The other was that a guerrilla army could not be maintained indefinitely while waiting for possible developments at an undefined future date. By their very nature guerrilla forces either grow by fighting and winning, or remain inactive and degenerate into dispirited and undisciplined bands.

Mihailovich eventually realized that his program and strategy were inadequate under prevailing conditions. In January, 1944, he called the Congress of St. Sava, named after the patron saint of the Serbs. The purpose of the gathering was to liberalize the program of the Chetnik movement in order to attract wider support. The Congress passed resolutions in favor of federalism, constitutional monarchy, and social and economic reforms. But by this time such resolutions were too late. The Allies already had discounted the Chetniks as a resistance force, while the Partisans were so strongly entrenched in so many parts of the country that Mihailovich could not hope to challenge them seriously.

Mihailovich now was forced by the circumstances of his position to collaborate with the enemy. He believed that the defeat of the Axis depended upon the Allied Powers rather than upon his Chetniks. Accordingly, he considered his primary duty to be the destruction of the Communists, whom he regarded a greater menace to Yugoslavia than the Germans, who in any case were doomed. But he was not strong enough to fight the Partisans alone, and the Allied Powers were unwilling to give him assistance. The only alternative was to collaborate with the Ustashi and the Axis forces, which were also anti-Partisan. Thus the course of events forced Mihailovich, who was both anti-German and anti-Croatian, to collaborate with the Germans, the Italians, and the Ustashi. As early as June 6, 1943, Prime Minister Churchill received the following report from his chiefs of staff: "It is clear from information available to the War Office that the Chetniks are hopelessly compromised in their relations with the Axis in Herzegovina and Montenegro. During the recent fighting in the latter area, it has been the well-organized partisans rather than the Chetniks who have been holding down the Axis forces." [11]

Tito's Triumph. The Partisans have defined seven main offensives launched against them by the Axis High Command. The first was in November–December, 1941, when they were driven out of Serbia and forced to retreat to Bosnia, Herzegovina, and Montenegro. The second was in January, 1942, when the enemy attacked their positions in Bosnia. The Partisans lost heavily but they managed to retain control of an area on either side of the headwaters of the Drina River. Tito used this as a base for resting his exhausted men and raising fresh recruits. In June, 1942, combined Chetnik-Italian forces launched the third offensive in Montenegro, driving the local Partisan units into Bosnia. Tito counterattacked with considerable success, liberating the territory along the Bosnia-Croatia border, including the city of Bihach, which became the Partisan political center.

The existence of Partisan-controlled territory near Zagreb and near important railway lines led the Axis authorities to organize a fourth offensive. This was an all-out operation that continued from January through March, 1943. The units included Germans, Italians, Ustashi, and Chetniks. Tito was able to break through the closing trap by attacking the Chetnik forces assembled along the Neretva River to block the way into Herzegovina. The Chetniks broke and fled, leaving behind many documents revealing their relations with the enemy. Brigadier Maclean examined these documents and then sent a report to Churchill that contributed to the cessation of British support for Mihailovich.

Tito regrouped his forces in the mountains of Montenegro, where he faced a fifth Axis offensive in the summer of 1943. This time the German and Italian high commands were determined that the Partisans should not escape destruction. They gathered a total of some 120,000 men against the 20,000 weary veterans that Tito could muster. In addition to this six-to-one numerical superiority, the Germans employed new techniques especially designed to cope with guerrilla warfare. These included the use of bloodhounds, the laying of ambushes, and the constant supplying of fresh troops to the front lines in order to maintain unremitting pressure against the exhausted Partisans. Another device was the construction of numerous small stone and steel fortresses designed to checkmate Partisan infiltration tactics. This offensive proved to be the bitterest test of Partisan strength and morale. The Germans expected Tito to try to break through to the southeast into the Sanjak. Instead, he attacked in the northwest and after severe losses was able to advance into Bosnia. The resilience and popularity of the Partisan movement was demonstrated now by the fact that by mid-August the influx of fresh volunteers had balanced the losses suffered during the fifth offensive. Furthermore, Tito immediately counterattacked and recovered much of the territory he had formerly held in Bosnia and Dalmatia.

The collapse of Italy in September, 1943, strengthened the Partisans immensely. They disarmed several Italian divisions, thereby acquring sufficient arms to increase their troops by 80,000. By November, 1943, they were able to liberate large parts of Slovenia, the Croatian littoral, Dalmatia, Macedonia, Bosnia and Herzegovina. By contrast, Mihailovich gained little from the Italian surrender because he had withdrawn his Chetniks to southwestern Serbia following his defeat during the fourth offensive. The mounting strength of the Partisans forced Mihailovich to cooperate more and more with the Axis and the Ustashi. His refusal to attack the important railway lines running through Serbia finally caused a breach between him and the Allies. He received no further supplies from the Allies after the summer of 1943, and in May, 1944, the British withdrew their mission from his headquarters.

Meanwhile, in December, 1943, the Axis launched the sixth offensive against the Partisan forces in Bosnia, Croatia, and Dalmatia. The Partisans were forced to abandon most of Dalmatia, the offshore islands, and certain inland regions. But, as in the past, they were able to counterattack, and in January, 1944, they regained much of the lost territory and made advances elsewhere. The seventh and final offensive in the summer of 1944 was on a considerable scale but was not confined to a restricted area. Its aim was to protect the German lines of communication that were being increasingly harassed by the resurgent Partisans. The offensive petered out by July except in Serbia, where the fighting was particularly bitter.

Serbia continued to be the center of operations henceforth because of its crucial importance for the crumbling German outposts in the Balkans. The German high command made every effort to retain control of the vital Morava-Vardar route against the Partisans and the Red Army advancing from the East. The Partisans converged upon Serbia from Macedonia, Montenegro, and Bosnia, winning important victories in August, 1944. By September 6, units of the Soviet Red Army reached the Yugoslav frontier. A few days later Bulgaria capitulated and Bulgarian troops joined the Red Army in the push into Serbia. On September 11 Partisan units reached the Danube. The following day Partisan and Soviet officers met to coordinate the campaign against the Axis armies. On September 28 the Partisan supreme command reached an agreement for joint operations with the Red Army, with the understanding that civil authority in the liberated areas should be vested in the Partisan National Committee of Liberation.

On October 20, 1944, after seven days of bitter fighting, Belgrade was taken by the Partisan First Proletarian Corps aided by Soviet tanks and artillery. The Germans now organized a new defense line at Srem, to the west of Belgrade. They defended this position tenaciously in order to keep open an escape route for their troops scattered in the Balkans. Not until April, 1945, were they driven back from the Srem front. By the middle of May the last Axis units were rounded up and the fighting on Yugoslav soil ended.

In the final stages of the war the Partisans received decisive aid from both the Soviet and Bulgarian armies. They could not have liberated Yugoslavia unaided because the Germans had concentrated in Serbia the units they had evacuated from Bulgaria, Greece, and Albania. Nevertheless, most authorities are agreed that the struggle for the liberation of Yugoslavia was to an overwhelming degree the work of the Partisans. Prime Minister Winston Churchill described the situation in Yugoslavia as follows in a report to the House of Commons on February 22, 1944:

> General Mihailovitch, I much regret to say, drifted gradually into a position where some of his commanders made accommodations with Italian and German troops, which resulted in their being left alone in certain mountain areas and in return doing nothing or very little against the enemy. . . . The Partisan movement soon outstripped in numbers the forces of General Mihailovitch. Not only Croats and Slovenes but large numbers of Serbians joined with Marshal Tito, and he has at this moment more than a quarter of a million men with him and large quantities of arms taken from the enemy or from the Italians. . . . These forces are at this moment holding in check no fewer than fourteen out of twenty German divisions in the Balkan Peninsula. . . . Of course, the partisans of Marshal Tito are the only people who are doing any effective fighting against the Germans now.[12]

Partisan Administration.   The Partisans developed an administrative system that they applied in the territories they liberated. When they occupied a village or town they first destroyed the existing political structure. They shot as quislings and traitors those gendarmes and civilian officials who had been particularly obnoxious. They burned police stations and all public records such as land registers, fiscal documents, and the archives of the police and law courts. The Partisans then set up their own state mechanism in the form of National Liberation Committees in villages, districts, and regions. In theory these committees were elected by the populace and reflected its views. But inevitably, under prevailing conditions, the voters and the candidates were limited to supporters of the Partisans, who in some areas constituted a majority and in others a minority. The committees discharged the functions of local government and represented the civilian arm of the Partisan movement. They directed agriculture and the primitive local industrial enterprises. They enrolled recruits and gathered supplies for the Partisan forces. They acted as organs of public safety, upholding law and order, and combating speculation and banditry. They also conducted anti-illiteracy and political propaganda campaigns, including the publication of several newspapers.

National Liberation Committees were also organized in enemy-occupied regions by the underground Communist party. Their duties were manifold and their contributions invaluable. They gathered funds and raised recruits for the Partisan armed forces. They organized sabotage in industrial centers and collected intelligence data concerning enemy operations and resources. One of their most spectacular achievements was the collection and smuggling of food supplies from the fertile plains areas to the Partisan brigades in the mountains. This operation was necessary because the mountain regions of Yugoslavia had never been able in peacetime to feed their own population, let alone the tens of thousands of additional consumers now gathered in the Partisan ranks.

The first nationally representative body organized by the Partisans met at Bihach in Bosnia on November 26 and 27, 1942. It was a congress attended by representatives from all parts of Yugoslavia, liberated and occupied, and the delegates included well-known members of most of the prewar political parties. The congress elected a body called the Anti-Fascist Council for the National Liberation of Yugoslavia, commonly known by its initials AVNOJ. The Communists conceived and called the congress in order to gain as broad a basis as possible for their Partisan movement. They calculated that they could entrust the nominal control of the Partisan organization to a representative body through which they could quietly and unobtrusively have their way while preserving the illusion of democratic procedure. In this manner they hoped that, without yielding control of the resistance movement, they would be able to attract wider support both within the country and from the Western powers.

This strategy succeeded brilliantly. The presidency of the AVNOJ was accepted by a prominent and respected figure, Dr. Ivan Ribar. He was known as the former speaker of the historic constituent assembly that had outlawed the Yugoslav Communist party more than twenty years earlier. It was not known that for some years he had been a close friend of Tito's. The

National Liberation Committees were nominally subordinated to the AVNOJ, though the dominant force and the binding cement continued to be the Communist party. The AVNOJ issued the so-called Bihach Manifesto, a program enumerating the six aims of the Partisan movement. These included "the liberation of the country," "the inviolability of private property," and "no radical changes whatsoever in the social life and activities of the people." In view of Tito's frank avowal to Brigadier Maclean that his aim was a Communist postwar Yugoslavia, these statements appear to be deliberately false and misleading. The manifesto also stipulated: "All the most important questions of social life and State organization will be settled by the people themselves through representatives who will be properly elected by the people after the end of the war." [13] Tito and his lieutenants undoubtedly were convinced that, in view of their leadership in the liberation struggle, they would be the "representatives of the people" at the end of the war. Thus there would be no real conflict between the plans for a Communist Yugoslavia and the promise of democratic procedure. The sixth point in the Bihach Manifesto was particularly important: "The National Liberation Movement fully recognizes the national rights of Croatia, Slovenia, Serbia, Macedonia and all other regions. . . . It guarantees that the national rights of all the peoples of Yugoslavia will be preserved." [14]

The Bihach assembly and its manifesto had a tremendous impact upon the country. Tito had already proved himself to be a genuine resistance leader. Now he appeared to be also a conciliatory statesman who offered a rational solution to Yugoslavia's basic nationalities problem and who proposed to deal with the other problems in a democratic and moderate fashion. Little wonder that increasing numbers of Yugoslavs now rallied to the side of Tito and his Partisans.

The sweeping victories of the Partisans following the collapse of Italy in September, 1943, induced them to call a second plenary session of the AVNOJ at Jajce in Bosnia. The meeting, which was held on November 29, 1943, transformed the AVNOJ into a legislative and executive body. A presidium of sixty-seven members, with Dr. Ribar as president, was established and invested with executive powers. Thirteen acting ministers were appointed, headed by Tito, who also served as acting minister of national defense. For the first time Tito's name, Josip Broz, was made public, and he was invested with the title of marshal. Finally, a resolution was passed forbidding the king and his government-in-exile to return to Yugoslavia until the people decided the form of government they preferred. "The so-called Yugoslav Government abroad," proclaimed the assembly, "is deprived of all the rights of a legal Government." [15]

In this manner Tito attained his goal of revolution through the fires of resistance. The struggle at home had been fought and won. The final outcome now awaited the readjustment of great power relationships that would follow inevitably with the crumbling of Hitler's Reich and the development of a power vacuum in the Balkans.

OCCUPIED GREECE

Occupation and Partition.   Greece, like Yugoslavia, was partitioned by the Axis conquerors. The Bulgarians took eastern Macedonia and Thrace, and the Albanians the northern part of Epirus. The Germans occupied the most strategic territories, including Athens, Saloniki, the province of Evros on the Turkish frontier, as well as Crete and certain other islands. The Italians occupied the rest of the country, which left them the rulers of most of Greece.

The Germans did not have the opportunity in Greece that they did in Yugoslavia of fomenting strife between religions and nationalities. Accordingly, they selected prominent Greek personalities to function as puppet premiers in order to make foreign rule more palatable. The first of these premiers was General George Tsolakoglou, who had surrendered the Epirus armies to the Germans * and who now remained in office from April 30, 1941, to December 2, 1942. His successor was professor Constantine Logothetopoulos, related by marriage to General von List, commander of the German Balkan campaign. Logothetopoulos was replaced on April 7, 1943, by a well-known royalist politician, John Rhalles, who remained premier until the liberation of Greece in October, 1944.

These officials, in order to win the support, or at least the toleration, of the Greek people, conducted a vigorous propaganda based primarily upon anti-Communism and anti-Slavism. They sought to exploit the traditional fear of Slavism in Greece, dating from the series of wars with the Bulgarians and the Russian espousal of Bulgarian territorial aspirations in the nineteenth century. Accordingly, the puppet officials in Athens branded their opponents in the resistance movement as "agents of international Slavic Communism." They pictured the war as a gigantic conflict between eastern hordes bent on establishing a Slavic-Communistic domination over Europe, and the German armies, which were waging a noble struggle to save European civilization from this double threat. It followed that every Greek patriot had the duty to cooperate with the Athens government and the German occupation authorities in combating the enemy within the gates, that is, the "Communistic" resistance groups. The following extract from a handbill distributed widely in occupied Greece in the summer of 1944 illustrates this propaganda campaign:

Come to your senses, Greek Andartes [guerrillas]. Open your eyes, recover your wits. Do not kill unjustly and do not strike your brothers in order to serve Britain and the Bolsheviks. The former writhes now like an expiring beast. The latter are nothing more than Slav nationalists who wish to absorb all Europe, drown its culture, assimilate us with the other Slavs of the Balkans, and put in practice Peter the Great's Satanic Pan-Slavic plans for making us helots, slaves, pariahs, minus religion, minus family, minus property, minus nationality.

Come to your senses, that we lose not the great name of Hellenes which we bear, that we lose not our life, our honor, our ground, and our precious liberty.

Let us extend our hands, let our slaughter of one another stop, and let

* See Chapter 37.

us join together like good brothers, helping Greater Germany to crush with every means, with every method, those two great enemies of the world, the Anglo-American-Jewish coalition and the Bolsheviks, the two evil demons of humanity, who tyrannize the world.

In the long run this propaganda proved ineffective. A major reason was the utter destitution of the Greek people, who were literally driven to resistance as a means of personal and national self-preservation. The basic difficulty was that Greece was of little economic value to the German war machine. Greece had nothing comparable to the Czech industries, the Danish dairy farms, or the Rumanian wheat fields and oil wells. Consequently, the Germans were little interested in the state of the Greek economy. In fact, they allowed their soldiers to strip the country clean by requisitioning or "buying" with freshly printed marks whatever caught their fancy. By October 10, 1942, Ciano was noting in his diary:

If we continue on the present basis the most complete bankruptcy will result within two months. Today the middle class is already obliged to give up its jewels, its beds, at times its daughters, in order to live. Hence, we are facing uprisings and disorders, the proportions of which it is impossible to estimate accurately at this time. But nothing can make the Germans change their absurd and idiotic attitude, and the worst of it is that we Italians must stand for 80 per cent of the consequences.[16]

The effect of this looting was accentuated by two other factors: the sharp decline in the productivity of the country and the almost complete cessation of imports. Agricultural production declined drastically because of the lack of fertilizer, draft animals, and equipment, and because of the general condition of insecurity in rural areas. Thus the average production of cereals during the years 1941–1944 was 60 per cent of the 1938 level. The two other most important crops, tobacco and currants, likewise fell to 89 and 66 per cent, respectively. Conditions were even worse in industry. The confiscation of machinery and the lack of raw materials cut down production to between 10 and 15 per cent of prewar levels and produced widespread unemployment.

Equally serious was the drop in imports with the enforcement of the Allied blockade against occupied Greece. Imports fell during the first year to 6 per cent of the prewar level. What this meant may be judged from the fact that before the war Greece imported 45 per cent of her wheat requirements, 57 per cent of the fish, 90 per cent of the rice, and 100 per cent of the sugar. The inevitable result was that actual famine conditions prevailed in Athens, Piraeus, and some of the islands in the winter of 1941–1942. The situation improved somewhat during the following years with the partial lifting of the Allied blockade and the rushing in of Red Cross relief supplies. Yet the diet of most Greeks continued to be totally inadequate in caloric intake and largely lacking in animal proteins and fats. The effect on the health of the population was described as follows in a confidential report prepared in April, 1943, by the General Director of Public Welfare and Hygiene:

The consequences of malnutrition have now taken a tragic form. Large numbers of persons are stricken with tuberculosis even in the higher classes, among lawyers, doctors, men of letters and science and public functionaries. . . . In certain localities every third child presents a case of tubercular glands. . . . Physical exhaustion and malnutrition have also increased other diseases. As shown by reports submitted by the Supreme Hygienic Council of the State and in special meetings of the Medical Society of Athens we are confronted with a terrific spread of malaria which has assumed a very virulent form. There are villages where no day goes by without at least one or two persons in every home being sick in bed with malaria. It is a tragic sight to see children yellow from anemia and with swollen abdomens. . . . Unless fundamental measures are taken to improve urgently and radically the health of the people, we will see the annihilation of a large portion of our nation.[17]

Such was the nightmare of occupation in Greece. During those three and a half years, 30 per cent of the nation's wealth was destroyed, 7 per cent of the population (500,000 out of 7,000,000) perished in battle or of starvation and diseases, while collaborationists and black marketeers added moral degradation to the material hurts of the nation. Such conditions were more eloquent than any amount of propaganda about the Slavic-Communist peril. Out of this misery emerged a resistance movement that attracted the support of a substantial portion of the population and attained a significance comparable to that of Tito's Partisans in Yugoslavia.

National Liberation Front (EAM). The Communist-controlled National Liberation Front was the leading resistance organization in Greece, corresponding to the Communist-controlled Partisans in Yugoslavia. The National Liberation Front, or EAM, as it was commonly called after the initials of the Greek words *Ethnikon Apeleftheretikon Metopon,* was organized in Athens on September 27, 1941. It rose to prominence for largely the same reasons that Tito's followers did to the north. The Communist party provided disciplined leadership and a nation-wide underground organization that had been tested during the years of the prewar Metaxas dictatorship. Also, the Greek Communists, like their Yugoslav counterparts, made their EAM a national rather than a party resistance organization. They invited into the EAM all Greeks regardless of political beliefs so long as they were opposed to the foreign occupationists. By 1944 the EAM had become a truly national organization in its composition. Several political groups had established affiliation, including the Communist party and four other minor Socialist and Agrarian parties. As for individuals, the EAM numbered in its ranks six bishops, several hundred priests, virtually all the labor leaders regardless of their political affiliations, and thirty university professors, including the president of the Polytechnic School and two members of the National Academy.

In addition to these personalities the EAM attracted large numbers of ordinary citizens into its various functional bodies. These included the National Popular Liberation Army (ELAS), United All-Greece Youth Organization (EPON), National Mutual Aid, or "Red Cross of the Resistance"

(EA), and Workers' National Liberation Front (EEAM). With this network of organizations the EAM was able to secure the active support of a large proportion of the population. The most militant and physically fit could join ELAS and fight in the mountains. The workers in the cities could organize and work through EEAM. The youth found social recreation and useful duties in EPON. All elements of the population could participate in the work of the "Red Cross of the Resistance." This was perhaps the most important achievement of EAM. It provided a program that was acceptable to all patriotic Greeks and established organizations suitable for citizens of all ages and backgrounds.

There is no agreement as to the size of the EAM and its subsidiary organizations. Estimates range from 500,000 to 2,000,000 members. Foreign Secretary Anthony Eden estimated that the armed forces, or ELAS, numbered 50,000 men and that the rest of the EAM apparatus included another 500,000 to 750,000 people. Whether these figures, or others that are considerably higher, are accepted, it is apparent that the EAM was a major force in a country of 7,000,000.

Nationalist Bands.   The EAM was not the only resistance organization in Greece. Several other groups existed, the most important being the Greek National Democratic League, or EDES. It was led by Colonel (later General) Napoleon Zervas, who might be compared to Mihailovich in the role that he played during the occupation. Neither the EDES nor the other so-called "nationalist" bands ever approached the EAM in popular following or effectiveness in resisting the Germans. They lacked the nation-wide organizational apparatus furnished the EAM by the Communists. Their leaders never showed any real grasp of the situation in Greece. They did not adopt or consistently follow a definite program based on the needs of the country. They wavered back and forth until their obvious weakness in relation to the EAM drove them to complete dependence on the British and to surreptitious collaboration with the Germans and the Italians.

This is well illustrated by the career of General Zervas. The EDES leader undoubtedly wished to rid the country of the invader. But he completely lacked the personal qualities and the organizational backing necessary to develop a strong resistance movement. He regarded EDES as his personal instrument that he was free to use as he wished to combat the Axis and also to advance his own fortunes. One of his chief lieutenants, who worked closely with him during the occupation, has described clearly his incapacity as a resistance leader:

> General Zervas' lack of a more general education, in the broad meaning of the word, and of ideological orientation, always was a basic obstacle to the development of psychological and spiritual ties among the guerrillas and members of EDES. . . . during the whole course of our endeavors we wavered between a superficial democratism and a superficial nationalism, without ever evolving a stable national political policy which could be used to arouse enthusiasm and militancy. We always met the stubborn opposition of General Zervas and of those

about him. . . . The centralization [of power] which General Zervas insisted on maintaining because of the circumstances of the struggle proved to be unwarranted and injurious. Nothing was heard but the slogan, "Faith in the Leader. All for the Leader. All from the Leader." [18]

It is not surprising that EDES was soon hopelessly outstripped by the EAM. When the British, for reasons which will be noted later, decided to back EDES as a counterweight to the EAM, Zervas eagerly accepted this aid and became completely dependent upon his supporters. Colonel C. M. Woodhouse, Chief of the British Military Mission to occupied Greece, observed that "without British support Zervas' army would never have existed . . . ." [19] There is also considerable documentary evidence indicating that Zervas had certain understandings with the Axis commanders. On August 10, 1943, the German chief of staff at Yanina in Epirus reported to Berlin: "At the conclusion of his operations Zervas has returned to a loyal position toward us and is being favorably received in Nationalist circles. British supplies helped Zervas carry out general mobilization and create new regiments. Zervas has now started fresh offensives against Communist bands." [20]

Despite British aid and German cooperation, EDES was never able to match the EAM and its ELAS forces in popular backing or military strength. At the time of liberation Zervas was found to have not more than 12,000 men and to control only a small area in Epirus, 35 miles long and 25 miles wide. Three months later when fighting broke out between ELAS and the British, Zervas' army was dispersed by ELAS in a brief four-day campaign. If it is remembered that Zervas' EDES was the only serious rival of ELAS, it becomes apparent why the EAM and ELAS could scarcely help becoming the mainstay of Greek resistance.

Resistance Struggle. The EAM's military arm, ELAS, was formally established in December, 1942. It was organized around a number of guerrilla chieftains who had taken to the mountains early in the year and waged individualistic, uncoordinated warfare against the invader. From the outset ELAS differed basically from the other resistance groups in that it was definitely subordinate to a parent political organization. Zervas' EDES and the other nationalist groups were commanded by military leaders who were free to pursue whatever policy they wished in either the political or the military field. By contrast, ELAS was created by the EAM and remained its subordinate military branch to the end.

All political matters were automatically referred to the EAM Central Committee. Military problems were entrusted to the ELAS High Command, but the Central Committee selected the personnel of this body. The Central Committee further ensured its control over ELAS by a multiple system of command. Each ELAS unit was led by a military commander, usually a regular army officer in the case of the higher ranks, and by a Kapetanios, the popular leader who frequently came from the ranks. The former made the final decision in military affairs while the latter took care of propaganda and morale within the unit and directed relations between the unit and the civilian population and organizations. In the top ELAS posts, such as general headquarters and division headquarters, the military commander and the Kapetanios were joined by a third person, a political representative of the EAM. The Kapetanios was a Communist as a rule and the political representative almost invariably. Thus, although the military men in ELAS were supreme so far as actual operations were concerned, nevertheless the army as a whole was firmly in the control of the EAM and ultimately of the Communist party.

In April, 1943, the prestige of ELAS rose considerably with the entry into its ranks of a well-known and distinguished regular army officer, Colonel (later General) Stephanos Saraphis. A month later, on May 19, 1943, a regular ELAS High Command was formed, consisting of Saraphis as military chief, Ares Velouchiotes, the redoubtable Communist guerrilla leader and the first organizer of ELAS bands, as the Kapetanios, and Vasiles Samariniotes, also a Communist, as the EAM representative.

At this time ELAS was strongest in central and northern Greece, that is Roumele, Thessaly, and Macedonia. Some 12,000 men belonged to the ELAS formations in these areas, and an undetermined additional number in the Peloponnesian and Thracian bands. In July, 1943, all these groups were reorganized by the new High Command along regular military lines. The prewar Greek army was used as the model in the internal organization of ELAS, the naming of the various units, and the adoption of military regulations and penal code.

In the summer of 1943 the new ELAS army carried out its first large-scale, coordinated operations. Up to this time it had gained control of the mountainous Pindus and Olympus areas and conducted hit-and-run operations in the plains. Now it received an order from General Headquarters, Middle East, to launch with EDES a coordinated series of sabotage operations. The reason for this order was the Allied invasion of Sicily scheduled for July 10. It was hoped that the diversionary operations would lead the Germans to anticipate landings in Greece rather than in Sicily. The plan was successful. During these weeks ELAS and EDES blew up trains and bridges, destroyed highways, cut telephone communications, and attacked Axis outposts. The Germans hurried two divisions to Greece, and on July 10 these forces were not available for the defense of Sicily.

Two months later Italy capitulated to the Allies and a large proportion of the Italian war matériel in Greece fell into the hands of ELAS. This provided ELAS with precisely what it hitherto had lacked. From the outset it had a surplus of manpower and a shortage of equipment. The Italian booty enabled ELAS to organize new artillery and cavalry units and to increase the number of armed regulars.

By the autumn of 1943 ELAS had become a rather formidable military machine. Its reserves in the cities and in the countryside were increasing rapidly and were gradually being armed. These reserves aided in the supply of the regular ELAS, gathered intelligence, attacked the enemy communication and transportation systems, and occasionally participated in pitched battles. The operations of ELAS were coordinated by a telephone network which was completed at this time and which connected virtually all the villages in the ELAS-controlled areas. Even barbed wire was used for this purpose. Equally impressive was the ELAS School of Reserve Officers, which graduated its first class of 136 cadets in September, 1943. British officers participated in the graduation ceremonies and delivered speeches praising the work of the school. The graduates were given commissions in ELAS with the rank of sublieutenant. The second class, consisting of 300 cadets, began its training the following month.

At this time ELAS demonstrated its strength by meeting successfully the severest test to which it was subjected. For various reasons which will be considered later, relations between ELAS and EDES had deteriorated to the point of armed conflict in October, 1943. At the moment when the ELAS attack was getting under way, German columns attacked the ELAS positions in the Pindus from five directions. This was a major offensive, the Germans using large forces equipped with planes, mountain artillery, and armored cars. They succeeded in reopening the strategic Kalambaka-Metsovo-Yanina highway connecting Thessaly with Epirus. Although ELAS was forced to retreat on a wide front and to surrender many villages, it retreated in good order and inflicted heavy losses on the enemy. By the end of December the German attacks petered out and ELAS began a counteroffensive. From January to April, 1944, it launched coordinated attacks at scattered points until finally the Germans abandoned the captured positions and returned to their original ones.

Having survived this test, ELAS was now the dominant resistance organization in all parts of Greece except for the small EDES force in Epirus and still smaller nationalist bands in isolated sections of Macedonia. During 1944 the Germans attempted only to retain control of the large towns and cities and the important transportation routes. In the Peloponnesus they held coastal cities such as Patras, Kalamata, Nauplion, and Corinth. In Macedonia and Thrace they remained in the largest cities, such as Saloniki, Kavalla, Serres, and Drama. In the rest of Greece they were concerned primarily in controlling and operating the vital railway running from Athens to Saloniki. They succeeded in keeping ELAS out of the towns along the route—Thebes, Levadeia, Lamia, and Larissa—but they were not able to prevent ELAS units from continually blowing up bridges and sections of track. In 1944 the Germans were able to transport along this line only a small percentage of the normal load. By the summer of that year, when the Germans began to evacuate Greece because of Russian pressure in the north, only about a third of the country was under German control. The remaining two thirds constituted "Free Greece," defended by the ELAS forces and administered by the EAM.

Much controversy persists concerning the role of ELAS in occupied Greece. Certain quarters tend to minimize the contribution of ELAS to the resistance struggle. The Germans are perhaps the best authorities as to who

was responsible for the resistance they encountered in Greece. In their propaganda efforts they invariably denounced the EAM-ELAS and warned the
Greek people that it was the enemy within the gates—the agency of international Slavic Communism. But in regard to EDES and the other resistance
bodies, both the Germans and their puppet Greek propagandists were eloquently silent. Similarly, the captured German documents invariably refer to
attacks by "communist" ELAS bands and to mopping-up operations against
these bands, but EDES and the other groups are very infrequently mentioned.
Typical is a German report bearing the date July 6, 1943, and entitled
"Political Situation in Greece, 4 June to 3 July 1943":

> "90 percent of the Greeks today are unanimously hostile toward the Axis
> Powers and are ready for open revolt. . . . the EAM with its combat organizations
> [is] the main bearer of the entire resistance movement against the Axis Powers.
> The greater part of the bands is subordinated to it. It is in a leading position, po-
> litically speaking, and, because it is very active and enjoys a coordinated leader-
> ship, it represents the greatest danger to the occupying powers." [21]

EAM Administration. The village was the base of the nation-wide
EAM structure. In each village there were four EAM groups: the EA for
relief work, the EPON youth body, the ETA (Epimeletes tou Andarte) or
guerrilla commissariat, and the general EAM committee. The duty of ETA
was to collect taxes throughout liberated Greece, and, when possible, in the
occupied territories. The levy was based on the principle of no taxation on a
specified minimum quantity necessary for sustenance, and progressive taxation
on the remainder. For example, the peasant paid nothing on his first 300 okas
(an oka equals 2¾ pounds) of grain, then 5 per cent on the next 1,500,
11 per cent on the next 2,000, and 13 per cent on the remainder. The same
principle applied for livestock, fish, olives, raisins, tobacco, and all other
produce.

About 20 per cent of the proceeds went to the various civilian bodies
to meet the expenses of village administration. The rest, usually foodstuffs,
went to the district ELAS headquarters and from there to the ELAS depots.
Thus ELAS units had food supplies available for them throughout the country and did not have to resort to unorganized and indiscriminate requisitioning, which would have antagonized the peasants.

The secretary of the general EAM committee was known as the
Ipefthinos, or responsible one. His duties were to check the identification
papers of travelers or newcomers to the village, furnish mules and guides
when needed by ELAS, and provide recommendations for local villagers who
wished to join ELAS. It was through the Ipefthinos that the Communists
controlled the EAM mechanism. When the occupation began, most of the
EAM organizers were members of the Communist party, which had kept a
nation-wide underground organization during the Metaxas dictatorship. Thus
it was almost always a Communist who arrived at a village, recruited as

many peasants as he could into the EAM, and stayed on as the leading EAM functionary.

The hierarchical form of the EAM further increased Communist influence. The Ipefthinoi of a group of villages elected the eparchia, or district EAM committee. The members of this committee in turn elected an Ipefthinos, and the Ipefthinoi of several district committees elected the nomos, or prefecture EAM committee. The process was repeated and the Ipefthinoi of several prefectures elected the regional committee, which represented a large area such as Thessaly or Macedonia. There were approximately a dozen such regions in Greece, and each had one representative in the national central committee.

Large cities, such as Athens, Piraeus, Saloniki, Patras, and Volos, had one delegate in the national central committee, each being the Ipefthinos of its city's central committee. The latter was elected by the Ipefthinoi of the neighborhood committees and of the functional groups—for lawyers, scientists, doctors, teachers, artists, civil servants, clerks, workers, and so forth.

In this way some twenty-five delegates were elected to the national Central Committee, the supreme policy-making body. These delegates represented the constituent political parties (Communist, Socialist, Agrarian, and so on), the functional groups (ELAS, EPON, EA, and so on), the central committees of the various regions, and the central committees of the large cities. It is apparent that the Communist control of the Ipefthinoi ensured a Communist majority on the national central committee, although only about a tenth of the total EAM membership were also members of the Communist party. It is also apparent that this organizational mechanism enabled the Communists to camouflage their control, at least so far as the majority of Greeks were concerned.

The final step in the evolution of the administration of the liberated territories was the creation by the EAM on March 10, 1944, of a five-man Political Committee of National Liberation, or PEEA. This body was entrusted with two tasks. One was to bring pressure to bear on the government-in-exile to agree to the formation of a representative national government. In this respect the Greek Communists differed basically from their Yugoslav comrades, who had specifically repudiated their exile government at their Jajce assembly in April, 1943. The Greek Communists, by contrast, were now endeavoring to force their way into their government-in-exile in Cairo. The significance of this difference will be analyzed in the following chapter. Suffice it to note here that it explains in part the entirely different course of events in the two countries following liberation.

The other task of PEEA was to supervise the administration of the liberated territories. Since these included by this date over one half the area of the country and about two and a half million people, PEEA decided that the time had come for the election of a National Council. The election was held on April 9, 1944. Elaborate measures were taken to secure a representative assembly, but the delegates inevitably reflected the EAM predominance in the liberated areas and in the underground resistance in the occupied territories. On May 7 a total of 250 delegates met from all parts of Greece. Athens was represented by 20 delegates, Saloniki by 10, Piraeus by 7, and so on to the provincial towns and rural districts. The delegates were a representative cross section of Greek society, including 2 bishops, 2 priests, 5 university professors, 8 generals, 20 civil servants, 5 industrialists, 15 doctors, 25 lawyers, 22 laborers, 23 farmers, 10 newspapermen, 10 scientists, 9 high school teachers, and others.

The National Council issued a proclamation on May 27 defining its objectives. It declared its "undaunted will to fight to the end for the liberation of the country, for the complete smashing of fascism and for the restoration of national unity and popular sovereignty." In the light of later events the significant feature of this proclamation is that it looked forward to an arrangement with the government-in-exile. The final article stated: "The work of the National Council will continue until the whole country is liberated. It may be dissolved before liberation if it decides itself on a motion by one third of its own members, or on a proposal by PEEA." [22] This meant that both PEEA and the National Council were ready to leave the stage if the EAM could secure representation in the royal cabinet in Cairo. We shall see later that in September, 1944, the EAM was allowed to participate in the cabinet, with far-reaching repercussions for the resistance movement and the entire postwar history of Greece.

In conclusion it is apparent that by the summer of 1944 the EAM had developed a complete state apparatus. It possessed a powerful army, an effective administrative organization, and a National Council with delegates from all parts of Greece. Needless to say, the EAM had many serious shortcomings. Criminal elements seized the opportunity provided by the years of turbulence to commit crimes in the name of resistance. Certain ELAS officers were also responsible for unnecessary excesses. Some of them were fierce guerrilla fighters who rose from the ranks of ELAS but who remained guerrilla chieftains at heart and gave no quarter and expected none. Others were fanatical Communists, imbued with the ideology of the class struggle and assuming that those who were not with them were against them and should be treated as enemies. In addition, certain ELAS units were guilty of executing suspects on inconclusive evidence or because facilities were lacking for their imprisonment.

Despite these shortcomings, the fact remains that the EAM represented Greece as much as any organization could during a period of foreign occupation. Colonel Woodhouse, the chief of the British Military Mission, who regarded the EAM as a tyrannical organization and who fought it as a menace to British imperial interests, nevertheless paid it the following tribute:

> The initiative of EAM/ELAS justified their predominance, though not their tyranny. Having acquired control of almost the whole country, except the principal communications used by the Germans, they had given it things that

it had never known before. Communications in the mountains, by wireless, courier, and telephone, have never been so good before or since; even motor roads were mended and used by EAM/ELAS. Their communications, including wireless, extended as far as Crete and Samos, where guerillas were already in the field. The benefits of civilisation and culture trickled into the mountains for the first time. Schools, local government, law-courts and public utilities, which the war had ended, worked again. Theatres, factories, parliamentary assemblies began for the first time. Communal life was organised in place of the traditional individualism of the Greek peasant. His child was dragooned into EPON, his nest-egg levied into EA, his *caique* commandeered to equip ELAN [EAM's naval arm]. . . . Followed at a distance by the minor organisations, EAM/ELAS set the pace in the creation of something that Governments of Greece had neglected: an organised state in the Greek mountains. All the virtues and vices of such an experiment could be seen; for when people whom no one has ever helped started helping themselves, their methods are vigorous and not always nice. The words "liberation" and "popular democracy" filled the air with their peculiar connotations. Uneasy stirrings were breaking the surface everywhere, but only the KKE [Communist party of Greece] knew how to give them direction.[23]

OCCUPIED ALBANIA

In Albania the Communist-dominated National Liberation Front, or LNC (Levisiya Nacional Clirimtare), was the counterpart of the Greek EAM and the Yugoslav Partisan movement. The situation in Albania was such that the LNC, as the National Liberation Front will be termed henceforth, was able to seize power with comparatively little opposition. There was no exile government to challenge the pretensions of the Communist resistance leaders. Also, the years of King Zog's dictatorship and of the Italian occupation left Albania with no political parties or leaders, thus presenting the Communists with an open field for their operations. And the LNC had the additional advantage of being supported by the powerful Partisan and EAM resistance organizations. Finally, the LNC did not have to contend with Allied forces as did the EAM in Greece after the Germans departed. Neither the Russians nor the Western powers bothered to send troops to Albania once the country had been evacuated by the Axis.

After the Italians had occupied Albania in April, 1939, they issued a constitution for the country on June 3, 1939. They defined Albania as an autonomous constitutional monarchy, hereditary in the house of Savoy. The constitution actually was designed to institutionalize Italian domination. King Victor Emmanuel was entrusted with executive, legislative, and judicial authority, and the Albanian armed forces and diplomatic corps were incorporated into those of Italy. Two years later, when the Germans overran Yugoslavia and Greece, Albania was given the Yugoslav province of Kosovo, which had a predominantly Albanian population, and the northern part of the Greek province of Epirus, which had a small Albanian minority. Axis propaganda now boasted that Albania at last had secured her just ethnic frontiers.

Despite these territorial gains, the Albanians did not resign themselves to foreign rule. They had always resented central authority, and now that it was foreign their resentment was greater. Also, their experiences of the past decade had shown that the main danger to their national independence came from Italy. The Italians sensed the general disaffection and made various concessions in June, 1941, allowing the Albanians greater autonomy. Despite these concessions, an organized resistance movement began to develop in the country in 1942.

The Albanian Communists during the prewar years had functioned in scattered and uncoordinated groups. The three most important had been in Scutari in the north, in Tirana in the center, and in Koritsa in the south. To the latter group belonged an obscure young *lycée* teacher, Enver Hoja (Hoxha), who was to become the president of the country after the war. The social basis of Communism in Albania was to be found in the landless peasants of the south and the disaffected, European-trained intellectuals in the cities. The peasants had long been ready for revolt: they lacked land and, in addition, the owners of the estates they tilled were Moslems, whereas they were Orthodox Christians. As for the intellectuals, they never numbered more than two or three thousand, but they constituted the mainstay of the Communist apparatus and provided the leadership necessary for the organization of the peasants. These young men were peculiarly susceptible to revolutionary ideas because they had no roots in landed property or among the tribes, and could find no satisfaction for their aspirations within the narrow limits of independent Albania. At one time ambitious young Albanians had gone to Constantinople and found a career in the Ottoman imperial bureaucracy. Now this outlet was closed and none other had taken its place. Under such circumstances, educated young men in other countries had turned to fascism. But in Albania this was the creed of the foreign overlord, so the young men turned instead to communism.

The Albanian Communists owed much to Tito, who, even before the war began, had sent agents to help build a party structure. On November 8, 1941, these Yugoslav organizers summoned a meeting in Tirana of the most promising Albanian Communists and thereby established the Albanian Communist party. A central committee of eleven was selected, with Enver Hoja as provisional secretary. In September, 1942, the party leaders organized the LNC when they persuaded a number of the northern chieftains to join forces with them. Soon after the LNC came into existence, a more conservative group of Albanian patriots formed the National Front, or Balli Kombetar. They were anti-Zogists of mildly liberal, republican, and strongly nationalist convictions. When some British and a few American agents arrived in Albania they strove to unite the Ballists and the LNC into one strong resistance organization. They arranged a meeting of representatives of the two bodies on August 2, 1943, and induced them to accept a plan for united action against the Italians. But the Supreme Committee of the LNC reversed its position and refused to ratify the agreement. The reaction of the British officers to the two Albanian groups is revealing:

The forces of the Balli Kombetar seemed to Maclean and Smiley weaker in numbers, organisation, and morale than those of the LNC. Some indeed of their leaders paid more heed to British advice than did the Communists, but their zeal for war was severely restrained by the enjoyment of their present riches. While, therefore, the British officers gave them some supplies of arms and money, and occasionally took part in their operations against the enemy, the greater part of their efforts were devoted to the training and supplying of the Partisans [of LNC].[24]

When Italy collapsed in September, 1943, the LNC disarmed two Italian divisions and obtained large quantities of supplies. With these it was able to increase its forces and occupy several large cities, including Koritsa, Argyrokastron, Berat, and Elbasan. The Germans then rushed in troops, captured the cities, and set up a four-man regency to help its forces rule the country. The Germans could spare only two and a half divisions for Albania, so they contented themselves with controlling the cities and main routes, leaving the rest of the country to the resistance bands.

By October, 1943, the two Albanian resistance groups were openly at war with each other after the manner of their counterparts in Yugoslavia and Greece. The reasons were basically the same as in the two neighboring countries. On the one hand, the Ballists were alarmed by the mounting strength of the LNC and some of their leaders resorted to collaboration with the Germans as the lesser of two evils. On the other hand, the LNC had regarded the Ballists as dangerous rivals and treated them accordingly. A British officer concluded that he "could not escape coming to the conclusion that the Communist leaders were more interested in eliminating their rivals and seizing political power after the war than in the immediate task of killing Italians." [25]

The Germans took advantage of the civil war to launch their first offensive against the LNC on December 19, 1943. The guerrillas successfully evaded the advancing Germans and were able to increase their numbers as a result of German terrorism. By the fall of 1944, when the Germans evacuated the country, the LNC leaders claimed to have nearly 70,000 men under their command.

In the political field the LNC followed the example of Tito. On May 24, 1944, it assembled a National Congress of two hundred delegates from all parts of the country. The Congress selected a supreme legislative body, the Antifascist Council of National Liberation, consisting of thirty members. The Congress also forbade Zog to return to Albania and resolved not to recognize any Albanian government that might be formed abroad. At the second meeting of the Antifascist Council on October 20, 1944, a provisional government was formed with Enver Hoja at the head. The following month the LNC forces drove the Germans out of Tirana and on December 4 Hoja formally proclaimed the complete liberation of Albania.

THE NEW SPIRIT

One of the most important developments in the Balkans during the war years was the undermining of the old order in most of the peninsula. Hitler was not able to establish his much advertised "new order," but he did succeed in destroying the old one. For all his avowed anticommunism, Hitler's historical role proved to be revolutionary because he demolished existing institutions—social, economic, and political. In Eastern Europe especially, Hitler proved to be the great leveler.

Even in the satellite countries he undermined the old order because the existing regimes were discredited by their association with him. Then in late 1944, the Red Army, whose entrance into Europe he made possible, marched in and forcibly swept away the remnants of the old regimes and imposed new ones. This revolutionary change was much more pronounced in the occupied countries, where powerful resistance movements attracted a wide following. The resistance organizations, by their very nature, not only shattered the existing institutions but also created a new atmosphere—a new spirit.

One manifestation of this new spirit was the awakening of the hitherto inert peasantry. The guerrillas who fought against the Axis armies were in the great majority of cases peasants turned fighters. These peasants learned that they could exist without the towns but that the towns could not survive without supplies from the countryside. They also discovered that they were physically and psychologically better equipped than the townsmen to meet the harsh conditions of guerrilla warfare. In fact, it was largely peasant armies that liberated the cities from the foreign invaders. Such experiences and triumphs inevitably affected the outlook of the peasantry profoundly.

Another manifestation of the new spirit was the marked change in the relationship of the sexes. Before the war the interests and activities of women had been strictly limited by traditional social conventions. During the occupation these conventions were to a considerable degree abandoned. With the absence of so many men, the women assumed responsibility for the family farms and the care of the children. The younger women also entered every branch of the resistance movements, including the fighting brigades. In Greece, for example, about 40 per cent of the members of the EPON youth organization were young women, and one of the crack ELAS battalions consisted exclusively of women. A Yugoslav woman leader described the changes in sex relationships in her country as follows:

Before any written law, women became equal with men during the course of the war. This came about through an accepted, almost unspoken agreement. . . . The right of women to take part with the men in the whole life of their people became the right of shepherdesses in the mountains, village women in Krajina and Lika, in the Slavonian villages and in the dugouts of Srem. . . . Before they knew what it meant, the right was theirs. . . . They attained it in a unique way, one only possible during a great liberation struggle. Before any law was written, women were already taking part in making laws. . . . No one any longer drove women out of doors while the men were consulting.[26]

The new spirit also found expression in the new position of youth. In all revolutionary periods it is natural that youth should come to the fore because it is less committed to the *status quo,* more receptive to new ideas, and more ready to take up arms. In the Balkan countries young men and women flocked into the youth organizations and played a prominent role in the resistance struggle. Teen-age guerrilla fighters were common, as were also commanders in their early twenties. This naturally shook the domination of the middle-aged and elderly men, which had been unconsciously accepted for generations as a normal condition of peasant life.

A final manifestation of the new spirit was the discrediting of the traditional political leaders. They had no aptitude or relish for underground work. They were apprehensive of the competition of the new leaders who were arising from the rank and file of the resistance movement and felt at home in it. Thus the great majority of the prewar political personages remained aloof from the struggle against the foreign invaders. They also proved incapable of comprehending the new forces and ideas at work in their countries. In Yugoslavia, for example, they continued to think along the traditional national-religious lines, with the Serb politicians determined to reimpose their hegemony at the end of the war, and the Croatians to maintain their independent Croatia. The same was true in Greece, where Colonel Woodhouse described the role of the old political leaders as follows:

> They lived in the past both socially and politically. . . . Most of them remained throughout the dictatorship of Metaxas, throughout the German occupation, and remain to this day oblivious of the social revolutions that have taken place in Western Europe. The retrogression of their political thought is still more marked: for the only lively political problem that divides them is still the constitutional question of Monarchy or Republic, which has been fruitlessly debated without intermission since it came into being in 1917.[27]

In this manner the old party chiefs forfeited their traditional leadership. In doing so they left a political vacuum which the Communists quickly exploited. They succeeded not only because they were well organized and disciplined but also because they astutely used nationalism for their own purposes. They took the lead in organizing revolutionary nationalist movements against the foreign invaders and thereby gained the positions and power necessary to realize the revolutionary social changes that were their ultimate aim. The following statement by Stalin offers a key to much that happened in the Balkan Peninsula during the occupation: "Leninism . . . recognizes the latent revolutionary capabilities of the national liberation movement . . . and it is possible to use these for the purpose of overthrowing the common enemy, for the purpose of overthrowing imperialism."[28]

39. Hidden War, Cold War and Peace Settlement in 1947

THE BALKAN COUNTRIES underwent entirely different experiences during the war years. Bulgaria and Rumania, not having offered resistance to the Axis Powers, were spared the ordeals of invasion and occupation. Consequently, they did not generate significant national resistance movements. By contrast, Yugoslavia, Greece, and Albania waged grueling struggles against the occupation forces and at the same time endured savage internecine fighting between the Communist-led groups and their rivals. In the end, the radical resistance organizations gained the upper hand and were the dominant power in their respective countries by the time the Axis forces withdrew.

These developments seemed to foretell that if the postwar Balkan regimes were to differ significantly from each other the dividing line would run north and south, with Bulgaria and Rumania on the one side and Yugoslavia, Greece, and Albania on the other. A dividing line did appear as soon as the Germans withdrew, but it ran from east to west. On the one side was Greece, who experienced the least institutional change despite her turbulent war record, and on the other were the remaining Balkan countries, which were subjected to Communist domination and social upheaval.

This unexpected outcome indicates that the course of postwar Balkan history was determined, in part at least, by external forces. The most important of these was, as usual, the interplay of conflicting great-power policies. Even during the war years the Allies were engaged in a covert struggle with each other at the same time that they fought against Hitler. They fought two wars during these years, a war against the Axis and a war, now hidden, now open, among themselves. They had a common cause against the enemy, but they kept in mind the postwar balance of power and jockeyed for position. The closer they came to victory the more they sacrificed unity for what they considered to be their national interests. And as soon as they defeated the

800

enemy their hidden war burst into the open and became the Cold War. In this chapter we shall trace the veiled course of the hidden war during the occupation period, and the flamboyant unfolding of the cold war between liberation and the signing of the peace treaties in 1947.

BRITISH AGENTS AND BALKAN GUERRILLAS

During most of the war period, Britain alone, of the Allied Powers, maintained contact with the resistance organizations in the Balkans. On October 23, 1943, for example, Prime Minister Churchill informed President Roosevelt: "We British have about eighty separate missions working with partisans and patriot bands scattered over these immense mountainous regions. . . ." [1] Until late in the war neither the United States nor the Soviet Union had sent missions of their own. The Soviet government apparently was too preoccupied to establish contact at a time when it was fighting for survival on the banks of the Volga. The United States government, on the other hand, regarded the entire Middle East, including the Balkans, as an area of British concern and deliberately avoided any involvement. Thus Britain was left with virtually a free hand, and her primacy was further strengthened by the fact that the Greek and Yugoslav governments-in-exile were located in London and were dependent on British financial subsidies. In fact, the British government had much more contact with, and influence over, the resistance groups than did the exile governments. The latter not only lacked the technical facilities for communication but also were estranged from the resistance bodies because of ideological and political differences.

Considering first British relations with the Yugoslav resistance movement, we find that the earliest British missions were assigned to Mihailovich as the representative of the government-in-exile. In May, 1943, Churchill sent a small group to Tito's headquarters to check reports of a powerful and growing Partisan movement. Captain F. W. Deakin, an Oxford don who commanded the group, sent back dispatches emphasizing the extent and significance of Tito's operations against the enemy. Churchill then decided to send a senior officer, Brigadier Fitzroy Maclean, to head the mission with the Partisans. Maclean arrived in September, 1943, to find the situation revolutionized. Tito had taken advantage of the Italian surrender to disarm six Italian divisions while two others had joined him voluntarily. The Partisans now numbered 200,000 men and Maclean reported that they were destined to be the future rulers of Yugoslavia. Churchill acted in accordance with this information and took the initiative at the Teheran Conference in November, 1943, to propose that Allied support be transferred from Mihailovich to Tito. The following month he withdrew all British personnel from Mihailovich's headquarters.

Churchill's general attitude toward developments in Yugoslavia at this time is made clear in the following account by Maclean of a conversation that he had with the prime minister shortly after the Teheran Conference:

I now emphasized to Mr. Churchill the other points which I had already made in my report, namely, that in my view the Partisans, whether we helped them or not, would be the decisive political factor in Jugoslavia after the war and, secondly, that Tito and the other leaders of the Movement were openly and avowedly Communist and that the system which they would establish would inevitably be on Soviet lines and, in all probability, strongly oriented towards the Soviet Union.

The Prime Minister's reply resolved my doubts.

"Do you intend," he asked, "to make Jugoslavia your home after the war?"

"No, Sir," I replied.

"Neither do I," he said. "And, that being so, the less you and I worry about the form of Government they set up, the better. That is for them to decide. What interests us is, which of them is doing most harm to the Germans?" [2]

Turning to British relations with the Greek resistance movement, we find that Churchill's attitude toward the Communist-dominated EAM was much less accommodating than it was toward Tito's Partisans. The explanation certainly does not lie in any substantive difference in the two organizations. Both were led and directed by Communists and both had the same ultimate objectives that Maclean had described to Churchill. Yet the British prime minister from the beginning was resolved to control the Greek resistance organizations in contrast to his acceptance of Tito's hegemony in Yugoslavia. It may be assumed that one reason for the difference in his policy was that Greece loomed more important in British imperial considerations than did Yugoslavia. Greece, with her numerous harbors and islands, was an essential factor in the balance of power in the eastern Mediterranean. If Britain was to retain her traditional primacy in that area it doubtless seemed essential to Churchill that postwar Greece should be ruled by a friendly, non-Communist government.

Another explanation for Churchill's Greek policy may lie in the fact that the EAM was not as powerful and militant an organization as its Yugoslav counterpart. Churchill was informed unequivocally that the Partisans would play a decisive role in postwar Yugoslavia. The reports from Greece, although stressing the pre-eminence of the EAM, did not accept its ultimate triumph as inevitable. Accordingly, Churchill, in giving arms to the EAM to fight the Axis, imposed throughout certain conditions and restrictions designed to make possible British supervision and control, and to prevent the EAM from consolidating and extending its predominance.

The first British mission to occupied Greece dropped by parachute on October 1, 1942. Twenty-five miles north of the landing spot were Thermopylae and the Gorgopotamos Bridge on the main Saloniki-Larissa-Athens railroad, which was then carrying supplies for Rommel's army in North Africa. The objective of this mission, headed by Brigadier Edward Myers, was to blow up the Gorgopotamos Bridge. After weeks of hiding in damp caves and struggling up and down snow-covered mountains, the mission made contact with two guerrilla groups and with their help demolished the bridge. When escape from Greece proved impossible, the mission was ordered to stay on as an official British Military Mission for liaison between the Greek guerrillas and General Headquarters, Middle East.

Myers now discovered that the Communist-led EAM, with its military branch, ELAS, was by far the strongest resistance organization in the country. It dominated central and northern Greece, while EDES, its only significant rival, controlled only a part of the province of Epirus.* The cooperation of EAM-ELAS was obviously essential if there was to be any substantial resistance in Greece. Under these circumstances Myers furnished ELAS with the minimum of arms necessary for specific operations and at the same time encouraged and bolstered EDES as a counterweight to ELAS. Myers also prepared in March, 1943, a document specifying how Greek resistance bodies should be organized and how they should operate in order to be eligible for British aid. The most important provisions were the following:

1. All andarte [guerrilla] bands are to be known for military purposes as "National Bands," which title will be the only one used by the Allies.

2. Greece is to be divided into areas. A competent leader, recognised by mutual agreement of Brigadier Eddie [Edward Myers] † as representative of GHQ, Middle East, and of the Greeks, will be appointed military commander of each area. Each commander will be solely responsible for all military decisions in his area. All "National Bands" in the same area will co-operate fully under the military commander's orders.

5. No member of any "National Band" is ever to mention politics in public. Every member is to be free to have his own political views.

9. If, in the opinion of the British Liaison Staff, there is any failure to carry out the above Agreement, GHQ, Middle East will immediately order the cessation of supply of war material until the failure is rectified.[3]

The effect of these provisions would have been to remove the resistance struggle from the political arena and place it under effective British control. The EAM leaders refused to accept these terms, and it was not until July, 1943, that an agreement was reached that was acceptable to all parties. This provided for the establishment of a Joint General Headquarters "for the better direction of the struggle and for the co-ordination of all military actions." This body was to be composed of "representatives of all guerrilla bands recognized throughout Greece or occupying large areas, as well as a representative of the Middle East." The ELAS High Command was to continue and it was clear from the negotiations and the terms of the agreement that it would operate as an autonomous unit in carrying out the orders of GHQ, Middle East. The provision for no politics was withdrawn, though it

---

* Various Greek resistance groups were described in Chapter 38.

† Members of the military missions used their Christian names, even for formal purposes, when operating in the occupied Balkan countries.

was still stipulated that supplies were to be cut off if the pact's provisions were violated.[4]

This agreement made possible the effective cooperation of all Greek forces in carrying out a far-flung series of diversionary operations in the summer of 1943. The Germans rushed two divisions to Greece to meet an expected Allied invasion which materialized, instead, in Sicily. Myers then received orders to "lie low . . . with a view, when the time came for the invasion of Greece itself, to carrying out another series of widespread sabotage operations. . . ."[5] Considerations of higher strategy prevented an invasion from being made before the Germans evacuated the country in the fall of 1944. During the interval Myers became increasingly involved in political entanglements. The basic reason was that all parties concerned—the British as well as the rival Greek resistance groups—were jockeying with an eye to the postwar balance of power.

The EAM, like the Yugoslav Partisans, had plans for social revolution following the war. They believed that the British would make every effort to stop them and would use King George as their tool. Accordingly, they conducted a propaganda campaign against the Glueksburg, as they invariably called the king. They accused him of responsibility for the prewar Metaxas dictatorship and denounced him for fleeing the country and living abroad in luxury while his people endured the hardships of occupation and resistance. Above all they warned that he would be foisted willy-nilly upon the people of Greece at the end of the war as a puppet of imperial Britain.

This propaganda proved so effective that Myers now proposed that the British government should persuade King George to announce publicly that he would not set foot on Greek soil until the people expressed in a free plebiscite their desire for his return. In this manner, Myers argued, "the bottom could be knocked out of EAM's basket of propaganda."[6] In order to settle this ticklish monarchy question Myers arranged for a meeting in Cairo between Greek officials and representatives of the resistance groups. In August, 1943, six resistance representatives, together with Myers, flew to Cairo from hidden airfields in occupied Greece. By coincidence there appeared in Cairo at the same time an official spokesman of the several political parties represented in the preMetaxas parliament. Thus there now gathered in Cairo representatives of all the Greek political parties and resistance organizations.

These representatives on August 17 submitted a memorandum to Premier Emmanuel Tsouderos, head of the Greek exile government which recently had moved from London to Cairo. The memorandum requested that "for the sake of national unity which alone can guarantee the success of our national struggle. . . . an authoritative statement be issued that the King will not return to Greece before the people have expressed themselves on the form of their government."[7] On August 19 the Tsouderos cabinet discussed the memorandum, approved its contents unanimously, and passed a resolution authorizing Tsouderos to "communicate this decision of the Council of Ministers to His Majesty the King."[8]

This placed the king in a difficult position. All the resistance groups, all the political parties, even the royal ministers, were agreed that the king should not return until after a plebiscite. King George already had declared publicly on July 4, 1943, that the Greek people would be free to elect a constituent assembly after liberation. But he refused to go further and state publicly that he would remain out of the country until after the people had expressed their wish.

The open conflict between the king and the Greek delegates and ministers served to bring to the fore a basic dichotomy in British policy. This dichotomy has been defined succinctly as follows by Colonel C. M. Wood-house, who shortly was to succeed Myers as commander of the British Mission in Greece: "Those who put the war effort first tended to have an adverse opinion of the King, because practically all resistance to the Germans in Greece was carried on by republicans; those who put long-term considerations first looked with favour upon the King as the most likely guarantee that Greece would not pursue an anti-British policy after the war." [9] More specifically, the proposal that the king should remain abroad was supported by SOE, or Special Operations Executive, the British counterpart of the American Office of Strategic Services. Because the SOE was directly in charge of the British missions in Greece it was concerned primarily with or-ganizing effective resistance operations. On the other hand, the Foreign Office, which was more interested in postwar power relationships, strongly supported the king as the most reliable guarantee of a friendly Greece. Churchill sup-ported the Foreign Office and the final decision therefore was to stand by the king.

The top British officials in the Middle East now met with the Greek ministers and resistance delegates and informed them that the British gov-ernment favored the return of the king upon liberation and opposed the de-mands being made upon him. The British officials also ordered the Greek delegates to leave Cairo at once and return to their homeland. Furthermore, Brigadier Myers, who had become identified with the plan to keep King George abroad, was not allowed to return to Greece, being replaced by Col-onel Woodhouse. The reaction of the resistance delegates was expressed by the EDES representative.

> After some days we received our answer: we were ordered to leave Cairo at once. This order was announced to us officially by Marshal Wilson. We pro-tested against the unheard-of-manner in which we were being forcibly expelled. We were transported like prisoners to the airdrome. Mr. G. Kartales [representa-tive of the political parties], suffering from acute malaria and fever, was forced to follow. . . . On the mountains of Greece, we, and the guerrillas we represented, were the "heroic Greeks." In Cairo, because we disturbed British policy and the plans of the King, we were "undesirables." [10]

These developments in Cairo marked a turning point in Greek affairs. Field Marshal Lord Wilson, the British commander in chief in the Middle East, has emphasized the significance of the decision to back King George.

The acute differences between our diplomats and S.O.E. arose over Myers, whom the former accused of getting too deeply committed to E.A.M. and ranging outside his province in the political sphere by encouraging the left wing leaders, whereas H. M. Government were backing the King and the refugee Government; Myers, on the other hand, claimed that E.A.M. held the greatest control of the resistance movement though some of our liaison officers differed about this; the Greeks recognized Myers as a leader and he had their confidence, thus enabling him to get the different parties to sit round a table and agree to work under one direction. The suggestion to defer the return of the King brought matters to a head; our diplomats were strongly averse to any encouragement being given to parties which might prejudice the return of the King and the existing Greek Government, while S.O.E. wanted to build up resistance regardless of the politics of any of the bands they had contacted. From the war effort point of view the latter course was preferable and I personally did not like the idea of tying our liaison officers exclusively to one political party. . . . I felt that the wisest course was to work with the left wing parties and endeavour to guide them rather than to resist them. Myers, nevertheless, was ordered to report to London and was not allowed to return to Greece.

The warm welcome of the six delegates by our Ambassador followed by a rapid cooling off as soon as their political demands were made known marked in my opinion the turning point in our relations with E.A.M. . . . since the six delegates who came to Cairo had returned with their demands not acceded to, a strong anti-British bias was noticeable; I therefore recommended the return of Myers, who was most likely to get them round to the right way of thinking; the diplomats, however, were too strong for me and I was overruled.[11]

A marked intransigence and hardening of policy was noticeable henceforth on the part of all participants in Greek affairs. The king naturally was more resolved than ever to return to his throne, secure in the knowledge of British support. The British were disturbed by the EAM's growing strength and were determined to forestall any developments in Greece that might jeopardize their postwar position in that country. Finally, the EAM-ELAS now considered its suspicions of the British and the king to have been confirmed, and henceforth acted with corresponding mistrust and harshness. It is scarcely surprising that developments in Greece from now on were marked by increasing violence.

When the Italians surrendered in September, 1943, ELAS seized most of their arms and supplies. The following month ELAS attacked EDES, partly because of provocation by the latter body and partly because the EAM-ELAS leaders wished to eliminate a rival organization which the British were fostering as a counterweight. The Germans seized this propitious moment to launch an offensive against the Greek guerrillas. At the same time the British rushed arms to EDES and denied them to ELAS. Under these circumstances ELAS failed to attain its objective and a peace settlement was negotiated by the two organizations on February 15, 1944. The following month the EAM leaders established a five-man Political Committee of National Liberation, or PEEA. The main objective of PEEA was to force the exile cabinet to offer seats to EAM representatives. It was not a provisional government like that already established by Tito when he repudiated the Yugoslav exile government. Nevertheless, the establishment of PEEA carried the threat that if Premier Tsouderos in Cairo did not accept resistance representation in his cabinet the EAM could follow the example of Tito.

The most spectacular example of EAM strength and influence came in April, 1944, when Greek army and naval units in Egypt revolted against the Tsouderos government. The revolt was a complex affair, being supported by irresponsible republican Greek politicians in the Middle East who were motivated by antiroyalist considerations. The leaders of the EAM in Greece did not instigate the mutiny, which, indeed, caught them by surprise. Nevertheless, members of the rank and file, whose disaffection made the revolt possible, were moved by EAM propaganda and slogans. In the end, the uprising was suppressed following decisive intervention by British military forces. Nevertheless, it had illuminated like a flash of lightning the deep fissures and violent passions that rent the Greek political world.

In retrospect it appears that the turbulence of Greek politics at this time arose from the fact that the policy Churchill followed in Greece was different from his policy in Yugoslavia. In the latter country he accepted Partisan predominance and cooperated with Tito as the future ruler of his country. In Greece, by contrast, Churchill refused to accept EAM predominance. Had he done so the EAM would have forged ahead to supreme power as easily as did the Partisans. The only rival organization was EDES, a British creation that remained dependent on British aid from beginning to end. Colonel C. M. Woodhouse, Myers's successor in Greece, has stated flatly that "it is perfectly correct to say . . . that without British support Zervas' army [EDES] would never have existed. . . . If Zervas had not been supported the whole of Greece would have been controlled by EAM-ELAS when the Germans left it." [12]

Such EAM control was precisely what Churchill was resolved to forestall. This explains his backing of King George in the face of unanimous Greek opposition. It also explains the following minute which he wrote on September 29, 1943, a month after the Cairo negotiations:

> Should the Germans evacuate Greece, we must certainly be able to send five thousand British troops with armoured cars and Bren carriers into Athens. . . . The Greek troops in Egypt would accompany them. Their duty would be to give support at the centre to the restored lawful Greek Government. . . . There may be some bickering between the Greek guerrilla bands, but great respect will be paid to the British, more especially as the saving of the country from famine depends entirely on our exertions in the early months of liberation.[13]

The contrast is apparent between this plan for armed intervention in Greece and the advice that Churchill gave to Maclean that "the less you and I worry about the form of Government they [the Yugoslavs] set up, the better."

"THE BRUTE ISSUES"

The turbulence of Greek politics and the manifestations of EAM strength would have been disturbing to British policy makers under any circumstances. They were particularly so at the time because the Teheran Conference of November, 1943, had rejected Churchill's proposals for Allied thrusts into the Balkan Peninsula. Churchill had been advocating such action for several months but had been steadfastly opposed by the American chiefs of staff. These military men from the beginning had placed first priority on Overlord, the cross-Channel invasion of Europe projected for the summer of 1944.

It should be added that Churchill did not wish to abandon Overlord, as some of his critics assert. Rather, he refused to accept the American view that Overlord and a Balkan campaign were mutually exclusive. He maintained that a series of diversionary attacks in the eastern Mediterranean might delay Overlord for a few months but would greatly enhance that operation's prospects for success. At the Teheran Conference Churchill presented this thesis to Roosevelt and Stalin on November 28, 1943. He pointed out that at the moment there were two surplus British and American divisions in the Mediterranean, as well as a powerful army maintained by the Turks, who probably could be persuaded to join the Allies. Under these circumstances, he asked, are there not possible operations in the eastern Mediterranean that should be considered even if they might involve a slight delay for Overlord?

Roosevelt intervened at this point to suggest an expedition across the Adriatic to help Tito in Yugoslavia. Churchill quickly accepted and supported the proposal. But Stalin now objected that it would be unwise to scatter Anglo-American strength by launching new operations. He also added that the Turks would never budge from their neutral stand. Stalin's negative reaction proved to be decisive because Roosevelt was unwilling to stand up against the Russian dictator. The president wanted above all else to ensure a comprehensive postwar settlement with the Russians, and if the way to get that was to accept their strategic plans (which agreed with those of his own chiefs of staff), then Roosevelt was willing to go along. Churchill argued his case stubbornly and persuasively for two days but to no avail. In the end he was forced to agree to a cross-Channel invasion scheduled for May 1, 1944, and to a supporting attack on the coast of southern France.

This decision obviously was of basic significance for the future of the Balkans. It ruled out the possibility of an Anglo-American invasion of the peninsula. The Red Army now was assured of a free hand in Southeastern Europe. Furthermore, obviously Yugoslavia would come under the rule of the Communist Partisans, while Greece also was likely to fall to the Communist EAM unless energetic measures were taken. Such was the grim outlook that Churchill faced at the beginning of 1944. These were the circumstances in which he wrote a memorandum to Foreign Minister Anthony Eden on May 4, 1944, requesting a reappraisal of the situation.

A paper should be drafted for the Cabinet, and possibly for the Imperial Conference, setting forth shortly—for that is essential—the brute issues between us and the Soviet Government which are developing in Italy, in Rumania, in Bulgaria, in Yugoslavia, and above all in Greece. . . . broadly speaking the issue is: are we going to acquiesce in the Communisation of the Balkans and perhaps of Italy? [14]

ANGLO-RUSSIAN DIVISION OF THE BALKANS: SUMMER 1944

The basic problem confronting the British was how to safeguard their interests in the Balkans with the Red Army advancing from the north and with an Anglo-American expedition ruled out at Teheran. The only course open was to attempt to reach an understanding directly with the Russians. On May 5, 1944, Anthony Eden proposed to the Soviet ambassador in London, F. Gusev, that they discuss a temporary arrangement whereby Rumanian affairs should be regarded mainly as Russia's concern, and Greek affairs should be Britain's concern. This suggestion set off a chain reaction of negotiations which also involved the United States and which ultimately led to the division of the peninsula into spheres of interest.

The Soviet ambassador informed the Foreign Office on May 18 that his government was willing to accept the British proposal but wished to know whether the United States had been consulted. Accordingly, on May 30, Lord Halifax, the British ambassador in Washington, asked Secretary of State Cordell Hull whether the United States would object to the proposed Anglo-Soviet agreement as a temporary wartime arrangement. Hull replied that he would give this proposal serious consideration, but added that he was opposed to spheres of influence in the Balkans because he feared they would sow the seeds of future conflict and weaken the postwar international security organization.

On the following day, May 31, Churchill sent a telegram to Roosevelt strongly urging the acceptance of the proposed agreement and explaining once more that it would apply only for the war period and did not involve spheres of influence. Churchill sent another message on June 8 repudiating again the idea of spheres of influence and adding that it seemed reasonable to him that Russia should deal with Rumania and Bulgaria, and Britain with Yugoslavia and Greece. This casual inclusion of Bulgaria and Yugoslavia in the proposed agreement meant that it would cover virtually the entire peninsula. Secretary Hull was convinced more than ever that the plan should be opposed. Accordingly Roosevelt on June 10 sent a negative reply to Churchill, expressing the opinion that even if the agreement were limited to military affairs it would lead to spheres of influence and engender future trouble. The president concluded that he favored consultative machinery for the Balkans to resolve misunderstandings and to prevent the development of exclusive zones of influence.

Churchill replied the following day in "a long and forceful telegram" to the president, stating that a tripartite arrangement would be too cumbersome. He urged instead that the proposed Anglo-Russian agreement, limited to Rumania and Greece, be given a three months' trial, after which it could be renewed or ended as seemed desirable. Roosevelt now decided to accede to Churchill's request. On the next day, June 12, he replied accepting the three months' proposal and adding that care should be taken to avoid the development of postwar spheres of influence.

Roosevelt did not inform Hull of his decision, the reason seemingly being that he disliked to communicate unwelcome news to personal friends. As a result, Hull did not learn of the president's action until eighteen days later, during which time there was considerable confusion. This became apparent when Churchill wired Stalin on July 11 requesting that the Balkan plan be tried for three months. Stalin replied on July 15 "that the American Government have some doubts regarding this question, and that it would be better to revert to this matter when we receive the American reply to our inquiry." [15] That same day the Russians asked Washington what had been decided and were informed that the Balkan arrangement had been endorsed with the three months' time limit. Stalin now failed to take up the matter again with Churchill. As a result, the proposed agreement never came into effect. "We were thus unable," relates Churchill, "to reach a final agreement about dividing responsibilities in the Balkan peninsula." [16]

It is important to note, however, that on certain critical occasions both governments acted in accordance with the terms of the proposed agreement. The British, for example, declined to intervene actively in Rumanian and Bulgarian affairs when, in the summer of 1944, envoys from those two countries attempted to bring Anglo-American forces on the scene as a counterweight to the Red Army. The Russians in the same spirit advised the Greek Communists in August, 1944, to join a British-sponsored government for Greece. Despite the lack of legal sanction, both Britain and Russia now acted as though they had divided the Balkans between them.

RED ARMY IN RUMANIA AND BULGARIA: FALL 1944

Rumania was the first Balkan country to fall to the advancing Red Army. As described in Chapter 37, Rumania had contributed heavily to the Axis war effort and had suffered severe losses on the Russian front. Following the disaster at Stalingrad in the winter of 1942–1943 the Rumanians began sporadic negotiations with the Western Powers in the hope of securing Anglo-American intervention to block the approaching Russians. These efforts were doomed to failure because of the Teheran decision against a

Western invasion and also because of the Anglo-Russian negotiations which had assigned Rumania to Russia.

The Red Army crossed the Pruth River and reached Rumanian soil in April, 1944. After pausing for consolidation and preparation it resumed its advance in the summer. The Rumanians sought frantically to obtain a cessation of hostilities. Negotiations were carried on by representatives of the National Democratic Bloc, a loose grouping that had been formed in June, 1944. It included the four leading opposition parties: the Liberals, Socialists, Communists, and National Peasants. The leader of the latter party, Iuliu Maniu, directed the negotiations. He proved to be so slow and indecisive that in the end it was not the Bloc but young King Michael who extricated Rumania from the Axis camp.

Michael had succeeded to the throne when his father abdicated in September, 1940. At first he had been completely dominated by the imperious Antonescu. But by 1944 he had begun to show a will of his own and to express distaste for the Germans and sympathy for the Allies. He was encouraged in these views by his mother, Queen Helen, and by certain Foreign Office officials. On August 23 Michael invited Antonescu to the palace and demanded his resignation. Antonescu refused and began to bluster. The king then summoned his guard and had him arrested. That evening Michael announced over the radio that Rumania had accepted the Allied surrender terms and that she no longer was at war with Russia.

The Germans retaliated the next day by bombing Bucharest, aiming especially at the palace. Michael then formally declared war on Germany on August 25. During the following months the Rumanian army fought alongside the Soviet, first forcing the Germans out of Transylvania and then driving into Hungary, Czechoslovakia, and Germany. After the grievous losses they had suffered on the Russian plains the hapless Rumanian soldiers now sustained 169,822 casualties fighting against their former allies.

Michael's coup was one of the decisive events of World War II. The "great historic act of 23 August 1944," as it was called by the Rumanians at the time, opened the way into the Balkans for the Red Army. The immediate effect was the collapse of the Axis-dominated regime in Bulgaria.

As described in Chapter 38, a change of government had occurred in Bulgaria in May, 1944, as a result of the Anglo-American air raids and the threat of the approaching Red Army. The new premier, Ivan Bagrianov, was an Agrarian, and his cabinet was composed mostly of "technicians." These men were neither pro-German enough to satisfy Hitler nor anti-German enough to suit Stalin. They tried to maintain a balance between the two dictators, but when Stalin's Red Army pushed into Moldavia their position became impossible. On September 2 Bagrianov was replaced as premier by another Agrarian, Kosta Muraviev. The latter formed a cabinet comprising political personages who belonged to the prewar democratic parties. These men had opposed the pro-German course of the war governments but they also distrusted the Communists and refused to join the Fatherland Front.

Their sympathies were with the West and they deplored the action of King Boris's government, which had declared war on the Western powers in March, 1941, while remaining neutral in the Russo-German struggle. Accordingly, the Muraviev government now declared itself no longer at war with Britain and the United States.

Moscow was highly suspicious of this move because it meant that future peace negotiations would be conducted directly between Bulgaria and the West. This distrust was unwarranted in view of the fact that the Bulgarian envoys in Cairo had been cold-shouldered by Britain and the United States, who were obviously waiting for Russian initiative in Bulgaria. Moscow, however, held that Bulgaria should have sought Soviet mediation in dropping out of the war. In order to make it quite clear that it was resolved to control Bulgarian affairs, the Soviet government, without informing its allies, suddenly declared war on Bulgaria on September 5, 1944.

Within five hours Premier Muraviev requested an armistice from Russia. The next day he declared war on Germany, neutrality no longer being feasible. Two days later, on September 8, the Red Army entered Bulgaria without encountering resistance. That same night the Fatherland Front grasped the opportunity it had long awaited. It seized power smoothly and quickly with the assistance of collaborators in the war ministry and in certain army units stationed near Sofia.

The new government included representatives of the four parties comprising the Fatherland Front. The prime minister, Colonel Kimon Geor giev, and four other members of the cabinet, belonged to the *Zveno* group The Communists held four cabinet posts, including the important ministries of interior and justice, while the Agrarians and Socialists held four and three seats, respectively. Under this new government Bulgaria participated actively in the war against Germany. Bulgarian troops fought beside the Yugoslavs and the Russians, taking Skoplje, Nish, Belgrade, and then fighting on through Croatia and Hungary to Vienna. In these operations some 30,000 Bulgarian soldiers were killed.

These developments in Rumania and Bulgaria left the Soviet Union in a dominant position in the northern Balkans. The Soviet success was due basically to the strength of the Red Army and to the Teheran decision against an Anglo-American invasion. This left the Western powers no alternative but to accept Russian responsibility in the northern Balkans as had been proposed in the summer negotiations. The predominance of the Soviet Union was formalized by the armistice agreements that it signed with Rumania and Bulgaria on September 12 and October 28, 1944, respectively. Representatives of the United States and Great Britain participated in the armistice negotiations. But since the two satellite countries were in the Russian sphere of military operations, the Soviet government took the initiative in preparing the armistice documents, both of which were signed in Moscow.

In regard to frontiers, Bulgaria was required to evacuate Greek and Yugoslav territory, while Rumania was forced to accept the loss of Bessarabia and northern Bukovina, which she had ceded to the Soviet Union in 1940. On the other hand, Rumania was to regain Transylvania from Hungary. Finally, Rumania was required to pay 300 million dollars in reparations to the Soviet Union as well as to meet the cost of Soviet operations on her territory.

The most important provisions, so far as the future of Rumania and Bulgaria was concerned, called for the establishment of Allied Control Commissions in Bucharest and Sofia. These commissions were to include representatives of all three allies, but their authority and functioning were defined as follows: "During the period between the coming into force of the armistice and the conclusion of hostilities against Germany the Allied Control Commission will be under the general direction of the Allied (Soviet) High Command." [17] This phrasing showed clearly where the preponderance of authority was to lie. Furthermore, it is significant that no corresponding provision was made for the period between the surrender of Germany and the coming into force of the peace treaties. Thus the Soviet Union acquired a legal basis for its predominance in Bulgaria and Rumania until the signing of the peace treaties, whose terms would require its approval.

BRITISH DIPLOMACY IN YUGOSLAVIA AND GREECE: FALL 1940

While the Soviet Union was establishing its dominance in the northern Balkans, Great Britain sought to strengthen her position in Yugoslavia and Greece. Britain was unable to act as decisively as the Soviet Union because her armies at this time were fighting in France rather than in the Balkans. Consequently, she was able only to exert her influence upon the Greek and Yugoslav exile governments and to utilize the various missions that she was maintaining throughout the peninsula.

Considering first Britain's policy in Yugoslavia, we saw earlier in this chapter that in December, 1943, Churchill had recognized the predominance of the Partisans and shifted his support from Mihailovich to Tito. Having made this basic decision, Churchill thereafter sought to promote a working arrangement between Tito and King Peter in Cairo. As a move in this direction Churchill persuaded Peter to dismiss the coterie of politicians who hitherto had surrounded him. These men had proven singularly unconstructive, being divided into quarreling factions because of conflicting personal ambitions and the traditional Serb-Croat feud.

On June 1, 1944, Peter accepted as premier the Croat Dr. Ivan Shubashich. Prior to 1941 Shubashich had served as governor of Croatia. During the years of exile he had kept aloof from the intrigues of the other politicians and had openly expressed his sympathy for the Partisans. Following his appointment to the premiership Shubashich held meetings with Tito on June 14–17, 1944. Shubashich promised that his government would cooperate as closely as possible with the Partisans, and both men agreed that "the final solution of the organization of the State shall be decided by the people after the liberation of the whole country." [18]

The next important development was a meeting held in Naples between Churchill and Tito on August 12, 1944. The British statesman was cordial to his guest, stating that he regarded "Marshal Tito and his brave men with the utmost admiration." [19] After discussing the future of Istria, a problem that was to cause much trouble later, Churchill expressed the hope that Tito would not introduce communism after the war. Tito replied that he had no intention of doing so. But when Churchill asked him to reaffirm this statement in public he refused on the ground that it would appear that it had been forced upon him.

Tito was similarly evasive when Churchill declared that he wanted a strong and united Yugoslavia, and hoped for a reconciliation between the Partisans and the exile government. Tito gave his usual response that the status of the monarchy could not be settled until the Yugoslav people expressed their wishes after the war. When Churchill proposed a meeting between King Peter and Tito, the latter replied that he had no objection in principle to the meeting but that the time was premature.

The outstanding feature of the Churchill-Tito meeting was the resolute independence of the Yugoslav leader. Churchill wished to promote the interests of the king in the hope of thereby furthering Britain's postwar position in Yugoslavia. Despite Tito's rebuffs, Churchill continued to provide aid to the Partisans. Even King Peter himself broadcast an appeal from London on September 12 urging his people to unite under Tito.

During this time Tito was pursuing an equally independent policy toward the Russians. On September 21, 1944, he suddenly departed by plane for Moscow, much to the annoyance of the British, whom he had not forewarned. The purpose of the Moscow trip was to coordinate the operations of the Red Army and the Partisans. In the ensuing negotiations with Stalin, Tito consented to the entry of Russian troops into Yugoslav territory. But in return he required Stalin to agree that the Russian troops should be withdrawn upon completion of their operations, and that Yugoslav civil administration should operate in Yugoslav territory where Red Army units were located. Following this arrangement the two men discussed a variety of other topics. Tito's account of the conversations is revealing, both for what was to happen in Yugoslavia at the time and also several years later:

. . . tension arose at this first meeting with Stalin. We were more or less at cross-purposes on all the matters we discussed. I noticed then that Stalin could not bear being contradicted. In conversation with the men around him he is coarse and touchy. Of all the members of the Politburo of the Soviet Central Committee it is only Molotov to whom he turns occasionally to ask for his opinion, but he never listens to him to the end, but goes on with his own line of thought.

I was not used to such conversation, which led to uncomfortable scenes. For instance Stalin said to me:

"Walter, [Tito's prewar party name in Moscow] be careful, the bourgeoisie in Serbia is very strong!"

I answered calmly:

"Comrade Stalin, I do not agree with your view. The bourgeoisie in Serbia is very weak."

He was silent and frowned and the others at the table, Molotov, Zhdanov, Malenkov, Beria, gaped.

Stalin then began to inquire after different bourgeois politicians in Yugoslavia, where they were, what they were doing, and I replied, "He is a scoundrel, a traitor, he worked with the Germans."

Stalin asked about another one. I gave the same answer. Stalin flared up: "Walter," he said, "to you they are all scoundrels!"

I replied, "Exactly, Comrade Stalin: anyone who betrays his country is a scoundrel."

Stalin frowned again, while Malenkov, Zhdanov, and the others looked at me askance.

The talk proceeded in a very painful atmosphere. Stalin began to assure me of the need to reinstate King Peter. The blood rushed to my head that he could advise us to do such a thing. I composed myself and told him it was impossible, that the people would rebel, that in Yugoslavia the king personified treason, that he had fled and left his people in the midst of their struggle, that the Karageorgević dynasty was hated among the people for corruption and terror.

Stalin was silent, and then said briefly:

"You need not restore him forever. Take him back temporarily, and then you can slip a knife into his back at a suitable moment."

At this moment Molotov returned to the room, which he had left a moment back. He carried a telegram from a Western news agency reporting that the British had landed in Yugoslavia.

I leaped to my feet: "That's impossible!"

Stalin, angrily: "Why impossible! It is a fact!"

I repeated that it was impossible and probably the agency was mistaken; that we had asked General Alexander to send us three batteries of heavy artillery to help our Fourth Army in its operations towards Mostar and Sarajevo, and the arrival of this artillery had probably been mistaken for an invasion of Yugoslavia by the British.

Stalin was silent, and then he asked the direct question: "Tell me, Walter, what would you do if the British really forced a landing in Yugoslavia?"

"We should offer determined resistance." [20]

One explanation for this remarkable scene is that Stalin may have been thinking along the lines of the June, 1944, Anglo-Russian negotiations which had assigned Yugoslavia and Greece to Britain, and Rumania and Bulgaria to Russia. If this be so, then Stalin presumably was testing Tito's reaction to such a division of the Balkans. In any case, whatever the explanation might be, Tito had made his position as clear to Stalin as he had to Churchill. It should be noted that we are depending here on Tito's version of his meeting with Stalin, and that we have no way of checking that version. On the other hand, Tito's observations do jibe with the following characterizations of Stalin by Nikita S. Khruschev, first secretary of the Soviet Communist party, at a secret session of the party's twentieth congress in Moscow on February 24–25, 1956: "Stalin absolutely did not tolerate collegiality in leadership and in work. . . . Stalin acted not through persuasion, explanation, and patient cooperation with people, but by imposing his concepts and demanding absolute submission to his opinion." [21]

Turning to Greece, we find that both the British and the Russians had much less trouble in that country, thanks to the comparative docility of the Greek Communist leaders of the EAM. We noted earlier in this chapter and in Chapter 38 the considerable turmoil among the Greeks, including the fighting between ELAS and EDES, and the mutiny of the Greek armed forces in the Middle East. Yet the EAM never made as far-reaching demands as the Yugoslav Partisans. When it established PEEA on March 10, 1944, its primary aim was to secure representation in the Greek exile government in Cairo. By contrast, Tito, some months earlier, at the Jajce Assembly of November, 1943, had specifically repudiated King Peter and his government.

A similar difference is noticeable in the relations between Tito and Moscow on the one hand and the Greek Communists and Moscow on the other. The subservience of the Greek Communists to Moscow became evident following the Anglo-Russian negotiations for the division of the Balkans into spheres of responsibility. On June 25, 1944, only ten days after the State Department had informed the Soviet government that it had accepted the British Balkan plan, a Russian military mission arrived at EAM-ELAS headquarters in occupied Greece. Immediately thereafter the EAM began to modify its conditions for entering the exile cabinet.

Negotiations had been going on for some time for the establishment of a national unity government. These negotiations began after the April, 1944, mutiny in the Greek armed forces in the Middle East. Following the suppression of the mutiny the British intervened energetically in Greek political affairs and selected George Papandreou, a well-known opponent of the EAM, to serve as premier of the exile government. Papandreou called a conference in Lebanon which was attended by representatives of all Greek political parties and resistance organizations. The conference adopted on May 20 a National Charter which was to serve as the basis for the establishment of a national unity government.

Although the EAM delegates to the conference accepted the charter they were repudiated by their superiors when they returned to Greece. Instead, the EAM leaders demanded more ministries and more important ministries as their price for joining the cabinet. This was the situation when the Soviet mission arrived at EAM headquarters. Soon afterward the EAM modified its conditions, and on September 2 it agreed to participate in the unity government. One may presume a connection between the EAM about-face and the appearance of the Soviet representatives.

This incident highlights the contrast between Tito and the Greek Communists. Tito had not only repudiated the exile government but also refused Churchill's request that he meet with King Peter. The Greek Communists, on the other hand, entered a cabinet headed by a premier who had been hand-picked by the British and who was an avowed and violent enemy of the EAM. And in return the Communists and the EAM received six ministries—labor, agriculture, public works, national economy, finance, and underministry of finance—all of which were useless as instruments of power manipulation. And this at a time when the Germans were beginning to evacuate Greece and when the EAM-ELAS, as the only national resistance organization worthy of the name, was assuming *de facto* control of the country without any opposition.

The submissiveness of the Greek Communists to the current Moscow "line" was even more strikingly manifested at a meeting held in Caserta, Italy, late in September, 1944. The meeting was called by the British and included representatives of EAM and EDES. The purpose of the meeting is to be found in a note that Churchill had addressed to his chiefs of staff the previous month, on August 6, 1944: "It may be that within a month or so we shall have to put 10,000 or 12,000 men into Athens, with a few tanks, guns, and armoured cars. You have a division in England which has above 13,000 troops. Such a force could be embarked now, and would probably be in time for the political crisis, which is of major consequence to the policy of His Majesty's Government." [22]

The crisis that Churchill foresaw was the power vacuum that would be created in Greece when the Germans evacuated the country, a development that was expected very shortly because of the advance of the Red Army in the north. This was a most serious matter for Churchill in view of the course of events elsewhere in the Balkans. The Russians were firmly ensconced in Rumania and Bulgaria, while Tito had made it clear that he would not tolerate any foreign intervention in his country. Thus the question now was whether the British would be able to take advantage of the impending German departure to secure their position in at least one Balkan country. The issue, in other words, was the new power situation that would develop in the Balkans now that Hitler's "New Order" was crumbling. Churchill made this clear in a dispatch to Anthony Eden on August 16: "Regarding our expedition to Greece, General Wilson and his staff are already taking action. . . . I have strongly emphasized that the operation must be regarded as one of reinforced diplomacy and policy rather than an actual campaign. . . ." [23]

Under these circumstances the Caserta meeting was held in order to persuade the EAM to agree to the landing of British troops in Greece when the Germans withdrew. It is significant that the only member of the EAM delegation who opposed the proposal was a professional military man, General Saraphis. He maintained that there was no need for British troops to enter Greece in view of the fact that the Germans were already retreating northward. The Communist members of the EAM delegation overruled Saraphis and signed the so-called Caserta Agreement by which they undertook to carry out the orders of the British General Scobie. The crucial clause provided:

> All guerrilla forces operating in Greece place themselves under orders to the Greek Government of National Unity. The Greek Government places these forces under the orders of General Scobie, who has been nominated by the Supreme Allied Commander as General-in-Command of the forces in Greece.[24]

In the light of later developments it is significant that the original version of the agreement included a paragraph defining the aim of the commanding general (General Scobie) as being "to restore law and order in Greece." When Saraphis refused to accept this clause it was omitted. Saraphis and the EAM-ELAS made it clear that they undertook to carry out General Scobie's orders only as they involved military operations against the Germans.

Despite the elimination of the "law and order" clause, the British were now in a strong position to safeguard their interests in Greece. The head of the Greek government was their man and the EAM not only had accepted a subordinate position in the cabinet but also had agreed to the landing of British troops in Greece.

DIVISION OF THE BALKANS CONFIRMED: OCTOBER, 1944

In October, 1944, Churchill and Stalin held a conference in Moscow that was to have momentous consequences for the Balkan Peninsula. The reason for the conference was the rapid advance of the Red Army up the Danube Valley and across the Polish plains. The new military situation called urgently for new political arrangements. Churchill, with his keen sense of political reality, saw the shifts that were taking place and the need for reappraisal at the highest level.

> The arrangements which I had made with the President in the summer to divide our responsibilities for looking after particular countries affected by the movements of the armies had tided us over the three months for which our agreement ran. But as the autumn drew on everything in Eastern Europe became more intense. I felt the need of another personal meeting with Stalin, whom I had not seen since Teheran. . . . The Russian armies were now pressing heavily upon the Balkan scene, and Rumania and Bulgaria were in their power. As the victory of the Grand Alliance became only a matter of time it was natural that Russian ambitions should grow. Communism raised its head behind the thundering Russian battle-front. Russia was the Deliverer, and Communism the gospel she brought.[25]

President Roosevelt was unable to participate in the Moscow Conference because he was involved in the presidential and congressional elections. He agreed, therefore, that Churchill and Stalin should meet alone, with the American ambassador in Moscow, Averell Harriman, attending as an observer. The first meeting was held in the evening of October 9. Churchill has left a vivid picture of the manner in which he settled Balkan affairs with Stalin.

The moment was apt for business, so I said, "Let us settle about our affairs in the Balkans. Your armies are in Rumania and Bulgaria. We have interests, missions and agents there. Don't let us get at cross-purposes in small ways. So far as Britain and Russia are concerned, how would it do for you to have ninety per cent predominance in Rumania, for us to have ninety per cent of the say in Greece, and go fifty-fifty about Yugoslavia?" While this was being translated I wrote out on a half-sheet of paper:

Rumania	
Russia	90%
The others	10%
Greece	
Great Britain	90%
(in accord with U.S.A.)	
Russia	10%
Yugoslavia	50–50%
Hungary	50–50%
Bulgaria	
Russia	75%
The others	25%

I pushed this across to Stalin who had by then heard the translation. There was a slight pause. Then he took his blue pencil and made a large tick upon it, and passed it back to us. It was all settled in no more time than it takes to set it down. . . .

After this there was a long silence. The pencilled paper lay in the centre of the table. At length I said, "Might it not be thought rather cynical if it seemed we had disposed of these issues, so fateful to millions of people, in such an off-hand manner? Let us burn the paper." "No, you keep it," said Stalin.[26]

This extraordinary episode reflects the rapidly shifting balance of power in the Balkans. When the British first proposed the division of the Balkans in June, 1944, they retained both Yugoslavia and Greece for themselves. Now they accepted equal Soviet representation in Yugoslavia while acknowledging continued Soviet predominance in Bulgaria and Rumania. The explanation for this change is that the Red Army now had overrun Rumania and Bulgaria, and had entered Yugoslavia and Hungary as well, while the British still had only their military missions in Greece and Yugoslavia. Furthermore, it had been agreed at the second Quebec Conference between Churchill and Roosevelt (September 11–19, 1944) that

as long as the battle in Italy continues there will be no forces available in the Mediterranean to employ in the Balkans except:

(a) The small force of two British brigades from Egypt which is being held ready to occupy the Athens area and so pave the way for commencement of relief and establishment of law and order and the Greek Government.
(b) The small land forces in the Adriatic which are being actively used primarily for Commando type operations.[27]

Thus the percentage figures that Churchill himself proposed at Moscow reflected the fact that he had negligible forces with which to counter the advancing Russians. In fact, we shall see now that the British were in such a weak position that they came within an ace of losing even Greece despite the loyal cooperation of Moscow and the submissiveness of the EAM in allowing them to land their two brigades.

CRISIS IN GREECE: NOVEMBER–DECEMBER, 1944

The Germans began to evacuate Greece in September, 1944, because the Russians were about to cut their only escape route, the Saloniki-Belgrade railway. "The testing time for our arrangements had now come," relates Churchill. "At the Moscow Conference I had obtained Russian abstention at a heavy price." [28] The price, of course, had been Russian domination of the northern Balkans. Churchill now took measures to ensure control of the part of the Balkans allotted to him at the Moscow Conference. In doing so he faced two major obstacles that the Russians in the north had been spared. One was the pitiful lack of armed forces, contrasting markedly with the massive power of the Red Army sweeping through the Danube Valley. The other was the pro-Russian orientation of the Communist-dominated EAM-ELAS, which would be by far the strongest organization in Greece upon the departure of the Germans.

The first British troops to arrive in Greece were small commando units which occupied Patras on October 4. They reached Corinth by October 10 and four days later were in Athens, which they found under ELAS control. During the remainder of the month they pursued the retreating Germans northward, fighting only a few skirmishes. They found that the ELAS had preceded them in all the towns and cities, but it made no attempt to seize control of the country or to block the British. In fact, on the eve of the arrival of the British, the Central Committee of the Greek Communist party issued a proclamation entitled "Forward for the Final Battle"—a proclamation that stands in striking contrast to Tito's response when Stalin suggested British landings in Yugoslavia.

Let us march united in one soul and one movement.
It is everybody's primary national duty to ensure order and a smooth political life for the country.
Avoid taking the law into your own hands, as the punishment of the collaborationists and other criminals rests in the hands of the United National Government. . . .
Communists, you stood as the champions of the national and popular up-

rising. Stand now as the vanguard for securing order and democratic freedom. Patriots all, unite in the struggle for the completion of the liberation of Greece along with the ELAS and OUR ALLIES under our United Government.[29]

On October 17 Premier Papandreou and his government returned to Athens on board a Greek warship. The capital and its port of Piraeus were a blaze of lights, thanks to an ELAS band that had fought off a German demolition squad ordered to dynamite the power plant. Three particularly large electric signs stood out above the rest. They spelled out the initials EAM, ELAS, and KKE (Communist party of Greece). These signs symbolized the dilemma facing the returning government, a dilemma described at the time by the London *Times* correspondent as follows: "Without a working administrative machine, with no revenue, with a civil service and a police force that had to be purged of collaborationist elements and completely reorganized before they could be either effective or trusted . . . the Government's authority does not extend beyond the principal cities, hardly beyond Athens." [30]

The basic problem henceforth was how to secure the transfer of power from the EAM-ELAS to the legal but impotent Papandreou government. This transfer obviously was essential not only for regular and orderly government but also for British interests. Churchill wrote to Anthony Eden on November 7: "In my opinion, having paid the price we have to Russia for freedom of action in Greece, we should not hesitate to use British troops to support the Royal Hellenic Government under M. Papandreou." [31]

The problem, specifically, was to secure the disarming of the resistance forces so as to transfer state power to the legal government. Failure to find a disarmament formula acceptable to all parties precipitated the battle of Athens in December. The forces involved in the disarmament dispute were 40,000 to 50,000 in ELAS, 10,000 to 15,000 in EDES, and a few thousand in the government's Mountain Brigade and Sacred Company. The last two consisted of hand-picked royalists, so the Papandreou government now maintained that these bodies should be preserved because they were official military organizations, while both ELAS and EDES should be disbanded because they were guerrilla organizations. The EAM leaders were suspicious of a plan that would leave royalist bodies as the only military forces in the country until a new national army could be organized.

The disarmament negotiations began in earnest on November 22 when Papandreou initialed a plan for the disbandment of the Mountain Brigade and the Sacred Company as well as ELAS and EDES. The EAM accepted this plan but Papandreou suddenly reversed his position and insisted that the government units remain intact. According to one source, "He [Papandreou] gave an EAM minister a letter from Scobie which said Prime Minister Churchill would not permit the royalist Mountain Brigade to be disbanded. This is why the attempt to disarm the political factions in Greece first failed, as confirmed by the American ambassador in Greece." [32]

General Scobie now intervened and presented an Order of the Day to Generals Saraphis and Zervas, commanders of ELAS and EDES, respectively, requiring the disbandment of their forces by December 10. Saraphis rejected the order, pointing out that Scobie's authority under the Caserta Agreement pertained only to operations against the Germans. The disbandment of an army and the formation of another, Saraphis maintained, were domestic matters that must be settled without foreign interference.

On November 27 the EAM ministers in the cabinet proposed a compromise to break the deadlock. They suggested the formation of a mixed division consisting of the Mountain Brigade, the Sacred Company, an EDES unit, and an ELAS brigade equal in men and arms to the combined strength of the other three units. They suggested also that there should be joint command of this division and that the men should be mixed in the squads.

Papandreou approved the plan except for the mixed squads. At this point, when the question seemed to have been settled peacefully, Papandreou made public a different plan which he claimed had come from the EAM ministers. This Papandreou plan kept the Mountain Brigade, the Sacred Company, an EDES brigade, and an ELAS brigade, but the latter was to equal only the EDES brigade in strength. Obviously this was quite different from the original EAM compromise. This left the ELAS brigade outnumbered two to one, while the EAM plan provided for an ELAS brigade equal in strength to all the other units combined.

The Communist ministers denounced as "a breach of faith" this attempt of Papandreou to present his plan as their own and now insisted on withdrawing the November 27 compromise plan and going back to their original position. On November 29 they informed Papandreou that the Mountain Brigade and the Sacred Company must be dissolved as well as EDES and ELAS.

General Scobie now brought the crisis to a head. On December 1 he issued an order for the disbandment of all guerrilla forces on December 10. The six EAM ministers denounced this as an interference in internal Greek affairs and resigned the same day. At the same time the EAM Central Committee revived the ELAS Central Committee, which had been disbanded upon liberation, and ordered a mass meeting in Athens' Constitution Square on December 3. Saturday afternoon, December 2, the EAM Central Committee asked for and received permission to hold the demonstration. Papandreou discussed the situation later in the day with Ambassador Leeper and General Scobie. Both impressed on him that this was the time to be firm with the EAM. They urged him to stop the demonstration. Papandreou agreed. His minister of the interior ordered the Athens police chief to tell the EAM leaders that they could not hold the demonstration. By the time this notification reached them it was almost eleven o'clock Saturday night. Telephones and radios are rare in Athens, especially among the poorer people. It was physically impossible to call off the demonstration at that late hour.

The next morning the EAM supporters poured out into the streets.

As usual in EAM demonstrations, the crowd was young, although there were thousands of old men and women and young children. They carried placards with typical EAM slogans: "America, send us soldiers to make a balance and avoid civil war"; "We want a real national unity government"; "We can solve our own problems"; "The people's will"; "Independence." The demonstration began peacefully. The marchers were unarmed. There was no fighting with the police. Then suddenly firing began and the bright December morning was transformed into Bloody Sunday.

One of the eyewitnesses of the shooting was the British officer, W. Byford-Jones. He described the scene as follows:

> During the next quarter of an hour I watched the demonstrators arrive in the square, carrying their banners and flags, British, American, Russian and Greek. As a large procession was lining up, megaphonists continued to shout their slogans. "Down with Papandreou," they cried in chorus. "Down with Intervention," "Try the collaborators," . . . .
>
> I took up my position outside Jannaki's bar, which is on the ground floor of the building which also houses the police headquarters, on one corner of the square and watched the procession move off. The head of it had reached the road in front of the old royal palace when my attention was attracted by the sound of voices to a group of police officers leaning on the balcony of the second floor of the building above the bar. To my surprise these officers had rifles at the ready. Some were standing, others kneeling, so that only their heads could be seen. One or two were taking aim at the head of the procession. I took it that this was merely a precaution, should the demonstrators attack the police station. The Greek police are an armed force.
>
> The procession approached: men, women and children marching eight to ten abreast. . . . There was nothing sullen or menacing about the procession. Some of the men shouted fanatically towards the police station and the hotel, but there was a good deal of humorous banter, and many jokes were exchanged between demonstrators and those who watched from the kerbs.
>
> My attention was again attracted to the balcony above by what sounded like an order, given in Greek. The head of the procession was at this time thirty yards away. Mr. S. Barber of the United Press, told me later that it was an order to fire. Next moment the police officers began to pull back the bolts of their rifles, not in unison like a disciplined body, but hesitantly, one after the other, as though some of the men were reluctant to obey. I still thought that this was a precautionary measure, and looked again at the approaching multitude.
>
> What happened next was so fantastically unreal I might have been watching a film. The squad of police above emptied their rifles into the procession. . . . I thought at first that the police were firing blanks, or that they were aiming far above the crowd. Many other people thought that. But the worst had happened. Men, women and children, who, a few moments before had been shouting, marching, laughing, full of spirit and defiance, waving their flags and our flag, fell to the ground blood trickling out of their heads and bodies either on to the road or on to the flags they had been carrying. . . . The shots continued to ring out, echoing and re-echoing among the high buildings, and between the volleys, there were screams of fear and cries of pain, a wild stampede of people who fell over bleed-

ing bodies. The police now seemed afraid to stop and the sight outraged the sense of decency of every British man who looked on. . . .

Every moment those of us who stood within the line of fire expected E.A.M. to use arms. On the roof of the K.K.E. [Communist party] headquarters in the square there was a machine-gun nest, and it could have raked the neighborhood with devastating fire. But E.A.M. contented themselves with cursing and threatening. I do not think anyone in the procession was armed. Such was the fury of the crowd that, if they had been, civil war would have broken out that moment.[33] *

About twenty demonstrators were killed and one hundred and forty wounded. The die was cast. Hostilities began which developed into the bloody and bitter battle of Athens. On the day of the demonstration Premier Papandreou broadcasted: "Today our conscience is clear. All responsibility before history and before the nation is upon the leaders of the extreme left." In reply the EAM retorted: "Henceforth Papandreou is an outlaw. The people will fight for liberty without counting the sacrifices." Two days later, on December 5, Churchill sent the following instructions to General Scobie:

You are responsible for maintaining order in Athens and for neutralising or destroying all E.A.M.-E.L.A.S. bands approaching the city. You may make any regulations you like for the strict control of the streets or for the rounding up of any number of truculent persons. Naturally E.L.A.S. will try to put women and children in the van where shooting may occur. You must be clever about this and avoid mistakes. But do not hesitate to fire at any armed male in Athens who assails the British authority or Greek authority with which we are working. It would be well of course if your commands were reinforced by the authority of some Greek Government, and Papandreou is being told by [Ambassador] Leeper to stop and help. *Do not however hesitate to act as if you were in a conquered city where a local rebellion is in progress.*[34]

When the fighting began in the streets of Athens Prime Minister Churchill encountered a storm of protest, both at home and abroad. Even the London *Times,* the Manchester *Guardian,* and the *Economist* contributed to the avalanche of criticism. Churchill himself was moved to declare that "there is no case in my experience . . . where a British Government had been so maligned and its motives so traduced in our own country by important organs of the Press or among our own people." [35] In answering his critics Churchill assailed the EAM-ELAS as "gangsters," "brigands," and "a gang of bandits from the mountains." He stressed above all else the alleged existence of a "fairly well organized plot or plan by which ELAS should march down upon Athens and seize it by armed force and establish a reign of terror. . . ." [36]

This contention fails to answer a number of crucial questions. If EAM-ELAS planned to seize power, why did it not do so during the weeks prior to the British arrival when the Germans were fleeing the country? Why

* From *The Greek Trilogy* by W. Byford Jones, by permission of Hutchinson & Co. (Publishers) Limited, London.

did it permit the landing of a handful of British troops in early October? Why did it not assume power in Athens during the three days between the departure of the Germans and the arrival of the British, when, in fact, it controlled the city? Finally, why was ELAS caught unprepared for battle, as we shall note shortly? Or to go further back, why did the EAM commit itself to the return of the exile government and to the landing of British troops by participating in the Papandreou government and signing the Caserta Agreement?

The diplomacy and the events preceding the battle of Athens suggest strongly that a decisive factor was Churchill's determination to disarm ELAS in order to establish Britain's position in Greece as provided for at the Moscow Conference. This is borne out by Churchill's dispatch to Scobie soon after the hostilities began: "The clear objective is the defeat of E.A.M. The ending of the fighting is subsidiary to this." [37] Because of their subservience to Moscow's directives, the Greek Communist leaders, far from plotting to seize power, had in fact relinquished the power that they actually held. In return they demanded only certain safeguards and assurances concerning the future, a demand that was absurdly modest in the light of what they had conceded in the past and in view of ELAS's strength compared to that of the handful of British troops. It has been pointed out that "if ELAS had elected to resist the British landing parties and refused to admit the Greek exiled Government, there would have been little Churchill could do. As it was, the British found it hard to scrape together the handful of troops actually assigned to the landing in Greece." [38]

The puzzling feature of the events leading to the outbreak of the battle of Athens is Churchill's rejection of the specific EAM proposal that an equal number of ELAS and non-ELAS troops be retained during the interval while a regular national conscript army was being trained. Acceptance of this plan would have led to the disbandment of most of the ELAS units and would have reduced the strength of that formidable force to the level of its rivals. This probably would have enabled Churchill to attain his objectives in Greece peacefully rather than by a costly and embarrassing armed struggle. Yet Churchill turned down the EAM terms and thereby precipitated the battle of Athens.

The explanation for this parodox perhaps lies in faulty intelligence reports from Greece which led Churchill grossly to underestimate and misjudge the EAM-ELAS. Captain Deakin and Brigadier Maclean sent realistic reports from Yugoslavia concerning the strength of Tito's Partisans. But the available evidence suggests that the reports from Greece were misleading. This would explain why, even before the Germans had evacuated Greece and before the crisis had developed, Churchill in private correspondence referred contemptuously to the EAM as "miserable Greek banditti." [39] But as soon as the fighting began, Churchill realized that the enemy had been underestimated, and he wrote complainingly to General Wilson, "You guaranteed most strongly that you had already sent enough soldiers. . . . I warned you of the paramount political importance of this conflict. At least two more brigades should hurry to the scene." [40]

It is noteworthy, in this connection, that M. W. Fodor, a correspondent with years of experience in the Balkans, commented that the events in Greece "leave this writer, who followed the aftermath of the last war [World War I], amazed by the deterioration of the British intelligence service, its one-sidedness and its complete failure to understand the Balkan mentality. This criticism applies to high and low officials alike, both here [in Athens] and in England." [41]

Similar observations were made by a well-known British journalist and Member of Parliament, Vernon Bartlett:

> I have a feeling that the Foreign Secretary is not as well informed by his representatives abroad as he should be, because they are not the sort of people who by training have much sympathy with these resistance movements. . . . I think that the Diplomatic Service at the present time is terribly out of touch with these developments inside Europe. If it were not so we should not have so misjudged the Greek situation. . . .[42]

BATTLE OF ATHENS: DECEMBER, 1944— JANUARY, 1945

The battle of Athens was unique; neither side was prepared to fight. There were no ELAS regulars in the capital when hostilities began. The headquarters and staff officers of the First ELAS Corps were in Athens but the men from the beginning had been kept outside in accordance with Scobie's orders. Only ELAS reserves were within the city—between ten and fifteen thousand men, armed mostly with rifles and untrained and unorganized. The nearest regular ELAS units were the Thirty-fourth Regiment at Eleusis and the Second Regiment at Thebes, totaling less than two thousand men. The main concentration of ELAS veterans was far to the north in Thessaly, where the men had come down from the mountains after liberation.

Between the departure of the Germans and the development of the crisis the ELAS forces had begun to demobilize. Its top policy body, the Central Committee, had been dissolved, leaving only the executive High Command. Orders had been issued to demobilize the reserves, to return requisitioned horses, mules, and vehicles to their owners, and to grant leaves to officers and men wishing to visit relatives. Thus, when the crisis came, the ELAS leaders were unprepared and confused. On December 2 the ELAS Central Committee was re-established, but when, on the following day, the High Command asked the Central Committee for a general plan of action, no answer was forthcoming. Such was the bewilderment and unpreparedness of the army that allegedly had been plotting to seize Athens.

General Scobie was equally unprepared for battle. He had available about ten thousand men: the paratroop brigade which had made the original landing in Greece, an armored brigade, and the Greek Mountain Brigade.

He also had about twenty-four tanks, two squadrons of armed cars, and a Spitfire squadron stationed at the nearby Hassani airfield. Scobie, who did not expect the EAM to fight back and thought ELAS incapable of serious resistance, had scattered his troops throughout Athens, unprepared for either attack or defense.

The first week's fighting was planless and desultory. Neither side had readied itself for large-scale action, for both were still hoping for a diplomatic settlement. It took ELAS leaders in Athens six days to get in touch with all their units and get their activities co-ordinated. But after the first week they began to press the British. In various parts of the city, reserve units were gradually consolidating under central control, and some ELAS regulars were seeping in from the outside. Still, ELAS was using only a fraction of its total strength, with the Royal Air Force patrolling the roads into Athens and forestalling large troop movements.

As the ELAS operations gained, the scattered British detachments fell back to the center of the city, leaving behind supply dumps which provided ELAS with much-needed food. By December 12, when the lines became fairly fixed, the British controlled only three small and isolated areas. One group held out on the tip of the peninsula in Piraeus. Another controlled the airfield at Hassani and the shore toward Phaleron Bay. The main body of British troops held a thin strip of central Athens, about two miles long and five or six blocks wide. Except for these three isolated areas, ELAS controlled not only Athens but all of Greece.

Meanwhile the British in Athens were growing stronger. On December 11, Field Marshal Alexander personally investigated the situation and ordered immediate reinforcements from Italy. During the next fortnight one hundred American troop carrier planes flown by American pilots rushed in two British divisions, a brigade of the Fifth Indian Division, and several miscellaneous battalions. When these reinforcements began to arrive, the ELAS High Command realized that it must strike at once or give up any hope of success. On the night of December 15–16 it launched an all-out attack on the British positions. But though it won some minor gains it could not drive the British out of Athens, partly because adequate reinforcements had not arrived from Thessaly and partly because the attack had not been properly synchronized.

This failure was the turning point. British air-borne troops were arriving in increasing numbers from Italy. The balance was turning against ELAS. On December 27, General Scobie launched his offensive. The British advanced steadily. In three days of raw and bloody fighting they cleared the southern half of Athens and much of Piraeus. After a few days' rest they resumed the attack on January 3. Still ELAS fought back bitterly. Its losses averaged thirty dead and twenty-four wounded for each street given up. British casualties were "above normal." Then suddenly it was all over. On the night of January 4–5, ELAS slipped out of the city in the darkness.

The victory in Athens did not end the Greek crisis for Churchill. He was warned by General Wilson that resources were lacking to challenge ELAS's domination of the rest of Greece:

> I earnestly hope that you will be able to find a political solution to the Greek problem, as I am convinced that further military action after we have cleared the Athens-Piraeus area is beyond our present strength. . . . During the German occupation they [the Germans] maintained between six and seven divisions on the mainland, in addition to the equivalent of four in the Greek islands. Even so they were unable to keep their communications open all the time, and I doubt if we will meet less strength and determination than they encountered.[43]

On Christmas Eve Churchill flew from London to Athens in search of the "political solution" that Wilson had urged. He was not able to restore peace but on his return to England he eased the controversial monarchy question by persuading King George to withdraw (December 30) and to appoint Archbishop Damaskinos as regent. At the same time Premier Papandreou resigned and Damaskinos appointed in his place the veteran republican General Nicholas Plastiras. These changes paved the way for armistice negotiations when ELAS withdrew from Athens. An armistice was signed on January 11, 1945, and a month later, on February 12, the Varkiza Peace Agreement was signed.

The principal provisions were that ELAS should surrender its arms within two weeks; the Communist party and the EAM be recognized as legal political organizations; elections and a plebiscite on the monarchy question be held within the year; the prosecution of those implicated in the uprising be confined to those who violated criminal law and not extend to political offenses; and the immediate purging of those in the civil and armed services who had collaborated with the Germans.

Thus ended the thirty-three days of fighting in Athens. The cost is estimated to have been 250 million dollars worth of property destroyed and 11,000 persons killed, 6,500 of them noncombatants. Churchill had finally secured Britain's position in Greece as the Soviet Union had done in the northern Balkans. Greece now was to be on the side of the West during the forthcoming Cold War of the postwar years.

YALTA

The fighting in Athens had barely ceased when, in February, 1945, the Big Three powers met at Yalta for the last of their wartime conferences. By this time Russia was in a particularly strong position in Eastern Europe. The principle had been established that until the end of the war each great power would supervise political developments in those areas through which its armies passed in pursuit of the foe, and for Russia this meant all the territory north of Greece. Moreover, as we saw earlier in this chapter, the armistice agreements concluded with Rumania and Bulgaria in the fall of 1944 gave the Soviet authorities almost unrestricted political power until the peace treaties were concluded. As for Yugoslavia, the Communist Tito was consolidating his position without any significant opposition. Thus when Stalin appeared at Yalta he was already the *de facto* master of Eastern Europe.

During the negotiations Stalin carefully respected the division of the Balkans arranged at the October, 1944 Moscow Conference. He raised no objections concerning the armed British intervention in Greece. Instead, he assured Churchill that he had "complete confidence" in his Greek policy, and added cynically that "since the Greeks had not yet become accustomed to discussion, they were following the practice of cutting each other's throats." [44] In regard to Yugoslavia, the Big Three placed themselves squarely behind Tito by endorsing an agreement he had concluded with Shubashich on November 1, 1944, for the establishment of a regency until a plebiscite could be held. King Peter naturally had been alarmed by this arrangement, but British pressure had compelled him to restrain his objections. Now the decision at Yalta undermined his position and reduced still further what little hope remained that he might return to his throne.

The three powers also agreed to assist the liberated peoples of Europe "to form interim governmental authorities broadly representative of all democratic elements in the population and pledged to the earliest possible establishment through free elections of governments responsive to the will of the people. . . ." [45] On paper, this Declaration on Liberated Europe represented a substantial concession on the part of the Soviets. Despite their domination of Eastern Europe they had consented to free elections which might well bring to office anti-Soviet governments. The substance of this concession, however, was negligible. The Declaration proved to be meaningless and barren because it was interpreted very differently by the various signatories.

The United States interpreted the Declaration literally, that is, free elections and no spheres of influence in Eastern Europe. The United States was free to take this position because it was not bound by the percentages arrangement made at Moscow. Britain, on the other hand, was ambivalent about the Declaration because the percentages agreement had enabled her to secure her position in Greece. On the other hand, the Declaration was alluring because, if literally enforced, it would enable Britain to regain positions in Rumania and Bulgaria that she had abandoned.

The Russians, by contrast, clung to the percentages agreement and regarded the Declaration as mere window dressing. They had scrupulously kept their hands off Greece while Churchill had battered the ELAS. Now they expected the Western powers in turn to respect their "90 per cent say" in Rumania and "75 per cent say" in Bulgaria. Consequently they were surprised and outraged when the British gradually and somewhat embarrassedly joined the United States in forgetting the percentages and insisting on fulfillment of the Declaration. The Russians refused to budge on this point because they regarded "friendly" governments in Eastern Europe as absolutely essential for their security. A few months later at the Potsdam Conference Stalin declared flatly: "A freely elected government in any of these countries [in Eastern Europe] would be anti-Soviet, and that we cannot allow." [46] This contradiction between "friendly" and "freely elected" governments was the rock on which the Big Three Grand Alliance foundered as soon as this rock was laid bare by the ebb of the tide of German conquest.

YALTA VIOLATED

The first conflict over "friendly" or "freely elected" governments took place in Rumania. King Michael had withdrawn his country from the Axis camp when he rid himself of Antonescu on August 23, 1944. The next day a coalition government was formed, representing the four main "democratic" parties: the National Peasants, the Liberals, the Social Democrats, and the Communists. The premier was General Constantin Sanatescu, Marshal of the Royal Court, who had been the connecting link between the king and the army in the coup against Antonescu.

The disparate elements in this coalition soon were at loggerheads. The Communists and Social Democrats combined with two smaller left-wing parties, the Plowmen's Front and the Union of Patriots, to form a National Democratic Front (FND) and to demand a greater voice in government. They accused Maniu and Bratianu of opposing reform measures and of failing to fulfill the armistice terms. These charges were to a certain degree justified because the conservative Rumanian leaders were strongly anti-Russian and assumed wishfully that the Western powers would somehow protect them against Soviet pressure. Having thus misjudged the power situation, they failed to purge the pro-Germans and war criminals, and they evaded the Russian demands for material assistance in the war against the Germans.

On November 5, 1944, the Sanatescu government resigned following a protest from the Russian General Vinogradov, vice-president of the Allied Control Commission, that the armistice terms were being violated. On the same day Sanatescu formed a second cabinet in which the FND had increased representation. But the FND remained hostile to the premier, and within less than a month he was forced to resign a second time. On December 2 a new government was formed by General Nicholas Radescu, chief of the Rumanian general staff.

In accepting the premiership Radescu stipulated that the Communist militia be disbanded and that agrarian reform be postponed until the Rumanian troops were home from the war. The Communists accepted these terms and entered Radescu's cabinet. But it soon became apparent that they had no intention of honoring their commitment and that their goal was a Communist-dominated government. On January 16, 1945, Gheorghiu-Dej, secretary-general of the Communist party and minister of communications, returning from a visit to Moscow, instructed the FND to overthrow the Radescu government and begin agitation for immediate land reform. Radescu had little chance against the coordinated sabotage of the Russians and the Communist-controlled FND. The Communist undersecretaries in various ministries sabotaged the work of their departments and refused to resign when

Radescu requested them to do so. Radescu was unable to reach the public because the Soviet Mission suppressed all opposition papers.

The crisis came on February 24, when mass demonstrations were organized against the government in Bucharest and in some provincial towns. That evening eight demonstrators were killed by a burst of firing in the streets of Bucharest. The Communists charged Radescu with responsibility, while the premier maintained that Communist *provocateurs* had done the shooting. The next day the Communist-controlled press denounced Radescu as a murderer and demanded his execution.

The turning point in Rumania's postwar history came on February 27, 1945. On that day Andrei Vyshinsky, the Soviet foreign minister, arrived in Bucharest and delivered an ultimatum to King Michael demanding Radescu's resignation. The following day Radescu complied with this demand. The king then proposed that Prince Barbu Stirbei, a high court functionary, assume the premiership. Vyshinsky reacted violently to this suggestion, slamming the door so forcibly as he left that he cracked the wall plaster. The Russian demanded and secured the appointment of Peter Groza, leader of the leftist Plowmen's Front. The cabinet, as announced on March 6, consisted entirely of members of the FND and of dissident Liberals and National Peasants who represented nobody but themselves. The Russians promptly strengthened the position of this government by transferring northern Transylvania to Rumania.

Obviously, these events in Rumania were gross violations of the Yalta Declaration on Liberated Europe, which had been enunciated only a month earlier. Churchill was nevertheless reluctant to intervene because of the percentages agreement:

> The Russians had established the rule of a Communist minority by force and misrepresentation. We were hampered in our protests because Eden and I during our October visit to Moscow had recognized that Russia should have a largely predominant voice in Rumania and Bulgaria while we took the lead in Greece. Stalin had kept very strictly to this understanding during the six weeks fighting against the Communists and E.L.A.S. in the city of Athens, in spite of the fact that all this was most disagreeable to him and those around him. . . . He had subscribed on paper to the principles of Yalta, and now they were being trampled down in Rumania. But if I pressed him too much he might say, "I did not interfere with your action in Greece; why do you not give me the same latitude in Rumania?" [47]

Roosevelt was not hampered by the percentages agreement but he was loath to press the issue. According to James F. Byrnes, who shortly was to become secretary of state,

> The President felt that the Rumanian situation did not offer the best test case of our relations with the Soviets. Great Britain and the United States had no armed forces in Rumania. It was under the exclusive control of the Red Army. The President knew that the Soviets had to maintain a line of communication

from the homeland through Rumania to their armies in Germany. He knew the Soviets would claim the action taken was necessary to protect their armies. . . .[48]

Soviet highhandedness in Rumania had its parallel in Bulgaria. On September 9, 1944, as noted earlier in this chapter, the Fatherland Front had executed its coup and established a government under Colonel Kimon Georgiev. The four parties comprising the Fatherland Front were all represented in the government. The *Zveno* group had the premiership and four ministries. The Agrarians, who enjoyed widespread peasant support, held four cabinet seats. The Social Democrats had three and the Communists four, including the key ministries of interior and justice.

One of the first tasks undertaken by the new government was to purge and punish all politicians associated with Bulgaria's pro-German policy since 1941. "People's Courts" with powers of summary trial and execution without appeal were established throughout the country. The Communist ministers of interior and justice did not exert a restraining influence. According to official figures, 10,897 had been found guilty by March, 1945, of which 2,138 had been sentenced to death and executed (including the three wartime regents), 1,940 had been sentenced to 20 years' imprisonment, 962 to 15 years, 727 to 10 years, and the remainder to shorter terms. Rumors spread that many more had been punished, but even if the official figures are accepted they indicate that the purge in Bulgaria was of a severity unparalleled in any other European country.

The next task after the purge was to prepare for the forthcoming elections. The Fatherland Front government was provisional, and it was agreed, in conformity with the Yalta Declaration, that a free election should be held as soon as conditions allowed. Friction developed during the campaign between the Communists on the one hand and the Agrarians and Social Democrats on the other. The Agrarians accused the Communists of interfering in the internal affairs of their party and of trying to unseat Agrarian leaders, such as Nikola Petkov, who were anti-Communist. In fact, the Agrarian party did split in May, 1945, during a party congress at which Petkov was ousted in favor of Alexander Obbov, who favored cooperation with the Communists. Petkov and certain Social Democratic leaders then resigned from the Fatherland Front and organized an opposition group whose main aim was to prevent the Communists from dominating Bulgaria. The contest was unequal because the Communists controlled the Fatherland Front, the press, the militia, and local government. And, more important, the Russians supported the Communists, whereas the Western representatives on the Control Commission could do little to aid Petkov. Thus it appeared that the Russians were assured of a Bulgarian regime as "friendly" as that in Rumania.

In Yugoslavia the Communists became the masters of the country before elections were held. As the Germans withdrew, the Partisans' National Liberation Committees took over control. Furthermore, the Big Three at Yalta endorsed the Tito-Shubashich agreement of November 1, 1944, providing for a regency to act for the king until a plebiscite could be held. The regency was established on March 5, 1945, and two days later a new government was formed with Tito as prime minister and minister of war, and Shubashich as foreign minister. Only five of the twenty-eight cabinet posts were held by non-Tito representatives. Loyal Partisans held all the strategic posts so that there never was any doubt about the outcome of the election of the constituent assembly scheduled for November 11, 1945.

In the field of foreign affairs Tito at this time was pressing his claim to the Italian province of Venezia Giulia with the city of Trieste. The Partisans had demanded the province as early as November, 1943, at their Jajce Assembly. By May 1, 1945, Partisan forces had occupied most of the province and were fighting inside Trieste itself. This led to acute friction with the Western powers, which insisted that the fate of the province be reserved for the peace conference. New Zealand troops were rushed to Trieste, and on June 9, 1945, the Yugoslavs yielded to a virtual ultimatum and withdrew their forces behind the so-called Morgan Line, leaving Trieste to the Allies. When Stalin complained to Churchill about the pressure on Tito, the British premier replied heatedly: "Our joint idea at the Kremlin in October was that the Yugoslav business should work out around 50-50 Russian and British influence. In fact it is at present more like 90-10, and even in that poor 10 we have been subjected to violent pressure by Marshal Tito." [49] This exchange is significant in reflecting the growing friction between the Western powers and the Communist states, and also in revealing that Churchill was still thinking in terms of the percentages agreement reached at Moscow.

These conflicts in the Balkans were considered at the Potsdam Conference held from July 17 to August 2, 1945. This was the longest and the least satisfactory of the Big Three conferences because the need for military cooperation was no longer an overriding bond and political differences were coming increasingly to the fore. The differences in the Balkans were discussed by Churchill and Stalin when they dined together at a preliminary meeting on July 18. Churchill again complained about the situation in Yugoslavia, protesting that Britain was being steadily eliminated in that country.

I then spoke of the difficulties in Yugoslavia, where we had no material ambitions, but there had been the fifty-fifty arrangement. It was now ninety-nine to one against Britain. Stalin protested that the proportions were 90 per cent British, 10 per cent Yugoslav and 0 per cent Russian interests. The Soviet Government often did not know what Tito was about to do. Stalin also said that he had been hurt by the American demand for a change of Government in Rumania and Bulgaria. He was not meddling in Greek affairs, and it was unjust of them. [50]

The implication of Stalin's remarks was clear: the percentages agreement should be followed and the Yalta Declaration ignored. When full negotiations began it was soon discovered that the problem could not be disposed of so simply. Stalin made it clear he expected the Western powers to recognize the "People's Democracies" of Rumania, Bulgaria, Yugoslavia, Albania, and other Eastern European countries. But the American delegates, President Harry S. Truman and Secretary of State James F. Byrnes, took their stand by the Yalta Declaration. They wanted free elections in the liberated countries and, if necessary, they were prepared in conjunction with Britain and Russia to send missions to observe and assist with the conduct of the elections. Furthermore, they produced a memorandum maintaining that the Yalta Declaration had not been observed in Rumania and Bulgaria. Stalin came back with the obvious rejoinder, attacking British behavior in Greece. The British heatedly rejected the Russian charges, and thus the Cold War lines were drawn with the Soviet Union on the one side and the Western powers on the other.

The Potsdam deliberations concerning Eastern Europe were doomed to failure because they were based upon two incompatible starting points, the percentages agreement and the Yalta Declaration. At one point Byrnes told Molotov: "The United States sincerely desires Russia to have friendly countries on her borders, but we believe they should seek the friendship of the people rather than of any particular government. We, therefore, want the governments to be representative of the people." [51] If Byrnes was unaware that his proposal was inherently contradictory, Stalin was ready to enlighten him with brutal frankness: "A freely elected government in any of these countries would be anti-Soviet, and that we cannot allow." [52]

PEACE SETTLEMENT

The Potsdam Conference was not altogether profitless so far as the Balkans were concerned. The negotiators did agree that the Council of Foreign Ministers should prepare peace treaties for Rumania and Bulgaria, and that these treaties were to be concluded with "recognized democratic governments." It was also agreed to "examine . . . the establishment of diplomatic relations . . . to the extent possible prior to the conclusion of peace treaties. . . ." This did not settle anything, but at least it arranged for continuation of negotiations at a lower level. Furthermore, the requirement for "recognized democratic governments" slowed down temporarily the Communist drive to power in the northern Balkans.

In Rumania King Michael declared that the Groza government did not meet the requirements stipulated at Potsdam and asked for British, American, and Russian assistance in forming a new cabinet. The Russians assured Groza he still had their backing, so he refused to tender his resignation. King Michael thereupon staged a royal sitdown strike, leaving Bucharest for his summer palace and refusing to sign any decrees. Meanwhile in Bulgaria Petkov had protested officially to the American and British representatives in Sofia that the Yalta free-election provision would not be observed if the election were held as scheduled on August 26. The United States and Britain in turn protested to both Sofia and Moscow, with the result that the Russian government agreed to inform the Bulgarian government that it would not object if the election were postponed. On the election day itself the Fatherland Front government announced the postponement of the election to November 18.

This upsurge of opposition to Communist domination proved ephemeral because the Soviet Union had the preponderance of power in that area and the Western powers were not ready to offer challenge. They did hold the line at the first meeting of the Council of Foreign Ministers in London in September, 1945. At this meeting the arguments heard at Potsdam were repeated. Molotov insisted that the "people's democracies" be recognized, while Byrnes reiterated that he wanted to see governments in Eastern Europe that were both friendly to the Soviet Union and democratic. The conference broke up on October 2 without any achievement to its credit.

The next meeting of the Council of Foreign Ministers was held in December, 1945, in Moscow. This time the Western powers gave way on Eastern Europe in return for concessions elsewhere. The Soviet Union agreed to accept an arrangement for Allied administration of Japan which did not significantly impair American control. The Western powers in turn agreed that "two truly representative members" of the opposition parties should be added to the Rumanian and Bulgarian cabinets. In the case of Rumania, free and unfettered elections were to be held as soon as possible, after which the Western powers promised to extend recognition to the remodeled Rumanian government. The election requirement did not pertain to Bulgaria because an election had already been held there on November 18, with the opposition abstaining and the government thus receiving an 86 per cent majority.

Groza in Bucharest did accept two minor opposition figures in his cabinet. But no one paid any attention to them and the formal promises of civil liberties and early elections proved entirely empty in the years to come. Before the unregenerate behavior of the Rumanian government had become fully apparent, Britain and the United States extended recognition on February 5, 1946. In Bulgaria, however, recognition was withheld because opposition representatives were not included in the government. The Soviet government forbade Sofia from making this concession, presumably because such opposition leaders as Petkov had too strong a following.

During the year 1946 protracted negotiations were conducted for the conclusion of a peace settlement. It had been agreed at the Moscow meeting of the Council of Foreign Ministers that the peace should be prepared in three stages. First the drafts were to be drawn up by those members of the Council of Foreign Ministers who were signatories of the armistice pacts. Next a conference of twenty-one Allied nations was to "consider" the drafts, and finally the Council of Foreign Ministers was to draw up the final texts of the settlements. This complicated procedure represented a compromise between the Russians, who wanted to restrict the number of powers participating in the peacemaking, and the Western powers, which wished to include all Allied nations.

The Council of Foreign Ministers met in Paris from April 25 to May

16 and from June 15 to July 12. It reached an accord on many questions, though a considerable number still remained unresolved. The problem now arose concerning the powers that were to be accorded the conference of Allied nations. The Soviet Union, which had accepted the plan for a conference with reluctance, now was determined to restrict its authority as much as possible. In the end, the Soviet viewpoint prevailed to a large extent. The conference could not change or even pass judgment on the large number of clauses that the Council had already formulated. On the twenty-six points which the Council had left open, the conference was merely to make "recommendations." Whether these recommendations were to be considered, let alone adopted, was left entirely to the discretion of the Council.

Despite these restrictions, the conference did give the smaller states an opportunity to discuss fully many controversial issues and to adopt fifty-nine recommendations by a two-thirds majority and forty-eight recommendations by a simple majority. These recommendations appreciably affected the final peace terms prepared by the Council of Foreign Ministers in New York from November 4 to December 16, 1946. The peace treaties, which formally ended the war between the Allies on the one hand, and Italy, Rumania, Hungary, Bulgaria, and Finland on the other, were signed in Paris on February 10, 1947.

The most important provisions, so far as the Balkans were concerned, had to do with reparations and frontier changes. Italy was required to pay 125 million dollars to Yugoslavia, 105 million dollars to Greece, 5 million dollars to Albania, in addition to other sums to Russia and Ethiopia. Likewise, Hungary was to pay 70 million dollars to Yugoslavia, as well as other sums to Russia and Czechoslovakia. Italy was required to surrender the Dodecanese Islands to Greece, Saseno Island to Albania, and a part of the province of Venezia Giulia to Yugoslavia. The latter cession represented a compromise between Russia and Yugoslavia, on the one hand, who had demanded the entire province, and Italy and the Western powers, on the other, who had insisted on an ethnic boundary. The final compromise gave to Yugoslavia the port of Pola, Izonzo Valley, and Istria, with a population of 225,000 Slavs and 128,000 Italians. Trieste, with its immediate hinterland, estimated at 300 square miles, was placed under international control. Hungary was reduced to the Trianon frontiers, yielding northern Transylvania to Rumania, southern Slovakia to Czechoslovakia, and Carpatho-Ukraine to Russia. Bulgaria restored the Greek and Yugoslav territories that she had occupied but she acquired southern Dobruja, which she had lost to Rumania in 1919. Finally, Rumania confirmed the cession of Bessarabia and northern Bukovina to Russia.

Superficially this peace settlement appears inconsequential. Both the financial provisions and the territorial changes were on a relatively minor scale. Yet the peace treaty represented a momentous turning point in Balkan history because it sanctioned the new Communist regimes in the northern Balkans. This meant revolutionary and far-reaching changes within the peninsula as well as a basic shift in the orientation of the northern Balkan countries from the Western capitals to Moscow. Churchill had frequently declared during the war that he did not propose to allow the Soviet zone to extend westward to a line from Stettin in the north to Trieste in the south. Yet this is precisely what the Western powers accepted when they signed the peace treaty at Paris.

The explanation for the Soviet advance has provoked much speculation and controversy since the war. It has often been asserted that the Russians could have been stopped if Churchill's proposal for a Balkan invasion had been followed. On the other hand, a well-informed authority, Dr. Philip E. Mosely, has pointed out that a Balkan invasion might have served to extend the Soviet zone still further instead of restricting it.

In recent years it has often been argued that, if the American leadership had accepted the Churchill-sponsored project for an invasion of the Balkans in 1943, the later fate of East Central Europe might have been a very different one, for the need and opportunity for Soviet-style "liberation" would have been averted. The plans for a Balkan approach have remained obscure, as to forces proposed and limits of advance and schedule, but there has been no indication that they called for more than an advance northward to the Danube-Sava line. If carried out, this plan would presumably have brought Bulgaria within the British safety-zone for the Mediterranean, but it is probable that Yugoslavia would have remained under the control of Tito's forces. In any case, Poland and Czechoslovakia, Hungary and Rumania would have remained within the Soviet military theater, with all the consequences derived therefrom. In addition, the SHAEF invasion of Western Europe could not have been carried out during 1944. It is possible that not only all of Germany, but also Denmark, the Netherlands, Belgium and perhaps France would have experienced Soviet-style "liberation."[53]

This analysis indicates that the fate of the northern Balkans was determined by the course of events outside the peninsula. Soviet domination was probably inevitable once the Wehrmacht was defeated in Russia and the Red Army began its relentless advance westward. An Anglo-American countermove into the Balkans, as Dr. Mosely suggests, might have simply deflected the Red flood into Western Europe and thus given Moscow control of the heart of the Continent. Theoretically, the Western powers might have attempted to roll back the Soviet zone immediately after the war when Russia was exhausted and devastated and the United States alone had possession of the atom bomb. This may have been militarily feasible but the fact remains that it was not so politically. Allied public opinion was not prepared to accept an anti-Soviet war at that moment. In Britain there was much warm feeling toward the Russians for having borne so long and so gallantly the brunt of the Nazi onslaught. And in the United States the public clamor was not to launch a crusade into Eastern Europe but rather to "bring the boys back home."

Epilogue

WORLD WAR II represents one of the great turning points in the long and variegated history of the Balkan Peninsula. Regardless of whether or not one is convinced that what has happened is desirable, the fact remains that there has been far-reaching and incalculably important change. Kings have been expelled from their thrones; traditional parties have been splintered into impotence or completely suppressed; and venerated political leaders have disappeared into retirement, exile, or grave. New men and new parties have appeared on the stage, with radical and all-embracing plans for social change, and with the organization and foreign backing necessary to effect such change. The institutions and traditions of a millenium have been revolutionized before our eyes during the brief period since the Balkan Peninsula was engulfed in World War II.

To find another such turning point in Balkan history it is necessary to go back to the Ottoman invasion in the fourteenth and fifteenth centuries. Indeed, the invasion and the half millenium of Ottoman rule that followed offer suggestions as to what might be expected in the present era of transition. The first parallel that comes to mind is the social cleavage and class conflict within the peninsula which paved the way for both Islam and Communism. To be sure, the decisive factor in each case was armed force, whether wielded by the Janissary Corps or the Red Army. But foreign invasion was facilitated by domestic dissension, especially because the invaders in both periods were able to proclaim themselves to be the deliverers of the common people against their exploitive rulers. Thus the Red Army found powerful allies in the Communist-dominated resistance movements in the Balkan Mountains, while the Turks likewise received assistance throughout their campaigning, beginning with the discontented Christian peasantry of Asia Minor in the early fourteenth century and ending with the Bogomils of Bosnia a century and a half later.

Following their conquest of the peninsula, the Turks remained mas-

839

ters until the twentieth century. Yet the several ethnic Balkan groups were able to retain their identity and to emerge finally as independent peoples with essentially unimpaired national cultures. A basic reason for this phenomenon was the loose structure of the Ottoman Empire, which remained a flabby congeries of peoples, religions, and conflicting loyalties. The subject groups were allowed to retain their institutions and cultures so long as they accepted the suzerainty of the sultan and continued to pay tribute. In this respect the Communist regimes in the northern Balkans are the complete antithesis of the old Ottoman imperial structure. They have subordinated every form of human activity to the interests of the official ideologies and programs. Furtermore, they possess the technological devices for realizing the regimentation they seek. The press, the radio, the stage, and the schools have been reduced to a degree of uniformity that suggests that the new Balkan regimes will leave a far deeper imprint than the Ottoman Empire.

This certainly will be the case if the Communist governments remain in power for any length of time. In this connection the reasons for Ottoman decline and disintegration are relevant. At a relatively early stage the Ottoman Empire was doomed to eventual extinction, even though European rivalries preserved it as a passive and impotent power until the twentieth century. The empire's ultimate fate was decided by its inability to keep pace with the dynamic West, which was being transformed by the Renaissance, the discoveries, the Commercial Revolution, the scientific advances, and the rise of the absolutist monarchies. The Ottoman Empire, by contrast, remained unaffected and unchanging. As a result it was incapable of either defending itself or providing its subjects with the prerequisites of modern life. The failure of the Ottoman Empire was, in the broadest terms, a failure in adjustment, a failure to respond to the challenge of the dynamic West.

This fact has a direct bearing upon the present situation because the underlying problem in the Balkans today is still one of the adjustment to the West. We have seen that the manifold difficulties that have beset the Balkan peoples in recent decades have arisen from the impact of the dynamic Western civilization upon an agrarian, self-contained, and relatively static culture. The result has been a crisis that has manifested itself in every aspect of Balkan life—economic, political, and cultural. The prewar regimes tried in vain to cope with this crisis. They failed to alleviate the plight of the peasants with their tiny plots, low productivity, and lack of capital. They also failed to attain political stability, so that the representative institutions established at the end of World War I gave way to authoritarian structures that prevailed in every Balkan country when World War II began. They failed, finally, to retain the allegiance of their own intellegentsia which, frustrated by social injustice and lack of opportunity, became the spearhead of a revolutionary movement. In this respect the Balkan intellectuals reacted in essentially the same manner as their counterparts in China or India or tsarist Russia. And the reason was that they were responding to a basically similar situation—

to the same complex of problems that is today facing all the underdeveloped regions of the world.

We are now witnessing in the Balkan Peninsula two different and rival approaches toward the solution of the traditional problems. One set of procedures is being followed in the Communist-dominated northern Balkans and a very different set in Western-oriented Greece. We have seen that the latter country was set firmly in the Western camp as a result of the Churchill-Stalin division of the Balkans in October, 1944, and the armed British action in Athens two months later. Greece was retained in the Western orbit by the enunciation of the Truman Doctrine in March, 1947, when a Communist-directed rebellion threatened to overthrow the Athens government. Today, in 1957, Greece remains a Western outpost in the Balkan Peninsula. Consequently, her efforts to cope with the basic problems noted above are typically "Western" in character. Greece is attempting not to create a new social order but rather gradually to reform existing institutions with Western financial and technical assistance.

This assistance has reached very considerable proportions. Between liberation and the summer of 1956 it amounted to 1.8 billion dollars from the United States alone. This sum, which does not include the large military grants, represents 214 dollars for every Greek man, woman, and child—a rate of per capita aid surpassing that given to any other European country. Greece has utilized this lavish assistance to cope with the ravages of occupation and of civil war, and also to increase the productivity of her economy. By the beginning of 1956 Greece was producing 40 per cent more farm crops than before the war, and her industrial output was 86 per cent higher. The greatest gains were in electric power output, which more than doubled, and in rice production—largely on reclaimed salty coastal lands—which skyrocketed nearly 700 per cent.[1] In the field of public administration efforts have been made, with less satisfactory results, to cope with long-standing issues such as an inequitable tax structure, a swollen bureaucracy, and an excessively centralized administration.

In striking contrast to this gradualism, the northern Balkan countries have experienced a thoroughgoing political and economic revolution. The political revolution has involved the establishment of so-called "people's democracies," which have been defined candidly as "the dictatorship of the proletariat though not in the Soviet form." [2] All pro-Western elements were ruthlessly eliminated from political life, especially after the signing of the peace treaties in February, 1947. Nikola Petkov was executed in Bulgaria, Iuliu Maniu was imprisoned in Rumania, and Ivan Shubashich was forced to resign in Yugoslavia. The process was completed with the organization of the Communist Information Bureau (Cominform) in September, 1947. Its purpose was to coordinate the activities of all the Eastern European Communist parties in their efforts to combat "Anglo-American imperialism." This made it plain that the period of "antifascist" coalitions was finished and that the

Communist parties were to act alone and forcefully against those whom they considered to be Western agents.

This political revolution was accompanied by—indeed it made possible—a corresponding economic upheaval. One feature of the economic change was the extension of state control over an increasing portion of the national economy—beginning with foreign trade and expanding to banking, industry, and wholesale trade. The other main feature was the launching of economic programs, the first ones being short-term reconstruction plans designed to regain prewar production levels, and the later ones being long-term development plans for industrial expansion. The plans called for heavy capital investment which in turn necessitated rigid curbs upon consumption. The authoritarian regimes had the power and the will to enforce the required curbs, with the result that the objectives of the plans have generally been reached. The following figures reveal the unprecedented growth of heavy industry which has been favored at the expense of consumers' goods production.

Output of Basic Materials in Yugoslavia, Bulgaria, and Rumania

Commodity	Unit	1939[a]	1951	1952	1953
Coal	Millions of tons	11.5	21.9	23.5	24.1
Pig iron	Thousands of tons	231.1	605.3	673.6	720[b]
Cement	Millions of tons	1.6	2.9	3.5	3.9
Electric power	Billion kilowatt hours	2.5	6.0	7.1	8.0

[a] 1939 figures for Yugoslavia and Bulgaria, 1938 figures for Rumania.

[b] This figure does not include Bulgaria's production, for which no information is available for that year.

Source: Compiled from Economic Survey of Europe in 1954 (Geneva, 1955), p. 265; and R. L. Wolff, The Balkans in Our Time (Cambridge, Mass., 1956), p. 440. The rate of industrial growth is equally impressive in Albania: see statistics in Economic Survey of Europe in 1955 (Geneva, 1956), p. B42.

The statistics concerning postwar industrial growth in Greece as well as the northern Balkans are impressive, but they should not be interpreted overoptimistically. In Greece, for example, unemployment in the industrial sector is estimated to be between one third and one quarter of the labor force actually engaged in industry, and disguised unemployment in the countryside is estimated to be close to 40 per cent of the population actively engaged in agriculture.[3] The ministry of welfare has reported that at the end of September, 1955, 29 per cent of the population (2,764,017 out of 7,900,000) were destitute, having an average monthly income of less than 240 drachmas or 8.40 dollars a month.[4] A competent observer analyzed the economic state of the country in January, 1956, as follows:

American money, despite all its benefits, has not revolutionized the nation. The mass standard of living is still probably the lowest in Europe this side of the Iron Curtain. Unemployment is so heavy that mere false rumors of jobs open on Greek ships have sent jobless men scurrying to distant ports in Northern Europe. Men who know Greece say that where 100 wealthy families formerly controlled its economy now the number is about 500.[5]

We may conclude that although the Greek economy has made gratifying progress in certain areas this has not alleviated the traditional and fundamental problems of low productivity, surplus labor, and inequitable distribution of national income. The northern Balkan countries also have experienced serious difficulties, the most dangerous being the perennial agrarian problem. The peasants are generally dissatisfied and are opposing their governments by limiting production. One of their grievances is the constant pressure for the collectivization of the land along the lines of the Soviet kolhozi. Another is the lack of consumers' goods because of the concentration on heavy industry. This has forced the Communist rulers to resort to compulsory delivery of agricultural produce, which in turn has further alienated the peasant masses. Furthermore, it should be noted that the Balkan countries all lack the great reserves of virgin land which existed in the Soviet Union and which provided leeway for trial-and-error experimentation. These difficulties are reflected in the fact that the increase planned by the northern Balkan countries in national production and in industrial production for the period 1955 to 1960 are substantially less than the increases actually realized for the period 1950 to 1955.[6]

In addition to these economic problems, the Communist governments must contend with the anti-Soviet proclivities of their nationalist-minded subjects. The Balkan peoples are uniformly antipathetic to foreign domination, direct or indirect, even if it emanates from Slavic Mother Russia. The Bulgarians dramatically manifested this tendency following the Berlin Congress when they rejected dictation by the Russians, even though the latter had just delivered them from Turkish rule. A more recent and significant expression of rugged Balkan nationalism was the 1948 split between Tito and Moscow.

The roots of the schism go back to the war years when Tito, as we noted, followed a much more independent course than the other Balkan Communist leaders. He continued to assert his independence after the end of the war. On a number of issues he took the heretical position that the Yugoslav state should be completely free and independent, and that the Yugoslav Communist party should be equal to the parent Soviet party. When he stubbornly refused to recant, the Cominform expelled the Yugoslav party in an angry proclamation in June, 1948. But Tito's government did not collapse as expected. Instead "Titoism," a new term in the Marxist lexicon, spread widely throughout Eastern Europe.

With the death of Stalin in 1953 Soviet imperiousness diminished and the ties binding the Eastern European states to Moscow were allowed to slacken. By the time of the Twentieth Congress of the Soviet Communist party in 1956 the new Soviet leaders were listing Yugoslavia as one of the "people's democracies" and were accepting autonomist formulas which they earlier had branded as deviationist and anti-Communist. Tito responded by addressing the Congress delegates as "Dear Comrades" and by referring to the Soviet Union as a socialist state rather than a bureaucractic dictatorship.

The *rapprochement* cooled off with the tumultuous events that convulsed Eastern Europe in the second half of 1956. Beginning with the riots in Poznan, Poland, in late June, they built up in October and November to the establishment of the "national communist" regime of Wladislaw Gomulka in Poland, and to the armed Russian intervention in Hungary. Tito welcomed Gomulka's advent enthusiastically, but he condemned the Red Army's bloody role in Budapest as "absolutely wrong" and a "fatal error." The Russians, in turn, used the columns of *Pravda* (November 11, 1956) to accuse Tito of "tendencies to interfere in the affairs of other Communist states." At the same time the devastation of Hungary sent tremors throughout the northern Balkans, causing the Communist regimes to make conciliatory gestures to their peoples in order to avoid further anti-Communist and anti-Soviet explosions.

These recent developments exhibit the same pattern as does the entire history of the Balkan Peninsula in the past two centuries. This pattern suggests that the present rulers of Bulgaria, Rumania, and Albania face a delicate and perilous task in reconciling the sturdy nationalism and individualism of their subjects with land collectivization, forced industrialization, and subservient relationships to the Soviet Union.

In conclusion, the half millennium of historical experience analyzed in this volume indicates the likelihood of certain general trends. In the first place, the Balkan Peninsula in all probability will retain its identity. It is very unlikely that it will become a carbon copy of the Soviet Union or of any other power. On the other hand, if we look ahead in terms of decades, there doubtless will be far-reaching and enduring institutional change throughout the peninsula. The deep-rooted crisis that the Balkan states have experienced will require more than minor adjustments. The decisive factor that will determine the precise course of future events, apart from an unpredictable and incalculable World War III, probably will be the outcome of the contest now being waged, wittingly or unwittingly, by Greece and the northern Balkan states.

Both sides face the same basic problems—rural overpopulation, low productivity, few industries, shortage of capital, and the traditional lack of rapport between rulers and ruled. We have seen that these difficulties stem, directly or indirectly, from the fact that the Balkan Peninsula is a part of the vast underdeveloped portion of the globe. It is not, to be sure, as underdeveloped as large areas of Asia and Africa. But it faces, like them, the same task of adaptation to the demands and challenges of a dynamic world economy. A Balkan society that is incapable of adaptation to its world setting is doomed irrevocably to the same fate that befell the Ottoman Empire. Consequently, the crucial question at present is whether the Communist-controlled regimes in the north or the Western type of society in Greece will, in the years to come, prove more adaptable and more capable of coping with the traditional problems that have plagued all underdeveloped areas.

A parallel may be drawn at this point between the Communist-Greek competition in the Balkan Peninsula and the China-India competition in

Asia. The latter contest has attracted wide attention because of its momentous implications. A British authority has presented the issue as follows:

> . . . the decisive struggle in Asia is quite simply the effort of the two most ancient and populous peoples of the Orient—China and India—to modernize their communities. . . . China, by submitting to the dictatorship of the Communist party, has in the short run provided itself with some formidable instruments of capital accumulation. India, on the other hand, by consciously adopting democratic procedures and Western standards of freedom and welfare, has left itself with virtually only one weapon—persuasion. . . . There can be little doubt that Asia as a whole—and perhaps underdeveloped peoples elsewhere—will watch with increasing absorption the development of these two fateful experiments. . . . The liberal method of advance, and the totalitarian method, will in the next decade be pursued side by side in starkest contrast, with the world watching and judging the results.[7]

This analysis applies perfectly to the Balkan Peninsula as well as to Asia. The contest in the Balkans obviously is insignificant compared to that between China and India. Yet the same vital issues are at stake, and the outcome will have decisive influence on the future course of events in the peninsula and perhaps in adjoining regions.

Notes

3. Coming of the Ottoman Turks

1. Cited by G. G. Arnakis, "Futuwwa Traditions in the Ottoman Empire: Akhis, Bektashi Dervishes and Craftsmen," *Journal of Near Eastern Studies,* XII (October, 1953), 237.
2. Cited by M. Spinka, *A History of Christianity in the Balkans* (Chicago, 1933), p. 66.
3. F. Braudel, *La Méditerranée et le monde méditerranéan à l'époque de Philippe II* (Paris, 1949), p. 510
4. C. Mijatovich, *Constantine: The Last Emperor of the Greeks* (London, 1892), pp. 11–12.
5. See F. Babinger, *Beiträge zur Frühgeschichte der Türkenherrschaft in Rumelien (14–15 Jahrhundert)* (Munich, 1944), pp. 29 ff., and G. Ostrogorsky, *History of the Byzantine State* (Oxford, 1956), p. 489.
6. Ducas, cited by A. A. Vasiliev, *History of the Byzantine Empire* (Madison, Wisc., 1952), p. 629.

4. Conquest of the Balkans

1. *Pero Tafur: Travels and Adventures 1435–1439,* tr. and ed. by Malcolm Letts (London, 1926), pp. 144–146; "The Travels of Bertrandon de la Brocquière, A.D. 1432 and 1433," in Thomas Wright, *Early Travels in Palestine* (London, 1848), pp. 334, 340.
2. Phrantzes, cited by C. Mijatovich, *Constantine: The Last Emperor of the Greeks* (London, 1892), pp. 201–202.
3. L. Pastor, *History of the Popes* (London, 1923, 5th ed.), II, 277–278.
4. Cited by T. W. Arnold, *The Preaching of Islam: A History of the Propagation of the Moslem Faith* (London, 1913), p. 198.
5. Cited by Mijatovich, *op. cit.,* p. 8.
6. F. Babinger, *Mehmed der Eroberer und seine Zeit* (Munich, 1953), p. 25, has decided affirmatively concerning the mystery of whether or not Mohammed had planned to advance from Otranto to Rome.

5. Ottoman Empire at Its Height

1. O. Ferrara, *Le XVIᵉ siècle vu par les ambassadeurs vénitiens* (Paris, 1954), p. 344.
2. J. F. von Hammer-Purgstall, *Des osmanischen Reichs Staatsverfassung und Staatsverwaltung* (Vienna, 1815), I, 98.

3. F. C. Lane, "Venetian Shipping during the Commercial Revolution," *American Historical Review,* XXXVIII (January, 1933), 228.
4. Cited by D. M. Vaughan, *Europe and the Turk: A Pattern of Alliances 1350–1700* (Liverpool, 1954), p. 135.
5. Cited by S. A. Fischer-Galati, "Ottoman Imperialism and the Lutheran Struggle for Recognition in Germany, 1520–1529," *Church History,* XXIII (March, 1954), 57–58.
6. Cited by Vaughan, *op. cit.,* p. 136.
7. *Ibid.,* p. 135.

6. Ottoman Institutions

1. *The Turkish Letters of Ogier Ghiselin de Busbecq. Imperial Ambassador at Constantinople 1554–1562.* Newly translated from the Latin . . . by Edward Seymour Forster (Oxford, 1927), p. 239.
2. H. Blount, "A Voyage into the Levant," in J. Pinkerton, ed., *A General Collection of the Best and Most Interesting Voyages* . . . (London, 1808–1814), X, 222.
3. S. Gerlach, *Tage-Buch* . . . (Frankfurt, 1674), p. 314.
4. Cited by G. L. Lewis, *Turkey* (London, 1955), p. 27. For different evidence, see S. Vryonis, Jr., "Isidore Glabas and the Turkish Devshirme," *Speculum,* XXXI (July, 1956), 439–442.
5. Busbecq, *op. cit.,* pp. 60–61.
6. *The Letters and Works of Lady Mary Wortley Montagu* . . . (London, 1893), I, 322.
7. E. J. W. Gibb, *A History of Ottoman Poetry* (London, 1900), I, 28–29.
8. A. Pallis, *In the Days of the Janissaries: Old Turkish Life as Depicted in the "Travel-Book" of Evliya Chelebi* (London, 1951), pp. 119 ff.

7. Balkan Peninsula under Ottoman Rule

1. E. S. Forster, ed., *The Turkish Letters of Ogier Ghiselin de Busbecq* . . . (Oxford, 1927), p. 14.
2. P. Rycaut, *The Present State of the Ottoman Empire* . . . (London, 1668), p. 212.
3. *The Letters and Works of Lady Mary Wortley Montagu* . . . (London, 1893), I, 283.
4. *Ibid.,* p. 321.
5. *Voyages du Sr A. de la Motraye en Europe, Asie et Afrique* . . . (Le Havre, 1727), I, 462.
6. R. Dalven, *Modern Greek Poetry* (New York, 1949), p. 52.
7. G. R. Noyes and L. Bacon, *Heroic Ballads of Servia* (Boston, 1913), pp. 172–173.
8. M. Konstantinović, *Istorija ili ljetopisi turski spisani oko godine 1490* . . . [*A History or Turkish Chronicles Written about the Year 1490* . . .] (Belgrade, 1865), pp. 22, 41, 156.
9. S. Gerlach, *Tage-Buch* . . . (Frankfurt, 1674), p. 123.

8. Decline of the Ottoman Empire

1. *The Negotiations of Sir Thomas Roe in His Embassy to the Ottoman Porte from the Year 1621 to 1628 Inclusive* . . . (London, 1740), pp. 66–67.
2. Matteo Zane, cited by A. H. Lybyer, *The Government of the Ottoman Empire in the Time of Suleiman the Magnificent* (Cambridge, Mass., 1913), p. 43.
3. W. L. Wright, Jr., ed., *Ottoman Statecraft: The Book of Counsel for Vizirs and Governors of Sari Mehmed Pasha* . . . (Princeton, N. J., 1935), pp. 88–89.
4. Roe, *op. cit.,* p. 206.
5. P. Rycaut, *The Present State of the Ottoman Empire* . . . (London, 1668), p. 209.
6. Wright, *op. cit.,* p. 126.
7. Roger North, cited by Wright, *op. cit.,* p. 58.
8. Cited by H. Pfeffermann, *Die Zusammenarbeit der Renaissancepäpste mit den Türken* (Winterthur, Swtz., 1946), p. 14.
9. E. D. Clarke, *Travels in Various Countries of Europe, Asia and Africa* (Cambridge, Eng., 1810), I, 689–691.
10. Cited by A. Pallis, *In the Days of the Janissaries: Old Turkish Life as Depicted in the "Travel-Book" of Evliya Chelebi* (London, 1951), p. 90.
11. Cited in manuscript by Lewis V. Thomas, "Ottoman Awareness of Europe, 1650–1800."
12. Cited by A. Adnan-Adivar, "Interaction of Islamic and Western Thought in Turkey," *Near Eastern Culture and Society,* ed. by T. C. Young (Princeton, N. J., 1951). p. 122.
13. Cited by A. C. Wood, *A History of the Levant Company* (Oxford, 1935), p. 230.
14. Cited by W. Eton, *A Survey of the Turkish Empire* . . . (London, 1809), p. 109.
15. W. Macmichael, *Journey from Moscow to Constantinople in the Years 1817, 1818* (London, 1819), p. 154.
16. W. Hamilton, "Notes on a Journey in Asia Minor in 1837," *Journal of the Royal Geographical Society of London,* VIII (1838), 156–157.
17. Eton, *op. cit.,* pp. 247, 248, 263.
18. Cited by Wright, *op. cit.,* p. 21.
19. P. Rycaut, *The History of the Turks Beginning with the Year 1679* . . . (London, 1700), preface. The same point was made by Obreskov, the Russian ambassador to Constantinople in the mid-eighteenth century: see A. F. Miller, *Mustafa Pasha Bairaktar: Ottomanskaia Imperiia v Nachale XIX Veka* [*Mustafa Pasha Bairaktar: The Ottoman Empire in the Beginning of the Nineteenth Century*] (Moscow, 1947), p. 36.

9. Balkan Peninsula during Ottoman Decline

1. H. Inalcik, "Land Problems in Turkish History," *Muslim World,* XLV (July, 1955), 224.
2. Acting Consul Calvert to Lord John Russell, July 23, 1860. *Great Britain. Accounts and Papers: State Papers,* LXVII (1861), 10–11.
3. *Early Voyages and Travels in the Levant,* ed. by J. T. Bent (London, Hakluyt Society, 1893), LXXXVII, 188.

4. W. Eton, *A Survey of the Turkish Empire* . . . (London, 1809, 4th ed.), pp. 263–264.

5. K. M. Koumas, *Historia ton anthropinon praxeon apo ton archaiotaton chronon heos ton hemeron mas* [*History of the Acts of Man from the Earliest Years to Our Days*] (Vienna, 1832), XII, 544.

6. Cited by A. F. Miller, *Mustafa Pasha Bairaktar: Ottomanskaya Imperiia v Nachale XIX Veka* [*Mustafa Pasha Bairaktar: The Ottoman Empire in the Beginning of the Nineteenth Century*] (Moscow, 1947), p. 102.

7. Cited by G. K. Kordatos, *Regas Pheraios kai he Balkanike homospondia* [*Rhigas Pheraios and Balkan Federation*] (Athens, 1945), p. 28.

8. S. S. Wilson, *A Narrative of the Greek Mission* (London, 1839), p. 206.

9. Cited by D. Mishew, *The Bulgarians in the Past* (Lausanne, 1919), p. 123.

10. Cited by G. P. Noyes, ed., *The Life and Adventures of Dimitrije Obradović* (Berkeley, Calif., 1953), p. 243.

11. *Ibid.,* p. 23.

12. *Ibid.,* p. 135.

13. Cited by A. Dascalakis, *Rhigas Velestinlis: La révolution française et les préludes de l'indépendance hellénique* (Paris, 1937), p. 85.

14. Cited by S. G. Chaconas, *Adamantios Koraïs: A Study in Greek Nationalism* (New York, 1942), p. 28.

15. Cited by L. Hadrovics, *Le peuple serbe et son église sous la domination turque* (Paris, 1947), p. 124.

16. Translated from Greek text in T. H. Papadopoullos, *Studies and Documents Relating to the History of the Greek Church and People under Turkish Domination* (Brussels, 1952), pp. 143–145.

17. Cited by Chaconas, *op. cit.,* p. 88.

10. Defeat by Austria

1. *The Turkish Letters of Ogier Ghiselin de Busbecq. Imperial Ambassador at Constantinople 1554–1562.* Newly translated from the Latin . . . by Edward Seymour Forster (Oxford, 1927), pp. 65–66.

2. Evliya Effendi, *Narrative of Travels in Europe, Asia, and Africa in the Seventeenth Century.* Translated from the Turkish by the Ritter Joseph von Hammer (London, 1850), Vol. I, Pt. II, p. 11.

3. *The Negotiations of Sir Thomas Roe in His Embassy to the Ottoman Porte from the Year 1621 to 1628 Inclusive* . . . (London, 1740), pp. 54, 114.

4. Evliya, *op. cit.,* Vol. I, Pt. I, pp. 138–139.

5. *Ibid.,* p. 141.

6. *Ibid.,* p. 131.

7. *Ibid.,* Pt. II, p. 12.

8. *The Turkish History . . . by Richard Knolles, with a Continuation to the Present Year MDCLXXXVII . . . by Sir Paul Rycaut* . . . (London, 1687), II, 89.

11. Defeat by Russia

1. A. N. Kurat, *The Despatches of Sir Robert Sutton, Ambassador in Constantinople (1710–1714)* [Royal Historical Society, Camden Third Series, Vol. LXXVIII] (London, 1953), pp. 25, 28.

2. Cited by B. H. Sumner, *Peter the Great and the Ottoman Empire* (Oxford, 1949), p. 46.
3. Kurat, *op. cit.*, pp. 48, 60.
4. Cited by A. Sorel, *The Eastern Question in the Eighteenth Century: The Partition of Poland and the Treaty of Kainardji* (London, 1898), p. 10.
5. *Ibid.*, p. 54.
6. *Ibid.*, p. 29.
7. M. S. Anderson, "Great Britain and the Russian Fleet, 1769–70," *Slavonic and East European Review,* XXXI (December, 1952), 149–150.
8. Cited by P. M. Kontogiannes, *Hoi Hellenes kata ton proton epi Aikaterines II rossotourkikon polemon (1768–1774)* [*The Greeks During the First Russo-Turkish War under Catherine II (1768–1774]* (Athens, 1903), p. 188.
9. Cited by Sorel, *op. cit.*, p. 25.
10. Text in T. E. Holland, *The Treaty Relations of Russia and Turkey from 1774 to 1853* (London, 1877), pp. 36–56.
11. Reports of Baron Thugutt, August 17 and September 13, 1774, cited by Sorel, *op. cit.*, pp. 250–251.
12. Terms in the introduction to A. von Arneth, *Joseph II und Katharina von Russland: Ihr Briefwechsel* (Vienna, 1869).
13. Cited by G. B. Hertz, *British Imperialism in the Eighteenth Century* (London, 1908), p. 156.
14. Cited *ibid.*, p. 158.

12. The Balkans, the French Revolution and Napoleon

1. Cited by B. Lewis, "The Impact of the French Revolution on Turkey," *Journal of World History,* I (July, 1953), 119.
2. Spiridon Foresti to Lord Grenville, July 5, 1797. Foreign Office 348/2.
3. G. Pautier, *Les Iles Joniennes pendant l'occupation française et le protectorat anglais* (Paris, 1863), p. 12.
4. Foresti to Lord Nelson, October 3, 1799. Foreign Office 348/2.
5. Cited by V. J. Puryear, *Napoleon and the Dardanelles* (Berkeley, Calif., 1951), p. 113.
6. Cited by E. Dard, "Les souvenirs napoléoniens en Yougoslavie," *Revue d'histoire diplomatique,* XLVII (January–March, 1933), 3.
7. Cited by Puryear, *op. cit.*, p. 195.
8. Cited *ibid.*, p. 191.
9. Cited *ibid.*, p. 236.
10. Cited *ibid.*, pp. 267–268.
11. Cited *ibid.*, pp. 287–288.
12. R. Adair, *The Negotiations for the Peace of the Dardanelles* (London, 1845), I, 206.
13. Cited by B. Mouravieff, *L'alliance russo-turque au milieu des guerres napoléoniennes* (Paris, 1954), p. 316.
14. Cited by J. Savant, "Napoléon et la libération de la Grèce," *L'Héllenisme contemporaine,* (July–October, 1950), p. 321.
15. Ch. Photios, *Apomnemoneumata peri tes Hellenikes Epanastaseos* [*Memoirs on the Greek Revolution*] (Athens, 1899), I, 1.

16. T. Kolokotrones and E. M. Edmonds, *Kolokotrones: Klepht and Warrior* (London, 1892), pp. 127–128.

17. Cited by F. Zwitter, "Illyrisme et sentimente yougoslave," *Le monde slave,* X (April, 1933), 364.

18. A. Boppe, *Documents inédits sur les relations de la Serbie avec Napoléon I, 1809–1814* (Belgrade, 1888), pp. 6–7.

19. H. Desprez, "La grande Illyrie et le mouvement Illyrien," *Revue des deux mondes,* XVII (March 15, 1847), 1017.

20. S. Lane-Poole, *Sir Richard Church* (London, 1890), p. 27.

13. Dynamics of Balkan Politics

1. A. Neale, *Travels through Some Parts of Germany, Poland, Moldavia and Turkey* (London, 1818), p. 266.

2. W. Hamilton to Lord Hawkesbury, May 6, 1803, cited by J. W. Baggally, *Ali Pasha and Great Britain* (London, 1936), pp. 87–88.

3. Article in *Eleftheron Vema* of Athens, September 2, 1931, cited by N. Moschopoulos, *La presse dans la renaissance balkanique* (Athens, 1931), pp. 130–131.

4. A. Boppe, *Documents inédits sur les relations de la Serbie avec Napoleon I, 1809–1814* (Belgrade, 1888), p. 63.

5. A. Gorovei, "Les peuples balkaniques dans le folklore roumaine," *Revue internationale des études balkaniques,* V–VI (1937–1938), 470.

6. M. A. Ubicini, *Letters on Turkey . . . Translated by Lady Stanhope* (London, 1856), II, 173.

7. W. Gell, *Narrative of a Journey in the Morea* (London, 1823), p. 65.

8. J. C. R. Broughton, *A Journey through Albania and other Provinces of Turkey . . .* (London, 1813), p. 597.

9. E. Hurmuzaki, ed., *Documente Privitóre la Istoria Românilor* (Bucharest, 1887–1922, 19 vols.), V, 484.

10. A. C. Wood, *A History of the Levant Company* (London, 1935), pp. 191–201; F. E. Bailey, "The Economics of British Foreign Policy 1825–50," *Journal of Modern History,* XII (December, 1940), 449–484.

11. P. Martens, *Recueil des traités et conventions conclue par la Russie avec les puissances étrangères: Tome III, Traités avec l'Autriche, 1808–1815* (St. Petersburg, 1876), p. 178.

14. The Serbian Revolution and the South Slavs

1. P. E. Mosely, "The Peasant Family: The Zadruga or Communal Joint-Family in the Balkans, and Its Recent Evolution," in C. F. Ware, ed., *The Cultural Approach to History* (New York, 1940), p. 95.

2. G. R. Noyes, tr. and ed., *The Life and Adventures of Dimitrije Obradović . . .* (Berkeley, Calif.: University of California Press; 1953), p. 107.

3. *Ibid.,* pp. 99, 100, 134.

4. *Ibid.,* p. 135.

5. Cited by T. R. Djordjević, *Srbija pre sto godina* [*Serbia One Hundred Years Ago*] (Belgrade, 1946), p. 167.

6. Cited by G. Yakschitch, *L'Europe et la résurrection de la Serbie, 1804–1834* (Paris, 1907), p. 27.

7. A. Boppe, *Documents inédits sur les relations de la Serbie avec Napoléon I, 1809–1814* (Belgrade, 1888), p. 6.

8. Cited by M. Gavrilović, "The Early Diplomatic Relations of Great Britain and Serbia," *Slavonic Review,* I (June, 1922), 88.

9. Cited by T. W. Riker, "Michael of Serbia and the Turkish Occupation," *Slavonic Review,* XII (July, 1933), 138, 139.

10. Cited by Gavrilović, *loc. cit.,* p. 100.

11. B.-S. Cunibert, *Essai historique sur les révolutions et l'indépendance de la Serbie depuis 1804 jusqu' à 1850* (Leipzig, 1855), II, 5.

12. Cited by E. Haumant, *La formation de la Yougoslavie, XVe—XXe siècles* (Paris, 1930), pp. 270–271.

13. Cited by Gavrilović, *loc. cit.,* p. 102.

14. Cited by S. Jovanović, *Druga vlada Miloša i Mihaila, 1858–1868* [*The Second Reign of Milosh and Michael, 1858–1868* (Belgrade, 1923), p. 216.

15. Cited by D. Stranjaković, "La collaboration des Croates et des Serbes en 1848–1849," *Le monde slave,* XII (June, 1935), 396.

16. Cited by O. Jaszi, *The Dissolution of the Hapsburg Monarchy* (Chicago, 1929), p. 310.

17. Cited by G. Y. Devas, "Les origines de l'unité yougoslave," *Le monde slave,* I (April, 1918), 540.

18. Cited by R. W. Seton-Watson, *The Southern Slav Question and the Hapsburg Monarchy* (London, 1911), pp. 34, 35.

19. Cited by C. E. Maurice, *The Revolutionary Movement of 1848–1849* (London, 1887), p. 38.

15. Greek Revolution and Independent Statehood

1. Nikola Luccari; cited by N. Iorga, "Raguse et les Turcs," *Académie Roumaine, Bulletin de la Section Historique,* XVIII (1931), 96.

2. A. C. Ypsilantis, cited by T. H. Papadopoullos, *Studies and Documents Relating to the History of the Greek Church and People under Turkish Domination* (Brussels, 1952), p. 55.

3. A. J. Toynbee, *A Study of History* (London, 1935), II, 225.

4. O. Shparo, "Rol Rossii v Borbe Gretsii za Nezavisimost" ["The Role of Russia in the Greek War of Independence,"] *Voprosy Istorii,* No. 8 (August, 1949), p. 54.

5. I. Juilliany, *Essai sur le commerce de Marseille* (Paris, 1842), I, 118.

6. W. M. Leake, *An Historical Outline of the Greek Revolution* (London, 1836), pp. 23–24.

7. M. B. Sakellariou, *He Peloponnesos kata ten deuteran Tourkokratian 1715–1821* [*Peloponnesus During the Second Turkish Rule 1715–1821*] (Athens, 1939), pp. 214–216.

8. H. Holland, *Travels in the Ionian Isles, Albania, Thessaly, Macedonia etc. during the Years 1812 and 1813* (London, 1815), pp. 148–149.

9. *Ibid.,* p. 151.

10. Cited by A. Dascalakis, *Rhigas Velestinlis: La révolution française et les préludes de l'indépendance hellénique* (Paris, 1937), p. 18.

11. Translation by Rae Dalven, in *Modern Greek Poetry* (New York, 1949), p. 65.
12. Cited by Rizo-Neroulo, *Cours de littérature grecque moderne* (Geneva, 1828), p. 48.
13. Holland, *op. cit.*, p. 530.
14. Cited by D. Mitrany, *The Land and the Peasant in Roumania* (New Haven, Conn., 1930), p. 24.
15. *Lettres inédites de Coray à Chardon de la Rochette, 1790–1796* (Paris, 1877), p. 122.
16. London *Post,* December 20, 1825, cited by J. H. Gleason, *The Genesis of Russophobia in Great Britain* (Cambridge, Mass., 1950), p. 72.
17. Cited by R. J. Kerner, "Russia's New Policy in the Near East after the Peace of Adrianople . . .," *Cambridge Historical Journal,* V (1937), 283–284.
18. L. Bower and G. Bolitho, *Otho I: King of Greece* (London, 1939), p. 106.
19. Cited by C. Webster, *The Foreign Policy of Palmerston 1830–1841* (London, 1951), I, 509.
20. Cited by E. Prevelakis, *British Policy towards the Change of Dynasty in Greece* (Athens, 1953), pp. 133, 134.
21. "The Euthanasia of the Ottoman Empire," *Blackwood's Edinburgh Magazine,* DXLVII (May, 1861), 581.
22. M. A. Ubicini, *Letters on Turkey* . . . (London, 1856), II, 18.
23. "The Euthanasia of the Ottoman Empire," *loc. cit.*, p. 583.
24. *Ibid.*, p. 586.
25. A. D. Sideres, *He georgike politike tes Hellados 1833–1933* [*The Agrarian Policy of Greece 1833–1933*] (Athens, 1934), pp. 58–59.
26. E. D. Clarke, *Travels in Various Countries of Europe, Asia and Africa* (London, 1816), VII, 366.

16. Ottoman Reform and Near Eastern Crises

1. Cited by J. E. Swain, *The Struggle for Control of the Mediterranean prior to 1848* (Philadelphia, 1933), p. 62; V. J. Puryear, *France and the Levant from the Bourbon Restoration to the Peace of Kutiah* (Berkeley, Calif., 1941), p. 129.
2. Cited by C. Webster, *The Foreign Policy of Palmerston 1830–1841* (London, 1951), I, 282.
3. *Ibid.*, I, 284.
4. Cited by F. S. Rodkey, *The Turco-Egyptian Question in the Relations of England, France, and Russia, 1832–1841* (Urbana, Ill., 1924), p. 18.
5. Cited by P. E. Mosely, *Russian Diplomacy and the Opening of the Eastern Question in 1838 and 1839* (Cambridge, Mass., 1934), p. 10.
6. Cited *ibid.*, p. 11.
7. Cited *ibid.*, p. 14.
8. Cited by Webster, *op. cit.*, I, 305.
9. Cited by H. Temperley, *England and the Near East: The Crimea* (London, 1936), p. 81.
10. J. H. Gleason, *The Genesis of Russophobia in Great Britain: A Study of the Interaction of Policy and Opinion* (Cambridge, Mass., 1950), p. 204.
11. Cited by Temperley, *op. cit.*, p. 89.

12. Cited *ibid.*, p. 96.
13. H. L. Bulwer, *The Life of . . . Viscount Palmerston . . .* (London, 1870), II, 145.
14. Cited by Webster, *op. cit.*, II, 628.
15. Cited by Temperley, *op. cit.*, p. 105.
16. Cited by Rodkey, *op. cit.*, p. 129.
17. Cited *ibid.*, p. 130.
18. Cited *ibid.*, p. 141.
19. Cited by Bulwer, *op. cit.*, II, 359–360.
20. Cited *ibid.*, pp. 327–328.
21. Cited by F. E. Bailey, *British Policy and the Turkish Reform Movement* (Cambridge, Mass., 1942), p. 182.
22. Full text of memorandum *ibid.*, pp. 271–276.
23. Full text of decree *ibid.*, pp. 277–279.

17. Crimean War

1. Cited by V. J. Puryear, *England, Russia, and the Straits Question 1844–1856* (Berkeley, Calif., 1931), p. 91.
2. Cited by V. J. Puryear, *International Economics and Diplomacy in the Near East* (Stanford, Calif., 1935), p. 213.
3. Cited by H. Temperley, *England and the Near East: The Crimea* (London, 1936), p. 251.
4. *Ibid.*, p. 257.
5. Cited *ibid.*, p. 267.
6. Cited by G. B. Henderson, *Crimean War Diplomacy* (Glasgow, 1947), pp. 6, 7.
7. Cited by Temperley, *op. cit.*, p. 314.
8. *Ibid.*, p. 321.
9. *Ibid.*, p. 342.
10. *Ibid.*, p. 345.
11. *Ibid.*, p. 355.
12. S. Lane-Poole, *The Life of Stratford Canning* (London, 1888), II, 299–300.
13. Cited by B. Kingsley Martin, *The Triumph of Lord Palmerston: A Study of Public Opinion in England before the Crimean War* (London, 1924), p. 215.
14. Cited by Temperley, *op. cit.*, p. 374.
15. *Ibid.*, p. 378.
16. Cited by Martin, *op. cit.*, p. 226.
17. Cited by Puryear, *England, Russia, and the Straits Question*, p. 448.
18. Cited by H. Temperley, "The Treaty of Paris of 1856 and Its Execution," *Journal of Modern History*, IV (September, 1932), 401–402.
19. G. H. Bolsover, "Nicholas I and the Partition of Turkey," *Slavonic and East European Review*, XXVII (December, 1948), 145.

18. Making of Rumania

1. L. Thouvenel, *Trois années de la question d'Orient, 1856–1859 . . .* (Paris, 1897), p. 570.
2. W. Wilkinson, *An Account of the Principalities of Wallachia and Moldavia . . .* (London, 1820), p. 155.

3. Cited by D. Mitrany, *The Land and the Peasant in Rumania* (Oxford, 1930), p. 24.

4. Cited by S. I. Samoilov, "Narodno-osvoboditelnoe vosstanie 1821 g. v. Valakhii," ["The National Liberation Uprising of 1821 in Wallachia,"] *Voprosy Istorii,* no. 10, (October, 1955), p. 101.

5. Cited by J. C. Campbell, "French Influence and the Rise of Roumanian Nationalism" (Harvard University unpublished doctoral dissertation, 1940), p. 16.

6. M. A. . . . de Bucharest, "La Valachie et la Moldavie," *Revue des deux mondes,* IX (January 15, 1837), 162.

7. Cited by Campbell, *op. cit.,* p. 210.

8. Cited by R. W. Seton-Watson, *A History of the Roumanians from Roman Times to the Completion of Unity* (Cambridge, Eng., 1934), p. 226.

9. Cited *ibid.,* p. 225.

10. Cited by M. Roller, "The Rumanians in 1848," in *The Opening of an Era 1848: An Historical Symposium,* ed. by F. Fejtö (London, 1948), p. 306.

11. Cited by Campbell, *op. cit.,* p. 360.

12. Cited by W. G. East, *The Union of Moldavia and Wallachia, 1859.* (Cambridge, Eng., 1929), p. 64.

13. Cited *ibid.,* pp. 104, 111.

14. Cited by T. W. Riker, *The Making of Roumania* (Oxford, 1931), p. 130.

15. Cited by Mitrany, *op. cit.,* pp. 50, 55.

16. *Ibid.,* p. 46.

17. *Ibid.,* p. 47.

18. Cited by Riker, *op. cit.,* p. 437.

19. Cited by Mitrany, *op. cit.,* p. 78.

20. *Ibid.,* p. 80.

21. J. de Witte, *Quinze ans d'histoire 1866–1881* . . . (Paris, 1905), p. 7.

22. *Aus dem Leben König Karls von Rumänien* (Stuttgart, 1894), I, 43.

23. *Ibid.,* II, 159.

24. Cited by Seton-Watson, *op. cit.,* pp. 177, 179.

25. *Ibid.,* p. 280.

26. *Ibid.,* p. 276.

27. E. Poujade, *Chrétiens et Turcs* (Paris, 1867), p. 305.

28. Seton-Watson, *op. cit.,* p. 560.

29. Cited *ibid.,* p. 561.

19. Bulgarian Awakening

1. E. D. Clarke, *Travels in Various Countries of Europe, Asia and Africa* (London, 1816), IV, 540, 543.

2. C. Robert, "Du mouvement unitaire de l'Europe orientale," *Revue des deux mondes,* VIII (November 1, 1844), 436.

3. C. Robert, *Les Slaves de Turquie* (Paris, 1844), p. 287.

4. Cited by L. Leger, *La Bulgarie* (Paris, 1885), pp. 55–56.

5. G. Trubetzkoi, "La politique russe en Orient: le schisme bulgare," *Revue d'histoire diplomatique,* XXI (1907), 186–187.

6. Cited by J. F. Clarke, "Protestantism and the Bulgarian Church Question in

1861," in *Essays in the History of Modern Europe,* ed. by D. C. McKay (New York, 1936), p. 97.

7. Cited by Trubetzkoi, *loc. cit.,* p. 177.
8. "Zapiski Grafa N. P. . . . Ignatieva (1864–1874)," *Izvestiia Ministerstva Inostrannykh Del* (1914), Bk. VI, p. 158.
9. Cited by B. H. Sumner, "Ignatiev at Constantinople, 1864–1874," *Slavonic Review,* XI (April, 1933), 571.
10. Cited by Trubetzkoi, *loc. cit.,* pp. 190, 191.
11. J. A. Blanqui, *Voyage en Bulgarie pendant l'année 1844* (Paris, 1845), p. 181.
12. Marco Antonio [Canini], *Vingt ans d'exil* (Paris, 1868), p. 263.
13. Full text in L. S. Stavrianos, *Balkan Federation: A History of the Movement toward Balkan Unity in Modern Times* (Northampton, Mass., 1944), pp. 275–276. See also pp. 89–94 for the other two schemes propounded at this time.
14. Cited by S. A. Nikitin, "Revoliutsionnaia borba v Bolgarii v 1875–1876 godakh i Aprelskoe Vosstanie," ["The Revolutionary Struggle in Bulgaria in 1875–1876 and the April Uprising,"] in *Osvobozhdenie Bolgarii ot Turetskogo Iga [The Liberation of Bulgaria from Turkish Rule]* (Moscow, 1953), p. 19.
15. Cited by A. Hajek, *Bulgarian unter den Türkenherrschaft* (Stuttgart, 1925), p. 262.

20. Reform and Revolution in the Ottoman Empire

1. Cited in unpublished doctoral dissertation by H. H. Davison, "Reform in the Ottoman Empire 1856–1876" (Harvard University, 1942), p. iv.
2. *Ibid.,* p. 56.
3. *Ibid.,* p. 59.
4. *Great Britain. Accounts and Papers. State Papers,* LXVII (1861), 3.
5. *Ibid.,* p. 12.
6. *Ibid.,* p. 43.
7. *Ibid.,* LXXV (1867), 34. This report was made in reply to inquiries made by Lord Lyons several years after Bulwer.
8. Davison, *op. cit.,* pp. 158–161.
9. *Ibid.,* pp. 213–214.
10. Cited by H. Temperley, "British Policy towards Parliamentary Rule and Constitutionalism in Turkey (1830–1914)," *Cambridge Historical Journal,* IV (1933), 175.
11. E. Pears, *Forty Years in Constantinople* (New York, 1916), p. 58.

21. Balkan Crisis and the Treaty of Berlin

1. Cited by W. L. Langer, *European Alliances and Alignments 1871–1890* (New York, 1931), p. 15.
2. Cited by G. Trubetzkoi, "La politique russe en Orient, le schisme bulgare," *Revue d'histoire diplomatique,* XXI (1907), 191.
3. From 1874 memorandum of N. P. Ignatiev in *Izvestiia Ministerstva Inostrannykh Del* (St. Petersburg, 1914), Bk. IV, p. 92.
4. Cited by R. W. Seton-Watson, "Les relations de l'Autriche-Hongrie et de la

Serbie entre 1868 et 1874; la mission de Benjamin Kállay à Belgrade," *Le monde slave,* III (August, 1926), 283.

5. N. Iorga, *Correspondance diplomatique roumaine sous le roi Charles I, 1866–1880* (Paris, 1923), p. 324.

6. Cited by A. Onou, "The Memoirs of Count N. Ignatyev," *Slavonic Review,* X (December, 1931), 390, 391.

7. A. Leroy-Beaulieu, "Les réformes de la Turquie, la politique russe et le panslavisme," *Revue des deux mondes,* XVIII (December 1, 1876), 530.

8. Cited by B. H. Sumner, *Russia and the Balkans 1870–1880* (Oxford, 1937), p. 582.

9. Hansard, *Parliamentary Debates,* 3rd Series, CCIV, 81–82.

10. Cited by D. Harris, *A Diplomatic History of the Balkan Crisis of 1875–1878: The First Year* (Stanford, Calif., 1936), pp. 107–108.

11. Cited *ibid.,* p. 120.

12. *Ibid.,* p. 379.

13. Iorga, *op. cit.,* pp. 128–129.

14. Cited by D. Harris, *Britain and the Bulgarian Horrors of 1876* (Chicago, 1939), p. 235.

15. W. F. Monypenny and G. E. Buckle, *The Life of Benjamin Disraeli* (New York, 1920), VI, 70.

16. H. G. Elliot, *Some Revolutions and Other Diplomatic Experiences* (London, 1922), pp. 285–286.

17. Cited by M. D. Stojanović, *Great Powers and the Balkans 1875–1878* (Cambridge, Eng., 1938), p. 134.

18. Monypenny and Buckle, *op. cit.,* VI, 111.

19. Gwendolen Cecil, *Life of Robert Marquis of Salisbury* (London, 1921), II, 139.

20. Monypenny and Buckle, *op. cit.,* VI, 217–218.

21. Cited by R. W. Seton-Watson, *Disraeli, Gladstone and the Eastern Question* (London, 1935), p. 450.

22. *Ibid.,* p. 445.

23. Cited by Langer, *op. cit.,* p. 160.

24. Cited by Seton-Watson, *Disraeli, Gladstone and the Eastern Question,* p. 490.

25. H. D. Wolff, *Rambling Recollections* (London, 1908), II, 265.

22. Dynamics of Balkan Politics

1. W. L. Langer, *Diplomacy of Imperialism 1890–1902* (New York, 1951, 2nd ed.), p. 67.

2. D. C. Blaisdell, *European Financial Control in the Ottoman Empire* (New York, 1929), p. 217.

3. Cited by H. Feis, *Europe the World's Banker 1870–1914* (New Haven, Conn., 1930), p. 276.

4. J. Tomasevich, *Peasants, Politics, and Economic Change in Yugoslavia* (Stanford, Calif., 1955), p. 176.

5. From Maksimov's novel *Tseliná [Virgin Soil],* cited by V. Pinto, "The Civic and Aesthetic Ideals of Bulgarian Narodnik Writers," *Slavonic and East European Review,* XXXII (June, 1954), 357.

23. Making of Bulgaria

1. Cited by C. E. Black, *The Establishment of Constitutional Government in Bulgaria* (Princeton, N. J., 1943), p. 75.
2. *Ibid.*, p. 78.
3. *Ibid.*, p. 116.
4. *Ibid.*, p. 119.
5. *Ibid.*, p. 181.
6. A. Koch, *Prince Alexander of Battenberg* (London, 1887), pp. 70–72.
7. Cited by Black, *op. cit.*, pp. 199–200.
8. *Ibid.*, p. 210.
9. *Ibid.*, pp. 238, 245.
10. E. C. Corti, *Alexander von Battenberg: Sein Kampf mit den Zaren und Bismarck* (Vienna, 1920), pp. 165–168.
11. Cited by G. C. Logio, *Bulgaria: Past and Present* (Manchester, Eng., 1936), p. 331.
12. A. H. Beaman, *M. Stambuloff* (London, 1895), p. 59.
13. *Ibid.*, p. 75.
14. *Ibid.*, pp. 99, 101.
15. Cited by V. Chirol, *Fifty Years in a Changing World* (London, 1927), p. 129.
16. T. G. Djuvara, "Souvenirs diplomatiques," *Revue des sciences diplomatiques,* LIII (January–March, 1930), 33.
17. H. R. Madol, *Ferdinand de Bulgarie: la rêve de Byzance* (Paris, 1933), pp. 102–103.
18. Paléologue to Pichon, May 12, 1907, in *Documents diplomatiques français,* 2nd series, X, 801–802.
19. Lady Grogan, *The Life of J. D. Bourchier* (London, 1926), pp. 41, 43.
20. R. W. Seton-Watson, *Europe in the Melting-Pot* (London, 1919), pp. 358, 360.
21. Cited by Logio, *op. cit.*, p. 356.
22. G. Buchanan to Foreign Office, January 1, 1907, in *British Documents on the Origins of the War 1898–1914,* V, 100, 102.
23. I. Sakazov, *Bulgarische Wirtschaftsgeschichte* (Berlin, 1929), p. 271.
24. W. K. Weiss-Bartenstein, "Uber Bulgariens volkswirtschaftsliche Entwicklung," *Zeitschrift für Volkswirtschaft, Sozialpolitik und Verwaltung,* XXII (1913), 414; N. Sakarov, *Die industrielle Entwicklung Bulgariens* (Berlin, 1904), p. 29.
25. L. Pasvolsky, *Bulgaria's Economic Position* (Washington, D.C., 1929), pp. 35–42; Logio, *op. cit.*, pp. 62–66; H. Feis, *Europe the World's Banker, 1870–1914* (New York, 1940), pp. 280 ff.
26. Cited by Logio, *op. cit.*, p. 370.

24. Serbia and the South Slavs

1. Cited by W. L. Langer, *European Alliances and Alignments 1871–1890* (New York, 1931), p. 329.
2. A. F. Pribram, *The Secret Treaties of Austria-Hungary, 1879–1914* (Cambridge, Mass., 1920), I, 61.
3. *Ibid.*, pp. 59–61.

4. C. Mijatovich, *A Royal Tragedy* (London, 1906), p. 121.

5. *Ibid.*, p. 123.

6. *Ibid.*, p. 149.

7. *Ibid.*, pp. 138, 141, 142.

8. C. Dumba, *Memoirs of a Diplomat* (Boston, 1932), p. 97.

9. Sir F. Plunkett to the Marquess of Lansdowne, June 18, 1903, in *British Documents on the Origins of the War 1898–1914*, V, 132.

10. Sir C. Scott to the Marquess of Lansdowne, June 18, 1903, *ibid.*

11. Cited by W. S. Vucinich, *Serbia between East and West: The Events of 1903–1908* (Stanford, Calif., 1954), p. 182.

12. *Ibid.*, p. 197.

13. By Josip Marich, in O. M. Utieshenovich, *Die Hauskommunionen der Südslaven* (Vienna, 1859), p. 128. Adapted from a translation kindly made available by Dr. Jozo Tomasevich.

14. Cited by A. J. May, *The Hapsburg Monarchy 1867–1914* (Cambridge, Mass., 1951), p. 442.

15. Cited by L. Albertini, *The Origins of the War of 1914,* tr. and ed. by I. M. Massey (London, 1953), II, 20.

16. *Ibid.*, p. 23.

17. *Ibid.*, p. 21.

18. Cited by B. E. Schmitt, *The Coming of the War* (New York, 1930), I, 150.

25. Greece

1. Cited by B. H. Sumner, "Ignatiev at Constantinople, 1864–1874," *Slavonic Review,* XI (April, 1933), p. 571.

2. W. L. Langer, *The Diplomacy of Imperialism 1890–1902* (New York, 1935), I, 378.

3. Sir G. Lowther to Sir Edward Grey, October 13, 1908, in *British Documents on the Origins of the War 1898–1914* (London, 1928), V, 439.

4. S. B. Chester, *Life of Venizelos* (London, 1921), p. 5.

5. Cited by T. Saloutos, *They Remember America: The Story of the Repatriated Greek-Americans* (Berkeley, Calif., 1956), p. 118.

6. N. Forbes, A. J. Toynbee, D. Mitrany, and D. G. Hogarth, *The Balkans: A History of Bulgaria, Serbia, Greece, Rumania, Turkey* (London, 1915), p. 249.

7. Saloutos, *op. cit.*, pp. 130–131.

26. Rumania

1. T. E. Holland, *The European Concert in the Eastern Question* (Oxford, 1885), p. 301.

2. R. W. Seton-Watson, *A History of the Roumanians . . .* (Cambridge, Eng., 1934), p. 385.

3. Bismarck to William II, September 20, 1888, in *Die Grosse Politik,* VI, no. 1351, 344.

4. Bülow to Caprivi, March 6, 1891, *ibid.*, VII, no. 1465, 154.

5. Cited by Seton-Watson, *op. cit.*, pp. 385, 386.

6. D. Mitrany, *The Land and the Peasant in Rumania* (London, 1930), p. 90.

7. Cited by Seton-Watson, *op. cit.,* pp. 394, 395, 401.
8. *Ibid.,* p. 414.
9. *Ibid.,* p. 428.
10. Henry to Delcassé, June 25, 1901, in *Documents diplomatiques français (1871–1914),* 2nd series, I, no. 301, 352.

27. Albanian Awakening

1. *The Albanian Struggle in the Old World and New.* Compiled and Written by Members of the Federal Writers' Project of the Works Progress Administration of Massachusetts (Boston, 1939), pp. 26–27.
2. *The Memoirs of Ismail Kemal Bey,* ed. by Somerville Story (London, 1920), pp. 13–14.
3. Cited by J. Swire, *Albania: The Rise of a Kingdom* (London, 1929), p. 42.
4. Goschen to Earl Granville, July 26, 1880, in *British Sessional Papers, House of Commons,* LXXXI (1880), 185.
5. Cited by S. Skendi, "Albanian Political Thought and Revolutionary Activity, 1881–1912," *Südost–Forschungen,* XIII (1954), 9.
6. *Ibid.,* p. 16.
7. *Memoirs of Ismail Kemal Bey,* p. 373.
8. Cited by Swire, *op. cit.,* p. 145.
9. Prince Lichnowsky, *Heading for the Abyss* (London, 1928), p. 249.
10. Cited by Swire, *op. cit.,* p. 231.
11. Bishop Fan Noli, cited *ibid.,* p. 195.

28. Diplomatic Developments

1. A. F. Pribram, *The Secret Treaties of Austria-Hungary, 1879–1914* (Cambridge, Mass., 1920), I, 50–55.
2. E. Driault and M. Lhéritier, *Histoire diplomatique de la Grèce de 1821 à nos jours* (Paris, 1926), IV, 200.
3. R. Graves, *Storm Centres of the Near East* (London, 1933), p. 100.
4. Driault and Lhéritier, *op. cit.,* IV, 291.
5. Pribram, *op. cit.,* I, 184–195.
6. G. Buchanan to Foreign Office, January 1, 1907, in *British Documents on the Origins of the War 1898–1914,* V, 101.
7. J. B. Whitehead to Foreign Office, April 2, 1908, *ibid.,* p. 118.
8. E. F. Knight, *Turkey: The Awakening of Turkey. The Turkish Revolution of 1908* (Boston, 1910), pp. 109–113.
9. Cited by H. Temperley, "British Policy towards Parliamentary Rule and Constitutionalism in Turkey (1830–1914)," *Cambridge Historical Journal,* IV (1932), 186.
10. Cited by W. D. David, *European Diplomacy in the Near Eastern Question 1906–1909* (Urbana, Ill., 1940), p. 92.
11. Aehrenthal memoir, August 9, 1908, in *Österreich-Ungarns Aussenpolitik von der bosnischen Krise 1908 bis zum Kriegsausbruch 1914,* I, 32.
12. J. B. Whitehead to Sir Edward Grey, September 30, 1908, in *British Documents,* V, 370.

13. Cited by B. E. Schmitt, *The Annexation of Bosnia 1908–1909* (Cambridge, Eng., 1937), p. 36, ft. 1.
14. Cited *ibid.*, p. 96.
15. *Ibid.*, p. 194.
16. *Ibid.*, p. 216.
17. Forgach report, April 3, 1909, in *Österreich-Ungarns Aussenpolitik,* II, 239.
18. Berchtold memoir, October 2, 1912, *ibid.*, IV, 528.
19. Lady Grogan, *The Life of J. D. Bourchier* (London, 1926), p. 134.
20. Sir Edward Grey to Sir A. Nicolson, December 28, 1908, in *British Documents,* V, 543.
21. Cited by S. B. Fay, *The Origins of the World War* (New York, 1934, 2nd rev. ed.), I, 433.
22. "Zapiski Grafa N. P. Ignatieva (1864–1874)," *Izvestiia Ministerstva Inostrannykh Del* (1914), Bk. III, p. 108.
23. Cited by E. C. Helmreich, *The Diplomacy of the Balkan Wars, 1912–1913* (Cambridge, Mass., 1938), p. 361.
24. Viscount Grey of Fallodon, *Twenty-Five Years, 1892–1916* (New York, 1925), I, 254.
25. H. H. Lamb to Sir Edward Grey, February 28, 1914, in *British Documents,* X, Pt. I, 104.
26. Cited by Fay, *op. cit.*, I, 488.

29. Sarajevo and War

1. Cited by R. W. Seton-Watson, *Sarajevo* (London, 1926), p. 80.
2. Cited by L. Albertini, *The Origins of the War of 1914,* tr. and ed. by I. M. Massey (London, 1953), II, 12.
3. Cited by Seton-Watson, *op. cit.*, p. 84.
4. Cited by Albertini, *op. cit.*, II, 49.
5. *Ibid.*, p. 68.
6. *Ibid.*, I, 297.
7. *Ibid.*, p. 298.
8. Cited by S. B. Fay, *The Origins of the World War* (New York, 1934, 2nd rev. ed.), II, 87.
9. Cited by Albertini, *op. cit.*, II, 34.
10. *Ibid.*, p. 87. This statement agrees with the account allegedly written by Dimitrijevich himself shortly before his execution following his trial in Saloniki in 1917 on charges of conspiring against the dynasty. See S. Gavrilović, "New Evidence on the Sarajevo Assassination," *Journal of Modern History,* XXVII (December, 1955), 410–414.
11. Cited by B. E. Schmitt, *The Coming of the War 1914* (New York, 1930), I, 276–279.
12. *Ibid.*, p. 305.
13. Cited by Fay, *op. cit.*, II, 471.
14. J. C. Adams, *Flight in Winter* (Princeton, N. J., 1942), p. 29.
15. Cited by Schmitt, *op. cit.*, II, 433.
16. H. Morgenthau, *Ambassador Morgenthau's Story* (New York, 1918), p. 225.
17. *Ibid.*, pp. 227–228.
18. A. Savinsky, *Recollections of a Russian Diplomat* (London, 1927), p. 250.

19. Cited by J. A. R. Marriott, *The Eastern Question: An Historical Study in European Diplomacy* (Oxford, 1940, 4th ed.), p. 505.
20. Cited by Schmitt, *op. cit.,* II, 454.
21. A. F. Frangulis, *La Grèce et la crise mondiale* (Paris, 1926), I, 195–196.
22. Cited by H. W. V. Temperley, *A History of the Peace Conference of Paris* (London, 1921), IV, 28.

30. Peace Settlement

1. Winston Churchill, *The Second World War: The Gathering Storm* (Boston: Houghton Mifflin Company, 1948), p. 10.
2. O. Czernin, *In the World War* (New York, 1920), p. 164.
3. H. W. V. Temperley, ed., *A History of the Peace Conference of Paris* (London, 1921), IV, 113.
4. Cited by R. J. Kerner, "Yugoslavia and the Peace Conference," in *Yugoslavia,* ed. by R. J. Kerner (Berkeley, Calif., 1949), p. 94.
5. Temperley, *op. cit.,* IV, 422.
6. Heck to the United States ambassador in France, January 4, 1919, *Papers Relating to the Foreign Relations of the United States, 1919: The Paris Peace Conference* (Washington, D.C., 1942), II, 280–282.
7. Mustapha Kemal Pasha, "Creating a Nation," *Living Age,* CCCXXXIII (December 1, 1927), 975.
8. Cited by A. A. Pallis, *Greece's Anatolian Adventure—and After* (London, 1937), p. 15.
9. *Ibid.,* p. 18.
10. *Ibid.*

31. Dynamics of Balkan Politics

1. W. E. Moore, *Economic Demography of Eastern and Southern Europe* (Geneva, 1945), pp. 63–64. Different figures are given for Rumania in H. L. Roberts, *Rumania: Political Problems of an Agrarian State* (New Haven, Conn., 1951), p. 44; for Yugoslavia, Bulgaria, and Rumania in J. Tomasevich, *Peasants, Politics and Economic Change in Yugoslavia* (Stanford, Calif., 1955), p. 316; and for Greece in G. Coutsoumaris, "Possibilities of Economic Development in Greek Agriculture" (University of Chicago, unpublished doctoral dissertation, 1953), p. 57. But all sources agree that a substantial proportion of the Balkan agricultural population was surplus.
2. Data on Balkan tax structures from *Economic Development in S. E. Europe* (London, 1945), ch. 6; D. Mitrany, *Marx against the Peasant: A Study in Social Dogmatism* (Chapel Hill, N. C., 1951), pp. 102–104, 236.
3. J. Tomasevich, "Foreign Economic Relations, 1918–1941," in *Yugoslavia,* ed. by R. J. Kerner (Berkeley, Calif., 1949), p. 521.
4. Cited by Roberts, *op. cit.,* p. 73.
5. *South-Eastern Europe: A Political and Economic Survey* (London, 1939), p. 203.
6. Ch. Evelpides, "Le revenu national des pays balkaniques," *Metron,* XIV (June 15, 1940), 169; *Economic Development in S. E. Europe,* pp. 14, 19.
7. Statement by Andreya Stampar, cited by Roberts, *op. cit.,* p. 71.

8. *Statistical Year-Book of the League of Nations 1940–41* (Geneva, 1941), p. 40.
9. Tomasevich, *op. cit.*, pp. 571–573.
10. Roberts, *op. cit.*, p. 339.
11. G. C. Logio, *Bulgaria Past & Present* (Manchester, Eng., 1936), p. 11.
12. H. Seton-Watson, *Eastern Europe between the Wars 1918–1941* (Cambridge, Eng.: Cambridge University Press, 1946), p. 146–147.
13. Cited by Mitrany, *op. cit.*, p. 138.
14. *Ibid.*, p. 118.
15. B. N. Peselj, "Peasant Movements in Southeast Europe" (Georgetown University, unpublished doctoral dissertation, 1951), pp. 437–438.
16. Tomasevich, *Peasants, Politics and Economic Change in Yugoslavia*, p. 260.
17. Seton-Watson, *op. cit.*, p. 259.
18. Cited by Roberts, *op. cit.*, pp. 115–116.
19. Mitrany, *op. cit.*, p. 122.
20. Cited by E. N. Mittleman, "The Nationality Problem in Yugoslavia: A Survey of Developments 1921–1953" (New York University, unpublished doctoral dissertation, 1954), p. 136.
21. Cited by E. Barker, *Macedonia: Its Place in Balkan Power Politics* (London, 1950), p. 65.

32. Yugoslavia

1. Cited by E. N. Mittleman, "The Nationality Problem in Yugoslavia: A Survey of Developments 1921–1953" (New York University, unpublished doctoral dissertation, 1954), p. 13.
2. *Ibid.*, p. 14.
3. *Ibid.*, p. 131.
4. Statistics obtained from J. Tomasevich, *Peasants, Politics, and Economic Change in Yugoslavia* (Stanford, Calif., 1955), pp. 241–242.
5. Cited *ibid.*, p. 241.
6. Cited by Mittleman, *op. cit.*, p. 82.
7. Cited by Tomasevich, *op. cit.*, p. 226.
8. L. Adamic, *The Native's Return* (New York, 1934), pp. 290–291.
9. Statistics on health conditions from Tomasevich, *op. cit.*, ch. 25.
10. R. Trouton, *Peasant Renaissance in Yugoslavia 1900–1950* (London, 1952), pp. 185–186.
11. H. Seton-Watson, *Eastern Europe between the Wars 1918–1941* (Cambridge, Eng., 1946), pp. 229–231.

33. Bulgaria

1. New York *Times,* April 10, 1921.
2. N. D. Petkov, *Aleksandr Stamboliiski: Lichnost i idei [Alexander Stamboliski: Personality and Ideas]* (Sofia, 1930), pp. 183–184.
3. L. Pasvolsky, *Bulgaria's Economic Position* (Washington, D.C., 1930), p. 18; *South-Eastern Europe: A Political and Economic Survey* (London, 1939), p. 167.

4. S. D. Zagoroff *et al.*, *The Agricultural Economy of the Danubian Countries 1935–1945* (Stanford, Calif., 1955), pp. 381–382.
5. *South-Eastern Europe*, p. 170.
6. G. C. Logio, *Bulgaria Past & Present* (Manchester, Eng., 1936), pp. 180, 186–187.
7. *South-Eastern Europe*, p. 169.
8. Zagoroff, *op. cit.*, p. 373.
9. I. T. Sanders, *Balkan Village* (Lexington, Ky., 1949), p. 32.
10. Cited by W. M. Kotschnig, *Unemployment in the Learned Professions* (London, 1937), pp. 110–111.
11. Cited by Logio, *op. cit.*, p. 42.
12. Sanders, *op. cit.*, pp. 179–181.
13. *Ibid.*, p. 13.

34. Greece

1. Cited by N. Kaltchas, *Introduction to the Constitutional History of Modern Greece* (New York, 1940), p. 155.
2. Cited by *South-Eastern Europe: A Political and Economic Survey* (London, 1939), p. 94.
3. *Le Messager d' Athènes*, January 10–11, 1939.
4. "Censor's Instructions," *Spectator*, CLXI (August 19, 1938), 293.
5. *Le Messager d' Athènes*, January 6, 1939.
6. G. Servakis and C. Pertountzi, "The Agricultural Policy of Greece," in *Agricultural Systems of Middle Europe,* ed. by O. S. Morgan (New York, 1933), p. 148.
7. *Ibid.*, pp. 148–152.
8. *Economic Development in S. E. Europe* (London, 1945), p. 43; *Report of the FAO Mission for Greece* (Washington, D.C., March, 1947), pp. 155–156.
9. G. Coutsoumaris, "Possibilities of Economic Development in Greek Agriculture" (University of Chicago, unpublished doctoral dissertation, 1953), p. 43.
10. A. Pepelasis, "Socio-Cultural Barriers to the Economic Development of Greece" (University of California, Berkeley, unpublished doctoral dissertation, 1955), p. 48.
11. *Report of the FAO Mission for Greece*, p. 136.
12. F. Hilgerdt, *Industrialization and Foreign Trade* (Geneva, 1945), pp. 137, 143.
13. Pepelasis, *op. cit.*, p. 76.
14. *South-Eastern Europe*, p. 78.
15. Pepelasis, *op. cit.*, pp. 101, 103.
16. *Ho Oryktos ploutos tes Hellados* [*The Mineral Wealth of Greece*] (Athens, 1947), p. 210.
17. *Report of the FAO Mission for Greece*, p. 3.
18. Pepelasis, *op. cit.*, pp. 225–229.
19. L. G. Allbaugh, *Crete: A Case Study of an Underdeveloped Area* (Princeton, N. J., 1953), pp. 145–158.

35. Rumania

1 Cited by H. L. Roberts, *Rumania: Political Problems of an Agrarian State* (New Haven, Conn., 1951), p. 24.
2. Cited by D. Mitrany, *The Land & the Peasant in Rumania* (New Haven, Conn., 1930), p. 101.
3. Cited by Roberts, *op. cit.,* p. 30.
4. *Ibid.,* p. 91.
5. H. Seton-Watson, *Eastern Europe between the Wars, 1918–1941* (Cambridge, Eng., 1945), p. 204.
6. Cited by Roberts, *op. cit.,* p. 136.
7. Seton-Watson, *op. cit.,* pp. 203–204.
8. Roberts, *op. cit.,* pp. 44–45.
9. International Labour Office, "Agricultural Credits in Rumania," *Industrial and Labour Information,* XLI (January–March, 1932), 22.
10. *Economic Development in S. E. Europe* (London, 1945), p. 121.
11. Roberts, *op. cit.,* pp. 68, 198.
12. C. M. Jordan, *The Romanian Oil Industry* (New York, 1955), p. 320.
13. *South-Eastern Europe: A Political and Economic Survey* (London, 1939), p. 126.
14. Cited by Roberts, *op. cit.,* p. 70.
15. *Ibid.,* p. 83.
16. Seton-Watson, *op. cit.,* p. 336.
17. Roberts, *op. cit.,* pp. 81–82.
18. P. E. Mosely, "The Sociological School of Dimitrie Gusti," *Sociological Review,* XXVIII (April, 1936), 163–165.
19. Roberts, *op. cit.,* p. 80.
20. *Economic Development in S. E. Europe,* p. 14
21. Mitrany, *op. cit.,* p. 524.
22. *Economic Development in S. E. Europe,* p. 15.

36. Albania

1. H. W. V. Temperley, ed., *A History of the Peace Conference of Paris* (London, 1921), IV, 340.
2. E. P. Stickney, *Southern Albania or Northern Epirus in European International Affairs, 1912–1923* (Stanford, Calif., 1926), p. 105.
3. Temperley, *op. cit.,* IV, 344.
4. Cited by J. Swire, *Albania: The Rise of a Kingdom* (London, 1929), p. 323.
5. *League of Nations Official Journal,* III (June, 1922), 574–575.
6. *Ibid.,* p. 576.
7. *Ibid.,* IV (May, 1923), 510.
8. *Ibid.,* III (June, 1922), 579.
9. *Ibid.,* IV (May, 1923), 502.
10. *Ibid.,* p. 501.
11. *The Albanian Struggle in the Old World and the New.* Compiled and Written by Members of the Federal Writers' Project of the Works Progress Administration of Massachusetts (Boston, 1939), p. 69.
12. S. Skendi, "The Political Evolution of Albania, 1912–1944" (New York,

Mid-European Studies Center of the National Committee for a Free Europe, Mimeographed Series, March 8, 1954), p. 7.

13. *League of Nations Official Journal,* IV (May, 1923), 497.
14. Swire, *op. cit.,* p. 435.
15. *Ibid.,* p. 444.
16. *League of Nations, Records of the Fifth Assembly,* 1924, plenary sessions, p. 101.
17. Cited by E. Staley, "Italy's Financial Stake in Albania," *Foreign Policy Reports,* VIII (June 8, 1932), 85.
18. *Ibid.*
19. Full text in "Albania: The Problem of the Adriatic," *Foreign Policy Reports,* III (June 22, 1927), 121.
20. *Near East and India,* XLI (September 15, 1932), 741–742.
21. *Ibid.,* XLI (November 10, 1932), 900.
22. *Ibid.,* XLVIII (February 11, 1937), 202.
23. *Ciano's Hidden Diary 1937–1938* (New York, 1953), p. 107.
24. *Ibid.,* p. 177.
25. *The Ciano Diaries 1939–1943* (New York, 1946), p. 43.
26. *Ibid.,* p. 52.
27. *Ibid.,* p. 60.
28. *Ibid.,* pp. 63–64.
29. *Ibid.,* pp. 64–65.
30. R. Almagia, "Modern Albania: A Review," *Geographical Review,* XXII (July, 1932), 470.

37. Diplomatic Developments

1. Cited by C. A. Macartney, *Hungary and Her Successors* (London, 1937), p. 249.
2. Cited by H. N. Howard, "Yugoslavia, the Little Entente, and the Balkan Pact," *Yugoslavia,* ed. by R. J. Kerner (Berkeley, Calif., 1949), p. 328.
3. Cited by M. H. H. Macartney and P. Cremona, *Italy's Foreign and Colonial Policy 1914–1937* (London, 1938), p. 93.
4. Cited by Arnold J. Toynbee and F. T. Ashton-Gwatkin, eds., *Survey of International Affairs 1939–1946: The World in March 1939* (London, 1952), p. 252.
5. A. P. Papanastassiou, *Vers l'union balkanique* (Paris, 1934), p. 46.
6. Cited by H. N. Howard, "Bulgaria and the Balkan Entente," *Journal of Central European Affairs,* I (January, 1942), 447–448.
7. Arnold J. Toynbee, *Survey of International Affairs, 1936* (London, 1937), p. 506.
8. Cited by J. A. Lukacs, *The Great Powers and Eastern Europe* (New York, 1953), p. 70.
9. New York *Times,* May 8, 1936.
10. G. Ciano, *L'Europa verso la Catastrofe* (Milan, 1948), pp. 153–160.
11. Cited by Lukacs, *op. cit.,* p. 120.
12. *Ibid.,* p. 245.
13. Cited by L. S. Stavrianos, *Balkan Federation: A History of the Movement toward Balkan Unity in Modern Times* (Northampton, Mass., 1944), p. 255.

14. Cited by G. L. Weinberg, *Germany and the Soviet Union 1939–1941* (Leiden, 1954), p. 115.
15. Royal Ministry of Foreign Affairs, *Greek White Book: Italy's Aggression against Greece: Diplomatic Documents* (Athens, 1940), no. 178.
16. Cited by S. Lavra, *The Greek Miracle* (New York, 1942), p. 17.
17. *Ciano's Diary 1939–1943* (London, 1947), p. 297.
18. M. Ascoli, ed., *The Fall of Mussolini: His Own Story* (New York, 1948), pp. 189–191.
19. Cited by Lukacs, *op. cit.,* p. 347.
20. D. Alfieri, *Dictators Face to Face* (London, 1954), p. 82.
21. *Trial of the Major War Criminals before the International Military Tribunal* (Nuremberg, 1947), X, 523.
22. Cited by Weinberg, *op. cit.,* p. 137.
23. Winston S. Churchill, *The Second World War: Their Finest Hour* (Boston, 1949), p. 587.
24. R. J. Sontag and J. S. Beddie, *Nazi-Soviet Relations 1939–1941* (New York, 1948), pp. 233, 242.
25. *Ibid.,* pp. 258–259.
26. Churchill, *op. cit.,* p. 589.
27. *Nazi Conspiracy and Aggression* (Washington, D.C., 1946), I, 780.
28. Sontag, *op. cit.,* pp. 260–261.
29. Winston S. Churchill, *The Second World War: The Grand Alliance* (Boston, 1950), p. 106.
30. *Nazi Conspiracy and Aggression,* I, 784–785.
31. Major-General Sir Francis de Guingand, *Operation Victory* (London, 1947), p. 55.
32. London *Times,* May 8, 1941.
33. Field Marshal Lord Wilson of Libya, *Eight Years Overseas, 1939–1947* (London, 1950), p. 75.
34. Ernest von Weizsäcker, cited by Weinberg, *op. cit.,* p. 163.

38. Occupation, Resistance, and Liberation

1. E. I. Tsouderos, *Hellenikes Anomalies ste Mese Anatole* [*Greek Anomalies in the Middle East*] (Athens, 1945), p. 112.
2. Office of Chief of Counsel for War Crimes, *Translation of Document No. NOKW–1762,* p. 18 of original.
3. P. Schmidt, *Statist auf diplomatischer Bühne, 1923–45* (Bonn, 1949), pp. 537–538.
4. Maniu and Bratianu to Antonescu, January, 1942, in *Documents on International Affairs 1939–1946:* Vol. II, *Hitler's Europe,* edited and selected by M. Carlyle (London, 1954), pp. 326–327.
5. B. M. Kolker, "Natsionalno-Osvoboditelnaia Borba v Rumynii v 1941–1944 Godakh," ["The War of National Liberation in Rumania 1941–1944,"] *Voprosy Istorii,* no. 8 (August, 1954), p. 85.
6. H. L. Roberts, *Rumania: Political Problems of an Agrarian State* (New Haven, Conn., 1951), p. 258.
7. *Ciano's Diary 1939–1943,* ed. by M. Muggeridge (London, 1947), p. 399.

8. Cited by J. A. Lukacs, *The Great Powers and Eastern Europe* (New York, 1953), p. 783.
9. F. Maclean, *Eastern Approaches* (London, 1949), pp. 324–325.
10. *Ibid.*, pp. 315–316.
11. Winston S. Churchill, *The Second World War: Closing the Ring* (Boston: Houghton Mifflin Company, 1951), p. 463.
12. *Parliamentary Debates (Hansard)*. *House of Commons,* 5th Series, XCDVII, 694.
13. *Hitler's Europe*, p. 333.
14. *Ibid.*
15. *Ibid.*, p. 334.
16. *Ciano's Diary*, p. 509.
17. *Health Centers for Greece* (New York, 1944), p. 6.
18. K. Pyromaglou, *He Ethnike Antistasis* [*The National Resistance*] (Athens, 1947), pp. 165–167.
19. C. M. Woodhouse, *Apple of Discord: A Survey of Recent Greek Politics in Their International Setting* (London, 1948), p. 82.
20. Leland Stowe in New York *Post*, February 20, 1945. See also document published in "Letters to the *Times*," New York *Times*, March 28, 1947.
21. *Translation of Document No. NOKW–1762*, p. 10 of the original.
22. *Archeio Ethnikes Antistases* [*Archives of National Resistance*] (Athens, 1946), I, no. 2, 91–92.
23. Woodhouse, *op. cit.*, pp. 146–147.
24. J. Amery, *Sons of the Eagle: A Study in Guerilla War* (London, 1948), p. 60.
25. *Ibid.*, p. 59.
26. Cited by R. Trouton, *Peasant Renaissance in Yugoslavia 1900–1950* (London, 1952), p. 225.
27. Woodhouse, *op. cit.*, p. 29.
28. J. Stalin, *The Foundations of Leninism* (Moscow, 1950), p. 101.

39. Hidden War, Cold War and Peace Settlement

1. Winston S. Churchill, *The Second World War: Closing the Circle* (Boston: Houghton Mifflin Company, 1951), p. 466.
2. F. Maclean, *Eastern Approaches* (London, 1949), pp. 402–403.
3. E. C. W. Myers, *Greek Entanglement* (London, 1955), pp. 130–131.
4. C. M. Woodhouse, *Apple of Discord: A Survey of Recent Greek Politics in Their International Setting* (London, 1948), p. 300.
5. Myers, *op. cit.*, p. 224.
6. *Ibid.*, p. 190.
7. E. Tsouderos, *Hellenikes Anomalies ste Mese Anatole* [*Greek Anomalies in the Middle East*] (Athens, 1945), p. 64.
8. *Ibid.*, p. 65.
9. Woodhouse, *op. cit.*, p. 49.
10. K. Pyromaglou, *He Ethnike Antistasis* [*The National Resistance*] (Athens, 1947), p. 111.
11. Field Marshal Lord Wilson of Libya, *Eight Years Overseas, 1939–1947* (London, 1950), pp. 167, 179–180.
12. Woodhouse, *op. cit.*, p. 82.

13. Churchill, *Closing the Circle,* p. 538.
14. Winston S. Churchill, *The Second World War: Triumph and Tragedy* (Boston: Houghton Mifflin Company, 1953, pp. 72–73.
15. *Ibid.,* p. 80.
16. *Ibid.,* p. 81.
17. Cited by P. E. Mosely, "Hopes and Failures: American Policy toward East Central Europe, 1941–1947," *Review of Politics,* XVII (October, 1955), 478.
18. M. Carlyle, ed., *Documents on International Affairs 1939–1946:* Vol. II, *Hitler's Europe* (London, 1954), p. 335.
19. Churchill, *Triumph and Tragedy,* p. 92.
20. V. Dedijer, *Tito Speaks* (New York: Simon & Schuster, 1953), pp. 233–235.
21. New York *Times,* June 5, 1956.
22. Churchill, *Triumph and Tragedy,* p. 109.
23. *Ibid.,* p. 110.
24. Woodhouse, *op. cit.,* pp. 306–307.
25. Churchill, *Triumph and Tragedy,* p. 208.
26. *Ibid.,* pp. 227–228.
27. *Ibid.,* p. 159.
28. Churchill, *Triumph and Tragedy,* p. 285.
29. *Ethnikos Keryx* [*National Herald*], October 20, 1944. This is a daily published in New York.
30. Cited in New York *Times,* December 7, 1944.
31. Churchill, *Triumph and Tragedy,* p. 286.
32. Leland Stowe, in New York *Post,* February 15, 1945.
33. W. Byford-Jones, *The Greek Trilogy* (London, 1946), pp. 138–140.
34. Churchill, *Triumph and Tragedy,* p. 289. Italics in original.
35. *House of Commons Debates,* January 18, 1945, col. 400.
36. *Ibid.,* December 8, 1944, col. 943.
37. Churchill, *Triumph and Tragedy* p. 291.
38. W. H. McNeill, *Survey of International Affairs 1939–1946: America, Britain, & Russia: Their Co-Operation and Conflict 1941–1946* (London, 1953), p. 495.
39. Churchill, *Triumph and Tragedy,* p. 109.
40. *Ibid.,* p. 291.
41. M. W. Fodor, in *PM* (New York), December 7, 1944.
42. *House of Commons Debates,* December 20, 1944, col. 1890.
43. Churchill, *Triumph and Tragedy,* p. 310.
44. E. R. Stettinius, Jr., *Roosevelt and the Russians* (New York, 1949), p. 218; *Foreign Relations of the United States: Diplomatic Papers: The Conferences at Malta and Yalta 1945* (Washington, D. C., 1955), pp. 780, 849.
45. *The Conferences at Malta and Yalta 1945,* p. 977. See also pp. 251–254 and 980 for documents concerning decisions on Yugoslavia.
46. P. E. Mosely, *Face to Face with Russia,* in *Headline Series,* no. 70, July–August, 1948, p. 23.
47. Churchill, *Triumph and Tragedy,* p. 420.
48. J. F. Byrnes, *Speaking Frankly* (New York, 1947), p. 53.
49. Churchill, *Triumph and Tragedy,* p. 560.
50. *Ibid.,* p. 636.
51. Byrnes, *op. cit.,* p. 73.

52. Mosely, *Face to Face with Russia*, p. 23.
53. Mosely, "Hopes and Failures," *loc. cit.*, p. 472.

Epilogue

1. *Wall Street Journal*, January 26, 1956.
2. "The Character of a 'People's Democracy,' " *Foreign Affairs*, XXVIII (October, 1949), 151.
3. *Economic Survey of Europe in 1953* (Geneva, 1954), p. 98.
4. New York *Times*, January 30, 1956.
5. *Wall Street Journal*, January 26, 1956.
6. *Economic Survey of Europe in 1956* (Geneva, 1957), ch. 2.
7. Barbara Ward, "The Fateful Race between China and India," New York *Times Magazine*, September 20, 1953, pp. 9, 66.

Bibliography

General

T HE MOST RECENT GENERAL BIBLIOGRAPHY of the Balkans was issued in 1943 by the United States Library of Congress, Division of Bibliography, in five installments, as follows: *The Balkans: I General; II Albania; III Bulgaria; IV Rumania; V Yugoslavia; Greece*. These bibliographies cover all aspects of the countries concerned, and in some cases provide summaries of the works listed. Only books and articles in Western languages are included. The most useful pre–World War II bibliographical guide was L. Savadjian, *Bibliographie balkanique* (Paris, 1920–1938, 8 vols.). See also R. J. Kerner, *Slavic Europe: A Selected Bibliography in the Western European Languages, Comprising History, Languages and Literatures* (Cambridge, Mass., 1918); R. J. Kerner, *Social Sciences in the Balkans and in Turkey: A Survey of Resources for Study and Research in the Fields of Knowledge* (Berkeley, Calif., 1930); N. V. Mikhov, *Bibliographie de la Turquie, de la Bulgarie, et de la Macédoine* (Sofia, 1908–1913, 2 vols.); N. V. Mikhov, *Sources bibliographiques sur l'histoire de la Turquie et de la Bulgarie* (Sofia, 1914–1924, 2 vols.); R. J. Odavitch, *Essai de bibliographie française sur les Serbes, Croates et Slovenes depuis le commencement de la guerre actuelle* (Paris, 1918); G. Bengesco, *Essai d' une notice bibliographique sur la question d' Orient, 1821–1897* (Paris, 1897); V. M. Yovanovitch, *An English Bibliography on the Near Eastern Question, 1481–1906* (Belgrade, 1909); *List of Works in the New York Public Library Relating to the Near Eastern Question and the Balkan States, Including European Turkey and Modern Greece* (New York, 1910); *Materials in the National Archives Relating to the Balkan States*. National Archives, Reference Information Circular no. 4 (Washington, D. C., 1942). In addition to these regional bibliographies, the *Foreign Affairs Bibliography* is indispensable for current publications. It is compiled by W. L. Langer and H. F. Armstrong for the period 1919–1932, by R. G. Woolbert for 1932–1942; and by H. L. Roberts for 1942–1952. Finally, there are numerous bibliographies on individual countries and special subjects, which are listed in the appropriate sections below.

Scholarly periodicals in the field of Balkan history have appeared in various countries but many have ceased publication. The most important of these defunct periodicals are *Affaires danubiennes* (Bucharest, 1938–1941); *Balkan-Revue: Monatsschrift für die wirtschaftlichen Interessen der südost-europäischen Länder* (Berlin, 1914–1918), title changed to *Südost: Balkan-Revue* (Berlin,

873

1918–1920); *Les Balkans: Revue mensuelle: Albanie, Bulgarie, Grèce, Roumanie, Yougoslavie* (Athens, 1931–1939); *Bulletin de l'Institut pour l'étude de l'Europe sud-orientale* (Bucharest, 1914–1924), title changed to *Revue historique du sud-est européen* (Bucharest, 1924–1940); *Le monde slave* (Paris, 1917–1938); *Revue des Balkans* (Paris, 1919–1933); *Revue internationale des études balkaniques* (Belgrade, 1934–1940). *Leipziger Vierteljahrschrift für Südosteuropa* (Leipzig, 1937–1943).

Scholarly periodicals now appearing in the various Balkan countries are listed in *Historical Abstracts*, I (June, 1955), 230–231 (Yugoslavia); I (September, 1955), 332 (Bulgaria); I (September, 1955), 333 (Rumania); II (September, 1956), 181–183 (Greece). Relevant periodicals being published in non-Balkan countries include the *American Historical Review* (New York, 1896–); *American Slavic and East European Review* (New York, 1945–); *Eastern Review* (Vienna, 1948–); *Journal of Central European Affairs* (Boulder, Colo., 1941–); *Journal of Modern History* (Chicago, 1929–); *Revue des études slaves* (Paris, 1921–); *Slavonic Review* (London, 1922–1927), title changed in 1928, 1939, and again in 1943 (since 1943 has been *Slavonic and East European Review*); *Südost-Forshungen* (Munich, 1936–).

Current developments may be followed in *The Near East: A Weekly Journal of Oriental Politics, Literature, Finance and Commerce* (London, 1911), title changed in 1925 and 1935 (since 1935 it has been *Great Britain and the East*); and the bimonthly *Ost Europa* (Stuttgart, 1951–). Considerable material on current developments is available in the official "information" publications of the various Balkan governments interested in presenting their viewpoints to the outside world. The most informative of these publications are *Free Bulgaria,* now *Bulgaria Today,* issued fortnightly from 12 Narodno Sobranie Square, Sofia; the *Greek Bulletin,* issued irregularly by the Greek Information Office at 34 Hyde Park Square in London; and the *Yugoslav Review* issued monthly by the Yugoslav Information Center of 816 Fifth Avenue, New York 21. In the same class is the organ of the Communist Information Bureau, *For a People's Democracy: For a Lasting Peace* (Belgrade, 1947–1948; Bucharest, 1948–1956).

A critical appraisal of current affairs is available in the publications of the *National Committee for a Free Europe, Inc.,* 110 West 57th Street, New York 19. This organization has issued useful special studies, mostly by *émigrés*, published by its Mid-European Studies Center. It has also published since 1952 the monthly *News from Behind the Iron Curtain.* The same viewpoint is presented in the *Monthly Bulletin: International Peasant Union* (New York, 1950–), also consisting largely of articles by *émigrés.*

The best and most recent study of the Balkans is by R. L. Wolff, *The Balkans in Our Time* (Cambridge, Mass., 1956). This is a solid and reliable study, but it does not include Greece, and 500 of its 600 pages are devoted to the post-World War I period. The Byzantine and Ottoman periods are covered in F. Schevill, *History of the Balkan Peninsula from the Earliest Times to the Present Day* (New York, 1922), but this work has long been outdated, even in its 1933 revised edition. The general history by the Rumanian historian N. Iorga, *Histoire des états balkaniques jusqu'à 1924* (Paris, 1925), is uneven, though containing valuable material on certain phases of Balkan history. A penetrating analysis of the nature and results of Turkish rule in the Balkans is given by Sir Charles Eliot, *Turkey in Europe* (London, 1908). More recent studies are by R. Ristelhueber, *Histoire des peuples balkaniques* (Paris, 1950), which does not add anything new to the subject; and G. Stadtmuller, *Geschichte Südosteuropas* (Munich, 1950), which includes the Magyars and Czechoslovaks and which concentrates mostly on the Byzantine period to the neglect of the Ottoman and post-Ottoman. Other general Balkan histories are in existence, though they have long ceased to be of value: W. Miller, *The Balkans, Rumania, Bulgaria, Servia and Montenegro* [*The Story of the Nations*] (New York and London, 1896); N. Forbes, A. J. Toynbee, D. Mitrany, D. G. Hogarth, *The Balkans: A History of Bulgaria, Serbia, Greece, Rumania, Turkey* (Oxford, 1915); K. Roth, *Geschichte der christlichen Balkanstaaten: Bulgarien, Serbien, Rumänien, Montenegro, Griechenland* (Leipzig, 1907); W. S. Davis, *A Short History of the Near East from the Founding of Constantinople, 330–1922* (New York, 1922).

The most important general histories of the period since the eighteenth century are by W. Miller, *The Ottoman Empire and Its Successors, 1801–1922* (Cambridge, Eng., 1922, rev. ed.); R. W. Seton-Watson, *The Rise of Nationality in the Balkans* (London, 1917); L. André, *Les états chrétiens des Balkans depuis 1815: Roumanie, Bulgarie, Serbie, Montenègre, Grèce* (Paris, 1918); and the brief survey of W. M. Gewehr, *The Rise of Nationalism in the Balkans, 1800–1930* [*Berkshire Studies in European History*] (New York, 1931).

In addition to these general histories, many surveys are available of Near Eastern diplomacy or the so-called Eastern Question. The most recent is the excellent study of F. Cognasso, *Storia della questione d'oriente* (Turin, 1948), which includes a comprehensive bibliography. Other diplomatic histories are by E. Driault, *La question d'Orient depuis ses origines jusqu'à nos jours* (Parıs, 1898); and J. A. R. Marriott, *The Eastern Question: An Historical Study in European Diplomacy* (Oxford, 1940, 4th ed.). For surveys of the Eastern Question since the eighteenth century, see J. Ancel, *Manuel historique de ia question d'Orient, 1792–1923* (Paris, 1923); and the two-volume study by M. Lascaris, *To Anatolikon zetema, 1800–1923* [*The Eastern Question, 1800–1923*] (Saloniki, 1948–1954), provides an excellent bibliography. Finally, note should be made of the extremely useful documentary collection by J. C. Hurewitz, *Diplomacy in the Near and Middle East:* Vol. I, *A Documentary Record: 1535–1914;* Vol. II, *A Documentary Record: 1914–1956* (Princeton, N. J. 1956).

While this work was in the press there appeared the first volume in the *Mid-European Studies Center Handbook Series, East Central Europe under the Communists.* The first volume by S. Skendi, *Albania under the Communists* (New York, 1957), provides basic factual data concerning Albania, and will be followed by other similar handbooks on Bulgaria, Rumania, and Yugoslavia, as well as on various countries in Central Europe.

1. The Land and the People

By all odds the most comprehensive and useful work on Balkan geography is the *Geographie universelle,* ed. by P. V. de la Blache and L. Gallois. The second part of Volume VII, by Y. Chataigneau and Y. Sion, is entitled *Pays balkaniques* (Paris, 1934), and deals with Albania, Greece, Bulgaria, Turkish Thrace, and Yugoslavia. Volume IV, Part II, *Europe centrale* (Paris, 1931), by E. de Martonne, deals with Rumania in pp. 699–825. The authors consider in detail the ethnography and economy, as well as the geography, of the Balkan countries, and provide excellent charts, maps, and bibliographies.

Other important works on this subject are J. Cvijič, *La péninsule balkanique: geographie humaine* (Paris, 1918), a standard analysis by a Serbian geographer; D. G. Hogarth, *The Nearer East* (London, 1905); M. I. Newbigin, *Southern Europe* (London, 1949), includes only Greece and Albania; C. Evelpidi, *Les états balkaniques* (Paris, 1930), a useful study by a Greek agricultural economist; and W. B. Turrill, *The Plant Life of the Balkan Peninsula: A Phytogeographical Study* (Oxford, 1929). H. Hodgkinson, *The Adriatic Sea* (London, 1955), is an interesting description and history of the sea and its coast lines, based on sound scholarship and extensive traveling. J. L. Myres, *Geographical History in Greek Lands* (New York, 1953), carries the geographic interpretations from antiquity to the present.

On Balkan ethnography the most useful works are M. E. Pittard, *Les peuples des Balkans* (Paris, 1920); and the more general studies by W. Z. Ripley, *The Races of Europe* (New York, 1899); and C. S. Coon, *The Races of Europe* (New York, 1939). For a political approach to Balkan ethnography, see C. A. Macartney, *National States and Minorities* (London, 1934). The population transfers following World War I are described in S. B. Ladas, *The Exchange of Minorities: Bulgaria, Greece and Turkey* (New York, 1932); those following World War II are described by J. B. Schechtman in *European Population Transfers 1939–1945* (New York, 1946) and in "Compulsory Transfer of the Turkish Minority from Bulgaria," *Journal of Central European Affairs*, XII (July, 1952), 155–169.

For the linguistic and general cultural affinities of the Balkan peoples, see K. Sandfeld, *Linguistique balkanique, problèmes et resultats* (Paris, 1930); A. Seliščev, "Des traits linguistiques communs aux langues balkaniques," *Revue des études slaves*, V (1925), 38–57; N. Iorga, *Le caractère commun des institutions du sud-est de l'Europe* (Paris, 1929); and J. Ancel, "L'unité balkanique," *Revue internationale des études balkaniques*, I (1934), 117–139.

2. Historical Background

The most up-to-date one-volume survey of Greek history is H. Bengtson, *Griechische Geschichte von den Anfängen bis in die römische Kaiserzeit* (Munich, 1950). A more detailed history of the Greek and Roman periods, with maps, illustrations and bibliographies, is provided by the *Cambridge Ancient History* (Cambridge, Eng., 1923–1939, 12 vols.), ranging from prehistoric man to A.D. 324. Briefer surveys are available in E. Eyre, ed., *European Civilization: Its Origin and Development* (New York, 1934–1939, 7 vols.), the first two volumes of which deal with Greece and Rome; and M. I. Rostovtzev, *History of the Ancient World* (Oxford, 1926–1927, 2 vols.). See also M. Cary, *The Geographic Background of Greek and Roman History* (Oxford, 1949). The above works provide bibliographical guides to specific aspects of ancient history.

The best one-volume histories of Byzantium are A. A. Vasiliev, *History of the Byzantine Empire* (Madison, Wisc., 1952, rev. ed.), and G. Ostrogorsky, *Geschichte des byzantinischen Staates* (Munich, 1940), tr. by J. M. Hussey as *History of the Byzantine State* (Oxford, 1955). In the *Histoire générale* series edited by G. Glotz, the Byzantine period is treated by C. Diehl and G. Marçais,

Le monde oriental de 395 à 1081 (Paris, 1936), and C. Diehl, R. Guilland, L. Oeconomos, and R. Grousset, *L'Europe orientale de 1081 à 1453* (Paris, 1945). In the series *L'évolution de l'humanité*, L. Bréhier is the author of *Le monde byzantin:* Vol. I, *Vie et mort de Byzance* (Paris, 1947); Vol. II, *Les institutions de l'empire byzantin* (Paris, 1949); Vol. III in preparation. See also the following cooperative histories: *Cambridge Medieval History:* Vol. IV, *East Roman Empire (717–1453)* (Cambridge, Eng., 1923); N. H. Baynes and H. St. L. B. Moss, eds., *Byzantium* (Oxford, 1948). A series of interpretive articles by C. Diehl, G. Ostrogorsky, N. Iorga, and I. Sakazov, dealing specifically with Byzantium's impact on the Balkan Peninsula was published in *La revue internationale des études balkaniques,* IV (1936), 377–419. These works provide bibliographical guides to specific aspects of Byzantine history.

3. Coming of the Ottoman Turks

The Oriental sources for Ottoman history are described in F. Babinger, *Die Geschichtsschreiber der Osmanen und ihre Werke* (Leipzig, 1924). Brief though revealing surveys of Turkish historiography are available in "Historical Studies in Turkey," *The Times Literary Supplement,* no. 2725, April 23, 1954, p. 270; and B. Lewis, "History Writing and National Revival in Turkey," *Middle Eastern Affairs,* IV (June–July, 1953), 218–277. A useful handbook and bibliographical guide to Western materials is provided by J. K. Birge, *A Guide to Turkish Area Study* (Washington, D. C., 1949).

Among Western sources, the first from the chronological viewpoint, and essential for early Ottoman history, are the Byzantine historians—Phrantzes, Ducas, Chalcondyles, and Kritobulos—the work of the last of these having been translated recently by Charles T. Riggs and published as *History of Mehmed the Conqueror* (Princeton, N. J., 1954). For the period after the fifteenth century, basic sources are the reports of the Venetian ambassadors, edited by E. Alberi, *Relazioni degli ambasciatori veneti al Senato . . . .* (Florence, 1839–1863, 15 vols.), and by N. Barozzi and G. Berchet, *Relazioni degli Stati Europei, lette al Senato degli ambasciatori Veneti nel secolo XVII° . . . .* (Venice, 1856–1878, 10 vols.). Another important source that has been inadequately exploited is the great mass of travel literature from the days of the Bavarian captive, Johann Schiltberger, in the early fifteenth century, to the ambassadorship of Henry Morgenthau during World War I, when the empire was in its death throes. In order to be used effectively the thousands of travel accounts need to be catalogued with data concerning the date of each journey, the route followed, and the chief interest of the traveler. The only significant analytical study of this travel literature is by R. Warnier, "La découverte des pays balkaniques par l'Europe occidentale de 1500 à 1815," *Journal of World History,* II, no. 4 (1955), 915–948. For other works about Western travelers in the Balkans, which have not been consulted for the present study, see M. Lascaris' bibliographical notice in *Revue historique du Sud-Est Européen,* XXI (1944), 288.

The first great history of the Ottoman Empire was written by J. von Hammer-Purgstall, *Geschichte des osmanischen Reiches* (Pesth, 1827–1835, 10 vols.). Based mostly on Turkish sources, this massive study still remains indispensable. It ends with the Treaty of Kuchuk Kainarji of 1774. The French edition, translated by J. J. Hellert, *Histoire de l'empire Ottoman depuis son origine jusqu'à nos jours* (Paris, 1835–1843, 18 vols.), corrects some minor errors in the German edition and is better indexed. Another study of equal scope is by J. W. Zinkeisen, *Geschichte des osmanischen Reiches in Europa* (Gotha, 1840–1863, 7 vols.), a work that uses many Western sources ignored by Hammer and which carries the story to 1812. From these two fundamental histories are derived several shorter works, including E. Creasy, *History of the Ottoman Turks* (London, 1854–1856, 2 vols.); Stanley Lane-Poole, *Story of Turkey* (New York, 1922, new ed.); and A. de la Jonquière, *Histoire de l'empire ottoman* (Paris, 1914, rev. ed., 2 vols.).

A more recent general history of the Ottoman Empire is by N. Iorga, *Geschichte des osmanischen Reiches* (Gotha, 1908–1913, 5 vols.). This study by the well-known Rumanian historian and statesman is, like all his works, hurriedly written, inaccurate in spots, poorly footnoted, yet frequently very illuminating, especially on social and economic subjects neglected by his predecessors. Sir Charles Eliot's *Turkey in Europe* (London, 1908, new ed.), is a briefer interpretive work that is still valuable because of the author's long residence in Turkey, his perceptive analyses and his engaging style. Two recent studies are noteworthy, though they concentrate on the nineteenth and twentieth centuries: G. L. Lewis, *Turkey* [*Nations of the Modern World*] (London, 1955); Sir Harry Luke, *The Old Turkey and the New: From Byzantium to Ankara* (London, 1955, rev. ed.). A final source of a general nature is the *Encyclopedia of Islam* (Leiden and London, 1913–1938, 4 vols. and supplement). This is an invaluable mine of information, though the articles are of uneven quality, the translations frequently poor, and the cross references inadequate. The reader has no way of discovering, for example, that Albania is considered under Arnauts, Moldavia under Boghdan, and Wallachia under Iflak. The article in the *Encyclopedia* under "Turks—History" by J. H. Kramers, provides an excellent introduction to the Ottoman Empire. A new edition of the *Encyclopedia of Islam* was planned at the 21st Annual Congress of Orientalists at Paris in July, 1948, and the first fascicles of Volume I appeared in 1954. Students will also find very useful the *Atlas of Islamic History* compiled by H. W. Hazard (Princeton, N. J., 1951).

The question of the origins of the Ottoman Empire was first investigated in detail in the monograph by H. A. Gibbons, *The Foundation of the Ottoman Empire* (New York, 1916). Later studies utilizing Oriental sources not used by Gibbons have thrown light on obscure phases of early Turkish history. The most important of these in the order of their appearance are W. L. Langer and R. P. Blake, "The Rise of the Ottoman Turks and Its Historical Background," *American Historical Review*, XXXVII (April, 1932), 468–505; M. F. Köprülü, *Les origines de l'empire Ottoman* (Paris, 1935); W. Barthold, *Turkestan Down to the Mongol Invasion* (London, 1938); P. Wittek, *The Rise of the Ottoman Empire* (London, 1938); V. A. Gordlevsky, *Gosudarstvo Seldzhukidov Maloi Azii* [*The Empire of the Seljuks of Asia Minor*] (Moscow, 1941); G. G. Arnakis, *Hoi Protoi Othomanoi: Symbole eis to problema tes ptoseos tou Hellenismou tes Mikras Asias* (*1282–1337*) [*The Early Osmanlis: A Contribution to the Problem of the Fall of Hellenism in Asia Minor* (*1282–1337*)] (Athens, 1947). The latter work, which stresses the contribution of the Anatolian Greeks to the early Turkish state-builders, includes a useful introductory essay entitled "The History of the Osmanli Problem: A Critical Review of Sources and Publications."

See also the important articles by G. G. Arnakis, "Futuwwa Traditions in the Ottoman Empire: Akhis, Bektashi Dervishes, and Craftsmen," *Journal of Near Eastern Studies*, XII (October, 1953), 232–247; J. A. B. Palmer, "The Origin of the Janissaries," *Bulletin of the John Rylands Library Manchester*, XXXV (March, 1953), 448–481; and S. Vryonis Jr., "Isidore Glabas and the Turkish *Devshirme*," *Speculum*, XXXI (July, 1956), 433–443. The latter article throws new light on the date of the introduction of the devshirme. F. Babinger, *Beiträge zur Frühgeschichte der Türkenherrschaft in Rumelien* (Brünn, 1944), clears up many obscure features of the early Turkish invasion of the Balkans. The following article is noteworthy for placing the Ottoman expansion into Europe in the general perspective of Near Eastern–Western relations: A. S. Atiya, "The Crusades: Old Ideas and New Conceptions," *Journal of World History*, II, no. 2 (1954), 469–475. On the Turkish expansion in the Balkans see also the book by St. Novaković, *Srbi i Turci XIV i XV veka* (Belgrade, 1893, not consulted). Also noteworthy is W. C. Brice, "The Turkish Colonization of Anatolia," *Bulletin of the John Rylands Library*, XXXVIII (September, 1955), 18–44, which analyzes the circumstances under which Asia Minor was Turkified following the battle of Manzikert.

4. Conquest of the Balkans

Turkish-Byzantine relations in the first period of Turkish expansion in the Balkans are critically reviewed by P. Charanis, "The Strife among the Palaeologi and the Ottoman Turks, 1370–1402," *Byzantion*, XVI (1942–1943), 286–314, who corrects a number of misconceptions and factual errors. Franz Babinger does likewise for the ensuing Turkish penetration of the Balkans in his *Beiträge zur Frühgeschichte der Türkenherrschaft in Rumelien (14–15 Jahrhundert)* (Munich, 1944). Babinger also deals with the reign of Murad II in his biography, *Mehmed der Eroberer und seine Zeit* (Munich, 1953), pp. 1–66. The European repercussions to Turkish expansion are conveniently and excellently summarized in D. M. Vaughan, *Europe and the Turk: A Pattern of Alliances 1350–1700* (Liverpool, 1954), ch. 1. See also J. D. le Roulx, *La France en Orient au XIV*e *siècle: Expéditions du maréchal Boucicaut* (Paris, 1886, 2 vols.) and M. Silberschmidt, *Das orientalische Problem zur Zeit der Entstehung des Türkischen Reiches* (Leipzig, 1923), the latter work being especially valuable for its use of Venetian materials and its detailed analysis of the Eastern Question from 1381 to 1400. For the efforts of the Byzantine emperors to obtain support from the West, see O. Halecki, *Un empereur de Byzance à Rome* (Warsaw, 1930); W. Norden, *Das Papsttum und Byzanz, die Trennung der beiden Mächte und das Problem ihrer Wiedervereinigung bis 1453* (Berlin, 1903); and N. Iorga, *Philippe de Mézières et la Croisade au XV*e *siècle* (Paris, 1896). Information on the role of Venice in Near Eastern affairs at this time is available in C. Diehl, *Venise: une république patricienne* (Paris, 1915); and in H. Kretschmayr, *Geschichte von Venedig* (Stuttgart, 1905–1926, 32 vols.).

On the Bogomil heresy and its significance for the Ottoman conquests, see J. Lavrin, "The Bogomils and Bogomilism," *Slavonic Review*, VIII (1929–1930), 269–283; J. A. Ilić, *Die Bogomillen in ihrer geschichtlichen Entwicklung* (Sremski Karlovci, 1923); M. Spinka, *A History of Christianity in the Balkans: A Study in the Spread of Byzantine Culture among the Slavs* (Chicago, 1933); V. N. Sharenkoff, *A Study of Manichaeism in Bulgaria, with Special Reference to the Bogomils* (New York, 1927); S. Runciman, *The Medieval Manichee: A Study of the Christian Dualist Heresy* (Cambridge, Eng., 1947); D. Obolensky, *The Bogomils: A Study in Balkan Neo-Manichaeism* (Cambridge, Eng., 1948) and D. Angelov, "Filozofskite vozgledi na Bogomilite," ["The Philosophical Views of the Bogomils,"] *Izvestiia* (Sofia), nos. 3–4 (1951), 113–147.

The individual campaigns are described in the Balkan national histories listed below, and in the following works: J. H. Kramers, "Skanderbeg," *Encyclopedia of Islam;* A. Gegaj, *L'Albanie et l'invasion turque au XVe siècle* (Louvain, 1937); Bishop F. S. Noli, *George Castrioti Scanderbeg (1405–1468)* (New York, 1947); and especially the following work, which presents all the original and secondary material on the subject: J. Radonić, *Djuradj Kastriot Skanderbeg i Albanija u XV veku* [*George Kastriotis Skanderbeg and Albania in the Fifteenth Century*] (Belgrade, 1942). See also G. Beckmann, *Der Kampf Kaiser Sigmunds gegen die werdende Weltmacht der Osmanen, 1392–1437* (Gotha, 1902); A. S. Atiya, *The Crusade in the Later Middle Ages* (London, 1938); and *The Crusade of Nicopolis* (London, 1934). The latter work should be read together with the comments of R. Rosetti, "Notes on the Battle of Nicopolis," *Slavonic and East European Review,* XV (April, 1937), 629–638. See also O. Halecki, *The Crusade of Varna: A Discussion of Controversial Problems* (New York, 1943), which presents one viewpoint concerning the truce of Szeged, but data supporting the other viewpoint are presented convincingly in G. Ostrogorsky, *History of the Byzantine State* (Oxford, 1956), p. 503, which gives a full bibliography. An interesting analysis of the various contemporary versions of what happened on the Kosovo battlefield is given in D. Subotić, *Yugoslav Popular Ballads: Their Origin and Development* (Cambridge, Eng., 1932), ch. 2.

The well-known Turkish historian, M. F. Köprülü, clears up the circumstances of Bayezid's death in captivity in the article "Yildirim Bayezid' in Intihari Mes' elesi," ["The Question of Yildirim Bayezid's Suicide,"] *Belleten,* VII (July, 1943), 591–599. The standard and indispensable work for the Ottoman recovery following the battle of Ankara is P. Wittek, "De la défaite d'Ankara à la prise de Constantinople (un demi-siècle d'histoire ottomane)," *Revue des études islamiques,* XII (1938), 1–34. This period is also treated thoroughly by N. Iorga, *Geschichte des osmanischen Reiches* (Gotha, 1908), I, 325 ff.

The most useful general work on the fall of Constantinople is the collection of essays by prominent Greek historians in *1453–1953. Le cinq-centième anniversaire de la prise de Constantinople,* published by the periodical *L'hellénisme contemporaine* in Athens in 1953. It includes several essays on the circumstances of the fall of Constantinople, the ideological cleavages among the Greeks before and after the fall, and the historical significance of that event. See also S. Runciman, B. Lewis, R. Betts, N. Rubistein, and P. Wittek, *The Fall of Constantinople* (London, 1955), and vol. XIV (1953) of *Byzantinoslavica,* which contains a very important collection of studies dealing with the fall of Constantinople. Both works have not been consulted for the present study. The diplomacy associated with the siege and the relations of Mohammed with Europe are traced by D. M. Vaughan, *Europe and the Turk: A Pattern of Alliances 1350–1700* (Liverpool, 1954), chs. 1, 2. R. S. Atabinen, "Les Turcs à Constantinople du Ve au XVe siècle," *Revue d'histoire diplomatique,* October–December, 1953, pp. 338–364, is an interesting article by a Turkish historian presenting the Ottoman penetration of Byzantium as a gradual process, similar to the barbarian conquest of Italy, with the difference that the Turks possessed a much higher civilization than had the German tribes.

A. A. Vasiliev, *History of the Byzantine Empire* (Madison, Wisc., 1952) provides an excellent analysis of the contemporary sources on the siege, including the Greeks Phrantzes, Ducas, Chalcondyles, and Kritobulos; the Catholic ecclesiastics Cardinal Isidore and Archbishop Leonard; the Venetian Nicolo Barbaro, and the Russian Nestor Iskinder. For the Turkish sources see F. Babinger, *Geschichtsschreiber der Osmanen und ihre Werke* (Leipzig, 1927), pp. 23–45 and *passim*. The kanuns or decrees of Mohammed are translated in J. F. von Hammer-Purgstall, *Des osmanischen Reichs Staatsverfassung und Staatsverwaltung* (Vienna, 1815), I, 87–101. Two Western travelers have left vivid accounts of the state of Byzantium on the eve of its fall: *Pero Tafur: Travels and Adventures 1435–1439,* translated and edited with an Introduction by Malcolm Letts (London, 1926); "The Travels of Bertrandon de la Brocquière, A.D. 1432 and 1433," in Thomas Wright, *Early Travels in Palestine* (London, 1848). For an estimate of their testimony see Izzedin, "Deux voyageurs du XVᵉ siècle en Turquie," *Journal asiatique,* CCXXXIX (1951), 159–174.

On the principals in the siege of Constantinople there is C. Mijatovich, *Constantine: The Last Emperor of the Greeks* (London, 1892); and F. Babinger, *Mehmed der Eroberer und seine Zeit* (Munich, 1953). The latter work, which filled a long-felt need, has also been published in a French edition: *Mahomet II le conquérant et son temps 1432–1481* (Paris, 1954). On this standard biography see the comments by C. Marinesco, "L'état et la société turque à l'époque de Mahomet II: A propos d'un ouvrage récent," *Revue historique,* CCXIV (July–September, 1955), 35–47. Barnette Miller has written admirable studies of Mohammed's Seraglio and Palace School in her two works: *Beyond the Sublime Porte: The Grand Seraglio of Stambul* (New Haven, Conn. 1931), and *The Palace School of Mohammed the Conqueror* (Cambridge, Mass., 1941). A Turkish viewpoint concerning Mohammed's attitude toward Byzantine learning is presented in A. Adnan-Adivar, "The Cultural Situation of Byzantines and Turks at the Time of the Conquest of Constantinople 1453," *Muslim World,* XLV (January, 1955), 61–71. See also L. Thuasne, *Gentile Bellini et Sultan Mohammed II* (Paris, 1888). Mohammed's repeopling of Constantinople is described by H. Inalcik, "Ottoman Methods of Conquest," *Studia Islamica,* II (1954), 103–130; and by O. L. Barkan, "Les déportations comme méthode de peuplement et de colonisation dans l'empire ottoman," *Revue de la faculté des sciences économiques de l'université d'Istanbul,* XI (October, 1949–July, 1950), 67–131. The standard secondary work on the capture of Constantinople is E. Pears, *The Destruction of the Greek Empire and the Capture of Constantinople by the Turks* (New York, 1903). G. Schlumberger, *Le siège, la prise et le sac de Constantinople par les Turcs* (Paris, 1922, 6th ed.), is of little value. The unsuccessful siege of Rhodes is interestingly described in Chapter 18 of S. Toy, *A History of Fortification from 3000 B.C. to A.D. 1700* (London, 1955).

5. Ottoman Empire at Its Height

For the reign of Bayezid II, the most useful work is by S. N. Fisher, *The Foreign Relations of Turkey 1481–1512* (Urbana, Ill., 1948), an excellent study which contains considerable information on internal as well as diplomatic developments. See also the same author's article "Civil Strife in the Ottoman Empire 1481–1503," *Journal of Modern History*, XIII (December, 1941), 448–466. Other aspects of this reign are covered in the following: L. Thuasne, *Djem Sultan* (Paris, 1892); and H. A. von Burski, *Kemal Re'is: Ein Beitrag zur Geschichte der türkischen Flotte* (Bonn, 1928).

By all odds the most important work for the period of Selim is by G. W. F. Stripling, *The Ottoman Turks and the Arabs 1511–1574* (Urbana, Ill., 1942). In addition to an exhaustive bibliography, this study presents important data concerning the Mameluke Empire, the invasion of Selim, and the efforts of the Turks to reopen the trade routes. On the latter topic the pioneer work was done by A. H. Lybyer, in "The Ottoman Turks and the Routes of Oriental Trade," *English Historical Review*, XXX (October, 1915), 577–588. Later writers have modified Lybyer's findings by stressing the continued use of the old routes throughout the sixteenth century. See F. C. Lane, "Venetian Shipping during the Commercial Revolution," *American Historical Review*, XXXVIII (January, 1933), 219–239; "The Mediterranean Spice Trade," *American Historical Review*, XLV (April, 1940), 581–591; N. Mirkovich, "Ragusa and the Portuguese Spice Trade," *Slavonic and East European Review*, XXI (March, 1943), 174–187; F. Braudel, *La Méditerranée et le monde méditerranéen à l'époque de Philippe II* (Paris, 1949), pp. 421–427. An early Venetian-Egyptian plan for a canal at the Suez as a reply to the Portuguese interlopers is described by F. Charles-Roux, "L'Isthme de Suez et les rivalités européennes au XVI° siècle," *Revue de l'histoire des colonies françaises*, XVII (1924), 153–192. See also W. H. Moreland, "The Ships of the Arabian Sea about A.D. 1500," *Journal of the Royal Asiatic Society*, January, 1939, pp. 63–74; and H. Wilberforce-Bell, "The Red Sea," *Journal of the Royal Asiatic Society*, April, 1939, pp. 415–426. For the Turkish-Portuguese wars, see M. Longworth Dames, "The Portuguese and Turks in the Indian Ocean in the Sixteenth Century," *Journal of the Royal Asiatic Society*, January, 1921, Pt. I, pp. 1–28. This article is corrected on certain points by E. Denison Ross, "The Portuguese in India and Arabia 1517–38," *Journal of the Royal Asiatic Society*, January, 1922, Pt. I, pp. 1–18. See also C. D. Ley, ed., *Portuguese Voyages 1498–1663* (London, Everyman's Library, 1947).

Selim's relations with the Persians are described in D. M. Vaughan, *Europe and the Turk: A Pattern of Alliances 1350–1700* (Liverpool, 1954), ch. 5, and in V. Minorsky, "The Middle East in Western Politics in the 13th, 14th and 15th Centuries," *Journal of the Royal Central Asian Society*, XXVII (1940), 433–448, an article which actually deals with the 13th, 15th and 17th centuries, the title having a typographical error.

The Turkish sources for Suleiman's reign are given in the article on this subject by J. H. Kramers in the *Encyclopedia of Islam*. A few of these sources are available in translation, including *Suleiman der Gesetzgebers Tagebuch auf seinem Feldzuge nach Wien*, tr. by F. A. Berhauer (Vienna, 1858), and *Die osmanische Chronik des Rustem Pasha*, tr. by L. Forrer in *Türkische Bibliothek* (Leipzig, 1923). The most important contemporary source is the *Relazioni* of the Venetian ambassadors, published by Albéri (Florence, 1839–1863).

Three biographies are available in English: F. Downey, *The Grande Turke* (New York, 1929); H. Lamb, *Suleiman the Magnificent* (New York, 1951); and R. B. Merriman, *Suleiman the Magnificent* (Cambridge, Mass., 1944), the latter being by all odds the best. Suleiman's grand vizir is treated inadequately by H. D. Jenkins in *Ibrahim Pasha: Grand Vizir of Suleiman the Magnificent* (New York, 1911).

A useful general survey of Ottoman military history at this time is given in C. Oman, *A History of the Art of War in the Sixteenth Century* (New York, 1937). For individual campaigns and military leaders, see W. Sturminger, *Bibliographie und Ikonographie der Turkenbelagerung Wiens, 1529 und 1683* (Cologne, 1955); Kemal Pasha Zadeh, *Histoire de la campagne de Mohacz,* tr. and ed. by A. J. B. Pavet de Courteille (Paris, 1859); *The Sieges of Vienna by the Turks, from the German of Karl August Schimmer and other Sources,* tr. by the Earl of Ellesmere (London, 1847); Haji Khalfah, *The History of the Maritime Wars of the Turks,* tr. by James Mitchell (London, 1831); S. Lane Poole, *The Story of the Barbary Corsairs* (New York, 1890); Jurien de la Gravière, *Doria et Barberousse* (Paris, 1886), *Les corsaires barbaresques* (Paris, 1887), *Les chevaliers de Malte* (Paris, 1887, 2 vols.); F. Braudel, *La Méditerranée et le monde méditerranéen à l'époque de Philippe II* (Paris, 1949), pp. 723–856; and P. Hubac, *Les Barbaresques* (Paris, 1949), which is vivid and well illustrated, if not always accurate.

The basic sources for the diplomacy of the period are E. Charrière, ed., *Négociations de la France dans le Levant* (Paris, 1848–1860, 4 vols.), in *Collection de documents inédits sur l'histoire de France;* and A. von Gévay, ed., *Urkunden und Actenstücke zur Geschichte der Verhältnisse zwischen Österreich, Ungarn, und der Pforte im XVI und XVII Jahrhunderte* (Vienna, 1838–1842, 3 vols.). See also the fine monograph by J. Ursu, *La politique orientale de François 1er, 1515–1547* (Paris, 1908); and the excellent study of Ibrahim's diplomatic adviser by H. Kretschmayr, "Ludovico Gritti," *Archiv für österreichische Geschichte,* LXXXIII (1896), 1–106, issued the same year in Vienna in book form. For the interaction of Lutheranism and the Ottoman Empire, see G. Simon, "Luther's Attitude towards Islam," *Moslem World,* XXI (July, 1931), 257–262; S. A. Fischer-Galati, "Ottoman Imperialism and the Lutheran Struggle for Recognition in Germany 1520–1529," *Church History,* XXIII (March, 1954), 46–67; S. A. Fischer-Galati, "The Turkish Impact on the German Reformation, 1520–1555" (Harvard University, unpublished doctoral dissertation, 1949). The changing attitude of Christendom toward the Ottoman Empire is well described in F. L. Baumer, "England, the Turk, and the Common Corps of Christendom," *American Historical Review,* L (October, 1944), 26–48. Finally, a comprehensive analysis of Ottoman relations with Europe during this period is given in D. M. Vaughan, *Europe and the Turk: A Pattern of Alliances 1350–1700* (Liverpool, 1954), pp. 104–156.

6. Ottoman Institutions

The standard work on Ottoman institutions has for long been A. H. Lybyer, *The Government of the Ottoman Empire in the Time of Suleiman the Magnificent* (Cambridge, Mass., 1913). This should be supplemented now by the following study, which is much more comprehensive than the title indicates: H. A. R. Gibb and H. Bowen, *Islamic Society and the West: A Study of the Impact of Western Civilization on Moslem Culture in the Near East:* Vol. I, *Islamic Society in the Eighteenth Century* (New York, 1950). For the evolution of the child-tribute see the article "Dewshirme" by J. H. Mordtmann in the *Encyclopedia of Islam.* For the janissaries there are the article on this subject by C. L.

Huart in the *Encyclopedia of Islam* and also the following works: Ahmed Djevad Bey, *Etat militaire ottoman depuis la foundation de l'empire jusqu'à nos jours:* tome I, livre I: *Le corps des Janissaires depuis sa création jusqu'à sa suppression* (Constantinople and Paris, 1882); N. Weissmann, *Les Janissaires, étude de l' organisation militaire des Ottomans* (Paris, 1938); and the definitive study by I. H. Uzunçarsīlī, *Osmanlĭ Devleti Teskilatĭna Medhal [Introduction to the Administration of the Ottoman State]* (Istanbul, 1941). The following article by an outstanding Turkish historian minimizes Byzantine influence on Ottoman institutions: Köprülü Zade Fouad Bey, "Les institutions byzantines ont-elles joué un role dans la formation des institutions ottomanes?" *Résumés des communications presentées au VIIᵉ congrès international des sciences historiques* (Warsaw, 1933), pp. 297–302. See also by the same author, *Aclune osservazioni all influenza delle istituzioni bizantine sulla istituzioni ottomane* (Rome, 1953, not consulted). For the composition and functioning of the Ottoman dynasty, see A. D. Alderson, *The Structure of the Ottoman Dynasty* (Oxford, 1956), which has invaluable genealogical tables; N. M. Penzer, *The Harem* (London, 1936); and the two works by Barnette Miller listed in Chapter 4.

The position of non-Moslems is treated in T. W. Arnold, *The Preaching of Islam: A History of the Propagation of the Muslim Faith* (London, 1913, 2nd rev. and enl. ed.) and F. W. Hasluck, *Christianity and Islam under the Sultans* (Oxford, 1929). For the position of the Jews, consult the biographies of the outstanding Ottoman Jewish family by C. Roth: *The House of Nasi: Dona Grãcia* (Philadelphia, 1948), and *The House of Nasi: The Duke of Naxos* (Philadelphia, 1948), which contain references to the numerous other studies of this subject. Works on the position of the Patriarchate and of Balkan Christianity are listed at the end of the following chapter.

By far the most interesting and revealing introduction to Ottoman culture is A. Pallis, *In the Days of the Janissaries: Old Turkish Life as Depicted in the "Travel-Book" of Evliya Chelebi* (London, 1951). This is based mainly on J. von Hammer-Purgstall, *Evliya Efendi: Narrative of Travels in Europe, Asia and Africa* (London, 1846–1850, 2 vols.), which in turn is a translation of only two of the original ten volumes. For Evliya's biography and a good bibliography, see F. Babinger, *Die Geschichtsschreiber der Osmanen und ihre Werke* (Leipzig, 1927), pp. 219 ff.

The first serious study of Ottoman literature was by Hammar-Purgstall, *Geschichte der osmanischen Dichtkunst* (Pesth, 1836–1838, 4 vols.), but this is more a dictionary of Ottoman poets than a history of Ottoman poetic art as the title suggests. It has been superseded by the standard work of E. J. W. Gibb, *A History of Ottoman Poetry* (London, 1900–1909, 6 vols.). This should be checked with the article on "Turks–Literature" in the *Encyclopedia of Islam* by Köprülü Zade Mehmed Fu'ad, who assigns more individuality to Ottoman literature than does Gibb. For the poetic craze in Ottoman society, see A. Navarian, *Les sultans poètes (1451–1808)* (Paris, 1936). For Ottoman music, see H. G. Farmer, *Turkish Instruments of Music in the Seventeenth Century* (Glasgow, 1937); the important long article by R. Yekta Bey, "La musique turque," in A. Lavignac, *Encyclopédie de la Musique* (Paris, 1923), II, 2485–3064; and the analysis of Islamic music in general in the article "Musiki" by H. G. Farmer in the *Encyclopedia of Islam.*

Ottoman institutions fascinated contemporary Western Europeans and stimulated numerous works by travelers and envoys. Most revealing are the four confidential letters addressed by the Hapsburg ambassador, Ogier Ghiselin de Busbecq, to his friend Nicolas Michault between the years 1555 and 1562. The two-volume edition, *The Life and Letters of Ogier Ghiselin de Busbecq,* ed. by C. T. Forster and F. H. Blackburne Daniell (London, 1881), contains notes and additional information lacking in the more convenient single volume, *Turkish Letters of Ogier Ghiselin de Busbecq,* ed. by E. S. Forster (Oxford, 1927). Some of the numerous other contemporary Western accounts of the Ottoman Empire are listed in Lybyer, *op. cit.,* pp. 307–330. Ottoman influence on contemporary Western literature and thought is described for the Elizabethan period in S. C. Chew, *The Crescent and the Rose* (New York, 1937); for the period to 1840, in B. P. Porter, *Islam in English Literature* (Beirut, 1939); for eighteenth-century English drama, in T. B. Clark, *Oriental England* (Shanghai, 1939); and for France, in C. D. Rouillard, *The Turk in French History, Thought, and Literature (1520–1660)* (Paris, 1938).

Finally, see the valuable bibliography on Ottoman-European cultural interaction in D. M. Vaughan, *Europe and the Turk: A Pattern of Alliances 1350–1700* (Liverpool, 1954), pp. 280–287.

7. Balkan Peninsula Under Ottoman Rule

No period of modern European history remains as obscure as the five centuries of Ottoman rule in the Balkans. The difficulty of languages, the scarcity of materials, and the tendency of Balkan historians to turn their backs to a period of subjugation have contributed to this situation. Yugoslav historians since World War II have made the most serious attempts to analyze the nature of Turkish institutions in the Balkans. Their works are listed and described in the bibliographical articles by W. S. Vucinich, "Postwar Yugoslav Historiography," *Journal of Modern History,* XXIII (March, 1951), 53–54; and "The Yugoslav Lands in the Ottoman Period: Postwar Marxist Interpretations of Indigenous and Ottoman Institutions," *Journal of Modern History,* XXVII (September, 1955), 287–305.

For studies in the Western languages see the general histories of Hammer-Purgstall, Zinkeisen, Iorga, and also the following: F. Giese, "Die geschichtlichen Grundlagen für die Stellung der christlichen Untertanen im osmanischen Reiche," *Der Islam,* XIX (1931), 264–277; H. A. R. Gibb and H. Bowen, *Islamic Society and the West: A Study of the Impact of Western Civilization on Moslem Culture in the Near East:* Vol. I, *Islamic Society in the Eighteenth Century* (New York, 1950); M. Braun, "Türkenherrschaft und Türkenkampf bei den Balkanslawen," *Die Welt als Geschichte,* VI (1940), 124–139; and S. N. Fisher, "Ottoman Feudalism and Its Influence upon the Balkans," *Historian,* XV (Autumn, 1952), 3–22. The favorable position of the Balkan peoples under Turkish rule in the early centuries is emphasized by G. Vernadsky, "On Some Parallel Trends in Russian and Turkish History," *Transactions of the Connecticut Academy of Arts and Sciences,* XXXVI (July, 1945), 25–36. Bibliographies of the various Balkan peoples during the Turkish period are given in the relevant chapters below. Special mention should be made of the following article which specifically compares Turkish and Venetian administration in Crete and emphasizes the preference of the inhabitants for the former: C. Tukin, "Osmanli

Imparatorluğunda Girit Isyanlari: 1821 Yilina Kadar Girit," ["Cretan Revolts in the Ottoman Empire: Crete to 1821,"] *Belleten*, IX (April, 1945), 163–211.

For the migrations of peoples during the Turkish period see the works on ethnography listed in Chapter 1, and also the following: T. Kowalski, "Les Trucs balkaniques," *Revue internationale des études balkaniques*, IV (1936), 420–430; E. Pittard, "Les peuples que les Turcs ont amenés dans les Balkans," *Revue internationale des études balkaniques* II (1935), 195–200; S. A. Birnbaum "The Jewries of Eastern Europe," *Slavonic and East European Review*, XXIX (June, 1951), 420–443; and T. Stoianovich, "L'économie balkanique aux XVIIͤ et·XVIIIͤ siècles" (University of Paris, unpublished doctoral dissertation, 1952), ch. 1. The latter is the most important single source.

General studies of the Orthodox Church are presented from three different viewpoints in A. D. Kyriakos, *Geschichte der orientalischen Kirchen von 1453–1898* (Leipzig, 1902); B. J. Kidd, *The Churches of Eastern Christendom from A.D. 451 to the Present Time* (London, 1927); A. K. Fortescue, *The Orthodox Eastern Church* (London, 1927). For the position of the Orthodox Church in the Ottoman Empire, see T. H. Papadopoullos, *Studies and Documents Relating to the History of the Greek Church and People under Turkish Domination* (Brussels, 1952); H. Scheel, *Die staatsrechtliche Stellung der ökumenischen Kirchenfürsten in der alten Türkei: Ein Beitrag zur Geschichte der Türkischen Verfassung und Verwaltung* (Berlin, 1942); G. G. Arnakis, "The Greek Church of Constantinople and the Ottoman Empire," *Journal of Modern History*, XXIV (September, 1952), 235–250. The relations of the Constantinople Patriarchate with the non-Greek peoples of the peninsula are presented from conflicting viewpoints in J. Konidaris *He Hellenike Ekklesia os politistike dynamis en te historia tes Chersonesou tou Aimou* [*The Greek Church as a Civilizing Force in the History of the Balkan Peninsula*] (Athens, 1940); L. Hadrovics, *Le peuple serbe et son église sous la domination turque* (Paris, 1947); I. Snêgarov, *Istoriia na Ochridskata arkhiepiskopiia patriarshiia ot padaneto i pod turtsitê do neinoto unishtozhenie (1394–1787g)* [*History of the Ohrid Archdiocese Patriarchate from Its Fall to the Turks to Its Abolition (1394–1767)*] (Sofia, 1931); and C. Jelavich, "Some Aspects of Serbian Religious Development in the Eighteenth Century," *Church History*, XXIII (June, 1954), 3–11. Finally, see T. W. Arnold, *The Preaching of Islam: A History of the Propagation of the Muslim Faith* (London, 1913), ch. 6, for a description of the spread of Islam in the Balkans and the position of the Christians under Moslem rule.

Balkan folk literature in general is described in A. Ognjanov, *Die Volkslieder der Balkanslaven* (Berlin, 1941); K. Dieterich, "Die Volksdichtung der Balkanländer in ihren gemeinsamen Elementen: Ein Beitrag zur vergleichenden Volkskunde," *Zeitschrift des Vereins für Volkskunde*, XII (1902), 145–155, 272–291, 403–415; G. A. Megas, "La civilisation dite balkanique: La poésie populaire des pays des Balkans," *L'hellénisme contemporaire*, IV (January–February, 1950), 8–30. For individual countries see C. Fauriel, *Chants populaires de la Grèce moderne*, (Paris, 1824–1825, 2 vols.); S. Michaelides, *The Neohellenic Folk-Music* (Limassol, Cyprus, 1948); D. Subotić, *Yugoslav Popular Ballads: Their Origin and Development* (Cambridge, Eng., 1922); G. R. Noyes and L. Bacon, *Heroic Ballads of Servia* (Boston, 1913); H. Rootham, *Kossovo: Heroic Songs of the Serbs* (Oxford, 1920); D. H. Low, *The Ballads of Marko Kraljević* (Cambridge, Eng., 1922); W. A. Morison, *The Revolt of the Serbs against the Turks (1804–1813)*: *Translations from the Serbian National Ballads of the Period* (Cambridge, Eng., 1942); A. Strauss, *Bulgarische Volksdichtung* (Vienna, 1895); G. Rosen, *Bulgarische Volksdichtungen* (Leipzig, 1879); R. A. Patterson, *Romanian Songs and Ballads* (London, 1919).

Excellent studies of modern Greek literature are available in C. Th. Demaras, *Historia tes neoellenikes logotechnias* [*History of Modern Greek Literature*] (Athens, 1948–1949, 2 vols.); C. A. Trypanis, *Medieval and Modern Greek Poetry: An Anthology* (Oxford, 1951); R. Dalven, *Modern Greek Poetry* (New York, 1949). The first is the standard work on the subject; the second gives a useful introductory survey of Greek literature since A.D. 330 together with selections in the original; and the third also provides a summary of modern Greek literary development together with selections in translation. For the written literature of the northern Balkans see M. S. Stanoyevich, *Early Yugoslav Literature (1100–1800)* (New York, 1922); E. Turdeanu, *La littérature bulgare du XIVe siècle et sa diffusion dans les pays roumains* (Paris, 1947); E. Turdeanu, "Le Livre grec en Russie: L'apport des presses de Moldavie et de Valachie (1682–1725)," *Revue des études slaves*, XXVI (1950), 69–87; and J. Torbarina, *Italian Influence on the Poets of the Ragusan Republic* (London, 1931). Finally, the problem of bilinguism is well summarized in K. Sandfeld and P. Skok, "Langues balkaniques," *Revue internationale des études balkaniques,* IV (1936), 465–481. See also J. M. Rife, "The Language Situation in Greece Today," *Classical Journal,* XXXVII (November, 1941), 65–76; W. K. Matthews, "Sources of Old Church Slavonic," *Slavonic and East European Review,* XXVIII (April, 1950), 466–485; and the two articles by W. R. Loader, "Spoken Greek," *Greece and Rome,* XIII (June, 1944), 73–80, and "Purified or Popular? A Note on the Language Promlem of Modern Greece," *Greece and Rome,* XIX (October, 1950), 116–122.

For Turkish cultural influence in the Balkans see P. Skok, "Restes de la langue turque dans les Balkans," *Revue internationale des études balkaniques,* II (1935), 247–260; S. S. Bobčev, "Notes comparées sur les hadjis balkaniques," *Revue internationale des études balkaniques,* III (1936), 1–12; W. S. Vucinich, "Yugoslavs of the Moslem Faith," in R. J. Kerner, ed., *Yugoslavia* (Berkeley, Calif., 1949), pp. 261–275; and R. S. Atabinen, *Les apports turcs dans le peuplement et la civilisation de l'Europe orientale* (Paris, 1952), the latter being a disappointing propagandist tract.

8. Decline of the Ottoman Empire

The decline of the Ottoman Empire has not received the attention it deserves. Apart from the references in the general histories of Hammar-Purgstall, Zinkeisen, and Iorga, there is the superficial and unsatisfactory study by A. Zeki, *Essai sur les causes de la décadence de l'empire Ottoman* (Paris, 1929). More rewarding are the accounts left by the Ottomans themselves in their Nasibat literature. An excellent example of this literature is available in English translation by W. L. Wright, Jr., *Ottoman Statecraft: The Book of Counsel for Vizirs and Governors of Sari Mehmed Pasha . . .* (Princeton, N. J., 1935). This work also provides in pp. 17–21 a useful description of this Nasibat literature as well as bibliographical references to French and English translations of Qochi Bey, Katib Chelebi, and other Turkish authors.

Another important source is the testimony of contemporary Western travelers and envoys. Perhaps the most outstanding of these is Sir Paul Rycaut, who served for eighteen years as English consul at Smyrna and then as secretary of the English Embassy at Constantinople. His observations on Ottoman history and institutions at the beginning of the decline rank with those of Busbecq when the empire was at its height. Of the numerous editions of his works, the following were used for this study: *The Present State of the Ottoman Empire* . . . (London, 1668), and *The History of the Turks Beginning with the Year 1679* . . . (London, 1700). Some of the numerous other Western accounts of the Ottoman Empire during the early period of decline are listed in the footnote references of Wright, *op. cit.*

A serious gap in the historiography of Ottoman decline is in the relationship and interaction of the Ottoman Empire and the West. For the intellectual relations see the revealing essay by Lewis V. Thomas, "Ottoman Awareness of Europe 1650–1800" (in manuscript); T. C. Young, ed., *Near Eastern Culture and Society: A Symposium on the Meeting of East and West* (Princeton, N. J., 1951), which has important relevant contributions by G. Sarton, E. E. Calverley, A. Adnan-Adivar, and L. V. Thomas; and, finally, the pioneer study by A. Adnan, *La science chez les Turcs ottomans* (Paris, 1939). A second enlarged edition of the latter work was published in Turkish in Istanbul in 1943. The additional material is described in the review by R. N. Frye in *Isis,* XXXVIII (November, 1947), 121–125. For Piri Reis's map of the world, see P. Kahle, "A Lost Map of Columbus," *Geographical Review,* XXIII (1935), 621–638.

The economic relations between the Ottoman Empire and the West are studied in several important works: M. Epstein, *Early History of the Levant Company* (London, 1908); A. C. Wood, *History of the Levant Company* (London, 1935); C. H. Matterson, "English Trade in the Levant 1693–1753" (Harvard University, unpublished doctoral dissertation 1936); and the classic studies of P. Masson, *Histoire du commerce français dans le Levant au XVIIe siècle* (Paris, 1896) and *Histoire du commerce français dans le Levant au XVIIIe siècle* (Paris, 1911). See also the more recent articles of A. L. Horniker, "William Harborne and the Beginning of Anglo-Turkish Diplomatic and Commercial Relations," *Journal of Modern History,* XIV (September, 1942), 289–316; "Anglo-French Rivalry in the Levant from 1583 to 1612," *Journal of Modern History,* XVIII (September, 1946), 289–305. Closely related are the studies of the capitulatory privileges, the most important being G. P. du Rausas, *Le régime des capitulations dans l'empire ottoman* (Paris, 1902–1905, 2 vols.); P. M. Brown, *Foreigners in Turkey: Their Juridical Status* (Princeton, N. J., 1914); N. Sousa, *The Capitulatory Regime of Turkey* (Baltimore, 1933). These and other works are written from the viewpoint of Western commercial relations without considering the effect of these relations on the Ottoman economy. An exception is the pioneer work of M. Akdag, "Osmanli Imparatorlugunun kuruluş ve inkişaf devrinde Türkiye' nin ikitsadî vaziyeti," ["The Economic Position of Turkey during the Foundation and the Rise of the Ottoman Empire,"] *Belleten,* XIII (July, 1949), 497–568, and XIV (July, 1950), 319–411. This valuable work emphasizes the injurious effect of Western trade upon the Ottoman economy and presents evidence which suggests a significant parallel between Ottoman and Spanish economic history, e.g., compare the Akdag article with E. Hamilton, "The Decline of Spain," *Economic History Review,* VIII (May, 1938), 168–179. The same author, M. Akdag, presents economic factors in the decline of the janissaries in his article "Yeniçeri ocak nizaminin bozuluşu," ["Decline of the Janissaries,"] *Ankara Üniversitesi, Dil ve Tarih-Coğrǎfya Fakültesi Dergisi,* V (May–June, 1947), 291–313. Another important work in this field is the unpublished doctoral dissertation by Traian Stoianovich, "L'économie balkanique aux XVIIᵉ et XVIIIᵉ siècles" (University of Paris, 1952), which is based on the French consular archives and which contains much valuable data and interpretation. See also L. Gucer, "Le commerce intérieur des céréales dans l'empire ottoman pendant la seconde moitié du XVIᵉ siècle, *"Revue de la faculté des sciences économiques de l'université d'Istanbul,* XI (1949), 179–182.

Another subject requiring serious research for an understanding of Ottoman decline is the location of power after the weakening of the sultans. Wright, *op. cit.,* pp. 56–60, states that the slave courtiers surrounding the puppet rulers controlled the empire, whereas Akdag, *loc. cit.,* p. 394, assigns more influence to the *eşraf* class consisting of big landowners and high officials. Closely related is the question of the influence of various national groups at various periods. It appears that the Serbs and Jews played a dominant role in imperial affairs to the seventeenth century and were replaced by the Greeks to 1821 and by the Bulgarians and Armenians for the remaining period. To what extent was this true and precisely what was the source and nature of their influence? Also, how did Western financial imperialism affect power relationships within the empire after the Crimean War? A study of these problems would throw much light on Ottoman history since the sixteenth century.

Another virgin field for research is the history and effect of the plague on the Ottoman Empire. The best general history and bibliography on the plague in general is G. Sticker, *Abhandlungen aus der Seuchengeschichte und Seuchenlehre* (Giessen, 1908, 2 vols.). Of the numerous accounts of contemporary observers the following are outstanding: A. F. Bulard, *De la peste orientale* (Paris, 1839); W. Macmichael, *Journey from Moscow to Constantinople in the Years 1817, 1818* (London, 1819); R. Walsh, *Narrative of a Journey from Constantinople to England* (London, 1829); and the first twelve volumes of the *Journal of the Royal Geographical Society of London,* which contain the journals of numerous British travelers in the Ottoman Empire in the early nineteenth century.

Finally, see the following bibliographical article for the valuable pioneer research by Yugoslav historians on Ottoman institutions in Yugoslavia and the peninsula as a whole: W. S. Vucinich, "The Yugoslav Lands in the Ottoman Period: Postwar Marxist Interpretations of Indigenous and Ottoman Institutions," *Journal of Modern History,* XXVII (September, 1955), 287–305.

9. Balkan Peninsula during Ottoman Decline

Most of the scanty bibliography concerning the Balkans during this period of Ottoman decline will be found above in Chapter 8 and below in the relevant "national" chapters in Part IV. No comprehensive survey of Balkan institutions and developments during this period is available, though a considerable amount of information may be found scattered in H. A. R. Gibb and H. Bowen, *Islamic Society and the West:* Vol. I, *Islamic Society in the Eighteenth Century* (London, 1950). Much material is also available in the numerous travel accounts, a few of which are mentioned in the Notes for this chapter.

The evolution and character of the chifliks are analyzed in the following works: R. Busch-Zantner, *Agrarverfassung, Gesellschaft und Siedlung in Südosteuropa in besonderer Berücksichtigung der Türkenzeit* (Leipzig, 1938); J. Tomasevich, *Peasants, Politics and Economic Change in Yugoslavia* (Stanford, Calif., 1955); H. Inalcik, "Land Problems in Turkish History," *Muslim World,* XLV (July, 1955), 221–228; T. Stoianovich, "Land Tenure and Related Sectors of the Balkan Economy 1600–1800," *Journal of Economic History,* XIII (Fall, 1953), 398–411; and the same author's essay in manuscript form: "Lost Villages, Recolonization, and Peasant Servitude: A Balkan Example." The Stoianovich articles are especially important in showing the economic and political repercussions of the rise of the chiflik regime.

The most important single work on the rise of commerce and industry in the Balkans during this period is the unpublished doctoral dissertation by T. Stoianovich, "L'économie balkanique aux XVIIᵉ et XVIIIᵉ siècles" (University of Paris, 1952). Material may also be found in Gibb and Bowen mentioned above, in F. Braudel, *La Méditerranée et le monde méditerranean à l'époque de Philippe II* (Paris, 1949); economic histories of individual Balkan states (listed in relevant chapters below) such as I. Sakazov, *Bulgarische Wirtschaftsgeschichte* (Berlin and Leipzig, 1929); and contemporary accounts by the consuls of foreign powers who followed economic developments—for example, F. Beaujour, *A View of the Commerce of Greece Formed after an Annual Average from 1787 to 1797* (London, 1800).

On the awakening of the Balkan peoples, see the materials given below on individual countries. Very little has been written that is Balkan-wide in coverage, an exception being the interesting study by N. Moschopoulos, *La presse dans la renaissance balkanique* (Athens, 1931). Similar studies on a peninsular scale are needed concerning the effect upon Balkan nationalism of foreign ideologies, the development of commerce, and the rise of merchant groups at home and in foreign cities. Analyses are needed also of the roles of various elements such as the primates, the outlaws, the church prelates, and the village priests.

A comparative study of the primates among the various Balkan peoples is attempted by S. S. Bobčev in his articles "Coup d'oeil sur le régime juridique des Balkans sous le régime ottoman," *Revue internationale des études balkaniques,* II (1935), 185–194, and "Notes comparées sur les çorbacis chez les peuples balkaniques et en particulier chez les Bulgares," *Revue internationale des études balkaniques,* V–VI (1937–1938), 428–445. These studies are so elementary, however, that this important subject may be considered virtually unexplored. On the outlaws, only restricted studies are available, such as G. Rosen, *Die Balkan Haiduken im Beitrag zur innern Geschichte des Slawenthums* (Leipzig, 1878); J. W. Baggally, *The Klephtic Ballads in Relation to Greek History 1715–1821* (Oxford, 1937); and P. S. Spandonidis, "Le Clefte," *L'Héllenisme contemporaine,* January–February, 1954, pp. 3–18. General studies of the Orthodox Church are given in Chapter 7. For conflicting interpretations of the attitude and role of the church concerning education and the new learning in general, compare the Marxist historian G. K. Kordatos, *Neoellenike politike historia* [*Modern Greek Political History*] (Athens, 1925), with the series of articles by the Greek church official and historian M. I. Gedeon, in *Ekklesiastike Aletheia* [*Ecclesiastical Truth*], July 6, August 17, and September 21, 1888.

10. Defeat by Austria

Three contemporary sources for the period 1566–1656 deserve special mention: *The Negotiations of Sir Thomas Roe in His Embassy to the Ottoman Porte from the Year 1621 to 1628 Inclusive* . . . (London, 1740), which consists of the reports of the ambassador during the years indicated; *The Turkish History* . . . *by Richard Knolles, with a Continuation to the Present Year MDCLXXXVII* . . . *by Sir Paul Rycaut* . . . (London, 1687, 2 vols.), which includes a detailed and valuable account of this period by Rycaut; and Evliya Effendi, *Narrative of Travels in Europe, Asia, and Africa in the Seventeenth Century*. Translated from the Turkish by the Ritter Joseph von Hammer (London, 1850, 2 vols.), which contains revealing firsthand accounts of the various rulers, particularly the author's idol, Murad IV. See also the report on the state of the Ottoman Empire, by Lello, the English ambassador in Constantinople from 1597 to 1606, edited by the Turkish scholar Orhan Burian, *The Report of Lello, Third English Ambassador to the Sublime Porte* (Ankara, 1952).

For the careers of Sokolli (Sokolovich) and of his rival, Nasi, see M. Brosch, *Geschichten aus dem Leben dreier Grosswesire* (Gotha, 1899) and C. Roth, *The House of Nasi: The Duke of Naxos* (Philadelphia, 1948). On the taking of Cyprus the standard version now is to be found in Sir George Hill's exhaustive three-volume *History of Cyprus* (Cambridge, Eng., 1940–1948), in the third volume of which there is a detailed and documented account of both the military and diplomatic aspects of the conquest. Important sources for the diplomacy of the period are E. Charrière, ed., *Négociations de la France dans le Levant* (Paris, 1848–1860, 4 vols.), in *Collection de documents inédits sur l'histoire de France;* and G. Tongas, *Les relations de la France avec l'empire ottoman durant la première moitié du XVIIᵉ siècle* (Toulouse, 1942), the latter being based on hitherto unpublished documents.

The naval engagements during these years, including Lepanto and the Cretan War, are described at length in R. C. Anderson, *Naval Wars in the Levant 1559–1853* (Princeton, N. J., 1952), which includes an extensive bibliography. This work is almost exclusively factual and needs to be supplemented by the more interpretive account in H. A. R. Gibb and H. Bowen, *Islamic Society and the West: A Study of the Impact of Western Civilization on Modern Culture in the Near East:* Vol. I, *Islamic Society in the Eighteenth Century* (New York, 1950), pp. 88–106, which analyzes changes in naval technology. See also W. Bigge, *Der Kampf von Candia in den Jahren 1667–69* (Berlin, 1899).

For the war on the Danube, see the relevant chapters on Michael the Brave and Transylvania in R. W. Seton-Watson, *A History of the Roumanians from Roman Times to the Completion of Unity* (Cambridge, Eng., 1934); C. Benda, "Les relations politiques entre la principauté transylvaine, la Moldavie et la Valachie," *Revue d'histoire comparée*, n. s., I (1943), 352–400; L. Hudita, *Histoire des négociations entre la France et la Transylvanie au XVIIᵉ siècle* (Paris, 1927); D. Angyal, "Gabriel Bethlen," *Revue historique*, CLVIII (May–June, 1928), 19–80; *Etienne Báthory: Roi de Pologne, Prince de Transylvanie* (Cracow, 1935); A. Lefaivre, *Les Magyars pendant la domination ottomane en Hongrie (1526–1722)* . . . (Paris, 1902, 2 vols.); and L. Fekete, "Osmanli Türkleri ve Macàrlar 1366–1699," ["Ottoman Turks and the Hungarians 1366–1699,"] *Belleten*, XIII (October, 1949), 664–743. The latter contains a summary of the

Turkish conquest of Hungary and a good account of all aspects of Hungarian life under the Hapsburgs.

For the Persian wars, there are the biography by L. L. Bellan, *Chah Abbas I. Sa vie, son histoire* (Paris, 1932); the fascinating and fully documented account of the Sherley brothers in S. C. Chew, *The Crescent and the Rose: Islam and England During the Renaissance* (New York, 1937), chs. 4–6; E. D. Ross, *Sir Anthony Sherley and His Persian Adventure* (London, 1932); and F. Babinger, *Sherleiana* (Berlin, 1932), the latter using Oriental sources. A related episode is described by E. Pears, "The Spanish Armada and the Ottoman Porte," *English Historical Review*, VIII (July, 1893), 439–466. The efforts of Elizabeth to gain Turkish aid at the time of the Armada are described also in D. M. Vaughan, *Europe and the Turk: A Pattern of Alliances 1350–1700* (Liverpool, 1954), pp. 166–175. This work also provides a valuable summary of the other aspects of Turkish-European relations during the century covered by this chapter.

General surveys of the second half of the seventeenth century are available in the relevant sections of Hammer-Purgstall, Zinkeisen, and Iorga; in the Knolles and Rycaut history listed in the preceding chapter; and in the following continuation of the latter work: P. Rycaut, *The History of the Turks Beginning with the Year 1679 . . . Until the End of the Year 1698, and 1699 . . .* (London, 1700). This important source contains much firsthand information and documentary material. For the Kiuprili family see M. Brosch, *Geschichten aus dem Leben dreier Grosswesire* (Gotha, 1899), which deals with Sokolli (Sokolovich) and the first two Kiuprilis; the article on the entire Kiuprili family in the *Encyclopedia of Islam* (Franz Babinger); and the excellent characterizations in Leopold von Ranke, *Die Osmanen und die spanische Monarchie im XVI und XVII Jahrhundert . . .* (Leipzig, 1877). No adequate history of this important family appears to be available in any language.

The first Russo-Turkish War arose from Sokolli's grandiose attempt in 1569 to build a canal between the Don and Volga rivers, recapture Astrakhan from the Russians, sail a fleet from the Black to the Caspian Sea, and thus open a second front against the Persians. The history of this project is given in H. Inalcik, "Osmanli-Rus rekabepinin menşei ve Don-Volga kanali teşebbüsü," ["The Origin of the Ottoman-Russian Rivalry and the Don-Volga Canal,"] *Belleten*, XII (April, 1948), 349–402. Various aspects of the struggle for the Ukraine are presented in J. von Hammer-Purgstall, *Geschichte der Chane der Krim unter osmanischen Herrschaft . . .* (Vienna, 1856); *Cambridge History of Poland from the Origins to Sobieski (to 1696)* (Cambridge, Eng., 1950); M. Hrushevsky, *A History of Ukraine* (New Haven, Conn., 1941); W. E. D. Allen, *The Ukraine: A History* (Cambridge, Eng., 1941); and C. B. O'Brien, "Russia and Turkey, 1677–1681: The Treaty of Bakhchisarai," *Russian Review*, XII (October, 1953), 259–268. See also N. Smirnov, *Rossiia i Turtsiia v XVI–XVII vv.* (Moscow, 1946), 2 vols. (not consulted).

An excellent summary of the military and diplomatic aspects of the siege of Vienna and of the following war of the Holy League is given by J. B. Wolf, *The Emergence of the Great Powers 1685–1715* (New York, 1951). The author makes clear the interrelation of the Turkish war and the Hapsburg-Valois feud, and also lists the most important sources in his footnotes and bibliography. A revealing Turkish account of the siege, left by the Master of Ceremonies for the Sublime Porte, has been recently translated and edited by R. F. Kreutel, *Kara*

Mustafa vor Wien, Das turkische Tagebuch der Belagerung Wiens 1683 [*Osmanische Geschichtsschreiber,* No. 1] (Vienna, 1955). For the Slavic sources see the fine little study by B. H. Sumner, *Peter the Great and the Ottoman Empire* (Oxford, 1949), which presents important data on Russian relations with the Tatars, the Turks, and the Balkan Slavs. This should be supplemented with P. M. Kontogiannes, *Hoi Hellenes kata ton proton epi Aikaterines II ·rossotourkikon polemon (1768–1774)* [*The Greeks during the First Russo-Turkish War under Catherine II (1768–1774)*] (Athens, 1903), which contains an introductory section on early Greco-Russian relations, and by R. C. Anderson, *Naval Wars in the Levant 1559–1853* (Princeton, N. J., 1952), for the Venetian and Russian naval campaigns. Finally, the most detailed study of the Karlowitz (Syemski Karlovci) peace settlement is the unpublished doctoral dissertation by W. B. Munson, "The Peace of Karlowitz" (University of Illinois, 1940). The following bibliography should be noted: W. Sturminger, *Bibliographie und Ikonographie der Turkenbelagerungen Wiens 1529 und 1683* (Cologne, 1955).

11. Defeat by Russia

For the defeat of Peter the Great the best account is given in B. H. Sumner, *Peter the Great and the Ottoman Empire* (Oxford, 1949). Sumner confines himself to Peter's relations with the Rumanians and Balkan Slavs, so his account should be supplemented by P. M. Kontogiannes, *Hoi Hellenes kata ton proton epi Aikaterines II rossotourkikon polemon (1768–1774)* [*The Greeks During the First Russo-Turkish War under Catherine II (1768–1774)*] (Athens, 1903), in which pp. 11–28 deal with Peter's relations with the Greeks. Also noteworthy is S. Bogoiavlenskii, "Iz russko-serbskikh otnoshenii pri Petre Velikom," ["On Russo-Serbian Relations at the Time of Peter the Great,"] *Voprosy Istorii,* nos. 8–9 (1946), pp. 19–41. An important source for this period is *The Despatches of Sir Robert Sutton, Ambassador in Constantinople (1710–1714),* edited for the Royal Historical Society by the Turkish historian, A. N. Kurat and published in the Camden Third Series, Vol. LXXVIII (London, 1953).

For the adventures of Charles XII in Turkey, see A. Stille, *Karl XII* (Stockholm, 1918); and A. N. Kurat, *İsvec Kirali XII Karl' in Türkiyede Kalişi ve Bu Sïralarda Osmanli İmparatorluğu* [*The Stay in Turkey of Charles XII, King of Sweden, and the State of the Ottoman Empire at That Time*] (Istanbul, 1943). Ottoman diplomacy during the early eighteenth century is critically reviewed in A. N. Kurat, "XVIII Yüzyil Başi Avrupa Umumî Harbinde Türkiye' Nin Tarafsizliği," ["The Neutrality of Turkey During the General European War in the XVIII Century,"] *Belleten,* VII (April, 1943), 245–272, in which the author maintains that the Pruth Treaty was a mistake and that Turkey should have taken advantage of the involvement of the Western powers in the War of the Spanish Succession to ally herself with Sweden and defeat Russia.

Various aspects of the Turkish reconquest of the Peloponnesus are considered in the following: Leopold von Ranke, *Zur venetianischen Geschichte* (Leipzig, 1878). pp. 277–361; M. B. Sakellariou, "He anakatalepsis tes Peloponnesou hypo ton Tourkon en etei 1715," ["The Reconquest of the Peloponnesus by the Turks in 1715,"] *Hellenika,* IX (1936), 241–260; G. Finlay, *A History of Greece from Its Conquest by the Romans to the Present Time B.C. 146 to*

A.D. 1864 (Oxford, 1877, rev. ed.), V, 216 ff.; and R. C. Anderson, *Naval Wars in the Levant 1559–1853* (Princeton, N. J., 1952), ch. 8.

For the remarkable influence of Villeneuve on Ottoman relations with Austria and Russia, see A. Vandal, *Une ambassade française en Orient sous Louis XV: La mission du Marquis de Villeneuve 1728–41* (Paris, 1887). The standard study of Eugene and his campaigns is A. Arneth, *Prinz Eugen von Savoyen* (Vienna, 1858, 3 vols.). The vast bibliography on the great general is collected in B. Böhm, *Bibliographie zur Geschichte des prinzen Eugen von Savoyen und seiner Zeit* (Vienna, 1943). The Austrian defeats following his death are described in M. E. von Angeli, *Der Krieg mit der Pforte 1736–1739* (Vienna, 1880). For Russian-Turkish relations during these decades, see H. Uebersperger, *Russlands Orientpolitik in den letzen zwei Jahrhunderten* (Stuttgart, 1913); and A. S. Tveritinova, "K Istorii Russko-Turetskikh otnoshenii v Elizavetinskoe vremia," ["On the History of Russo-Turkish Relations in the Time of Elizabeth,"] *Sovyetskoe Vostokovedenie,* VI (1949), 312–326, the latter being based on the reports of Veshniakov, the Russian resident in Constantinople. A convenient summary is available in B. Nolde, *La formation de l'empire russe* (Paris, 1953), Vol. II, ch. 8, which contributes nothing new to the diplomacy of the period but does describe Russian colonization efforts in the southern territories. A detailed analysis of the negotiation and provisions of the Kuchuk Kainarji Treaty is given in E. I. Druzhinina, *Kiuchuk-Kainardzhiiskii Mir 1774 goda* (*Ego Podgotovka i Zakliuchenie*) [*The Kuchuk Kainarji Peace Treaty of 1774* (*Its Preparation and Signing*)] (Moscow, 1955). The "Introduction" in the latter work contains an analysis from a Marxist viewpoint of earlier works on this subject.

The standard work on Persian-Turkish relations during this period is Mohammed-Ali Hekmat, *Essai sur l'histoire des relations politiques irano-ottomanes de 1722 à 1747* (Paris, 1937), which is based on French, Persian, and Turkish sources. See also L. Lockhart, *Nadir Shah: A Critical Study Based Mainly upon Contemporary Sources* (London, 1938); P. Sykes, *A History of Persia* (London, 1930, 2 vols.); and M. L. Shay, *The Ottoman Empire from 1720 to 1734 as Revealed in the Despatches of the Venetian Baili* [*Illinois Studies in the Social Sciences,* Vol. XXVII, no. 3] (Urbana, Ill., 1944), which gives the shrewd comments of the Venetian envoys on Turkish relations with Persia and Russia.

The most important works on Turkish-Prussian relations are R. Porsch, *Beziehungen Friedrichs des Grossen zur Türkei 1740–1763* (Marburg, 1896), and S. Tansel, "Büyük Friedrich Devrinde Osmanli-Prusya Münasebetleri Hakkinda," ["Concerning Ottoman-Prussian Relations at the Time of Frederick the Great,"] *Belleten,* X (January, 1946), 133–165; and X (April, 1946), 271–292. The latter work shows that it was Sultan Mustafa who was opposed to intervention in the Seven Years' War, rather than Raghib Pasha, as commonly asserted.

The most brilliant, vivid, and concise analysis of Near Eastern diplomacy during the time of Catherine still is the old study by A. Sorel, *La question d'Orient au XVIIIe siècle: Le partage de la Pologne et le traité de Kainardji* (Paris, 1889), also available in translation as *The Eastern Question in the Eighteenth Century: The Partition of Poland and the Treaty of Kainardji* (London, 1898).

The most useful work on the Polish partitions and their background is the cooperative *Cambridge History of Poland from Augustus II to Pilsudski (1697–1935)* (Cambridge, Eng., 1941). See also the standard study by R. H.

Lord, *The Second Partition of Poland: A Study in Diplomatic History* (Cambridge, Mass., 1915), which includes an excellent introduction on prepartition Poland and the first partition.

For Prussia's role in the diplomacy of this period an important new work is by C. V. Easum, *Prince Henry of Prussia: Brother of Frederick the Great* (Madison, Wisc., 1942), which throws a new light on the origins of the first Polish partition and corrects the older study by Lord. The definitive biography of Frederick the Great is the four-volume work by R. Koser, *Geschichte Friedrichs des Grossen* (Berlin, 1921–1925, 7th ed.), which is more sympathetic than the critical interpretation of P. Gaxotte, *Frederick the Great* (New Haven, Conn., 1942). On Prussia and the Triple Alliance of 1788 there is P. Bailleu, "Graf Hertzberg," *Historische Zeitschrift*, XLII (1879), 442–490.

Austria's role in the diplomacy of the first Polish partition is examined in the unpublished doctoral dissertation by S. K. Padover, "Prince Kaunitz and the First Partition of Poland" (University of Chicago, 1932). A summary of the dissertation is published under the same title in the *Slavonic Review*, XIII (January, 1935), 384–398. The same author has written a sympathetic biography of *The Revolutionary Emperor: Joseph II* (New York, 1934). More relevant to Ottoman affairs is G. Ritter von Arneth, *Joseph II und Katharina von Russland. Ihr Briefwechsel* (Vienna, 1869).

British policy toward Russia and the background economic factors are analyzed in the important study of D. Gerhard, *England und der Aufstieg Russlands* (Munich, 1933). The Anglo-Russian crisis of 1791 is examined in G. B. Hertz, *British Imperialism in the Eighteenth Century* (London, 1908), ch. 5. See also Sir Richard Lodge, *Great Britain and Prussia in the Eighteenth Century* (Oxford, 1923). Finally, see the excellent, thoroughly documented articles by M. S. Anderson, "Great Britain and the Russian Fleet, 1769–70," *Slavonic and East European Review*, XXXI (December, 1952), 148–163; "Great Britain and the Russo-Turkish War of 1768–74," *English Historical Review*, LXIX (January, 1954), 39–58. The following study shows that Britain at this time was not interested in Poland or Turkey: D. B. Horn, *British Public Opinion and the First Partition of Poland* (Edinburgh, 1945).

For the principal figures in Russian foreign policy see the biographies by A. Brückner, *Katherine der Zweite* (Berlin, 1883); by G. S. Thomson, *Catherine the Great and the Expansion of Russia* (New York, 1950); and by G. Soloveytchik, *Potemkin: Soldier, Statesman, Lover and Consort of Catherine of Russia* (New York, 1947). The latter work contains important material on Potemkin's influence on Russo-Turkish relations and on his activities in the newly conquered areas. The Bruckner biography of Catherine is still the best available in a Western language, being based on original sources and providing full documentation. Russia's expansion to the Black Sea during Catherine's reign is described in B. Nolde, *La formation de l'empire russe* (Paris, 1953), chs. 9–10, which includes many quotations from Russian sources and also an analysis of the colonization and development of the new territories.

The repercussions of the Russo-Turkish wars in Greece are described in the Kontogiannes study cited above, and in M. B. Sakellariou, *He Peloponnesos kata ten deuteran Tourkokratian, 1715–1821* [*Peloponnesus During the Second Turkish Rule, 1715–1821*] (Athens, 1939), pp. 146–204; Auriant, "Les corsaires grecs alliés de la Russie 1787–89," *L'Acropole*, IX (January–March, 1934), 20–

28; and R. C. Anderson, *Naval Wars in the Levant 1559–1853* (Princeton, N. J., 1952), chs. 10, 12. The Sakellariou study is the latest and the best on the Peloponnessian revolt, but the Kontogiannes study deals in addition with developments among Greek communities in the islands, Constantinople, and Asia Minor. The role of Montenegro during Catherine's wars is presented in the interesting article by M. B. Petrovich, "Catherine II and a False Peter III in Montenegro," *American Slavic and East European Review,* XIV (April, 1955), 169–194. W. Persen, "The Russian Occupation of Beirut 1772–74," *Royal Central Asian Journal,* XLII (July–October, 1955), 275–286, describes the circumstances under which Russia for the first time ruled an Arab area and made no effort to establish durable ties with the Arab world. See also E. Tarle, *Chesmenskii voi i pervaia russkaia ekspeditsiia v Arkhipelag* (Moscow, 1945, not consulted).

12. The Balkans, the French Revolution, and Napoleon

The most recent and useful work on Napoleon and the Ottoman Empire is by V. J. Puryear, *Napoleon and the Dardanelles* (Berkeley, Calif., 1951), which is based almost exclusively on documentary sources. Puryear covers the period from 1802 to 1815. His work might be supplemented by B. Mouravieff, *L'alliance russo-turque au milieu des guerres napoléoniennes* (Paris, 1954). This study of Russia's Near Eastern policy from 1799 to 1815 is written from a strongly nationalistic viewpoint, is based only on French and Russian published materials, and needs to be checked with other works.

For Napoleon's invasion of Egypt in 1798 the most useful single work is by S. Ghorbal, *The Beginnings of the Egyptian Question and the Rise of Mehemet Ali . . .* (London, 1928), which makes clear the effects of Napoleon's expedition upon Egypt's development. For more detail on the expedition itself see the documentary work of C. de la Jonquière, *L'expédition d'Egypte* (Paris, 1899–1907, 5 vols.); and also the studies by F. Charles-Roux, *Les origines de l'expédition d'Egypte* (Paris, 1910), and *Bonaparte, gouverneur d'Egypte* (Paris, 1936). An interesting summary is available in the recent biography by J. M. Thompson, *Napoleon Bonaparte: His Rise and Fall* (New York, 1952), ch. 5.

For Selim's intervention on the side of Napoleon there are the detailed study by P. F. Shupp, *The European Powers and the Near Eastern Question 1806–1807* (New York, 1931), and the older pro-Napoleonic work by E. Driault, *La politique orientale de Napoléon 1806–1808* (Paris, 1904). On Admiral Duckworth's forcing of the Straits, see J. H. Rose, "Admiral Duckworth's Failure at Constantinople," in *The Indecisiveness of Modern War and Other Essays* (London, 1927), ch. 10; and R. C. Anderson, *Naval Wars in the Levant 1559–1853* (Princeton, N. J., 1952), ch. 15, which also deals with the other naval engagements in Egypt and elsewhere during this period. The abortive British expedition to Egypt is described in G. Douin and E. C. Fawtier-Jones, *L'Angleterre et l'Egypte: La campagne de 1807* (Cairo, 1928); and G. Douin, *Mohamed Aly: Pacha du Cairo, 1805–1807* (Cairo, 1926).

For the negotiations between Napoleon and Alexander there are, in addition to Puryear, S. Tatishchev, *Alexandre Ier et Napoléon, 1801–1812* (Paris, 1891), and A. Vandal, *Napoléon et Alexandre Ier* (Paris, 1891–1894, 3 vols.). The various projects for Ottoman partition that appeared during these years are summarized in L. S. Stavrianos, *Balkan Federation: A History of the Movement toward Balkan Unity in Modern Times* (Northampton, Mass., 1944), ch. 2. For Russian-Turkish-British relations there are the authoritative monograph of S. M. Goriainov, *Le Bosphore et les Dardanelles* (Paris, 1910), and the documentary account of Robert Adair, *Negotiations for the Peace of the Dardanelles . . .* (London, 1845, 2 vols.). The negotiation of the Bucharest Treaty is vividly described in S. Lane-Poole's biography of *Stratford Canning* (London, 1858), Vol. I, ch. 4. Finally, the guarantee issue at the Vienna Congress is discussed in C. K. Webster, *The Foreign Policy of Castlereagh 1812–1815* (London, 1931).

There is need for a solid, comprehensive study of the impact of the French Revolution and of Napoleon on the Balkans as a whole. The following studies contain general data: N. Iorga, *La révolution française et le sud-est de l'Europe* (Bucharest, 1934); F. Thierfelder, *Ursprung und Wirkung der französischen Kultureinflüsse in Südosteuropa* (Berlin, 1943); N. Moschopoulos, *La presse dans la renaissance balkanique* (Athens, 1931); *1789: Eveil des peuples: La révolution française, l'Europe centrale et les Balkans* (Paris, 1939).

French influence in Dalmatia has been studied intensively because of the aftereffect of the Illyrian movement. First should be noted the excellent analysis of economic policies and results: M. Pivec-Stele, *La vie économique des provinces illyriennes, 1809–1813* (Paris, 1930). Yugoslav works on this subject are given in J. Tomasevich, *Peasants, Politics and Economic Change in Yugoslavia* (Stanford, Calif., 1955), p. 114. Then see the following: P. Pisani, *La Dalmatie de 1797 à 1815* (Paris, 1893); V. Kisovec, "Aperçu historique de l'Illyrie jusqu'à la révolution française," *La revue slave*, VI (September–October, 1909), 105–123; F. Zwitter, "Illyrisme et sentiment yougoslave," *Le monde slave*, X (April, 1933), 39–71; II (May, 1933), 161–185, 233–243; and II (June, 1933), 358–375; E. Dard, "Les souvenirs napoléoniens en Yougoslavie," *Revue d'histoire diplomatique* XLVII (January–March, 1933), 1–9; V. Kisovec, "La révolution française et le royaume de l'Illyrie," *La revue slave*, VI (November–December, 1909), 253–287; P. Skok, "Le mouvement illyrien et les Français," *Le monde slave*, XII (June, 1935), 426–438; G. Cassi, "Les populations juliennes-illyriennes pendant la domination napoléonienne, 1806–1814," *Revue des études napoléoniennes*, XXXI (October, 1930), 193–212; XXI (November, 1930), 257–275; XXI (December, 1930), 355–369; and C. E. Black, "Fouché in Illyria," *Journal of Central European Affairs*, II (January, 1943), 386–396.

On French rule and influence in the Ionian Islands see P. Gratsiatos, *He Heptanesos hypo ten xenokratian . . . [The Ionian Islands under Foreign Rule . . .]* (Cephalonia, 1878); P. Chiotes, *Historika Apomnomoneymata*: III, *Historia tes Heptanesou kai idios tes Zakynthou [Historical Reminiscences: Vol. III, History of the Ionian Islands and Particularly of Zante]* (Corfu, 1863); G. Pautier, *Les Iles Ioniennes pendant l'occupation française et le protectorat anglais* (Paris, 1863); Comtesse Dora d'Istria, "Les Iles Ioniennes sous la domination de Venise et sous le protectorat britannique," *Revue des deux mondes*, XVI (July 15, 1858), 381–422; E. R. Rangabè, *Livre d'or de la noblesse ionienne* (Athens, 1925); and the standard economic studies by A. M. Andreades, *Peri test oikonomikes dioikeseos tes Heptanesou epi Venetokratias [Concerning the Economic Administration of the Ionian Islands under Venetian Rule]* (Athens, 1914, 2 vols.), and *He Heptanesiake demosia oikonomia kata ten periodon 1797–1814 [Ionian Public Economy During the Period 1797–1814]* (Corfu, 1936).

Napoleon's influence on Greece is considered in the following works: C.

Kerofilas, "Napoléon et la Grèce," *Les études franco-grecques,* II (June, 1919), 145–155; II (July, 1919), 202–211; II (August, 1919), 273–281; and II (September, 1919), 324–333; C. Rados, *Napoléon Ier et la Grèce* (Athens, 1921); E. Driault, *Napoléon et la résurrection de la Grèce* (Paris, 1924); the series of five articles by J. Savant, "Napoléon et la libération de la Grèce," *L'Hellenisme contemporain,* July–October, 1950, pp. 320–341 ff.; and the account by the Stephanopoli brothers, members of the Greek colony in Corsica, who were sent by Napoleon on a political mission to the Peloponnesus: Dimo and Nicolo Stephanopoli, *Voyage en Grèce* (Paris, 1800, 2 vols.).

For French influence on other regions of the Balkans at this time, see A. Boppe, *L'Albanie et Napoléon 1797–1814* (Paris, 1914); J. D. Ghika, "La France et les principautés danubiennes, 1789–1815," *Annales de l'école libre des sciences politiques,* XI (1896), 208–229; and the documentary article of A. Dumaine, "Un consulat de France en Bosnie sous le premier empire: Pierre David," *Revue d'histoire diplomatique,* XXXVIII (April–June, 1924), 129–169; XXXVIII (July-September, 1924), 301–328. For the influence of the French Revolution on the Turks, see the following article, which uses Turkish sources: B. Lewis, "The Impact of the French Revolution on Turkey," *Journal of World History* I (July, 1953), 105–125.

13. Dynamics of Balkan Politics

The best systematic studies of the state of the Ottoman Empire in the early nineteenth century are the recent work by H. A. R. Gibb and H. Bowen, *Islamic Society and the West: A Study of the Impact of Western Civilization on Moslem Culture in the Near East:* Vol. I, *Islamic Society in the Eighteenth Century* (London, 1950); and the contemporary work by I. M. D'Ohsson, *Tableau general de l'empire Othman* (Paris, 1788–1824, 7 vols.). D'Ohsson was an Armenian who served as the Swedish minister in Constantinople from 1796 to 1799 and his massive study is the standard work on the subject. The numerous accounts left by travelers are listed in S. H. Weber, *Voyages and Travels in the Near East Made During the Nineteenth Century: Being a Part of a Larger Catalogue of Works on Geography, Cartography, Voyages and Travels in the Gennadius Library in Athens* (Princeton, N. J., 1952); and F. W. Hasluck, *Christianity and Islam under the Sultans* (Oxford, 1929), I, xxi–lxiv. The following three reports are noteworthy in presenting different interpretations of the empire: W. Eton, *A Survey of the Turkish Empire . . .* (London, 1809, 4th ed.); J. C. Hobhouse, *A Journey through Albania and Other Provinces of Turkey in Europe and Asia to Constantinople During the Years 1809–1810* (London, 1813); and T. Thornton, *The Present State of Turkey . . .* (London, 1807). A striking description of the open insubordination in the empire is given by Napoleon's ambassador to Constantinople, A. F. Andreossy, *Constantinople et le Bosphore de Thrace* (Paris, 1841, 3rd ed.). An excellent analysis of conditions in the mid-nineteenth century based on travel accounts is given by B. Jelavich, "The British Traveller in the Balkans: The Abuses of Ottoman Administration in the Slavonic Provinces," *Slavonic and East European Review,* XXXIII (June, 1955), 396–413.

Ali Pasha and Pasvan-Oglu are the subjects of several studies. The following biographies of Ali Pasha are available: R. A. Davenport, *The Life of Ali Pasha* (London, 1837); S. Christowe, *The Lion of Yanina* (New York, 1941);

W. Plomer, *Ali the Lion: Ali of Tebeleni, Pasha of Yanina 1741–1822* (London, 1936); and G. Romerand, *Ali de Tebelen: Pacha de Janina 1744–1822* (Paris, 1929), the last two works being the most trustworthy. Many travelers and some diplomatic representatives have left accounts of Ali and his court, outstanding being the works of the French representative at Ali's court, F. C. H. L. Pouqueville, *Voyage en Morée, à Constantinople, en Albanie* . . . (Paris, 1805, 3 vols.); *Voyage dans la Grèce* . . . (Paris, 1820, 5 vols.); and of the British representative W. M. Leake, *Travels in the Morea* (London, 1830, 3 vols.), and *Travels in Northern Greece* (London, 1835, 4 vols.). Less detailed but exceptionally revealing and perceptive are the travel accounts of Hobhouse listed above, and of H. Holland, *Travels in the Ionian Isles, Albania* . . . *During the Years 1812 and 1813* (London, 1815). See also the following studies for the important impact of Ali Pasha on Greek affairs: I. Lamprides, *Epeirotika Meletemata* [*Epirote Studies*] (Athens, 1887–90), Pts. I–X; S. P. Aravantinos, *Historia Ale Pasa* . . . [*History of Ali Pasha* . . .] (Athens, 1895); F. Michalopoulos, *Ta Giannena kai he Neoelleniki Anagennesis 1648–1820* [*Yanina and the Modern Greek Renaissance 1648–1820*] (Athens, 1930); D. A. Zotos, *He dikaiosyne eis to kratos tou Ale Pasa* [*Justice in the State of Ali Pasha*] (Athens, 1938).

The most important source for Pasvan-Oglu is the correspondence of Baron de Mériage, the French agent in Vidin from February, 1807, to the end of 1808. His voluminous reports to Paris have been published piecemeal in A. Boppe, *La mission de l'adjudant-commandant Mériage à Vidin* (Paris, 1886); G. Iakichitch, "Notes sur Passvan-Oglu 1758–1807 par l'adjudant-commandant Mériage," *La revue slave*, I (May, 1906), 261–279, and following issues; I. Pavlovitch, "Documents inédits concernant la péninsule Balkanique et la Serbie (1795–1813)," *Mémoires de l'Académie Royale de la Serbie* (Belgrade, 1890), Vol. II; and A. J. Odobescu, "Documente culese din Achivele Ministeriului Afacerilor Straine din Paris," *Documente Privotore la Istoria Românilor* (*1781–1814*) (Bucharest, 1895), Vol. II. The most important other contemporary sources are the first volume of G. A. Olivier, *Voyage dans l'empire Othoman* (Paris, 1801); "La Bulgarie à la fin du XVIIIᵉ siècle: Mémoires de Sofroni, Évêque de Vratsa," transl. from the Bulgarian by L. Leger in *Mélanges orientaux: Textes et traductions* (Paris, 1883); and the above-mentioned works of Pouqueville, who makes penetrating comparisons of Pasvan-Oglu and Ali. See also the article in the *Encyclopedia of Islam* by F. Bajraktarević, who provides a good bibliography, and also the study by M. Teofilova, *Buntŭt na Pazvan-Oglu i negovoto znachenie za Bŭlgarskoto ozvoboditelno dvizhenie v XIX vĕk* [*Pasvan-Oglu's Insurrection and Its Significance for the Bulgarian Liberation Movement of the Eighteenth Century*] (Sofia, 1932). The latter, reviewed favorably as an important interpretation of Pasvan–Oglu's career, was not available for this study. An excellent interpretation of Pasvan-Oglu is available in D. Pantelić, *Beogradski pashaluk pred prvi srpski ustanak, 1794–1804* [*Belgrade Pashalik before the First Serbian Revolt, 1794–1804*] (Belgrade, 1949), which makes effective use of Austrian reports on Pasvan-Oglu.

The two most important works on Selim and his reform efforts are the eyewitness account of the French officer Juchereau de Saint-Denis, *Les revolutions de Constantinople* (Paris, 1819, 2 vols.), and the critical monograph by C. Schlechta-Wesehrd, *Die Revolutionen in Constantinopel* (Vienna, 1880). The Greek historian N. Moschopoulos places the Selim episode in its cultural setting in his revealing article "Le despotisme éclairé en Turquie," *Bulletin of the International Committee of Historical Sciences,* IX (1937), 147–180. Also useful is the survey of the janissaries in Theodor Manzel, "Das Korps der Janitscharen," *Beiträge zur Kenntnis des Orients,* I (1902–1903), 47–94. Finally, see the article and bibliography on Selim III in the *Encyclopedia of Islam* by J. H. Kramers. In Turkish there is the article by E. Z. Karal, "Tanzimattan evvel garplilasma hareketleri," ["Westernization of Turkey before Tanzimat,"] in the volume *Tanzimat* (Istanbul, 1940), pp. 13–30.

A basic work on this period of Ottoman history is by the Russian historian, A. F. Miller, *Mustafa Pasha Bairaktar: Ottomanskaia Imperiia v Nachale XIX Veka* [*Mustafa Pasha Bairaktar: The Ottoman Empire in the Beginning of the Nineteenth Century*] (Moscow, 1947), who gives a valuable analysis of the state of the empire, and a new appraisal of the roles of Selim and Bairaktar.

Works concerning the various economic and cultural forces responsible for the rise of Balkan nationalism are given above for Chapter 9. Greek-Slav conflict is frequently described by contemporary travelers but has not been systematically studied apart from indirect references in works like A. Gorovei, "Les peuples balkaniques dans le folklore roumain," *Revue internationale des études balkaniques,* II (1938), 469–485. The opposite trend is well described in M. Lascaris, *Hellenes kai Serboi kata tous apaleytheretikous ton agonas 1804–1830* [*Greeks and Serbians During Their Wars of Liberation 1804–1830*] (Athens, 1936). Cooperation among the Balkan peoples in the early nineteenth century requires more study, particularly because each nationalist movement seems to have had an early peninsular phase before becoming exclusive and antiforeign because of territorial disputes. Class conflict within the various subject nationalities is another basic but largely ignored problem, though contemporary travelers frequently noted evidence of it. Apart from the Marxists, the only historian who has considered this matter extensively is R. H. Davison in his valuable unpublished doctoral dissertation, "Reform in the Ottoman Empire 1856–1876" (Harvard University, 1942).

For the early phase of great-power policies in the Near East, see W. Fritzemeyer, *Christenheit und Europa* (Leipzig, 1931); F. L. Baumer, "England, the Turk, and the Common Corps of Christendom," *American Historical Review,* L (October, 1944), 26–48. For the changing relations between Britain and Russia in the Near East, see D. Gerhard, *England und der Aufstieg Russlands* (Munich, 1933), and J. H. Gleason, *The Genesis of Russophobia in Great Britain* (Cambridge, Mass., 1950). Commercial factors in Near Eastern diplomacy may be noted in C. Geblesco, *La question d'Orient et son caractère économique* (Paris, 1904); S. Costopoulo, *L'empire de l'Orient: aspects économiques et sociaux de la question d'Orient* (Paris, 1925); P. Masson, *Histoire du commerce français dans le Levant au XVIIIᵉ siècle* (Paris, 1911); A. C. Wood, *A History of the Levant Company* (London, 1935); G. B. Hertz, *British Imperialism in the Eighteenth Century* (London, 1908), ch. 5, for a study of commercial factors during the 1791 Anglo-Russian crisis; V. J. Puryear, *International Economics and the Diplomacy of the Near East: A Study of British Commercial Policy in the Levant 1834–1853* (Stanford, Calif., 1935); F. E. Bailey, "The Economics of British Foreign Policy, 1825–50," *Journal of Modern History,* XII (December, 1940), 449–484.

14. The Serbian Revolution and the South Slavs

A comprehensive survey of Yugoslav bibliography is given by E. Haumant in his article "Yougoslavie," in *Histoire et historiens depuis cinquante ans: Bibliothèque de la revue historique* (Paris, 1947), I, 454–468. The important post-World War II historical publications in Yugoslavia are thoroughly analyzed by W. S. Vucinich, "Postwar Yugoslav Historiography," *Journal of Modern History,* XXIII (March, 1951), 41–57, and "The Yugoslav Lands in the Ottoman Period: Postwar Marxist Interpretations of Indigenous and Ottoman Institutions," *Journal of Modern History,* XXVII (September, 1955), 287–305. See also *Ten Years of Yugoslav Historiography, 1945–55,* edited by J. Tadić (Belgrade, 1955, not consulted). The two most valuable studies of the South Slavs in Western languages are E. Haumant, *La formation de la Yougoslavie (XVᵉ–XXᵉ siècles)* (Paris, 1930) for the general historical development, and J. Tomasevich, *Peasants, Politics and Economic Change in Yugoslavia* (Stanford, Calif., 1954) for the economic and social evolution. Haumant may be supplemented by H. Wendel, *Der Kampf der Südslawen um Freiheit und Einheit* (Frankfort, 1925); and by G. I. Maur, *Die Jugoslawen einst und jetzt* (Leipzig, 1936, 2 vols.).

For the Hapsburg Slavs the best general study remains R. W. Seton-Watson, *The Southern Slav Question and the Hapsburg Monarchy* (London, 1911). See also the excellent chapters in R. A. Kann, *The Multinational Empire: Nationalism and National Reform in the Hapsburg Monarchy 1848–1918* (New York, 1950, 2 vols.); and O. Jaszi, *The Dissolution of the Hapsburg Monarchy* (Chicago, 1929). On Serbia alone there are no satisfactory general histories, the following being outdated: H. W. V. Temperley, *History of Serbia* (London, 1917); G. Y. Devas, *La nouvelle Servie* (Paris, 1918); and C. Mijatovich, *Servia and the Servians* (London, 1908).

For the intellectual and literary renaissance the most revealing work in English is the fascinating *Life and Adventures of Dimitrije Obradović,* translated and edited by G. R. Noyes (Berkeley, Calif., 1953). A more meaningful analysis of Obradovich is given in M. Kostić, *Dositej Obradović u istoriskoj perspektivi XVIII i XIX veka* [*Dositej Obradović in the Historical Perspective of the XVIII and XIX Centuries*] (Belgrade, 1952). On Karajich, a useful summary is available in V. Ćorović, "Vuk Karadžić," *Slavonic and East European Review,* XVI (April, 1938), 667–677. The most important full-length study is by L. Stojanović, *Život i rad Vuka Stef. Karadžića* [*The Life and Works of Vuk Stef. Karadžić*] (Belgrade, 1924).

For the role of the church in the Serbian renaissance see L. Hadrovics, *L'église serbe sous la denomination turque* (Paris, 1947); and D. Jelavich, "Some Aspects of Serbian Religious Development in the Eighteenth Century," *Church History,* XXIII (June, 1954), 3–11, which includes an excellent bibliography of Yugoslav materials. Worth noting here is an excellent study of the Serbian church in the later years by J. Mousset, *La Serbie et son église (1830–1904)* (Paris, 1908). A revealing article on Serbian historiography and general intellectual development is by M. B. Petrovich, "The Rise of Modern Serbian Historiography," *Journal of Central European Affairs,* XVI (April, 1956), 1–24.

An important study of the conditions in the Belgrade pashalik before 1804 and of the steps leading to the revolt is provided in the following work, which uses Austrian archival materials: D. Pantelić, *Beogradski pašaluk pred prvi srpski ustanak, 1794–1804* [*Belgrade Pashalik before the First Serbian Revolt 1794–1804*] (Belgrade, 1949). The most important works in Western languages on the Serbian revolution are S. Novakovich, *Der Wiedergeburt des serbischen Staates* (Sarajevo, 1912); Leopold von Ranke, *A History of Servia and of the Servian Revolution* (London, 1874, English ed.) based on materials provided by Vuk Karajich; B.-S. Cunibert, *Essai historique sur les révolutions et l'indépendence de la Serbie depuis 1804 jusqu'à 1850* (Leipzig, 1850, 2 vols.), by a well-informed Sardinian who was Milosh's private physician; and W. A. Morison, *The Revolt of the Serbs against the Turks (1804–1813): Translations from the Serbian National Ballads of the Period* (Cambridge, Eng., 1942). The standard work on the diplomacy of the revolution remains G. Yakschitch, *L'Europe et la résurrection de la Serbie, 1804–1834* (Paris, 1907). See also B. von Kállay, *Die Geschichte des serbischen Aufstandes, 1807–1810* (Vienna, 1910); P. F. Shupp, *The European Powers and the Near Eastern Question 1806–1807* (New York, 1931); A. Boppe, *Documents inédits sur les relations de la Serbie avec Napoléon I, 1807–1814* (Belgrade, 1888); and M. Lascaris, *Hellenes kai Serboi kata tous apeleutherotikous ton agonas, 1804–1830* [*Greeks and Serbians During Their Wars of Liberation, 1804–1830*] (Athens, 1936). Finally, see the excellent bibliographical article which includes Yugoslav materials: I. Avakumović, "Literature on the First Serbian Insurrection (1804–1813)," *Journal of Central European Affairs,* XIII (October, 1953), 256–260. The entire issue of *Istoriski Glasnik,* nos. 1–2 (1954), consisting of eleven articles, was devoted to the 1804 Serb revolt, in celebration of the 150th anniversary. This issue was not utilized during the preparation of this study.

An excellent brief description of everyday life in Serbia in the early nineteenth century is given in D. P. Subotić, "The Serbia of Prince Miloš," *Slavonic Review,* III (June, 1924), 156–165. For more details see the excellent study by T. R. Djordjević, *Srbija pre sto godina* [*Serbia One Hundred Years Ago*] (Belgrade, 1946). Valuable material is to be found in travelers' accounts, some of the most important being C. Robert, *Les slaves de Turquie* (Paris, 1844); A. Ubicini, *Les Serbes de Turquie* (Paris, 1865); A. Boué, *La Turquie d' Europe* (Paris, 1840, 4 vols.); A. M. L. de Lamartine, *Souvenirs, impressions, pensées et paysages pendant un voyage en Orient 1832–1833* (Paris, 1845).

On the political developments to 1878 the basic works are the monumental and unequaled studies of Slobodan Jovanović: *Ustavobranitelji* [*Defenders of the Constitution*] (Belgrade, 1912); *Druga vlada Miloša i Mihaila, 1858–1868* [*The Second Reign of Milosh and Michael, 1858–1868*] (Belgrade, 1923); *Vlada Alexandra Obrenovića* [*Reign of Alexander Obrenovich*] (Belgrade, 1936, 3 vols.); *Vlada Milana Obrenovića* [*Reign of Milan Obrenovich*] (Belgrade, 1934, 3 vols.).

There is no diplomatic history of Serbia in the nineteenth century comparable to that of Driault and Lhéritier for Greece. The following works are listed in the order of the period covered: M. Gavrilović, "The Early Diplomatic Relations of Great Britain and Serbia," *Slavonic Review,* I (June, 1922), 86–109; I (December, 1922), 333–351; and I (March, 1923), 552–560; T. W. Riker, "Michael of Serbia and the Turkish Occupation," *Slavonic and East European Review,* XII (July, 1933), 133–149; XII (January, 1934), 409–429; and XII (April, 1934), 646–658; H. Wendel, *Bismarck und Serbien in Jahre 1866* (Berlin, 1927); J. A. von Reiswitz, *Belgrad-Berlin, Berlin-Belgrad, 1866–1871* (Munich,

1936); R. W. Seton-Watson, "Les relations de l'Autriche-Hongrie et de la Serbie entre 1868 et 1874: la mission de Benjamin Kállay à Belgrade," *Le monde slave* III (February, 1926), 211–230; III (May, 1926), 186–204; III (August, 1926), 273–288; S. Jovanović, "Serbia in the Early Seventies," *Slavonic Review*, IV (December, 1925), 385–395; V. Trivanovitch, "Serbia, Russia, and Austria during the Rule of Milan Obrenovich, 1868–78," *Journal of Modern History*, III (September, 1931), 414–440; J. Ristić, *Diplomatska istorija Srbije za vreme srpskih ratova za oslobodjenje i nezavisnost 1875–1878* [*Diplomatic History of Serbia during the Serbian Wars for Freedom and Independence 1875–1878*] (Belgrade, 1896–98, 2 vols.).

The best general source for Serbian and South Slav economic development to 1878 is in J. Tomasevich, *Peasants, Politics and Economic Change in Yugoslavia* (Stanford, Calif., 1954). Contemporary travelers have left important accounts, including A. Boué, *La Turquie d' Europe* (Paris, 1840, 4 vols.) which has data on agriculture and commerce; and W. Richter, *Serbiens Zustands unter dem Fürsten Milosch bis zu dessen Regierungs—Entsagung im Jahre 1839* (Leipzig, 1840), which describes the atmosphere in Serbia in these years. Valuable monographic studies are by M. L. Stanojevich, *Die Landwirtschaft in Serbien* (Halle, 1913), and J. Krikner, *Industrie and Industriepolitik Serbiens* (Halle, 1913). On the zadruga see D. Novakovich, *La Zadrouga* (Paris, 1905); E. Sicard, *La Zadruga sud-slav dans l'évolution du groupe domestique* (Paris, 1943); and the preliminary findings of Philip E. Mosely presented in his articles "The Peasant Family: The Zadruga or Communal Joint-Family in the Balkans and Its Recent Evolution," in C. F. Ware, ed., *The Cultural Approach to History* (New York, 1940), pp. 95–108, and "Adaptation for Survival: The Varžić Zadruga," *Slavonic and East European Review*, XXI (March, 1943), 147–173. Yugoslav sources on the zadruga are given in the Tomasevich study cited above.

Works concerning Illyrism during the French Revolution and Napoleon are given in the relevant chapter above. Good material on the contributions of Kopitar, Karajich, and Gaj is available in the general studies by A. Fischel, *Der Panslawismus bis zum Weltkrieg* (Stuttgart, 1919); H. Wendel, *Der Kampf der Südslawen um Freiheit und Einheit* (Frankfort, 1925), and *Aus dem südslawischen Risorgimento* (Gotha, 1921). See also A. Wenzelides, "Liudevit Gaj, réformateur de la littérature croate, 1809–1872," *Les Balkans*, VII (November–December, 1935), 328–338; P. E. Mosely, "A Pan-Slavist Memorandum of Liudevit Gaj in 1838," *American Historical Review*, XL (July, 1935), 704–706. The latter article emphasizes Gaj's connections with Russia in the light of new documents.

South Slav cooperation during the 1848 revolution is described in the following: G. Y. Devas, "Les origines de l'unité yougoslave," *Le monde slave, I* (April, 1918), 532–549; D. Stranjaković, "La collaboration des Croates et des Serbes en 1848–1849," *Le monde slave*, XII (June, 1935), 394–404; L. S. Stavrianos, *Balkan Federation: A History of the Movement toward Balkan Unity in Modern Times* (Northampton, Mass., 1944). For the Magyar–South Slav war, see M. Schlesinger, *The War in Hungary, 1848–1849* (London, 1850, 2 vols.). Since World War II Yugoslav historians have paid attention to the role of the South Slavs in 1848, their general interpretation being critical of the "counter-revolutionary" activities of Patriarch Rajachich and Baron Jellachich. See V. Bogdanov, "Uloga podunavskih slavenskih naroda 1848–49 u svitejlu novih istraživanja sovjetske historiografije," ["The Role Played by the Danubian Slavic Peoples in 1848–49 in the Light of New Investigations in Soviet Historiography,"] *Historijski zbornik,* I (1948), 43–66; and also the monograph by the same author *Društvene i političke borbe u Hrvatskoj 1848–1849* [*Social and Political Conflicts in Croatia 1848–1849*] (Belgrade, 1949).

15. *Greek Revolution and Independent Statehood*

Although Greek historians have tended, for understandable reasons, to concentrate on the ancient and Byzantine periods of their history, a vast amount of published material is available on the Turkish and national periods. Before the bibliographical guides are considered the following article should be mentioned: P. W. Topping, "The Public Archives of Greece," *American Archivist,* XV (July, 1952), 249–257. The standard bibliography is E. Legrand, *Bibliographie hellénique* (Paris, 1885–1928, 11 vols.), which reaches 1790. For the years 1790–1800 there is A. P. Bretos, *Neoellenike Philologia* [*Modern Greek Literature*] (Athens, 1854); and for the following period, D. S. Ghines and V. G. Mexas, *Hellenike Bibliographia 1800–1863* [Greek Bibliography 1800–1863] (Athens, 1939–1941, 2 vols.). For later publications the bibliographical articles of William Miller are indispensable. These are scattered in the following journals: *History,* X (July, 1925), 110–123; *Cambridge Historical Journal,* II (1928), 229–247, and VI (1938), 115–120; *Journal of Modern History,* II (December, 1930), 612–628; *American Historical Review,* XXXVII (January, 1932), 272–279, and XL (July, 1935), 688–693; and *Journal of Modern History,* IX (March, 1937), 56–63. See also S. H. Weber's article which continues the survey, in *Journal of Modern History,* XXI (September, 1950), 250–266; and also P. W. Topping, "Historical Studies in Greece, 1940–1946," *Byzantina Metabyzantina,* I (1949), 113–127. For publications since 1945 see the invaluable *Bulletin analytique de bibliographie hellénique,* published by the French Institute of Athens. The following bibliography is useful for publications in Western languages: A. D. Brown and H. D. Jones, *Greece: A Selected List of References* (Washington, D. C., Library of Congress, 1943).

By far the most meaningful history of Greece since 1453 in a Western language is N. G. Svoronos, *Histoire de la Grèce moderne* (Paris, 1953). It is unfortunately very brief, yet more revealing than works many times its length.

The most important studies of Greece under Turkish rule are W. Miller, "Greece under the Turks," *Westminster Review,* CLXII (August, 1904), 195–210, and CLXII (September, 1904), 304–320; T. H. Papadopoullos, *Studies and Documents Relating to the History of the Greek Church and People under Turkish Domination* (Brussels, 1953); D. A. Zakythinos, "La commune grecque: Les conditions historiques d' une décentralisation administrative," *L' hellénisme contemporaine,* II (July–August, 1948), 295–310, and II (September–October, 1948), 414–428; N. Moschovakis, *To en Helladi demosion dikaion epi Tourkokratias* [*Public Law in Greece under the Turks*] (Athens, 1882); A. Andreades, *L'administration financière de la Grèce sous la domination turque* (Paris, 1902); T. Evangelides, *He paideia epi Tourkokratias* [*Education under Turkish Rule*] (Athens, 1936, 2 vols.). H. D. Bourazelis, *Ho bios tou Hellenikou laou kata ten Tourkokratian* [*The Life of the Greek People under Turkish Rule*] (Athens, 1939); G. Finlay, *A History of Greece* (Oxford, 1877, new ed.), Vols. VI and

VII; and the special number of *L'hellénisme contemporaine,* issued on May 29, 1953, under the title *1453–1953: Le cinq-centième anniversaire de la prise de Constantinople.* Half the articles in the latter work deal with the Greek people and institutions under Turkish rule.

For favorable and unfavorable interpretations respectively of the Phanariotes, see N. Iorga, "Le despotisme éclairé dans les pays roumains au XVIIIe siècle," *Bulletin of the International Committee of Historical Sciences,* IX (1937), 100–115; and M. P. Zallony, *Essai sur les Fanariotes* (Marseilles, 1824). The history and the role of both the church and the Phanariotes during the Turkish period require further study. See also D. Russo, *Studii istorice greco-române* (Bucharest, 1939, 2 vols.); R. Ortiz, "Sull 'importanza della dominazione fanariota in Rumania," *Studi Bizantini i Neoellenici,* V (1939), 252–283; L. Galdi, *Les mots d'origine neogrecque en roumain à l'époque des Phanariotes* (Budapest, 1939); J. Gottwald, "Phanariotische Studien," *Leipziger Vierteljahrschrift für Südosteuropa,* V (1941), 1–58 (not consulted), and the informative article by P. A. Argyropoulos, "Les Grecs au service de l' empire ottoman," in *1453–1953: Le cinq-centième anniversaire de la prise de Constantinople* (Athens, *L'hellénisme contemporaine,* 1953), pp. 151–178.

The economic revival of the eighteenth century is another important but neglected field. A few excellent regional studies have appeared, the most important being M. B. Sakellariou, *He Peloponnesos kata ten deuteran Tourkokratian 1715–1821 [Peloponnesus During the Second Turkish Rule 1715–1821]* (Athens, 1939); two works by N. Svoronos, *Le commerce de Salonique au XVIIIe siècle* (Paris, 1952) and *Salonique et Cavalla 1686–1792* (Paris, 1951); A. Lignos, *Historia tes nesou Hydras [History of Hydra Island]* (Athens, 1946, 1953, 2 vols.); and E. Georgiou, *Historia kai synetairismos ton Ambelakion [The History and the Cooperative of Ambelakia]* (Athens, 1951). Contemporary accounts are important in this connection, particularly those of consuls who followed and reported on economic developments, e.g., F. Beaujour, *A View of the Commerce of Greece, Formed after an Annual Average from 1787 to 1797* (London, 1800).

For the intellectual awakening, the observations of Koraïs are revealing, A. Coray, *Memoire sur l'état actual de la Grèce* (Paris, 1803). See also N. Moschopoulos, *La presse dans la renaissance balkanique* (Athens, 1931); T. E. Evangelides, *He paideia epi Tourkokratias [Education under Turkish Rule]* (Athens, 1936, 2 vols.); F. Michalopoulos, *Ta Giannena kai he Neoellenike Anagennesis 1648–1820 [Yanina and the Modern Greek Renaissance 1648–1820]* (Athens, 1930); and the first volume of C. Dimaras, *Historia tes neoellenikes logotechnias [History of Modern Greek Literature]* (Athens, 1948), which covers the period from 1453 to 1820. The standard biography of Koraïs in English is S. G. Chaconas, *Adamantios Koraïs: A Study in Greek Nationalism* (New York, 1942); a thorough study of Rhigas is by A. Dascalakis, *Rhigas Velestinlis* (Paris, 1937), and *Les oeuvres de Rhigas Velestinlis* (Paris, 1937). See also L. Branousis, *Regas* (Athens, 1953), not consulted.

There is need for a comprehensive history of the Greek revolution which will include the economic and intellectual antecedents, the attitude and role of the various classes and interests, the connections with the other Balkan peoples, and the impact on the empire as a whole. The Philike Hetairia also remains obscure in important respects, though several studies have been published recently, the outstanding being T. Ch. Kandiloros, *E Philike Hetereia [The Philike Hetai-*

ria] (Athens, 1926). The Balkan ramifications of the Philike Hetairia are considered in M. Lascaris, *Ellenes kai Serboi kata tous Apeleutherotikous ton Agonas 1804–1830 [Greeks and Serbians during Their Wars of Liberation 1804–1830]* (Athens, 1936).

A fair number of participants in the revolution left memoirs, including Makregiannes, Kolokotrones, Papadopoulos, Chrysanthopoulos, Margarites, Phrantzes, Metaxas, Dragoumes, and Kassomoules, whose works may be found in the bibliographies listed above. Recent Greek studies range from the Marxist interpretation of G. Kordatos, *Koinonike semasia tes Epanastaseos tou 1821 [Social Significance of the Revolution of 1821]* (Athens, 1946, rev. ed.); to the factual, multivolume study of D. A. Kokkinos, *He Hellenike Epanastasis [The Greek Revolution]* (Athens, 1931–.). The most recent general study in English is by C. M. Woodhouse, *The Greek War of Independence: Its Historical Setting* (London, 1952).

There is a considerable body of literature on the philhellenic movement which aided the Greek revolution, the most important works being M. A. Cline, *American Attitude toward the Greek War of Independence* (Atlanta, 1930); V. Penn, "Philhellenism in England," *Slavonic Review,* XIV (January, 1936), 363–371, and XIV (April, 1936), 647–660; "Philhellenism in Europe, 1821–28," *Slavonic Review,* XVI (April, 1938), 638–653; D. P. Whitehill, "The Philhellenic Movement in France, 1821–1830" (Harvard University, unpublished doctoral dissertation, 1939); T. Spencer, *Fair Greece Sad Relic* (London, 1954), which is a masterly study of English literary philhellenism before Byron; and finally D. Dakin, *British and American Philhellenes* (Saloniki, 1955). The latter work is especially important because it traces carefully the contributions of the philhellenes after their arrival in Greece, and presents the Greek secondary works on this subject. See also S. Larrabee, *Hellas Observed* (New York, 1957, not consulted).

For the diplomacy of the revolution see Vols. I and II of E. Driault and M. Lhéritier, *Histoire diplomatique de la Grece de 1821 à nos jours* (Paris, 1925); C. W. Crawley, *The Question of Greek Independence* (London, 1930); C. K. Webster, *The Foreign Policy of Castlereagh 1815–1822* (London, 1925); H. Temperley, *The Foreign Policy of Canning 1822–1827* (London, 1925); C. K. Webster, *The Foreign Policy of Palmerston 1830–1841* (London, 1951, 2 vols.); J. H. Gleason, *The Genesis of Russophobia in Great Britain* (Cambridge, Mass., 1950); V. J. Puryear, *France and the Levant from the Bourbon Restoration to the Peace of Kutiah* (Berkeley, Calif., 1941); Vols. I and II of T. Schiemann, *Geschichte Russlands unter Kaiser Nikolaus I* (Berlin, 1904–1909), and O. Shparo, "Rol Rossii v borbe Gretsii za nezavisimost," ["The Role of Russia in the Greek War of Independence,"] *Voprosy Istorii,* VIII (August, 1949), 52–78. The latter has revealing data on the effect of the Greek uprising on Russian Black Sea commerce, but its polemical claims concerning the initiative and contribution of Russia to Greek independence need to be checked. For the Polignac plans and other Ottoman partition projects of this period, see L. S. Stavrianos, *Balkan Federation: A History of the Movement toward Balkan Unity in Modern Times* (Northampton, Mass., 1944), ch. 2. For the 1829 definition of Russia's Near Eastern policy, see R. J. Kerner, "Russia's New Policy in the Near East after the Peace of Adrianople; Including the Text of the Protocol of 16 September, 1829," *Cambridge Historical Journal,* V (1937), 280–290. A detailed analysis of the negotiation, provisions, and significance of the Adrianople Treaty is given in S. Turan,

"1829 Edirne Antlasmasi," [Treaty of Adrianople 1829,"] *Ankara Universitesi, Dil ve Tarih-Cografiya Fakultesi Dergisi,* IX (March–June, 1951), 111–151. See also S. Lascaris, *Diplomatike historia tes Hellados, 1821–1914* [*Diplomatic History of Greece, 1821–1914*] (Athens, 1947).

Fresh and interesting material on the postrevolution developments in Greece may be found in the firsthand accounts published frequently in periodicals like *Blackwood's Edinburgh Magazine* and *Revue des deux mondes.* The reports of the French ambassador in Athens have been published by J. Poulos, "La Grèce d'Othon: textes et documents," *L'hellénisme contemporaine,* IX (September–October, 1955), 321–351, and IX (November–December, 1955), 408–447. See also the general histories of W. Miller, *A History of the Greek People 1821–1921* (London, 1922); J. Mavrogordato, *Modern Greece: A Chronicle and Survey 1800–1931* (London, 1931); and E. S. Forster, *A Short History of Modern Greece 1821–1940* (London, 1941). The standard work on Greek international relations is the diplomatic history of Driault and Lhéritier cited above.

A considerable amount of material in Western languages is available on Greek economic development. The best introduction is the detailed analysis of the social background in G. L. von Maurer, *Das griechische Volk in offentlicher, kirchlicher und privatrechtlicher Beziehung* (Heidelberg, 1835, 3 vols.). Then see A. M. Andreades, *Les progres économiques de la Grèce* (Paris, 1919); E. Tsouderos, *Le relévement économique de la Grèce* (Paris, 1919); P. Papageorgiou, *Agricultural Greece* (Athens, 1915); P. A. Decasos, *Die Landwirtschaft im heutigen Griechenland* (Berlin, 1904); X. Zolotas, *Griechenland auf dem Wege zur Industrialisierung* (Leipzig, 1926); P. Moraitinis, *La Grèce telle qu' elle est* (Paris, 1877); and E. Rochetin, "Les premières associations coopératives en Grece," *Revue politique et parlementaire,* XIX (1899), 91–110. Important data may also be found in the following journals: *The Board of Trade Journal; Weltwirtschaftliches Archiv;* and *L' économiste français.*

16. Ottoman Reform and Near Eastern Crises

For the circumstances of Mahmud's accession, see the works cited for Chapter 13 concerning Selim's career. The best brief survey of Mahmud's reforms is in H. Temperley, *England and the Near East: The Crimea* (London, 1936), which also provides an excellent bibliography. The most thorough work on Mahmud's greatest accomplishment, the elimination of the janissaries, is the excellent unpublished doctoral dissertation by H. A. Reed, "The Destruction of the Janissaries by Mahmud II in June, 1826" (Princeton University, 1951). An interesting work is B. A. Martin, *The Veiled Empress* (New York, 1933), which considers inconclusively the influence upon Mahmud of his French Creole mother.

On Mehemet Ali's career see the works reviewed by H. L. Hoskins, "Some Recent Works on Mohamed Ali and Modern Egypt," *Journal of Modern History,* IV (March, 1932), 93–103. The standard general biography is by H. Dodwell, *The Founder of Modern Egypt: A Study of Muhammad Ali* (Cambridge, Eng., 1931). An important study of Mehemet's work to 1812 is by S. Ghorbal, *The Beginnings of the Egyptian Question and the Rise of Mehemet Ali* (London, 1928). The best analysis of Mehemet's attempt at economic reconstruction is in A. Bonné, *State and Economics in the Middle East* (London, 1948), and in F. S. Rodkey, "Colonel Campbell's Report on Egypt in 1840, with Lord

Palmerston's Comments," *Cambridge Historical Journal,* III (1929), 103–114. S. Altundag has utilized Turkish, Egyptian, and Syrian archival materials in his study *Kavalali Mehmet Ali Pasa isyani: Misir-Meselsi 1831–1841* [*The Revolt of Mehemet Ali Pasha of Kavala: The Egyptian Question 1831–1841*] of which the first volume, carrying the story to 1833, was published in Ankara in 1945. Parts of this study have been published in *Belleten,* VI (1942), 229–251, on the Ottoman mission to London in 1832 to obtain aid; and VIII (1944), 231–243, on the administration of Syria by the Egyptians. See also the articles by J. H. Kramers in the *Encyclopedia of Islam* on "Muhammad Ali" and "Khediw."

On the Algerian episode of 1830 there are G. Douin, *Mohamed Ali et l'expédition d' Alger (1829–1830)* (Cairo, 1930); V. J. Puryear, *France and the Levant from the Bourbon Restoration to the Peace of Kutiah* (Berkeley, Calif., 1941); and J. E. Swain, *The Struggle for Control of the Mediterranean Prior to 1848* (Philadelphia, 1933).

The most important works dealing with the crisis period 1831–1841 as a whole are M. Sabry, *L'empire égyptien sous Mohamed-Ali et la question d'Orient (1811–1849)* (Paris, 1930); F. S. Rodkey, *The Turco-Egyptian Question in the Relations of England, France and Russia 1832–1841* (Urbana, Ill., 1924); H. Temperley, *England and the Near East: The Crimea* (London, 1936); S. Goriainov, *Le Bosphore et les Dardanelles* (Paris, 1910); V. J. Puryear, *International Economics and Diplomacy in the Near East* (Stanford, Calif., 1935); and C. Webster, *The Foreign Policy of Palmerston 1830–1841* (London, 1951, 2 vols.).

The following more specialized works are also important: P. E. Mosely, *Russian Diplomacy and the Opening of the Eastern Question 1838–9* (Cambridge, Mass., 1934); E. Guichen, *La crise d'Orient de 1839 à 1841 et l'Europe* (Paris, 1922); F. Charles-Roux, *Thiers et Méhémet-Ali: La grande crise orientale et européenne de 1840–1841* (Paris, 1951); A. Hasenclever, *Die orientalische Frage in dem Jahren 1838–1841* (Leipzig, 1914); E. Driault, *L'Égypte et l'Europe: La crise de 1839–41* (Cairo, 1930–1934, 4 vols.); G. H. Bolsover, "Nicholas I and the Partition of Turkey," *Slavonic and East European Review,* XXVII (December, 1948), 118–145; F. S. Rodkey, "Lord Palmerston and the Rejuvenation of Turkey, 1830–41," *Journal of Modern History,* I (December, 1929), 570–593, and II (January, 1930), 193–225; and M. Vereté, "Palmerston and the Levant Crisis, 1832," *Journal of Modern History,* XXIV (June, 1952), 143–151. The latter corrects a misconception concerning Palmerston's attitude to Turkey, a point that Webster also refers to in his work cited above, I, 284, ft. 1.

On the significant influence of public opinion during the crisis see the careful study by J. H. Gleason, *The Genesis of Russophobia in Great Britain* (Cambridge, Mass., 1950); and also G. H. Bolsover, "David Urquhart and the Eastern Question, 1833–37: A Study in Publicity and Diplomacy," *Journal of Modern History,* VIII (December, 1936), 444–467. On the significance of the routes through the Near East the standard work is H. L. Hoskins, *British Routes to India* (New York, 1928).

A general but uneven survey of the Ottoman reform movement is available in E. Engelhardt, *La Turquie et le tanzimat: histoire des réformes dans l'empire ottoman depuis 1828 jusqu'à nos jours* (Paris, 1882–1884, 2 vols.). The following article is largely a summary of Reshid's memorandum to Metternich of March 10, 1841: N. Milev; "Réchid Pacha et la réforme ottomane," *Zeitschrift für osteuropäische Geschichte,* II (May, 1912), 382–398. See also the useful survey of the *Tanzimat* in the *Encyclopedia of Islam* by J. H. Kramer. In Turkish there is the important volume *Tanzimat* (Istanbul, 1940), published under the auspices of the Ministry of Education and consisting of 29 articles on various aspects of the reform movement.

For the relationship between the *Tanzimat* and the European powers see F. E. Bailey, *British Policy and the Turkish Reform Movement: A Study in Anglo-Turkish Relations 1826–1853* (Cambridge, Mass., 1942); S. Lane-Poole, *The Life of Stratford Canning* (London, 1888, 2 vols.); the works by Temperley and Webster cited above, and the article by Rodkey on the "Rejuvenation of Turkey," also cited above. Bailey and Temperley may be compared for contrasting estimates of the effectiveness of foreign influence on the *Tanzimat*. There is need, as indicated in the text, for a study of the nature and the operations of the vested interests opposed to reform. This might obviate such frequent recourse to the mysterious mind and soul of Orientals as is to be found, for example, in Temperley.

17. Crimean War

Serious study of the diplomacy of the Crimean War did not begin until 1910, with S. M. Goriainov's analysis of the Russian documents in his *Le Bosphore et les Dardanelles* (Paris, 1910). An excellent brief survey was presented next by B. E. Schmitt, "Diplomatic Preliminaries of the Crimean War," *American Historical Review,* XXV (January, 1919), 33–67. In recent years three historians have presented basic full-length studies: V. J. Puryear, *England, Russia, and the Straits Question 1844–1856* (Berkeley, Calif., 1931); H. Temperley, *England and the Near East: The Crimea* (London, 1936); and E. Tarle, *Krimskaia Voina* [*Crimean War*] (Moscow, 1945, 2 vols.). Puryear has a chapter on "Commercial Preliminaries," which presents new material on the diplomacy which in general is most critical of Stratford Canning. Temperley begins with Mahmud II and stops with the outbreak of the war, and he takes issue with Puryear on many points, such as the role of Stratford Canning and the significance of the 1844 Nesselrode Memorandum and the Seymour Conversations. Tarle has new data on British-Russian economic rivalry and considers in detail the military campaign which the other two ignore, but his analysis of the diplomacy is tendentious and replete with unsupported charges. Another important recent study is by G. B. Henderson, *Crimean War Diplomacy and Other Historical Essays* (Glasgow, 1947), a memorial volume of articles published in various journals. The articles clear up many obscure points, particularly on the diplomacy during the war, when the British and the French, as Henderson shows, were quite as devious as the Austrians. The high standard of these articles is a tribute to the author, whose premature death in 1945 was a signal loss to historical scholarship. An excellent and useful analysis of Russian diplomacy is given by G. H. Bolsover, "Nicholas I and the Partition of Turkey," *Slavonic and East European Review,* XXVII (December, 1948), 115–145.

Other significant works are H. Friedjung, *Der Krimkrieg und die oesterreichische Politik* (Stuttgart, 1911), poorly documented but a sound exposition; Vicomte de Guichen, *La guerre de Crimée (1854–6) et l' attitude des puissances européennes* (Paris, 1936), based on archival sources but poorly done; F. A. Simpson, *Napoleon III and the Recovery of France* (London, 1923) strongly biased against Stratford Canning; and the old classic by A. W. Kinglake, *The Invasion of the Crimea* (London, 1863–1880, 8 vols.), well written but also biased against Stratford Canning and particularly Napoleon, the author being an unsuccessful rival for the favor of the French Emperor's English mistress, Miss Howard.

The best account of the war is by C. Rousset, *Histoire de la guerre de Crimée* (Paris, 1877, 2 vols.). See also the firsthand account by E. I. Todleben, *Défense de Sébastopol* (St. Petersburg, 1863–1874, 2 vols.). Most of the second volume of Tarle's above-mentioned work is devoted to the Crimean campaign and the Kars siege. A good summary of the Kars siege is in W. E. D. Allen and P. Muratoff, *Caucasian Battlefields 1828–1921* (Cambridge, Eng., 1953). The atmosphere of the Crimean War and the personalities involved are recaptured in the sprightly and absorbing works of C. Woodham-Smith, *Florence Nightingale 1820–1910* (New York, 1951) and *The Reason Why* (New York, 1954).

An excellent and indispensable study of the influence of public opinion in Britain is provided by B. Kingsley Martin, *The Triumph of Lord Palmerston: A Study of Public Opinion in England before the Crimean War* (London, 1924). The peace conference itself is analyzed in H. Temperley, "The Treaty of Paris and Its Execution," *Journal of Modern History*, IV (September, 1932), 387–414 and IV (December, 1932), 523–543.

An excellent analysis of the commercial background of the Crimean War is given in V. J. Puryear, *International Economics and Diplomacy in the Near East: A Study of British Commercial Policy in the Levant 1834–1853* (Stanford, Calif., 1935); and in F. E. Bailey, *British Policy and the Turkish Reform Movement: A Study in Anglo-Turkish Relations 1826–1853* (Cambridge, Mass., 1942). A convenient summary of the commercial material in the latter work is available in F. E. Bailey, "The Economics of British Foreign Policy, 1825–50," *Journal of Modern History*, XII (December, 1940), 449–484.

Most important is the following thorough bibliographical survey that appeared after the completion of this chapter: G. D. Gooch, "A Century of Historiography on the Crimean War," *American Historical Review*, LXII (October, 1956), 33–58.

18. Making of Rumania

An excellent and very comprehensive bibliography for Rumania's history is given in two articles by Paul Henry: "Histoire roumaine," *Revue historique*, CLXXVI (July–December, 1935), 468–537, and "Histoire de Roumanie," *Revue historique*, CXCIV (January–March, 1944), 42–65, CXCIV (April–June, 1944), 132–150, and CXCIV (July–September, 1944), 232–252. The Communist regime of Rumania following World War II published a nineteen-volume collection of documents on Rumanian history since the eleventh century: M. Roller *et al.*, eds., *Documente Privind Istoria Romaniei* (Bucharest, 1952–1953). This collection, which was not used for this study, is reviewed, together with other publications of the Communist regime, by S. A. Fischer-Galati, in the June, 1955, issue of the *Journal of Modern History*.

The only extensive history of Rumania in English is by R. W. Seton-Watson, *A History of the Roumanians from Roman Times to the Completion of Unity* (Cambridge, Eng., 1934), which carries the story to the Trianon Treaty.

Important works in other Western languages are by N. Iorga, *Geschichte des rumänischen Volkes* (Gotha, 1905, 2 vols.), and A. D. Xenopol, *Histoire des Roumains de la Dacie Trajane, depuis les origines jusqu' à l'union des principautés en 1859* (Paris, 1896, 2 vols.). The most extensive histories in Rumanian are by C. C. Giurescu, *Istoria Românilor* (Bucharest, 1935–1937, 4 vols.), and N. Iorga, *Istoria Românilor* (Bucharest, 1936–1939, 10 vols.). See also L. Galdi, *et al., Geschichte der Rumänen* (Budapest, 1942), not consulted.

Among the more important contemporary sources for the pre-union period are W. Wilkinson, *An Account of the Principalities of Wallachia and Moldavia* . . . (London, 1820); M. Ubicini, *Valachie et Moldavie* (Paris, 1856); and J. A. Vaillant, *La Romanie, ou histoire, langue, littérature, orographie, statistique des roumains* (Paris, 1844–1845, 4 vols.). For contrasting interpretations of Phanariote rule in the principalities, see the favorable analysis by the Rumanian historian N. Iorga, "Le despotisme eclairé dans les pays roumains au XVIIIᵉ siècle," *Bulletin of the International Committee of Historical Sciences,* IX (March, 1937), 110–115; and the critical by the contemporary Greek observer, M. P. Zallony, *Essai sur les fanariotes* (Marseilles, 1824). See also the informative article by P. A. Argyropoulos, "Les Grecs au service de l'empire ottoman," in *1453–1953: Le cinq-centième anniversaire de la prise de Constantinople* (Athens, *L'hellénisme contemporaine,* 1953), pp. 151–178. An interesting account of Rumanian society is provided by L. Sainéan, "Le régime et la société en Roumanie pendant le règne des Phanariotes (1711–1821)," *Revue internationale de sociologie,* X (October, 1902), 717–748. A noteworthy interpretation of Vladimirescu's revolt in 1821 is given in S. I. Samoilov, "Narodno-osvoboditelnoe vosstanie 1821 g. v Valakhii," ["The National Liberation Uprising of 1821 in Wallachia,"] *Voprosy Istorii,* no. 10 (October, 1955), pp. 94–105.

The most thorough study of the development of Rumanian nationalism is the unpublished doctoral dissertation by J. C. Campbell, "French Influence and the Rise of Roumanian Nationalism" (Harvard University, 1940). See also his article on "The Influence of Western Political Thought in the Rumanian Principalities, 1821–1848: The Generation of 1848," *Journal of Central European Affairs,* IV (October, 1944), 262–273. On the 1848 revolution there is the brief study by M. Roller, "The Rumanians in 1848," in *The Opening of an Era 1848: An Historical Symposium,* ed. by F. Fejtö (London, 1948), pp. 298–311; and also J. C. Campbell, "The Transylvanian Question in 1849," *Journal of Central European Affairs,* II (April, 1942), 20–34. Two excellent studies of the unification of the Principalities are available: W. G. East, *The Union of Moldavia and Wallachia, 1859: An Episode in Diplomatic History* (Cambridge, Eng., 1929); and the more comprehensive work of T. W. Riker, *The Making of Roumania: A Study of an International Problem, 1856–1866* (Oxford, 1931). An important documentary source is *Trois années de la question d' Orient, 1856–1859, d' après les papiers inédit de M. Thouvenel* (Paris, 1897). A good picture of Franco-Russian relations after the Crimean War is given in F. Charles-Roux, *Alexandre II, Gortchakoff et Napoléon III* (Paris, 1913).

For the postunion years there is the careful study by Paul Henry, *L' abdication du Prince Cuza et l'avènement de la dynastie du Hohenzollern au trône de Roumanie* (Paris, 1930). The memoirs of Charles I are available in the German edition *Aus dem Leben König Karls von Rumänien* (Stuttgart, 1894–1900, 4 vols.), which is preferable to the expurgated French edition *Notes sur la vie du roi Charles de Roumanie* . . . (Bucharest, 1894–1901, 4 vols.). On Rumanian foreign policy during these years see N. Iorga, *Correspondance diplomatique roumaine sous le roi Charles Ier (1866–1880)* (Paris, 1923); and chs. 4 and 5 of L. S. Stavrianos, *Balkan Federation: A History of the Movement toward Balkan Unity in Modern Times* (Northampton, Mass., 1944).

On the agrarian question in Rumania, two first-rate studies are available in English: D. Mitrany, *The Land and the Peasant in Rumania* (London, 1930), and H. L. Roberts, *Rumania: Political Problems of an Agrarian State* (New Haven, Conn., 1951). The first carries the story to the agrarian reforms of the World War I period; Roberts concentrates on the twentieth century and includes a study of reforms during and after World War II.

An excellent analysis of the Rumanians in Transylvania, Bukovina, and Bessarabia is to be found in chs. 4, 7, 10, 13, and Appendix I of Seton-Watson's Rumanian history listed above, which also provides a bibliography.

19. Bulgarian Awakening

The standard bibliography of materials on Bulgaria in Western European languages is R. J. Kerner, *Slavic Europe* (Cambridge, Mass., 1918). See also P. E. Mosely, "The Post-War Historiography of Modern Bulgaria," *Journal of Modern History,* IX (September, 1937), 348–366; H. Trenkov, "Bulgarian Bibliography," *Slavonic and East European Review,* XXVIII (December, 1948), 259–277; and the articles on Bulgarian historians by J. F. Clarke, "Bobchev and Bulgaria (1853–1940)," *Slavonic and East European Review,* XXI (March, 1943), 188–193, and "Zlatarski and Bulgarian historiography," *Slavonic Review,* XV (January, 1937), 435–439. For bibliographies in Bulgarian, see the titles listed in the above article by Trenkov. An interesting account of the early Bulgarian books and the national revival is given in J. F. Clarke, "The First Bulgarian Book," *Harvard Library Notes,* no. 30 (March, 1940), pp. 295–302.

The best general accounts of Bulgaria under the Turks are A. Hajek, *Bulgarien unter der Türkenherrschaft* (Stuttgart, 1925); H. Wendel, *Der Kampf der Sudslawen um Freiheit und Einheit* (Frankfort, 1925); the second part of N. Stanev's *Geschichte der Bulgaren* entitled *Vom Beginn der Türkenzeit bis zur Gegenwart* (Leipzig, 1917); F. Hýbl, *Dějiny Národa Bulharského [History of the Bulgarian People]* (Prague, 1930, 2 vols.); and N. S. Derzhavin, *Istoriia Bolgarii [History of Bulgaria]* (Moscow, 1947), of which Vol. III is on the Ottoman period. Nothing in the English language approaches the above works; D. Mishew, *The Bulgarians in the Past* (Lausanne, 1919) is strongly nationalist and polemical but contains a good deal of material. The following works by S. S. Bobchev are suggestive but too brief: *La société bulgare sous la domination ottomane* (Sofia, 1935), and "Notes comparées sur les çorbacis chez les peuples balkaniques et en particulier chez les Bulgares," *Revue internationale des études balkaniques,* III (1938), 428–445. Interesting source material is to be found in the work of M. Leo, *La Bulgarie et son peuple sous la domination ottomane tels que les ont vus les voyageurs anglo-saxons (1586–1878)* (Sofia, 1949).

The most important study of the Bulgarian cultural awakening is the unpublished doctoral dissertation by J. F. Clarke, "Bible Societies, American Missionaries and the National Revival of Bulgaria" (Harvard University, 1937), which is more broad in scope than the title suggests. The following articles are based on this dissertation: "Father Paisi and Bulgarian History," in *Essays in Honor of Lawrence B. Packard,* ed. by H. Stuart Hughes (Ithaca, N. Y., 1954), pp. 258–283; and "Serbia and the Bulgarian Revival (1762–1872)," *American Slavic and East European Review,* IV (December, 1945), 141–162. A brief but useful study of the Bulgarian awakening is L. Leger, *La Bulgarie* (Paris, 1885). A valuable analysis of the role of writers in the Bulgarian awakening is given in V. Pinto, "The Civic and Aesthetic Ideals of the Bulgarian Narodnik Writers," *Slavonic and East European Review,* XXXII (June, 1954), 344–366, which is based on the author's doctoral dissertation, *The Narodnik Movement in Bulgarian Literature and the Influence on That Movement of Russian Literature and Thought* (University of London, 1952). See also the following biographies of two important leaders of the renaissance: M. Arnaudov, *Aprilov: Zhivot, deinost, sŭvremenitsi (1789–1847)* [*Aprilov: Life, Work, Contemporaries*] (Sofia, 1935); and M. Arnaudov, *Neofit Hilendarski Bozvali, 1785–1848* (Sofia, 1930).

The fullest Bulgarian account of the exarchate struggle is by P. Nikov, *Vŭzrazhdane na bâlgarskiia narod: Tsŭrkovno-natsionalni borbi i postizheniia* [*The Renaissance of the Bulgarian People: The Achievements of the Struggle for a National Church*] (Sofia, 1929). Other Bulgarian accounts are S. Zankow, *Die Verfassung der bulgarischen orthodoxen Kirche* (Zurich, 1918); and T. S. Burmov, *Bâlgaro-grtskata tserkovna raspria* [*Bulgarian-Greek Church Struggle*] (Sofia, 1902), the latter being a detailed and important exposition by a leader of the moderate Bulgarian nationalists in Constantinople who was also in close touch with the Russian embassy. An excellent Greek survey is available in the article by the erudite archbishop of Athens, Chrysostomos, "Bulgaria, Church," *Megale Ellenike Egkyklopaideia,* VII, 672–682, and in E. J. Karpathios's article on the "Bulgarian Church," in *Religious and Christian Encyclopedia* (Athens, 1937), II, 628–686, the latter providing an extensive bibliography. More details are available in M. I. Gedeon, *Eggrapha patriarchika kai synodika peri tou boulgarikou zetematos (1852–1873)* [*Patriarchal and Synodical Documents concerning the Bulgarian Question (1852–1873)*] (Constantinople, 1908). An important Russian source is the text in French of Ignatiev's memorandum written in 1874 reviewing his ten years in Constantinople, and published in *Izvestiia Ministerstva Inostrannykh Del* (1914), Bks. I–VI, and (1915), Bks. I–VI. Russian material is also used in the following articles: G. Trubetzkoi, "La politique russe en Orient: le schisme bulgare," *Revue d'histoire diplomatique,* XXI (1907), 161–198, 394–426; and B. H. Sumner, "Ignatiev at Constantinople, 1864–1874," *Slavonic Review,* II (January, 1933), 341–353, and II (April, 1933), 556–571. The following article contains data concerning Protestantism in Bulgaria and also references to works concerning Catholicism in Bulgaria: J. F. Clarke, "Protestantism and the Bulgarian Church Question in 1861," *Essays in the History of Modern Europe,* ed. by D. C. McKay (New York, 1936), pp. 79–97. See also L. S. Stavrianos, "L'institution de l'exarcat bulgare: Son influence sur les relations interbalkaniques," *Les Balkans,* IX (1939), 56–69.

For conditions in Bulgaria in the 1860's and the reform efforts of Midhat Pasha, see the excellent account in the unpublished doctoral dissertation by R. H. Davison, "Reform in the Ottoman Empire, 1856–1876" (Harvard University, 1942), chs. 4–6; and *The Life of Midhat Pasha . . . by His Son Ali Haydar Midhat Bey* (London, 1903), ch. 2. The relationship between the spread of the chifliks and peasant unrest is demonstrated in the following important work utilizing

Turkish materials: H. Inalcik, *Tanzimat ve Bulgar Meselesi* [*The Tanzimat and the Bulgarian Question*] (Ankara, 1943). On this subject see also N. G. Levintov, "Agrarnye otnosheniia v Bolgarii nakanune osvobozhdeniia i agrarnyi perevorot 1877–1879 Godov," ["Agrarian Relations in Bulgaria on the Eve of the Liberation and the Agrarian Revolution of 1877–1879,"] in *Osvobozhdenie Bolgarii ot Turetskogo Iga* [*The Liberation of Bulgaria from Turkish Rule*] (Moscow, 1953), pp. 139–221.

For a brief survey of the revolutionary movement and a bibliography of Bulgarian sources, see C. E. Black, *The Establishment of Constitutional Government in Bulgaria* (Princeton, N. J., 1943), and also the same author's "The Influence of Western Political Thought in Bulgaria, 1850–1885," *American Historical Review*, XLVIII (April, 1943), 507–520. A fuller account of the revolutionary movement from Rakovski to 1876 is available in A. Burmov, *Bŭlgarski Revoliutsionen Tsentralen Komitet 1868–1876* [*The Bulgarian Revolutionary Central Committee 1868–1876*] (Sofia, 1943). See also N. T. Obretenov, *Spomeni za bŭlgarskitě vŭzstaniia* [*Memoirs of the Bulgarian Uprisings*] (Sofia, 1943). Post-World War II developments in Bulgaria have stimulated studies of Bulgarian-Russian relations, including the following on the period before 1878: N. I. Kazakov, "Iz istorii russko-bolgarskikh sviazei v period voiny Rossii s Turtsiei (1806–1812 gg.)," ["From the History of Russo-Bulgarian Ties During the Russian War with Turkey (1806–1812),"] *Voprosy Istorii,* no. 6 (June, 1955), pp. 42–55; and A. Burmov, "Kŭm istoriiata na rusko-bŭlgarskite vrozki prez 1876 g.: Bâlgarsko Chelovekoliubivo Nastoiatelstvo v Bukureshch," ["On the History of Russo-Bulgarian Relations in 1876: 'The Bulgarian Philanthropic Society' in Bucharest,"] *Izvestiia* (Sofia), nos. 1–2 (1951), pp. 81–98. The May, 1876, Bulgarian revolt and the resulting massacres are thoroughly analyzed by D. Harris, *Britain and the Bulgarian Horrors of 1876* (Chicago, 1939). Finally, see L. S. Stavrianos, *Balkan Federation: A History of the Movement toward Balkan Unity in Modern Times* (Northampton, Mass., 1944), ch. 5, for the relations of the Bulgarian revolutionaries with their neighbors, and their views concerning inter-Balkan relations.

The color and atmosphere of the Bulgarian revolutionary movement may be gained from the following works in English: Z. Stoyanov, *Pages from the Autobiography of a Bulgarian Insurgent* (London, 1913); A. H. Beaman, *M. Stambuloff* (London, 1895); and the novel by the Bulgarian poet Ivan Vazov, *Under the Yoke: A Romance of Bulgarian Liberty,* first published in English in 1893 and revised in 1912.

20. Reform and Revolution in the Ottoman Empire

By far the best work on Ottoman history after the Crimean War is the unpublished doctoral dissertation by R. H. Davison, "Reform in the Ottoman Empire, 1856–1876" (Harvard University, 1942). This study is much broader than the title suggests and was leaned on heavily in the preparation of this chapter. Less comprehensive and perceptive is E. Engelhardt, *La Turquie et le Tanzimat* (Paris, 1884, 2 vols.). The best contemporary sources are A. Ubicini, *Letters on Turkey* (London, 1856, 2 vols.); and A. D. Mordtmann, *Stambul und das moderne Türkenthum* (Leipzig, 1877–1878, 2 vols.). In Turkish there is the important volume *Tanzimat* (Istanbul, 1940) published under the auspices of the ministry of education and consisting of 29 articles on various aspects of the reform movement.

For the literary and intellectual awakening see the excellent summary in ch. 7 of Davison, and also the standard work of E. J. W. Gibb, *A History of Ottoman Poetry* (London, 1900–1909, 6 vols.). See also A. Emin, *The Development of Modern Turkey as Measured by Its Press* (New York, 1914); the recent biography by V. Heyd, *Foundations of Turkish Nationalism: The Life and Teachings of Ziya Gökalp* (London, 1950); and the memoirs of the successive presidents of Robert College: C. Hamlin, *Among the Turks* (New York, 1878); G. Washburn, *Fifty Years in Constantinople and Recollections of Robert College* (Boston, 1909); and C. F. Gates, *Not to Me Alone* (Princeton, N. J., 1940). The connection between Turkish nationalism and historiography is revealingly outlined by B. Lewis, "History-Writing and National Revival in Turkey," *Middle Eastern Affairs,* IV (June–July, 1953), 218–227.

On the reform of the millets, Davison presents the only consecutive account in ch. 5. For more details see L. Arpee, *The Armenian Awakening: A History of the Armenian Church, 1820–1860* (Chicago, 1909); H. J. Sarkiss, "The Armenian Renaissance, 1500–1863," *Journal of Modern History,* IX (1937), 433–448; A. O. Sarkissian, *History of the Armenian Question to 1885* (Urbana, Ill., 1938); A. D. Kyriakos, *Geschichte der Orientalischen Kirchen von 1453–1898* (Leipzig, 1902); M. Franco, *Essai sur l'histoire des israélites de l'empire ottoman depuis les origines jusqu'à nos jours* (Paris, 1897).

Ottoman economic history is a neglected topic, but the foreign-loan aspect is well covered by A. Du Velay, *Essai sur l'histoire financière de la Turquie* (Paris, 1903); C. Morawitz, *Die Turkei im Spiegel ihrer Finanzen* (Berlin, 1903); and D. C. Blaisdell, *European Financial Control in the Ottoman Empire* (New York, 1929).

The diplomacy of the Balkan crisis will be considered in the following chapter. For domestic Turkish developments in 1876 and 1877 see *The Life of Midhat Pasha . . . by His Son Ali Haydar Midhat Bey* (London, 1903); *The Memoirs of Ismail Kemal Bey* (London, 1920); H. Temperley, "British Policy towards Parliamentary Rule and Constitutionalism in Turkey (1830–1914)" *Cambridge Historical Journal,* IV (1932), 156–191; H. G. Elliot, *Some Revolutions and Other Experiences* (London, 1922); E. Pears, *Forty Years in Constantinople* (New York, 1916). Works on Abdul Hamid are listed in chapter 28.

21. Balkan Crisis and the Treaty of Berlin

The best account of the Balkan crisis from the viewpoint of European diplomacy is the admirable study by W. L. Langer, *European Alliances and Alignments 1871–1890* (New York, 1931), chs. 1–2. The second edition (1950) contains supplementary bibliographies. The Balkan diplomatic background and particularly the first Balkan alliance system are considered in L. S. Stavrianos, *Balkan Federation: A History of the Movement toward Balkan Unity in Modern Times* (Northampton, Mass., 1944), ch. 5. The most detailed study of the crisis is by D. Harris, *A Diplomatic History of the Balkan Crisis of 1875–1878: The First Year* (Stanford, Calif., 1936), though it has not been continued beyond the first year. The entire three-year period is covered adequately by M. D. Stojanović, *Great Powers and the Balkans 1875–1878* (Cambridge, Eng., 1938). A large number of excellent studies have appeared in recent years on particular aspects of the crisis, the most important being D. Harris, *Britain and the Bulgarian Horrors of 1876* (Chicago, 1939); W. Jahrmann, *Frankreich und die orientalische Frage 1875–1878* (Berlin, 1936); D. E. Lee, *Great Britain and the Cyprus Convention Policy of 1878* (Cambridge, Mass., 1934); G. H. Rupp, *A Wavering Friendship: Russia and Austria 1876–1878* (Cambridge, Mass., 1941); R. W. Seton-Watson, *Disraeli, Gladstone and the Eastern Question* (London, 1935); B. H. Sumner, *Russia and the Balkans 1870–1880* (Oxford, 1937); the public opinion study by W. G. Wirthwein, *Britain and the Balkan Crisis 1875–1878* (New York, 1935); and S. Goriainov, *La question d'Orient à la veille du traité de Berlin, 1870–1878* (Paris, 1948).

On the role of the Balkan states during the crisis there are M. Lhéritier, *Histoire diplomatique de la Grèce* (Paris, 1925, Vol. III); S. T. Lascaris, *La politique extérieure de la Grèce avant et après le congrès de Berlin* (Paris, 1924); N. Iorga, ed., *Correspondance diplomatique roumaine sous le roi Charles I* (Paris 1923); third volume of *Aus dem Leben König Karls von Rumänien* (Stuttgart, 1897); R. Rosetti, "Roumania's Share in the War of 1877," *Slavonic Review,* VIII (March, 1930), 548–551; R. W. Burks, "Romania and the Balkan Crisis of 1875–78," *Journal of Central European Affairs,* II (July, 1942), 119–134, and II (October, 1942), 310–320; J. Ristić, *Diplomatska Istorija Srbije za vreme srpskih ratova za oslobodjenje i nezavisnost, 1875–1878* (*Diplomatic History of Serbia in the Time of the Serbian Wars for Liberation and Independence, 1875–1878*) (Belgrade, 1896–1898); V. Georgévitch, *La Serbie au congrès de Berlin* (Paris, 1891), which was published the same year in *Revue d'histoire diplomatique;* R. W. Seton-Watson, "Les relations de l'Autriche-Hongrie et de la Serbie entre 1868 et 1874: la mission de Benjamin Kállay à Belgrade," *Le monde slave,* III (February, 1926), 211–230, III (May, 1926), 186–204, and III (August, 1926), 273–288; V. Trivanovitch, "Serbia, Russia and Austria during the Rule of Milan Obrenovich," *Journal of Modern History,* III (September, 1931), 414–440; S. Jovanović, "Serbia in the Early 'Seventies," *Slavonic Review,* IV (December, 1925), 384–395.

An excellent account of the campaigns is given in P. K. Fortunatow, *Der Krieg 1877–78 und die Befreiung Bulgariens* (Berlin, 1953), which includes an analysis of the Caucasian as well as Balkan campaigns. See also the *"Daily News" War Correspondence* (London, 1878, 2 vols.); F. V. Greene, *The Russian Army and Its Campaigns in Turkey in 1877–1878* (London, 1879); C. B. Norman, *Armenia and the Campaign of 1877* (London, 1878); C. Williams, *The Armenian Campaign: A Diary of the Campaign of 1877 in Armenia and Koordistan* (London, 1878); and W. E. D. Allen and P. Muratoff, *Caucasian Battlefields: A History of the Wars on the Turco-Caucasian Border 1821–1921* (Cambridge, Eng., 1953), Bk. III.

Finally, there are the excellent detailed study by W. N. Medlicott on *The Congress of Berlin and After: A Diplomatic History of the Near Eastern Settlement 1878–1880* (London, 1938), and the same author's recent study of *Bismarck, Gladstone and the Concert of Europe* (London, 1956).

22. Dynamics of Balkan Politics

A brief but comprehensive analysis of imperialism, with excellent bibliographical references, is available in ch. 3 of W. L. Langer, *Diplomacy of Imperialism 1890–1902* (New York, 1951, 2nd ed.). A summary of the material in this chapter is given in his article "A Critique of Imperialism," *Foreign Affairs,* XIV (October, 1935), 102–115.

For a general analysis of railway construction in both the Balkans and the Middle East, see chs. 13 and 15 of H. Feis, *Europe the World's Banker 1870–1914* (New Haven, Conn., 1930). The political rivalries behind railway building in the Balkans are well brought out in the articles by A. J. May, "The Novibazar Railway Project," *Journal of Modern History,* X (December, 1938), 496–527, and "Trans-Balkan Railway Schemes," *Journal of Modern History,* XXIV (December, 1952), 352–367; and also in W. S. Vucinich, *Serbia between East and West: The Events of 1903–1908* (Stanford, Calif., 1954), pp. 210–230. The standard works on railway construction in Asiatic Turkey are E. M. Earle, *Turkey, the Great Powers, and the Bagdad Railway* (New York, 1923); and W. B. Wolf, *The Diplomatic History of the Bagdad Railroad* (Columbia, Mo., 1936).

An excellent general survey of the finances of Turkey and the Balkan states is given in chs. 12 and 14 of Feis, *op. cit.* For more detailed information, see D. C. Blaisdell, *European Financial Control in the Ottoman Empire* (New York, 1929); A. Levandis, *The Greek Foreign Debt and the Great Powers 1821–1898* (New York, 1944); K. C. Popov, *La Bulgarie économique* (Sofia, 1920); D. Kastris, *Les capitaux étrangers dans la finance roumaine* (Paris, 1921); M. Simitch, *La dette publique de la Serbie* (Paris, 1925).

There is no study of the origins, evolution, and effects of capitalism in the Balkans as a whole. The best introduction to the subject is given by D. Warriner, "Some Controversial Issues in the History of Agrarian Europe," *Slavonic and East European Review,* XXXII (December, 1953), 168–186. This article, which refers to all of Eastern Europe, brings out some of the basic problems and advances stimulating theories. For detailed information it is necessary to turn to national economic and social histories which are given below in the bibliographies relating to individual countries. Outstanding among these histories are I. Sakazov, *Bulgarische Wirtschaftsgeschichte* (Berlin, 1929); I. T. Sanders, *Balkan Village* (Lexington, Ky., 1949); J. Tomasevich, *Peasants, Politics and Economic Change in Yugoslavia* (Stanford, Calif., 1955); R. Trouton, *Peasant Renaissance in Yugoslavia 1900–1950* (London, 1952); D. Mitrany, *The Land and the Peasant in Rumania* (London, 1930); H. L. Roberts, *Rumania: Political Problems of an Agrarian State* (New Haven, Conn., 1951); Ch. Evelpides, *Oikonomike kai koinonike historia tes Hellados* [*Economic and Social History of Greece*] (Athens, 1950); G. Kordatos, *Eisagoge sten historia tes hellenikes kephalaiokratias* [*Introduction to the History of Greek Capitalism*] (Athens, 1930), the latter being a Marxist interpretation.

Noteworthy also are these studies of specific topics: E. Zaleski, *Les courants commerciaux de l'Europe danubienne au cours de la première moitié du XXᵐᵉ siècle* (Paris, 1952), and W. Moore, *Economic Demography of Eastern and Southern Europe* (Geneva, 1945).

23. Making of Bulgaria

For bibliographies and general histories of Bulgaria see the works given for Chapter 19. There is need for a comprehensive history of Bulgarian political and economic development since 1878. Nothing is available comparable to the works of R. W. Seton-Watson, D. Mitrany, and H. Roberts in the Rumanian field. In Bulgarian there is the work of N. Stanev, *Istoriia na nova Bŭlgariia 1878–1928* [*History of Modern Bulgaria 1878–1928*] (Sofia, 1929). The study by G. C. Logio, *Bulgaria Past and Present* (Manchester, Eng., 1936) is fresh and perceptive but scrappy and strongly opinionated.

Two informative biographies of Prince Alexander are available, both having considerable documentary material: E. C. Corti, *Alexander von Battenberg: Sein Kampf mit den Zaren und Bismarck* (Vienna, 1920), and A. Koch, *Prince Alexander of Battenberg* (London, 1887). See also the short appreciation by the London *Times* correspondent J. D. Bourchier, "Prince Alexander of Battenberg," *Fortnightly Review*, LXI (January, 1894), 103–118; and the accounts by the German correspondent A. von Huhn, *The Struggle of the Bulgarians for National Independence* (London, 1886) and *The Kidnapping of Prince Alexander of Battenberg* (London, 1887). The best works on the domestic developments under Alexander are C. E. Black, *The Establishment of Constitutional Government in Bulgaria* (Princeton, N. J., 1944) and A. Hajek, *Bulgariens Befreiung und staatliche Entwicklung unter seinem ersten Fürsten* (Munich, 1939). The former uses the British and Austrian archives and carries the story to 1885; the latter is a more general analysis of the same period and a valuable source despite the references in the Preface to "world poisoning internationalism" and to Hitler's "New Order," reflecting the date of publication. See also C. E. Black, "The Influence of Western Political Thought in Bulgaria, 1850–1885," *American Historical Review*, XLVIII (April, 1943), 507–520. Also noteworthy is K. S. Vasilev, "Borba bolgarskogo naroda protiv reshenii berlinskogo kongressa 1878 goda," ["The Struggle of the Bulgarian People against the Decisions of the Berlin Congress in 1878,"] *Voprosy Istorii*, no. 8, August, 1955, pp. 119–130, which includes an analysis of the economic and social effect of the Berlin decisions upon the Bulgarian lands.

For diplomatic developments during Alexander's reign see W. L. Langer, *European Alliances and Alignments 1871–1890* (New York, 1931), ch. 10; J. V. Fuller, *Bismarck's Diplomacy at Its Zenith* (Cambridge, Mass., 1922), chs. 2, 3; A. M. Hyde, *A Diplomatic History of Bulgaria from 1870 to 1886* (Urbana, Ill., 1927), which is mostly outdated; W. N. Medlicott, "The Powers and the Unification of the Two Bulgarias 1885," *English Historical Review*, LIV (January, 1939), 67–82, and LIV (April, 1939), 263–284; M. Lascaris, "Greece and Serbia during the War of 1885," *Slavonic Review*, XI (July, 1932), 88–99.

A satisfactory biography of Ferdinand of Saxe-Coburg is not available. H. R. Madol, *Ferdinand de Bulgarie: la rêve de Byzance* (Paris, 1937) is apologetic, while J. Macdonald, *Czar Ferdinand and His People* (London, 1913) is a useless panegyric. A. H. Beaman, *M. Stambuloff* (London, 1895) is by an admirer of the Bulgarian statesman yet informative and useful. Bulgarian foreign policy under Ferdinand may be traced in the short though important study by K. Kratchounov, *La politique extérieure de la Bulgarie 1880–1920* (Sofia, 1932), and in A. Stancioff, *Recollections of a Bulgarian Diplomatist's Wife* (London, 1930);

C. Jelavich, "Russo-Bulgarian Relations, 1892–1896, with Particular Reference to the Problem of the Bulgarian Succession," *Journal of Modern History,* XXIV (December, 1952), 341–351; E. Walters, "The Serbo-Bulgarian Secret Treaty of 19 February 1897," *Slavonic and East European Review,* XXVIII (April, 1950), 493–499; E. C. Helmreich and C. E. Black, "The Russo-Bulgarian Military Convention of 1902," *Journal of Modern History,* IX (December, 1937), 471–482; and L. S. Stavrianos, *Balkan Federation: A History of the Movement toward Balkan Unity in Modern Times* (Northampton, Mass., 1944), chs. 6, 7. For works dealing with the Macedonian question and Bulgarian diplomacy during the Bosnian crisis, the Balkan Wars, and World War I see the bibliographies of the appropriate chapters below.

The most important general economic histories are I. Sakazov, *Bulgarische Wirtschaftsgeschichte* (Berlin, 1929); W. K. Weiss-Bartenstein, "Uber Bulgariens volkswirtschaftsliche Entwicklung," *Zeitschrift für Volkswirtschaft, Sozialpolitik und Verwaltung,* XXII (1913), 407–428, and the same author's *Bulgariens volkswirtschaftsliche Verhaltnisse* (Berlin, 1917), which parallels the earlier work; A. Iaranoff, *La Bulgarie économique* (Lausanne, 1919), which has many statistical tables; and the short section on the pre-1914 period in L. Pasvolsky, *Bulgaria's Economic Position* (Washington, D. C., 1929).

For special aspects of Bulgaria's economy see the short doctoral dissertation on the guilds by S. S. Kalpakchiev, "Die Zunft Bulgariens im XIX Jahrhundert" (Greifswald, 1900); the study of zadrugas in J. E. Guechoff, "Les associations agricoles et ouvriers en Bulgarie," *Nouvelle Revue,* LXIV (1890), 381–391; the short dissertation by N. Sakarov, "Die industrielle Entwicklung Bulgariens" (Berlin, 1904); another dissertation by the brother of Prince Alexander and consisting mainly of government statistics—Franz Joseph, Prinz von Battenberg, "Die volkswirtschaftliche Entwicklung Bulgariens von 1879 bis zur Gegenwart (Leipzig, 1890); and the study of government tax policy by J. Raudnitz, "Die staatswirtschaftsliche Entwicklung Bulgariens," *Zeitschrift für Volkswirtschaft, Sozialpolitik und Verwaltung,* XXII (1913), 429–462. Finally, there is the indispensable article by N. Levintov, "Agrarnyi perevorot v Bolgarii v 1877–1879 godakh," ["The Agrarian Revolution in Bulgaria in 1877–1879,"] *Voprosi Istorii,* no. 12 (December, 1951), 55–76, which utilizes the archives of the Russian occupation forces and the personal correspondence of Prince Dondukov-Korsakov.

24. Serbia and the South Slavs

A general bibliography on Serbia and the South Slavs is given above in Chapter 14. For the reigns of Milan and Alexander Obrenovich, the basic sources are the unequaled multivolume works by S. Jovanović, *Vlada Milana Obrenovića* (Belgrade, 1934, 3 vols.); and by Z. Zivanović, *Politička istoriija Srbije u drugoj polovini devetnaestog veka* [*Political History of Serbia in the Second Half of the Nineteenth Century*] (Belgrade, 1923–1925, 4 vols.). For the change of dynasty in 1903 and the consolidation of the new regime to 1908 the definitive work is W. S. Vucinich, *Serbia between East and West: The Events of 1903–1908* (Stanford, Calif., 1954). See also the interesting account of C. Mijatovich, *A Royal Tragedy* (London, 1906), who is sympathetic to Alexander.

In the field of Serbian foreign relations there is nothing comparable to Driault and Lhéritier's diplomatic history of Greece, though a good brief survey is available in V. Popović, *Evropa i srpsko pitanje u periodu oslobodjenja 1804–1918* [*Europe and the Serbian Question in the Period of the Liberation 1804–1918*] (Belgrade, 1938). The general histories by Jovanović and Zivanović cited above contain detailed information on foreign relations. See also the important works of J. Ristić, *Diplomatska istorija Srbije za vreme srpskih ratova za oslobodjenje i nezavisnost 1875–1878* [*Diplomatic History of Serbia during the Serbian Wars for Liberation and Independence 1875–1878*] (Belgrade, 1896–1898, 2 vols.), and *Spoljašnji odnošaji Srbije* [*Foreign Relations of Serbia*] (Belgrade, 1897, 3 vols.). For the later period see V. Ćorović, *Odnoši izmedju Srbije i Austro-Ugarske u XX veku* [*Relations between Serbia and Austria-Hungary in the Twentieth Century*] (Belgrade, 1936), and D. Popović, *Borba za narodno ujedinjenje od 1908 do 1914* [*Struggle for National Unification from 1908 to 1914*] (Belgrade, 1938). Apart from Serbian sources there is an excellent synthesis of Serbian diplomacy during Milan's subservience to Austria in W. L. Langer, *European Alliances and Alignments 1871–1890* (New York, 1931), ch. 10. For more details see A. F. Pribram, "Milan IV von Serbien und die Geheimverträge Österreich-Ungarns mit Serbien, 1881–1889," *Historiche Blätter*, I (1921–1922), 464–494; and the same author's *The Secret Treaties of Austria-Hungary 1879–1914* (Cambridge, Mass., 1920, 2 vols.). Serbian foreign policy between 1903 and 1908 is thoroughly covered by Vucinich in his work cited above. See also the interesting memoirs of the Austrian envoy in Belgrade, C. Dumba, *Memoirs of a Diplomat* (Boston, 1932); and also C. Mijatovich, *The Memoirs of a Balkan Diplomatist* (London, 1917).

The best general source for Serbian and South Slav economic development between 1878 and 1914 is J. Tomasevich, *Peasants, Politics and Economic Change in Yugoslavia* (Stanford, Calif., 1954). The best account of both the economic and the diplomatic aspects of the "Pig War" is given in ch. 7 of the Vucinich study cited above. See also the analysis of handicraft and factory developments in J. Krikner, *Industrie und Industriepolitik Serbiens* (Halle, 1913); the excellent general survey in M. L. Stanojevich, *Die Landwirtschaft in Serbien* (Halle, 1913); M. Simitch, *La dette publique de la Serbie* (Paris, 1925); and the invaluable survey of social and cultural trends in R. Trouton, *Peasant Renaissance in Yugoslavia 1900–1950* (London, 1952).

General studies of the Hapsburg Slavs are listed above in Chapter 14. An important analysis of the problem of Bosnia-Herzegovina on the eve of the war is given in J. M. Baernreither, *Fragments of a Political Diary* (London, 1930). The author, a broad-minded Bohemian German, favored the creation of a triune Hapsburg state, to which he believed the kingdom of Serbia would be drawn like a filing to a magnet. Another important work is V. Masleša, *Mlada Bosna* [*Young Bosna*] (Belgrade, 1945), a study, from a Marxian viewpoint, of the activities, objectives, and leadership of the revolutionary youth movement in Bosnia before and during World War I. Convenient summaries of the Yugoslav revolutionary movement are also available in D. Lončarević, *Jugoslaviens Entstehung* (Zurich, 1929); L. Albertini, *The Origins of the War of 1914,* tr. and ed. by I. M. Massey (London, 1953), Vol. II, ch. 1; R. W. Seton-Watson, *Sarajevo* (London, 1926), ch. 3; and S. B. Fay, *The Origins of the World War* (New York, 1934, rev. ed.), Vol II, ch. 2. Works on the 1908 Bosnian crisis and the 1914 Sarajevo crisis are given in the relevant chapters below.

25. Greece

The basic works on nineteenth century Greece will be found in the bibliography for Chapter 15. The outstanding authority on Greece at the turn of the century is William Miller, who lived there at the time. See especially his *Travels and Politics in the Near East* (London, 1898). An important source is the biography by D. Pournaras, *Charilaos Trikoupes: He zoe kai to ergon tou* [*Charilaos Trikoupes: His Life and Work*] (Athens, 1950, 2 vols.), which provides much background material on the preceding decades of Greek history. There are several biographies of Venizelos, the most recent and the best being by D. Alastos, *Venizelos: Patriot, Statesman Revolutionary* (London, 1942). See also S. B. Chester, *Life of Venizelos* (London, 1921); H. A. Gibbons, *Venizelos* (New York, 1923); V. J. Seligman, *The Victory of Venizelos: A Study of Greek Politics, 1910–1918* (London, 1920).

The 1909 revolution of the Military League has been described by the leader of the League, Colonel N. K. Zorbas, *Apomnemoneumata* [*Reminiscences*] (Athens, 1925); and by A. Theodorides, *He epanastasis kai to ergon tes* [*The Revolution and Its Work*] (Athens, 1914). For the constitutional issues involved, see N. Kaltchas, *Introduction to the Constitutional History of Modern Greece* (New York, 1940).

On the international relations of Greece during these decades, the most detailed and authoritative work is the fourth volume of E. Driault and M. Lhéritier, *Histoire diplomatique de la Grèce* (Paris, 1926). On specific issues, see S. T. Lascaris, *La politique extérieure de la Grèce avant et après le congrès de Berlin* (Paris, 1924); and the same author's "Greece and Serbia during the War of 1885," *Slavonic Review*, XI (July, 1932), 88–99. On the Cretan question and the Greco-Turkish War, the best survey, and one on which I have leaned heavily, is W. L. Langer, *The Diplomacy of Imperialism 1890–1902* (New York, 1935), Vol. I, chs. 10, 11, which provides a very extensive bibliography of Western sources. Materials published more recently, such as Vol. XIII of the first series of *Documents diplomatiques français* (Paris, 1953), do not alter the account as given in Langer. Of the Greek materials, the most important is A. Ainian-Mazarakes, *Historike melete 1821–1907 kai o polemos tou 1897* (*Meta parartematos 1898–1908*) [*Historical Study 1821–1907 and the War of 1897* (*With a Supplement on the Years 1898–1908*)] (Athens, 1950, 2 vols.), which provides much background material on the earlier decades as well as a 500-page analysis of the political and military aspects of the war. On Crete after the 1897 war, see J. S. Dutkowski, *L'occupation de la Crète, 1897–1909; une expérience d'administration internationale d'un territoire* (Paris, 1953).

The basic works on Greek economic development in the nineteenth century are listed in the bibliography for Chapter 15. For the financial difficulties of the 1890's there is the excellent study by J. A. Levandis, *The Greek Foreign Debt and the Great Powers 1821–1898* (New York, 1944). On the agrarian question there are available in English the following: "Agrarian Reform," *International Review of Agricultural Economics,* XII (August, 1921), 462–472; G. Servakis and C. Pertountzi, "The Agricultural Policy of Greece," in O. S. Morgan, ed., *Agricultural Systems of Middle Europe* (New York, 1953), ch. 4; and K. A. Doukas, "Agrarian Reform in Greece," *American Journal of Economics and Sociology,* V (October, 1945), 79–92. The basic work remains that of D. Zographos, *Historia tes hellenikes georgias* [*History of Greek Agriculture*] (Athens, 1922–1924, 3 vols.). For a colorful account of the struggles of the Thessalian peasants by one of their leaders, see D. Bousdras, *He apeleutherosis ton sklavon agroton* [*The Liberation of the Enslaved Peasants*] (Athens, 1951). On the currant problem there is J. Kipps, "The Greek Currant Trade," *Economic History,* II (January, 1930), 137–153.

The best study of Greek emigration to all countries is by N. J. Polyzos, *Essai sur l'émigration grecque* (Paris, 1947). H. P. Fairchild's *Greek Immigration to the United States* (New Haven, Conn., 1911) remains the best work on the subject. See also T. Saloutos, *They Remember America: The Story of the Repatriated Greek-Americans* (Berkeley, Calif., 1956), an analysis of why Greek-Americans returned to their homeland and of their ideas and influence. On the significance of emigrant remittances, see E. G. Mears, "The Unique Position in Greek Trade of Emigrant Remittances," *Quarterly Journal of Economics,* XXXVII (May, 1923), 535–540.

26. Rumania

For bibliographies, sources, and general histories, see the works given for Chapter 18. The Communist regime in Rumania following World War II published a three-volume collection of documents on the period 1877–1878: M. Roller, V. Cherestesiu, V. Maciu, and S. Stirbu, eds. *Documente Privind Istoria Romaniei: Razboiul Pentru Independenta* (Bucharest, 1952–1953). This collection, which was not used for this study, is reviewed by S. A. Fischer-Galati in the June, 1955, issue of the *Journal of Modern History.* An analysis of Rumanian diplomacy during the Russo-Turkish War is given in R. V. Burks, "Romania and the Balkan Crisis of 1875–78," *Journal of Central European Affairs,* II (July, 1942), 119–134, and II (October, 1942), 310–320. For a broader picture of Rumanian foreign policy, see E. Ebel, *Rumänien und die Mittelmächte von der russisch-türkischen Krise 1877–78 bis zum Bukaresten Frieden vom 10 August 1913* (Berlin, 1939). A convenient summary of the steps leading to the 1883 secret alliance is given by W. L. Langer, *European Alliances and Alignments 1871–1890* (New York, 1931). See also the data in *Aus dem Leben König Karls von Rumänien* (Stuttgart, 1894–1900, 4 vols.); and the brief review in the pamphlet by G. I. Bratianu, "La politique extérieure du roi Charles I de Roumanie" (Bucharest, 1940).

For domestic developments after 1878 see the general histories given under Chapter 18. The indispensable secondary works for the 1907 Peasant Revolt are D. Mitrany, *The Land and the Peasant in Rumania* (London, 1930), and H. L. Roberts, *Rumania: Political Problems of an Agrarian State* (New Haven, Conn., 1951). The Communist Rumanian government has published a three-volume collection of documents on the revolt: M. Roller, ed., *Rascoala Taranilor din 1907* (Bucharest, 1948–1949). This collection, which has not been used for this study, is also reviewed in the June, 1955, issue of the *Journal of Modern History.* A revealing account of the plight of the peasantry at this time and of their revolt is given in the novel by Leo Katz, *Seedtime* (New York, 1947). For a contrast see the memoirs of Princess Anne-Marie Callimachi, *Yesterday Was Mine* (New York, 1949), which portrays the life of the Greco-Rumanian aristocracy in the nineteenth century.

For the economic development of Rumania apart from agriculture, see C. N. Jordan, *The Rumanian Oil Industry* (New York, 1955); D. Kastris, *Les capitaux étrangers dans la finance roumaine* (Paris, 1921); S. Radulesco, *La politique financière de la Roumanie* (Paris, 1923); A Theveneau, *La Roumanie économique et le change roumain au lendemain de la guerre* (Paris, 1928); and *Rumania: An Economic Handbook* by United States Department of Commerce, Bureau of Foreign and Domestic Commerce, Special Agents Series, no. 222 (Washington, D. C., 1924). On emigration there is C. A. Galitzi, *A Study of Assimilation among the Roumanians in the United States* (New York, 1929).

An excellent account of the Transylvanian Rumanians after 1878 is given by R. W. Seton-Watson, *A History of the Roumanians* (Cambridge, Eng., 1934). For the Rumanian interest in the Vlachs see the memoirs of the Rumanian diplomatist, T. G. Djuvara, *Mes missions diplomatiques* (Paris, 1930), excerpts of which were published in installments in the 1929 and 1930 issues of *Revue des sciences politiques*.

27. Albanian Awakening

Albanian historiography is in a rudimentary state, careful studies being needed in almost every phase of the country's history. Several bibliographies are available: F. Manek, G. Pekmezi, A. Stotz, *Albanesische bibliographie* (Vienna, 1909); E. Legrand, *Bibliographie albanaise: description raisonnée des ouvrages publiés en albanais ou relatifs à l'Albanie du quinzième siècle à l'année 1900* (Paris, 1912); N. B. Jopson, "A Survey of Albanian Studies," *Slavonic Review,* III (1924–1925), 412–418; J. G. Kersopoulos, "Albanie: ouvrages et articles de revues parus de 1555 à 1934," *Les Balkans,* V (1934), 377–424, 651–712.

The best general history is by J. Swire, *Albania: The Rise of a Kingdom* (London, 1929), although it is very spotty and has an abominable reference system. The following surveys are also useful, but the authors are ardent nationalists and write accordingly: C. A. Dako, *Albania: The Master Key to the Near East* (Boston, 1919); C. A. Chekrezi, *Albania: Past and Present* (New York, 1919). The Dako work is the more important, containing revealing autobiographical sections. R. Almagia, *L'Albania* (Rome, 1930) is a useful general handbook with a bibliography. See also the very revealing chapters on Albania in H. N. Brailsford, *Macedonia: Its Races and Their Future* (London, 1906); and C. Eliot, *Turkey in Europe* (London, 1908). A vivid picture of customs and manners is given by two well-known English authorities: Margaret Hasluck, *The Unwritten Law in Albania* (Cambridge, Eng., 1954), and Mary E. Durham, *High Albania* (London, 1909).

The only work analyzing the social structure in Albania at the time of the Turkish conquest is by N. D. Smirnova and I. G. Senkevich, "Osvoboditelnaia Borba Albanskogo Naroda Protiv Turetskikh Porabotitelei v XV Veke," ["The Albanian People's War of Liberation against the Turkish Oppressors in the Fifteenth Century,"] *Voprosy Istorii* no. 12 (December, 1953), pp. 80–97. For the career of Skanderbeg see Bishop Fan S. Noli, *George Castrioti Scanderbeg (1405–1468)* (New York, 1947); A. Gegaj, *L'Albanie et l'invasion turque au XVᵉ siècle* (Louvain, 1937); J. H. Kramers, "Skanderbeg," *Encyclopedia of Islam;* and J. Radonić, *Djuradj Kastriot Skenderbeg [George Kastriotis Skanderbeg]* (Belgrade, 1942). The latter work, published under the auspices of the

Serbian Academy of Sciences, was not available for this study. See also F. Pall, "Die Geschichte Skanderbegs im Lichte der neuren Forschung," *Leipz. Viertel-jahrschrift f. Südosteuropa,* VI (1942), 85–96 (not consulted).

There is no careful history of events and institutions in Albania during the centuries of Turkish rule. Most accounts concentrate on outstanding person-alities like Skanderbeg and Ali Pasha—see bibliography on Ali Pasha in Chapter 13. There is especial need for a study of the land system and social structure in the Turkish period, including an analysis of the few dominant families, their rela-tions with each other and with the imperial government.

On the Albanian national awakening there is S. Skendi, "Beginnings of Albanian Nationalist Trends in Culture and Education (1878–1912)," *Journal of Central European Affairs,* XII (January, 1953), 356–367, which is useful but of a survey nature. There is need for a detailed study of the national awakening in its educational, literary, and political aspects. Another gap is the history of the Albanian colonies, which played so important a role in the renaissance. There is the excellent account of the Albanians in the United States by the Federal Writers' Project of the Works Progress Administration, *The Albanian Struggle in the Old World and New* (Boston, 1939), as well as some studies of the communities in Italy—see references in the Skendi article cited above. But there do not appear to be histories of the important colonies in Constantinople, Sofia, Egypt, Bucharest, and elsewhere.

The first impact of Albanian nationalism on European diplomacy is well described in S. Skendi, "Beginnings of Albanian Nationalist and Autonomous Trends: The Albanian League: 1878–1881," *American Slavic and East Euro-pean Review,* XII (April, 1953), 219–232. For the period between 1881 and the Balkan Wars there is the revealing study by S. Skendi, "Albanian Political Thought and Revolutionary Activity, 1881–1912," *Südost-Forschungen,* XIII (1954), 1–40. See also I. S. Galkin, "Iz Istorii Natsionalnogo-osvoboditelnogo dvi-zheniia v Albanii v 1910–12 Godakh," ["From the History of the National Libera-tion Movement in Albania in 1910–12,"] *Voprosy Istorii,* no. 11 (1954), pp. 35–46; *The Memoirs of Ismail Kemal Bey* (London, 1920); M. E. Durham, *The Struggle for Scutari* (London, 1914); H. C. Woods, *The Danger Zone of Europe* (London, 1911); and R. W. Graves, *Storm Centres of the Near East* (London, 1933). Chapter 13 of the latter work is a revealing account of a journey through-out Albania on the eve of the Balkan Wars.

28. Diplomatic Developments

Much has been written on the Macedonian question, yet there is no adequate comprehensive study. Most available works are either frankly partisan or else general and superficial with much emphasis on the anarchy and conflicting claims but without careful research and analysis. A definitive work remains to be written on the basis of the Balkan materials, traveler and missionary accounts, and Western archive materials. Monographic studies are also needed: for exam-ple, an analysis of the relations between the IMRO and the External Organiza-tion, and also an analysis of the work of the exarchate in Macedonia to determine the extent to which it was responsible for the Bulgarophil sentiments of the Mace-donian population as reported by most contemporary travelers.

A good introduction to the Macedonian question may be obtained by reading first H. R. Wilkinson, *Maps and Politics: A Review of the Ethnographic Cartography of Macedonia* (Liverpool, 1951), a valuable study by a geographer who traces the evolution of ethnographic theories and national claims regarding Macedonia; and then H. N. Brailsford, *Macedonia: Its Races and Their Future* (London, 1906), which is the best general study available. Among the best of the recent studies are G. Weigand, *Ethnographie von Makedonien* (Leipzig, 1924); J. Ancel, *La Macédoine* (Paris, 1930); W. Jacob, *Die makedonische Frage* (Berlin, 1931); K. Koitscheff, *Mazedonien geschichtlich, staatspolitisch und völkerrechtlich in Verbindung mit der Entwicklung des bulgarischen Staates bis zum Balkankrieg 1912* (Heidelberg, 1948). Contemporary Western accounts include R. von Mach, *Die Macedonische Frage* (Vienna, 1895); V. Bérard, *La Macédoine* (Paris, 1897); and W. Miller, *Travels and Politics in the Near East* (London, 1898). See also the references to Macedonia in W. S. Vucinich, *Serbia between East and West: The Events of 1903–1908* (Stanford, Calif., 1954), which includes important information on recent research and interpretations on the Macedonian question by Yugoslav historians. A comprehensive survey of Macedonia's development, with emphasis on the geographic background, is available in the unpublished doctoral dissertation by H. L. Kostanick, "Macedonia: A Study in Political Geography" (Clark University, 1948).

The Bulgarian viewpoint is presented in I. Ivanov, *La question macédoine* (Paris, 1920); S. Radeff, *La Macédoine et la renaissance bulgare* (Sofia, 1918); Historicus [S. Panaretoff], *Bulgaria and Her Neighbors* (New York, 1917); and V. A. Tsanov, *Reports and Letters from American Missionaries Referring to the Distribution of Nationalities in the Former Provinces of European Turkey 1858–1918* (Sofia, 1919). For the Serbian viewpoint, see T. R. Georgevich, *Macedonia* (London, 1918); J. Cvijić, *Remarks on the Ethnography of the Macedonian Slavs* (London, 1906); and the pioneer Serbian claim for Macedonia in S. Gopčević, *Makedonien und Alt-Serbien* (Vienna, 1888). The Greek claims are set forth in C. Nicolaides, *La Macédoine* (Berlin, 1899); N. Stroumzi, *La question macédonienne, étude d'histoire diplomatique et de droit public* (Lyons, 1932); V. Colocotronis, *La Macédoine et l'hellénisme: étude historique et ethnographique* (Paris, 1919); S. P. Phocas Cosmetatos, *La Macédoine: son passé et son présent* (Lausanne, 1919); N. Kasasis, *L'hellénisme et la Macédoine* (Paris, 1903); and N. B. Vlachos, *To Makedonikon os Fasis tou Anatolikou Zetematos, 1878–1908* [*The Macedonian Problem as a Phase of the Eastern Question, 1878–1908*] (Athens, 1935). The latter is the only significant work in the Greek language on the Macedonian problem, the others being either polemical tracts or restricted local histories. Finally, on the Vlachs there is G. Weigand, *Die Aromunen* (Leipzig, 1895); for the use Rumania made of the Vlachs see the account of the Rumanian diplomat T. G. Djuvara, *Mes missions diplomatiques* (Paris, 1930), and "Souvenirs diplomatiques," *Revue des sciences politiques,* LII (April–June, 1929), 205–229 and continued in three following issues.

For the Balkan policies of the great powers after 1878 see the brief but lucid and well-documented survey in W. L. Langer, *European Alliances and Alignments 1871–1890* (New York, 1931), ch. 10. For special aspects see A. F. Pribram, *The Secret Treaties of Austria-Hungary, 1879–1914* (Cambridge, Mass., 1920, 2 vols.); G. Yacktchitch, "Le traité secret austro-serbe du 28 juin, 1881 et du 9 fevrier, 1889," *Revue d'histoire diplomatique,* LI (October–December, 1937), 429–466, and LII (January–March, 1938), 65–105; M. C. Wren, "Pobedonostsev and Russian Influence in the Balkans, 1881–1888," *Journal of Modern History*, XIX (June, 1947), 130–141; W. N. Medlicott, "The Powers and the Unification of the Two Bulgarias," *English Historical Review*, LIV (January, 1939), 263–284; C. Jelavich, "Russo-Bulgarian Relations 1892–1896," *Journal of Modern History*, XXIV (December, 1952), 341–351.

For inter-Balkan relations from 1878 to 1914 see the general survey in L. S. Stavrianos, *Balkan Federation: A History of the Movement toward Balkan Unity in Modern Times* (Northampton, Mass., 1944), chs. 6, 7, which provides a full bibliography. See also M. Lascaris, "Greece and Serbia during the War of 1885," *Slavonic Review*, XI (July, 1932), 88–99; E. Walters, "The Serbo-Bulgarian Secret Treaty of 19 February, 1897," *Slavonic Review*, XXVIII (April, 1950), 493–499; E. C. Helmreich and C. E. Black, "The Russo-Bulgarian Military Convention of 1902," *Journal of Modern History*, IX (December, 1937), 471–482.

Most accounts of Abdul Hamid are of the "bloody Sultan" variety. Typical is E. Pears, *Life of Abdul Hamid* (London, 1917), and his *Forty Years in Constantinople* (New York, 1916). Better balanced though far from adequate are G. Roy, *Abdul Hamid, le sultan rouge* (Paris, 1936) and A. Wittlin, *Abdul Hamid: The Shadow of God*. Tr. from the German by N. Denny (London, 1939). The only comprehensive study of the origins of the Young Turk movement is by E. E. Ramsaur, Jr., *The Young Turks: Prelude to the Revolution of 1908* (Princeton, N. J., 1957). A Marxist interpretation is given in Kh. Z. Gabidullin, *Mladoturetskaia revoliutsiia* [*The Young Turk Revolution*] (Moscow, 1936). Unfortunately this is not based on original research but interprets well-known facts to show that the Young Turks were bourgeois in outlook and "against the proletariat" (p. 225). The most important work on the Young Turks in Paris before 1908 is P. Fesch, *Constantinople aux derniers jours d' Abdul Hamid* (Paris, 1907). This contains much documentary material on the struggle between Riza and Sabaheddin. The author, a French priest, interested himself in Sabaheddin and is partial to him.

Once the revolution occurred, numerous contemporary accounts were written by Western travelers and journalists attracted by the sensational news. These accounts vary greatly and reflect several viewpoints—pro–Young Turk, pro–Liberal Union, pro-nationalities, but none of them pro–Abdul Hamid. Taken together they constitute a valuable source. G. F. Abbott, *Turkey in Transition* (London, 1909); V. Bérard, *La révolution turque* (Paris, 1909); H. Diamantopoulo, *Le réveil de la Turquie* (Alexandria, 1909); A. Durand, *Jeune Turquie, vieille France* (Paris, 1909); Y. Fehmi, *La révolution ottomane* (*1908–1910*) (Paris, 1911); E. F. Knight, *Turkey: The Awakening of Turkey: The Turkish Revolution of 1908* (Boston, 1910); R. Pinon, *L'Europe et la jeune Turquie* (Paris, 1911); A. Sarrou, *La jeune Turquie et la révolution* (Paris, 1912); A. Graf von Sternberg, *Die türkische Revolution* (Berlin, 1909); W. M. Ramsay, *The Revolution in Constantinople and Turkey* (London, 1909); F. McCullagh, *The Fall of Abd-ul-Hamid* (London, 1910). Also worth noting are the diplomatic reports on the Young Turk revolution in *Die Grosse Politik der europäischen Kabinette 1871–1914*, XXV, Pt. II, 557–626; and *British Documents on the Origins of the War 1898–1914*, V, 247–320.

The standard works on the Bosnian crisis are B. E. Schmitt, *The Annexation of Bosnia 1908–1909* (Cambridge, Eng., 1937) and N. Nintchitch, *La crise bosniaque (1908–1909) et les puissances européennes* (Paris, 1937, 2 vols.), the latter work being written by a former Yugoslav foreign minister who employs Serbian archive material. See also W. D. David, *European Diplomacy in the Near Eastern Question 1906–1909* (Urbana, Ill., 1940); and W. M. Carlgren, *Iswolsky und Aehrenthal vor der bosnischen Annexionkrise: russische und öster-reichisch-ungarische Balkanpolitik, 1906–1908* (Uppsala, 1955).

The indispensable study of the Balkan wars is E. C. Helmreich, *The Diplomacy of the Balkan Wars 1912–1913* (Cambridge, Mass., 1938), which includes a clear summary of the military campaigns and full documentation. See also the *Report of the International Commission to Inquire into the Causes and Conduct of the Balkan Wars* (Washington, D. C., 1914), which contains interesting data and which appears quaint in retrospect after two world wars. Another work of this type that is worth note is by Diplomatist [George Young], *Nationalism and War in the Near East* (Oxford, 1915).

The most detailed account of Balkan diplomatic developments on the eve of World War I is in the unpublished doctoral dissertation by M. Faissler, "European Diplomacy in the Balkan Peninsula, August 10, 1913–June 28, 1914" (University of Chicago, 1938). See also the valuable material in "war origins" books such as S. B. Fay, *The Origins of the World War* (New York, 1934, 2nd rev. ed., 2 vols.); B. E. Schmitt, *The Coming of the War, 1914* (New York, 1930, 2 vols.); and L. Albertini, *The Origins of the War of 1914* (London, 1952, 2 vols.), the latter work having been published first in Italy in 1942 and then translated and edited by Isabella M. Massey.

29. Sarajevo and War

Works on the Yugoslav revolutionary movement and on the situation in Bosnia are given in Chapter 24 on Serbia and the South Slavs, 1878–1914. The best and most recent analysis of the Sarajevo murder and of the responsibility for the crime is given in L. Albertini, *The Origins of the War of 1914,* tr. and ed. by I. M. Massey (London, 1953), Vol. II, chs. 1–3, which presents new material based on personal interviews. This should be supplemented by recent Yugoslav interpretations of the Black Hand which are described in W. S. Vucinich, *Serbia between East and West: The Events of 1903–1908* (Stanford, Calif., 1954), pp. 102–105. See also S. Gavrilović, "New Evidence on the Sarajevo Assassination," *Journal of Modern History,* XXVII (December, 1955), 410–414, which gives the text of a statement that Dimitrijevich allegedly wrote concerning his role in the Sarajevo murder. In addition there are the standard studies of the *Kriegs-schuldfrage.* The best German statements are by A. von Wegerer, *Der Ausbruch des Weltkrieges* (Berlin, 1939, 2 vols.); H. Lutz, *Die europäische Politik in der Julikrise, 1914* (Berlin, 1930); and E. Anrich, *Europas Diplomatie am Vorabend des Weltkrieges* (Berlin, 1937). For French interpretations see P. Renouvin, *Les origines immédiates de la guerre* (Paris, 1937); C. Bloch, *Les causes de la guerre mondiale* (Paris, 1933); and J. Isaac, *Un débat historique* (Paris, 1933), the latter author criticizing his French colleagues. The best American studies are by S. B. Fay, *The Origins of the World War* (New York, 1934, rev. ed., 2 vols.), which is most critical of Russia, Austria, and France; and B. E. Schmitt, *The Coming of the War, 1914* (New York, 1930, 2 vols.), which is most critical of Germany and Austria. Finally, there is R. W. Seton-Watson, *Sarajevo* (London,

1926), which is valuable for the Yugoslav nationalist movement and which seeks to exculpate Serbia. Its conclusions should be checked with the more recent evidence presented by Albertini.

The Serbian victory in 1914 and defeat in 1915 are described eloquently by J. C. Adams, *Flight in Winter* (Princeton, N. J., 1942), who recaptures admirably the atmosphere of those years. For the intervention of Turkey, see the fully documented account of H. N. Howard, *The Partition of Turkey: A Diplomatic History 1913–1923* (Norman, Okla., 1931), ch. 3. On the Dardanelles and Gallipoli expeditions, see M. Larcher, *La guerre turque dans la guerre mondiale* (Paris, 1926), which is based on official Turkish documents; C. F. Aspinall-Oglander, *Military Operations, Gallipoli* (London, 1929), based on official British documents; the personal reports of Winston Churchill, *The World Crisis* (New York, 1928) Vol. II; and Liman von Sanders, *Dardanellensieg* (Munich, 1920). For the diplomatic aspects of the Straits problem, see R. J. Kerner, "Russia, the Straits and Constantinople, 1914–1915," *Journal of Modern History*, I (September, 1929), 400–415; and the same author's "Russia and the Straits, 1915–1917," *Slavonic Review*, VIII (March, 1930), 589–593. Two recent publications are relevant here: C. J. Smith, Jr., *The Russian Struggle for Power, 1914–1917: A Study of Russian Foreign Policy During the First World War* (New York, 1956), which throws much light on the roles of all the Balkan countries at this time; and A. Moorehead, *Gallipoli* (London, 1956), an absorbing and well-written account that is comparable to Cecil Woodham-Smith's works on the Crimean War.

The best monographic study on Bulgaria's intervention is the unpublished dissertation by J. M. Potts, "Russian Diplomacy and Bulgaria, 1914–1915" (Columbia University, 1951), which gives a full bibliography of Slavic and Western sources. A briefer but more available analysis is given in Howard, *op. cit.*, pp. 152–166. Important personal accounts may be found in V. Radoslavov, *Bulgarien und die Weltkrise* (Berlin, 1923); and N. and C. R. Buxton, *The War and the Balkans* (London, 1915). A Marxist interpretation is given by T. Vlakhov, "Bolgariia i Tsentralnite Sili v Nadvecherieto na Pervata Svetovna Voina," ["Bulgaria and the Central Powers on the Eve of the First World War,"] *Izvestiia* (Sofia), nos. 1–2 (1951), pp. 39–80. The latter work denounces Ferdinand and the bourgeois politicians for intervening in the war for "chauvinist-revanchist" reasons, and praises the "Narrow" Socialists for opposing the war, as did Lenin.

There is no full-scale study of Rumanian diplomacy during World War I. A comprehensive and convenient account is given in R. W. Seton-Watson, *A History of the Roumanians* (Cambridge, Eng., 1934), chs. 5–6. On the Bessarabian dispute, see C. Uhlig, *Die Bessarabische Frage* (Breslau, 1926); G. I. Bratianu *La problème des frontières Russo-Romaines* (Bucharest, 1928); and, for the Soviet viewpoint, A. Dolnik, *Bessarabiia pod vlastiu Ruminskikh boyar 1918–1940* [*Bessarabia under the Rule of the Rumanian Boyars*] (Moscow, 1945).

Much material has been published on Greece in World War I because of the controversy involved. For the diplomatic aspects, see Vol. V of E. Driault, *Histoire diplomatique de la Grèce* (Paris, 1926), which uses the Greek Foreign Office archives and which seeks to steer a middle course between the Venizelists and the Royalists; and the unpublished doctoral dissertations by J. H. Lehmann, "Greece and Salonica: A Study in Allied Cooperation 1914–1917" (Northwestern University, 1949), and by J. K. Warren, "The Diplomatic Relations between Greece, France and England 1914–1917" (Ohio State University, 1924). The outstanding pro-Constantine accounts are by A. Frangoulis, *La Grèce et la crise mondiale* (Paris, 1926) and S. Phocas-Cosmetatos, *The Tragedy of Greece* (London, 1928), both of which present ·many documents from the Greek archives. The Venizelist viewpoint is presented in the numerous biographies of the statesman, of which the best are by W. H. Crawfurd-Price, *Venizelos and the War* (London, 1917), and D. Alastos, *Venizelos* (London, 1942). See also Venizelos' own speeches in the chamber, published in *Greece in Her True Light as Expounded by E. K. Venizelos,* tr. by Xanthaki and Sakellarios (New York, 1916); and also the account by a member of the Greek royal family: Prince Nicholas, *Political Memories 1914–1917* (London, 1928). Finally, see the excellent bibliographical essay on this topic in A. A. Pallis, *Greece's Anatolian Adventure—and After . . .* (London, 1937), App. I.

Finally, for the Saloniki campaign which ended the war in the Balkans there is the well-written official British history by C. Falls and A. F. Becke, *Military Operations in Macedonia* (London, 1933, 2 vols.), and the outspoken account by the French commander, General M. P. Sarrail, *Mon commandement en Orient 1916–1918* (Paris, 1930).

30. Peace Settlement

By all odds the best general account of the peace settlement is H. W. V. Temperley, ed., *A History of the Peace Conference of Paris* (London, 1920–1924, 6 vols.), which does not, however, cover the treaties with Turkey. See also S. Saucerman, *International Transfers of Territory in Europe* (Washington, D. C., 1937) for convenient statistical data concerning territorial changes. For the breakup of Austria-Hungary, see D. F. Strong, *Austria (October 1918–March 1919): Transition from Empire to Republic* (New York, 1939); F. Déak, *Hungary at the Peace Conference: The Diplomatic History of the Treaty of Trianon* (New York, 1942); C. A. Macartney, *Hungary and Her Successors: The Treaty of Trianon and Its Consequences 1919–1937* (New York, 1937); and H. W. V. Temperley, "How the Hungarian Frontiers Were Drawn," *Foreign Affairs,* VI (April, 1928), 432–447, the latter being a vigorous defense of the Trianon Treaty against the revisionists.

An excellent summary of Rumania in the war and peace conferences is given in R. W. Seton-Watson, *A History of the Roumanians from Roman Times to the Completion of Unity* (Cambridge, Eng., 1934), chs. 15–17. A considerable number of works have been published on the making of Yugoslavia, the best being E. Holzer, *Die Entstehung des Jugoslawischen Staates* (Berlin, 1929); Z. S. Tomitch, *La formation de l'état yougoslave* (Paris, 1927); R. J. Kerner, *The Jugo-Slav Movement* (Cambridge, Mass., 1918); R. J. Kerner, "Yugoslavia and the Peace Conference," in *Yugoslavia,* ed. by R. J. Kerner (Berkeley, Calif., 1949), ch. 6; and C. Jelavich, "Nikola P. Pašić: Greater Serbia or Jugoslavia," *Journal of Central European Affairs,* II (July, 1951), 133–152. Various participants have also left accounts because of the controversies involved: S. Pribitchevich, *La dictature du roi Alexandre* (Paris, 1933); A. Pavelić, *Aus dem Kampfe um den selbständigen Staat Kroatien* (Vienna, 1931); Count Carlo Sforza, *Fifty Years of War and Diplomacy in the Balkans* (New York, 1940); and the "Autobiography of Stephen Radich," *Current History,* XXIX (October, 1928), 82–102. See also the excellent detailed account in the unpublished master's thesis by D. N.

Ristic, "Foreign Relations of Yugoslavia 1914–1934" (University of California, Los Angeles, 1953), chs. 1, 2.

On the Neuilly Treaty there is, in addition to the chapters in the Temperley volumes cited above, the study by L. Kratchounov, *La politique extérieure de la Bulgarie 1880–1920* (Sofia, 1932), which is excellent though brief. Interesting details are given by K. Todorov, *Balkan Firebrand: The Autobiography of a Rebel, Soldier and Statesman* (Chicago, 1943), who served at the time as minister to Belgrade. See also "Dnevnikot na Mikhail Sarafov za Sklinchvaneto na Mirniia Dogovor v Noii pres 1919g.," ["The Diary of Mikhail Sarafov on the Signing of the Peace Treaty of Neuilly in 1919,"] *Izvestiia*, nos. 3–4 (1951), pp. 314–365. This article, published in the journal of the Bulgarian Academy of Sciences, includes a preface by Khristo Khristov (pp. 314–319), which presents the current Communist interpretation of the Neuilly Treaty, including an attack upon the American consul in Sofia on the grounds that he aided the Bulgarian bourgeoisie to suppress the army rebellion, save capitalism, and use Bulgaria as a base for intervention against the Soviet Union.

The relations of the United States to these treaties are analyzed in the following works by V. S. Mamatey: "The United States and Bulgaria in World War I," *American Slavic and East European Review*, XII (April, 1953), 233–257; "The United States and the Dissolution of Austria-Hungary," *Journal of Central European Affairs*, X (October, 1950), 256–270; "The United States and the Origins of the Adriatic Question, 1918," *Florida State University Studies*, no. 4 (1951), pp. 45–60.

The best comprehensive account of the Sèvres Treaty and of the preceding secret treaties is H. N. Howard, *The Partition of Turkey: A Diplomatic History 1913–1923* (Norman, Okla., 1931). An interesting and revealing personal account of the Turkish nationalist movement is given in Halidé Edib, *The Turkish Ordeal* (New York, 1928). See also Kemal's marathon speech to the People's Party Congress in which he reviewed the nationalist movement from 1919 to 1924: *A Speech Delivered by Ghazi Mustapha Kemal . . . October 1927* (Leipzig, 1929). Valuable data on the conditions in Turkey, out of which the nationalist movement developed, are given in Ahmed Emin, *Turkey in the World War* (New Haven, Conn., 1930). Finally, the Soviet Orientalist, A. F. Miller, has written *Kratkaia Istoriia Turtsii* [*A Short History of Turkey*] (Moscow, 1948), in which he presents the Marxist interpretation that the Anatolian peasant was the main foundation of the Turkish struggle for independence; that the proletariat was too weak to head the struggle; that the bourgeoisie consequently headed the movement; and that the revolution therefore did not proceed beyond the winning of independence, leaving class relationships and land arrangements largely untouched. For further references see M. D. Mercanligil, *Catalogue of Books on Ataturk and the Turkish Revolution* (Ankara, 1953).

The best single volume on the Greek crisis is by A. A. Pallis, *Greece's Anatolian Venture—and After* (London, 1937). More detailed accounts are available in A. Frangoulis, *La Grèce et la crise mondiale* (Paris, 1926) which is anti-Venizelist; G. Ventires, *He Hellas tou 1910–20* [*Greece in 1910–20*] (Athens, 1931), which is pro-Venizelist; and the fifth volume of E. Driault and M. Lhéritier, *Histoire diplomatique de la Grèce contemporaine jusqu'à nos jours* (Paris, 1926). The latter work takes an independent position, and as a result the Greek government of 1925 attempted to prevent its publication. This episode is described in E. Driault, *Le roi Constantin* (Paris, 1930). Finally, see the excellent biblio-graphical essay on this topic in Appendix I of the Pallis work listed above.

The best account of the Greco-Turkish war in a Western language is by J. L. E. Bujac, *Les campagnes de l'armée héllenique, 1918–1922* (Paris, 1930). For the Lausanne Treaty, see the relevant chapters in the Howard study cited above, and also the excellent analysis by R. H. Davison, "Turkish Diplomacy from Mudros to Lausanne," in *The Diplomats 1919–1939*, ed. by G. A. Craig and F. Gilbert (Princeton, N. J., 1953), ch. 6.

Finally, on the refugees and population exchange, there are several fine studies: *Greek Refugee Settlement* (Geneva, 1926); H. Morgenthau, *I Was Sent to Athens* (New York, 1929); C. B. Eddy, *Greece and the Greek Refugees* (London, 1931); and S. P. Ladas, *The Exchange of Minorities: Bulgaria, Greece and Turkey* (New York, 1932). These accounts should be checked with the more critical analysis of the ethnographic effect of the population shifts upon Macedonia given in H. R. Wilkinson, *Maps and Politics: A Review of the Ethnographic Cartography of Macedonia* (Liverpool, 1951), pp. 260–273.

31. Dynamics of Balkan Politics

The most valuable source for data on interwar Balkan economic develop-ments is *Economic Development in S. E. Europe* (London, Political and Economic Planning, 1945). This includes much statistical material compiled during World War II by experts from all the Eastern European countries except Russia. Much material is also given in the two studies by the Royal Institute of International Affairs: *The Balkan States: I. Economic* (1936), and *South-Eastern Europe: A Political and Economic Survey* (1939). The distinguished Greek agricultural economist, C. Evelpidi, who has written authoritatively on Greek economic de-velopment, has also analyzed the wider Balkan scene in *Les états balkaniques* (Paris, 1930), and "Le revenu national des pays balkaniques," *Metron*, XIV (June 15, 1940), 159–169. The studies of the English authority, Doreen War-riner, are also noteworthy, especially *Economics of Peasant Farming* (New York, 1939), and "Some Controversial Issues in the History of Agrarian Europe," *Slavonic and East European Review*, XXXII (December, 1953), 168–186. An early study that still is of some value is L. Pasvolsky, *Economic Nationalism of the Danubian States* (New York, 1928), though it deals mostly with international economic matters such as trade, debts, and reparations. Equally specialized is S. D. Zagoroff, J. Vegh, and A. D. Bilimovich, *The Agricultural Economy of the Danubian Countries 1935–45* (Stanford, Calif., 1955), whose main concern is agriculture and food in Hungary, Rumania, Bulgaria, and Yugoslavia during World War II, though considerable data are given on the 1930's. Finally there is the disappointing unpublished doctoral dissertation by M. K. Begdes, "Balkan Economic Problems" (Indiana University, 1944). The author, a Turkish student, is enthusiastic and diligent, but his lack of historical background, together with the broadness of the topic, has resulted in a superficial compendium of well-known facts.

Excellent studies have been published on the population problem in Eastern Europe, the most important being W. E. Moore, *Economic Demography of Eastern and Southern Europe* (Geneva, 1945); and D. Kirk, *Europe's Popula-tion in the Interwar Years* (Geneva, 1946). See also the more theoretical analysis by D. Warriner, "The Population Question in Eastern Europe," *Slavonic Review,* XVI (April, 1939), 629–637. German economic domination on the eve of World War II is analyzed by H. W. Arndt, *Economic Lessons of the Nineteen-Thirties* (London, 1944) and A. Basch, *The Danube Basin and the German Economic Sphere* (New York, 1943). The latter work emphasizes the sinister aspects of German economic penetration while the former points out the benefits derived by the Balkan states.

Social conditions are presented in the statistical data given in the above works by Zagoroff and by Political and Economic Planning of London. See also *Nutrition: Final Report of the Mixed Committee of the League of Nations on the Relation of Nutrition to Health, Agriculture and Economic Policy* (Geneva, 1937), which has a section on "Central and Eastern Europe." See also the article by the famous Yugoslav health expert, A. Stampar, "Observations of a Rural Health Worker," in the October, 1939, issue of the *International Journal of Agrarian Affairs.* Educational conditions and problems are considered in scattered passages of W. M. Kotschnigg, *Unemployment in the Learned Professions* (London, 1937).

Political developments in the Balkans in the interwar period were first analyzed in a meaningful manner by H. Seton-Watson, *Eastern Europe between the Wars 1918–1941* (Cambridge, Eng., 1945), especially ch. 5. Agrarianism is considered briefly by the Bulgarian peasant leader G. M. Dimitrov, "Agrarianism," in *European Ideologies,* ed. by F. Gross (New York, 1948), ch. 10. For a full-length study, see D. Mitrany, *Marx against the Peasant: A Study in Social Dogmatism* (Chapel Hill, N. C., 1951); and the unpublished doctoral dissertation by B. N. Peselj, "Peasant Movements in Southeast Europe" (Georgetown University, 1951). The latter analyzes the political, social, and economic doctrines of Agrarianism in general, and summarizes the histories of the individual Peasant parties.

Works dealing with the Communist parties of individual Balkan countries are given in the bibliographies for the relevant chapters below. All the Balkan parties are covered in Khr. Kabakchiyev, B. Boshkovich, and Ch. D. Vatis, *Kommunisticheskie partii balkanskikh stran* [*Communist Parties of the Balkan Countries*] (Moscow, 1930). The attitude of the Balkan Communist parties toward Balkan federation is analyzed in L. S. Stavrianos, *Balkan Federation: A History of the Movement toward Balkan Unity in Modern Times* (Northampton, Mass., 1944); and their attitude toward the Macedonian problem is traced in E. Barker, *Macedonia: Its Place in Balkan Power Politics* (London, 1950). There is need for objective studies of both the Agrarian and Communist movements in the Balkan Peninsula, including an analysis of such broad problems as the origins of their ideologies, the reasons for Communist predominance over the Socialists, the reasons for Agrarian weakness in Greece and Serbia, relations with the Soviet Union, as well as detailed presentations of the programs and histories of the individual Agrarian and Communist parties.

32. Yugoslavia

For the early constitutional struggle leading to the adoption of the 1921 constitution, see R. J. Kerner, *The Jugo-Slav Movement* (Cambridge, Mass., 1918); the collection of documents in *The Jugo-Slav Movement,* Handbook Prepared under the Historical Section of the Foreign Office, no. 14 (London, 1920); and the excellent analysis by C. Jelavich, "Nikola P. Pašić: Greater Serbia or Jugoslavia?" *Journal of Central European Affairs*, XI (July, 1951), 133–152. Considerable material on the first days of the Yugoslav state may be found in the reports of American official observers published in *Papers Relating to the Foreign Relations of the United States: Paris Peace Conference, 1919*, especially Vol. II (Washington, D. C., 1942), and Vol. XII (Washington, D. C., 1947).

There is no satisfactory political history of Yugoslavia in the interwar period. One work covering the ground is the unpublished doctoral dissertation by E. N. Mittleman, "The Nationality Problem in Yugoslavia: A Survey of Developments 1921–1953" (New York University, 1954), but this describes only the constitutional conflict between the centralists and federalists and throws little light on the forces behind the scenes that moved the political leaders. Another survey of constitutional developments is available in the chapters on the "Yugoslav Movement" and "Constitutional Development 1914–1941" by R. J. Kerner and M. W. Graham, respectively, in R. J. Kerner, ed., *Yugoslavia* (Berkeley, Calif., 1949). The constitutional and administrative issues are analyzed in Charles A. Beard and G. Radin, *The Balkan Pivot: Yugoslavia: A Study in Government and Administration* (New York, 1929). For various interpretations of the political developments in the interwar period see H. Seton-Watson, *Eastern Europe between the Wars 1918–1941* (Cambridge, Eng., 1946), which is critical of the dictatorship; and Stephen Graham, *Alexander of Yugoslavia* (New Haven, Conn., 1939), a sympathetic biography. See also the valuable information concerning the Saloniki trial and its recent historiography, in W. S. Vucinich, *Serbia between East and West: The Events of 1903–1908* (Stanford, Calif., 1954), pp. 104 ff.

The economic development of Yugoslavia has been analyzed in the masterful study by J. Tomasevich, *Peasants, Politics, and Economic Change in Yugoslavia* (Stanford, Calif., 1955). This basic work is essential for the political and social as well as economic growth of Yugoslavia, and consequently has been used heavily in the preparation of this study. The condition of the Yugoslav lands during World War I is well described in ch. 12 of Tomasevich's book, which contains a full bibliography on this topic on p. 217. For those aspects of Yugoslav economic development not considered fully in the Tomasevich study, see his article on "Foreign Economic Relations 1918–1941," in R. J. Kerner, ed., *Yugoslavia* (Berkeley, Calif., 1949), ch. 11; S. D. Obradović, *La politique commerciale de la Yougoslavie* (Belgrade, 1939); and S. M. Kukoleča, *Industrija Jugoslavije 1918–1938* [*Industry of Yugoslavia 1918–1938*] (Belgrade, 1941); and relevant chapters in S. D. Zagoroff *et al.*, *The Agricultural Economy of the Danubian Countries 1935–45* (Stanford, Calif., 1955).

For social and intellectual developments see the relevant chapters in Tomasevich, plus R. Trouton, *Peasant Renaissance in Yugoslavia 1900–1950* (London, 1952); O. Lodge, *Peasant Life in Jugoslavia* (New York, 1942); O. Lodge, "Infant and Maternal Mortality in Jugoslavia, with a Background of General Conditions," *Population*, I (November, 1934), 55–82, and II (November, 1935), 111–148. L. Adamic, *The Native's Return* (New York, 1934); and the articles in Kerner's *Yugoslavia* by A. N. Dragnich, "Social Structure"; by S. K. Turosienski, "Education"; by M. Spinka, "Modern Ecclesiastical Development"; and by W. S. Vucinich, "Yugoslavs of the Moslem Faith." Finally, the history of the socialist and communist movements in Yugoslavia is described in D. Lapchevich, *Istorija Socializma u Srbiji* [*History of Socialism in Serbia*] (Belgrade, 1922); and in Josip Broz Tito's *Report Delivered at the V Congress of the Communist Party of Yugoslavia* (Belgrade, 1948). The latter work includes a survey of the history of the socialist and communist movements in all parts of Yugoslavia from their origins to the present. The beginnings of Slovenian trade unionism are described in J. G. Polach, "The Beginnings of Trade Unionism among the Slavs of the Austrian Empire," *American Slavic and East European Review,* XIV (April, 1955), 239–259. A bibliographical survey of this topic is given by Ivan Avakumović, "Literature on the Marxist Movement in Yugoslavia," *Journal of Central European Affairs,* XV (April, 1954), 66–70.

33. Bulgaria

There is need for a comprehensive history of Bulgarian politics comparable to R. W. Seton-Watson's work on Rumania, and of Bulgarian economics comparable to J. Tomasevich's work on Yugoslavia. For bibliographies see the works given for Chapter 19.

There is a considerable periodical literature on Stambuliski because of the attention he attracted, and some of the articles are excellent, e.g., J. D. Bourchier, "Alexander Stambolisky," *Contemporary Review,* CXVIII (November, 1920), 784–789; P. Gentizon, "Stamboulisky et le peuple bulgare," *Revue de France,* V (October 1, 1923), 593–608. Full-length studies are available in N. D. Petkov, *Aleksandr Stamboliiski: Lichnost i idei* [*Alexander Stambuliski: Personality and Ideas*] (Sofia, 1930); and the biography published in Serbian in Belgrade by one of his followers, K. Todorov, in 1930. Todorov has also published his memoirs, which throw light on various aspects of Bulgarian history in the interwar years—*Balkan Firebrand* (Chicago, 1943). Stambuliski's Agrarian party is described briefly in A. Omelianov, "A Bulgarian Experiment," in *A Systematic Source Book in Rural Sociology,* ed. by P. A. Sorokin, C. C. Zimmerman, and C. J. Galpin (Minneapolis, 1931), II, 638–647; G. M. Dimitrov, "Agrarianism" in F. Gross, *European Ideologies* (New York, 1948), pp. 396–451; and in more detail in P. Kiranov, *Bŭlgarskoto zemledelsko dvizhenie* [*The Bulgarian Agrarian Movement*] (Sofia, 1927). For Stambuliski's efforts in behalf of a "Green International," see M. Hodza, *Federation in Central Europe: Reflections and Reminiscences* (London, 1942); and for the compulsory labor service the best account is by B. G. Djimreff, *Le service obligatoire de travail en Bulgarie* (Toulouse, 1936). Full Bulgarian sources are given in the excellent summary of Stambuliski in XIV, 317, of the *Encyclopedia of the Social Sciences,* by V. Sharenkoff. Worth noting here is the very opinionated work by G. C. Logio, *Bulgaria Past & Present* (Manchester, Eng., 1936), which is strongly anti-Stambuliski and pro-Velchev, but which does contain much valuable material.

The fullest study of the IMRO is by J. Swire, *Bulgarian Conspiracy* (London, 1940) which is pro-Stambuliski and pro-Federalist. S. Christowe, *Heroes and Assassins* (New York, 1935), is strongly anti-Stambuliski and rather pro-Mihailov. A brief but clear and balanced account is available in E. Barker, *Macedonia: Its Place in Balkan Power Politics* (London, 1950). For the role of Stambuliski and the IMRO in Balkan affairs, see L. S. Stavrianos, *Balkan Federation: A History of the Movement toward Balkan Unity in Modern Times* (Northampton, Mass., 1944).

The history of the Communist and Socialist movements in Bulgaria is described in T. Tchitchovsky, *The Socialist Movement in Bulgaria* (London, 1931); Khr. Kabakchiev, "Bolgarskaia Kommunisticheskaia Partiia," in Khr. Kabakchiev, B. Boshkovich, and Ch. D. Vatis, *Kommunisticheskie Partii Balkanskikh Stran* [*Communist Parties of the Balkan Countries*] (Moscow, 1930); and George Dimitrov's Report to the Fifth Congress of the Bulgarian Communist party, December, 1948, which gives an official history of the party.

For Bulgaria's economic development see, first, G. T. Danailov, *Les effets de la guerre en Bulgarie* (Paris, 1932); and then L. Pasvolsky, *Bulgaria's Economic Position* (Washington, D. C., 1930). For the later years, see the periodic reports on "Economic Conditions in Bulgaria" issued in London by the British Department of Overseas Trade—*i.e.,* C. Bramwell report in 1928; S. Harrison report in 1930; T. C. Rapp report in 1932; R. B. B. Tollinton reports in 1935 and 1937; and T. V. Brenan report in 1939. See also the general survey and interpretation in L. P. Savadjiev, *Les caractères et les effets de la politique du nationalisme économique en Bulgarie* (Lyons, 1939). The best studies of Bulgarian agriculture are by J. S. Molov, ed., *Die sozialökonomische Struktur der bulgarischen Landwirtschaft* (Berlin, 1936); the same author's "Bulgarian Agriculture," in *Agricultural Systems of Middle Europe*, ed. by O. S. Morgan (New York, 1933), pp. 41–86; and the relevant chapters in S. D. Zagoroff, *et al., The Agricultural Economy of the Danubian Countries 1935–45* (Stanford, Calif, 1955). Special aspects of Bulgaria's economy are covered by T. S. Kosaroff, *La dette publique extérieure de la Bulgarie (1879–1932)* (Paris, 1933); A. Beshkov, "Tobacco in Bulgaria," *Economic Geography,* XVI (April, 1940), 188–194; and T. Chipkoff, *L'industrie de la rose et de l'essence de roses en Bulgarie* (Strasbourg, 1937).

By far the best analysis of Bulgarian peasant life is presented by the American scholar I. T. Sanders, *Balkan Village* (Lexington, Ky., 1949), a detailed and revealing sociological study of the village of Dragalevtsy near Sofia. See also T. Tchitchovsky, "Political and Social Aspects of Modern Buglaria," *Slavonic Review,* VII (January–March, 1929), 272–287, 594–603, and VIII (June, 1929), 176–187; H. Leslie, *Where East Is West: Life in Bulgaria* (Boston, 1933); W. F. Russell, *Schools in Bulgaria* (New York, 1924); K. S. Chandan, *La presse Bulgare de son origine à nos jours* (Paris, 1933); O. Lodge, "Infant and Mortality Rates in Bulgarian Villages, with a Background of General Conditions," *Population,* II (December, 1937), 60–80; and I. Golosmanoff, *The Public Health Services of Bulgaria* (Lyons, 1926).

34. Greece

Probably more has been published in Western languages on modern Greece than on any other Balkan country, presumably because of the traditional interest in the homeland of ancient civilization. But most publications are fragmentary or superficial, and emphasize cultural topics or local regions. There is no solid comprehensive political history comparable to that of R. W. Seton-Watson on Rumania, or an adequate economic survey comparable to the Mitrany and Roberts studies on Rumania and the Tomasevich study on Yugoslavia. These are serious gaps in Greek historiography, which the factual, anecdotal, and uninterpretive works of William Miller and others have done little to fill.

For bibliographies and general histories see the bibliography for Chapter 15.

Political developments in the interwar period are described by W. Miller, *Greece* (London, 1928); J. Mavrogordato, *Modern Greece: A Chronicle and a Survey 1800–1931* (London, 1931); and E. S. Forster, *A Short History of Modern Greece 1821–1945* (London, 1946). On constitutional developments there are N. Kaltchas, *Introduction to the Constitutional History of Modern Greece* (New York, 1940); P. J. Zepos, *Greek Law: Three Lectures Delivered at Cambridge and Oxford in 1946* (Athens, 1949); and G. T. Bacopoulos, *Outline of the Greek Constitution: Political Systems Since the Greek Revolution of 1821* (Athens, 1950). The following biographies are all positive toward their subjects but do provide important materials: D. Alastos, *Venizelos* (London, 1942); P. N. Pipineles, *Georgios II [George II]* (Athens, 1951); I. A. Pepones, *Nikolaos Plasteras sta gegonota 1909–45 [Nicholas Plastiras in the Events of 1909–45]* (Athens, 1947, 2 vols.); D. Gatopoulos, *Andreas Michalakopoulos, 1875–1938* (Athens, 1947), the latter being based on the premier's personal papers.

For the Metaxas dictatorship there is the general's *[Personal Diary] To prosopiko tou hemerologio* (Athens, 1951–1952, 2 vols.), which reaches only to January, 1921. The dictatorship is defended by M. Malainos, *4 Augoustou: Pos kai diati epeblethe he diktatoria tou I. Metaxa [4th of August: How and Why the Dictatorship of J. Metaxas Was Imposed]* (Athens, 1947); and attacked by I. G. Koronakes, *He politeia tes 4 Augoustou [The Polity of the 4th of August]* (Athens, 1950). An Australian journalist who visited the islands where the political prisoners were kept wrote an interesting and very critical account: B. Birtles, *Exiles in the Aegean* (London, 1938).

The crisis that developed in Greece during and following World War II, leading to the enunciation of the Truman Doctrine and to massive American aid, stimulated considerable study of the ailing Greek economy. The most important study of a general nature is the unpublished doctoral dissertation by A. Pepelasis, "Socio-Cultural Barriers to the Economic Development of Greece" (University of California, Berkeley, 1955), which analyzes the economic development of Greece as well as the retarding influence of the administrative system, the church, the schools, and so on. Several prominent Greek economists are writing on the evolution and the problems of their economy, outstanding being A. Angelopoulos, Ch. Evelpides, and X. Zolotas. Each has written a number of works which are cited in the Pepelasis study. For the economic state of Greece during World War I and immediately thereafter, see A. Andreades, ed., *Les effets économiques et sociaux de la guerre en Grèce* (Paris, 1926), and E. G. Mears, *Greece Today: The Aftermath of the Refugee Impact* (Stanford, Calif., 1929), the author of the latter work being formerly American Resident Trade Commissioner in Greece.

The standard work on the natural resources of Greece is by the UNRRA Committee on the Development of the Productive Resources of Greece. Its Subcommittee on Mineral Resources published *Ho oryktos ploutos tes Hellathos [The Mineral Wealth of Greece]* (Athens, 1947). The most important general study of Greek agriculture in English is the *Report of the FAO Mission for Greece* (Washington, D. C., March, 1947). A more analytical study is given by G. Coutsoumaris, "Possibilities of Economic Development in Greek Agriculture" (University of Chicago, unpublished doctoral dissertation, 1953). For the evolution of Greek agriculture in the interwar years, see "Greece: The Agrarian Reform," *International Review of Agricultural Economics,* XII (August–September, 1921), 463–472; G. Servakis and C. Pertountzi, "The Agricultural Policy of

Greece," in *Agricultural Systems of Middle Europe,* ed. by O. S. Morgan (New York, 1933); and K. A. Doukas, "Agrarian Reform in Greece," *American Journal of Economics and Sociology,* V (October, 1945), 79–92.

The standard study of Greek industrial development is by G. Anastasopoulos, *Historia tes Hellenikes biomechanias* [*History of Greek Industry*] (Athens, 1948, 3 vols.). See also *Report on Economic and Commercial Conditions in Greece* (London, 1938); and S. R. Jordan, *Report on Economic and Commercial Conditions in Greece* (London, 1937). The standard work on Greek labor is by the Marxist historian G. K. Kordatos, *Historia tou Hellenikou ergatikou kinematos* [*History of the Greek Working Class Movement*] (Athens, 1931–1932, 2 vols), which reaches 1918. For the later years see the section on the Greek Communist party in Khr. Kabakchiev, B. Boshkovich, and Ch. D. Vatis, *Kommunisticheskie partii balkanskikh stran* [*Communist Parties of the Balkan Countries*] (Moscow, 1930); and the official history issued by the Central Committee of the Greek Communist party: *Deka chronia agones 1935–1945* [*Ten Years of Struggle 1935–1945*] (Athens, 1945). Labor legislation and government–trade union relations are analyzed in *Labour Problems in Greece* (Geneva, 1949). Finally, there is the revealing study sponsored by the Rockefeller Foundation: L. G. Allbaugh, *Crete: A Case Study of an Underdeveloped Area* (Princeton, N. J., 1953), which analyzes in detail industry, commerce, agriculture, and government as well as social conditions, and thereby sheds light on the general problem of Greece as well as that of Crete.

On social developments see the relevant chapters in the Pepelasis study listed above and also Dorothy Lee, "Greece," in *Cultural Patterns and Technical Change,* ed. by Margaret Mead (New York, 1952). On education in Greece, the best and most recent study is by K. D. Antonakaki, *Greek Education* (New York, 1955), which has a good bibliography. A convenient and excellent summary of literature and the arts in modern Greece is available in the *Encyclopedia Americana,* "Greece—Modern Culture" by E. P. and B. M. Panagopoulos. The standard history of literature, which is also a history of intellectual development, is by K. Th. Dimaras, *Istoria tes Neoellenikes Logotechnias* [*History of Modern Greek Literature*] (Athens, 1948–1949, 2 vols.). An anthology of modern Greek poetry in English translation is by Rae Dalven, *Modern Greek Poetry* (New York, 1949). See also "Perspective of Greece," *Atlantic Monthly Supplement,* June, 1955, which contains a bibliography of works in English on modern Greek literature. The standard work on the language problem is by M. A. Triantaphyllides, *Neoellenike Grammatike* [*Modern Greek Grammar*] (Athens, 1938), which is written from the vernacular viewpoint and contains a lengthy historical introduction with specimens of the language from the earliest inscriptions down to the present-day colloquial. See also on this matter J. M. Rife, "The Language Situation in Greece Today," *Classical Journal,* XXXVII (November, 1941), 65–72; "Greek Literary Life," *The Times Literary Supplement,* August 5, 1955, p. xxi; and the two articles by W. R. Loader, "Spoken Greek," *Greece and Rome,* XIII (June, 1944), 73–80, and "Purified or Popular? A Note on the Language Problem of Modern Greece," *Greece and Rome,* XIX (October, 1950), 116–122.

35. Rumania

By far the most important study of Rumania in the interwar years is by H. L. Roberts, *Rumania: Political Problems of an Agrarian State* (New Haven, Conn., 1951). This work, upon which this chapter is largely based, provides a penetrating analysis of economic and political developments as manifestations of the adjustment of a self-sufficient agrarian society to the intrusion of Western industrial civilization.

For the World War I period, see N. Basilescu, *La Roumanie dans la guerre et dans la paix* (Paris, 1919–1923, 2 vols.); G. Antipa, *L'occupation ennemie de la Roumanie et ses conséquences économiques et sociales* (Paris, 1929); and G. Ionescu-Sisesti, *L'agriculture de la Roumanie pendant la guerre* (New Haven, Conn., 1929). For the interwar years there are, in addition to Roberts, J. S. Roucek, *Contemporary Roumania and Her Problems* (Stanford, Calif., 1932), which contains useful data but is weak on interpretation; G. C. Logio, *Rumania: Its History, Politics and Economics* (Manchester, Eng., 1932), which is valuable for the author's experiences; and the excellent chapter on Rumanian interwar politics in H. Seton-Watson, *Eastern Europe between the Wars, 1918–1941* (Cambridge, Eng., 1945).

For economic developments there is, in addition to Roberts, D. Mitrany, *The Land & the Peasant in Rumania* (New Haven, Conn., 1930), the definitive study of the land reforms and their repercussions. Another important source is the Department of Overseas Trade (London), which published annual reports from 1919 to 1936 (except 1920 and 1925) on economic conditions in Rumania. For various aspects of Rumanian economic development see X. Netta, *La dette publique de l'état roumain* (Paris, 1935); A. Pantazi, *Contribution à l'histoire monétaire de la Roumanie* (Paris, 1934); P. G. Razus, *Les entreprises économiques de l'état* (Paris, 1939); A. P. Iancoulesco, *Les richesses minières de la nouvelle Roumanie* (Paris, 1928); and C. N. Jordan, *The Romanian Oil Industry* (New York, 1945).

The important Rumanian sociological studies of peasant life are described by P. E. Mosely, "The Sociological School of Dimitrie Gusti," *Sociological Review,* XXVIII (April, 1936), 149–165. See also J. Berkowitz, *La question des Israélites en Roumanie* (Paris, 1923); H. Schuster, *Die Judenfrage in Rumänien* (Leipzig, 1939); L. Feraru, *The Development of Rumanian Poetry* (New York, 1929); and G. Oprescu, *Roumanian Art from 1800 to Our Days* (Malmö, Sweden, 1935).

36. Albania

For bibliographies and general histories of Albania, see the bibliography above for Chapter 27. To this should be added two general histories of Albania in the twentieth century: V. Robinson, *Albania's Road to Freedom* (London, 1941), and S. Skendi, "The Political Evolution of Albania, 1912–1944" (New York, Mid-European Studies Center of the National Committee for a Free Europe, Mimeographed Series, March 8, 1954). The diplomatic history of the period is surveyed in the unpublished doctoral dissertation by G. M. Self, "Foreign Relations of Albania" (University of Chicago, 1943), which covers the period 1912 to 1939. This is a useful study, though tending at times to accept uncritically the Albanian viewpoint.

The period 1912 to 1914 is well treated by J. Swire, *Albania: The Rise of a Kingdom* (London, 1939), who makes use of materials provided by Prince William and other participants. Swire's viewpoint is strongly pro-Albanian and pro-Italian, and anti-Greek and anti-Yugoslav. Another pro-Albanian account is by Mary E. Durham, *The Struggle for Scutari* (London, 1914), the author being an Englishwoman who was engaged in relief work in northern Albania from 1911 to 1913. The diplomacy of these prewar years is considered most thoroughly in the unpublished doctoral dissertation by C. R. Salit, "Albania as an Index to European Pre-War Diplomacy" (Harvard University, 1938).

The diplomacy of the World War I period and the Peace Conference is treated in Self's dissertation listed above, and in the thorough and valuable study by E. P. Stickney, *Southern Albania or Northern Epirus in European International Affairs, 1912–1923* (Stanford, Calif., 1926). The latter study provides an excellent bibliography, particularly of the voluminous propaganda materials issued during the Peace Conference. For domestic developments during this period, see Swire's history and, above all, the valuable reports of the League Commission published in the *League of Nations Official Journal,* especially III, 491–510, and IV, 572–582. See also the reports of the League's financial adviser to Albania in the *Official Journal,* IV, 162–168, 727–728, 761–763.

Zog's rule during the interwar years is presented sympathetically by Swire. The views and activities of the anti-Zog Albanian organization in the United States are described in *The Albanian Struggle in the Old World and the New.* Compiled and Written by Members of the Federal Writers' Project of the Works Progress Administration of Massachusetts (Boston, 1939). Considerable data on all aspects of Albania's development are to be found in the weekly British periodical *The Near East and India.* See also "Albania: The Problem of the Adriatic," *Foreign Policy Reports,* VIII (June 8, 1932), 80–86. For the Italian invasion of Albania, see, in addition to Self's dissertation, *Ciano's Hidden Diary 1937–1938* (New York, 1953) and *The Ciano Diaries 1939–1943* (New York, 1946).

The Italians understandably have published the best works on Albania's economic development, outstanding being G. Lorenzoni, *La questione agraria albanese* (Bari, 1930) and A. Baldacci, *L'Albania* (Rome, 1930), the latter work emphasizing economic matters. More up-to-date is D. Zavalani, *Die landwirtschaftlichen Verhältnisse Albaniens* (Berlin, 1938). Excellent surveys of all aspects of Albania's economy are available in the reports of the American representatives: M. Blake, "Economic Conditions in Albania," *Commerce Reports Issued by the Bureau of Foreign and Domestic Commerce, United States Department of Commerce,* no. 83, (April 2, 1923), pp. 1–10; and J. C. Holmes and R. R. Jordan, "Economic Developments in Albania," *ibid.,* no. 32 (August 11, 1930), pp. 372–374. A valuable account of health conditions is given in the report of Dr. W. E. Haigh, who was in Albania in 1923 and 1924 for the League of Nations: "Malaria in Albania" (Geneva, League of Nations Health Organization, Mimeographed, C. H. 272, February, 1925).

Social organization and customs have been analyzed in several excellent works, these being in chronological order: J. G. von Hahn, *Albanesische Studien* (Jena, 1854), and *Griechische und albanesische Märchen* (Leipzig, 1864); A.

Dozon, *Contes albanais* (Paris, 1881); Mary E. Durham, *High Albania* (London, 1909), and *Some Tribal Origins, Laws and Customs of the Balkans* (London, 1928); and M. Hasluck, *The Unwritten Law in Albania* (Cambridge, Eng., 1954).

37. Diplomatic Developments

There is no full-length study of Balkan diplomacy between the wars. Developments may be traced in the yearly *Survey of International Affairs,* edited by Arnold J. Toynbee and published by the Royal Institute of International Affairs since 1925. See also the yearly *Documents on International Affairs* published under the same auspices. The period after 1934 is analyzed in detail in J. A. Lukacs, *The Great Powers and Eastern Europe* (New York, 1953). Briefer surveys of interwar Balkan diplomacy are to be found in L. S. Stavrianos, *Balkan Federation: A History of the Movement toward Balkan Unity in Modern Times* (Northampton, Mass., 1944), chs. 8, 9; H. Seton-Watson, *Eastern Europe between the Wars 1918–1941* (Cambridge, Eng., 1946), chs. 8–10; E. Barker, *Macedonia: Its Place in Balkan Power Politics* (London, 1950), ch. 2; *South-Eastern Europe: A Political and Economic Survey* (London, 1939), chs. 2–3; and the excellent interpretive essay by H. L. Roberts, "International Relations between the Wars," in *Challenge in Eastern Europe,* ed. by C. E. Black (New Brunswick, N. J., 1954), ch. 9.

The Balkan conferences and entente are considered in the following works: A. P. Papanastassiou, *Vers l'union balkanique* (Paris, 1934); N. J. Padelford, *Peace in the Balkans: The Movement towards International Organization in the Balkans* (New York, 1935); R. J. Kerner and H. N. Howard, *The Balkan Conferences and the Balkan Entente 1930–1935* (Berkeley, Calif., 1936); T. I. Geshkoff, *Balkan Union: A Road to Peace in Southeastern Europe* (New York, 1940); and Stavrianos, cited above, the latter work being the only one tracing inter-Balkan relations since the eighteenth century. See also two journals inspired by the Balkan federation movement: *Les Balkans* (Athens, October, 1930–1939), and *Revue internationale des études balkaniques* (Belgrade, 1934–1940).

The history of German ascendancy in the Balkans in the late 1930's is inseparable from the general European diplomatic history. Bibliographies for specific events such as the *Anschluss* and the Munich Agreement are to be found in Lukacs cited above. Noteworthy is the following study based on official Yugoslav sources: J. B. Hoptner, "Yugoslavia as Neutralist: 1937," *Journal of Central European Affairs,* XVI (July, 1956), 156–176. The rise of German influence in the Balkans is well analyzed in *Survey of International Affairs 1939–1946: The World in March 1939,* ed. by Arnold Toynbee and F. T. Ashton-Gwatkin (London, 1952), pp. 206–292; and more briefly in H. Seton-Watson, *The East European Revolution* (London, 1950), ch. 3.

For the German-Russian Nonaggression Pact of 1939, the basic source is the documentary collection by R. J. Sontag and J. S. Beddie, *Nazi-Soviet Relations 1939–1941* (New York, 1948). The best and most recent analysis of the hectic diplomacy between 1939 and 1941 is by G. L. Weinberg, *Germany and the Soviet Union 1939–1941* (Leiden, 1954). See also A. Rossi, *The Russo-German Alliance August 1939–June 1941* (Boston, 1951); D. Dallin, *Soviet Foreign Policy 1939–1942* (New Haven, Conn., 1942); the first part of G. Gafencu, *Prelude to the Russian Campaign, from the Moscow Pact (August 21, 1937) to* the *Opening of Hostilities in Russia* (*June 22, 1941*) (London, 1945); and the same author's *Last Days of Europe: A Diplomatic Journey in 1939* (New Haven, Conn., 1948).

The dismemberment of Rumania is described in the second part of Gafencu's *Prelude to the Russian Campaign*, cited above; A. Hillgruber, *Hitler, König Carol und Marschall Antonescu: die deutsch-rumänischen Beziehungen, 1938–1944* (Wiesbaden, 1954); and the two articles by P. E. Mosely: "Is Bessarabia Next?" *Foreign Affairs*, XVIII (April, 1940), 557–562, and "Transylvania Partitioned," *Foreign Affairs*, XIX (October, 1940), 237–244.

The diplomatic background of the Italian invasion of Greece on October 28, 1940, is given in Royal Ministry for Foreign Affairs, *Greek White Book: Italy's Aggression against Greece: Diplomatic Documents* (Athens, 1940). The unprovoked aggression thesis of this collection is supported by postwar Italian accounts: *The Ciano Diaries, 1939–1943* (New York, 1946); the account of the Italian minister in Athens, E. Grazzi, *Il principio della fine* (Rome, 1945); and of the military attaché, L. Mondini, *Prologo del conflitto Italo-Greco* (Rome, 1945). The most important secondary accounts of the diplomacy of the Italian invasion are by E. S. K. Schramm (von Thadden), *Griechenland und die Grossmächte im zweiten Weltkrieg* (Wiesbaden, 1955); and E. Wiskemann, *The Rome-Axis* (New York, 1949), ch. 14. See also P. Pipinelis, *Historia tes exoterikes politikes tes Hellados, 1923–1941* [*History of the Foreign Policy of Greece, 1923–1941*] (Athens, 1948, not consulted).

For the military aspects of the Italo-Greek War, see the accounts of the rival commanders: A. Papagos, *Ho polemos tes Hellados 1940–41* [*The War of Greece 1940–41*] (New York, 1941); U. Cavallero, *Commando Supremo* (Bologna, 1948); S. Visconti Prasca, *Io ho aggredito la Grecia* (Milan, 1946); and P. Badoglio, *L'Italia nella seconda guerra mondiale* (Milan, 1946). Noteworthy also are the strongly critical accounts of the Greek conduct of the war by certain Greek generals: N. Gregoriades, *Ho pankosmios polemos 1939–1945: A. Helleno-italo-germanikos polemos 1940–41* [*The World War 1939–1945: I. Greek-Italian-German War 1940–41*] (Athens, 1945); and D. Katheniotes, *Ai kyrioterai strategikai phaseis tou polemou 1940–1941* [*The Main Strategic Phases of the War 1940–1941*] (Athens, 1946).

For the circumstances of the German invasion of the Balkans in 1941, see the works cited above concerning the German-Russian pact, and especially Weinberg's study, which has been followed closely for this chapter. Weinberg's thesis is criticized and defended in the following exchange: G. L. Weinberg, "Der deutsche Entschluss zum Angriff auf die Sowjetunion," *Vierteljahrshefte für Zeitgeschichte*, I (October, 1930), 301–318; and H.-G. Seraphim and A. Hillgruber, "Hitlers Entschluss zum Angriff auf Russland," in the same journal, II (July, 1954), 241–254. See also W. L. Langer and S. E. Gleason, *The Undeclared War 1940–1941* (New York, 1953), chs. 5, 13, which reveals admirably the interrelationship between events in the Balkans and other parts of Europe as well as Asia. For Yugoslavia's involvement, see C. Fotich, *The War We Lost* (New York, 1948); R. L. Knejevitch, "Prince Paul, Hitler and Salonika," *International Affairs*, XXVII (January, 1951), 38–44, and the reply by D. Tsvetkovich, "Prince Paul, Hitler and Salonika," *International Affairs*, XXVII (October, 1951), 463–469. For Turkey's role at this time, see H. N. Howard, "Germany, the Soviet Union and Turkey during World War II," *Department of State Bulletin*, July 18, 1948;

C. Acikalin, "Turkey's International Relations," *International Affairs,* XXIII (October, 1947), 477–491; and E. R. Vere-Hodge, *Turkish Foreign Policy 1918–1950* (London, 1951). Greece's role, diplomatic as well as military, is made clear by Winston Churchill, *The Second World War: The Grand Alliance* (Boston, 1950), chs. 1, 6, 9, 12, 15, 16. See also Field Marshal Lord Wilson of Libya, *Eight Years Overseas 1939–47* (London, 1950); Sir Francis De Guingand, *Operation Victory* (London, 1947); G. Long, *Australia in the War of 1939–45* (London, 1954); C. Buckley, *Greece and Crete, 1941* (London, 1953); and R. de Belot, *The Struggle for the Mediterranean 1939–1945* (Princeton, N. J., 1952).

Finally, much material may be found in the fourteen volumes and appendices of the Nuremberg transcript, International Military Tribunal, *Nazi Conspiracy and Aggression* (Washington, D. C., 1947); and in Vols. XII–XIV of the subsequent *Trials of War Criminals before the Nuremberg Military Tribunals* (Washington, D. C., 1949–1953, 15 vols.).

38. Occupation, Resistance, and Liberation

The best general surveys of the Balkan countries under Axis rule are to be found in R. L. Wolff, *The Balkans in Our Time* (Cambridge, Mass., 1956), ch. 8; H. Seton-Watson, *The East European Revolution* (London, 1950), chs. 4–7; and in Arnold Toynbee and V. M. Toynbee, eds., *Survey of International Affairs 1939–1946: Hitler's Europe* (London, 1954), Pt. VI. A good analysis of the patterns of occupation and resistance is given by J. Amery, "Of Resistance," *Nineteenth Century,* CXLV (March, 1949), 138–149. The military characteristics of the Balkan resistance struggle are described from different viewpoints by A. Papagos, "Guerrilla Warfare," *Foreign Affairs,* XXX (January, 1952), 215–230; and D. Kveder, "Territorial War: The New Concept of Resistance," *Foreign Affairs,* XXXII (October, 1953), 91–108.

Few sources are available concerning Rumania during World War II because there were no resistance exploits to be recounted and no Allied agents to leave accounts. An "official" pro-Communist and pro-Soviet version is given in B. M. Kolker, "Natsionalno-osvoboditelinaia borba v Rumynii v 1941–1944 Godakh," ["The War of National Liberation in Rumania 1941–1944,"] *Voprosy Istorii,* no. 8 (August, 1954), pp. 79–85. Documents concerning the history of the Rumanian Communist party have been published by the postwar regime: *Documente din Istoria Partidului Muncitoresc din Romania, 1917–1922* (Bucharest, 1953); *Documente din Istoria Partidului Communist din Romania, 1923–1928* (Bucharest, 1953); and *Documente din Istoria Partidului Muncitoresc din Romania* (Bucharest, 1951), the latter work covering the years 1917 to 1944. One of the few solid works on Rumania during the war years is by A. Hillgruber, *Hitler, König Carol und Marschall Antonescu: die deutsch-rumänischen Beziehungen, 1938–1944* (Wiesbaden, 1954). On the same subject considerable material is to be found in the memoirs of the chief interpreter in the German Foreign Office at that time: P. Schmidt, *Statist auf diplomatischer Bühne, 1923–45* (Bonn, 1949). See also the laudatory biography by H. Laeuen, *Marschall Antonescu* (Essen, 1943). The agrarian developments during the war are analyzed by H. L. Roberts, *Rumania: Political Problems of an Agrarian State* (New Haven, Conn., 1951). Postwar developments are summarized in the Roberts study, and are described at length by an informed and very critical correspondent: R. H.

Markham, *Rumania under the Soviet Yoke* (Boston, 1949). The same critical viewpoint is shared by two observers, R. Bishop and E. S. Crayfield, *Russia Astride the Balkans* (London, 1949). An enthusiastic pro-Communist account is given by J. Lindsay and M. Cornforth, *Rumanian Summer* (London, 1953). The government viewpoint is also set forth in *Trial of the Former National Peasant Party Leaders Maniu, Mihalache . . . after the Shorthand Notes* (Bucharest, 1947).

A considerable number of "official" accounts of Bulgaria during World War II and of the resistance movement have been published under the postwar Communist regime. Some of these are analyzed by L. Valev, "Knigi o natsionalno-osvoboditel nom dvizhenii v Bolgarii v period vtoroi mirovoi voiny," ["Books on the National Liberation Movement in Bulgaria During the Second World War,"] *Voprosy Istorii*, no. 12 (December, 1950), pp. 134–138. See also N. Gornenski, "Pregled na Partizanskite Deiistviia u nas prez 1941–1943 g.," ["Review of the Activities of Our Partisans 1941–1943,"] *Izvestiia na Instituta za Bŭlgarska Istoriia*, nos. 3–4 (Sofia, 1951), pp. 181–230. The latter account reveals clearly the difficulties under which the Bulgarian guerrillas operated and the hit-and-run nature of their operations. A briefer survey of guerrilla activities is given in ch. 1 of F. T. Konstantinov, *Bolgariia na putik sotsializma* [*Bulgaria on the Road to Socialism*] (Moscow, 1953).

Among Western accounts the most useful are by E. Barker, *Macedonia: Its Place in Balkan Power Politics* (London, 1950), which describes Bulgarian policy in the occupied territories; I. T. Sanders, *Balkan Village* (Lexington, Ky., 1949), which analyzes events before and during the war in the village of Dragalevtsy near Sofia; and *There Is a Spirit in Europe: A Memoir of Frank Thompson* (London, 1948), which concerns a British officer who lost his life fighting with the Bulgarian Partisans, and provides an excellent picture of the type of struggle conducted by the bands. Official and hostile accounts of postwar developments in Bulgaria are available in *The Trial of Nikola D. Petkov* (Sofia, 1947); and M. Padev, *Dimitrov Wastes No Bullets* (London, 1948).

The violent and revolutionary course of Yugoslav history during World War II has evoked a great volume of literature, much of it as controversial as the events it describes. The flood of Yugoslav writings on the Communist party before the war and on the Partisan movement during the war years is conveniently summarized in the bibliographical article by I. Avakumović, "Literature on the Marxist Movement in Yugoslavia (1872–1944)," *Journal of Central European Affairs*, XV (April, 1955), 66–70. The most important "official" sources available in English are the biography *Tito* (New York, 1953) by one of Tito's close associates, V. Dedijer; the official record of the Mihailovich trial, *The Trial of Dragoljub-Drazha Mihailovich* (Belgrade, 1946); and Josip Broz Tito's *Report Delivered at the V Congress of the Communist Party of Yugoslavia* (Belgrade, 1948).

The Mihailovich cause is strongly defended by D. Martin, *Ally Betrayed: The Uncensored Story of Tito and Mihailovich* (New York, 1946); by the Yugoslav ambassador to Washington, C. Fotitch, *The War We Lost: Yugoslavia's Tragedy and the Failure of the West* (New York, 1948); and in King Peter's autobiography, *A King's Heritage* (New York, 1954). See also E. Yourichitch, *Le procès Tito-Mihailovitch* (Paris, 1950), the author, a former Chetnik, is very critical of the Partisans.

Important accounts have been written by members of the British military missions in Yugoslavia: the head of the British mission to Tito, F. Maclean, *East-*

ern Approaches (London, 1949); a liaison officer in Hungarian-occupied territory, B. Davidson, *Partisan Picture* (Bedford, Eng., 1946); a liaison officer with Chetnik units in northeast Serbia, J. Rotham, *Miss Fire: The Chronicle of a British Mission to Mihailovich, 1943–1944* (London, 1946); a liaison officer to the Partisans in Slovenia, W. Jones, *Twelve Months with Tito's Partisans* (Bedford, Eng., 1946); a member of the mission to Tito, S. Clissold, *Whirlwind: An Account of Marshal Tito's Rise to Power* (London, 1949); a liaison officer to the Chetniks in Serbia in 1941–1942, C. Lawrence, *Irregular Adventure* (London, 1947).

Among the numerous secondary accounts, the most important pro-Partisan works are by K. Zilliacus, *Tito of Yugoslavia* (London, 1952), and L. Adamic, *The Eagle and the Roots* (New York, 1952). Anti-Tito accounts are provided by A. N. Dragnich, *Tito's Promised Land: Yugoslavia* (New Brunswick, N. J., 1954); and by R. H. Markham, *Tito's Imperial Communism* (Chapel Hill, N. C., 1947). More balanced versions may be found in H. Seton-Watson, *The East European Revolution* (London, 1950), ch. 6; W. S. Vucinich, "The Second World War and Beyond," in *Yugoslavia,* ed. by R. J. Kerner (Berkeley, Calif., 1949), ch. 20; and R. L. Wolff, "Mihailovich: A Post-Mortem," *Atlantic,* CLXXVIII (October, 1946), 43–49. See the reply to the latter article by Constantin Fotitch in the December, 1946, issue of the *Atlantic,* and Wolff's response in the same issue. The impact of the war and the resistance struggle upon village life and the peasant mind is analyzed by R. Trouton, *Peasant Renaissance in Yugoslavia 1900–1950* (London, 1952), Bk. III.

For the critical split between Tito and the Kremlin in 1948 see *The Soviet-Yugoslav Dispute* (London, 1948); H. F. Armstrong, *Tito and Goliath* (New York, 1951); and A. B. Ulam, *Titoism and the Cominform* (Cambridge, Mass., 1952).

Bibliographies of materials on occupied Greece are provided by L. S. Stavrianos and E. P. Panagopoulos, "Present-Day Greece," *Journal of Modern History,* XX (June, 1948), 149–158; and by F. A. Spencer, *War and Postwar Greece: An Analysis Based on Greek Writings* (Washington, D. C., Library of Congress, European Affairs Division, 1952).

Works on occupied Greece reflect the controversial nature of their subject. Secondary studies representing divergent viewpoints are by W. H. McNeill, *The Greek Dilemma: The War and Aftermath* (New York, 1947); and L. S. Stavrianos, *Greece: American Dilemma and Opportunity* (Chicago, 1952). For divergent viewpoints of British officers in occupied Greece, see C. M. Woodhouse, *Apple of Discord: A Survey of Recent Greek Politics in Their International Setting* (London, 1948); and C. W. Myers, *Greek Entanglement* (London, 1955). Compare also the accounts of one of the EDES leaders, K. Pyromaglou, *He ethnike antistasis* [*The National Resistance*] (Athens, 1947); and of the ELAS military leader, S. Saraphis, *Ho ELAS* [*ELAS*] (Athens, 1946).

The program and ideology of the EAM are presented in the famous and widely distributed booklet by D. Glenos, *Ti einai kai ti thelei to EAM?* [*What Is the EAM and What Are Its Aims?*] (Athens, 1942). The most complete account of the resistance struggle is given in the Saraphis book listed above, which has been translated in abridged form as S. Sarafis, *Greek Resistance Army: The Story of ELAS* (London, 1951). An invaluable documentary source for the organization of the EAM and the administration of its liberated territories is the *Archeio ethnikes antistasis* [*Archives of National Resistance*] (Athens, 1946).

Two numbers of this publication, which appeared in April and August, 1946, together provide 104 pages of basic documentary material. Equally valuable is D. Zepos, *Laike dikaiosyne eis tas eleutheras periochas tes ypo katochen Hellados* [*People's Justice in the Liberated Territories of Occupied Greece*] (Athens, 1945), a careful technical study by a lawyer of the administrative and legal system introduced by the EAM in its liberated territories. A convenient analysis and survey of the organization and administrative policies of the EAM is given in L. S. Stavrianos, "The Greek National Liberation Front (EAM): A Study in Resistance Organization and Administration," *Journal of Modern History,* XXIV (March, 1952), 42–55.

The best picture of Albania during World War II is given by the head of a British mission to the Ballist forces: J. Amery, *Sons of the Eagle: A Study in Guerilla War* (London, 1948). More than a story of personal adventure, it analyzes with considerable insight the historical and social background in Albania as well as the general characteristics and problems of Balkan guerrilla warfare. A British officer with the Albanian Partisans has also left an account: Brigadier Edmund "Trotsky" Davies, *Illyrian Venture: The Story of the British Military Mission to Enemy-Occupied Albania 1943–44* (London, 1952), but this is not as informative as the Amery work because the author was captured before he was able to operate widely. See also the novel by Anthony Quayle, *Eight Hours from England* (London, 1945), based on personal experiences in occupied Albania. Useful secondary accounts are available in W. S. Vucinich, "Communism Gains in Albania," *Current History,* XXI (October, 1951), 212–219; and in S. Skendi, "Albania within the Slav Orbit: Advent to Power of the Communist Party," *Political Science Quarterly,* LXIII (June, 1948), 257–274. Finally, see the important account by V. Dedijer, *Jugoslovensko-albanski odnosi (1939–1948)* [*Yugoslav-Albanian Relations (1939–1948)*] (Belgrade, 1949), which is based on official Yugoslav materials and statistics, describes the role of the Yugoslav Communist party in uniting the Albanian party, and claims that after the war Yugoslavia gave more to Albania than she received. Some of the materials in this book have been republished by the same author in "Albania: Soviet Pawn," *Foreign Affairs,* XXX (October, 1951), 103–111.

39. Hidden War, Cold War, and Peace Settlement

Because of the many controversies involved, a good deal of material has appeared concerning post–World War II developments in the Balkans and also the inter-Allied conflicts during the war years. The most recent and detailed study is by R. L. Wolff, *The Balkans in Our Time* (Cambridge, Mass., 1956). Much data are also available in two publications of the Royal Institute of International Affairs: W. H. McNeill, *America, Britain, & Russia: Their Co-Operation and Conflict 1941–1946* (London, 1953), and Arnold and Veronica M. Toynbee, eds., *The Realignment of Europe* (London, 1955), the first of these works emphasizing great-power policies and the second the domestic developments within the European countries. H. Seton-Watson, *The East European Revolution* (London, 1950) is valuable and informed. Other noteworthy works dealing with this period are R. R. Betts, ed., *Central and South East Europe 1945–1948* (London, 1950); J. A. Lukacs, *The Great Powers & Eastern Europe* (New York, 1953); A. Gyorgy, *Governments of Danubian Europe* (New York, 1949); C. E. Black, ed., *Chal-*

lenge in Eastern Europe (New Brunswick, N. J., 1954); C. E. Black, ed., *Readings on Contemporary Eastern Europe* (New York, Mid-European Studies Center of the National Committee for a Free Europe, Inc., 1953); E. Barker, *Truce in the Balkans* (London, 1948); and D. Warriner, *Revolution in Eastern Europe* (London, 1950).

For developments within the Balkan countries during the war and postwar years see the bibliography for the preceding chapter. Here we are concerned with great-power policies, and since the Russians do not take to the pen we must depend on American and British sources which throw considerable light on Russian actions. By far the most important British contribution is the six-volume history by Winston Churchill, *The Second World War* (Boston, 1949–1953). Most of the British works naturally deal with developments in Greece, the most important of these being Field Marshal Lord Wilson of Libya, *Eight Years Overseas 1939–1947* (London, 1950); Sir Reginald Leeper, *When Greek Meets Greek* (London, 1950); C. M. Woodhouse, *Apple of Discord: A Survey of Recent Greek Politics in Their International Setting* (London, 1948); and E. C. W. Myers, *Greek Entanglement* (London, 1955). These British accounts should be balanced by EAM materials, especially the *EAM White Book* (New York, 1945); and S. Saraphis, *Ho ELAS [ELAS]* (Athens, 1946), which has been translated in abridged form as *Greek Resistance Army: The Story of ELAS* (London, 1951). Different interpretations of the origins of the battle of Athens are presented by W. H. McNeill and L. S. Stavrianos in the December, 1949, issue of the *American Slavic and East European Review*. See also W. H. McNeill, *The Greek Dilemma* (Philadelphia, 1947), and L. S. Stavrianos, *Greece: American Dilemma and Opportunity* (Chicago, 1952).

On the American side there is no counterpart to Churchill's massive contribution. A number of Roosevelt's close associates have left accounts, including R. E. Sherwood, *Roosevelt and Hopkins: An Intimate History* (New York, 1948); W. D. Leahy, *I Was There* (New York, 1950); and Elliott Roosevelt, *As He Saw It* (New York, 1946). Also, three secretaries of state have left memoirs: Cordell Hull, *Memoirs* (New York, 1948, 2 vols.); James F. Byrnes, *Speaking Frankly* (New York, 1947); Edward R. Stettinius, Jr., *Roosevelt and the Russians: The Yalta Conference,* ed. by Walter Johnson (New York, 1949). Most recent are President Harry S. Truman's *Memoirs* (New York, 1955, 2 vols.), which should be consulted together with Byrnes's volume for the Potsdam Conference and the following events, especially the Truman Doctrine. Finally, there is a useful collection of articles in R. Dennet and J. E. Johnson, *Negotiating with the Russians* (Boston, 1951), which contains the account by Mark Ethridge and C. E. Black, "Negotiating on the Balkans, 1945–1947." Other noteworthy books are J. L. Snell, ed., *The Meaning of Yalta . . .* (Baton Rouge, La., 1956); and the documentary collection *Foreign Relations of the United States: Diplomatic Papers: The Conferences at Malta and Yalta 1945* (Washington, D. C., 1955).

Excellent summaries of the peacemaking at the end of World War II are given by C. E. Black, "The Axis Satellites and the Great Powers," *Foreign Policy Reports,* XXII (May 1, 1946), 38–52; W. N. Hadsel, "The Five Axis Satellite Peace Treaties," *Foreign Policy Reports,* XXIII (April 15, 1947), 22–32; and S. Lowery, "The Peace Settlement in Eastern Europe," in Arnold and Veronica M. Toynbee, *The Realignment of Europe,* cited above, pp. 332–352.

Index

Index